ALSO BY RICHARD KLUGER

History

SIMPLE JUSTICE:
A HISTORY OF BROWN V. BOARD OF EDUCATION AND
BLACK AMERICA'S STRUGGLE FOR EQUALITY

THE PAPER: THE LIFE AND DEATH OF
THE NEW YORK HERALD TRIBUNE

Novels

WHEN THE BOUGH BREAKS

NATIONAL ANTHEM

MEMBERS OF THE TRIBE

STAR WITNESS

UN-AMERICAN ACTIVITIES

THE SHERIFF OF NOTTINGHAM

Novels with Phyllis Kluger

GOOD GOODS

ROYAL POINCIANA

ASHES TO ASHES

ASHES TO ASHES

America's Hundred-Year
Cigarette War,
the Public Health, and
the Unabashed
Triumph of Philip Morris

RICHARD KLUGER

ALFRED A. KNOPF   *New York*   1996

THIS IS A BORZOI BOOK
PUBLISHED BY ALFRED A. KNOPF, INC.

Copyright © 1996 by Richard Kluger
Published in the United States by Alfred A. Knopf, Inc., New York,
and simultaneously in Canada by Random House of Canada Limited, Toronto.
Distributed by Random House, Inc., New York.

http://www.randomhouse.com/

Grateful acknowledgment is made to Warner Bros. Publications U.S. Inc. for per-
mission to reprint an excerpt from "Smoke, Smoke, Smoke That Cigarette" by
Merle Travis & Tex Williams Copyright © 1947 (Renewed) Unichappell Music
Inc. (BMI) & Elvis Presley Music (BMI) All Rights Reserved. Reprinted by
Permission of Warner Bros. Publications U.S. Inc., Miami FL 33014

Library of Congress Cataloging-in-Publication Data
Kluger, Richard.
Ashes to ashes : America's hundred-year cigarette war, the public health,
and the unabashed triumph of Philip Morris / Richard Kluger.—1st ed.
p.   cm.
Includes bibliographical references and index.
ISBN 0-394-57076-6
1. Cigarette habit—United States—History.   2. Tobacco habit—
United States—History.   3. Cigarette industry—United States—History.
4. Tobacco industry—United States—History.
I. Title.
HV5760.K58   1996
394.1'4—dc20   95-42103
CIP

Manufactured in the United States of America
First Edition

With love for Phyllis, my life's companion,

who is all too familiar with the subject

Tobacco, I do assert . . . is the most soothing, sovereign and pre-cious weed that ever our dear old mother Earth tendered to the use of man! Let him who would contradict that most mild, but sincere and enthusiastic assertion, look to his undertaker. . . .

BEN JONSON

For thy sake, Tobacco, I would do anything but die.

CHARLES LAMB

Smoke, smoke, smoke that cigarette.
Puff, puff, puff, and if you smoke yourself to death,
Tell Saint Peter at the Golden Gate
That you hate to make him wait
But you've got to have another cigarette.

"SMOKE! SMOKE! SMOKE!"
1947 SONG BY MERLE TRAVIS
AND TEX WILLIAMS

Contents

Foreword: A Quick Drag

AS THE twentieth century wanes, we may marvel justifiably at the triumphs of the human intellect in the course of this span over the visitations of nature at its unkindest. We have largely overcome the savaging effects of infection and contagion, of extreme climates and turbulent weather, of famine and peril from other species. We have attacked the vastness of our planet's distances, even the force of gravity itself, while unlocking the earth's elemental secrets. We have generated creature comforts and pleasures on a scale undreamed of by our forebears and doubled our expected life span.

Yet, as if to reassure the overseers of the universe that we have not attained godlike status but remain in essence creatures of folly and victims of our darker natures, we have also ingeniously crafted fresh forms of misery and death-dealing. We have generated vile effluents with our life-enhancing technology, fouling soil, waters, and skies in ways only beginning to be understood. We have fashioned doomsday weaponry. We have promoted mindless tribal hatreds into genocide and rationalized it in the name of profane statecraft. And worst of all, if we are to credit the number of fatalities as calculated by public-health authorities, twentieth-century man has embraced the cigarette and paid dearly for it.

The stated toll is horrific. Americans are said to die prematurely from diseases caused or gravely compounded by smoking at the rate of nearly half a million a year; a multiple of that figure is put forward as the world toll, approaching several million. The number claimed has risen appallingly as the century has lengthened, population and wealth have grown, and social customs have turned more permissive. No one can make more than an informed guess at the total loss of life, but those decrying it most urgently assert that the mortality figure from smoking for the century as a whole rivals the multimillions who have fallen in all its wars.

Yet there has been little outrage at the appalling statistics—only a dirgelike, loosely orchestrated, and inconstant chorus of protest over the continuing practice of the custom and, increasingly of late, restrictions on where it may be undertaken. At mid-century, nearly half the adult American population smoked; near the end of the century, despite massive indictment of the habit by medical science, more than a quarter of all Americans over eighteen continues to smoke—nearly 50 million people. And while overall consumption has declined somewhat, those who cling to the custom smoke more heavily than ever: an estimated twenty-seven cigarettes a day on average. Meanwhile, in Asia, Africa, and Eastern Europe, tobacco is a growth industry. There the cigarette is widely regarded as a sign of modernity, an emblem of advancement, fashion, savoir-faire, and adventure as projected in images beamed and plastered everywhere by its makers. And, in a case of supreme irony, not to say perversity, the more evidence accumulated by science on the ravaging effects of tobacco, the more lucrative the business has become and the wider the margin of profit.

Why should this be? Did mankind simply become putty in the hands of the master manipulators who ran the cigarette business? Were we so charmed by the iconography with which these marketing Svengalis enriched our popular culture—a fantasyland populated by heroically taciturn cowboys, sportive camels, and an array of young lovers, auto racers, and assorted bons vivants all vibrantly "alive with pleasure"—that we exonerated them from all charges of capital crimes?

Or have we been convinced by these merchants' unyielding insistence that peddling poison in the form of tobacco is no vice if (a) it is freely picked by its users and (b) its dangers have not yet been conclusively, to the last logarithm of human intellect, proven? Or perhaps our complicity in this man-made plague stems from our very familiarity with the subject; the product has become so ubiquitous and the case against it so clear that we are plain bored by the whole matter. Or perhaps it is the circumstances of death from smoking. The toll is slowly exacted, in the form of seven or eight years of lost life to the average smoker, who, like the rest of us, succumbs mostly to the degenerative diseases of old age: cancer, failing hearts, blocked arteries, dysfunctional lungs. Death from such causes comes singly, and usually at hospitals, not in spectacular conflagrations or crashes obliterating hundreds at a time and capturing the world's attention and sympathy. The smoker's death is banal, private, noticed only by family and friends, and, in the final analysis, self-inflicted.

Doubtless there is an element of plausibility in each of these explanations, but the persistent sway of the cigarette may be equally understood by dwelling not on the consequences of the habit, as its detractors naturally do, and why these people *ought* to have curtailed it, but on the reason for the phenomenon in the first place. Simply put, hundreds of millions worldwide have found smoking useful to them in myriad ways, subconscious or otherwise.

The proverbial visitor from a distant planet would likely find no earthling custom more pointless or puzzling than the swallowing of tobacco smoke followed by its billowy emission and accompanying odor. Told that the act neither warms nor cleanses the human interior, that it neither repels enemies nor attracts lovers, our off-planet visitor would be still more baffled. The utility of the exercise, he/she/it would be informed, is traceable to the changing pace, scale, and nature of daily living in this century. Our lives used to be simpler and shorter, given over largely to the struggle for survival. But the technological marvels of our age have provoked attendant stresses from congested living and our often grating interdependence; from the irksome nature of our duties and lack of time to accomplish them; from a welter of conflicting values and emotions born of unattainable expectations and unmanageable frustrations; and from the often careening velocity of life. Many of us have lacked the inner resources to get through the battle and gain a little repose without help wherever and however we could find it, and no device, product, or pastime has been more readily seized upon for this purpose than the cigarette. It has been the preferred and infamous pacifier of the twentieth century, even as—or if—it has been our worst killer. Its users have found it their all-purpose psychological crutch, their universal coping device, and the truest, cheapest, most accessible opiate of the masses.

Let us consider, then, this protean usefulness of the cigarette, which, practically speaking, *is* the tobacco business in the United States, accounting for some 95 percent of the industry's revenues. The unique value of the cigarette to its users has resided in its perceived dual (and contradictory) role as both stimulant and sedative. Clinically, smoking has been found to speed up a number of bodily functions, most notably the flow of adrenaline, with its quickening effect on the beat of the heart, but the smoker when questioned will most often characterize the cigarette as a relaxant. This seeming paradox is the essence of the product's appeal, for in fact, the smoker uses it to meet both needs.

The smoker smokes when feeling up or in the dumps, when too harassed and overburdened or too unchallenged and idle, when threatened by the crowd at a party or when lonely in a strange place. A smoke is a reward for a job well done or consolation for a job botched. It can fuel the smoker for the intensity of life's daily confrontations yet seem to insulate him from the consuming effects of any given encounter. It defines and punctuates the periods of the smoker's day, and nothing helps as much in dealing on the telephone with trying people or unpleasant matters. The cigarette, in short, has been the peer-less regulator of its user's moods, the merciful stabilizing force against the human tendency to overrespond to the infinite stimuli that inescapably impinge upon us.

Abetting this admirable, if illusory, versatility of the cigarette have been its obvious virtues as an item of merchandise. It is remarkably convenient: small, portable, readily concealable though highly visible, for sale all over, easy to operate and swiftly disposable, a quick fit into respites throughout the day, us-able—until recent years—almost anywhere indoors or out, interchangeable with any other brand of like strength, as blindfold tests have demonstrated (de-spite company claims of unique flavorfulness, smoothness, and goodness), and cheap. Even at ten or so cents apiece, or a bit over a penny per minute of en-joyment—or of relief, perhaps—the butt has ranked as one of life's least costly indulgences.

Though a mere article of merchandise, the cigarette is a uniquely intimate possession. It is everywhere about you—in your hand, in your mouth, in your pocket close to your heart, and its smoke is down your throat, in your lungs, in your hair, on your skin, and ineradicably on your clothes, not to mention breath unless you are an equally assiduous consumer of mints or mouthwash. Necessarily, one's cigarette has come to take on a persona, a character, a standing as a companion, and an especially valued one at that: it is always on call, reliably there when needed, a friend who never answers back or slaps you around. How many other stress-free friendships are there in life—unless, of course, one grasps the antitobacconists' killjoy contention that smoking com-pounds rather than allays stress. The cigarette has been perhaps most gratefully embraced when the smoker is alone and afraid, to fill "all the dreadfully ordi-nary intervals and the great gulfs of silence before the Showdowns," as the poet-smoker John Hollander has written. And in that ultimate loneliness of wartime, it has been the soldier's solace as he endures boredom, fatigue, and the prospect of imminent obliteration.

Whatever its utility otherwise, smoking is essentially a physical and highly sensual experience. Among the senses, that of touch is most apparent. Tactility begins with the snug fit of the pack in the palm, followed by all the little rituals of crackling off the wrapper, neatly tearing open the pack, surgically extracting the first snow-white tube, percussively tapping its tobacco end against the wrist or any convenient flat surface, deftly inserting it between barely parted lips, and lighting it with the absolute minimum of pyrotechnics—the quintes-sence of cool. It is, of course, the perfect plaything for nervous hands that cling to it like an anchor, fondle it, and wave it about as a prop to enhance one's words or dramatize one's feelings. Add, then, its raptures to the taste (bitter-sweet, acrid, tingling), the smell (an autumnal pungence, an organic mellow-ness), the feel (the small, sharp hit at the back of the throat, teasingly raspy and enlivening on the way down, the sudden fullness and completeness deep within, the final swift, satisfying surge of emission), and the sight (the little blue-gray cloud proclaiming one's *Lebensraum* and, between puffs, the lazy, sinuous ribbon wafting upward, signaling that the smoker exists). Here, for the habitué is the very meaning of instant gratification. And was there ever a more ideal complement to those other two sinful non-nutrients, coffee and booze, or a perfect nightcap following an exquisite meal or even average sex?

That smoking is equally a boon to the soul as to the body, few partakers would claim, but most believe it helps them think. Samuel Johnson, among the eighteenth century's more celebrated pipe-puffers, modestly praised the practice as "a thing which requires so little exertion and yet preserves the mind from total vacuity." Freud went a good deal further: "I owe to the cigar a great intensification of my capacity to work"—this was written in his seventy-second year after thirty agonizing operations for cancer of the jaw, by which time the connection between the two was not likely lost on him. Molière, with a certain Gallic vagueness, waxed most rhapsodic of all on the transcendent efficacy of smoke: "It not only refreshes and cleanses the brain, but also leads the soul to virtue and teaches honesty."

Is there clinical support for smoking as brain food? Some experimenters have found, though the evidence is equivocal at best, that nicotine, tobacco's psychoactivating ingredient, excites the brain waves, can increase vigilance in the performance of repetitive (one might say mindless) tasks, and may improve the processing of sensory stimuli—provided, that is, one keeps on smoking. Does any of this amount to a boost in productive mental energy? Some scientists have theorized that smoking creates an apparent heightening effect by neutralizing (one might say numbing) the edges of one's consciousness and thereby reducing distractions. Translation: Smoking may help you concentrate by emptying the mind of all but the subject of the moment.

In the even murkier realm of the subconscious, smoking has been arguably credited with filling needs and registering impulses not conceded or even guessed at by the smoker. The cigar-loving Freud contended that smoking was an oral autoerotic manifestation of inadequate breast-suckling, presumably in infancy, and likened it to thumb-sucking. Lesser sages have ascribed overeating to this same "orality," but the smoker is far busier with his fix if measured in mouth-hours. Some Freudian followers, licensed and otherwise, have hypothesized that cigars, cigarettes, and pipes are all phallic substitutes, or possibly supplements, and smoking a surrogate form of sexuality. Higher-minded cultural anthropologists have attributed to male smokers a yearning for the primal power of Man as Fire-Conqueror or for the magical potency of the fire-breathing shaman or, when not on those particular power trips, for the comforts of hearth and home evoked by their little portable tobacco furnaces. And many social commentators have concluded that smoking for women is both a badge of would-be equality with smoky men and a sanctioned outlet for the frustrated expression of combativeness and other impulses that men are allowed to vent but that are forbidden to the female of the species, always supposed the gentler and more nurturing of the two.

Nor to be minimized, either, has been the usefulness of smoking as coded defiance—of authority, of the hand fate has dealt you, of sweet reason itself. It is most favored, in the first instance, by juvenile smokers as an initiator into the mysteries and empowerment of the adult world; the accompanying displeasures of nausea and dizziness assaulting the novice inhaler are tolerated as rites of passage and the price to be paid for partaking of forbidden fruit. And how easy to defy the tyranny of grown-ups by illicitly taking up a favorite habit of theirs, all the better for its reek of sensuousness with no risk of rejection by a pined-after sex object. For youth or adult alike, the habit may serve to compensate for profound feelings of inadequacy, inferiority, or an abiding bitterness that stems from degraded social status, low occupational achievement, certifiable injustice, or paranoid delusion. Such victims of social pathology are suspected of smoking not in spite of the hazards associated with it but *because* of them.

Even better-adjusted smokers, though, are susceptible to the perverse condition that behavioral specialists call "cognitive dissonance," acting in direct and self-destructive contradiction of known truths or indisputable fact. And all smokers are gifted at rationalizing their habit. Many smokers, for example, readily acknowledge, even insist, that they are hopelessly hooked. But as addictions go, they may argue, it is pretty benign. Even as the mild kick of the inhaled cigarette does not compare with heroin's euphoric high or the giddiness induced by marijuana or the sudden brightening of spirits that alcohol can bring on, neither does smoking result in any of the acute physical impairments or social disruptions of those more powerful narcotics. Smokers, moreover, rarely rob to feed their entirely legal habit or in a crazed trance beat their families. Yes, tobacco seduces you to a dependency upon it, but just as surely, the knot can be undone; millions, after all, have freed themselves.

For those millions enslaved by nicotine, the weightier charge that the addiction can ultimately prove lethal inspires a lot of fast talking and whistling by the graveyard. The catechism of the hopelessly habituated runs something like this: (1) Even if those busybody biostatisticians are right, only one of four smokers will die due, more or less, to smoking, so the odds are on my side. (2) Besides, you've got to die of something, so why not from a source of pleasure? (3) Anyway, it takes decades for the diseases linked to smoking to develop, and those years I might lose aren't exactly quality time, coming late in life when many human faculties and the yen for living are diminished. (4) Life is full of dangers—to live is to take risks of all sorts every day; I may get hit by a truck tomorrow. I'm here and want to enjoy myself to the fullest extent possible, and cigarettes help me do that. And (5), let's face it, I might have gone cuckoo a long while back without smoking or stressed out terminally, as they say. So, (6) if you don't mind—or even if you do—please get out of my face and tend to your own garden. P.S. (7) When your number's up, it's up; you can't mess with your karma.

Why, given the enormity of the crimes against humanity with which it has been charged, the cigarette has not been outlawed or its ingredients and design modified by government command is thus explainable in the first place by the immense and continuing consumption of the product for all the above uses and excuses. It must then be added at once, without excessive moralizing, that the tobacco industry, understandably devoted to its own survival ahead of all others', has labored prodigiously to reassure its customers, disarm its foes, purchase allies in high places, and minimize government intrusion into its gravely suspect business. But the success of that industry cannot be facilely dismissed as greedy capitalism at its most predatory, for in many nations, capitalist and socialist alike, the manufacture and sale of tobacco products have been reserved as an operation of the state, carried out in the name of the public interest if not the public health. Among these nations have been China, Japan, the constituent states of the former Soviet Union, France, Spain, Italy, all the Eastern European countries before their liberation from totalitarian rule, Kenya, both Koreas, Taiwan, and Thailand.

Around the world, moreover, the pro-smoking cause is championed by millions dependent on the tobacco industry for their livelihood. Most numerous among these are the growers of what the industry claims is the most widely cultivated non-food plant on earth. In the United States, tobacco remains the most profitable cash crop on a per-acre basis, and in many places throughout Latin America, Africa, and Asia, where subsistence farming is the obligatory way of life for the masses, pending the creation of viable domestic industry, tobacco has been considered a godsend. Even in Japan, every leaf grown was long guaranteed purchase by the state-backed tobacco enterprise, and the American government has vitally helped support tobacco cultivation since the 1930s. Can all these national governments be justly accused of callous indifference to the well-being of their peoples, or might it be argued instead that, in Darwinian terms, economic survival has gained priority over mere physical fitness, to the chagrin of public-health advocates?

Beyond growers, the ranks of those with a prominent vested interest in sustaining smoking are swollen by machinists operating state-of-the-art cigarette makers that spit out 10,000 units per minute; by distributors and vendors, including supermarket managers who hawk Marlboros by the carton, state-store operators in Burgundy pushing Gauloises by the pack, men on bikes traveling the Ugandan bush country, and street urchins in Calcutta selling smokes by the single stick; by Madison Avenue dream merchants dependent on the U.S. tobacco trade's more than $5 billion annual advertising and promotion outlay as well as by newspaper and magazine editors keenly aware that cigarette ad linage helps determine the size of their news hole; by auto-racing drivers and their pit crews, dance troupes and symphony orchestras perennially on the edge of extinction; by professional women tennis players (until recently); by museum directors, colleges, and minority-member social action groups, all gratefully accepting cigarette manufacturers' largesse without perceptible qualms of conscience.

With such a mammoth and influential constituency in place, it is no surprise that would-be tobacco regulators are scarce in the political arena. Governments, furthermore, have themselves become addicted to the cigarette because of the taxes it harvests for them. Cigarettes are the most heavily taxed consumer product in the world. About twenty industrialized nations tax cigarettes more heavily than the U.S., some of them five times more. In China, they have been the largest source of capital formation for broadening the country's industrial base. Few politicians have been willing to forgo such revenues, as well as the votes and support of smokers and all those battening on the habit. Even the World Health Organization, a unit of the United Nations, has been hamstrung in its efforts to combat tobacco by the indifference of member-nation governments and the pressures applied by the private international goliaths, Philip Morris Companies, Inc., British-American Tobacco, RJR Nabisco, and Rothmans.

And so, near the end of the century, the debate over smoking rages on. The cigarette makers argue that the smoking of tobacco has persisted in civilized places for 500 years now, never without its loud detractors; that science may have incriminated the practice but has not found it guilty beyond a shadow of a doubt—and that, regardless of how definitive the findings to date, every smoker knows, whether from warning labels, public reports, media attention, or word of mouth, that there are risks attached. Antismoking activists respond that most smokers begin at an immature and suggestible age—90 percent of them in the U.S. by the time they are twenty—when they are incapable of weighing the prospect of an early grave and believe they can break the habit at will; that the perceived benefits of smoking are in reality a delusion induced by a drug, which when consumed at the rate of 70,000 or so hits a year (twenty or twenty-five cigarettes a day X eight or ten puffs each X 365 days) causes deeply conditioned behavior and a corrosive effect on human tissue, and that the medical case is proven—except to the extent that science is only just beginning to grasp the precise mechanics by which all diseases assault the body's intricate defense and immune systems. But that tobacco smoke is a ruthless pathological agent provocateur, there remains no doubt.

The question, then, is whether cigarette merchants are businessmen basically like any other, selling a product judged to be highly hazardous long after its usefulness to millions was well established, and are now sorely abused by "health fascists" and moralizing busybodies, or are they moral lepers preying on the ignorant, the miserable, the emotionally vulnerable, and the genetically susceptible?

ASHES TO ASHES

1

Adoring the Devil's Breath

TOBACCO is a hard plant to love. Man-sized or taller, demanding at every stage of its growth, sticky to the touch during hot weather, highly inviting to unsightly and voracious pests, tobacco prompted one of its more eminent growers, Thomas Jefferson, to call it "a culture productive of infinite wretchedness" in view of the hundreds of hours of backbreaking labor per acre that it required—and still does, despite advances in mechanization and agronomy.

The tobacco plant is something of an anomaly of nature in that its unprotected leaves rather than its blossoms, fruit, or shielded seed are what man values. Native to the Western Hemisphere but now grown worldwide, *Nicotiana tabacum* is rarely found in the wild. It has a limited life expectancy without cultivation but sprouts spectacularly when tended. If unchecked, the plant grows as high as nine feet, with wide-spreading leaves in the shape of a rounded arrowhead, sixteen to eighteen inches in length and attached to the wrist-thick stalk in an ascending spiral so that the ninth leaf overlaps the first. The leaves and stalk are covered with soft, downy hair that emits gums and aromas; these oils, resins, and waxes increase as the leaf matures and accumulate on the surface in a viscous sheen. The whole point, when raising it commercially, is to force the growth into no more than fifteen or twenty leaves per plant, which, if properly selected, harvested, and cured, will bulk nicely and prove rich in nicotine, a potent compound that, unless absorbed in small doses, can be lethally toxic and is generally acknowledged as the source of the habit-forming property of inhaled tobacco smoke. Just how it addicts, nobody knows for certain.

So labor-intensive is tobacco that its growth and processing may be said to resemble horticulture more nearly than agriculture; it is practically handcrafted from the first. Until about midway into the twentieth century, American farms raising tobacco typically grew no more than four or five acres of it, given all the time and effort it commanded. For a crop that size, a seedbed of about a hundred square yards is carefully disked, plowed, harrowed, and sterilized with ashes or gas to rid the soil of insect or plant contaminants. Late in winter the bed is spread with tobacco seed so tiny that only an ounce, containing some 300,000 seeds, is needed. Covered with hay or cloth to protect them from the cold, the seedlings incubate for several months until they reach five to eight inches in height and are transplanted to the field one at a time, 6,000 to 10,000 per acre, three to four feet apart atop little ridges to allow for optimal drainage. The soil surrounding each must be kept loose and weed-free, especially in the early growing stage, and then the more intensive cultivation, with its painstaking stoop labor, begins.

The hot, moist climate of the American South, with its especially hospitable porous clay soil, is ideal for tobacco, but the farmer can only pray that the heavens will provide proper rainfall. Too much, and the tobacco leaves will end up thin and washed-out; too little rain yields a heavy, coarse, poorly flavored leaf. The success of the rest of the process is in human hands. First the plant must be "topped" at the right height, for if cut off too low, it will produce too few leaves, and if too high, there will be too many small and immature ones. Then the plant must be constantly suckered for five to six weeks to remove the small new growths between the leaves and the stalk and thus force the growth into the surviving leaves, which begin to take on a waxy sheen as they mature. Most unpleasant of all is the vigil against insatiable, leaf-loving pests, of which the hornworm, naturally camouflaged a vivid green, thick as a farmer's little finger, and several inches long, is the worst menace; they must be plucked and stomped ruthlessly. And considering that an acre of tobacco holds between 100,000 and 150,000 leaves, each oozing sap as the hot, drier midsummer weather comes on, it is one messy, endless chore.

Each leaf on the plant, moreover, may differ from every other in size, shape, color, thickness, and the amounts and distribution of its chemical constituents—e.g., the farther up the stalk, the lower the potassium content and the greater the proportion of nicotine. The commonest variety of American tobacco is harvested in stages, three or four leaves at a time from the bottom up, over a five- or six-week period beginning about mid-July in a process called "priming". The redolent, sticky, chemically active contents of the gargantuan leaves combined with the baking sun have been known not infrequently to induce nausea and dizziness in the pickers. And the most perilous part of the process remains.

Lugged by mule-drawn sleighs in the pre-tractor days, the leaves were brought to special steep-roofed, airtight curing barns, roughly sixteen to twenty feet per side and twenty-five or so feet high, where the farm women traditionally tied three of the large leaves together into "hands" and looped them over sticks that were hung on tiered wires or poles. There the leaves remained for from five to seven days while their water content, making up between 80 and 90 percent of their weight, was bled out of them at temperatures reaching as high as 140 degrees, depending upon the source of the heat. In the process, the chlorophylls were decomposed and the underlying xanthophyll and carotene emerged, and the leaves turned to shades of brown and yellow. Then the barn was thrown open to allow the leaves to reabsorb sufficient moisture—about 10 percent of their weight—to make them pliable enough to be handled, graded, and carted off to the auction warehouse without cracking or crumbling. Poor oversight of the whole operation, requiring round-the-clock supervision of the curing fires, could easily ruin a whole barnful of leaf. Overcooking impaired its taste, aroma, and color, while undercuring left it prone to ruin by mold and other agents of spoilage. The occasional wayward leaf that fell from its place and landed on the flue could burst into flame and send the whole barn up if those tending it grew lax. The entire process of growth, harvesting, and curing would consume well over 400 hours per acre before the modern era (*i.e.*, post-1950), when mechanization began to speed the transplanting, fertilizing, and hauling procedures, sprays facilitated the suckering and worming, and metal barns and containers of stacked trays to hold the leaves improved the curing. Even so, with the best of equipment and economies of scale, it takes more than 200 hours of tending to bring an acre of typical North Carolina tobacco to market.

For roughly two centuries, from the time English settlers began to grow the plant in the rich, loamy soil of tidewater Virginia in the early years of the seventeenth century in competition with the Caribbean plantations cultivated by Spain at its imperial height, the growing process was essentially unaltered. But then an important change occurred that brought with it immense consequences in the nature of tobacco use and its potential impact on the health of its users.

During the first few decades of the nineteenth century, open, smoky, and dangerous fires were increasingly abandoned as the heat source for the curing process and were replaced by a low brick flue with metal stripping on the top that ran the length of the barn floor and had an exterior opening of about a foot or eighteen inches at either end for the fuel, usually firewood. These flues had the advantage of providing a more intense, easier-to-control, and smokeless heat. The change did not greatly alter the appearance of the strong, pungent, dark leaf that flourished in the coastal regions of Virginia and had long been the preferred variety in America and England for pipe smoking, chewing tobacco, and snuff. It was a different story, however, in the inland Piedmont region of Virginia and North Carolina, where a 150-mile-wide swath was given over to tobacco-raising after the richer coastal lands had become exhausted and farmers moved west. A less heavy, more sallow leaf grew in the thin, sandy, grayish soil of the Piedmont, which was good for growing little else. In contrast to the heavy, dark leaf with high nicotine from the lowland soil, the new leaf, lighter in both weight and color, had a less harsh taste and more pleasing flavor, thanks in part to the soil's lower nitrogen content. The difference was accentuated when, in 1839, on a farm in Caswell County, North Carolina, just south of Virginia's prime inland tobacco market in Danville, charcoal was by chance introduced as the fuel for flue-curing. Not only did the method consume one-eighth as much fuel as the wood fires, but the intense heat it produced turned the thinner Piedmont leaf a brilliant golden color that delighted the eye as much as smokers' taste. The "Bright" leaf would soon become the bellwether American variety. Besides its appealing flavor and appearance, Bright tobacco had one other feature that gladdened the user: its smoke was far easier to swallow. Indeed, its very mildness, when compared to the smoke from the darker leaf, very nearly obliged the smoker to inhale it for a satisfying experience.

In determining the affinity of substances for one another at the molecular level—whether they bind or absorb or are soluble with one another, that is, or whether they repel or irritate one another—chemists gauge them on a spectrum measuring their degree of acidity or alkalinity. Acid substances may generally be thought of as more watery and astringent, like vinegar; alkaline substances as more oily or fatty in nature. A common instance of the uncongeniality of the two extremes is the eroding effect of an excess of certain gastric acids on the alkaline-rich membranes of the stomach, resulting in an ulcer. Smoke is a mixture of gases and infinitesimal droplets of several thousand compounds—4,000 or so have been identified to date—ranging in diameter from ten to forty millionths of an inch. Among these compounds is the nicotine molecule, an alkaline substance, that arrives within the body amid the smoke aerosol suspended in a solid particle of partially burned tobacco that has been given the imprecise, catchall name of "tar". For a foreign material like nicotine to gain passage through the cell membrane walls and thus be absorbed by the human system, fatty or oily substances like the alkaline lipids of the mucous membranes lining the mouth are a highly receptive medium. The darker leaf tobacco that was commonly used for pipe, cigar, and chewing tobacco as well as snuff was alkaline in nature, while in the flue-cured processing of Bright leaf, chemical changes yielded a smoke that was more acidic in nature and not so readily absorbed by the mouth. Thus, in one of nature's myriad little ironies, the nicotine in each mouthful of the stronger dark-tobacco smoke would be absorbed slowly and in modest quantity through the oral membranes and the saliva, eventually being metabolized without any remarkable effect on the internal tissues, whereas the other harsh compounds in the dark-leaf smoke, upon reaching the back of the throat, triggered a reflexive rejection in the form of cough-ing and irritation and, if swallowed, nausea or worse. By contrast, the lighter, gentler, more acidic smoke of Bright tobacco, unabsorbed by the alkaline mouth membranes, traveled readily down the throat and deep into the bron-chial tree of the respiratory system, until it eventually reached the tiny air sacs, or alveoli. Here the nicotine droplets and other compounds in the smoke passed easily through the thin membrane walls and directly into the blood system.

The impact of this distinction can be better appreciated if one understands that the absorptive surface of the lungs' intricate pathways is several hundred-fold greater than the absorptive area of the mouth. Thus, the lighter smoke of Bright tobacco, because it is far more easily admitted to the internal human system, ironically causes a far profounder reaction than the smoke from the heavier, dark leaf used in cigars, pipes, and chewing tobacco, which generally is not taken in beyond the mouth. As a result, 50 percent of the Bright leaf smoke, its acidity diluted, is retained by the lungs, 80 percent of the tars are de-posited in the respiratory tract, and 90 percent of the nicotine is passed into the blood. It is a transient but powerful hit, momentarily suffusing an entire cross section of the bloodstream.

Within seconds of each puff, the chain reaction sets in, affecting both the nervous and cardiovascular systems in ways not yet totally understood. It may be safely said that nicotine-sensitive receptors in the brain activate neurotrans-mitters that cause the release of enzymes that in turn increase the heart rate by between ten and twenty-five beats per minute, raise the blood pressure, and constrict the blood vessels. The combined effect of these and related reactions is that, for each inhaled puff and particularly the first, the smoker experiences a systemic bite or sting; the reward of these tiny "highs" is swift, complex, and mildly narcotic, as the soldiers who began rolling cigarettes from Bright to-bacco during the Civil War were pleased to discover. A craving for these inter-mittent little highs would become the basis for a cumulatively heightening addiction unless the smoker could avoid inhaling; latter-day surveys disclosed that only 5 to 10 percent of cigarette smokers believed they did not inhale.

But none of this was well understood in the mid-nineteenth century, as flue-cured Bright leaf began slowly to gain popularity. It would not be until the early twentieth century that the American blended cigarette, more than half consisting of Bright tobacco, came into its own. Meanwhile, other varieties en-joyed their heyday. Prominent among these was Burley, an adaptive hybrid of the old dark, heavy Virginia leaf, now being grown less and less in the de-pleted lowland soils. Burley did especially well in rich, if hilly, Kentucky soil and offered growers several important advantages. A somewhat smaller but bulkier leaf than the Virginia and Bright varieties, it took perhaps one-third less time to tend; instead of being harvested a few leaves at a time, each stalk was taken down whole, and instead of being fire- or flue-cured, it was left to dry in the open air for thirty or forty days. During that time, the enzymes that would have been killed by heat-curing survived in the Burley and slowly, steadily consumed the sugars in the plant and left it, when smoked, with a strong, bitter taste. Fortunately, the Burley leaf had a loose, porous cellular structure that allowed it to absorb a considerable quantity of flavorings—rum, licorice, molasses, and chocolate the most popular—that made it a favorite component of pipe and chewing tobacco. Burley also eagerly accepted humectants that kept the tobacco moist—no small advantage in the pre-motorized age, when store inventories were infrequently replenished. A second mainstay of the pre-twentieth-century tobacco market was "Oriental" or "Turkish" leaf, grown mostly in countries bordering the eastern Mediterranean. While sun-cured like Burley, it had a lower nicotine content than American tobacco but a more distinct and pungent aroma that made it attractive for blending with domestic leaf; by itself, especially in the form of "Turkish" cigarettes toward the end of the nineteenth century, it was regarded as a luxury import. Minor but continued use was made, too, of Maryland tobacco, a light-textured leaf valued for improving the evenness of the burning quality of blended products.

In sum, those who took their tobacco in pipes or cigars (the latter mostly made of the dark, highly alkaline tobacco from Caribbean plantations and Connecticut River Valley farms) or by chewing it or putting it up their noses derived gradual, low-level doses of nicotine, but none of these forms of smoking proved to be intensely addicting. The drugging dependency invited by nicotine and the effects of its suspect partners in pathology were not prominently evident until the full flowering of Bright leaf and, with it, the arrival of the readily inhaled cigarette.

II

B EFORE the white man's arrival in the New World, tobacco was grown, used, and revered there from Brazil to the St. Lawrence River. Typically its dried leaves were crumbled and chewed or smoked in pipes, while in the more tropical regions smaller leaves were wrapped within larger ones or with corn husks and consumed as an early and doubtless potent form of cigar. Each tribe or nation of the native peoples likely evolved its own uses and blends, improving the flavor of the imperfectly cured leaf with pungent herbs and such additives as sumac leaves and dogwood bark. And how better to enhance the efficacy of their prayers than to send up tobacco's aromatic vapors into the great void where the Spirit of Manitou dwelled and might be persuaded to bless the efforts of warriors and hunters and make the earth and tribal loins fruitful. No object was more sacred among the Indians of North America than the calumet, the shared pipe of peace and greeting, and no substance served so well as tobacco smoke for a magical palliative or a cloak for the medicine man's illusory arts. More profanely, it was chewed and smoked as a narcotic in an age lean on diversions beyond sex and blood sport.

Within a week of their landfall, Columbus and his crews took notice of the natives' fondness for chewing the aromatic dried leaves or drinking their smoke through a Y-shaped pipe the Indians called the *toboca* or, possibly, *to-baga,* commonly claimed by etymologists to be the origin of the name of the plant. In short order, his sailors were sharing in the local custom, and in a fore-shadowing of both the delight and danger attributable to the plant, Columbus scolded his men for sinking to the level of the savages by partaking of the smoky pastime, only to discover, as he was reported to have said, "it was not within their power to refrain from indulging in the habit."

Within a century and a quarter, for better or worse, tobacco was spread throughout the globe, eventually recognized along with coffee, chocolate, and cane sugar as one of the treasured and unanticipated gifts of the New World to the Old.

The Spanish, Portuguese, and Italian sailors who manned the early trans-atlantic voyages were eager bearers of the exotic leaf to their home ports, where its use took hold in the demimonde as a notorious heathen import, then followed the trade routes east to the Levant and on to Araby, Persia, and India. Dutch and Portuguese mariners are credited with extending the leaf's sway to China, Japan, and the East Indies, where it took root. Turkish soil was also soon found hospitable, and a regional variant won ready consumers despite the strictures of Islam against its use as a defiler of body and soul. In Western Europe, tobacco quickly gained astounding acceptance among the better classes, thanks in no small measure to its two most eminent patrons, the Frenchman Jean Nicot and the English courtier Walter Raleigh. As ambassador to Portugal in the mid-sixteenth century, Nicot learned that the court physicians prized the Indian leaf for its healing powers, and when a tobacco poultice was credited with curing the chronic ulcer of a relative of one of his aides, Nicot wrote home to Paris rhapsodizing about its curative powers and sending seed sam-ples from his own garden in Lisbon to acquaintances at the royal court, thereby assuring its prompt fame in France. Within two generations, tobacco smoke was widely accepted as an antitoxin and disinfectant, a panacea reportedly so versatile that it could fend off the plague, cure gonorrhea, and serve potently as an unguent, a laxative, a styptic, a gargle, and even as a dentifrice in the form of its ashes, said to be a superior whitener of teeth. Only a bit less persuasive was the claim for tobacco's psychic powers; its smoke was said to drive off melancholy and other foul humours and improve the memory. Little wonder Nicot's name has passed down to posterity linked to the narcotic substance unique to his beloved plant. In comparable fashion later in the sixteenth century, Raleigh became fixated with the leaf that the sea marauder Francis Drake brought home to Elizabethan England as booty from Spanish holds and so avidly encouraged its enjoyment and cultivation that he was said to have persuaded the queen herself to try a smoke. Courtiers and lesser dandies followed, regarding tobacco's alleged medicinal uses as a ready rationale, and despite the almost prohibitive cost of the leaf, its smoke was soon rising everywhere from Cheapside alehouses to the soaring interior of St. Paul's Cathedral during the liturgy.

It should have come as scant surprise, however, when a plant of such storied curative and prophylactic qualities but of no known nutritional value soon ran afoul of the authorities, both temporal and ecclesiastical. Smoking officially became "the Indian vice," a barbaric custom offensive to God, the pope, and the Koran; an invitation to debauchery; a peril to the public safety at a time when fire was a constant threat to crowded and closely built cities; and a usurper of cropland that would better have been devoted to grain or other nutrients than to tobacco, the idler's plaything. It was denounced in Europe as a form of pagan savagery and in the Levant and the Orient as a wanton and seductive visitation of Christianity. Repressive steps shortly followed. Among the least of them, King James I of England raised the import duty on tobacco brought in Spanish galleons by 4,000 percent, the papacy banned smoking in its basilicas, and the czar of all the Russias exiled users of the illicit substance to Siberia. Deeper into the seventeenth century, more rigorous measures were employed: the Mogul emperor of Hindustan ordered smokers' lips split; in China, traffickers in tobacco were executed; and in Turkey, Sultan Murad IV, greatly perturbed that Constantinople had gone up in flames and convinced that careless smoking was the cause, conducted a rudimentary sting operation on the streets of his empire—those he seduced with tobacco were made an example of by having a pipe driven through their noses, either immediately before or after their beheading.

And yet the custom thrived, like all forbidden fruit. In England, the better-heeled taverngoer had his favorite long "churchwarden" pipe or short "nose warmer" awaiting his arrival. In France, nicotine-cravers began joyfully exploring their nostrils as a suitable venue for the pleasure. In Turkey, wary minstrels covertly sang of tobacco as one of "the four cushions of the couch of pleasure," and in China, with exquisite understatement, poets referred to the plant as the "smoke-blossom". What most of all spared tobacco from the scourges of xenophobia and righteousness, though, was the discovery by rulers in all lands that the commodity, beyond suppression now, could greatly enrich their treasuries with serious taxes on its import and sale. And nowhere was this more so than in England, whose North American colonies had become one of the world's two prime suppliers.

The influence of tobacco on prerevolutionary America and particularly on its largest and wealthiest colony, Virginia, cannot be overstated. The leaf grown in the new Spanish colonies of Mexico, Cuba, and the West Indies was of a high quality and fine flavor that won it a flourishing European market in the sixteenth century before English colonists settled in the New World. It was only natural, then, that early in the seventeenth century, the colony at Jamestown should turn to tobacco as its savior. The leaf grown there by the Powhatan tribe was a weak, bitter, and otherwise inferior variety of the Spanish staple, and so John Rolfe, one of the leaders of the Jamestown settlement and surely better known to history for his second marriage, to the Powhatan princess Pocahontas, managed to acquire tobacco seed from Spain's New World colonies, probably from Trinidad, and at a stroke laid the economic base for the Virginia colony. The strong, dark leaf Rolfe had introduced was soon contending with its Spanish progenitor for the home English market and a foothold in the continental competition with Dutch and Turkish leaf as well.

Unhappy at seeing its silver siphoned off by imported Spanish leaf, the British crown encouraged its fledgling colony, with an ideal climate and soil for the plant, to grow as much tobacco as it could manage. Generous land grants were offered to gentry and yeomen willing to brave the wilds; ocean passage was available on easy terms, and London merchants gladly provided credit for supplies. Soon English farmers were prohibited from growing the leaf in the home country, punitive duties were imposed against tobacco imported from elsewhere than Virginia, and in time the American colonies were granted a monopoly on all leaf shipped to England. As the seventeenth century lengthened, every jetty and dockside in the Maryland and Virginia tidewater clattered and rumbled with half-ton hogsheads of the prized leaf being rolled aboard British ships bearing them back to a nation stricken with tobaccomania. Virginia flowered, and tobacco became the mainstay of nearly every phase of the colonists' lives: wages were paid in it, goods bartered for it, wives purchased with it—120 pounds of cured leaf was the going rate for a healthy spouse from the mother country. The only problem was the shortage of hands to tend the demanding crop, and so the African slave trade grew under Dutch transport, the dark cargo purchased mostly with the lush harvests of the leaf.

In return for Virginia's privileged status as tobacco supplier to Great Britain, the colonial crop could be shipped nowhere else and only on craft flying the British flag; the growing continental demand for Virginia leaf was gladly satisfied by London merchants who reshipped the leaf at a healthy markup. Still, colonial growers felt sufficiently compensated to expand their tobacco crop at a steady pace—and to the exclusion of any other crop beyond what was needed for their subsistence. Thus, their dependency on the exclusively British tobacco market deepened, and with it, their indebtedness to English merchants who supplied them on terms deemed ever harsher by the colonists. In time, it grew painfully clear to the American growers that they were captives of the crown and its domineering mercantile policies. Virginians were saddled with lower prices for their leaf, higher shipping charges, steeper duties, and more onerous credit arrangements than would have prevailed if the colonies had enjoyed access to the world market. The growers' reflexive response to this dilemma was to plant more tobacco, buy more slaves, ask for more credit, and hope for the best. But this single-mindedness in time resulted in a chronic excess of tobacco and an increasingly irritable colonial mentality. "Our thriving is our undoing, and our purchase of negroes, by increasing the supply of tobacco, has greatly contributed thereto," observed Virginia's Governor Thomas Culpepper late in the seventeenth century.

The tobacco boom also brought with it political patterns and social values that contrasted markedly with those prevailing in New England and other Northern colonies. The proliferating tobacco plantations and farms caused the still sparse population to be widely dispersed; few towns larger than crossroads hamlets existed; and the expansive use of slave labor helped promote aristocratic pretensions, even in the least lordly of masters. The agrarian paradise being built by the planter class was only remotely related to the democratic yearnings that manifested themselves elsewhere in the colonies. Economic grievance, not political high-mindedness, was what animated tobacco country. By the eve of the American Revolution, tobacco represented some 75 percent of the total value of goods exported from Virginia and Maryland, and among the reasons least loudly but most tellingly advanced in support of the rebellion in those bellwether colonies was the expectation that victory would allow the tobacco growers to ignore the heavy debts they had incurred with exploitive British creditors.

The long, draining war with the mother country and its chaotic aftermath produced mostly economic travail for tobacco interests. Credit vanished, currency was debased, the British market turned cool, and the Napoleonic wars and additional ongoing international tensions made the transatlantic trade increasingly problematic. Instead, the infant nation turned inward for economic development, and tobacco as an export staple receded as land and labor were increasingly given over to that new commercial star of the plant kingdom—cotton.

III

A FORM of tobacco smoking long practiced in the Spanish colonies of the New World grew in favor in Europe during the first half of the nineteenth century. Produced from the dust of the cured leaf and the sweepings of rolled cigars, the miniature smokes were wrapped with plant husks or, by the seventeenth century, crude paper and provided a cheaper and quicker pleasure than a pipe or cigar. The *cigarito* first attained popularity in Spain, with production centered in Barcelona, where dexterous workers became adept at rolling tan paper around the shredded tobacco, twisting it at the lighting end, and folding it back neatly into a smooth cylinder. But it was time-consuming, costly work, and most smokers preferred to save money by buying the makings and rolling their own.

In neighboring France, the cigarette was taken up during the Revolution by the antiroyalist masses as the tobacco product least like snuff, that elaborately boxed and ceremoniously taken powder so beloved by the monarchists. There was nothing fancy about French cigarettes, notorious there as elsewhere for being cheap and made from the leavings of other tobacco products—and further adulterated, it was rumored, by spit, urine, and dung. By the time the government began licensing their manufacture around 1840, cigarettes had been sufficiently improved to have a bourgeois appeal as well. A new, much whiter kind of wrapper, extracted from rice straw, was developed that did not stick to the lips the way earlier cigarette paper had, and a tasteless vegetable paste made the rolling quicker and easier. By mid-century, the prominent tobacco merchant Baron Joseph Huppmann had opened a factory in St. Petersburg and brought the cigarette in quantity to the Russian upper class and intelligentsia, always keen on French style and *objets*.

The cigarette was little seen in England until after the Crimean War (1854–56), when its soldiers had been heavily exposed to the short smokes, which seemed ideally suited to wartime use, by their French and Turkish allies and were even proffered them by captured Russian officers. The English veterans of Crimea took their new yen for the cigarette home, where the product had previously been degraded as suitable mainly for the poor and so weak-tasting as to invite the suspicion that those smokers who preferred it were effeminate.

Among those catering to the new fashion in smoking was a Bond Street tobacconist named Philip Morris, about whom little is known personally other than that he died at a relatively young age in 1873 and the business was carried on for a time by his widow, Margaret, and brother Leopold. In his early days Morris discreetly sold fine Havana "seegars" and Virginia pipe tobacco to the carriage trade, but when returning Crimean veterans began asking for cigarettes, he quickly accommodated. Stressing to his select clientele that he had the cleanest factory and used the best paper, the purest aromatic tobaccos, and the finest cork tipping to keep the cigarette from sticking to the lips, Philip Morris helped lend to the product a cachet it had not previously enjoyed. He called his brands Oxford and Cambridge Blues, later adding Oxford Ovals, and thus attracting as customers the young elite attending those preeminent universities and holding on to them afterward when they went off to run the empire and wrote to Bond Street to have their favorite smoke forwarded to them. But even for a merchant as successful as Morris, cigarettes remained a cottage industry. The most skillful rollers could not turn out more than 1,500 or 2,000 units in a ten- or twelve-hour day.

The pipe had been the most common way to consume tobacco as the United States began to beat back the wilderness and shape a continental nation. Virginia and locally grown leaf were abundant; and in a frontier society, pipes were made from whatever was at hand—wood, clay, stone, bone, corncob, or metal—and often worked into wondrous shapes during long winter nights. In certain patrician and mercantile circles, Americans aped the grand manner of European swells in their fondness for snuff. Rather than employing it as nostril candy in a ceaseless quest for the perfect sneeze, American snuffers preferred the moist dip, using a twig or stick to bring it to the mouth for chewing or depositing a pinch in the cheek, where it would slowly dissolve. Far more popular, if still less sanitary, was chewing tobacco. Since Columbus's day, the chew was a great favorite with sailors who would otherwise have had the wind and dread of shipboard fires to contend with in taking their tobacco pleasures. The smokeless chewing variety was widely adopted by the less exalted sector of American society that wanted to enjoy tobacco while at work in occupations unconducive to the pipe, cigar, or snuff. It was splendidly suited to the outdoor life and immune from such vagaries of nature as the raking prairie winds. At first the untreated dried leaf was sold loose in bulky bags, but then, especially with the wider cultivation of Burley tobacco, the chew was moistened with a variety of sweeteners and molded into lumps more convenient for pocket-carrying. A veritable stream of tobacco juice filled the American air throughout much of the nineteenth century, targeted at the ubiquitous cuspidor but at least as frequently darkening carpets, walls, draperies, and trousers, demonstrating to foreign visitors that they were among a slovenly people.

The cigar did not seriously awaken American smoking tastes until after the war against Mexico (1846–48), with its exposure to that strong form of tobacco preferred by Latin cultures. By the midpoint of the nineteenth century, cigars were a goodly manufacturing business in New York and Philadelphia, another 100 million of them a year were being imported from Cuba, and among those sturdy pioneers trailblazing westward, foot-long cigars called "stogies" after the Conestoga wagons in which they rode were a prized time killer. As for the cigarette, it was scarcely more than an American curio at mid-century, and while it began to show up occasionally on the streets of New York in the ensuing decade as travelers abroad brought the custom home with them, the little smokes did not begin to exert any real appeal until the Civil War.

It remains to be said that in the 369 years between Columbus's discovery of tobacco and the war, the sentiment against smoking never remotely approached the level of scientific coherence. The early assaults were couched largely in moral, xenophobic, and economic terms. Of all those semi-hysterical admonishments against smoking in its pre-cigarette era, none was more passionate, or would be more often cited by posterity, than the treatise by the Scottish-rigid British monarch James I, published in 1604. In *A Counter-Blaste to Tobacco*, King James professed high concern for the moral degeneracy of his subjects, whom he found softened by new wealth, "which makes us wallow in all sorts of idle delights and soft delicacies," the worst of them being tobacco smoke, the concoction of "these beastly Indians." If England was set on taking up the savages' ways, "[w]hy do we not as well imitate them in walking naked . . . yea, why do we not deny God and adore the Devil, as they do?" Dismissive of the medicinal claims made for tobacco on the ground that it was always praised when smokers recovered from their illnesses but always exonerated if a man died after smoking, the king reserved his fiercest rhetoric for the closing lines of his assault upon

> a custom loathsome to the eye, hateful to the nose, harmful to the brain, dangerous to the lung, and the black stinking fume thereof, nearest resembling the horribly Stygian smoke of the pit that is bottomless.

Not only would James's fuming countrymen not abjure the pastime, but by 1665 they were fiercely embracing it as a defense against the great plague that devastated London that year. It was near the end of the seventeenth century when smoking first faced the rigorous scrutiny of authentic science, as authorities at the leading school of medicine in Paris began reporting their suspicion that tobacco consumption shortened lives. Early death, though, was still so familiar a companion that the possible destructive effect of tobacco was not a pressing concern. Indeed, the first recorded clinical data on the subject was not published until 1761, when a London physician reporting ten cases of cancer, nine afflicting the nostrils and one the esophagus, among habitual snuff-takers, noted that the hard, black, malignant "polypusses" were indeed cancers "as dreadful and as fatal as any others," and warned against the overuse of snuff. Fourteen years later, another London physician, Percival Pott, observed the frequent occurrence of cancer of the scrotum in chimney sweeps and theorized that the cause was their constant immersion in soot (and no doubt a scarcity of bathing facilities). But neither snuff nor soot was smoke itself, though the former was a product of tobacco and the latter of combustion, hinting that each had properties deleterious to human tissue.

Still, the relationship of tobacco to health lay deep in the shadow of ignorance. By the end of the eighteenth century, the most respected physician in the New World and the author of a learned tract on chemistry, Benjamin Rush of Philadelphia, was warning of the effects of tobacco on the mouth, stomach, and nervous system and linking it to drunkenness—this at the same time he was prescribing profuse bleedings as the preferred treatment for almost all illnesses.

Little of truly scientific note was added as tobacco use spread in the first half of the nineteenth century, despite the scorn of polemicists like Horace Greeley, founding editor of the New York *Tribune*, who defined the cigar as "a fire at one end and a fool at the other." There began to emerge now, however, critiques of smoking that were more medical than moral in their carping. Among the shrewdest and more prescient of them was *The Beauties and Deformities of Tobacco-Using*, a slender volume issued in Boston in 1853 by a physician named L. B. Coles, who argued without a shred of documentation that tobacco was "a deadly narcotic" that stifled the brain's reasoning and perceptive powers, impaired the hearing, vision, liver, and lungs, and shortened smokers' lives by 25 percent. Coles also hypothesized that many tobacco-caused afflictions were not recognized as such because they did their fatal work gradually. The habit so weakened the internal system, he concluded, that the smoker was easy prey to many diseases. Yet the scientific consensus of the time was better represented in the pages of *The Lancet*, the leading English-language medical journal, which devoted much space in the years 1856–57 to a running debate among its readers on the possible dangers of smoking. The tenor was still nearly as much moral as medical, dwelling on the alleged connection between smoking and the increase in street crime and other forms of social pathology no less than on its unsubstantiated link to dimmed vision, loss of intellectual capacity, and "nervous paralysis". The prevailing view, however, was perhaps most succinctly stated by a former military surgeon in London who wrote in 1857 that "tobacco-smoking may be indulged in with moderation, without manifest injurious effect on the health for the time being, or on the duration of life." But he did not attempt to define "moderation" as applied to the smoking habit, nor could he foresee the revolution in the marketplace that would profoundly undermine the very notion.

I V

G IVEN their soil, climate, vast arable acreage, and slave labor to work it, Americans had become the world's heaviest per capita users of plentiful tobacco by the middle of the nineteenth century. But that common usage of the commodity hardly constituted a major domestic industry. American society was overwhelmingly rural; its typical citizen was a native-born outdoorsman, short on cash and uneager to spend what he earned on things he could grow himself or swap with a neighbor or a traveling peddler. He tended to take his tobacco Indian-style, either chewing it or smoking it in a pipe, in an age when brand-name goods hardly existed.

By far the most extensive commercial use of the leaf as a manufactured good was the chew, flavored with sweeteners for Yankee taste but left in a more natural state for Southern tongues, and sold by every town tobacconist and every rural crossroads storekeeper. To the extent that so common a product could claim a manufacturing center, Richmond was it, close enough to the source of supply and with enough access by rail and ship to serve major markets. On the eve of the Civil War, Virginia's capital city boasted more than fifty tobacco factories, astir with the chants and spirituals of their slave workers. But the heyday of the chew passed with the war, as factories were used to make military supplies or were converted into hospitals and prisons. Yet so deeply ingrained was tobacco in the agrarian society of the Confederate states that the leaf was often included among the Johnny Rebs' regular food rations. And no form of smoking was better suited to warfare, here as in the Crimea, than the cigarette. With neither time nor money for pipes or cigars, soldiers liked the quick narcotic kick of the mild, inhalable little smokes now being made from the Bright leaf of the Virginia and Carolina Piedmont. Freed of family strictures against the vaguely notorious product and prone to imitate their colleagues in wartime misery, more and more men tried the cigarette and found it pleasing. For the first time, Americans began to think of it as something other than a poor substitute for the real thing.

No one capitalized more on the virtues of flue-cured Bright than John R. Green, a farmer who set up shop granulating the leaf in the little railroad-junction village of Durham, close by Raleigh, North Carolina's capital, and accessible to the students who, on their way to the public university at Chapel Hill, sampled Green's mild mix and made it a favorite. Green's wares proved popular with the forces of both armies who encamped in the vicinity during the course of the conflict, but with the end of the fighting and an easing of the tensions of everyday life, the vogue for cigarettes passed. Recalling a bull's-head insignia embossed on the jar of his favorite mustard, manufactured in Durham, England, Green now adopted it as the trademark for the smoking tobacco he began to produce under the name of Bull Durham. It had just the right sound for a decidedly masculine product, and Green merchandised it as no other tobacco manufacturer had done. He advertised it widely, gave away gifts to frequent users and premiums to aggressive dealers, won unlikely endorsements for it from such litterateurs as Tennyson and Carlyle, and proceeded to erect signs and posters of the mighty bull, sometimes with the imposing stud's reproductive equipment tastefully obscured by a gate or fence post. At his death fifteen years later, ownership of Green's enterprise passed to his protégé, William T. Blackwell; by then the Bull Durham plant had become the largest tobacco factory in the world, employing 900.

But the manufactured cigarette was rarely seen outside of a few Northern cities. Its most common form was in roll-your-own little sacks that Bull

Durham and others produced as a sideline. Only one ready-made brand, Sweet Caporals, a blend of Virginia and imported Turkish leaf with a dash of the aromatic Louisiana perique, made by the New York City firm of F. S. Kinney and sold for far less than the imported straight Oriental brands, had anything approaching a national clientele. The depression of 1873 helped boost the penny-apiece Sweet Caps and other inexpensive regional cigarette brands and fueled the thinking of Lewis Ginter, a gifted entrepreneur who had moved to Richmond from his native New York and gone into tobacco manufacturing with the already established John F. Allen. At a time when no other Richmond firm was producing cigarettes, Allen & Ginter seized the day.

Ginter quickly discovered the virtues of both the Bright and Burley tobacco, which included, in the latter case, an absorptive quality that allowed cigarettes skillfully made from it to resemble, in taste, color, and aroma, the more expensive products of leaf imported from the Levant and Cuba. By 1875, national figures based on tax fees showed that sales of manufactured cigarettes had climbed to 42 million units from 20 million a decade earlier—still a pittance compared to other forms of tobacco use but a sign of stirring consumer interest. Previously sold in loose, bulky rolls or clumps from which it was sometimes hard to separate a single stick, Allen & Ginter brands were put inside tight paper wrappers with attractive labels that bespoke contents of quality. And to stiffen the pack, the company inserted a small, lithographed cardboard that doubled as a promotional reward for the buyer. The colorful little cards, designed in sets, depicted among other subjects "Fifty Scenes of Perilous Occupations," "Flags of All Nations," famous battles, foreign dignitaries, Indian chiefs, baseball players and boxers, actresses, and a whole bestiary of rarely seen animals. The gimmick caught on at once at a time when newspapers were rarely illustrated and books were still a luxury item. Fathers turned the cards over to their children, who saved them in miniature albums that Ginter's company offered. At the American Centennial Exposition in Philadelphia in 1876, Allen & Ginter's handsomely displayed cigarettes vied for popularity with the ice-cream soda and helped overcome the standing prejudice against the small smokes as an adulterated product that lacked the virtues of the honest if messy chew, the dignified and aromatic pipe, and the rich, manly cigar. By 1880, sales of ready-made cigarettes reached 500 million and probably twice that many were consumed in the roll-your-own form. Ginter had taken the national lead in cigarettes, pushing his Richmond Straight Cut No. 1 and Pet brands, made from the "brightest, most delicate flavored and highest cost Gold Leaf Tobacco grown in Virginia." But the larger, costlier cigar was still outselling the manufactured cigarettes by two and a half times in units and twenty to thirty times in tobacco tonnage consumed.

From 1880 to 1910, the United States underwent an extraordinary transformation. Its population nearly doubled, due in large part to the influx of the poor and degraded masses from abroad who flocked to the cities, where work was more abundant and life proceeded at a quickened pace. In this faster-moving world of electric lighting, transportation, and communication, as the midday dinner gave way to the quick lunch away from home and the horse moved over for the automobile, old ways of smoking lost favor. Chewing tobacco was no longer merely messy but socially disagreeable in more crowded urban America, and its inevitable by-product, spitting, was now identified as a spreader of tuberculosis and other contagions and thus an official health menace. The leisurely pipe all at once seemed a remnant of a slower-tempo age, and cigar fumes were newly offensive amid thronged city life. The cigarette, by contrast, could be quickly consumed and easily snuffed out on the job as well as to and from work.

This watershed period marked the beginning of the consumer age of trademarked, mass-produced, and nationally distributed products. From about 1880, Americans of all social classes began to eat, drink, chew, smoke, dress, and clean themselves and outfit their homes with factory-made goods available at moderate prices because they were identically produced in a continuous process that used plentiful low-wage labor. Flowing from this mechanized cornucopia were soups, soaps, cereals, toothpaste, safety razors, cameras, canned comestibles of all sorts, chewing gum, and the cigarette. To spur a demand for these new products based on something other than the lowest possible price, merchandisers created attractive packaging and alluring advertisements. The settling of a continental nation was bringing an unprecedented prosperity to the common man, and with it dollars for goods beyond necessities. The cigarette, though, had proven highly resistant to mass production for this beckoning marketplace.

As of 1876, the cost-per-thousand for the standard factory hand-rolled cigarette was ninety-six cents, of which all but ten cents went to pay the rollers. Allen & Ginter was employing hundreds of girls as rollers; no matter how comely and moral, they presented a chronic supervisory problem and a highly variable quality of labor. The softness of the materials that went into a cigarette greatly complicated the development of a machine efficient enough to replace human hands. The filler was often too loosely packed and the final product too irregularly shaped; the continuous roll of the paper wrap also was subject to tearing at the slightest irregularity in the applied tension. And with stray tobacco bits flying about and so many moving parts for them to lodge in, the contraption broke down regularly.

To overcome these obstacles, Allen & Ginter offered the then enormous prize money of $75,000. A teenage tinkerer named James Albert Bonsack, son of a plantation owner near Lynchburg, had been working on the problem for years, and in 1880, when he was twenty-one, finally obtained a patent. The Bonsack machine had an improved feeding mechanism, forming tube, and cutting knives that allowed it, at peak efficiency, to turn out between 200 and 212 cigarettes a minute, the equivalent of what forty to fifty workers could produce among them. The one-ton behemoth rarely reached its top-rated output, usually managing 70,000 units each ten-hour day.

Still, Bonsack's machine promised major savings in the cost of production, and Allen & Ginter ordered a model installed on its premises on an experimental basis. Contemporary reports suggest that there was more involved than its operating efficiency in the company's final rejection of the Bonsack machine. There was the prize money, of course, but along with other tobacco companies that had considered the Bonsack, Ginter's firm feared high buyer resistance to a machine-made version of a product that had traditionally been thought of as handcrafted; perhaps the taste of the machinery would be perceived as somehow clinging to the tobacco. Then, too, there was the fear that the machine would prove too efficient, leaving the company with mountains of cigarettes that exceeded the demand. And finally, perhaps Allen & Ginter reflected the managerial timidity and fear of technological advances, with their accompanying risks and dislocations (*e.g.*, the dismissal of unneeded workers), which afflicted Richmond industrialists of this period and doomed the once prosperous city to becoming an economic backwater.

What is certain is that Allen & Ginter, with the leadership of the infant cigarette business in hand and dominance over its promising future within grasp, let the Bonsack machine go. A young, ruddy giant from North Carolina, lacking Ginter's refinement but full of resolve, was waiting to snatch it away and, in so doing, create one of America's great fortunes. The not incidental cost to the nation's physical well-being would prove incalculable.

V

A WIRY, taciturn widower of forty-five, Confederate gunnery officer Washington Duke had watched Richmond burn under pounding by Union cannon before being taken prisoner in the closing weeks of the war. Freed after Appomattox, Duke made his homeward trek of 135 miles on foot, through the scarred countryside he had gone off to defend, though he was a foe of slavery and had voted for Abraham Lincoln in 1860. On reaching his 300-acre farm near Durham, he found that Sherman's marauding troops had stripped the place of crops, tools, and livestock. All that was left to him were a pair of blind mules, a small batch of cured tobacco leaf, and his three children, a daughter and two sons, who had stayed with his late wife's folks while Wash was off fighting.

His older son was just nine, the namesake of the man elected fifteenth President of the United States the year the boy was born, but even then it was plain that James Buchanan Duke, whom everyone called Buck, was a lad of uncommon size, strength, and wits. He helped haul out the leftover leaf that his father managed to find machinery to grind and press, and the two of them set out behind those bedraggled mules to peddle their home-grown chew. Some took Wash Duke's long silences for wisdom, others disagreed, but all concurred that he could do the work of two men, and with his boy Buck, who joined him in the dawn-to-dusk labor, the family eked out a subsistence living from their Bright leaf.

With the success of John Green's Bull Durham operation almost right before his eyes, Wash Duke gauged that he could make a better living by processing and selling tobacco than by growing it. He opened a little factory on Durham's Main Street and made Buck his right-hand man. Early in his teens, the boy had turned into a tall, broad-shouldered hulk, hard to miss with his red hair and pale blue eyes under a floppy straw hat, his pigeon-toed walk that approached deformity, and a bulge of tobacco perpetually in his cheek. A pugnacious streak drove him on occasion to lord it over his older sister and frail younger brother, but otherwise, Buck Duke was an astonishingly disciplined youth, dutiful, hardheaded, and resourceful—a study in applied energy. When not directing the hired help, he was repairing the machinery, labeling the burlap sacks with the Dukes' brand name—Pro Bono Publico—or off on a far-flung wagon route to deliver goods to storekeepers and gather new orders. Sent with his siblings to a Quaker academy for some formal learning, the big boy found the Latin, poetry, and much else in the curriculum lacking in any vocational relevance and after a couple of months came squawking home. A stay at a business school in Poughkeepsie, New York, better suited to his aptitudes, allowed Buck to master double-entry bookkeeping and other practical skills. Back home again, he applied his fresh tools to the Duke factory books and by sundown each day knew to the penny how their operations were faring. Wash Duke knew an unpolished gem when he saw one and made Buck, just eighteen, his full partner in the business.

The three-story, false-front Duke establishment with its little bell tower had become a Durham fixture by now, and under Buck it grew into a well-run, steadily expanding business, but always well within the shadow of the mighty Durham Bull, which was spreading the town name across America and overseas. The Duke of Durham brand pipe tobacco, successor to Pro Bono Publico, prospered in no small measure due to the Bull's reflected glory; little love was lost between the two establishments.

Buck could see, though, that he and his father were in a fight that in time they would have to lose. Then he hit upon the one area in the Bull Durham product line that the far bigger company was neglecting, and surely not by oversight—the ready-made cigarette. Capitalizing on the growing fame of its name, the Bull sold the makings for cigarettes that buyers rolled themselves, and saw no reason to forgo its profit by absorbing the painfully high cost of labor to sell them pre-rolled. But Buck also knew of the progress Allen & Ginter was making with cigarettes in Richmond, and that several New York firms were beginning to move the low-priced product in volume. Here was a new kind of smoke for a new age, and, in view of their location in the heart of the Bright belt, with its potential advantage of a cheap supply of tobacco ideally suited for cigarettes, why shouldn't the Dukes plunge vigorously into the fray? Wash was persuaded by Buck's conviction, and in 1881 Duke of Durham cigarettes debuted.

Buck threw all the company's limited resources into the effort. Customers were presented with a package that not only matched Allen & Ginter's inclusion of lithographed picture cards but notably improved on the Richmond firm's offerings by selling the Duke line in sturdy, brightly colored little cardboard boxes. This "slide-and-shell" package, which worked like a miniature bureau drawer, was more costly than their competitors' soft paper packs, but the added protection it lent the cigarettes at once distinguished the Duke brand. In Buck's mind, though, the real battleground was not the package or the premiums inside but the price.

Cigarettes were essentially a two-tiered market. At the top were the luxury imports, like the Egyptian brand, made of all Oriental leaf, which sold at fifty cents for twenty smokes, and the still tonier Huppmann Imperiales of Havana manufacture, which fetched six cents apiece. At the bottom were the cheap all-domestic brands like the Dukes', which sold for a dime for a pack of ten or, at the least, a nickel for a pack of eight of a somewhat trashy blend. The federal cigarette tax on manufacturers of $1.75 per thousand made it difficult to bring down the price and sustain any profit. But in 1883, the tax, instituted as a revenue measure midway into the Civil War, was slashed to fifty cents per thousand, and Buck Duke was prepared to pass the savings on to the customer. That same year, he caught wind of the woes Allen & Ginter was experiencing with the Bonsack machine, which had been rejected by all other leading manufacturers as well. Buck hurried to Lynchburg to have a look at the mechanical contraption, and he liked what he saw well enough to have two of the Bonsacks brought to the Duke factory floor for a trial installation—at a properly reduced cost.

Still smarting from their dashed hopes, Bonsack and his backers were determined enough now to offer the services of their very best mechanics, who worked for months with Duke and his hired hands to get the bugs out of the machines. Finally, on the last day of April 1884, the machine operated perfectly for a full ten-hour shift, manufacturing some 120,000 cigarettes. Duke now demanded his reward—a special deal for the Bonsacks: Duke would always enjoy a royalty charge at least 25 percent under what any future competitors using Bonsacks would pay. In return, he agreed to take as many of the

Bonsacks as his company could keep busy. Toward that end, Buck calculated that he could cut his retail price in half, charging a nickel for a pack of ten Duke of Durham cigarettes. Against his price of four dollars per thousand to the jobbers, Buck had to pay 87.5 cents for tobacco (3½ pounds @ 25 cents), 17.5 cents for packaging and shipping, 50 cents in taxes, and 30 cents for manufacturing (including a 24-cent royalty to Bonsack), for a total of $1.85. Even at the standard discount of 10 percent for prompt payment by jobbers, Duke could achieve nearly a 100 percent profit.

The whole strategy made sense only if the company could generate far more sales. And in the new age of branded packaged goods, price advantage alone would not be adequate incentive to assure sales, especially for goods in a nonessential category. The manufacturer had to catch customers' eyes, arouse their curiosity, and suggest a need or use where none was apparent.

Duke began by adding new entries with snappy names to his brand stable and putting them in bright packages with distinctive lettering and easily recognized images. The front of Duke's Cameo brand pack, for example, was devoted almost entirely to the name and likeness of a large cameo ring depicting an elegant, dark-curled beauty in a buoyant floral chapeau. Some Duke brands now offered buyers coupons redeemable for pleasing collectibles like miniature college pennants and Oriental rugs. To dealers Duke offered free clocks and folding chairs among other practical inducements to push his brands. And he started advertising on a scale and in places new to the trade.

Even with thousands of potential outlets for his attractive new goods, Duke knew he ought not to rely on jobbers alone to stimulate sales; in many cases they handled competing brands as well and could not be expected to pitch Duke brands to the detriment of the rest. To carry his case directly to the retail trade and promote it vigorously to the public, he engaged the services of Edward F. Small, a smooth-talking young Southerner with a decided knack for razzle-dazzle. Small started in his hometown of Atlanta, where Allen & Ginter's brands held sway, by obtaining—for a price—the endorsement of a sensuous French actress called Madame Rhea and posing her for an advertisement at a lectern piled high with packs of Duke's brands. Then Small flooded the city with samples, all including picture cards of leading ladies of the stage from a set that had been newly lithographed for the Duke line. Although local newspapermen were skeptical about Madame Rhea's use of the product, as well as her talents and virtue, dealers loaded up and the stock moved; pulchritude sold cigarettes.

Small was a veritable fount of invention. He had fresh ideas for new sets of picture cards that proved highly popular, like the "Rags to Riches" series featuring prominent businessmen who had risen from obscure origins—surefire role models for impecunious young smokers—and the still more alluring "Sporting Girls" set that revealed rather more leg than modesty then permitted.

The latter may not have qualified as pornography, but it plainly struck male smokers, who then constituted 99 percent of the cigarette market, as the next best thing. Homing in on the national craze for roller skates, Small got Duke to pay for a touring team, called the Cross Cuts (after one of the new brands), which played exhibition matches—a sort of polo on wheels—against all comers. One contest in Cincinnati drew 12,000 spectators, all properly besieged with leaflets proclaiming the qualities of Duke's cheap, mild smokes. And as he ranged west from the Great Lakes to the Rio Grande, the indefatigable Mr. Small was only too happy to have Mr. Duke underwrite the cost of life-size carved Indians and turbaned Turks who stood beside the front door as a beckoning sentinel at leading tobacconists, carrying the proprietor's name and, in small but still prominent lettering, the names of Duke's brands.

But Duke knew in his heart that he had to be his own best salesman. And so as soon as the Bonsack was operating smoothly in Durham, he brought his wares to the nation's biggest and most tumultuous bazaar. New York, with its flood of newcomers who could afford only the cheapest tobacco products if any at all, was plainly the most promising arena for Duke's huge gamble on the cigarette. Not without misgivings by his family and associates back home, Buck came north in 1884—a tall, awkward, ruddy rube of twenty-eight with a Southern accent that did not soothe the ear in this citadel of Yankee commerce. He took a two-dollar-a-week room in a boardinghouse, opened a tiny office on Chambers Street, and hit the sidewalks, buttonholing every dealer who would give him the time of day.

The competition was intense, to be sure, but no one company and no single brand had gained anything approaching dominance. Buck opened a small factory on Rivington Street with four Bonsacks and doubled as production supervisor and sales chief. He already had the cheapest and best-looking product on the market, and his premiums to buyers and retailers were a match for any, but in that pre-electronic time he could not rely on word of mouth to spread the Duke name. He enlisted top talent and paid for quality printing to make a splash as the Duke brands were pictured everywhere: in the papers and periodicals, on the billboards that blighted the cityscape, in the programs distributed to theatergoers, in handbills at ballfields and boxing matches, on posters littering every fence and wall and storefront they let him use and on many they didn't.

Duke was at his factory first thing in the day to greet his laborers and when the machines fell silent at night; in between he was in the field, opening up new accounts like drugstores and groceries that had not previously offered his cigarettes or any at all. And invariably he walked, in that gawky, pigeon-toed gait, avoiding the grandeur and expense of a hansom. "Walk when you're young," he would counsel in one of the pithier aphorisms attributed to him, "so that you can ride when you're old." To cover outlying communities and the Hudson River Valley, Duke dispatched jobbers and drummers selling strictly his brands from wagons heaped with merchandise and free clocks and folding chairs for every merchant who placed a substantial order. By the end of 1885, the company's volume had tripled from its pre-Bonsack days, and the New York operation was narrowly in the black. Soon the Duke factory moved to larger quarters on First Avenue at Thirty-eighth Street, housing fifteen Bonsack machines and a labor force of 750, with 40 in the printing department alone. "I hated to close my desk at night," Duke would later recall, and when he did lock up, the inveterate bachelor would often haunt the shops that stayed open late to ask clerks what brands were moving and smokers the reasons for their preferences.

His four principal rivals, led by the Ginter and Kinney firms, still viewed Duke as a provincial vulgarian, but they could hardly gainsay the impact he was making. Duke's growing capital needs were now being filled by the New York financial houses, only too glad to advance him thirty- and sixty-day lines of credit that were punctiliously met. With the industry leadership in the offing, Duke began displaying another trait of character besides the shrewd judgment and unstinting energy that had marked his advancement—a relentlessness that turned momentum into inevitability.

Thanks to his notably lower production costs, Duke slashed his prices further, handed out under-the-table rebates to dealers who pushed his line the hardest, and showered them with premiums from floor mops to ersatz diamond stickpins. His placards seemed to be up on every wall and building side, not infrequently obscuring those of his competitors, as he plowed back an extraordinary twenty cents of every sales dollar into advertising and promotion—a proportion that overwhelmed his rivals' resources. Now, for the first time, he was exhibiting the *modus operandi* that was to power his triumphant, brutal career: "Hit your competitors in the pocketbook," he later explained. "Hit 'em hard. Then you either buy 'em out or take 'em with you."

At about that time, Duke also disclosed a supreme self-confidence that took the form of intolerance of any subordinate who supposed himself indispensable. Flashy Edward Small, for all his sales wizardry, had taken to living higher, at Duke's expense, and talking louder about his inspired conquests and perfected art of persuasion than the dogged Duke could abide. And when Small's figures for 1888 suggested that he was doing more talking than selling, he found his service abruptly terminated. Allen & Ginter in Richmond quickly grabbed Small in a display of defiance amid growing reports that Duke was eager and ready to buy up his competitors. Indeed, the president of Kinney, makers of the popular Sweet Caporals, confided that he was "most eager to get out of the advertising madhouse" and what he called "the damned picture [card] business" that was squeezing his profit margin unmercifully. But Major Lewis Ginter, contemptuous of the upstart North Carolinian who was muscling his company out of key urban markets, put out word that his operations were not for sale, and claimed that Duke neither had nor could borrow enough to meet his price. But perhaps Duke would like to sell instead? It was a forlorn wish. From New York came the reply: a further price cut that gave retailers a full 50 percent higher margin selling Duke brands than others.

It was left to the Bonsack company's president, D. B. Strouse, apparently foreseeing higher profits as purveyors to a monopoly, to promote the notion of a peaceable consolidation among the five leading cigarette manufacturers as a means of both ending the cutthroat contest among them and shutting the door on potential future competitors. Duke would be glad to meet his rivals at any time, he wrote Strouse, "to discuss any matter for our common good, but if you mean by a consolidated cigarette company that there is to be another factory started or a trust formed, and want us to take stock in them, I am opposed to anything of the kind, as we want the full control of our business, which we could not have with a trust." Unless, of course, it was a trust he controlled. And so Buck poured it on. By 1889, he was churning out well over 2 million cigarettes a day and let it be known that he was prepared to toss the entire 10 percent profit he claimed to be making on annual sales of $4 million into advertising—on top of the $800,000 he was already spending. It was too much for the proud Ginter. No, he would not sell to Buck Duke, but in the interest of survival, he would make his pact with the devil. The heads of the five leading cigarette makers, of which W. Duke Sons & Company was by now the undisputed leader with a 40 percent share of the market, gathered at a hotel on lower Fifth Avenue the afternoon of April 23, 1889.

Throughout the course of his mastery of the tobacco business, Duke would buy or absorb some 250 companies, and in his dealings with the first four of them, he displayed the trait that would distinguish him as a takeover artist par excellence—a relative generosity to the vanquished. Thus, Duke's 30 percent slice of their freshly baked pie was no bigger than Ginter's; Kinney got 20 percent, and the other two firms 10 each. But it was Buck Duke, to be sure, who emerged from the meeting room as president of the new American Tobacco Company, as they styled their joint venture, capitalized at $25 million. No one supposed his title was in the least honorary; at thirty-three, just five years after he had gambled the family business on a balky machine no one else wanted, Buck Duke was king of the cigarette business in America.

V I

I N the same year that Duke went into partnership with his father, Richard Joshua Reynolds fled from his overbearing father and, some eighty miles due west of the Dukes' establishment, went into the tobacco business on his own.

Like Buck Duke, Dick Reynolds was a big, rawboned farm boy with little formal schooling. Where young Duke had a nearly crippling foot disfigurement, young Reynolds suffered from a lifelong stammer and what is now known as dyslexia, which left him a painfully slow reader and poor speller and often invited people to underestimate his native intelligence. Both young fellows were go-getters with the grit and resolve to match their brightness. They would go off in opposite geographical directions and choose different products to exploit at first, but it was this pair who would emerge in time as the pioneering giants of the cigarette business and their companies as its leading rivals for dominion until the last third of the twentieth century.

Reynolds, who was six years older than Duke, started with more material advantages. His family homestead in the shadow of No Business Mountain in the Blue Ridge foothills of Patrick County, Virginia, abutting the state boundary with North Carolina, was the centerpiece of an 11,000-acre spread that was farmed, on the eve of the Civil War, by perhaps as many as ninety slaves. Prime among its crops was Bright tobacco, processed by the family in a small log factory and sold as plug for a generation before Richard Reynolds was born. A handsome, powerful teenager, Dick worked the fields alongside the family's former slaves and other hands when the war was over, knew tobacco from the ground up—and just about all there was to know about turning it into flat goods by the time he was sent off for a couple of years of schooling at a small local college. He was quick enough with numbers but floundered in his other subjects due to his reading disability. Pressed into the family enterprise, Dick spent much of his time on the road, peddling chew, his speech impediment notwithstanding. And he was good at it. Pleased, his stern Methodist father sent Dick farther afield, to Baltimore, where he established relationships with jobbers that would later stand him in good stead. While there, he furthered his education, both in and beyond the classroom, acquiring enough of city ways to allow him to move with confidence through the larger world of commerce. That exposure was likely instrumental in his coming to grasp the severe limitations of his family's business. Its remoteness made transportation of goods slow and expensive and labor hard to attract, and like his older brother, who had been given a stake and allowed to cut loose, Dick Reynolds asked his father to bankroll him in his own business. Dick got half of what his brother had, plus the big licorice kettle from the old family factory, and headed due south.

He went only fifty miles, to the dusty little town of Winston, North Carolina (population 500), close by the more picturesque Moravian settlement at Salem. The sweet smell of licorice hung in the Winston air from the fifteen or so plug makers already settled there, but rather than discouraging Reynolds, the competition served his ends. There were better rail and road connections, and all the plants were a magnet for cheap black labor from the surrounding countryside. He bought a lot the size of a tennis court, put up a two-story building, painted it red, moved into the second floor, rolled up his sleeves, hired thirty pairs of dark hands to work beside his, and went into the tobacco business.

Like Buck Duke, Dick Reynolds worked as if possessed. To flavor his plug and twist, he cooked up "sauces" to his liking—blends of sugar, licorice, rum, and sweet oils—and bargained shrewdly for leaf with the fast-talking auctioneers, many of whom preached for their main vocation, and the predatory "pin-hookers," as the tobacco speculators were called. Then he assembled a network of jobbers who handled all his sales over a territory that would eventually range as far as Georgia to the south, Tennessee and Kentucky to the west, and Pennsylvania to the north, with Baltimore as the urban hub of his trade. To woo the best wholesalers, he turned out private-label brands, sometimes named for them or their loved ones. He kept wages low and the factory clean and efficient, adding the latest equipment, like a gas-burning leaf dryer, which was far more economical than climbing to the factory roof and laying out the sugar-laced leaf in the sun. What he may have been best at, though, was inventing memorable and homey names for his brands of chew, like Brown's Mule, Golden Rain, Dixie's Delight, Zeb Vance, Yellow Rose, Live Indian, Purity, City Talk—and Dick Reynolds's Best.

Within two years, he had doubled the size of the factory. By 1883, his ninth year as an entrepreneur, he had 110 hands, and the local newspaper, in recognition of his preeminence among the town's manufacturers, referred to him as "R.J.R." The next year, Dick's younger brother Will, a college man, joined the sprouting company and relieved the boss of much of his leaf-buying duties. Soon "R. J.," as he was known more familiarly around his own premises, freed himself to solidify his sales program; before long he had nearly fifty accounts in Baltimore alone. By 1886, the industry registry listed close to a hundred trademarked names in the Reynolds stable, and two of them, Maid of Athens and Schnapps, were among the trade's top sellers.

He had become a very big, vibrant fish in a small, drab pond. As if to spite his abstemious father's strictures, R. J. played as hard as he worked. The roseate glow of his cheeks bespoke his bottomless capacity for liquor, and his weekend-long poker games were famous locally. A bachelor married to his work just like Buck Duke, Reynolds lacked the former's city diversions and devoted himself, when not gambling at cards, to fast horses and pliant women. His pair of matched white steeds was rated among the finest in the state, and he liked nothing better than galloping them through Winston's dusty streets.

Yet he was regarded not as a notorious roué but as the community's fore-most industrialist, wearing a patriarchal beard by now, and notably civic-spirited at that. He took the lead in upgrading Winston from a frontier pesthole through the installation of sewers, establishment of a reliable fire department, and improvement of rail service, all of which served, of course, to enhance and safeguard his own business. In 1889, as the American Tobacco Company was being organized in New York, Richard Reynolds was erecting a six-story, block-long, electric-powered, fireproof factory, the largest plug plant in North Carolina. He was well on the way to becoming the biggest manufacturer of sweet chewing tobacco in the entire South, and it would not be long before his enterprise would whet the omnivorous appetite of Buck Duke.

2

The Earth with a Fence Around It

I N T H E same year that the American Tobacco Company began to operate under the whip hand of Buck Duke, the Congress of the United States passed its first major piece of legislation aimed at checking the unbridled exercise of corporate might. But in seeking to temper the behavior of any enterprise that attempted to restrain trade or commerce, the Sherman Antitrust Act of 1890 spoke in broad and ill-defined language even as the tentacles of gigantic, monopolistic operations were reaching out to seize a growing portion of the furiously expanding American marketplace.

The corporation had proven an invaluable tool of the industrial age because it permitted the accumulation of capital on a scale never before contemplated, easier access to credit, and limited personal liability without which the risks inherent in the entrepreneurial system would likely have been unbearable. The "trust" carried the concept one logical step further. Taking the form of one corporation owning or controlling another corporation or several of them, trusts were ideal vehicles for the creation of wealth because they facilitated supervision of geographically dispersed activity and economies of scale.

But in their very potential to improve productivity, trusts carried the seed of great mischief-making. To invite their growth in the name of economic expediency was to hope for benign limits to the exploitation of highly vulnerable markets. The peaceable amalgamation of businesses to advance their joint interests was plainly progress over the old law of the jungle, where the fight was to the death unless the vanquished accepted enslavement. What if, though, economic expediency invited alliances that created immense opportunity for plunder, as in the building of the American railroads, ventures so chancy that their operators felt entitled to extract from their dependent customers all that the traffic could bear? With flaring resentment, the people turned to the frail reed of government to check such abusive profiteering and to tame it without quashing the go-getting spirit.

Such was the genesis of the Sherman Act. Besides far-flung railroad systems, trusts or trustlike combinations had won command over petroleum, sugar refining, whiskey, meatpacking, copper, lumber, and, lately, cigarettes. And the trend was growing; the boom that followed the depression of 1893 would lead, in the year 1899 alone, to the registered formation of eighty-seven new combinations capitalized at an average of $20 million, an immense sum for the time.

If competition and combination were polarizing drives in U.S. society, Buck Duke had brilliantly exemplified the virtues of the former. Competition served to create markets, propagate goods, consume labor, and, ideally, yield profits to reward the investor and plant new growth. For Duke's rivals, however, the competition proved withering, and combination with him was their only salvation. But where competition created markets, combination was logically intended to control them. Was such control necessarily tantamount to an illicit restraint of trade or commerce within the meaning of the broad Sherman antitrust language and therefore undesirable on its face? Weren't there "good" combinations that, by curbing the excesses of competition, promoted prosperity for all participants? Buck Duke's conduct as helmsman of the cigarette business would not advance that argument.

To meld five hotly competing companies into one organization, Duke lost no time in picking the ablest employees from the collective pool and discarding the rest. No one could call that cruelty—only prudence. Similarly, American Tobacco's cigarette manufacturing was now centralized at the former Allen & Ginter factory in Richmond, closest to the source of the basic commodity and an abundant supply of labor. The Bonsack company, which had promoted the cigarette combination in order to help achieve economies of scale and a more popular and profitable product, was rewarded by having its royalty rate driven down to about one-third its former level—but where else could Bonsack turn except abroad? Duke's distributors, too, now had to accept a profit margin ceiling of 10 percent, like it or not, and monitor the prices fixed by the company for retailers to charge the public. Those jobbers who did so vigilantly were rewarded with a rebate, while those who failed in their oversight risked temporary or permanent blacklisting. Advertising and promotional costs could now be cut sharply without fear of losing customers to waiting competitors. And the cigarette combination was big enough now to avoid competitive bidding at auction for the raw leaf; tobacco farmers, having hauled their perishable crop long distances to market, were thus often at the mercy of take-it-or-leave-it bids by American Tobacco. Against his few surviving competitors Duke employed comparably grinding tactics, cutting prices selectively by brands and locations until the smaller independents died off or could be absorbed on the cheap.

All of these steps netted Duke's combination high profits—$2.5 million after the first year of its joint operation—amounting to 58 percent on tangible assets and a 27 percent profit margin on net sales, and served to feed Buck's autocratic tendencies. These were rarely exhibited demonstratively, for all his forbidding physical presence; rather, he maintained remarkable self-control and a calm manner behind those chilly blue eyes. "Don't ever ask me for a raise," he would tell his subordinates. "I know what my people are worth, and when they earn a raise, they'll get it." He rarely squandered his emotional reserves on personal confrontations and never reprimanded an offending employee in public; you were simply dispensed with if you disappointed the boss one time too many.

Despite the great and rapid success he had achieved with cigarettes, Duke calculated early in 1891 that they were not enough to sustain the enterprise he now envisioned. The little smokes were a relatively small piece of the whole tobacco business. He would use them as the lever to move into the much larger and potentially far more profitable sectors of the business, even as his social ambitions were being propelled upward. The overgrown country boy was now received with outward respect by New York's café society and financial community; further advancement required new initiatives and a clientele beyond the déclassé.

There were twice as many chewers as smokers of tobacco in America, and so Duke summoned to his office the head of the substantial Louisville firm of Pfingst, Doerhoefer & Company, purveyors of several leading brands of Burley-based chewing tobacco, including Battle Ax and Newsboy. Duke painted a rosy picture for the Kentuckian showing what would happen if he joined forces with American Tobacco. The deal, soon consummated, was marked by three features that would come to characterize so many of the transactions that followed. First, the price of nearly $2 million was paid for with only one-third cash and the balance in American Tobacco stock. Second, Doerhoefer and his colleagues were to be retained to operate their beloved business. And third, if any of the principals chose to resign from the Louisville operation or in the unlikely event that they were asked by their New York overseers to step aside, none of them would be allowed to engage in the tobacco business for at least the next ten years.

Two months later, under similar terms, Duke bought a Richmond company that was the leading maker of cheroots. Then Duke added two Baltimore companies with strong lines of plug and snuff, paying for all but 5 percent of the $5 million purchase price with American Tobacco stock and, following the pattern he had initiated upon merging his cigarette-manufacturing units, he closed down the smaller Baltimore acquisition. Now American Tobacco salesmen had a much broader line of merchandise to peddle, and fewer of them were needed. By 1894, company profits had surged to $5 million.

But as the 1890s lengthened, the cigarette business began to tail off perceptibly. Reformers and moralizers routinely referred to cigarettes as "coffin nails," distinguishing them from other forms of tobacco mainly on the ground they were all too accessible to boys and damaging to their health. By 1893, agitation had reached the point where the state legislature of Washington outlawed the sale of cigarettes, and other states were considering similar action. Plainly American Tobacco had to expand its other tobacco lines at an accelerated pace. Duke proposed a compact of leading plug makers along the lines of the cigarette combination he had forged, but when they declined the honor, he declared war on them and waged it with a ferocity that made his campaign to dominate the cigarette business look tame. Jobbers were given big rebates to push the American Tobacco line of chews, and those who did not were likely to find their cigarette orders going unfilled. The company spent lavishly on premium giveaways and staged showy promotions, but most of all, Duke employed "fighting brands" to slay his foes. Some lines had their prices cut in half or even below their manufacturing cost in order to win buyers in a war of attrition that was not merely ungentlemanly—it was downright ruthless.

Several of American Tobacco's ranking directors, Lewis Ginter among them, argued that Duke was acting rashly and squandering company capital in reaching for control of the entire tobacco universe. These rebels approached the Standard Oil multimillionaire Oliver H. Payne, by then a prominent Wall Street investor, and sought his aid to wrest control of American Tobacco. Payne had an audience with Duke, who persuaded him of the necessity of these slashing tactics that, in variant forms, Standard Oil itself had pioneered. Payne came aboard as an ally of Duke, not to check him.

With a major Wall Street player in his camp for the first time, Duke undertook still heavier cannonading in his plug war and soon was practically giving the stuff away. By 1898, his cumulative losses in the plug struggle had reached $3 million and were depressing American Tobacco profits. But the warfare eased that year as five sizable plug companies caved in to Duke, who promptly packaged them with his own properties as the new combination of Continental Tobacco. It was much easier, then, for Duke to entice the young scion of the P. Lorillard Company, probably the nation's oldest continuing tobacco business, with its big plug and snuff works across the Hudson River at Jersey City, to join up as well for $6 million, payable largely in Duke's paper. For good measure, Duke also picked up the New York outfit that made the popular Between the Acts brand of little cigars, giving him more than half that market; among the rest of American Tobacco's holdings now were 22 percent of the

U.S. plug business, 26 percent of its smoking tobacco sales, 6 percent of its snuff trade, and 85 percent of the cigarette market.

The aptly named Thomas Fortune Ryan, Virginia-born moneyman who had gained control of practically every street railway line in New York through his infinitely manipulable Metropolitan Traction Company, saw in Duke's bludgeoning ambition the chance for a killing. A far more suave operator, Ryan moved noiselessly, as was his wont, to buy up for $4 million in cash Blackwell's Durham Company, the still prospering makers of Bull Durham smoking tobacco, then married the Bull to the National Cigarette and Tobacco Company, one of the few remaining independents outside of Duke's web. Ryan named the yoked units Union Tobacco and then, as the guiding figure in a syndicate including his powerful financial allies William C. Whitney and Peter A. B. Widener, traveled to St. Louis to meet with the supremely conservative rulers of the world's largest chewing tobacco manufacturer, Liggett & Myers. Vowing his hatred of predatory trusts in general and Duke in particular, Ryan found a receptive ear among the St. Louisians, whose profits had been badly hurt by Duke's all-out price war to capture the plug market. For $200,000, Ryan came back to New York with an option to buy Liggett for $11 million; dovetailed with Union Tobacco, it would constitute a formidable rival indeed to Duke's spreading empire.

Buck saw red when Ryan spelled out his alleged intentions. If the Wall Streeter's swift thrusts into the tobacco business were a ploy, they were a good one; Ryan's lineup was a viable enterprise, and Duke dared not call the bluff. He also did not fail to see the opportunity that Ryan was inviting him to share with his syndicate. For one-third of American Tobacco's stock, Union Tobacco came into the fold; for one-third of Continental's stock, Duke got Liggett & Myers, $5 million in cash, and sway over the U.S. plug business. Ryan, Whitney, and Widener, who may have made as much as $20 million in paper profits on the deal among them, joined Duke's board of directors. He was keeping company now, beyond any doubt, with the movers and shakers of Gotham.

There were two bonuses in the Ryan encounter for Duke. Out of it he obtained the services of Percival Smith Hill, a Harvard man who had been slated to assume the presidency of the Bull Durham operations when Ryan took them over. A solid and imperturbable manager, Hill would soon prove second to nobody in his reverence for Buck Duke, who brought him to New York as his most trusted lieutenant; Hill's son, George W. (for Washington), was to become still more important to the company.

II

A MONG the detractors of Buck Duke, no one took a back seat to Richard Joshua Reynolds. From his provincial outpost at Winston, center of the Bright plug industry (if nothing else), Dick Reynolds looked north with grudging admiration for the seemingly insatiable monster Duke had nurtured into being. Yet he lamented over the creature Buck himself had become: a highfalutin Yankee big shot who had shaken the Carolina soil from his boots and embraced the gospel of Mammon and lucre-loving Republicanism.

Not that Reynolds was in the tobacco business for philanthropic reasons. But he did not stomp on people to get ahead, the way Buck Duke did, especially on the struggling farmers whose leaf prices were now being virtually dictated out of the fancy New York offices of American Tobacco. And the prickly Reynolds, proud of his own steadily growing company, did not hesitate to speak out publicly against Duke, though the latter's leaf-buying policies surely saved him considerable money as well. The difference between them was that Dick Reynolds did not care to advance on the backs of others, and if that meant playing the tortoise to Duke's hare, so be it.

As American Tobacco grabbed up the "navy" plug business, the sweet chewing tobacco made from Burley that was the staple west of the Appalachians, the R. J. Reynolds Tobacco Company persistently extended its lead in the crowded Bright plug category. There was no magic in his method, just a lot of small innovations that added up, like the Schnapps Kicking Machine, a little item of homespun humor that was the company's hottest promotional gimmick. Named for one of its top-selling brands, the gadget consisted of a metal foot attached to a pulley device with a string to activate it for use by any plug customer foolish enough to prefer a rival brand—and sorry, only one Schnapps kicker per store. Reynolds achieved a comparably nice folksiness in the advertising he now began to place in the trade journals. One of the first ads, quietly extolling the goodness of his products, was headlined "How the Bottom Rail gets on Top and all be Benefited by the Shuffle," and cast the proprietors as country fellas purveying their honest goods. But not so honest as to cavil at describing Reynolds products as consisting of "Naturally Sweet Tobaccos" when every hundred pounds of chew had mixed into it ten pounds of licorice root paste and five pounds of sugar.

By now he was no longer dependent on jobbers to do his selling. A cadre of young Reynolds salesmen roamed throughout the Southeast, at $5.75 a week, ever exhorted by the boss's letters from Winston to push the new brands, stick to the listed prices, and send back daily—or weekly, at the very least—sales reports so that production at the factory might be better geared to the realities of the marketplace. Between 1892 and 1898, Reynolds's output grew fourfold, reaching 6 million pounds for the latter year. Even so, he was dwarfed by the 84 million pounds of plug manufactured that year by Duke's new Continental Tobacco combine. But Reynolds's operations were all his, and though he was constantly strapped for capital to build the business, he would not trade control of it for outsiders' cash input. But the threat from Duke was growing. By the early part of 1899, he had taken control of both Liggett and Lorillard, the national leaders in the navy plug trade, and when Duke picked up the Hanes plug works in Winston, the second largest in town, Dick Reynolds knew his days of independence were numbered if the New Yorker tried to bring him to heel with his usual price-slashing terrorism.

Accounts of the Duke-Reynolds negotiations vary, but it can be safely ventured that Reynolds went to Duke's office at 111 Fifth Avenue not hat in hand but in order to ask if the tycoon was interested in investing personally in the best plug business in the South. He did not want to surrender his company to the American Tobacco leviathan but wouldn't mind having Buck buy in if the alternative was likely to be a protracted pissing contest. No, said Duke, he was not interested in a personal stake, but his company might buy two-thirds of Reynolds's business if the latter would take a fair price for it and agree to continue running it. Duke knew that Reynolds ran a tight ship and sold a lot of chew of the type Continental Tobacco was missing from its lineup. More resigned than resentful, Reynolds apparently stated his reluctance to deal on bended knee with any master, and Duke must have assured him that it was Reynolds's knowledge and drive he was willing to invest in, not a lot of machines. The price was set at $3 million, a slight premium for two-thirds of a business with a book value of about $4 million, and the deal was done.

Reynolds was hardly grateful, though he cannot be said to have sold under duress, and felt it essential to tell the world that the transaction was not what it seemed. Soon afterward, he told his friend Josephus Daniels, North Carolina's leading newspaper editor and a populist Democrat who had railed in print against Duke's autocratic ways, "Sometimes you have to join hands with a fellow to keep him from ruining you and to get the under hold yourself. . . . I don't intend to be swallowed. Buck Duke will find out he has met his equal. . . . I am fighting him now from the inside." Such public posturing by the defiant underdog skirted the truth—by a goodly margin—but it suited Reynolds, who knew full well the growing hatred that Duke's tobacco trust had engendered among farmers, jobbers, shopkeepers, and certain segments of the consuming masses. He was now skillfully playing the fox to the wolfish Duke. He took Duke's capital, raised his own salary to $10,000 a year from one-quarter of that, paid off his debts, built a new processing plant, and set out to dominate the Bright plug business in North Carolina and Virginia in a miniaturized replication of Duke's stratagems.

In short order, Reynolds Tobacco absorbed some fifteen smaller competitors and became the largest employer in his state. And the devil he had leagued with did his best to keep distance between them, not setting foot in Reynolds's office until four years after their deal was sealed. But Duke's auditors were regular visitors in Winston, and from time to time Reynolds would appear at 111 Fifth Avenue for business discussions. Duke had little reason to disabuse the world regarding Reynolds's noisy protestations that he was an untethered proprietor; after all, the Winston brawler was ringing up profits for him, and Buck now controlled two-thirds of the plug trade.

I I I

N OT content with domination of the cigarette and chewing tobacco business, Duke devoted the opening years of the twentieth century to rounding out his tobacco trust. He was set upon both horizontal and vertical integration of the industry; his targets for takeover included the snuff business, cigars, and stogies; the sectors of the tinfoil, wooden-box, and cotton-sacking industries devoted to the packaging of tobacco goods; the licorice paste business, dealing in the chief flavoring ingredient for many forms of tobacco; and the tobacco retailing trade. Only cigars eluded his throttling grasp.

For one thing, the cigar business was enjoying boom times while cigarettes were lagging. By the late 'Nineties, each was selling about 4.5 billion units; but while cigarettes slipped to 3.5 billion annually during the first few years of the new century, cigar sales had risen to 6 billion by 1901 and added another billion in the next three years, at which point they represented 60 percent of the total value of all manufactured tobacco products. Yet the very nature of the product did not lend itself to monopolization. Cigars came in a wondrously varied array of sizes, forms, and strengths, and their bunching, shaping, binding, wrapping, and boxing—particularly for the more luxurious styles—had to be done by hand. Because economies of scale were hard to realize and profit margins per unit were attractive, many small cigar factories were able to thrive by catering to a regional clientele. Duke sank tens of millions into cigars, buying up major producers in Florida and Cuba, but never controlled more than one-sixth of the total U.S. business.

Why the cigar and cigarette businesses had gone in opposite directions was not a mystery. The great burst of prosperity that showered the country promoted sales of the cigar, costliest of tobacco products and symbol of financial well-being. At the other end of the economic spectrum, the plug war, for which Duke was responsible, had made chewing tobacco a better buy than cigarettes. A heavy contributor as well to the cigarette slump was the social stigma that had become attached to it as to no other tobacco product.

The assault on smoking in antebellum America did not differentiate as to the delivery system; the leaf was simply an unmitigated evil. Among the most ardent of the antitobacco reformers was the Reverend George Trask, whose *Thoughts and Stories for American Lads* of 1859 was subtitled "Uncle Toby's Anti-Tobacco Advice to His Nephew Billy Bruce" and counseled that smoking did away with some 20,000 souls a year, a statistic unsupported by even remotely credible data. A more temperate view was expressed by Ralph Waldo Emerson, who, without pretense of scientific specificity, took note of the debate over whether smoking was medically harmful, but concluded only that "the habit once established gives rise to more or less craving for this form of indulgence." He was not dwelling, though, on the lure of the cigarette, which was hardly more than a novelty item until the mid-1870s. Nor were the few scientists who reported serious data in Europe, where the cigarette was better established. A French physician, for example, studied sixty-eight patients with cancer of the mouth and lips and noted in 1859 that all the victims were tobacco users and all but two of them preferred a short-stem clay pipe, suggesting that the heat from it, not the specific ingredients of the bowl, was causative. In England, Langley and Dickinson had by 1889 published their landmark studies on the effects of nicotine on the ganglia and hypothesized that there were receptors and transmitters on these bunched nerve cells that responded functionally to stimulation by specific chemicals. Their concern, though, was with the properties of nicotine without regard to the form of smoking or chewing by which it was absorbed. Near the end of the century, a German investigator found a high proportion of lung cancer among the tobacco-manufacturing workers of Leipzig, but when animal studies failed to replicate the phenomenon, little more was said of the cause-and-effect hypothesis.

Agitation against the cigarette per se began in earnest with the mass production of the cheap little smokes and was surely abetted by cigar makers and plug manufacturers who feared the competition and spared no hyperbole in painting the product as debased and degrading. The heart of the stated moral argument against cigarettes was that their low price and mild taste made them uniquely tempting to boys, whose use of them arrested their mental and physical development and led inexorably to a life of depravity. The outcry was most righteously raised by an indefatigable spinster schoolteacher from Illinois, Lucy Gaston, whose parents had been active in both the abolitionist and temperance movements and whose own strident rectitude and physical ungainliness—she bore a beardless resemblance to Abraham Lincoln—made her an easy butt of ridicule. But she was a formidable crusader.

Gaston's fervent opposition to the cigarette was empirically based, she said: her worst students had invariably been the boys who stole off for a clandestine smoke and then fell prey to the habit. She concluded that the most damaging ingredient in cigarettes was not nicotine but a compound called furfural, which was formed in the combustion process from glycerine, long used as a moistening agent in tobacco products. The wasting effects of furfural led to an affliction Miss Gaston termed "cigarette face," with its telltale dissipation evident to any trained observer. A still greater cause for alarm was the widespread testimonial evidence she avidly collected of immoral and heinously criminal behavior by cigarette users, from little fiends to adult murderers. There was, of course, nothing approaching a careful study of any sizable population sample that remotely suggested an objective statistical basis for this stated proneness to depravity. But she ladled out this stew of pseudo-science and evangelism at church and school meetings across the land, and soon her legions grew. They began besieging city halls and state legislatures, the National Anti-Cigarette League was established with state affiliates, and Lucy published a monthly broadside called *The Boy*, urging young fellows who suffered cigarette face and related afflictions to use a mouthwash with a weak solution of silver nitrate after every meal for three days running, eat a bland diet, and, least welcome of all, take plenty of warm baths.

In 1898, Congress pushed up taxes on the sinful cigarette 200 percent as a source of badly needed revenue to pay for the Spanish-American War; the effect was to raise the cost of a ten-for-a-nickel pack of cigarettes by 20 percent—a considerable disincentive to the poorest buyers. By the end of the century, Iowa, Tennessee, and North Dakota had outlawed the sale of cigarettes in response to lobbying by the Gastonites and their allies, and by 1901 a dozen more states were weighing a ban on the sale of cigarettes, already in serious decline.

Before 1900, then, the pillorying of the cigarette was almost entirely lacking a rational basis. But in the opening years of the twentieth century, advances in chemical analysis brought the earliest glimmers of scientific insight into the peculiarities of cigarette smoking. *Harper's Weekly*, for example, could report in a May 1906 issue that due to imperfect combustion, the "little furnace" each smoker carried in his mouth produced smoke that on laboratory analysis revealed a measurable amount of oxide of carbon and 2 percent nicotine and that cigarette filters made from cotton or wool and impregnated with salts of iron succeeded in retaining "the greater part of the toxic qualities of tobacco as freed by combustion." This finding seemed to imply that it was the burning process itself rather than the form of the tobacco that might cause problems. A clearer understanding was offered by *Education* magazine in early 1909 in an article on boys and smoking. The cigarette was a much more insidious smoke than the cigar, it contended, even though it was smaller and milder, because these two advantages were "more than offset by the early age at which [cigarettes] are used and the practice of inhaling the smoke." Cigarette smoke entered the mouth with "less purification and filtration than from either a pipe or a cigar"—an effect often compounded by the great numbers in which they were consumed. Still more telling was the quoted comment of a professor from the New York School of Clinical Medicine, noting that precisely because cigarettes were taken in such small doses, "no form of tobacco is so cumulative in its action. . . . The absorption is more rapid and the resistance by nature is less active. The cigarette smoker is slowly and surely poisoning himself, and is largely unconscious of it." By mid-1912, *Harper's* was telling its readers that pipe smoke was less dangerous than cigarette smoke because the former was not inhaled and reporting methods then under study to modify the suspected hazards of cigarette smoking, including filters made from porous cellulose and steeping tobacco leaves in water for several hours to dilute their nicotine content. Continuing concern was voiced in many quarters over the effects of burned cigarette paper and traces of arsenic and other compounds found in smoke that in sufficient quantity were undeniably deadly.

Still, all this amounted to little more than guesswork, essentially devoid of knowledge of specific organic interactions. Yet an intuitive consensus had emerged that filling the lungs repeatedly with smoke from any source was not a practice likely to improve bodily functions. The pioneer botanical geneticist Luther Burbank captured the growing distress among serious scientists of the day, remarking that cigarettes were "nothing more or less than a slow but sure form of lingering suicide. . . . Would you place sand in a watch? Would you smudge a house full of beautiful pictures?"

The vested interests of the American Tobacco trust were not powerless against this mounting chorus of concern. Duke fielded a small army of lawyers, lobbyists, and other persuaders who appealed to the hearts, minds, and pocketbooks of legislators being asked everywhere to crack down on cigarettes. By century's end, most states had laws on the books proscribing the sale of cigarettes to minors, but so long as they remained more honored in the breach than the practice, Duke's people were not greatly distressed. Total prohibition of the product was a much graver matter, and the industry's operatives largely succeeded in preventing the passage of such measures in the populous Eastern states and the heavy-smoking South. To improve the dwindling profit margin of cigarette sales, industry agents reached a forceful arm toward the Senate Finance Committee, which, in secret session, rolled back the wartime excise tax on the short smokes. The prevailing level of political ethics may be inferred from the fact that three members of the key Senate committee owned tobacco stock, including its chairman, Nelson W. Aldrich of Rhode Island, who held more than a million dollars' worth. When the tax cut became law, Duke pocketed the savings, thus bringing a nice extra 2 to 3 percent of his gross to the bottom line.

Senator Aldrich and other federal lawmakers happy to do Buck Duke's bidding were very much around four years later when Congress passed the epochal Pure Food and Drug Act and a companion law to monitor meatpack-

ing practices. As the culmination of a twenty-year reform drive to curb manufacturers who believed that having enough money was a license to operate beyond the public's scrutiny, no matter what their abuses, these laws were
championed by President Theodore Roosevelt and won wide public support.
For too long, milk had been watered, meat adulterated by filth, flour "extended" by chalk, and artificial flavorings, colorings, and preservatives added
to food products untested for their safety. No ingested products were subjected
to heavier processing, more additives, or as many known or suspected toxins
as tobacco products, but when the long and acrimonious debate over the Food
and Drug law came to an end, tobacco was egregiously excluded from regulation. The industry would argue forever after that tobacco was neither a food
nor a drug and thus properly exempted; others have said the exemption was the
result of pure economic and political might. The ingredients and processing of
tobacco products in the United States would remain beyond serious government oversight for the rest of the twentieth century.

I V

As if to greet the bright new century by setting his vast, somewhat ram-
shackle holdings in good order, Buck Duke fused his two principal units,
American and Continental, into a single monolithic holding company, Consolidated Tobacco. Its sales were running at an annual rate of $125 million, and
its workforce numbered 100,000. He was well on the way to dominating
almost the entire U.S. tobacco business. As befit his new rank as a major industrial baron, Duke lived in a Fifth Avenue mansion and had begun the
process of converting a 300-acre farm he had bought along the Raritan River in
New Jersey's Somerset County into an Elysian showplace. Still, he needed
new worlds to conquer—or, more precisely, the Old World.

The Consolidated colossus shipped a billion cigarettes a year to sales offices
in Canada, Australia, China, and Japan—next to nothing compared to what
Duke had achieved in America. The chief problem was that most foreigners
preferred dark Oriental leaf or some domestic variant thereof. The notable exception was Britain and its empire, which at that time happened to occupy a
major portion of the earth's landmass. Cigarettes made from barely sweetened
Bright leaf imported from America were much in vogue in England. John
Player & Sons, operating out of Nottingham, had introduced its cheap Gold
Leaf Navy Cuts in the mid-'Eighties, and the larger firm of W. D. & H. O.
Wills, out of Bristol, had soon followed with its popular Wild Woodbine. Here
was an immense market, if one counted the empire as a whole, where a little
American ballyhoo could go a long way.

The problem, of course, was the historically high British tariff walls meant

to repel predators precisely like Duke, even as they had driven off Spanish tobacco products three centuries earlier. Exporting finished American goods to
Britain would thus be prohibitively expensive. But Buck was a much better
merchant than the Spaniards, had the grit and wherewithal to stage a far more
effective invasion than their armada had managed, and he even spoke a semblance of the same language as the British. Within a fortnight of their landing,
a pair of Duke's top lieutenants had bought up for $5.3 million the sizable to-
bacco operations of Ogden Ltd. of Liverpool, whose Taps brand was a serious
competitor of Woodbine and Navy Cut. The whole British tobacco industry
went into an overnight frenzy. The American tobacco king, whose bullyboy
shenanigans were well known to them, seemed the very embodiment of the
brawling young nation across the Atlantic which by now had turned into the
industrial prodigy of the world. The prospect was even more frightening when
word emanated from Ogden's that the Duke from Durham intended to reinvest
every ha'penny he reaped in England, slash prices, and flood the island with
cheap smokes until the established native firms sued for peace on terms that
exalted him.

The full measure of Duke's cheek became manifest soon after the chiefs of
the thirteen ranking tobacco companies in Britain gathered for six days of intensive soul-searching in Birmingham, pledged to one another that none would
sell to the marauding buccaneer, and under the leadership of seventy-one-year-
old William Wills agreed to pool their fortunes in a corporate confederacy. But
when they sought to register their compact under the name of the British Tobacco Company, they discovered that Duke's people had already claimed it.
Instead, they settled on the Imperial Tobacco Company of Great Britain and
Ireland, Ltd., chartered at the close of 1901 and at once among the nation's
largest enterprises. They promptly made a show of running up the flag by offering a bonus to every retail shop that agreed not to stock any brands made by
American Tobacco or its British affiliates.

Duke, a master at this sort of game, managed to make Imperial—or "Imps,"
as The City crowd took to calling the tobacco amalgam—look unsporting by
counteroffering to distribute any profits his Ogden's unit ran up over the next
four years among all the dealers that handled its brands, with no requirement to
boycott Imperial brands in the bargain. Such boldness astonished the sedate
British tobacco trade, soon showered with gifts and souvenirs by the interlopers, who also unleashed an unprecedented flurry of advertising and price cuts.
This courtship of the British cigarette market would only grow more ardent,
the rough-hewn Duke let it be known.

This goading threat did not sweeten the considerable West Country charm
of Sir William Wills. The Imps head quickly maneuvered to take over the
United Kingdom's leading tobacco retail chain, shutting out Ogden's product

line, and countered Duke's efforts to corner the market in Bright leaf, mainstay of the top British brands. When the Wills family put out a peace feeler, Duke turned standoffish, claiming he was occupied just then with the landscaping of his New Jersey Shangri-la. But when Imps signaled that it would be a lively bidder for any worthy tobacco business in the States, Buck understood he was facing a formidable adversary and that an armistice was the only prudent alternative to a financial bloodbath for all.

The agreement as worked out at Wills's home off Hyde Park in effect created the first global trust. Duke sold Ogden's to Imperial for a 14 percent stock interest in the British combine; Imps and American Tobacco agreed not to conduct business in each other's home terrain and indeed swapped exclusive trading rights to each other's brand names in their domestic markets. With regard to the rest of the world, the two giants joined to form the British-American Tobacco Company (BAT) to sell the Imperial and American brands globally. But Duke, as was his wont, got the lion's share: two-thirds of the BAT stock and chairmanship of the board.

In short order, British imperial outposts were being surfeited with BAT cigarette brands, and a big new plant was rising in Shanghai to bring cheap smokes to the Asian masses.

V

THE larger he got, the less charitable Buck Duke became. It was not enough, for example, to buy three-quarters of the window display space from the Bewlay chain of tobacco shops; Duke wanted outlets of his own that were unquestionably loyal to his brands and perpetually pushing them and no one else's. Toward that end, he engaged the services of the Whelan brothers, whose small chain of United Cigar Stores headquartered in Syracuse, New York, was a welcome departure from the dingy old shops, haphazardly stocked and often inconveniently located, that typified much of the retail tobacco trade.

Correctly anticipating that the rest of the retail business would not embrace news of the trust's entry into the field, the United Cigar deal was consummated secretly. But word of it could not be contained, and dealers were alternately furious and tremulous; mutterings about leagued boycotting of Duke's brands were detected by the trust managers, who elected to ride out the storm or, in some cases, try to lie their way out. To allay alarm among Boston retailers, for example, Percival Hill, by now Duke's ranking henchman, wrote toward the end of 1902 to the owners of Estabrook & Eaton, the city's leading tobacco wholesaler and retailer, that American Tobacco "would be very much pleased if your firm were to become even more influential than it is at present, in a retail way, as a protection against this new company in Boston. . . . Of course all rumors to the effect that our company is in back of the United Cigar Stores Co. are entirely without foundation." Six months later, First Vice President Hill was writing to George J. Whelan, president of United Cigar, of his displeasure regarding "the disposition on the part of some of your employees at certain of your stores to further the sale of goods competing with similar goods of our manufacture." Hill reminded Whelan of the latter's pledge that "you would always further, as far as you possibly could, the sale of our products; in fact, we have stated to you that unless this was done we would consider it in our interest to hamper your enterprise in every way we could." Lest Whelan remain in doubt as to how closely the trust was policing their agreement, Hill then cited the place, date, and precise nature of the infractions that prompted the menacing protest, *e.g.*, at a store on New York's Sixth Avenue a customer requesting a ten-cent packet of pipe tobacco was given Mastiff, a rival brand.

To assure United's spread and success, American Tobacco operatives worked to drive competing shops out of business. That many of these were very modest establishments run by pensioners, invalids, or aging war veterans was of small concern at 111 Fifth Avenue. Whatever was necessary to drive them from the vicinity of the newly arrived United Cigar emporium was done, whether that meant simple price-cutting or dispensing free merchandise to the clientele or pressuring their landlords to increase their rents or, as a last resort, buying up the property and pushing the rival proprietor off the premises. Ruthlessness had grown into brutality. And arrogance had become so routine that Percy Hill did not hesitate to write to one of the trust's largest independent retail chain customers, Acker, Merrall & Condit, objecting to a delivery to its prominent Forty-second Street outlet of rival Silko cigarettes, remarking, "As this is a brand for which there cannot possibly be any demand, I cannot understand why in the world they should be purchased."

It was a short step from deception and oppression to outright skullduggery. A series of interoffice letters surviving from 1903 disclose a system of underhanded activities involving aliases, spies at rival companies, and fake "independent" outfits whose true purpose was to damage the operations of the trust's remaining competitors. That this villainy was clandestine by design is shown by a letter from mastermind Hill to a San Francisco agent regarding a formerly hostile independent now being harnessed as a front for the trust. Hill urged that this development be kept "a very confidential proposition" since the whole point of it was that there not be "any suspicion that we are connected with it in any way." To discomfit the independent People's Tobacco Company in New Orleans, Hill set up Craft Tobacco, whose puppet proprietor eagerly reported his plans not only to try to hire away from "the People's their principal [work] force" but also to "endeavor to cause a strike within their factory."

When inside sources told Hill that the Ware-Kramer Company, one of the few surviving sizable independents, had just shipped 5 million cigarettes to China, Hill was alarmed in view of the ambitious plans in the Orient for newly formed British-American Tobacco. He wrote at once to the head of Wells-Whitehead Tobacco in Wilson, North Carolina, the trust front nearest to the Ware-Kramer operation, asking to be advised from what port the rival cigarettes were shipped, where they were due to be landed in China, and either the brand name or the markings that the enemy cargo containers bore; a plot to shanghai the goods was readily inferable.

Eventually Duke's high command grew so determined to crush all remnants of competition that any substantial jobber who was willing to discontinue handling competitors' merchandise would receive a 6 percent discount on top of all other existing inducements. When this freeze-out arrangement was prevented by the courts, the trust simply began making payments for "special attention" to its products, the nature of which it did not have to spell out, and before long more than 250 distributors across the country had signed up for the program.

The trust's iron hand finally met firm resistance from its most crucial suppliers: the tobacco farmers. Dominant in all but the cigar trade, the trust did not have to bid at all at leaf auctions; it dictated prices, with disastrous effects on farmers who, for too long, tried to compensate with more abundant harvests. Prices eventually hit rock bottom, and farmers were making less than thirty cents a day. Desperate, they united, as the Grangers had out west a generation earlier to fight freight rates set by the railroads. The tobacco farmers formed cooperatives and "pools" to process and store their leaf until the trust was willing to pay a marginally humane price for it. In the Bright belt of North Carolina and Virginia, such efforts were stymied with pathetic ease by the trust's buyers, who had only to offer a modestly higher price to a few farmers all too willing to break ranks; the cooperatives' boycott soon became an exercise in futility. But the Burley growers of Kentucky and Tennessee were a more rugged breed. In the Black Patch region, where the dark leaf grew in greatest profusion, the cooperatives were animated by defiant pride; those who declined to sign up and instead trafficked with the hated trust soon found themselves spat upon, shot at, beaten, and the targets of night riders who thought their grievances justified terror toward any who would not join with them. Storage barns went up in flames, and the trust's facilities suffered the farmers' wrath as well. It was close to all-out war.

When called on to defend his company's merciless treatment of the tobacco farmers, Buck Duke labeled the fiercely resistant growers "socialist agitators" who were not, after all, indentured servants, and if they did not like the prices they were offered, they could either learn to plant less, thereby benefiting from the law of supply and demand, or use their land for other crops. But eventually he edged his offering price up to eight or so cents a pound—about half a living wage.

VI

THEODORE ROOSEVELT was a patrician, a puritan without being a prude, and an ardent patriot with a stern sense of duty. He had an instinctive hatred of unfair, undercover, and otherwise unscrupulous dealings. Here was an honorable man who devoted most of his life to unselfish public service. None of this could have been—or was—said of his fellow New York Republican James B. Duke, no admirer of the twenty-sixth President. In truth, Duke was among those party plutocrats who worked to deny Roosevelt the Republican renomination to his high office in 1904, the year that may be said to have launched his reputation as The Trustbuster.

Teddy Roosevelt's beliefs about the evils of economic combination were far more nuanced, though, than history's facile labeling would suggest. Indeed, his antitrust philosophy was something of a rationalized muddle, mirrored in the Supreme Court's inconstant readings of the 1890 Sherman Act outlawing "unreasonable restraints" of trade or commerce. For Roosevelt, the size and power of corporations or any combination thereof were secondary to whether they served public as well as private ends. The monstrousness of a trust resided not in its scale or musculature but in exploitive self-aggrandizement that failed to contribute to the material quality of American life overall and was indifferent to the pernicious consequences of its acts on society. That is, there were "good" and "bad" corporations; to distinguish required careful weighing.

On succeeding McKinley, beloved by big business for a worshipful laissez-faire permissiveness, Roosevelt acted on his conviction that the social utility of the trusts was best determined in Washington by honest public officials and not left to the mercy of Wall Street. His key tool was the new Bureau of Corporations, set up in the Department of Commerce and Labor to assist contemplated Justice Department actions against restraint of trade. Seven such antitrust actions were initiated in Roosevelt's first term, and their first fruits were the 1904 Supreme Court ruling to dissolve the Northern Securities Company, the vast iron web of railroads including the Northern Pacific and Great Northern roads carpentered into a single holding company. The "reasonableness" of the enterprise was not much debated, only its deleterious impact on the public. Once re-elected, Roosevelt instituted thirty-seven new antitrust actions directed at, among others, Standard Oil, du Pont, Union Pacific, and the American Tobacco Company.

In the wake of the Northern Securities dismemberment, Buck Duke had moved to make his goliathan creation less of a sitting target for Roosevelt's trustbusters. The labyrinthine structure of Consolidated Tobacco, as his two principal divisions had been called since their fusion in 1901, was somewhat simplified, making less devious the control exercised by Duke and five Wall Street associates and spreading the rewards of the enterprise in a fashion more equitable to the minority stockholders, many from units long since bought out by the trust; the whole apparatus was renamed American Tobacco. But such a reshuffling of the deck did not alter the commanding hand Buck Duke held. The tobacco trust's profits and dominance only grew. In the span between 1890 and 1908, American Tobacco netted 33 percent yearly overall on its tangible assets, profit margins on the sale of cigarettes averaged 40 percent, and an investment of $1,000 at the beginning of that eighteen-year period had produced a total return—*i.e.*, enhancement plus dividends received—of $36,000 by the end of it.

The Justice Department action filed against American Tobacco in mid-1907 named twenty-nine individuals, sixty-five American corporations, and two British companies. The government's goal was not "punishment of immorality, but prevention of mischief consequent upon unification of control and destruction of competition." Duke's defense lawyers were far from apologetic. American Tobacco, they insisted, was innocent of antitrust activity, because it had neither cornered nor tried to corner the industry's raw material supply, had not enjoyed rebates or other preferences in transportation, had not had exclusive use of manufacturing machinery (especially since the Bonsack patent had been vacated in 1895), and had not excluded others from the avenues of distribution. Nor was there anything intrinsically wrong or illegal about underselling competitors or pricing goods below cost to drive out weaker rivals or secret agreements or partnerships or arranging for exclusive distributorships or buying out competitors and pledging them not to reenter the fray. All these were characterized as "ordinary methods of competition" sanctioned under common law. Duke himself, testifying in federal court without notes or a regiment of attorneys attending him, was by turns refreshingly blunt and flagrantly artful. Every deal he ever made, he said, was intended not to destroy competition but only to "round out" his own company and to "get our fair share of the trade" or just to flat-out "make some money". His audacity and defiance converged as he concluded, "We happen to have more of the brands that please the people and consequently we sell more tobacco."

Of such guff, Duke's most outspoken press critic, Josephus Daniels, wrote in the Raleigh *News & Observer* that the desires of Duke's company were modest, after all: "All it wants is the earth with a barbed wire fence around it. The Tobacco Trust is a hog, and wants all the swill." The federal trial court was less troubled by its greed than by its methods and found American Tobacco in violation of the law, but the final judgment was to come from the

Supreme Court in 1911. Meanwhile, the question remained: By Teddy Roosevelt's standard, was American Tobacco a "bad" trust? Why pillory Buck Duke for having proven himself a master manager of men, money, machinery, and markets? His company, monopolistic or not, was not charging the public outrageous prices for its products, which were not, bear in mind, among the necessities of life. Should he have been indicted as a malefactor of wealth by a meanness of antitobacco spirit?

V I I

B UCK DUKE'S legal woes were Dick Reynolds's manna.
As the new health laws began to catch up with public spitting, sales of chewing tobacco declined, and smoking tobacco, which had accounted for about 60 percent as much per capita use of the leaf as plug at the turn of the century, surpassed it eight years later. Aware of the trend, R. J. Reynolds Tobacco pushed up its pipe tobacco sales tenfold in the first half-dozen years of the new century, but it was still a minor contender against such nationally known brands as Bull Durham and Duke's Mixture. Reynolds needed a big winner and experimented with several new brands. One of them changed the entire course of Reynolds's business.

The new product differed from other Reynolds merchandise in two notable ways. First, the boss finally put aside his regional chauvinism, in the form of exclusive use of Bright leaf in the company's products, and tried a blend of Burley, with its greater tolerance for flavorful additives. To sterilize the Burley and cut its rougher smoking qualities, they bathed the leaf in a licorice infusion and applied for a patent for the process on the claim that it produced a less irritating smoke. No data or authority was provided to support the claim, and of course calibrating the gentleness of taste is a highly subjective matter, but the government granted the patent all the same, and the company would soon exploit it. The other notable departure was the name of the new entry. Reynolds brands usually had decidedly American names, simple, gritty, maybe a bit saucy. This one, doubtless in an effort to reach a higher class of customer, they named for the reigning king of England—well, almost. There was a risk in christening your brands after a living person; dignitaries had a way of going in and out of fashion with the public or, worse still, of dying. So they called the new pipe tobacco Prince Albert, as the monarch had been known all those years while waiting to ascend to the throne, and just so there could be no doubt that the company meant Edward VII and not his father, who as Victoria's consort had the same name, the rounded tins that carried the picture of the prince in the mid-thigh-length overcoat he had made fashionable bore the words "Now King" in large letters just beneath the oval bearing his likeness.

Reynolds himself fussed endlessly with the blend and the package, hesitating to move Prince Albert into the national marketplace for fear of the reaction from the trust for his breaking out of the product niche to which his company had been confined. But once the government filed its antitrust action against his parent company, Reynolds likely felt Duke's high command could not afford to crack down on him without strengthening the hand of the trustbusters at the Justice Department. The public responded to the handy two-ounce red tins that made such an eye-catching package. The trust moved surreptitiously to hamper Reynolds's supply of Burley leaf, but Reynolds was seen as the farmers' friend, and the supply was forthcoming. For the first time now, the Winston-based company moved beyond its regional redoubt and hired a big-city advertising agency, N. W. Ayer of Philadelphia, to make a splash in national magazines. Touting Prince Albert as "the Joy Smoke" and "A Smoke Without a Sting," the advertising campaign revealed that Dick Reynolds, when given half a chance, had more than a bit of the snake-oil peddler in him. To call attention to the patented process by which the tobacco in Prince Albert had supposedly been tempered, Reynolds's ads explained that "we control the process that takes the tongue-blistering bite out of the tobacco—so there can't be even a near substitute." There was not a shred of documented evidence in support of the claim, but the product had a pretty container, a pleasing taste, and the right price. Reynolds pipe tobacco sales doubled between 1909 and 1910.

The brand's momentum threatened to slow after King Edward had the ill grace to die. Wags at the Winston factory proposed changing the "Now King" line beneath the Prince Albert oval to read, "Now Dead". The product soon proved to be anything but dead; sales doubled again during 1911 and an additional 40 percent in 1912, by then representing one-third of the entire Reynolds output that year. Even so, the company held less than 3 percent of the U.S. pipe tobacco market. But the introduction of Prince Albert demonstrated that the Reynolds company had enough drive and flair to become something more than a provincial plug maker.

VIII

REYNOLDS was not the only tobacco company to capitalize on the celebrity of the former Prince Albert. In 1902 the new king appointed as his royal tobacconist the firm of Philip Morris, Ltd., thereby reaffirming a relationship that had begun a quarter-century earlier when, as H.R.H. the Prince of

Wales, he had dubbed the Bond Street boutique his main supplier of cigarettes, his favorite form of smoking and one which he made popular in Britain's fashionable circles.

By then the Morris family had long disappeared as proprietors. On Philip's death in 1873, his widow, Margaret, and brother Leopold took over the business, soon boosted by the cachet of Prince Albert's patronage. Leopold Morris bought out his sister-in-law in 1880 and was joined in the ownership by a Joseph Grunebaum; their advancing prosperity was confirmed the following year, when a public offering of stock ownership for £60,000 was oversubscribed sixfold, allowing the company to open manufacturing facilities at Poland and Marlborough streets. Their Bond Street shop by that time had a well-established competitor nearby, operated by Messrs. Richard Benson and William Hedges. By 1889, the year Buck Duke was forging his American Tobacco combine, little Philip Morris, Ltd., was offering free samples of its patented cork-tip brands by post and promising that they brought "Luxury to the Lips and Prevent all Tongue and Throat Irritations."

The company gained ground until Leopold Morris was smitten by an opera singer whose attractions were matched by her expensive tastes. By 1894, the firm was in the hands of its creditors, and when it emerged from receivership, it was controlled by William Curtis Thomson and his family. The Thomsons nursed Philip Morris back to health, but it was still far too small a business to rate inclusion among the leading British manufacturers who united as Imperial Tobacco in 1901. But, its standing newly enhanced by the appointment as tobacconists to the crown, Philip Morris grew more prominent and began advertising in chic English periodicals. In a discreet 1907 ad, for example, the company called itself manufacturers of "highest grade Turkish cigarettes," of which the most popular were "Philip Morris original London cigarettes," which came in a little brown cedarwood box. Another British ad of that period depicted a uniformed pageboy in a pillbox hat who was proffering the reader a tray bearing cigarette packs; the headline read "Call for Philip Morris."

The upturn in cigarette sales in the United States in the first decade of the new century prompted the Thomson family to open a small American branch. Imports accounted for only 4 percent of the U.S. market, and tariff levels assured that only luxury-priced brands were worth shipping in. The more sensible way to penetrate the American market was to manufacture finished goods there, and so Philip Morris & Company, Ltd., was incorporated in New York in April of 1902; half the shares were held by the parent company in London, and the balance by its U.S. distributor and his American associates. Its overall sales in 1903, its first full year of U.S. operation, were a modest 7 million cigarettes. Among the brands offered, besides Philip Morris, were Blues, Cambridge, Derby, and a ladies' favorite named for the London street where the home company's factory was located—Marlborough.

I N mid-May of 1911, Chief Justice of the United States Edward Douglass White read the Supreme Court's opinion on the legality of the Standard Oil trust's operations. While the net effect of the ruling was the dismemberment of the oil trust, the Court's reading of the antitrust statute seemed hazily permissive. "[I]n every case where it is claimed that an act or acts are in violation of the [antitrust] statute the rule of reason, in the light of the principles of law and public policy which the act embodies, must be applied," White wrote. The reasonableness of the degree of restraint on trade exercised by a trust was to be determined by viewing the alleged misconduct in light of its observed effect on competition; the Sherman Act was intended not to limit the freedom to contract but to expand it by outlawing only those contracts that unduly constrained the rights of others. And by that measure, Standard Oil had unreasonably restrained trade. Two weeks later, the Court similarly ruled against American Tobacco.

Regarding the tobacco trust's contention that its every assailed act was "but a legitimate and lawful result of the exertion of honest business methods . . . for the purpose of advancing trade," the Court found such a view "a plain misconception of both the letter and the spirit of the Anti-trust Act." From the first, the Justices said, American Tobacco had demonstrated its purpose to be the "dominion and control of the tobacco trade, not by the exertion of the ordinary right to contract . . . but by methods devised in order to monopolize . . . [and] by driving competitors out of business. . . . [W]e think the conclusion of wrongful purpose and illegal combination is overwhelmingly established. . . ." The opinion divined "a conscious wrongdoing" demonstrated by the form in which the buyout transactions were embodied from the start, "ever changing but ever in substance the same . . . so as to obscure the result actually attained . . . to restrain others and to monopolize and retain power in the hands of the few who, it would seem, from the beginning contemplated the mastery of the trade." American Tobacco was ordered to be broken up and the constituent parts reassembled in smaller units.

Buck Duke had sat at his desk, awaiting telegraphic word of the Court's decision. When it came, he looked over at the photograph he kept of his father in front of the little log farmhouse in which Buck had grown up and, according to one of his biographers, remarked (to whom, it was not stated), "In England if a fella had built up a whale of a business out of *that*, he'd be knighted. Here they want to put him in jail." No one answered him that in class-ridden England, a fella almost certainly could never have accomplished what Duke had in free-spirited America. But he had overreached, and his countrymen had finally whacked him for it.

In fashioning the breakup remedy, the federal courts paid Duke an ironic tribute by turning to him to show how the reorganization might best be accomplished with minimal disruption of the economy and the lives of all involved. Simply put, nobody else knew his monstrous offspring half so well as the man who had sired it. Within eight months, Duke's plan was completed and approved. Under it, a number of the more independent subsidiaries were cut loose to operate on their own, including United Cigar Stores, British-American Tobacco, and the R. J. Reynolds company. But the core of the enterprise was parceled out unevenly among three new companies. The largest retained the American Tobacco name; its assets included one-third of the total U.S. cigarette and smoking tobacco business, a quarter of the plug trade, and about 6 percent of the cigar market. Liggett & Myers, about two-thirds the size of the the new American Tobacco, was assigned one-third of the plug market and about 20 percent each of the cigarette and smoking tobacco trade. Lorillard, reborn at about half the size of the new American Tobacco, got 26 percent of the nation's cigarette market, 23 percent of the pipe tobacco market, 5.7 percent of the cigar business, and 3.7 percent of plug.

A key element in the court-approved formula was the effort to dilute the dominant Duke interest in the restructured companies by reducing the holdings of the twenty-nine individual defendants from 56 percent of the common stock in the dismembered trust—the only shares with voting rights—by limiting the amount of stock in the three new companies that any defendant might acquire and awarding voting power in them to the formerly voteless holders of preferred stock, the only classification the minority holders had been permitted under the trust. The defendants, moreover, were forbidden for three years to increase their holdings in the new companies, which themselves were not allowed any financial transactions with one another for five years and were permanently enjoined from recombining any of their brands, offices, or manufacturing facilities or jointly owning any subsidiaries or requiring jobbers to carry one product in order to obtain another. The covenants restricting those who had sold out to the trust from engaging in the tobacco business for a long span of years were dissolved, as was the agreement to divide the world tobacco market among American Tobacco, Imperial, and British-American. The tobacco business was thus converted overnight from monopoly to oligopoly as a "reasonable" and court-sanctioned restraint of trade.

Duke, morose and drinking heavily now, had tens of millions to console him for his country's rebuke and moved away from tobacco to devote the last thirteen years of his life to a whole new career building the electric power industry in his native region. To earn the high regard of posterity that contemporary North Carolinians declined to extend him, he turned to philanthropy on a major scale, most notably by endowing little Trinity College, not far from his Durham birthplace, when the school agreed to exchange its name for his and the money to become a university of national rank.

Generally overlooked in the tumult over the reshaping of the tobacco trust was the liberation of Dick Reynolds's company. It gained none of American Tobacco's assets and spun free with what it had, namely, about 18 percent of the U.S. chewing tobacco business, 2.7 percent of the pipe tobacco market on the strength of Prince Albert's ascent, and none of the cigarette industry. Its assets were valued at about one-third the amount of Lorillard's, the smallest of the three new successor companies carved from the trust. But Reynolds himself was euphoric over the breakup. Within a week of the court's approval of it, he was sending his salesmen "News of Freedom" in a letter that reiterated for a final time that his company had always remained separate and distinct from the trust. If so, then why the gleeful proclamation of freedom? With the hated Duke out of his life now, Dick Reynolds at the age of sixty-two underwent a rejuvenation. Released from captivity, he decided to put R. J. Reynolds Tobacco into the one part of the business that he liked least and had no experience in—cigarettes. The results would soon turn his industry upside down.

3

It Takes the Hair Right Off Your Bean

ONE immediate result of the breakup of the tobacco trust was the onset of authentic competition among the newly independent parts of the former monolith. Each began to fill in its product lines so that it could sell across the board against the others. Nowhere was this new competitive zest more apparent than in Winston-Salem, North Carolina, as Reynolds Tobacco's home was now called.

Ever the opportunist, Richard Reynolds now used his chronic shortage of working capital as leverage to diminish the control over his enterprise by Duke and his Wall Street cronies, who still held the biggest voting bloc of his shares. Possibly because his operations were still relatively small and they had so much else on their collective minds, the New York crowd did not object when Reynolds proposed a new stock issue that would increase the number of shares outstanding by 25 percent, none of which the former trust insiders were allowed to purchase under the terms of the federally mandated dismemberment. Even so, outsiders, mostly Northern, still held some 55 percent of the Reynolds stock five years later. To rid itself of this protracted hold, Reynolds devised a second or "B" category of common stock, which gave its holders no voting rights but a hefty dividend undiluted by the profit-sharing feature of the regular common. Available on a swap basis for the old issue, the "B" stock was naturally more attractive to outsiders, and before long Reynolds people and their fellow North Carolinians were in absolute control of the state's biggest company.

Fresh funds in hand, Dick Reynolds was chiefly concerned with how to expand his business best and fastest. The cigarette field, he knew, was the most promising area in the tobacco industry. Unit sales, which had been only 4 billion a decade earlier, were now more than three times that figure. There were at least fifty prominent brands on the market, ranging in price from a nickel to a quarter for a pack or box of twenty. The leading seller was Liggett & Myers's Fatima, a blend of Turkish and domestic leaf, which at fifteen cents was most popular in the Eastern urban sector of the nation. But cheaper brands held sway regionally, like Piedmont, the all-Bright leaf entry that dominated in the Southeast, and the straight Burley brand, Home Run, a New Orleans favorite; both sold for five cents.

Before taking the plunge, Reynolds had to satisfy himself regarding the charges that cigarettes, unique among tobacco products because their smoke was so readily inhaled, were a danger to their users. A plug man from the first, he had long since been persuaded that smoking was a more hazardous habit than chewing, which he had convinced himself was a preservative of the teeth. Comfortable with the purity of tobacco, he was susceptible to the claim, voiced most notably by the nation's genius of electrical invention, Thomas A. Edison, that the white paper cigarette wrapper was the culprit, releasing toxic substances in the combustion process. Only when three separate laboratories hired by Reynolds reported back with negative findings did he resolve to proceed.

But with what sort of cigarette? First he and his blenders tried to mix Turkish with the local Bright and a dash of imported Latakia, an Oriental of keen aroma, calling the brand Osman after a heroic Turkish general and pricing it at twenty for ten cents. Neither it nor an all-Bright they called Reyno and sold for five cents made much of a dent in test markets. Plainly something different was needed. And the answer was to adapt for a cigarette the formula behind Reynolds's booming Prince Albert pipe mixture—a blend predominantly of Bright and western Burley, with its high tolerance of flavoring additives, supplemented by perhaps 10 percent Turkish leaf and, in a later reformulation, a touch of Maryland leaf for its even-burning character. The mix was not precisely revolutionary, but it did have a taste detectably different from what was then on the market: the Reynolds formula had a richer flavor than the all-domestic blends and a lighter quality on inhalation than the Turkish brands and their American imitators. Reynolds elected to price the new entry in the middle range—a dime for a pack of twenty—and to throw the company's full resources into this single brand, as none of his competitors did.

Some thought was given, in the wake of Prince Albert's success, to naming the new brand for another foreign royal—Germany's Kaiser Wilhelm, who would be pictured in full imperial regalia on a white horse. But Reynolds hesitated to name the product after a living figure because "you never can tell what the damned fool might do." World events would shortly bear out his canny caution. What was wanted, rather than celebrity with its built-in riskiness, was a short, memorable name that alluded to the exotic appeal of Turkish cigarettes without seeming to be just another entry in that crowded field. Having set his sights on Fatima, the market leader, which called itself "TURKISH Blend CIGA-RETTES" (with the "Blend" in much smaller type on the package), Reynolds would style his brand a "TURKISH & DOMESTIC BLEND" in a co-billing that greatly overstated the minor proportion of Oriental leaf in his blend. But if that was the fashion, he would hew to it, and the leading contenders for the new brand were winnowed to three, all redolent of the Near East—Kismet, Nabob, and Kamel.

Reynolds opted for the last, possibly because no other prominent brand was named for an animal. The only obstacle to its selection was a tiny independent brand called Red Kamel, on the market for just a few years. For $300, Reynolds bought the name, good will, and last 5,000 sticks the brand's New York manufacturer claimed were in existence. Always a poor speller, Reynolds nevertheless recognized that the more familiar English usage was better for the American market: "Camel" it was to be.

It would be sold not in a little box like many of the fancier Turkish brands but in a cheaper tinfoil-and-paper cup like Fatima, and the pack was to be as clean and simple as the name yet distinctive from the field. The result was a front panel consisting mostly of one riderless camel of the single-hump variety in a limitless desert landscape broken by two pyramids and three palm trees, all in pleasing yellow and reddish brown tints under a white sky across which the brand name, in silvered blue capital letters of vaguely Arabic styling, formed a gentle arc. The back panel offered a sketchy oasis with the obligatory mosques and minarets, and both front and back were framed along the edges by twin pillars with flared crowns and bases that gave each scene a rounded, picture-book look. On the back panel, the sky was imprinted with Reynolds's inspired message to customers: "Don't look for premiums or coupons, as the cost of the tobaccos blended in CAMEL cigarettes prohibits the use of them."

The only trouble with the finished design, as presented to Reynolds by his illustrator in the fall of 1913, was the camel. It looked sad, with a shaggy pelt, awkward stance, and drooping neck, suggestive of a somewhat zestless product within. A perkier version was required. As chance (and company lore) had it, the Barnum and Bailey circus came to Winston-Salem just then, with a camel among its menagerie. When asked if the dromedary could be prevailed upon to pose for a local photographer, the circus superintendent balked, citing the notoriously cranky nature of the species. Reminded that Reynolds had traditionally given its workforce the afternoon off to attend the visiting big top—a highly reversible policy—the circus man changed his tune, and the animal was trotted forth. But Old Joe, as the camel was called, proved less than entirely obliging, stretching his neck sideways in a quizzical and most unphotogenic gaze at the camera. Joe's keeper thereupon attracted his attention with a

smart whack on the nose that succeeded in producing a look somewhere between astonishment and displeasure. His neck straightened, his tail lifted, and
the photographer captured a forthright, albeit still ungainly, likeness of Joe,
which was dispatched at once to the illustrator, who faithfully reproduced
the pose.

Reynolds's advertising agency, N. W. Ayer, kicked off the big introduction with a three-part teaser campaign in selected newspapers across the country. The first showed a picture of Old Joe and read, simply, "Camels." The
second was headlined "The Camels Are Coming" and its text said, "Tomorrow
there'll be more CAMELS in this town than in all Asia and Africa combined."
The clincher exulted, "Camel Cigarettes Are Here!", and went into detail
about the special new blending for keen flavor and the allegedly high-grade
tobaccos used. The new brand was snapped up, and by mid-1914 Reynolds Tobacco was operating overtime to keep up with the demand. People liked the
pronounced flavor, and the package itself became the object of fond scrutiny
and parlor tricks. In the swirls of Joe's textured hide, you might detect—depending on your imagination—the form of a lion or a naked woman or a man
with an erection. When you held the pack's side panel, bearing only the all-
capitalized words "CHOICE QUALITY," upside down in front of a mirror, the
first word mysteriously still appeared right side up while the second was seen
upside down (because, it happens, all the capitalized letters in the former word
look identical upside down while in the latter, only the "I" appears un-
changed). And when a favorite uncle came to visit, he might produce a pack of
the new brand and a dime and tell his nephew the coin would be his if he could
cover all the animal's four legs with it. Try as he might, the youngster would
be baffled—the space was just too great for the small coin to fill; the uncle
would then merely place the dime over Joe's forelegs, explain the feeble wordplay with a laugh, and, if he was any kind of an uncle, surrender the dime, anyway. Within a year, the new brand had captured 13 percent of the market.

Reynolds pushed hard now, advertising Camels in newspapers everywhere,
including specialized journals that ranged from *The Wall Street Journal* to
New York's Yiddish-language *Daily Forward*; on billboards; and in magazines like *The Saturday Evening Post*, where a double-page spread for the
brand in December of 1914 was the first cigarette ad to appear inside that popular weekly. Promising "no cigarette after taste (you know what that means) in
the mouth," Camel kept growing. At American Tobacco's offices on lower
Fifth Avenue, where news of the new brand had at first been greeted with
snickers, nobody was laughing now. The company's sales director (and eventually president), George Washington Hill, would later recall, "I worked the
road in those days, and it was very discouraging. Territory after territory
swung over in the Camel column. . . . [E]veryone was talking about this new
taste in cigarettes."

The price-slashing tactics of the old trust were unavailable now to Reynolds's competitors, none of whom could afford to sacrifice one of their better lines as a "fighting brand," and no secondary brand could blunt Camel's sensational advance. War in Europe, moreover, seriously interrupted Oriental leaf shipments to the United States and turned public sympathy against Turkey and things Turkish as the inheritors of the Ottoman Empire leagued themselves with the Central Powers. And when America readied for and then entered the war, cigarettes were categorized as military supplies, and the government allocated its purchase orders along existing market-share lines—a bonanza for Reynolds, since Camel by then accounted for well over one-third of the nation's cigarette sales. By 1916, Reynolds had surpassed Liggett & Myers to become the second most profitable tobacco manufacturer; by 1917, its net earnings of $10.3 million were only $3 million shy of industry leader American Tobacco's.

When Richard Joshua Reynolds died in 1918 at the age of sixty-eight, he was not mourned with unalloyed reverence. Something of a penny pincher and slave driver, he was nonetheless admired as a stalwart defender of his workers, few of whom were ever fired except for the most flagrant of causes, and a battler against monsters to the north. By keeping costs low, centralizing output in one location, and concentrating his sales and promotion efforts on a few brands in the pioneering age of mass production, he prospered hugely in the end. At his death, the company held some 40 percent of the country's soaring cigarette trade and 20 percent of both the chewing and smoking tobacco business.

II

IN the aftermath of the trust breakup, the new, leaner American Tobacco Company had on hand the ideal successor to Buck Duke in the person of his longtime first vice president and order-taker, Percival Hill. A low-key manager moderate in all ways but his loyalty to Duke, Hill never buckled during his testimony at the antitrust trial by blaming the company's brutal tactics on orders from above. Rewarded with the presidency of the diminished American Tobacco in 1912, he proved an able if undynamic chief, a details man with an agile mind for figures. His most useful contribution to the company's fortunes was the steady advancement of his son, George.

Young Hill, possessed by a driving impatience that radiated from his fierce eyes and truculent manner, had dropped out of Williams College after two years and joined the old tobacco trust in 1904 at the age of twenty. He learned the business the hard way, training in the leaf department and on the factory floor for several years and displaying a serious-mindedness in all things, including the habit of inscribing in a small notebook his every gain and loss at the penny-ante card games that provided his prime recreation in the boarding-houses of Durham. His precocity won him the managership of a dawdling all-Turkish brand called Pall Mall, which he swiftly built into the leader in the deluxe market through Anglophilic snob appeal.

Hill had a real flair for advertising that boosted him up the corporate ladder. His method was to find or invent an attribute in each product that could be conveyed in an arresting fashion; just to showcase the brand with bland, dignified copy was a waste of money. The headline that asked a question was a device he favored for winning consumers' attention. At his best, he pushed the forty-year-old brand of Sweet Caporal, still a strong seller, in an ad asking, "Who smoked 'Sweet Caps' when Garfield and Hancock ran for President?" and answering, "Ask Dad, *he* knows." Even when his fertile brain misfired, his ads had a grabbing if goofy liveliness, as in one headlined "Where was Moses when the light went out? Groping around for a pack of Mecca"; boxed in small print below was the message "The price of Mecca cigarettes is not even a hint of their quality. Don't let that nickel mislead you."

George Hill was more than a phrasemaker; he was a salesman of such single-mindedness that he was affronted by store managers who failed to share his enthusiasm for American Tobacco products. Placed in charge of the company's sales force, he expected his drummers to display no less dedication than he did. To maximize their efforts, he got the company to invest early in that new wonder of the age, the automobile, allowing his field men to reach even remote sales outlets on a regular route and keep a close eye on dealer stocks. A skilled packager as well, he developed such innovations as vacuum-packed tins for pipe tobacco, cigarette cartons wrapped in glassine paper, and dating on all shipping cases and boxes so that freshness of product could be maintained systematically.

For all his efforts, it became plain to Hill and his father that since Camels gave no sign of slowing their surge, American would have to compete with its own blended brand. But badly shaken by upstart Reynolds's sudden success in a field where it had had no prior record, the Hills would not rush out just any old brand; it had to be as special as Camel yet readily distinguishable from it.

From the first, the new brand was conceived of as proudly American; there was to be nothing Turkish or foreign in the name, package, or blend. The Hills put the company's best blender of plug to work in their Brooklyn factory on a formula that had even more Burley in it than Camel, while George scoured the long list of trademarks that the old trust had accumulated over the years for a striking name. He found it in a long-abandoned pipe tobacco brand once made in Richmond and registered in 1871 when memories of the California Gold Rush were still fresh—Lucky Strike. The old package had had a nice, unfussy look to it: a deep hunter green background and a bright red central disk bearing the brand name. George had an artist clean up the lettering so that the name appeared all in bold, black capital letters without serifs and the disk was set off with a double band, gold on the inside and black on the outer edge. On one of the side panels a small Indian chief's head was introduced—in time it would become the company symbol—and on the back, to counter Camel's self-serving assertion that it had substituted a better grade of tobacco for customer premiums, Lucky Strike carried a money-back guarantee to buyers.

Still, George Hill did not rush to introduce Luckies, as the brand was informally called. It was in dire need of a talking point, something the advertising could seize upon. His field people, though, were haranguing him now almost daily to give them a brand to sell against Camel, and while dwelling more urgently on the problem, George one day headed for the manufacturing plant where the new blend was being processed in anticipation of the imminent launching. Within a few blocks of his destination Hill was bathed in the intoxicatingly rich aroma of the tobacco, not unlike mouth-watering baked goods or some similar confection by a master chef. On his return to the company's Fifth Avenue offices, George reported his olfactory arousal to his father and thought it might hold the key to their missing sales gimmick. There was something about the way they were processing the leaf that George could not quite find the words for—it was as if they were cooking the tobacco. His father mused, "What is it that you use . . . where heat is applied in an appetizing way that will react quickly on a person's mind?"

While the pair of them pondered, a mutual acquaintance from the cigar business wandered into the executive suite and was invited to share the Hills' problem of how to express applied heat in an appetizing fashion. "I always have toast in the morning," the visitor quickly answered. Percy Hill's face grew incandescent. "That's it—it's toasted!"

That all other companies similarly "toasted" their tobacco during the drying and sterilization process before the leaf was shredded was no impediment to a true huckster like George Hill. He knew a winning phrase when he heard it. "IT'S TOASTED" went on the package right under the brand name—quotation marks included, as if the incantation of some celebrated sage—and became the sales mantra as Lucky Strike finally reached the market in 1916. "You'll enjoy this *real* Burley cigarette. It's full of flavor—just as good as a pipe," George Hill's early ads declared, adding that the Burley was toasted and this "makes the taste delicious. You know how toasting improves the flavor of bread. And it's the same with tobacco exactly." To one side of the copy within a heavily outlined circle, as if to explain this technological miracle, was an illustration of a hand holding a toasting fork with a piece of bread speared to it. Later versions would note how steak "broiled and buttered" or the lowly potato was similarly and wonderfully transformed by heat—so common a piece of intelligence that Hill's competitors supposed that the buying public would see through the bogus claim of a nonexistent distinction.

But it worked, probably more because of the catchy name and the smart package so easily visible on dealers' shelves than the virtues of toastiness. George poured in the advertising dollars, and within a year of its debut Lucky Strike had gained 11 percent of the market. But America's entry into the great war in Europe put a sudden brake on Luckies' advance. The government's allocation formula for military purchases locked in the prewar market shares—a heavy disadvantage for Lucky Strike and the price the Hills paid for their dilatory launching of it.

George returned from war service in the Red Cross with some fresh promotional ideas, and Luckies pioneered advertisement by skywriting. People would stop at street corners and gawk upward at the mile-long letters being formed 10,000 feet overhead. Smoke in the sky, George reasoned, would suggest smoke in gawkers' mouths. Slowly Luckies regained their drive, reaching a 16 percent market share by 1925. Camels, though, grew faster, thanks in part to a slogan rather more robust than Luckies' "Toasted". An outdoor advertising specialist hired early in 1921 to expand Camel's billboard presence was playing golf one day when his foursome ran out of cigarettes and sent a caddy off to replenish their supply. Awaiting his return, one of the adman's colleagues remarked that he would gladly "walk a mile for a Camel." Within weeks, in the press and on billboards coast to coast, Americans were greeted by devoted smokers telling them why "I'd Walk a Mile for a Camel." Reynolds Tobacco spent more than $8 million on its advertising that year, among the largest outlays yet made by any company. By the following year, its profits moved past American Tobacco's to gain the industry leadership; by 1925, Camels held well over 40 percent of the burgeoning cigarette market.

Lucky Strike was not even the distant runner-up. Well out ahead of it by the mid-'Twenties, though still far behind the Reynolds pacesetter, was the Liggett & Myers blend, Chesterfield, which had appeared on the market in 1912, one of the first moves by Liggett upon being cut loose from the trust. The reins at Liggett had been handed to another Duke henchman and confidant, Caleb C. Dula, who gave the old-line St. Louis plug maker competent and consistent leadership that was neither aggressive nor inventive. But Liggett knew how to make a good cigarette, and the Chesterfield, sold in a slide-and-shell box under the bland slogan "They do satisfy," made a small splash when introduced. Dula, however, was quicker than the American Tobacco bosses to recognize the threat to the conventional blends posed by the Burley-heavy Camel. In 1915 Liggett reconstituted Chesterfield's formula, adding Burley with few flavorings so that the taste was less sweet than Camel and could be proclaimed as more "natural". The new brand was then repackaged in a paper-and-tinfoil cup to bring down its price to Camel's level, but it had an altogether different and rather more dignified look, as befitted a product with so English a name. It was printed in somewhat delicate Old English lettering on an upward slant, with many calligraphic loops and flourishes and the "Ch" enclosed in an odd heraldic device; below was a sketch of a small, dreamy harbor nowhere in particular. Mostly, one saw the whiteness of the pack, which suggested the mildness that became the brand's watchword. With its understated slogan shortened to "They satisfy," Chesterfield had a British refinement to it that appealed to conservative and better-educated smokers. Liggett advertised the brand with a quiet elegance that helped it capture nearly one-quarter of the U.S. cigarette market by 1925.

At the end of that year, Percival Hill died, just two months after his lord and master, Buck Duke. American Tobacco's new leader, George Hill, cut more in Duke's mold than in his father's, would soon prove a holy terror.

III

THE spurt in cigarette sales during the first quarter of the twentieth century was attended by a detectable shift in the American social attitude toward the product that spared it from the outbreak of puritanism dooming alcohol to prohibition and scoring its use as by far the worse sin.

That pugilistic folk hero of the late nineteenth century John L. Sullivan served as a spokesman for his times when he dismissed the cigarette as a smoke suitable only for "dudes and college misfits" and decidedly un-American, an allusion to the foreign origin of both the leaf used in many brands and the immigrant masses favoring them, especially in New York, which as late as 1910 accounted for 25 percent of all cigarettes sold in the U.S. Men of substance and virility smoked cigars; besides paupers, only the effeminate, the effete, or the affected chose cigarettes, according to the charge against them. The adult per capita consumption of cigarettes, while edging up, was still only 138 in 1910, a year when *The New York Times*, in hailing the new Non-Smokers Protective League, remarked that anything that could be done to allay "the general and indiscriminate use of tobacco in public places, hotels, restaurants, and railroad cars, will receive the approval of everybody whose approval is worth having."

Therein lay the making of the cigarette and the decline of the cigar and pipe. For in the relative mildness of its aroma and convenience of its use, the smaller, quicker smoke was proving a good deal less objectionable to an increasingly urbanized society. In busy, crowded offices, on public conveyances, at cultural and recreational gatherings, the cigarette was simply less obtrusive, requiring less paraphernalia and skill to use than the pipe and less space and leisure than the cigar in a culture that was coming to understand that time was human currency. By the second decade of the century, the cigarette was becoming the smoke of choice in high as well as low society, as testified to by the press reports on the sinking of the great ocean liner *Titanic* on its maiden voyage in 1912: many of the tuxedoed male passengers were said to have awaited their watery graves while drawing stoically on a cigarette. And Sullivan's "college misfits" were taking up the habit in great numbers. As Camels and Chesterfields were attaining almost instant popularity, Penn State's *Froth*, the campus humor magazine, ran a little poem in 1915 that passed quickly into the popular culture: "Tobacco is a dirty weed. I like it. / It satisfies no mortal need. I like it. / It makes you thin, it makes you lean, / It takes the hair right off your bean, / It's the worst darn stuff I've ever seen. / I like it." These elegiac lines are notable for their insouciance toward the health hazards attributed to cigarettes uniquely among tobacco products. People simply did not believe that the milder smokes were a greater peril than the more traditional uses of tobacco. This new toleration was greatly abetted by two unfolding events, each of consuming importance to one of the sexes—the coming of the world war and the climax of the women's suffrage movement.

Any lingering notions of the unmanliness of cigarette smoking were blown away by the First World War. Pipes and cigars were manifestly unmanageable in the battle lines, and chewing tobacco was a menace to sanitation. Cigarettes were no bother, small insult to the nostrils in close quarters, and a perceived aid to vigilance, and so quickly became the universal emblem of the camaraderie of mortal combat, that consummate male activity. There was no better way to discharge tension on the brink of battle, no readier solace for the prospect of imminent doom; here was the perfect narcotic to numb the senses to the misery of the trenches, the witnessed horrors of mutilation, and the tedium of the endless interludes. Not by accident did one of the jauntier ballads of the war urge the young combatants to smile in the face of death "while you've a Lucifer to light your fag." The cigarette, in short, served as the essential sustainer of morale. Doctors spoke of its soothing effect on the wounded. In answer to an inquiry from the home front, General John J. ("Black Jack") Pershing, commander of the American Expeditionary Forces, stated, "You ask me what we need to win this war. I answer tobacco as much as bullets." Organizations like the Red Cross and the Young Men's Christian Association that before the war had opposed the propagation of cigarettes among the nation's young manhood did their best now to supply them liberally.

Wrapping themselves in the mantle of patriotism, the cigarette companies savored the boom. Fellows they would likely never have enlisted as paying customers fell into their laps through military conscription, and the windfall was all the sweeter because soldiers smoked 60 to 70 percent more butts on average each day than civilians, whose own use was now up 15 to 20 percent as the stresses and dislocations of wartime took their emotional toll. Almost all cigarette factories were working double or even triple shifts, and with Turkish leaf now unavailable, American tobacco farmers who in the heyday of the trust were lucky to fetch ten or twelve cents a pound were now commanding as much as seventy cents. Profits, though, did not keep pace with the soaring volume, because the manufacturing costs for almost everything leaped—the leaf, paper, labor, fuel for machines, heating, and transportation.

In the din of war and its accompanying tumult at home, hardly a whisper of protest was lodged against the triumphal march of the cigarette. Even the staunch Lucy Gaston, veteran pillar of antitobacco rectitude, had to await the armistice to denounce the cigarette makers for wily propaganda that had led to the forced doping of formerly wholesome young men on a scale without precedent. Such laments were lost in the wind at the very time alcohol was being officially demonized by Congress and outlawed with the concurrence of three-fourths of the states; Johnny marched home to a nation about to become legally boozeless, but at least he and his countrymen had their smokes for consolation. By 1919, cigarettes had surpassed smoking tobacco in the poundage of leaf consumed; by 1922, they passed plug to become the nation's highest grossing tobacco product.

Nearly as essential as the war to this phenomenon was the reluctant male acquiescence in political equality for American women, enshrined by the ratification of the Nineteenth Amendment in 1920. To express the need for and then the attainment of this liberation from second-class citizenship, the cigarette was a valuable tool.

Just as men who smoked them had been denounced as unmanly and degenerate, so women who used cigarettes were widely perceived as unladylike and exhibitionist. In polite circles, tobacco was taken as fit only for the "sporting girls" of the demimonde and other professional performers of their sex. Increasingly, though, women themselves came to recognize in the cigarette a far more aesthetically pleasing experience than any other form of tobacco use, especially the cigar. The latter was long, strong, dark, thick, aromatically overwhelming, and took forever to consume. The cigarette, by contrast, was short, mild, white, lean, a fraction as smelly, did not cling ineradicably to clothing and draperies, and could be taken briefly in the interstices between the numberless tasks that made up a woman's day. Here was a product that could be enjoyed equally by both sexes. But women who did so too publicly continued to be stigmatized in the early years of the twentieth century as possessors of dubious character.

Within a few years, however, the social currents of modernity and the industrial age were forcing a change. While the intensifying drive for the vote was the catalyst, women came to view their degraded status in a broader context; as they had been disenfranchised from the first, so, too, had they been disembodied and dishonored by men's denial of their right to sexuality and refusal to recognize their human worth. With such immense stakes involved, the little cigarette—"friendly, sociable, light," as the *Atlantic Monthly* called it in April of 1916—became for women in that leading literary journal's view "the symbol of emancipation, the temporary substitute for the ballot." The approach of war intensified the outpouring of feminist fervor in various forms. Women were needed more in the workplace, and offices, clubs, and the new department stores drew them away from home, while the spread of the telephone, mass transit, the automobile, the phonograph, and motion pictures helped spring them from a sequestered existence defined largely by the many services they were expected to render their families. "Women were newly *public* people and needed, more than before, social currencies acceptable in the public world defined by men," the acute sociologist Michael Schudson noted in a study of emerging consumer patterns of this period. "The cigarette was one such social coin and a particularly convenient one: cheap, visible, an identifying mark, both easily flaunted and easily hidden, a topic of talk, a token of comradeship and, to boot, a comfort in anxious moments."

Thus, the long-nailed hand that at last held the ballot now took up the cigarette far more openly. Women who were more socially and culturally secure led the way, among them the Eastern urban society set, which began to be offered cigarettes in the more sophisticated shops they patronized. College women took up the custom more clandestinely as a sign of youthful daring. Most egregious among the fledgling female smokers were those flaming hedonists, the flappers, for whom the flaunted cigarette was as *de rigueur* as bobbed hair, bared knees, rouged cheeks, and teasing lips. Not everyone applauded. The *Ladies' Home Journal* commented acidly in June of 1922 that female smokers differed from men, who did so to calm "restlessness or emotional inquietude," whereas "women smoke nervously, they cannot smoke moderately," and dismissed the practice by women as "another fetching stratagem of sex attraction." To the *Journal*, at least, The New Woman was no lady.

Only one taboo remained—women who smoked on the street were still considered trollops; men who did never invited a second glance. Thus cabined, female smokers were often more avid about pursuing the practice indoors than men, who, for example, were far less inclined to smoke in the shops they frequented, like haberdasheries and hardware stores, while women often and conspicuously indulged in department stores, millinery shops, ice-cream parlors, and railroad dining cars. In setting aside a pair of common rooms for smoking at Smith College, the president of that distinguished women's institution said in 1930 that his students' claims for social equality with their male counterparts dictated the step, but added, "The trouble is, my dear young ladies, you do not smoke like gentlemen."

Nevertheless, women helped the per capita consumption of cigarettes sustain its exponential growth. By 1930, it was twice what it had been ten years before.

IV

HARD evidence of the ravages of tobacco smoke upon the human body did not exist during the first quarter of the twentieth century, as the cigarette found increasing favor. What new evidence there was remained largely anecdotal—random and widely dispersed personal observations and impressions in an age when biostatistics were just beginning to be gathered in a systematic way. Fragmentary data from insurance companies suggesting that regular tobacco use, like alcohol, reduced the life span by as many as eight years, and a growing sense among doctors that smokers enjoyed only half the recovery rate after surgery that nonusers did, in no way marked cigarettes as a deadlier form of tobacco than any other.

The absence of documented danger hardly concerned those most outspoken against the cigarette in the period just preceding the Great War. The line between moral and medical objections to smoking, blurred from the first, grew even hazier now. No one in America spoke out more forcefully against cigarettes in particular than the scientist-industrialist Thomas Edison, who was sure the problem lay not with the tobacco itself but with acrolein, a compound released by "the burning paper wrapper," as he wrote in 1914 to fellow industrial titan Henry Ford, and that foul substance "has a violent action on the nerve centers, producing degeneration of the cells of the brain, which is quite rapid among boys." The clinical evidence for this assertion was never forthcoming, but the celebrated inventor was sure that the damage caused was permanent and uncontrollable and thus, "I employ no person who smokes."

That was good enough for the straitlaced Henry Ford, who supposed that his mastery in the new automobile business qualified him as the nation's moral mentor, and in 1916 he had issued under his name *The Case Against the Little White Slaver*, a widely disseminated broadside that spread the anticigarette gospel according to Edison and Miss Gaston. Anyone who examined the clues of pathologic behavior in the typical criminal, Ford insisted, "will find that he is an inveterate cigarette smoker. Boys, through cigarettes, train with bad company. They go with other smokers to the pool rooms and saloons. The cigarette drags them down." Ford's views were challenged by American Tobacco's president, Percival Hill, who wrote the carmaker to assure him that cigarette paper had been carefully tested for toxicity and the tobacco it held was pure and contained less nicotine than other forms of smoking, so that "their temperate use is in no way injurious to normal smokers." But no tobacco company officer then—or since—ever spelled out the meaning of moderation in smoking.

Spurred by Edison, Ford, and other business leaders, a number of large U.S. companies began to actively discourage cigarette smoking, among them the Cadillac Motor Car Company, business-machines maker Burroughs, the giant Marshall Field and Wanamaker department stores, and Montgomery Ward, the mail-order merchandiser. Eminences in other spheres joined in the denunciation, including the labor union chieftain Samuel Gompers, the black educator and inspirational force Booker T. Washington, and the swift scourge of the baseball diamond, Ty Cobb.

Probably no more comprehensive or conscientious summation of the case to discourage cigarette use was produced in this period than *Tobacco and Human Efficiency*, a 1918 book-length study by Frederick J. Pack, a geologist at the University of Utah, a Mormon stronghold where tobacco smoking was considered, as by Islam, to be an ungodly defilement of the flesh. Pack's book, a collage of clinical observations, suppositions, and moral bias, noted that cigarette smoke, while containing less nicotine than cigar or pipe smoke, had the unfortunate tendency upon being inhaled of mixing the highly toxic gas carbon monoxide into the bloodstream; the precise consequences of this introduction were not yet clear. And because inhaled cigarette smoke came into contact with "hundreds of square feet of mucous membrane in comparison with the square foot or two on the surfaces of the oral cavity when inhaling is not indulged in," Pack stated that the injury inflicted by cigarettes was "almost directly proportional to the area reached by the poisonous fumes." But the nature and extent of such injury as well as the data to support this sweeping conclusion were not provided.

Congressional passage of the Eighteenth Amendment outlawing alcoholic beverages early in 1919 set off alarm bells in the tobacco industry. The war boom had peaked, and powerful reform groups like the Women's Christian Temperance Union and charismatic religious spokesmen like the Reverend Billy Sunday, needing fresh targets to sustain their tumescent moralism, turned now from the demon rum to the demon weed. With such allies, the ceaseless crusader Lucy Gaston made one last charge against the smoky citadel of sin and, since women were now voters, announced her candidacy for President. Her victorious opponent was that handsome "cigarette face," Warren G. Harding, to whom she wrote asking that, for both his own sake and the youth of the nation, he give up using the little smokes. Under Gaston's harangue, Harding may well have cut down on his smoking—at the least he no longer flaunted the habit in public—but too late if indeed it had compromised his health; he died of a stroke midway through his term of office. Any facile linkage, though, between smoking and mortality that might have been inferred from Harding's case was frayed when Gaston herself died a year after the President; the cause in her case—cancer of the throat—was then considered far more likely to have been tobacco-induced, but so far as was known, Miss Gaston had never been kissed and never smoked.

Her death seemed to draw to an end the campaign to proscribe cigarettes. Ironically, the product gained stature now when contrasted with alcohol. Tobacco in general and cigarettes in particular neither intoxicated nor excited the passions, and, far from being a destructive influence on family life, as booze most emphatically could be, a good smoke lured men home for contemplative lingering by their hearth, argued the tobacco industry. Leading intellectuals, moreover, like the philosopher John Dewey and political conservatives like former President William Howard Taft, warned that if the so-called reform process that had begun with the fruitless effort to halt the sale of alcohol was extended to other purportedly harmful practices, such as smoking, it would fuel a misguided puritanism that would run roughshod over American liberties. The disastrous experience that Prohibition was proving to be—an open invitation to criminal pandering to backdoor licentiousness—was, for many, evidence enough of the ineffectuality and imprudence of government intrusion upon privately exercised pleasures, however offensive to bluenoses.

The ironical enhancement of tobacco's position *vis-à-vis* alcohol was well captured just before Harding's election in an article in the *Atlantic* entitled "Is a Tobacco Crusade Coming?" and predicting that "the present gale of vilification will blow itself out and die unnoticed at the feet of scientific truth. . . . That the claims of those who inveigh against tobacco are wholly without foundation has been proved time and again by famous chemists, physicians, toxicologists, physiologists, and experts of every nation and clime." A more judicious reading of the social climate was made in 1921 by the journal *Current Opinion* when it stated that while science might suspect that smoking was injurious to the throat, heart, and nerves—no mention was made of the lungs—the state ought not casually to prohibit the practice "unless it makes out a better case against tobacco than it has done up to the present. . . ."

True to the highly pragmatic strain in the American character that has always run as deep as its soaring principles, the nation then adopted a more immediately useful policy toward cigarettes than clamoring about their alleged nastiness and undemonstrated peril to health: it began taxing them more heavily. There was a world of difference between branding their use a sin and making it a crime. If the former, a user's fee could be imposed with relatively good conscience; if the latter, government could succeed only in immersing itself in a fresh swamp, its police powers failing hopelessly against human nature. Thus, the federal excise levy on cigarettes was boosted to six cents a pack, and in 1921 Iowa became the first state to tax cigarettes, charging two cents a pack on top of the U.S. rate. Other states shortly followed, even as Kansas, in 1927, became the last state to drop its prohibition against cigarette sales. By 1930, federal tax collections on tobacco products, which had amounted to $58 million in 1910 (13 percent accounted for by cigarettes), had risen to nearly ten times that figure—and 80 percent came from cigarette sales. So embedded in American life had the product become that *The New York Times* wrote in a rhapsodic editorial in 1925, "Short, snappy, easily attempted, easily completed or just as easily discarded before completion—the cigarette is the symbol of a machine age in which the ultimate cogs and wheels and levers are human nerves." H. L. Mencken's *American Mercury* that year commended the cigarette as "the most democratic commodity in common use" since both the banker and his bootblack could share a brand, the *Mercury* scoffed, as was its wont, at all "the appalling charges" lodged against the little smokes and wound up, "A dispassionate review of the [scientific] findings compels the conclusion that the cigarette is tobacco in its mildest form, and that tobacco, used moderately by people in normal health, does not appreciably impair either the mental efficiency or the physical condition." This view would prevail as the American consensus for another twenty-five years.

V

B Y the end of the 1920s, as the per capita use of cigarettes by Americans eighteen or older reached four a day, a few medical investigators reported, more with curiosity than alarm, on the faintly measurable increase of a disease that had been quite rare—cancer of the lung. A special study by the U.S. Census Bureau in 1914 had found a death rate from the disease of 0.6 per 100,000 living Americans; by 1925 the lung cancer mortality rate had risen to 1.7, a threefold increase that was nevertheless still quite low in absolute terms and relatively unnoticeable when compared to such still virulent contagious diseases as influenza and tuberculosis. But in various urban centers sampled over selected time periods, the death rate was noticeably higher than the overall national figure for lung cancer. In Albany, New York, the number was 2.5 for 1919–23, and across the state in Buffalo it was 3.2 for 1922–26; in Boston for 1920–24 the rate had been 3.9, and in San Francisco for the same period it reached 4.7. In England and Wales, where cigarette smoking had also grown greatly, the rate had been 1.0 for the first decade of the century but had risen to 2.33 by 1926.

The phenomenon was still too minor to qualify as a trend, and even as the figures continued their upward movement, some observers were quick to attribute them to better diagnostic tools, of which the X-ray machine was among the most prominent. Deaths, that is, that had been wrongly attributed to other diseases earlier were likely to have been due in fact to lung cancer. But sites other than the lung, examinable by the same new diagnostic methods, were not revealing a comparable rate of rise in cancer. Nor were the mortality rates climbing comparably for other diseases, as advances in immunology were beginning to add significantly to human longevity, largely by reducing infant deaths. Frank E. Tylecote, a British investigator reporting in *The Lancet* in 1927, found it notable that the climb in lung cancer rates was by no means limited to the working classes, "as might be assumed," and then added, "I have no statistics with regard to tobacco, but I think that in almost every case I have seen and known of the patient has been a regular smoker, generally of cigarettes."

The first sizable and systematic study comparing cancer patients with those suffering from other diseases, undertaken by a pair of investigators from the Massachusetts Public Health Department and the Harvard School of Public Health, was reported in April of 1928 in the *New England Journal of Medicine*, the nation's most highly regarded publication devoted to comprehensive coverage of the healing arts. Herbert Lombard and Carl Doering examined the histories of 217 cancer victims statewide and a comparable number of patients free of the disease but closely comparable in age, gender, and economic status. Their study, aimed at considering potential causes of cancer, dwelled on their subjects' dietary and exercise habits and their use of alcohol (though illegal at the time), laxatives, and tobacco. Perhaps the most revealing discovery in their study was that in sites generally considered most susceptible to harm from smoking—the lips, cheeks, jaw, and lungs—all but one of the thirty-five cancer sufferers were heavy smokers. But certifiable tobacco users in the group with cancer outnumbered only slightly users in the control group free of the disease. The findings were therefore open to at least two varying interpretations: the use of tobacco was (1) irrelevant to the incidence of cancer or (2) a necessary contributor to the disease but not sufficient in and of itself to be the cause of it.

A more free-ranging exploration of the lately detected increase in lung cancer, by a Prudential Life Insurance Company statistician, Frederick Hoffman, writing in 1929 in the *American Review of Tuberculosis*, contrasted the 50 percent decline over four decades of tuberculosis, the vastly more prevalent lung disease. Because lung cancer occurred mostly in men, speculation arose that it might be linked to certain occupations in which possible irritants were unavoidable, such as wood dust in carpentry and millwork and mineral particles in mining and metals processing. At least as likely a contributor, though, was the immense increase in automobile road traffic, with its emanations of gasoline vapors, oil particles, and coal tar; a growing number of studies were showing that tar products and coal combustion, then the most common heating fuel source, had "a unique carcinogenic efficacy," as Hoffman put it, and so other petrochemical products were naturally suspect. Not quite as an afterthought, he also noted, "There is no definite evidence that smoking habits are a direct contributory cause toward malignant growths in the lungs."

V I

THE scientific consensus that had thus far exonerated the cigarette of any demonstrable harmful effect on human tissue served as a license in the late 'Twenties for tobacco manufacturers to push the ever more successful product with growing resources and commitment.

R. J. Reynolds Tobacco, purveyors of the industry-leading Camel brand, was now spending some $10 million a year in advertising, most of it on the one brand. And unlike most medical commentators, RJR, as Reynolds came to be familiarly called, sounded no cautionary note about the desirability of moderate or temperate use of cigarettes. Quite the opposite. "Each successive Camel you smoke brings a fresh pleasure no matter how constantly you smoke," declared a typical ad. Another from 1927 saluted "experienced smokers" who "have paid Camel the highest compliment: 'No matter how liberally we smoke them, Camels never tire the taste. They never leave a cigaretty after-taste.' "

Anxious to improve Camel's appeal to better-heeled customers, ads for the brand now spoke of the quality and mildness of its tobacco and depicted smokers of presumably good taste and breeding, in evening attire at dinner parties or on ocean liners or more informally garbed for a tennis or polo match, all of whom were urged to "HAVE A CAMEL," the Ayer advertising agency's notion of a catchy slogan. Reynolds's approach to the market seemed to be that of a winner eager not to make a mistake by any display of flamboyance. The company's prosperity and high standing were splendidly embodied by the opening in 1929 of its $2 million new headquarters in Winston-Salem, a twenty-two-story structure sheathed in Indiana limestone with Art Deco detailing designed by Shreve & Lamb and resembling the next major edifice that firm would fashion—the Empire State Building. The Reynolds tower was among the tallest structures in the South and surely its handsomest office building.

The very blandness of the Camel approach all but invited an intensified onslaught by competing brands. While Reynolds, with a cultural conservatism reflective of its regional base, declined openly to seek female smokers or display them in their ads—the women in them smilingly *watched* the men enjoy their Camels—even cautious Liggett & Myers began to explore the distaff market, albeit with a style and subtlety that eluded the RJR admakers. "Blow some my way," implored a fetching young woman nestled by her devoted companion on some idyllic crag as he puffed away in a 1926 Chesterfield ad considered daring for its day. The Chesterfield ads in general were the smartest-looking in the cigarette business, with their elegant drawings and type styling, tight copy blocks and abundance of white space, constant promise of mildness "without a hint of harshness or irritation," and cryptic yet pleasingly suggestive slogan—"They Satisfy". By decade's end, Chesterfield was selling three-quarters as much as Camel.

The appeal of "mildness" became a watchword in cigarette advertising in this period, as if the industry recognized that despite the absence of condemnation by the legitimate scientific community, the chronic inhalation of tobacco smoke could hardly help being an irritant and that likelihood had to be implicitly counteracted, if not openly denied. A brasher approach to this sensitive subject was taken now by a new brand that was to become the most successful cigarette arrival of the decade, and in the nick of time for its manufacturer, P. Lorillard.

Handed the bulk of the tobacco trust's Turkish brands, representing about one-quarter of the industry's cigarette revenues in 1912, Lorillard did not flourish as an independent operation. As war and the xenophobic impulses it triggered cut heavily into its Turkish brands, Lorillard responded far too timidly to sustain or build market share. Its 1915 introduction of Tiger was so transparently imitative of Camel and so ineptly mounted that the brand quickly vanished. Even the company's pathbreaking pursuit of women customers, to whom Lorillard pitched as early as 1919 with ads for its Murad and Helmar brands showing or strongly implying their use by women, was viewed in industry circles as foolhardy. It was the very moment when Prohibitionists, fresh from their triumph over alcohol, were hot on the trail of tobacco. By 1925, the company had lost all but 2 percent of the cigarette market and was staying in business on the strength of its other tobacco products.

Raising $30 million, Lorillard ended its slide in 1926 by leaping afresh, if ten years late, into the Burley blend competition with a new brand, Old Gold, which it promoted with vigor and imagination that surprised its rivals. But they could hardly admire the newcomer's bravura slogan, "Not a cough in a carload," a claim of innocence from an affliction tacitly imputed to Old Gold's competitors—smoker's cough. Its ads made prominent use of the "blindfold test," a self-serving technique authoritatively discredited only a few years earlier by the big J. Walter Thompson agency, which had shown that panels of smokers, asked to judge cigarette brands with their imprinted identities masked, correctly identified their own no more frequently than the law of averages would have dictated. Still, the company flaunted its claims, hiring artist John Held to draw his famous flapper girls for Old Gold ads, featuring in others the equally famous Petty girls posed as lithesome pirates in short pants and similarly coy guises, and making imaginative use of the comic-strip form in ads based on Ripley's "Believe It or Not" wowsers and the gifts of illustrator Winsor McKay, whose "Little Nemo" creations were the Sunday comics' nearest approach to high art. Old Gold, promoted as well on the newest ad medium, radio, and by inventive contests, had expensively gained 7 percent of the cigarette market by 1930. Advertising, it seemed, could achieve almost anything if you did enough of it and with verve.

V I I

Y ET another brand made its appearance during this period, and while it would prove modestly profitable, there was little about its style or performance to foreshadow the magnitude, in a reincarnated form, of the success it would one day score. The company that produced it was a pygmy in the field.

Marlboro was the brainchild of a personable native Alabaman named Reuben Morris (no relation) Ellis, who in 1924 had been named president of the Philip Morris Company, Ltd. Ellis had made his mark in sales as a youngster first with the tobacco trust in Philadelphia and then in New York with the leading independent firm of Miltiades Melachrino, an Egyptian whose Turkish brand, named for himself, had a considerable following in America's great portal city. With a colleague, Leonard Burnham McKitterick, a Nebraskan ten years his senior, Ellis put Melachrino on the map in the heyday of the Turkish brands. While they worked the whole country, their main effort was focused on New York itself, where they ceaselessly sampled hotel and theater lobbies, society balls, Bowery boxing clubs, and the racetracks. "We never knew what it was like to have a night to ourselves," McKitterick would later recall. One of his basic sales preachments, delivered to a young drummer he enlisted by the name of Alfred Emanuel Lyon, who would one day forge a fateful union with him and Ellis, was "People don't buy your product—they buy you and then sell your product."

When the trust was broken up, one of its quasi-independent parts, the United Cigar Stores, survived intact under its president, George Whelan, who at once used his chain as the basis for a holding company he called Tobacco Products Corporation. With financial help from Wall Street, he tried to snatch up any good little independent company he could find, now that the trust no longer threatened to strangle every operator outside its web. Among Whelan's first purchases in 1912 was Melachrino, whose stars, Ellis and McKitterick, he made Tobacco Products directors and handed major operating responsibilities. Though the Turkish market rapidly eroded, Whelan kept wheeling and dealing, and since every brand he could get his hands on had the advantage of favored treatment in his stores, the holding company's survival was not imperiled. In 1919, Whelan picked up Philip Morris as his final acquisition for Tobacco Products, and a nice little plum it was.

Since its American incorporation in the first years of the century with stockholders on both sides of the Atlantic, Philip Morris had puttered along unspectacularly, trading on its English name and resonance, which enhanced its standing during the war years even as the Turkish brands lost favor. Its makes still bore the royal coat of arms, though the king who had appointed its parent firm as tobacconist to the crown had been dead for almost a decade by the time Whelan used a group of Tobacco Products stockholders including Ellis and McKitterick to buy the little outfit and tether it closely to his holding company. Whelan put Reuben Ellis in charge of Philip Morris, whose brands held a collective half of one percent of the cigarette market in 1925, and told him to build it.

Aware of the growing female sector of the market, somewhere in the 10 to 15 percent range, Ellis reached into the Philip Morris trademark list for the Marlboro name and positioned it as a premium-priced smoke for women by putting it in a white pack with heavy foil, the royal crest in black and the Philip Morris signature scrawled across it in script, and a little arrangement of scrolls surrounding the motto "The Mildness of America's Best." In case anyone missed the point, the advertisements from the first bore the prominent slogan "Mild as May," the drawing of an obviously female hand holding a cigarette, and a smart text saying that no less outdated than the mustache cup, the overstuffed parlor, and the lapdog was the notion that "decent, respectable women do not smoke. . . . Has smoking any more to do with a woman's morals than has the color of her hair?" No other company had put the matter so boldly yet so artfully. By 1927, Ellis's company grew more aggressive, melding the snobbish and feminist appeals: "Women—when they smoke at all—quickly develop discerning taste. That is why Marlboros ride in so many limousines, attend so many bridge parties, repose in so many hand bags." To lend elegance, an "ivory tip," a little laminated wrap around the unlit end, was added to keep the cigarette paper from clinging to lipsticked mouths.

For all its *soigné* lure, Marlboro sold only a few hundred million units a year, barely one-fifteenth of what Old Gold managed. Even so, it helped Philip Morris turn a tidy profit—a lot more than could be said for the rest of the Whelans' Tobacco Products empire, which in 1929 crashed a few months before the stock market. When the separate units were sold off to satisfy creditors, on hand to pick up control of Philip Morris was Rube Ellis, who had gradually added to his holdings in the operation and now summoned his erstwhile colleague Leonard McKitterick from a long sabbatical in Europe. Between them, and despite an economy gone suddenly haywire, they would turn their little British-American hybrid of a duckling into a lustrous, if tobacco-stained, swan.

VIII

UPON succeeding his father as president of American Tobacco at the beginning of 1926, George Washington Hill seemed possessed by a need to show the world that he had not gained his position through nepotism, as if his more than two decades of service to the company had not adequately testified to his abundant skills. At that moment, Chesterfield was outselling Lucky Strike by 50 percent and Camel was 150 percent ahead of it. The new president, at the age of forty-one, vowed to end American's third-place humiliation. He did so with a single-mindedness indistinguishable from monomania.

George Hill, to put it charitably, was not a lovable man. He had few close friends outside of American Tobacco, and fewer still within it. A poor delegator of responsibility, he ruled like a paranoid dictator, energizing the company through tension and fear of his explosive temperament. He was forever issuing orders, now in a strong staccato, now in a high-pitched whine, and woe be it to whoever failed to execute his demands as prescribed. In some ways a throwback to the rugged individualism Buck Duke had embodied in the company's early days, Hill brought a truculence and eccentricity to his leadership that made it unnervingly volatile.

There was the matter, for instance, of The Hat. Inside the company's bastion on the east side of Fifth Avenue at the corner of Eighteenth Street, Hill always wore a hat. Sometimes it was a Stetson sombrero, sometimes a felt fedora, sometimes even a trout fisherman's rumpled number. The in-house joke, never uttered above a whisper, was that the hat was the boss's crown, always worn so none would forget who ruled. There were a few other trappings of kingly omnipotence, like the bodyguard patrolling the corridor outside his throne room and the Rolls-Royce perpetually parked close by the palace entrance, on standby to whisk him wherever the royal whim might dictate— usually lunch at the Vanderbilt Hotel near Grand Central Terminal. He was also reported to spit on his desk from time to time, though this may have been no more than a discharge of saliva accompanying an overzealously given command. To the outside world he was a mystery man. He rarely gave speeches or press interviews, avoided stockholders' meetings, and directed that the company's annual reports disclose as little as possible about its operations.

All that said, there was no denying Hill's obsessive devotion to the task before him. He put in endless hours with his sales executives, for example, trying to perfect his field force's presentation to retailers on the superiority of American Tobacco products. The marketplace had changed, of course, from the one in the days when Duke barged in on a still embryonic cigarette trade. Now the battle required sales acumen as well as muscle—no easy matter when dealing with competing brands that were practically all the same, save for their packaging and advertising. But Hill insisted on a rote script that would surely have put off all but the most pliant customer if delivered precisely as handed down from the mount.

He was satisfied that in Lucky Strike's cool green wrapper, he had the most distinctive and attractive package on the market. But Hill's advertising was not working well enough. Higher expenditures for it helped raise Luckies' sales about 7.5 percent during Hill's first year at the helm, but the brand still lost ground to Camels and Chesterfields. Frustrated because he considered himself an advertising virtuoso who often wrote his own copy, Hill had to reexamine his thinking on the subject. It amounted to a simplistic set of assumptions: (1) Your product must have a real or claimable difference from others of its kind, and (2) if it does and you drum it home loud and often enough, it will sell. Missing from such a reductive formula was the belief that consumer persuasion might be more a form of art than an exercise in arm-twisting. Since Hill ate admen for breakfast, it was no easy matter for him to concede he needed talent beyond his own to help Lucky Strike, but having so concluded, he hired the man widely regarded as the best in the business.

Starting in the mail room of Chicago's Lord & Thomas agency in 1902, Albert D. Lasker rose to its presidency in just eight years, and over the next thirty built such brands as Kleenex, Frigidaire, Sunkist, Pepsodent, and Quaker Oats into household, indeed almost generic, names. Lasker was a shrewd and somewhat cynical foil to George Hill's evangelical style of hucksterism, but they shared a basic belief in "reason why" advertising that relied more on a product's selling point of difference than brawny breast-beating. Between them they surveyed how rival cigarette makers were exploiting the themes of mildness and feminism, coded appeals to the fear of smoking irritation, and proceeded to outdo them gaudily.

Step one was to resuscitate the old "Toasted" flimflam, which Lasker's people now cloaked with the trappings of scientific legitimacy. Research chemists reported that the "toasting" in the Lucky Strike manufacturing process, by heating the leaf to between 260 and 300 degrees, did indeed reduce the nicotine and ammonia content and other acidic irritants, thus producing a "milder" smoke. Milder than what, was left to the imagination—surely than whatever the Aztecs had smoked in pre-Columbian Mexico. That the tobaccos in other leading brands were comparably handled was irrelevant to the Lord & Thomas scheme. "AN ANCIENT PREJUDICE HAS BEEN REMOVED," claimed the headline in a typical new Lucky Strike ad, which depicted a hand marked "American Intelligence" breaking free from the shackles of ignorance, elaborated thus in the copy:

YEARS AGO, when cigarettes were made without the aid of modern science, there originated that ancient prejudice against the cigarette. That criticism is no longer justified. LUCKY STRIKE, the finest cigarette you ever smoked, made of the choicest tobaccos, properly aged and skillfully blended— "It's Toasted."

"TOASTING," the most modern step in cigarette manufacturing, removes from LUCKY STRIKE harmful irritants which are present in cigarettes manufactured in the old-fashioned way. . . . LUCKY STRIKE'S extra secret process . . . removes harmful, corrosive ACRIDS (pungent irritants) . . . which in the old-fashioned manufacture of cigarettes cause throat irritation and coughing. . . .

To glorify this nonsensical claim, the hoary practice of soliciting celebrity endorsements was given a new twist. Moving beyond opera stars whose vocal cords were presumed uniquely sensitive to smoke irritants, Lasker's people signed up attractive stage and screen stars like Helen Hayes and Billie Burke, song-belter Al Jolson, heroic aviatrix Amelia Earhart, socialite home decorator Elsie De Wolfe, and then a slew of leading business executives, their egos fanned by public exposure in formal photographic portraits that bore their signatures as if to certify the goodness and unirritability of Lucky Strike. In a masterstroke Lasker then achieved the apotheosis of endorsements by soliciting doctors across America to try Luckies, and if they agreed that the manufacturer's miraculous, secret heating process made them the least abrasive brand on the market, they would receive five free cartons. The response allowed Hill's new ads to assert raucously what his competitors only implied in their velvet references to mildness: "20,679 Physicians Say Luckies Are Less Irritating. . . ."

The Lasker-Hill team truly hit its stride, though, with the sales proposition that smoking promoted slenderness, a pitch that deftly mated health concerns and female vanity. Who thought up the idea was beside the point, but the company's version of the famous campaign naturally credited George Hill, who was being chauffeured up Fifth Avenue one day on the way to his marble-pillared home on the Hudson in suburban Westchester when his car paused for a traffic light and he noticed a heavy woman on the corner chewing gum. Alternate versions have this rounded pedestrian wolfing down some sort of fattening refreshment, but all agree that when Hill swung his gaze to a taxicab waiting next to his car headed downtown, he noted that its passenger was a svelte woman sipping at her cigarette holder. Eureka! Already convinced without a morsel of documented evidence that smoking cigarettes was an effective appetite suppressant, Hill got on the phone with Lasker at the earliest possible moment, and soon thereafter the new campaign was exhorting, "Reach for a Lucky instead of a sweet." After the candy industry protested loudly, took ads out to complain that tobacco was a far worse health peril than candy, and pressured affiliates like the Schrafft's restaurant chain with its big candy-counter business to ban the sale of Luckies on its premises, the slogan was modified to "When tempted to over-indulge, reach for a Lucky instead." Lucky Strike sales raced ahead by 5.7 billion units in 1927, by an additional 8.3 billion in 1928 to surpass Chesterfield for the runner-up spot, and with a gain of nearly 10 billion in 1929 pulled within 200 million of Camel's stagnant sales.

At this point, American Tobacco lawyers were summoned to the Federal Trade Commission offices, where competitors had charged Hill and Lasker with concocting an ad campaign that amounted to an unfair business practice. The company was kindly invited, in the FTC's gentlemanly fashion of reprimand, to lay off the implicit claim that smoking cigarettes was a suitable way to diet. The Hill-Lasker response was ingenious. In a new series of ads, the drawn figure of a trim man or woman in the prime of life was shown in an athletic posture—a swimmer toeing the edge of a diving board or already in graceful descent, a horseback rider taking a jump, or a tennis or golf player completing a perfect swing—and hovering immediately adjacent in ghostly silhouette was a blob recognizable as the distended likeness of the original figure, striking a grotesquely similar pose. The ads bore headlines like "Is This You Five Years from Now?" or "Before It's Too Late" or "Face the Facts," followed in each case by: "When tempted to over-indulge, reach for a Lucky instead . . . (and) Avoid the Future Shadow." To hush the FTC, a line in small type across the bottom of the ads read, "We do not say that Luckies reduces [sic] flesh. We do say when tempted to over-indulge, 'Reach for a Lucky instead.' "

The Lucky Strike campaign of the late 'Twenties had none of the dull dignity of the Camel ads, the smart looks of the Chesterfield ads, or the occasional charm of the Old Gold ads; instead, it was strident, alarmist, numbingly repetitious in words but not graphics, and almost joyfully vulgar. No one would have mistaken these ads for art, but they worked.

To strengthen his hand further, Hill also hired the best publicists money could buy, in the persons of Ivy Lee and Edward Bernays. The latter was particularly adept at reading Hill's moods and broadening his outlook. When, for instance, the company wanted to do something dramatic in 1929 to counter the taboo against women smoking on the street, Bernays was allowed to engage the services of psychiatrist A. A. Brill, who counseled Hill that cigarettes were symbols of freedom for women as well as "a sublimation of oral eroticism; holding a cigarette in the mouth excites the oral zone," as Bernays recounted this flash of profundity. Thus, Brill concluded, "Cigarettes, which are equated with men, become torches of freedom." This last phrase sounded so uplifting that Bernays, with Hill's blessing, organized a "freedom march" led by ten debutantes and some prominent feminists who strode up six blocks of Fifth Avenue while smoking extravagantly as part of the Easter Sunday parade of finery. The stunt won enough publicity for Hill to seek analyst Brill's renewed counsel a few years later for a billboard campaign to show women smoking. One favored version presented a woman offering a smoke to two men, but Brill reminded its creators that the cigarette was of course a self-evident phallic symbol, thus the men ought to be offering it to the woman. Such was the motivational research of the day.

Superintending all this hoopla turned Hill into an obsessive autocrat. When a Luckies ad did not get preferred placement in a magazine or dominate its newspaper page, the Lord & Thomas team on the American Tobacco account might receive a furious tongue-lashing at any hour. Or Hill, who was said to have a radio constantly turned on in every room of his palatial home in order to monitor the Luckies commercials, would protest promptly if he didn't approve of the way an announcer delivered his paean to the brand. His expensive suits were tailored to conceal half a dozen packs of Luckies, which he used for impromptu sampling. The windows of his limousine were turned into miniature showcases for the brand. And in the garden of his Westchester home, tobacco grew.

During his first five years as head of American Tobacco, George W. Hill boosted the sales of Lucky Strike by 230 percent; by 1930, the brand was more than 8 billion units ahead of Camel. A mad hatter he may have been, but he could sell cigarettes with Buck Duke any day.

4

The Golden Age of Malarkey

A MONG those envious of R. J. Reynolds Tobacco's success it was some-times snidely suggested that the initial letters of the company's home-town stood not for Winston and Salem but for Work and Sleep, the principal, if not exclusive, activities in that torpid backwater. To this list they might chari-tably have added Prayer, all but obligatory in a town where the Methodist and Baptist congregations vied avidly for predominance, and Golf, the preferred recreation of the local upper crust. In truth, Winston, however suffocatingly parochial, had become a boomtown on the strength of RJR's rising fortunes.

In sharp contrast with the big-city ways of that consummate flimflam artist George Washington Hill, who had pushed Lucky Strike ahead of Camel, Dick Reynolds's successors were a diligent but lackluster lot, devoted to his mem-ory and precepts—perhaps slavishly so—and disinclined to risk much. Will Reynolds continued to stalk the warehouse floors during the leaf auction sea-son, heading a corps of one hundred Reynolds buyers and overseeing the pro-duction end of the business. The driving force, though, since the founder's death in 1918 was the tireless Bowman Gray, who rose to the presidency from the sales side and was respected for his mastery of detail. A certain brusque-ness of manner was attributed to Gray's shyness, a trait rare but not unknown among former salesmen; his penny-pinching was admired as tight manage-ment, and his idea of culture—having whole rooms removed from Touraine châteaux and shipped for inclusion in the manse he was having erected outside of town just across from Reynolda, the showy homestead R. J. had put up in his later years—inspired local awe. Nor was Gray hesitant to elevate his nephew, James, who had worked for the Wachovia Bank, the local Moravians' financial house, into a ranking post as RJR's chief money-watcher.

What this team lacked in innovative spirit they made up for in doggedness, and the Reynolds coffers overflowed in the late 'Twenties. The company had no bonded indebtedness, had retired its preferred stock in 1926, and raked in enough cash to pay out 84 percent of its net in dividends, so attractive a ratio that its stock price advanced steadily. Indeed, reports abounded that of the company employees and outside locals who had bought in under the favorable arrangements R. J. had set in motion to remove his enterprise from New York's control, some fifty now had Reynolds holdings worth a million or more dollars at prevailing market prices.

Still, American Tobacco under Hill had lately stolen Camel's thunder, and the nation's growing economic distress added to the sense that fresh blood might be a tonic for RJR as Will Reynolds retired as chairman in 1931 and Bowman Gray succeeded him. Installed as president and whip hand now was lawyer S. Clay Williams, who after fourteen years with the company, ten of them as its general counsel, was still viewed as something of an outsider. Much of this had to do with Williams's differences in background and temperament from the rest of Reynolds's lockstep managerial crew. For one thing, he was Presbyterian and thus suspiciously High Church by the local standard. He was also better educated than his colleagues; once a hulking guard on the University of Virginia football team, he had finished up college with a Phi Beta Kappa key from small but selective Davidson, while those few at the company who attended university went to the state institution at Chapel Hill. Then there was his profession: Williams was a funny, quick-witted, and somewhat long-winded attorney who loved the intrigues of state and national politics, often traveled for business and pleasure to Washington and New York—Sodom and Gomorrah to pious Winstonians—and was chauffeured to work at a company whose top executives had made it a point of honor to drive themselves in cars below the luxury line.

All that was petty stuff when stacked beside American Tobacco's advance, which Williams promptly moved to counter. Reynolds began to put a cellophane sheath around the Camel package to assure greater freshness, and dubbed it a "humidor wrap" in ads proclaiming the innovation. But the advantage was short-lived as Luckies and then the rest of the industry matched the move. And Luckies' advertising now grew even more cheeky as George Hill turned a lately acquired fascination with ultraviolet heat lamps for facial tanning into a new sales tool. "Don't Rasp Your Throat with Harsh Irritants. . . . Consider Your Adam's Apple," his brash ads hectored, reminding smokers that Luckies were " 'toasted' including the use of Ultra Violet Rays. . . . Sunshine Mellows, Heat Purifies. . . ." As if to distinguish them still further from its competitors, American's ads now also ascribed to the company a candor unique among cigarette makers: " 'Keep that under your hat,' said the cigarette trade when first we raised the question—'Do you inhale?'. . . . [E]veryone else inhales—whether they realize it or not," but "Luckies' famous purifying process removes certain impurities concealed in every tobacco leaf. Luckies created the process. Only Luckies have it!" Infuriated by now, Reynolds struck back with a series of combative ads cryptically mocking the Luckies claim by declaring that Camels were "NEVER PARCHED OR TOASTED" and urging smokers to switch to them for maximum freshness. But Lucky Strikes continued to gain ground, and Williams, in his annoyance, ordered the Camel ad budget pared back. And then he did something far worse.

In June of 1931, despite leaf costs that were the lowest they had been in two decades and a mere 25 percent of their wartime high, despite laborsaving developments such as a new type of ball bearing that raised the speed of production conveyor belts and helped cut industry payrolls to half of what they had been in 1914, despite continued strong sales of a product that proved cheap solace in a time of economic chaos, and despite profits that were annually netting Reynolds stockholders 23 percent on their equity—5 percent above the tobacco industry average and nearly double the return for American industry as a whole—Clay Williams ordered a penny-a-pack rise in the price of Camels. At the time, they and rival Luckies, Chesterfields, and Old Golds were selling for fourteen cents a pack or two for twenty-seven cents; the A&P markets, the nation's biggest food chain, was selling them at two packs for a quarter, putting heavy pressure on tobacco shops and other retailers to shave their sales price. Reynolds had exercised the pricing leadership in the cigarette business ever since Camel had raced out ahead some fifteen years earlier, but why it chose this moment, as the nation was tobogganing into full-scale depression and the company's costs were low and under control with profits still strong, was a mystery. Williams would later explain somewhat lamely that the 7 percent price hike to wholesalers, forcing the selling price in the stores to fifteen cents a pack, was needed to cover the added expense of the cellophane wrapper and to help hard-pressed retailers improve their profit margin. Some accused Reynolds of sheer profiteering, others thought the move a form of muscle-flexing in the face of Luckies' advance, but what was most remarkable about the ill-advised move was that the company's competitors followed its lead.

George Hill, by then the market leader and paying himself around a million dollars a year, would later explain that he felt American Tobacco had done its bit for the nation's growing legion of impoverished smokers by cutting the price of the Bull Durham roll-your-owns from eight cents a bag to a nickel for twenty smokes. But he conceded that Luckies' acquiescence in Camels' price rise had been sheer profit-seeking opportunism and, in view of the deepening economic crisis, had not been "the right thing" to do. Why, though, hadn't third-place Liggett & Myers held the price line with Chesterfield and sought converts? Its executives later rationalized that if they, too, hadn't boosted the price, the brand's revenues would have lagged still farther behind the leaders' and denied the company the dollars needed to sustain its advertising at a competitive level; furthermore, even if the company had held back, retailers would likely have raised their asking price to smokers anyway and pocketed the larger differential. Whatever the reasoning, the industry-wide decision, which smacked of price-fixing, though no evidence of collusion ever surfaced, was shortsighted, if not blind to the reality of the turbulent social landscape, and reaction to the callous step was swift.

Within two months, a small, old-line Richmond tobacco firm, Larus & Brother, put out a new brand called White Rolls, to sell for just ten cents a pack. It could afford to do this because leaf prices were severely depressed, and by letting the bargain price serve as the brand's chief sales inducement, Larus could save the 15 to 20 percent of production and marketing costs (exclusive of the six-cent-per-pack federal revenue stamp) that the top-selling brands spent on advertising. Then Philip Morris dropped the price of the troubled Paul Jones brand it had inherited from the old Whelan-owned Tobacco Products combine, and within several months the two new ten-cent brands had 4 percent of the national market. Seeing this, two Louisville-based outfits followed suit; Brown & Williamson, purchased in 1927 by big British-American Tobacco, dropped the price of its Midwest regional Wings brand, and Axton-Fisher, whose mainstay was the twenty-cent mentholated Spud brand, came to market with Twenty Grand. And other ten-centers followed, so that by the end of 1931 the Big Four had lost 6 billion units and almost 10 percent of the market to the bargain brands, which along with the roll-your-own lines were operating overtime to meet the demand.

Anxious, partly because the manufacturers of the cheap brands were no fly-by-night operators, the market leaders began denigrating the ten-cent cigarettes as inferior goods, made from low-grade leaf, and certain to vanish soon because at a dime per pack they could not generate the cash for advertising, the industry's vital nutrient. The upstart proprietors fought back within the trade, insisting that their tobacco was as good as the majors used, that cigarette advertising was mostly wasteful ballyhoo, and that with their manufacturing know-how and absence of greed of the sort that had inspired the Big Four to jack up their prices without justification, they could survive very nicely, thank you, on sliver-thin margins if the public bought enough of their bargain brands. And the public did, for a time. By the end of 1932, the cheapies had grabbed nearly 20 percent of the market. Almost panicky now, Clay Williams slashed the Camel ad budget again, from $9 million to $5 million, thereby compounding the problem, but his chief rivals were also hurting as a result of their colossal pricing error.

Rumors flew now about how the leaders would act to quash the surge by the dime brands. One report had it that they would soon market ten-cent "fighting brands" of their own. Another held that the majors would shortly begin bidding higher during the leaf auction season to drive up costs in the one area where the bargain brands were most vulnerable. While RJR dithered over how best to recoup, George Hill up in New York saw the national economy as well as his own market share plunging and knew it was time to admit a mistake. Over the first two months of 1933, American Tobacco slashed the price of Lucky Strike by 20 percent. It was enough to allow the brand to be priced on a par with or close to the ten-centers, though it meant that retailers were realizing less than one-third of a cent in profit per pack. For the major cigarette houses, all of which followed George Hill's lead, the slash meant operating at breakeven or actually in the red for a large part of that year. But in the process they succeeded in driving down the cheap brands' market share to 7 percent and regaining a substantial piece of their lost volume. Fat with profits as they had been, however, the leaders could not survive a price war indefinitely, and so, at the beginning of 1934, American Tobacco again broke ranks and edged the price of Luckies back up to two packs for a quarter. Profits improved, but at the cost of granting the bargain brands about 11 percent of the market over the rest of the 'Thirties.

Actually, it was less the hammering tactics of the major companies than the humane economic programs of the New Deal that squelched the rise of the ten-cent brands. By the beginning of the 1930s, tobacco farmers, for the most part poorly instructed in the ways of agronomy, had been reduced to near peonage. Strapped for cash as prices eroded, they were forced to pay a full year's interest charge for credit, although they needed loans for only half a year or less; the result was murderous rates as high as 37 percent for fertilizer and 27 percent for other supplies. And farmers were in a perpetual quandary as to how much and what grades of tobacco to grow—whether, for example, to fertilize heavily for a high yield of lower-grade leaf or lightly for a medium yield of high-grade leaf. Of vital help, of course, would have been some clue from the manufacturers as to the likely extent of their production needs, but given their tremendous concentration of buying power, the companies were hardly inclined to yield their bargaining advantage. Thus subject to chronic uncertainty as to how the auction market would greet their harvest, tobacco growers were unmercifully buffeted by the vagaries of the cigarette industry's needs of the moment. The reality was that the manufacturers maintained two- to three-year leaf inventories precisely to insulate themselves against gyrating prices and keep the growers at bay. By early 1933, this hardfisted policy had devastated the farmers. In North Carolina, the heart of tobacco country, 25 percent of all families were on relief; credit facilities were crumbling; and faced with ruin, the growers turned to state and local government for relief while threatening to withhold their harvest from the market altogether unless their most elemental needs were met.

The new Roosevelt administration was sympathetic, and the big cigarette makers reluctantly recognized they had suffered a setback in their public standing by the pricing maneuvers they had now abandoned. The new, vigorous Secretary of Agriculture, Henry A. Wallace, threatened to put cigarette prices under government control and open up the industry's books for inspection against profiteering if the manufacturers did not bend in recognition of the farmers' desperate condition. With Clay Williams as their spokesman, the majors did what they could readily afford to do—agree to pay at least seventeen cents a pound for leaf in the coming auction season, up from ten cents the previous year. From this commitment the federal tobacco price support system was fashioned under the Agricultural Adjustment Act. The essence of the program was the growers' agreement to limit their output by accepting acreage (and later poundage) allotments—violators faced a stiff 33 percent penalty tax if they brought over-quota leaf to market—in exchange for the government's agreement to buy up any leaf not bid for at a preset parity price pegged to the farmers' costs for doing business at the average prices prevailing during the 'Twenties. For their part, the manufacturers, besides displaying a willingness to pay a fairer price for leaf, agreed to advise the Department of Agriculture of their approximate supply needs in advance of the planting season so government administrators could better gauge where to set the guaranteed support level.

It worked. By 1936, leaf prices were twice what they had been a few years earlier—good news for everyone but the producers of the economy cigarette brands. Higher tobacco costs left them with nearly invisible profits as demand for their product continued strong. Philip Morris's Paul Jones was now moving 2 billion units a year, but at a dime a pack, it was a pyrrhic victory. As one Philip Morris sales official wrote in 1935 in commendation of his company's late president: "Paul Jones . . . stepped forward with a speed that took our breath away, and Rube Ellis, God bless him, quickly saw the dangers of allowing the brand to step into heavy volume and [he] put the brakes on, thereby saving our manufacturing life. . . . There is no profit in ten-cent cigarettes."

I I

I N an industry in which rival products were essentially identical, packaging innovations were readily copied, and lockstep prices were all but inevitable, Clay Williams came to see that his chief weapon in the battle to put Camels back into the lead that Lucky Strike had seized was more vigorous advertising.

The brand's starved ad budget was plumped up, and the bland Ayer agency's approach, featuring a covert denial of Luckies' "Toasted" blarney and the belated introduction of women smokers in the layouts, was abandoned. A new agency headed by a young, unorthodox New Yorker who had campaigned for the assignment was given the coveted Reynolds account.

William Esty, dark and intense, was the scion of a long line of New England ministers. An Amherst dropout and World War I machine gunner, he had taken a turn as a boardwalk barker on Coney Island and become an amateur magician before going to work as a space salesman for *The New York Times* and later as a copywriter for the big J. Walter Thompson agency, pushing Lux soap. After only seven years in the ad business, Bill Esty raised $100,000 and laid siege to Winston-Salem, claiming he could boost sagging Camels sales. His first suggestion was to pretty up the Camel pack; the brand name and the package colors tended to put off women, now a prime sales target. RJR executives, swallowing their indignation, said any tampering with the Camel look would raise concern among customers that the brand's quality had also been tampered with; Esty was told to do the job he was hired for.

"It's Fun to Be Fooled" was the theme of his earliest effort, a series of cartoon panels stemming from Esty's fascination with magic tricks and subtly urging smokers not to be hoodwinked by Lucky Strike's fake claims. "To avoid illusion about cigarettes remember this: Camels are made from finer, more expensive tobaccos than any other popular brand." It was an unverifiable claim and one that Will Reynolds, that savvy leaf-buyer, could not have relished, since his prime function on earth was to obtain good tobacco for Camels at the lowest possible price. Strict veracity, though, was not a serious inhibition for Bill Esty, and Reynolds's high command was too anxious to put George W. Hill in his place to be sticklers for the truth. RJR would fight malarkey with malarkey now.

The magic-show ads won a following but did not notably advance Camel's sales figures, so Esty launched a more daring series of campaigns characterized by inelegant layouts—a jumble of headings, photos, drawings, captions, and text blocks in boxes and reverse (white type on a black background), all clamoring for the reader's attention—and product claims that made George Hill's advertising read as if it had been crafted by Eagle Scouts. Esty's first sortie was his least adventurous flight of fancy: the cigarette as sedative, especially for those in tense or risky occupations. "It Takes Steady Nerves to Fly the Mail at Night," said one headline, and the text block had the plucky pilot elaborating, "That's why I smoke Camels. And I smoke plenty! Camels never ruffle or jangle my nerves, and I like their mild, rich flavor." That "mild" and "rich" may have been opposite qualities as applied to flavor was a quibble. What mattered was that "Camel's Costlier Tobaccos NEVER GET ON YOUR NERVES, NEVER TIRE YOUR TASTE," and a procession of big-game hunters, broncobusters, and bridge champions testified to as much at high decibels. And even if you were no daredevil or professional competitor but just a habitual nail-biter, pencil-chewer, or hair-puller, as Esty's snappy copy therapeutically prescribed, "Get enough sleep and fresh air—find time for recreation. Make Camels your cigarette. You can smoke as many Camels as you please" since they would never jangle your nerves. It did not matter that there was hardly a scintilla of evidence that habitual smoking had any calming effect beyond preventing those hooked on the habit from spinning out of orbit if they were too long deprived of their next smoke.

And Esty was just warming up. Determined to outdo Luckies' confected benefits from being "toasted," the adman searched high and low for clinical evidence to help Camels, and finally found an article in *Science* magazine, an exceedingly serious journal, by a pair of Yale physiologists who reported that smoking raised the body's blood sugar level, taken by some to be an index of human energy. Inquiring whether their studies had involved the use of Camels, Esty found the Yale scientists ill disposed to such exploitation; they suggested he enlist a commercial laboratory to do his bidding. While awaiting positive results from a New York food research lab, Esty's continual search yielded another article, this one by a pair of Swedish scientists reporting on the effects of smoking on diabetes—essentially negative, since it stimulated the adrenal glands, which in turn triggered the release of blood sugars (not to mention— which Esty did not in his ensuing copy—speeding up the heartbeat). As it happened, the Swedish investigators had used Camels in their tests. Esty went back to the Yale researchers with the Swedish data in hand but was told nobody knew if constant stimulation of the adrenal glands from smoking was healthful or harmful for the human organism. A trivial caveat for Bill Esty, who from these few threads fashioned a campaign that exclaimed, "YOU GET A LIFT WITH A CAMEL," adding, "A FACT: Science Advances New Data That May Completely Change Your Ideas of Cigarettes." Accompanying were little graphs and pseudo-scientific language that never bothered to explain how slight and transient the blood sugar rise was from smoking, that it was contraindicated for diabetics, that its connection with relieving muscular fatigue was hazy at best, or that even if Camels had this marginal tonic effect, so did every other brand. It was as outrageous and phantom a claim as Luckies' "toasted" boast, but it made for rousing ad layouts. One version spoke of "A HARMLESS RESTORATION OF THE FLOW OF NATURAL BODY ENERGY" from Camels which had been "confirmed by a famous New York research laboratory."

Camel sales climbed 8 billion units that year, while Luckies slumped by 4.5 billion and fell a fraction behind RJR's resurgent brand. Now Esty was hitting his stride. His 1935 marvel was "THEY DON'T GET YOUR WIND," a shrill endorsement by leading sports stars, with a virtual warranty of harmlessness in the supporting claim, "So mild . . . you can SMOKE ALL YOU WANT." Typical was an ad built around the then forty-two-year-old nonpareil of the net, Bill Tilden, who was quoted as saying, "Playing competitive tennis day after day, I've got to keep in top physical condition. I smoke Camels, the mild cigarette. They don't get my wind or upset my nerves. I've smoked Camels for years, and I never tire of their smooth, rich taste." Combining "smooth" and "rich" was an improvement, at least, over "mild" and "rich," but scientists by then were well aware that the faster heartbeat and reduced oxygen-carrying capacity of the blood which were a result of smoking, when combined with the higher oxygen demands of the body due to athletic exertion, were highly likely to induce breathlessness in the chronic smoker pursuing sports. Nevertheless, the latest Camel claim helped push its sales further ahead of Luckies.

Emboldened by his early success, Esty reached even further in 1936 by asserting, "For Digestion's sake, smoke Camels!" The subheading of this most dubious of all departures from scientific legitimacy read, "Camels make mealtime more pleasant—digestion is stimulated—alkalinity increased." Authorities cited for these claims were the maître d' of the Louis XVI dining salon at Washington's deluxe Shoreham Hotel, the most valuable baseball player in the National League during the previous season, and an "on-the-go" salesman of unspecified affiliation who confided to readers, "I smoke Camels as an aid to my digestion." To the extent that science understood anything at all at this time about the relationship of smoking to digestion, the prevailing view was that the custom might cause an excess of acidity, which is harmful, not beneficial, to digestion. In his mastery of mendacity, Bill Esty threw in a few other tricks that he supposed nobody was likely to learn about or call him on, such as the claims that Camels were lower in nicotine—than which competitors, the ads did not indicate—and left no aftertaste when in fact Camels were higher in nicotine than some rival brands, such as Lucky Strike, and *all* cigarettes left an aftertaste. Esty also wangled endorsements from celebrities like photographer Margaret Bourke-White, who would later concede that they had never smoked the brand.

It was no wonder, then, that *Fortune* magazine, the most astute chronicler of American business, labeled William Cole Esty the "Whizz and Whoozle Man." His technique, full of energy and visual pyrotechnics, left Luckies' pitch sounding muted and Chesterfields' genteel in the extreme. By the close of 1937, Camels were outselling Luckies and Chesterfield by some 40 percent. The Winston-Salem millionaires had put it to the city slickers at American Tobacco.

III

Iɴ Slicktown itself, an aging, thickening, and somewhat mellowed George Hill, still wearing his hat, sat in his plush, thirty-foot-square office on the second floor of 111 Fifth Avenue and, with less histrionics than a decade earlier, plotted how to halt the Camel resurgence. He was not given to small talk or foolery, but the new man from the Lord & Thomas agency on the American Tobacco account—Emerson Foote, who would one day become a principal in Foote, Cone & Belding, the successor firm to Lord & Thomas—found Hill's reputation as a man-eater somewhat overstated. "But Mr. Hill did have a unique faculty for creating tension in a meeting," Foote would later recall, and people at the agency on the American account "did have a way of disappearing without a trace."

If a touch more benign now, Hill still ran the company in an unorthodox fashion and very much as his own fiefdom. He installed his personal barber, Vincent Riggio, as the sales chief, after a spell of training, on the theory that he was very much in touch with the common man. As his chief aide and liaison in the all-important advertising department Hill designated his son, George, Jr. In 1931, he added, amid a cadre of yes-men vice presidents, a slight, soft-spoken attorney out of Columbia Law School who had been with the firm handling American Tobacco's legal problems, and before long Paul Hahn became Hill's shadowy amanuensis, a hired brain he trusted and tutored in the tobacco business. In time, he became the chief planner and rival to Riggio and George, Jr., as Hill's would-be successor.

Possibly Hill's most useful aide was a young former copywriter with the Young & Rubicam agency, brought in to energize American's creative marketing efforts. Sylvester Weaver, called Pat, was anything but a yes-man to the redoubtable huckster, who found in the irreverent newcomer a bold jester able to say things that made him laugh and think as few others in the place managed. Weaver, who would later have a notable career in broadcasting as the creator of the "Today" and "Tonight" shows for NBC television (and father of the actress Sigourney Weaver), found American Tobacco in the later 'Thirties a dream place for a bright young man to work at. Even though Lucky Strike was struggling to regain supremacy in the marketplace, morale was excellent. Weaver remembered, "you didn't have to work very hard—at least I didn't—and the pay was very, very good." As a junior executive, Weaver earned $35,000 a year in those still Depression-weary days, with an additional $10,000 for expenses. All the vice presidents were pulling down a quarter of a million or more at a time when that was a small fortune, and Hill held out the lure to Weaver. "He dangled the prospect in front of me, and I listened."

Lucky Strike advertising had become tiresomely repetitive, and to free it from Hill's heavy, strangling hand, Weaver had to be adroit enough, in developing fresh strategies, to present them in such a way that the boss either thought of them as his own or came out where Weaver and the agency people wanted him to. Part of the problem was weaning Hill away from media that were no longer cost-effective, like newspapers and billboards, which by definition were local and expensive. Weaver, Foote, and other young people on the Luckies account pushed for more play in national media, like magazines and radio. And in place of Hill's insistence on back-cover, black-and-white use only of the leading weekly publications, Luckies ads began to run in four-color reproduction inside the magazines on a biweekly basis, which, for a comparable outlay, created a far more striking appearance. The ads themselves moved away from the old sensationalism to a higher plane in a kind of lyric salute to the romance of tobacco, of which Lucky Strike was the ultimate embodiment. Leading artists, among them Thomas Hart Benton, were hired to paint handsome, heroic farmers lovingly examining the great golden leaves they had coaxed fecund Nature to bring forth. If the poetic copy partook of the fatuous and was less grabbing than the artwork, the net effect was nonetheless pleasing, and Luckies began to narrow Camels' lead.

Weaver and other younger aides scored their principal marketing victory not in the print media but in radio, the sensation of the age. A chief ingredient in this expanded effort was the sponsorship of more appealing and varied programs beyond Hill's own narrow and insistent preference for sweet, up-tempo dance bands. Musically superior groups like those led by Wayne King, Eddie Duchin, and Kay Kyser were put on the air, and the Lucky Strike "Hit Parade" now became vastly more successful as the weekly dispenser of the nation's top new popular tunes. In the comedy field, just opening up, Luckies backed the popular Jack Benny, whose arch voice and willingness to make himself the verbal butt of the show's humor worked well in a medium without visual cues. For the more cultivated listener, the company put on the air broadcasts from the New York Metropolitan Opera, the social and political commentary of newspaperwoman Dorothy Thompson, and "Information Please," a panel of cerebral types lightly parading their considerable learning. The company's commercials, too, showed a better understanding of how to use the broadcast medium. The most arresting of its devices were snatches of the tobacco auctioneer's twangy singsong, a nonstop recitation of the offered prices that served to spare the speaker's voice and baffle everyone but the buyers. The only decipherable part of the melodic babble as aired were the concluding words called out in triumph, "Sold A-mer-ican!" (as in American Tobacco). The delivery was inimitable and seemed to bond the company and all of tobaccoland inextricably.

The centerpiece of Luckies advertising in the late 'Thirties and early 'Forties was a refinement of the endorsement technique that American Tobacco had pioneered in the late 'Twenties when it lured thousands of doctors into supporting its claim that Lucky Strike was less irritating than rival brands. This time, unworried by medical concerns, the company came up with another group whose collective endorsement of the brand was likely to be seen by smokers as still more expert and persuasive—the leaf men, those in the business who were closest to the raw commodity. The new ads sang out in a ceaseless anthem, "Sworn Records Reveal That: WITH MEN WHO KNOW TOBACCO BEST, IT'S LUCKIES 2 TO 1." And here was a photograph, so you knew he was real, of Mr. Billie Branch, veteran of 2,000 tobacco auctions, stating, "Like most other independent tobacco experts, I smoke Luckies." He and his *confrères*, denizens of the auction warehouses across the South, testified that American bought the cream of the tobacco crop, and as a result, Luckies were less acidic and irritating.

This inspired campaign of persuasion unfortunately proved, upon close examination by government regulators a few years later, to be claptrap, a tissue woven from lies and gross exaggeration. The company claimed to have interviewed some 2,210 "experts," of whom it said 1,184 were exclusive Luckies smokers. Of these, federal investigators tracked down 440 and discovered that more than 100 denied smoking Luckies exclusively, 50 did not smoke at all, and some smoked other brands exclusively, some did not recall having ever been interviewed on the subject by American Tobacco, and some had no connection with the tobacco industry. Such details aside, the campaign and the company's new media-buying strategy were hugely successful, and by 1941 Lucky Strike would narrowly reclaim the market share lead from Camel and widen it dramatically in ensuing years.

"He was a dictator, of course," Pat Weaver recalled of the newly triumphant George Hill of this period, but now he invited the input of others. "His strength," said Weaver, "was his tremendous conviction about the importance of the business he was in. His weakness was tunnel vision—he was really obsessed with Lucky Strike, I'm afraid." But not to such a degree that he failed to recognize the danger of his company's dependence on a single brand amid the vicissitudes of a fickle marketplace. "One day, I came into his office," Weaver remembered, "and I said, 'Mr. Hill, I have a good idea.' He said, 'Great, what is it?'—he loved ideas." Weaver's was a not entirely harebrained scheme to get around the federal excise tax of six cents per pack of twenty cigarettes by putting out a brand in which each smoke was twice the normal length and the package would include a razor blade for slicing each one in two, thereby saving the customer the equivalent of three cents a pack.

Hill listened and nodded, then told young Weaver the government was not stupid and assumed that some smart aleck like him would dream up such a scheme and so had put a weight limit of three pounds of tobacco per thousand cigarettes manufactured to qualify for the federal excise of six cents per pack. As it happened, this limit provided leeway for about 17 percent more tobacco than was actually being used in the standard-sized cigarette. Weaver retired in chagrin but succeeded better than he knew. Several months later he was summoned to Hill's office, where he discovered to his astonishment its occupant sitting hatless at his desk. The hat sat on a table nearby, and Weaver was instructed to lift it. "That is how long a cigarette can be under the rules," Hill told him as Weaver's eyes feasted upon a carmine red package with an ersatz royal British crest in white and the name in slender, aristocratically elongated letters to emphasize the length of the cigarettes inside—PALL MALL.

It was the very brand that Hill, as a young executive under the tobacco trust thirty years earlier, had ushered from the mutt of the all-Turkish breed into the top position in the premium twenty-five-cent field. Now reblended, placed in a paper wrap instead of a deluxe box, and made longer—85 millimeters instead of the standard 70 (or about 3⅓ inches rather than the normal 2¾)—but a bit smaller in circumference to exaggerate its length, Pall Mall was handed to Hill's right-hand man, Paul Hahn, who was charged with edging it into the marketplace starting in 1940. Two decades later, long after emphysema and its complications had put George Hill in his grave, Pall Mall would reign for half a dozen years as the leading U.S. cigarette.

IV

THE pricing blunder made by the big three brands at the onset of the great 'Thirties Depression might well have eroded the oligopoly they had constructed over the previous dozen years, but as the threat of cheap cigarettes receded along with the hard economic times, it became plain that the industry leaders had weathered the storm well. Their most obvious challenger, Lorillard, had been unable to advance its Old Gold brand much beyond its initial successful incursion in the late 'Twenties. By 1940, Old Gold had faltered badly, selling one-third fewer units than it had a decade earlier. Two other cigarette makers had come forward, however, and each would become a major player in the business.

The more likely contender, given the resources behind it, was Brown & Williamson. Formed as a partnership in 1894, B&W was a small Winston-Salem maker of plug, snuff, and pipe tobacco that branched out by opening a factory in Louisville, close by a ready supply of Burley leaf. Looking to establish a presence in the growing U.S. cigarette market, British-American Tobacco picked up Brown & Williamson in 1927 and launched a new brand that bespoke its English ownership—a fifteen-center called Raleigh. It soon did well enough to become the No. 5 brand, behind Old Gold, but was suffering as the Depression hit, so its management cut the price and adopted a strategy that the industry had all but abandoned since Camel loped onto the scene. Each pack of Raleigh began to carry a coupon on the back, redeemable for playing cards, a card table, and later other prizes like electric toasters and irons that, in a sliding economy, were available cheaply enough to be factored into the selling price while keeping the brand both competitive and profitable.

The couponing of Raleigh became typical of the B&W marketing game: instead of trying to compete with the industry leaders by riding a single, strong entry and putting all the company's resources behind it, the Louisville-based company developed a stable of specialty brands, each different in some notable way from the majors. In 1933, B&W brought out a mentholated brand to compete with Spud, marketed by its Louisville neighbor, Axton-Fisher. Menthol, a chemical compound extracted from the peppermint plant and classified by medical science as a mild local anesthetic sometimes used in veterinary medicine, served to mask the harsher taste of nicotine and other elements in cigarette smoke by, in effect, numbing the throat to the irritating effects without diluting them. The menthol additive gave Spud's taste a kind of cooling, faintly medicinal quality that some buyers believed made smoking a less unhealthy habit. Brown & Williamson's new menthol entry, at fifteen cents, was a nickel cheaper than Spud and had a much more suitable name—Kool. Its ads featured a playful penguin and copy that narrowly skirted the sort of blatant malarkey peddled by the big brands. "GIVE YOUR THROAT A KOOL VACATION!" a typical ad was headlined, and its text followed up: "Like a week by the sea, this mild menthol smoke is a tonic to hot, tired throats. The tiny bit of menthol cools and refreshes, yet never interferes with the full-bodied flavor. . . ." Kool remained a specialty brand for the time being, as did B&W's 1936 novel entry, Viceroy, the first serious brand to feature a filter made from cellulose acetate, a highly malleable substance and more effective in certain configurations than the crimped paper and cotton wadding filter offered by Parliament, another premium brand introduced a few years earlier by a small, New York independent, Benson & Hedges, better known as tobacconists to the upper crust.

While none of its brands had made a big splash, Brown & Williamson's entries were selling half as many units as Liggett & Myers's by 1940 and held the No. 4 spot in market share. Closing in behind it by then, however, was a company with an old name that it had lately resuscitated with notable success.

Operating out of the lower floors of an inelegant, eight-story building with balky elevator service on New York's Fifth Avenue, a few doors north of giant American Tobacco's relatively palatial headquarters, little Philip Morris had found itself trapped by the price wars of the early Depression years. American descendant of the old London firm and the new breakaway independent from bankrupt Tobacco Products, Philip Morris relied for most of its business on its twenty-cent premium brand, Marlboro, which was stuck on a plateau of half a billion or so units a year and going nowhere in those hard times, and its ten-cent entry, Paul Jones, which was going great guns but, given its low profitability, rapidly depleting the company's limited capital. The luxury market, where the company had historically been strongest, had such bleak prospects in the early 'Thirties that its proprietors halted all imports, including the company's old English namesake, Philip Morris, in the brown, simulated cedar box.

But Philip Morris was run by a pair of wily, highly experienced men determined to make a go of the small enterprise they had liberated from fallen Wall Street titans. Its president, Reuben Ellis, had made a lot of friends in the industry with his surface joviality and a habit of wiring congratulations to dealer customers when they placed healthy new orders and, for good measure, on their birthdays. Underneath there lurked a shrewd, stubborn penny pincher whose credit-consciousness helped keep the company afloat by reassuring leaf buyers who continued to supply the cash-short outfit. Ellis's close associate Leonard McKitterick was the more cerebral of the pair; his patience and undemonstrative mien did not entirely cloak strongly held opinions and intense drive. The third and junior-most member of the company's ruling triumvirate was the master salesman Alfred Lyon, a feisty and voluble native Londoner whom McKitterick had hired twenty years earlier to sell Melachrino cigarettes and who for the past dozen years had been globe-trotting as the chief international purveyor of Tobacco Products' melange of brands. By now fluent (or so he said) in six languages including Hindustani and able to double-talk in English to the great amusement of those in on the gag, Al Lyon was full of jokes, tricks, and wonderful stories in which truth and apocrypha were so inextricably blended that even he no longer could distinguish them. He loved to recite the perils of his swaying voyage by camelback from Baghdad to Tehran, where he successfully sold his wares to the shah of Persia. And there was the time after the Great War when Al arrived in cash-poor Poland and to clinch a sizable sale had to barter his cigarettes for a considerable flock of geese. Since the birds were highly perishable and not readily transportable, the enterprising Lyon hired a bunch of local maidens who, for a modest ration of coffee he had previously acquired in a similar fashion, plucked the geese, whose feathers were shipped to Paris, where a well-heeled upholsterer converted the deal to cash. On enlisting Lyon's services, Ellis and McKitterick sent him to the fast-growing West Coast market to raise the Philip Morris standard, threadbare as it was.

To stay afloat and then prosper, the company plainly needed a new product, and while its distinctive features eluded them for the moment, Ellis and McKitterick were sure of one thing—it had to sell for fifteen cents and remain at that price, whatever the battering or temptation to lower it. At above fifteen cents, no new brand, or even an established one, could sell in volume during a depression; at a lower price, the new entry would be caught up in a glutted battlefield, where jobbers and retail dealers alike were being crushed by what they saw as the tyrannical domination of the big three brands, which in their zeal to stamp out the economy brands had slashed prices and, with them, dealers' margins. If distributors' livelihoods were unmercifully squeezed in the process, that was their hard luck, and for a time they might have to sell cigarettes as break-even goods or loss leaders. At Philip Morris, though, Ellis and McKitterick calculated that a new brand retailing for fifteen cents, or two and a half cents higher than the Big Three, would allow vendors as much as a 15 percent profit margin per unit, while wholesalers, for only a penny and a half more per pack than the major brands charged them, could realize a relatively vast 4 percent net. There was every reason to believe, therefore, that a new Philip Morris brand might win preferential treatment within the trade if it could generate sufficient demand.

But how, in those parlous times, to justify the existence of any new brand, let alone one selling at a premium? Philip Morris floated out a prosaic brand called Unis at the magic price, but nothing happened. Then Ellis and McKitterick devised a brand with claimed smoking qualities and an aura that gave it a chance for survival.

While in semi-retirement, McKitterick had found himself in a golf foursome on the Riviera one day in 1928 with a retired industrial chemist who six years earlier had filed a patent for a new kind of humectant, a humidifying agent that was proving useful in the manufacture of cosmetics, antifreeze, and explosives. The substance, a synthesized organic compound called diethylene glycol, might also be advantageous in the making of cigarettes, the chemist pointed out, because it avoided the irritating effects of glycerine, the humectant currently used in cigarettes to prevent their drying out and burning with a harsher than normal taste. Glycerine, an alcohol-like compound that neither hardened nor evaporated, had a nasty way, when heated, of producing acrolein, a form of tear gas, the irritant that Thomas Edison had wrongly suspected of being produced by burning cigarette paper. Diethylene glycol, McKitterick was told, gave off no acrolein and thus would contribute to a milder smoke. McKitterick promised to explore the possibility if he ever returned to the tobacco game.

When he did so the following year at Rube Ellis's request, McKitterick remembered the conversation about glycol, and put Philip Morris chemists to work in the old brick factory on Richmond's Tobacco Row blending the new humectant into a batch of Marlboro, the premium brand aimed at women smokers and promoted as "mild as May". The company's panel of eleven taste-testers reported that the glycol seemed not only to reduce the expected irritating bite of the inhaled smoke but also to bring out the Turkish content in the blend. But with the economy going bust, Philip Morris did not dare to experiment with one of its new fifteen-cent brands.

By 1932, though, when the search was on for a new fifteen-cent brand with a marketable difference, the glycol humectant was reexamined, and the company chemists tested, within their highly limited competence, to see whether it was safe for human consumption. At the same time, the leaf blenders elected to replace the 5 to 10 percent of the mix composed of Maryland tobacco in most leading brands with Latakia, a small-leafed variety grown mostly on Cyprus that took on a rich, earthy aroma yet yielded a mild, even bland smoke. Worked into the new Philip Morris blend, the Latakia contributed to a darker, more pungent tobacco that the company leaf men left free of most of the sweeteners used in the best-selling brands. This somewhat neutral taste struck Ellis and McKitterick as a highly marketable commodity, with perhaps particular appeal to women smokers.

All the blend needed was a name and a package. The solution to both lay right in front of their eyes, but they had been too close to see it. After hosting a dinner in Pittsburgh for jobbers and retailers at which he confided the company's plans for a distinctive new brand, McKitterick was approached by the proprietor of a hotel tobacco counter and urged to name the newcomer after the distinguished old-timer that for some thirty years had been associated with quality cigarettes—the tiny Philip Morris brand. Put it in a paper-cup package like other popular brands but let it closely resemble the old brand's attractive sepia-brown box with the simulated wood grain imprinted on it, and smokers would be more inclined to believe they were being offered a premium brand at a reasonable price than just another flashy suitor for their affections.

How better to overcome price resistance than to suggest that the new brand was a bargain, not a deeper reach into the customers' pockets? McKitterick and Ellis would advertise the new Philip Morris as costing "Now Only 15 Cents," though in fact it was a totally different product in its mix of tobaccos from the old twenty-five-cent British import made from Turkish leaf. To stress its Old World roots, the words "English Blend" would be added prominently to the front of the brown package, though there was nothing English about it except the nationality of the man after whom the brand and the company were named. To further emphasize its pseudo-Englishness, the new paper-cup package retained all the old elements that did not apply to the American variation, including the British royal coat of arms; the company's name with the abbreviation "Ltd." printed in type six times larger than its American counterpart, "Inc.," which followed it; and the words "London W." positioned in such a fashion as to imply that it was the company's home address, along with the added misinformation that the manufacturer had factories there and in Cairo and Canada, in addition to one in Richmond. To achieve instant lineage, the package also declared that the makers had been "Established Over 80 Years."

In-house, the Philip Morris people quickly took to calling the new product "English Blend" by way of distinguishing its name from the company's, but as soon as it began being floated out to the public early in 1933, everyone called the brand Philip Morris. If the name, the whole English getup, and its pricing at "Now Only 15 Cents" were part and parcel of a single, calculated deception—well, it was harmless enough—and as William Esty's ads for Camel were about to point out to smokers, "It's Fun to Be Fooled." In their introductory advertising pitch, Ellis and McKitterick were slightly less disingenuous than in the naming and packaging of the new brand. "Play it safe," the Philip Morris ads advised smokers, by buying the only brand that didn't produce irritating acrolein. The new smoke had "a natural, distinctive mildness found only in this new cigarette. . . . Philip Morris taste [*sic*] different because they're made different." McKitterick, however, was not entirely persuaded by the company's testing that the brand's distinctive humectant in fact created no acrolein or comparably irritating ingredient upon combustion, so he ordered the advertising to drop for the time being any direct references to the alleged chemical benefits in the manufacture.

Now the only problem was to spur the nation's 5,000 jobbers and 600,000 retailers to place the new Philip Morris into smokers' mouths. Ellis and McKitterick drew on every ounce of the considerable reservoir of good will the pair had built up during their combined sixty years in the tobacco trade. In consideration of the higher margins that the fifteen-cent price would provide them and the company's fervent pledge to cut out any dealers who refused to hold the line, many retailers across the country gave Philip Morris free window and counter display space during its debut month. Certain key dealers, it was whispered within the company, were presented with small parcels of Philip Morris stock to assure that the new brand, on which so much was being staked, received preferential display treatment. Such help was essential because the company lacked cash to grease dealers' palms and could not afford a massive advertising campaign to compete in the top sellers' league. And what they did spend on advertising had to pay off. A small New York agency run by Milton Biow was hired to conceive a campaign that had to sing out memorably above the din generated by the trade's heavy hitters. Biow's chief contribution to the process was to discover precisely the right singer.

Johnny Roventini was much like any other lad growing up in Brooklyn's tough Bay Ridge section. He played ball and roller-skated, hawked newspapers along the waterfront, and spoke the harsh argot of the neighborhood. But Johnny was unmistakably different from other teenagers; he had grown to a height of only forty-three inches. His mother, puzzled because she, her husband, and their three other children were of normal stature, took the nice-looking boy to every doctor she could find who might unlock the mystery. In despair, she counseled Johnny to eat well and get plenty of exercise, and eventually he would outgrow his affliction. But Johnny was to remain vertically disadvantaged. In his late teens he went to work as a pageboy in New York hotels, where his high, clear voice was an asset.

One morning in April of 1933, twenty-two-year-old Johnny was at his job in The New Yorker hotel, in his uniform of knickerbockers and an English tweed jacket, earning ten dollars a week in wages and another ten in tips, when adman Biow approached him. In his quest for an attention-getting but inexpensive gimmick to implant the Philip Morris name in the American psyche, Biow had rummaged through the company's file of old English journals from the turn of the century and come upon ads that featured a bright pageboy in pillbox hat, brass-buttoned jacket, and smartly striped pants who was offering readers a silver tray with a box of the distinctive Philip Morris brand and a card that said, "Call for Philip Morris." Pageboys seemed to suggest hotels and resorts that attracted wealthy guests—of the sort who could afford a fifteen-cent brand even in hard times—and now, Biow thought, with the arrival of electronic broadcasting, a page's call could become manifest, hammering on the national eardrum until the new brand's name was firmly registered within. Biow's inquiries for a page with an unusual voice brought him to the lobby where little Johnny Roventini worked.

Biow gave the page fifty cents and asked him to announce a message for Philip Morris—"without the 'Mister' "—and Johnny scurried all over the lobby, up to the mezzanine, into the barbershop, and through the dining room, emitting a vibrant, even piercing, but never shrill cry: "Call-l-l-l for-r-r-r Philip Maw-reeeees!" It was a pure, unforgettable sound, without a hint of the Brooklyn sidewalks from which its owner had sprung. Biow knew he had his pitchman.

Johnny was hustled over to the NBC studio, where Philip Morris's weekly radio program, a musical variety show under the supervision of orchestra conductor Ferdinand Rudolf Grofé, was in rehearsal. On testing, Johnny's call proved to be a perfect B-flat pitch and worked well harmonically with the "On the Trail" section in E-flat of the *Grand Canyon Suite*, which had established Ferde Grofé as a serious composer and served as the musical signature for the Philip Morris radio show. Johnny was put on the air at the first opportunity a few days later. McKitterick, who was on the West Coast, had thought the whole pageboy concept pretty silly; he changed his tune the moment he heard Johnny's piping call across the network's coast-to-coast hookup.

Johnny not only sounded good, but with his small, even features, which gave him a porcelain-doll prettiness, and his slender form, he looked good, too, especially when marched into the Brooks costume shop and outfitted in a tight scarlet jacket with bright gold buttons, black trousers with a red stripe, white gloves, and black pillbox hat. Actually, with his full, ruddy cheeks, which seemed androgynously rouged, he was *adorable*. Before long 100,000 life-size cardboard-cutout likenesses of the uniformed Johnny and foot-high statuettes of him were on their way to cigarette vendors all over the country for display purposes. When the announcer introduced Johnny as "stepping out of the store windows and showcases all over America" to deliver his patented call at the beginning and end of each weekly radio broadcast, the sound of tinkling glass was all but palpable. The little man was about to become the world's first living trademark, and the brand he pushed began to sell seriously.

V

W HE N Rube Ellis died at fifty-four toward the end of 1933, Philip Morris cigarettes were off to a promising start, but in the face of such a key loss in the company's leadership, new president Len McKitterick recalled Al Lyon from the West Coast, where he had been earning $5,000 a year while performing wonders for the company and especially the new brand. Lyon had opened up with just two salesmen in his charge, but within two years he had forty hard at work and had organized a network of college representatives, unique in the trade, to push Philip Morris with schoolmates.

Installed as vice president for sales, Lyon supplied the dynamism that would fuel the company for the better part of twenty years. An extroverted, debonair charmer, he was nearing the apex of a career that would be crowned by his inclusion in the book *America's Twelve Master Salesmen*, published in 1950 by *Forbes* magazine. Lyon, a self-instructed and omnivorous reader with a prodigious memory for passages he loved to spout, was full of gab and a disarming inquisitiveness that became his most useful sales tool. His trick was to probe lightly in an effort to learn all he could about his prey—where and how did his customer live, what were the names of his wife and children, which were his favorite foods and drink—or anything else that was grist for a chat. "A business deal doesn't have to be a dull, cut-and-dried operation," he would write. Superintending the now enlarged Philip Morris field force and gladhanding his way around the country, Lyon insisted that the company's representatives be courteous even when thwarted, make a good appearance because good grooming lent an air of authority to a man, and above all, never ask for an order until they had done a service that the customer had not expected, even if that meant helping the dealer open up his shop at seven-thirty, sweeping the floors, taking inventory, and/or buying his twin girls dresses for their third birthday.

With his sales apparatus well in hand, McKitterick addressed anew his flagship brand's purported health advantages as a result of the humidifying agent, diethylene glycol. If the substance was so beneficial, why weren't other manufacturers using it, too?

To find the answer, Philip Morris engaged the services of Michael Mulinos, an associate professor of pharmacology at Columbia University's medical school, the College of Physicians and Surgeons. Mulinos had performed earlier tests on the potency of various irritants by applying them in solution to the delicate tissues that formed the linings of rabbits' eyelids and then measuring the edema, or amount of swelling. For Philip Morris he prepared three batches of cigarettes made from the same tobacco: one batch had a humectant consisting of a 3.65 percent concentration of glycerine, the substance used in most other brands; the second had a 2.74 percent concentration of glycol, the humectant used only by Philip Morris, while the third batch had no humectant added. The smoke from the three batches was dissolved by being bubbled through three different liquids: water, a saline solution, or a preparation called Ringer's fluid, the latter two approximating the salt content of the blood and other chemical constituents of bodily fluids and tissues used in experiments. The outcome, as measured by the rabbits' edema, was that the smoke with the glycol added was rated "much less irritating" than the smoke with the commonly used glycerine—and, *mirabile dictu*, less irritating even than the smoke with no humectant at all.

The limitations of Mulinos's study, however, ought to have left the company's technical people wary. To start with, the two humectants were of differing strengths, and the results might have been less favorable if each had been applied at the same concentration. Worse, no distinction was made among the three differing fluids in which the three kinds of smoke were dissolved, even though there was a distinct possibility that plain water, without the saline solutions, was more of an irritant than the prepared solutions. Here, then, were two important sets of what scientific researchers call "confounding factors," which muddied the results. Furthermore, there was no objective standard for measuring the degree of swelling of the rabbits' eyelids—only the momentary visual observation of the investigators. And whether the human tissue in smokers' throats was comparable to that of rabbits' eyelids in susceptibility to the effects of the humectants was anybody's guess. Finally, a certain skepticism prevailed even in that period regarding research subsidized by any party with a vested interest in the outcome.

All of that notwithstanding, the Mulinos study was published in the October 1934 *Proceedings of the Society for Experimental Biology*. His test was repeated the following year by a pharmacology professor from the New York University Medical School, and while he cured one of the flaws of the Mulinos study by dissolving the smoke from all three tobacco batches in the same saline fluid, the same laboratory assistant who had made the visual appraisals of the edema in the earlier experiment was employed in the new one, compromising clinical objectivity. More to the point, other laboratories that investigated the subject failed to confirm the claims made for glycol.

Understandably uneasy at relying on the rabbit test, McKitterick commissioned a new kind of test. Frederick Flinn, head of the public health and hygiene department at Columbia's Physicians and Surgeons, was a throat specialist who asked ten colleagues in his field to enlist the cooperation of ten patients each, who among them had smoked for an average of twelve years and were then consuming twenty-eight cigarettes a day. Three-quarters of them were suffering from a congested larynx or pharynx, two-thirds had coughs, and seven had irritated tongues. All agreed to quit their former brands and smoke only cigarettes with the glycol humectant. After just three to four weeks, according to Dr. Flinn, the symptoms of irritation presumably caused by the subjects' smoking had disappeared in nearly two-thirds of the cases, while all the rest enjoyed a "considerable improvement"; three-quarters lost their cough altogether, and every case of irritated tongue vanished. Then the process was reversed: the subjects were fed cigarettes with the usual glycerine humectant, and before long some 80 percent of the subjects displayed renewed irritation, and many declined to continue smoking the obviously harmful cigarettes.

These truly astonishing results, while understandably inspiring exultation at the Philip Morris office, were clouded in the view of outsiders because there were no stated standards for what constituted "irritated" tissue, there were no data given on the differences in the subjects' smoking habits—*e.g.*, how many cigarettes per day they smoked, or how far down the butt, how many inhaled, and to what extent—and there was no way of telling if all the sore throats and coughs were due to smoking. The perfection of the results from the manufacturer's point of view was, on the face of it, cause for concern, and while the Flinn results, when published in the February 1935 issue of *Laryngoscope*, a professional journal, indicated that the research "was made possible through a grant by Philip Morris & Company, Ltd., Inc.," the company's vested interest in the outcome was not explained.

Such cavils were swept aside now by McKitterick, who ordered a rise in the decibels of the claims made in behalf of the Philip Morris brand. The clinical details were omitted from the consumer advertising, but the company hired nine publicists to roam the country distributing reprints of the Mulinos and Flinn studies to every medical practitioner they could find. They haunted doctors' conventions, sent out mass mailings, and placed ads in some forty national and state medical journals, arguing the case for Philip Morris's less irritating effects and offering copies of the experimental results to any doubters. The brand's sales moved ahead steadily.

The drumbeat grew louder after the relatively cautious McKitterick died in August of 1936. His successor, Otway Hebron Chalkley, a lanky, reticent native of Richmond, had served as secretary-treasurer of Philip Morris for a dozen years, knew the leaf and manufacturing end of the business inside out, and was judged a somewhat safer choice for president than the flamboyant Alfred Lyon, elevated to executive vice president and more than ever the catalyst of the company's growing sales strength. Chalkley deferred to Lyon in the marketing area, and the latter lost no time in charging up the advertising with breast-beating hyperbole. Diethylene glycol, at best a dubious benefit to smokers, was touted as "the greatest achievement in cigarette manufacture since the introduction of cigarettes themselves," while Flinn's hazy study was said to have "*proved conclusively* that on changing to Philip Morris, every case of irritation due to smoking cleared completely or definitely improved" (italics in the original text). An asterisk indicated that the conclusive studies had appeared in "leading medical journals," and it was further stated, "These facts have been accepted by eminent medical authorities." Actually, the medical journals were obscure ones, no "eminent medical authorities" had embraced the findings, and there had never been any evidence that the throat irritation so swiftly cured by the glycol additive was "due to smoking."

By 1938, even the company's ads in medical journals were indulging in such rash statements as "Our research files contain exhaustive data from authoritative sources," when in fact there was no new clinical support for the Mulinos and Flinn claims. That year, *Consumer Reports*, the monthly magazine of the two-year-old Consumers Union, a nonprofit organization devoted to objective assessment of product quality and claims, performed taste and chemical tests on thirty-six cigarette brands. The magazine noted in its July number that the makers of Philip Morris "lay great stress in their advertising upon their substitution of glycol for glycerine. The aura of science surrounding their 'proofs' that this makes a less irritating smoke, does not convince many toxicologists that they were valid. Of the many irritating combustion products in tobacco smoke, the modification of one has probably little more than a psychological effect in reducing irritation felt by the smoker." All that Philip Morris had really proven was that in the creation of deceptive advertising, it could compete toe to toe with the big boys.

VI

THE battle to put the new brand on the map was now joined in hand-to-hand combat, literally in some cases, in every store that sold cigarettes. Philip Morris had a unique asset in little Johnny, who was turning into a great door-opener for the sales force as parents brought their children to attend the pageboy's personal appearances. These had become so successful and numerous that the company hired four understudy Johnnies to travel the country, but only the original continued to give the call on radio that some in the business press said snidely was beginning to produce "an international earache." Johnny's celebrity compensated to some degree for the company's relatively small marketing muscle, flexed mostly in the big cities on the East and West coasts, where two out of every three packs of Philip Morris were sold. The most hotly contested turf was, of course, New York City, where 20 percent of the brand's sales were recorded.

Salesmen were dirt-cheap then, and the company put on some ninety men, most of them earning twenty to twenty-five dollars a week, to try to get the young brand into New York stores and displayed competitively. Unlike the big, rich companies that gave their field men a car to drive, the Philip Morris crew walked or used public transportation, lugging their samples and display materials with them. The full complement mustered early every morning at the company's 119 Fifth Avenue offices, with their battered leather furniture and poky elevator, and, while standing, endured a harangue delivered by the sales manager, John Switzer, a terror who had worked for the Schulte cigar store chain and drilled his troops constantly on the price lists, how to cope with tough customers, and the need to save their empty packs of Philip Morris for conspicuous littering—the cheapest form of advertising. Switzer was said to have a weekly quota of men to fire in order to keep his salesmen inspired by dread at a time when it was hard to find any kind of a job. Woe be it, then, to any man called upon at the morning meetings, where the day's routes were assigned, who did not give crisp answers and satisfactory reports on how many store visits he had logged, how many displays he had placed, and how many reorders he had written the previous day. The quickest way to be booted out the door was to refer to any rival brand by name—circumlocutions were mandatory; thus, Lucky Strike was "the brand with the green pack and bull's-eye."

"There was a terrific turnover rate," recalled Max L. Berkowitz, who as a youngster from the Bronx came to work for Philip Morris in 1937, hid in the back of the room to avoid Switzer's terrible lash, and survived forty years, eventually to direct the company's sales operations. The Berkowitz sales technique, more suited to the New York tempo than Al Lyon's more folksy and leisurely approach, became a company legend. "You had to talk fast and hard," he would recount long afterward. "People had to be trained—you had to know how to open—you just couldn't say hello." His typical opening was to lay out a few packs of Philip Morris on the counter until he caught the eye of the store owner or manager and would remark, "Everyone else in the area tells me they're selling an awful lot of Philip Morris—how are you doing with it?" If the answer was positive, Berkowitz pushed for a bigger order or an earlier reorder. If the answer was negative, he would ask why and offer to improve the situation by putting up a display carton on the counter or in the window.

Usually the offer was curtly rejected, and Berkowitz would begin to fast-talk. What was the problem—the push money from Liggett for a window display? How much were they paying? "None of your business," the owner answered. Berkowitz persisted: "So what is it—three bucks? Seven bucks? Whatever it is, you're tying up your window for—so how long is the deal? What, *three weeks*! The cigarettes get stale sitting in the window that long—make it two weeks, and put us in there for a week—people don't want to keep looking at the same thing for too long, anyway." If the window was out, he would push for the countertop. "Here, let me put up a carton on display for a week—what, a week is too long? Two days, then—you can spare the space for two days, can't you?" If the answer was still no, Berkowitz would practically have to beg for one day of free display, and if he succeeded, there was every chance that the next salesman through the door from a rival brand would take down the Philip Morris carton. Sometimes out of desperation, Berkowitz recounted, "we became prosecutors, saying things like 'Why are you doing this, putting in so much two-for-a-quarter stock when you can do better with us at fifteen cents a pack?' " The key was to ready a comeback for every situation. "You see, the salesman actually has the upper hand—it's like a pitcher in a ball game. He knows what pitch he's going to throw, and the batter doesn't."

Such dauntless prodigies of salesmanship began to pay off. Philip Morris sales were now doubling annually, and by 1938 the brand had swept by Old Gold to take fourth place among the cigarette industry's top sellers. And the profit margins were strong, thanks to the flagship brand's fifteen-cent retail price, a highly effective advertising campaign—the company spent only two-thirds as much per unit sold as Reynolds did on Camels and half as much as Liggett did on Chesterfields—and a generally tight, no-frills operation. Al Lyon's selling prowess was celebrated in a *Time* magazine cover story in April of 1938, and Wall Street took notice as net income that year reached $5.6 million, as much as the company was grossing in sales just before the launch of the "English Blend" Philip Morris. *Financial World* called the company "a coming blue chip," and its new issue of preferred stock was snapped up.

About the only setback the company suffered as the 'Thirties wound down was a slap on the wrist by the Federal Trade Commission, lately empowered to police deceptive advertising and business practices. The brazen, ersatz Englishness in the packaging and presentation of the Philip Morris brand was no longer acceptable. The prominent "London W." on the package front was replaced by "Made in the U.S.A.," the "Inc." in the company name was made the same size as the "Ltd.," and the unicorn facing the rampant lion on the imitation British royal crest lost its horn to become a plain horse.

More nervy by far than the company's counterfeit Englishness in introducing its bread-and-butter brand was the original pricing decision. Based on nothing intrinsic to the product—no fancier tobaccos or flavors or packages or greater length of smoke—the fifteen-cent price was imposed on a marketplace in upheaval. By 1940, due almost entirely to the performance of that stodgy little brown pack, the company had won 7 percent of the U.S. cigarette market. The other top shares by brand were held by Camel, with 24 percent (and about to lose the lead to Luckies); Lucky Strike, 22.6 percent; Chesterfield, 18 percent; the ten-cent brands combined, 12 percent; Raleigh, 5.1 percent; Old Gold, 3 percent; and Pall Mall, 2.2 percent. It had been a remarkably skillful piece of marketing for Philip Morris to have penetrated the Big Three oligopoly—and done so with the gusto of a practiced mountebank.

V I I

To label the cigarette makers of the 'Thirties as knowing charlatans, as unconscionable purveyors of a wicked product, would amount to unfair revisionist history. It would be closer to the truth to note that Americans were in love with smoking at a time when their collective life was low on other consolations. If the habit was bad for their health, so was hunger, and the latter seemed the more pressing peril by far.

Even the most responsible journals in the periodical press were moderate in their criticism of smoking, which on balance was held to be a marginal social benefit. *Fortune* magazine, in a late 1935 appraisal of the medical effects of tobacco and alcohol, reported that much mystery on the subject remained and "[i]t is only certain that the cigarette evil has been exaggerated." Although some medical men claimed that oral and bronchial cancer were more common among smokers, "the prevailing opinion is that they are not," and while some practitioners believed that chronic bronchitis linked to the habit ("smoker's cough") made the subject more susceptible to pulmonary disease, "this belief is now discounted. . . ." That same year, *Forum & Century*, a prominent journal of social commentary, gushed over how Nature, "to protect the delicate tissues of the breathing organs . . . places around the system a screen, as it were, which assures the normal function of breathing and yet permits indulgence in smoking to a considerable extent, with little, if any, damage to the mechanism." In its June 1936 issue, the highly regarded *Scientific American* ran a piece by one of its editors who stated, "Most smokers—probably all smokers—are doubtless harmed to some extent, usually not great, by smoking." But the article went on to contend that cigarettes represent "a packet of rest" that quiets the nerves, that "the average intelligent smoker knows when he is smoking too much because he does not feel well . . . and eases off, almost unconsciously," and that even if smoking were truly risky, it is also dangerous "to climb mountains and stepladders, play football, cross the street, or merely to exist, but the risk is so small that we willingly accept it. . . ."

Such nonchalance was even echoed in *Consumer Reports*. The scrupulously objective journal said in mid-1938 that many readers had asked its staff to render a technical judgment of cigarettes, "one of the most widely used and most misrepresented products," because, for all their common usage, their quality was unregulated by government. After running chemical and taste tests on thirty-six top brands, *CR* reported: (1) There was little perceptible difference between brands of cigarettes of the same type, and in blindfold tests smokers could "little distinguish" between brands; and (2) ". . .[c]igarette smoking is probably slightly deleterious to the human machine," and none of the popularly advertised brands appeared to be any more or less harmful than the rest. It gave the back of its editorial hand to "the obvious bias of cigarette manufacturers, as well as of the 'scientists' whom they directly or indirectly subsidize," and, with regard to claims of mildness, listed the concentration of nicotine it had found among the market leaders. Chesterfield, the least clamorous in its advertising, was rated as strongest with 2.3 milligrams of nicotine per cigarette, tied by Philip Morris's specialty premium brand, Marlboro—"mild as May" it wasn't. Philip Morris itself was close behind with 2.2 mg. of nicotine, followed by Old Gold, 2.0 mg.; Camel, 1.9 mg.; and last—*i.e.*, lowest in nicotine among the leaders and thus making partially good on its many boasts of superiority—Lucky Strike at 1.4 mg.

The same year that *Consumer Reports* ran the first of what would later become a regular battery of comparative tests intended to keep the cigarette industry honest in its ad claims, a widely respected biostatistician at Johns Hopkins announced perhaps the most troubling data yet on the relationship of smoking and health. Raymond K. Pearl had long been fascinated by why some members of the same species live longer than others and, after studying rats, roosters, vinegar flies, mice, and—now near the end of his career—men, he had concluded that "the duration of life in general varies inversely with the rate of living." The heart that beat faster, the organism with the higher metabolism, did not survive as long. In exploring the subject, Dr. Pearl constructed life tables for 6,813 men whose medical histories he found in the Johns Hopkins files, complete with their smoking habits. These revealed that smoking "is associated with a definite impairment of longevity," that only 45 percent of smokers lived until age sixty, compared with 65 percent of nonsmokers who did so, and that the disparity held at every age level up to seventy, even for those who smoked moderately—not the case with moderate drinkers. Pearl was not prepared to argue conclusively that smoking *caused* poor health; indeed, it might have been a manifestation of a faster "rate of living" that took its toll in many ways, with smoking an incalculable factor inseparable from the rest. Pearl was a bit vague, moreover, about the source of his data and the uniformity of its collection, and his sample was hardly random or representative of the whole population.

If the effects of smoking on the human system remained unclear, in one area of pathology, at least, cigarettes were beginning to be seen as a discrete and likely agent of harm—cancer of the lung. Only 371 cases had been reported throughout the United States in 1914; by 1930 the figure was 2,357, and by 1940 it would reach 7,121. Here was a growing incidence of a subspecies of a disease long regarded as so mysterious and shameful—in part because it was dreaded as the incurable prelude to a lingering and painful death—that it was rarely even mentioned in obituaries; its victims were said to have succumbed "after a long illness."

For medical science, cancer represented a rebuke to man's limited curative powers. The disease rarely manifested itself until those harboring it were too far gone to save, and even then, the surgeon's art had not sufficiently progressed to cope with the immense energy of the virulent invader. Cancer was the single name for a disease of baffling complexity, producing more than one hundred kinds of tumors with rogue cells that never ceased the process of mitosis—subdividing—in contrast to normal ones with a finite number of divisions programmed into their genetic code. Cancer cells were known to steal oxygen and other nourishment from surrounding cells for their own malignant needs and to use their support systems to create a network of connecting tissue, blood vessels, and nerves, all of which starved the body and gave its victims a wasted look. In time, the cancer expropriated the body's blood and lymph systems for growth and waste removal, voyaged around the body, and colonized, with fatal results.

The arrival of radiology and the X ray near the end of the nineteenth century improved cancer diagnosis, but chemotherapy was as yet unknown. Surgery was the only treatment, and often the size of the tumor was so massive that its attempted removal was almost always fatal. In lung cancer, before the development of the artificial respirator, surgery was complicated by the need to avoid collapsing the lung on incision and shutting down much or all of the body's breathing apparatus. By 1926, there were 800 clinics for venereal disease in the U.S., 600 tuberculosis sanitoria, and 100 heart clinics, but hardly a single institution devoted solely to cancer care. To bring the disease out of the closet, the American Society for Control of Cancer—later called the American Cancer Society, the nation's largest voluntary health organization—was formed in 1913 and devoted itself primarily to educating the public on the need for early detection of the condition. But only when the cancer society began enlisting women from the Social Register to spread the word about this disease that did not distinguish among the socioeconomic classes in settling on its victims did public awareness of it intensify. In 1937, the federal government established the National Cancer Institute at Bethesda, Maryland, but it was a shoestring operation.

Still, researchers were coming to understand how normal cells turned malignant by stages—in a protracted metamorphosis of unknown cause or causes. The initial phase, hyperplasia, was commonly attributed to chronic irritation either chemical or mechanical (*e.g.*, by rubbing or some other form of abrasion) in nature which caused the cells to divide in a defensive reaction, so that the one or two layers of cells lining, say, the breathing passages would become aggravated by cigarette smoke and grow protectively to five or six layers. Hyperplasia in itself was a benign enough process, a toughening of tissue like the formation of a callus where a part of the foot or hand was constantly rubbed. The second phase of the cancer cycle—metaplasia—was more menacing. Cells became altered in their structure as they proliferated; their nuclei typically enlarged while the life-sustaining cellular fluid, or cytoplasm, was diminished. The reasons for this basic alteration remained obscure. The third and critical phase of cancer—neoplasia, meaning a new growth—generally referred to the development of a tumor. But there were tumors of varying degrees of virulence. Some grew and stopped; some enlarged continually but remained in their original organ or tissue site; some burst through the body's retaining structures, began devouring anything in their path, and spread their deadly reach via the body's circulatory systems. Learning why tumors behaved in their differing ways and whether medical science could do anything about them had to await the arrival of better tools and more knowledgeable investigators.

Laboratory experiments were under way in earnest by the early 'Thirties, and a few scientists were beginning to conclude that whatever other effects nicotine triggered in the body, cancer was not among them. The far more likely agent was one or possibly several of the chemical compounds in the tobacco that underwent changes during the combustion process and, upon inhalation, blanketed the bronchial system. Most prominent among these investigators was an Argentinian, A. H. Roffo, director of the new cancer institute in Buenos Aires, who pioneered in distilling from tobacco smoke the tarry residue—with the nicotine removed—of the burning process and applying it to the ear linings of rabbits. The resulting tumors were produced by the tar distilled from tobacco burned at high temperatures. And the most carcinogenic, or cancer-causing, compounds, Roffo's laboratory learned through chemical analysis by use of the new spectroscope, were a category known as hydrocarbons, of which the coal-tars were typical. Just how these compounds grew unstable in their internal atomic configuration when heated and turned into marauding irritants of peril to human cells could hardly be guessed at. But by the late 1930s, Roffo had come to believe that the menace of lung cancer from tobacco was so serious that antismoking measures ought to be undertaken by government. But some believed his dosages of tobacco tar distillate for animals was too large and hardly comparable to human exposure to cigarette smoke.

American clinicians, building on their direct experience and intuition, were coming to be persuaded in small but growing numbers of a causal link between smoking and lung cancer. One of them was Boston thoracic surgeon Richard H. Overholt, who, faced with the reality that removing the visible portion of a lung tumor often left intact its microscopic outcroppings and the promise of a fresh malignancy, took out his first whole lung in 1933. Lungs ravaged by cigarette smoke, he found, were not as black, certainly, as those of afflicted coal miners, but they were heavily pigmented and felt heavier and stiffer than normal ones. They behaved differently as well during surgery, taking longer to collapse—the standard procedure, surgeons had learned, before attacking the tumor—and longer to reinflate afterward, a plain indication of loss of the elastic, bellows-like function of the organ and its efficiency as the body's prime oxygenating agent. Firsthand knowledge of this condition, along with a keener awareness that cigarette smoke somehow overstimulated the mucus-producing cells of the bronchial system and generated congestive phlegm inviting to infectious microorganisms, helped Overholt understand why smokers fared so much more poorly postoperatively than nonsmokers. He began to refuse accepting patients for surgery unless they stopped smoking; in time he became a vigorous opponent of smoking and lost friends over it in the medical profession, too many of whom, Overholt was convinced, let their own smoking addiction warp their judgment about the true pathological nature of the habit.

Perhaps the best known of the outspoken medical critics of cigarette smoking at this time was New Orleans surgeon Alton Ochsner, who as a third-year student at Washington University's medical school in 1919 was summoned to observe a lung cancer surgery then considered so rare that he was told he might never see another in his career. And indeed, seventeen years passed before he confronted his second lung cancer patient—and then, as a professor of surgery at Tulane, he saw eight cases within six months, all smokers who had contracted the habit during the world war. This pattern struck Ochsner as far more than coincidence and suggested that the incubation or latency period of the wasting process might well be twenty or more years. By 1939, Ochsner was reporting in the journal *Surgery, Gynecology, and Obstetrics* on seventy-nine cases of pulmonary malignancy he had treated which left him in little doubt that the inhalation of smoke was a prime factor because of the chronic irritation it caused throughout the bronchial tract.

Probably the best-informed and most persuasive scientific paper of the decade on the smoking and health question was "Tobacco Misuse and Lung Carcinoma," written in 1939 by Franz Hermann Müller of the University of Cologne's Pathological Institute. He observed that the great increase in the consumption of tobacco starting before the First World War and accelerating since "runs parallel with the increase in primary lung cancer" (*i.e.*, cancer originating in the lung) and, given the smoking habits of the sexes, explained why the disease was six times more prevalent among men. Müller added that the incursion of the disease was probably linked to the breakdown of "the physiological defense mechanisms of the lung, particularly the action of the ciliated epithelium," a reference to the concerted sweeping action of the cilia, tiny hairlike projections lining the bronchial tubes and pushing along the protective film of mucus that trapped waste and abrasive foreign matter. In a defective body or one malfunctioning "due to continuous excessive strain (smoker's catarrh), the accumulation of carcinogenic substances which enter into the lungs from the outside occurs much more readily. . . ."

Müller had conducted the first careful study of its kind on the clinically observed relationship of smoking to lung cancer. Comparing the case histories of eighty-six men so afflicted with another eighty-six men of comparable backgrounds who were healthy, he found that only three of the lung cancer victims were nonsmokers—a correlation so high that in and of itself it was suggestive of a close link. Yet all but fourteen of the healthy cases were also smokers, so that the habit could hardly be said to constitute a sufficient cause of the disease. When the *amount* of smoking, rather than the mere fact of it, was taken into consideration, however, half of the lung cancer victims turned out to have smoked twenty-five or more cigarettes a day, while only about 10 percent of those unaffected by the disease smoked that heavily, suggesting a clear dose-response relationship.

A year after a translation of Müller's seminal study was published in the *Journal of the American Medical Association* (*JAMA*), that journal carried a report by three investigators at the Mayo Clinic entitled "Tobacco and Coronary Disease." It was largely statistical and did not speculate on the possible agents or mechanics of the disease, but the data were the first to suggest with authority a systemic pathological impact of cigarette smoke beyond the lungs. A cohort of 187 men between forty and forty-nine with coronary heart disease (CHD) included 80 percent who smoked; in a comparable group of 307 free of the disease, 62 percent were smokers—meaning that smokers in the study were about one-third likelier to contract the disease. In larger samples of 1,000 in each category, the Mayo investigators found that 5.4 percent of smokers in the forty-to-forty-nine age category suffered from heart disease compared with 1 percent for nonsmokers; in the fifty-to-fifty-nine age bracket, 6.2 percent of smokers had CHD vs. 2.6 percent of nonsmokers.

The public, unaware for the most part of these technical reports and serenaded by manufacturers about how benign their brands were, was taking to smoking as never before. By 1940, Americans eighteen and over were annually smoking 2,558 cigarettes per capita, nearly twice the 1930 level of consumption, even during the nation's worst economic catastrophe. The industry as a whole was earning 17 percent on its invested capital in 1940, or nearly twice the overall rate for publicly held American corporations.

The tobacco companies, therefore, had no need now to compete in pricing or leaf purchasing; only disastrous internecine warfare would ensue. Tobacco, no longer a monolithic trust, had become a classic cartel, prompting the U.S. Department of Justice to undertake a two-year investigation that culminated in a mid-1940 antitrust suit against the industry. But in the course of a twenty-week trial in a Kentucky federal court the following year, the government failed to produce any explicit evidence of collusion and proved only that it was in the companies' joint interest to act identically, except for their advertising, in what they paid to make, and charged for, their product. A jury found the industry guilty of unfair competition, even though during the immediately preceding years two companies had emerged as profitable new competitors to the established entries and a whole new tier of economy brands had come into existence beneath the leaders' price level. The fact was that the cigarette business, like most American industries now, was ruled by major players whose economies of scale were lifting the nation's standard of living. And nobody thought of the lords of tobacco as deadly predators.

5

"Shall We Just Have a Cigarette on It?"

THE December 1941 issue of *Reader's Digest*, the only mainstream periodical of the time to crusade against the alleged perils of tobacco, carried an article entitled "Nicotine Knockout" and attributed to Gene Tunney, in which the retired, undefeated heavyweight boxing champion, then running the U.S. Navy's physical fitness program, noted three likely consequences of serious smoking: "[Y]ou smell so strong and dogs will never bite you," you will cough in your sleep and so robbers "will not try to steal your belongings," and "you will have many diseases . . . and die young."

Within days of the article's appearance, many would be dying young from more acute causes than smoking as the world plunged into its first truly global bloodletting. In light of the imminent carnage, any risk attached to consuming cigarettes seemed irrelevant, and they became as never before the drug of choice to allay the chronic stresses of wartime. The U.S. military machine would eventually require 12 million bodies to operate it, and they smoked an average of thirty cigarettes a day, or about 30 percent of the total output, which soared to half again as much as its prewar level during the almost four years of American involvement. The classic renderings of weary, dirt-caked G.I.'s by cartoonist Bill Mauldin invariably showed young soldiers with butts dangling from their grimly wisecracking lips. The leaders of the Big Three nations in the antifascist coalition were heavy smokers, and the supreme commander of the Allied military effort in the Pacific theater, a corncob pipe clenched with resolve in his firm jaw, replied to home-front aeronautical workers who had wired him asking how best to spend the $10 million they had raised to help the

fighting forces: "The entire amount should be used to purchase American cigarettes which, of all personal comforts, are the most difficult to obtain here."
Earlier, President Roosevelt had ennobled smoking by declaring tobacco an
essential wartime material and granting military exemptions to those who grew
it. And women, supplementing the depleted civilian labor pool, took up heavy
manufacturing jobs with their attendant pressures and smoked as never before,
if not quite as heavily as men. The forced separations and other emotional exigencies of wartime added further to the perceived usefulness of the cigarette as
a sublimating device to soothe the nation's arrested sex drive and promote
fidelity until the troops came marching home. Could any product, lethal or
otherwise, be more patriotic?

As the New Deal's public works projects had vitally helped save the
nation's economy from hemorrhaging fatally during the 'Thirties, so now
the massive armaments required to win World War II had the deeply consol-
ing effect of restoring the country to prosperity. There was work for everyone,
and if profits shrank due to inflation, higher costs of labor and supplies, price
controls, and new taxes against profiteering, consumption of nearly all goods
soared. As particular beneficiaries of wartime demand, cigarette makers might
theoretically have sold all they could produce, even as the price per pack
advanced to fifteen cents and finally twenty before peace came. In fact, the
ingredients that went into the manufacture of cigarettes were all in short
supply, along with equipment and skilled workmen to run it. Since military
purchases were given priority, exacerbating the shortage as demand outstripped supply, the hoarding of cigarettes by civilians became inevitable,
along with a black market that included many consumer goods. Distributors
were put under tight allocations by the manufacturers to prevent the situation
from growing ugly, and while cigarettes were never officially rationed like
gasoline and meat, smokers grabbed any brand they could if their favorite was
out of stock.

World War II guaranteed a vastly expanded future customer base, as millions of previously nonsmoking youngsters in the service sampled the product,
available either free as part of their combat ration or for a few pennies a pack at
commissaries behind the lines, and became addicted to it. American soldiers,
furthermore, passed out the smokes from their abundant supply to civilians in
lands they liberated as a good will gesture or for services granted them in return. For several years after peace came to those war-shattered societies,
American cigarettes became part of a quasi-official currency in barter economies, and ten smokes could buy a soldier a full meal or a night with a woman.
A decade was to pass before the U.S. cigarette makers began actively to exploit the war-nurtured taste for the American blended product that would eventually become the world standard.

Wartime prosperity also reestablished and indeed deepened the dominance of the leading cigarette manufacturers. The *raison d'être* of the bargain brands all but disappeared in the full-employment economy, and while the huge growth in demand might have lured new competitors into the field, the outlay for leaf, equipment, and advertising to establish a viable presence would have required capital in heavy demand by the rest of the booming economy. Within two years of the war's end, the top three companies commanded more than 80 percent of the market, as most older buyers went back to their prewar, pre-Depression favorites, and new smokers gravitated toward the market leaders. Not only were the manufacturers beginning to prosper notably as wartime controls receded, but their distributors and tobacco growers were doing far better as well. Leaf farmers, who saw prices for their crops jump threefold between 1940 and 1949, were at a point where, so long as they abided by the strict acreage allotments set for them by the federal government, which bought up all unsold tobacco at no less than 90 percent of the annually adjusted support price, tobacco growers were raising the single most valuable crop per acre. *Fortune* magazine, no enemy of free enterprise, commented that the growers had now joined the tobacco manufacturers as an integral part of "the tightest little monopoly you ever saw."

During the war years, the cultural habituation of Americans to their cigarettes was seductively advanced by Hollywood. In that pre-television age, the movies were at their apex as an entertainment medium, and actors had discovered the protean uses of smoking on celluloid to enhance their craft. To convey callow anxiety, you lit up fumblingly, whereas the powerful, controlling screen personality did so with a masterful flick—always toward the smoker himself if a male, as if manfully impervious to the flame, and away from herself with caution if a woman. The little burst of fire signaled a moment of supreme self-awareness, often full of portent, and how the performer handled the emotion-laden prop thereafter spoke volumes. Quick puffs and repeated tapping of the ash meant irritation or nervousness. The lovingly cupped butt, slow draw, and billowy exhalation might signal profound contemplation or the cagey bluff. The stubbing out, depending how emphatic, might register menace or relief but announced at any rate that a decision had been reached and action was imminent.

No one smoked on screen to greater purpose than Humphrey DeForest Bogart, son of a New York society doctor and star of the 1942 film *Casablanca*, in which the hero is first encountered through a shot of his hand signing his name to a check and reaching for a half-smoked cigarette in a nearby ashtray. In that hand and in his mouth, the cigarette became endowed with a kind of ironic nobility as Bogart used it to make a moral statement about a world gone awry. He was that self-contradictory figure, the contemplative man of action, with a somehow tarred past, living dangerously in a present beset by corrupt authority and social injustice, toward which his every considered drag and expelled puff of smoke seemed to represent a mocking laugh of bitter defiance. Cool under pressure, Bogey characteristically—and *Casablanca* set the mold—wielded his smoke as a swordsman or gunslinger would his weapon in a pirate film or a Western, but instead of slaying his tormentor, he was more likely to resolve matters ambiguously by deftly discarding his still burning butt in a low, flat trajectory that ended in life's gutter. *Now Voyager*, first exhibited the same year as *Casablanca*, featured that prototypical female screen smoker Bette Davis, for whom the cigarette was laden with unspoken sexual language. She seemed to smoke with a seething intensity and, when she spoke, used the cigarette to punctuate her words; when she stubbed it out with ferocious finality, the vixen was ready to strike.

Yet it was Davis's co-star, Paul Henreid, who stole the show at the end of *Now Voyager* with the most intimate light-up in the annals of filmmaking. As the lovers hug the rail, this suavest of all screen smokers, to mark the unfulfilled outcome of their shipboard affair, placed two fresh butts in his mouth, lit them effortlessly, remarked, "Shall we just have a cigarette on it?" and delivered one to Davis, as if to bond them in the knowledge that love is perilous, and often as ephemeral and uncontainable as smoke.

I I

T HE war years and the one immediately after marked the swan song of George Washington Hill, whose rambunctious career at American Tobacco dated back to the beginning of the century and established him as the cigarette industry's most skillful pitchman. Hill never performed better than during those last years when Luckies flew by Camel to become anew the nation's favorite smoke.

Famed photographer Yousuf Karsh captured Hill's essence in a portrait at the time that revealed not a handsome man but a highly purposeful one, his by then fleshy face framing full lips, a beaked nose, and eyes shrewd, narrow, and not a little distrustful, surmounted by thick, demonically unruly brows; he wore his customary dark suit, solid dark bowtie, and trademark dimpled fedora, cocked slightly as if to declare his insistently eccentric personality. His hand, a heavy gold signet ring on the pinkie, held a lit cigarette, its smoke in a sinuous curl. He looked, all in all, like someone vastly enjoying himself.

And well he should have been. As a showman, he was in rare form, glad to shell out $22,000 a week for the talent alone—airtime was a lot extra—on Lucky Strike's top-rated Jack Benny comedy show and to impose, though more lightly than he had been wont, his regressive musical taste on "Your Hit Parade". At Hill's insistence, the latter dispensed with the services of a hot young singer named Frank Sinatra, whose style the cigarette baron judged too

slow and swoony, and hired basso profundo Lawrence Tibbett from the Metropolitan Opera to belt out "Accentuate the Positive," "Mairzy Doats," and other
such ignoble ditties. It was as a sloganeer, though, that Hill continued to enjoy
his greatest success. You did not have to be Sigmund Freud to detect the sexual overtones of the Luckies slogan "So round, so firm, so fully packed . . . so
free and easy on the draw." Hill had his share of duds, of course, like "Lucky
for you, It's a Light Smoke" and "Have You Tried a Lucky Lately?" and his
misguided venture into anthropomorphism, "I'm Your Best Friend" (said the
talking cigarette). But even one of his most banal slogans hit pay dirt: "Lucky
Strike Means Fine Tobacco." Repeated endlessly on the air and in print, it took
on the quality of a profound mantra, and by 1944 had become familiar enough
to be abbreviated—"L.S./M.F.T."—and thus gain telegraphic urgency. Hill
was so taken with the letters-only slogan that he ordered it placed at the bottom
of every Luckies pack. He had an indisputable knack for arresting the attention
of the consuming public without actively offending it, though he did not hesitate to grate on its nerves by endless repetition of that season's talismanic
slogan.

His nerviest, probably most effective, and possibly most fraudulent slogan
dealt with nothing more vital than the color of the Lucky Strike pack. For
years, close advisors like Eddie Bernays and Pat Weaver had been counseling the boss that the brand's dark green color against the brilliant red disk
bearing the Luckies name was an impediment to sales to women. The color,
however pleasing, was strong and would necessarily clash with or poorly complement a woman smoker's outfit and accessories on any given day. A more
neutral color, preferably white, would be smarter and more appealing, the way
the Chesterfield pack drew women to the brand. But Hill, having been a major
player in the creation of the brand and the original pack, was loath to depart
from it beyond a slight streamlining of the lettering and other small changes at
the time of the 1939–40 New York World's Fair.

But by early 1942, war needs had cut the availability of the copper powder
used to make the gold ink in which the inner circle of the bull's-eye disk and
the side panels of the package were printed, so a grayed tan had to be substituted. Soon after, according to the official company version, its vice president
for purchasing advised Hill that the chromium used to make the brand's basic
green ink was down to a three-month supply, because it was in great demand
for camouflage paint on military equipment. When Hill was shown a washed-
out green-yellow pastel as a possible substitute, he asked the vice president if
that was the best the production people could manage. His subordinate
shrugged and replied, "Just like the soldiers, green ink has gone to war." Hill's
palm came slapping down on his desktop, the Luckies pack was at once ordered changed to mostly white, and the ad agency hurried out the newly

minted (or deminted) slogan, "Lucky Strike Green Has Gone to War . . . so here's the smart new uniform for fine tobacco." Competitors and skeptics questioned the authenticity of the claim. Emerson Foote, who as a young ad-man worked on the Luckies account, probably came closest to the truth when he recalled, "If it was not an outright lie, the claim was surely overblown. It was pure Hill, done simply to attract attention, with possibly a shred or two of fact connected to it. But the agency liked it." The public liked it even more; Lucky Strike sales surged.

A longer-lasting demonstration of Hill's genius for investing the banal with sales appeal was the revival of American Tobacco's Pall Mall brand. The company became the first of the major cigarette manufacturers to field two strong entries, and in doing so, took pains lest the newer one cannibalize the mainstay. Pall Mall was differentiated from Lucky Strike by its British name, packaging, class appeal, and advertising, but for all its patina of elegance, the pitch was still vintage George Washington Hill in its shameless hyperbole and dubious allegiance to fact.

The chief distinction of Pall Mall was that it had been lengthened into a "king" size, a fact explicitly illustrated in all the 1939–40 ads by a little boxed diagram comparing it with standard-brand lengths and implying that you enjoyed more puffs for the same money. Then there was that gorgeous red pack with the gracefully elongated white letters of the name, the royal crest larger and bolder than on the Philip Morris pack, and beneath it, in case you hadn't got the message of its snob appeal, was the slogan "Wherever Particular People Congregate." For good measure, the crest bore *two* Latin mottoes, vying hard for the honor of being the more preposterously inappropriate: *"In hoc signo vinces"* ("Under this sign you triumph"), the divine message reported by the Roman emperor Constantine after dreaming he saw a Christian cross in the sky and later adopted as the banner and motto of the Crusaders; and *"Ad astra per aspera"* ("To the stars through adversity"), the state motto of Kansas. Hill and his dapper aide, Paul Hahn, assigned to take the refurbished brand big-time, were just warming up. The key sales argument was nothing so direct as Pall Mall's greater length but an insistence that its shape represented "Modern Design," the product of the very technology, claimed the ads, that was now bringing the world such wonder weapons of war as streamlined tanks, speedy aircraft, and the semiautomatic Garand rifle. "On the land, in the air, on the sea," intoned the radio commercials in a baffling allusion to the ubiquitous charms of Pall Malls, the words followed by a triple beep of a warship's horn. It may have made no sense, but it drew your attention. And then the crowning appeal: Pall Mall's greater length, it was said, "gentles the smoke" and made it milder, cooler, and less irritable to the throat. "It is a scientific fact that tobacco is its own true filter," the spiel claimed with Hill's usual wave at the truth, but the ads and commercials omitted that unless the smoker stubbed out the Pall Mall when he normally quenched his standard-length brand, he would absorb more, not fewer, irritants.

Hahn successfully sampled the new brand at 500 superior hotels, put on seventy-five salesmen to push it nationwide, and in 1940, the first full year it was broadly marketed, sales hit nearly 4 million packs a week. By war's end, the figure was nearly a million packs a day; five years later, the total would be three times higher, nicely compensating for the slump in Luckies.

But Hill did not live long enough to see his beloved Lucky Strike in sharp decline. Indeed, 1946, the year he died, was a banner one for American Tobacco, which added 36 billion units to its sales total—a 47 percent gain on top of the 41 percent advance during the previous four years together and the largest one-year gain ever by a U.S. cigarette maker. True, its profit margin was just over half the prewar level, due to higher costs and price controls, and below the net rate on sales achieved by R. J. Reynolds. But American Tobacco was selling one-third more units than RJR, and so, despite its lower profitability, brought substantially more dollars to the bottom line. When Hill died at sixty-one that fall at his fishing camp in Quebec, the house he left behind was the envy of the industry. Its factories were cleaner and more modern, their grounds meticulously landscaped, their tobacco stored in spotless warehouses that the company owned—not rented, as its competitors did—and its flatbed delivery trucks, made of aluminum and half again as costly as everyone else's carriers, were regularly washed in the company's oversize garages and emerged with the sparkling look of winners.

With Hill's departure, Buck Duke's legacy of rugged individualism came to an end at American Tobacco, which thereafter became a closely orchestrated organization instead of the one-man band it had so long been. Hill was succeeded by a caretaker president, Vincent Riggio, an able but overaged Hill loyalist who had directed American's sales operations but lacked the scope and tools to pilot the company through the choppier waters just ahead. After four years the reins were passed over early in 1950 to Hill's soft-spoken protégé, Paul Hahn, whose achievement with Pall Mall suggested that he was far more than a competent technician. This hopeful assessment would prove to be mistaken.

III

BILLBOARDS were not considered exactly avant-garde advertising by 1942, but it could not have done George Hill's blood pressure much good when his chief competitor, the North Carolina crowd at Reynolds Tobacco, invaded American Tobacco's headquarters town that year and put up a huge sign for Camel in Times Square. Overnight it became the nation's most famous billboard.

It was a model of simplicity. Two stories high and running half a block between Forty-third and Forty-fourth streets on the east side of Broadway, the sign had just three elements: the brand name in giant letters, its old slogan "I'd Walk a Mile for a Camel," and the huge head and shoulders of an American serviceman—a soldier one season, a sailor the next, an airman the one after that—who had for a mouth a perfectly round hole about a yard wide. Behind the hole and the surface of the sign was a chamber with a synthetic rubber backing that a cam would pull taut as the chamber filled with piped-in steam; a second gear would then cause the elastic membrane to relax with a whooshing sound and propel out the hole several times a minute a perfect simulated smoke ring that would grow to about fifteen feet in width as it wafted over the heart of the nation's premier entertainment district. Countless millions gawked at the Camel "smoking" sign during the twenty-five years it remained in place, serving as the prototype for some two dozen smaller versions around the country.

The famous sign, however, was an anomaly in RJR's otherwise lackluster advertising program during the 'Forties, as Camel fell further and further behind Lucky Strike and in 1944 even dropped below Chesterfield's sales. Its drab campaigns featured the report that in a poll of more than 11,000 doctors by three independent organizations, Camel was the preferred brand—a shopworn version of Hill's brainstorm of some fifteen years earlier—and urged smokers to try the "T-Zone Test" to see if Camel was not kinder to their taste and throat.

This pedestrian advertising was emblematic of what Reynolds Tobacco had become: a sound, profitable, unadventurous outfit, largely dependent on a single product that appealed mainly to males in rural and small-town America. Wary of outsiders by tradition, the company remained provincial by design and grew inbred by habit. In 1939, it had fewer than 2,500 stockholders, the largest twenty of whom controlled 60 percent of the common. By 1944, as management and ownership grew ever more tightly bound, 78 percent of the common stock was held by RJR employees, and its board of directors consisted entirely of company officers and department heads.

The company ran Winston-Salem like a classic corporate fiefdom; the town's chief manufacturer, bank, utilities, board of trade, politics, and religious institutions were under tight, interlocking control, and potential major employers who might raise the demand for labor, and with it the local wage scale, were not avidly solicited. As a result, Reynolds's pay to factory hands averaged less than at the notoriously stingy textile mills domiciled in the proudly, fiercely antiunion Carolinas. Not averse to progressive policies under its founder, RJR had turned stodgy and almost antiquarian. There were few college men in its employ, except at the very highest level, as if too much learning might soften a man and make him unfit for the hard practicalities of the tobacco business. Private offices were rare, telephones were scarce (and the chief executive officer had to approve of every new one installed), the accounting department still featured high stools and green eyeshades of Dickensian quaintness, and there was no air-conditioning despite the dank summer climate. Other than the close surveillance it exercised over just who was buying the company's stock, Reynolds operated with dispassionate leadership under the somewhat aloof board chairman, Clay Williams, and his chief operating overseer, the acidic ex-banker James Gray, who served as president from 1934 to 1946 and whose universe was bound by the company, his family, the Methodist church, and the University of North Carolina athletic teams.

Guided largely by short-term effects on the bottom line, Reynolds policies in this period reflected a small-mindedness that was nevertheless able to justify itself by the company's sustained prosperity. During the war, it had not been willing to risk profitability to pursue higher sales volume, and so its loss of market share was readily rationalized by a return on its relatively narrow equity base which remained 20 percent above the industry's average, thanks to RJR's low wages, absence of debt service, and generally cheaper costs of doing business. Once the war ended and pricing began to catch up with costs, Reynolds grew more aggressive in its selling practices. But its social consciousness was slow to awaken. The company's employment policies, not unique for the South in that era, were white supremacist; blacks were denied skilled, better-paying jobs and relegated largely to the dusty, often stifling leaf-processing rooms. By maintaining a two-tier wage scale for a workforce split about equally between white and black employees, the company effectively stymied union-organizing efforts across the whole rank and file. Reform efforts to improve wages and living conditions in the community, led by teachers, black preachers, and white union organizers, were promptly labeled as communistic by the company, dedicated to maintaining its cheap labor supply. After a boisterous, five-week strike in 1947, marked by standard repressive tactics like confiscation of the organizers' sound truck and arrest of its occupants as agitators, the house union emerged stronger than ever. Intermittent efforts to organize continued over the next eight years until the union movement was finally routed by an eight-to-five ratio when 13,000 RJR workers voted on the issue in 1955. The company would remain the only non-union shop in the industry.

Reynolds's lackadaisical marketing notwithstanding, Camels had nearly overtaken Luckies for the brand leadership by the end of 1948, but American Tobacco was still selling a healthy 20 percent more cigarettes than RJR, due partly to the rise of Pall Mall. Clay Williams decided that the moment was ripe—a whole decade after his main foe had taken the plunge—for RJR to market a king-size brand of its own and end its dependency on Camel. But as American had done, Reynolds wanted the new entry to differ markedly from its bellwether. Williams himself, while on a trip to Canada, had become taken with the Players brand, an all-Virginia smoke, as the British styled the Bright leaf cigarettes with very little flavoring that the Commonwealth preferred. Why not an all-Bright king for the new Reynolds entry, Williams suggested; the unblended tobacco was near at hand, minimal flavoring additives would further reduce costs, and nobody would mistake the product for a Camel. In effect, he was proposing that Reynolds go back to the pre-Camel days before the company had invented the American blended cigarette, and few in the RJR upper echelon chose to argue with the boss. The new brand was christened Cavalier to evoke the Virginia origin of its Bright leaf ingredients, and after promising test-market results, the new king was rolled out nationally in 1949. RJR salesmen, dressed up in swashbuckling seventeenth-century "musketeer" costumes, marched in promotional parades with local celebrities to kick off the first new Reynolds product in thirty-six years.

There was just one thing wrong—RJR had devoted those thirty-six years to habituating American smokers' taste to the highly flavored blended cigarette. Cavalier tasted bland by comparison, and the harshness of "natural" tobacco that sweeteners usually masked was unwelcome. Reorders failed to materialize, and there was no inventive advertising pitch to jar smokers loose from their old brands. RJR scrambled to adjust the taste, revamp the package, and juice up the advertising, but to no avail. Cavalier was a $30 million dud that its sire, Clay Williams, did not live long enough to see skewered. But the experience so soured James Gray, the new RJR chairman, on risky new products that the company had to await his death four years later before moving decisively into the new age of smoking.

In one area of its operations, however, Reynolds took the industry leadership in the late 'Forties. Cigarettes were perceived as a product that by and large sold itself on the strength of the advertising "pull" generated by company marketers and the creative agencies they hired. Industry salesmen in the field could do little beyond sampling to push brands individually with the millions of faceless customers; instead, their job was to hobnob with distributors, place point-of-sale displays, and do their best to see that retailers' stocks were regularly replenished. American Tobacco's more forceful advertising further diminished the importance of its footmen, who served primarily as order-takers. The Reynolds field force had to work harder, and it was not an easy life. There was much physical work involved as they drove their cars, often poorly equipped for cold weather, to even the most remote outlets to show the RJR flag, lugged fresh stock and signage in shabby canvas bags, got paid low wages and bare subsistence travel allowances, and were nagged by communiqués from company headquarters often sharply critical of their performance but rarely dispensing constructive advice. Those who made it up the ranks to division and regional managerships enjoyed little authority under the company's highly centralized operations. As a reward for their efforts, top sales personnel were likely to be mercilessly summoned to Winston-Salem for an annual strategy session over the Christmas holidays, presumably a time when little business could be booked. Morale was understandably low, and it was hard to retain good men in cigarette sales.

But as postwar margins improved with the lifting of price controls, selling cigarettes took on the rudimentary aspects of a profession. Manufacturers at that time sold mainly through some 3,000 wholesalers, many of them small, family operations that were inefficient and chaotic and fought endlessly over territory in a business without exclusive dealerships. And since all manufacturers' shipments were on consignment—returnable if unsold—it took little capital to go into tobacco jobbing. The typically overcrowded warehouse was a jumble of incoming shipments and outgoing orders, often colliding in the same space, and a lot of dusty, flyspecked, and ignored display materials; profits, not surprisingly, were measured in fractions of a percentage point. But since wholesalers were the industry's lifeline to the smoking public, company sales reps could hardly dwell on the inadequacies of the jobbing system; what they could and did begin to do, though, was revise the thinking of the million or so cigarette retailers toward the product. For them profit margins fluctuated widely, depending on their competitive situation: Chicago outlets, for example, might net as much as 18 percent per pack against only 10 percent in the more crowded New York City market. But because the markup for cigarettes was lower than for almost all other merchandise, the impression had crystallized in dealers' minds that the main value of the product was to create store traffic as smokers fed their daily habit and, it was hoped, bought other goods in the process. By the late 1940s, however, close analysis disclosed a quite different picture.

If dealers paid proper attention and gave adequate display space to cigarettes, gross profits on their sale were very high relative to the capital invested in their inventory, thanks to the product's remarkably high turnover rate and frequent, reliable deliveries by wholesalers. Per dollar of inventory investment, in fact, cigarettes were found to be almost five times as profitable as any other item on the store shelf; none moved as fast as, or in the volume of, smokes. One ideally located New York drugstore, plainly an extreme example of the phenomenon, was able through daily deliveries to post cigarette sales of $36,450 for 1949 on an average inventory investment of only $155. Though they accounted for just 3 percent of retailers' sales and storage space, cigarettes produced a disproportionate 5 percent of profits and, according to a 1950 survey of food retailers by Curtis Publishing researchers, the cigarette department delivered ten times as much profit per square foot of floor space occupied as any other grocery item. Cigarettes, moveover, were about the least troublesome product to handle: they were lightweight and durably packed, rarely spoiled, were hard to steal since they were usually sold from behind the counter, underwent few price changes, and required almost no selling effort.

To impress more firmly on retailers the virtues of this dream product, Reynolds now systematically upgraded its field force. Beyond better wages and travel allowances, its salesmen began to be regarded as professionals. Closer and more instructive communication with the home office became routine, better-educated salesmen were enlisted, given more sensitive training, and, when promoted, had more authority over their territory, which they might hold for many years, thereby gaining an intimacy with dealers well beyond any their transient competitors could achieve.

A classic example of the benefits of this more highly motivated and enterprising Reynolds sales force took the form of a simple discovery by one of the company's Seattle area representatives in 1948, a time when carton sales were growing in popularity amid postwar prosperity. Heavily loaded with the usual sales paraphernalia, the RJR rep happened to rest a small Camel display rack on an upended orange crate as he began pitching the store manager on the advantages of self-service cigarette displays. Noting how nicely the Camel display fit, the salesman proposed that the raw sides of the crate be covered with Camel posters to form an eye-catching base to support the display stand. But on reflection, and because he was supposed to help the store sell cigarettes in general, not just Camel, he suggested that the crate itself be turned into an all-brands carton dispenser, with Camels stacked above the central crate divider and competing brands below it. The store manager agreed to give it a try in view of Camels' rising market share, and the device worked like a dream. Soon RJR designed sturdier, more attractive racks and began giving them to retailers in exchange for the preferred display position and more generous space allocation than any other brand.

Eventually the Reynolds hardwood racks, prominently featuring the Camel and later RJR brand placards, became permanent store fixtures holding several hundred cartons and giving the company an enormous selling advantage that its salesmen worked hard to defend. "They saw the opportunity, they had the product and the capital to do the fixturing, and they cleaned up while the rest of us looked on," one rival salesman recalled. By 1950, Camel was again the best-selling brand, and Reynolds stood on the verge of its second golden age.

IV

WORLD War II treated no cigarette maker more kindly than Philip Morris. Sales were up by a third in 1941, by just under a quarter in 1942, and by more than a quarter in 1943—the biggest proportionate gains in the industry—and if profit margins were thinned, the company's market share hovered in the 10 to 11 percent range for a solid No. 4 position, well behind the majors but on top of the second flight.

By 1944, as demand continued strong, Philip Morris elected to drop the cellophane wrapping on its packs rather than curtail production due to supply shortages, figuring as some other companies also did that the brisk sales pace would prevent the product from turning stale on dealers' shelves. When the inevitable shortage of tobacco leaf itself hit, PM's executive vice president and supersalesman Alfred Lyon could not bear the thought of his company's loss of sales momentum. Lyon lived for sales; no other numbers mattered to him but sales figures, on the premise that if you could sell enough units, the profits would materialize sooner or later. Behind his desk hung a sign bearing the inveterate salesman's creed: "There are a hundred thousand reasons for failure but not a single excuse." It was not surprising, then, that when an opportunity appeared in 1944 to pick up a huge cache of aged tobacco leaf, Lyon urged Philip Morris's President Otway Chalkley to seize it, even if the tobacco came only with a whole manufacturing company attached to it.

Besides the 26 million pounds of tobacco in its warehouse and a serviceable plant in Louisville, the Axton-Fisher Company sold a pair of brands that Lyon rationalized might be far better marketed by Philip Morris. One was a king called Fleetwood, launched in 1942, that seemed a more promising entry than the deluxe Dunhill king that Philip Morris had offered in 1940 but attracted few takers. Axton-Fisher's other exploitable brand was Spud, the modestly successful, pioneer menthol that had been far outstripped by Brown & Williamson's Kool. Still, Al Lyon thought he saw potential in this pseudo-medicated kind of smoke that would eventually capture more than one-quarter of the entire market.

The cautious Chalkley thought that the $20 million asking price for Axton-Fisher was prohibitive, but Lyon, with Philip Morris on a roll, argued long and hard for the company to take the plunge. He finally prevailed. There was simply no other way to get the leaf—at any price—to keep Philip Morris's wartime sales growing. The newly acquired leaf allowed Philip Morris sales to hit a record 32 billion units—5 million packs a day as its creaking factories were pushed to the limit of their two-shift-a-day operations—by the close of the company's fiscal year in March of 1945. Its market share had reached 11.5

percent, its stock was at a record high, and on the next day—April Fool's Day—Lyon was installed as Philip Morris's $100,000-a-year president upon Chalkley's designation as board chairman.

Lyon did not have a good first year at the helm. In fact, he nearly ruined the company.

Because Philip Morris sales had advanced practically nonstop through some very hard times since the introduction of the "English Blend" brown pack a dozen years earlier, Lyon the happy warrior saw even brighter days ahead now. Explosive growth could be expected in the civilian market, long restrained by wartime priorities and shortages, and with victory in Europe at hand and the end in sight in the Pacific as well, distributors began placing heavy orders, partly in anticipation of an imminent lifting of price controls by the government; inventories assembled when the retail price was under wraps would of course yield considerably higher profits if the over-the-counter price was to climb by the time smokers bought them. Military purchase orders were sure to drop with the coming of peace and a reduction of the armed forces, but Lyon reasoned that the higher orders for the rejuvenated civilian market would naturally compensate. Thus, by mid-1945 he ordered jobbers' allocations increased by 50 percent and the flood of new orders to be expedited, even if Philip Morris cigarettes had to be shipped in their wartime packaging (*i.e.*, without cellophane or foil). The pragmatic overseers of the company's manufacturing operations at Richmond warned Lyon that the new orders were unrealistically high and brought with them a decided risk that the new shipments would go stale if demand fell off. Other companies were moving more cautiously, it was noted, holding allocations in line longer or easing them only modestly in the hope that supply shortages would lift with the end of hostilities and new cigarette shipments could thus be packaged to assure sustained freshness, should postwar demand turn soft. Lyon was unpersuaded. Philip Morris could steal a march on its timid rivals by not slowing down output to repackage as the war ended. He ordered Richmond to roll ahead full speed.

All of the company's unbroken progress, which Lyon had come perhaps subconsciously to view as divinely ordained, came at a price. Leaf inventories had to be steadily enlarged, production equipment purchased, and the big acquisition of Axton-Fisher paid off. Philip Morris was highly solvent, to be sure, but its short-term debt had risen to $40 million by 1945. Its Wall Street banking house, Lehman Brothers, proposed a $30 million trip to the financial markets, consisting of a $15 million new issue of preferred stock and another $15 million in twenty-year $2^5/_8$ percent debentures, both of which, considering the company's stellar record, Lehman felt would be quickly and fully subscribed.

But within weeks of the Japanese surrender in August 1945, cigarettes went from a state of black-market scarcity to one of sudden abundance. Hoarders stopped hoarding, smokers returned to their prewar favorite brands, wholesalers' shelves were loaded (especially with Philip Morris), and to compound the situation, the U.S. military, which had stockpiled cigarettes as a necessity of war, now stopped ordering altogether and would not reenter the market until the year's end. Other brands, in shiny postwar wrapping, were now readily available and selling nicely while Philip Morris, in its dull brown war dress, piled up. Customers complained that the product seemed stale, and switched to fresher brands. Telegrams went out from Philip Morris headquarters, reluctantly inviting wholesalers to return any stock they felt might have turned stale. All that autumn, the boxcars pulled up in Richmond and disgorged the oversupply—by the billions. For weeks the factory was getting back more cigarettes than the fresh ones—in cellophane wrap again, finally—it was shipping. Lyon made matters worse by ordering some of the stale returns to be wrapped in cellophane and reshipped as if new merchandise. When word of that gambit was leaked to the trade, the reaction was so furious that the practice was instantly halted and leaf inventories were invaded beyond normal to rush out replacement stock, accompanied by point-of-sale signs proclaiming, "Just arrived—FRESH!—Philip Morris cigarettes." But the damage had been done. In November of 1945, Philip Morris operations ran $57,000 in the red; December, usually a high-profit month, showed a net of just $12,000, and the prospect for 1946 was highly uncertain, considering the brand's tarnished reputation.

Lyon now made his final mistake in a string of miscalculations. While registering its planned $30 million financing with the Securities and Exchange Commission in mid-January of 1946, the company failed to mention the sudden downturn in Philip Morris's fortunes; the financial data in the disclosure statement covered only the first half of the current fiscal year, which had ended with the figures for October, before sales collapsed. Lyon would later lamely explain that the November–December numbers were not included for investors' consideration because management thought them a temporary aberration, due entirely to the economy's shift of gears from wartime and unlikely to persist into the new year. Word of the trouble at Philip Morris soon reached Wall Street, the stock price plunged, and the SEC ordered the company to tell all to the subscribers of its new issues and offer them their money back. Most of the investors accepted the offer, and the financing was humiliatingly withdrawn. Stale cigarettes were bad enough, but dishonest dealing with the investment community threatened quick ruination.

Lyon, true to his salesman's creed, offered no excuses. He conceded that he had been "a damn fool in trying to do everything, including many tasks I didn't know anything about. . . . I realized for the first time Philip Morris was no longer a baby, that we had grown up and not been aware of it." Lyon, the exemplary "street man," the drummer who could sell ice to Eskimos, was a victim of his own limitations, and his ambition had threatened to take the company down.

The basic soundness of the business and its primary product soon reasserted itself, and the crisis eased. Lyon was able to unload 5 billion stale units in cigarette-starved Europe, the volume loss for fiscal 1946 was limited to 8 percent below the record performance of the previous year, and Lehman Brothers was able to place the company's entire new financing package, now at $32 million and more needed than ever, in a private deal with Equitable Life Assurance. But it was clear to all concerned, including the beleaguered company president himself, that Lyon needed serious help, especially on the financial side, and fast.

Oliver Parker McComas had ancestors who once grew tobacco near the Maryland tidewater of Chesapeake Bay, but offered few other credentials to serve as rescuer of a troubled cigarette manufacturer. A big man with easy, polished manners, McComas had graduated from Princeton, won the Silver Star for gallantry during World War I, gone to work on Wall Street as a foreign-exchange trader, and in time nicely advanced himself at Bankers Trust, heading the Paris office for a while and then, back in New York, serving as the bank's chief commercial lending officer. Among his clients was Philip Morris, and Lehman Brothers, knowing of McComas's reputation for square dealing and tough-mindedness, urged Lyon to bring the banker on board, even if he had to be paid three-quarters as much as Lyon himself. Never an operations man, McComas relished the challenge of stabilizing Philip Morris's wobbly position; he came over late in 1946, and during the next eleven years would do much to set in motion the company's eventual rise to predominance in its industry.

The first two years were devoted to repair work, as sales remained in a trough and Philip Morris stock tailed off to 27, little more than a third of what it had been before the 1945 fiasco. McComas began by imposing far stricter budgetary and inventory controls and ordering full financial disclosure in company reports to Wall Street lest its reputation be further tainted. The headquarters staff was chopped by one-third in an economy move that allowed the company to correct the disastrous 200 percent annual turnover in its salesmen's ranks; better pay and benefits were offered to attract more skilled field men. A major planning and communications gap between sales and manufacturing was addressed by McComas in bringing to New York the chief of Philip Morris's production, Clark Ames, a bluff, profane, and very direct man who had run the Richmond operation, one semi-admirer would recall, "as if in charge of a cockfight." Younger and vitally needed new talent, also from the manufacturing side, advanced soon after Ames's arrival, including a pair of native Richmonders who caught on fast in New York. Robert P. Roper was the epitome of the courtly, witty, and sweet-tempered Southern gentleman, well connected in Virginia social circles and to the gentrified crowd that ran Universal Leaf, the big Richmond brokers who bought, financed, and partially processed Philip Morris's tobacco. Roper displayed a good deal more ambition and energy than the stereotypical progeny of the faded Dixie aristocracy as he reshaped the personnel and operations departments in New York. His close friend Ross P. Millhiser belonged to a family that owned a large box-making plant in Richmond and had sent him to Yale—a pair of distinctions he shied away from proclaiming upon joining Philip Morris as a factory hand before the war. Blessed with a questing mind and a love of words that had quickly made him useful to factory superintendent Ames, Millhiser reluctantly accompanied his boss to New York, where, after a checkered apprenticeship, he began to show a decided knack for marketing. McComas also now brought more professionalism to the company's public relations, hiring the firm of Benjamin Sonnenberg, a flamboyant, social-climbing, and highly gifted publicist. Sonnenberg assigned to the Philip Morris account a wry, smooth young native New Yorker, George Weissman, whose craggy good looks and resonant voice made him welcome at the company office, where McComas soon put him to work writing more forceful speeches and adroit press releases. Among them, Roper, Millhiser, and Weissman would form the operational core of the far larger enterprise Philip Morris was about to become; only their catalytic agent was yet to appear on the scene.

Within a year of his arrival at the company, Parker McComas, who all agreed was personable—for a banker—as well as skilled, was promoted to executive vice president. In 1948, the sales slump ended, Philip Morris's volume gained 20 percent, and sales and production had become well coordinated. By 1949, sales gained an additional 27 percent, earnings per share doubled, the company's market share was back up to 9 percent, and it was aggressively pushing its advertising on both daytime radio, as sponsor of popular shows like "Queen for a Day," and the hot new medium of television, where it was paying for programs with uniquely visual appeal like "Candid Camera" and "This Is Your Life." Philip Morris advertising itself, though, seemed to be suffering from fatigue. The little pageboy Johnny Roventini's shrill call was all too familiar, and nothing better was substituted for the tired claims of no throat irritation than the still more dubious promise of "No Cigarette Hangover" and the almost plaintive pitch that Philip Morris cigarettes ought to grace even nonsmoking homes for the benefit of visitors.

In 1950, the company picked up a further 25 percent gain in sales, which passed $250 million for the first time, and could claim 11 percent of the market, still well behind but now within sight of No. 3 Liggett & Myers, with its 18 percent share. McComas was by then president, as Lyon was shifted upstairs to board chairman upon Chalkley's retirement. That spring, the company moved from its beat-up offices on lower Fifth Avenue to color-coordinated, air-conditioned quarters on three lower floors at 100 Park Avenue, a short walk south of Grand Central Terminal—a sure sign of growing confidence and affluence. Yet the 'Forties had been a roller-coaster decade for the company; its earnings per share were still shy of the 1941 figure, and there were tensions now between McComas and the sixty-five-year-old Lyon, whose role at the company was now largely ceremonial. What neither man knew yet and would shortly inflame the growing gulf between them was that the Philip Morris brand had peaked, and no managerial finesse could compensate for a product whose time had come and gone.

V

A FTER breaking up the tobacco trust, the American government took no substantive regulatory action for the next thirty years against the manufacturers of what was probably the most profitable, among the most heavily and deceptively advertised, and arguably the least healthful consumer product in common usage. And when the government did act, with a pair of measures in the 1940s, these proved to be casebook studies in bureaucratic futility.

The two-year Justice Department investigation that culminated in a misbegotten antitrust suit argued in 1941 was prompted by political and social considerations in reaction to perceived economic injustice. Anger festered toward the cigarette makers throughout the 'Thirties for the millions they were garnering while tobacco growers and distributors of the finished product counted their profits, if any, in pennies. Though this disparity had been partially alleviated by New Deal programs, the antitrust case was still filed. But the long trial failed to yield any hard evidence that a collusive oligopoly had conspired to fix prices, wages, and the cost of supplies, and the cigarette industry's six leading manufacturers were found guilty only of their *potential* to conspire and destroy competition. A measure of the fruitlessness of this exercise in knight errantry was that the courts finally mandated no structural remedies and issued no cease-and-desist orders against any given practices by the industry, whose members' principal crime evidently was that they had learned they had more to gain by acting largely in concert than in combat. Only token fines were levied against the defendants, including Philip Morris, which had succeeded in doing precisely what the government antitrusters had presumably wanted would-be challengers of the oligarchs to do—namely, push their way to a profitable share of the market.

A far more legitimate blow to the industry was landed by *Reader's Digest* against the tobacco manufacturers' passion for the bogus sales come-on. Continuing its lone-wolf tracking of the industry, the *Digest* tested two dozen cigarettes from each of the leading brands—too few to be valid, the manufacturers cried—and reported the results in a July 1942 article entitled "Cigarette Advertising Fact and Fiction" by Robert Littell. Only very small differences were found between the brands with regard to their irritating properties, so that the smoker "need no longer worry as to which cigarette can most effectively nail down his coffin. . . ." The next month, whether fortuitously or goaded by the *Digest*'s exposé, the Federal Trade Commission filed a series of complaints against four of the top cigarette makers for continually offering health reassurances that skirted intolerably close to express warranties of harmlessness.

Established by Congress in 1914 to compensate for the perceived weakness of the Sherman Antitrust Act to combat the abuses of industrial concentration, the FTC had devoted itself mainly to policing unfair restraints on competition by manufacturers. Only in 1938 was the commission's scope widened to deal with certain concerns expressed by the object of industry's ardent pursuit—the American consumer. On the face of it, the FTC was handed broad powers to move against unfair and deceptive business practices, emphatically including advertising; the commissioners could now conduct investigations, hold hearings, subpoena documents, lay down fair-practice guidelines, issue cease-and-desist orders, and seek civil penalties in the federal courts of up to $10,000 per day per violation. Alas, Congress had whelped a toothless tiger, because the commission was denied the power to enjoin the suspect practice throughout the course of proceedings against alleged wrongdoers. In cases brought in 1942 against the cigarette makers, the industry lawyers, through endless motions, hearings, trials, and appeals, caused the adjudication to drag on for between eight and thirteen years.

In the case against Reynolds Tobacco, decided in March of 1950, the FTC found that Camel advertisements had been worded in such a way as to declare or imply that using the brand was harmless to all smokers regardless of their health, harmless to all parts of the body, and harmless no matter how many cigarettes were smoked, and, as such, were false and deceptive. It added that "for one to smoke as many cigarettes 'as he likes,' " as Camel ads invited, "is to smoke to excess," which, "like eating or drinking in excess, is harmful, not only to an athlete, but to others as well." And the claim that smoking Camels "renews and restores bodily energy" and like phrases were "clearly false and deceptive, there being in tobacco smoke no constituent which could possibly create energy."

With regard to American Tobacco's ads, "[i]n truth and in fact . . . Luckies are not toasted as that term is commonly understood by the purchasing public," the FTC found after endless deliberation, and they were no less irritating or acidic or lower in nicotine than their competitors. On the claim that tobacco buyers, auctioneers, and other such professionals preferred Lucky Strike by a two-to-one ratio and believed that American Tobacco bought the finest leaf, "there are no records sworn to and verified by such so-called experts which establish that such is the fact"—and besides, given the many auction sites and the proprietary nature of the blending process, these claimants "do not know the grade, quality, type, or prices of all varieties of tobacco making up Luckies, or any other brand of cigarettes on the market."

Lorillard was castigated for having gravely distorted the 1942 *Reader's Digest* study by stressing that its Old Gold brand was found to be the lowest in nicotine while failing to note that the difference between it and the brand with the most nicotine was only two-fifths of 1 percent—a margin that was found to be physiologically without significance. Indeed, the whole thrust of the article had been that there were no significant differences among the brands in terms of their likely impact on health.

The action against Philip Morris was potentially the most devastating because the brand had been built largely around the Johnny-One-Note claim of lower or nonexistent throat irritation due to the use of the humidifying agent diethylene glycol. The company had exacerbated the problem by clinging fiercely to the claim despite criticism of it both within and outside the industry; its advertising even included statements like "No other cigarette can give this proof. No worry about throat irritation even when you inhale!" and "Recognized laboratory tests have conclusively proven the advantage of Philip Morris over other cigarettes."

The government challenged the methodology, findings, and objectivity of the company-run tests in the mid-'Thirties that had formed the basis for these sweeping claims, and noted that no outside investigators had corroborated the reported results. When Philip Morris protested the FTC complaint and submitted further supporting test data from between 1944 and 1950, the government undertook similar studies and found the company claims wanting. In one company-backed test, for example, an investigator measured the size of a single blood vessel in the uvula, the pendant fleshy lobe in the upper throat, before and after subjects smoked various brands, in order to gauge the degree of irritation caused. But an independent investigator of the same phenomenon found varying and inconclusive responses among several blood vessels of the same uvula. In another before-and-after test run by the company, an investigator used a pharyngeal colorimeter to measure the intensity of redness in the throat caused by various brands, and found that the glycol humidifier used in Philip Morris was less irritating than glycerine. But outside investigators reported that throat redness was not a static phenomenon even without the introduction of irritants like tobacco smoke, that there were sharp variations for each individual tested, that the degree of redness differed within any given thirty-second period, and thus more redness readings had to be taken before and after smoking. In sum, the FTC held that the company had insufficient bases for its extreme health claims.

Philip Morris lawyers were so adroit at countering the government's case, however, that the matter was not finally resolved until 1955, when the company had long since dropped the health claim. The practices complained of in the other protracted government actions had similarly long since ceased. As *The Consumers Union Report on Smoking and the Public Interest* deftly put it several years later, "Like astronomers studying stars millions of light years away, the FTC commissioners were constantly coming to conclusions about phenomena that were no longer in existence."

VI

THROUGHOUT the 1940s, whatever the true health peril presented by smoking seemed trivial. Cigarette smoke was understood to contain irritants and toxins that were low-level and slow-acting, and the diseases in which they might be implicated struck mostly in old age. And anyway, after years of privation, Americans felt entitled to dissipate a bit without being nagged about their naughtier habits.

And so they smoked with growing abandon. Authoritative surveys in 1949 found that between 44 and 47 percent of all Americans eighteen or older smoked—more than half of all men and about one-third of all women. And they smoked a great deal: ten cigarettes per capita in 1950, which translated into more than a pack a day for those who actually smoked. Doctors, too, smoked like everybody else. Even some who concerned themselves with the possible connections between smoking and health were far from certain about the magnitude of the peril. Alton Ochsner, the eminent New Orleans clinician who before the war had been so outspoken on the matter, reported in the May 1947 *Annals of Surgery* on 129 lung cancer patients whose tumors he and his associates had removed, but noted, "Neither occupation nor smoking habits, which some reports, including our own, have stressed as of possible significance, seemed of any special significance in this particular series." In a population nearly half of which consisted of smokers, the finding that three-quarters of his lung cancer patients smoked did not then seem to constitute enough of a disparity to Dr. Ochsner to be strongly suggestive of a causal link. The *Journal of the American Medical Association* (*JAMA*) remarked editorially the following year that "more can be said in behalf of smoking as a form of escape from tension than against it. . . . [T]here does not seem to be any preponderance of evidence that would indicate the abolition of the use of tobacco as a substance contrary to the public health."

There had thus been few notable new findings on the smoking and health issue until 1950, when three important studies appeared. Collectively, they may be said to have marked the end of the age of innocence about the blithe charms of the cigarette.

Medical investigators had been coming to understand that the disease process was neither inevitable nor uniform but most likely the result of an interplay of environmental influences and bodily resistance that varied with individual genetic codes, themselves intricately differentiated, which some researchers were just beginning to decipher. Others continued to pursue the identity and behavior of the causative agents of disease and to assess the contributing roles of environment and human conduct. In short, nature and nurture were probed in tandem now.

But no disease continued to be more elusive—and fearsome—than cancer, the death rate from which doubled in the United States during the first half of the twentieth century. But because twenty years were added to the average American life span during that same period, the disease—so resistant to treatment and whose suspected causes were so numerous—was widely perceived as part of the aging process and beyond any hope of early conquest. Cancer of the lung, however, appeared increasingly to some observers to be a separable phenomenon. It had grown in the U.S. at five times the rate of other forms of the disease between 1938 and 1948, trailing only stomach cancer as the most common form of the affliction. Something—or things—was behind it. Air pollution, of which tobacco smoke could be considered a variant, was the most obvious suspect. Because the disease, whatever its cause, was usually so far advanced when detected and because even surgically treated victims survived only briefly, the scientific focus now began to shift from cure to prevention. What precisely was there in man's modern environment or his own unwitting behavior that was contributing to the sudden growth of this generally fatal disease? Here truly was a fit subject for the emerging science of epidemiology, the study of all the factors that distinguish those who contract a given disease from those who do not.

Among these early cancer physician-detectives was Johns Hopkins–trained public-health specialist Morton L. Levin, working on the epidemiology of the scourge's elusive causes at the State Institute for the Study of Malignant Diseases (later called Roswell Park Memorial Institute) at Buffalo during the 1930s and serving jointly as assistant director of New York's new state bureau of cancer control, a unit of the health department at Albany. Levin's discipline was so new, actually, that he was the sole investigator in the area at a time when only lip and tongue cancer had been definitely linked to smoking. "They didn't know what to do with me," Levin recalled, and much of his time was devoted to lecturing women's groups on the need for early detection of cervical cancer.

But the data on smokers' shorter life span reported in 1938 by Dr. Levin's former Hopkins mentor, biostatistician Raymond Pearl, and Franz Hermann Müller's still more troubling study in Germany set the epidemiologist thinking, even though as a longtime pack-a-day smoker of Lucky Strike he was reluctant to probe the perils of the cigarette habit. He ordered the staff at Roswell Park to begin the systematic collection of data on the smoking habits of every entering patient, regardless of complaint and before any ailment had been diagnosed—in order to prevent unintended bias. Levin accumulated his data over a ten-year period, during which he encountered heavy skepticism from fellow physicians who were used to dealing with individual cases rather than representative samples of people and comparing multiple factors related to their pathology. Besides, many of his associates in the high-stress medical profession liked to smoke as much as he did and were not eager to be disabused about the effects of a favorite pleasure. But his findings were hard to ignore, if hardly conclusive. Among 236 cancer hospital patients who had smoked for twenty-five years or longer, the lung cancer rate was nearly 21 percent compared to an 8.6 percent incidence among patients who were nonsmokers; among those smoking a pack of cigarettes a day, the relative risk of lung cancer was ten times as high, Levin found, as among those who did not smoke.

He wrote up his painstakingly gathered data and, while serving as director of a temporary national Commission on Chronic Diseases installed at the American Medical Association's national headquarters in Chicago, submitted his paper on smoking and cancer to the AMA's *Journal*. Rejected without explanation and returned to his regular office in Albany, the paper caught up with the highly regarded epidemiologist in Chicago, where he traveled a few floors within the same building to ask the editor of *JAMA* why his paper had been turned down. "Oh," said the red-faced editor, "the statistician did that," and the latter was consulted. Surprised that the paper's author was the same eminent Dr. Levin heading a national commission installed at the AMA, the statistician explained that he had trouble with the concept of "smokers" versus "nonsmokers" since the two could trade places at any moment. Levin satisfied the balky editor that this problem had been addressed by careful interrogation to determine the subjects' smoking histories, but he was then presented with a second paper on the same subject that was about to meet the same fate as his own. Levin read it, recognized its value at once, reassured the statistician that it had been properly adjusted to account for the ages of the subjects, and urged that it be run in the same issue as his own study. It would be this second paper that led off the May 27, 1950, number of *JAMA* and gained far more attention than Levin's useful study.

Ernst L. Wynder was the son of a Jewish physician in the Westphalian town of Herford, where his father, though viewed as somewhat leftist politically, had been socially prominent before Hitler came to power. The family fled Nazi persecution and settled in suburban New Jersey, where the senior Wynder re-

sumed his practice while young Ernst, now Ernest—he would alternate between the two spellings as part of his lifelong ambivalence toward his native
Germany—graduated from New York University in 1943 and served in the
U.S. Army intelligence section. As a medical student at Washington University in St. Louis, he wore his dark hair long, and his angular face often bore a
dour, world-weary, even distasteful expression that looked to some as if he had
just detected an unpleasant aroma in the vicinity. If his high opinion of himself
was not entirely endearing, there was no gainsaying Ernie Wynder's brains,
energy, and ambition.

In the course of a summer internship at NYU after his second year at medical school, Wynder attended an autopsy of a lung cancer victim and was
struck by the absence of any report of smoking in the deceased's medical history. Inquiring of the widow, he discovered that the man had been a two-pack-
a-day smoker, and Wynder began to suspect that the relationship between
smoking and lung cancer had been underestimated due to such faulty reporting. With Bellevue Hospital right across the street, he approached the head of
the chest service there and obtained permission to conduct in-depth interviews
with those stricken by the disease, seeking not only his subjects' smoking
history in detail but information on such other possibly related factors as
occupational exposures and the cause of parents' death. "After twenty or so
interviews," Wynder recalled, "I knew I had something."

Returning to medical school, Wynder asked his anatomy professor to approach famed thoracic surgeon Evarts Graham, head of chest service at Barnes
Hospital, which was closely affiliated with the Washington University medical
program, to inquire whether the precocious investigator could continue his
data-gathering with the patients in Graham's charge. The surgeon, renowned
for having performed one of the first successful removals of an entire cancerous lung, was primarily a clinician with what struck young Wynder as somewhat limited curiosity about the causes of the diseases he sought to check with
his scalpel. Besides, Graham was a heavy smoker and dubious about the ciga-
rette-lung cancer connection. Other faculty members thought Wynder's questionnaires a waste of time, but Graham saw no harm in the undertaking. Once
the results began to accumulate, Wynder remembered, "Graham became quite
supportive. It was a great break in my life."

During his last two years at medical school, Wynder kept collecting his
data, traveling to widely separated sites whenever possible. Among them was
California, where he showed up one day in the state's Department of Health
office occupied by Dr. Lester Breslow, an alert young epidemiologist who
believed the smoking-cancer link was more anecdotal than clinically demonstrable. He had his doubts, furthermore, that an investigator as brash and inex-
perienced as Wynder could perform reliable field work. But Breslow gave him
access to state hospital patients and by way of monitoring his technique sent

along a health department examiner. "Our man reported back that Wynder's work was just awful—the questioning was crude and the record-keeping inconsistent," Breslow recounted. But Wynder apparently learned some lessons from his first serious brush with public health professionals, and so did Breslow, who as a result ordered his department to undertake its own investigation into the subject, the findings of which eventually proved almost identical to those in Wynder's 1950 *JAMA* report.

That article, "Tobacco Smoking as a Possible Etiologic Factor in Bronchiogenic Carcinoma: A Study of 684 Proved Cases," with Dr. Graham tactfully listed as the second author, came to be regarded as a classic in epidemiology due to the size and geographic spread of its sample, the fact that its data derived from personal interviews and not from hospital records or other second-hand sources, and its breakdown of subjects into five clearly calibrated categories of smoking dosage, ranging from none (meaning less than one cigarette daily over the previous twenty years) to chain-smoking. Among its chief findings were that 96.5 percent of the lung cancer patients interviewed were moderately heavy to chain-smokers (compared with 73 percent of the 780 patients with diagnoses other than lung cancer), that almost all those stricken had smoked for twenty or more years, and 98.7 percent of the cigarette smokers were conscious inhalers (compared with 62.5 percent of the cigar smokers and only 18 percent of pipe smokers). There were no nonsmokers among the lung cancer victims in his collective sample—but then only 14 percent of the noncancer hospital patients covered in the study were nonsmokers, suggesting that smoking was merely an incidental factor in the formation of the disease or that it had a major impact as well on diseases other than lung cancer. All of this invited far deeper suspicion about the cigarette habit.

Four months after the Wynder-Graham study appeared, the *British Medical Journal* carried the first preliminary report on the same subject by an Englishman who would in time rank with Wynder and one other scientist as among the world's foremost investigators on the relationship of smoking to health. Dr. Richard Doll, ten years Wynder's senior and a far more reserved personality, was a well-regarded scholar-biostatistician on Britain's Medical Research Council when he and a colleague, A. Bradford Hill, made a study of 1,732 cancer patients at twenty London hospitals and compared them with 743 noncancer patients. While somewhat more ambiguous than Wynder's findings, the Doll-Hill results were still more incriminating when examined closely for the dose-response relationship: heavy smokers (twenty-five cigarettes or more a day) in the British study were found fifty times as likely as nonsmokers to contract lung cancer.

V I I

HARDLY noticed at the time but of major consequence to the future of the cigarette industry was the 1940s entry into the field by Joseph F. Cullman, Jr., a short, plump, high-spirited tobacco grower, broker, and investor, already in his sixties. Possessed of an old-shoe ease of manner and reputation for straight dealing, Joe Junior, as he was widely called, was among the best-loved men in his business, though his dealings had been mainly in the cigar end of the trade. It did not hurt that one of his family enterprises, Tobacco and Allied Stocks, a publicly held company but controlled by the Cullmans, had sizable holdings in many of the big cigarette manufacturers, including Reynolds.

Joe Junior traced the family's interest in tobacco to his grandfather, Ferdinand Kullman, who in the wake of the social revolutions sweeping Europe in 1848 left his German Jewish ancestors in a Rhine River town and voyaged to America on the same ship with countryman and social reformer Carl Schurz. Kullman had less exalted business to conduct, trying to continue in the family wine trade but having better luck in the new and booming U.S. cigar trade. The powerful smokes the first Kullman manufactured and purveyed, family lore held, did more damage to the Union troops during the Civil War than Rebel bullets and bayonets. A mediocre businessman, he was kept afloat by cash infusions from the old country, but his son Joseph, a more vigorous and personable sort, built speedily and well on his father's beginnings.

Starting out at fifteen in a New York tobacco merchant's Water Street offices, he quickly absorbed the dynamics of the business, became an expert cigar roller in the bargain, and proved an accomplished salesman, known as "Piano Joe" for his aptitude on the ivories. Taken into partnership while in his early twenties, the first Joe also had the good fortune to marry into money, brought his relatives into the business, outlived his original partner, and soon commanded a sizable leaf brokerage enterprise. Business travel broadened his horizons, and he was a bold enough operator to buy up almost all the Dutch East Indian leaf offered at auction in Holland in 1890, just before the U.S. erected a steep tariff wall against such imports, and thereby made a killing that added to his hefty holdings.

His firstborn and namesake was given the best of everything, including an education at New York's elite Collegiate School, where Joe Junior was captain of the football team; a horse of his own, stabled near the Cullmans' West Seventy-first Street home a block from Central Park, where he exercised the animal; and membership in Yale's class of 1904. Though physically unprepossessing—he was a bull of a man, with a large head and neck, bushy brows, powerful arms, and short legs—he was popular in college, jocular, and little inhibited socially by his religious affiliation. Indeed, his father had turned from Judaism to the Ethical Culture Society, and Joe Junior was very much the assimilationist, at ease in almost any social sphere. Indoctrinated early in the tobacco business and as a youngster attending leaf auctions abroad with his father, Joe Junior worked for a while after college in the tobacco fields of Wisconsin and on Cuban plantations before sharing a rolltop desk with his father in the family office. Over time, he would master the horticulture of cigar tobacco to the point where he could tell by the look, feel, taste, and smell of a leaf just where it grew, the nature of the soil that had nourished it, the density of the yield per acre, and what kind of fertilizer had been applied to it. He also moved the family beyond the business of buying and reselling Sumatran leaf for wrapping cigars and Cuban leaf for filling them by pushing his father in 1910 into buying land in the Connecticut River Valley to raise their own "shade" tobacco, grown under a veil of protective cheesecloth, for sale to cigar makers. With that effort blooming, the family began investing in the stock of other, larger tobacco companies, among the nation's most prosperous businesses.

Throughout the 'Twenties, Joe Junior worked and played hard, enjoying the great loves of his life: a growing family (four sons and a daughter), food (mostly heavy German, which did nothing to improve his stocky shape), liquor (speakeasies were part of his regular cigar-sales territory), dance (including the conga, learned at Havana night spots), sports (he regularly hunted, fished, swam, sailed, played tennis, and most of all rode horseback—the friskier the mount the better he liked it), gambling (for fun), and the ladies (unflagrantly but an open secret, even to his wife, who was not robust). At Cedar Lodge, the Cullmans' substantial though unpretentious country place in Stamford, Connecticut, Joe was an expansive host in his jodhpurs, loud jackets, and outlandish hats. Among those regularly entertained was fellow tobacco industry leader Al Lyon of Philip Morris, whose own country place was only a few miles away in Greenwich; the pair often rode together.

Most of all, Joe Cullman, Jr., minded his business. He bought to hold, was never a speculator, and nicely weathered the great Wall Street crash in 1929. But the 'Thirties were not kind to the cigar business, and Joe Junior grew moody now, seized by frequent bouts of depression brought on by fears that the Cullman enterprises would soon be pauperized. Except while at play with them, he treated his sons as a stern Victorian father, fearful that heaping them with luxuries or overt love might spoil them. He was best at preaching the work ethic to the boys. His third son, Edgar, once was to accompany his father on a business trip to Tampa but elected to stop off en route a day early to attend a friend's wedding in Georgia. Plane service was less than reliable in those days, and foggy weather forced Edgar to phone his father to say he feared he might not arrive on time for their appointment. "He hung up on me," Edgar remembered, "and when I finally got there, my father had completed the business call and gone." Nothing further was ever said about his truancy, "but the episode made an impression on me."

Among other companies represented in the Cullmans' investment portfolio was little Benson & Hedges, offspring of the early Bond Street tobacconists who had competed for the carriage trade with Philip Morris's old London shop in the mid-nineteenth century. An import branch had been opened in New York at the close of the century and sold out to American interests in 1928. B&H's principal place of business by then was a swank shop on Fifth Avenue near Thirty-ninth Street that offered such boutique items as monogrammed, gold-tipped, hand-rolled Turkish cigarettes and customized boxes embossed with family crests. The store staff wore morning coats, even the deliverymen were uniformed, and English tea was served to the clientele each afternoon. The operation expanded in 1931 from the customized cigarette business to a new premium ready-made brand, Parliament, a Turkish-American blend featuring a recessed European-style mouthpiece that kept tobacco shreds away from the mouth; later a combed-cotton filter was inserted in the mouthpiece to reduce the intake of irritants in the smoke. Making and attaching the filter were slow work—it took ten times as long to make one Parliament as it did to turn out one standard-brand smoke—and the cigarettes had to be hand-packed in their fancy tan-gray slide-and-shell box. Priced at thirty cents and little advertised, only 20,000 boxes of Parliament were sold that introductory year, mostly in New York.

But the brand slowly built up a following and was selling 95 million units by 1941 when the marginally profitable company was being offered for sale. Philip Morris briefly considered it, but fearful of antitrust implications after the company had been included among the defendants in the government's sweeping suit filed that year, Chalkley and Lyon let it go. But the latter urged his close friend Joe Cullman, Jr., to look into the company as a complement to the family's flagging cigar volume. The manageably small size of the operation, its snobbish affectations, and the jewel-like profit in such retail items as a fifty-unit glass jar of cigars selling for $25 appealed to Joe Junior, who put up $850,000 for control of Benson & Hedges and remarked that he would gladly take the crumbs off Big Tobacco's table.

Even under wartime wraps, the little outfit grew, grossing more than $5 million by 1945. And then, with ads in magazines catering to the affluent, like *The New Yorker* and *Cue*, the product's ritzy tone caught on and outpaced all competitors in the deluxe field. The little B&H factory on Water Street was soon humming as never before, packing a million Parliaments a day.

Joe Junior now had to divide his workday between overseeing Benson & Hedges operations in the morning and the family's leaf and investment interests in the afternoon. He ran a tight ship at B&H, and by the late 'Forties, demand for Parliaments, which netted their maker 3 cents per box compared with about 1.2 cents for every standard-brand pack, was happily outstripping the company's capacity to supply them. Sales surged 25 percent in 1948, 47 percent in 1949, and 66 percent in 1950. Even so, B&H's share of the cigarette trade was only three-tenths of a single percentage point. Joe Junior told *Fortune* magazine that year that he was "happily married to the carriage trade" and had no intention of deserting it at his age—nearing seventy—for the rough-and-tumble of the mass market. The photograph accompanying the story showed Joe Junior with his oldest son, Joseph F. Cullman III, at his side, a hand resting on his father's shoulder in filial devotion. Joe Third, as his son was known to the trade, was by then running B&H and, at thirty-eight, was unfazed by the perils of the big-time tobacco business. His ambition was soon to be tested—and the future course of the whole industry altered as a result.

6

The Filter Tip and Other Placebos

WHILE a precocious lad of seven, Clarence Cook Little began studying and breeding mice, an interest that in time led him to the field of biology at Harvard, where he won his doctorate in the subject. But there was no mistaking "Pete" Little, as he preferred to be called, for an antisocial researcher chained to his laboratory. A Boston Brahmin of Huguenot ancestry, descended from Paul Revere on his mother's side, he was a large man of magnetic charm, with an impeccable Harvard accent that could, on certain lubricated occasions, transform itself into a hilariously salty Down East dialect for folksy joke-telling. As he pursued his dissertation on genetics and raised his personal colony of mice, he managed to serve Harvard in a variety of junior administrative posts, including secretary to the corporation. Upon his completion of a four-year fellowship studying experimental evolution, Little's outgoing and high-toned personality, his training in academic management, and credentials as a serious scientist earned him appointment in 1922, at the age of thirty-four, as president of the University of Maine.

Three years later, Little became the youngest head of a major American center of higher learning by assuming the presidency of the University of Michigan, and his mice followed him west. But after only four years in Ann Arbor, Little was hounded from his post for his outspoken views in favor of birth control, his permissiveness toward unorthodox student conduct, and continuing reports of an adulterous relationship. Among those who had befriended him in Michigan was a wealthy automotive executive, Roscoe B. Jackson, who put up the funds for a research institute in his name and under Little's supervision in Bar Harbor, Maine. His well-established colony of purebred mice found their ultimate home and usefulness there, for the spartan brick compound, affectionately dubbed "Mousetown" by its staff, was essentially a facility for the breeding of mice. The fastidious conditions Little insisted upon helped create worldwide demand for his mice for experimental uses. But Jackson Memorial Laboratory was an austere operation: Little himself was paid only $3,000 and had to ask his staffers to go fishing once a week to help keep themselves fed.

Little's reduced circumstances and geographic remoteness were somewhat alleviated by his 1929 appointment, simultaneous with the establishment of the Jackson laboratory (and mouse factory), as managing director of the still fledgling American Society for the Control of Cancer (ASCC). Very much under the sway of the medical profession, itself in continuing dread of the disease and its impotence to cure it, the ASCC paid Little $9,000 a year to commute from Maine to its New York office for a few days a week and help reduce the public's phobic attitude toward cancer through education and the message that early detection was the chief, if not only, hope of beating the affliction. And big, personable Pete Little was the perfect messenger, especially among society matrons whose idle hours he enlisted to help spread lifesaving word about how to spot uterine cancer early. Among his writings was the book *Civilization Against Cancer*, typical of his efforts to explicate the disease, the enormous complexity of which fascinated him. Cancer was "not a unity," he wrote, "and many factors must be considered in attempting to blot it out—heredity, sex, hormones, diet, sunlight, vitamins. . . ." While not on the forward edge of the new field of oncology, Little grasped early on that the carcinogenic process was probably not initiated by a germ or virus, as were most infectious diseases, but came, as he wrote in 1933, "from some as yet mysterious 'derangement' within a single body cell." As to the growing incidence of lung cancer and its possible causal link to smoking, he wrote in a 1944 ASCC pamphlet, "Cancer: A Study for Laymen," that although there was as yet "no definite evidence" of such a relationship, "it would seem unwise to fill the lungs repeatedly with a suspension of fine particles of tobacco product. . . . It is difficult to see how such particles can be prevented from becoming lodged in the walls of the lungs and when so located how they can avoid providing a certain amount of irritation. . . ."

While he enjoyed occupying the platform as the cancer society's chief spokesman and popular educator, Little did not succeed in nurturing the organization beyond its larval stage. Its prewar staff had just a few publicists, its fund-raising netted scarcely $100,000 a year, and its managing director seemed to lack any vision of an enlarged role for the cancer society. And so its leadership was wrested from him in 1944 by a group of prominent New Yorkers, who renamed it the American Cancer Society (ACS).

Principal agent of Pete Little's unseating was Mary Woodard Lasker, second wife of legendary advertising man Albert Lasker, who had helped turn Lucky Strike cigarettes into the nation's leading smoke. Mrs. Lasker's housemaid had contracted cancer in 1943, and the more her employer, a Radcliffe honors graduate, looked into the disease and the primitive stage of its treatment and research, the more appalled she grew. An attractive woman of wealth, social grace, and considerable self-assurance, with a wide circle of influential friends, Mrs. Lasker approached Pete Little with a plan to turn the cancer society into a big-time volunteer health organization. They would enlist nationwide movers and shakers in industry, finance, law, education, labor, and government to reinforce the doctors and scientists who were the frail society's present leaders and the socialite women who formed its rank and file. Instrumental in this process that Little embraced were Emerson Foote, head of Foote, Cone & Belding, the successor firm to Albert Lasker's agency, and investment banker James Adams, a partner at Lazard Frères, who turned to a number of executives he knew in the pharmaceutical industry and urged them to get into the fight against cancer both on humanitarian grounds and as smart business in view of the unfolding research on chemotherapy as a weapon for halting the spread of the disease. Adams's chief recruit was Elmer H. Bobst, the ex-druggist who had made a fortune in the vitamin business as head of the Hoffman-La Roche company. Word spread from the Laskers' swank salon on New York's Beekman Place, the de facto fund-raising nexus of the ACS, and within a few years the society's annual appeal was netting $10 million, as industrialists and other large givers found the cause irresistible and the publicity for its benefactors not a little self-serving. Soon the society had a sizable new headquarters with a permanent staff of several hundred, including a dozen highly adept publicists, and was reaching out to schools and colleges, offices and factories, churches and fraternal orders in virtually every community.

With such growth inevitably came tensions and jealousies, especially between the medical and scientific people and the laymen at the top of the organization. Bobst, a vain but energetic and highly committed catalyst, became chairman of the ACS in 1949 and helped devise a new structure for the organization's directors to avoid divisive policy battles. By design the board of fifty-six would be split evenly between professionals and lay people, with one of the former serving as president and one of the latter as chairman. The working heart of the effort would be its enlarged professional staff, whose new young medical-scientific director, the complex and eloquent Charles S. Cameron, a breast cancer specialist, brought a passion to his task of a sort that Pete Little had never managed. His departure from the ACS was understood to have been prompted in large measure by Mary Lasker's deep disapproval of both his professional conduct within the organization and an attitude toward women said to be alternately patronizing and predatory. If Little was embittered by his removal, he gave no overt sign, but events a decade later would suggest that the scar never healed.

II

AMONG the professional newcomers to the American Cancer Society staff under Charles Cameron's command was a young epidemiologist of impeccable academic credentials, an elegant bearing that revealed his patrician roots among Maryland's Chesapeake gentry, and a singular dedication to the intellectual task he had been assigned—namely, the strengthening and broadening of the ACS's statistical research section. Although the society did not itself undertake biological research into the nature of the disease but rather made grants to individuals and institutions for that purpose, it turned in 1946 to thirty-four-year-old E. Cuyler Hammond, a tall, slender Yale graduate with a doctorate from the Johns Hopkins public-health school, to coordinate the nationwide effort of ACS branches, cancer registries, and other agencies gathering data on the disease in all its insidious forms: you had to know your foe in order to conquer it.

There was an exterior coolness to Cuyler Hammond, but below a surface courtliness lurked a nervous energy and a hungrily questing intellect that did not readily embrace received wisdom. He smoked three to four packs of cigarettes a day—yet, as if ruled by some divine monitor, inhaled only lightly. A perfectionist about his work who sometimes grew impatient with and a bit arrogant toward those he perceived as his intellectual inferiors, he had apprenticed before the war as a biostatistician with the National Institutes of Health; his wartime service was capped by extensive on-site gathering of data among the survivors of the first atomic bomb at Hiroshima. His training won him a part-time post teaching biometry at Yale while working at the cancer society in New York, where he was known for scrupulous attention to the accuracy of his department's statistical computations.

The first major fruit of Hammond's presence on the ACS staff was the 1948 publication of "Trends in Cancer Mortality," which confirmed the startling rise in lung cancer and concluded that it had become, at about that time, the most prevalent and deadly form of the disease. Pressed by Dr. Alton Ochsner, the New Orleans surgeon who had early on pointed to cigarettes as the likeliest villain and was then serving as president of the ACS, Hammond set to work devising a comprehensive study of the problem. But he was a good deal more skeptical than Ochsner that smoking was the answer. It seemed too facile an explanation. The trouble with the 1950 studies of Drs. Wynder and Graham and Morton Levin in the U.S. and Doll and Hill in England, which provided the weightiest evidence yet of a link between the disease and smoking, and Müller's pathbreaking report eleven years earlier was that they were all based on the disparity between hospital patients who had already contracted lung cancer and comparable groups of patients free of the disease. Their smoking histories were collected and analyzed retrospectively, and the higher prevalence of smokers among the diseased subjects was interpreted as no accident. Hammond was too much a purist, though, not to grasp the potential weaknesses in this methodology. Hospital patients, to start with, were anything but typical of the population as a whole, and most of them were gathered in clinics or wards on the basis of symptoms diagnosed by their physicians; the underlying systemic causes of their sicknesses could vary widely and produce misleading diagnoses. The taking of smoking histories from those already suffering with lung cancer, moreover, was not the most reliable basis for scientific judgments. Beyond the fallibility of memory, especially among those of advanced age, afflicted smokers were prone to shade the truth, albeit unconsciously, when questioned about their lifelong habits. The heavy-smoking patient, hoping that his painful coughs were due only to an overindulgence he could curb, might be tempted to exaggerate his daily intake of tobacco by way of trying to ward off the dreaded diagnosis, whereas the patient already diagnosed with the disease and grieving over his foolhardy surrender to the habit might understate the amount he had smoked, as if to demonstrate that fate and not his own conduct had betrayed him. To avoid these and other such biases built into the sampling of hospital patients, Hammond realized, it was necessary to reverse the process: the sample population under study ought to consist of asymptomatic smokers and nonsmokers—that is, without lung cancer and equally free of other known symptoms of fatal diseases—who would be followed for a number of years to see which group the disease hit harder.

But how to manage such a study, especially with a massive cohort of the size Hammond had in mind—100,000 or more? Hospital populations were by definition confined, and data on them readily gathered through institutional staffs. It was a far more daunting task to monitor a healthy, at-large multitude over a number of years and across a broad geographic stage. Hammond consulted the Gallup and Roper polling organizations and learned they would charge about fifty dollars a head to undertake the four-to-five-year tracking he had in mind—a prohibitive price for a voluntary, non-profit health organization. Hammond's wife then came up with a brainstorm. Why not enlist the ACS's huge corps of well-educated and underutilized housewives?

Immediate objections were lodged against this inspired notion. How could untrained volunteers be relied on in the first place to conduct interviews and record answers correctly? At least as worrisome, could they be depended upon to follow up on a regular basis and over a protracted period of time? Actually, interviewers employed by even the foremost polling companies—not to mention the U.S. Census Bureau—were often not highly trained professionals. Why couldn't Hammond and his ACS colleague Daniel Horn, a Harvard-trained psychologist, provide what training was needed? The essential task, after all, was not terribly complex. Each of the ACS interviewers would be asked to find ten men in their community, preferably though not necessarily of their acquaintance, between the ages of fifty and sixty-nine—the span when lung cancer was most likely to appear; it did not matter whether the enlistees were smokers, only that they were not chronically ill at the time they were signed up for the study. The ACS volunteers had to do no more than fill out the original questionnaire with each subject, check back with him annually, and be aware of any major intervening medical event, in particular the subject's death, to be reported promptly to the ACS.

The plausibility of the plan brought on an attack of cold feet in the ACS directorate. Such a massive study might be mismanaged and harm the society's reputation as a noncontroversial entity devoted to educational ends. It did not exist to undertake research of its own—that was best left to independent experts. And why dwell on smoking as the prime suspect? There was arguably as much reason to blame the gas-guzzling automobile culture, with its ubiquitous spread of noxious fumes and asphalt dust. While automotive pollution might well be contributing to the rise in lung cancer, Hammond and Horn noted, it could not explain why the retrospective studies to date were revealing a disproportionately high incidence of the disease among smokers; if cars were at fault, smokers and nonsmokers ought to be affected equally. Unspoken in all this was the concern that many ACS contributors were, like Hammond and Horn, serious smokers who did not want their habit impugned.

"Dr. Hammond had to tread very carefully," recalled Lawrence Garfinkel, a statistician-sociologist not long out of New York's City College and assigned to the Hammond-Horn project. "A lot of people in the organization were nervous, and Cuyler had to get his funding one stage at a time." Among those disinclined to make cigarettes the subject of an intellectual lynching was ACS scientific director Charles Cameron, himself a pack-a-day smoker who thought that smokers might well be in some fashion constituted differently from nonindulgers and thus prone to the ravages of lung cancer. Cameron was "not overly enthusiastic" about the proposed giant study, according to Garfinkel, who became a career epidemiologist with the ACS, but Cameron himself would insist long afterward that he never wavered in his support of Hammond—a view confirmed by Dr. Arthur I. Holleb, a successor in Cameron's post. "It would not have happened without Cameron," Holleb stated.

Cameron, though, was undoubtedly subjected to cautionary pressure from the society's chairman, Elmer Bobst, the pharmaceutical heavyweight who had friends in the tobacco industry and on at least one occasion brought Cameron along to a luncheon with Reynolds Tobacco operatives warning against the premature indictment of their product. But Bobst, by most accounts, was judicious and nonobstructionist in the use of his power at the ACS, and so Hammond, professing keen skepticism and stressing the need for unequivocal evidence before tobacco could be charged with causing lung cancer or other diseases, was given the green light. He, Horn, and Garfinkel visited ten cities, enlisted 200 volunteer interviewers, trained them, and ran them through practice sessions gathering data before everyone was satisfied that ACS volunteers could serve adequately. During the first half of 1952, the study, perhaps the largest of its kind ever undertaken by a single private group, began in earnest.

Some 22,000 volunteers spread among 394 counties in eleven states, including New York, Illinois, and California, were engaged in the effort. The sampling of white men over fifty, it would later be argued, was not representative of the whole nation, since it had a disproportionately high enlistment of subjects east of the Mississippi, their average age far exceeded that of the population as a whole, and their socioeconomic and educational level—only one-fourth of them had not finished high school—was also well above the U.S. norm. But Hammond had reasoned that the states selected for the test all had substantial rural as well as urban populations; his sample was not necessarily intended to represent the whole nation. And if he had not limited his subjects to those in the most cancer-prone age bracket, the study might have to run twenty years before it yielded enough data for a realistic judgment. The above-average socioeconomic standing of his subjects, furthermore, might arguably serve to make the study's findings more conservative and thus reliable, not less so, since sickness and death rates were generally higher among lower-income and less educated people.

As the first data began to flow in, the need for keen vigilance was underscored. The questionnaires collected in one Minnesota county, for example, were found to have all been filled out in the same handwriting and had to be tossed out. Some of the subjects listed were under fifty or female or not white—racial susceptibility to the disease was thought to be a possibly confounding factor and so the sample base was all-white by design—and had to be eliminated. As the first subjects began to die off, Hammond's staff wrote away for a copy of their death certificates and then followed up for as much detail as possible in the form of autopsy reports and, in the case of cancer deaths, histological classification of the form of the disease—*i.e.*, categorizing it by microscopic examination of the lethal cells. The first major test of the likely reliability of the whole enterprise came in the autumn of 1952, when all the volunteer interviewers were asked to conduct their first follow-up sessions; an astonishing 99.4 percent of the subjects were located and their health status accounted for.

As Hammond and his associates at the ACS were gearing up for their effort, a similar prospective study, smaller and far less varied in its sampling but uniquely reliable, was being undertaken by the leading British investigators on the subject, Richard Doll and Bradford Hill. They sent a "questionary" to the nearly 60,000 doctors in Great Britain, inquiring about their age, health, and smoking habits, among other things, with the intention of following up periodically on their subjects' health status. About two-thirds of the recipients responded; Doll and Hill suspected that a substantial number among the doctors electing not to reply were already stricken with lung cancer or some other, likely terminal disease, the presence of which might skew the validity of the study. Women doctors and practitioners under thirty-five were also excluded from the sampling in order to limit the subject base to those most likely to become afflicted with lung cancer.

While their doctor study was under way, Doll and Hill published the final report on their retrospective study of London hospital patients. It so persuasively pointed the finger of suspicion at smoking that the *British Medical Journal* was prompted to editorialize late in 1952 that it was now "surely incumbent on tobacco manufacturers" to undertake intensive research on the chemical constituents of smoke, for if the carcinogenic agents could be isolated, then they might also be removed "so that smoking will become a less dangerous occupation than it appears to be now." The journal's blithe suppositions—that profit-making industrialists would without duress intently examine the perils inherent in their highly lucrative product, that science could neatly calibrate the potency of cancer-causing or cancer-spreading agents, and that even if investigators were able to achieve as much, the cigarette could then be rendered harmless and yet remain a cigarette—were to prove wildly wishful.

III

IF the reports and suspicions being generated in the early 'Fifties by the scientific community on the documentable relationship between smoking and health were unwelcome to the leading cigarette manufacturers, the companies on the lower rungs of the industry ladder saw in this menacing news an opportunity to make hay, so to speak, while the clouds gathered.

Brown & Williamson, smallest of the top six cigarette makers, found a growing demand for its mentholated Kool and filter-tip Viceroy brands, both with supposedly therapeutic qualities vaguely hinted at in their advertising. But it was sleepy Lorillard that awoke first to the chance to reverse its lagging fortunes by exploiting the public's slowly spreading apprehension that the old wives' tales and busybody moralizers' warnings about cigarette smoking might be scientifically verifiable.

The 1950 breakthrough studies could not have come as a big surprise at Lorillard, where as early as mid-1946 one of its leading staff chemists, Harris B. Parmele, sent a memorandum to the secretary of the company's committee on manufacturing in which he noted that certain scientists and medical authorities "have claimed for many years that the use of tobacco contributes to cancer development in susceptible people. Just enough evidence has been presented to justify the possibility of such a presumption." But he was not yet alarmed by the evidence and saw no reason to believe smoking was any more implicated than many other possible causative factors. Five years later, however, by which time Dr. Parmele had been advanced to Lorillard's director of research, his concern over the health issue had grown and was shared by the company's tough, street-smart sales director, Lewis Gruber. The latter believed that the moment was ripe for Lorillard to market a new brand that specifically and with scientific authenticity addressed the fear factor. Since nobody knew just what it was in tobacco that might be doing the damage, let alone whether it could be selectively removed, the most plausible way to allay the health-conscious smoker's alarm was to put a truly effective filter tip on the product that substantially reduced the total intake of smoke without entirely depriving the user of its taste and jolt. Concurring, Parmele began to study seriously the dynamics of smoke filtration.

For a product as simple as a cigarette, no more than a short stick of cured, shredded, flavored, and paper-wrapped leaf, devising a true filter to reduce intake of its combustible by-product was a surprising technological challenge. Cigarette tobacco, burning in the range of 700 to 900 degrees Fahrenheit, produced hundreds of volatile compounds in a smoky aerosol composed of millions of microscopic particles of incompletely burned organic matter ejected into a gas stream by the burning cone and condensing as they cooled to room temperature in the two-tenths of a second required to travel from the ember to the smoker's mouth. In the process many physical and chemical changes occurred, so that the inhaled smoke was quite different molecularly from the cured tobacco of the unlit cigarette. How and what to filter from this immensely complex mixture? Possibly the toxic gases within it could be absorbed chemically by the filter, but such a technique would have to await precise analysis of the volatile gases by equipment just then becoming available. The only practical form of filtration available at Lorillard was the primitive one of mechanical intervention. And since a sievelike narrowing of the smoke's passageways would cause it to clog up at the openings and greatly increase resistance, thereby requiring the smoker to draw in with far more force, the most practical form of filtration would be fibrous in nature—that is, a weblike arrangement dependent upon the chance collision of smoke particles held to the fibrous filaments by the adhesive forces of nature. The choices of material that would best lend itself to this end were greatly limited by the requirements that the substance be nontoxic, tasteless, pliable, adaptable to swift fabrication, and, above all, cheap.

While filters had been made of materials ranging from permeable leaves to porous crepe paper dating as far back as Montezuma's time, the first modern, reasonably effective American cigarette filter in noticeable commercial use was the one on the premium Parliament, introduced in 1931. It was made from spun-cotton fiber soaked in a solution of caustic soda that made it swell and grow shiny with tension; in the washing and drying process, the fibers crisscrossed to form a highly absorbent web suitable for trapping minute particles in smoke. But the cotton filter material had to be carefully inserted in a little wad by hand; faster, cheaper, and infinitely more malleable was the cellulose acetate filter, a form of which was first used in the 1936 Viceroy. Cellulose, a proteinlike vegetable material that lends structure to whatever it is mixed with, was found to be highly manipulable when blended with the acidic solvent acetate, run through a sieve, and extruded spaghetti-fashion in a wide, soft ribbon called a "tow," the form in which it was sent to the cigarette manufacturer. The latter fluffed it, shaped it, twisted the filaments—infinite variations of crimping were possible—and then recondensed it, coated it with a plasticizer to harden it, and sliced it into little plugs joined to the tobacco by a paper overwrap. The cellulose filter was one reason Viceroy could be offered to smokers at a premium of only one or two cents more than the regular unfiltered brands while the Parliament cost nearly 50 percent more.

But settling upon some form of cellulose acetate, which could also be supplemented with other substances to heighten its blockage efficiency, was only part of the puzzle. The efficacy of the cellulose could vary depending on the degree of fineness or coarseness of the fibers, on whether they were packed densely or loosely, on how much and in what shape they were twisted, on what pattern they were arranged in—whether parallel, at right angles, or randomly—and on the length and circumference of the filter. All of these factors could affect how much smoke actually penetrated the filter. As it would evolve, the typical cellulose acetate cigarette filter of about 20 millimeters in length would, at any given cross section, present an amazingly large total surface area, calculated to be on average about 27,000 millimeters, or enough to collect slightly more than half of the hundreds of millions of passing microscopic particles in a typical 500-milligram cigarette.*

As Parmele was pondering his design options, he became aware of a filter material said to be uniquely efficient and just declassified as a wartime secret

---

* A milligram is 1/1,000 of a gram, or 1/28 of an ounce.

by the U.S. military. Used in gas masks and at atomic fuel plants to prevent the escape of radioactive dust, the material was called crocidolite or "African blue," a form of asbestos, the rocklike mineral highly resistant to heat and corrosion, which when crushed into fine fibers could be easily woven and matted for use in automobile brake linings and clutch pads, roofing, flooring, plumbing, and electrical insulation. That free-floating filaments of the stuff might, if inhaled, prove gravely harmful to human tissue was not common knowledge outside the asbestos industry itself. Crocidolite was a remarkable form of asbestos in that its fibers were so thin that they could be arranged to trap particles as small as one micron, or 1/25,000 of an inch. The man most responsible for finding military uses for the asbestos material was summoned to Lorillard's New York offices and demonstrated how smoke pumped into a pair of glass vessels was so effectively barred entry to the one with the crocidolite filter that the water in it displayed not a trace of brownish discoloration.

No more than 30 percent of the new Lorillard cigarette filter was fabricated from the asbestos, lest the device should prove impenetrable; the balance was a blend of crimped paper and cotton acetate, and the whole gadget was dubbed the "Micronite" filter, after the microscopic unit of measurement the asbestos was capable of blocking. Since surveys disclosed that women were the most health-conscious smokers and thus the most promising customers for the new filter tip, the brand was given a clean white package with faint horizontal striations so that it would appear a bit less antiseptic; a stronger color hinted at a stronger, possibly more hazardous smoke. Named for Lorillard's retiring president, Herbert A. Kent, the new product was marketed in March of 1952 as a major scientific accomplishment and priced accordingly at eight or nine cents a pack above the price of regular brands.

Introduced at the very time the Federal Trade Commission was cracking down on the older brands for false claims of mildness and nonirritability, the Kent was positioned by Lorillard as, in effect, the first authentically safeguarded cigarette on the market and its Micronite filter proclaimed "The Greatest Health Protection in Cigarette History." In truth, the Kent filter permitted only about half as much tar and nicotine to reach the smoker's mouth as any other brand, and because, after testing it, research director Parmele had assumed the asbestos to be so tightly bound into the filter that it could not escape from the smoke, the first Kent ads stated that the Micronite was made of "a pure, dust-free, completely harmless material," so safe it was used to filter air in hospitals.

Lorillard lost no time in trying to drive home the new brand's big alleged advantage, even if that meant tarring all competitors by inference. It was said that "rigorous scientific studies . . . put Kent in a class by itself where health protection is concerned" and that "The Difference in Protection Is Priceless." Two problems, though, prevented the new brand from becoming an instant hit.

First, if a smoker was so concerned about the possible harm he was doing to his health, the safest course was plainly not to smoke at all—and for the first time in memory, smokers began to cut back or quit or started to think hard about the practice and what it might be doing to them. Thus, Lorillard's flush competitors at the top of the industry found the Kent, and especially the way in which it was advertised, most unwelcome. Second and of more immediate concern, many who tried the new Kent found it very hard to draw upon, and when they did, were rewarded by an almost flavorless smoke. The miraculous Micronite might be doing its job too well. The brand sold fewer than 100,000 packs a day in its first year.

But long-standing habits are not reversed overnight. Kent had made its point, and the public's attention was further captured at the end of 1952 when the nation's largest-circulation magazine, *Reader's Digest*, which at the time accepted no advertising whatever and was thus immune from pressure by the free-spending tobacco industry to go easy on its products, ran a two-page article entitled "Cancer by the Carton." Although it offered no fresh findings, the article induced chills by charging the cigarette industry with covering up the real peril of smoking through all its advertising claims of mildness and references to such relatively benign side effects of the habit as throat irritation and "cigarette hangover". The far graver worry was lung cancer, a disease never mentioned or alluded to in the cigarette ads. The *Digest* had taken the unmentionable subject out of the medical journals and laid it bare for the masses.

I V

K ENT's arrival and the interest it had sparked pushed the two established filter-tip brands to more blatant claims of prophylactic value.

Viceroy, the leader, sought to double its appeal as the most healthful cigarette available by offering itself in a king-size as well as regular-length model in 1953, the year that American Tobacco's long, unfiltered Pall Mall claimed 10 percent of the market and surpassed the Philip Morris brand as the fourth best-selling product in the industry. There was not a shred of serious evidence that the king-length cigarette might be less hazardous than the standard 70-millimeter—only the dubious claim that tobacco was its own best filter—yet the perception was fed, and besides, women liked the longer, more slender shape of the king. Viceroy's ads, while smaller than its rivals', now proclaimed a "double-filtering action" of longer length, illustrated with a blowup drawing of the unwrapped device featuring "20,000 tiny filter traps" so that tars and nicotine "cannot reach your throat and lungs." For the first time, a major cigarette maker implicitly conceded that the lung was an organ that smoking might damage.

Conservative Benson & Hedges, while far from a major player in the business, tried to cash in on the emerging health appeal in pitching its Parliament. With unabashed overstatement, Parliament, it was now asserted, "filters 100 percent of the smoke—recessed filter keeps trapped tars and nicotine from touching lips and mouth." The implication that all the smoke was thus rendered harmless distorted the truth. The brand, moreover, was said to have been "[c]ertified superior and attained consistent filtering efficiency at the laboratory of the U.S. Testing Company," which sounded like a governmental agency. But when tested in independent labs, Parliament fell far short of all these claims.

It was Kent, though, in its second year and frantically trying to carve a place for itself in the increasingly clamorous marketplace, that set the pace for stridency. "Here's How Science Solved Your Problem of Sensitivity to Nicotine and Tars," proclaimed a typical double-page Kent ad in *Life* magazine in May of 1953, the implication clearly being that the product had thus been rendered harmless. Kent's Micronite filter, it was said, removed "seven times more nicotine and tar"—more than what, it did not state. More pointed still, the brand's ads asked in their headline, "Do you like a good smoke but not what smoking does to you?" and spoke consolingly of the one in three smokers who happened to be sensitive to tars and nicotine and "[a]s a result, he is usually left with a persistent cough, a nervous feeling, or frequent headaches"—not to mention cancer of the lung, the possibility of which was indeed not mentioned.

However wildly its benefits were exaggerated, Kent's filter was found to be more effective than its competitors in test results published in *Consumer Reports* early in 1953. With a yield of 7 mg. of tar and 1 mg. of nicotine, Kent generated less than half as much of these now strongly suspect substances per cigarette as Viceroy, with its yield of 14 mg. of tar and 2.4 mg. of nicotine, and Parliament with 12 mg. and 2.7. The yield of king-length Pall Mall at 15 mg. and 2.6 was similar to that of its regular-length stablemate, Lucky Strike, at 16 mg. and 2.1, rendering the alleged Pall Mall advantage illusory. Reynolds's regular Camel, at 15 mg. of tar and 1.9 mg. of nicotine, was found to yield less than the Viceroy and Parliament filters, while the Chesterfield king version was higher than the regular Chesterfield. Most of the ad claims, in short, were bunk.

If the smaller players in the industry were trying to outdo one another with poorly founded health claims and thereby improve their market shares, the smallest of the three leaders—Liggett & Myers—was apparently a bit more ambivalent about the wisdom of making implicit health claims for its expanded line. Normally tight-lipped Benjamin Few, the tall, slender South Carolinian who had worked his way up on the manufacturing side to head L&M, remarked that the arrival of the king cigarette was "the worst thing that has happened to this industry," because the long smokes would inevitably cannibalize their shorter versions and reduce profit margins. Yet he had no choice, Few added, because "if Chesterfield consumption is to be drained off by king-size and filter-tip cigarettes, let it be by our own brands."

Accordingly, Liggett undertook a remarkably retrogressive series of campaigns that seemed a collective warranty of product safety for all its brands. "Play Safe, Smoke Chesterfield," ran the banner for the staple brand in the Liggett product line, as buyers were told of a six-month study of smokers consuming between ten and forty cigarettes daily and undergoing thorough examinations before and after the test period of their nose, throat, "and all accessory organs"; the results were that "all participating subjects" were found to be "not adversely affected." So pleased was the company with this test that its leading radio shill, Arthur Godfrey, in his inimitable chummy manner, reassured listeners of the safety of Chesterfields by citing the study results and commenting to listeners of his "Arthur Godfrey and His Friends" broadcast of, for example, September 24, 1952:

> Now that [the six-month test results] ought to make you feel better if you've had any worries at all about it. I never did. I smoked two or three packs of these things every day—I feel pretty good. I don't know. I never did believe they did you any harm and we—we've got the proof.

Liggett & Myers, he went on, was a trustworthy outfit, and "[f]or years and years they have been advertising, you never heard 'em make an unsubstantiated claim—ever!" And for the twenty-three years he had been on the air, Godfrey stated, "I have never misled you with advertising. . . ." The engaging redheaded schmoozer was later found to be suffering from lung cancer, though he survived it for some years and succumbed to another form of the disease.

Such egregiously self-serving disclaimers caused the FTC to go beyond its usual cease-and-desist efforts and ask the federal courts in late 1952 to issue an injunction against Liggett's nervy new advertising on the ground that the company was now engaging in precisely the same sort of deceptive practices as its competitors which the regulatory commission had struggled ten years to halt. To allow Liggett to ignore the findings of the other four cases and exhaust its remedies over years of legal maneuvering was, by the FTC's reasoning, to reward a malefactor. The company soon after compounded the transgression when it came to market in 1953 with its filter-tip brand, L&M. Liggett's President Few, in an apparent spasm of candor, had commented to *Fortune* magazine that his chemists "say filter-tip cigarettes can't be made with less irritating factors than Chesterfields. But if the public wants it, so long as it isn't harmful, we'll give the public what it wants."

The ads for the new L&M brand went even further. Typical was one featuring a picture of actor Fredric March declaring: "THIS IS IT. L&M Filters Are Just What the Doctor Ordered!" Subsequent ads left the statement in quotations but failed to attribute it to any speaker; other ads removed the quotes and left the bald assertion, with its unmistakable implication that the new L&M filter was of medically prescriptive value. The closest the company came to specifying which doctor did the ordering was a statement on the Liggett & Myers corporate letterhead and reproduced in the Fredric March ad in which the company's research director, Dr. Frederick R. Darkis—with a doctorate in chemistry, not medicine—told of Liggett's search for the "purest material" it could find for its new filter and how it allowed the L&M smoker to "draw into [his] mouth much less smoke with much less nicotine and nitrogenous constituents." Tests failed to validate the claim that the new L&M filter was in any way significantly more effective than its rivals.

By the end of 1954, the truth-stretching L&M was selling 6.1 billion units, 50 percent ahead of Kent and more than twice the Parliament total but less than half of Viceroy's nearly 15 billion units for the clear industry lead. But by then Reynolds Tobacco had brought out its filter entry that studiously avoided the health issue, and would shortly run away with the industry leadership.

v

LICKING its wounds from the marketing fiasco of the king-size, unfiltered Cavalier, RJR Tobacco took solace in the early 'Fifties as its Camels continued to surge well ahead of Lucky Strike as the nation's best-selling brand. By 1953, however, American Tobacco held a solid 25 percent lead in unit sales over Reynolds on the strength of its two king brands, Pall Mall and the cork-tipped Herbert Tareyton, the latter also cast as an elegant smoke in ads with a monocled, top-hatted, and presumably very British gent proclaiming the brand's virtues. RJR was plainly in need of a successful new product to challenge American Tobacco's stable, but the effort was not truly mounted until the death in 1953 of the company's hypercautious head, James Gray, and his succession by a man universally regarded around Winston-Salem as a caring human being and the ablest Reynolds chieftain since the death of The Founder.

Nobody supposed that John C. Whitaker, a nephew of Will Reynolds and graduate of the university at Chapel Hill, would long remain in overalls when he began his RJR career on the factory floor in 1913, running a cigarette-making machine on the very same shift, company legend had it, that produced the first Camel. But Whitaker remained on the factory side for twenty-five years, the genial and warmhearted "Mr. John," who knew everybody in the place, pushing top management into more enlightened personnel policies, such as health and burial insurance, and hiring a minister to counsel drunks and burnouts among the nonunionized working force so that they would not have to be fired. Whitaker's door was always open, and he answered his own phone, even as he finally rose in the executive ranks. His ascent may have been hampered by his unprepossessing looks; he bore a certain physical resemblance to the stage, screen, and broadcasting funnyman Ed ("The Perfect Fool") Wynn. And Whitaker indeed loved collecting jokes, preferably off-color ones, and reciting them, just as he was fond of devoting his off-hours to playing the zither, performing locally as a ham actor, and deeply involving himself in political and civic affairs such as the construction of a substantial county hospital.

Beneath the joviality and kindness was a steely will that functioned with the persistence of water wearing away stone. Whitaker hewed to the small-town virtues of hard work and a frugality that had allowed cost-conscious RJR to achieve the highest profit margins in the business—a good 20 to 25 percent ahead of its two chief rivals. In contrast to American Tobacco's big-city spending ways, Reynolds prided itself on continuing to pay less for its supplies, credit, and labor. Its wages were 10 to 15 percent below its rivals' and a little more than half as high as those paid to a union autoworker. Free from organized labor's tighter manning rules, RJR could assign two "making" machines to each operator's oversight, while American, rationalizing that it thereby gained more "quality control," used one man per machine.

One of Whitaker's pet projects, the use of reconstituted tobacco leaf, proved a major economy for the company. About 30 percent of the tobacco leaf, in the form of the woody stem (chopped out during the shredding process), scraps, and tobacco dust, used to be wasted routinely, prompting RJR to begin exploring in the late 'Thirties how to salvage this costly loss. It took a dozen years of seat-of-the-pants secret research to realize the savings by pulverizing the stems in an old-fashioned coffee grinder, draining the resulting pulp over a wire screen, adding the scraps and tobacco dust, and pressing the mess flat with a felt mat in a process that resembled papermaking. The trick was to get the resulting sheets to gain enough tensile strength so they did not shatter when cut for the blending process. Known also as RTS (reconstituted tobacco sheet), the homogenized leaf, when blended into the "natural leaf," had no loose pieces and so was said to burn more evenly and provide a more uniform draw. It also readily absorbed flavorings, which allowed further savings because a cheaper grade of tobacco could thus be bought for the new filtered brand the company had begun to contemplate. Not incidentally, the heavy stems comprising the bulk of the RTS were lower in tar and nicotine content than the rest of the leaf.

Comfortable with who and what he was, John Whitaker was no domineering chief executive on taking the Reynolds chairmanship. In the critical sales and marketing area, where he was least experienced, Whitaker deferred to his second in command, Edward A. Darr, in many ways his opposite. A big, opinionated, stubborn man whose autocratic manner inspired dread among underlings, Darr had come into RJR after working the wholesale tobacco trade out of Baltimore, and from the late 'Thirties began urging the company to broaden its cigarette line. But he long found himself swimming upstream against the cautious, tightfisted Reynolds veterans, and when Cavalier laid an egg, Darr concentrated his efforts on energizing the sales force and pushing Camel back to the top. With supermarkets accounting by then for nearly half of all cigarette sales, Darr directed his field men to cultivate store managers, even if it meant circumventing the line of command with the chains' home offices. As a result, Reynolds won wide placement of its racks, with their assured preferential display of Camel cartons, and many takers for its dealer-service plan, so the store managers were relieved of having to place cigarette orders and Reynolds was assured that Camels would never be out of stock at any subscribing market. "Nothing happens till somebody sells the product" was Darr's anthem, and he got the sales executives out from behind their desks and into the field, constantly monitoring, demonstrating, and problem-solving. His field corps, whose managers averaged fifteen to twenty years with RJR, was the envy of the industry.

On a trip abroad in 1951, Darr was impressed by the fact that in the health-conscious Swiss market, filter-tip cigarettes were winning half the business. Convinced that filters were the wave of the future, he got nowhere back in Winston-Salem, where the old-timers mocked the innovation as an effeminate smoke and dubbed them "Tampax" for their absorbent qualities. But when named RJR president at the age of sixty-two, two years older than new chairman Whitaker, Darr at last had the power to move the filter. He was determined to avoid another Cavalier-like flop.

Essential to the company's thinking was avoidance of the health claims that the smaller manufacturers were making for their filter-tip entries in a misguided attempt to steal market shares from the industry leaders. Banging the health drum loudly and incessantly would inevitably hurt them all; smokers might be risk-takers, but they were not certifiably suicidal. Thus, the Reynolds filter brand would have to be a far more flavorful smoke than the rest—a Camel with a filter attached, more or less—which would require a looser and thus less intrusive filter and invite the use of the cheaper, reconstituted leaf. Darr knew, too, that the new product had to be both king-size and priced at the level of Viceroy, just a penny or two above the standard brands, if it was to have mass appeal; the long length and filter would make it attractive to women and urban smokers, the sectors of the market in which Camels fared most poorly, while men, thanks to a filter that was not too tight, could enjoy the Camel-like taste. Consistent with these basic considerations, Darr and his makers reached for nothing fancy or tricky in presenting the new entry. The first half of the company's hyphenated hometown provided a perfectly service-able name for the brand, one with a British tone to it like Kent, Viceroy, and Pall Mall, all enjoying strong acceptance in the U.S. market. The package it-self was classically simple and inoffensive: the top and bottom third were pure fire-engine red with the midsection in white and the name "Winston" in black, easily legible, and uninteresting lettering. The pack also bore the no-nonsense message "Finer Filter, Finer Flavor" by way of implying that the taste of the product mattered as much to the manufacturer as any enhancement in safety.

There was no shortage of problems as the company geared up for the brand introduction. Lorillard and Brown & Williamson, for one thing, had tied up the supply of filter-making machines manufactured by the Molins company of England, the nonpareil of the business, so Reynolds had to wait its turn. And when the machines finally came in, the cigarettes they produced had far too many "broken necks," where the filter join was imperfect. The blend itself proved complicated; the flavor had to be strong enough to penetrate the filter without overwhelming it, otherwise the unspoken reason for the device as a health safeguard would be defeated. Concern grew within the company that unless the Winston could be hurried along, it would reach the market too late to make a serious impact, especially with the L&M now out there and doing well. Charles B. Wade, Jr., a Reynolds vice president and director and, as a Duke man, the company intellectual, stopped Ed Darr on the street one day to urge him politely to bring out Winston soon, preferably within the month. Darr grabbed the smaller Wade by his tie, lifted him a bit, and snarled, "Not one damned day before it's ready—and from what I've tasted so far, it's not."

When the day came in the spring of 1954, the Winston launch was most no-table for the way its otherwise banal advertising giddily perverted the English language. A typical early ad showed a smiling mature couple, hands lovingly intertwined, with each also clutching a cigarette, and the headline "New filter cigarette: WINSTON brings flavor back to filter smoking!" Below the drawing of the smokers was a smaller heading that would turn into the unlikeliest suc-cessful slogan since "L.S./M.F.T."—"Winston tastes good—like a cigarette should." Countless literate folk were offended by this brutish usage of "like" as a conjunction, a linguistic gaucherie that made the new product the butt of sneering jokes. But the RJR marketers in Winston-Salem, never exactly a citadel of high culture and flawless grammar, were delighted with the atten-tion, made the offending slogan the lyric of a bouncy little jingle on television and radio, and wryly defended their syntax as a colloquialism rather than bad grammar. In this they were supported by the nation's best-known philologist, Northwestern's Professor Bergen Evans, later editor of *A Dictionary of Contemporary American Usage*, who pointed out that Shakespeare, Keats, and the King James Version of the Bible had committed the very same sin.

The unanticipated flap served to spotlight both the brand and its chief distinguishing feature—that Winston had more taste than other filter tips—and with the muscle of the Reynolds sales force behind it, the newcomer had little trouble racing past Parliament, Kent, and L&M into second place behind Viceroy by the end of 1954.

At American Tobacco's New York headquarters, meanwhile, they watched the filter phenomenon unfold, and waited. The ten-year headstart the company had enjoyed in the king-size market had made it fat, happy, and a bit complacent as the only cigarette maker with sales in excess of a billion dollars. Its quiet, dapper boss, Paul Hahn, was one of the new breed of organization men who used his high-priced vice presidents to administer the company in collegial fashion. The lack of flair showed in the steady decline of the flagship brand, Lucky Strike, but the slack was more than picked up by American's soaring king brands, Pall Mall and Herbert Tareyton. It was a conservative time for the nation, with a patriarchal Republican administration running the federal government for the first time in twenty years, and the female star of Lucky Strike's popular Saturday night television show, "Your Hit Parade," was a pretty blonde named Dorothy Collins, who wore blouses with virginally high collars and seemed to embody the prevailing mood of propriety and orderliness. Why worry about reports from a few obscure scientists that smoking was a serious threat to the public's health?

By the end of 1953, filters had claimed only 3 percent of the cigarette market, and American Tobacco's Hahn nonchalantly told the press, "If we can find a good filter—a really good one that doesn't take all the taste and flavor out of the cigarette—we'll have a serious look at it." But as AT's two closest runners-up for market share pushed actively into the filter arena in 1954 and little Brown & Williamson, on the strength of its hot Viceroy, moved past Philip Morris into the No. 4 slot in the industry, the filter market share reached 10 percent by the end of that year. To hedge his bet ever so slightly, Hahn ordered a filtered version of his king-size Herbert Tareyton brought out; its unfiltered version, though, outsold it heavily. American Tobacco commanded one-third of the cigarette market, while RJR, even with its new Winston off and running, held no more than a quarter of the market. Hahn saw no point in dashing into the increasingly crowded filter market. It was a major blunder.

VI

A T the annual clinical congress of the American College of Surgeons, held in October of 1953 and attended by 11,000 of the nation's most eminent sawbones, heightening suspicion was voiced about the possible deleterious effects of smoking. Among those most concerned was a University of Pennsylvania surgical professor named L. S. Raydin, one of the organizers of the convention program, who used the platform to assert that "in a matter which involves public health to such a degree, the tobacco industry has a moral obligation to pay for the research necessary to prove or disprove the suspected relationship. . . . Who else should be more interested?"

If the cigarette makers scoffed privately at the notion that they should underwrite serious studies of the health issue which might prove their undoing, a report appearing in the journal *Cancer Research* not long after the surgeons' 1953 conclave forced tobacco manufacturers to rethink the proposal. The lead investigator was once again Dr. Ernst Wynder, the young epidemiologist whose 1950 retrospective study with St. Louis master surgeon Evarts Graham had initiated the new age of scientific scrutiny of smoking. Wynder, by now the one-man staff of the new division of clinical investigation at the Sloan-Kettering Institute of New York's Memorial Hospital for Cancer, took the question to a level beyond the statistical association of smoking and disease with a two-year experiment on the susceptibility of mice to the growth of cancerous tumors on their backs after being painted with a distillate of cigarette tobacco smoke. The reported results were not good news for the industry.

Since a definitive experiment with human subjects was ethically impermissible, the next best thing would have been to try to replicate man's smoking with large animals of comparable anatomy. But large animals were hard to handle and expensive to maintain, and their use would have required long years to measure the effects of slowly developing cancer, even assuming the subjects could be taught to puff and inhale like humans. The problem with inhalation experiments was compounded by the fact that most species in the animal kingdom, and especially small creatures, are, unlike man, obligatory nose-breathers, with a highly articulated filter system built in to block the passage of foreign matter or to absorb it, thus preventing whole smoke from ever reaching their lungs in a quantity remotely approximating the human experience. Heavy doses of smoke would be needed to compensate, but since oxygen-robbing carbon monoxide makes up about 3 percent of tobacco smoke, heavy repeated doses were found to asphyxiate small animals early in the experimental procedure or otherwise induce fatal diseases. Some animals buried their snouts in their own fur or that of their cage-mates to avoid the smoke bath, thereby limiting their intake and foiling the point of the exercise. The most practical method, therefore, was to swab the shaved backs of mice—the preferred experimental model because they were small, short-lived, and comparable enough anatomically to humans—with tobacco tars derived from whole smoke and see how many developed tumors. While the results could not be readily extrapolated to humans, they might indicate to investigators if they were on the right track—"to give you some insight into the mechanisms of how cancers occurred in people," as Wynder later put it.

Perhaps the most questionable element in the mouse-skin experiments was not the obvious differences between animal and human species or between the chemical constituents of whole inhaled fresh smoke and a tarry distillate of it, but the nature of the cells to which the tar was applied. Wynder of course understood that the cells composing the tough epidermis of a mouse's back skin were different from the complex, thinly layered, and more sensitive epithelial cells lining the lungs. But Wynder would later contend that in the unfolding stages of the cancer-forming process, the lung epithelium under assault by tobacco smoke first underwent hyperplasia and metaplasia, thickening phases in which the cells revert to a more primitive form in a kind of protective reaction against the repeated insults by the irritants in the smoke; in that altered state, said Wynder, the lung cells did in fact resemble those of the mouse skin, thus allowing the cancer-forming process to be legitimately analogized.

Wynder's experiment, performed in league with Adele Croninger, a coworker from Toronto who handled the animals, and Dr. Graham, the reformed smoker who continued to lend his prestige to the research of the nervy Wynder, used a tarry condensate derived from fifty-carton batches of Lucky Strike, smoked by specially designed rhythmic suction machines attached to a series of glass beakers and approximating the human smoking cycle. The dark brown viscous fluid that resulted after condensation was mixed, in order to avoid inducing toxic shock when applied to the mice, one part to three of acetone, a naturally occurring, noncarcinogenic dilutant; after a while, the solution was changed to equal parts of tar and acetone. The subjects were 156 mice purchased from Clarence Little's Jackson Memorial Laboratory in Maine, 86 of which had their backs electrically shaved from the nape of the neck to tail and painted three times a week with a saturated camel's-hair brush. The dose was 40 milligrams of the tar distillate, the rough equivalent of the tar and nicotine yield of a pack of cigarettes.

Of the 62 mice in the painted group surviving after a year into the experiment, 58 percent developed tumors proven to be cancerous upon microscopic examination; 44 percent of the overall painted group got cancerous tumors, suggesting that some animals had died from other causes before the carcinogenic effects might have taken hold. Only 10 percent of the painted animals survived the full twenty months of the experiment, compared with 58 percent of the unpainted controls. As Wynder reported in *Cancer Research*, the "suspected human carcinogen has thus been proven to be a carcinogen for a laboratory animal"—an outcome that provided "a working tool which may enable us to identify and isolate the carcinogenic agent(s) within the tars." Dr. Graham, in remarks to a news magazine after the results were published, was less cautious; the experiment, he said, "shows conclusively that there is something in cigarette smoke which can produce cancer. . . . Our experiments have proven it beyond a doubt." Such certitude was spoofed in *Forbes* magazine, which noted, "Graham gave no estimate of the number of smokers who distill the tar from their tobacco and paint it on their backs in concentrated form."

More substantive skeptics of the skin-painting technique would remain unpersuaded by Wynder's contention that the mouse epidermal cells exposed to the tar were comparable to the bronchial cells after undergoing metaplasia. The more fervent criticism was that the dosages applied to the mice were so massive, in order to obtain speedy results, that the organism's defense mechanisms naturally collapsed. But defenders of the skin-painting said it was far from clear that the mice had been overdosed to produce cancers, since in human smoking the surface of lung tissue exposed to the small but continuous assaults by carcinogenic irritants was exponentially greater, due to the highly ramified structure of the bronchi, than the back area on the mice from which the tar could be readily sloughed off—in short, the whole smoke was much more efficiently absorbed by the human lung cells than the tar could be by the mouse epidermal cells. Tobacco industry defenders would further claim a few years after the Wynder mouse-skin report that 25 percent of all known chemical compounds, including simple sugars occurring in nature, caused some type of carcinogenic reaction in certain laboratory animals. For decades, industry scientists argued that while the tarry condensate was prepared by collecting the smoke in a freezing cold trap, then extracting it with acetone and concentrating the extract by evaporation before applying it to the back of the test mouse, all kinds of chemical reactions were taking place among the smoke components and confounding factors that further undercut the validity of the skin-painting study.

Yet for all of these objections, cigarette manufacturers and government and private laboratories would long afterward persist in using the skin-painting technique, because however flawed it might have been, however imperfect the analogy to human smoking, and however inconclusive, no more reliable form of bioassay has ever been developed. Wynder's experiment may not have indicted cigarette smoke as a killer, but it surely served to place the substance at the scene of the crime. Publication of his findings at the end of 1953 was enough to persuade the American Medical Association to stop accepting cigarette ads in its main scientific journal, *JAMA*, and nine smaller medical magazines.

VII

THE wide media attention paid to Wynder's graphic findings in the mouse-skin experiment stirred a petulant response by the tobacco industry, so long coddled in the news and editorial columns of the press, whose owners had grown flush with revenues from cigarette advertising. Paul Hahn, head of the industry pacesetter, American Tobacco, offered a rare public statement, lamenting "much loose talk on the subject [of smoking and health] in the press during recent months" and contending that nothing had been proven either statistically or in laboratories. A company statement added that "[u]nwarranted attacks on tobacco products are as old as the industry itself. . . ."

Such a reflexive denial and the counterargument that a suspected major menace to the public health must remain at liberty until proven guilty were no doubt understandable. But in their facile reassurance to a customer base composed of nearly half the nation's adult population, industry officials displayed insensitivity to the public's dawning comprehension of the enormity of the issue. Their dismissive tone was even more pointedly sounded by Reynolds's president, Edward Darr, who revealed his own and his company's combativeness with the remark, "One of the best ways of getting publicity is for a doctor to make some startling claim relative to people's health regardless of whether such a statement is based on fact or theory." Here was a blatant instance of the pot calling the kettle black; it ill behooved a company lately chastised by the Federal Trade Commission for fraudulent health claims in its advertising to malign the studies of highly qualified scientific investigators.

Behind the bravado, the cigarette barons had become increasingly uneasy if not yet panicky. Their mood was suggested by a memorandum circulated among them on December 14, 1953, by Brown & Williamson's president, Timothy V. Hartnett, a veteran of more than forty years in the tobacco business. Hartnett was of the opinion that the investigators on the smoking and health issue included men of "unquestioned integrity and sincere in their belief," so he urged "[e]xcessive caution . . . in the methods we adopt to counteract these claims." With remarkable candor he added that it was important for the industry leaders to recognize "we may be embarrassed by page after page of *pseudo*-scientific selling over the years. As one manufacturer says, we've perhaps too often been unlicensed medicine men rather than honest tobacco men" (italics in original text). Hartnett then called for a two-pronged counterattack "to get the industry out of this hole": (1) "unstinted assistance to scientific research," the most difficult part of this effort being "how to handle significantly negative research results if, as and when they develop," and (2) "the best obtainable" public-relations counsel since none "has ever been handed so real and yet so *delicate* a multimillon dollar problem" (italics in original).

Hartnett's candid concern was heeded. Shortly thereafter, the tobacco industry retained the services of Hill & Knowlton, among the most highly regarded U.S. public-relations firms. In a December 24, 1953, memorandum to the cigarette makers' chieftains, H&K offered sobering counsel: "It is important that the industry do nothing to appear in the light of being callous to considerations of health or belittling medical research which goes against cigarettes." Moreover, the tobacco moguls ought to understand that their past advertising "may have created a degree of skepticism in the public mind" that could initially hamper a public-relations effort to mitigate the health scare. In endorsing an industrywide research initiative, the New York–based publicists called for the formation of a scientific advisory board of men "whose integrity is beyond question."

Moving with a dispatch that reflected concern over a more than 3 percent decline in cigarette sales for 1953, fourteen leading tobacco manufacturers and allied groups among the growers and warehousemen opened the new year with a full-page announcement in 448 newspapers of the establishment of the Tobacco Industry Research Committee. Headlined "A Frank Statement to Cigarette Smokers," the ad's text began, "Recent reports on experiments with mice have given wide publicity to a theory that cigarette smoking is in some way linked with lung cancer in human beings," and while not regarded as conclusive, the results ought not to be "lightly dismissed"—a decided change of tune by the industry within a few weeks of the Wynder revelations. After this opening concession, the ad dispensed a torrent of reassurances: Research had shown there were many likely causes of lung cancer, there was no proof that smoking was one, and—in an unjustifiable claim—the biostatistics so far produced "could apply with equal force to any one of many other aspects of modern life. We believe the products we make are not injurious to health," the signers of the ad continued—a statement of creed, not a warranty, they would later contend, suggesting that the text had been meticulously lawyered. And then, revealing the fine hand of master publicists, the "frank statement" sought to blur any distinction between earlier denunciations of smoking without empirical evidence and the troubling new scientific data. For more than 300 years, tobacco "has given solace, relaxation and enjoyment to mankind" even while being held "responsible for practically every disease of the human body. One by one these charges have been abandoned for lack of evidence. . . ." Nevertheless, the industry was undertaking joint financial aid to research efforts on the smoking and health question and would soon appoint "a scientist of unimpeachable integrity and national repute" to oversee the program.

Liggett & Myers alone of the major players in the cigarette industry held itself aloof from this joint undertaking. The company may have feared renewed antitrust action against the industry for this combined effort or merely been registering deep distrust of its competitors, but at least as likely an explanation was that, obtuse as Liggett's advertising seemed to have been on the health issue (*e.g.*, "Just What the Doctor Ordered"), intramurally the company conceded that the public's awakening alarm was not groundless. According to the minutes of a March 29, 1954, meeting of Liggett scientists and advisors, for example, research chief Frederick Darkis remarked that "if we can eliminate or reduce the carcinogenic agent in smoke we will have made real progress," and that while the company had indeed made real progress in the reduction of the nicotine content of its brands through filter tips and leaf selection (*i.e.*, the lower the leaf on the stalk, the less nicotine it contained), the blenders still "have a ways to go." Here was acknowledgment that the product probably contained harmful ingredients that ought to be removed or reduced.

Toward that end Liggett undertook, without public announcement, its own ongoing research effort by hiring the leading industrial consulting firm of Arthur D. Little, Inc. (ADL), of Cambridge, Massachusetts. The ADL team on the Liggett account met regularly with the company scientists at their laboratory in Durham, North Carolina, where a pair of top chemists from Duke now joined the research program on a consulting basis. While the rest of the tobacco industry was slowly gearing up for health research funding, Liggett scientists gathered at Cambridge that spring heard ADL consultant Louis Fieser of Harvard, author of perhaps the most widely used textbook on organic chemistry, tell them that the first step in their program ought to be an effort to replicate Ernst Wynder's mouse-skin experiment. In charge of that project, to which Liggett promptly agreed, and the company's future efforts was prominent toxicologist Charles J. Kensler, a bluff, cigar-smoking authority on liver cancer who had lately left Cornell to take a joint appointment at the Arthur Little labs, where he was to become chief of life sciences, and in the pharmacology department at Harvard. The attempt to reproduce Wynder's skin-painting study—or, better yet from Liggett's standpoint, to repudiate his findings—was based, Dr. Kensler recalled, "on the assumption it had something to do with the human condition, but you couldn't be certain." That such an investigation by a cigarette manufacturer bespoke a seriousness of purpose and not simply an effort to whitewash its own brands was evident to Kensler, who long afterward remarked, "You can't brag about getting fewer tumors" than other brands produce in a skin-painting bioassay. "If you get one, you're in trouble."

That the Tobacco Industry Research Committee (TIRC) effort would, by contrast, be aimed in significant part at rebutting the health charges against smoking became evident three months after the announcement of the program, when the joint committee issued an eighteen-page pamphlet that amounted to a brief for the defense. A compilation of pro-industry statements by cancer researchers, medical school faculty members, and private practitioners, the TIRC's first publication included the view of none other than Clarence "Pete" Little, former executive director of the American Cancer Society, who stated that from the perspective of the laboratory clinician, no definite cause-and-effect relationship between smoking and lung cancer had been established on "a basis that meets the requirements of definitiveness, extent, and specificity of data, which the seriousness and implication of the problem deserve." But nobody among the health investigators had suggested that the case against smoking was closed—only that it ought to be fully ventilated. The American Medical Association's president-elect, Walter B. Martin, was quoted in the TIRC document to the effect that the evidence thus far gathered was not convincing enough "to establish as a positive fact that cigarette smoking is necessarily the cause" of lung cancer. But nobody authoritative had proclaimed smoking to be "*the* cause" of anything other than a high level of corporate profit. A Chicago surgeon, Dr. Max Cutler, offered a gem of sophistry in declaring press statements of a "causative" relationship to be "absolutely unwarranted" and adding, "Simply because one finds bullfrogs after a rain does not mean that it rained bullfrogs."

The moral dilemma beginning seriously to confront the cigarette makers at this time was perhaps best, if unintentionally, rendered by Philip Morris's chief executive, Parker McComas, who, in his capacity as temporary chairman of the TIRC, stated, "If the industry leaders really believed that cigarettes cause cancer, they would stop making them." But what McComas or any other tobacco industry official believed or chose to believe was less to the point than what their responsibility was as far as uncovering and reporting scientific information that the smoking public ought to possess when deciding to buy and use their product. Indicative of how they viewed that responsibility, the industry chiefs in mid-1954 selected as scientific director of the TIRC and chairman of its Scientific Advisory Board an apparently sterling catch: Pete Little, founder and retiring president of the Roscoe B. Jackson Memorial Laboratory and at age sixty-six an internationally known, bona fide cancer-fighter. Ten years earlier, while he was the director of the nation's top anticancer organization, he had written about the imprudence of smoking; now he was a hireling of an industry facing charges that it was intimately implicated in the spread of the most virulent form of cancer. Here supposedly was "a scientist of unimpeachable integrity" who the tobacco industry had promised the public in its "frank statement" would head its research.

If Pete Little's science was of "unimpeachable integrity," his character was not quite so free of tarnish, given previous accusations of moral misconduct at the University of Michigan and the American Cancer Society. While some at the ACS remembered Little as a rather emotional man, somewhat distant and

formal—one publicist termed him "a self-conscious bigshot"—his appointment to run the tobacco industry's research program came as a shock to many
at the society. The suspicion was that he had taken the job out of lingering bitterness over having been jettisoned by the cancer society after his clash with
Mary Lasker. Others who knew him felt that Little, fearing a kind of intellectual impotence with his pending retirement from the Maine laboratory he had
built, was highly susceptible just then to the tobacco industry's invitation and
currying; a restorative pride accompanied the power to distribute the research
funding of a major American industry. ACS medical director Charles Cameron
thought that Little "must have been pretty hard up" and that his accepting the
new position was "purely a mercenary kind of thing," to survive financially in
his old age. Whatever the reason, Cameron added, "Nobody at the society admired him for it."

VIII

"I WAS very dubious—and personally a heavy smoker—when we went into
it," explained American Cancer Society epidemiologist Cuyler Hammond
as he faced the press after delivering his paper, readied at the last moment,
before the annual convention of the American Medical Association in San
Francisco near the end of June 1954, just twenty months after he, co-
investigator Daniel Horn, and their support staff of thousands of ACS volunteers had launched their massive prospective study on the effects of smoking
on health. One measure of their preliminary findings was that both Hammond
and Horn had switched from smoking cigarettes to pipes.

They had not intended to make their first interim report for another year or
two, but the numbers tumbling out of the data-processing punch cards in the
second annual follow-up on the 187,766 subject white men between ages fifty
and sixty-nine documented a trend too apparent to withhold from the public.
The mortality figures for the 4,854 men who had already died showed significantly higher rates for cigarette smokers: 65 percent more smokers than nonsmokers had died in the fifty-to-fifty-four-year-old range; 60 percent more in
the fifty-five-to-fifty-nine range; 102 percent more in the sixty-to-sixty-four
range; but only 30 percent more in the sixty-five-to-sixty-nine range, presumably because the most susceptible smokers were dead by then. The death rate
for those who smoked cigars only was slightly above that for nonsmokers,
while the rate for pipe smokers was not at all elevated. And the more you
smoked, the greater your chances of dying prematurely. Among those smoking
under a pack daily, the overall death rate was 52 percent higher than that of
nonsmokers; for those smoking a pack or more a day, the rate was 75 percent
higher.

Since air pollution, especially what was generated by urban automobile traffic, had been a prime suspect along with cigarettes for the big jump in lung cancer rates, the ACS findings were particularly revealing, because they showed that there were proportionately fewer rural than urban smokers, that rural smokers consumed fewer cigarettes than urban smokers, and that in the rural and urban categories alike, smokers posted significantly higher death rates than nonsmokers. If air pollution, not smoking, was the prime culprit in lung cancer, why did nonsmokers, breathing the same fouled air, enjoy a notably lower death rate in general and lung cancer rate in particular? And by way of suggesting seriously for the first time that the ravages of smoking might not be limited to lung cancer and bronchial diseases, the Hammond-Horn data showed that pack-a-day smokers in the fifty-to-sixty-four age category died from coronary heart disease at a rate twice as high as that for nonsmokers.

Finally, and most overwhelming of the ACS statistics, was the analysis of the 167 men who had died of lung cancer in the twenty-month period. Depending on their age category, smokers were struck down by the disease at a rate from three to nine times as frequently as nonsmokers, while those smoking a pack or more a day died of lung cancer at a rate from five to sixteen times higher. All of their evidence, Hammond and Horn declared in concluding their bombshell report, was consistent with the hypothesis that the association between smoking habits and elevated death rates from lung cancer and heart disease was not coincidental. "We know of no alternative hypothesis that is consistent with all of the known facts," they wrote. On almost the same day, the *British Medical Journal* carried a preliminary report by Richard Doll and Bradford Hill on "The Mortality of Doctors in Relation to Their Smoking Habits." Of the 789 British doctors who had died during the first twenty-nine months of their prospective study, 35 had succumbed to lung cancer—all of them smokers, and the more they smoked, the greater their chances of dying sooner than nonsmokers of the same age.

The gravity of the Hammond-Horn numbers was evident from the industry's instantaneous rejection of all that they implied. Timothy Hartnett, the acting chairman of the TIRC who half a year earlier had cautioned his fellow tobacco executives against intemperate reaction to their scientific critics, now went off like a loose cannon. The preliminary ACS findings, notwithstanding the immense scale and scholarly care that went into the effort that produced them, were "biased, unscientific, and filled with shortcomings," declared the heated Hartnett. A few weeks later, Hartnett, by then retired from Brown & Williamson and named the first full-time chairman of the TIRC, had cooled off enough to issue a statement that would serve for years, with slight variations to meet the need of the moment, as the industry's standard response to the growing critical mass of evidence against it. There was "no conclusive scientific evidence" against cigarettes, said Hartnett from his Louisville office, adding, "The millions of people who derive pleasure and satisfaction from smoking can be reassured that every scientific means will be used to get all the facts as soon as possible." Implicit in that pledge was a specifically targeted, carefully coordinated, authoritatively supervised, and amply funded program. Not even a shadowy resemblance to such an effort would materialize.

By the first autumn of its existence, the industry research committee's chief scientific spokesman had already perfected the scripted remarks that would be invoked to repulse the health community's escalating onslaught. Consider Dr. Little's response to a statement issued by the executive board of the Public Health Cancer Association, a professionally dominated offshoot of the American Public Health Association, at its eighty-second annual meeting in October of 1954. There was enough evidence, said the board, "to justify advising the public to stop smoking cigarettes," and youth in particular to ponder the risks of taking up the habit. Little stated in reply that "unreasoning fear based on incomplete information is not a constructive force . . ." and that "No convincing clinical or experimental evidence" had materialized to indict smoking as the positive cause of lung cancer.

More curious than Little's pitch in behalf of his new employers were the ambivalent remarks by his opposite number at the ACS, Charles Cameron, in the immediate wake of the first Hammond-Horn report. The hazards of smoking "do not appear to differ significantly in degree from lots of other calculated risks to which modern man exposes himself," said Dr. Cameron, who then registered his sympathy with those "willing to shuck off this mortal coil a few years ahead of schedule as the price for a carefree, full-blooded—some would say undisciplined—life." But within a few months, Cameron had apparently thought better of such expansive tolerance of a dire health hazard that the organization for which he worked was conceived to combat. At his and Cuyler Hammond's urging, the ACS board that October issued its first formal warning about the possible peril of smoking: The "presently available evidence" indicated "an association" between smoking and lung cancer—nothing was said of a causal relationship—and the U.S. Public Health Service ought "to devise and pursue public health education and other measures" to check the rising tide of lung cancer. Hardly a rush to judgment. Officials with the American Heart Association were still less outspoken, primarily because the ACS-funded report on smoking by Hammond and Horn had had the audacity to disclose its findings in connection with heart disease as well as cancer.

Such caution and territorial bickering seemed absurd to Ernst Wynder, the Sloan-Kettering investigator who by the age of thirty had established himself as the nation's, and perhaps the world's, boldest scientific assailant of cigarette smoking. Writing in the November 1954 issue of the *Pennsylvania Medical Journal*, Wynder laid out his case witheringly. Doubtless such peripheral factors as air pollution and occupational hazards contributed to carcinogenesis, and surely genetic and hormonal factors with their systemic effects abetted an "internal disposition" to lung cancer among some of its victims, but such susceptibility was "a factor affecting all human diseases" and could hardly serve to explain away the relatively high frequency of this disease among serious smokers. While no one study or factor had yet conclusively incriminated cigarette smoking, the emerging pattern of evidence was cumulatively persuasive to Wynder: "The established statistical association . . . is a causative one." The cigarette makers, rather than going out of business, ought to respond to the evidence already at hand—and not wait until it became conclusive—"by modifying the manufacture of tobacco products," perhaps with truly effective filters that selectively removed the offending agents in the smoke as these were identified.

The public seemed to agree. By the end of 1954, one of every ten cigarettes bought was a filter tip, and per capita cigarette consumption dropped another 6 percent that year, making a falloff of about 10 percent over the two years in which the Wynder skin-painting experiment and Hammond-Horn population study were reported.

IX

JOSEPH FREDERICK CULLMAN III was well into his thirties before he began working closely with his father in managing Benson & Hedges, the manufacturing end of their family's various tobacco businesses. Joe Third was a short, lively fellow, but notably less earthy and demonstrative than Joe Junior. There was little at first to suggest that he would one day emerge as the most successful tobacco merchant since Buck Duke.

Young Joe was not a stellar student at the elite Hotchkiss School or in Yale's class of 1935 nor a leader among his peers in an era when youngsters of the Jewish faith, whatever else their background, were not eagerly received on the playing fields of the Eastern social establishment. But Joe Third had a pragmatic mind, keen curiosity, plenty of energy, a superior athlete's grace and channeled aggressiveness, and an infectious personality with a natural knack for storytelling. "He was just fun to be with," said his brother Edgar, the third of the four Cullman boys and the one who went into Culbro, the family's tobacco-growing and brokerage business. Yet there was a perceptible, guarded quality about Joe Cullman and the self-possession of a skilled cardplayer working the game of life.

Fresh out of college in the middle of the Depression, he went to work as a fifteen-dollar-a-week clerk at the Schulte tobacco counter in the lobby of an office building behind the New York Stock Exchange. It was a sixty-hour work week during which he was obliged to try to foist "push items" on his customers in accord with their manufacturers' payment for same. Then came a stint at the Upmann cigar factory in Cuba, learning the leaf and manufacturing end of the trade, followed by a more intensive spell as a traveling salesman for the Webster-Eisenlohr company, peddling their line of cigars on the East Coast. Although the Cullmans sold the Webster people the tobacco they used as wrapper for their cigars and his father later became involved in its management while the company was in bankruptcy, Joe Third was spared little of the pain of the drummer's life. Essentially a quite private person, he applied a native optimism and self-confidence that are essential to effective salesmanship. For all his advantages of upbringing, moreover, Joe was no high hat and mingled easily with those below his social station.

His taxing five-year apprenticeship was not a merry one, and it was hardly surprising that Joe Third jumped the gun on World War II by enlisting in the U.S. Naval Reserve in 1940, serving first in Washington but spending much of the war as the chief air defense officer on the light cruiser U.S.S. *Montpelier.* Struck by how little his young wartime colleagues understood about what they were fighting for, Joe gave thought to becoming a history teacher at war's end and did in fact take some history courses at Columbia upon his return to civilian life. But by then his father badly needed him at Benson & Hedges. Young Joe proved a less lovable but more orderly executive than his father, so much so that when he would reduce his thoughts and concerns to memos, as he had routinely done in the navy, Joe Junior balked, preferring face-to-face communication. "There is nothing easy about working for your father," Joe Third recalled.

As the smoking and health issue gathered momentum in the early 'Fifties, Benson & Hedges's Parliament brand, with its recessed filter, continued to grow steadily. In 1951, it became the twelfth best-selling U.S. brand; by the next year, its market share reached one-half of 1 percent—tiny, to be sure, but lucrative since Parliaments sold at a premium nearly 50 percent above the standard brands. By 1953, as the filter field grew more crowded, the company's volume surpassed $20 million, and Benson & Hedges was a bustling little business with 600 employees and a 4 percent net profit.

But the solid standing of the prosperous little company was precisely why Joseph Cullman III decided that the moment was ripe to end Benson & Hedges's existence as a tiny independent in a field of giants. The major companies were now muscling in on the Cullmans' turf with filter-tip brands, and since industry leaders Reynolds and American Tobacco were likely to market popularly priced versions in the imminent future, the premium price that Parliament had been commanding was in peril. Parliament's cotton filter, moreover, needed fixing. As its fibers swelled during the manufacturing process, they formed loose twists of irregular sizes and configuration, resulting in an inconsistent performance that was no longer tolerable when measured against the effectiveness of the cellulose, acetate-based filters coming into common use among the big cigarette makers. Such competitive pressures as well as "developments in the field of public health," stated a 1953 B&H status report on its research needs for the following year, doubled the need to "search for the responsible agents for carcinogenic action of cigarette smoking. . . . The overall outlook for a small firm with limited resources is not bright when viewed against the background of current research budgets of some of the large manufacturers." B&H would earmark only $31,000 for such purposes in 1954.

Mindful of these realities, Joe Third raised the idea of seeking a purchaser with his brother Edgar, who saw its merits but suspected that their father, full of pride over how Benson & Hedges had been built up, would strongly object. They agreed, though, that there was one potential buyer who, if interested and willing to pay generously, might overcome Joe Junior's understandable reluctance to sell—Cullman's longtime friend, Philip Morris chairman Al Lyon. Indeed, Lyon had practically become a member of the Cullman family, clowning with the youngsters and growing especially close to Edgar, whom he would take out on early morning fishing trips and regale with tales of his career as a globe-trotting drummer.

Not long after, Edgar, not directly connected with Benson & Hedges, found himself on the same Stratocruiser, returning to New York from Nassau, with Lyon. The two repaired to the bar in the belly of the craft, and Edgar asked if Philip Morris might have an interest in taking over B&H. "Talk to your father," Lyon urged, "and if he'll consent, come see me at the Carlyle," the fashionable upper Madison Avenue hotel where the Philip Morris chief kept a suite. The task of persuasion fell to Joe Third, then B&H's executive vice president. "My father was very proud of our progress—of his watch-charm jewel of an operation," young Joe remembered. But Joe Junior, in his seventies by then, was swayed by his son's conviction that the day of the popularly priced filter brand was at hand. "I told him I didn't think we could compete much longer with the resources and technology available to us. Still, he was really opposed." But the negotiations were allowed to proceed, no doubt on the premise that a sufficiently high price would ease the senior Cullman's unhappiness.

A perceptible drift had settled over the executive offices of Philip Morris, occupying the fourth floor at 100 Park Avenue and running the entire block between Fortieth and Forty-first streets. President Parker McComas had brought order and stability to the company, which was now comfortably in the black. But the patriarchal McComas, essentially an inside man and a numbers specialist with an ex-banker's reserve, deferred in the crucial marketing area to Chairman Lyon, who, nearing seventy, was a spent force.

Reflecting a lack of direction, the Philip Morris product line was stagnant in the early 1950s. Sales were flat in 1951, slid 6.6 percent in 1952, and dipped an additional 3 percent in 1953. Surveys by rival companies disclosed the main reason: a public perception that the flagship Philip Morris brand had "a sort of musty taste" and its simulated wood-grain package a dreary look that attracted few switchers. Philip Morris loyalists, moreover, were proving not all that loyal. Composed disproportionately of East and West Coast urbanites, college students (thanks to an aggressive network of campus sales representatives), and women who were light smokers, Philip Morris users were also more concerned than others about the health question and all too inclined to switch to Pall Mall, Kent, and Viceroy, then being pitched as virtually therapeutic smokes. Lyon's advertising now seemed dated. In a desperate bid to exploit the growing chorus of industry advertising on the health question but lacking a product on which to base a plausible claim, Lyon lamely authorized ads urging buyers to make "The Switch That Takes the Fear Out of Smoking." Urged by younger subordinates to bring out a king-size Philip Morris, Lyon opted instead to dress up the company's old filterless king brand, Dunhill, with a cork-like tip and offer it to the health-conscious with the slogan "King Dunhill Screens Out Irritants." But when buyers tried it and found it had no filter to do the screening, Dunhill fizzled despite a costly ad campaign. And when Lyon finally kinged the Philip Morris brand in 1953, it did not attract enough buyers to compensate for the drop in sales of the standard-length staple. The company was going nowhere.

Emblematic of its problem was that even when it made an inspired media buy, the marketplace did not respond. Lyon had been summoned to the little theater in the mansion of his company's savvy publicist, Benjamin Sonnenberg, in 1951 and shown the pilot film for a new situation comedy, then a new format in television programming. Lyon liked the sample of the planned series, about a zany Cuban bandleader and his nutcake of a wife, well enough to agree to the $19,000-per-episode cost, but declined to pay an extra $2,000 per show for Philip Morris to retain the rights in perpetuity to "I Love Lucy". The show promptly scaled the heights of TV hilarity, and when co-stars Desi Arnaz and Lucille Ball were caught up in the Red-baiting frenzy of the day after signing an ad for a cause said to be sympathetic to communism, McComas asked only, "Are they guilty?" Upon being reassured they were political naifs, Chairman Lyon got on the telephone to the Desilu studio to advise their inspired clowns, faced with the prospect of blacklisting, that the company would stick firmly by them. By 1953 "I Love Lucy" was the top-ranked show, seemingly well worth the $3.5 million a year it was costing the company. Yet surveys showed that while almost everyone knew about the boffo show, relatively few could identify the sponsor, with its lackluster commercials.

The dearth of fresh marketing ideas was painfully evident to the field sales force, especially in the Southern territories worked by native North Carolinian Paul Jeblee, who as a boy had helped raise tobacco and would later become a ranking Philip Morris sales executive. Jeblee was finding it so tough to get the company's brands into stores that he resorted to outfitting a panel truck with old "Call for Philip Morris" placards, parking just outside plant gates at closing time in factory towns, and selling cartons to departing workers. He might move four or five dozen cartons on a good day, then go over to the leading local cigarette retailer, pay him what he would have earned if he had sold the cartons from his shop, and with that inducement ask for an order and the chance to put up a display. At the company's own factories in Richmond, meanwhile, manufacturing had been cut to three or four days a week as PM brands slumped. "It was an operation run by poor boys and strong men," recalled one veteran Philip Morris hand, "and everyone felt damned glad to have any kind of job."

McComas brought in a new sales manager from Pepsi-Cola and a strong finance man from American Airlines, promoted from within, and sparked up PM advertising. But the change that paid the quickest dividends was the 1952 hiring away of the easy-mannered George Weissman from Ben Sonnenberg's public-relations shop.

A product of the best public education that New York City could offer— Townsend Harris high school for the gifted and City College's Bernard Baruch School of Business—the Bronx-born Weissman found that junior accountants were in oversupply, and, given his gift for clear written expression, went to work as a newspaperman in New Jersey. After wartime service as the commanding officer of a subchaser, the mellow-voiced Weissman worked for a while for Hollywood producer Samuel Goldwyn's New York publicity office and then caught on with Sonnenberg's crew of smooth flacks. He did so well in his four years on the Philip Morris account, building up the hardly colorful Parker McComas through speeches, press releases, annual reports, and special events, that Weissman was offered the post of executive assistant to the PM president.

After only six months on the job, he was asked by McComas to put down on paper what he thought the company needed most to energize itself. Not without hesitation, Weissman produced a thirty-two-page memorandum which would prove the making of a career that was to carry him to the pinnacle of New York corporate and cultural power. The memo contained two main suggestions. The first was for a marketing department to help frame PM's sales and advertising decisions. Weissman had been appalled by the lack of sales data and absence of research in the field. "Everything just sort of funneled in to Al Lyon," he recalled of the idiosyncratic decision-making process. Nor was there even the semblance of a product research program until McComas ordered the creation of a small laboratory in the rear of the fourth floor of one of the company's auxiliary red-brick factory buildings, where old Richmond production hands were less than delighted when the water would occasionally overflow and damage the leaf stored on the floor below. Weissman's second suggestion was that since filter-tip cigarettes were clearly the coming thing— "I was seeing more and more Parliament and Kents around town"—Philip Morris ought to develop its own entry promptly.

Weissman was told to explore a market research apparatus for the company. Through friends he obtained invaluable access to Procter & Gamble's marketing people in Cincinnati, who were in the vanguard of consumer testing of products and advertising and preached the virtues of intensified brand management over the traditional centralized approach. "The main lesson I learned from them," Weissman recalled, "was that if you try ten new ideas and nine of them flop, you can still make it all back and a lot more on the tenth one. But if you stand still in product development, you're going nowhere but down." He then turned to the Elmo Roper polling firm, whose gifted Louis Harris worked out a detailed questionnaire with him and PM colleague Ross Millhiser. There followed probably the largest consumer study ever paid for by a cigarette maker—10,000 at-home, in-depth interviews with smokers on their preferences and phobias. "We were trying to find out the potential depth of the filter market," said Weissman. What they found was that 61 percent of their subjects had tried a filter brand and abandoned it either because its smoke lacked taste or they felt it was effeminate to use such a safety-first product— or both.

Weissman told McComas that Philip Morris had to create a filter brand with a strong enough taste to overcome the prevailing notion that filters were for sissies, and then create a virile image for it. Named vice president with oversight of marketing, packaging, and new products, Weissman, who was still a newcomer and no trained tobaccoman, was given a license to range widely in assembling the pieces for the crucially needed product, with the final decision to be left to the top brass. Development of the new cigarette could not be left primarily to the blending and manufacturing people in Richmond, where they lacked technical expertise on filters and what they were supposed to remove from the smoke, not least because industrywide efforts to determine exactly what cigarette smoke was composed of were only just beginning in earnest. Thus, it was clear to Weissman that he would have to seek supplemental talent outside Philip Morris. The ensuing eighteen-month effort, launched in mid-1953, would involve eight consulting firms, six testing laboratories, and the Roper polling organization as well as twenty-five technicians in Richmond and nearly every executive at the company's New York headquarters. Lyon and McComas told jittery stockholders that the company was working on a filter brand but, virtually acknowledging that the competitive situation was too precarious to risk a flop, added, "It may be wise to wait a while and see how the trend develops." By "trend" they meant what Reynolds and American Tobacco were going to do.

Before a blend and a filter were developed for the new brand, two key elements in its presentation were settled upon—its name and the nature of the package. Among the possible names tested in the original Roper survey of 10,000 smokers, the old Marlboro brand had scored well. Still selling some 12.5 million packs a year as a premium brand, it was widely associated with quality merchandise, and the name had a masculine ring to it even though it had long been promoted as a mild, woman's smoke. The name also had a British resonance that the industry seemed to find *de rigueur* for filter brands (and that would soon be reemphasized with the arrival of RJR's Winston). To perform what amounted to a sex-change operation on the Marlboro and market it massively as a popularly priced filter with a pronounced flavor instead of one with an effete image might have seemed risky to outsiders. But starting late in the filter game, the ad hoc Philip Morris marketing team felt that Marlboro's established name recognition was a valuable base to build on and worth sacrificing the quarter-billion units the old brand was selling yearly.

The new hairy-chested Marlboro, company hands agreed, had to offer a highly visible, toutable point of difference, beyond the abstract claim of full flavor, when it reached the market. Accordingly, fresh attention was paid to the discovery, made by production chief Clark Ames during a 1952 trip to Europe, of a cardboard cigarette package with a hinged lid. Fiddling with the foreign prototype, in a "twin bundle" configuration of two rows of ten cigarettes each, Ames saw how it could be readily adapted to the American standard pack of three rows consisting of seven, six, and seven cigarettes, respectively, and could be made to close tight with a snug little snap. No U.S. company had yet ordered the machinery to form the hinged-lid boxes from Molins, the world leader in cigarette-manufacturing equipment, and so the Philip Morris Marlboro team began weighing the virtues of Ames's idea. There was a certain masculine quality to the hard-edged cardboard box when compared to the standard "soft" pack, a kind of protective firmness that would guard against the crushing or distorted shape that cigarettes often suffered in the flimsier paper-cup wrapping. The box also prevented tobacco from escaping into a smoker's pocket or purse while making it easier to extract a cigarette because the hinged lid offered easy access by exposing the top of the package. The sharp edges made for a bulkier, less malleable shape, but the distinctiveness of the trim package outweighed such drawbacks in the minds of the PM team. Molins agreed to give the company exclusive U.S. rights to the machinery to make the box through mid-1956.

Now the focus of the Marlboro effort became the cigarette itself. McComas remained uneasy about the know-how of his Richmond people when it came to filters, with which they had no experience. Al Lyon's report to him at about this time that Philip Morris could greatly strengthen its capability in the filter area, as well as pick up a profitable premium brand, by buying out Benson &

Hedges, fell on receptive ears. The Cullmans were well regarded; B&H had some talented younger managers, including Joe Third, who could only bolster Philip Morris if they agreed to come over as part of the buyout, and 10 percent of the Cullman-dominated Tobacco & Allied Stocks holding company portfolio was composed of PM stock. This last news invited pause on McComas's part, for what if the Cullmans used their previous Philip Morris holdings and the stock they received in exchange for handing over Benson & Hedges as the basis for a campaign to seize control of PM? While the Cullmans were hardly known as predatory, the possibility could not be discounted altogether.

One solution, of course, would have been to buy B&H outright instead of merging the smaller outfit into the larger one. But McComas preferred the approximately 5 percent dilution of Philip Morris stock that the transaction cost him to the heavy cash payment of $22.4 million in PM stock that the Cullmans were asking. There was no haggling over the terms, as it was made clear to McComas that B&H was not about to be shopped around the industry to the highest bidder. The Cullmans knew and liked Philip Morris and its people; they had something of value to offer the larger company; and that was the price—take it or leave it.

McComas took it, paying a steep twenty-five times B&H's current earnings to add the Parliament to his faltering stable of brands and, he hoped, useful personnel and key technological skills. To protect against any immediate possibility of a takeover bid by the Cullmans, their Philip Morris stock, now amounting to about 10 percent of the company's total equity, was placed in a non-voting trust for three years, so that Wall Street would understand that the transaction was a friendly one, and Joe Junior and Joe Third joined the PM board of directors early in 1954 when the deal became official.

X

IT did not take the Philip Morris manufacturing people long to realize that the Benson & Hedges crowd could provide no real help with the development of the new Marlboro filter. The acquired company had actually been struggling with the inadequacies of its cotton-fiber Parliament filter and had lacked the financial resources to address the problem seriously. The real benefit of the B&H purchase, then, would be the managerial skill that came over to PM at a time it badly needed some. Joe Junior brought the sagacity of three generations in the tobacco trade; Joe Third brought vigor, broad knowledge, and persistence. And then there were Joe Third's cousin, Hugh Cullman, nine years younger with a dogged conscientiousness that seemed surprising in one with such adept social skills; Clifford Goldsmith, a crack operations man who had run the B&H factory; and B&H treasurer John Cookman. All four of the younger men would play central roles in the future of Philip Morris, especially Joe Third, who came in as the new senior marketing man.

The arrival of Reynolds's Winston in the spring of 1954, with its stress on rich taste and studied omission of all references to any health advantages beyond the fact of its "finer" filter tip, drew Philip Morris's attention to the need to hasten development of the new Marlboro. The Winston, everyone in Richmond and PM's New York offices recognized, was a very good cigarette indeed and threatened to steal the thunder from the new PM filter entry. Thus, the key Philip Morris player now became its veteran chief blender, Wirt Hargrove Hatcher.

A cob-rough country boy whose land-rich, cash-poor family lived on a farm not far from Richmond, Wirt Hatcher had come to town to attend business school and in 1914 joined the old Whelan-dominated Tobacco Products Corporation, with production facilities in Richmond. Born with a love for the land and everything on it, Wirt became the company's leaf specialist and in time its chief blender, cooking up the formula for the old Marlboro after Tobacco Products took over Philip Morris, and later putting together the English Blend, as the Philip Morris brand was called in-house. Now a gimpy old-timer with a soft drawl, ripe language, a crusty on-the-job manner, and, it was said, four cents of the first nickel he ever earned, Hatcher had to come up with a blend superior to the bland Kent, the lackluster Viceroy, and what the PM factory people perceived as the "off" taste of the L&M, which they believed was suffering from Liggett's rumored purchase of cheaper leaf for the brand— on the apparent premise that since the filter dimmed the taste of top grades, their proportion could be cut back. To create a blend as pleasing as Winston's with its vaguely wine-and-raisin taste, Hatcher had to depart from the lightly flavored but aromatic English Blend, with its preponderance of Bright leaf, and make more use of Burley, the new reconstituted leaf, and their absorptive capacity for licorice, honey, and chocolate. The resulting blend was so delicious to Hatcher that he walked around the factory chewing a jawful of the granulated stuff. "We were the test panel," recalled factory engineer Joseph Lloyd, part of the most discerning group of tobacco people in the place, who gathered after work each evening between five and seven o'clock to try the various batches of the new Marlboro blend Hatcher was concocting. "The Winston was a formidable target, but that was the one we knew we were aiming at."

Hatcher's handiwork then had to be yoked to the cellulose acetate filter designed for Philip Morris by the American Enka company and packed loosely enough for the full flavor and bouquet of the master's blend to penetrate the barrier. What would be the point if the filter did its job too well? In order to "maximize taste," as Weissman would later describe the basic engineering solution to the product's design, "you had to compensate at the other end," with the result that the tar and nicotine yield of the initial version of the Marlboro was only slightly less than for the unfiltered Philip Morris brand.

The final essential ingredient, the package design of the hinged-lid box, while the work of many hands, was perhaps most zealously overseen by Ross Millhiser, the young native Richmonder named brand manager of the new cigarette. Rarely alluding to his Yale degree or wartime heroics as a foot soldier who escaped from his Nazi captors, the expansively voluble Millhiser was less reluctant to remind listeners that he had begun at Philip Morris before the war with an oil can in his hand and instructions to keep a row of cigarette-making machines operating throughout his shift. He was, from the first, a passionate and demanding judge of the reincarnated Marlboro and would ride with it to prominence.

Assigned at the time to coordinate the company's advertising efforts, Millhiser worked closely with the packaging design firm of Frank Gianninoto & Associates, located in the Graybar Building on Forty-second Street around the corner from PM's offices, to create a distinctive look for the new Marlboro pack. Their one guideline came from Louis Cheskin's Color Research Institute in Chicago, which had urged prominent use of red on the package to signify a product with a strong flavor; Millhiser, who had always liked the warm look and quality image of the Campbell's Soup can label, concurred. Gianninoto's artists offered Millhiser several designs for the Marlboro, but one stood out in his judgment. The bottom half of the box had a white background, but just above the midpoint the white portion began tapering until it formed a right-angle point that thus created an overall white shape resembling a traditional house as a child might render it; the "roof" portion, comprising most of the top and lid, was in bright red. This simple but striking geometric design served as backdrop for the brand name, rendered entirely in slender and rather elegant lowercase letters in a serif-style typeface: even the initial "M" in Marlboro was done in lowercase to lend the whole a more casual and stylized look. The ascending portions of the two middle letters—the "l" and the spine of the "b"— were given an exaggerated height, and behind them rose a drawing of a cigarette, surging perpendicularly toward the apex of the "house" portion of the design. For visual interest the red "roof" portion had thin white chevrons added to it, achieving a kind of candy-stripe look.

Every element of the design underwent intense in-house scrutiny. The only major modification made at that point, though, was the removal of the may-pole-like cigarette drawing; it seemed too blatantly phallic. But what would replace it in the white "second-story" portion of the house design? Consumer polls showed a favorable reaction to the Philip Morris "crest," the ersatz likeness of the royal British coat of arms that had lent pedigree, albeit illegitimate, to the original Marlboro and English Blend packs, and so a cruder, miniaturized version in gold was now proposed for the space above the brand name on the new Marlboro pack—to signify continuity, class, and a hint of elegance lacking in the dirt-plain Winston design. But brand manager Millhiser objected fiercely. "I was for our purposely dodging the elegance," he recalled, but though outvoted on the inclusion of the crest, Millhiser was so strongly against embossing it in gold—the company had too long "catered to the tastes of the effete East and West coasts," he felt, and ignored the more primal appeal to the heartland—that he persuaded the company to print the crest in a dark grayed blue. As if to surpass the Pall Mall crest with its pair of nonsensically pretentious Latin mottoes, the Marlboro crest bore the same Caesarian boast that had adorned the Philip Morris brand—*"Veni, vidi, vici"*—perhaps to convey company hopes for the product.

With two important exceptions, everyone at Philip Morris was now pleased with the look of the design. Manufacturing boss Ames was unhappy because the bottom of the hinged lid cut right across the middle of the top part of the white house, so that unless the printing and dye cut were precisely right, the roofline image would not line up evenly and the whole look of the design would be destroyed. Joe Cullman, Jr., in his advisory capacity as board member and senior tobaccoman, thought the Marlboro logo lettering was distinctive and elegant to a fault—*i.e.*, hard to read. Both objections were overridden when test-marketing results showed that the pack design scored well on supermarket shelves.

The last element in product design was the form and color of the filter tip: should it be recessed like the Parliament or flush like all others, and should it be an antiseptic white or of simulated cork? The former in each case was seen as an implicit appeal to the health-conscious, while the latter was thought rather more masculine in appeal. The various combinations were tried out toward the end of 1954 in four test markets—Providence, Rochester, Dallas, and Denver. While the tests, in which the flush-end, cork-tipped version used in Dallas would prove most successful, were being carried out, the small New York ad agency given the Marlboro account for its introductory campaign went broke, and Millhiser led the scramble to find a replacement in time for the scheduled end-of-the-year debut in the New York market.

In the winnowing task, it was perhaps inevitable that Millhiser would turn his colleagues away from the big East Coast and Madison Avenue agencies and urge consideration of a small, nineteen-year-old Chicago agency with fewer than thirty accounts but a rising reputation for homespun craftsmanship. Its presiding genius was founder Leo Burnett, a small, dumpy, and authentically shy native Midwesterner of sixty-three, with cigarette ashes perpetually spilling down his rumpled suit jacket. His appearance, manner, and philosophy of advertising were the polar opposite of the usual Madison Avenue huckstering. Among his first accounts had been the Minnesota Valley Canning Company, for whom Burnett's agency had created the symbol of a jolly green giant.

The image worked so well that the company changed its name accordingly and stayed on ever after as a client while Burnett became the embodiment of the "Chicago school of advertising," which in contrast to New York–style slickness stressed what its roly-poly exponent called "finding the inherent drama in the product and writing the ad out of that drama rather than using mere cleverness. . . . You have to be noticed, but the art is in getting noticed naturally, without screaming and without tricks." He favored directness, horse sense, and conversational language over the mannered and cute. From such values were fashioned the classic campaigns featuring Allstate Insurance's "good hands," United Airlines' "friendly skies," the Pillsbury "doughboy," Kellogg's "Tony the Tiger," and Maytag's "dependability people." To Philip Morris in New York, betting heavily that its new Marlboro brand could keep the company in the big leagues of cigarette manufacturing, Burnett seemed like someone with his finger on the nation's pulse—a native small-town Michigander who once worked as a police reporter in Peoria, Illinois, and *knew* what played in Hometown, USA.

The Burnett agency was sent the projected Marlboro package and the hurry-up call to develop an ad campaign redolent of virility yet not offensive to women. Joseph Cullman III and Philip Morris ad director Roger Green entrained for Chicago shortly thereafter and at once got two pieces of advice about the Marlboro package. American consumers expected their brand names to begin with a capitalized letter; the lowercase "m" at the beginning of the Marlboro logo as presented on the package may have been different, but the differentness served to trivialize the product—it had to go. Similarly, the diagonal peppermint stripes that formed the chevrons on the red "roof" of the pack were too fussy and distracted from the clean, strong basic design.

The conviction and confidence with which Burnett made his presentation left Joe Third even more receptive to the first proposed ad for Marlboro that the agency unveiled the next morning. The most striking, graphically demonstrable feature of the new cigarette was without doubt its hinged-lid package. Yet as Burnett himself would later comment, the container was "very handy for carrying buttons and fish hooks, [but] people don't smoke boxes." The innovative package was modestly displayed in the bottom left of the layout, lid lifted, but the only written reference to it was a small-type mention of the product's "NEW FLIP-TOP BOX," and "flip-top" it would be called forever after. Most of the black-and-white ad was devoted to a photograph of a cowboy.

"We asked ourselves what was the most generally accepted symbol of masculinity in America," Burnett said in recounting the creative process. The runner-up candidate was a taxi driver, that crusty, embattled, and quintessential urbanite. But to succeed, the Marlboro had to reach out beyond the old Philip Morris citified constituency, and who better to embody the appeal of the new brand than that mythic figure so deeply etched in the American grain—the cowpoke? So Burnett's people hired a model with marginally rugged, squinty-eyed good looks, stuck a black wrangler's hat on him and a cigarette in his mouth, and proclaimed, "New from Philip Morris" across the top of the picture and, in much bigger type below, the Marlboro brand name in letters resembling, but thicker and more visible than, those on the package logo. The brief, clean text block explained, in an approximation of cowboy-straight lingo: "The new easy-drawing cigarette that delivers the goods on flavor. Long size. Popular filter price. Light up a Marlboro and be glad you've changed to a filter." There was not a word about smoking and health, no false promise of mildness or protection against evil irritants. Marketing head Joseph Cullman liked the cowboy idea right away because, as he remembered, it conveyed "a certain gritty honesty and flavor." The cowboy, however incongruous to metropolitan sensibilities, was approved as chief pitchman for the New York kickoff at the close of 1954.

At Richmond, the pace became frenetic. There had been endless problems with the Molins box-making machines when they arrived at the Stockton Street factory, where the initial Marlboro run was under way. The dye cut for the box kept breaking down, so that only two of the six machines were operative for much of the time. And the fiberboard content of the Marlboro box was absorbing moisture from the cigarette tobacco inside, producing a soggy feel that could be cured only by laminating the box—a further complication in the tricky packaging operation. The manufacturing crew, tinkering endlessly, worked a seven-day week now, racing to get out enough of the new brand to meet the hoped-for demand in the introductory market. "We worked late every evening," engineer Joe Lloyd remembered, "going home for a shower break—there were no such facilities at the plant—and coming back in. Everyone knew there was an awful lot riding on it."

Truly, the whole future of Philip Morris was at stake. Its sales had slipped another 13 percent in 1954, or nearly twice the industrywide loss for that year. Even the newly and expensively acquired Parliament, after a long run of unbroken sales gains, suffered a 10 percent loss under the PM aegis as the company's overall market share fell to 8.7 percent, dropping it to No. 5 in the industry.

But down in Winston-Salem, where a few of the first, strikingly different packs of the new Marlboro had been snatched from New York tobacco counters and shipped for close examination, Reynolds's vice president for sales, Bowman Gray, Jr., took a few deep drags of their much smaller rival's cigarette, fingered the flip-top package, and was said to have remarked to his associates, "Philip Morris will have to be watched closely from here on in."

7

The Anguish of the Russian Count

IF THE emerging scientific evidence left smokers throughout the 'Fifties
with the choice of altogether abandoning their precious and protean source
of instant gratification in this life of endless travail or switching to a modified
form of it possibly less menacing to their health, plainly they would opt for the
latter course. The result was a remarkable transformation in the cigarette business in the second half of the 'Fifties. At the outset of that period, about one of
ten smokers used filter-tip cigarettes; by the close, more than five in ten were
using filters, medicinal-tasting mentholated brands were booming, and unfiltered Pall Mall had become the No. 1 best-seller, partly on the strength of the
absurd premise that its greater length somehow made it less noxious.

To stay competitive, all six of the major manufacturers were now offering a
stable of brands—unfiltered regulars and kings, filtered regulars and kings, and
menthols—and clamorously advertising in a marketing free-for-all dubbed the
"tar derby," in which conflicting and unsubstantiated claims abounded. For a
time it seemed that any filter would serve: they all took away some of the bad
stuff, didn't they? The fact was that the brands combining the least effective
filter with the strongest tobaccos sold the best, as if the public were just going
through the motions. Surveys showed that while 70 percent of the switchers
said they had taken up filters out of concern for their health, more than half of
them doubted that the change would make any real difference. To judge by the
sales figures alone, the scare over smoking seemed to have passed by the end
of the 'Fifties, when total consumption was up 18 percent over the mid-decade
figure; in 1960, per capita annual consumption of cigarettes for all Americans

age eighteen and over reached a record 4,171, or eleven and a half smokes for every person every day.

The tidal shift in brand choice by smokers was accompanied by technological changes in the industry which improved its profitability even as they were supposed to reduce the risks to its customers' collective health. Filter material was 15 to 20 percent cheaper than the equivalent length of the tobacco it replaced, and the stronger-tasting leaf used to counteract the filtering effect was less costly than the milder leaf. Reduced use of nitrogen-based fertilizers helped cut nicotine yields, as did the industrywide adoption now of reconstituted leaf, which also reduced tar intake and, due to its lower density and the development of puffed leaf in the following decade, cut the amount of tobacco used per cigarette by one-third—a major advance in cost-cutting. Changes to reduce the suspected hazards of smoking included advances in the configuration of the filter and the introduction of new materials, like activated charcoal; perhaps still more important by the end of the 'Fifties was the use of smoke dilution in the form of more porous cigarette paper and, in subsequent years, smoke ventilation through microscopic holes punched mechanically or electrically in the tipping paper around the filter's circumference. The porous paper, admitting more oxygen, helped the manufacturer by quickening the burn rate (so smokers bought more packs to sustain their puff level) and may even have benefited the smoker by producing a somewhat cleaner burn with fewer resulting toxic wastes from incomplete combustion.

Despite the industry's public disavowals of any profound health consequences from smoking, work being done in company laboratories evidenced sophisticated knowledge of the biochemistry of the process and its grave potential to do harm. By way of example, Philip Morris's research director, Robert DuPuis, sent a memo dated July 20, 1956, from Richmond to the company's top officers in New York reporting in ventilated cigarettes "a proved decrease in carbon monoxide and carbon dioxide plus an increase in oxygen content of the smoke"; the former, he explained, was "related to decreased harm to the circulatory system as a result of smoking," while the latter meant there would be less chance of depriving cells of oxygen "and of starting a possible chain of events leading to the formation of a cancer cell."

So long as the medical evidence against cigarettes remained soft and anecdotal, the industry did not hesitate to use specious or highly suspect scientific claims to sell its product. But as the scientific case against smoking began to crystallize in the 'Fifties, industry leaders American Tobacco and Reynolds backed away from the health pitch in the belief that any talk of the hazardous nature of cigarettes and relief therefrom through the miraculous new filters being purveyed noisily by the industry's also-rans would serve only to amplify the apprehensions of smokers.

This division in industry ranks was narrowed in 1955, when the toothless regulators at the Federal Trade Commission promulgated a seven-point guide for advertising by cigarette makers aimed at eliciting their voluntary compliance. To avoid becoming embroiled in ten-year legal battles to defend their spurious come-ons, the manufacturers were asked to refrain from their most egregiously deceptive claims, starting with any representation of "medical approval of cigarette smoking," like Liggett's L&M ads promising "Just What the Doctor Ordered," Camel's "T-Zone Test," or the smiling presence of white-coated medicos. The guide explicitly ruled out any claims concerning the effects of smoking "on the (a) nose, throat, larynx or other parts of the respiratory tract, (b) digestive system, (c) nerves, (d) any other parts of the body, or (e) energy." Nor was any claim to be allowed of lowered tar and nicotine yields due to the length of the cigarette, the addition of a filter, "or for any other reason . . . when it had not been substantiated by competent scientific proof . . . that the claim is true, and if true, that such a difference or differences are significant." Thus, Brown & Williamson could continue to describe its Viceroy brand as containing "20,000 filter traps" and American Tobacco could shortly introduce its Tareyton "dual filter" with "activated charcoal" so long as both descriptions were factual and no health advantage was explicitly claimed as a result; what the smoker inferred was his problem. Meanwhile, the companies were free to rhapsodize about the taste, flavor, and pleasure of their product.

Not surprisingly, highly flavored brands with the least filtration fared best in the marketplace. Winston's filter left it with a tar and nicotine yield as high as its RJR stablemate, unfiltered Camel, still the top seller among all U.S. brands. In 1955, its second year on the market, Winston sales tripled; another 50 percent gain the next year made it the runaway leader among filter tips. Marlboro made up for its late start with superior packaging and a sales pitch steeped in testosterone. Beyond its telegraphic pitch of "Filter . . . flavor . . . flip-top box," Philip Morris peopled its Marlboro ads with the most virile-looking guys it could find, whether cowboys, longshoremen, or grizzled tennis players, all possessing a hand tattooed with a winged shield, the insignia of the sort of man who led a more adventurous life by, among other manly acts, smoking Marlboro because "the filter doesn't get between you and the flavor." Typical ads in the brand's early years stated with practically orgasmic zeal that "the man-size taste of honest tobacco comes full through"—does taste have a size and what size is a man?—and pictured a rugged hunk captioned "a lot of man . . . a lot of cigarette" or displayed an adoring younger female in the background under the headline "Where there's a man, there's a Marlboro" (and, apparently, women who like men who like Marlboro). By 1956, its second full year on the market, Marlboro was outselling Kent by four to one; another 44 percent jump in 1957 brought it closer to No. 2 filter brand Viceroy and No. 3 L&M.

The most instructive performance in the 'Fifties tar derby was turned in by

Lorillard's Kent brand, which after early misadventures scored a triumph confected chiefly—in about equal measure—of perseverance and cynicism. Following a flurry of interest in 1952 based on its alleged health advantages, Kent made little headway against the new, lower-priced, and more highly flavored filter brands. Its prime asserted virtue, a truly effective "Micronite" filter, had proven its undoing; smokers complained that puffing on a Kent was like smoking through a mattress. To make matters worse, Lorillard's research director, Harris Parmele, had determined from tests by two independent laboratories that Kent smoke contained "[s]harp little fibers" of asbestos, tiny barbs that, as one of the research reports visualized it, implanted in smokers' lungs precisely those irritants that the filter was designed to screen out. Four decades later, researchers would learn that of thirty-three workers at a Massachusetts factory where "Micronite" filter material was made for Lorillard for almost five years, nineteen had died of cancer—five from mesothelioma, the form associated with the inhalation of asbestos fibers.

Parmele, in an age still largely unaware of the perils of asbestos, nevertheless took the laboratory reports seriously and set to work seeking a substitute filter material. But the company did not advise the public of its quest and indeed kept advertising the Micronite filter as entirely harmless. Nor did it announce, having flaunted Kent as a brand low in tars and nicotine and, accordingly, less hazardous to its users' health, that it was loosening the filter to allow more flavor—and irritants—through it. By 1955, the original yield of 2 milligrams of tar had been increased sixfold and the 0.5 milligram of nicotine had quadrupled. Still, there was no pickup in Kent sales.

When hard-boiled Lewis Gruber, who had been instrumental in Kent's creation, was named chief executive of Lorillard in mid-1956, he immediately ordered the brand's price slashed four cents, in line finally with rival filters, and its tar and nicotine yields heightened still further—to no avail. But by mid-1957, Parmele was ready with the "New Micronite," *sans* asbestos and very like other filters in its composition but more tightly crimped and supplemented by porous cigarette paper. The result was about a 35 percent drop in its strength, enough to place it one-third below the yields of most leading brands. Fortunately for Lorillard, *Reader's Digest* was then running an exposé of misleading filter-cigarette advertising and raved about the new Kent's lowered numbers. On the strength of the publicity via the *Digest*'s massive circulation—at 14 million copies sold a month, it was the nation's largest periodical—Kent skyrocketed to a strong No. 2 position in the filter field, and Lorillard passed Philip Morris and Brown & Williamson to gain fourth place in the industry.

A more enduring phenomenon than Kent's comeback—and equally without evidence that they were less hazardous than any other form of smoke—was the rise in the later 'Fifties of the mentholated brands. These represented only 3 percent of all cigarette sales in 1956, when Reynolds, in the full flush of its success with Winston, launched its companion brand, Salem, the first filter-tip menthol. It had the same size, format, and packaging look as Winston, but instead of the torrid red banding, Salem was done up in a chilly blue-green to suggest its taste. It reached the marketplace, by dint of an accelerated push from the production people, shortly before the filter version of Brown & Williamson's Kool and a repackaged version of Philip Morris's laggard menthol, Spud. But Salem enjoyed two advantages over its established rivals. First, it had a much lighter menthol taste than Kool and so appealed more to women, especially the heavy smokers among them who were uneasy about the health risks of their habit. (Ironically, the erroneous belief that the cooling sensation of menthol brands made them less hazardous, if not actually medicinal, invited deeper and longer inhalation, thus likely promoting rather than retarding disease formation.) Second, RJR mobilized a massive marketing effort for the new brand, combining a powerful push by its giant sales force with the pull of big advertising dollars in a campaign featuring softly colored scenes of inviting nature and a slogan that proclaimed Salem to be "Refreshing as Springtime Itself"; there were none of the medicinal overtones that Kool had always emitted. By its second year on the market, Salem was selling twice as many packs as Kool. Salem soon introduced high-porosity paper that its copywriters said "breathes new mildness into the smoke . . . new freshness into the flavor," and the artwork grew as lush as Impressionist landscapes, with hand-entwined lovers traipsing over upland meadows, their tumescent hearts doubtless set on a pristine kiss and a Salem to soothe whatever followed. By 1960, the brand had tripled Kool's rising sales and was largely responsible for the menthols' 11 percent share of the market; by the 'Eighties, the category would command more than one-quarter of all cigarette sales and become the preference of perhaps as many as three-quarters of African-American smokers. Nobody could adequately explain this latter peculiarity; some market researchers saw it simply as a cultural preference, even as blacks disproportionately favored fruit-flavored sodas to colas in the soft-drink field, while others theorized that the Kool brand name stemmed from jazz argot, of black origin, in which "cool" was the essential term of approval.

An intentional laggard in the tar derby was American Tobacco. On the strength of its unfiltered brands—Lucky Strike, Herbert Tareyton, and still climbing Pall Mall—American clung to first place in industry sales ahead of onrushing Reynolds, but plainly it needed a new freestanding filter entry, not just its indifferently promoted filter version of Tareyton, to remain on top.

The result, late in 1956, was Hit Parade, a brand utterly devoid of a unique selling proposition, to use the term adman Rosser Reeves popularized in that era. Hit Parade had the same full flavor, easy draw, flip-top box, and red-and-white packaging as Winston, L&M, and Marlboro, leaders in the filter field, but it was a tardy copycat. The company's rescue effort, by recasting it as a quasi-health brand with a sharply lowered tar and nicotine yield and "400,000 filter traps," twenty times the Viceroy claim, could not save it.

As if in compensation, American's filterless Pall Mall in the beautiful red pack, by making a virtue of its strong flavor ("No flat, filtered-out taste") and the remarkable fact that "you can light either end," overtook Camel in 1960 as the best-selling individual brand and held the top spot for half a dozen years—a temporary anomaly in the age of the filter and a diversion from the reality that, despite later desperate efforts to recoup, American Tobacco's long hegemony in the cigarette trade was over.

II

B Y disallowing the most blatant health claims of cigarette makers' advertising while permitting them to offer descriptions of filter tips with their implied efficacy—they had to be filtering out *something*—the FTC unwittingly validated the grand deception being foisted on the public. To compensate for the taste robbed from them by filters, the new brands used stronger tobaccos that yielded about as much tar and nicotine as the old unfiltered brands—a fact never noted in the industry's advertising. The filters, by and large, were merely cosmetic mouthpieces.

The whistle-blowing began in earnest in March of 1957, when small but influential *Consumer Reports*, in its biannual survey of cigarette brands (based on its own laboratory tests), disclosed that the tar and nicotine yields of the filter brands had been rising steadily for several years and now approximated the level of the older and presumably more hazardous unfiltered brands. Four months later, *Reader's Digest* confirmed, in a report based in part on the findings of an independent laboratory, that smokers were being deceived in their hope to allay health concerns by switching to filter brands. RJR's filterless Camel, for example, yielded 31 mg. of tar and 2.8 mg. of nicotine per cigarette compared with 32.6 mg. and 2.6 mg. per Winston. American Tobacco's new Hit Parade had yields about one-third higher than its regular Lucky Strike, while Liggett's filter brand, L&M, was comparably higher than its old Chesterfield. The *Digest*'s praise for the new Kent filter stemmed solely from evidence that, by having reduced its yields by about one-third (after having raised them considerably in the immediately preceding years), it was acting counter to the industry's shameless practice.

While the *Digest*'s two-part exposé was running, Congress for the first time probed the same terrain, albeit in a tangential and short-lived gesture. John Blatnik, a boyish-looking, five-term liberal representative from Minnesota—and a devoted smoker—led his subcommittee on government operations through a four-day set of hearings on the FTC's oversight of cigarette advertising. Blatnik bristled as the testimony, the first ever presented to federal lawmakers on the relationship of smoking to health, revealed the dimensions of the industry's deception in increasing the strength of its filter brands.

Among the examples Blatnik cited in his report and later article on the hearings was how Liggett, after having boosted its nicotine yield by 70 percent over the previous three years and its tars by one-third, claimed in 1958 to have a "much more effective filter"—than what, it did not say—but tests revealed that eleven of seventeen rival brands had lower yields than the Liggett filter. Such licentious advertising was going unpunished—and at one point during 1958, six brands were simultaneously claiming the lowest tar and nicotine content on the market. If the FTC was guilty of laxness in protecting the consumer, as Blatnik charged, more glaring still was the smugness of the tobacco industry, which declined to send any company officials to testify, as Blatnik had requested. Its avoidance was understandable, for the placebo nature of the filters was both transparent and indefensible, but the industry was not made to answer for it. The closest it came to an official statement was the testimony of the Tobacco Industry Research Committee's scientific director, Dr. Clarence Little, who said the industry had never told him anything about its use of filters or shown him any research on filters in their laboratories and, furthermore— despite the fact that smokers were switching over to filters massively and the manufacturers were singing their praises—"I have no opinion about . . . the filter at all. I don't know why it was done, and I frankly—if you don't think I am in contempt—care very little."

In the aftermath of the hearings, Blatnik introduced a bill in the House of Representatives that would have limited the tar and nicotine yields of cigarettes and granted the FTC injunctive powers against deceptive tobacco advertising instead of requiring the regulators to jump through legal hoops for years before obtaining relief. So powerful was the tobacco industry, however, and so well placed were its home-state legislators that not only was the Blatnik bill denied a hearing in the House, but its sponsor was stripped of his subcommittee chairmanship and the subcommittee itself dissolved.

Blatnik's effort was not entirely in vain, though. Stung by his and others' criticism, the FTC convened a two-day conference in February of 1958 aimed at developing a single reliable test standard for measuring tar and nicotine yields in order to bring an end to the wild and conflicting brand claims that were making a mockery of the commission's 1955 ad guidelines. But the last thing the cigarette makers wanted was to replace the test results obtained by their own unmonitored scientists or pet outside laboratories with a single, authoritative, and well-publicized rating system sanctioned by government by which the buying public could measure the presumptive degree of hazard in any given brand. This was especially true of the front-running companies with the highest-yielding brands. In a bravura display of disdain for the collective scientific evidence, Reynolds's new president, Bowman Gray, Jr., told the FTC gathering, "We attach no significance to the measurable quantities of solids and nicotine reported to have been found in the smoke of cigarettes."

Unsurprisingly, no agreement was reached with the industry on a standard test for the strength of its cigarettes. But the message had registered. Even haughty RJR now joined with its competitors, all of them newly anxious over the public disclosure of their numbers game, in dramatically lowering the tar and nicotine content of their filter brands. Between 1955 and 1960, the yields were slashed by an average of 40 percent. But to call attention to their turn-about would have been to concede their past transgressions and admit they feared that the growing health charges against them might be true. Lowered yields, on the other hand, due to milder tobaccos, filters that actually filtered, and other precautionary manufacturing techniques provided uneasy smokers with what to them was an acceptable alternative to quitting, and implied to youngsters considering the habit that the peril was reduced.

As the cigarette yields were dropping—without explanation—and claims of the implied miraculous powers of the filters—without proof—were escalating, the chairman of the FTC struck a statesmanlike pose and pressured the industry into adopting what he hoped would be an advertising policy in the public interest. It would shortly prove to be just the opposite.

Earl W. Kintner, a twelve-year FTC veteran and its general counsel before assuming the chairmanship, exultantly reported in February of 1960 that the tobacco companies had voluntarily agreed to "a drastic change in the tone of cigarette advertising." Henceforth, there were to be "no more tar and nicotine claims," which were being "eliminated simultaneously and on an industry-wide basis, because the individual claims were confusing to the public and possibly misleading in view of the absence of a satisfactory uniform testing method and proof of advantage to the smoker." Where the 1955 FTC cigarette ad guide had ruled out unsubstantiated health claims (which nonetheless continued to be implied by allowable descriptions of filter styles and yield data attributed to reputable sources), the 1960 agreement ended all mention of the smoke yields since their health effects could not be proven. "In my view," said the FTC head, patting himself on the back, "this is a landmark example of industry-government cooperation in solving a pressing problem."

Like most forms of censorship, the FTC edict succeeded mainly in promoting ignorance—in this case, on the part of consumers—and retrogression—on the manufacturers' part. Having somewhat modified their product in order to appear to have reduced its health hazards (that they nevertheless continued to deny existed), the companies now saw no value in continuing the trend. If they could not even imply a reduction in the perils of smoking, under the new FTC rules, further slashes in tar and nicotine strength offered them no possibility of competitive advantage and might even, if they weakened their brands too much, destroy the addictive power of cigarettes that sustained their economic existence. Soon the yields leveled off or, in some cases, began creeping upward again.

III

HAVING reduced their intake marginally in the preceding two years, smokers in 1955 resumed their indulgence in cigarettes, as if reassured by the arrival of many new filter brands designed—or so they chose, and were led, to suppose—to diminish whatever health hazard their habit fed. One prominent poll reported that nearly two-thirds of all adult men smoked cigarettes, one-third of all adult women, and half of all eighteen-year-olds. The health "scare" seemed to have eased. Cigarettes were barely linked to the No. 1 killer, heart disease—"the available evidence is not sufficient" to make the connection, said the American Heart Association's scientific committee, except in the case of those already afflicted with a cardiac condition, and if there was a causal connection, "it is only one of many factors."

While more convincing evidence had been developed regarding the likelihood that regular use of cigarettes was a major contributor to lung cancer, the February 1955 issue of *Consumer Reports* contended that the case "is still inconclusive." By the end of 1960, when the death toll from lung cancer surpassed 35,000 a year, or twice the 1950 figure, a different verdict was reaching consensual proportions. The change, based on the extension of the earlier findings from surveys on death rates and laboratory experiments on mice, was due mainly to the work of pathologists and other investigators engaged in microscopic studies of human and animal tissue chronically exposed to tobacco smoke.

If epidemiologists, who had conducted most of the smoking studies in the early 'Fifties, were widely viewed in the medical profession as practitioners of "soft" science, pathologists enjoyed an exalted standing among their peers. Their interpretation after microscopic study of diseased tissue, usually undertaken just before surgery or immediately after death, represented science's last word on the ravages of nature and how well doctors had coped with them. Pathologists knew better than anyone else the mistakes in diagnosis and treatment common to the healing arts. One such practitioner, in his fiftieth year when he started examining the smoking question, was Dr. Oscar Auerbach, by then a paunchy little pipe smoker admired within his field for a compulsively meticulous work ethic. Where others examined three or four "sections" of tissue before rendering judgment on the precise nature of the suspected disease, Auerbach might examine a dozen or two dozen slides. Well liked and unassuming (for a pathologist, it was generally added), he was an exuberant and bouncy man who seemed to run rather than walk when outside his laboratory, as if to compensate for the largely sedentary nature of his work, which left him hunched for endless hours over a microscope. He wore thick glasses to correct severe myopia, which, while not affecting the accuracy of his microscopic vision, made him an uneasy motorist who, for his own safety and everyone else's, commuted to work during off hours. Drawn to pathology while in Vienna for part of his student training because "it seemed to give you all the answers to so many diseases," Auerbach specialized in lung disease early in his career and so had naturally grown familiar with cancer as it replaced tuberculosis as the prime bronchial menace.

Stationed at the Veterans Administration hospital in East Orange, New Jersey, Auerbach had a thought following one of his regular Tuesday morning clinical conferences in 1953. Part of the session had been devoted to a lung cancer victim whose tissue samples clearly illustrated the progressive stages of the disease. Why not undertake a study at autopsy of the lung cells of smokers who had succumbed to the same disease to see if a comparable progression could be tracked? The implications of such a finding might be profound.

The normal trachea, or windpipe, is divided into two main tubes, or bronchi, which en route to the lungs subdivide into ever smaller air tubes called bronchioles, ending in tiny air sacs, or alveoli, numbering perhaps 400,000 and surrounded by blood vessels with semi-permeable walls through which the vital life function of exchanging inhaled oxygen for exhaled carbon dioxide waste from the bloodstream is conducted. The interior surface of this intricate bronchial system, from the nostrils to the tiniest airways, is lined with a layer of sticky mucus, excreted by deep-lying glands and goblet-shaped cells along the surface to protect the breathing system from infection. The inner lining (or epithelial) cells are topped with a whiplike fringe of hairy filaments called cilia that beat back and forth rhythmically, propelling the carpet of mucus upward and outward in a protective mechanism that traps up to 99 percent of the irritants and toxic substances invading the body; scavenger cells called macrophages generally catch and consume unwelcome invaders not mired in the mucus. Any intrusive force, such as inhaled smoke, that might disrupt this chief line of the body's defenses against disease was of keen interest to pathologists like Oscar Auerbach.

His lung tissue study, begun with a small grant from the Pfizer pharmaceutical company, would eventually involve four primary researchers who over an eight-year span microscopically examined more than 100,000 samples from some 1,500 cadavers, whatever their cause of death. To assure objectivity, the specimens were examined in a "blind" test, whereby each individual slide was identified only by a serial number so the investigators would have no prior knowledge of the subject's cause of death. The sole condition in selecting the subjects was that a reliable history of each one's smoking habits be made available.

When his initial funding ran out and was not renewed, Auerbach took his project to the American Cancer Society, where chief epidemiologist Cuyler Hammond saw at once how such a careful pathological study might be an ideal complement to the biostatistics emerging from the ACS field survey of nearly 200,000 subjects. If the population study confirmed a close relationship between smoking and health, a microscopic examination at the cellular level might add the vital dimension of explaining how the disease process unfolded. Hammond got Auerbach ACS funding and the added expert counsel of Columbia's famed pathologist Arthur Purdy Stout, who reviewed Auerbach's slides and readings. By 1956, the first preliminary findings were reported.

Auerbach and his colleagues found three kinds of cell changes affecting the bronchi of smokers that rarely, if ever, showed up in nonsmokers' lungs—and the more heavily the subjects had smoked, regardless of their ultimate cause of death, the more frequent and prominent the cell changes. First, some 95 percent of smokers had undergone hyperplasia of the epithelial cells lining their bronchi—an excessive growth (*i.e.*, anything more than two layers) in reaction to chronic irritation of the walls lining the airway and thus thickening them and narrowing the passage. In a number of cases, this had advanced to metaplasia, the abnormal proliferation of cells of altered shape and arrangement, which in turn, if unchecked, sometimes became tumorous lesions that drained nutrients from normal cells and formed what Auerbach and other pathologists called "carcinoma in situ," meaning cancerous growths that had not yet broken through the underlying tissue of the membrane floor and started traveling to other body sites. Auerbach thus felt justified in terming such lesions "preinvasive," by way of suggesting that if the subjects lived long enough, the chronic irritants inducing the disease process (*i.e.*, smoking) would cause the fatal spread.

A second phenomenon Auerbach observed in the cells of smokers was the destruction, shrinkage, or paralysis of the cilia during and after hyperplasia. The immobilized mucous lining, its flow arrested by the dysfunction of the cilia, allowed irritants from tobacco smoke, infectious bacteria, and other disease-bearers to accumulate and become ever more deeply embedded to do their mischief against the lungs' now overmatched other defense mechanisms. Third, Auerbach found atypical cells in disproportionate numbers in the smokers' lung tissue. The cell nucleus, visible under a microscope in normal cases as a little dark dot that served as the cellular brain directing the chemical processes in the cytoplasm, the surrounding fluid, began to enlarge and grow very dark in smokers' cells because, as further studies would disclose, they were accumulating abnormal quantities of DNA and RNA, the critical gene materials affecting cell division and mutation. Belief grew that the carcinogens in smoke constantly assaulting the epithelial cells eventually succeeded in penetrating the nucleus and altering or damaging the genetic material and thus promoted the disease process. The loss of cilia and presence of atypical cells were not found at all in the lungs of Auerbach's nonsmoking subjects, whereas all lesions found in the heavy smokers' lungs showed the atypia. In the latter, 11.4 percent of the subjects had all three kinds of changes, and in 14.3 percent of the lung cancer victims, *all* the epithelial cells were atypical. Such numbers were consistent with the emerging epidemiological studies that would show about one in ten heavy smokers contracting lung cancer.

Of further corroborative, or at least highly suggestive, value was the location of the tumorous lesions Auerbach found. As was the case in laboratory experiments using Y-shaped glass tubing to collect smoke condensate, the heaviest collection of which occurred at the joint where the tube bifurcated, so the branching points where the human airways are widest and the surface exposure is greatest proved the prime gathering site for the suspiciously precancerous changes in smokers' cell samples. Still more persuasive as Auerbach's studies lengthened was the finding that these cell changes in smokers' lungs declined markedly after they quit the habit, and the longer they had stayed off it, the fewer cell changes were observed, suggesting that the disease process could be arrested and reversed.

Auerbach's key investigation was substantiated by smaller contemporaneous studies by others working independently of him, especially on how cigarette smoke interfered with the critical function of the cilia. Anderson C. Hilding, a Minneapolis ear, nose, and throat specialist, used cows' lungs to show how smoke inhibited ciliary action and that tars and other substances tended to accumulate on the lungs' surface in places where the cilia had been destroyed and the clearance mechanism thus impaired. Paul Kotin and Hans Falk, working at the University of Southern California, used rabbits and rats to confirm that tobacco smoke curtailed ciliary activity and increased mucus secretion. And at the Arthur D. Little labs in Cambridge, in studies with rabbits paid for by Liggett & Myers, Charles Kensler, Sam Battista, and their co-workers found that the cilia were destroyed or stunted not only by tar solids but also by such toxic compounds in the gas phase of tobacco smoke as ammonia, hydrogen cyanide, formaldehyde, and acrolein. The net effect of these studies was to demonstrate that when one of the body's chief defense mechanisms was deactivated by smoke, foreign materials of whatever origin—auto exhaust fumes, industrial dust, air pollutants, tobacco smoke carcinogens, or any other airborne pathogenic irritants—readily collected and remained in contact with the bronchial lining for far longer periods in smokers than in nonsmokers. This process greatly enhanced the likelihood that smokers would suffer more diseases, regardless of the specific agent or the precise and not yet understood nature of the mutation process at the cellular level.

In short, smoking was a major promoter of health damage, and probably in a wide variety of forms. This likelihood was underscored, though the investigators did not say it in so many words, by the husband-and-wife team of Cecile and Rudolf Leuchtenberger, pathologists at Western Reserve in Cleveland, working with a grant from the tobacco industry's own research committee (TIRC) and using mice exposed to tobacco smoke. Their findings included cell changes in lung tissue markedly similar to those Auerbach was finding in human tissue of smokers at autopsy; no such signs were observed in the Leuchtenbergers' unexposed control animals. However—and to their tobacco industry sponsors it was the saving feature of their investigation—in none of the 600 mice exposed over a two-year study did they uncover any case of invasive carcinoma, thereby casting doubt upon Auerbach's contention that "carcinoma in situ," the sizable tumors found in smokers' lungs, was necessarily "preinvasive" and that such lesions were necessarily a stage in an unstoppable death march. Others argued, with Auerbach, that the only reason the Leuchtenbergers' mice and other animals comparably exposed did not suffer from invasive cancers was that they died from related or other elements in the smoke before the ineluctably malignant process could play itself out.

To his dismay, Oscar Auerbach was not greatly embraced when he reported his findings at professional gatherings, "where I had to wade through clouds of smoke—it seemed as if 90 percent of doctors were smoking then." After a typical presentation, he would be assaulted by thoracic surgeons asking him, "How come my pathologists don't find what you do?" The answer, though he was too polite to say it, was probably that the smoke kept getting in their eyes.

I V

FINAL results of three major epidemiological studies on the relationship between smoking and health now showed not only a statistically significant linkage but, in the case of heavy users of cigarettes, a ratio of peril so large as to indict the habit as causally connected, even if nobody could yet say for certain just how the damage was inflicted.

After fifty-three months, the study of British doctors by investigators Doll and Hill recorded 81 lung cancer deaths among the 1,714 subjects who had succumbed, with a mortality rate for that disease among heavy smokers of twenty times that for nonsmokers. For those who had quit the habit, the rates declined in proportion to the length of time they had been off tobacco. The 1956 Doll-Hill findings were dwarfed the following year by the final report from American Cancer Society investigators Hammond and Horn, who, after close analysis of the 11,870 deaths among nearly 200,000 subjects during a forty-four-month study, found that cigarette smokers had a 68 percent higher mortality rate than nonsmokers, while cigar smokers had an elevated rate of 22 percent and pipe smokers a 12 percent higher rate. Among the most persuasive ACS data were the risk figures for quitters. For those who had smoked up to a pack of cigarettes daily, the death rate was 104 percent higher than for non-smokers within the first year after they had quit, but dropped to only 30 percent higher between one and ten years off the habit and to just 8 percent higher after ten years of not smoking. For those who had smoked more than a pack, the contrast was equally dramatic, but even after having quit for a decade, heavy users had a mortality rate half again as high as those who had never smoked. Of the 448 lung cancer deaths recorded during the ACS study (80 percent of them confirmed by microscope diagnosis), only 15 victims had never smoked. Regular cigarette users had a lung cancer death rate eleven times higher than nonsmokers, while those who smoked two packs a day were struck down by the disease sixty-four times as frequently as those who did not smoke. So con-scientious had the ACS's volunteer interviewers been that almost 99 percent of those who had been enrolled in the study were accounted for at the end, prompting chief investigator Cuyler Hammond's wife, Marian, to handwrite a note of gratitude to all 22,000 interviewers.

A still larger population, using federal government data, was investigated for the toll smoking took upon it by biostatistician Harold F. Dorn of the Na-tional Cancer Institute (NCI). Dorn had hit upon a relatively easy way to accu-mulate a massive data base through readily accessible government records: he enlisted a quarter of a million veterans of American military service who had signed up for attractively priced life insurance policies that the U.S. had of-fered its soldiers between 1917 and 1940 and, at the outset of the study, asked them to report their smoking habits (or absence of same). During the thirty-month tracking period, Dorn learned of the deaths of his subjects through the insurance benefit claims filed on their policies with the Veterans Administra-tion and obtained details on the causes of death from forms that were required to be filed with the U.S. Public Health Service before the claims could be hon-ored. Dorn's findings, reported in 1957–58, tallied closely with the Hammond-Horn and Doll-Hill results. Smokers suffered a 58 percent higher death rate than did those who had never smoked, while heavy smokers had an excess rate twice that high, and regular smokers had a chance of contracting lung cancer 9.35 times higher than nonsmokers in the Dorn study. The earlier you started smoking, Dorn also found, the poorer your health prognosis.

On many fronts, and in many laboratories, the case against smoking grew in the late 'Fifties. Half a dozen labs, for example, reported confirming Ernst Wynder's success in producing cancerous tumors on the backs of mice painted with tobacco tar condensate, though most were less numerous than in Wyn-der's study, while other labs reported that they had not been able to replicate Wynder's results after following his method. One confirming laboratory, the

Arthur D. Little program for Liggett & Myers, had consulted closely with Wynder and succeeded in 1955 in its own skin-painting effort, albeit at a lower tumor level than Wynder's, but did not report the results publicly until 1962— and did so then in an offhand manner. A timely report of its findings by a research institution as well regarded as ADL might have contributed significantly to the ongoing health debate.

Wynder himself continued to turn up important new evidence. By way of assessing the possible role of air pollution in causing lung cancer, the Sloan-Kettering epidemiologist arranged a four-year study of some 8,700 patients admitted to hospitals run by the Seventh-Day Adventists in highly polluted Southern California. About 8 percent of the subject patients were adherents of the Adventist faith, which forbids smoking. If air pollution and not smoking were a major causative factor in lung cancer, the nonsmoking Adventist patients could have been expected to contract the disease in about the same proportion as the other patients since they all had been breathing the same fouled air. A proportionate death toll from lung cancer during the course of Wynder's study would have taken the lives of 10 or 11 Adventists; in fact, only one died from the disease, and that victim had been a pack-a-day smoker for twenty-five years before joining the Adventist church thirteen years earlier. For other body sites, the Adventists fell victim to cancer in comparable proportion to the rest of the subject group, according to Wynder's 1958 report.

Gifted at attracting publicity for his findings, Wynder further demeaned the air pollution argument a few years later by testing the level of airborne toxic substances in New York City's thronged Herald Square and finding it to be the equivalent of the intake from seven cigarettes, not the two packs that skeptics of the smoking and health relationship had suggested. Nasal breathing of the city air, moreover, Wynder noted, allowed the body to filter out a sizable portion of the contaminants, whereas inhaled cigarette smoke bypassed the nose's natural filtration system.

By the late 'Fifties, Wynder had taken on an invaluable ally in his smoking studies. Where Wynder had fled from Nazi anti-Semitism, fellow German Dietrich Hoffmann had fought for Hilter's Wehrmacht before beginning his career as a gifted bench chemist. Despite their deep-seated differences, there was mutual respect between the flamboyant Wynder and the methodical Hoffmann, and the pair would collectively publish more papers of a substantive nature than any other investigators of the smoking peril. With Hoffmann doing most of the laboratory work on the fractionation of smoke, breaking down the immensely complex substance into its component parts, the team had by 1959 isolated no fewer than seventeen carcinogenic compounds in cigarettes. But these were present only in trace quantities, unlikely in a given individual to be adequate to trigger carcinogenesis, though nobody knew if there might indeed be a minimum threshold dosage for any cancer-inducing substance. The

Wynder-Hoffmann chemical analysis fed speculation that the true carcinogen in cigarette smoke still eluded investigators or, alternatively, that the various carcinogens might behave synergistically (*i.e.*, combining their potency), or might become far more carcinogenic in the presence of such suspected promoters of the disease as phenol or carbolic acid, a crystalline distillate found in tobacco smoke.

V

WHY people smoke became a legitimate topic of social research as the evidence piled up against the prudence of the custom. Psychologists were naturally reluctant to label as abnormal behavior or a personality disorder a practice indulged in by nearly half of the adult population. The most that could plausibly be advanced by way of a rational theory to explain the popularity of smoking was that the stresses of modern life induced a form of self-destructive behavior that seemed to stabilize the emotions and prevent many forms of dysfunction.

A mock-Freudian analysis of the habit, appearing in the April 1955 issue of the *Harvard Medical Alumni Bulletin* under the title "Smoke Gets In Your Id" by Boston University psychiatrist Peter Knapp, offered a tongue-in-cheek analysis of the mental state of smokers. Four percent of them, Knapp suggested, confecting the numbers, were social smokers, most of them women, from whom "[l]arge puffs of smoke are emitted rapidly, sometimes with an audible squeal"; 26 percent were "neurotic or reactive" smokers, responding to stresses of a usually minimal nature, like "the strain of waiting for a cocktail to chill in a shaker"; and 50 percent were addictive, for whom the main motive to light up was to relieve "the stress of finishing a prior cigarette." Smoking was a highly useful behavior, he noted, because it allowed the practitioner to express a variety of drives and resolve conflicts as part of "an individual's web of ritualized activity"—solving, for example, the pressing problem of what to do with one's hands. The habit was rooted in "orality," Knapp hypothesized, meaning that it was no mere case of emotional deprivation from insufficient breast-feeding but a kind of respiratory eroticism linked to "the biphasic nature of the breathing act," *i.e.*, the luxuriating nature of inhalation followed closely by the satisfying relief of exhalation.

Among the first to posit that smoking might provoke rather than allay stress was researcher Charles MacArthur, who followed 250 Harvard students for many years after enrolling them in his study during their sophomore year. After finding that anxiety and heavy smoking "are not as clearly related in our data as we had expected," MacArthur added: "It seems likely that heavy smoking is best used as a tension reducer after it is already established high in one's habit hierarchy"—in other words, as a way to counter the stressful symptoms of withdrawal.

The ambivalence of heavy smokers toward their habit was well and variously reflected in a 1957 motivational research study of 750 subjects, each of whom submitted to two-hour interviews with the Market Planning Corporation at the behest of Liggett & Myers. Many of the subjects believed that smoking did them no good, caused coughing and shortness of breath, made them feel awful upon awakening, stained their teeth, and burned their clothing; indeed, "a majority of those we interviewed <u>said they wished they could stop smoking</u>" (underscoring in original text) and earnestly hoped that their children would not begin. Yet most subjects also dreaded the supposed adverse effects of quitting, fearing that they "would not be able to cope with life" without their cigarettes. Among the cited gratifications of the practice were "pleasure at will," the draining of tensions and aggressions, the company it provided in times of loneliness, relief from boredom and social pressures, and a sense of adulthood, independence, vigor, and the thrill of risk-taking, so that the prospect of living dangerously was thus an inducement, not a deterrent, to the smoking habit.

A leading epidemiologist at Johns Hopkins—Abraham Lilienfeld—studied some 4,500 adults in the Buffalo, New York, region in an effort to isolate emotional and behavioral characteristics that might explain why so high a proportion of smokers contracted lung cancer. Reporting in 1959 in the *Journal of the National Cancer Institute*, Lilienfeld found that smokers tended to marry, change jobs, move their home, play sports, and enter the hospital more than nonsmokers and were more "neurotic," though he did not define that condition, but these differences were too marginal, in his judgment, to matter much. At about the same time, a leading British psychologist, Hans Jurgen Eysenck, began publishing in what would amount to a three-decade campaign of denial that cigarette smoking was a prime cause of disease. Eysenck argued instead that personality configuration held the key to disease formation; repressed emotions and hopelessness, for example, promoted cancer just as hostility and aggression did heart disease—tendencies that he believed, not surprisingly, could be reversed by psychotherapy. In a 1960 study of 2,300 males, he found that smokers were decidedly more extroverted than nonsmokers—the act itself, with its great billowy clouds, was essentially a form of public display and extremely sensual in nature—but were neither less rigid nor more neurotic than those who refrained from the habit.

Perhaps the most telling behavioral study of smoking habits in this period was a survey directed by ACS psychologist Daniel Horn, who in association with Cuyler Hammond had run the cancer society's big prospective study. Horn, at least Hammond's mental equal but lacking his looks, social graces, organizing ability, and drive, had split with him after coming to feel that he had been relegated to a decidedly secondary position behind the epidemiologist. Now he applied his talents to a study of 22,000 high school students in Portland, Oregon, in a quest for clues as to why and how the smoking habit took hold. In findings published in 1958, Horn reported that three out of four smokers had begun the practice before they finished secondary school—in the most suggestible years of adolescence. One-third of all the Portland high school students smoked—38 percent of the boys and 29 percent of the girls. Said one youngster in the Oregon contingent, cutting to the core of smoking's perilous attraction: "Nobody young worries much about some disease they might get forty or fifty years from now." Family role models were deemed the most influential factor in starting them on the custom: 40 percent of the students both of whose parents smoked became smokers themselves, as did 36 percent of those with an older sibling who smoked and 33 percent with one parent who did. By contrast, only 8 percent of the surveyed high schoolers smoked against the wishes of both parents. Horn estimated that for about 25 percent of smoking high schoolers, the practice was "a compensatory form of behavior" that reflected "failure to achieve peer-group status or satisfactions" whether academically, socially, or extracurricularly. The third main reason youngsters smoked, said Horn, was rebellion against authority or discipline, a motive particularly common at Portland's five Catholic high schools.

A semi-official consensus now began to emerge in the professional medical and public-health community. It was first voiced in a 1957 report sponsored by the two federal agencies most closely linked to the smoking and health issue—the National Cancer Institute and the National Heart Institute—although neither was exactly a hotbed of agitation against the tobacco industry, along with their counterpart voluntary private agencies, the American Cancer Society and the American Heart Association. The four organizations had designated a seven-man ad hoc Study Group on Smoking and Health, composed of leading academicians like Abraham Lilienfeld who held six two-day conferences to review the swiftly growing body of literature on the subject. Their conclusion was that the "sum total of scientific evidence establishes beyond reasonable doubt that cigarette smoking is a causative factor in the rapidly increasing incidence of human epidermoid carcinoma of the lung." The group called for intensified research, especially in the area of heart disease, where evidence was more cryptic.

After he had helped frame the ad hoc Study Group's report in March of 1957, NCI pathologist Michael Shimkin approached the nation's nominally top health officer and chief medical advisor to the federal government, U.S. Surgeon General Leroy E. Burney, and urged him to speak out on the smoking problem. Burney, a conservative Indianan who liked to smoke, recognized the gravity of the matter. The Surgeon General, though, while he had line oversight of the Public Health Service and the National Institutes of Health (NIH), derived his power entirely from the Secretary of Health, Education, and Welfare and so had to proceed with great caution in any matter that might prove politically explosive. Still, Burney was persuaded by the earnest Shimkin, whose outspokenness had not made him the darling of the NCI bureaucracy. "I knew I was dealing with an honest and candid man," Burney recalled, and after obtaining several other advisory opinions on the smoking issue from people he trusted both within and outside the government, the Surgeon General asked Shimkin to draft an appropriate statement for him on the burning subject. The cautious statement Burney delivered in July of 1957, which marked the first official position on the question to be taken by any U.S. administration, noted that while the case against smoking was still "largely epidemiological in nature," many past public-health advances were based on statistical data, and, at any rate, supporting biological findings had lately emerged so that "the weight of the evidence is increasingly pointing in one direction . . . that excessive smoking is one of the causative factors in lung cancer."

The telltale cautionary words in that initial statement were "excessive" and "one". What constituted "excessive smoking"? And if it was just one of several factors in causing the disease, what were the others that deserved mention at the same level of culpability?

NCI director John R. Heller, an irresolute careerist who ran his fiefdom for a dozen years with surpassing concern about offending powerful congressmen who might trim his agency's budget, was even more cautious. Asked shortly after the release of Burney's statement what he considered an "excessive" amount of smoking, the nonsmoking Dr. Heller replied two packs a day, leaving the inference that any smaller quantity was biologically tolerable. The truth was that nobody knew how many cigarettes of whatever strength any individual's physical constitution could withstand. At the House subcommittee hearings chaired by Congressman Blatnik a few weeks later, Heller and Burney said it was premature to place health warning labels on cigarette packs, and called for further research before the government contemplated so rash a step.

Burney was emboldened to speak out more pointedly two years later by the intervening publication in the January 1959 *Journal of the National Cancer Institute* of a thirty-page article that represented the culminating scientific paper of the decade on the smoking issue. Credited as lead author of the article in the alphabetical listing was Johns Hopkins's highly regarded biostatistician Jerome Cornfield, who was joined in the effort by faculty colleague Abraham Lilienfeld, NCI's William Haenszel and Michael Shimkin, Cuyler Hammond of the ACS, and Ernst Wynder from Sloan-Kettering—an all-star lineup of epidemiologists steeped in the subject. One by one, they shredded the arguments of skeptics, diehards, and the cigarette companies' apologists.

For those clinging to the view, for example, that the disparity in lung cancer rates between men and women undermined the conclusion that smoking could be causal in the formation of the disease, Cornfield *et al.* hammered at the hard data: in the over-fifty-five age category, where most lung cancer deaths occurred, only 0.6 percent of American women smoked more than a pack of cigarettes daily, compared with about 7 percent of men. Observation and interviews, moreover, had disclosed clearly, if with less explicit data, that women not only had smoked less for fewer years than men but also inhaled less deeply, did not smoke as far down the butt, and were more frequent users of filter-tip brands, reflecting a more health-conscious attitude generally than found among men. As the century wore on, the fact was, women's lung cancer rate rose—to the point in the mid-1980s where it would surpass breast cancer as the most virulent form of the disease among women.

Cornfield and his co-authors waxed most ardent in countering the argument that it was "incredible," as one critic had put it, that smoking should be held accountable as a prime causal agent in such a wide variety of diseases. "We see nothing inherently contradictory," they replied, in such multiple causation, and noted, for example, how the Great Fog of London in 1952 had been linked causally with a measurable rise in both the respiratory and coronary disease rate; other public-health advocates had pointed out that unpasteurized milk had been found to host bacteria implicated in a number of infectious diseases. Given that tobacco smoke was such "a complex substance and consists of many different combustion products," the Cornfield article argued, "[i]t would be more 'incredible' to find that these hundreds of chemical products all had the same effect than to find the contrary." The authors concluded that if the collective findings that had to date incriminated cigarette smoke as a health peril had been made against a different agent "to which hundreds of millions of adults were not already addicted, and . . . which did not support a large industry, skilled in the arts of mass persuasion, the evidence for the hazardous nature of the agent would be generally regarded as beyond dispute."

Later in the year, with the Cornfield demolition in hand, Surgeon General Burney offered a careful six-page statement in the name of the U.S. Public Health Service that reviewed the findings, which had grown substantially since his hedged comment two years earlier, and concluded, "The weight of the evidence at present implicates smoking as the principal etiological factor" in the increased incidence of lung cancer. But the Burney statement did not amount to a policy position or a call to action by the federal government. The most that could be said of the Eisenhower administration's involvement with this pervasive and increasingly recognized public-health problem was that it did not force its chief medical officer to remain altogether silent on the subject.

If Burney's position expressed less leadership on the smoking issue than a probable majority of public-health advocates thought appropriate, it also went further than conservative elements in the medical community liked. Two weeks after the Surgeon General's statement appeared in *JAMA*, the journal most widely read by U.S. physicians, an editorial in that magazine shocked Burney by insisting that there were not yet enough facts in the debate over smoking to "warrant the assumption of an all-or-none authoritative position" on causation. It went on to repeat the discredited arguments that lung cancer rates were higher among men than women "even when smoking patterns were the same," and likewise were higher in urban than in rural areas, in disregard of the far more telling fact that smokers' mortality rates were notably higher than those of nonsmokers no matter where they lived—and the more they smoked, the greater the disparity.

Many observers felt that the AMA and its medical journals were downplaying the smoking issue due to the need for allies to face the rising tide of national sentiment favoring publicly financed health care for citizens over sixty-five. Similar to the Social Security retirement benefits, a "Medicare" program was dreaded by a sizable portion of the medical profession as an unwelcome intrusion by the welfare state. Morton Levin, the top New York state health officer who had reported early on his findings regarding smokers' elevated mortality rates, recalled attending an executive session of AMA eminences at the organization's 1960 convention and hearing a powerful trustee insist that the AMA remain mute on the smoking issue because "the Senators from the tobacco states have threatened to vote against us on Medicare if we take any formal stand whatever—and, gentlemen, we simply cannot have Medicare."

Foremost of the establishment groups on the other side of the smoking debate, and growing stronger now in its anticigarette position, was the American Cancer Society. The ACS leaders had long hesitated to antagonize millions of their contributors by denouncing their cherished smoking habit as arrant folly. Nor were the society's chiefs anxious to tangle with a major U.S. industry, especially one with great influence over the media, which provided gratis vital publicity for the ACS's fund-raising efforts. But it was the ACS that, however cautiously, had funded the crucial studies by Hammond, Horn, Auerbach, and, early on, Wynder. In the late 'Fifties, under the impetus provided by Howard Taylor, Jr., a Columbia professor of obstetrics and gynecology, and ACS executive director Mefford Runyon, the society began pushing doctors to take a more active role in discouraging their patients from smoking. "We are all looking for a breakthrough in cancer," Taylor would evangelize, adding, "We already have it—through prevention we can control most of the lung cancer problem."

The climactic clash within the upper strata of the ACS leadership over how activist a role the organization could risk taking on smoking occurred toward the end of 1959, as the board considered issuing an unequivocal indictment of smoking. At one stage in the heated intramural debate, ex-ACS president and longtime director Alton Ochsner took the floor and regaled his eminent colleagues with a tale intended to disarm those still unpersuaded by the proof against smoking. There was a certain Russian count, Ochsner told them, who, suspecting his attractive young wife of infidelity, advised her that he was leaving their home for an extended trip, but in fact posted himself at a nearby residence to spy on her. The very first night after his leave-taking, the count watched by moonlight as a sleigh pulled up to his house, a handsome lieutenant from the Czar's Guard bounded out, the count's wife greeted the hussar at the door and led him inside, and in a moment the couple was seen through an upstairs bedroom window in candlelit silhouette as they wildly embraced; after another moment the candle was blown out. "Proof! Proof!" said the anguished count, smiting himself on the brow. "If only I had the proof!"

Ochsner's colleagues got the message. In January 1960, the ACS board declared that, based upon all clinical, epidemiological, experimental, chemical, and pathological evidence, it was now "beyond any reasonable doubt" that smoking was *the* major cause of lung cancer and ought to be addressed as such. The society soon began producing pamphlets and filmstrips with titles like *Is Smoking Worth It?* for distribution to schools and any other interested organizations, and it placed further resources in the hands of Cuyler Hammond, who had launched a new investigation he termed a "cancer prevention study" which dwarfed his previous effort. Where his first prospective study had enlisted an all-male population sample of about 200,000, now he conscripted more than a million subjects, of both sexes, using 68,000 ACS volunteers in twenty-nine states. And instead of inquiring almost exclusively about their smoking habits, the far more intricate questionnaire sought some 300 pieces of information from each participant, covering their work, dietary, sleep, and exercise habits. Hammond was out to clinch his case.

The enormity of the stakes in the heated controversy over smoking was fully recognized at a two-day symposium on the subject held in September of 1960 at the New York Academy of Medicine. The conference chairman remarked, not without a hint of incredulity, that should the causation charge be substantiated, "it would indicate that cigarettes cause more deaths than any other recognized lethal agent, including all the known bacteria, known viruses, bullets, wild animals, chemical poisons, or even the American automobile."

V I

IT is instructive to contrast what the cigarette manufacturers did and what they said in the course of the 'Fifties as the health controversy intensified.

The companies had three courses of action open to them, theoretically. They could have accepted the evidence against them as conclusive and gone out of business rather than further risking the public's health. They could have emphatically denied that their product was lethal and gone sullenly about their trade. Or they could have solemnly proclaimed their concern, decried any rush to judgment, and joined in the study of the problem, hoping that it would either exonerate their product or isolate the harmful agent. As prudent men purveying a legal, popular, and highly profitable product, they elected this third course, promising that if science could definitively identify a nasty ingredient that indisputably harmed smokers, their laboratories would remove it forthwith.

Meanwhile, the tobacco industry took action by offering many new brands with a filter tip. True, it was a largely cosmetic measure in most cases, but at the first real show of government concern and outcry in the print media, the industry reduced the strength of tobacco smoke reaching customers' lungs. Nobody knew whether the reduction would make any difference, but since the studies were unanimous in finding a dose-response relationship—*i.e.*, the more smoke you consumed, the greater your risk—the logic of the measure was irrefutable. Yet the industry, other than Lorillard with its Kent brand, never said or would concede what it was in fact doing and why; to do so would have been tantamount to a confession that it was selling an inherently dangerous product. All it said about its product innovations was that it was offering smokers a wider variety of cigarette styles because that was what they seemed to want. If the industry had left it at that, it might reasonably have been accused of nothing more than disingenuousness.

But the cigarette industry did not leave it at that. Instead, it proceeded during the last half of the 'Fifties to dispute, distort, minimize, or ignore the unfolding evidence against it. Throughout, the companies reassured the smoking public that they were hot on the trail themselves and more anxious than anyone to settle the health question.

Their chosen instrument to do so was the Tobacco Industry Research Committee, which geared up in the last half of the 'Fifties under its scientific director, Clarence Little. That he fully understood the dual nature of his charge was disclosed in an April 1955 memo in which he wrote, "Essentially, the major purposes of the T.I.R.C. are Research and Public Relations. Our job is to maintain a balance between the two." To facilitate the balancing act, the TIRC offices were moved to Rockefeller Center in quarters separated by just a few floors from the lair of Hill & Knowlton, the tobacco industry's public-relations counselors. Back in the limelight now, Pete Little, that mercurial extrovert, with his social charms very much intact, had logged many years studying and fighting cancer and in the process had gained a healthy respect for that relentless adversary. To get anywhere on the subject of tobacco and health, Little argued, science would first have to unravel the mysteries of the human cell; only then could it begin to understand the basic causes of cancer and try to devise ways to come to grips with them.

The scientific enterprise he headed, Little wrote in the March 1956 issue of *Cancer Research*, was left "completely free from suggestions or pressure by the industry in any form whatsoever" and could initiate as well as respond to requests for study grants—the tobacco companies had set up a kitty of about $1 million a year for these purposes. The TIRC had but "one objective," Little asserted, "namely, to find the whole truth and to see that it is made known as quickly and effectively as possible." But what if "the whole truth" was incorrigibly elusive in an age when science was opening up many more questions with every answer it uncovered? In the TIRC's 1956 annual report, Little displayed the rhetorical usefulness of his utopian "one objective," writing, "We have learned much in the past two years, but perhaps the most important thing we have learned is how much more must be done before definite answers can be given" on the relationship of smoking to health. The next year his report began, "Progress of medical research is slow and painstaking. Many promising avenues must be followed before finding one that opens the way to new and useful knowledge. . . ." Here was rapturous music to the ears of Little's tobacco industry patrons: while science inched ahead, you could sell one helluva lot of cigarettes.

Was the TIRC program a serious scientific effort or an elaborate exercise in temporizing, an industry-sponsored masquerade funded by a fistful of conscience money—and as tight a fist as the manufacturers could get away with, at that? For every dollar spent on its joint research effort in those early years of the program, the industry spent nearly $200 on advertising and promoting its product. Certainly the TIRC was not, despite Clarence Little's claim in his 1956 report, listing grants to fifty-five investigators, "a carefully planned, well integrated scientific endeavor to help in the solving of important questions." There was nothing structured or programmed about it. And it initiated practically nothing in the way of a sustained or substantive inquiry, preferring to dispense funds for scattershot studies sometimes only remotely connected to smoking or devoted to tilling fields already overharvested.

The TIRC did have, though, an aura of plausibility in the form of competent and, in some cases, distinguished scientists contributing to the effort. Chosen as Little's full-time assistant in running the TIRC's Scientific Advisory Board (SAB) was MIT Professor Robert C. Hockett, an expert in sugar chemistry. A short, shy, gentle man lacking Little's magisterial manner and appearance, Hockett had a serviceable, encyclopedic, and somewhat plodding mind and played the dutiful Sancho Panza to his superior's Quixote and his quest for "the whole truth." Among their early recruits for the SAB, whose main business was to meet periodically to evaluate grant applications for research somehow related to smoking and health, were McKeen Cattell of Cornell Medical College, a distinguished pharmacologist; Julius Comroe, a cardiovascular expert from the University of California; Leon Jacobson of the University of Chicago Medical School, who directed the Argonne Cancer Research Hospital; and Kenneth Lynch, dean of South Carolina Medical College at Charleston.

A pioneer member of the SAB was a young pathologist from the University of Southern California—Paul Kotin—whose motives for serving at the behest of a highly suspect industry suggest the shrewdness of the enterprise. Having previously acted as a consultant to Ford, Sears, and Standard Oil of New Jersey (now Exxon), Kotin felt that private industry had contributed more to the understanding of carcinogenesis than the scientific academy had and so he did not dread Mammon's money. More to the point regarding tobacco dollars, "You weren't going to change their policies by calling them murderers," Kotin reasoned, "but as an advisor, you could work from within." As the only SAB member deeply involved in lung cancer research, he was able to direct funds to investigators who otherwise would not have been kindly disposed to accept tobacco industry money. The material rewards for his services—an honorarium of several hundred dollars per day for the grant review meetings plus travel expenses—were hardly an inducement to "sell out" to a rogue industry, but its invitation represented a different kind of seduction for Kotin. As an associate professor at USC, a liberal in a profession dominated by conservatives, and a poor boy from an unfashionable neighborhood in Chicago, he found it irresistible to be asked to sit among the scientific elite at collegial sessions presided over by the genial Pete Little and afterward drink and socialize and listen to Little's second wife mock Ernst "Vynder" and his German accent. After an initial period of uncertainty about tobacco's role in causing cancer, Kotin liked to think of himself as something of a subversive on the SAB, but he nevertheless served for a dozen years, by the end of which he had become a ranking official at NCI and found it professionally untenable to keep taking the cigarette makers' money.

Less defensive about his SAB membership was Richard J. Bing, a St. Louis heart surgeon on the Washington University medical school faculty and experimental cardiologist, who served more than three decades as a tobacco industry advisor. Bing said he was drawn by the intellectual challenge of the smoking questions because of "the terrible discrepancy between the epidemiological data" and the ambiguous chemical findings of only traces of carcinogens in the cigarette smoke. Fascinated by Clarence Little, whom he found to be "an artist, a truly great man," Bing nevertheless was eventually convinced that cigarette smoking was causal for bronchitis and compounded the health perils of anyone already stricken with a heart ailment, but he claimed never to have been persuaded of tobacco's role as an instigator of cardiac disease. A latter-day SAB member, Harvard biochemist Manfred L. Karnovsky, explained that he was inclined to believe that heavy cigarette smoking "increases the possibility of lung cancer, but I don't know why. . . . It's a very complex thing." He was

deeply suspicious of the validity of skin-painting experiments and animal inhalation studies due to "the forced level" of the dosage, which unnaturally
sped up organic processes, while "we don't know what the true pace of these
changes is in the human lung." As to the TIRC sponsorship, the Harvard professor said he had "no fear of taint. If this was a group of gangsters from New
York, that would be a different thing, but I feel that smoking is a thing that
people do voluntarily—like driving—and that's their business." In acknowledging that much of the funding by the TIRC and its renamed but otherwise
identical successor, the Council for Tobacco Research (CTR), went for studies
at best remotely related to the smoking question, Karnovsky said the CTR
might better have been named the Biochemical Research Council. But, he
added, "no one ever said to us that we should in any shape, manner or form defend the tobacco industry."

Yet there were many in academia and the public-health community who
faulted both the TIRC's scientific advisors and the recipients of their largesse
for legitimizing the tobacco industry's position, even if there were no visible
strings attached to the funding. A representative expression of disapproval of
such consorting with an industry that had a clear vested interest in the exonera-
tion of its product by respectable scientists from distinguished institutions was
offered by Lester Breslow, former director of the California State Department
of Public Health, dean of the UCLA School of Public Health, and longtime
advisor to NCI. "Do not impute villainy to them," Breslow said of well-
intentioned scientists who accepted tobacco money to conduct their research,
"but they do not understand how the industry uses them—it's terrible."

While some of the early TIRC grants, like those for the Leuchtenbergers'
smoke inhalation studies and Kotin's work in ciliary toxicity, helped shed corroborative light on the health issue, these were exceptions to an unfocused program that implicitly ran the risk of closing itself down if it discovered too
much. Even the industry's own scientists recognized early on the shortcomings
of the TIRC effort. Philip Morris research director Robert DuPuis called in
1958 for an improved and enlarged effort by the SAB, with its grants better
targeted. Frederick Darkis, research chief of Liggett & Myers, which had chosen to remain outside the TIRC and pursue strictly smoking-related research
on its own and through the Arthur D. Little laboratory, was quoted as saying in
a 1963 publication of Consumers Union that the TIRC was "mostly a publicity
organization. They have given millions to various research analysts, but it is
very difficult to know what purpose the money has served."

Despite Clarence Little's insistence that the TIRC research was entirely free
of the industry's oversight, there were early signs that studies too critical of the
product would not be encouraged. Officials of the Rand Development Corporation in Cleveland, who had received a grant to study tobacco for carcinogens,
testified at the 1957 Blatnik hearings in Congress that after their investigation

had found benzpyrene in burned cigarette paper and, to a lesser extent, the tobacco—and after they had then been visited by Clarence Little, who praised
their facilities and research effort and agreed that benzpyrene ought to be removed from the product—their research grant was not renewed. A similar experience was disclosed by Boston University investigator Peter Knapp, who in
1962 with a TIRC grant wrote a paper he titled "Addictive Aspects in Heavy
Cigarette Smoking." Knapp recalled that TIRC officials "were very sensitive
about not putting pressure on us, but they definitely did not want that word 'addictive' to be used in the title—it was a low-key but unambiguous request. We
said no—there were real withdrawal symptoms and a morphine-like effect
from smoking." Knapp published his paper after reading it at the 1962 American Psychiatric Association meeting; his grant was not renewed.

V I I

O F far more public prominence than the health research funded by the
tobacco industry were the statements by its hired scientists and less qualified officials, ceaselessly denigrating or trivializing every new study and report by truly independent investigators who found cigarette smoking to be
mortally perilous.

Apparently unchastened by the public-relations counsel he got from Hill &
Knowlton, the TIRC's president, nonscientist Timothy Hartnett, served as the
industry's lead attack dog. For example, after the second interim report in the
huge, ACS-sponsored prospective study by Hammond and Horn had disclosed
in 1956 that quitters improved their life expectancy compared to that of continuing smokers, Hartnett asserted that it would be "tragic if an overpublicized
allegation that lacks scientific support were to divert and impede public or
private support of sound research in such an important field of health."
Clarence Little's approach was, by contrast, simply more cautioning, except
when he chose to carp at emerging evidence that he found to be gravely
flawed. After the final Hammond-Horn report in 1957, for example, Little objected because the investigators' questionnaire had not probed beyond the subjects' age, residence, smoking habits, and cause of death and because it would
amount to "a scientific gymnastic feat" for smoking to serve as a prime causal
agent in all the diseases claimed in the study. That same year, when Surgeon
General Burney issued his first tepid statement that excessive smoking was *a*
likely cause of lung cancer, Little answered that the TIRC's funded studies had
so far produced nothing to justify such a claim and that most of the "statistical
studies," as he styled the epidemiological surveys, had "so far failed to consider adequately many variables in human habits, environments and constitution. . . ." And writing in the December 1957 *Atlantic*, Little sounded his

anthem in declaring that since even cynics would admit the tobacco industry could not afford as a practical matter "to offer products which have been so definitively attacked without making every effort to find out the whole truth," he and his patrons "claim merely the right to pursue knowledge through scientific research, the right to hold our point of view, and the right of the public to be aware of it."

But Little and his backers did more than pursue the truth in their fashion; what they continued to exercise most strenuously was their First Amendment right to degrade the findings of others at least as dedicated and far more disinterested. Thus, when in 1958 the NCI's Harold Dorn published the results of his massive investigation of the mortality rates of smokers who as veterans had bought life insurance from the U.S. government, Little remarked only that "statistical association does not prove cause and effect." And when Oscar Auerbach reported at the AMA's annual convention in Dallas in 1959 on his findings after reviewing more than 20,000 slides from 402 cadavers for cell changes common in smokers and exceedingly rare in nonsmokers, Little's chief aide, Robert Hockett, said that these highly suggestive findings were merely more of the same sort of thing Auerbach had reported earlier and that they "had not since been accepted by many other pathologists"—a dismissive slur devoid of substantiation and disregarding the fact that Auerbach's papers on the subject had been published in the *New England Journal of Medicine* and other top peer-reviewed journals.

The integrity of such rebuttals can be inferred from an advisory memo written in July 1959 by the TIRC's publicity consultants, Hill & Knowlton, to Reynolds Tobacco's new chief executive, Bowman Gray, Jr., serving as chairman of the industry's lately formed Tobacco Institute, the heart of its future lobbying and public-relations activities. The H&K memorandum underscored the industry's need for intensified measures "to cope with attacks based on 'scare' charges" and to reaffirm "through all means possible the position that the role of tobacco in health and particularly lung cancer is not proved and that evidence mounts to dispute the broad charges made against tobacco. . . . The health of the nation is constantly improving, along with increased use of tobacco. The 'scare' campaign . . . has developed nothing new since the statistical studies. . . ."

This sort of jabberwocky, doubtless soothing to the publicists' clients but as detached from reality as Alice in Wonderland, also characterized the industry's response a few months later to Surgeon General Burney's long, careful statement firmly implicating smoking in lung cancer causation. Attributed to Clarence Little and likely prepared in Hill & Knowlton's offices a few floors below his, the rebuttal argued that experimental animals exposed to tobacco smoke had not contracted lung cancer (but had, it failed to note, undergone many serious and likely precancerous cell changes); that human lung tissue in heavy smokers was often normal (even as, it might have been noted with about equal relevance, many who were exposed to tuberculosis did not contract the often deadly disease); and that there was recent evidence that air pollution might be a bigger menace to the lungs than smoking—a statement as false as the Hill & Knowlton suggestion that there was mounting evidence to discredit the broad charge against smoking.

This ceaseless, groundless, and distorting combativeness reached its full flowering in the 1960 TIRC report by Little's Scientific Advisory Board. Headed "Causation Theory of Smoking Unproved," the text contended that "[t]he continued failure of evidence which is qualitatively different or of increased significance to appear leaves the causation theory of smoking in lung cancer, heart disease and other ailments without clinical and experimental proof. . . . The result is that the tobacco theory is rapidly losing much of the unique importance claimed by its adherents at its original announcement." What "tobacco theory"? What "adherents"? What "original announcement"? Here was nothing less than wholesale dismissal of a decade of findings by many separate and independent investigators of good standing, often smokers themselves, examining a major health issue in a variety of ways—not the keening of a cabal of pointy-headed prohibitionists. Little's statement went on: "[T]he one hard fact that we must face up to is that there is so much more to find out. . . . It is [as] important to know . . . why the overwhelming majority of heavy cigarette smokers do not develop lung cancer as it is to know why the comparatively small percentage of smokers do." Little might as logically have called for a study on why most motorists who speed do not die as a result while many who do not speed are still killed in auto accidents.

To give the cigarette makers a pulpit from which to sound a more positive note instead of simply naysaying after each new critical scientific report, they opened the Tobacco Institute (TI) in Washington in 1958 and funded it in proportion to each company's share of the market the year before. In addition to the producers and distributors, the TI proclaimed itself a united front also representing 600,000 tobacco-growing families, some 30,000 factory workers, and multitudes in the retailing end of the tobacco trade. The TI catechism stressed the contribution of tobacco to the national economy and the preservation of the endangered American farm, the inconclusiveness and inconsistencies in the antismoking findings, and the rights of individual smokers to disregard killjoy public-health investigators. Like any trade organization, the institute lobbied Capitol Hill, managed even with a rudimentary staff in those early years to keep a lid on the federal cigarette tax (eight cents a pack since 1951), and helped prevent tobacco products from being explicitly included in the 1960 federal Hazardous Substances Labeling Act.

As a defensive strategy, the Tobacco Institute reassured its customer base by minimizing the alleged hazards of smoking and mocking those who reported them. Its quarterly (later monthly) broadside, *Tobacco & Health Research*, distributed free to some 200,000 doctors and others in the medical community, hewed closely to the TIRC line in casting doubt on any and all antismoking revelations and publicizing studies that linked everything but smoking to cancer. The TI's first president, James Richards, a former U.S. representative from South Carolina, set the tone for sensitivity to the health issue with remarks like "There have always been a few people who are fanatically prejudiced against tobacco. Not liking it themselves, they are opposed to its use by others." Richards was succeeded in 1960 by a suaver industry spokesman, native North Carolinian George V. Allen, a former ranking State Department official and lately retired director of the U.S. Information Agency. Allen ratcheted the propaganda machine up to a new level of paranoiac shrillness, declaring soon after his installation: "We must learn to distinguish the real facts of tobacco from unjustified emotional campaigns, based on the 'health scare'—a technique that was not successful one hundred or three hundred years ago and, we are confident, will not be successful today."

If their hired mouthpieces were intemperate in operating their disinformation agencies, the industry's own executives were even more confrontational. Howard Cullman, head of the Cullman Brothers cigar leaf business and the more polished and political brother of Joseph Cullman, Jr., whom he succeeded on the Philip Morris board upon Joe Junior's death in 1955, denounced "recurrent attacks of do-gooders . . . announcing what they think should be our way of life. . . ." When Cullman's nephew, Joe Third, took over as Philip Morris chief in 1958, he was quick to comment, "The health scare is receding—the worst is over," as if describing the swelling from a pesky but decidedly minor irritant. Liggett & Myers was guilty of, at the very least, grievous hypocrisy in its 1957 annual report, in which it quoted remarks made by a Yale Medical School pathologist that since nothing in cigarette smoke was carcinogenic, there was nothing for a filter to remove—a proposition that Liggett-paid scientists at the Arthur Little laboratories had discarded two years earlier, after replicating the Wynder skin-painting experiment and in other smoke analysis research. And when *Time* magazine featured recently elected Reynolds chairman Bowman Gray, Jr., on its April 21, 1960, cover, he was quoted as saying of the cancer charges: "I just don't believe it. People are hearing the same old story, and the record is getting scratched."

VIII

I F only by virtue of becoming chief executive of the new sales leader in the cigarette business, RJR's Bowman Gray, Jr., was regarded by 1960 as the tobacco industry's leading statesman. His claim to the title was further strengthened by the Reynolds tradition of dynastic rule; Gray's father and namesake had once presided over the company, as had his uncle, James. Yet most people at Reynolds felt that freckled "Red" Gray had won the top post less on his pedigree than on merit.

He had begun working for the company in the factory as a schoolboy during summer breaks and after college had lived out of a suitcase for six Depression years as a crack RJR salesman. Installed at Reynolds's Winston-Salem headquarters, he displayed a sponge-like mind for absorbing facts and figures and strongly championed the field sales force, helping hone its calculatedly downhome counterside manner. For all his detectably patrician attitude, Gray insisted that his phone line be open at all hours for a direct call from any member of the Reynolds 2,000-man sales force with a problem in the field. As befit one who was on record in his disdain for the health charges against the industry, he smoked four packs of Winston a day, but he could not ignore the spinal disease that was atrophying his muscles and would force him into a wheelchair during much of his tenure running the nation's top tobacco company.

At the bottom end of the industry, another change occurred in the executive suite in the late 'Fifties that was to have a far more profound effect on the cigarette business. Parker McComas had reinvigorated slumping Philip Morris by buying Benson & Hedges, launching the reinvented Marlboro as a filter brand in its strikingly designed box, and bringing along a new crop of junior executives. The most prominent and visible of these was the new executive vice president, Joseph Cullman III, the senior marketing man. Conscious that he was something of a privileged character who had not exactly struggled to the top at Benson & Hedges before his family sold it to Philip Morris, Cullman did not take his position for granted. No one had promised him a rose-petaled path to the top, and so, in his early forties now, he seemed to be all over the place, trying to learn about every aspect of the company operations even if he put some noses out of joint in the process. There was the day, for example, when Cullman in shirtsleeves breezed into an office temporarily occupied by John Vance Hewitt, the deeply formal senior partner of the law firm handling Philip Morris's business, Conboy, Hewitt, O'Brien & Boardman. Hewitt and an associate were busy questioning a PM sales executive on an FTC-related pricing matter when Cullman appeared, wanting to know what was going on, and when apprised, indicated that the salesman should not be tied up for too long and that perhaps a junior man would serve as well—as if the interview were not a serious matter. "Joe gave you the sense of a scrappy little guy who didn't hesitate to toss his weight around," one Philip Morris veteran recalled of Cullman. But he was usually upbeat and disarming, forever questioning and listening closely to the answers he got, mixing widely and well, yet maintaining a measured manner and authoritative presence that would make him the inevitable choice to succeed stately Parker McComas.

The company, meanwhile, had been greatly buoyed by the Marlboro launch. A 1955 ad in New York's *Daily Mirror* offering a free pack of the new brand to anyone who showed up at the company's 100 Park Avenue headquarters that day drew 15,000 takers, and the excitement generated elsewhere was such that production could not catch up with demand for nearly a year. The flip-top box was proving so appealing that the company repackaged all its brands in that style and, while it was at it, retired the old Philip Morris brown package for a spiffy new red-white-and-gold one. But the change seemed only to accelerate the flagship brand's rate of decline, which, when added to the high start-up costs for Marlboro, kept company profits anemic. Advertising dollars were not stinted, though, in establishing the presence in the tobacco firmament of that two-fisted worthy, The Marlboro Man. Sometimes portrayed as a wistful wrangler, sometimes as a professional athlete or a naval officer or just a guy in a trenchcoat, he was always an older, rugged-looking fellow who knew the ropes and sported as testimony to his adventurous past a tattoo on the back of his hand in the shape of a winged shield. These stigmata, a writer for *The New Yorker* suggested in a jocular 1958 appreciation of this fanciful persona, made the Marlboro Man, for all his swagger, seem "encrusted with anxieties." By 1957, its third year on the market, Marlboro was the No. 8 best-selling cigarette and had surpassed the Philip Morris brand as the company's bellwether and main hope for advancement.

Philip Morris's profit pinch was exacerbated in the mid-'Fifties by what came to be known within the company as The Dixie Dilemma. Ordered in 1955 to desegregate its public schools, the surly and largely white-supremacist culture of the South was snappish toward any perceived Yankee intrusions. At the likely instigation of one or more of its competitors, Philip Morris was painted throughout the old Confederacy as a warm friend of black America because it had made a modest charitable contribution to the Urban League, it employed one Negro as a minor sales executive, and its main manufacturing facilities in Virginia were somewhat more integrated than those of the other tobacco companies, most with factories in North Carolina. The result was a boycott of Philip Morris brands. Recalled Paul Jeblee, the company's division manager in Georgia, Alabama, and Florida in this period, "I encountered a very discouraging scene. There were towns where you couldn't park your car if it had Philip Morris stickers on it . . . places where you couldn't even get your fuel tank filled." Jeblee retained vivid memories of a day in Hayneville, Alabama, when he and the company's sales representative visited twenty-three stores, "of which twenty-two had no Philip Morris brands when I arrived, and twenty-two had none when I left, the exception being a store with a single dusty carton of Philip Morris high on an out-of-the-way shelf. So I thanked the man for supporting Philip Morris, and he said, 'Hell, I'm not supporting Philip

Morris, but I'm damned if those other sons-of-bitches in town are going to tell me what I can and can't sell.' "

Philip Morris's comparative weakness in the domestic market allowed President McComas to take a chance that none of his more prosperous rivals was interested in pursuing. American cigarettes had gained worldwide acclaim in the wake of World War II but were hard and expensive to come by abroad. Reynolds and Liggett & Myers, somewhat provincial if not actively xenophobic in outlook, had scant interest in the foreign market. American Tobacco had ceded international selling rights to its brands to British-American Tobacco under the old trust arrangement dating back to the beginning of the century, while Brown & Williamson was a BAT subsidiary and thus strictly limited to the U.S. market. And Lorillard was pumping all its money into salvaging Kent. That left the door open to McComas, a former international banker, to give Philip Morris a crucial headstart overseas.

The start, in 1955, was inauspicious enough and largely experimental, with little capital available to subsidize foreign operations for long. The first two efforts were a small manufacturing unit in Australia, from which Philip Morris hoped eventually to supply all of the sterling market in Asia, using native leaf and local brands, and a joint venture in oil-rich Venezuela with a local manufacturer who would turn out domestic brands with local leaf and distribute Philip Morris's imported brands. Comparable ventures were soon set up in Canada and the Philippines, but McComas's keenest interest was in Europe, where tariff walls and currency exchange problems made exporting a dubious strategy. The only sensible arrangement was to license foreign nationals to make Philip Morris brands, an even trickier business in terms of taste and quality control. To avoid giving away too many trade secrets, the company shipped in preblended U.S. tobacco, starting small with a solid but not dominant Swiss firm, Fabriques de Tabac Réunies (FTR), which began making Marlboros in the lakeside city of Neuchâtel in the late 'Fifties. It became the catalyst that would one day make Philip Morris Europe's largest cigarette purveyor.

As McComas's final contribution to the salvaging and reshaping of PM, he diversified the company's product line with the purchase in 1957 of Minneapolis-based Milprint, Inc., a manufacturer of flexible packaging materials and a supplier to Philip Morris of foil, laminated cigarette-carton cellophane, and the little red "tear tape" for opening packs. Here, through vertical integration, was a way for PM to cut its supply costs while also ending its total dependency on cigarette sales. The new unit added some 15 percent to Philip Morris's gross revenues, but its low profit margins, characteristic of highly competitive industries like packaging, did nothing to lift PM's net, stuck in the range of 4 percent of revenues, the lowest in the tobacco industry and only one-third as high as top-earning RJR's figure.

IX

Parker McComas never regained consciousness after exploratory surgery for pancreatic cancer at New York's Lenox Hill Hospital the last week in November of 1957; he suffered a postoperative heart attack in his room and died at sixty-two. For all his success in righting the company, though, Philip Morris under his presidency had essentially been running just to stay in place. Its share of the cigarette market—9 percent—was less than it had been a decade earlier, and had not advanced in five years.

His successor, Joseph Cullman, age forty-five, was chosen within a week. His first task on picking up the reins was to attend to Marlboro's slowing progress after the brand's spectacular debut. Most of the new filter-tip brands were slumping now, in the wake of poor publicity about their misleading advertising and the largely cosmetic nature of the filters. Cullman, who had had relatively little to do with devising the reconceived Marlboro but hovered over it like an adoring guardian for the rest of his Philip Morris career, was urged by some at the company to bring the brand's tar and nicotine numbers way down, out of the running, really, against Winston and L&M, and position it against Kent as a tastier choice for health-conscious smokers. "I rejected that," Cullman recalled. "I thought it was a short-term fix. I didn't want to get into a derby with Kent—we would have succeeded only in prostituting ourselves."

Instead, the Marlboro filter was reengineered to make it more effective and the tobacco was given an infusion of reconstituted leaf that both lowered the numbers and allowed for the smoother blending of flavorants. The rejiggered Marlboro, as a result, had a tar and nicotine yield only two-thirds of Winston's, which Reynolds would not bring down for another year or so. Cullman also overruled Marlboro's passionate brand manager, Ross Millhiser, in making several changes in the pack. The little ersatz royal crest above the brand name was altered from dark blue-gray to gold to class up the image a bit. More important, Cullman had long been urging his colleagues to offer Marlboro in a soft pack as well as the flip-top box, which had been so useful in establishing the brand. A Roper poll showed that one in four soft-pack users of other brands had tried a boxed brand and rejected the harder-edge package; Kent in the soft pack was outselling its own boxed version by four to one, while Winston's ratio was ten to one. "It was like having a car company that sold only roadsters," recounted Cullman, who ordered the creation of the alternate package.

It was not Marlboro, though, that showed a sales spurt after its fix-up but Parliament, which the company elected to position against Kent in the lower-yield sector of the market. Its premium price differential dropped, Parliament was put in a smart new white and blue package prominently featuring a Cadillac-like chevron device to suggest it was a high-quality product, and its numbers were brought down very close to Kent's. Parliament sales surged 122 percent in 1958 and an additional 54 percent the next year, to place it No. 15 in overall sales, with a unit volume nearly half that of Marlboro, which picked up a mere 3 percent in 1959 and slipped to No. 10 in the market, leaving Cullman and his company in the industry's sales basement by decade's end. The Marlboro Man ads seemed spent as criticism rose over his omnipresent tattoo, actually drawn on the models' hands with a ballpoint pen shortly before each shoot but suspected of being a permanent disfigurement with the attendant risk of blood poisoning. Instead, Marlboro customers were now urged to "take a tip from [professional football star] Sam Huff—settle back and have a full-flavored smoke." But the "settle-back" campaign, displaying a series of bulky males stretched supine while luxuriating in their favorite smoke, was not the tonic the brand needed.

Nor was the company scoring well in trying to penetrate the hot new mentholated market, where Salem was running wild and B&W's Kools and Lorillard's new Newport entry were also gaining. To replace its old Spud menthol, never a winner, Philip Morris brought out Alpine in 1959 and gave it a package that mimicked the Marlboro design, only in green instead of red and with a snowy mountain peak instead of the peaked roof. Alpine began promisingly but quickly turned into a me-too brand, and the company, at any rate, did not have the cash to spare to sustain yet another major marketing effort.

Even while struggling to improve his share of the cigarette market, Cullman also saw the virtues of diversification, which his predecessor had set in motion. Philip Morris picked up Polymer Industries, a maker of adhesives, and put Milprint, its packaging components producer, into play in Europe. Cullman remarked with candor to the press, "The cigarette industry is strong today, but the situation may not continue indefinitely." The health issue never crossed his lips. Instead, he added: "Besides, there are very few one-product companies around today." Thus hedging his bet and trying to lift Philip Morris's laggard profit margin, Cullman made his first major move to diversify in the consumer products field in 1960 by buying out ASR, formerly called the American Safety Razor Company, for about $22 million in PM stock—the same price his family got for selling Benson & Hedges six years before. ASR, maker of Gem and Pal razor blades, other shaving products, and surgical equipment, was a distant third behind Gillette and Schick in its field, but Cullman had served on its board, knew its owners well, and saw a ripe growth opportunity for building up a product line that, like cigarettes, consisted of low-priced goods, in daily use, readily disposable, and sold over many of the same counters. Strengthened by Philip Morris know-how in sales, packaging, and advertising, it was hoped, ASR would soon vault into the big time.

But the company's 1960 net, adjusted for cost-of-living rises, was hardly above what it had been in 1950, when cigarettes were its only product. Hungry for higher margins and new markets, Cullman now looked hard at Philip Morris's overseas operations, which, though hardly out of the incubator, were still far ahead of the rest of the tobacco industry, preoccupied as it was with domestic challenges. As the world recovered from its postwar trauma and markets everywhere revived, Cullman envisioned global possibilities for his Marlboro brand if it could be made to a uniform standard of quality and taste and marketed vigorously, though priced at a premium over domestic brands.

To move deeper into this complex marketplace, Cullman turned to two key aides. One was Paul Smith, a pudgy, irascible attorney whom Cullman had brought in from the Conboy, Hewitt firm in order to have a strong legal counselor at his elbow. Smith, whose behavior ranged narrowly between the cantankerous and the abrasive, made no secret of his conviction that most company executives sat around all day with their thumbs up their bungs, and he thought even peppy Joe Cullman was still pretty wet behind the ears and badly in need of an avuncular hand to guide him. Among Smith's pet peeves was the international cigarette business if it meant that Philip Morris had to put itself at the mercy of foreign licensees and distributors, with whom it had to share marketing and technological expertise but from whom it gained very little in return beyond a show of the company flag. Far better to take the plunge, Smith argued, by going in with real partners over whom the company could exercise a degree of control or by opening up independent operations using foreign nationals—if competent ones could be found.

Smith's view entailed a far larger commitment of capital and attention than Philip Morris had thus far allotted. Real diplomacy would also be required, which meant that direction of an expanded overseas operation could not be vested in the crotchety Smith. Instead, Cullman turned to his chief marketing hand, the versatile and imaginative George Weissman, whose affability Smith viewed as the smooth facade of a P.R. man—than which, on the lawyer's index of certifiable callings, there was nothing lower.

Weissman, by then a corporate director, had taken a combined-business-and-pleasure trip to Europe in 1960 and brought along a number of cartons of Marlboro. "Everywhere I went in Europe," he recalled, "people were grabbing my Marlboros—they were intrigued by the box and flavor." He came back raving to Cullman and Al Lyon about the brand's European potential, especially in Germany, where a large contingent of American occupation forces could provide a solid foundation for locally made Marlboros. Cullman decided to harness Weissman's enthusiasm and offered him the presidency of PM Overseas, a newly created entity to coordinate all the company's foreign tobacco operations. Weissman, who had been close to the core of the company's domestic operations, feared that the assignment might actually be a ploy to get rid of him. Reassured of his value to Philip Morris, he took up the new job and saw major problems everywhere he looked. The Australian plant was teetering at breakeven. In Venezuela, the government was cracking down on imports, so Philip Morris had the choice of getting out or getting in more deeply with C.A. Tabacalera Nacional (CATANA), in which it already had a controlling interest, to make both domestic and Philip Morris brands. At Smith's urging, they got in all the way. A foray into the Canadian market was complicated by Philip Morris's lack of rights to the Marlboro name, because the company's British ancestor had retained them for Commonwealth nations. And in Britain, with its strong preference for all-Virginia light tobaccos without sweeteners, PM's output was finding few takers. More promising from the first, as Weissman had forecast, was the German market, which Philip Morris entered through a licensing deal with the big Brinkmann firm. But before long, the arrangement in Germany would bear out Smith's caveat against bedding down with partners who could not tolerate competition from an increasingly popular American brand.

Cullman's tapping of Weissman to give Philip Morris true global reach would prove over time to have been a masterstroke, one that disclosed perhaps his greatest gift as a chief executive—how to deploy the diverse talent at his disposal and make it mesh productively even when his operatives, as in the case of Smith and Weissman, did not care much for each other. He was also given to stopping a subordinate from any department when he passed him in the hall or ran into him on the elevator, where he would confront him with a proposed new pack design and ask for an opinion or what he thought of the latest Marlboro commercial. Cullman's effect on the place was electric, even if it did not produce instantaneous results.

"Everyone who came into contact with him was impressed by how much Joe knew about the business," recalled Hamish Maxwell, then a young Briton who had joined the company the same year as Cullman and worked in sales and marketing. "He was excellent at establishing his priorities and dealing with people—he didn't get bogged down in nitpicking and chickenshit." And while he could flash his temper, he was never gratuitously cruel nor did he invite bootlicking. "You felt you were going to do well or not at Philip Morris on the merits," said Maxwell, who would do very well indeed.

Among those from whom Joe Cullman sought counsel was his tobacco research director in Richmond, Robert DuPuis. In a memo to the company brass late in 1959 regarding desirable future product developments, DuPuis urged the high command to permit his department to "[c]orrelate our chemical knowledge with medical knowledge" in product modification that could combine both substantially lowered tar and nicotine yields and "good flavor and burning properties. . . . We must consider not only what is technically sound, but what is forced on us by the press, enemies and competitors. . . . The health problem overrides all of our research work and is probably the most important and most difficult problem facing the industry."

Such a conviction stood in marked contrast with Cullman's pop-off comment the year before that "the worst is over" with regard to public fears over the health issue. With Paul Smith's cautionary hand hovering nearby, Cullman would rarely put his foot in his mouth like that thereafter. Nor, though, would he share DuPuis's candor with the public. Rather, Philip Morris, along with the rest of the cigarette trade, kept on assiduously reassuring its customers that their product was, if not entirely harmless, certainly not guilty of manslaughter.

8

Grand Inquisitors

A s STUDIES multiplied on the manner and immensity of disease formation from smoking cigarettes, just what role government as guardian of
the public health could or should play remained debatable. Was smoking a
public or private matter? What right did the state have to intrude upon the personal behavior of its citizens, even if they chose to indulge in bad habits that
threatened their own survival? How would this differ from interfering in their
choice of speech, dress, diet, recreational activities, or any other legal conduct?
Freedom to live life as one chose, so long as others were not materially affected in the process, was the essence of each American's birthright.

The argument that smoking was not a freely chosen activity because it typically began before the onset of awareness of how brief at best is life's candle—
and was for many devilishly hard to shake thereafter—did not command
widespread support. The use of cigarettes, on the contrary, was granted a favored status and exempted from government scrutiny at the opening of the
century—a tribute to the power of federal legislators from the leaf-growing
states and their allies in the Midwest Farm Belt. Given the congressional seniority system and the long sway of the one-party South, tobacco-state lawmakers only added to their potency during the Democrats' New Deal era and
retained it when the activist era of government waned, thus accustoming the
cigarette industry to unique liberty from bureaucratic oversight.

As the 1960s dawned, a young Democratic President faced a crowded social
agenda on which a preventive public-health policy against the dangers of cigarettes was among the least pressing items. The product was hugely popular,

consumed by 60 to 70 million Americans—a record number—in 1963. Tobacco was an immensely profitable industry, and several million drew at least
part of their livelihood from it. The delights of smoking were hammered into
the popular consciousness through advertising that saturated the electronic and
print media, and were fiercely defended in the political citadels, which themselves mined billions in excise taxes from the habit that greased the wheels
of government. Who, moreover, could get greatly exercised about a product
that nobody accused of killing children and rarely struck at people in their
prime? A 1962 Gallup survey found that only 38 percent of respondents
believed that smoking caused lung cancer. The following year the Food and
Drug Administration, empowered by the 1960 Federal Hazardous Substances
Labeling Act to determine whether suspect substances—toxic, irritating, corrosive, flammable, strongly sensitizing and pressure-generating—required
regulations, ruled that cigarettes were not hazardous in any of those ways.

The American Cancer Society continued to provide the spearhead—
somewhat dulled by now and never very pointy—for the antismoking movement at the beginning of the new decade. But in the 'Sixties, the giant agency
was at pains to enlist as allies three other prominent private health groups: the
American Heart Association, the National Tuberculosis Association, and the
American Public Health Association. Together, the four voluntaries addressed
a letter on June 1, 1961, to President Kennedy, still reeling from the Bay of
Pigs fiasco and struggling to frame a coherent legislative program, to appoint a
national commission on smoking, "seeking a solution to this health problem
that would interfere least with the freedom of industry or the happiness of individuals" yet address the responsibilities of business, government, and the
health community.

The President bucked the letter to Health, Education, and Welfare Secretary
Abraham Ribicoff, whom the voluntaries then asked to meet with to explore
the subject. When, after four months, no formal reply had been received, the
ACS-led coalition flexed its muscles uncharacteristically and threatened to advise the press of the administration's foot-dragging. The result was a meeting
in the first week of 1962 between officials of the four voluntaries and the new
top government health officer, Surgeon General Luther L. Terry, a honey-
voiced Alabaman who, as a youngster, had picked tobacco. Terry was named
after his father's physician, Luther Leonidas Hill, whose son, Lister, became a
U.S. senator chairing the subcommittee in charge of health matters. A beneficiary of Hill's patronage, Terry was a Public Health Service careerist with a
record of competence in hospital administration and some research work in the
treatment of hypertension. As Surgeon General, he promised to consider the
proposed commission on smoking and health but failed to act with dispatch.

At about that time, Oregon's junior senator, Democrat Maurine Neuberger,
introduced a joint congressional resolution directing the President to name a

group to formulate a comprehensive program to check smoking-caused disease. When Neuberger's husband, Richard, a liberal idealist, died before completing his first Senate term, she ran for and won his seat. Plucky and principled, she nevertheless proved an ineffectual lawmaker, unwilling to bend to the Senate's clubby ways. Neuberger won six co-sponsors for her resolution on the smoking problem, but it went nowhere in Congress. Still, hers was a persistent voice, the first in Congress since Representative John Blatnik five years earlier to speak out clearly on the smoking issue. Neuberger's proposed resolution helped push Surgeon General Terry to suggest to the HEW Secretary in April 1962 a national commission that would make a rigorous assessment of the scientific case against the cigarette. Senator Neuberger, meanwhile, pursued the subject in an adroit letter to the new chairman of the Federal Trade Commission, Paul Randall Dixon, an affable Tennessean, who, like Luther Terry, owed his appointment to the influence of powerful Southern lawmakers. Neuberger urged the FTC not only to rescind what most public-health people now took to have been the commission's ill-advised ban on any mention of tar and nicotine strengths in cigarette advertising but also to hold as inherently deceptive all such advertising that failed to include a warning on the health hazards of smoking. In mid-May, Neuberger carried her case to Terry, urging the Surgeon General to take a more forceful stand on the smoking peril.

When the President himself was finally asked at his May 23, 1962, press conference about the growing concern over smoking and health and what his administration intended to do to address the issue, Kennedy replied, "That matter is sensitive enough and the stock market is in sufficient difficulty without my giving you an answer which is not based on complete information, which I don't have." Confronted with the Cold War, civil rights, Medicare, and other monumental issues, the President was conceding a low rank to the smoking issue but promised to answer the question at his next meeting with the press. Two weeks later, Surgeon General Terry announced that it was indeed "timely to undertake a review of all available data" on the smoking question and that he planned to appoint a committee of experts to advise him on their findings. The cigarette makers, he said, would be allowed to blackball nominees so long as there were substantive grounds for the objection.

Just how weighty the judgment of the Surgeon General's committee would prove was foreshadowed by the response Senator Neuberger finally received in July to her appeal to FTC chairman Dixon to mandate health warning labels in cigarette advertising. "If the Commission is able to secure competent probative scientific evidence including that furnished by the Public Health Service" of the harmful effects of smoking, Dixon wrote, then an FTC order to include health warnings in cigarette ads would likely "be upheld in appellate courts." In short, the FTC wanted the official backing of the government's chief health officer before it would consider such a bold initiative.

THE closest thing to an official endorsement of the medical case against smoking had come earlier that spring from Great Britain. A nine-member panel chosen by the 444-year-old Royal College of Physicians (RCP), an honorary society numbering some 7,000 of the kingdom's most prominent practitioners, issued a seventy-page report to a nation in which three-quarters of the men and half of the women smoked. Stressing that the high statistical association between smoking and disease had lately been strengthened by compatible if not conclusive laboratory evidence, the RCP said the weight of the findings in some 200 studies was that smoking was a major cause of lung cancer, was causal in bronchitis, and probably contributed to the development of coronary heart disease. And while air pollution intensified the health problems induced by smoking, the toll in disease and death was proportionate to the level of cigarette use, regardless of where an individual lived in the United Kingdom. Among the therapeutic measures proposed were a ban or limits on cigarette advertising, curbs on smoking in public places, and the stamping of tar and nicotine yields on every pack accompanied by the caveat that no brand was necessarily safer than any other.

British cigarette manufacturers were minimally responsive to the doctors' urgings by agreeing to cease broadcast advertising before 9 p.m. The American industry, through the Tobacco Institute, brushed off the British report, saying it was based on old data. But more objective students of the subject were struck by the implications of two investigations soon reported in the *New England Journal of Medicine*, which dealt a punishing blow to the industry's defense.

The April 16, 1962, issue of the *NEJM* disclosed results from the thirteen-year-old continuing study established in Framingham, Massachusetts, by the Public Health Service and later expanded to include a cohort from Albany, New York, to monitor the long-term health histories, especially cardiac, of more than 4,000 subjects. The new report focused on the association between smoking and heart disease, long suspected but little documented. Both the total death rate and the fatal toll from coronary heart disease among smokers in the Framingham-Albany cohort were five times higher than the rate among nonsmokers. The disparity with regard to heart attack in the forty-to-forty-nine-year-old category was greater still. And the more one smoked, the greater the incidence of disease. The article concluded, however, that the "mechanism" behind these striking figures "is obscure".

But the numbers, combined with findings in microscopic studies at autopsy by Oscar Auerbach, were enough to prompt his ACS collaborator, epidemiologist Cuyler Hammond, to tell the annual American Medical Association meeting in July that the lung cancer toll exacted on cigarette smokers might prove "relatively unimportant" compared with the damage to them from other forms of disease, in particular those of the heart. In that month's *Scientific American*, Hammond wrote a long article in which he hypothesized a systemic, interlocking pathology that frighteningly suggested how the heart and lungs were mutually affected by cigarettes. Smoke irritants thickened the walls of the small blood vessels and pulmonary veins carrying the oxygenated blood from the lungs to the heart, thus making the heart muscle work harder to obtain and distribute the vital oxygen the body needed for survival. The smoke also made thicker and less elastic the linings of the alveoli, the grapelike cluster of tiny air sacs used to feed oxygen to the cardiopulmonary system, greatly reducing their efficiency. Smoke toxins that additionally destroyed the cilia also triggered an apparently compensatory hypersecretion of the mucous cells and glands. This excess discharge often plugged the smaller airways, making it harder to breathe and forming a seedbed for infectious diseases, especially pneumonia. To clear these clogged passages, the sufferer coughed and sneezed, sometimes causing so great an increase in the pressure of the trapped air that the alveolar walls ruptured, further reducing the lungs' capacity to process oxygen. Since normal lungs house some eight times as many alveoli as they need, a minor loss could be easily compensated for, but in smokers experiencing chronic insults to their tissues, the eventual loss in this vital function was both large and irreparable. When these functional complications were added to the previously known biochemical effects of tobacco smoke—in particular, a loss of 5 to 6 percent in the oxygen capacity of heavy smokers' hemoglobin because of the high binding with it by carbon monoxide from the burned cigarette, the quickening of the heartbeat during and up to twenty minutes after smoking, and the constricting of the peripheral blood vessels—it was clear why smokers' chronically overworked hearts often broke down prematurely.

That same month, Hammond co-authored a report in the *New England Journal*, for which Auerbach was the lead investigator, adding clinically explicit evidence of the part smoking played in the development of cancer. Examining the dissected tissue from 1,522 bodies autopsied at twelve hospitals over a seven-year period, Auerbach found obvious changes in the structure and arrangement of the bronchial cells four times as often in male smokers and three times as often in female smokers as in nonsmokers, regardless of their causes of death. Hyperplasia, the abnormal thickening of the airway walls, occurred in 88 percent of the male smokers and 83 percent of the female smokers, compared to 11 percent and 18 percent respectively in nonsmokers. Atypical cells with enlarged and darkened nuclei were found in an overwhelming 97 percent of male smokers and 81 percent of female smokers, compared to less than 1 percent among nonsmokers of either sex. Cell changes closest in form to frank invasive carcinoma—lesions composed entirely of atypical cells with their cilia absent—were found in lung cancer victims and almost as frequently in the bronchial epithelium of heavy cigarette smokers who died first of other causes. Thus, Auerbach's use of the term "preinvasive" for such tumors gained credibility.

A still more striking finding, this one unexpected, grew out of a subsidiary study Auerbach had included in his investigation in order to learn what effect, if any, quitting the habit had on the pathogenic condition of smokers. Observing the cell changes in three sets of seventy-two subjects—smokers, ex-smokers (defined as those who had quit five years or longer before their deaths), and never-smokers, with none in any of the groups having died of lung cancer—Auerbach found hyperplasia in 93 percent of the smokers, 57 percent of the ex-smokers, and 12 percent of the nonsmokers. The contrast was still greater with regard to atypical cells: they were present in 93 percent of the smokers, only 6 percent of the quitters, and 1.2 percent of the nonsmokers.

But there was something else. In 43 of the 72 ex-smokers, Auerbach observed a condition present in none of the 144 other subjects, whether smokers or not: lung cells with nuclei that appeared to be shrinking, fading, or just disintegrating. It was not clear whether these had been atypical cells before their hosts had quit smoking, but it was noted that the number of atypical cells in continuing smokers increased until their terminal illness. Thus, Hammond and Auerbach hypothesized that smoke might alter the environment of the bronchial passages in a way that favored the survival and reproduction of cells with atypical nuclei once the mutation process that generated such cell changes had been set in motion. And by extension, they reasoned, an environment in which smoke had ceased its steady assault was unfavorable to sustaining such atypical cells, so quitting caused them to atrophy or disintegrate, thereby reducing the number of cells present that might evolve into invasive cancer. Such a suspected sequence of events would help explain the drop in lung cancer rates in quitters and led Auerbach and Hammond to write:

> Persons who have smoked cigarettes for many years sometimes express the opinion that the harm has already been done and that they might as well continue to smoke since it will do them no more harm. The evidence is completely contrary to that point of view.

III

As the medical case against smoking accumulated, the American tobacco industry seemed to grow fiercer in its declarations of defiance.

After dismissing the Royal College of Physicians report, for example, the Tobacco Industry Research Committee took a harsher whack at the British doctors' effort by asserting in its 1962 annual report, "The unquestioning, unreserved endorsement, as conclusive, of each such repetitive report, which contains no new or original data but amounts to a statement of opinion, is a disservice to scientific research." Not only did the industry's spokesmen ignore the highly suggestive, if not altogether incriminating, findings on cell change in smokers' lungs by Oscar Auerbach, but they also conceded nothing as a result of studies funded by the TIRC itself. Its 1962 report, for example, was virtually silent on the extended findings of the Leuchtenbergers with regard to cell alterations in the bronchi of mice exposed to whole smoke— further corroboration of Auerbach's observed changes in human smokers' epithelial tissue. Another TIRC-backed study, dealing with 139 lung cancer deaths out of 915 autopsies, noted that all of those so stricken had been smokers. The emerging awareness of smoking as a prime promoter of heart disease was underscored in a report by industry-funded investigator Alvan Kershbaum, who, extrapolating from animal studies on the effects of nicotine, noted: "An eventual, delayed increase in serum levels of cholesterol and other lipoprotein lipids . . . is a conceivable result in humans after smoking. . . . If, as many investigators believe, a disturbance of lipid metabolism is a factor in the development of atherosclerosis, the effect of cigarette smoking on lipid metabolism should be given attention in considering the pathogenesis of this disorder."

Instead of giving ground in the health debate or falling silent in the face of such findings, the tobacco industry snatched at any study, however dubious, that minimized the pathogenic impact of smoking. The Tobacco Institute's now monthly newsletter, *Research Reports on Tobacco and Health*, typically carried articles with headlines like "Human Virus Induces Animal Lung Cancers" and "Study Questions Accuracy of Death Certificates" and reprints of pro-industry articles like "Heavy Smokers with Low Mortality." Amid this steady drumbeat of denial and disinformation, there was no crueler instance of reassurance to the industry's customers than the one in a letter of rebuttal by the TIRC's new president, W. T. Hoyt, in the February 1963 issue of *The New Englander*, in which he wrote: "Our scientific advisers tell us that the causes of lung cancer are still not known and that, as a matter of fact, recent research has tended to point up many new possible causes. . . ."

Despite propagating such indefensible humbug, the cigarette makers' operations from 1960 onward were increasingly attuned to the health issue, which could no longer be dismissed as a mere "scare". Ever more concerned with the possible legal liability to which their perceptibly hazardous product might expose them in court suits, tobacco executives grew dependent on lawyers in framing their every public move and in the sort of research they undertook privately. In his unpublished corporate history of Philip Morris, Jerome E. Brooks, son of the prominent Harvard social historian Van Wyck Brooks, reported that during the 1962–65 period "no move of a public nature was or could be made without the special approval of legal advisors, a control which was to become more restrictive" as a result of the liability suits beginning to plague the industry at that time.

The growing realization that they would all sink if they did not swim together, regardless of which company was bearing the brunt of litigation at the moment, led to the adoption of a siege mentality among the cigarette makers. They leagued their efforts through four jointly wielded instruments: the industry's executive committee, composed of the chief executive officers of the leading companies; the "Secret Six," composed of the general counsel of each company; a parallel but more venturesome ad hoc committee of younger lawyers from outside firms that were of counsel to the industry members; and the industry's chief publicists as well as those at Hill & Knowlton assigned to the tobacco account. Collectively these four groups exercised control over the industry's statements on the health charges against smoking as issued by the Tobacco Institute and TIRC.

Yoked strictly by expediency, the tobacco executives and their costly hirelings were not exactly in love with one another. American Tobacco's lawyers, for example, were viewed by others in the tobacco camp as tradition-bound and "tight-assed," querulous within industry councils, die-hard on the health issue, and the last to reach for the dinner check. Liggett's contingent from a white-shoe New York firm were rated as more gifted socially than as legal strategists. Reynolds's legal corps, headed by wary, Harvard-trained house counsel Henry Ramm and manned mostly by operatives from the crack Wall Street firm of Davis, Polk, Sutherland & Wardwell, was considered competent if less than brilliant. Lorillard's officers and lawyers were the most suspiciously viewed of any in the industry because the marketing of their lead brand, Kent, had been most dependent upon exploiting the health issue, studiously downplayed by its larger competitors.

Probably the ablest and most enlightened of the legal representatives was the team assembled by Philip Morris, which as a result wielded power within the industry's councils disproportionate to the company's modest market share. Their passionately protective general counsel, Paul Smith, moved regularly and with the full joy of combat between New York, Washington, foreign parts, and even Winston-Salem, where he might suddenly show up for a *tête-à-tête* with RJR's boss, Bowman Gray, Jr., whom Smith much admired as a true gentleman. Smith had able reinforcements from the Conboy, Hewitt firm, of which he had formerly been a member, and, to deal with regulatory and legislative matters, the Washington firm of Arnold & Porter, a powerhouse in Democratic political circles with a high-profile New Deal pedigree. The firm's top strategist and behind-the-scenes wire-puller, Abe Fortas, would shortly gain immortality in American jurisprudential annals with his pro bono 1963 victory in *Gideon v. Wainwright*, expanding indigents' right to counsel. The embattled tobacco industry, while hardly paupers, also felt the need for illustrious representation in the law courts as well as the court of public opinion, and Arnold & Porter's liberal lawyers were hardly in a position philosophically to turn down the cigarette makers now being accused of purveying death to multitudes. "People here felt intensely about the importance of the right to counsel," recalled Arnold & Porter partner Abe Krash, who was on the Philip Morris account from the start. ". . . [I]t's not necessary that our views be congruent with our clients'."

As public-relations counselors, Hill & Knowlton exercised a dual role. On the one hand, it cautioned the industry against excessive displays of truculence or just plain putting its foot in its mouth, as in the case of a proposed statement to the effect that 97 percent of smokers never contracted lung cancer. Aside from being inaccurate, the claim was tantamount to conceding that at least several million current customers would get the disease. When, on the other hand, H&K proposed measures that the industry might take to demonstrate sensitivity to rising criticism, such as voluntarily adopting an advertising code, urging customers to smoke in moderation, and putting warnings of a health hazard on each cigarette pack, the suggestions were coolly received. To urge moderation on cigarette users, the companies' lawyers argued, implied that there was a safe level of smoking and, logically, an area beyond it that was excessive when in fact there was no known standard that could be applied generally, so why open Pandora's box? The idea of voluntarily placing a warning label on the pack seemed to have the double virtue of easing public pressure on the industry and helping fend off future liability suits, since forewarned smokers could thereafter be said to have assumed the risk of their decision to begin or continue smoking—a valid legal defense. But the industry lawyers worried that such warnings were an admission that might invite lawsuits as well as deflect them. One who strongly pushed the warning labels as an enlightened preemptive measure by the industry was Hill & Knowlton account executive Edward DeHart. DeHart's persistent advocacy of conceding at least a sliver of ground in the health controversy almost cost him his job. He was confronted in a hallway one day by RJR's Henry Ramm, then serving as unofficial chairman of the Secret Six, who said to the public-relations man, referring to placement of health warnings on cigarette packs, "I want you to stop talking about it." The industry, DeHart recalled, "was in no mood those days to do anything it didn't absolutely have to do."

IV

ONE day early in his tenure as president of Philip Morris, Joseph Cullman was bustling through the corporate offices on Park Avenue when he passed the desk of a new star recruit and noticed that Helmut Wakeham was neither smoking nor in possession of an ashtray.

Smoking was not exactly obligatory for industry employees, but ranking officials who harbored career ambitions were well advised to make at least a pretense of smoking or risk the suspicion that they were not totally loyal to the product. In the case of Wakeham, momentarily apprenticing to PM operations vice president Robert Roper but hired as a physical chemist with a doctorate from Berkeley to work in research and product development, there were extenuating circumstances. As the son of a German mother and a father who was a native Nebraskan adhering to and actively teaching the tenets of the Seventh-Day Adventist church, Wakeham had grown up with the belief that smoking was a desecration of the temple that was the human body. While not unduly freighted by such dogma, the urbane and well-traveled Wakeham deferred to parental wishes during a career that included research in the oil, tire, and textile industries, and so arrived at Philip Morris as a lifelong abstainer from tobacco.

"I see you're not a smoker," Cullman remarked to him in a nonconfrontational way as he stopped at Wakeham's desk. "Well, maybe you can be more objective that way," he added and moved on.

It was a quick, shrewd read, of the sort Cullman was skilled at. Helmut Wakeham, his full head of blond hair going gray now in his early forties, saw himself above all as a man of science and cultivation. Blessed with a probing mind able to dissect technical subjects like the intricacies of cigarette filtration, he was equally at home discussing a play by Schiller, music from Bach to Debussy, or the politics of the Indian subcontinent, where he had worked for several years as a consultant to the International Cooperation Administration and the indigenous textile industry. He did not see himself as a tobacco chemist any more than he had seen himself as a textile chemist earlier. "I am simply applying scientific facts and methodology to tobacco problems," he told a reporter for the Richmond *Times-Dispatch* soon after being transferred to the Philip Morris research center across the James River from the company's main manufacturing facilities. Candid, precise in his speech, skilled at translating technical concepts into laymen's words, Wakeham was tapped in 1960, two years after his arrival at the company, to be director of research and development. It was not long before he found himself occasionally at swordspoint with Philip Morris's testy house counsel. "Paul Smith had been made company czar of the smoking and health question," Wakeham recalled, "and, being a very ambitious man, saw it as the key to his gaining and holding power. He continuously raised the specter of the tobacco companies' losing a lawsuit" that might prove ruinous, "but I didn't altogether buy that view."

Deferential though he was to his resident legal counselor, Cullman mandated an openness of expression among his chief subordinates which was the hallmark of his management; he did not favor yes-men or lockstep thinking. Wakeham was thus free to speak his mind and did so without excessive concern about his prospects for corporate advancement; his prime ambition seemed to revolve around the growth of his department, which within five years of his taking charge numbered 500 scientists and technicians. One of Wakeham's principal forums for self-expression was a monthly seminar he conducted for the company brass on technical aspects of the business, often touching upon the health area. Attendance was high, if not mandatory, and was usually boosted by Cullman's presence, though he would typically arrive a few minutes after the appointed starting time, scan the crowded room that had respectfully waited for him, and ask Wakeham with an impatience more detectable now as his power and duties grew, "How long is this going to take?" Wakeham would answer, "About forty-five minutes—if you don't ask me a lot of questions." But Cullman was a champion questioner, and Wakeham's seminars often ran twice the allotted time.

One of the new research director's early initiatives was to enlist Archer Martin, who had won the Nobel Prize for developing gas chromatography, to help train Philip Morris scientists in the new techniques for tracking down the thousands of constituent compounds released by burning cigarettes. Wakeham thought it elementary that "only by knowing the chemistry of tobacco and smoke could we ever hope to control the composition of our ultimate product."

With the aid of the latest equipment, Wakeham was able to report to the PM research and development committee, in a memorandum dated November 15, 1961, that his lab people had confirmed at least trace amounts of forty-two compounds in cigarette smoke identified as carcinogens. "Present evidence suggests," he added, "that smoking has a stronger <u>tumor-promoting</u> than <u>tumor-initiating</u> effect . . ." (underscoring in original text). Other portions of this memo also revealed high familiarity with health considerations and acknowledgment that the company could and should take measures to modify its product in response. Wakeham spelled out a three-part "Research and Development Program Leading to a Medically Acceptable Cigarette," which long afterward he would explain referred to a product that the health community would concede to pose minimal risk to users. "I was a little bit naïve," he commented more than thirty years later, "in thinking that our critics would really like us to find a more acceptable product. I was forced to come to the conclusion after many years that they weren't really interested in such a thing"—that health investigators and antismoking advocates, in short, wanted the cigarette to disappear, not to be fixed.

Wakeham's three avenues of pursuit, as elaborated in his 1961 memo, were "Reduction of Irritating Factors in Smoke," better control over the nicotine content of PM cigarette brands, and "Reduction of the General Level of Carcinogenic Substances in Smoke," the last goal likely to consume seven to ten years since it "will require a major research effort, because . . . [c]arcinogens are found in practically every class of compounds in smoke. . . . The best we can hope for is to reduce a particularly bad class, i.e., the polynuclear hydrocarbons, or phenols." The problem, he noted, was compounded because "[f]lavor . . . and carcinogenic substances come from the same class, in many instances." What Wakeham characterized as a low-irritation, low-nicotine cigarette could be developed within two to five years in the normal course of R&D programs, he believed, but on an almost plaintive note he concluded, "A medically acceptable low-carcinogen cigarette may be possible. Its development will require TIME[,] MONEY[, and] UNFALTERING DETERMINATION" (underscoring and capitalization in original text).

Confronted by this telling document nearly twenty-seven years after it was written, Philip Morris lawyers contended that "Nothing in the memorandum indicates that Dr. Wakeham believed these animal carcinogens were carcinogenic in men." But then why was he urging his company to undertake a major new research program? The latter-day lawyers, eager to explain away the Wakeham memo after a liability trial at which it had been disclosed, added that it was no secret that the listed forty-two carcinogenic compounds existed in smoke "in minute amounts." But nobody knew in 1961—or in 1988, for that matter—whether those trace quantities, singly or in some combination, had lethal effects over time and when taken in the steady dosages to which heavy smokers grow accustomed. And if the amounts were trivial, as the company's lawyers implied, why did Wakeham think it worthwhile to reduce or eliminate them and thereby create a "medically acceptable" cigarette?

Two years later, in 1963, in response to a request from top management to advise as to where he thought the next thrust against smoking by health investigators would be directed, Wakeham expressed concern about "the cocarcinogen idea. With the hundreds of compounds in smoke, this hypothesis will be hard to contest." Another new concern, which had been raised recently at an industry conference in Hamburg, Germany, was posed by nitrosamines, a likely carcinogen or cocarcinogen—a promoter of cancerous growth—formed by nitrogen oxides and nitrogen bases, "both of which are present in smoke." The cigarette industry, Wakeham continued, "ultimately may be in greater trouble" because of the product's association with emphysema and bronchitis than with lung cancer—and he did not deny or minimize the smoking link to any of the three, though he thought the threat posed by heart disease, to which nicotine had been linked, was relatively smaller, adding, "If forced to, we could produce a fairly tasty low nicotine product."

In a memo sent the day before President Kennedy's assassination, Wakeham sketched out the research department's goals for 1964, still citing the hope to "develop a 'medically acceptable' cigarette in light of the present health attitude." He spoke of his department's past accomplishments in reducing nicotine content by leaf selection and irritating phenols by the use of cellulose acetate filters and cited as continuing targets the removal of hydrocarbons and nitrosamines.

The R&D effort under Wakeham and its frank discussions intramurally are of particular interest historically because of how they contrasted with what Philip Morris officials, under advice of counsel, were telling the public about smoking and health. Within a few weeks of the release of the 1962 report by the Royal College of Physicians, for example, President Cullman was reassuring stockholders at the Philip Morris annual meeting in Richmond, "So far, there is no clinical proof to support the theory that smoking causes carcinoma of the lung. There is evidence that smoking has pharmacological and psychological effects that are of real value to smokers." This was the kind of calculated wordplay that lawyers relish, for while it was quite true that there was still no certifiable *proof* in the idealized form of what Clarence Little referred to as "the whole truth"—and would likely never be in the lifetime of anyone then on earth—there was a great deal of *evidence* that smoking caused lung cancer and other fatal diseases. Far more fanciful was Cullman's contention that smoking had intrinsic benefits beyond keeping smokers temporarily glued together against the stresses induced by their addiction.

At the annual meeting a year later, Cullman stated, "While I do not minimize the health question, I think that eventually cigarettes will be exonerated." That November, even while research director Wakeham was sending memos to company headquarters acknowledging the gravity of the health peril, Cullman commented to *The New York Times*, "I don't think the present product will prove to be a major health hazard. I also believe that changes can be made in the product if they are indicated." This was a somewhat toned-down version of a statement attributed to an unnamed Philip Morris official in an article in *Business Week* two months earlier, when the industry was girding for the overdue report by the Surgeon General's Advisory Committee: "If they tell us tomorrow that a cancer-causing element has been identified in tobacco smoke, we could remove it by the day after." In fact, what Philip Morris and everyone else in the industry knew was that cigarette smoke did contain cancer-causing elements; what they did not know was how to remove them without destroying the product in the process.

Some of Cullman's public remarks suggested a man who, while hardly conscience-stricken over the hazardous product he was purveying, was uncomfortable with the contradictory stances the tobacco manufacturers felt they had to assume in their own defense. Interviewed for a *Forbes* cover story on the embattled cigarette business in July 1963, in which he was called "one of the industry's least dogmatic, most forthright minds," Cullman remarked disingenuously, "No company is working specifically on the health question. We're trying to make a cigarette that smokes mild and tastes good." Yet later in the story he conceded, "Of course this whole filter business has been triggered by the health issue." But then he made light of recent moves by Philip Morris to bolster its non-tobacco business by buying Burma-Shave toiletries as a companion to its ASR line of shaving products and Clark chewing gum, a nontoxic alternative to smoking. Although with these new products PM's non-tobacco revenues were now approaching 20 percent of total sales, Cullman nevertheless insisted, "But none of this is related to the health thing. We acquire other companies only because we like their future." In what other industry, confronted with a threatened catastrophic drop in sales because of health charges against it, would a leading executive so transparently deny the truth—namely, that his company was taking prudent measures (a) to modify the suspect product and (b) to lessen corporate dependency on it?

Even to admit that the filter revolution was a response to the health charges against the industry, as Cullman did to *Forbes*, was enough to send Philip Morris general counsel Paul Smith into a tantrum. The whole subject, explained Alexander Holtzman, one of Smith's younger legal associates and later a long-term lawyer with the company, "was a no-win situation for the industry, because there's absolutely no evidence that filters are any safer than regular [non-filter] cigarettes. It was the kind of situation where you were damned if you do and damned if you don't confront the health subject." More precisely, the industry lawyers felt that the companies could not risk claiming any health advantage in lowering tar and nicotine yields because that would have amounted to conceding that the core of the scientific case against them—the dose-response data, showing that the more toxins you absorbed from smoke, the greater your health risk—was valid, opening the door to massive liability actions.

Thus, Cullman usually buttoned his lip on the health question and let the company's professional spokesmen field such inquiries. Perhaps the most gifted of these, and the most defiant, was James Chandler Bowling, Cullman's executive assistant and PM's de facto public-relations chief, whatever his title of the moment. Like many of the smart, talented, and ambitious younger men surrounding Cullman throughout his long tenure, Bowling was a complex figure and not a little cunning. After having served as a model campus representative for Philip Morris while attending college at the universities of Kentucky and Louisville, Bowling brought to the company the wavy-haired good looks, dapper dress, and silken tongue of a riverboat dandy, nor was he shy about his ties to the socially and politically powerful. In many ways he was the perfect corporate man, immoderate in his love of the product, willing to do whatever was needed to defend his company's honor.

When interviewed on the health issue in 1963 by Thomas Whiteside for *The New Yorker*, Bowling said his company's researchers were hard at the task of modifying the product to make it more "medically acceptable," but he spoke of "the health scare" as if the data were spectral and the charges born of animus. Of the link between smoking and disease, Bowling asserted, "We believe there is no connection, or we wouldn't be in the business," and later defended the industry's executives as "people with a social conscience." The antismoking case was established, Bowling claimed, "without a full understanding of the facts. Gosh, we're awed how a story can be told and retold by the anticigarette people, and how little attention is given in the press to claims *for* cigarettes." As an example of the latter, he cited a remark he had heard recently from a physician that if smoking were suddenly halted, there would be "more wife-beating and job dissatisfaction than people's natures can tolerate."

Remarks made to *The New Yorker* at that time by another rising young star at Philip Morris, tall, curly-headed John T. Landry, then company director of brand management and soon to blossom into its resident advertising genius, conveyed a craftier way of dealing with the health issue. Landry, who grew up in Saratoga Springs, New York, and from boyhood hung around the stables during the fashionable summer horse-racing season, was a bluff, engagingly profane transferee to Philip Morris from Blue Coal, where his advertising and promotional skills were wasted. A marketing man who enjoyed consorting with professional athletes and the sporting crowd in his hard-drinking off-hours, Landry had little use for the sort of research and surveys favored by George Weissman and relied instead on his instincts and street wisdom. Nor was he good at double-talk of the sort perfected by corporate apologists. He told reporter Whiteside that like their boss, Joe Cullman, Philip Morris people believed cigarettes would eventually be acquitted of the health charges against them but that they would never try to convince anyone that cigarettes were physically good for him, although he felt smoking eased tension—"and if I didn't smoke, I'd probably develop a tic or something."

Public statements aside, Philip Morris was at work trying to make its cigarettes less risky, even if the company had convinced itself that legal considerations and FTC strictures did not permit it to proclaim what was behind the effort. Nor were these attempts rewarded by commercial success in the early 'Sixties, when the company brought out the charcoal-filter Paxton and the yet more elaborately designed Multifilter to appeal to health-conscious smokers. A major role in the development of both brands, neither of which gained more than a fractional market share, was played by Philip Morris's No. 2 operations man, engineer Clifford Goldsmith, future czar of the company's entire tobacco operations. Goldsmith, with a sophisticated grasp of the smoking and health issue not unlike Helmut Wakeham's, personified the PM position; as he would put it long afterward, "To this day we don't know what the harmful elements are in smoke. But whether you trust us or not, we were trying to be responsive to what appeared to appeal to the public." If the strategy was to reassure the public, the tactic was to provide smokers with the most taste for the lowest tar and nicotine. "That was the game—more flavor and less tar," Goldsmith added.

Eager to soften criticism from the health community, Philip Morris did not balk at buying support from useful sympathizers. And none was better placed to suit the company's ends than Dr. Frank Horsfall, Jr., director of the cancer-fighting Sloan-Kettering Institute. Partial to Marlboro cigarettes, at least when he showed up at PM headquarters soliciting a corporate contribution to his institution, Horsfall assured company officials asking about the smoking-cancer link that, as one who heard him recalled, "There are more carcinogens in a tomato than in a pack of cigarettes." Starting in 1962, Philip Morris made a three-year, $25,000 annual gift to Sloan-Kettering, and other cigarette manufacturers soon followed suit.

In urging the company to extend these grants in 1964, James Bowling wrote, "Dr. Horsfall's opinion . . . has been beneficial. As head of the nation's principle [sic] cancer research organization, he has tremendous influence." Specifically, Horsfall had the power to muzzle the tobacco industry's most outspoken detractor, Ernst Wynder, now installed with co-investigator Dietrich Hoffmann at Sloan-Kettering and producing a steady flow of damaging and well-publicized studies that documented the growing number of body sites imperiled by smoking. Bowling's memo to his PM colleagues termed Wynder's studies "attacks" on smoking and alleged that once the Philip Morris grants were flowing to the cancer institute, its officials "began subjecting Wynder to more rigorous screening procedures before letting him speak in the name of the institute. This had a proper and pleasing effect. . . . The deductible contribution to Sloan-Kettering is probably the most effective of all health research contributions." Here was the genesis of the company's later, perfected program of acquiring allies in the health debate by helping meet the financial needs of prominent social and cultural institutions, whose vulnerabilities complemented the tobacco company's own.

v

LIGGETT & MYERS, still No. 3 in the cigarette business but fading now at an accelerated pace, was ahead of its competitors in research on the health issue and in its willingness to put out a technologically advanced prod-

uct. By holding itself aloof from the rest of the industry's scattershot grant program and instead funding research by Arthur D. Little, Inc. (ADL), Liggett enjoyed the fruits of a focused effort by a first-rate industrial laboratory.

In the late 'Fifties and early 'Sixties, ADL scientists under Charles Kensler
working with rabbit tissue discovered that cilia exposed to tobacco smoke
were more affected by toxic substances in the gas phase than by those in the
tarry materials that could be effectively blocked by cellulose acetate filters. To
counteract this ciliatoxic effect, the ADL team developed a filter using granulated charcoal. Because the granules presented the smoke with an extensive
surface area, due to the extremely porous structure of the charcoal, they
trapped the gases rather like a sponge taking in water and scrubbed off the
toxic molecules by absorbing them. When the charcoal granules were fit into a
tiny compartment combined with the cellulose acetate filter designed by Duke
chemist Charles Keith, the resulting product, which Liggett would dub its Lark
brand, was said to remove an estimated 60 percent of the ciliatoxic materials in
the smoke, according to a 1963 article in the *New England Journal of Medicine* by Kensler and colleagues. Without making explicit health claims, the
article said that while the findings "may not be directly extrapolated to the
effects of cigarette smoke on human pulmonary tissue, the use of the charcoal-
granule filter will obviously reduce the level of exposure of . . . bronchial and
alveolar cells to potentially harmful smoke components."

But months before the article appeared—and a likely factor in its being
written at all and submitted to a leading scientific journal, thereby disclosing
the particulars of ADL's confidential work-product for Liggett—Kensler had
been contacted by Harvard's Professor Louis F. Fieser, then serving as a member of the Surgeon General's ten-man advisory committee on smoking and
health, in the midst of its closed-door deliberations. Fieser, whose link to the
tobacco industry as a consultant to ADL while it worked for Liggett was unknown to the Surgeon General's office or to his colleagues on the special study
panel, asked Kensler to submit, with Liggett's full blessing, a detailed report
on its work for the cigarette maker. In acquiescing, Liggett and ADL were
open to suspicions that they hoped the new Lark would be commended in the
report by the Surgeon General's committee, thereby gaining a priceless advantage in the marketplace. In retrospect, Kensler said such a charge was "to
impugn our motives and our integrity, and I deeply resented it."

Whatever the motives, the ADL-Liggett documents submitted to the Surgeon General's Advisory Committee in 1963 were a classic example of the tobacco industry's wanting it both ways—the right to deny that there was a real
health problem due to smoking, but just in case there did happen to be one, to
claim that it could be readily fixed, and indeed the manufacturers were doing
so prophylactically. "We find much of the reported work relating cigarette
smoke to death rates or lesser impairments to have been unreliably con-

ducted," the ADL-Liggett report stated gratuitously and went on to question the validity of Wynder's mouse-skin-painting studies on the arguable ground that the dosages were equivalent to a thousand times what two-pack-a-day human smokers might absorb. This cavil begged the question why, if the Wynder investigation was so flawed conceptually, ADL-Liggett undertook to replicate it—and, to a significant degree, succeeded. And if smokers' elevated mortality rates were based on such shaky methodological grounds, why was Liggett working so hard to develop the charcoal-granule filter?

One measure of the disingenuous nature of the ADL-Liggett report was that its extensive discussion of how ciliatoxicity could be combated with a charcoal filter failed to elaborate upon the deeply suspect relationship between the destruction of the cilia and the occurrence of lung cancer and chronic obstructive pulmonary disease. More pointedly, the ADL-Liggett document argued that the mortality rate studies behind the association between smoking and disease were "conducted upon populations using products significantly different from those used by most American smokers today." But then it concluded that if the ciliatoxic substances in smoke have actually "contributed to a health hazard, the use of filter cigarettes should reduce the risk to the user, and would maximally benefit new smokers." In short, the report conceded no health hazard while claiming that there was now a way to reduce it.

All of which availed Liggett little. The final report by the Surgeon General's panel barely alluded to the claims for the new charcoal-granule filter and did not mention Lark by name. Even so, Lark sales for 1964 reached nearly 10 billion units, some 20 percent of Liggett's total for the year, but ebbed thereafter, and it never became a major U.S. brand, though it would achieve that rank in Japan, where the charcoal filter became a national cultural preference.

V I

WHILE Liggett's presentation to the Surgeon General's panel may have lacked candor, it did not take the path that the managers of Brown & Williamson elected, revealing nothing whatever to the government committee about what it knew of the perils of smoking as a result of recent studies undertaken for it and its parent company, British-American Tobacco (BAT), by Battelle Laboratories in Switzerland.

By the late spring of 1963 BAT had shared with B&W executives in Louisville the mixed bag of findings by Battalle. The British-owned tobacco giant's scientists had probably delved deeper into the psychopharmacological aspects of smoking than any other company up to that time. Among its studies was one entitled "A Tentative Hypothesis on Nicotine Addiction," noting the need for chronic intake of the drugging element in cigarettes to maintain the user's physiological and emotional equilibrium. Other in-house studies ventured that cigarettes "cause or predispose" their users to lung cancer, "may well be truly causative in emphysema," and might initiate or exacerbate heart disease. But BAT researchers saw a silver lining. Research executive Charles Ellis, for example, in conceding the addictive nature of nicotine at a 1962 company conference in Southampton, also characterized it as "a very remarkable beneficent drug that both helps the body to resist external stress and can also as a result show a pronounced tranquilizing effect."

This claimed therapeutic aspect of smoking was seized upon by Brown & Williamson's general counsel and senior vice president Addison Yeaman as a justification for the habit that might carry weight with the Surgeon General's advisory committee. "We are, then, in the business of selling nicotine, an addictive drug effective in the release of stress mechanisms," he wrote in a memo to his company colleagues, and asked permission of his company's overseers in London to share the Battelle lab's candid findings with the SGAC, along with news of a new filter B&W was developing, which like Liggett's Lark could screen out various toxic substances. If it was forthcoming in this bold manner, Yeaman suggested, the company would then be able to speak out in public about its health-oriented research and be free to analyze and criticize the report to the Surgeon General when it materialized, although such a step would run the risk of exposing the company to liability suits that charged it with knowingly marketing a hazardous product.

When BAT's cautious directors turned down the idea, Yeaman drafted an extraordinary internal memorandum in which he urged the company to abandon its defensive policy of asserting that the health charges against cigarettes were unproven and, instead, to "accept its responsibility" by conceding the problems with the product and disclosing everything it was doing to try to solve them; the alternative was to remain largely silent. Dismissing the Tobacco Industry Research Committee as "a public relations operation," he proposed that it be replaced by a "massive and impressively financed" research program that would be "self-perpetuating and uncontrolled" by the industry and that it enlist the cooperation of the American Cancer Society and other public-health organizations; the goal would be to discover and eliminate the chemical compounds in tobacco smoke that caused disease.

Nothing came of Yeaman's ideas until they surfaced before a congressional committee thirty years later to document what tobacco industry officials knew about the dangers of their wares and when they knew it. Probably the most extreme disparity, though, between what cigarette manufacturers were saying about the health problem and what they knew and were doing about it was the case of American Tobacco, laggard in the filter field while resting on its laurels in the wake of Pall Mall's rise as the best-selling brand.

New blood arrived in the AT executive suite, once occupied by Buck Duke and George Washington Hill, in the person of Robert Barney Walker, a rough-and-ready sort without formal education beyond high school, who had begun with the company as a route salesman in the Bronx and had worked his way up the sales side to win the presidency in early 1963 at the age of forty-nine, succeeding the less robust Paul Hahn. Possessed of good looks that were said to have advanced him well beyond where his brains and brassy manner might have carried him, Walker habitually wore a pink rose in his buttonhole—an incongruous adornment for a tough-talking Luckies chain-smoker. "There isn't a mounting weight of evidence," he said of the health charges against smoking in an interview with Thomas Whiteside of *The New Yorker* not long after taking charge at American Tobacco. "There is a mounting wave of propaganda." He and his fellow tobaccomen were "dedicated to the good of the country" and had "made a contribution to humanity," which entitled the industry to fair play and a presumption of innocence until proven guilty. After all, he added, "Cholesterol may be the killer of us all. But until it's proved, should the whole dairy industry be condemned?" The question, intended to liken the two industries, facilely disregarded the essential differences between them: dairy products, however problematical, had high nutritional value and could be consumed in moderate portions; the redeeming value of cigarettes resided, if anywhere, in the mind of the smoker, and they were, by pharmacological conditioning, consumed immoderately.

Shortly after winning the top job at AT, Walker dispatched his resident intellectual, former *Forbes* writer Robert Heimann, who held a doctorate in sociology from New York University and was later named executive vice president, to address the New York Society of Security Analysts. Heimann was a master dispenser of denial and disinformation. The health issue was a red herring, he asserted, "and clinical and experimental research do not bear out the anticigarette theory. . . . Nor has any substance been found in cigarette smoke in any quantity known to cause cancer in humans." This argument glossed over the dire possibility that no single substance but a combination of substances lurking in the product was lethal over time and, furthermore, that nobody knew the threshold, if any, of carcinogenic activity for the substances in smoke. The industry, nevertheless, had slashed the tar and nicotine content of its filter brands by some 40 percent in the past several years, Heimann noted, and then proceeded to make light of the health charge by describing to the Wall Streeters a study that had followed 11,000 American Tobacco employees for nearly fifteen years and found that the mortality rate for the cohort, who smoked more heavily than the national average, nonetheless showed a mortality rate 29 percent below the national norm. But the study of AT employees flew in the teeth of what epidemiologists called the "healthy workers' rule," which held it invalid to base sickness and death rates on any fully employed group of subjects for the simple reason that employers tend not to hire workers with acute or chronic diseases, while those who develop them in the course of their employment or become otherwise handicapped are usually discharged or retire early. Thus, the most health-imperiled have been stripped away from any group of the actively employed, who would naturally show a lower mortality rate than the average for all people in the same age bracket. And at any rate, smokers in all studies showed notably higher lung cancer rates than the non-smokers within their respective cohorts—which Heimann failed to point out.

Whether mere artifice or, to judge them less charitably, prodigies of deceit, such public disclaimers would have been easier to justify as partisan advocacy in defense of its realm if American Tobacco had not at the same time been laboring strenuously to develop a cigarette much milder than any competitor's. Barney Walker was eager from the first to make up the ground lost to his company due to its past failure to exploit smokers' health concerns by offering them an attractive and effective filter brand. "We should have come into the filter market with both feet," he told *The New York Times*.

To win its fair share of the filter market, American Tobacco throughout the 'Sixties launched an unprecedented number of new entries to compensate for the slipping sales of Luckies and Pall Malls. The effort seemed so frenzied at times that the industry took to calling Walker "Brand-a-Month Barney." His first attempt, while never a big hit, was the most daring and would prove the only enduring brand launched under his presidency. Debuting at the end of 1963, on the eve of the anxiously awaited report from the Surgeon General's committee, Carlton had the least tar and nicotine of any popularly available cigarette. By combining all the new technology—high-porosity paper, a dual cellulose acetate and charcoal filter, a heavy paper overwrap to secure the filter and create a longer butt, and two rows of tiny vent holes in the overwrap to allow greater air dilution of the passing smoke—AT got the Carlton yield down to 2.4 mg. of tar and 0.4 mg. of nicotine, about one-sixth of the Kent numbers. To circumvent the FTC ruling against advertising the yield numbers lest the smoking public infer a health benefit that was only wishful so far as science knew, Walker ordered the sensationally low figures to be printed on the Carlton package itself.

If rivals fumed at this bold move and its implicit concession to the rebuke that many in the industry expected to suffer momentarily from the Surgeon General, at least one vocal critic of the industry praised American Tobacco for lowering the yield numbers so dramatically. Senator Maurine Neuberger, whose new book, *Smoke Screen: Tobacco and the Public Welfare*, had denounced the tobacco industry for reaping record profits of late by "suppressing, distorting, and overcoming by psychological manipulation, the truth about smoking," introduced a bill into Congress requiring all cigarette brands to follow the Carlton lead by listing their strength on the package. More than thirty years later, by which time almost all products taken into the human body were required to carry a notice on the package listing their ingredients—unhealthful ones in particular—cigarettes remained implausibly exempt from the requirement.

VII

MIDWAY through the first gathering, on November 9, 1962, of the Surgeon General's Advisory Committee on Smoking and Health (SGAC), the panel members were treated to a bit of comic relief in the form of a new record featuring the routines of stand-up comedian Bob Newhart, who would become a bigger success later as the star of several situation-comedy shows on television. Newhart's most effective comedic device was the one-sided telephone conversation, in this case re-creating an imagined exchange between Sir Walter Raleigh, credited not entirely without foundation as the prime promoter of tobacco in England, and the nameless chief executive of a London-based importer of the New World's exotic commodities. In Newhart's inspired anachronism, the transatlantic exchange ran in part:

> Things are fine here, Walt. . . . Did we get the what? That boatload of turkeys. Yeah, they arrived fine, Walt. As a matter of fact, they're still here, Walt. They're wandering all over London as a matter of fact. . . . See, that's an American holiday, Walt. What is it this time—you got another winner for us, do ya? . . . Tobacco. What's tobacco, Walt? . . . It's a kind of leaf. And you bought eighty tons of it. Let me get this straight, Walt—you bought eighty tons of leaves. This may come as kind of a surprise to you, Walt, but come fall in England we're kind of up to our—it isn't that kind of a leaf? What is it, a special food of some kind, is it, Walt? . . . Not exactly. It has a lot of different uses. Like what are some of the uses, Walt? . . . Are you saying "snuff"? What's snuff? . . . You take a pinch of tobacco [*laughing*] and you shove it up your nose. And it makes you sneeze. I imagine it would, Walt, yeah. Goldenrod seems to do it pretty well over here. . . . It has some other uses, though. You can chew it or put it in a pipe, or you can shred it and put it on a piece of paper and roll it up and—don't tell me, Walt, don't tell me—you stick it in your ear, right, Walt? . . . Oh, between your lips? Then what do you do to it, Walt? . . . You set fire to it, Walt? Then what do you do, Walt? . . . You inhale the smoke? You know, Walt, it seems offhand that you could stand in front of your fireplace and have the same thing going for you. . . .

A laughable perversion when seen outside of its historical context, the smoking of tobacco—and of cigarettes in particular—was a deadly serious concern to that roomful of blue-ribbon scientists convened by Surgeon General Luther Terry. Although disparaged as a political appointee, selected to head the 33,000-member U.S. Public Health Service from outside the ranks of the commissioned officers' corps at the heart of the PHS, Terry brought an innate decency and the reassuring bedside manner of the old-time family physician to the task of administering fourteen government hospitals and some 200 federal institutes and programs. He had the competent administrator's essential knack of picking able assistants—in this case, his Assistant Surgeon General, James Hundley, a more severe and brighter man than himself, to serve as chief liaison with the advisory committee on smoking, and as scientific coordinator for the project that would prove Terry's monument, a young star from the officers' corps, Dr. Peter Van Vechten Hamill. Brilliant and intense, Hamill was a University of Michigan–trained chest physician with an advanced public-health degree from Hopkins, who had done useful work for the PHS in the areas of frostbite and air pollution. All three of them—Terry, Hundley, and Hamill—were serious cigarette smokers at the outset of the SGAC's deliberations, and at Hamill's suggestion, it was agreed that all of them ought to quit the habit then and there or stick with it throughout the committee's existence in order not to tip off outside observers prematurely about any emerging consensus within the study group. The same course was prescribed for the five regular smokers among the ten committee members, three of whom used cigarettes heavily and two a pipe or cigar. None of them quit until their report was completed—and indeed, several increased their tobacco intake amid the growing tension of the undertaking.

The Surgeon General insisted on one other rule of conduct: the deliberations of the advisory committee were to remain absolutely secret until their report was issued. Their subject, after all, was of surpassing interest to nearly half the adults in America and affected the very existence of a major U.S. industry. When, after his first weeks on the job, the advisory committee's staff director commented to a newspaper reporter that current knowledge on the subject "definitely suggests tobacco is a health hazard," Terry fired him before 9 a.m. the next morning. The staff director's job was added to the responsibilities already being handled by the driven and ambitious Peter Hamill.

Hamill's initial task had been to sift through the list of 200 names proposed by government and private health officials and the cigarette makers to find the ten most able and willing to serve on the committee. Their seniormost member and unofficial chairman was one of the grand old men of American medicine, Stanhope Bayne-Jones, then a seventy-four-year-old bearded savant with still twinkly eyes that made him seem a kind of Santa Claus in mufti to some of the committee's younger staff people. An eminent bacteriologist and the author of a leading textbook on that subject, Bayne-Jones had served as dean of Yale Medical School before World War II and later presided over the administrative board of New York Hospital, among the nation's top health-care facilities. "B-J," as almost everyone connected with the SGAC effort referred to him affectionately, had the intellectual toughness and openness of mind to serve as the committee's conscience, urging his colleagues—men from many varying medical specialties and of unequal intellectual acumen—to educate one another as they proceeded.

The youngest and probably most efficient committeeman was its sole Southern representative, pulmonary specialist Charles LeMaistre, a full professor by age thirty at the University of Texas's Southwestern Medical School and now, eight years later, medical director as well at Woodlawn Hospital in Dallas. Cautious in judgment and politic in manner, "Mickey" LeMaistre carried himself with an air of authority that would in subsequent years earn him the chancellorship of the entire University of Texas system and directorship of the largest U.S. cancer treatment and research center west of the Mississippi.

Perhaps the single most useful of Hamill's enlistees for the SGAC owed his selection to a decision by the Metropolitan Life Insurance Company, the nation's largest insurer, preventing its chief actuary, Mortimer Spiegelman, a pioneer in the development of life tables and the ideal choice to evaluate the population studies at the core of the medical case against smoking, from accepting the Surgeon General's invitation. But Spiegelman recommended a Harvard mathematician, William G. Cochran, whose textbook on statistics was rated among the very best and whose remarkable technical skills had been applied to solving problems in Corn Belt agronomy as well as to critical calculations for the famed Norden bombsight that had allowed pinpoint targeting by Allied aviators during World War II. A somewhat bleak Scotsman and devoted cigarette smoker, Cochran was less than overjoyed at the prospect of joining the Surgeon General's panel, but Hamill traveled to Cambridge and, beside the fireplace after a meal at the Harvard Faculty Club, succeeded in thawing the wintry Cochran. Although the only member of the committee who was neither a physician nor a Ph.D., he brought a rock-hard rigor to their joint intellectual analysis, along with an ample portion of horse sense—qualities that led one of his SGAC colleagues to say of Cochran long afterward, "He kept us honest."

Probably the most original thinker in the group was the chairman of the pathology department at the University of Pittsburgh, Emmanuel Farber, whom Hamill recalled as "a volatile little guy with a highly superior I.Q." While not a cancer specialist, Farber had undertaken experimental studies on the growth and destruction of cells which won him some keen admirers at NCI. Possessed of a sweet manner and clear mind, he was far more open than many pathologists to the uses of epidemiology and thus served the critical function of integrating the statistical and microscopic evidence before the panel.

The most disappointing performance by a committee member would be turned in by the scientist among them certainly most eminent in his field—Harvard's Louis Fieser, a towering figure in organic chemistry. The author of eight books and some 300 articles, Fieser had done pathbreaking work on vitamin K and cortisone as well as less ennobling wartime research vital to the development of napalm as an incendiary weapon. Perhaps because he was ten years past his prime, he seemed somewhat bemused by and almost indifferent to the review process engaged in by his SGAC colleagues. Nobody among them knew of his prior consulting work with Arthur D. Little, Inc., for Liggett & Myers or that he was one of the two panelists endorsed by the cigarette manufacturers.

Presumed to be as knowledgeable on the biology of cancer as Fieser was supposed to be on the carcinogenic chemistry of hydrocarbons was Columbia pathologist Jacob Furth, who rejected the committee's initial overtures but whom Hamill pursued in his New York lair. Furth, though, once captured, would turn out to be more a conciliator than a stringent critic of the evidence, leaving Hamill with the feeling that the Columbia scholar had come to the task perhaps five years too late.

The most sociable and heaviest-smoking member of the committee was University of Minnesota epidemiologist Leonard M. Schuman. A specialist in venereal diseases and other communicable afflictions, like polio, which were the original terrain of public-health investigators, Schuman was a gabby raconteur and a bit full of himself, but when finally mobilized would turn into the SGAC's workhorse in shaping consensually acceptable language for its final report. By that point, his tobacco consumption was up to two and a half packs a day. "I was such an inveterate smoker that I don't think I wanted to believe there was a relationship," Schuman remarked of the smoking and health connection. "The chance for me to review the literature was a challenge to my scientific integrity."

Staff director Hamill's eventual selection as the panel's authority on the likely effects of smoking on the intimately connected heart and lungs system was a relatively uncelebrated clinician, John. B. Hickam, chairman of Indiana University's department of internal medicine. Straightforward, knowledgeable, and conscientious, Hickam was hungry for a better understanding of the underlying mechanisms in the pathology of cardiovascular heart disease as compounded by smoking. But since the evidence took the forms primarily of statistical association and reasonable inference rather than clear pathogenic pathways, Hickam urged his colleagues not to venture beyond a statement expressing a strong suspicion that tobacco was a cardiac killer.

A far more egregious protector of the industry's interests was the second committee member to be put forward by the tobacco manufacturers—Maurice H. Seevers, chairman of the pharmacology department at the University of Michigan and an expert on habit-forming drugs. A lusty, two-fisted type fond of liquor, cigars, and bawdy jokes not always appreciated by his committee colleagues, "Mo" Seevers was, despite appearances, a complicated man who had been dean of the medical school at his university when Hamill attended it. But his former mentor disappointed the young public-health official now for what seemed an adamant refusal to consider labeling the use of tobacco as addictive behavior. The fault, if any, lay with the user, not the substance, by Seevers's reckoning.

Equally useful to the industry's defense, if unwittingly so, was the final member of the Surgeon General's committee—Walter J. Burdette, head of the surgery department at the University of Utah, ironically a state where smoking was widely frowned upon due to the precepts of the Mormon church, the dominant religious group. Perhaps the least brilliant bulb on that panel of luminaries, Burdette struck some SGAC colleagues as an opinionated and somewhat narrow-minded egoist who fancied himself an expert on genetics because he had written a book on the subject. This credential left him highly susceptible to the tobacco industry's most fervent argument—the "constitutional" theory that certain people were born prone both to smoking and to the development of lung cancer, but that the two were not necessarily causally related. Of Burdette, Hamill would later remark, "He never really understood what we were doing"—a view that also revealed Hamill's reluctance to restrict his own role to the mere gathering of materials for the committee's consideration; instead, at times he played the undesignated eleventh member of the panel, eager to exercise a shaping hand in its deliberative process.

All in all, the Surgeon General's committee was as sensible a panel of scientists not predisposed against smoking as the tobacco industry could have wished for. From the first, it was clear that the committee's basic challenge was to define its task, for discerning public-health officials understood that no truly comprehensive, critical overview had yet been attempted on the relationship of smoking to health, even though the subject had already generated some 6,000 reported studies and scholarly articles. Even the Royal College of Physicians report, issued a few months before the SGAC first met, had dealt with only a fraction of the literature, and in the view of some at the U.S. Public Health Service and on the SGAC staff, the British doctors seemed almost to have made up their minds beforehand; their findings were, at any rate, less than a meticulously argued exegesis of the case against tobacco.

The Surgeon General's panel had three choices. It could go through the motions but essentially just rubber-stamp the British report—plainly an inadequate procedure as this was the first full-fledged inquiry into the subject by appointees of the U.S. government. Or the SGAC members could farm out the review work to the Public Health Service staff and other expert consultants outside the federal bureaucracy, letting them work up reports that the committee members could then sit in judgment of and approve or modify as they saw fit. Or somehow, in a manner hard for such busy and already heavily committed men to conjure, the committee could itself do the deep thinking and investigating, albeit with ample staff support. "Many of us were naïve about the amount of time and work it would consume," said LeMaistre. It would take them six months to grasp that to do the task right—*i.e.*, not delegating the intensive scrutiny of evidence to others—would amount to what LeMaistre characterized as "a massive and overwhelming job." Yet, after considerable foot-dragging, the committee concluded that this was the only scientifically justifiable course.

The result was a consuming thirteen-month voyage of self-education and discovery. The committee sat as a whole for nine sessions, running from two to four days each, and in between there were numerous subcommittee gatherings, endless telephone communication, and many specially convened conferences, seminars, and commissioned reports involving 155 outside consultants. The immense task was necessarily parceled out to the committee members and the resulting assessments shared with the whole group. They also entertained with equal attention the findings on smoking and ciliatoxicity of industry-supported researcher Charles Kensler, "a first-rate pharmacologist who gave us a first-rate report," in Hamill's words, and the American Cancer Society–backed investigations of Oscar Auerbach, whose laboratory was visited by several SGAC members for a firsthand look at his slides of cell changes found in cigarette smokers.

The locus of the SGAC's efforts was the new National Library of Medicine, on the sprawling campus of the National Institutes of Health in Bethesda, just north of Washington. Full committee sessions were occasionally held at the Public Health Service headquarters downtown in the capital, but more typically the ten men gathered on the mezzanine of the Library of Medicine, an ultramodern structure with an odd, pagoda-like roof, or in the third subbasement of the library, where, because construction on the building had not been completed, it was possible to arrange a makeshift compound of desks, tables, filing cabinets, and partitions that enclosed a temporary clerical staff of from fifteen to thirty while typewriters clattered and copying machines hummed at all hours of the day and night. That subterranean redoubt, though inelegant and characterless—also windowless but well ventilated and thus effectively removing telltale cigarette smoke from the premises—served to isolate the committee and its working papers from the rest of the world. As committeeman Schuman remembered, they were "so removed that nobody could ever find us down there. Sometimes we felt like moles." Armed guards were stationed at the library entrances and patrolled the corridors; all committee members, their staff, and consultants had to obtain government clearance, and all the materials and internal documents generated by the study were under lock and key. These measures were aimed at preventing leaks to Wall Street, where the manipulation of tobacco stock prices might result. The hush-hush atmosphere added to the building awareness that the committee's business was of surpassing international significance.

VIII

THE proceedings of the Surgeon General's Advisory Committee on Smoking and Health were notable on three accounts—for the care its members took in examining the evidence, the quest for explicitly stated criteria in reaching their collaborative judgment, and their willingness to engage the counter-arguments put forth by spokesmen for the tobacco industry. The last of the three was essential, if any truly fair appraisal was to be reached, because even the most outspoken critics of smoking had to admit that the health case against regular tobacco use was not a single, clear scientific proposition, like a geometry theorem, but an untidy mosaic of evidence.

The SGAC staff, while striving to keep the members insulated from the industry, nevertheless welcomed the vast amounts of material that the cigarette companies provided in historical and scientific mitigation of the alleged health perils of smoking. But the committee's sense of duty went further and was perhaps best exemplified by the attentive ear that staff director Hamill gave to the industry's chief scientific representative, Clarence Little, who at seventy-five was performing his final well-paid services for the tobacco manufacturers. He was seeking assurance that the Surgeon General's panelists would take into account all the possibly confounding variables in the evidence before them. He and Hamill proceeded as wary performers, if not open antagonists, in a high drama, with Hamill recognizing what he called Little's "blind spot"—an almost dismissive attitude toward the laws of statistics and probability. "You had to see a thing happen in the laboratory to convince him it was true," Hamill recalled of their exchanges. And as a certified expert in genetics, Little carried great weight with committeeman Burdette, who was inclined at the outset to believe that smokers contracted lung cancer mainly because they were genetically programmed to do so.

The most articulate and persistent proponent of this "constitutional" theory of lung cancer causation was the British mathematician Ronald A. Fisher, who had argued throughout the 'Fifties that heavy smokers were of a distinctly different genotype from nonsmokers, whose genes in effect immunized them from the disease. In the view of the Surgeon General's panel, such a theory logically dictated that those who quit smoking or smoked a pipe or cigar—categories that registered sharply reduced rates of lung cancer—had to make up still another genotype, closer to nonsmokers than smokers in their predisposition to both the habit and the disease. Indeed, Fisher when challenged would so argue and be joined by fellow Briton Hans Eysenck, the psychologist who claimed that those who quit smoking were different psychologically and emotionally from continuing smokers. But given the glacial rate of human mutation, was it plausible that such genotypes could have evolved within just two generations, prior to which cigarettes were not in common usage and lung cancer was scarcely known among the list of diseases fatal to mankind? If lung cancer was not greatly exacerbated by the inhalation of tobacco smoke, why was the disease—and the genotype promoting it—all but nonexistent before the worldwide mass-merchandising of cigarettes?

Advocates of the constitutional theory were reduced to answering these questions by claiming that prior to the twentieth century, most people simply did not live long enough to contract lung cancer, essentially a degenerative disease, and that diagnostic techniques did not exist to recognize the disease in those who did contract it. Far more plausible to the SGAC members was the likelihood that some smokers were indeed genetically more susceptible than the rest of the population to the carcinogenic and toxic substances in tobacco smoke, but this unfortunate proneness in no way reduced the culpability of cigarettes in inducing disease—quite the opposite in the case of those who, not knowing their genetic makeups, indulged in the habit. By the same token, those whose genetically determined personalities made them likely to take up smoking may indeed have been betrayed by their genetic constitutions—for it was the smoke, not the genes, that served as the pathological agent.

Far more resistant to dismissal than the theories of Fisher and Eysenck, contrarians who availed themselves of research grants and consulting fees from the tobacco industry, were the relentless objections raised over the course of a dozen years to the findings of the population studies on smoking by the chief of biostatistics at the famed Mayo Clinic in Minnesota. Joseph V. Berkson, a bouncy, combative, highly excitable man whose wiry red hair seemed to grow more vivid as he charged that there were methodological flaws in the findings of heightened risk of disease and death from smoking, had to be taken seriously because he was widely recognized as a first-rate mathematician on the staff of one of the nation's most highly regarded diagnostic centers. Hospital patients, Berkson argued, were self-selected populations, choosing their medical-care facilities in accord with their symptoms and presumed causes; the diagnoses they received were thus far more likely to be compromised by circumstances. A thoracic surgeon, therefore, confronted by lung cancer in a smoker was prone to assume that the tumor was primary when in fact it might well have metastasized from another site, where its origin might in no way have been linked to the victim's smoking habit. In fact, such a misdiagnosis occurred perhaps in one case out of twenty, and the reverse mistaken diagno-

sis—*i.e.*, labeling as primary a tumor at a distant site that had actually originated in the lung—likely occurred about as often, thus nullifying the argument.
But this did not dissuade Berkson.

When, partly in response to Berkson's constructive carping, the prospective
studies on smoking were launched, drawing on a vast population of subjects
who were not only outside of hospitals but also ostensibly in good health at the
time, Berkson continued to rail against the dependability of the results. The cohorts were not randomly selected, he insisted, and reflected the biases of the
volunteer interviewers, who may unwittingly have signed up a disproportionately high number of sick smokers or of well nonsmokers, thus skewing the results. He also insisted that the massive study undertaken by Cuyler Hammond
at the American Cancer Society was of limited value because it failed to take
into consideration other health habits and factors in the subjects' histories besides smoking. Some in the biostatistical field whispered that Berkson was envious of the acclaim greeting Hammond, perhaps a less gifted mathematician,
who had been a subordinate of his while both were working for Army Air
Force intelligence during World War II. Whatever the motive, Berkson sustained a drumbeat of naysaying as the statistical evidence piled ever higher. At
Mayo Clinic staff meetings he would rail that the ACS smoking studies and
others like them "proved too much" (*i.e.*, blamed smoking for being causally
linked with too many diseases) and were based on "a spurious statistical phenomenon." In the *British Medical Journal* in 1959, Berkson began sounding
like the tobacco industry's scientific spokesman, Clarence Little, as he argued
that before the case against smoking could be conclusively established, it was
essential for scientists first to understand "the physiobiological factors which
are involved and how they operate." By mid-1963, as the Surgeon General's
committee was hard at its task, Berkson was still writing in *The Cancer Bulletin* that the case against smoking was built on "a statistical fallacy"; he then
added, almost spitefully in the face of massive evidence to the contrary, "Even
strong contenders of the smoking-lung cancer theory no longer believe that
the cancer is produced by carcinogens . . . contained in tobacco smoke. . . .
The whole fabric of the original theory has broken down and virtually been
abandoned."

Berkson tirelessly tried to press these views on the Surgeon General's committee, asking repeatedly to appear before the panel and frequently telephoning its nearest member, Leonard Schuman, eighty miles away from the Mayo
Clinic at his University of Minnesota office in Minneapolis. "I'd listen to his
tirades for a while and then drop a hint that this was costing a lot of money,"
Schuman recalled, "but Joe would say, 'That's okay, I've got a WATS line.' "
Berkson's views were so well known to the SGAC and had been so satisfactorily repudiated by others that the committee members had no further interest in
having him lobby them in person. "Berkson and Fisher were discussed at great

length," SGAC member Emmanuel Farber remembered, "with seriousness and respect," but for all Berkson's vehemence, his views were unpersuasive—except with his colleagues in the biometry department at the University of Minnesota, where he taught, and at the Mayo Clinic, where he was lionized as brilliant, entirely honorable, and right on the smoking question.

The twenty-nine major retrospective and seven prospective population studies on smoking and health that Berkson had found fatally flawed were of the essence to the investigation undertaken by the Surgeon General's committee, and especially to its stellar mathematician, William Cochran of Harvard. The dour Scotsman intently scrutinized this mountain range of data and undertook cumulative computations after transforming their statistical findings into common coinage. The task was complicated by the widely varying sizes of the groups sampled and the categories of data collected in each study, but there was no gainsaying what SGAC staff director Hamill characterized as "the uncanny consistency" of the thirty-six studies. Collectively, they formed a large central core of data, like three dozen overlapping circles of different sizes and textures. To avoid top-weighting the biggest of the seven prospective studies in calculating a cumulative mortality ratio, Cochran gave each study equal standing, arranged their death rates in ascending order, and settled on the median, or fourth one on the list, as the standard for the lot; thus, the death rate from lung cancer for smokers was found overall to be 10.8 times as high as that for nonsmokers—a ratio of overwhelming significance.

"He generated excitement by the rigor of his discussion," Mickey LeMaistre recalled of Cochran's explications in the SGAC skull sessions, the Scotsman's burr thickening as he got caught up in his presentment. "He gave us confidence," added Emmanuel Farber. But what was of overriding importance to the committee was, as Hamill would later put it, "There is no major finding in the whole corpus of work in smoking research that is of an acceptable quality and jars or is discordant—that flies in the face of the main body of findings." The closest thing to such an anomalous piece of evidence was a finding in the first Doll-Hill retrospective study of London hospital patients that self-reported inhalers of cigarette smoke had a slightly lower lung cancer rate than smokers who said they did not inhale. This finding was contradicted in three subsequent studies and was likely mitigated by the ambiguous wording in the original Doll-Hill questionnaire, which asked its subjects, "Did you inhale—that is, take the smoke deeply into the lungs?" That qualifying adverb "deeply," some public-health investigators speculated, may have made the smoking habit seem foolhardy, so that many inhalers simply denied doing so. At best, calibrating the degree of inhalation is a tricky business, more subjective than objective, and at any rate, almost every smoker inhales, intentionally or not.

If the statistical association between smoking and damaged health was found to be overwhelming, the SGAC's next key challenge was to define the criteria for determining whether the undeniable association was causal in nature. What they were after was a set of standards comparable to the postulates set out by Robert Koch, the famed nineteenth-century German bacteriologist, in determining the causative agent in such contagious diseases as typhus, tuberculosis, anthrax, and Asiatic cholera in a period when such single-cause diseases exacted a ravaging toll on humanity. But in the case of chronic, multicausal killers like cancer and heart disease, formulating the criteria to determine the most prominent contributory agents was a far more complex challenge.

To help Leonard Schuman, the SGAC's epidemiologist, frame the case for causality by testing the statistical association as rigorously as possible, Hamill spirited him and Cochran away for a few days of concentrated brainstorming in the tonic atmosphere of Saratoga Springs in mid-June of 1963. The three were joined by two of the nation's most respected epidemiologists, the University of Pennsylvania's Johannes Ipson and the dean of the University of California's School of Public Health, Reul A. Stallones. After much shooting of pool and talking shop, the little group had its final dinner together, wreathed in smoke from all their cigarettes, and at the end it was Stallones, a witty companion and incisive thinker, who pulled it all together. The question before them had been what criteria had to be met before medical science could conclude that the statistical case against smoking as the prime cause of lung cancer had been proven. "This is what I think we've been talking about," Stallones said and, taking an empty pack of Luckies from his pocket and tearing it apart, scrawled on the inside surface of the wrapper: "The consistency of the statistical association, the strength of the association, specificity of the association, and the coherence of the association."

The consistency of the association was beyond dispute, Berkson's mad-dog objections aside. Despite the differences in the sizes of the sampled cohorts, their whereabouts, their social customs and economic status, and the purity or impurity of the air they breathed, the findings were uncannily similar. And the strength of the association was no mere 20 or 30 percent higher for smokers than nonsmokers but on the order of fifty to sixty times higher than that, and even more for the heaviest smokers—a magnitude made all the more persuasive by the dose-response data (*i.e.*, the more one smoked, the greater the chance of contracting lung cancer). The specificity of the association, meaning the precision with which one element in an associated pair (smoking and lung cancer) can be depended upon to predict the occurrence of the other, was of particular concern because lung cancer *did* occur, in twelve to fifteen cases out of one hundred, in nonsmokers while it did *not* strike the majority of smokers—or, to put it another way, it had not struck them at the time of their deaths from some other cause. But since the risk ratio was more than ten times higher in smokers, to attribute lung cancer to another causative factor would have required its presence in a comparably high ratio (and its absence in nonsmokers); no such factors were ever demonstrated by the defenders of tobacco. The specificity argument was also enhanced when the dose-response factor was more closely examined: it was not only how much one smoked that raised one's lung cancer risk but how early one began to smoke and how long one kept at it.

Finally, as to the coherence of the association, the committee members had to be satisfied that the statistical case was of a piece with the known facts in the natural history and biology of the diseases as well as environmental and social considerations. For Leonard Schuman, the coherence criterion required determining, for example, upon finding that blue-collar workers suffered more from lung cancer than other groups, whether they in fact smoked more heavily as well. They did. Similarly, if women got the disease a good deal less than men, did they in fact smoke fewer cigarettes a day than men, inhale less, leave longer butts, and as a group begin the habit in earnest several decades later in the century than men had? They did. And if Britons got more lung cancer than Americans but smoked fewer cigarettes per day, did they smoke them further down the butt, where the toxic materials collected in intensified strength, possibly because each fag they drew on was far more heavily taxed than the American cigarette? They did. It was all of a piece.

In the wake of such a searching analysis, as detailed in the SGAC report, to dismiss the case against smoking as "merely statistical" was a preposterous denial of reason itself. The numbers, hard logic, and human experience behind them fused to build a conclusive case.

I X

T HE Surgeon General's panel had only one lingering concern about the population studies indicting smoking as the most prominent cause of lung cancer. Cuyler Hammond's results in his big American Cancer Society study seemed almost too perfect. And Hammond himself did not help much by evidencing what the SGAC panel and its staff felt to be a rigid personality and a highly controlling attitude toward sharing the backup materials for his announced results. "He spoke as if he were God, without any doubts about the accuracy of his studies," Peter Hamill recounted. "And he spoke as he wrote, as if life were predigested and predetermined."

Pathologist Emmanuel Farber, while enthralled with the stringent analysis by his committee colleague William Cochran of Hammond's numbers and those in the other studies, nevertheless wanted to see the supporting clinical evidence for himself. That insistence drew him, Cochran, and Hamill to the East Orange, New Jersey, laboratory of Oscar Auerbach for two days of inspecting the slides that the VA pathologist had painstakingly assembled over seven years and that showed severe changes in the lung cells of smokers. The hovering Auerbach, his mass of work under intense scrutiny now, struck the visitors as inarticulate, obsessive, and opinionated, though hardly close-minded, as Hammond was thought to be. But after two days, the second one beginning at 4:30 a.m and ending at 10 p.m., Farber concluded that his fellow pathologist was honest, dedicated, and very careful in his microscopic tissue examination. The inference to be drawn from Auerbach's massive studies disclosing the grim cellular metamorphosis in smokers was unmistakable. Comparable cell changes found in experimental animals dosed with smoke were enough to compensate, most SGAC members felt, for the failure to produce frank, metastasized tumors in the animals, which frequently died first from other toxins in the smoke. The case against smoking as the chief perpetrator of lung cancer was closed, and two of Auerbach's microphotos were borrowed for inclusion in the committee's report, along with extensive citation of his findings.

Whatever uneasiness may have remained over the almost too precise symmetry of Hammond's earlier study was routed in the late fall of 1963 as the SGAC knuckled down to committing its judgment to writing. After thirty-four months, Hammond's second massive population study under the ACS banner—this one involving 1,078,894 men and women, with a 99 percent follow-up rate—had progressed sufficiently to allow the preliminary results to be rushed to the Surgeon General's committee. Beyond its unprecedented size, what distinguished this project, known as Cancer Prevention Study No. 1 (CPS-I) to epidemiologists, was the way in which Hammond had designed it to counter the criticism of Berkson and others that the first ACS population study was based only on the factors of smoking, age, and residence. This time, using a computer, Hammond matched some 37,000 pairs of subjects, each composed of a smoker and a nonsmoker of a comparable age and otherwise identical or very similar with regard to two dozen possibly confounding factors, including height, weight, race, national origin, marital status, drinking, sleeping, dietary and exercise habits, longevity of parents and grandparents, and occurrence of cancer in other family members.

In Hammond's paired subsampling, 1,385 of the smokers had died after nearly three years of follow-up, compared with only 662 of the nonsmokers. And in every category examined, whether the subjects had been tall or short, white or black, married or single, those who smoked a pack of cigarettes a day or more died of lung cancer at an appreciably higher rate. The overall risk for the disease among Hammond's huge sample was nearly eleven times higher than that for nonsmokers, or almost exactly the median figure that Cochran had calculated in his cumulative computations for the seven prior prospective studies.

This last-minute infusion of clinching data only added to the advisory committee's unanimous finding on lung cancer. From the first, their hope had been to issue a single consensual document, and that sentiment had grown over the course of their deliberations even as certain irreconcilable differences among them surfaced. All of them conceded that a minority report would emasculate the whole effort. "It was a matter of credibility," recalled Leonard Schuman, who did more of the writing than any other committeeman. "We didn't want to be second-guessed, and a minority report would have invited that, with people saying, 'See, even they had their doubts and misgivings.' "

As a result, the SGAC's 387-page report had to omit certain judgments that a majority but not all of its members would have endorsed. Every nuanced word was reviewed scrupulously, assuring the most cautious possible language consistent with the evidence. Thus, the panel's single most indicting judgment read: "Cigarette smoking is causally related to lung cancer in men; the magnitude of the effect of cigarette smoking far outweighs all other factors. The data for women, though less extensive, point in the same direction." With regard to the cardiovascular peril posed by tobacco, the committee would go no further than to state: "Although the causative role of cigarette smoking in deaths from coronary disease is not proven, the Committee considers it more prudent from the public health viewpoint to assume that the established association has causative meaning than to suspend judgment until no uncertainty remains." Indeed, such an assumption was the central thrust of the entire document, which was and could be no more than an interim judgment, not a conclusive statement about a subject in which science was constantly generating new evidence. Science, as embodied by the Surgeon General's learned committee, was saying to the smoking public, "Better safe than sorry."

For all its collegiality, the SGAC had to settle two substantive clashes within its ranks as the writing proceeded. One involved a disagreement between its two youngest members, LeMaistre and Farber. The former, in charge of drafting the chapter on the effects of smoking on chronic obstructive lung diseases, was satisfied that cigarette smoking was the most important cause of bronchitis, triggering both the inflammation of the bronchial walls that reduced air flow and the hypersecretion of mucus that caused chronic smoker's cough. But the case against emphysema was a tougher call, even though some 80 to 85 percent of the cases occurred in smokers. Farber thought the evidence was sufficiently clear-cut to call the connection causal, and his concern was intensified by the belief that emphysema was "a far worse sort of disease than lung cancer." The latter struck down its victims generally within a few years of their turning symptomatic, but with emphysema "you choke to death for twenty years."

Little mystery remained about the dysfunctional nature of emphysema, the term applied to the destruction or loss of elasticity of the walls of the alveoli, the tiny air sacs at the end of the bronchioles where the body exchanges carbon dioxide, its chief gaseous waste matter, for life-fueling oxygen. The irreparable damage was rarely discovered until some 60 percent or more of the alveoli were gone, producing chronic shortage of breath and the eventual choking sensation. But just how tobacco smoke broke down the alveoli could only be theorized at the time. One theory held that some toxic substance in smoke turned the macrophages, scavenger lung cells that normally thrived on foreign matter not trapped in the mucus and expelled from the body by the beat of the cilia, into cannibals that devoured the alveolar walls. A second theory posited a smoking-induced imbalance of enzymes in the bronchial cavity which destroyed the elastic nature of the alveolar walls, causing them to rupture when the air pressure got too high. "My opinion was clear," LeMaistre recounted, "but the corroborative evidence—the proof—was simply not there yet. . . . We had to put credibility first, not our personal beliefs." Thus was the reach of the SGAC report shortened in order, as LeMaistre later put it, "to meet the body of evidence then available—it had to conform to what we felt we could justify." Accordingly, and despite Farber's fury that LeMaistre was being overly cautious, the consensual language read, "A relationship exists between cigarette smoking and emphysema but it has not been established that the relationship is causal." A mellower Farber would concede nearly three decades later that LeMaistre had probably been right.

A more serious clash developed after committee members read Walter Burdette's draft of chapter 9, which dealt with cancer and would make up one-third of the final version of the report. Burdette, the nonsmoking surgeon from tobacco-hating Utah, angered his heavy-smoking colleague, Leonard Schuman, by larding the key chapter with material on the genetics of cancer, inferentially lending substance to the constitutional theory of lung disease favored by the tobacco industry and its apologists while shortchanging the hard epidemiological, chemical, biological, and clinical evidence. If the victims of cancer—bronchial along with other kinds—were foreordained from birth, then environmental and behavioral factors like cigarette smoking were beside the point. To the outraged Schuman, who stopped smoking soon after the SGAC report was issued, this was close to quackery. He told the top staff people and the Surgeon General's office that he would part company with the committee if the punch was to be pulled so blatantly. Burdette, at first supercilious in his response to the criticism, was diplomatically massaged by the staff until he conceded that perhaps he had not taken into account the full range of evidence.

Schuman was invited to redraft the chapter; his version, as fine-tuned by others on the panel and editors from the Public Health Service staff, became the centerpiece of the report.

But neither Schuman nor other uneasy committee members could do anything to sway the judgment put forward by Maurice Seevers, the pharmacologist among them, in his chapter on the possible addictive nature of tobacco. Without a psychologist or other specialist in human behavior on board, there was no panel member with the credentials to combat Seevers, whom Schuman remembered as "one tough hombre". To Seevers, addiction meant an overpowering desire to continue using a drug, a tendency or need to keep increasing the dose, a physical dependency, withdrawal symptoms that could be life-threatening, and the user's willingness "to obtain it by any means"—a none too thinly veiled reference to antisocial acts like robbery to pay for the habit. The alternative term, habituation—which was how Seevers characterized cigarette smoking—did not involve constantly escalating dosages, implied a psychological rather than physical dependency that could be rather more easily broken, and was not associated with antisocial acts. This last observation, Seevers's text failed to acknowledge, may have been valid with respect to cigarette-craving because the product was cheap, ubiquitous, and legal, none of which was true for most drugs acknowledged to be addictive. Instead, Seevers repeated the standard psychiatric view of the day: that addiction was "based upon serious personality defects from underlying psychologic or psychiatric disorders which may become manifest in other ways if the drugs are removed." How, then, could smoking be branded as addictive unless the SGAC was prepared to ascribe "serious personality defects" to nearly half the adults in America?

A more measured analysis of the addictive hold of cigarettes might have found that some smokers were able to quit cold-turkey while others trying to do so suffered long and painfully in a variety of ways and eventually gave up, with most would-be quitters falling somewhere in between—the difference depended possibly as much on the pharmacological hold and behavioral conditions of the habit as on any flaw of character or want of willpower on the part of the smoker. But Seevers would not entertain any such nuances. "None of us were well versed enough in the field to pass judgment on his judgment," Schuman recounted in explaining the committee's deference to Seevers. "He was cocky enough to impose his view on us without ever once conceding, 'This is a controversial area,' or that the weight of the evidence is such-and-such." Thus, smoking was decreed a habit, not an addiction, and the tobacco industry was rewarded for its championing of Seevers as a member of the Surgeon General's elite panel.

What emerged, finally, was a highly detailed, closely reasoned, but far from combative report, that was substantially compromised. Understated and embodying the lowest common denominator of agreement among them, the report nonetheless offered as its final finding, "Cigarette smoking is a health hazard of sufficient importance in the United States to warrant appropriate remedial action." With eloquent simplicity, the social challenge was put forth, but there was not a word about what form such a remedy might take. That was left, for the time being, to the politicians, who were in no hurry to address the consequences of a custom, however self-destructive, that so many of their constituents clung to fiercely.

X

A s the advisory committee's report to the Surgeon General was being assembled under conditions of extreme secrecy in the closing months of 1963, public and industry speculation about the contents intensified. At the committee's makeshift headquarters in the bowels of the National Library of Medicine, pestering inquiries from the outside were mounting by the day, along with staff tension as the drama grew amid that swirl of underground activity. "It was almost a Manhattan Project mentality," recalled John T. Walden, brought in during the late stages of the work to help edit the report and head up the arrangements to reveal it to the public. The armed guards were instructed to be more vigilant; an editor who leaked some of the findings to *Newsweek* was summarily dismissed; and Surgeon General Luther Terry was more visible now, outwardly affable as always but his eyes on red alert. The momentous nature of the pending report was not lost on any of the SGAC staffers, including their youngest member, Donald Shopland, a high school student who smoked two packs of Pall Malls a day while working as a stockboy and gofer. "We were all aware of the scientific and political implications," recalled Shopland, who would quit smoking as soon as the report was issued, drop out of school, and devote his career as a federal employee to fighting cigarettes as a health peril.

The report, for all its urgency, could not be rushed unduly, for it would prove, in that era before computerized word-processing, a highly complex printing job, impossible to complete with the mandatory care before the year was out. While the report included a synopsis and boldface type to make its more important passages accessible to laymen, it was in fact a highly technical document. Chapter 8 alone, on the mortality of smokers, contained thirty tables set in agate type; chapter 9, on cancer, running 136 pages, cited 396 studies as its sources, including 21 attributed to Ernst Wynder and his associates, the most credited to any single investigator in the field. The type was composed behind a fenced section of the U.S. Government Printing Office, where the printers were used to dealing with sensitive federal documents, and the chapters were sent separately to outside peer-reviewers, so that no one beyond the committee and its staff ever saw the document as a whole until it was made public.

The whole world discovered those contents on the morning of Saturday, January 11, 1964, when some 200 members of the press were admitted to the State Department auditorium, the same room in which President Kennedy, slain less than two months earlier, had been questioned on the smoking issue, and were handed the 150,000-word report by the Surgeon General's advisory committee. A Saturday was chosen for the press conference to minimize the impact of the report on the stock markets and to maximize its coverage in the Sunday papers. What the reporters read was the language of cautious, prudent scientists who were convinced by the converging lines of evidence that "many kinds of damage to body functions and to organs, cells and tissues occur more frequently and severely in smokers" than in those who abstained.

To rebuke the tobacco industry's contention that no carcinogenic substance had yet been found in cigarettes in sufficient quantity to be held responsible for lung cancer, the report noted that (1) seven cancer-causing compounds had thus far been found in a heavy enough concentration to arouse concern; (2) these compounds were so volatile that perhaps half of their potency was vitiated during the fractionation and purification process used to measure them, suggesting that they were likely present in heavier amounts than scientific instruments could calibrate; and (3) "Whether there is a threshold for effective dosage of a carcinogenic agent is controversial at the present time," meaning that nobody could tell for certain, regardless of the tobacco industry's reassurance to the contrary, how small a dose of a cancer-causing substance was enough to plant the disease. As to the crucial microscopic findings by Oscar Auerbach, on whose exhaustive studies the committee relied heavily, the report concluded that "some of the advanced epithelial lesions with many atypical cells, as seen in the bronchi of cigarette smokers, are probably pre-malignant."

Unlike other prior inquiries, the report to the Surgeon General gave the tobacco industry at least brief consideration of the possible benefits of smoking. It seemed to promote "good intestinal tone and bowel habits," *i.e.*, had laxative effects, and served to counter obesity, but these were scarcely adequate to counterbalance the "significant health hazard" posed by cigarettes. And while smoking appeared useful to stimulate smokers when fatigued or to calm and sedate them when tense or excited, the cigarette was found to be predominantly a tranquilizing agent—but it was impossible to determine with any objectivity whether smoking "induces pleasure by creating euphoria or by relieving dysphoria." The report had the grace—or bad manners, depending on one's perspective—to note the utility of cigarettes for "a large fraction of the American population to satisfy the total need of the individual for a psychological crutch."

Press coverage of the panel's report was immense and accepting. The nation's foremost daily, *The New York Times*, called the findings by the committee "a severe blow to the rear-guard action fought in recent years by the tobacco industry. It dismisses, one by one, the arguments raised to question the validity of earlier studies." The New York *Herald Tribune*'s astute science writer, Earl Ubell, in the paper's leading story headlined "It's Official— Cigarette Smoking Can Kill You," found the report "far harsher than anticipated" and said that it emphatically shifted "the burden of disproof" to the industry. The Washington *Post* gave the story top billing but provided tobacco industry spokesmen almost as much front-page space to answer the charges. Perhaps the most obtuse—or at least industry-friendly—coverage in the popular press ran in *Newsweek*, which wrote that the report, while exhaustive, "carefully buried the argument that the evidence . . . is largely statistical." Rather than burying that criticism, the report had by any standard met and massively rebutted it.

The immediate response by the tobacco industry and its allies varied from moderate to shamelessly dismissive. The Tobacco Institute's George Allen was the most guarded spokesman, saying that the report deserved and would get careful study but hardly constituted the last word on the subject. At the other extreme was Howard Cullman, president of Cullman Brothers and the Tobacco Merchants Association, a board director of Philip Morris, and uncle of Joseph Cullman, that company's president. Like an obstinate envoy from the Flat-Earth Society spurning the survivors of Magellan's crew on returning from their round-the-world voyage, Cullman asserted, "We don't accept the idea that there are harmful agents in tobacco." Dr. Kenneth Lynch, then chairing the Tobacco Industry Research Committee's scientific advisory board, nicely encapsulated the bias of his region by trivializing the SGAC report as mostly epidemiological and claiming "some kind of an association between any and all of these [pathological] conditions and the use of tobacco. But what it means, nobody knows. Such diseases can occur without any use, or exposure to use, of tobacco." Terry Sanford, governor of North Carolina, the leading tobacco-producing state, called the report "a review of previously existing evidence, none of which is conclusive and much of which is based on statistical studies."

In fact, the careful, temperate, and comprehensive report of the Surgeon General's panel had but one glaring fault—an omission that was never admitted or subsequently corrected. At the press conference following the release of the report, Assistant Surgeon General James Hundley commented that "there was not enough evidence to make a judgment that filters do any good." But this almost casual remark skimmed over a central fact of all the population studies: The elevated mortality rates of smokers, so neatly corresponding to dose-response measurements, were entirely or largely based upon the use of pre-filter cigarettes. During the five years prior to the report, the industry had reduced the tar and nicotine yields of the filter brands by an average of 40 percent; half the smoking population, moreover, was now using filter brands.

When U.S. Senator Sherman Cooper from Kentucky, the No. 2 tobacco state, wrote the Surgeon General two days after the report was issued to point out this potentially significant shortcoming, Terry backed away from Hundley's airy comment at the press conference. It was erroneous to conclude from the report, the Surgeon General wrote Cooper, that cigarette filters had no effect; indeed, filters then in common use "do remove a variable portion of the tars and nicotines. . . . [T]he committee felt that developing better filters or more selective filters is a promising avenue for further development." But he did not concede the key point—that nobody knew with any certainty whether the product had been modified sufficiently by its manufacturers to negate the whole thrust of the advisory committee's report. Cigarettes with a filter that was more than cosmetic simply had not been on the market long enough for epidemiologists to conduct a meaningful population study—and the better part of another generation would be required before the mortality rates of those who smoked high-filtration brands exclusively could be calculated. In fact, such a study has never been made in the three decades since the original report to the Surgeon General, doubtless because the public-health community has long since considered the case against cigarettes conclusively proven. That the preponderance of the evidence strongly supports that judgment does not alter the validity of the objection that the bedrock statistical data used in reaching that judgment stemmed largely from a product—the unfiltered cigarette— swiftly going out of use at the time of the first Surgeon General's report. The industry elected to protest only meekly at the time; a more vigorous denunciation would likely have been taken as the companies' tacit acceptance of the SGAC's findings with regard to unfiltered cigarettes, as well as an undemonstrable health claim for the filter brands that might have invited the Federal Trade Commission's wrath. In hindsight, the decision not to make a major point of the possible efficacy of the filter was probably one of the industry's two worst mistakes in dealing with the health issue. The other was its insistence on reflexively and incessantly denying every shred of scientific evidence against it, in the process insulting the intelligence of smokers and nonsmokers alike.

At the close of its business, one member of the Surgeon General's committee acted in a way he would live to regret soon thereafter. When asked at the panel's press conference whether he still smoked and what brand, Louis Fieser, who continued to consume four packs of cigarettes a day despite a chronic cough and poor sleeping habits, believing that tobacco would surely have done him in already if he was fated to succumb to it, replied, "I still smoke Larks, the cigarette with the activated charcoal filter." Ten days later, he told the *Harvard Crimson*, the undergraduate daily at his university, that the Lark filter "represents a definite encouraging advance." In neither case did Fieser reveal a conflict of interest stemming from his position as a consultant to Arthur D. Little, Inc., and through that firm to Liggett & Myers, makers of the Lark. His endorsement of the product under such circumstances was ethically reprehensible. Less than two years later he was operated on for a tumor in his right lung; heart disease, bronchitis, and emphysema were also discovered to be present.

A few months after surviving his surgery and finally casting cigarettes aside, Fieser wrote in *Reader's Digest*, the world's most doggedly antitobacco publication, "Perhaps my experience will convince others that *the time to quit smoking is now!*" (italics in original text). For his belated repentance, the Lord—and an amazingly durable constitution—let Louis Fieser live another eleven years, to the age of seventy-seven. His chemistry textbook, as co-edited by his widow, continues in print as of this writing.

9

Marlboro Mirage

IN CALLING for "appropriate remedial action" to correct the immense insult to Americans' collective health as a result of their long affair with the cigarette, the Surgeon General's learned advisory committee had not suggested what form that massive dose of medicine might take or who should administer it.

Plainly the tobacco industry itself was not about to undertake sweeping reforms in its way of doing business unless compelled to—it was making too much money for that, and in America making money ranked as an exalted social good. Cigarettes, moreover, had taken hold as a mass consumer product and socially acceptable habit more than a full generation *before* their adverse health effects were authoritatively established. To urge the nation, as its official policy, to abandon or even curb the smoking habit was to expect a display of iron self-discipline among close to 70 million of its citizens and of nearly divine altruism among those who thrived economically off tobacco—including 300,000 stockholders and perhaps six times as many farmers, factory workers, shopkeepers, innkeepers, and restaurateurs, as well as closely affiliated beneficiaries like those in the broadcasting business, which derived 10 percent of its advertising revenues from cigarette manufacturers.

Tobacco's hold extended even to those whom society expected to serve as its prime preceptors in matters of health and hygiene. Doctors, especially those who indulged themselves, hesitated to prescribe abstinence to their patients, partly out of fear of offending and thereby losing them, just as the American Cancer Society, the nonpareil among private voluntary health agencies, would

not risk its survival by too harsh an assault against the tobacco menace for fear
it would anger contributors who smoked. Even schoolteachers who had just
finished a lecture to their pupils on the evils of smoking often beelined to the
faculty lounge for a cigarette break.

The dilemma facing antismoking advocates was aptly noted by British
scholar Thomas McKeown in his book *The Role of Medicine*, in which he argued that the healing sciences would prove far more efficient if they devoted
themselves to preventing rather than treating diseases. Mankind's most destructive habits, McKeown wrote, "commonly begin as pleasures of which we
have no need and end as necessities in which we have no pleasure. Nonetheless we tend to resent the suggestion that anyone should try to change them,
even on the disarming grounds that they do so for our own good." Indeed, only
a generation earlier the United States had witnessed, in the form of the Eighteenth Amendment, the travesty of mandated abstinence from alcoholic beverages, a scourge then viewed as no less debilitating than cigarettes were now
said to be. The lesson of Prohibition seemed clear to all: it was one thing to
condemn a vice and quite another to try to eliminate it by unenforceable laws.
Government, the American masses perceived, did not exist to perfect human
nature.

But it could, at least, instruct the citizenry. And there were clear precedents
for governmental measures against disease-causing agents of epidemic proportion—as smoking had now been judged by the report to the Surgeon General.
Most commonly, these measures of disease control were undertaken before the
precise pathogenic mechanisms were fully understood—smallpox, typhus, pel-
lagra, and poliomyelitis, for examples, were all best combated not by treatment
but by prevention. If smoking could not be outlawed, its practice could surely
be discouraged by governmental policies. But someone would have to adopt
and implement them, and the collective might of the tobacco business stood in
the way.

The national political muscle exercised by the cigarette companies and their
allies was rivaled only by that of the oil and textile industries; no others were
so compactly concentrated in geopolitical terms. Tobacco, while grown in 12
percent of the 435 U.S. congressional districts in the early 'Sixties, was king in
just two dozen of them spread among just six states. In North Carolina, some
47 percent of cash receipts from farm commodities was produced by tobacco;
in Kentucky, the comparable figure was 40 percent; in South Carolina, 25 percent; and in Virginia, 19 percent—numbers that served wonderfully to concentrate the attention of those states' congressional representatives. Furthering the
industry's strength was Washington's legislative seniority system under which
one-third of the chairmen of the standing House committees and one-fourth of
the Senate committees came from the six leading tobacco states, where conservative Democrats had controlled the political machinery for more than a cen-

tury, except during the Reconstruction period. The tobacco bloc, in defense of its realm, enjoyed a natural affinity with other Southern lawmakers, who tended to unite in matters of regional concern, and with congressional Republicans, by and large pro-business and anti-governmental intervention—except when protecting, indeed subsidizing, the farmers in the G.O.P.-dominated Midwest. Northern liberals partial to government efforts to ameliorate pressing social problems found themselves susceptible to tobacco-state congressmen willing to trade off their votes on measures they would ordinarily oppose but were dear to liberal hearts—like urban renewal funding—in return for keeping government regulators away from the cigarette business. As consumer advocate Ralph Nader commented, "Any group of really cohesive congressmen can have disproportionate power like the tobacco bloc . . . [and become] a proverbial battering ram, saying in effect to their colleagues, 'This is our particular bailiwick, and if you ever want us to defer to you someday, you'd better go along with us on this issue.' "

Tobacco's sway was no less apparent in the White House, where Lyndon Johnson had become the first President from a state of the old Confederacy since the antebellum era (not counting Wilson, a transplanted Virginian). Johnson was much in need of votes from his fellow Southerners to put across his ambitious social programs, including the broadening of civil rights, medical care for the elderly, and a war on poverty—none of them issues likely to stir an outpouring of affection in Dixie. A heavy smoker himself until he suffered a serious heart attack while serving as Senate majority leader in 1955 and was ordered by his doctors to quit the habit, the President told reporters a few months after the Surgeon General's panel had reported, "I've missed it [smoking] every day, but I haven't gone back on it, and I'm glad that I haven't." He would say no more about the subject throughout his five years in office. In this respect President Johnson was no different from any other political officeholder who avoids antagonizing those he does not have to among the electorate, about 40 percent of whom were smokers at this time.

It was not without justification, then, two months before the Surgeon General's committee recommended remedial action on the smoking problem, that *Advertising Age*'s Washington columnist, Stanley Cohen, wrote that suppression of the tobacco industry by the political process would prove "a painful and thankless assignment" representing "one of the most difficult regulatory challenges ever faced by government and industry." The first serious effort nonetheless began almost at once and came from a thoroughly unlikely source—one of the government's most torpid backwaters.

II

As the scientific evidence against it gathered throughout the 1950s, the tobacco industry did not merely deny, dispute, and mock it as a defensive
strategy; it also spent heavily on advertising as its prime offensive weapon to
convince its customers that the product was well worth any risk that might accompany their use of it. In achieving a 30 percent rise in unit sales during the
decade, the tobacco companies nearly tripled their advertising and promotional
outlays—a trend that continued into the 'Sixties. True, the Federal Trade Commission had acted to halt the industry's explicit health claims and most offensive innuendos, but it seemed disinclined to stay the hand of Madison
Avenue's dream-spinners, so adept at making cigarettes desirable by portraying them in words and pictures as pleasure-producing, compatible with physical well-being and fitness, and conducive if not indispensable to professional,
social, and sexual success—without the merest hint to the consumer of the serious health hazards of smoking.

This omission struck the tobacco industry's detractors as precisely the sort
of deceptive advertising practice against which the FTC had been authorized to
act by Congress in the 1938 expansion of its powers. Such a failure to disclose
pertinent characteristics of the product was no less of a deception than false
claims in its behalf—and seemed especially regrettable now, in the immediate
wake of the judgment by the Surgeon General's committee. But just what initiatives the FTC could take on its own in such cases had not been clearly
spelled out by Congress, nor was the FTC, by its nature, history, and dependency on the lawmakers for its financial lifeblood, inclined to strike out boldly
on its own.

Given its own limitation of time, personnel, and expertise, Congress turned
increasingly to the "independent, quasi-judicial regulatory agencies" it had
created to shape rules and regulations interpreting how federal statutes were to
be applied to the business community, especially in technical matters. This
arrangement was working well enough where Congress had established regulatory bodies with watchdog authority over specific industries, as in the cases
of the Securities and Exchange Commission, the Federal Communications
Commission, the Federal Power Commission, and the Food and Drug Administration, and the courts had by and large upheld their delegated oversight powers. But no sooner had the FTC been created under the Wilsonian reform
movement in 1914 than the First World War reduced its mission; any brake on
the national industrial engine bordered on the unpatriotic. When the Republicans ruled Washington throughout the 'Twenties and into the Great Depression, they had scant interest in the FTC as an interventionist tool to further

economic justice. And so its regulatory machinery atrophied, and Franklin Roosevelt found that the agency had become a dumping ground for political patronage; when he wanted to control the wayward impulses of businessmen in critical industries, he created new agencies specifically for that purpose. Without the will to move aggressively against suspect industrywide practices, the FTC almost never acted on its own initiative but moved against one transgressor at a time in cases brought to it by a wounded competitor or aggrieved consumer. Without statutory power to impose serious punitive or compensatory fines—only slaps on the wrist in the form of cease-and-desist orders after protracted investigations and hearings—the commission functioned cumbersomely, if at all. A typical action consumed four years, and sixteen were required to get the "Liver" out of deceptively named Carter's Little Liver Pills. Besides dwelling on trivial problems, the agency was hospitable to cronyism, absenteeism, alcoholism, and lethargy—almost nobody there worked late or on weekends—and reflected a Southern courthouse bias against fancy Ivy League lawyers. The result was institutionalized mediocrity, at best, and, as U.S. Representative Blatnik had shown when investigating deceptive filter-cigarette advertising in the late 'Fifties, massive default of its public charge.

When John Kennedy took office in 1961, eager to revitalize the federal regulatory agencies, he was leaned on heavily by popular and powerful Senator Estes Kefauver to name a fellow Tennessean, Paul Randall Dixon, to chair the FTC. Dixon, who had begun his career there as a trial lawyer and won his epaulets as chief counsel of Kefauver's headline-grabbing subcommittee investigating corrupt business and labor practices, pledged to bring a new broom to the agency and end its futile pursuit of malefactors long after their corrupt practices had been abandoned. "We are going to use a squad car instead of a hearse," he promised. But the amiable, easygoing Rand Dixon, nicknamed "Windy" for his conversational excesses, talked a better game than he played. Most of the commission's deadwood remained unpruned, and although Chairman Dixon staked out a claim in 1962 to industrywide rule-making authority without additional congressional empowerment—he cited the general authorizing language at the time the FTC was created—by early 1964 the agency had laid down rules for only two very small fish, makers of sleeping bags and "leakproof" dry-cell batteries.

This sort of toe-testing in troubled waters was hardly the hearty plunge into serious regulation being urged on Dixon by one of his four fellow commissioners, Philip Elman, perhaps the agency's closest brush with brilliance in its lackluster history. A Harvard-trained lawyer who had clerked for U.S. Supreme Court Justice Felix Frankfurter, the peppery and opinionated Elman was anything but the usual cautious civil servant even after fifteen years in the Justice Department, where he had helped shape the government's position in favor of striking down segregated public schools. Plucked from the Solicitor

General's office by Attorney General Robert Kennedy to galvanize the FTC, Elman used his acid and sometimes rude tongue to call upon the agency to spot problem areas, undertake searching investigations into abuses, and lay down industrywide remedies. In the case of the tobacco industry, Elman's impulses were contested by Commissioner Everette McIntyre, a twenty-five-year careerist at the agency, whose conservatism was buttressed by his origins: he was a native of North Carolina, heart of the cigarette business. The other two commissioners were moderates, like Dixon, and pliable to Elman's coaxing.

Having been primed by Senator Neuberger's 1962 plea to the agency to move against cigarette advertisements for their failure to include health warnings, the FTC had all but invited the U.S. Public Health Service to draft an authoritative assessment of the medical case against smoking, and now, in the report to the Surgeon General, it had done just that. Commissioners Dixon, Elman, and McIntyre had gathered at the FTC offices on the Saturday morning the SGAC report was made public and read through it together. "The report made a tremendous impression on him," Elman recalled of Dixon's reading. " 'Jesus, Phil, listen to this,' he'd say and read out an excerpt, and before long he stubbed out his smoke and said, 'That's my last cigarette—I've got to talk to my boys,' meaning his two sons, who were also heavy smokers." When Dixon reached the part of the report calling for "appropriate remedial action," he said to his colleagues, "They're talking about us"—and Elman knew the iron was hot. "Let me get going on this, Rand," he said, arguing that even if the tobacco industry were to take the FTC to court for inadequate statutory authority to regulate it, the commission was sure to prevail eventually before the Supreme Court under its activist chief justice, Earl Warren. Nor was there any point in the commissioners' consulting first with congressional leaders, given their demonstrated indifference to the smoking peril; besides, the FTC was supposed to be an independent body that had no need to kowtow to Capitol Hill. The chairman gave Elman the nod. It was Rand Dixon's shining hour.

Before that Saturday was over, Elman and Richard Posner, one of the gifted assistants he had brought in from outside the commission (and later to become a highly regarded University of Chicago law professor and federal appeals judge), had drafted a three-part regulatory rule, the chief feature of which was a mandatory warning label to appear on every cigarette pack and advertisement with either of two wordings:

a. CAUTION—CIGARETTE SMOKING IS A HEALTH HAZARD. The Surgeon General's Advisory Committee has found that "cigarette smoking contributes to mortality from specific diseases and to the overall death rate";

or

b. CAUTION: Cigarette smoking is dangerous to health. It may cause death from cancer and other diseases.

No pack or ad, moreover, was to state or imply "by words, pictures, symbols, sounds, devices," or in any other way that the brand promoted health or well-being or was less hazardous than any other cigarette in the absence of "substantial and reliable evidence" to back up such a claim. Finally, no pack or ad was to state the tar and nicotine contents unless verified in accordance with "a uniform and reliable testing procedure" approved by the FTC. The proposed rule was approved that same week by the commission and a press conference scheduled for the following Saturday, just a week after the Surgeon General's report was released, to announce the FTC initiative.

That Friday afternoon, Elman was greeted by Dixon, just back from the White House. "They want us to hold off," the chairman told his spirited fellow commissioner, who was not entirely surprised, considering that Lyndon Johnson's closest confidant and unofficial legal counselor was Abe Fortas, still a private practitioner representing, among other clients, Philip Morris. The President, Dixon was led to understand, felt that no single agency ought to go off on its own on the smoking problem, as the FTC now threatened to do; instead, it ought to act only as part of a coordinated government program.

To Elman, the White House directive sounded like a plan to sink the health warning in a bottomless quagmire of bureaucratic bickering. "Rand, it's too late—we can't pull it back," Elman said, arguing that the press had already been alerted for a major announcement by the FTC, which, if canceled, would give the appearance that the agency, a supposedly independent watchdog of the public interest, could be dictated to by the White House. Maverick Elman also intimated to Dixon that if the chairman backed down, he himself would go public and the President would be made to appear tobacco's "boy". Anyway, the proposed rules were only proposals; the commission would hold full-dress hearings in March, so there was time to trim sails if necessary.

Dixon, with an uncontrollable agent provocateur in his midst, held his ground against the White House and announced the proposed health measure.

I I I

THE FTC's sudden show of strength set off even louder alarm bells than the Surgeon General's report, which, according to Abe Krash at Arnold & Porter, legal counselors to Philip Morris, had come as a great shock to the tobacco industry. While the only really new aspect of the FTC proposal was the mandatory warning label, the very notion was, as Krash put it, "greatly troubling" to many in the business who fiercely resented being asked to disparage their product on its own package and to include the same confession in their paid advertising.

To cushion the blow, if not evade it altogether, the cigarette manufacturers formed a united political front. Suddenly, Philip Morris's decision to hire Abe Fortas well before the Kennedy assassination had the look of a providential act. There was now no more highly placed attorney in the capital than Fortas, with his easy access to the presidential ear; Fortas's word in and of itself had immeasurable influence, which he exercised, without having to invoke the President's name, in tobacco's behalf until confirmed for a Supreme Court seat in mid-1965.

But the industry also needed a more active and visible power broker suited to the rough and tumble of congressional horse-trading, a role not much savored by the obvious candidate for the job, the Tobacco Institute's president, George Allen, a rather formal—some said stiff—gentleman at ease with Cabinet officers and diplomats. Instead, the industry turned, largely on Fortas's advice, to another Johnson intimate, Earle Clements, a canny old warrior and superb strategist who knew where all the levers were that operated Washington's political machinery. A former Kentucky governor and U.S. senator who had been majority leader Johnson's whip and most trusted lieutenant, a marvel of indirection in his dealings, he was known for such down-home Machiavellian maxims as "Never ask a man to vote for something that isn't good for him." Ousted from office in the 1956 Eisenhower landslide, he was called back to Washington to work for the Democratic National Committee during the 1960 election. After several years in the political wilderness as a lobbyist, he was buoyed by LBJ's sudden accession to the White House, where Clements's daughter began serving as Lady Bird Johnson's appointment secretary and the old pol himself was welcomed at private movie screenings. Nearing seventy now and in need of income, Clements was a lovely catch for the moguls of tobacco. Rounding out the industry's team of political maneuverers was H. Thomas Austern, a tough-talking, chain-smoking senior partner at Covington & Burling, considered by some to be Washington's top legal shop, and a specialist in antitrust law and trade regulations.

In consultation with the cigarette companies' "Secret Six" panel of general counselors, Austern orchestrated a three-part salvo in response to the FTC's proposed regulation. First, no tobacco company officer asked to appear before the FTC at its formal hearings—by way of registering their view that the commission was acting without statutory authority from Congress in framing its rule-making on cigarettes and health. If Congress had wanted to empower the agency in such an explicit fashion, it would have done just that. Here was a matter too important to be decided on unilaterally by a mere administrative agency instead of the people's elected representatives in Congress. Second, the industry produced spokesmen, appearing both at the commission's three-day hearing and wherever they were welcomed around the U.S., who argued that tobacco had played a prominent role in the development of the American nation since colonial times, that it was of surpassing economic importance to the South, and that its manufacture was entirely legal—among the very arguments used to justify slavery until the Civil War; the moral context of the practice went unmentioned, just as Austern elected not to confront the substance of the health charges against his clients. Finally, the tobacco advocates pursued the where-will-all-of-this-end defense by declaring, as North Carolina's Governor Sanford had in a speech a month before the FTC hearings, "The automobile is the most dangerous machine ever invented, but we don't require a warning on the steering wheel. Nor do we require airlines to put a warning on their tickets that accidents sometimes happen. It makes no more sense to require a skull and crossbones on a cigarette package."

None of the foregoing arguments swayed the FTC. When formally issued in June 1964, with only Commissioner McIntyre dissenting, the regulation stood essentially as it had been drafted and was accompanied by an explanatory report that raked over the cigarette manufacturers far less tenderly than the Surgeon General's advisory committee had. Included was a pointed discussion of cigarette advertising themes and appeals "which tend to allay anxiety about the dangers of smoking." Typical was the ballyhooing of filters, which, despite earlier FTC decrees accepted by the industry, were being promoted as health devices. As one example, the report cited ads for Winston that spoke of its "pure white modern filter," words which, while claiming nothing explicit, "could imply to many people . . . that [it] is sufficiently 'modern' to cope with any dangerous properties in cigarette smoke." Similarly, the boast that Parliament "puts the filter where it does you the most good" could be interpreted as a thinly veiled health claim. Overall, said the FTC indictment, it was the industry's practice "to transport the smoker to a world so well insulated from any suggestion of health hazards that the effect is to assure the smoker that smoking is safe." This form of deception was compounded by the magnitude and pervasiveness of cigarette advertising, so that "virtually all Americans, including most children, are continually exposed to the portrayal of smoking as desirable and to reassurances respecting the safety and healthfulness of cigarette smoking." In its most excoriating language, the FTC added:

> To allay anxiety on the . . . hazards of smoking, the cigarette manufacturers have made no effort whatever, and have spent nothing, to inform the consuming public of the mounting and now overwhelming evidence that cigarette smoking is habit-forming, hazardous to health, and once begun, most difficult

to stop. On the contrary, the cigarette manufacturers and the Tobacco Institute have never acknowledged, and have repeatedly and forcefully denied, that smoking has been shown to be a substantial health hazard.

Finally, the FTC dismissed the industry's "slippery slope" defense by effectively distinguishing cigarettes from other hazardous products. Alcohol and rich foods could safely be consumed in moderation, it noted, whereas "[t]here is no known moderate or safe level of cigarette consumption." The sale of liquor, moreover, was "subject to an elaborate network of public and private regulation that has no parallel in the cigarette industry"; commercials for hard liquor were no longer broadcast, its print ads avoided the themes of romance, contentment, and sociability, and all liquor products, unlike cigarettes, were labeled to disclose alcoholic content. As for automobiles, which killed and maimed tens of thousands annually, society had taken many measures to protect consumers from injury through such regulations as driver licensing, car inspections, speed limits, and restrictions on driving by minors. There were no comparable strictures governing cigarettes.

The final FTC rule as issued did not specify the precise language on the health label—only substantive disclosure in a form of the industry's devising. Elman was uncomfortable with the First Amendment implications of mandated wording. But as for the rest of the FTC cigarette regulation, he recalled, "My hope was that the industry would immediately take us to court," anticipating that the Supreme Court would uphold it as it had various SEC and FCC rule-making measures without any explicit congressional directive.

The warning labels were to appear on packs and in ads at the beginning of 1965, according to the FTC regulation, but well before that date, the industry flexed its biceps, and Rand Dixon blinked. Word reached him that the President wanted the commission to befriend and not harass the captains of the nation's industries, tobacco included. Representative Oren Harris, the Arkansas Democrat who chaired the House Commerce Committee, formally asked the FTC to postpone the effective date of its rule on cigarettes until the middle of the following year, so that the new Congress would have the chance to consider the matter. Unspoken in this request by Harris was the threat of reprisals against the commission if it persisted in an action that not a few in Congress believed was an overreach by the long-docile agency. A congressionally mandated health warning, furthermore, was far more likely to withstand judicial review, Dixon was told, than one imposed by the FTC. Besides, it would take effect immediately upon its passage and not be tied up in court for years, as the industry threatened if the FTC failed to yield to Congress.

With such powerful arguments marshaled against him, the FTC chairman retreated. The commission had made its point, in thunderous words, but it was, in the final analysis, a creature of Congress. Dixon's shining hour had come and gone.

I V

O N the morning the Surgeon General's report was made public, a group of Philip Morris executives and lawyers trooped a block and a half from their offices to Grand Central Terminal, where the Columbia Broadcasting System had arranged a closed-circuit telecast of Luther Terry's press conference in Washington for the network's major advertisers. Among those in the Philip Morris party was outside counsel Alexander Holtzman, who remembered, "The mood as we walked over was serious but not grave—we knew it was going to be a watershed event and that things might never be the same again." As the Surgeon General read aloud from the report, Holtzman said, "I had a sort of sinking feeling"—more of bafflement than anger over how the panel could have reached such conclusions.

Joseph Cullman, the Philip Morris chairman, understood that the news from Washington represented "a setback for the industry," as he would later acknowledge. "It was the first really professionally competent group report—it had to be recognized and taken seriously. We had expected a more evenhanded report," as the company had been advised, he said, by people on or connected with the advisory committee. "We thought it would be rather noncommittal, not as specific . . . and fairer from our viewpoint. We took it as a very serious adverse development."

Consideration was given to protesting in public that the Surgeon General's panel had not based its findings on a fair model (*i.e.*, smokers of filter cigarettes), but such a step was deemed "ill advised," Cullman recounted, because it both conceded too much to the health charges and lacked enough credibility to blunt the report's main thrust. Despite the company's suspicions about much of the medical evidence, it was "ready to devote large sums," as Cullman put it, to determine if cigarettes were truly a health menace and, if so, what should be removed from the product to make it safe. "But unfortunately . . . we didn't know what was or wasn't a hazard, and no one's ever proven what the problem really is. . . . All we did know is that we could lower the tar and nicotine yields."

George Weissman, then Cullman's executive vice president for overseas operations, was less inclined to concede an inch to the Surgeon General's panel. "I read the whole report—we all read it—and marked it up," he recalled, but found nothing in it to suggest that Philip Morris ought to mend its ways. "Until then we'd always had the philosophy—and we still have it so far as I'm concerned—that there is no clinical evidence, no smoking gun, that it was impossible for one item to cause so many diseases and that more research has to be done. . . . We didn't say we were innocent—or that we were guilty. . . . Being prudent men, though, we did everything in our power to ensure the quality and safety of our product. If there was a problem with the tar and nicotine, we kept reducing the yields."

But among those committed to the industry position, some were able privately to separate their personal from their professional reaction to the landmark report from Washington. "As someone who had to be confronted by this document for the rest of my career," said one Philip Morris insider, "the Surgeon General's report was a remarkably fine . . . effort to deal conscientiously with some of the objections we had raised." He found the report well organized and intellectually substantive and was particularly struck by how the advisory committee had "devised those criteria for attributing causation [to a statistical association]—it was very clear—it lent force and authority to what might have been a readily attackable conclusion. They made it very hard to challenge." What made the essence of the indictment so unsettling, they acknowledged among themselves, was that "we had no countervailing data to present, only methodological objections. There was no silver bullet the industry could fire back—nothing to show, then or now. . . ."

None of the Philip Morris executives was more concerned with the implications of the government-sponsored report than Helmut Wakeham, vice president for research and development since 1962. In his corner office in the McComas Research Center at Philip Morris's Richmond complex, its two paneled walls covered with abstract art, the other two composed entirely of windows that commanded a view of the Virginia countryside, Wakeham pondered how to respond to a request from the company brass to suggest appropriate policy in the wake of the Surgeon General's report. His integrity as a professional scientist as well as a corporate loyalist was being tried.

Wakeham's formidable personality and confident manner made him controversial within the company. Cultivated, imaginative—even visionary on occasion—and not wanting in ego, he could not mask a no-nonsense manner that went straight to the point and an intolerant streak that could cut a slower-witted subordinate with a remark like "You may not do much, but what you do doesn't make sense." Said one of Wakeham's longtime ranking lieutenants, "You had a love-hate relationship with him, but you couldn't help respecting his intellect."

Ruminating on the smoking and disease link asserted in the report from Washington, Wakeham took heart from the way the Surgeon General and his advisors had fudged the issue of the efficacy of filter cigarettes. In his memo of assessment to Philip Morris officials in New York, Wakeham called the report a "perfunctory treatment of a major industry effort to meet objections to its product." Since the central implication of the Surgeon General's report was plain—*i.e.*, the health risks of smoking stemmed from the constituents in tobacco smoke—it followed that, as he would put it in private correspondence years later, "those risks would be decreased if the constituents were removed or reduced." But Philip Morris's effort to create such a modified product "does not mean that we in research and development or the company as a whole accepted the Surgeon General's committee's interpretations or criticisms as scientifically valid, or that we believed it had been established that cigarette smoking produces lung cancer and similar diseases in human beings."

But such an unwillingness to concede the case against smoking was not reflected in Wakeham's remarkable February 18, 1964, memorandum to his corporate superiors. In it he wrote, "Positive programs to cure ills cited in this [Surgeon General's advisory committee] report, whether real or alleged, are recommended, as little basis for disputing the findings at this time has appeared." He noted that the report had been widely taken "rather as a verdict against cigarette smoking" and was thus likely to promote "a shift in the onus of proof from the accusers to the tobacco industry." His latter-day disclaimer aside, Wakeham's true regard for the report to the Surgeon General may be inferred from his remark in the February 1964 memo: "The professional approach of the advisory committee furthermore may serve to force future arguments to a more scientific basis." As his first recommendation to top management, then, Wakeham urged the view that "greater benefit will accrue from accepting the report's findings on face value and proceeding to the cure of ills, real and alleged as they may be, than from engaging in disputation and refutation of these claims."

As head of R&D, Wakeham now asked for increased corporate support for "[d]evelopment by year end of a superior filter cigarette with acceptable taste having high gas phase absorption and very low TPM [total particulate matter, the residual post-combustion solids generally referred to as 'tar']" as well as expanded knowledge within the PM Research Center "through intelligence effort in epidemiology, bioassay, lung cancer research," and other areas. Wakeham added, "The hoped-for result of these efforts will be cigarettes with distinguishing new product properties which are biologically approved on all major health questions," and would therefore provide "a substantive basis for vigorous health advertising by publication of articles in the technical literature. . . ." He understood, in short, though others in his company and the industry would continually claim otherwise, that a truly innovative and possibly less hazardous cigarette could be advertised as such under standing FTC regulations if a manufacturer with the skills to create one also had the courage to face liability claims that its older brands were, by definition, more hazardous to the smoker.

That Wakeham may have been a self-deluding dreamer rather than the hardheaded scientist his colleagues preferred to picture is one possible inference to be drawn from the concluding hortatory remarks of his 1964 memo: "The industry must come forward with evidence to show that its products, present and prospective, are not harmful. Medical research must be done for this purpose. . . . The industry should abandon its past reticence with respect to medical research. Indeed, failure to do so could give rise to negligence charges" against the manufacturers. He even urged the company to undertake its own prospective study of the health effects of filter cigarettes on smokers.

But such proposals and thinking, however enlightened from the scientific standpoint, produced instant teeth-gnashing by Paul Smith, Philip Morris's ultraprotective general counsel. "I'd hear from Smith every day," Wakeham said. "His department recognized the legal hazard and felt that the activities of R&D would or could weaken their case and did everything they could to discourage [our] effort. We had our share of confrontations." But Philip Morris's top scientist clung to the Baconian precept that knowledge is power and that the cigarette industry's health problem could not be met without understanding it better. "The legal department's view of it," Wakeham recounted, "was that you couldn't be criticized for not knowing something." And strictly from the perspective of corporate safety, the lawyers had the better argument, for what if the company had undertaken a long-term study of the mortality rates of filter-cigarette smokers and found no reduced peril? Wasn't it better never to know than to find out and have to choose between suppressing the data or disclosing it at the high risk of financial suicide? Lawyerly prudence argued for letting others draw the reasonable inference that lowered tar and nicotine yields reduced the health hazard. That train of strategy only deepened Wakeham's dilemma. How could his department ever satisfactorily demonstrate to the FTC that it had developed a truly less hazardous product if to do so required his scientists to prove a negative—*i.e.*, no biological activity resulting from the experimental brands? "You can't prove the absolute safety of anything," he remarked. "How can you say what is a 'safe' cigarette?"

Although company officers worried that an ambitious R&D program might cost their enterprise its very existence, Wakeham's budget kept growing—indeed, his annual requests were never cut, he claimed. But the company leadership was ever wary of him. Recalled one twenty-year Philip Morris veteran who supervised overall operations at Richmond including research and development, "Wake [Wakeham's intramural nickname] always wanted to make a contribution [on the smoking and health issue], but the company executives didn't want him to. . . . The industry always felt that the research into the health question needed to be done by third parties . . . and was prepared to support that research effort generously." If adverse conclusions emerged, "it was more the government's responsibility to reach a conclusion on the subject"—meaning the continued legality of a lethal product. "The industry couldn't act any differently from the way it did." Indeed, what profit-seeking entity would place the public interest ahead of its own self-aggrandizement and voluntarily put itself out of business?

Just how nervous Wakeham's idealized goals made the ledger-watchers at corporate headquarters may be surmised from the appraisal of the R&D head by one veteran financial officer, Shepard Pollack, who in time rose to the presidency of Philip Morris's domestic tobacco business. "I never trusted him," said Pollack, finding in Wakeham "a certain intellectual stiffness" and in his department a set of "priorities that were unmugged by reality." Pollack, no by-the-book bean counter but a wily Harvard graduate who had apprenticed in Ford Motor's financial department during the company's "Whiz Kid" days, doubted that Philip Morris or any of its competitors could ever market a "medically acceptable" or "biologically approved" cigarette—as Wakeham had called for—"without exposing ourselves to totally bankrupting liability claims. . . . R&D didn't understand that." None of Wakeham's superiors worked harder to achieve the ends he championed than Clifford Goldsmith, the engineer who emerged as the company's mainstay on the manufacturing side in this period. But while Goldsmith held Wakeham in high regard as a scientist, "We didn't necessarily agree with his memos"—or at least with how the goal of a modified cigarette could be presented for public or even internal consumption. "We had to be extremely careful not to mislead the public," Goldsmith recounted. "We don't have the knowledge of the [health] effects of low-tar cigarettes."

But Wakeham loyalists took a different view from that of those who disparaged him. Said one, a chemist with a background in cancer research before coming to Philip Morris for a twenty-seven-year career in which he worked closely with Wakeham: "There was a conflict in the company between science and the law that's never been resolved." In his February 1964 memo, his longtime subordinate added, Wakeham "was addressing the issue purely as a scientist—lawyers look at the problem in a different way, and so we go through this ritual dance—what's 'proven' and what isn't, what's causal and what's just an association—and the lawyers' answer is, 'Let's stonewall.' . . . If Helmut Wakeham had run things, I think there would have been some admissions. But he was outflanked by the lawyers, led by Paul Smith, who some people felt walked on water. The lawyers were saying, in effect, 'My God, you can't make that admission' without risking liability actions against the company. So there was no cohesive plan—when critics of the industry speak of a 'conspiracy,' they give the companies far too much credit. . . . None of us at that time was sure what we could do, what we should or shouldn't do—or say. If there had been a way to detect cause and effect through biological testing, as there was in administering vinyl chloride to test animals [to determine its carcinogenicity], that would have clarified things. There were some who thought there might really be a 'magic bullet' cause—a single substance in the smoke—as the fractionating [chemical analysis by spectrometry] went on and on. There was much groping, looking at catalysts [for cleaner burning tobacco], additives to the filtration, devices like the Strichman filter [a Columbia University–sponsored invention], which gave you a hernia to draw on. . . . So these memos by Wakeham reflect a pretty smart scientist-businessman's point of view. And he stood his ground."

Just how narrow a territory the scientists commanded within the Philip Morris corporate realm could be divined from top-management statements in the months soon after Wakeham sent his memo to New York. In remarks at the annual meeting in April 1964, President Cullman said the company's scientists and outside experts who studied the report to the Surgeon General felt that its prime conclusion causally linking lung cancer to smoking was unjustified—not at all what Wakeham's memo had stated. And it was indeed regrettable, Cullman added, that the SGAC study was made without due regard for smokers of filter cigarettes, which then made up 60 percent of the overall market and 85 percent of Philip Morris sales. The company's 1964 annual report assured its stockholders (and the public) that the government document "was studied with great care by your management," which found that "it contained no specific recommendations . . . which could be usefully employed by our scientists, and no significant reports have been issued subsequently to clarify the question of tobacco and health"—as if to imply that the SGAC had only fogged the issue.

Such were the dismissive public remarks, lacking in candor and unreflective of the internal dissension on the subject, by perhaps the most enlightened management in the cigarette industry.

V

THE cigarette makers had a full-scale crisis on their hands as the new Congress, perhaps the most liberal in history as a result of Lyndon Johnson's landslide victory the previous November, convened in January 1965. Without congressional intervention, the FTC regulation mandating a health warning label on all cigarette packs and in all print advertisements and broadcast commercials would go into effect at midyear unless the industry moved against the requirement in the courts, where a satisfactory outcome was far from certain.

Some in the tobacco business wanted to head for the bunkers, shouting defiantly that their product remained innocent until proven guilty and was much loved by the public despite the woeful chorus of criticism on health grounds. But Earle Clements, the industry's wily chief lobbyist, had convinced its leadership that the scientific case was compelling enough that if the industry did not give ground voluntarily, Congress would have no choice but to impose harsh measures on the tobacco interests. What was wanted, Clements persuaded them, was a congressional bill that had at least the appearance of a health regulation yet effectively dismantled the FTC's pending version and would prevent, through the preemptive power of federal legislation, a multiplicity of warning labels from being slapped on cigarette packs by state and local governments, forcing the manufacturers to absorb the cost of doing business in a fragmented marketplace.

Many in the tobacco camp had believed that the most dire threat to their continued prosperity was the part of the FTC regulation requiring a health warning in all cigarette advertising. A warning repeated out loud countless times a day on television and radio and plastered on every pretty print ad like a figurative Jolly Roger might well have a chastening effect on would-be smokers. In an effort to head off the imposition of such a galling regimen, the industry had with some fanfare announced the previous spring, even as the FTC regulation was being debated, the establishment of formal machinery to police its own excesses in huckstering. Called the Cigarette Advertising Code, to take effect at the beginning of 1965, the program seemed to be a serious response to the industry's critics. All cigarette ads would now have to be approved by an all-powerful administrator, whom industry wags soon tagged "the tar czar," with the unappealable power to impose a fine of $100,000 for every infraction.

The main purpose of the new code was to blunt the charge that the industry was massively seducing minors to take up smoking at an age when they were indifferent to the possible ultimate consequences of the step. The code prohibited advertising in publications like comic books, school newspapers, and college athletic programs and on television and radio programs "directed primarily to persons" under twenty-one. It further forbade the distribution of free cigarette samples to the underaged, the use of models in ads or commercials who were or appeared to be under twenty-five years old, and testimonials by athletes or entertainers—categories thought to hold a special appeal for youngsters. Perhaps the most telling provision in the code was the one against any representation "that smoking is essential to social prominence, distinction, success or sexual attraction," but permitting pretty, robust models, or drawings of such people, to be used provided "there is no suggestion that their attractive appearance or good health is due to cigarette smoking." And no health claim could be made unless it was based on "adequate, relevant and valid scientific data" as determined by the code administrator.

The loopholes in the industry code soon became apparent. Millions of younger children and teenagers watched or heard programs sponsored by cigarette companies, like "The Beverly Hillbillies" and the broadcast of baseball and football games, and read daily newspapers, fan and fashion magazines, and other publications jammed with cigarette ads—and none of these was "directed primarily" at those under twenty-one. And what a Solomonic mind would be needed to weigh artful copy and glowing countenances implying that smoking Brand X was contributory to, or at least compatible with, success in love, business, or scuba diving. Nor was it necessary to suggest that physical attractiveness and well-being were "due to cigarette smoking"—just associating them within the confines of the same advertisement served to undercut reports of the debilitating effects of smoking. And how could even conscientious distributors of sample cigarettes be expected to interrupt their efforts on thronged sidewalks to demand proof of age from would-be recipients?

Because the efficacy of the new code would obviously depend on the zeal with which the administrator operated, the industry gained early credibility by enlisting as its advertising czar pack-a-day-smoker Robert B. Meyner, the retired, well-regarded two-term Democratic governor of New Jersey. Meanwhile, the mere announcement of the code prevented adoption of a similar measure by the National Association of Broadcasters, who, in view of the estimated $135 million in annual billings from cigarette advertising, were just as happy to let the tobacco industry try to police itself. To persuade the FTC of its good intentions before the commission decided whether to include a health warning requirement in cigarette advertising as well as on the pack in its pending regulation and to convince the Justice Department that the industry's own voluntary ad code should not be discouraged on antitrust grounds, Abe Fortas headed a delegation of tobacco lawyers at a joint meeting with FTC and Justice officials in early June 1964. Fortas assured the government group that the code was "an honest job, there is nothing but what appears." Washington's most powerful private legal practitioner went on, "We can't expect companies acting individually to regulate their own advertising—one overstates, then another. We must have pre-scrutiny with muscle. The only way is to set up this private system." The Justice Department raised no objection to the self-policing scheme. The FTC, fed up with past industry circumvention of its guidelines, declined to set aside its requirement for warnings in cigarette ads.

V I

B EYOND the unwelcome prospect of government-mandated warning labels was the tobacco industry's heightened dread that the Surgeon General's report would provide decisive authority to sway the outcome of product liability suits against the cigarette makers. Five such suits had already gone to trial and were proving difficult to defend. But they had to be defended, and fiercely, because the industry was convinced that even a single defeat would open the floodgates of litigation to every smoker who chose to blame his physical afflictions on his favorite brand of cigarette. Some of the first wave of liability suits, involving multiple trials and appeals, consumed a dozen years before the industry at last prevailed—or exhausted the energies and wallets of plaintiffs who dropped their claims.

In a front-page article the day before the Surgeon General's report was issued, *The Wall Street Journal* speculated on the possible legal consequences of the expected government conclusion that cigarettes were indeed a deadly product for some smokers. Despite the industry's shunning of health warning labels, the *Journal* observed, some experts believed that such a step would notably reduce the companies' liability exposure because no potential plaintiff could thereafter claim that he or she had not been forewarned.

Intensifying the tobacco companies' worries over costly, endless litigation was the timing of an effort within the legal profession to rethink the fairness of product liability law and redress the balance that had long seemed to favor sellers—not infrequently big, rich, faceless, and callous corporations—over individual consumers ill equipped to combat them. The prevailing doctrine of *caveat emptor* (let the buyer beware) had been softened by the evolution of social justice in the twentieth century, but its essence was still detectable in the outcome of the liability suits that had been brought against the cigarette makers based on two kinds of claims. The first was for negligence in failing to warn buyers of the danger, known to the sellers, from the use of the product. The other was for breach of warranty, whereby the manufacturers assured buyers either explicitly or implicitly that their cigarettes were safe to smoke; a plaintiff claiming otherwise was obliged to prove that the illness suffered was caused by the product. The industry was successfully rebuffing such claims by arguing that (1) no conclusive proof existed that smoking cigarettes caused disease, but (2) even if it did, there was no way the manufacturers could have been aware of it before the plaintiffs contracted their illness or were discovered to be sick. And (3) since the use of tobacco had long been alleged to be a health hazard regardless of the industry's expressed doubts about the charges, smokers were guilty of contributory negligence and could not shift to the cigarette makers the responsibility for their informed and freely taken lifestyle choices, any more than an alcoholic who overindulged in liquor or a motorist who drove too fast could blame the manufacturers of those products for the resulting harm.

Even in the case thus far most favorable to a plaintiff—*Pritchard v. Liggett & Myers*—the legal hurdles confronting the victims of smoking had proven towering. Claiming he had long smoked while relying on Liggett's negligently made statements that its cigarettes were no danger to his health (as in the company's 1952 ad headlined, "Play Safe / Smoke Chesterfield," statements such as "Nose, Throat, and Accessory Organs Not Adversely Affected by Smoking Chesterfields," and broadcasting entertainer Arthur Godfrey's reassurances along these same lines), plaintiff Pritchard and his surviving family endured two trials and two reversals of the verdict in their favor by a federal appellate court. In the second trial the jury had found that smoking was responsible for the claimant's illness but that Pritchard was not shown to have relied on any express warranty by the manufacturer and, at any rate, he had voluntarily assumed the risk. In ordering still a third trial, the appeals court held that under the laws of Pennsylvania, where Pritchard lived, he did not have to show reliance on such warranties—only that they were there—but, more to the point, how could the plaintiff have been found to assume a risk that the manufacturer explicitly advertised did not exist? The Pritchards nevertheless elected, after more than a decade of litigation, not to go on.

It was precisely to avoid such endless wrangling that judges, juries, and state legislatures were at this time formulating a new legal doctrine, most commonly referred to as strict product liability. Under this theory of action, a plaintiff was not required to dwell on the defendant company's actions or justify his or her own; what mattered was whether the product involved was "unreasonably dangerous," regardless of the manufacturer's awareness of that condition. The business community strongly objected to the doctrine of strict liability on the ground that it turned manufacturers into absolute guarantors of their customers' health and safety.

Such concerns grew out of the legal profession's ongoing effort to clarify and codify often conflicting common-law adjudications by the courts. The American Law Institute (ALI), frequently cited by courts and scholars around the nation as an arbiter in settling contentious legal questions, had examined the state of liability law governing wrongful civil acts and in 1939 issued its authoritative *Restatement of the Law of Torts*. In 1961, the ALI undertook a series of philosophical debates as part of a revision of the earlier work, and in 1964, just as the FTC and Congress were exploring the need for cigarette warning labels, produced its *Second Restatement* of American tort law, this time dealing with the emerging and highly controversial doctrine of strict liability. As reported by William Prosser, who had gained renown as a California law professor and author of the leading treatise on torts, the new *Restatement* as drafted described the special or strict liability of one "who sells any product in a defective condition unreasonably dangerous." Did that apply to cigarettes in their normal manufactured condition? How were they "defective" unless they were somehow adulterated by additives or unintended foreign substances? And who could say whether a cigarette was "unreasonably dangerous"? In deliberations by the ALI Council in 1962, commentary refining the limits of liability exposure and adopted in the final version of the *Restatement* would be widely invoked by judges and law schools over the ensuing three decades. In "Comment i" of Section 402A, an "unreasonably dangerous" product was defined as "dangerous to an extent beyond that which would be contemplated by the ordinary consumer who purchases it, with the ordinary knowledge common to the community as to its characteristics." That seemed to say that if most people knew a product was dangerous, it could not be deemed "unreasonably so"—an impression strengthened by Comment i's further remark: "Good tobacco is not unreasonably dangerous merely because the effects of smoking may be harmful; but tobacco containing something like marijuana may be unreasonably dangerous." Comment i added that a dangerous product might not be "unreasonably" so if consumers had received a proper warning of its condition. Prosser himself wrote in his 1971 *Handbook on Torts* that when danger from the use of a product like whiskey was "generally known," it could not be regarded as "unreasonably unsafe merely because it is capable of doing harm," and he added that "it is quite possible that cigarettes are to be placed in this category, even though they may cause lung cancer."

But such a line of thought by some of the most learned theorists in the profession was tantamount to rewarding a highly hazardous product for its notorious condition by exempting its producer from any resulting damage claims on the ground that most people were aware of its potentially lethal nature. *Caveat emptor*, indeed. Was that equitable, though? The implication seemed to be that so long as the product was legal, it did not matter how lethal it was, provided the community understood the danger. Why, however, should manufacturers of egregiously hazardous products be allowed by the judicial branch of government to evade liability claims merely because the legislative branch had declined to outlaw those products? Under the American common-law system, judges and juries are lawmakers as much as legislators are, free to remedy civil wrongs by awarding reparations to victims where the situation was not clearly covered or anticipated by statute. And what statute could determine whether a given brand of cigarettes might be dangerous to an extent beyond what "would be contemplated by the ordinary consumer who purchases it"? And if the producer warned of the danger, was the warning adequate to define the peril? And could even an adequate warning be undermined by the conduct of the producer—for example, through public statements denying or minimizing the degree of danger attributed to the product by others and through advertising that presented the product in an entirely attractive context without the least hint of the alleged danger? All of these considerations, which judges and juries might fairly take into account in adjudicating a liability claim, were left unresolved by the *Restatement*.

What tobacco industry lawyers strongly suspected by mid-1964, however, was that a federally mandated warning on a hazardous product already commonly known to be one was unlikely to hurt its sales and likely to help shield its makers from liability claims. Thus, cigarette makers were reluctantly ready to accept a soft warning label—one without the words "death" or "cancer," as one of the FTC's versions would have read as originally proposed—and, in-

deed, wanted one, but for them to have conceded as much early in the game
would have been poor tactics. Instead, industry spokesmen continued to mutter
against the fairness of being asked to disparage their own product and to claim
that the warning label was unnecessary, all the while using their apparent intransigence as a bargaining chip to extract other forms of legislated protection.
Such a strategy was confirmed by Abe Fortas at his June 1964 meeting at the
Justice Department on the Cigarette Advertising Code when he remarked,
"The companies want legislation. For your own knowledge only, we hope legislation will come through this session. A requirement that packages be labeled
would be helpful in civil litigation." And so the sly tobacco lobbyist Earle
Clements said to the industry's lawyers and executives, referring to the health
warning label: "Let's us write it."

VII

B ESIDES their own economic might, the tobacco manufacturers had one
other large advantage as Congress addressed the health question in
1965—there was no coherent force ranged against them.

True, cigarette sales had slumped in 1964 following the release of the Surgeon General's report, but only by 2 percent or so, and most of the loss was
recorded during the first few months of the year, when the findings were fresh
in the public mind. The authoritative medical indictment of smoking had
plainly not set off a national panic among smokers. To the extent that the
health risk posed by cigarettes was perceived as a serious concern, it was
largely taken to be a private and personal matter, up to each smoker to decide
upon; the communal conscience had not been aroused in a way demanding legislative remedies against a rascally industry. Indeed, in the months and years
immediately following, the issue of tobacco and health had a relatively low
standing on the national agenda as Americans underwent a social upheaval
in the 1960s. If smoking was a peril during the civil rights and Vietnam fer-
ment, it was not tobacco that raised concern but the rebellious younger generation's widespread use of marijuana and other illicit and far more fearsome
mind-altering substances, taken not so much to reduce the stresses of life,
as cigarettes were believed to do by most smokers, but as a euphoric escape
from them.

In this age of domestic turbulence, there was no discrete "health lobby"
with its champions in Congress—only a far-flung and unorganizable assort-
ment of individual Americans worried about the cigarette habit. And there was
no leadership on the issue from Lyndon Johnson's administration, engaged in
the fight for social justice and its war on poverty. "We were in monumental
battles," recalled Joseph A. Califano, Jr., then a key (and heavy-smoking)

White House aide. "Our focus in the South was on desegregation—we were making enough enemies as it was," and so to have pushed for regulation of the tobacco industry would likely have compounded the problems besetting the administration. The President's 1964 Republican opponent, Barry Goldwater, was still more indifferent to the smoking issue. He said a health warning label on cigarette packs "would interfere with freedom"—whose and how, he did not explain. Nowhere in the federal government was there an official prepared to lead a fight against the tobacco industry. Secretary of Agriculture Orville Freeman opposed the health warnings, because they might have an adverse effect on tobacco crop sales. At HEW, only Surgeon General Terry was allowed to come before Congress and speak in favor of the health warnings. At the Public Health Service, no bold champion emerged to take on the cigarette peril.

The closest approximation to a national voice urging action on the issue was the Interagency Council on Smoking and Health, an ad hoc group formed in mid-1964 by public and private organizations of professional health and education workers, among them the big voluntaries like the American Cancer Society and the American Heart Association, occupational and industrial groups like the American Dental Association and the American Pharmaceutical Association, government agencies like the U.S. Children's Bureau and the Public Health Service. This leviathan, however, was all bulk and no brain or muscle. It had neither money nor power to challenge the tobacco interests, and its chairman, former advertising executive Emerson Foote, a convert to the embryonic anticigarette cause, was more well-meaning than effectual. *Barron's*, the pro-business financial weekly, used the first anniversary of the Surgeon General's report as the occasion to charge that Surgeon General Terry had "made a mockery of the scientific method" and to belittle Foote as a mere exhuckster and turncoat fanatic.

The only national organization effectively involved in combating the smoking peril, the American Cancer Society, pointedly declined to invest its high standing in the Interagency Council. Lane W. Adams, for twenty-three years the executive director of the ACS, conceded in retrospect that the cancer society was not then prepared to subordinate its leadership role. "Having pioneered in the area [of smoking and health] and having the resources to pursue the matter, we thought we'd get more done moving independently," Adams recounted. It was "too early" to work cooperatively with so many other groups with different missions and priorities. As a result, longtime ACS public-relations director Irving Rimer noted, "Nobody wanted to cede [the Interagency Council] any power. . . . It didn't do much of anything except publish a newsletter—it was window-dressing."

The one powerful group that might have been expected to weigh in heavily to counter the tobacco industry was the American Medical Association. But the AMA had been standing in angry vigil since the early 1940s against a proposal by New Deal congressmen to extend the Social Security program to cover government-financed medical and hospital care for the elderly under an approved fee schedule for doctors' services. This plan, now embraced by the Johnson administration, was to be voted on shortly by Congress, much to the displeasure of the AMA, which viewed so-called Medicare as a form of socialized medicine and a menace to its livelihood. Anxious for the anti-Medicare votes of tobacco-state lawmakers, the AMA announced soon after the release of the Surgeon General's report that, as the first undertaking of its newly established Education and Research Foundation (ERF), the medical association had accepted a $10 million, no-strings grant from the tobacco industry for a five-year study of smoking.

This grand gesture served the cigarette makers by suggesting that in the AMA's minds the question of the relationship between cigarettes and disease had not been definitely answered by the Surgeon General's report; indeed, three members of the advisory committee were enticed to serve on the AMA-ERF's grant-dispensing panel, lending credence to the effort. For its investment the industry received an almost immediate dividend in the form of a letter from Dr. F. J. L. Blassingame, the AMA's executive vice president, to the FTC's division of trade regulation rules, stating:

> [w]ith respect to cigarettes, cautionary labeling cannot be anticipated to serve the public interest with any particular degree of success. The health hazards of excessive smoking have been well-publicized for more than ten years and are common knowledge. . . .

Besides, Blassingame claimed, 72 million Americans smoked cigarettes in support of a major industry and contributed important tax dollars to various levels of government, so that the FTC's proposed step ought to be dropped in favor of action, if any were in order, by Congress. A handful of congressional idealists denounced the AMA's deal with the cigarette makers, but on Capitol Hill as elsewhere, few were aroused by the smoking issue.

Accordingly, a highly pro-industry labeling bill sailed through the House Commerce Committee, eleven of whose thirty-three members were from the South and four others from border states. The bill had an announced dual purpose of ensuring that "the public may be adequately informed" of the risks associated with tobacco use by requiring the warning label "Caution. Cigarette Smoking May Be Hazardous to Your Health" on every pack—but *not* in any advertising—and that the national economy would not be "impeded by diverse, nonuniform, and conflicting cigarette labeling and advertising regulations with respect to any relationship between smoking and health." To lock in the latter goal, the House bill permanently denied to all federal and state agencies, the FTC included, the power to act in this area. Thus, in mandating the softest possible language on the warning label as the only form permissible nationwide, the House bill enhanced the tobacco companies' ability to fend off future product liability suits by strengthening their assumption-of-risk defense yet prevented the sovereign states from acting more forcefully in the face of a perceived major health peril to their citizens. In granting cigarettes this unaccountably privileged status, the House measure flew further in the face of logic by requiring the warning on the pack when the "more realistic and responsible approach," as California Representative John Moss, the one vocal antismoking spokesman in the House, put it, would have been to warn in cigarette advertising "before the product is purchased."

The story was different in the United States Senate, where the eighteen members of the powerful Commerce Committee were closely divided on the cigarette labeling proposal. Further complicating the picture was the recent arrival on the committee of the tobacco industry's chief (and only) Senate tormentor, Oregon's Maurine Neuberger. At the outset of the term she had put into the legislative hopper a labeling law that essentially confirmed the FTC's regulatory rule. If the Senate's bill was to prove as much of a valentine to the tobacco industry as the House version, Neuberger indicated she might oppose it as worse than no bill at all.

The fate of any Senate bill rested in the hands of the Commerce Committee's entrenched chairman, Warren Magnuson of Washington State. In his twentieth year in the Senate by 1965, Magnuson remained little known to the public but was perhaps the best liked, if not most admired, and surely one of the most powerful figures in the upper chamber. Gruff but kindly, with dark-rimmed glasses prone to slip down his prominent ruddy nose and an unlit cigar habitually clenched in his teeth, he was everyone's Dutch uncle and let even strangers call him "Maggie" to his face. A diffident public speaker given to gaucheries like calling France's stuffy president "Poopidoo," in private Magnuson was a prodigious joke-teller, Scotch drinker, cardplayer, and womanizing widower. He devotedly serviced the commercial interests of the timber, canning, and transportation industries vital to his Northwest base, and as he gained seniority in the Senate, he saw to it that his home state, with but 2 percent of the U.S. population, reaped 15 percent of the public-works funds allocated by Congress. Above all, "Maggie" was a horse-trading pragmatist and a pawn of special interests, whose name was attached to few pieces of significant legislation.

In 1962, Magnuson had narrowly held on to his Senate seat in a campaign against a political novice. A remarkable intellectual and moral metamorphosis followed, as the frightened "Maggie" transformed his Commerce Committee staff, long the darlings of lobbyists who were used to writing the regulatory laws for their own industries, into a team of crack young legal eagles bent on reforming economic abuses and elevating Magnuson's stature. Suddenly, there were Magnuson and his boys floor-managing the highly sensitive public-accommodations section of the 1964 Civil Rights Act, framing the fair labeling and packaging bills, and for the better part of the next decade pushing public-spirited laws through Congress. Remarked one veteran Washington public-relations man about Magnuson's young staffers, "They turned that cigar-smoking, wenching old man into Mr. Consumer." Some said he was too pliable to the wishes of his power-hungry young handlers, but insiders felt he knew precisely how long a leash to give his aides and could detect far better than they the feints and bluffs of other Senate heavyweights and their staffers.

Prominent among Magnuson's new reform-minded assistants was Michael Pertschuk, a brainy and amiable lawyer who had come to America at the age of five from London, where his Russian-born father had been a successful furrier. Raised on New York's Long Island, Pertschuk earned his college and law degrees at Yale, clerked for a civil-liberties-minded federal judge in Oregon, and, on his recommendation, joined the Washington legislative staff of that state's liberal senator, Maurine Neuberger, providing much of the energy for her anti-smoking efforts and the prose for her lucid, muckraking book, *Smoke Screen*. When Neuberger gained a seat on the Commerce Committee, Pertschuk was made a staff lawyer and stayed thirteen years, rising to chief counsel. Blessed with acutely tuned political antennae, adroitness at exchanging confidences, and an unstudied puckishness that softened his high purposefulness, Pertschuk served Magnuson so well that he was delegated great authority in drafting legislation and thus became one of the most powerful appointees on Capitol Hill.

But as a novice, charged with riding herd on what was to become known as the Federal Cigarette Labeling and Advertising Act, Pertschuk was not entirely unwitting clay in the hands of Earle Clements. Tobacco's chief lobbyist, with his peerless political connections, at first seemed to Magnuson's young aide to be the embodiment of evil—until Clements turned his flattering attention to Pertschuk, took him to lunch, and charmed him with political war stories and his exploits in trying to bring civil rights to Kentucky. At one point, referring wryly to the medical evidence and the alleged mortality toll of smoking, Clements commented confidentially, "You know, Pertschuk, when you're on the side of the angels, it's easier to stretch the truth."

Eager to be taken for a political realist and no posturing idealist, anxious to get Magnuson's name affixed as sponsor of a pro-health measure even if it had more gravy than meat in it, Pertschuk gave ground to Clements and his cadre of industry lawyers. The cautionary language in the Magnuson bill was even softer than in the House version: "Warning: Habitual Cigarette Smoking May Be Hazardous to Your Health"—"habitual" was a close cousin to "excessive," a vague term avoided in the medical lexicon since no health investigators could authoritatively define the threshold of risk from smoking. While

Pertschuk yielded on the critical congressional power to preempt any federal or state requirement for a health warning and omitted a warning requirement in cigarette advertising, Magnuson's bill did call for the listing of tar and nicotine strengths on each package. By contrast, Maurine Neuberger's bill had kept faith with the public-health community by requiring a warning label in ads as well as on packs that said smoking "is dangerous," not merely "may be hazardous," and did not bar further regulatory steps by the federal and state governments. Right after formally submitting Magnuson's version, Pertschuk went out to a dinner party to celebrate his thirty-second birthday and confessed his uneasiness to a close friend, Stanley Cohen, the chief capital reporter for *Advertising Age*, who, upon hearing the details, called it a "shocking" bill. Pertschuk went to Magnuson's top Commerce Committee counsel the next day and got the preemptive concession stripped from the bill as submitted.

At the Senate Commerce Committee hearings on the labeling bill, though, the public-health community was passive while the tobacco industry was permitted by Magnuson to parade as witnesses thirty-eight scientists, most paid for their services by the cigarette makers and some recipients of Tobacco Industry Research Committee grants, who did their best to cast doubt on the findings of the Surgeon General's committee. By contrast, the antitobacco forces' chief spokesman, Emerson Foote of the Interagency Council on Smoking and Health, expressed his doubts about the value of warning labels on cigarette packages instead of in advertising. "I don't think any real gain will be made on the health front," said Foote, "until you make the advertising self-defeating." This remark was pounced on by the cigarette companies' sole spokesman at the hearings, Reynolds's courtly chairman, Bowman Gray, Jr., who chain-smoked his way through several hours of masterful testimony. With what seemed more like sorrow than bitterness, Gray denied the need for any regulatory legislation and assured the Senate panel that his company and its competitors were "profoundly conscious" of the health allegations against them and had committed millions to medical research in view of "the lack of definitive clinical and laboratory scientific evidence on the relationship between smoking and health."

As the Senate version of the bill reached the markup stage, the seemingly manipulable Pertschuk, in behalf of his affable boss, accepted the House version's wording for the warning label, which Clements said the industry would buy, provided there was no further mention of warning labels in cigarette advertising. Broadcasters and magazine publishers pushed the same point. Pressure by the industry kept rising as the vote neared. Pertschuk would later remember seeing a pink telephone-message slip on Magnuson's desk saying, "Abe Fortas called—he wants you to vote for the House version of the cigarette labeling bill"—an unsubtle implication that the attorney was speaking for Magnuson's erstwhile congressional colleague, President Johnson. Not surprisingly, the inclusion of tar and nicotine content on cigarette packs was stripped from the Magnuson bill, in part because the industry's ad code administrator, Robert Meyner, told the Commerce Committee, "No one has given me any testimony that removing tar and nicotine makes the cigarette safer." Regarding the size and location of the warning labels, which the House bill directed to appear on one side of the pack, the Magnuson bill insisted only that the warning be in "conspicuous and legible type" somewhere on the pack.

But with regard to one vital ingredient in the House measure Magnuson drew the line—that no statement other than the warning required by the act "shall be required" on any cigarette pack nor would any other "relating to smoking and health . . . be required in the advertising of any cigarettes" labeled in conformity with the act. That would have meant a permanent ban on such measures by the FTC, any other federal agency, and all state and local governments. "Maggie" said that a four-year ban was as far as he would go, and meanwhile everyone could watch what effects, if any, the warning labels on the packs and the industry's self-imposed ad code would have.

Left up in the air was the question, growing more important by the year with the proliferation of product liability suits, of precisely what Congress meant in the labeling bill when it said no other health warnings "shall be required". Required by whom and for what? Normally the adequacy of a warning by the manufacturer and the purchaser's subsequent assumption of risk of the disclosed health hazard would be left to a jury to determine. But the congressional preemptive language in the 1965 labeling act could be interpreted to mean that no smoker afflicted after the warning label was put on the packs could bring a liability suit for tort under the common-law provisions or statutes of his or her state. "It was not brought to my attention in that way," Philip Morris President Joseph Cullman would later recall. The bill, Cullman said, was intended only to avoid "insurmountable logistical problems" that would have arisen if the federal warning label had not been the only one permitted. Lorillard's chief executive at that time, Morgan Cramer III, concurred; the labeling law, he said, "was never intended to protect us from lawsuits," though it was no secret that it might help the industry defend them, once filed.

But neither Cullman nor Cramer was a lawyer, and their hired counselors were far more attentive to the nuances of the preemption language and how far it extended the industry's protection. Lorillard's Washington attorney, Robert Wald, recalled that while the labeling law did not explicitly preclude state liability suits from being filed, it came close to providing the industry with an ironclad defense: "It got us assumption of risk—the warning label would do that. This was the [industry's] major motivation in accepting the legislation," and even as the tobacco spokesmen kept saying for the record that they opposed the warning label, "privately we desperately needed it." And privately some in the tobacco legal corps foresaw the day when judges would grant motions to throw out liability suits against the industry under state tort common law because all plaintiffs had been adequately forewarned under the preemptive federal labeling statute. "You bet," remarked Philip Morris attorney Alexander Holtzman, who was on the scene when the 1965 law was crafted, "but we didn't do much crowing about it." If recovery under common-law actions had been allowable, other industry lawyers added, Congress would have said so.

Precisely the opposite reading, however, was also possible: if Congress had intended to remove the right of smokers to claim that they had been damaged by an unreasonably dangerous product, warning or no warning, the lawmakers would have said so. "It would be like pickling fuzz from the universe to find in the labeling act an intention in Congress to preempt the states from enforcing product liability common law," said Pertschuk. "There was no such intention expressed in any of the debates at that time. The preemption was designed very simply to prevent the states from requiring more than Congress did in the interest of [labeling] uniformity." Even if Congress had not so intended, though, its language was sufficiently ambiguous so that twenty-six years would pass before the U.S. Supreme Court settled the question, more or less.

The 1965 labeling law was widely seen at the time of its passage as "an unabashed act to protect private industry from government regulation," as Elizabeth Drew wrote in her probing analysis of the law's odyssey, "The Quiet Victory of the Cigarette Lobby," in the September 1965 *Atlantic Monthly*. Over at the FTC, the agency's most spirited commissioner, Philip Elman, thought the new law "one of the dirtiest pieces of legislation ever." Senator Frank Moss, Democrat of Utah, remarked that in exchange for a few tepid cautionary words on the side of the pack, "Congress exempted the cigarette industry from the normal regulatory process." Michael Pertschuk would later concede that "it was quite a cynical bill."

Yet given the times and the realities of political power, a tougher law would not likely have been enacted. "That bill was in the interests of mankind," remarked Edward DeHart, the Hill & Knowlton publicist perhaps closest to the lawmaking process. And arguably, the substance of the labeling law mattered less than the fact of it: for the first time, the federal government had acted against the perils of cigarette smoking. The product now would bear the stigma of being officially labeled a hazard, and the lethal risk smokers ran had passed from the realm of folklore into state notification of their folly.

All but lost sight of in the bickering over the fine print in the labeling law was a provision, thought to be harmless by the industry lawyers, that the FTC and the HEW Department, through the Surgeon General's office, would report annually to Congress on cigarette advertising and the relationship of smoking to health. That sop to the two agencies would in time help turn smoking into a pressing public issue.

VIII

EVEN as medical and political forces were conspiring to narrow the appeal of smoking, one cigarette manufacturer was making a major marketing decision that would dramatically alter the future course and control of the industry.

Philip Morris, under the steadying hand of Parker McComas and the whip hand of Joe Cullman, had earned good grades for enlightened corporate leadership. The first cigarette maker to diversify seriously, PM in the early 1960s was working to expand the appeal of its non-tobacco consumer products by, for example, putting its ASR shaving products line early into the stainless steel razor blade market and adding flavors to its Clark chewing gum business. As the first American tobacco company to go hard after foreign sales, it had gotten a toehold in Europe in 1963 by buying up a strong Swiss manufacturer that would shortly become its base for a worldwide drive. And in defending tobacco against the growing threat of federal regulation, PM was the clear industry leader.

But Philip Morris was still the smallest of the six major cigarette companies in sales. Its leading brand, Marlboro, after a strong send-off, was in a rut. Winston's volume was nearly triple the Marlboro figure. To stir a little life into sales, singer Julie London in her smoky, come-hither voice began crooning, "Where there's a man, there's a Marlboro," as if summoning every red-blooded fellow within hearing range to share one with her. But neither she nor comedian Jackie Gleason—in his prime and exclaiming after a deep drag on a Marlboro, "Ah, how sweet it is!"—could get the brand moving. The rest of the Philip Morris stable was doing no better.

The Marlboro slump had been aggravated at the outset of the 'Sixties by a smear campaign that its field force traced to slanders spread by rival salesmen. The brand was said to be so deadly that the government had banned it from military bases and VA hospitals, and some states were reportedly quarantining Marlboro on health grounds. Rumormongers said that two little red coding dots on the Marlboro tax stamp signified that the brand had been banned in certain regions. The crude calumny hurt sales. Heavy sampling and promotional contests were launched to combat the slippage, followed by an ad campaign in 1961 to blunt the charges of any kind of regional taboo. "Wherever you travel this summer," ran the copy, "from the Klondike to Key West . . . in any state . . . in every state you're in Marlboro Country."

That phrase, "Marlboro Country," lodged in the collective consciousness of the Leo Burnett ad agency team as it struggled over the next several years to break Marlboro out of its lethargic numbers. The Burnett people would fly into

New York from Chicago almost every Tuesday night for two brainstorming days and fun-filled nights with Philip Morris marketers, most notably Jack Landry, the irreverent, hard-drinking Marlboro brand manager, who recalled that many blue-sky ad schemes got scribbled down on cocktail napkins, only to be discarded as hopeless by dawn's sobering light. But the Burnett-PM ad team could not ignore results from the advertising industry's regular monitoring of the effectiveness of individual ads and larger campaigns: Of all the two-fisted incarnations they had given the Marlboro Man since the brand's launch, one stood out by far. "Every time we ran a cowboy," recounted Burnett account executive John Benson, "there'd be a blip in the research, saying, 'Hey, people like seeing cowboys.' " Landry especially, having grown up in Saratoga Springs, with horses on the brain, noted that none of the vocations and avocations depicted scored better than ranching: "We had pretty well determined that, if we could make it work, what we wanted to go with was a campaign that focused strictly on the cowboys."

Since Marlboro sold best in big cities, the cowboy campaign began as a city-Western hybrid. Cowpokes were incongruously posed against famous city backdrops—Wall Street and Yankee Stadium in New York, Philadelphia's Liberty Bell, or the Hollywood Bowl—and the image bore in large, stenciled lettering the words "Marlboro Country." The voice-over on the television version intoned: "From the canyons of New York to the canyons of Colorado . . . a man's world of flavor in this cigarette." When sales failed to respond, the Marlboro ad team devoted months trying to figure out how to take the final step, putting the cowboy in his natural environment without making him seem irrelevant to city smokers. Production crews shot fresh TV footage of galloping cowboys against a rugged Western landscape and gave an off-camera narrator such full-throated lines as, "This is my country—big, open—makes a man feel ten feet tall" and "This kind of place takes a special breed of man," and his choice of cigarette was "like this country—it has spirit!" Even so, as Landry remembered, "it still didn't come off—there was an ingredient missing."

Then one day a member of the Burnett creative team brought to New York a recording of the score for the 1960 Western film *The Magnificent Seven*, by veteran Hollywood composer Elmer Bernstein. The Philip Morris conference room was darkened, the video footage rolled, and the narrator spieled to the rousing movie music, a pastiche part Aaron Copland, part Rossini's overture from *William Tell*, part Grofé's *Grand Canyon Suite*. The net effect was electrifying: a cigarette as larger-than-life hero, its virtues made manifest by thundering hoofbeats and soaring brass horns. "There was an almost immediate reaction," Landry recalled ever after. "The music made it all come off."

Rights to the movie music were purchased from United Artists, and the spirited strains at once became the Marlboro national anthem. Although Philip

Morris executives approved the musical glorification of their leading brand, fears lingered over putting all their Marlboro advertising into cowboy gear. "Quite a few top management people felt it was too macho and limited in scope," Landry remembered, risky in terms of attracting city dwellers and women smokers. Two marketing studies were ordered, and both indicated that if the all-Western campaign continued, the brand might die within five years.

But Landry refused to be scared off. He operated by instinct, not by the book, and felt that great advertising was more art than science. Of the dooms-day prospects for the cowboy campaign revealed in the research studies, he said, "I didn't believe it—I didn't think research truly reflected the impact the advertising had on consumers. People are very reluctant to tell you they've been impacted by advertising—the questioner will think they're patsies if they've been led down the path by advertising." The tendency was exacerbated in the case of cigarette advertising, in the view of Burnett's Marlboro account man, John Benson: "When you ask people why they smoke a particular brand, the answer is, 'I like it—the flavor.' " In-depth interviews disclosed little more; cigarette marketers, in short, were blind probers through a jungle of irrational impulses, trying to peddle a product that medical science was condemning more loudly by the day.

Landry persevered in the face of mounting criticism of the cowboy campaign. The advertising was steadily refined, the pitch sharpened. The theme line of 1963, "Wherever there are men who like a flavor smoke with character—that's Marlboro Country," was tightened and became 1964's simple breakthrough sell, "Come to where the flavor is. . . . Come to Marlboro Country." It was no overnight sensation. The brand's 1964 sales actually dipped by nearly a billion units, but Landry stuck to his guns. The campaign, he would say, "wasn't designed to make you run to the corner store and buy a pack." The numbers, though, made Landry's chief backer, President Joe Cullman, shaky about the cowboy theme. "And who wouldn't be," Landry asked in retrospect, "if he heard things all week like 'You're going to ruin this fucking company if you run with it'?"

Because the cigarette business lost ground in 1964, it was easy to miss the fact that Marlboro lost less than its competitors. The following year, its sales spurted 10 percent, and would jump by that percentage or more annually for the rest of the decade as it galloped past Kent and Salem to become the industry's second-best-selling brand. Winston was still selling twice as many units, but there was a glow now at Philip Morris headquarters.

Thirty years later, even though restricted by law to print media only, "Marlboro Country" survived as one of the longest-running and most successful advertising campaigns ever devised. Its enduring appeal was an overworked metaphor that generated its resonating power in direct proportion to the distance from the reality in which most smokers dwelled and by the passionate attention to detail with which the imagery was rendered. "Marlboro Country" seemed to beckon Americans to an earlier, simpler, morally unambiguous time, to the frontier irretrievably lost to the encroachment of thronged modernity. In the final third of the twentieth century, the nation too often found its cities increasingly blighted and violent, its suburbs sterile and conformist, its offices glazed and hermetic boxes, its work programmed and dehumanizing, its government inept when not corrupt, its faith bereft of nobler instincts, and life in general more alienating than fulfilling. As Norman Muse, then a Burnett copywriter for Marlboro and later chairman of the agency's international operations, capsulized it, "People don't want to be in the city, smelling all that crap." "Marlboro Country" transported them past smug suburbia and the cloying sweetness of Norman Rockwell's small towns, out beyond the tidy Arcadia and pastoral prettiness pictured in the Salem and Newport ads, to an immense, indeed limitless, landscape, awesome in its rugged yet serene beauty, where the menaces of nature were ultimately manageable, the mountain streams pure, the chuckwagon fare hearty and unfattening, and the skies were not sooty all day. "Marlboro Country" was what Bruce Lohof, in a 1969 paean to commercial iconography in the *Journal of Popular Culture*, trenchantly called "an environmental memoir, reminding Americans of where they had been and inviting them vicariously to return." Above all, "Marlboro Country" was unpolluted, free of hazards to one's moral and physical health—precisely the opposite of what science and the government were saying about smoking cigarettes.

And there was the correlative appeal of the Marlboro cowboy himself, as far a cry as possible from Woody Allen with all his urban hang-ups and psychic dysfunction. This ultimate Marlboro Man was a throwback hero, strong, stoic, self-reliant, free (though not without responsibilities), potent—the kind of man women are drawn to—and he never punched a time clock. He was capable of both repose, kneeling pensively beside a campfire, say, while drawing on his smoke with satisfaction, and of action gracefully executed, whether shown heading up a canyon after a thirty-mile ride shaking cattle out of the mesquite, scattering a threatened stampede, or just lugging his saddle past the corral gate. And he was classless, purposely neither a boss nor a hand, though his white hat, confident gait, and effortless handling of his mount tagged him as a leader and no grubby bunkhouse malingerer. He was also an apolitical man of peace who was never armed and had no enemies, a knight errant patrolling his craggy Eden and embodying what Frederick Jackson Turner had termed, in writing of the frontiersman, "that dominant individualism . . . that buoyancy and exuberance which comes with freedom."

And what sort of cigarette would such a fellow smoke—as smoke he surely would with all that time and space on his hands? "For me, always, the cowboy contains the expression of flavor," commented David Dangoor, an articulate latter-day head of Philip Morris's marketing. "I could not think of anything more convincing." And indeed one was convinced that the Marlboro cowboy liked his coffee strong, his horse powerful and fast, and his smoke with a full-bodied taste—to hell with its tar and nicotine content or the harping of the sissy Surgeon General.

It all may have worked because there was so little text—when you got right down to it, how much was there to say in praise of cigarettes that was neither gross exaggeration nor an outright lie?—and the page-filling pictures had a grainy, almost documentary immediacy enhanced by the attention to every detail of the composition. In an age when "plastic" became the dismissive adjective of choice for the fake and insubstantial, nothing plastic was allowed in "Marlboro Country," starting with the cowboys themselves. "Young cowboys look like they're in costume," remarked Hall Adams, who worked on the Marlboro account starting in 1961 and later became chairman of the Burnett agency. Added Jack Landry, "You needed guys who looked comfortable on a horse, men who had lived outdoors in all weather—whose lives showed in their faces." At one shoot early in the campaign, Adams recalled, by way of vouching for the Burnett team's insistence on authenticity in their models, they imported a good-looking rodeo star to the location ranch, where the hands had supposed that the stranger was an armchair cowboy from Hollywood, and so they produced the nastiest stallion on the spread for him to struggle with during the filming. The rodeo rider took one look at the archetypal White Lightning, got the picture at once, and gave the horse a wicked clout across the snout that made him rear in fear and then settle down tamely—to the wide-eyed amazement of the resident hands. All understood thereafter the code of "Marlboro Country": no dudes wanted.

There were no town shots, no modern machines, no glossy products, only natural materials—soil, wood, leather—and all inanimate objects were no mere props but working tools, the cowboy's spurs worn and dented, his fleece-lined Marley coat a necessity against the stinging wind and cold, his camp's pots and pans blackened from use. And all of this was caught by perfectionist photographers, unafraid of horses and thunderstorms, who like painters brought out mood and tonality by how they framed and arranged their compositions, whether in the angle of a horse's silhouetted head, the conformation of mount and rider, the play of a rope, a texture of a slab of wood, even the sense of a driving wind from the fullness of the cloud banks working overhead. It was poetic and thrillingly escapist—and what, finally, was a cigarette but a form of escape?

According to Landry, the man most credited with sustaining the idea, "Marlboro Country" sold cigarettes because the product "lived up to what we say or imply it's going to deliver. Because it's a good, flavorful cigarette—and that's all we say about it." If the campaign was, as one Burnett executive called it, "dumbbell simple," it was also inoffensive. In the words of Thomas C. Littleton, then a Philip Morris salesman and later director of the Southeast region, where the company's fortunes had long languished, "It played everywhere"—except in Texas and other parts of the Southwest, where real ranch hands did not relish being seen as Marlboro cowboys. Most of all, the Western metaphor gave Marlboro a firm identity that front-running Winston had always lacked. Even in Winston-Salem, Reynolds people were inclined to think of Winston as "a Camel with a filter," as veteran RJR sales executive Yancey Ford called it, and the catchy little jingle about its tasting "good like a cigarette should" did not do much for the brand's personality, any more than did the fun-and-games approach of its mentholated companion brand, Salem. Their airy, recreational approach struck a discordant note in 'Sixties America, with all its social upheaval, and unlike the toothsome smokers in the ads for Reynolds brands, the Marlboro Man never smiled—true heroes didn't. For life just then was earnest and not a little painful, and smoking, while pleasurable, had its perils, as all the world was now being advised. Maybe the Marlboro cowboy knew it, too, but indulged nonetheless, fatalistically, as if in possession of the core secret of the great happy hunting ground he roamed: Life is a terminal disease.

10

Three-Ton Dog on the Prowl

THE tobacco industry late in 1964 installed its "tar czar," former New Jersey Governor Robert Meyner, and a staff of six investigators in a thirtieth-floor suite in a midtown Manhattan office building and gave them broad powers to enforce its new code for advertising. In its first thirty months, Meyner would proudly report later to the skeptical Federal Trade Commission, his staff threw out 1,025 of the 16,000 or so ads submitted to it for approval, and more than half of the 154 campaign themes presented to them were denied unqualified approval. His job, he said, was neither "to increase the sale of cigarettes nor to depress them" but to quash ads that made health claims explicitly or implicitly or that appealed primarily to those under twenty-one. Testimonials by athletes were dropped, tobacco sponsorship of certain family comedy shows and fantasies on television like "Gilligan's Island" and "I Dream of Jeannie" ended, and Philip Morris had to dispense with the services of Julie London, whose husky-voiced spots were used as a break from the musky "Marlboro Country" ads, because the singer was (a) a celebrity, (b) an entertainer, and (c) feeding the sexual fantasies of underage viewers (leave aside those of male adults). The trouble arose when the advertising people for the industry, with company lawyers in tow, showed up before Meyner bearing storyboards for ads and commercials of a more marginal nature.

"He was a tough enforcer," recalled a Philip Morris lawyer on the team that dealt with the code administrator, "but a pretty arbitrary guy—you'd never know what you might run into with Meyner. He and his staff wanted to alter the whole complexion of cigarette advertising by making it lower key." In practice, their censorship was more curious than consistent or principled. A girl pictured in a sweater might be deemed to look unsuitably young, so the sweater had to be replaced by a dress, but the next pretty nubile miss might pass muster. You could show a smoker out sailing or trout-fishing, but in a waterskiing scene the smoker had to be the one driving the towboat. It was permissible to show someone wearing tennis garb and/or sitting near the court and smoking, and to show the same person in the locker room afterward in a fresh nonathletic shirt and lighting up, but it was *verboten* to picture anyone playing and smoking in tandem.

Yet in many cases Meyner's reading of health claims into ads was almost laughably broad. Scenes that showed a cigarette turning a smoker's foul mood into contented bliss or a smoker dragging too deeply in a quest for euphoria were stricken. And linkages of smoking and sex made the censors nervous; thus, "Camel time is pleasure time" had to be changed to "Camel time is flavor time," and "Happiness is the taste of Kent" was censured for equating happiness with good health, whereas no objection was raised to "I changed to Winston, and I changed for good," with health among the possible readings of that "good". Winston, though, was not allowed to refer to its filter as "modern," "pure," or "white" on the ground that they all connoted a therapeutic quality. More puzzling still, Tareyton's "charcoal filter" had to become "filter of charcoal," and despite the mandated taboo against linking smoking with social success, no objection was raised when Parliament was said to suit "the right time . . . the right place . . . the right people." For such inconsistencies, Meyner was soon said by the tobacco lawyers to have "a whim of iron."

There was nothing whimsical, though, about the code administrator's directives to Philip Morris's resident ad genius, Jack Landry, zealous guardian of the authenticity of "Marlboro Country". "Meyner would tell you to slow the horses down, there was too much action," Landry recounted of the ad czar's sweeping interpretation of athleticism. More to the point, Meyner was convinced that the Marlboro cowboys were highly attractive to youngsters and enticed them to begin smoking, and when Landry protested, fearing that the whole campaign might be endangered, Meyner ordered a survey of New Jersey high school students to assess the impact of Marlboro ads. The study did show a marked and growing preference for the brand among the teens, but, as Landry recalled, "Not one kid mentioned our advertising or the cowboy. It was 'My friends like it' or they thought the package was attractive." Meyner backed off, but not before disallowing the cowboy to be shown delivering the sales pitch or heard in a first-person voice-over. Nor could the cowboy be presented in too heroic a pose, as from a very low camera angle aimed upward. "We used to shoot the Marlboro Man as if he were the Jolly Green Giant, Paul Bunyan, Jack Gonads—now we had to work him down to life size," said one member of the Leo Burnett agency production team.

The serious displeasure within the industry over Meyner's conduct was reflected in a memorandum written late in 1965 by Lorillard's outside counsel, Washington lawyer Robert Wald, complaining of the code office's lack of impartiality and its permissiveness in allowing Marlboro to proceed with "a great campaign with probably the greatest appeal to kids: the gnarled, weatherbeaten cowboy—the hottest virility, sexual symbol going," and Winston "to use all the gimmicks proscribed for kids: romantic, daring, imitative figures, excessive pleasure, fun, fun, fun. . . ." Particularly objectionable to Wald was Salem's springtime-in-the-woods theme implying that a nice smoke was a passport to health and romance and a mentholated one was bursting with the freshness of youth in nature's season of renewal. The Lorillard lawyer asked of the young lovers displayed in these bosky idylls, "Where had this couple been? Where are they going? Wherever, it is plain Salem is the reward—or the essential prelude." Yet these smoke-clad romances evaded Meyner's ax. As one ad agency executive catering to a tobacco client told *Harper's* in March 1966, "That's the reason no one [on Madison Avenue] is really worried about the code. They can't stop us from showing good-looking people doing good-looking things." And so millions continued to be lavished on ads linking cigarettes with hillside romps, picnics at the beach, and the whole gang gathered around the family piano, laughing over a half-witted pleasantry.

If Meyner's enforcement rulings often seemed governed by caprice, he consistently maintained that since smoking cigarettes had not been proven to cause disease, it followed that brands with lowered yields of tar and nicotine could not be said to be safer than others, even if segments of the public leaped to that supposition; brands with reduced numbers were merely catering to a marketplace demand. By the same thinking, Meyner outdid the FTC in stringency with regard to references to filters, holding it improper "to identify or describe the structure, characteristics, function, or performance of a filter, to use qualifying adjectives . . . or in any way to represent that a filter has a function or purpose other than to affect tobacco taste" because such assertions constituted an implied health claim.

Such a reading of the 1960 FTC ruling that effectively halted the "tar derby" was a blow to the marketing efforts of brands aimed at the health-conscious smoker, including American Tobacco's lowered tar Carlton, Philip Morris's Parliament, and especially Lorillard's Kent, the industry leader, selling 3 million packs a day and inspiring the company to ready for market an even lower-yielding brand, to be called True. In a sharp letter to Meyner, Lorillard asserted that "if manufacturers can't identify, describe, or differentiate the specific unique distinguishing characteristics . . . of their filters in advertising, they cannot effectively compete—either with other filter brands or with nonfilter brands." But that was a desirable limitation for the makers of the best-selling, "full-flavor" brands like Winston and Marlboro, on which the filter was essentially a placebo-like appendage. Meyner's approval of ads for brands that claimed to "put taste back into filter smoking" prompted Lorillard's counselor Wald to grumble intramurally, "If Meyner had ears to listen with, someone might tell him the only way you can do this is by piling more tar and nicotine in. . . ." Meyner even threatened Lorillard's continued use of the "Micronite" name for its filter on the ground that it and others, like Marlboro's "Selectrate" filter, were little more than science-fiction labels. With tens of millions invested in the name, Lorillard battled to keep the "Micronite" name but agreed to separate it from the word "filter" on the package.

As the leading pursuer of health-conscious smokers, Lorillard mounted a largely clandestine offensive in Washington that aroused its competitors' darkest suspicions—namely, that Lorillard was in effect conceding the health charges against cigarettes. Lorillard's president, Manuel Yellen, became a poker-playing crony of Warren Magnuson, while attorney Wald would meet with Magnuson's key aide on the issue, Michael Pertschuk. Magnuson, Pertschuk, and antismoking activists like Senator Maurine Neuberger and ex-adman Emerson Foote, who had, in the end, supported the soft 1965 labeling law and then been burned by criticism that they had caved in to the tobacco industry, were highly susceptible to Lorillard's argument that brands like theirs, with reduced tar and nicotine, were in fact a less hazardous smoke and ought to be encouraged by steps like requiring that yields be listed on the packages and in the ads of every brand, as the original Magnuson bill had proposed.

Pertschuk in particular was responsive to Lorillard's position when it was embraced as well by two of the most authoritative investigators in the field, Daniel Horn and Ernst Wynder. Horn, the behavioral psychologist at the American Cancer Society who had parted company unhappily with Cuyler Hammond and then been let go by the cancer society for his erratic work habits, landed on his feet as the first director of the National Clearinghouse on Smoking and Health, a tiny unit added to the U.S. Public Health Service late in 1965 as an afterthought to the labeling legislation. The Clearinghouse was created to be a repository for all data and studies dealing with smoking and to assist in educating the nation to the attendant health peril. Horn cultivated Pertschuk and, like Wald, urged him to push Magnuson to get the FTC, which received its funding through Magnuson's committee, to rescind its 1960 ruling against advertising tar and nicotine numbers as an unsubstantiated health claim. Wynder, meanwhile, was passing to Magnuson's office test results from his laboratory at Sloan-Kettering, showing that the yields from most filter brands remained as high as those from unfiltered brands.

The upshot of this backstage campaign was that FTC chairman Rand Dixon readily accepted Magnuson's offer of congressional funding for a small testing laboratory under the commission's aegis to monitor the tar and nicotine yields of all widely available brands on a quarterly basis, with the results made public so that, as Magnuson put it when the first list was issued in the latter part of 1967, smokers could thereafter "choose their poison" more intelligently and the industry would be inspired to develop less hazardous brands. With the planned laboratory available to establish an objective factual basis for claimed tar and nicotine yields, the FTC could then roll back its 1960 order against advertising the numbers. Pertschuk went to the manufacturers to advise them, not to ask their approval—"I'd grown up by then," he said—of what was coming, and in the late spring of 1966 the FTC sent a terse letter to the industry ending the ban on the yield figures in cigarette ads, "which may be material and desired by the consuming public."

But cigarette advertising code czar Meyner, in a holier-than-thou ruling that reflected the strong preference of industry leader R. J. Reynolds, declared that his office would continue to regard the listing of tar and nicotine yields in cigarette advertising as "inherently deceptive." That was enough for Lorillard, which halted its voluntary compliance with the code and brought out its new True brand, lower-yielding than Kent. Company President Yellen explained, "We felt it was in the public's interest to inform smokers about True's filter—any manufacturer ought to be able to do this without having to consult with a code." Thus, the industry's united front on advertising policy was broken, amid growing rancor toward Lorillard for trying to advance at the expense of its competitors by feeding public apprehension over the safety of their common product.

II

IN the immediate wake of the 1964 advisory report to the Surgeon General, the broadcasting industry, beneficiary of some 70 percent of the cigarette makers' advertising budgets, registered cautious concern about its own role in transmitting messages that might mislead millions of listeners and viewers. The National Association of Broadcasters' Code of Television Advertising adopted a resolution stating that cigarette advertising carried by its member stations "should not be presented in a manner to convey the impression that smoking promotes health or is important to the personal development of the youth of our country." Stricter guidelines of acceptability, however, were put aside pending actions taken by the tobacco industry's newly announced Cigarette Advertising Code. At the TV Code Authority's New York office, where cigarette ads were screened for stations seeking the NAB's judgment, the early impression was that cigarette code czar Meyner was no flunky of his employers and meant business.

But in the wake of Meyner's adversarial response to the FTC's 1966 about-face, the NAB Code's New York office concluded that he was a captive of the tobacco companies and, without asking the permission of its parent headquarters in Washington, compiled a report which found that smoking was still depicted as "universally acceptable, attractive and desirable" and part of "a world to which the adolescent aspires." When the New York report was sent to NAB executives along with proposals that the broadcasters' own code be stiffened by eliminating from cigarette ads all sports settings, springtime imagery, heroic types including cowboys, and any depiction of the act of smoking, NAB President Vincent Wasilewski ruled that such toughening measures were "premature," and the New York office's report was pigeonholed for biting the nicotine-stained hand that was feeding his industry. Indeed, word reached the New York office from the TV Code's board chairman, Clair McCullough, regarding requests by NAB member stations for approval of cigarette ads: "When in doubt, okay it." And when American Tobacco followed Lorillard in withdrawing from the cigarette industry's code agreement because the company was already submitting its ads to the broadcasters' code office for vetting, no NAB official disclosed that such submissions were not occurring systematically, as the industry code required.

Frustrated, Warren Braren, principal author of the New York office's report, took to transmitting under-the-table advisories of his office's findings on the unreformed nature of cigarette advertising to the FTC's enforcement division, which retained its power under the 1965 labeling law to move against false or misleading ads for smoking. But Braren never drew a response from the FTC, whose oversight practices struck him as "a charade. It was like putting down atrocities on a piece of paper and filing it."

The FTC, as it turned out, was not quite so passive. In mid-1967, the commission issued the first of its annual reports to Congress on the tobacco industry as required by the labeling law, and it proved highly critical of the cigarette makers' efforts at self-policing. The companies' collective advertising pitch "continues to promote the idea that cigarette smoking is both pleasurable and harmless," the regulatory commission found, and it was no great trick for the industry to comply with both its own and the NAB ad codes "without making known the health hazards of smoking." The eighteen-month-old health warning on cigarette packs, moreover, was proving ineffectual, the FTC noted, citing as evidence 1966 unit sales, which reached a new high, and per capita use just under the 1963 record level. The commissioners urged Congress to draw up a stronger warning label and require it, along with disclosure of tar and nicotine yields, in all advertising as well as on the product itself.

As the FTC was signaling that it had not entirely caved in to pressure from the tobacco industry and its congressional agents, its sister regulatory body, the Federal Communications Commission (FCC), issued a ruling that jarred the cigarette companies and broadcasters alike.

The FCC was a more vibrant and focused bureau than the FTC, because it was empowered by statute to oversee a single industry deriving its very existence from access to the airwaves that the country had decided were the joint possession of all Americans. Accordingly, the FCC had a specific constituency, and its rules and regulations applied across the board to all broadcasting licensees; it did not merely respond to alleged infractions on a case-by-case basis as the FTC for the most part did. In this period the FCC was chaired by a Republican careerist, Rosel Hyde, an unscintillating figure who had been with the bureau since the early days of radio. The true locus of the seven-member commission's administrative power was its forty-year-old general counsel, Henry Geller, regarded in Washington as one of the town's most able public servants. A Northwestern law school graduate who had served as a trial attorney with the National Labor Relations Board and as an appellate lawyer in the Justice Department's antitrust division before joining the FCC, Geller was convinced by the 1964 report to the Surgeon General that the broadcasting industry was "hawking a product causing an enormous health risk." This view was thoroughly shared by Chairman Hyde, a Utah Mormon who did not require much persuasion about the perils of tobacco to body or soul, and most of the other commissioners.

Thus, Geller was primed when a letter was referred to him in the first few days of 1967 from a twenty-five-year-old New York City resident named John F. Banzhaf III, a Columbia law graduate who had lately finished clerking for a federal appellate judge on the District of Columbia Circuit and was about to join a New York firm specializing in patent law. After majoring in electrical engineering at MIT, Banzhaf had posted a strong record at Columbia as an argumentative student who, when assigned to write a law review note on whether copyright protection could be extended to the emerging field of computer programming, decided not just to theorize on the issue but to invent a program and try to usher it through the U.S. Patent Office; his success in this process won him a front-page notice in *The New York Times*, an appearance before a congressional committee exploring the subject, and a yen for publicity that would animate his ensuing career. At his Bronx home on Thanksgiving Day of 1966, Banzhaf was struck by the cigarette commercials on the pro football telecast that his family was watching: the cowboys and other figures seemed to glamorize the habit, which both his parents practiced but he himself did not. "If you had asked me to list the top twenty things I was concerned about or wanted to change then, smoking would not have been on it," Banzhaf recalled. But he was aware of the FCC's "fairness doctrine," requiring broadcasters to allow free time to state opposing views on matters of public controversy dealt with on the air. While the doctrine was almost always invoked in connection with the programming sector, Banzhaf did not see why it shouldn't apply with equal force to commercials, which consumed nearly one-fourth of the broadcast day.

As a charged-up youngster with technical training eager to see if he could put his new legal learning to practical application, Banzhaf wrote to the FCC for a pamphlet explaining how the fairness doctrine worked and then fired off a letter in December to WCBS-TV in New York, the station that had carried the football telecast with the offending cigarette commercials. Banzhaf argued that sponsored messages were equally covered by the FCC rule and that the station ought therefore to provide free airtime roughly in proportion to that spent "on your station promoting the virtues and values of smoking."

The station's letter in response a month later stated that since May the CBS network's evening news show anchored by Walter Cronkite had carried six reports on the smoking issue and that since September the network's New York outlet had run six segments by its science editor on the local news presentation, so it was plainly unnecessary to provide free airtime to antismoking adherents. This answer cut no ice with Banzhaf, who, in complaining now to the FCC, noted that by its own admission the TV station gave both sides of the subject on its news reports while commercials, of course, did not—and in view of the heavy volume of the latter, the station's news coverage did not "begin to offset the effects of paid advertisements, prepared by highly skilled experts. . . ."

When Banzhaf's request for free airtime to present the antismoking case arrived, a majority of the FCC members were "already there," as general counsel Geller put it, convinced that a medium regulated in the public interest ought not to be facilitating the sale of life-threatening products. True, the commission could have acted on its own without the goad of an unknown young attorney, "but when his letter came in, it struck a responsive chord, and I thought why not use it."

Geller drew up a draft ruling ordering WCBS-TV and all other stations to meet Banzhaf's petition and brought it to commission chairman Rosel Hyde. The rule, Geller knew, would be a bombshell and immediately provoke a "slippery slope" rebuttal: If you do this with cigarettes, don't you have to make a similar provision for a lot of other products capable of harming consumers? But Geller argued that cigarettes, unlike any other legal product, posed a peril to the health of millions when used normally and in the way intended by their manufacturers. Television and radio, moreover, were manifestly different from print media; broadcast messages were "in the air" and absorbed subliminally or even subconsciously by those tuned in, and what with most homes in that era possessing a single television set that was often the focus of family attention, TV was a pervasive and uniquely mind-shaping, not to say brainwashing, medium. Congress, of course, could have outlawed cigarettes, Geller conceded, but its not having done so on pragmatic grounds did not affect the FCC's statutory power to impose the fairness doctrine on tobacco products. Hyde and all his colleagues agreed.

Early in June 1967, WCBS-TV received a three-page letter from the FCC stressing in a preliminary ruling that "our holding is limited to this product," the normal use of which was so hazardous that "a station which presents such advertisements has the duty of informing its audience of the other side of this controversial issue" and must provide "a significant amount of time for the other viewpoint." While outraged broadcasters and tobacco industry lawyers scrambled to protest, Banzhaf was told by his new employer, a law firm located in the same building that headquartered Philip Morris, for which it handled matters concerning patent law, that it might be a good idea if he turned the FCC matter over to others interested in public-health issues. Banzhaf approached the Interagency Council on Smoking and Health for help, but it failed to agree on any coordinated action, in large part because its most powerful constituent members, the big health voluntaries, felt that their continued existence depended on annual fund-raising drives that were publicized by public-service announcements carried without charge by TV and radio stations. If the health organizations sided against the cigarette industry, they feared that their fund-garnering free ads would be halted by the aggrieved station owners.

As the plump briefs from the broadcasting and tobacco companies opposing the FCC ruling accumulated over the summer, Banzhaf grew anxious that his temporary victory would be overturned unless the objections to it were parried in effective lawyerly fashion—and he saw his role as central in this effort. At the FCC, where a loud squawk had been anticipated from the industries directly affected, the staff felt fully equipped to defend its position if, as seemed likely, litigation ensued. Of Banzhaf himself, Geller recalled, "We never gave him a further thought—he was somebody we were using," and so the youthful lawyer was never called in.

Banzhaf, a bulky six-footer well endowed with self-esteem, was not to be denied. One Washington antismoking activist who dealt with him in later years once remarked of Banzhaf, "He is the sort of person who, upon arising in the morning and seeing the sun shining, assumes there must be a connection between the two events." Convinced that the FCC needed significant outside support to sustain its ruling but fearful that he did not have the skills, time, or money to go up against the big law firms attacking the commission's application of the fairness doctrine to cigarette ads, Banzhaf kept after the Interagency Council. He was granted an audience by Emerson Foote, who found the young man "too brash" and advised him afterward that the council could be of no useful assistance to him. The other agencies Banzhaf approached were likewise uncooperative. "They were all very sympathetic, but they felt themselves dependent on the good will of the broadcasters," Banzhaf recounted. Alone, then, and at dire risk to his continuing employment by a firm with tobacco industry billings, the young lawyer filed his own brief with the FCC to parry the broad-casters' and cigarette makers' objections to the new ruling he had triggered.

Leaving his law office late one Friday evening early in September, Banzhaf picked up an early edition of the next morning's *Times* and read that the FCC had upheld its preliminary ruling on cigarette ads and prescribed one public-service announcement on the perils of smoking to run in prime time for every four cigarette ads carried on the air. Since the ruling in no way prevented broadcasters from carrying cigarette ads and required no warnings during or adjacent to such commercials—and mandated no particular language for the antismoking announcements—the FCC said its action ran afoul of neither the First Amendment nor the 1965 labeling law from Congress, which had pro-scribed any other form of required warning. Congress, the commission said in rejecting industry arguments to the contrary, had surely not meant to foreclose broadcasting "as an effective means of informing the public of the potential hazards of smoking."

Suspecting that broadcasting and tobacco companies would promptly ap-peal the FCC ruling, and in a Southern jurisdiction likely to be hospitable to their case, Banzhaf returned at once to his office and spent the rest of the night there, drawing up a notice of his own appeal to foil the industry effort. Trying to concoct a plausible ground for appealing so that he would have legal stand-ing, he argued that the FCC had failed to mandate equal or adequate free air-time to present the antismoking announcements, and then took the first available plane to Washington the next morning, a Saturday, and filed his no-tice in person with a judge from that tribunal, among the most liberal of the appeals courts—an irregular but permissible procedure. When the industry lawyers filed their own notice of appeal in Richmond on Monday morning, they learned they had lost the race to the courthouse to the vexing Banzhaf. They moved to have his appeal set aside on the ground that he was not truly an aggrieved party and, in shopping for a favorable venue to file, had acted ex-tralegally. In his first courtroom appearance, Banzhaf by himself opposed the industry motion, facing a phalanx of highly paid corporate lawyers—and won.

More than ever now, Banzhaf believed that the fate of the FCC ruling hung on the effort he could mount against the industry's appeal, which was in effect joined with his own case for hearing by the circuit court. Emboldened by his success to date, he crashed the first World Conference on Tobacco and Health held in New York under the Interagency Council's sponsorship and persuaded keynote speaker Senator Robert F. Kennedy, a new recruit in the antismoking crusade, to insert a few sentences in his address urging the health voluntaries to help prevent the FCC ruling from being set aside.

The key to Banzhaf's hopes was the American Cancer Society, the largest and best-funded member of the loose confederation ranged against the tobacco industry. Accounts vary, but several in the society recall that Banzhaf approached the ACS with a request for about $50,000 to represent its interests in the appeal he was bringing. But the society's executive director, Lane Adams, viewed litigation as an improper activity for the ACS: "We were a medical and research institution, and I felt we should stick to our knitting." Adams also feared that filing an *amicus* brief in behalf of the FCC position might imperil the cancer society's tax-exempt status, though it was lobbying rather than litigation that was forbidden to such organizations. More to the point, Banzhaf's was not the sort of personality likely to endear itself to the ACS, a huge, consensual organization not about to hand over its banner to a brash young man, however bright and well intentioned, for storming the barricades. Nor did the society's elders believe that Banzhaf's efforts were necessary after Clifton Read, a veteran ACS executive, canvassed the ACS legal advisors. "The report we got back was that Geller of the FCC was one of the brightest guys in Washington," Read remembered, "and we didn't have to go into this." Banzhaf retained a different memory of the ACS's standoffishness: "They didn't like being controversial . . . didn't want to step on any toes. It was the bureaucratic instinct." Precisely and perhaps understandably, but it was not like Banzhaf as a lone-wolf operator to abide by the basic institutional imperative against offending. "He had the capacity," remarked another antismoking activist, "to say by a sneer that everyone else in the room is a sellout."

Whatever Banzhaf's limitations, his effort to place the FCC ruling before a friendly court seemed justified when Judge David Bazelon of the District of Columbia Circuit ruled late in 1968 that Congress may have thought that the cautionary label it had mandated on each cigarette pack "was adequate *warning*. It surely did not think the warnings were themselves adequate *information*." To accept the industry's argument that the 1965 statute had preempted the FCC initiative, Bazelon wrote, his court would have had to conclude that Congress "legislated to curtail the potential flow of information lest the public learn too much about the hazards of smoking for the good of the tobacco industry and the economy." Regarding the applicability of the fairness doctrine, the judge added:

> [W]here, as here, one party to a debate has a financial clout and a compelling economic interest in the presentation of one side unmatched by its opponent, and where the public stake in the argument is no less than life itself, we think the purpose of rugged debate is served, not hindered, by an attempt to redress the balance.

III

WHEN the FCC ruling went into effect, America was suddenly confronting prime-time images that sent the anxiety level of smokers—and surely that of the tobacco moguls—spiking. The American Cancer Society, with abundant free airtime assured for unfurling its banner, now willingly took the lead in the effort by public-health agencies to decry the perils of smoking via television and radio. ACS publicist Irving Rimer received offers of free help from Madison Avenue in creating the antismoking commercials, provided the cancer society picked up the direct production costs. This top talent crafted a number of haunting messages that underscored how ineffectual, by comparison, the warning labels were on the pack.

Among the simpler efforts was a picture of a pensive fellow smoking while the voice-over asked, "Have you ever wondered what happens when you smoke a cigarette?" There was a pause while the smoker cogitated, and the background voice continued, "We have," as the picture faded and the screen was filled with the words: "American Cancer Society". Another instantly affecting message featured New York advertising guru Tony Schwartz's children, shown dressing up in adult clothes beside an old attic trunk as the narrator intoned, "Children love to imitate their parents—don't smoke." A more elaborate effort, aimed at Marlboro's prized metaphor, showed a saloon-ful of smoking, unshaven villains in ten-gallon hats eyeing a wholesome, smoke-free fellow at the bar. Suddenly, another foul dude barged through the swinging doors, smoking butt adangle from his lip, and proclaimed, "We figured [cough] you'd [cough] be here," but before he and his accomplices could draw, they all fell into an uncontrollable fit of coughing, allowing the stalwart nonsmoker to push by them easily. The barroom faded, replaced by the single word "Cancer," and the voice-over intoned, "Cigarettes—they're killers."

Perhaps the single most moving of the antismoking commercials during the two years they were aired in prime time featured actor William Talman, who had played the prosecutor who always lost to Raymond Burr in the "Perry Mason" television series. After seeing the first of the antismoking messages under the ACS aegis, Talman telephoned Rimer, revealed that he was dying from lung cancer, and asked if a camera crew and scriptwriter could be dispatched at once to his home in California. The commercial showed a drawn and obviously sick man who spoke of his wife and children and the good life he had had, then added: "I have lung cancer. Take some advice about smoking and losing from someone who's been doing both for years. If you don't smoke, don't start. If you do smoke—quit. Don't be a loser." By the time the message aired, Talman was dead.

"We were scaring the bejesus out of the tobacco industry," Rimer said, harking back to that period that was "the most exhilarating time" of his thirty years with the cancer society. Few in the cigarette business would concede the cumulative effectiveness of the estimated $75 million worth of free airtime that the public-health forces were granted under the FCC's fairness doctrine. "I never heard anyone in the industry who said, 'These [antismoking] ads are ruining us,' " recalled Rimer's counterpart then at the Tobacco Institute, William Kloepfer. What truly irked the industry, he said, was that the messages backed by the ACS and other health organizations were "propagandistic rather than factual"—as if cigarette commercials had ever been fair and square and the industry's refutations of the health charges against it were justified.

If Banzhaf's efforts were not overly appreciated at the FCC and the ACS, Henry Geller conceded that the young lawyer performed a singularly useful service in monitoring broadcasters' compliance with the requirement for adequate airtime for the antismoking commercials—a task the FCC's limited staff simply could not accomplish. When Banzhaf, by then out of his law firm and trying to put together his own organization, Action on Smoking and Health (ASH), tabulated the airtime being allotted by New York's WNBC-TV for the antismoking commercials, he found that it came to far less than one-fourth of the time consumed by paid cigarette commercials, the ratio set by the FCC's guideline. He promptly petitioned the commission to strip the NBC network's flagship outlet of its broadcast license—a move that caught all broadcasters' attention and notably improved compliance.

A few years later, as a member of the law faculty at George Washington University specializing in tort law and consumer advocacy, Banzhaf continued his crusade against the tobacco industry, leading the way, for example, in the effort to obtain separate smoking and nonsmoking sections in airplanes. As a frequent public speaker and expert witness before Congress, he had a gift for dramatizing the antismoking case and made telling use of props of his own devising, like an ashtray he distributed to congressional offices that was topped by a plastic model of a pair of human lungs, one of which turned black when it had absorbed enough cigarette smoke. But ASH served in large part as a vehicle for Banzhaf, and his unwillingness to share the spotlight and build an organization would ultimately keep him from becoming what he liked to bill himself as in the early days of the antismoking movement—"the Ralph Nader of the cigarette industry."

IV

AMERICAN TOBACCO, then ranking second in sales in its industry, and last-place Philip Morris faced different challenges in the late 'Sixties.

American, under its new president, ex-salesman Barney Walker, vowed to reverse a seven-year slippage in market share by dramatically altering its product
mix, which was 90 percent in unfiltered brands when Walker took over in
1963. Philip Morris, with 90 percent of its sales already in filter brands, was in
danger of becoming a one-horse stable—only its Marlboro brand was displaying friskiness.

Walker was a whirlwind. He markedly increased the advertising budget,
strengthened the sales force, putting his field men on a pay-for-performance
basis, and installed a companywide profit-sharing plan to spur initiative. He
also cut production costs in ways that old-timers felt were cheapening the company's brands, like making use of less expensive foreign leaf and reconstituted
tobacco sheets, and replaced twelve of the company's seventeen directors, previously all American Tobacco officers, with outsiders. He introduced many
new cigarette brands and, though last in the industry to do so, undertook a vigorous drive to diversify the company, all the while enjoying the fast corporate
lifestyle, seeing his name in the papers, and office perks like a chef who prepared no fewer than four daily specialties for the officers' dining room. But in
the end, American Tobacco only lost ground in the cigarette business as
Walker mistook motion for progress and favored the broadside volley over the
sharpshooter's aim.

The trouble began with Carlton, his first new brand, introduced just before
the first report to the Surgeon General. Walker could not get himself to acknowledge that Carlton, by far the lowest-yielding brand on the market, had
been designed to allay fears of health-conscious smokers. Caught between
Meyner's idiosyncratic application of the industry ad code, fickle FTC rules,
and Walker's own reluctance to risk carving a niche for the brand among
health-conscious smokers by conceding anything to the medical evidence,
Carlton went nowhere. Nor did any of the other filter brands Walker introduced, at the rate of seven a year during the first three years of his tenure,
among them Half & Half, a hybrid derived from one of the company's leading
pipe tobacco blends; a batch of mentholated brands; Waterford, with a water
capsule in the filter; old-timers Sweet Caporal, with a new simulated cork tip,
and Bull Durham, fattened to 27 mm. in circumference from the standard 25
mm.; Colony, with a coupon premium to compete with Raleigh; Silva Thins,
aimed at women smokers; and a filter-tip version of Lucky Strike to try to rescue that aging star from encroaching oblivion. None of these entries was presented with compelling verve or charm.

Riskiest of all was the line extension of American's jewel, No. 1 seller Pall
Mall, which Walker decided to market in the spring of 1966 in a "luxury
length" of 100 mm., about half an inch longer than the standard "king" length
of 85 mm. The company gave it what its president called "the Tiffany touch," a
glossy gold pack with white lettering, which was floated into the market at

swank hotels and fancy restaurants—rather more cautiously than Walker's other efforts, most of them rolled out quickly and almost promiscuously without resort to test-marketing because the company still had surplus cash to burn in its drive for market share. But the beautiful-looking product called Pall Mall Gold 100s, the first major entry of that length to come to market, was not blessed with either aura or image. Instead, the company took a nuts-and-bolts sales approach, stressing that the brand offered more puffs per cigarette than any other and "filters farther for a milder smoke"—which happened not to be true in terms of the brand's tar and nicotine content, among the highest on the market. Indeed, American suffered from uninspired advertising; only Tareyton's "Unswitchables" campaign, featuring a proud smoker with an egregiously blackened eye and the caption beneath, "I'd rather fight than switch," displayed a modicum of sprightliness and briefly lifted the brand onto the list of top ten sellers. Before 1966 was over, RJR's Winston had overtaken Pall Mall as the top-selling brand.

By the end of the 'Sixties, Walker had pushed American Tobacco's noncigarette business up to 23 percent of the company's volume, moving into the food field by buying up famous names like Sunshine Biscuit, runner-up to Nabisco in the cookie-and-cracker business, and Mott's leading line of apple products. Its higher take from non-tobacco revenues, though, reflected American's continued erosion in the cigarette market, where, after six years of Walker's frenetic efforts, unit sales were off by 20 percent and headed south.

Joe Cullman at Philip Morris, meanwhile, was playing tortoise to Walker's hare. Though Marlboro was finally making sustained strides by 1965, the company's second best brand, Parliament, was on a plateau, and the rest of the PM stable was lame. There was a need for new brands that would broaden the company's representation on store shelves as well as in vending machines, which accounted for nearly one out of five cigarette packs sold. But Cullman was not exactly awash in surplus cash to chance the savagely competitive cigarette market on a whim. Profits in his still fragile international operations were almost invisible, and whatever materialized was plowed back in and not repatriated to the parent company. The domestic diversification program was proving no great shakes, either. The ASR unit, after grabbing a full quarter of the new market in stainless steel razor blades, was getting rocked now by industry leader Gillette; the Burma Shave line had failed to generate new products to broaden its sales base; and Clark Gum, while tripling its volume in just a few years under PM ownership, still held only 5 percent of the market.

Never particularly innovative, preferring to learn from others' mistakes before taking the plunge itself, Philip Morris closely tracked Barney Walker's frenetic moves. Only the debut of Pall Mall Gold 100s caused their eyes to widen, and the idea of a new "luxury length" brand elegantly presented to the public was brought to Cullman's attention. He liked it and proposed introducing a competitor using the name of his family's old company, Benson & Hedges, then adorning a low-selling boutique brand. The name had a nice pedigree, paralleling Philip Morris's own. Now the game was to present the reborn brand in a way arresting enough to move it beyond the specialty category.

Although many had a hand in packaging decisions, no one at Philip Morris came to exercise more suasion in this area than its manufacturing overseer, Clifford Goldsmith, who achieved a quantum leap in power with the sudden death of affable operations chief Robert Roper, the victim of a heart attack at age fifty during the company's 1965 Christmas party. Goldsmith was a driving administrator with a perfectionist bent who kept after problem areas indefatigably. Nothing captivated him more than the look of the products he was superintending. "I always felt that a cigarette pack on your table in a restaurant was something you ought to be proud of and therefore should look good," Goldsmith recounted. But the notion of good looks, Goldsmith understood, varied with a brand's mission. What was wanted for the B&H package was a look of refinement suited to an upscale market yet not pretentious. The result was a darkly burnished gold package with simulated wood-grained flecks running vertically to enhance the elongated height. The Benson & Hedges name appeared in small navy blue capital letters under an equally diminutive, embossed coat-of-arms that had become the company hallmark; at the base of the pack was the line "Park Avenue New York," site of the manufacturer's headquarters and, more pointedly, America's foremost metropolitan boulevard of ritz. It was a mere cigarette pack, but it had a muted elegance more tasteful than Pall Mall's glossy Gold 100s. "Philip Morris was appreciative that customers don't need to be hit over the head with a brand name, but can be attracted by the uniqueness of the imagery and design that come with it," remarked Walter Landor, San Francisco–based industrial designer, who entered a long-standing relationship with the cigarette maker as a packaging consultant about this time.

Pack design in hand, Philip Morris advertising chief Jack Landry decided to turn away from the Burnett agency, its hands full with the booming Marlboro account, and try a tiny new firm, Wells Rich Greene, to invent an altogether different sort of pitch for Benson & Hedges. The agency was headed by one of Madison Avenue's few women stars, Mary Wells, who had made her mark at New York's innovative Doyle Dane Bernbach. The latter's trademark was the witty transformation of a product's liabilities into a chief selling argument, as with Volkswagen's funny-looking little beetle of a car, presented as a marvel of efficiency and economy.

After being rebuffed by the company for requesting that the B&H package be redesigned to have more "pop" in ads, Wells Rich Greene did the unthinkable in the tobacco business—it proposed a funny ad campaign based on the disadvantages of an extra-long cigarette. Infinite variations on the idea, many of which eventually appeared in print and on the air, were sketched out for Landry: how elevator doors closed on a protruding B&H 100, how it got mashed against a car window when a male smoker drew too close to ogle a good-looking female on the far side, and why a reader should "please hold this magazine a little further away if you're smoking Benson & Hedges 100s." Like the Pall Mall 100s, the B&H ads spoke of more puffs per pack, but made little of it, proclaiming instead a still greater advantage of the ultra length: "You'll never have to worry about lighting your nose."

Joe Cullman, who did not lack a sense of humor, was presented with the unprecedented B&H campaign in mid-1966. "He made clear that he didn't admire this approach," Landry recalled. "He didn't think you could sell a product by making fun of it." Instead, Cullman urged a campaign featuring a pretty girl in a gold dress, an allusion to the brand's gold pack, with the hemline 100 mm. above her knee, an alluring way to illustrate the magic dimension. And off the Philip Morris president went on a summer safari in Africa, leaving Landry and his colleagues despondent. They thought that Cullman's proposal was a far too blatant use of sex appeal for what was intended to be a classy smoke. But with a post–Labor Day launch fast approaching, there was little time to dream up something else, so Landry, with his boss incommunicado, chose insubordination over mindless compliance. He ordered the "disadvantages" campaign to proceed, with the first TV commercial showing elevator doors closing on an unwary B&H customer's smoke. "We just thought our idea was better," Landry said.

What happened next depends on whose memory is consulted, but by some accounts, Cullman returned home over a weekend, switched on his television set, saw the funny Benson & Hedges commercial, got furious, but held his fire. Returning to the office on Monday, he left word for Landry to be in his office at 5 p.m. that Friday—a time that the ad director took to be his moment of dismissal, especially since nothing further was said to him about the B&H commercial. A glum Landry spent the week cleaning out his desk and drinking heartily in wait for the executioner's ax. Upon arriving at Cullman's office at the appointed hour, Landry was told by the president's secretary that her boss had left two hours earlier, with no plans to return. "Don't worry," said Landry, "he'll be back." So he sat and fretted, but Cullman never showed up. The following Monday, it was business as usual. The two most plausible explanations were that (1) Cullman had attended a cocktail party Thursday night, on the eve of his intended sacking of Landry, had had his ears filled with a chorus of praise for his witty new B&H campaign, and naturally had thought better of his decision to dismiss the disobedient ad director, or (2) the party at which this happened was held on the weekend he returned, but Cullman, prepared to concede that perhaps Landry's advertising instincts were superior to his own, nevertheless felt he had to teach his subordinate a lesson for defying him and so made him sweat it out for a week.

What is indisputable, though, is that the brand took off fast, largely on the strength of the novel ads; Cullman forgave Landry; and within a year of Pall Mall Gold 100s' debut, there were twenty-seven brands of that length on the market, commanding 15 percent of all cigarette sales—and B&H 100s was the top seller among them.

An equally striking marketing victory came out of Philip Morris's response to American Tobacco's introduction of a women's specialty brand. Silva Thins, brought out in 1967, was a plausible notion not only because women comprised a growing proportion of the cigarette market but also because they had participated heavily in both the move to king-length cigarettes, which women liked for being more stylish, and the massive switchover to filter-tip brands, which women, as the more health-conscious sex, were quicker to take up than men. With the onset of the women's liberation movement in the 'Sixties, why not offer a brand with explicit feminist appeal? But American Tobacco's execution of Silva Thins was even more misbegotten than its handling of Gold 100s, particularly its advertising, which seemed to go out of its way to offend those at whom the product was aimed. "Cigarettes are like girls," declared the copy in one early Silva Thins ad, "the best ones are thin and rich."

Philip Morris entered the women's field a year later and bested American's entry in every way, starting with the name, Virginia Slims. "Virginia" was a woman's name, and also that of a prime tobacco state. And while "Thins" suggested the appetite-suppressing virtues of smoking, "Slims" was a more nuanced and pleasing synonym, implying grace and beauty. Then there was the smart Virginia Slims package, a soft and creamy off-white with a band of vertical stripes in autumn colors, and narrower than any other because the cigarettes inside were more slender—100 mm. long and 23 mm. in circumference compared with 25 mm. for most ultra-long brands; the brand name was printed in lean, discreet letters.

What made Virginia Slims click, though, was the brand's advertising, in particular the look of the women shown and, more important, their attitude. The models were young, pert, strikingly slim, and tailored with flair, often in pants suits that emphasized their long-stemmed beauty. Their poses were gymnastic, and their sassy looks had an in-your-face boldness that proclaimed a free spirit and robust health. The ad copy was pitched at the newly independent social status of women, exuberantly declaring their progress and needling men for having long exploited them as cooks, laundresses, and floor scrubbers. The most amusing and telling ads were worked around simulated vintage photographs of Victorian-era scenes in which, for example, a girl in a stifling swimming costume was dreaming aloud, "Just you wait. Someday we'll be able to wear any bathing suit we want. Someday we'll be able to vote. Someday we'll be able to smoke just like a man. Someday we'll even have our own cigarette." No longer were women men's "loving pets," the Slims ads asserted, and all of them featured the clinching brand slogan "You've Come a Long Way, Baby" at the bottom of print ads or delivered in a brassy, driving contemporary beat on broadcast media.

That "Baby" at the end of the slogan ignited a fierce debate between the Burnett ad agency team, which played a vital role in the whole conception of the new brand, and the marketing crew at Philip Morris. The agency people from Chicago feared that the word would be taken as offensive or derisive, close in meaning to "babe," with its connotation of a cheap or readily available woman *qua* sex object—and anyway, babies may have been cute and cuddly but they weren't equal to men in community standing. At the Philip Morris office in more cosmopolitan New York, "Baby" was understood to be a term of studly affection, the way Bogart called his film women "baby" and "sweetheart," and besides, since the whole point of the brand and its pitch was pro-feminist, the slogan would surely be taken as endearing recognition of women's liberated state. The Burnett people persisted in presenting the jingle *sans* the tag "Baby," but it fell flat—until one of the agency executives reluctantly put on the "Baby" version, and, as Landry remembered, "It was the shade of difference that lifted the whole thing a hundred feet in the air."

The slogan keyed the launch. The secret of it all, suggested Ellen Merlo, an early Slims brand manager and the first woman to advance as high as the second managerial tier at PM, was that "it was never strident, almost always tongue-in-cheek, and not feminist so much as liberationist, in the sense that the slogan really meant, 'You've got a lot of options now.' " It was fun, flattering, and effectively promoted through merchandise that underscored the equality angle, like little black books for listing men's phone numbers (since women, too, were allowed to play the field now), jogging shorts, and a bright yellow box for "serious" tools for women ("Because now you've got a lot more to fix than your face").

When the whole enterprise was laid out for his approval, Cullman pulled Landry aside and said he thought it was crazy to create a brand that intentionally eliminated half of the smoking market. But appreciative of Landry's savvy in embracing the "Marlboro Country" campaign against much internal opposition and the Benson & Hedges self-mocking approach against Cullman's own wishes, he okayed a market test in San Francisco, the likeliest place to accept the attitudinizing women's brand.

Sales executive Tom Littleton, newly transferred to the Bay City about the time of the Slims launch, remembered it as "a very slick piece of business" featuring audiovisual filmstrips, jazzy point-of-sale placards, and cartons instead of packs as samplers. "You knew right away it was a winner, the way it jumped off the shelves," said Littleton. "The copy in the Slims ads was so up-scale, so fashionable, so much on the cutting edge, and the models were absolutely, totally right—they just had it. It was all just as right in its way as 'Marlboro Country.' " Virginia Slims took a few years but soon ran away from all rivals as the leader within its niche in an increasingly fragmented market-place. Though never among the top-selling brands, Slims got up to a nearly 3 percent market share in a business where a single percentage point was enough to earn sizable profits. Within half a dozen years of the Slims launch, the percentage of teenage women who smoked had doubled. And Philip Morris was riding a hot streak: between 1964 and 1969, its unit sales climbed 63 percent—this at a time when industry leader RJR's volume barely held its ground—and the company had moved into fourth place in the industry, hard on the heels of No. 3 Brown & Williamson.

V

I N March of 1965, on the brink of Philip Morris's explosive growth, the brokerage house of E. F. Hutton presciently advised its clientele that the company was "the most attractive investment" in the tobacco business and "exceptionally well managed". Everybody in the industry knew that the driving force behind PM's superior management was Joseph Cullman.

He had a boyish enthusiasm that made him seem younger than his age and turned him into a charismatic motivator whom everyone in his burgeoning company wanted to please. Like most successful chief executives, Cullman was more reactive than creative, and he was self-confident enough to know his own limits and be willing to canvass broadly, all the while melding disparate talents and tolerating ornery but gifted subordinates like Jack Landry as he sought to build a consensus.

Near his desk and later moved to his trophy room was a pair of elephant tusks about seven curving feet in length that Cullman had bagged on one of his African hunting trips. Upon minimal inquiry, the sometime hunter would avidly narrate how he had set out in the bush wearing shorts and sneakers and toting a 456 Winchester with a 270 2.5-power scope, and by the time he pursued the retreating pachyderm through the thorny underbrush and delivered the coup de grâce at fourteen yards, he was down to his Jockey shorts. The huge ivory souvenirs of the adventure that he kept on nearby display gave rise to the company gag that Joe Cullman, though on the diminutive side, was for all practical intents a three-ton elephant who slept wherever he wanted on the premises (*i.e.,* got his own way with minimal resistance). "But they were wrong," remarked Shepard Pollack, later president of Philip Morris USA. "Joe was more like a three-ton dog—a dog walks around and around before he settles down to sleep, checking out the terrain carefully to be sure he won't be lying on bristles."

Cullman earned the respect of his colleagues not for any piercing intellect or excessive sweetness of disposition—indeed, he could be intense, impatient, and very tough on staffers who hadn't done their homework—but because he had absorbed and synthesized a great deal of knowledge about the tobacco business. He had grown up in the industry and had built on long family friendships with dealers across the country. While he could be highly guarded and private, he had an extroverted side that kept him from ever becoming a cloistered, above-the-battle commander. He made the rounds faithfully, showing the company banner at every major industry meeting, convention, and trade show and stopping by frequently at wholesalers' offices, with his regional sales manager in tow, to shoot the breeze and then ask pointed questions about how his brands were performing. If these visits smacked a bit of a royal audience, inferentially flattering to the big jobbers who were pleased to have an industry mogul drop by, so much the better. Cullman's visits were vividly recalled by Stephen J. Bloom, whose Chicago-based family tobacco distribution business was one of the nation's largest before being sold to giant Core-Mark: "Joe was a warm, outgoing individual with a high energy level who never became enchanted with his own success." Veteran Philip Morris sales executive Max Berkowitz saw the dual aspects of Cullman's winning ways with customers and subordinates alike: "He had the aura of class—his people were part of society—the German-Jewish equivalent of the Kennedys. Yet he was also a regular guy . . . who didn't pretend to be the smartest fella in the world—but he listened."

Never constrained by lines of authority, Cullman prided himself on running a big company, bulking up by the month now, with the management mentality of a small business. But by 1967, he had to step away from the day-to-day direction, taking the title of chairman of the board and CEO and naming as president George Weissman, who had been running the international operations for seven years; at the same time, he elevated Ross Millhiser, vice president for marketing and overseer of the fortunes of the company's bellwether product, Marlboro, as president of Philip Morris USA, and Hugh Cullman, Joe's cousin and junior by eleven years, as president of Philip Morris International. In the process he put in place the likeliest contenders to succeed him, particularly advancing the hopes of Millhiser, a man more like Cullman than the smooth and genial Weissman, the up-from-poverty City College graduate from the Bronx, whom Millhiser (among others at the company) was said to regard as something of an operator, more knowledgeable about the glad-handing arts than the tobacco business. Like Cullman, Millhiser was a Yale man from a well-off family of German-Jewish extraction. Unlike his boss, Millhiser was a complex man of boundless intellectual curiosity, reading up on subjects often remote from the tobacco trade, quick to question pat assumptions, forever verbalizing new ideas, and carrying it all off with a self-dramatizing quality that made him eminently quotable within the company walls.

Whatever their differences, Millhiser and Weissman typified the sort of executive whom Cullman particularly valued: not organizational politicians or business-school generalists but men with an entrepreneurial spirit, hungry to build the company as well as their own bank accounts, with expertise in a given field but gladly reaching out to learn the whole business—and willing to take calculated risks. Cullman had a true gift for attracting such people, deploying them shrewdly in jobs they themselves might not have thought they were suited for, and assembling a management team with extraordinary continuity. "He built a great cadre of managers," said Hugh Cullman, "and lost very few people he didn't want to lose." Those who stayed developed an abiding loyalty, unsullied by infighting common to large organizations, and Cullman reciprocated in kind with a personal interest in his people, immersion in all major decisions, and acceptance of setbacks without recrimination, even as he celebrated triumphs without gloating.

If he could be moody and mercurial at times, Cullman almost always kept his emotions in check, never drank in public beyond his capacity, and enjoyed a growing celebrity and widening range of interests. If there was a complaint about him, it was that he was becoming too busy with outside affairs and sometimes was just not around when his counsel was sought. But even those outside preoccupations had a way of advancing Philip Morris's cause. His passion for tennis was a prominent case in point. After arriving at his office by 8:15 each morning from suburban Briarcliff Manor, Cullman often went to the West Side Tennis Club in Forest Hills at 11 for a fast doubles match. This recreation grew into deep involvement with the business affairs of the U.S. Lawn Tennis Association, assisted by Philip Morris accountants. When the tennis organization entered into a five-year deal with CBS television to cover the U.S. Open tournament staged at the club, it was Cullman as tournament chairman who engineered the pact. As a payback, Philip Morris was visible everywhere at Forest Hills, the prime showcase for tennis in America, beginning with a donated $165,000 electric scoreboard beckoning spectators, on the premises and over television, to "Marlboro Country".

In only one area did Cullman show an iron hand, and it would turn into an often invoked company creed—an insistence on quality control of the product. To oversee the worldwide presentation of his broadening cigarette lines and maintain a consistency of look, taste, and quality, Cullman set up an elite Products Committee, composed of ten to a dozen top people, that met monthly and had to approve every introduction or innovation no matter how slight, whether the lettering on the packs or an alteration of a blend or, at the other extreme, a whole new brand. It was the same way with sales materials, whether ad layouts or point-of-sale posters. This compulsive oversight was intended not to dictate so much as to assure the maintenance of what Cullman conceived of as a high-class operation, notwithstanding the serious health charges levied against it.

His understanding of the uses and limits of advertising was also exemplary. Philip Morris advertising proved effective in the 'Sixties largely because it did not say more than it had to—a prudent as well as artful policy in view of the possible liability exposure from any too explicit claims or promises. As James Morgan, an earnest articulator of the company's marketing creed, put it, "Philip Morris advertising was especially good at getting the consumer to fin-ish the sentence. It says, 'This is what I am, you can understand it and decide for yourself how and why I'm relevant to you.' What does 'Marlboro Country' mean literally? Not much—but it lays out a proposition and lets the consumer absorb the message. . . ."

Once the advertising "pull" for Marlboro, Benson & Hedges 100s, and Vir-ginia Slims began to generate sizable cash flow, Cullman turned to the one area he and his marketing staff had neglected—the "push" by the company's undersized, underpaid, and undertrained sales force. "New York headquarters didn't quite understand the interplay between the customer and the sales repre-sentative," said Paul Jeblee, a Carolina country boy with a handlebar mustache and no college education who struggled up through the company sales ranks, partly by learning to bone up on every conceivable piece of data that Joe Cull-man might quiz him about. Cullman proved receptive to a laundry list of re-forms on the sales side which Jeblee was instrumental in urging, starting in the late 'Sixties as stores all over now regularly ran out of Philip Morris stock, though the fixtures that Reynolds provided free to most supermarkets remained loaded with RJR brands, which commanded twice the shelf space of any com-petitor's products. For a time it had been left to store managers to assign the shelf space to the non-Reynolds brands, presumably on the basis of sales movement, but when other companies began to pay for preferential placement, Philip Morris, the most reluctant to pay, was hit hardest. "RJR had the hard-ware," recalled Tom Littleton of his travails as a Philip Morris salesman, "so we were literally down on our knees to service the bottom shelves. To look at my pants, you'd have thought I spent my life in church."

The Reynolds lock on fixturing was costing Philip Morris sales. A Marlboro smoker unable to find his brand on, say, the fourth shelf down might well grab a carton of Winston from the shelf at shoulder level rather than go down the block or drive five miles for his favorite smoke. By 1969, Philip Morris began to pay for preferred space on the supermarket racks—sixty dollars a year, typi-cally, which did not amount to much per store but, when multiplied nationally, represented a considerable cash outlay. Even where "plan-o-grams" had been contracted for, allotting PM brands fixed footage on the second or third shelves, salesmen had to defend the space fiercely, so great was the pressure from competitors in an era of proliferating brands and line extensions. "You could never depend on the store managers or distributors to service the accounts—you had to mind the stores yourself," recalled Richard Schoenkopf, a middle manager in sales and merchandising with PM for a dozen years.

Jeblee's efforts to upgrade the sales program went well beyond boosting manpower and pay. A new sales manual was created and more sophisticated selling and servicing techniques were taught, as the big retail chains took over an ever larger share of the tobacco market from the little mom-and-pop stores. Malls were beginning to dominate, especially in California and the booming South and Southwest, and a new breed of salesman and sales manager was required to handle big orders and negotiate hard for adequate display on inelastic shelves. Newcomers who showed high managerial promise were put on the fast track to advancement. Jeblee pushed the company into high-speed market analysis with newfangled computers so that every wholesaler and retail outlet could be instantaneously rated on its performance with PM brands and management could know, as never before, what was selling where.

All of this purposeful motion set the company aglow. At its 1969 national sales meeting in Tierra Verde, Florida, the vice president for sales, Max Berkowitz, told his assembled troops: "The present climate at Philip Morris is . . . dynamic—growing—changing—shifting—innovating—you can supply your own words to describe a company whose sales have tripled in less than ten years. . . . [A]t no time in my thirty-two years with the company has the flavor of success—the sight of the top—been so close. At no other time . . . has the thought occurred to me that American [Tobacco] and Reynolds could be caught—and yet now it has to be obvious to all of you—we could be No. 2 before long."

V I

D URING the four years between the passage of the federal cigarette labeling law and its expiration date, June 30, 1969, the tobacco industry had three courses open to it. It could lie low, bide its time, and hope that the storm over the health charges against smoking would subside with the appearance of the warning on each pack. Or it could move quietly behind the scenes to head off still more serious government regulation by negotiating an orderly and gradual retreat. Or it could continue to deny the legitimacy of the health issue and act provocatively in defense of its highly lucrative domain.

Shaken by the 1964 indictment from the Surgeon General's office and stigmatized by the congressionally imposed warning label, however mild, the cigarette makers watched and waited a bit, saw the rising line on their sales graphs stutter only briefly, and chose intransigence as their response to medical science's declared war against them. Their unstated reason was the belief that any substantive concession—for example, that lowered tar and nicotine contents made a cigarette less hazardous—would doom them to expulsion from the legitimate marketplace. Thus, their anointed spokesman on the health issue, Clarence C. Little, scientific director of the Tobacco Industry Research Committee, by then renamed the Council for Tobacco Research (CTR), was, at the age of eighty, sounding like a badly broken record in asserting the same things in 1969 that he had fifteen years earlier about the hazards of cigarettes: (1) "there is no demonstrated causal relationship between smoking and any disease"—in direct contradiction of the conclusions of the Surgeon General's panel; (2) many factors were "significantly associated with cancer"—but none, he omitted, was so manifestly linked to cancer of the lung as smoking; (3) an individual's genetic makeup largely determined his or her susceptibility to cancer—a strong argument, actually, against smoking at all, since those susceptible had little way of knowing until it was too late; (4) although a few investigators claimed the inhalation of tobacco smoke might be followed by "certain changes in the tissue of lung surface," there was "definite disagreement among pathologists as to the significance of such changes"—a disagreement found preponderantly among those in the industry's hire; and (5) "the whole field of smoking and health requires a great deal more research and information before a proper evaluation can be made."

Earle Clements, the wise old pol who now headed the Tobacco Institute, may never have been a total captive of the industry that paid him, but he dealt with the health charges in a fashion complementary to Little's. He told the Illinois Association of Tobacco Distributors in 1967, for example, that through the $20 million in grants distributed over the past thirteen years by the CTR and the American Medical Association, "every facet of the charges against smoking is being evaluated, studied, and researched. . . . If there is something harmful, I am confident that scientists can remedy it." Meanwhile, he added by way of rallying the troops, "We can protect our industry by vigorously and accurately presenting the facts." But it was the facts that the tobacco industry was shying away from, if not actively trying to hide. At about the time Clements was defending the industry's efforts before the Illinois distributors, PM research director Helmut Wakeham was writing to the TI president to complain of the Council for Tobacco Research program, saying that "much of the grant work has little or no relevance to smoking and health, in my opinion" and adding, "[W]e should be prepared to admit the possibility of some risk . . . and to counsel moderation [in tobacco use]."

But there were few scientists in the industry as enlightened and willing to speak up as Wakeham, whose views, at any rate, went largely unheeded. The principal reason for this, to judge by internal industry documents during the mid and late 1960s, was that the joint research program, particularly the one administered by the CTR, was being used as much to protect the tobacco manufacturers as to advance any allegedly disinterested search for the scientific truth about smoking. Rather than being operated at arm's length from the industry's scrutiny, as tobacco spokesmen liked to boast, the CTR program and its associate scientific director, Robert Hockett, were directly linked to the "ad hoc committee" of younger company lawyers on global lookout for friendly or pliable scientists willing to testify for the industry and/or undertake studies that might cast doubt on the health charges against smoking. Such "special projects," as these helpful investigations were euphemistically tagged, would generally be offered first to the CTR's Scientific Advisory Board for funding, but if that panel declined them, they would be approved by the ad hoc committee and funded through a "Central File," as the high-priority kitty was termed in a January 3, 1966, memo by Addison Yeaman, vice president and general counsel of Brown & Williamson, to his fellow members of the "Secret Six," the industry's top in-house lawyers. Once funded, these projects were assigned to the supervision of New York attorney Edwin Jacob, who was not directly employed by any of the cigarette makers and so enjoyed the protection of confidentiality in his dealings with these scientist "clients". As Roy Morse, a former research director at R. J. Reynolds, disclosed long after, "As soon as Mr. Jacob funded [a scientific study], it was a privileged relationship, and couldn't come into court . . . So they could do projects that they could bury if they chose."

Examples of such undertakings were a small grant to a radiologist at the University of Cape Town in South Africa to investigate "population pockets" with a high incidence of lung cancer and low consumption of cigarettes and a $5,000 grant to Yale Medical School biostatistician Alvan Feinstein, who had investigated what he said was a selection bias in hospital diagnoses of cancer patients who smoked. Feinstein now solicited money to pursue a "multivariable analysis" of disease, contending in his grant application to Jacob, "If cigarette smoking is as harmful as has been alleged, it should not only 'cause' these diseases but should also make their manifestations and outcome worse" in smokers, but his preliminary findings did not show that. Feinstein's effort appealed to Jacob, who in endorsing it for ad hoc committee approval wrote that if the Yale investigator's early finding of no correlation between smoking and the clinical course of lung and laryngeal cancer was borne out, "it would be of assistance in disputing the assertions of aggregation and acceleration of cancer by smoking made in certain of the [product liability] law suits." That these "special projects" were conceived largely as lawyers' tools to defend the industry was further testified to by Yeaman's January 1966 memo in which he spelled out the priorities for such grants. "Category A" was "projects essentially of 'adversary value,' " the B category covered those "having a generally defensive character," and C, the lowest priority, referred to "basic research."

One "Category A" project referred to in this document was to be handled directly by the CTR, with "Dr. Hockett to submit preliminary plan for implementation." So much for claims of hands-off research.

This prejudicial selectivity in dealing with the medical case against smoking to bolster the industry's legal defense and public-relations efforts was a part of the companies' studied campaign of denial and deflection, if not outright deceit. Carl Thompson, the executive in charge of the Tobacco Institute account for public-relations consultants Hill & Knowlton, sent a memo on October 18, 1968, to the institute's new P.R. head, William Kloepfer, on how best to angle the contents of *Tobacco & Health Research*, the industry propaganda sheet masquerading as a legitimate newsletter and distributed massively to doctors and scientists around the country: "The most important type of story is that which casts doubt on the cause and effect theory of disease and smoking. . . ." Eye-grabbing headlines were the key, Thompson counseled, and "should strongly call out the point—Controversy! Contradiction! Other factors! Unknowns. . . ."

Hill & Knowlton's counseling was too benign for a number of die-hard tobacco industry executives—H&K, in fact, would shortly resign the account after fifteen years partly because the cigarette makers' stonewalling attitude embarrassed the firm with other clients—and some of its public-relations business went to the new Tiderock Corporation, run by Rosser Reeves, the legendary apostle of hard-sell advertising when he headed the Ted Bates agency. One of Tiderock's early inspirations was to plant an article by freelancer Stanley Frank in the January 1968 issue of *True* magazine (circulation: 2 million copies), ridiculing the smoking-health link, and then call attention to the issue with a big newspaper ad campaign. The month afterward, some 600,000 reprints of the article were distributed with a note attached signed by "The Editors" and saying, "As a leader in your profession and community, you will be interested in reading this story"; nowhere was there any indication that the reprints were paid for by tobacco money. Frank's article, nothing more than a rehash of the industry line (*e.g.*, "Statistics alone link cigarettes with lung cancer"), was then made yet more simplistic, given a pseudonymous byline, retitled "Cigarette Cancer Link Is Bunk," and run in a March issue of the *National Enquirer*, the nation's foremost scandal sheet, thus exposing another million or more readers to the disinformation campaign fueled by the tobacco companies.

Not only was the industry unapologetic about the health hazard it was selling to the public, but in launching 100 mm. brands with higher tar and nicotine yields than anything then on the market, it blithely compounded the medical peril. And when reputable parties like the FTC, Consumers Union, and the Roswell Park cancer institute called the public's attention to the heightened yields, the industry claimed that inadequate test samples and undependable measuring techniques had been used and invoked the straw man of science's continuing failure to prove that "any particular ingredient as found in cigarette smoke actually causes any human disease." This last contention had become the industry's favorite—and most transparent—ruse, for although no single ingredient among the several thousand compounds detectable in tobacco smoke may have been the culprit in and of itself, the combination of some of them or the entire accumulation almost surely was implicated in disease formation.

Individual companies in their occasional public statements remained equally hard-nosed. American Tobacco, perhaps the most unyielding member of the industry on the health charges, stated flatly at its 1967 annual meeting that "no clinical or biological evidence has been produced which demonstrates how cigarettes relate to cancer or any other disease in human beings." And Philip Morris was no more conciliatory. About a year after the American Tobacco statement, PM's new president, George Weissman, disdainfully told *Dun's Review* that the health issue had proven a major distraction to the company: "A great deal of our time is consumed by this harassment—time we could be using to build up our business." He went on to declare that "[n]o clearcut case against cigarette smoking has been made despite millions spent on research" and added indefensibly, "The longer these tests go on, the better our [the industry's] case becomes. . . ."

One informed and highly skeptical insight into such statements by Weissman and other industry executives was given by Paul Kotin, pioneer member of the CTR's Scientific Advisory Board and longtime tobacco industry consultant (even for several years after joining the National Cancer Institute as a ranking official). Betraying a deep ambivalence about his relationship with the cigarette makers' research programs, which he had helped dignify by his presence, Kotin recalled how he had hit it off over the years with Weissman, who he believed was "basically a decent, generous guy. But I became greatly disillusioned by him." The suave Philip Morris executive would light up a lot of cigarettes, Kotin noticed, "but he always stubbed them out after a few puffs," as if acknowledging that the longer he dragged on each one, the worse his exposure to its hazardous contents. Kotin came to feel insulted by Weissman's refusal to own up to the health peril—"and the same way with Pete [Clarence] Little. They knew the real relationship [between smoking and disease formation], and they were denying it. And who was I to tell them off?"

VII

REGARDLESS of the cigarette manufacturers' efforts, signs were appearing everywhere that Americans had begun to accept the truth about smoking. A Gallup poll reported in 1968 that 71 percent of the country believed that smoking caused cancer; only 44 percent had ten years before. A

Louis Harris poll found that the percentage of Americans over twenty-one who smoked had fallen from 47 to 42 in the four years following the first report of the Surgeon General. Four million were said to be quitting the habit every year, the American Cancer Society was passing out "I.Q." buttons (for "I Quit Smoking") in a national campaign featuring film actor Tony Curtis and thousands of posters by Peter Max proclaiming, "Life Is So Beautiful—Stay Alive—Don't Smoke," and U.S. mail trucks were adorned for a time with placards that said, "100,000 Doctors Have Quit Smoking—Do They Know Something You Don't?" Programs and clinics to help smokers through the ordeal of stopping began to open, some of them free, some charging several hundred dollars for courses running as long as eight weeks, like SmokEnders; success rates were said to range between 20 and 40 percent, but verification of claims was difficult since relapse was common. The anticigarette commercials mandated by the FCC appeared to be having an arresting effect on the nation's consciousness of the perils of smoking. Nearly half of those surveyed reported recalling at least one of the cautionary broadcast messages, and one-third of the viewing smokers said they had cut down or were thinking about it as a result. Annual per capita consumption slipped from 210 cigarette packs in 1967 to 205 in 1968 and just under 200 in 1969.

Although elected officials hesitated to call out for stronger regulatory efforts, the federal bureaucracy grew increasingly outspoken. The "sleeper" provision of the 1965 labeling act providing for annual reports to Congress on the smoking question by HEW and the FTC went into effect in 1967 and served at once as a prominent platform for trumpeting "official" annual reminders of the growing severity of the health problem and the need for action to allay it. U.S. Surgeon General William H. Stewart's mid-1967 report for HEW noted that none of the 2,000 scientific articles published on smoking since the 1964 report contradicted the main thrust of that document, which, if anything, "may have understated" the relationship between smoking and diseases of the lung and heart. Stewart's report placed new emphasis on heart disease, which accounted for one of every three deaths in the U.S.; underscored how smoking caused an increased demand for oxygen by the heart even while the intake of carbon monoxide in cigarette smoke reduced the flow of oxygen to the heart muscle; and noted new studies suggesting that smoking might accelerate the formation of blood clots. Smokers were also given memorably jarring statistics, such as that their chances of contracting heart disease were 70 to 200 percent higher than those of nonsmokers and that smoking claimed one American life every 105 seconds. HEW Secretary John Gardner urged Congress to toughen the warning label on packs, add the tar and nicotine yields, and put them on all cigarette advertising as well. A study of 42,000 households by the U.S. Public Health Service found that smokers lost 27 percent more work hours than nonsmokers. In his 1968 report, the Surgeon General referred to smoking as "the main cause of lung cancer" and to "the increasing convergence of epidemiological and physiological findings relating smoking to coronary heart disease." A special task force on smoking reported to the Surgeon General that same year and vilified the tobacco industry for "encouraging death and disease" through its advertising and for its "inability or unwillingness . . . to face up to the health hazards of smoking or even to admit that they exist"—a charge the Tobacco Institute called a "shockingly intemperate defamation of an industry which has led the way in medical research to seek answers in the cigarette controversy."

Over at the Federal Trade Commission, sentiment was growing for stronger measures than HEW was urging, since the commission had found, in its 1967 report to Congress, "no evidence that the warning statement on cigarette packages has had any significant effect," and the industry's advertising, despite claims of rigorous self-policing, continued to stress the desirability and "the relative safety of smoking" and "totally ignore the health hazards." The proliferation of 100 mm. brands was lamented as a "serious and disturbing trend," which the commission facetiously suggested might be advertised with the slogan "Extra Health Hazard at No Extra Cost." When the FTC released its first report on tar and nicotine yields in the fall of 1967, the Tobacco Institute airily dismissed the numbers as meaningless.

By the following year the FTC, noting that every U.S. household with a TV set was being exposed to some 800 cigarette commercials a year, made a bold call for the total elimination of tobacco advertising on broadcast media. Still more ringing was the announcement in February 1969 by the FCC that six of its seven commissioners favored putting an end to cigarette commercials—a measure they were permitted to impose after the federal labeling act expired four months later, unless Congress acted in the interim. The commission minimized First Amendment concerns over such a ban on commercial speech by arguing that it was "at odds with the public interest for broadcasters to present advertising promoting the consumption of the product posing this unique danger . . . measured in terms of an epidemic of deaths and disabilities."

Attracting four out of every five promotional dollars spent by cigarette makers, television was the tobacco industry's star salesman. All the claims about taste and flavor notwithstanding, cigarette brands were hard to distinguish except by their packaging and advertising, and the prospect of blacking out the most pervasive ad medium cast the industry into deep gloom. As attorney Abe Krash, long in charge of Arnold & Porter's counseling of Philip Morris, recounted, "The driving, central people in the business were the advertising and marketing executives, and the television ban would take away their modus vivendi." And no company had a greater stake in TV just then than Philip Morris, which was using the medium brilliantly. "Marlboro Country" commercials were full of sound, motion, and music: you saw the cowboys in action and heard the thundering gallop of the horses, the lowing of cattle, the crackle of the campfire. And there was a comparable allure and vivacity in the funny Benson & Hedges "disadvantages" campaign and the saucy beauties purveying Virginia Slims. "Television was where the big money was," one Philip Morris insider recounted, "where the creativity went, and it was putting our brands over."

The FCC's proposed TV ban hardly came as a surprise to the tobacco industry, but now, supported by the ACS and Consumers Union and advanced by Robert Kennedy in the last months of his life and Senator Frank Moss, Democrat from antitobacco Utah, the idea was on the congressional burner. The tobacco people had not sufficiently taken into account the need to cement their alliance with the politically potent broadcasters, who were growing ever more fretful that restrictions on cigarette commercials could lead to possibly ruinous slashes in their revenue. Gathering in Palm Springs for their annual convention in December 1968, the NAB clung to its contention, as voiced by its president, Vincent Wasilewski, that its own TV Code office was competently monitoring cigarette and all other forms of on-air advertising. But network and station owners were asking themselves by then if they would not be better off recognizing that tobacco products were indeed a public-health menace unlike any other.

There were cracks as well within the tobacco industry's formerly united front, as hardliners and accommodationists struggled for a single strategy in the impending legislative showdown. Lorillard especially had distanced itself from the herd. Its bright young Washington counsel, Robert Wald, had seen what was coming for several years and believed that the two big law firms advising the industry, Arnold & Porter and Covington & Burling, were giving it shortsighted, perhaps suicidal guidance. In a May 4, 1969, article in *The New York Times Magazine* by Elizabeth Drew, Wald went public by stating, "It is inevitable that television advertising [of cigarettes] is going to end, one way or the other," and that by failing to work for a compromise solution, the tobacco industry would wind up a heavy loser.

The industry, however, was still ruled by militants, like the American Tobacco executives who argued that since most smokers did not get lung cancer, the cause must lie elsewhere—and so their product should not be persecuted. Even more sophisticated industry people, like Joseph Cullman, were disinclined to be conciliatory. In remarks to *Newsweek* the week before he testified as the tobacco manufacturers' prime spokesman before the House Commerce Committee in April 1969, he said, "It's a hazardous world we live in—and cigarettes are far down the list of hazards. . . ."

VIII

A FEW weeks before Joseph Cullman presented the industry's position on continued or extended regulation of cigarettes before a friendly House committee, big tobacco had lost its ranking statesman, R. J. Reynolds's recently retired chairman, Bowman Gray, Jr. At sixty-two, Gray had succumbed to the chronic muscular disease that had hobbled him for twenty years.

"Red" Gray had been the epitome of the Southern gentleman, a fine speaker, and something of a wit. Joe Cullman, who greatly respected Gray, was none of those, and, according to some close to him at the time, the Philip Morris chairman did not relish stepping into the spotlight as the newly anointed industry spokesman. The task fell to him in part because he was then serving as board chairman of the Tobacco Institute, but his donning of Bowman Gray's mantle—it was Gray who had testified for the industry during Congress's deliberations over the 1965 labeling law—was fitting because Cullman's company was now the industry's rising force. Eleven of the twenty-five members of the House Commerce Committee came from big tobacco-growing states and, allied with antiregulatory Republicans from other regions, they formed a solid pro-industry majority that eased Cullman's anxiety as he took center stage during the thirteen-day hearing.

At first Cullman gave a forceful statement of why the cigarette companies were prepared to live with the warning label after its June 30 expiration date but would not accept anything more stringent. The public knew all about the health charges against smoking, he said, and since there had been no new scientific developments to justify stronger language, the current warning was entirely adequate. But to include it in cigarette advertising, as several government agencies had proposed, would, as a practical matter, lead to the elimination of cigarette advertising—which was no doubt what those who urged it had in mind. The public would not be served by such a measure, Cullman argued, since it would reduce competition and deny consumers information about any new and possibly improved brands.

By then it was widely understood that one reason the tobacco industry was no longer bemoaning the presence of a compulsory warning label on its product was that it served as what Representative John Moss, California Democrat and one of the few outspoken critics of the industry, called a "fringe benefit" that greatly bolstered the companies' assumption-of-risk defense in liability suits against them—didn't it, Moss pointedly asked Cullman. The Philip Morris chief denied that characterization, saying that the industry had not asked for such a warning label even though it had been involved in product liability cases when Congress considered the measure. "Oh, friend, it was a clearly identifiable benefit, and you know it as well as I do," Moss shot back. Cullman, growing feisty, snapped, "I will have to take exception to that." But Representative John D. Dingell, Democrat of Michigan, waded in by asking Cullman if as a layman he did not feel that the mandated label provided "all the warning that a prudent man could expect that . . . cigarettes are harmful to health." Cullman replied that since he was not a lawyer, he could not competently comment. Dingell persisted, but Cullman held fast. The tough Michigan congressman finally said, "I think, fundamentally, you are obfuscating the issue," and repeated his question. Cullman, toughing it out, answered, "I am not prepared to answer that." Dingell would not back off, though. "What is your best judgment?" he asked, meaning was the warning all that a prudent man could expect. Cullman, fearful of seeming unduly slippery, yielded: "I believe it is." Dingell at once pounced upon the concession: "In other words, one of the functions of the [1965 labeling] law . . . is to strip potential litigants of the privilege of going in and asserting that they have been injured."

Cullman soon got in worse trouble. Asked why the industry objected to including the health warning in advertising if the label on the packs had not adversely affected cigarette sales, Cullman said, "I think that is quite different. By the time that someone buys a package of cigarettes, that person had decided to smoke that pack of cigarettes"—to which his interrogator replied, "You are the best witness for why this needs changing that I have heard." Finally, liberal Democrat Bob Eckhardt of Texas began grilling Cullman about the efficacy of filters on cigarettes, asking if their very presence did not imply a health hazard from the tar and nicotine. Cullman replied that the industry might discuss filters and tar and nicotine yields in its advertising but did not make any health claims in the process. "You feel they [filters] really don't do any good, but they do cater to the public?" Eckhardt asked. "No, I didn't say that," Cullman shot back, and added, revealingly, "They do considerable good." And he elaborated, in a way that seemed to undermine his opening statement about the alleged lack of evidence relating tar and nicotine yields to any health risk, by pointing out the sharp drop in those yields over the preceding decade. Eckhardt wondered what the significance of that product modification was, but Cullman clung to the industry line: "We don't think it is significant. But we do know people want cigarettes of lower tar and nicotine."

Such moments of high discomfort aside, the House hearings were a pro-industry whitewash; there was no orchestrated outcry from the public-health community, and antismoking forces on the Commerce Committee were powerless to do much more than heckle. What emerged was a bill calling for a six-year extension of the 1965 labeling act as well as for a marginally tougher message on the pack—"Warning: The Surgeon General has determined that cigarette smoking is dangerous to your health and may cause lung cancer and other diseases." Even this the industry found oppressive; to concede that their product "is dangerous" was going a good deal further than to admit that it "may be hazardous," as the expiring law had worded it. And the very mention of cancer, even as possibly linked to smoking, was unacceptable to the manufacturers, ever more wary of their vulnerability to product liability suits. A ban on cigarette advertising on television was barely whispered about in the House.

Closely tracking the House proceedings was the tobacco industry's most dangerous opponent on Capitol Hill—Senator Magnuson's key legislative aide on consumer affairs, Michael Pertschuk. In regular contact for several years with staff members at the National Clearinghouse on Smoking and Health and its director, Daniel Horn, Pertschuk was determined that the cigarette makers would not escape serious regulation as they had four years earlier. His hand was notably strengthened by the rising recognition in Congress that legislation backing consumer interests was becoming good politics, as Magnuson's rejuvenated career and the emergence of Ralph Nader as a serious and widely admired independent consumer advocate were demonstrating.

To slow the momentum of the pro-industry bill due from the House Committee, Pertschuk worked behind the scenes to introduce a telling piece of testimony that had fallen into his lap and argued for congressional intervention in television advertising. After several years of watching the NAB's Advertising Code Authority permit its oversight of cigarette advertising to turn into a travesty, Warren Braren, head of the code's New York office and chief author of the 1966 report critical of the tobacco industry's own effort to curb its advertising, had quit in disgust. Upon hearing NAB President Vincent Wasilewski testify before the House that the broadcasters were rigorously vetting cigarette commercials, Braren decided to blow the whistle. He contacted his friend Stanley Cohen, *Advertising Age*'s top Washington correspondent, who put him in touch with his friend, the delighted Pertschuk, who prevailed upon Oregon's Representative Brock Adams to pry open the formally adjourned House hearings on the ground that the NAB had seriously misled the lawmakers about its own and the tobacco industry's self-regulation of cigarette advertising. Braren's extensive testimony caused a sensation and was an embarrassment to Wasilewski, who, when recalled to justify his earlier statements in light of Braren's revelations, tried limply to explain away the disregarded 1966 report by his New York office and denied all charges of nonfeasance by his Code Authority. The House committee gave a brief tsk-tsk, then voted 22 to 5 to extend the labeling law with the change in wording but no further restriction on the industry. (Braren, for his trouble, was effectively blacklisted by the broadcasting industry but found useful work with Consumers Union.)

A majority on Magnuson's Senate Commerce Committee found the House committee's measure offensive. Indiana's Vance Hartke, who had done the tobacco industry's dirty work when the original cigarette labeling bill was considered, was no longer willing to, and Utah's Moss, named to chair Commerce's consumer affairs subcommittee and facing reelection the following year, threatened to filibuster the weak House version of the labeling law extension if a Senate majority formed behind it—a stratagem that would then allow the regulatory agencies to step in with sterner measures. And the FTC showed every sign of doing just that, convening hearings the very day after the old bill expired to consider a tough regulatory rule including a ban on broadcast advertising, already embraced by the FCC. A highlight of the FTC session, symptomatic of the unraveling fortunes of an industry that had overplayed its hand, was a gaffe by the Tobacco Institute's usually deadly hired gun, attorney Thomas Austern. In ridiculing the need for a tougher label on the perils of smoking, Austern said that "anybody who is not deaf and blind knows it's a hazard"—he had forgotten to insert the lawyerly disclaimer "alleged to be" before the final two words and was immediately lashed for it by Philip Elman, the commission's most ardent antismoking member.

By then the broadcasters' association, its credibility shaken by the Braren testimony and fearful that the Senate Commerce Committee was about to come down hard on unchastened cigarette commercials, went to Magnuson with a deal it had chosen not to tell the tobacco companies about: Tobacco ads would be phased off the air over a four-year period, so that the broadcasting industry would not be badly bruised in the process; only brands with tar and nicotine yields ranking in the lowest quarter could continue to be advertised; and antismoking commercials being carried gratis in prime time by the stations could therefore, because of the fairness doctrine, continue, albeit on a reduced basis. It was a tempting offer to Magnuson, Pertschuk, and especially Daniel Horn at the Clearinghouse on Smoking and Health, where the belief prevailed that low-yielding brands were a useful way station to quitting and the broadcast antismoking messages were having a definite dampening effect on cigarette sales. In the end, though, the offer was rejected. "It sounded too much like a deal to Magnuson," Pertschuk recalled, and as Clearinghouse staff lawyer Edward Merlis remembered the decision, "The moral imperative dictated giving the television ban priority." If the antismoking commercials had to be sacrificed, then so be it.

Rebuffed, the broadcasters announced during the FTC hearings that they would curtail all cigarette advertising over a three-and-a-half-year period. The news did not sit well with the tobacco companies, who had not been consulted and felt betrayed. But by then the cigarette makers were facing up to the political readout they were getting from Earle Clements, retiring Tobacco Institute president: the industry's position in the Senate was hopeless; better to surrender on favorable terms than to be shot down in flames.

Cullman, now due to present the industry's position before the Senate Commerce panel, was feeling intense heat even within his own company over the prospective TV ban. As one company lawyer recalled, "He was hearing in particular from Jack Landry, who was saying, 'Joe, you can't let this happen—you've got to lie on the tracks and let them roll over you before you cave in. . . .' " But pride in tobacco and anguish over its stigmatized standing did not blur Cullman's calculating mind. He saw there was a silver lining on the dark cloud directly over the industry's head if it stood up now and voluntarily took its advertising off the air. The move would effectively end the possibility that any new competitors would ever enter the cigarette business in the future, however profitable the product, since without television advertising, the introduction of new brands would prove prohibitively expensive. If all the companies agreed to get out together, moreover, they would surely save many millions of advertising dollars, which could be used in non-tobacco diversification efforts or simply be brought down to the bottom line in the form of higher profits and dividends. And a timely retreat now would likely stave off still more mortifying measures by Congress, such as requiring the warning labels in print advertising along with the listing of tar and nicotine yields, and would mean the end of the barbed antismoking commercials.

"Joe was very patient, hearing all sides of the argument," one company counselor recounted. "Nobody was more disappointed than he was at the prospect of giving up television—he liked the medium, it had been good for the company, and quitting it seemed to stigmatize the product" even more than accepting the warning label had done. And there was the distinct possibility that the end of TV advertising would help freeze company market shares within the industry—a prospect that probably served to bring pacesetting Reynolds into line, for it looked to have the least to lose from the prohibition.

The Senate hearing on the cigarette bill on July 22, 1969, began with a twenty-minute film spliced together for the occasion and intended to crystallize antitobacco sentiment in the upper chamber. Assembled by Pertschuk, Merlis, and Clearinghouse publicist Richard Hutchings from clips of commercials provided by the industry and shown in the auditorium of the new Senate office building to attract a wide audience, the film featured beautiful people puffing happily away in a variety of settings. "We were enthralled by the skill that went into their making," Merlis recalled of the assemblage. "It was a very entertaining and alluring collection when viewed all together—you could see how they meant to create images of success and accomplishment that were seductive to kids." Hoist with their own petard, as it were, the tobacco companies then accepted the inevitable. Cullman read the industry's statement of concession: All cigarette commercials would cease as of September 30, 1970.

As part of the bargain, specific reference to cancer or other diseases was removed from the new warning label language, leaving it marginally more cautionary than the previous wording, but the FTC was empowered to consider the inclusion of warning labels in all surviving forms of advertising within six months of the onset of the broadcast ban—a second clear victory for the anti-smoking position. All but lost sight of, though, was a change in the preemption section of the act engineered by the industry lawyers that would have an effect not fully grasped by its adversaries for the better part of twenty years. The warning in the 1965 labeling law had been termed by its own statutory language to be "adequate" for its dual purpose—namely, alerting the public to the health hazard of smoking while preventing any government measures or enactments in conflict with the congressionally mandated wording, of the sort that the FTC and several state legislatures had been considering at the time, in order not to hamper the interstate operations of the tobacco industry. The law's reach did not on its face foreclose adjudicative proceedings carried out under state common law governing torts in general and product liability in particular. But the 1969 bill was worded a bit differently:

SECTION 5 (b). No requirement or prohibition based on smoking and health shall be imposed under State law with respect to the advertising or promotion of any cigarettes the packages of which are labeled in conformity with the provisions of this Act.

The phrase "imposed under State law" was far more sweeping in its reach than the earlier wording, as Supreme Court watchers might have detected from a decision by that body ten years earlier which held damages awarded under state common law of torts to be a form of regulation. Did this mean that a smoker sick from the habit could no longer even bring suit under state law, asking a jury to decide whether the claimant had been adequately put on notice by the warning label and thus had assumed whatever risk was entailed by use of the product? In the 1959 Supreme Court decision of *San Diego Building Trades Council v. Garmon*, the justices had said state regulation "can be as effectively asserted through an award of damages as through some form of preventive relief. The obligation [by a tortious defendant] to pay compensation can be, indeed is designed to be, a potent method of governing conduct and controlling policy." In other words, if product liability suits filed under state common law were a way of circumventing a congressional mandate that said no other "requirement or prohibition . . . shall be imposed under State law," then damage claims by smokers falling ill after the federal warning label went into effect were arguably blocked by the wording of the new bill. But since the chronic diseases associated with smoking had long incubation periods, dating back years and probably decades before the warning label had been affixed by law, the whole issue was too new and its legal consequences too far in the future to worry public-health advocates, delighted to achieve the more urgent objective of getting cigarette ads permanently removed from television's spellbinding eye.

In their bitterness over the tobacco industry's sudden withdrawal from combat, the broadcasters now raised a Fifth Amendment argument they would not have dared to broach before they and the cigarette makers had parted company: If cigarettes were so dangerous that they deserved to be taken off the electronic media, why were they deemed fit for advertising in any other media? The product, if Congress were acting rationally and not prejudicially denying broadcasters equal protection of the law, ought not to be allowed to be advertised at all—and if cigarette sales did not then materially diminish, perhaps the product itself should be outlawed as a public-health measure.

The federal courts, though, did not agree with this line of reasoning. In the 1971 ruling of *Capital Broadcasting Company v. U.S.,* the District of Columbia federal circuit tribunal said Congress was within its rights to impose the cigarette ad ban selectively since the Fifth Amendment did not compel legislatures to "prohibit all like evils, or none. A legislature may hit at an abuse which it has found, even though it has failed to strike at another." In an eloquent dissent, however, Judge J. Skelly Wright, an eminent civil libertarian, registered free-speech concerns that would continue to echo several decades later, when Congress began to weigh seriously a ban on all cigarette advertising. Wright wrote that he had no doubt that the girl in the Salem ads was "in fact a seductive merchant of death and that the real 'Marlboro Country' is the graveyard. But the First Amendment does not protect only speech that is healthy or harmless."

As a final reward to the tobacco manufacturers for yielding to the inevitable, Congress pushed back the date when the TV ban would take effect to midnight of January 1, 1971, thereby allowing the industry one final fling in the form of heavy cigarette advertising during the college football bowl games. No company bought more airtime that day than Philip Morris. "It was going to be a whole new world now," recalled the company's acknowledged ad wizard, Jack Landry. As his farewell gesture to the medium he had used so effectively, Landry scheduled a ninety-second Marlboro commercial, to begin at 11:58.30 and end precisely at the stroke of midnight. He sat home alone by his television set, watched four of his beloved cowboys gallop off into the sunset for the last time, and wept. "A lot of the excitement went out of the business then," George Weissman recalled.

IX

PERHAPS the truest measure of Philip Morris's advance toward the leadership of its industry in the 'Sixties was how it positioned itself in overseas markets as no other American company had. But the dream of establishing Marlboro and several other Philip Morris brands as the world standard in cigarettes, rather like Swiss watches or Italian leather goods, was burdened by the daunting reality that there was no such thing as a single global market for tobacco products, but a myriad of them, each distinguishable by national, cultural, political, and economic considerations.

Most obvious of the problems was the need to achieve a massive transformation in the taste preferences of non-American smokers. Just as those in British Commonwealth lands had a decided affinity for "Virginia flue-cured leaf," unflavored and more natural than the U.S. staple blended with sweetened Burley, so did most smokers on the European continent and in Latin America favor "black" air-cured tobacco blended with "Oriental" (in fact, Levantine) leaf for its strong aroma and a smoking quality that seemed rather harsh to American and British tastes. Nor did most smokers elsewhere yet share the American vogue for filter-tip brands, viewed abroad as interfering with true tobacco taste. Even though American brands had been widely sampled overseas as a result of the two world wars when production of domestic brands had been curtailed in many countries, U.S. smokes remained largely a high-priced novelty or tourist item abroad.

A huge portion of the potential world market, of course, was beyond Philip Morris's reach, locked away under Communist regimes that held sway from East Germany across the Eurasian landmass to the China Sea. But even many countries outside of the Communist sphere operated state tobacco monopolies to bolster domestic industry and employment and reap tax revenues often difficult to collect through income levies. France, Italy, Spain, Japan, and most Pacific Rim countries gave their state-owned cigarette brands nearly invulnerable advantages in the marketplace, slapping steep tariffs and excises on imported U.S. or other foreign brands that, after adding in generally much higher labor, leaf, and shipping costs, could be sold only at premium prices beyond most consumers' range, even if they liked the American blends. Even when manufactured by the state monopolies under a licensing arrangement, American brands were invariably penalized by being taxed at a higher rate than domestic brands were, and were usually locked into their premium price category, unable to adjust to changing economic conditions.

Other nations also burdened U.S. cigarette makers invading their shores with a variety of discriminatory devices, born out of self-protective impulses or simple xenophobia—or both. These impediments ranged from the required use of domestically grown tobacco (100 percent in most Latin American countries and at least half in Australia) to a limit of one-half or less of the ownership in a domestic tobacco company by foreign nationals (as in India and Nigeria) to more narrow prohibitions like Austria's ban on the advertising of foreign (but not domestic) cigarette brands. Withal, most free-world governments welcomed efforts by U.S. tobacco companies to operate within their borders if only because taxes from cigarette sales of any kind fattened their treasuries.

Although no other U.S. company was nearly so active in exploring this thorny international thicket, London-based British-American Tobacco, the world's largest private maker of cigarettes, loomed as Philip Morris's most formidable global competitor. BAT was barred by the terms of its turn-of-the-century charter from selling in Great Britain or the U.S., but it held worldwide rights outside those two countries to all American Tobacco and Imperial Tobacco brands and, catering to national and regional tastes with the domestic brands it produced, accounted for more than half the cigarette market in the fifty or so countries in which its subsidiaries were operating in the 1960s. Even in developing or pre-industrial nations, where the average smoker could afford only a package or less a week, BAT thrived by using cheap local labor and leaf and antiquated but serviceable machinery in manufacturing its brands, so that even a modest rise in the standard of living in such places could yield great profits. Except when faced with disasters like the shutdown of its operations by Red China—a nation where BAT had been the dominant cigarette purveyor before Japan occupied it in the 1930s—or the temporary seizure of its plants by Indonesia's Sukarno in 1964, BAT had learned to cope. In a poor, small nation like Malawi, it tailored its product to reality, offering an eight-stick cigarette pack called Tom Tom that sold for three and a half cents. On the Asian subcontinent, its India Tobacco Company held half the cigarette market, much of it in the form of one-stick sales by street wallahs who bought a pack at a time and resold the contents in competition with *bidi*, the crudely made, all-tobacco product that outsold cigarettes about eight to one despite their poor burning quality, which required them to be puffed twice a minute and accounted in large part for the nation's astronomical rate of oral cancer. Perhaps the best example of BAT's ability to extract some 35 percent of its net profits from developing nations was its performance in Brazil, a vast land with a volatile economy and unstable government but whose people loved to smoke. Thanks in part to a complex pricing system that penalized imported brands, limiting their appeal to the nation's rich, BAT's locally made brands grabbed a heavy majority of the market where cigarettes had to be distributed on a door-to-door basis for cash only. So extensive was BAT's delivery network that it could reach every urban *favela* with beat-up trucks paid for long ago and remote settlements off Amazon tributaries by canoe.

When not struggling against entrenched BAT or subsidized state monopolies, Philip Morris had to worry about smaller local competitors who could obtain supplies and labor at lower cost and had cheaper access to the marketplace. In the global market, George Weissman was guided by a single strategy: Try to sell as many units as possible, with market share and not profitability the first goal. The game was to stay at it patiently, enlist skilled local talent, learn native marketing techniques, soft-soap the authorities—short of bribing them, a never-ending form of blackmail—and in time the profits would materialize. But even if profits accumulated, it was at times difficult to repatriate them from foreign countries reluctant to be drained of wealth by America. Often the best U.S.-owned foreign operations could manage was to negotiate with finance ministries and central banks to recoup a percentage of their investment base, reinvesting the rest of their profits while gaining a nice credit on their parent company's consolidated earnings statement for taxes paid abroad.

Forced to run what amounted to a bootstrap operation, since Philip Morris was putting most of its money into building domestic brands, Weissman turned to licensing foreign manufacturers as the most economical and least aggravating way to gain a toehold in overseas markets. For a royalty in the neighborhood of forty cents per thousand units sold—less than a penny per pack after recovering costs—Philip Morris supplied the foreign licensee with blended U.S. tobacco (formula withheld), filters, flavorings, and troubleshooters from its Richmond manufacturing center to help achieve uniformity of quality and a taste indistinguishable from that of the American version.

One of Weissman's first moves, accordingly, had been to sign a ten-year deal with the house of Martin Brinkmann, third biggest cigarette maker in West Germany, the most promising and sizable market in Europe for U.S. brands, where younger people were taking avidly to such other American imports as jazz, blue jeans, and Coca-Cola. Brinkmann, well behind German market leader Reemtsma, once favored by the Nazi regime, and BAT, whose brands accounted for one out of four German cigarette sales, found Marlboro a useful addition to its line. But it insisted that it knew better than Philip Morris marketers how to sell to Germans: more Oriental leaf had to be added to the Richmond blend to appeal to the Teutonic taste, and instead of Western cowboys, Marlboro ads in Germany featured cozy family settings that Brinkmann claimed were the ultimate aspiration of its bourgeois customers. And they were right, up to a point. "They were very successful in selling the cigarette—they just restricted its sale to the exact minimum needed to satisfy the royalty arrangement—1 percent of the market—and they kept it there," Weissman recounted. "I mean, they really screwed us for ten years."

Soon Weissman willingly got himself entrapped in a licensing arrangement with a government-owned tobacco monopoly. In 1962, he found himself lunching with the head of the Italian state-owned manufacturer of M.S., the cheap, poorly made domestic brand that was by far the nation's top seller and a major source of the government's tax revenues. Increasingly, though, imports were cutting into his sales, the Italian executive complained, especially German brands that were being advertised heavily in Milan and other cities in the north. Why not make Marlboros for us, Weissman proposed. "We'll teach you how to make them—it's the best cigarette in the world." The deal was struck, but the Italian monopoly had a love-hate relationship with foreign brands, craving the higher revenues and tax receipts but resenting M.S.'s loss of market share, particularly as Marlboro soon proved highly popular as a status smoke, to the point where the costlier American brand became a weekend favorite, its flip-top box saved and filled with the cheaper domestic brand the rest of the week. Ostensibly to blunt the sale of German brands, the Italian government banned all cigarette advertising, a move that slowed Marlboro's progress. Nor would the state monopoly produce enough Marlboros to meet the demand. As a result, a black market began to grow in smuggled foreign brands, sold without the heavy domestic tax. Philip Morris, frustrated by shortsighted and emotional Italian government policies, averted its eyes from the increasing Italian traffic in unlicensed Marlboros.

At the mercy of overseas distributors who were also its prime competitors, Philip Morris gradually concluded that licensing was a penny-wise and pound-foolish expedient, and it would be better to conduct its own manufacturing operations abroad, preferably with a local partner in the early years while learning the cultural differences in doing business abroad and training a staff of competent nationals to run the operation. But Philip Morris's early experiences in overseas production had not been encouraging.

In Australia, for example, the company thought it saw a small, relatively wealthy, and stable market, where cigarettes were said to be in short supply and Yank tastes and a national tradition of rugged independence were thought to be well regarded. And it would theoretically be a good place to establish a manufacturing base for penetrating huge Asian markets, where U.S. brands were barely visible. But there were problems. For one thing, Philip Morris had no famous brand of all-Virginia leaf, the British smoking legacy to its old prison colony, to compete with Australian and English makes. And Marlboro's cowboy pitch was off-key in a society not long removed from its own frontier days. Nor was it easy to simulate the Richmond recipe with tobacco that by law had to be half Australian-grown, and labor costs were unduly high because of permissive "manning" rules, effectively killing chances of using Australia as a base for competing in Asian markets with their far lower production costs. "A dismal failure," Joe Cullman later termed the early Australian effort.

In oil-rich Venezuela, with a slightly larger middle class than most Latin American societies, the Philip Morris effort was handicapped by BAT's long headstart but abetted by the hands-on presence of Weissman's top legal expert, John A. Murphy, a hulking native of New York City. Murphy, who combined a sharp legal mind honed at Columbia, a head for numbers, the raffish appeal of an outsized leprechaun, and as much bully and bluster as the occasion required, put together a pair of local Venezuelan manufacturers under Philip

Morris control after earlier efforts had made scant headway. With the help of company technicians from Richmond like Joseph Lloyd, manager of manufacturing services who began to roam the globe solving production problems at facilities far less sophisticated than at home, the expanded operation opened in a rural community close by tobacco fields sixty-five miles from Caracas, Venezuela's capital. The plant grew by bits and pieces over two decades, as sales rode a roller coaster, first cresting in a period when the company enjoyed the blessing of a friendly dictator, then receding, partly by design, in the face of threats of nationalization by a less benign government, and partly due to a resurgence by BAT. The success of the enterprise depended, as Lloyd recalled, on "a bunch of poorly educated guys, busting their asses in quonset huts," struggling to overcome lax work habits, inadequate training, and the language barrier. Progress could be measured visibly at the work site, where in the early days laborers arrived on the job on foot, then by bike as the company's domestic brands began making sizable gains in market share, and finally by cars that required carving a parking lot out of the adjacent jungle. Profits were slow in coming and irregular at best.

Most perilous of all was the effort to penetrate the Dark Continent toward the end of the 'Sixties by opening operations in Nigeria, the richest and most populous of the black African nations. Yet it was still a land of wrenching poverty. A black Philip Morris sales executive named Tom Shropshire, whose job had been to push exports of the company's brands throughout West Africa, told the peripatetic Murphy that a local tobacco company owned by Unilever some 250 miles inland from the capital could be bought. No sooner was the takeover accomplished, with Shropshire placed in charge, than the Biafran war of secession began, shattering the country's tenuous stability. Smuggled British cigarettes undercut Philip Morris's legitimate prices because the contraband was tax-free. "Dash," the local term for payoffs to officials, was a way of Nigerian business life. "You couldn't even get out of the airport at Lagos without paying a small bribe," one Philip Morris executive recalled. And labor relations at the factory were a tangle of strife-ridden rivalry spilling over easily into animosity among workers from different tribes. Advancement was gained more often by purchase than merit, and the hierarchy of authority was so rigidified that, as Richard Vail, a Philip Morris lawyer who specialized in labor relations, remembered, "You had to teach the workforce not to prostrate itself every time the personnel manager walked in the door." When Vail tried to put in place a fringe benefit common in other countries where Philip Morris operated plants—accident insurance worth $50,000 for each of the company's traveling salesmen—the exasperated Shropshire intervened. "You want to start another civil war here?" he demanded, pointing out to Vail that this was a place where every cigarette salesman who rode the back country on his bike led a precarious existence and for the kind of money Vail was proposing as the insurance benefit, each one's life expectancy would be brief indeed.

Life in the tropics was not without its buoyant moments, to be sure. As a tribute to Shropshire's managerial patience and kindness to his workers (by helping them, for example, obtain beef, a commodity in short supply), a party was arranged at which the Philip Morris boss was to be presented with a cow. John Murphy, in one of his regular swings through the provinces from the company's overseas headquarters in Switzerland, was asked to make the presentation. Showing up for the occasion in a bright yellow blazer, Murphy was advised at the critical moment to step outside of Shropshire's house and latch on to the gift, said to be standing in wait "just up the block." The distance turned out to be quite a ways up a dusty street, past a military post, and the cow turned out to be a bull on a rope held by a waif. Murphy took highly tentative possession of the line, managed to tangle it around a telephone pole within a few steps, and, after sweatily extricating himself and his snorting charge, marched as unobtrusively as it is possible for a huge white man in a yellow blazer leading a bull to look while passing an army barracks and fearing he might be mistaken for a cattle rustler. The randy animal, presented to Shropshire before a houseful of admiring subordinates, proved a bit of a problem later that evening on being penned up in the rear yard. It shredded fencing with its horns, lured a cloud of flies with its stench, and, all in all, created an unmanageable uproar. "You son of a bitch!" Shropshire snarled on the telephone the next day to the departed Murphy, who, though innocent of the ruse, soon found the company's spotless headquarters in Lausanne the beneficiary of a very messy caged pig, air-freighted via Lagos and generating instantaneous chaos until the Great Philip Morris Animal War was called to a halt.

For years the Nigerian operation made no money but at least kept the Philip Morris flag aloft long enough to establish familiarity with its brands. Not until a generation later, after the company withdrew from controlling ownership, selling off to local proprietors and retaining about 25 percent of the equity, did it begin to realize a small return on its investment.

X

ITS early misadventures abroad left Philip Morris wiser and on the alert for less hazardous opportunities to establish a profitable operating base. One arose unexpectedly in 1963, when the owners of the company's Swiss licensee, Fabriques de Tabac Réunies (FTR), fell out with one another. FTR, which held about 20 percent of the Swiss cigarette market and had done well with Marlboro and other licensed PM brands, especially in the southern, Italian-speaking section of the country, invited Philip Morris to bid for it.

George Weissman, sensing a gem in the offing, opened the talks with the tradition-minded Swiss in his relaxed manner, but soon turned the real bargaining over to John Murphy. One of Weissman's strengths was that, like his superior, Joe Cullman, he knew his own limits and understood how to delegate to technically trained subordinates. One of Murphy's first moves was to hire a blond, ruddy young Scotsman named Ronald Hew Thomson, who had read law at Cambridge and, after becoming a chartered accountant, had worked for a large Swiss bank and in the Geneva office of the international accounting firm of Coopers & Lybrand.

Thomson, whose hiring would prove a fateful step in Philip Morris's climb over the ensuing quarter-century to leadership in the European market, was not an ordinary bean counter. Armed with a hair-trigger brain, a surfeit of self-confidence, and a fierce competitive instinct that had made him a nationally ranked rugby player, he began sifting through FTR's ledgers. The three sets of company books—standard operating procedure on a continent where entrepreneurs historically parted with tax payments grudgingly (if at all)—disclosed that FTR's assets were, by American accounting methods, worth a good deal more than the Swiss calculated. And Thomson at once saw one of the major advantages for Philip Morris in owning FTR rather than licensing it: "Its cash flow was dramatic," he recalled. Acting as a collector of excise taxes, U.S. cigarette companies had long been the beneficiary of a practice unique to their industry; since cigarette taxes were so much higher relative to prices than sales imposts on almost all other products, and the manufacturers, furthermore, were not required to turn over their tax receipts from wholesalers to the government for weeks or sometimes months, they had a ready reservoir of cash to help meet their daily costs of doing business and to avoid interest charges on loans they did not have to take. This bottom-line benefit was greater still in Europe, where cigarette tax rates were so much higher than in the U.S.

FTR was also attractive because it was manageable. Switzerland was a prosperous, compact marketplace with a population slightly smaller than New York City's, excellent air and rail connections from its central location on the continent, a large tourist trade to present U.S. blended cigarettes to, and ready access by its nationals, thanks to the country's long tradition of neutrality and international banking, to markets and financiers everywhere. And FTR itself was a profitable company with strong financial controls and a hardworking labor force.

For all that, Philip Morris almost lost the deal because of the unleashed pugnacity of its designated chief negotiator, crotchety general counsel Paul Smith, who flew in from New York to drive the hardest possible bargain. "His creed was that you've got to be prepared to lose a deal to get a deal," Thomson recalled. "You couldn't tell if he was brilliant or just cuckoo." On arriving for the negotiations, Smith separated himself from the rest of the Philip Morris legal team for a few days and worked himself into a state of advanced contentiousness. Once the talks began in earnest with the FTR officers, he kept them off balance through two ploys: displaying his mastery, to the letter, of their governing rules, such as asking precisely which paragraph of the Swiss code of corporate obligations applied to the point at hand, and retreating into total silence when questions were put to him—and the longer he held his tongue, the more bewildered and tense the Swiss negotiators became. "It was as if there were a one-sided dialogue being conducted," said Thomson. Smith turned up the heat so much at times that the Swiss, slow to rage but finally on the brink of fury, had to be calmed by Weissman and Murphy in a classic good cop/bad cop scenario. In the end, Philip Morris walked away with FTR for a bargain price of about $12 million.

The contrast between the hierarchical Swiss way of doing things and American informality was immediately apparent when the Philip Morris brass winged over for a celebratory bash, held at a picture-perfect auberge outside Lausanne, to which the top three levels of FTR management were invited along with their wives. Such inter-strata mingling, along with the entirely uncustomary inclusion of the women, added to the discomfiture of the Swiss, already dreading that their new American overseers would arrive with the swagger of conquering heroes. But Joe Cullman confirmed that that was the way he wanted the party run—democratically—and so the chill in the air in the rathskeller where the pre-dinner cocktails were served matched the frosty temperature outside. Instead of the easy mingling of guests that marks such occasions in the U.S., the Swiss lined up strictly as protocol dictated, by rank and seniority, as if at a diplomatic reception, and so had to be greeted in proper order by their hosts amid much bowing and scraping. The mood remained frostbitten through the meal and until Cullman's after-dinner remarks. They had all been employees of a Swiss company, he told them, "but now you are part of a growing international operation. Someday I'll be seeing some of you working for our Venezuelan affiliate or in Australia or at our New York office, because you are good managers."

After their new lord and master excused himself, the FTR people, who had taken hardly a sip of fermented liquid, began to relax a bit and confessed their bafflement over Cullman's meaning to Philip Morris underlings who remained on hand. As the company's vision of a truly global enterprise, staffed by the most deserving employees regardless of their country of origin, was explained to them by the likes of James Bowling, Philip Morris's public-relations virtuoso, the Swiss grew excited at the prospect of inhabiting a less parochial world. "Their sense grew not that they had been captured and were about to be occupied," Bowling recalled, "but that they had been freed—and they got drunk as lords."

From the beginning, FTR's performance outstripped Philip Morris's expectations. A few kinks had to be worked out, not always to the pleasure of the Swiss, such as curtailment of the long-standing acceptance of kickbacks from suppliers, perceived as a courtesy by the FTR people but as a masked expense—and less than entirely ethical—by their Philip Morris watchdogs. Most of the company's traditional ways of operating, though, were admirable. "The Swiss are remarkable—they just get things done," recounted Ronald Thomson, who remained on the scene for two years as the company's chief financial monitor and liaison between Neuchâtel and New York.

With unabashed pragmatism, FTR pushed sales with certain wholesalers who, upon duly paying their Swiss excise taxes, smuggled the cigarettes, especially Marlboros, in ever-growing numbers by truck over the Alps into Italy. There they quickly found their way onto the street and thus deprived the Italian government, which taxed smokers more heavily than the Swiss did, of considerable revenue. Unwilling or unable to crack down on this illicit transalpine traffic, in part because a sizable number of its citizens were making their livelihood from it, the Italian government's tobacco monopoly was receptive when FTR's Aleardo Buzzi, a suave, handsome Swiss of Italian extraction, urged them to counter the problem—obviously beyond FTR's control as well, Buzzi noted, since the wholesalers had strictly abided by Swiss rules—by stepping up their own licensed production of hard-to-get Marlboro and other FTR brands, even at the expense of lower sales for M.S., the Italian national brand. Buzzi's persuasiveness helped open the door to more aggressive marketing of Philip Morris brands, which a generation later would command one-third of the Italian cigarette market. FTR, meanwhile, was soon earning as much each year as Philip Morris had paid to buy it.

The Swiss and Italian ventures contrasted sharply with the Philip Morris effort in France, where the government monopoly, known by its acronym, SEITA, distributed the U.S. imports through strictly regulated and state-run tobacco shops. Marlboros sold for a 25 to 33 percent premium above the French brands, Gauloises and Gitanes, the state-subsidized "black" smokes favored by nearly 95 percent of the French market as much for a symbol of national pride as for their taste. Even so, the Philip Morris brands were kept at too low a price to pay their way; the company would lose money for fifteen years in France before it began winning large numbers of converts to the milder and sweeter Marlboro blend.

XI

GEORGE WEISSMAN, whose bold initiatives abroad helped get him named president of Philip Morris in 1967, was succeeded as head of international operations by Hugh Cullman, a more cautious, buttoned-up kind of

executive. He was experienced in the leaf and manufacturing end of the tobacco business but less familiar with and adept at the marketing side. He tried
to compensate for his shortcomings by working hard and absorbing as much
data as he could cram into his briefcase for overnight review. "Hugh was an information maniac," one company associate remarked. "All facts and factoids
were equal to him." But everyone agreed that Hugh Cullman had dedication,
an admirable range of knowledge, and the ambition (which he kept well dis-
guised) to succeed his older cousin Joe as CEO. If Joe favored his younger
cousin's aspirations, he gave little sign of it.

Hugh Cullman was smart enough not to try to run the international operation by the numbers out of New York. Instead, he gave the able subordinates
he inherited, like Murphy and Thomson, enough running room. Thomson especially, after an obligatory and unhappy stint in the New York home office,
felt unleashed on returning to Lausanne, by then the coordinating point for the
company's European, African, and Middle Eastern efforts.

Not long after Thomson took charge of that territory, he and Murphy, with
whom he had a tigerish but mutually respectful relationship, apprised New
York of an opportunity to reverse Philip Morris's lagging, indeed nearly invisible, presence in Great Britain, a cigarette market about one-fifth the size of the
U.S. pie. Without a serious Virginia-leaf contender in the field and aware that
its "Marlboro Country" theme evoked an impression more of savagery than
rugged individualism among Britons, Philip Morris could only nibble at a market in which Imperial Tobacco brands held a massive two-thirds share and its
only real competitor, Gallaher Limited, had 27 percent as of 1967. Under an
arrangement that would have been prevented by U.S. antitrust regulations, Imperial held a 36 percent piece of Gallaher's equity, which it decided to
unload in the spring of 1968 at twenty shillings a share, using the receipts to
diversify out of tobacco.

But the public offering was only 65 percent subscribed, partly because Gallaher's fortunes had ebbed. As recently as 1964, it had held 37 percent of the
market, but in the interim it had paid for its slow entry into both filter and
coupon brands, the latter becoming the promotional rage with the demise of
cigarette ads on British TV in the early 'Sixties. To compensate, Gallaher had
bought up a small British firm that specialized in coupon brands—Julius Wix
& Son—from American Tobacco for just under 13 percent of Gallaher's common shares. If American, which was not allowed to peddle its U.S. brands in
Great Britain under the terms of the original BAT charter, had wanted to make
a serious play for position in the international market, here was an opportune
moment to gain virtual control of the second ranking British cigarette maker.
But American Tobacco, apparently consumed by its travails in the U.S. market, did not enter the Gallaher picture—quite yet. Instead, Philip Morris now
inspected the situation closely and liked what it saw.

True, Gallaher was in a marketing slump, but the company was well regarded as a quality manufacturer, and its leading seller, Benson & Hedges, had a name of great value to Philip Morris, off and running now with its own 100-millimeter version in the U.S. market; Gallaher's lower-yielding Silk Cuts brand was also showing signs of life. Gallaher, moreover, would give Philip Morris a solid base for invading the Commonwealth and European markets with strong Virginia-leaf brands as well as a far more powerful marketing vehicle in Britain for Marlboro and its other U.S. brands. Gallaher profits ran to about $19 million in 1967, roughly one-third of the Philip Morris consolidated net, so the acquisition would represent a very large but not indigestible bite and one that, unlike most of its other foreign investments, would begin to earn back a goodly return from the first. In a late May 1968 memorandum from Philip Morris International in which Hugh Cullman, his legal counselor John Murphy, and his quick-witted young European ace Ronnie Thomson concurred, the company's executive committee was urged to appropriate the funds necessary to buy up control of Gallaher—in the $100 to $125 million range—at a tender price of twenty-five shillings a share, 25 percent above what the unsuccessful Imperial offering price had been. For Philip Morris, the memo said, such an acquisition would represent "a major step to becoming a significant force in the world tobacco trade," but the Gallaher management, of course, would have to be replaced with fresh blood invigorated by the new U.S. owners' marketing flair.

There was one unsettling aspect, however, to any move Philip Morris would make now in London. Unless the company went in after first buying out American Tobacco's 13 percent interest, Murphy pointed out, Philip Morris could find itself with a big minority position but no working control of Gallaher. On the other hand, to buy out American Tobacco at whatever price it took before tendering for the rest of Gallaher's shares in London would have meant skirting or directly violating a recently enacted provision of the rules of The City, Britain's financial community. More a club whose members agree voluntarily to abide by their own rules than an industry under government regulation like the U.S. securities business, The City had only a few months earlier issued a little green booklet containing its new "Code on Take-Overs and Mergers," a key tenet of which frowned on tender offers for less than all the stock outstanding. To prevent loss of public confidence and any suspicion of manipulation by management insiders, "all shares of a class of an offeree company shall be treated equally"—meaning tendered for at the same price. Murphy's strategy of negotiating first and separately with American Tobacco and then tendering in London at the twenty-five-shilling price, surely lower than American would be paid, would likely be perceived as conflicting with The City rule. But Murphy, his Hibernian soul awakened with a bit of up-the-English-establishment zeal, was prepared to play hardball. He scrawled on the front of his copy of the green booklet, "What authority does this have? How is it enforced? What is the penalty for violation?"

Philip Morris's chairman, though, was not eager to play Buck Duke reincarnated. Murphy was doubtless correct—it would have been far better to take American Tobacco out of the picture—but Philip Morris's chief London financial advisors, the merchant banking house of S. G. Warburg & Company, told Joseph Cullman that The City would turn its back on Philip Morris if it offered a premium for the American Tobacco shares and less to Gallaher's U.K. shareholders. Sir Siegmund Warburg had just been knighted and was not about to counsel underhandedness by a foreign investor, and most especially not by an American company. "Warburg was the establishment," Murphy recounted, "and Joe Cullman felt we had to be guided by their strong advice."

And so Philip Morris hewed to the line. Its management team, headed by the two Cullmans, arrived in Britain toward the end of June, dutifully apprised The City's officials of the company's planned tender bid for Gallaher, and asked for a meeting with the British cigarette maker's management to assure them that if the takeover bid succeeded, the New York company would work earnestly to expand their sales horizons and guarantee their tenures of employment and their pensions. But the Philip Morris delegation was welcomed icily. Gallaher's officers sat up on a dais, and, as Murphy remembered the session, "their managing director, Mark Norman, looked down his nose at Joe." The meeting did not last beyond half an hour; afterward, Gallaher announced that it would urge its shareholders not to accept the Philip Morris offer.

While the Cullmans and company contemplated their next move, American Tobacco roused itself. If taking over Gallaher was attractive to Philip Morris—which had swept past AT's Pall Mall Gold 100s with its newly minted Benson & Hedges brand, was beating it badly in the women's brands niche with Virginia Slims, and was posting global cigarette sales just a bit behind American Tobacco's now—then it had to be good business for American Tobacco to get into the act, especially since it already had a goodly stake in the British company.

An American Tobacco team headed by hard-liner Robert Heimann, executive vice president and heir apparent to Barney Walker's throne, arrived in London on a Sunday while Philip Morris's tender was still on the table and The City was waiting to see if it would sweeten its offer. Heimann's team met all that sabbath with the same financial team that had brokered Imperial's initial offering of its Gallaher shares—Morgan, Grenfell, headed by Viscount Harcourt, an Eton and Oxford man, and Cazenove & Company, under senior partner Sir Anthony Hornby, of Winchester and the Grenadier Guards, the ultimate in City suzerainty. The Morgan, Grenfell–Cazenove team had lost a decade earlier to the house of Warburg in a battle for ownership of British Tube, the big aluminum outfit; they did not intend to lose again. They started with one big advantage in that they knew precisely who the buyers had been of the Gallaher shares Imperial had offered a few months earlier—mostly institutions that liked the low price and the idea of holding a prudent speculation on a Gallaher turnaround. After Heimann had assured Gallaher management that it would be infinitely better off under American Tobacco, which would keep its hands off the British operation, than Philip Morris, it was no trick at all for the brokerage team to carry out a lightning strike the next morning, privately buying up 12 million shares within a few hours at an average price of thirty-five shillings, or 40 percent higher than the Philip Morris tender. The strike gave American some 28 percent of Gallaher's shares; as Heimann announced, "We are here . . . to preserve, protect, and defend a fine investment," and that his company was ready to buy at least half—not all, as requested by The City's new code—of other holders' shares at the same thirty-five-shilling price it had paid on average that morning, thereby obtaining outright control. It was a grievous breach of The City's code on takeovers, but despite much clucking in the press and among London's more ethical tycoons about the wickedness involved, the irregular deal was not undone.

"Philip Morris played by the rules—and it lost," Ronnie Thomson said with some disgust. The eagerly sought prize would now be prohibitively expensive for Joe Cullman and his colleagues to pursue, and so instead they turned, in consolation, to London's far smaller Godfrey Phillips company, which it won with a preemptive bid. The acquisition substantially bolstered the U.S. company's position in Australia, where Phillips had a strong Virginia-leaf brand, and gave it a foothold in the tumultuous market in India. But its gentlemanly conduct in seeking Gallaher would prove costly. In time, Gallaher surpassed Imperial as the top cigarette seller in the nation; its Benson & Hedges and Silk Cuts would become the leading brands in their categories; and in Great Britain, whence Philip Morris had sprung, that company would not play a serious role in the cigarette business—true in few other industrialized nations by the closing years of the twentieth century.

11

Stroking the Sow's Ear

FOR twenty years medical science had been building the case against smoking by small, incremental steps, which in the aggregate formed a judgment beyond reasonable doubt to most disinterested investigators. But the tobacco industry, its survival at stake, fought tirelessly to minimize the charges and insisted that unless and until living creatures were shown to contract cancer of the lung by the inhalation of fresh whole smoke under laboratory conditions, the case against cigarettes remained unproven. Thus, it was front-page news when *The New York Times,* on February 6, 1970, reported an alleged breakthrough that panicked tobacco apologists: "12 Dogs Develop Lung Cancer in Group of 86 Taught to Smoke."

It had been difficult to find an animal that could serve as an anatomically satisfactory stand-in for humans. The animals closest to man in their breathing apparatus were the horse, the pig, and the simian family, but given the unwieldiness of handling any of these because of their size and cancer's long incubation period, working with them for smoking experiments would have proven prohibitively time-consuming and expensive. Suitably small animals, like rodents and dogs, on the other hand, came with built-in differences that made their usefulness problematic. Chief among these were nasal passages far more intricately developed than those in humans; they were able, especially under stress, to trap and absorb a large portion of any inhaled life-threatening substances—like tobacco smoke. And when force-fed smoke, they often exhibited avoidance reactions: rabbits held their breath, hamsters treated in groups buried their snouts in one another's fur, and rodents altered their breathing to slower, smaller, and shallower intakes of smoke that tended to penetrate no deeper than their throats, so that only minute amounts ever reached their lungs. And if stronger doses of smoke were administered to overcome these reflexive safeguards, the animals' far lower tolerance for carbon monoxide than the human system led to death from asphyxiation, bronchial infection, and other causes well before cancers had time to form.

Among the clinicians with firsthand knowledge of the ravaging effects of smoking was New York thoracic surgeon William G. Cahan at Memorial Sloan-Kettering, who had encouraged Ernst Wynder's work on smoking while a resident researcher at the institute and was well aware of Oscar Auerbach's studies of cell changes in the lungs of smokers observed at autopsy. As a sideline of his surgical practice, Cahan began to track the deterioration in the structure of cells taken from the lungs of living human smokers—definitive confirmation, he believed, of the progressively destructive process Auerbach had persuasively hypothesized. Instead of lung tissue itself, too fragile for repeated biopsy, Cahan used sputum taken from his subjects by catheter, but this proved time-consuming, costly, and painful. It would be more practical to try to train dogs to smoke, Cahan decided, and set to work with beagles, tractable by size and disposition and possessing a bronchial system close enough to man's. His experiments, intended to bypass the dogs' nasal filtering system, involved tracheostomy, incisions in the animals' throats through which smoke could be pumped into their bronchi by a mechanical apparatus—a form of forced inhalation closely resembling human smoking. But developing the technique took far more time, space, and money than Dr. Cahan and the Sloan-Kettering administrators had bargained for, and so the surgeon turned to Auerbach, the bustling little pathologist at the VA hospital in nearby East Orange, whose decade-long study of lung cells had been perhaps the single most persuasive corroboration of the population studies on the health risk from smoking.

Auerbach—and his chief funding collaborator at the American Cancer Society, Cuyler Hammond—knew full well the graphic value of successfully inducing lung cancer in animals with smoking as the only variable factor: in the public's mind, the case would be clinched against tobacco, its manufacturers' bitter protests notwithstanding. Auerbach enlisted David Kirman, a mechanically gifted researcher on the VA staff and experienced at working with animals, and after obtaining a $97,000 grant from the Veterans Administration, then anxious to broaden its reputation for research capability at its hospitals, they began refining Cahan's earlier efforts. Kirman developed a nylon-Teflon collar that fit over the surgically cut hole in the beagle's neck and could not be chewed off. A small socket on the collar over the incision allowed a hose to be attached through which the smoke could be force-fed or, after the dog grew accustomed to the smoke, drawn in voluntarily by the animal. In a preliminary fourteen-month study of twenty beagles, with half of them taught to smoke and the rest kept as unexposed controls, the animals displayed many of the symptoms of novice human smokers—nausea, vomiting, and apparent dizziness—until they became habituated, and then it was hard to keep them away from the stuff. Their tails would begin wagging as they were brought to the smoking apparatus, and some were inclined to bite a handler who distracted them during the process. Half of the smokers died prematurely in the course of the experiment, mostly from pulmonary embolisms, but autopsy of the whole smoking cohort disclosed early signs of excessive and abnormal cell growth in the bronchial system, a bursting or fibrous thickening of the tiny air sacs in the lungs of many of the animals, and a 50 percent enlargement of their hearts compared to those of the nonsmokers, who did not exhibit the other symptoms, either.

On the strength of these findings, Auerbach and Hammond—after a disagreement with Cahan over who was to run the show—took over the beagle experiments and obtained $750,000 from the ACS to erect a laboratory building with five air-conditioned wards and carry out, with a staff of thirty lab technicians, a longer and larger study. Begun in May 1967, the study, by far the most ambitious of its kind ever tried, involved ninety-four pedigreed male beagles, in their physical prime, all purchased from the same breeder in the Adirondacks. The animals, exercised daily, checked regularly for worms and other doggy afflictions, and visited every day by Auerbach, who was constantly concerned about their sanitary conditions, were divided into five categories: eight controls, who were sham smokers (*i.e.*, underwent the tracheostomy and visited the smoking apparatus but were exposed to no smoke); twelve who smoked only filter-tip cigarettes; twenty-four who smoked only unfiltered cigarettes; thirty-eight heavier dogs who smoked only unfiltereds; and twelve who smoked half the number of unfiltered cigarettes as the rest. The cigarettes were all the same filter-tip brand that had 17.8 mg. of tar each; the filter was broken off from the cigarettes used for beagles consuming only unfiltered smoke, each yielding about twice the tar content of the intact filter version. Hammond calculated that the ideal length for the experiment would be 875 days, or the equivalent of about sixteen human years—long enough to produce many of the signs of smoking-induced disease, if not frank cancer, without killing most of the subject animals. The daily average dosage was seven cigarettes—the equivalent of a few cigarettes under two packs a day for a 150-pound man—except for the dozen lighter smokers on half-rations.

Such an exercise could hardly be carried out in a residential neighborhood without public awareness of it. When some of the details were reported by the media, including that all the dogs would be sacrificed at the end, Auerbach and his colleagues received written and telephoned death and bombing threats, and one day two busloads of picketers arrived for a protest march in front of the laboratory, with signs likening the place to Auschwitz. Given the enormity of the human health peril he was investigating, Auerbach suffered neither fear nor pangs of conscience.

Twenty-eight of the beagles died during the course of the study—about 30 percent of the total—nineteen of them from blood clots in the lungs, but none of the nonsmokers succumbed prematurely. Tumors were found in thirty-six of the ninety-four beagles when autopsied, including some in several of the nonsmokers, but the key finding in Auerbach's view was that twelve of the smokers—but none of the eight nonsmoking controls—were found to have what Auerbach called "invasive" or malignant tumors, by which he meant a proliferation of basal cells of the bronchial lining, with atypically enlarged nuclei, which had penetrated the underlying framework of connective tissue, blood vessels, and nerves that hold hollow organs in place. Some of the dozen beagles so stricken had twenty or more such tumors in a single lobe. The heavier smokers had more tumors than the lighter smokers, and 72 percent of the beagles who smoked unfiltered cigarettes showed tumors, compared with only 33 percent of those smoking the filtered cigarettes, suggesting a prophylactic effect from use of the latter.

"I knew what we had," Auerbach later recounted. "We'd been able to duplicate all the changes we'd found earlier in human beings who smoked and suffered from lung cancer. And so the hypothesis [that smoking can induce cancer] was answered in the affirmative."

What the beagles study had not produced, although Auerbach believed it would have if the experiment had continued, were massive tumors; only microscopic ones were found, and none had metastasized to other sites through the blood or lymph vessels. But the findings had been reviewed and confirmed by three outsiders: one a veterinary specialist, and two well-regarded pathologists, John Berg of the National Cancer Institute and Raymond Yesner of Yale Medical School. Visiting Auerbach's lab, Yesner was satisfied that the beagle slides showed "local invasion of the pleura" and cellular abnormalities, though no masses of traveling cancer. Thus corroborated, the findings were deemed sufficient to take them public with a flourish. The cancer society, which had paid for the study, was headed then by William H. Lewis, retired chairman of the Kenyon & Eckhardt advertising agency and a fierce foe of the tobacco industry who had risked losing business for his firm by outspokenly favoring the broadcast ban on cigarette commercials. Having thrived in a world where hoopla was routine, Lewis saw no reason not to stage a big press conference at the Waldorf-Astoria early in February 1970 to break the news of the beagles study findings. Auerbach was on hand for the occasion, using a pointer to indicate to lay reporters the tumors in his blown-up microphotos. On its front page the next day, *The New York Times* stated that the study marked the first time that malignant tumors had been produced in large animals by exposing them to cigarette smoke and quoted the cancer society's claim that the findings "effectively refute" the contention by tobacco manufacturers that there was no proven link between cigarettes and cancer. Every television network news show that evening led with the story of the smoking beagles.

Caught off guard by the news, the Tobacco Institute initially appealed to offended animal-lovers and then befogged the findings as unrelated to human smokers. The tobacco industry's "institute" professed intense interest in Auerbach's experiment but said wide agreement prevailed in the scientific community that "there is no satisfactory animal model for smoking experiments." In other words, the tobacco industry declined to concede the cancer peril from smoking unless it could be confirmed by laboratory experiments, but unfortunately such confirmation was impossible since no animal could properly serve as a human surrogate.

Such a transparent dodge could not cushion the blow. The industry lawyers and their hired scientific consultants felt their chief hope for damage control lay in the fact that the beagles study was disclosed to the general populace prior to publication in a scientific journal, the usual outlet for reporting serious medical findings. No doubt the ACS was confident that the Auerbach-Hammond paper would be published by a top journal, as all their other work had been; the staged press show at the Waldorf had been arranged to extract maximum publicity for the findings—and until Auerbach's data and slide photos were published, it was supposed, the tobacco people could not begin punching holes in them. Although Auerbach was liked and respected by his peers, there were some who felt he had a tendency to "overinterpret" by making excessive claims for his findings on the effects of smoking. Perhaps he had done so once more, the industry's scientists hopefully speculated.

First choice to publish the beagles study was the *New England Journal*, perhaps the nation's most highly regarded general medical periodical, which had carried some of the earlier smoking studies by both of the prime investigators. But only six months before the ACS press conference at the Waldorf, the *Journal* had carried an editorial on its policy of accepting only previously "unpublicized results" on the ground that articles in reputable scientific journals had been reviewed by competent editorial boards of peers, allowing the lay press "to guard against impropriety and inspiring false hopes." Studies that were ventilated without benefit of such a review process made it far more difficult "to sustain such probity." Accordingly, the *Journal's* editor, Franz Ingelfinger, returned the smoking beagles paper to its authors a few weeks after its receipt, saying that the decision to reject it on procedural—not substantive—grounds had been "agonizing" since the pair of them were "frequent and esteemed contributors" to the *Journal*, their work was unquestionably important, and "the *Journal* is emotionally involved in the anti-smoking campaign."

The paper was dispatched at once to the *Journal of the American Medical*

Association, whose editors asked for a copy of the Auerbach-Hammond correspondence with Ingelfinger and extra sets of the microphotographs. After three months of silence, a letter from *JAMA* senior editor Therese Southgate advised that no decision about publication had yet been reached because an extraordinary number of reviewers were being consulted in view of "the controversial nature of the work." But since the authors were scheduled to present their paper at the annual convention of *JAMA*'s parent, the AMA, later that month, she thought they might find it useful to consider the comments thus far received, which showed, as Southgate put it, "a certain consensus."

The two dozen or so reviewers who would ultimately evaluate the beagles paper for *JAMA* had a good many reservations, chief of which were that the number and quality of the microphotographs inadequately illustrated the authors' claims of invasive tumors; that neither emphysema nor fibrous thickening of the alveolar walls was shown "in a convincing way." One reviewer wrote, "I think it would have been better for the authors to wait until they could demonstrate at least one true, unequivocal, grossly recognizable mass of neoplastic tissue." The distinction between benign and malignant tumors, noted another reviewer, "is difficult in the absence of lymphatic or blood vessel invasion." Added a third reviewer, who claimed "the highest regard for Dr. Auerbach's ability" and asserted that he himself was "absolutely convinced as to the etiologic relationship between cigarette-smoking and human lung cancer," the beagles paper "as presently presented . . . could be used as a demonstration again of the failure to produce cancer comparable to the human disease in experimental animals."

Meanwhile, the Tobacco Institute executive committee, chaired by Philip Morris's Joseph Cullman, was hearing from its lawyers and the industry's scientific hirelings that the beagles study findings would prove attackable, once the details were available. Their strategists felt that an independent panel of experts to review Auerbach's findings was likely to come up with a mixed and ambiguous assessment, allowing the cigarette makers to argue that despite the ACS claims, the case remained unproven.

Cullman put his professional and personal credibility on the line three weeks after the Waldorf press conference by writing to ACS chairman William Lewis that the tobacco industry was "entitled to have a full understanding of the nature and significance of the [Auerbach] findings as quickly as possible." He proposed that "several highly qualified scientists" chosen by the Tobacco Institute and acceptable to the ACS be granted access to all relevant materials and data for independent review—and at the industry's expense. Lewis replied—somewhat wishfully, as it developed—that the beagles study would be "published in the very near future" and would speak for itself.

Soon, however, word reached the industry from its paid agents in academia and its allies at the AMA that the *New England Journal* had spurned the author's submission of the beagles paper, albeit for a reason unrelated to its merits, and that *JAMA*'s peer-reviewers were somewhat skeptical of the bold conclusions reached by the investigators. Like the cat all but tasting the canary that had dozed off outside its cage, Cullman wrote Lewis a second time to say that publication of the beagles paper did not appear imminent, that the ACS's exploitation of an unvalidated study was regrettable, and that mere publication of the Auerbach-Hammond findings would not satisfy the industry, given the sweeping claims made for the experiment; only open access to the beagles data and review by independent outsiders would do. Lewis fired back that the study had in fact been reviewed by distinguished pathologists and others who praised it; that the beagles slides were available for inspection by qualified observers at Auerbach's VA laboratory; and that the cancer society did not "intend to ask that these two eminent men [Auerbach and Hammond] submit their findings to any . . . committee chosen by the Tobacco Institute. . . ."

Lewis's huffy letter served Cullman's purpose. At an April 30, 1970, press conference, he revealed his exchange with the ACS chairman and wondered aloud why, if the beagles study was as sound as its patrons claimed, there was any objection to an impartial review. If the ACS, Cullman charged, continued to deny access to the data and hewed to its unexamined claim that cigarette smoking had been definitively indicted, "we believe this will serve as convincing evidence to the public, lay and scientific, that the data will not support the allegations made. . . ." Ten days later, *The New York Times* in an editorial said the industry's request was understandable and the beagles findings were undoubtedly "path-breaking and important, but like all pioneering investigations they must be scrutinized with particular care." Incensed, Lewis wrote to the *Times* charging that the implication that the ACS had perpetrated a publicity stunt in the form of the beagles study "comes from an industry that for years relied on publicity and advertising to obscure the fact that cigarette smoking is the main cause of lung cancer in man."

But the ACS was getting outmaneuvered by the industry the longer it took to find a journal to publish the beagles paper. Thus, in a June 3 letter, Auerbach and Hammond invited the new director of research for the Council for Tobacco Research—Sheldon C. Sommers, chief of pathology at New York's Lenox Hill Hospital—to the VA hospital to examine the beagles' tissue himself directly under a microscope. Sommers, who was traveling abroad at the time, wired back acknowledgment of the invitation on June 16 and added that he thought it desirable for other outside experts to see the slides, since "review by me alone might be considered biased," and concluded that he would appreciate the opportunity for further discussion on his return at the end of June.

But Sommers never did get back to Auerbach and Hammond. Instead, as he would explain long afterward, he relied on discussions he had had with a number of the *JAMA* reviewers who found the authors' conclusions invalid. Fifteen years later, while being deposed in a product liability suit in Texas, Sommers stated, "I made every reasonable effort to be permitted to examine the microscopic slides" in the beagles study, and denied that Auerbach had ever invited him to his laboratory to view the slides.

The ACS also asked Jesse B. Steinfeld, the Nixon administration's young and surprisingly activist Surgeon General, to order a corroborative review of the beagles study. A former cancer specialist at the University of Southern California, Steinfeld knew Auerbach to be a dedicated and meticulous investigator and felt that accepting the ACS request, as he later put it, "would have been playing into the tobacco industry's hands" and would have left the Surgeon General open to second-guessing every controversial medical study that came along. Since the beagle slides had been reviewed by a National Cancer Institute pathologist and were open for review by any legitimate investigator, Steinfeld told the ACS that he was satisfied to let things stand, in the belief that the new Auerbach-Hammond study offered fresh insight into the nature of the dose-related pulmonary changes caused by smoking.

Following through now on the industry's drive to besmirch the beagles study even before it saw print, James Bowling, in his dual capacity as Philip Morris publicist and head of the Tobacco Institute's public-relations oversight committee, and company attorney Alexander Holtzman traveled to Chicago on the eve of the annual AMA convention toward the end of June and tried to get the presentation of the Auerbach-Hammond paper on the smoking dogs struck from the program. Visiting AMA President Gerald Dorman in his hotel room, the Philip Morris operatives reached *JAMA* editor Hugh Hussey on the telephone and asked him to corroborate for Dorman that the reviewers of the beagles paper had serious reservations about its validity. They also presented Dorman with a letter from Cullman arguing that the beagles data were "unpublished and unsubstantiated in any way" and that if the AMA permitted the authors to take the platform at its convention, it would be "lending its facilities and authority to providing additional publicity for a study which has been and is being seriously questioned by the scientists who are reviewing the findings for the AMA's official journal."

Although unsuccessful in its effort to have the beagles paper muzzled at the convention, the industry had helped shake the confidence of AMA hands. Soon after the convention, the paper was returned to Auerbach and Hammond with the balance of the reviewers' comments and a request for revisions if they wished the study to be freshly considered. *JAMA* editor Hussey later told a reporter from *Nature* magazine that the beagles paper was not worthy of publication "in the form in which it was received" and that the suggestions for revision were "quite fundamental". The authors would concede only that the microphotographs could benefit from reshooting, but they were not otherwise prepared to tone down their conclusions in the vain hope of satisfying two dozen reviewers, some of them paid by a rogue industry with its knives out.

Soon thereafter, Auerbach received a letter from an old friend, Dr. Katharine Boucut, editor of the *Journal of Environmental Health*, a second-string but creditable AMA publication. Boucut said she was aware of the travail the authors had been enduring, and if they were willing to bring the beagles slides to her office in Philadelphia, where they could be examined by reviewers of her choice, she would gladly publish the paper as soon as possible. This turned out to be in December; in the interim, tobacco industry publicists toured the nation trying to plant articles on what they characterized to the press as the beagles fiasco. Kentucky Congressman Tim Lee Carter, a bare-knuckled champion of the industry and his state's Burley tobacco growers, claimed in the *Congressional Record* for August 14 that the *New England Journal* "had rejected the [beagles] research papers outright"—even *JAMA* had not done that—and lashed out at Surgeon General Steinfeld for his "uncritical acceptance of this research . . . a clear reflection of the superficial and biased manner in which the information which goes into these [Surgeon General's] reports is evaluated." In mid-October the new president of the Tobacco Institute, North Carolina country lawyer Horace Kornegay, a former district attorney and three-term U.S. representative from his state's sixth congressional district, its tobacco-growing heartland, did his part in the operation to trash the beagles study. Kornegay, who, as one top tobacco industry publicist put it, had "a puppy-dog likability" in private, revealed a quite different persona as successor to the velvet-gloved Earle Clements. With a painful shrillness that would typify his pronouncements on the smoking and health issue, Kornegay declared that the as yet unpublished beagles study as showcased at the Waldorf "may be one of the great scientific hoaxes of our time," was a publicity stunt to attract the attention of Congress (then considering a ban on broadcasting cigarette commercials and other regulations) and "is not the first time that tobacco products have been unfairly accused and the public misled by such misuse of science"—he did not cite other alleged instances.

As if eager to deliver the coup de grâce in an onslaught he had initiated nearly a year earlier, Joseph Cullman appeared on the CBS television interview show "Face the Nation" at the beginning of 1971, just after the TV ban had gone into effect, and used the occasion to try to bury the beagles study for good. As finally published, he claimed, the findings had been "materially changed," as a result, he implied, of all the criticism aimed at them. Challenged on this statement by CBS science editor Earl Ubell, one of the interviewers, Cullman said the original number of reported cancers—twelve—had been reduced in the published version to two. Ubell produced the published paper and cited its findings of twelve beagles "with invasive lung tumors."

That was not the same thing as cancer, Cullman insisted; Ubell disagreed. Besides, Cullman said, some of the nonsmoking dogs developed tumors as well. Only two of them, Ubell parried, and neither case was invasive. The investigators, Cullman went on, "did not claim, as they originally had, that they got any lung cancers from smoking cigarettes"—precisely the point of the whole study. In a more sweeping rebuttal still, Cullman stated, "We do not believe that cigarettes are hazardous; we don't accept that." In short, one of the tobacco industry's leading spokesmen was denying the validity of the "dangerous" label that the U.S. government had affixed to his product. And in his ultimate display of brass that Sunday morning, Cullman remarked, when asked about a recent study which found that smoking mothers gave birth to smaller babies than nonsmoking mothers, "Some women would prefer having smaller babies."

This cavalier, not to say brutal, attitude was further demonstrated several months later in the Philip Morris annual report, which crowed about the company's role in discrediting the beagles experiment. Yet in an interdepartmental memorandum on February 17, 1971, by Philip Morris research and development director Helmut Wakeham—shortly after Cullman's "Face the Nation" appearance and shortly before publication of the annual report—the beagles study was hardly dismissed as worthless science. Wakeham noted that "the so-called tumors were microscopic neoplasms. So the test was not conclusive, but it was a lot closer than skin-painting."

Auerbach himself came to regret only his complicity in the ill-advised ACS decision to hold the press conference in advance of scholarly review and publication, but at the time he had felt beholden to the organization for funding his studies on smoking. His corporate detractors, though, he felt were venal: "Anyone could have come to our place to review the slides. . . ." Perhaps the most even-handed judgment on the beagles episode was offered by Ernst Wynder's close associate in tobacco research, chemist Dietrich Hoffmann, who considered Oscar Auerbach "a wonderful human being, beyond corruption," who had accomplished "fantastic pathology" in his studies of cell changes in human smokers. "But I would not have done the beagles study," Hoffmann remarked long afterward. Science cannot replicate the human smoking experience with laboratory animals, he said, nor was it necessary to, as the die-hard tobacco industry insisted. "Even so," Hoffmann added of Auerbach's labors with the dogs, "he did get some lung tumors, so the study was added evidence."

II

I F the Tobacco Institute's Horace Kornegay needed instruction from the resident staff in the strategy the industry had adopted to deflect the health charges against it, he got it in a revealing memorandum to him on May 1, 1972, from the institute's assistant vice president for public relations, Frederick Panzer. A former presidential aide in the Johnson White House, Panzer wrote to Kornegay to register his dissatisfaction with the industry's defensive tactics. These, he said, "while brilliantly conceived and executed over the years helping us win important battles," had not been a vehicle for victory. Instead, they amounted to no more than "a holding strategy, consisting of creating doubt about the health charge without actually denying it; advocating the public's right to smoke, without actually urging them to take up the practice; encouraging objective scientific research as the only way to resolve the question of health hazard. . . ."

Just how "objective" and effective the industry-sponsored research was, Panzer may not have known. But others in the cigarette manufacturers' pay surely did. One of them was R. J. Reynolds Tobacco's general counsel, Henry Ramm, who in a November 30, 1970, memorandum to the Council for Tobacco Research executive committee wrote that while in no way wishing to disparage "the stalwart work" done by the council under its first scientific director, Clarence Little, asked for a more conscientious effort from that time forth. Many of the industry's joint research grants in the early years, Ramm thought, had "little if any direct application to the use of tobacco," and "[i]n view of the millions of dollars of annual sales of our industry our expenditures for health research have been of a minimal order." The RJR counsel asked the CTR "to program the research more specifically than has been possible in the past," and in a spasm of conscience added, "When the products of the industry are accused of causing harm to users, certainly it is the obligation of that industry to endeavor to determine whether such accusations are true or false."

But just eight months earlier, Ramm's company, presumably with the knowledge of its chief lawyer, had abruptly fired twenty-six research scientists and shut down their four-year effort with laboratory animals that were being tested for the effects of tobacco smoke. The researchers' notebooks were seized, and no explanation was given for the shutdown, which occurred just a month after the ACS press conference on the smoking beagles.

The RJR biological studies had been the source of heated intramural debate in Winston-Salem. Most of the lawyers and many of the managers opposed the program based on the fear that serious research might in fact conclude that smoking was detrimental to health and thereby put the company and the rest of the industry in an indefensible position when embroiled in product liability suits. But company chairman Bowman Gray, Jr., while publicly disparaging the health charges, had supported a conscientious effort to learn the truth, and so the Reynolds research building at the corner of Chestnut and Belews streets in downtown Winston-Salem was converted into a sprawling, yellow-brick complex that included a room with special drainage and ventilation for animal experiments. The facility, soon dubbed the "mouse house," was staffed by eager beavers like biochemist Joseph Bumgarner, then in his late twenties, who recalled, "We were young and idealistic, and we were going to change the world. . . . I never remember thinking we were going to hurt the company. That was not a consideration. Our goal was: if there is a problem, let's try to fix it— if there is a fix. . . ."

The major Reynolds biological study, involving rabbits, had suggested that emphysema may have been due in part to the effect of cigarette smoking on surfactant, a substance in the lungs that prevented the tiny alveoli from sticking together each time they exhaled air. Fifteen years after closing down the biological lab, Reynolds officials would claim that this effort was halted because the nasal tubes delivering smoke to the rabbits caused infections and thus made the results unreliable. Why halting the whole enterprise was preferable to just remedying the problem with the tubing was not explained. According to another scientist who worked on the rabbits project, Johns Hopkins–trained Anthony Colucci, a fourteen-year RJR veteran before being let go, "It wasn't about bad science or a business decision. The decision . . . was made because Reynolds did not at that time want to be collecting information that might be detrimental to itself—which would be telling the public what its product does. Ignorance is bliss."

Nor was Reynolds an exception to the tobacco industry's baleful attitude toward pursuit of the truth about smoking and health, especially by outside investigators whom they funded. The closer they came to damaging findings, the more likely the industry was to withdraw its backing. In that vein, nothing could have pleased the tobacco manufacturers more than the laggard project under the certified aegis of the American Medical Association that the industry was funding to the tune of $15 million—two-thirds of it authorized at the outset in 1964 and the balance as the inquiry dragged on into the 1970s without producing a hint of structured findings. By far the largest outside research effort paid for by the cigarette makers, the AMA's Education and Research Fund project on tobacco drew the fire of the industry's own research directors when they gathered at Scottsdale, Arizona, in May 1970 to hear the progress report. According to James Mold, assistant director of the Liggett R&D program, too much of the AMA-ERF effort was being devoted to the retilling of old ground, like the properties of nicotine, and far too little attention paid to carcinogenesis. The consensual memo produced by the industry research heads on July 7 following the 1970 evaluative process found that not more than half the program was relevant to smoking and that "little of scientific significance" would emerge from the program.

Why did the lushly financed AMA-ERF project yield so little? Part of the answer resided in the attitudes of even the most highly regarded scientists connected with the undertaking. Among these was the NCI's Paul Kotin, no longer a member of the Council for Tobacco Research advisory board but suspected by some at AMA headquarters of being an industry partisan on the AMA-ERF guiding board in charge of dispensing grants. The whole effort, Kotin conceded a dozen years after the project breathed its last, was "a total fiasco. We were chasing the obvious in terms of the state of knowledge." But they were not chasing the causes of lung cancer, because, to Kotin's way of thinking, there was no further point to it after the definitive findings of the 1964 report to the Surgeon General. Nor were they exploring the nature of tobacco's addictive properties, because the chairman of the AMA-ERF project, Maurice Seevers, was on the same pro-industry hobbyhorse he had been riding while a member of the original Surgeon General's Advisory Committee—namely, that smoking was purely and simply a habit from which withdrawal could be readily achieved without notable metabolic changes. "And Mo [Seevers] got real unhappy when challenged on his position," Kotin recalled.

There was the further problem of finding well-qualified researchers to accept the tobacco-tinged grants from the AMA. According to Charles LeMaistre, another original SGAC member who agreed to serve on the AMA-ERF grant-doling panel in order to advance the cause of research into his specialty, chronic lung disease, the enterprise proved "not very productive" during the two years he was connected with it, largely because "the flood of competent investigators we had hoped would occur" never did. Dr. LeMaistre, however, apparently did his best to counteract this problem; some $2 million or a full 20 percent of the original grant was directed to researchers at the University of Texas's Southwestern Medical School in Dallas, where LeMaistre served as dean.

Finally, there was no driving force at the scientific heart of the AMA-ERF endeavor. The meetings of the advisory board were, above all, pleasurable social occasions, often held at resorts with deluxe accommodations, and Kotin, for one, a liberal who had long found the AMA's social policies and political positions less than enlightened, was pleased to accept the organization's money and courtesies while enjoying exchanges with intelligent fellow scientists. "We were also indictable for having relaxed for the last 30 percent of our tenure," he confessed, "but those meetings were delights."

The AMA directorate was by no means unaware of the boondoggle being perpetrated under its banner. In 1971, the Tobacco Institute's public-relations head, William Kloepfer, had a conversation with the AMA's executive vice president and chief operating officer, Ernest B. Howard, who told him that the AMA had come to regard the tobacco research program as "a great liability" that had caused only "further blackening of the AMA's image." Howard wanted to see the project ended but would not terminate it unilaterally, because, as Kloepfer wrote to his boss, Horace Kornegay, the AMA was "most anxious to avoid any incident that will create displeasure with AMA among tobacco area Congressmen—he said AMA needs their support urgently." And so the program trudged on seven more years, during which the tobacco industry continued to point to its existence as a measure of its bona fide desire to get to the bottom of the cigarette "controversy".

An authoritative and withering inside assessment of the industry's joint research efforts was offered by Lorillard's R&D head, Alexander W. Spears, in a June 24, 1974, memorandum to his company's president, Curtis H. Judge. Spears, widely regarded along with Philip Morris's Helmut Wakeham as a genuine man of science as well as a strong company loyalist, summarized for Judge the whole range of tobacco research, from the CTR grants to industry-backed studies at individual universities, like those at Harvard (on the effect of smoke on host genetics, among other subjects), UCLA (on the nature of macrophages, the lung's scavenger cells), and the University of Kentucky (where tobacco studies were a whole subdepartment), to the U.S. Department of Agriculture's experiments to reduce the tar and nicotine yields of tobacco plants, to the efforts of the industry's own ad hoc committee of lawyers whose grants, as Spears put it, "primarily aimed at seeking alternate hypothesis [*sic*] of disease causation," *i.e.*, other than tobacco-induced. The studies had "historically" not been selected with specific scientific goals in mind, and so were not closely relevant to the health issue. "In general," Spears added, "these programs have provided some buffer to public and political attack of the industry, as well as background for litigious strategy." In short, the overall industry effort may have been more than lip service to tobacco executives' avowal of concern about the health charges against their product, but they fell far short of an earnest crusade for what their exalted scientific spokesman, Clarence Little, liked to call "the whole truth".

Most troubling of all were industry-funded researchers who came too close to the truth for their patrons' comfort and were abruptly dropped. Perhaps the most egregious instance was the experience of Swiss-born pathologist Freddy Homburger, who enjoyed nearly a million dollars of tobacco funding over almost twenty years, largely through grants to his commercial laboratory, the Bio-Research Institute, in Cambridge, Massachusetts. In the early 1970s, Homburger and his associates began a one-hundred-week inhalation study with 200 Syrian hamsters under a CTR contract, which, in contrast to the terms of outright grants to researchers, preserved the funding group's right to review, but not suppress, any papers on the investigators' findings submitted to scientific journals. At the close of the study, Homburger's team found that 90 percent of the exposed hamsters showed severe hyperplastic and neoplastic changes in the epithelium of the larynx, greatly similar to the changes Oscar Auerbach had observed in the lung lining tissue of his smoking beagles several years before. More revealing still, 47 percent of his animals showed either cancer or what Homburger termed "lesions that are known to precede cancer," which greatly resembled those in the cancer-stricken human larynx.

He wrote up his group's findings and submitted the draft to the Council for Tobacco Research. Before long, Homburger was paid a visit by a member of the CTR's scientific advisory board, who read him the riot act for alleged viral infections he said the council had heard were affecting his hamsters. Homburger hotly denied the charge, later proved fallacious, but the accusation as perpetuated by the CTR and some of its paid consultants would tar the reputation of Homburger's Bio-Research lab long afterward. Homburger was then descended upon by the CTR's associate scientific director and its outside counsel, who made clear their unhappiness with his paper, because it claimed that the experiment had at long last achieved what his lab had been repeatedly paid to accomplish—cancer in smoke-exposed animals. Long, technical discussions followed in which the CTR representatives asked for changes that, in Homburger's estimation, "would have completely castrated the paper. They didn't want us to call anything cancer. They wanted it to be 'pseudoepitheliomatous hyperplasia,' a euphemism for lesions preceding cancer. And we said, 'No, that isn't right. It is cancer.' " The discussions continued until, according to Homburger's testimony in court fourteen years later, Jacob told him point-blank, "You realize if you publish [this paper], you will never get a penny more from the Council for Tobacco Research"—no idle threat, as Homburger soon learned.

To avoid possible CTR intervention in the publication of his hamster study, which ultimately ran in the October 1974 issue of the *Journal of the National Cancer Institute*, Homburger had to resort to minor subterfuge by making changes in galley proofs at the last minute after the CTR had signed off on them. His chief concession to his longtime funders was to call the laryngeal lesions "microinvasive cancer," but this was not enough to allay the CTR's wrath. Having burned his bridges to the industry and grasping now the nature of its scientific integrity, Homburger attended the April 1974 annual meeting of the American Federation of Biological Societies in Atlantic City to deliver his hamsters paper and arranged for a press conference afterward at which he intended to tell the world of the tobacco interests' attempted censorship of his findings.

But knowing that it had a potential loose cannon in the now defunct Homburger, the CTR bird-dogged him in Atlantic City in the person of its outside publicist, Leonard Zahn, who, in an April 22, 1974, memo to the CTR labeled

"Confidential," boastfully described what happened next. On learning of Homburger's planned press conference, Zahn looked up an old friend of his who was the public-information officer for the American Society of Experimental Pathology, one of the organizers of the convention, and advised her that Homburger's censorship charges were bunk and that, "on the contrary, he'd been asked to publish," that Homburger "had not lived up to the terms of his contract," and that his contract was not renewed "because its intended goal had not been attained"—all lies. And Homburger was reporting old material, to boot, Zahn went on, and told his acquaintance that the CTR had never had such a charge leveled against it before. Zahn's friend promised to check up on the situation and soon came back to him with word that Homburger was perceived to be "an operator" and that his charges violated professional courtesy and decency, and thus his scheduled press conference would serve "no useful purpose". Accordingly, "and with her [the organization press officer's] okay, I arranged for it to be canceled ... because of scheduling difficulties in the press room," Zahn wrote with detectable pride in his achievement. When Homburger showed up there anyway under Zahn's watchful eye, he "was given a cordial welcome and nicely hastened out the door."

III

THE Nixon administration was no more eager to involve itself in the issue of smoking and health than any of its predecessors, but through benign neglect—its chief policy instrument for addressing the problems of poverty—it also performed two useful services for the public-health camp.

First, it did not try to derail congressional passage of the ban on broadcasting cigarette ads. And it tolerated, at least during Nixon's first term, two employees within the HEW Department complex who were avowed, active foes of smoking. One of these was the outspoken Surgeon General, Jesse Steinfeld, whose public remarks on smoking were far more passionate and sweeping than those by any of his predecessors. The other was the director of one of the smallest fiefdoms in the federal bureaucracy—the quirky, rumpled intellectual Daniel Horn, now running the National Clearinghouse on Smoking and Health, which never employed more than thirty or had an annual budget much above $2 million throughout the nine years he ran it.

Coming from USC to the National Cancer Institute as a ranking administrator in 1968, Steinfeld had been tapped by the Nixon White House to be deputy assistant secretary of HEW, with oversight of the National Institutes of Health and the Food and Drug Administration. Although beset by the war in Vietnam and problems of crime, drugs, racial and generational strife, and inflation, the Nixon administration did not ignore health issues. It put major new funding into cancer research, helped launch the Environmental Protection Agency, and countenanced such un-Republican measures as a federal role in fluoridation of the U.S. drinking water supply and the banning of cyclamates, the widely used artificial sweetener, because it had been found, in dosages fifty times the equivalent of human use, to cause bladder cancer in laboratory rats. Steinfeld was deeply involved in these last two issues, showing himself to be an aggressive government interceder in the public-health area and overcoming resistance at the FDA to his conviction that there was no safety threshold, or tolerable minimum, for carcinogens ingested by humans—a view that also made him keenly attentive to the perils of smoking. "But I had no mandate on the smoking issue," Steinfeld recalled, and he did have plenty of other pressing matters to deal with when named Surgeon General, including the hazards of pesticides, a widespread infestation of fire ants, restrictions on phosphate detergents, and the effects of television on children.

But Steinfeld did ally himself with the U.S. Clearinghouse on Smoking and Health, and especially its most visible achievement, the annual Surgeon General's report to Congress. Unlike the initial 1964 report by a panel of outside experts, the later reports were carpentered by the Clearinghouse staff and amounted to little more than a synthesis of old and new studies and data, issued under the Surgeon General's signature. Steinfeld ordered an upgrading of the report, and the result in 1971 was a 488-page document, the largest ever, calling attention to important new developments in smoking research. Among these was the matter-of-fact—and quasi-official—endorsement of Oscar Auerbach's beagles study, so assiduously assaulted by the tobacco industry: "Lung cancer has been found in dogs exposed to the inhalation of cigarette smoke over a period of more than two years." Findings were noted that paralleled the secret and by then aborted studies by Reynolds Tobacco researchers on an enzyme known as $alpha_1$-antitrypsin, which counteracted substances in the lung that attacked the linings of the air sacs and thus promoted emphysema. Maternal smoking during pregnancy now stood accused of a retarding effect on fetal growth (manifested by low birth weights), and contributing to the chances of premature delivery. Most striking of all was a number of new studies on the possible effects of carbon monoxide (CO) in smoke as a promoter of heart disease, in particular atherosclerosis. Animal studies, most prominently those by Danish investigator Paul Astrup and his associates, were now showing that heightened levels of CO in the bloodstream of smokers were associated with increased permeability of blood vessels, inviting infiltration by fatty lipoproteins that accumulated on arterial walls and led to the buildup of obstructive plaque, a major cause of heart attacks. Related studies suggested that insufficient oxidation caused by smoking, due to CO's affinity for—and, in effect, molecular replacement of—oxygen in hemoglobin, had complex metabolic consequences for human tissue, such as a decreased ability to break down carbohydrates. Building on these studies over the 1970s, other investigators concluded that CO levels in smokers of filter brands might actually be higher than in those who used the unfiltered product because the filter material and wrapper were less porous than plain cigarette paper, which allowed more of the gas to escape. This phenomenon prompted manufacturers to add tiny holes around the filter in compensation.

Despite this substantive new contribution by the 1971 Surgeon General's report, the Tobacco Institute's Horace Kornegay dismissed the document by asserting, "The question of health and smoking is still a question," and noting the rise in cigarette consumption the previous year; the latter suggested to Kornegay that the American public was not so gullible as to buy the Public Health Service's "high-priced publicity campaign." Such denigration of the findings of the nation's highest-ranking health officer represented a new level of scorn heaped by the tobacco industry's designated spokesmen upon the labors of scientists around the globe who were dedicated to learning the truth about smoking and not, like the industry's paid and unclean hands, to hiding it.

Steinfeld's 1972 report on smoking and health was worse news yet for the industry. In it, for the first time, the Surgeon General dwelled on the likely hazards of secondhand smoke—the stuff in the air either exhaled by smokers or emitted from the burning tip between smokers' puffs. This was a daring initiative—possibly even imprudently premature—because there was as yet very little scientific evidence to support it, and there seemed to be no practicable way to measure exposure levels and dilution rates. Steinfeld was caught up with the dangers of environmental pollution, now an official target of federal public-health guardians, and to him, secondhand smoke was precisely that—an environment pollutant—and an obvious peril to those already impaired with heart or respiratory disease. "Biologically it had to be," Steinfeld recounted, "and laboratory experiments showed that no animal smoked voluntarily—there was systemic resistance and histologically observable [by microscope] changes in the cells of exposed animals," which were, in effect, passive (or secondhand) smokers. He was convinced that secondhand smoke was also implicated in the deaths due to lung cancer of nonsmokers—"not a trivial problem," he commented, since as many as 15 percent of the overall lung cancer toll of about 65,000 a year at that time occurred among nonsmokers, a sizable portion of whom were no doubt environmentally exposed to tobacco smoke by their spouses or co-workers. Wherever he spoke, Steinfeld called for a serious investigation of the effects of secondhand smoke and proposed a ban on smoking in such enclosed public places as restaurants, theaters, and mass transit systems—recommendations added at the end of the Surgeon General's annual reports but regularly removed by Nixon's Office of Management and the Budget (OMB).

Steinfeld distanced himself from the tobacco industry by closing his office

door to their tireless missionaries. "I would not see the Tobacco Institute lobbyists," he recalled, despite their eagerness to wine and dine him and wave
their data under his nose. Invariably, though, he would run into their representatives at Nixon administration functions or in the office of Steinfeld's chief,
HEW Secretary Elliott Richardson, a man known to harbor presidential ambitions and not above currying favor with allies wherever he might find them. On
such occasions, "the tobacco people would give me the business, saying in effect, 'See, we can meet with the Secretary or top people in government without
worrying about the Surgeon General,' " Steinfeld felt. "There was a message
there." It was manifested in the disappearance of the tiny allocation for the
Clearinghouse on Smoking and Health from the 1971 and 1972 budgets until
Steinfeld forcefully intervened with the HEW Secretary to have it restored.
The Surgeon General, though, would not blunt his attack. His 1972 report
stated, "There is no disagreement—cigarette smoking is deadly."

Steinfeld's unflinching candor was his political undoing. When the commission under his charge on the effects of TV violence on children made its findings known in 1972, the White House considered them too critical of the
broadcast industry and ordered the Surgeon General not to testify on the matter
before Congress. But Steinfeld was subpoenaed to appear, and rather than
clear his proposed testimony with the administration, which had in the past required him to attest to views he did not fully endorse, he spoke his mind, raking over the broadcasters. For his troubles, Steinfeld was not reappointed for
Nixon's second term. The ouster was strongly endorsed by the tobacco companies, at least one of which reminded the White House of its campaign contributions and urged that the Surgeon General be sent packing. He became head of
oncology at the Mayo Clinic, and four years passed before a new Surgeon
General was named.

IV

No other agency or office throughout the entire federal bureaucracy was
devoted to combating what was increasingly recognized by the public-
health community as the nation's leading preventable cause of death, yet
HEW's Clearinghouse on Smoking and Health had to sweat out every penny
of its pitiably small appropriation and justify its previous year's expenditures
under intense scrutiny by tobacco-state congressmen. Operating at first out of a
warren of small offices in a nondescript building in Arlington, the Clearinghouse bounced around the Washington area for eight years beginning in late
1966—an unwanted orphan and political lightning rod that was sustained by a
sense of mission among its mostly youthful staffers.

The Clearinghouse's core function, as its name implied, was as a technical information center, collecting all the studies, articles, and data on smoking it could and serving as a reference service and bibliographic tool to researchers everywhere. This material, which provided the essence of the annual updated Surgeon General's reports to Congress, was overseen by Donald Shopland, the self-taught young man who had been so caught up in his work as an aide to the original Surgeon General's panel on smoking that he stayed on at the National Library of Medicine, became the keeper of the smoking and health archives when they were turned over to the Clearinghouse, and, though he lacked a college education, made himself a walking encyclopedia on the subject. In time, his would become a prominent voice in the allocation of tens of millions of dollars aimed at combating the perils of smoking.

The Clearinghouse's other principal function was to alert the public, to the extent that its meager dollars could be stretched, to the smoking problem. That it did so with notable success was due to the talents of its chief publicist, Robert Hutchings, a low-key charmer who was adept at cajoling more powerful federal agencies to approve of the pointed material he and his staff generated. These included pamphlets on quitting, posters distributed to public school classrooms ("If you smoke, you're a turkey") and affixed to the sides of U.S. mail trucks, placards that appeared in the New York subways and other public transit systems, and unpaid antismoking television commercials when they were ordered by FCC edict during the late 1960s.

But the heart and soul of the place was its director, Daniel Horn, the Harvard-trained psychologist who seemed far more the research professional polishing his ivory tower than the administrator of a politically sensitive government program surrounded by a clutch of charged-up youngsters. A stocky figure wearing his trademark bowtie, a nearly threadbare suit, and Hush Puppies shoes often caked with mud (or, according to office whispers, dog excrement from the prizewinning Chesapeake retrievers that he and his wife raised and showed as amateur breeders), Horn might hole up in his office for days to tinker with a report based on a public survey he had commissioned on smoking habits. Or he might go off for a two-day seminar somehow linked to the issue and forget to tell his subordinates where he was. Once, much to Hutchings's anguish, Horn failed to show up for a filmed shoot with the crew from "60 Minutes," one of television's most widely watched shows.

Yet for all his head-in-the-clouds idiosyncrasies, Horn had a deeper understanding of the smoking problem than any other federal employee. He knew full well that the value of his enterprise lay in figuring out not merely how to put a fresh spin on the ever-accumulating body of statistical data but how to transform that indictment into a program to help the smoking public modify its self-destructive behavior. An example of Horn's strengths and limitations was a twelve-page pamphlet he developed, *The Smoker's Self-Help Kit*, available for ten cents from the Government Printing Office, which included a series of tests that allowed would-be quitters to grasp, on the one hand, how their tobacco habit seemed to help them manage their emotions and structure their lives yet discover, on the other hand, their feelings of self-disgust over their enslavement to smoking and its nasty by-products, like reeking clothes, breath, and hair. As a behaviorist little interested in the pharmacological aspects of tobacco *qua* drug, Horn was a proponent of quitting by going cold turkey, once an unhappy smoker fully understood the nature of his addiction. The key to success, he wrote, was for the reluctant smoker to ask with each new smoke, "Do I really want this cigarette?" Yet Horn's "kit" had disappointingly little impact because, in shying away from scare tactics, it intellectualized the problem and lacked shock value.

Horn made up for his want of flashiness by perseverance and an ability to draw from the data in the field surveys he ordered sociological insights into the nature of smoking. In 1970, for example, he elaborated on the alarming rise of teenage smoking by noting that the phenomenon, most marked in households where one or both parents were no longer present, was a manifestation of the disintegrating structure of the American family. Other findings led him to suggest, earlier than almost any other observer, the reasons that women found it harder to quit and stay off cigarettes than men: smoking seemed to help them reduce tensions in a culture in which they played more roles than men and had fewer sanctioned outlets for venting their aggressions and frustrations; women were more worried about gaining weight, as quitters often did. In capsulizing a 1971 survey of 5,000 adults, Horn reported that 36 percent of the population still smoked, that three out of five Americans favored a total ban on cigarette advertising, and that, by way of endorsing compassion over contempt as a curative, "We have in the population a lot of people who simply feel that they are incapable of changing their smoking behavior—[and] need encouragement and help rather than a collection of sermons on how great it is to be a nonsmoker."

Soon after Jesse Steinfeld was dropped as Surgeon General, Dan Horn found his little agency zeroed out of the 1973 federal budget and had to beg for an emergency allocation of $900,000 to sustain even its basic data-gathering function. Begging got him nowhere in 1974. The Clearinghouse was swallowed up as a subsection of the Centers for Disease Control and moved to Atlanta, where its public-health message became a plaintive, all but inaudible whisper and its passionate staff, with the exception of Shopland and a few others, got reassigned. Lacking a Surgeon General, HEW's annual report to Congress on smoking and health became an emaciated and unnoticed document. Frustrated and disappointed, Horn left Washington to work for the World Health Organization.

V

ALTHOUGH fifteen years would pass following the ban on broadcast advertising of cigarettes before Congress would impose any new regulations on the tobacco manufacturers, the industry was not quite out of the woods, particularly at the outset of that relatively blissful spell.

The Federal Trade Commission, severely whacked in 1969 by reports from two sharply different sources—consumer advocate Ralph Nader's "Raiders" and a special study committee of the American Bar Association—for frittering away its energies on trivial pursuits, was in the process of reenergizing itself. Among the new, younger talent enlisted was Robert Pitofsky, named director of the FTC's bureau of consumer protection (and later to serve as a commissioner and chairman of that agency and dean of the Georgetown law school), who set about implementing several key features originally proposed in the 1964 regulatory rule for cigarettes that Congress had severely emasculated with the 1966 labeling law. Backed by a fragilely balanced commission and thus a moderately activist mandate at best, Pitofsky pushed the tobacco industry in the early 1970s to accept the inclusion of the tar and nicotine contents on cigarette packs and as part of the warning labels to be included in all advertising. The industry did not precisely roll over at the snap of Pitofsky's fingers.

Allowed to list their tar yields by the FTC's 1967 policy reversal, the cigarette makers did so only on a few brands aimed at the health-conscious smoker. Their reasons for hesitating were not baseless. To state the numbers in ads or on the packs was to risk their being taken as a kind of undeclared index of safety (or danger). Thus, a high-yielding Winston might be perceived by the public as a dozen times more perilous than a Carlton when there was inadequate scientific support for such a supposition. The problem was even more pertinent in the case of small differences between brand yields, since the FTC insisted that no health advantage could be claimed for any such differential without valid scientific backing. Furthermore, the two items to be listed differed in important ways from the ingredients to be disclosed by manufacturers under the 1960 Federal Hazardous Substances Labeling Act and other regulations. "Tar" was technically not a discrete substance but a distillate extracted from the combustion process; it was an amalgam of several thousand volatile compounds. Nicotine, the other alleged chief culprit in smoke, had been largely absolved as a health menace by the 1964 report to the Surgeon General, which found its effects to be mostly transient and its pharmacological impact to be habituating rather than addicting. While indicating the industry's reluctant willingness to deal with the FTC on this matter in 1970, Tobacco Institute chieftain Kornegay recited the companies' lawyer-sanitized understanding:

"There is, of course, no way to know that any given levels [of tar and nicotine] are of any relevance beyond simple matters of taste to individual smokers."

But the FTC had grown impatient by now with an industry that insisted, to protect itself against product liability suits, that any modifications it was making in the strength of cigarettes were not necessarily related to its customers' health. Particularly offensive to the federal regulators were ads like those for the charcoal-filter brands Lark and Tareyton, which plugged their alleged efficacy in reducing "certain harsh gases" without ever disclosing the condition the charcoal was supposedly ameliorating, namely, the ciliatoxicity of smoke that damaged one of the bronchial system's principal weapons of defense. Instead, typical ads read, "If you like the taste of gas, you'll hate the taste of Lark," and "If you could put Tareyton's charcoal filter on your cigarette, you would have a better tasting cigarette." Requiring a disclosure of tar and nicotine yields would serve at least as a partial antidote to this sort of pussyfooting on the health issue.

In the end, it was not the FTC determination that settled the numbers game so much as the industry's knack for turning a sow's ear into a silk purse. Listing the FTC-measured tar and nicotine yields in the companies' ads invited an inference by the public that (1) the federal government was now exercising oversight of the cigarette industry and therefore (2) the yields listed were not likely to represent a terrible health hazard—or else the government would not be permitting the product to be marketed in the first place. And there was the further tacit acknowledgment by the industry of the point made by one of its most ardent veteran detractors, New Orleans surgeon Alton Ochsner, in his 1970 book, *Smoking: Your Choice Between Life and Death:* "By resisting the FTC, the industry may find itself confronting the FDA, which will demand laboratory proof that the product is safe for human consumption—and that can put an end to the tobacco business overnight."

This industry nightmare of strict federal oversight of cigarettes as a drug— even if their manufacturers made no health claims for them—was at about this time also on the mind of *The New Yorker*'s Thomas Whiteside, one of the few U.S. journalists who fully grasped the smoking and health issue. He wrote to the FDA to ask why it was not timely for the agency to include cigarettes on the list of products it was empowered to deem hazardous under the 1960 congressional act, covering any substance the FDA found to be toxic or to cause illness or injury "through ingestion, inhalation, or absorption through a body surface." Since cigarettes had been judged to be a hazardous substance "beyond any doubt," Whiteside wondered why the FDA still hesitated in a posture "grotesquely inconsistent" with the agency's recent decision to ban cyclamates, a marginal peril when compared to the dangers of tobacco smoke. At the least, Whiteside urged, the FDA might require cigarette makers to reduce tar and nicotine yields and impose "strict and meaningful restraints" on cigarette promotions the same way the agency regulated claims made for prescription drugs.

FDA commissioner Dr. Charles Edwards responded that the 1966 labeling law prevented the FDA from requiring a different or additional warning on cigarette packs. He also claimed that his agency had no power to regulate product advertising, and all it could frankly do, if it found cigarettes to be a drug, was to ban the product outright—so serious a step that, as a practical matter, it would have to be taken by Congress. But all of that begged the point Whiteside was trying to make—that the FDA could have found cigarettes a health peril and, accordingly, placed limits on the tar and nicotine yields. Such a muscular posture, however, was entirely at odds with the prevailing mood at the FDA, according to John T. Walden, one of its top-ranking public-information officers throughout the 'Seventies. His agency "turned flips out of abject fear," said Walden, at the idea of clashing with the tobacco industry and its congressional champions, even though "a damned good case could have been made for the FDA's claiming jurisdiction over cigarettes."

After two years of protracted negotiations, the tobacco companies agreed to list the yields in their ads but not on the cigarette packs themselves—a compromise that the FTC swallowed, probably because it did not want to test its strength in the courts by imposing the requirement on packs as well. Half a loaf was better than none. By 1972, the FTC was even opposing a bill by anti-smoking stalwart Senator Frank Moss calling for a ceiling on the tar and nicotine yields. The FTC reasoned that a congressionally enacted ceiling on the yields might imply that any numbers below it were safe and represented a tolerable health risk. By then, too, the industry had indicated its willingness to carry the warnings in its ads.

The final agreement, after nine months of negotiations between the industry's lawyers and the FTC team led by Pitofsky, called for nothing so crass—and effective—as a skull and crossbones or similarly alarming emblem on the warning, only a minimal ruled box, black print on a white background, with two lines of text identical to the language on the packs, in print 10 to 16 points in height, scaled upward with the size of the ad, and to constitute a separate element in the layout, not blended invisibly among surrounding elements. It was a good deal less than the new young Turks at the FTC had wanted, "but more than we thought we would get at the start," Pitofsky recalled.

VI

SPURRED by Surgeon General Steinfeld's call, federal regulatory agencies began for the first time to address the health and comfort of nonsmokers under unwitting assault by smokers' irresistible impulse to light up. In any collision between their right to satisfy that impulse and the damage it might inflict on others, smokers rarely doubted whose interest ought to prevail. But their ranks were now thinning as a proportion of the overall population, and they were plainly outnumbered by a nonsmoking majority increasingly impatient with other people's smoke getting on their clothes, into their food, in their eyes, and inside their bodies.

The government, when goaded, slowly began to address the matter as a readily manageable irritant, not openly antisocial conduct. Public interstate transit, on which nonsmokers were captive victims of tobacco users, was the obvious place to begin, and airplanes, where the oxygen supply was most critical, was the first target for reformers. Ralph Nader launched what would become the nonsmokers' rights movement at the end of 1969 by petitioning the Federal Aviation Administration (FAA) to ban the use of cigarettes, cigars, and pipes on all passenger flights, arguing that the smoke annoyed nonsmokers, distracted the flight crew, and posed a danger to health and a fire hazard for all aboard. That same week, John Banzhaf, the Nader wannabe, called for a drastic measure: separate sections for smokers and nonsmokers on all domestic flights.

But was smoke in airplane cabins truly a health hazard or merely a visible, smellable annoyance for nonsmokers? A joint FAA-HEW study of that question failed to produce "persuasive evidence that exposure to tobacco smoke, in concentrations likely to occur [in aircraft] (assuming normal ventilation rates) is injurious to the health of nonsmokers," so the FAA declined to respond to the Nader and Banzhaf pleas. The reformers had better luck with the more consumer-oriented Civil Aeronautics Board, which in September 1972 responded positively to a Nader petition to require separate passenger sections, noting that while the health evidence justifying such a step was scanty, 60 percent of all passengers indicated they were bothered by smoke on flights. This figure was almost identical to the findings in a national poll a few years earlier, when three of five responded that they found it annoying to be next to a smoker in almost any circumstance, and a survey in *Nation's Business* in 1974 found overwhelming sentiment in favor of separating smokers. When the airline operators pointed out to CAB regulators that the air in their craft was ventilated completely every five minutes and was thus cleaner than the Environmental Protection Agency required in public buildings, the CAB replied that the high-density seating on planes made such standards inapplicable, and ordered separate seating.

The order was often grudgingly executed. Complaints were common about an inadequate number of seats being set aside for the nonsmoking sections and the hazy nature of the boundary between the sections. Enforcement, too, was lax, as the government relied on the private carriers to satisfy the wishes of the preponderant number of their customers, but the airlines were not about to punish the tobacco-addicted among their clientele when the rest had nowhere else to turn for timesaving travel. The CAB never did crack down on casual enforcers of the segregated seating solution, though it did order tougher restrictions, such as an in-flight ban on the smoking of cigars and pipes. Banzhaf's stalking horse, Action on Smoking and Health (ASH), sued the CAB in 1979 seeking diligent enforcement of the separated sections, and while the federal courts supported him, the agency temporized. And when the avowedly deregulatory Reagan administration took power in 1981, it rolled back even mild CAB reforms, and devotees of cigars and pipes were returned to the smoking sections.

A few weeks after his initial petition to the FAA, Nader called on the Interstate Commerce Commission to establish nonsmoking rules for buses. Within two years—lightning speed in the bureaucratic universe—smokers were confined to the rear 20 percent of vehicles traveling interstate routes. (In 1976, they were given an additional 10 percent of the seats.) Smokers were segregated in interstate railroad travel beginning in 1973, but their habit was permitted in one-half of the car space on any given train.

Before restricting smokers in places less confined than the interiors of public carriers, federal officials required persuasive scientific evidence that secondhand smoke was anything more than a nuisance. A few of the less populous Western states, however, undertook early initiatives, starting with Arizona, the first to enact serious antismoking rules. The crusade was led by a Scottsdale woman, Betty Carnes, better known as an ornithologist than a political operative. After succeeding in having three floors of the hospital that she partly administered set aside for the exclusive use of nonsmoking patients, Carnes laid siege to the Arizona legislature for its 1972 and 1973 terms, studying the smoking habits of every member to help her garner allies. She made numerous television appearances, sent off 300-word telegrams to resistant lawmakers, and dispensed thousands of her "Thank You for Not Smoking" signs, one of which made its way to Surgeon General Steinfeld's desk. After two tireless years, she won, as Arizona banned smoking in elevators, libraries, theaters, museums, concert halls, and buses.

Two years later, at its 1975 legislative session, Minnesota enacted its far more sweeping Clean Indoor Air Act, based on a Swedish model, which made it illegal to smoke in almost all confined public places unless explicitly permitted. Among the sites omitted from the Arizona statute but affected by the Minnesota law were restaurants, meeting rooms, and workplaces, where separate smoking areas were mandated. Belatedly, the tobacco industry awoke to this new threat at the state level. Its lobbyists flocked to state capitals and argued that smoking restrictions were unfair, unjustified by scientific findings, and unenforceable, given the heavy burden of local law officers dealing with serious crimes. From the first, though, most smokers, as if in recognition of their own thralldom to a habit that did them no good, willingly put out their butts when advised that they were violating the law.

Throughout the 1970s, though, the antismoking effort was hardly a groundswell as the industry installed an effective political apparatus at the state level. While Utah, Nebraska, and Montana passed clean-air laws in the wake of the Minnesota statute, theirs were less comprehensive; meanwhile, similar restrictive measures were vetoed by the governors of Illinois and Maine. The failure of the tobacco-control movement to gain momentum early on was plainly traceable to the softness of the scientific case against second-hand smoke. In 1975, a pair of investigators at Harvard measured the intake by nonsmokers in restaurants, bars, and railroad cars and reported that the dosage, depending on the duration of the exposure, ranged from 1/100 to 1/1,000 of the tar and nicotine yield of a filter cigarette smoked directly. At an international conference on cancer that same year, Cuyler Hammond of the ACS stated that there was as yet "no shred of evidence" that nonsmokers could contract cancer from environmental tobacco smoke. And Ernst Wynder, the most assiduous investigator in the field, added, "Passive smoking can provoke tears or can be otherwise disagreeable, but it has no influence on health [because] the doses are small."

V I I

IF state governments were slow to restrict consumption of tobacco in public, the U.S. Congress was avid about exempting it altogether from the spate of consumer protection laws passed during the 'Sixties and 'Seventies. Only the 1960 Federal Hazardous Substances Act had not explicitly excluded tobacco products, and the FDA had insisted several times, fearing a battle with the political forces that held its purse strings, that the law was not meant to apply to tobacco. The 1963 Clean Air Act mandated federal monitoring of airborne pollutants, but that power applied only to the outdoors, where environmental tobacco smoke readily dissipated. And while the Occupational Safety and Health Administration (OSHA) later set limitations on work-site exposure to twenty-four of the airborne pollutants and substances present in tobacco smoke, including carbon monoxide and acrolein, that agency declined to regulate tobacco use without evidence that a health hazard existed from secondhand smoke. Without explanation, tobacco products were then excluded from the 1966 Fair Labeling and Packaging Act, the 1970 Controlled Substances Act, the 1972 Consumer Product Safety Act, and the 1976 Toxic Substances Act.

Illustrative of the stranglehold the tobacco lobby and its congressional water carriers had on the federal legislative process was the fate of the effort by Utah's Senator Frank Moss to find a chink in the bureaucratic ramparts erected in defense of cigarette use. Moss, chairman of the Senate subcommittee on consumer affairs, had joined in 1974 with the American Public Health Association to petition the Consumer Product Safety Commission to ban as hazardous all cigarette brands that yielded more than 21 milligrams of tar—20 percent of the market. Moss *et al.* argued that under the 1972 act establishing the commission, Congress had transferred to it the HEW Secretary's former power to administer the 1960 hazardous substances act, which had *not* excluded tobacco products, and that this transfer superseded the tobacco exemption spelled out in the 1972 act—in short, a conflict seemed to exist between the statutes, and Moss was trying to charge through the loophole.

Moss's argument that the FDA's failure to impose controls on tobacco in no way curtailed the Consumer Product Safety Commission's authority to do so lost by a 32-to-2 vote. Moss then found a friendly U.S. federal district judge, Oliver Gasch, who in April 1975 held that the consumer product commission could exercise its sway over tobacco—a potentially grave setback for the industry.

But it wasted little time in exorcising the menace. Rather than appealing Gasch's ruling and risking a more conclusive defeat, the cigarette makers went to their newest champion on Capitol Hill—freshman Democratic Senator Wendell Ford of Kentucky. Not the usually diffident fledgling lawmaker, Ford had been a highly popular governor of his tobacco-rich state and an outgoing, statesmanlike figure. On reaching Washington, he asked for a seat on the powerful Senate Commerce Committee, which was already two members over its allotment of fifteen slots, thanks to senatorial rule-bending. When approached by semi-retired tobacco lobbyist (and by now longtime friendly adversary) Earle Clements to make room for Ford, who he said had been a strong consumer advocate while governor, Commerce Committee chief of staff Michael Pertschuk said he was sure the new Kentucky senator was an upright soul but there was simply no way to wedge him aboard.

When the Senate organized, however, Ford was assigned a place on the now grossly distended Commerce Committee—testament to tobacco's might within the Capitol's marbled halls. Among the items the committee was addressing early in the term was a revision of the Consumer Product Safety Act to exclude guns, ammunition, and pesticides from the safety commission's purview. There had been no mention during the committee deliberations of the tobacco loophole that Moss's lawsuit had found—until Judge Gasch's ruling was handed down. Within weeks, and under Ford's lash, the loophole was sealed; by a vote of 76 to 8, the Senate in July 1975 approved an amendment to the 1960 Hazardous Substances Act to exclude tobacco products, thereby definitively eliminating them from the Consumer Product Safety Commission's jurisdiction.

In the closing years of the decade, the enduring power of the tobacco forces in Washington was still further evidenced. When John Banzhaf's dogged ASH petitioned the FDA once again to rule that cigarettes were drugs and ought to be so regulated, the agency steadfastly held that unless health claims were made by the tobacco companies—who by now were all studiously avoiding any such explicit avowal—cigarettes could not be classified as drugs. And when Congress reconvened in 1979, Senator Frank Moss was gone and in his place as chairman of the Senate Commerce Committee's subcommittee on consumer affairs, with its oversight of tobacco products, was Wendell Ford.

V I I I

DESPITE steadily growing pressure against it from the health community, if not the public at large, the tobacco industry proved remarkably resilient and spectacularly profitable during the early 1970s. For the first three years after the loss of broadcast advertising, per capita cigarette sales to Americans over eighteen rose, leading to the suspicion that the antismoking commercials of the late 1960s, when cigarette sales dropped fractionally, were a more effective damper than the TV ban. Others in the health camp argued that it would take a decade, if not a generation, for the ban to eradicate the effects of the industry's deeply etched images of smoking as socially desirable.

The cigarette money that had flowed into TV was now heavily diverted to print and outdoor media; "placement allowances" for preferential treatment on retail shelves; merchandising that ranged from standard items like free cigarette lighters to new gimmicks like cut-rate dictionaries; and especially promotions such as the sponsorship of sports events, in which Reynolds, with its backing of rodeos, auto racing, and bowling tourneys, and Philip Morris, underwriting the women's professional tennis tour and big-stakes horse racing, led the way. Profit margins bounded ahead thanks to the supreme irony that evolved from the campaign against smoking: lower-yielding brands cost less to make and spurred heavier per capita use among some smokers who switched to them. Ever greater use was being made of reconstituted tobacco leaf, composed of scraps, and less costly grades lower in nicotine content, as smokers were coming to tolerate less tasty smoke than from the higher-yielding "full flavor" brands. Chemically expanded or "puffed" tobacco, with twice the filling power and reduced yields, was a further economy measure. And the widespread use of microscopic holes in cigarette paper and around the filters to allow more oxygen to enter the fuel mix, quickened the burn rate, as did the looser packing of the tobacco by some manufacturers. The result was that about one-third of smokers turning to the "low-tar" brands actually increased the number of cigarettes they consumed each day to sustain their usual intake of nicotine.

For industry leader R. J. Reynolds, the net effect of these changes could be seen in the profit margin it was achieving on its flagship brand, Winston. Of the fifty-three cents a consumer paid for a pack of Winston sold in New York City in 1970, twenty-seven cents went to meet federal, state, and local excise and corporate income taxes; fifteen cents was the combined bite taken by the wholesaler and retailer; and of the remaining eleven cents accruing to the manufacturer, seven went for production and shipping, two for marketing and advertising, and two cents represented profit—or a return on net sales of 18 percent, an extraordinary margin for almost any product. With daily sales at nearly 23 million packs for all RJR brands and higher margins in the post-TV era, Reynolds had more cash than it knew what to do with, and a sense that it had become an impregnable fortress took hold. "The comfort level here was too high," recalled David Fishel, then a young RJR publicist and later senior vice president for public relations. "Reynolds was very, very arrogant about its position in the market," concurred Ronald Sosnick, whose family-owned business was the largest wholesaler of tobacco products in central California. "The company's route men and rackers were dynamite—very well trained, like an army—but they didn't give you a warm, fuzzy feeling."

The company's easygoing helmsman was now Alexander H. Galloway, Jr., another courtly figure and a cousin of the Grays, who had run the company for nearly half a century. Galloway's tenure, while relatively brief, gave the company dynastic continuity but not much more. In the words of one longtime RJR executive on the financial side, "Alec seemed to walk around in a daze much of the time." But Galloway had enough knowledgeable crewmen whom he kept at their posts to ensure his craft's continued smooth sailing. As Philip Morris charged into the runner-up spot in cigarette sales in 1971, just ahead of American Tobacco, its market share reached 18 percent. Still far in the lead, RJR held 32 percent of the market and, if not oblivious to the gains being achieved by the inventive tobacco purveyors on New York's Park Avenue, the Winston-Salem pacesetters were satisfied that Philip Morris was advancing at the expense of the rest of the industry and not its own. The waters around them, though, were in fact growing choppier.

The end of television advertising had been thought likely to freeze brand shares of the market—a welcome benefit to front-running Reynolds. But things did not work out that way, especially for top-selling Winston. Without its peppy little jingle (". . . tastes good / like a cigarette should") filling the airwaves, Winston had trouble adapting itself to print media. The brand had neither personality nor image, just a good, strong taste in a boring red pack that nicely suited unfinicky older smokers, especially in the nation's Southern region. The company tried a lot of advertising ideas—the best it came up with was a paean to the brand's "Down Home Taste," suited to its Dixie bastion but not much farther afield—and kept changing them when none seemed to catch on.

Worse still, Reynolds was cheapening its products and, in the case of Winston, failing to keep up with changing tastes. Smokers may at first have craved the "bite" of Winston, but by the later 'Sixties and into the 'Seventies, a preference was growing for a smoother taste, of the sort achieved by its onrushing chief competitor, Marlboro. A detectably greater use of reconstituted tobacco sheet (RTS), of which RJR had been a pioneer developer and user, along with what its rivals heard was increased importation of cheaper Brazilian and Guatemalan leaf, was also perceptibly affecting the quality of the brand. "There was a feeling here that Winston and Camel had been loaded with G-7," the company name for the reconstituted leaf, one top Reynolds executive conceded. Other cost-cutting measures by a profit-hungry management also hurt. Among these were starvation-level budgets for the maintenance of plants, which were thirty years old in some cases and beginning to run down, so that faulty temperature-control equipment, for example, permitted frequently dried-out leaf and a harsher-smoking product. Blending, too, was less fastidiously carried out in that period, and economies like limiting intensive quality control to only one of the three daily manufacturing shifts caused too many packages to reach the public with cigarettes that had battered, wrinkled, or torn ends. The condition would not have developed if the cutters on the "makers" had been kept constantly sharpened. Even the RJR foil and cellophane packs seemed to have a certain mushy feel to them.

To compound Winston's deepening woes, RJR was reluctant to risk its reputation as a full-flavored smoke by extending the line into the low-tar field. Thus, it was not until late 1974, or two and a half years after Philip Morris took the step with Marlboro, that Winston Lights were marketed—with the stupefyingly bland slogan "A new cigarette that's lighter in taste, low in tar." During the 1970s, the Winston brand line, in all its variants (soft pack, boxed, 100 mm., menthol, and low tar), registered no increase in the number of units sold. Marlboro gained 134 percent over the same span and had taken from Winston its title as America's top-selling brand.

Whatever its failures with regard to Winston, Reynolds was by no means asleep at the switchover to low-tar brands, as yields for the industry dropped an average of 40 percent between 1967, when the FTC sanctioned their renewed listing in ads and on packs, and 1981. Only Lorillard, staking its survival on the low-tar segment, was well out in front when RJR recognized that the more moderate-yielding brands were more profitable to sell and would be the key to both holding on to health-conscious smokers and enticing the next generation of consumers, aware of the medical charges against the product.

In the belief that brand introductions would become much more difficult after television advertising ended, Reynolds rushed out a pair of lowered-tar entries. The first, in 1969, was Doral, with 15 milligrams of tar, the industry's arbitrary dividing line between "low tar" and "full flavor" brands. Initially it was presented like a brand left over from the old "tar derby" days, with its filter pictured in a cutaway diagram showing baffles and air channels that seemed to imply a space-age technology behind it. The brand's later advertising was a bit more inspired. Typical was a text quoting the ideal new Doral buyer: "I'm not too big in the willpower department. But I lost 700 milligrams of 'tar' the first week on what I call 'The Doral Diet.' Now I can still enjoy smoking, and cut down on 'tar' and nicotine, too." The brand managed to gain a 1 percent market share within a few years but as a full-priced brand would climb no higher.

More subtle and successful was the 1970 debut of Vantage just a few months before the TV blackout took effect. The white package featured a big bull's-eye with navy and sky-blue rings surrounding a coral-colored center; it was not very attractive but scored high in "shelf awareness" tests among consumers. Vantage's chief claim was an 11-milligram tar yield made possible by an innovative, densely packed filter, with six times the absorbent area of leading competitors. The Vantage filter was also twice as long as the one on True, the leading low-tar brand at the time, allowing Reynolds to announce a technological "breakthrough" with the new brand and pitch its introductory advertising "to every cigarette smoker who enjoys good taste but who's concerned about 'tar.' "

Vantage got off to a respectable start, but Reynolds sales chief Billy Smith, in a notable departure, brought in the small, imaginative New York ad agency of Lieber-Katz Partners, which handled Seagram's liquor and such luxury products as Lenox china and Baccarat crystal. The agency came up with a cerebral approach that forsook all imagery other than a picture of the bull's-eye pack and instead seemed to dare consumers with provocative headlines like "Smoking. What are you going to do about it?" and "To smoke or not to smoke," and a text that, at least relatively speaking, broke new ground for candor by cigarette makers. For example:

> Many people are against smoking cigarettes. You've heard their arguments.
> And even though we're in the business of selling cigarettes, we're not going to advance arguments in favor of smoking.
> We simply want to discuss one irrefutable fact.
> A lot of people are still smoking cigarettes. . . .
> Now if you're one of these cigarette smokers, what are you going to do about it? . . . If "tar" and nicotine has become a concern to you, you may consider changing to a cigarette like Vantage. . . .

Suddenly, Vantage began to score in urban markets among better-educated and obviously health-oriented smokers, previously *terra incognita* for RJR brands. By 1975, with the help of steady, heavy advertising disproportionate to its sales, the brand climbed to a 3 percent market share and had soared past True to take the lead in the low-tar category. And yet when Philip Morris brought out Merit the following year, using much the same sell—rich flavor and lowered numbers, thanks to a technological breakthrough, and showcased in largely text ads similar to those by Lieber-Katz, Reynolds failed to defend its low-tar turf, as the New York entry heavily outspent it and, despite Vantage's seven-year lead, Merit surpassed it in sales by 1979.

Two other mid-'Seventies brand launches by Reynolds reflected a half-heartedness born at least as much of marketing ineptness as of a front runner's understandable reluctance to risk making a major mistake. American Tobacco's Carlton had been the only major entry in the ultra-low field, dating from its 1964 rollout, until RJR brought out its Now brand in 1975. With nothing to recommend it but minuscule yield numbers, Carlton had gone nowhere in the marketplace, never attaining even one-half of 1 percent of the market. If ever there was a vulnerable target, Carlton was it. But Reynolds, as if incapable of rousing itself for a product it could not claim was bursting with flavor, merely repeated American's mistake with Carlton, selling Now strictly by the numbers and entirely avoiding the unspoken—and unspeakable—reason for smokers to switch to the brand: as a health measure.

In a more interesting, and ultimately baffling, case, Stanley Katz, a principal of the Lieber-Katz ad agency, proposed to Reynolds a long, thin, brown-paper cigarette that had the jaunty look of the slender cigars once smoked by riverboat dandies. Because the proposed brand was to be 120 millimeters, longer by 20 percent than any other on the market, it was dubbed More and, perhaps appropriately, dosed with more tar—22 milligrams—than almost every brand introduced since the first filter tips in the 'Fifties. "Full flavor is what people want," explained William Hobbs, president of Reynolds Tobacco, "and that's what Reynolds is going to give them." This, of course, flew directly in the face of the rationale behind the company's almost simultaneous launch of ultra-low Now and the massive evidence that more and more of the industry's customers were beginning to "smoke down". RJR's ad copy for More suggested that the smoker got more puffs per cigarette from the brand—thus its name—than any other, but this sort of quantitative sell failed to give the brand a persona or image in keeping with its strikingly different appearance. To the closely following eyes of Virginia Slims brand manager Ellen Merlo at Philip Morris, More had "verve" and real potential, "but their advertising didn't come near positioning it." The pitch was flat, and even when a milder version in a paler color was brought out to appeal more to youthful female smokers, it stayed flat: "It's beige. It's slender. It's special. . . ." Despite reports showing More to be especially popular with urban black women, no effort was made to turn them massively toward the brand as Kool and Newport had scored with black males. "They never did anything with it—never put any real horsepower behind it," lamented Katz, More's creator. "They got it up to a 1 percent market share and then let it go."

Within the trade RJR's shortcomings as marketers were no secret but did not become manifest until Philip Morris came on with a surge. In the analytical view of a leading wholesaler, Peter Strauss, at one time president of Metropolitan Tobacco Distributors, a giant in the New York area: "Reynolds took far too many years to shed its isolation down in Winston-Salem. They didn't even bother to appear at tobacco industry charity affairs—they were a world unto themselves, and any place more than five hundred miles from Winston-Salem might as well have been the moon. Everything about their merchandising, especially the packaging and advertising, reflected small-town thinking. They failed to respond to the changing demographics of smoking and smokers and to the Philip Morris challenge. Instead, they concentrated on the hardware in supermarkets, and in so doing, failed to win the fight for the minds of consumers. . . ."

IX

REYNOLDS, for all its lumbering, unstylish performance as cigarette pitchman, was awash in profits, which qualified it as a prime takeover target in the late 'Sixties for such trophy-hunters as Harold Geneen, who had built International Telephone & Telegraph into a mammoth conglomerate. RJR had to put its excess cash flow to work by moving into non-tobacco ventures and in the process acquiring what the company's financial people spoke of as "constructive debt". But what sort of sizable new business made sense to hypercautious North Carolina tobacco people?

Reynolds's earlier diversification moves had been small, careful sallies into the packaged foods business, buying up narrow but well-known brand lines like Hawaiian Punch fruit drinks, Vermont Maid maple syrup, My*T*Fine puddings, and Chun King Chinese cuisine. But these purchases had hardly made a dent in RJR's wallet and produced profits that were meager in comparison to margins in the cigarette business. When the company made a major move in 1969, its officers looked like country boys come to town with too much cash in their overalls and just waiting to be taken by a hustler—in this case, a bushwhacker largely of their own creation.

Malcolm McLean was a rough-hewn and little-educated industrial buccaneer who came from Fayetteville, about 120 miles southeast of Winston-

Salem, and had become a multimillionaire partly by hauling RJR cigarettes across the nation, in the process winning many lucrative truck routes from the Interstate Commerce Commission. Presentable enough to get elected to the Reynolds board of directors, he was smart enough to move out of conventional trucking with an idea that revolutionized the long-haul freight business—containerized shipping. The idea was to move crated products in huge containers that traveled overland on flatbed railroad cars or fit onto specially rigged trucks and could then be lifted by derrick and deposited directly in the holds of ships. Among the advantages of the method were lower handling costs, less damage, and much less pilferage (since the containers were never opened until they reached their destination). McLean's Sea-Land Corporation owned a fleet of nearly forty swift, allegedly very profitable ships by the time he came to his colleagues on the Reynolds board with a proposal that they take over the capital-intensive operation and use their excess cash to finance an expanded fleet of superswift, state-of-the-art ships.

The idea captured the imagination of the Reynolds brass. For one thing, they knew and liked the dynamic McLean, admired him because he was native to those parts yet was so different from them—a free-drinking high roller whose gambles had paid off big—and trusted him to the point that they relied on the financial data and analyses he gave them on Sea-Land's performance. There was something liberating about the whole idea, perhaps having to do with the romance of the sea, which was not visible from even the uppermost floors of the RJR headquarters building in Winston-Salem. There were skeptics among them who feared entry into a business so alien to their traditional ways of operation and so likely to sop up their profits, but the moment had come, Alec Galloway was persuaded, to take the plunge.

The Sea-Land buy-in cost $550 million, and the meter never stopped clicking thereafter. In 1970, the Reynolds board concurred with the suggestion that it spend an additional $55 million to buy American Independent Oil (Aminoil), doing business out of Saudi Arabia and Kuwait and specializing in bunker fuel, a thick grade used by ships, in order to assure the Sea-Land fleet of a reliable supply of cheap fuel. The new investment added to the anxieties of board members like Charles Wade, who remarked, if none too loudly, "What on earth do the bunch of us down on Fourth and Main in Winston-Salem know about oil in Kuwait, where they've got all kinds of intrigue and eat goat?"

Such misgivings did not take long to be borne out. After a brief spell of strong Sea-Land profits, a West Coast shipping strike hit late in 1970 and spread to Gulf and East Coast ports, badly hobbling operations. But such labor difficulties, domestic and foreign, including costs swollen by the need to pass out bribe money to bureaucrats on a regular basis to get any given ship landed, were only the tip of the iceberg. All at once there were new competitors everywhere—German, Dutch, and Japanese especially—many benefiting from government subsidies, and state-owned cargo fleets launched by Eastern European nations desperately hungry for hard Western currencies and thus willing to undercut Sea-Land's rates. Gyrating currency exchange rates over the five years it took to expand the Sea-Land fleet helped drive up the cost from a budgeted $38 million to $55 million per ship. And once in operation, their powerful engines used too much oil at their rated 32-knot maximum speed, and so it was dropped to 27 knots, defeating the whole point of their superfast design. On top of which they were now operating only half-full or less, as Japanese electronics makers, among Sea-Land's biggest early customers, switched to cheaper carriers. As a result, Sea-Land, soon the world's biggest private shipping fleet, showed profits that varied from narrow to invisible, leaving the Reynolds board with a wretched return on its investment and a corporate sore that would not heal for more than a decade.

A far more prudent use of Reynolds's surplus cash would have been to build up its efforts in the international tobacco business, but the company lacked the confidence to take the plunge in a serious way, as Philip Morris was then doing. Even a relatively sophisticated executive like "Red" Gray had hesitated to put RJR brands into international play in a decisive way, partly from an unwillingness to risk exporting its expertise and placing its blending skills in the hands of foreign nationals. "Philip Morris was beating our brains out in Europe," one Reynolds officer recounted, "but you couldn't send a good old boy to run things over there." Without a truly European operation in place and a nucleus of its own people to oversee it, Reynolds was in no position, as Philip Morris surely was, to exploit crumbling trade barriers when the Common Market began its operations and a vast continental market took shape.

X

R. J. REYNOLDS faltered under Alexander Galloway because for too long it had been ruled by nepotism and cronyism instead of merit, of which, at any rate, there was an insufficient supply. Among the few who recognized the root problem was the house intellectual, Duke man Charles Wade, vice president for personnel and labor relations and a company director. Because he harbored no illusions about ever becoming head of Reynolds and had built a reputation for being smart and politically adroit—skills that got him elected as well to the boards of such Carolina institutional strongholds as the Wachovia Bank, Duke Power, and Duke University—Wade was freer than most of his colleagues to speak his mind, and one of the things he told them was that their badly depleted pool of talent needed to be replenished by outsiders with a less parochial point of view. Especially needed were people to run the non-tobacco subsidiaries, which were in limbo as disparate entities and essentially out of the parent company's control. "I love you all," Wade would tell his fellow officers when the moment seemed right, "but I don't think we can run all of this with our present people." It was not an opinion that greatly endeared him to his colleagues, but the message was received.

In 1968, Wade succeeded in bringing on to the Reynolds board an outsider—one of only two non-employee directors at the time—with the wintry aspect of a white-thatched, bespectacled New England schoolmaster. At the time, J. Paul Sticht had been chief operating officer of Cincinnati-based Federated Department Stores, the nation's premier chain, and brought with him a national outlook and marketing skills that everyone agreed could be useful to RJR. Sticht, once a steelworker in his native Pittsburgh, had risen to shop steward and then pushed himself into the executive ranks by attending Harvard Business School and working in personnel at TWA and Campbell Soup before building his career in retailing at Neiman Marcus in Texas and Filene's in Boston.

Sticht, anxious not to get himself pegged a Yankee carpetbagger, was respected on the Reynolds board as an amiable, knowledgeable, no-nonsense sort, one who would not risk exploding the tight collegiality among his RJR colleagues by, for example, too vigorously questioning the wisdom of the Sea-Land deal, which was stuck under his nose, as he recalled it, as pretty much of a *fait accompli.* Only when Galloway announced he was stepping aside as chairman in 1972 and indicated that his choice as new chief executive was the financial vice president, David Peoples, did Sticht speak out forcefully. Peoples was perceived by Sticht and others in the company as not much more than a competent accountant with a narrow, bottom-line mentality; in short, he lacked the vision Reynolds so badly needed.

Sticht, who had taken early retirement at Federated Stores at fifty-five—some close to the Lazarus family, who controlled the department-store chain, suggested that Sticht had outlived his usefulness to the company—now found himself one of a four-man search committee of directors to pick a chairman other than Peoples. Surprisingly, except to those who knew that the fires of ambition had not been altogether banked within him, Sticht emerged as the committee's choice. But to allay latent xenophobia among veteran Reynolds people, Sticht was designated chairman of the board's executive committee and named co-equal with the new chief operating officer, Reynolds careerist Colin Stokes, whose father had once run the company's leaf department and had worked with The Founder himself. This "team concept" of leadership may have soothed local sensibilities, but as one prominent Winston-Salem businessman close to Reynolds people put it, "Everyone knew soon it was a lot of bullshit. Colin was like everybody's grandfather and down-to-earth, while Paul was just the opposite—not warm." Though they did not embrace Sticht socially, and vice versa—he tended to pass his spare time during the winter in Palm Beach and during the summer in New Hampshire, and no one pushed to get him speedily accepted at Winston-Salem's best country club—he was respected as the new broom in the house. Everyone deferred to him, including President Stokes, who, as Sticht recounted, "did go along" with the stronger man's directives.

In his first years of trying to run Reynolds without audibly cracking the whip, Sticht found himself preoccupied with a pair of problems that antedated his arrival on the scene. One was how best to correct the Sea-Land mistake. "We had a lot of other opportunities far more compatible with Reynolds's tobacco business," he recalled, "and we were deprived of the chance to explore them because of the monies tied up in Sea-Land, which was so foreign to the basic skills of the company." By the time Sticht concluded that Sea-Land had to be sold off, there were few potential takers—at any price.

Sticht's other draining problem was how to deal with a pair of messy corporate scandals that had attracted the attention of federal authorities. One involved some $25 million in questionable payments—namely, bribes—that the Sea-Land accounting ledgers carried as legitimate business expenses to get their ships unloaded in foreign ports. The other, over far less money, was a good deal more embarrassing: RJR officials were charged with making $90,000 in illegal campaign contributions to Republican presidential candidates from 1964 through 1972. The monies were said to have been paid in the form of personal gifts as high as $10,000 each from individual corporate officials, who were repaid from a company "slush fund," off-the-book monies drawn from RJR's overseas accounts. The charges required Sticht to make many trips to Washington in search of a solution that would bring the company a minimum of embarrassment. "It was a major distraction," he said.

The matter was finally settled in 1976, when, in place of fines or jail terms, three of the company's top veteran tobacco-side executives were forced to resign. For Sticht, these resignations had a silver lining—he was free now to bring in fresh talent from the outside—and used the opportunity. Most of the newcomers were Northerners, and few of them would share Sticht's reservations about throwing his weight around.

12

Let There Be Light

A s ITS marketing momentum propelled Philip Morris into second place in the cigarette business at the beginning of the 'Seventies, the company appeared to have more to lose than any of its competitors from the disappearance of television advertising of its product. But what soon became apparent was that Marlboro, its vivid Western imagery having already gained the status of instant folklore, would translate far better into print media than imageless Winston. Magazines, offering better reproduction than newspapers, were soon getting almost 40 percent of the Marlboro budget, as still greater care was lavished on the brand's presentation. A story line had to be implicit now—no longer could a wrangler be shown just leaning against a bunkhouse and lighting up—and every detail of the graphic, from the patina of the leather to the glow of the campfire, had to be just so. Costly formats, like double trucks, foldouts, and gatefolds, were introduced to accommodate spectacular panoramas of "Marlboro Country" that beckoned to the reader even more vividly than television had managed. The brand also moved vigorously into promotions and premiums as never before. A five-trailer Marlboro "Chuckwagon Caravan" toured the nation, serving as many as 2,000 Western dishes a day at state and country fairs, while the company was giving away millions of copies of a sixteen-page booklet, *Chuckwagon Cooking from Marlboro Country.* Another mail-order device, the Marlboro Country Store, offering merchandise from coffee mugs to sheepskin coats, further enhanced the brand image.

Marlboro was not the only Philip Morris brand to benefit from inventive merchandising in the post-TV era. Ellen Merlo, one of the bright young brand managers in Jack Landry's marketing shop, came to him with the idea for a Virginia Slims *Book of Days,* a witty appointment calendar chronicling women's long, slow rise from social degradation, as a giveaway. The chief marketer grasped at once how the pictured vignettes of feminists' bygone battles would advance the product. "Jack preached that everything you did for a brand had to be relevant to our audience," Merlo recalled. "The appointment calendar would be in front of the customer every day of the year and thus reinforce the brand's imagery."

Landry's department had a boisterous, raffish tone—nobody thought much of it that he sometimes referred to Merlo as "Poon" (as in poontang), which she chose to take as a rowdy term of endearment, even as Landry himself came to be known as (but not called to his face) "Loon." The long, liquid lunches at his favorite steakhouse became a ritual; his indifference to market research data deepened; and his attention at staff skull sessions seemed to dwindle as he sat in a corner, feigning sleep or on occasion trying to balance a quarter on his nose. Yet when everyone else had had his or her say, Landry would put in the final word, often the most cogent of any uttered during the session.

Emerging as a valuable prop to Landry's performance as the industry's marketing Merlin was his chief acolyte, James J. Morgan, the office golden boy out of Princeton, who had been recruited by Joe Cullman himself, a friend and admirer of Morgan's father, an executive at Exxon. Morgan, turning thirty in 1972, was nearly twenty years Landry's junior but had early on become a glib propagator of the marketing gospel according to St. Jack, also known in-house as "The Transcendence of Brand Imagery." "They were the yin and yang of each other," Merlo recounted of Landry and Morgan, totally different in their approaches to business and life. Morgan was the strategic thinker and devoted young family man; Landry, the creative force and hell-raiser. "Jimmy handled everything that Jack didn't want to be bothered with," Merlo added.

Spectator sports events emerged in this era as the prime venue for promoting cigarettes. Landry himself capitalized on his passion for horses by persuading the New York Racing Association to name a major new thoroughbred event, with an unprecedented purse of $150,000 donated by Philip Morris, after the company's stellar brand. In its first running in 1973, the Marlboro Cup was won in world's-record time for the mile-and-an-eighth distance by arguably the greatest racehorse of the century—Secretariat—all of which attracted great attention in the press and blazoned the brand name.

If a showcase horse race was the ideal promotion for a brand that got famous using Western iconography, an even more useful device was hit upon to promote Virginia Slims, which unlike Marlboro had not won a vast consumer base before the TV blackout of cigarette ads. The idea for Slims to sponsor a women's tennis tourney—and in time a whole circuit of them—was foisted on a not altogether delighted marketing department by the company chairman.

Joe Cullman, a nationally ranked tennis player in the senior age bracket, numbered among his friends the female publisher of the magazine *World Tennis*, who had urged the concept on him as a way to advance the cause of women's professional tennis, a poorly organized and sparsely attended version of the men's sport. And how better to push a cigarette brand built on the premise that women had come a long way toward parity with men?

What began as a single experimental event in Houston in 1970 soon blossomed into a twenty-two-event tour, as Ellen Merlo jumped into a station wagon and, with a stack of press releases and one or another of the female net stars in tow, bearded newspaper editors in their dens, pleading for ink for a sport they generally neglected. The early enlistment of the top women's player of the day—Billie Jean King—brought glitter to the Slims lineup, and a rift with the U.S. Lawn Tennis Association over the prize money brought more of the strong players into the Philip Morris camp. Soon some sixty world-class women were touring, and what had begun as the company's indulgence of the boss's passion for the game was building fame for its hot new women's brand and "star value," as Merlo termed it, for the players. The promotion worked in large part because Philip Morris took pains to see that it did. "All parts of the presentation had to be right," Merlo recounted, from the publicity to the look of the arena to the outfits the players and officials wore, especially since at first some of the less successful competitors showed up in ragged shorts and looked to Merlo "as if they were coming to a pickup game at a public park." The company hired a top designer to create new outfits each season for the athletes, and they were not the traditional all-white uniforms but done in pastels and stripes like those on the Slims package.

That the athletes on the Virginia Slims tour, eventually earning millions in prize money, were being willingly exploited to help sell a product likely detrimental to the achievement of excellence in that sport was a contradiction that seemed to bother neither the players, anxious for a living from the game and for its glamour, nor the sponsoring company. Merlo, who had more to do with establishing the tour than anyone else at Philip Morris, would always deny that wearing the brand's colors and bannering its name by participation in a Slims event was implicit endorsement of the product, even though to others they seemed a tacit denial that smoking was incompatible with the vigorous physical demands of tennis. "That's a very simplistic interpretation," Merlo argued. "Adults are capable of making decisions in their lives, especially about their own health and bodies, whether it's smoking or having an abortion or whatever."

The company's claim of clean hands was often supported by the Slims tour participants, whose loyalty to Philip Morris seemed to grow fiercer whenever it was attacked by antismoking critics. More than twenty years after the association began, Billie Jean King defended the company on the editorial page of

The New York Times by stating: "Not one of the Virginia Slims players has ever been asked by those who work for Philip Morris to smoke, to appear in cigarette advertising or otherwise endorse smoking." But surely King and her sister tennis stars were open to the charge of "otherwise" endorsing a product harmful to health generally, let alone athletic prowess. In her *Times* letter to the editor of December 2, 1993, King also wrote, "The Philip Morris executives I know . . . are enlightened people who understand and acknowledge the possible hazards of smoking." *Possible* hazards?

For all their collective smarts as marketers, Landry, Morgan, Merlo & Company had one serious blind spot. Philip Morris brands were running at an accelerated pace now, but retail shelves were not kept adequately stocked. What, then, was the point of all the advertising and promotional skills that were pulling in the customers? Monitoring stores to prevent out-of-stock situations and pushing for large enough orders by store managers took warm bodies, and Philip Morris still did not have enough of them in the field. In the late 'Sixties, the company's field force numbered fewer than 500—about one-third as many as the fearsome Reynolds sales phalanx. By 1973, Philip Morris had doubled its field force, advanced salaries by about 20 percent, notably improved its data-gathering and training techniques, and was paying for preferential placement on the Reynolds-owned racks, but such measures were viewed by some on the sales side as still inadequate. "I was concerned and parted company with Landry and Morgan," recalled Richard Schoenkopf, manager of sales personnel and planning and later head of merchandising. "I felt that in-store was where we had to be strong. . . . It wasn't just that they were unwilling to spend money—it was a mentality left over from the days of TV advertising," *i.e.*, the barker would pull the customers into the tent.

To counter the big advantage Reynolds had enjoyed by virtue of its supermarket racks, Schoenkopf talked Landry into experimenting with a Philip Morris version, an improved, spring-loaded model in which a replacement slid neatly into place each time a customer bought a carton. The point of the investment was to end the second-fiddle placement of the surging Philip Morris brands, and in the early test results, its brands in fact improved their sales by more than 25 percent. A second test was somewhat grumpily ordered by the marketing overseers, and though it, too, produced favorable results, Morgan began to nitpick in analyzing the added expenditure ("Look, Alpine lost business"). Finally, Morgan admitted to Schoenkopf that Landry had no heart for spending big on anything so prosaic as in-store fixtures, "even though," as Schoenkopf put it, "we were getting our asses eaten on the existing racks by Reynolds." He later brought the marketing team a second promotional scheme—the chance to pick up from fading Liggett & Myers a two-dollar-per-unit annual charge for auditing vending-machine sales, allowing vendors to get paid accurately, in exchange for preferential placement in the machines. But while Philip Morris hesitated, Reynolds jumped in to pick up the auditing expenditure for appreciative vendors, thereby adding to its great field strength.

I I

ALTHOUGH Philip Morris was not exactly spendthrift in its retail servicing tactics, it did not hesitate long to make a major commitment in the vital area that Reynolds was neglecting. As PM brands kept registering annual sales gains of about 15 percent, churned out from antiquated plants in Richmond and Louisville, operations chief Clifford Goldsmith prevailed on the board to believe the company's own marketing projections and build the largest and most technologically advanced cigarette plant in the world. And to make it, as well, one of the most beautiful factories on earth, a working advertisement for the company's burgeoning success.

Urged on by corporate President George Weissman, its resident culture maven, who argued that good architecture was no more expensive than the bad kind, the company chose Gordon Bunshaft of the top New York firm of Skidmore, Owings & Merrill to design the new manufacturing center, originally budgeted for $80 million in 1970 but costing over $200 million by the time it opened in 1974—the largest outlay for a single purpose in Philip Morris history but just part of the half-billion dollars it would spend on cigarette-making facilities in the U.S. and abroad over the course of the 1970s.

The easiest part of the huge capital investment was the decision to keep the core of the manufacturing operation in the Richmond area, the company's traditional production base. The Virginia capital had recently upgraded its port and communications facilities and remained the home of ultra-discreet Universal Leaf, the world's largest tobacco broker and independent leaf-processor, which continued to handle all of Philip Morris's purchases and gave the cigarette makers from New York access to the state's—and thus the region's—financial, political, and social elite. Thus, the giant new Philip Morris manufacturing complex, with forty acres of in-plant floor space, was set down a few miles south of the city, across the James River and hard by U.S. Interstate 95, the most heavily trafficked north-south artery in the Eastern half of the nation. The monumental horizontality of the immense structure, broken by ten towers each rising nearly a hundred feet and proclaiming the structure a titanic bastion of modern commerce, seemed the product of a totalitarian sensibility.

Whatever it lacked in external charm, the dark brick leviathan made up for with a gleaming interior that was indeed the last word in efficient, user-friendly production facilities. Some 15 percent of the budget had been set aside for workers' amenities, to the point where Goldsmith, overseer of the entire project, happily claimed, "You couldn't tell where the executive offices ended and the factory proper began." The latter had an airy, spacious feel to it, as far as imaginable from the dark, grimy, satanic mills of the past. The very floor of the plant, of a polished maple laid in parquet, was chosen to be easy on workers' feet and seemed more appropriate for a living room or a gymnasium. The place was bathed in glare-free light; the soaring walls were painted in cheery blues, greens, and yellows, and each worker had his own locker, access to comfortable, sound-muffled lounges overlooking the production facilities, and a view of floor-to-ceiling, glassed-in vaults full of trees, plants, and flowers native to Virginia. The manufacturing equipment itself had a beige or other light finish to it and was relatively quiet, and—at the workers' explicit request—the air was not incessantly aquiver with the sound of piped-in music. When challenged to justify such heavy expenditures to create a veritable workers' paradise, Goldsmith answered that people who labored in such surroundings would take pride in them and themselves and turn out more and better work.

It was less the grace notes of the manufacturing center, however large their contribution to worker morale, than the plant configuration itself that enlarged Goldsmith's reputation as a superb technician with skills that fattened the corporate bottom line. Equipped with a precision of manner, certitude of opinion, and icy look behind his thin-framed glasses which made him almost a caricature of the Erich von Stroheim film German, that embodiment of iron command, Goldsmith was known around the Richmond operation as "the U-boat captain," and even his admiring superior, Ross Millhiser, teasingly called him "Klaus"—a bittersweet irony for the refugee from Hitler who fought against the Third Reich in the U.S. Army and, when taken prisoner, had to play dumb lest his Nazi captors detect his German accent and guess his Jewish origins. Goldsmith had determined that to pay its way, the new plant design had to invite dramatic cuts in the high expenditure of time and manpower traditionally required by the movement of millions of cigarettes from one stage of production to the next across busy factory floors.

Goldsmith's innovation was to break up the main plant floor into five giant "bays," each an acre or more in size and containing some thirty "modules," each one in effect a complete, miniaturized manufacturing and packaging factory, integrating makers, tippers, pasters, cutters, wrappers, boxers, and cellophane-appliers, all funneling into cartons that were automatically loaded onto little freight cars and carried off on overhead tracks to the shipping platforms. The key to making these intricately coordinated units operate at a sufficient laborsaving speed was to gear them to a pace achievable by the fastest-rated machines available. The latest "making" models could turn out 5,000 cigarettes a minute, but no packaging machine could match that pace until an Italian company in Bologna came up with a high-precision design that Goldsmith was willing to try. The remaining problem, though, was that the more processes that were tightly meshed for maximum output, the greater the chance for a breakdown, and a bottleneck anywhere along the line would defeat the entire scheme.

Goldsmith's solution was the "OSCAR," an acronym for Overhead Storage Conveyor And Reservoir. If a packer broke down, the making unit in the integrated module would keep spitting out cigarettes but piling them up in the OSCAR for the twenty or so minutes that it took to make the average packer repair; and likewise if the maker got bollixed, the packer could just turn to the surplus cigarettes stored in the OSCAR to keep operating. To minimize downtime elsewhere in the system, Goldsmith installed electronic diagnostic charts and television screens that monitored trouble spots and scanners that, at the incredible rate of eight packs per second, could detect tears in cigarette paper, uneven seams, and loose filters and kick out the flawed butts. The net effect of the company's $50 million investment in these ultrasophisticated machines was a factory that produced 25 million packs of cigarettes per day at double the industry's per-man-hour rate of output.

III

WITHOUT television to bring instantaneous celebrity to a new brand, the Philip Morris marketing team was convinced that the best way to build sales was to extend its existing lines by offering them in different lengths, hard and soft packages, and menthol versions. Starting from scratch, even with a world-beater of a selling proposition, would be exceedingly costly now.

Still, few at the company's Park Avenue headquarters were enthusiastic when Joseph Cullman came in all hot and bothered one day early in 1971 with an idea that had seized him over the weekend after he had heard New York's mayor, John Lindsay, propose a cigarette sales surtax of four cents per package for brands high in tar, meaning above 15 milligrams. Such a measure, inspired by the reform-minded mayor's concerns about smoking as a health risk, could, Cullman feared, have a swift negative impact on Marlboro, the top-selling brand in the nation's biggest metropolitan market, and give milder rival Kent, also very popular with health-minded New Yorkers, a major boost. Why not bring out a weaker version of Marlboro, Cullman proposed, allowing the new entry to escape the proposed surtax? Call the line extension Marlboro Milds, the boss suggested.

Pandemonium reigned. The brand in all its existing versions accounted for 60 percent of the company's U.S. sales. The very thought of spawning a weak-kneed, degenerate offspring of a product that had billed itself as a full-bodied taste treat for real men and the sort of women who craved them seemed misguided to many, to say the least. "You were talking about Marlboro, the franchise itself," James Morgan recounted. But Jack Landry, like the rest, saw that "Joe was pretty damned serious," and so there followed a six-month intramural donnybrook over every aspect of the proposition, starting with the name of the low-tar line extension. To Landry, calling it "Milds" suggested that "the parent brand was strong and harsh, and I didn't want us to imply that. 'Lights' made a better statement, I said—and Joe took it. I think he was throwing me a bone, because he knew I didn't care for the idea."

And so Marlboro Lights, yielding 13 milligrams of tar compared to 17 for the regulars, hit the Philip Morris drawing boards, as Cullman sought the input of everybody whose opinion mattered in order to make the risky proposition work. The basic strategy that emerged, as Morgan put it, was: "Don't rip the legs off Red [Marlboro regulars] to launch Lights." All that followed, then, was done to make the distinction clear. Instead of the sharp-edged box with the bold red roof, Marlboro Lights came out first only in a soft pack featuring an inset roof of gold with a black-dot screen overlay. Instead of the simulated-cork tip on regulars, Lights had a white-wrapped filter, and where the ads for Reds showed palominos in gritty, almost documentary-style, photographs, Lights had white horses in them or consisted of Remingtonesque line drawings one degree of starkness removed. The sell was soft: "For smokers who prefer the lighter taste of a low-tar cigarette"; no Vantage-like promises were made about offering smokers the best-tasting low-tar brand ever or the flavor miracle of the century. "The scenario was never ever to talk about Lights without reinforcing what the Reds were about," said Morgan.

The new entry got off to a limping start. When Virginia Slims debuted with saturation advertising in its test market of San Francisco just three years earlier, some 78 percent of area residents polled reported familiarity with the new brand, but in the fall of 1971, after Marlboro Light was rolled out in a New England market without benefit of television, only 32 percent said they were aware of the product after a comparable time. But the company let the line extension plug along to the point in 1979 where it accounted for 15 percent of all Marlboro sales. By the end of the decade, Marlboro in all its various packages was outselling the Winston line by 25 percent, and while Winston Lights were still doing marginally better than Marlboro Lights, they had cannibalized the parent brand in the process, while Marlboro's regular Reds had grown a bit, vindicating the investment.

But even with Marlboro Lights on retail shelves, Philip Morris had been a laggard in the low-tar field. Lorillard had established an early lead with its Kent and True brands, and then Reynolds had made its presence felt with Doral and Vantage, as more and more smokers began switching to brands with lowered yields. Never an industry leader in basic developments, largely because it had not been financially strong enough in the past to risk pioneering, Philip Morris made its way upward by learning from the triumphs and mistakes of its competitors, and now, with the low-tar trend established, Ross Millhiser, president of the company's domestic tobacco business, urged operations head Clifford Goldsmith to develop a new, freestanding brand in that field.

This was no easy trick, since smokers by then constituted, in James Morgan's words, "a very skeptical marketplace." By the mid-'Seventies, an estimated 90 percent of all smokers had tried one or more low-tar brands, and only 10 percent of them had so far made the switch permanently. To overcome such resistance, Philip Morris would have to become more innovative than was its wont. Though there was little love lost between Goldsmith and his research and development director, Helmut Wakeham, the team worked closely on a plan under which the principal effort would go not into new filter technology, as Reynolds had done with Vantage, but into an intensification of the flavoring process which would neither boost tar yield nor junk up the taste by saturating the tobacco with additives.

"The worst thing you can do is overflavor the product," explained Frank Daylor, longtime manager of flavor development in Philip Morris's research department. Loading on sweeteners and other additives could have caused the aroma to overpower the smoker or even sicken him or her upon opening the pack, for smell is the key to taste—the tongue can distinguish only sweet, sour, salty, and bitter—but the quantity of any given flavoring substance does not necessarily govern the strength of its detectable smell. In developing what the company tagged "Enriched Flavor" for its new low-tar brand, Philip Morris scientists contributed nothing really new in terms of the additives but changed how the elements of flavor were combined for enhancement.

The detective work required identifying the best-smelling of the thousands of compounds and combinations thereof that made up tobacco smoke, a task facilitated by R&D's purchase of newly sensitive and very expensive instrumentation. The plodding task led to the discovery of what Wakeham called "basic flavor units that deliver taste way out of proportion to tar." These were then run through olfactometers, which measured the intensity of the smells that contributed to these flavor elements, and the most efficacious were analyzed for their chemical structure. Finally, the lab searched out or synthesized substances with a chemical structure identical to or closely corresponding with these high-flavor, low-tar components of smoke. "These chemical additives, or flavorings, were then added to the tobacco blended into Merit," Wakeham explained to the press when the resulting brand appeared at the end of 1975. He insisted that "in this entire procedure nothing new or foreign has been added—just more of the preferred elements that already existed in tobacco smoke." He did not say whether they had been tested to determine if "the preferred elements" promoted carcinogenesis or any pathology.

When submitted in blind tests to some 3,000 smokers, the 9-milligram Merit scored beautifully, and when Philip Morris salesmen sampled the brand, they guessed that it had twice its actual tar yield and excitedly asked the manufacturing department to get the product to market as soon as possible. "Everyone knew lower numbers were going to sell if they had taste," Philip Morris sales executive Tom Littleton recalled. "Vantage didn't really have it—there was a difference between night and day in the taste of the two brands." But how to persuade a jaded smoking public that Merit was something new under the sun? Step two after the taste hurdle had been cleared was a distinctive pack for Merit, a task turned over to the San Francisco shop of industrial designer Walter Landor. The outcome was a white background for a central geometric design that conveyed movement and modernity yet hinted at the tasty reward within by the use of the traditional tobacco colors, brown, orange, and yellow.

More important still was the marketing department's plan for how to present Merit. Perhaps its truest believer was the young marketing ace, Jimmy Morgan, who recalled, "After a year of test-marketing we had documentable, FTC-proof evidence that Merit tasted as good as brands with twice as many milligrams of tar. . . . We decided to position Merit as if General Motors had just developed a brand-new car. . . ." The plan was to play the brand's arrival as a major news event, with a big press conference presided over by Cullman and featuring the company's scientists to explain their prodigy of milder yet lip-smacking enticement. The print ads, sporting large, newslike headlines, much more text than traditional cigarette advertising, and no imagery besides the package itself, were highly reminiscent of the Vantage approach, but the text was less coy and the volume much heavier, especially in newspapers, to stress the newsiness of the event, with headings such as "Tar/Taste Theory Exploded . . . New 9 mg. MERIT with Enriched Flavor proves taste no longer depends on amount of tar" and "National Smoker Study Hails Merit."

The immensely costly send-off for Merit, with ads appearing in newspapers as often as three times a week and running up a $40 million space outlay in the brand's first year, dwarfed anything the tobacco industry had seen before. But as long as the Merit sales trend headed upward, the company kept spending. The new brand got a sizable if unwitting push from the health community just as the low-tar entry was reaching the market. The American Cancer Society's Cuyler Hammond reported the results of a twelve-year study concluded in 1972 during which smokers of what were then categorized as low-tar brands— the breakpoint was put at 17.6 milligrams of tar—showed a reduced risk rate for lung cancer of 26 percent and for heart disease of 14 percent, assuming no change in the number of cigarettes consumed. Accordingly, Hammond urged government health officials to order all high-tar brands off retail shelves—a step the FDA might have taken at any time. But Hammond's data failed to account for one phenomenon that *Consumer Reports* and other trackers of smoking patterns had begun to observe: as tar and nicotine yields were reduced by manufacturers, many smokers compensated by taking deeper and more frequent puffs, so that actual yields could not be determined solely through tests using automatic smoking machines.

All that was nuance so far as soaring Merit was concerned. By 1979, the brand was accounting for one of every five cigarettes sold by Philip Morris, moving well past Virginia Slims and Benson & Hedges, which had run into trouble translating its witty sell from electronic to print media.

I V

WHEN Marlboro was on the verge of passing Winston as the best-selling U.S. cigarette toward the end of 1975, Philip Morris people made a pact among themselves, as national sales director Jack Gillis recalled: "There wouldn't be any skyrockets or celebrations when it happened. The prevailing sense was 'Let's see how far we can ride this thing.'"

Even with the new national sales leader in its stable, Philip Morris had work to do. Reynolds still held one-third of the U.S. market, compared to PM's quarter. By then, though, the New York organization had surpassed RJR in global cigarette sales, thanks to its far better performance overseas. International sales were accounting for one of every five dollars Philip Morris brought to the bottom line.

The company's chief overseas go-getter, the fiercely independent and aggressive young Scotsman Ronnie Thomson, who commanded European operations from 1968 to 1976, combined manufacturing and marketing know-how, financial acumen, and lawyerly skills as a cool tactical negotiator and dealmaker. He tried to impress upon New York headquarters—and to an extent succeeded—that for all its national differences, Europe ought to be conceived of as one big market that could be penetrated by carefully orchestrated, centralized policies and planning, undertaken from the company's European base in Lausanne. There, on the shore of Lake Geneva, Thomson put up a little gem of a modern office building and brought to it a cadre of superior talent, among them Swiss, German, Swedish, Australian, and Israeli nationals who would one day assume top jobs in the Philip Morris hierarchy, just as Joe Cullman had forecast in his welcoming remarks to the uneasy employees at FTR a decade earlier. In the view of Walter Thoma, one of the Swiss whom Thomson enlisted and who would in time inherit his post as head of European operations, the ruddy Scotsman was "a very bright, talented, analytical, and motivating executive." But in a company that prided itself on a consensual system of management more than a top-down, inspirational brand of leadership, Thomson was a fish out of water. He hated organizational folderol and hewing to the chain of command that served merely to slow the moves conceived by his lightning mind. "He was a young man who thought he knew everything," Thoma added, "and that everyone else was an asshole."

As Thomson watched the lineaments of the European Economic Community take shape, he pushed his company into buying up small cigarette manufacturers in the Benelux countries and setting up an efficient production center in Holland, turning out 2 million packs a week at first for the Belgian, Dutch, Italian, and French markets and giving Philip Morris a strong potential presence in the Common Market. Thomson simultaneously addressed the troubling situation in the German market, where the disastrous ten-year licensing agreement with Brinkmann was expiring not a moment too soon. While the German licensee had brought Marlboro to a 1 percent market share that netted Philip Morris $600,000 a year, the far lusher rewards of Western Europe's largest single market eluded the company, and Reynolds was making headway there with Camel. The only solution, Thomson insisted, was for Philip Morris to establish its own operations in Germany, and after failing to strike a deal to take over Brinkmann or fashion a joint venture with Reemtsma, the top German tobacco manufacturer, he picked up the shell of an old printing plant in West Berlin and took full advantage of the generous write-offs allowed on equipment brought in to save the divided city's economic life. Soon he set up a managerial team operating out of a suite of three rooms off a dentist's office in Frankfurt, but both sites were quickly outgrown, and the German effort was centered in a former Reemtsma plant in Munich, where within a decade of its establishment, Philip Morris would be employing 1,500.

Manufacturing capability, with its enhanced profit potential, was one thing, but the key to overcoming European resistance to American blended brands in general and Marlboro in particular was an understanding that consumer preferences could not be brutally forced on the Continent. As Thomson recounted it, "Philip Morris management in New York was wise enough not to send over a bunch of Americans who couldn't understand the markets and the cultures" and instead let European nationals do the job. In Europe, the Wild West imagery of "Marlboro Country" stood for America, political freedom, and social mobility—an attractive message, especially for younger smokers. But it was not an unalloyed message. For the French, Marlboro was an impingement on their culture and an affront to the nationalized product, Gauloises. "To toss a pack of them on the table was to declare, 'I'm French,' " Thomson remarked, and the smoother, filtered Marlboro was by comparison a pallid smoke, and the dirty horses and cattle in "Marlboro Country" were less than totally picturesque to the fastidious natives of Germany and Switzerland.

The real breakthrough form of promotion that Thomson seized upon and that was still more ardently embraced by his Swiss-Italian colleague at Philip Morris—the dashing Aleardo Buzzi—was to put the Marlboro brand into sports sponsorship, especially cross-country or "Formula 1" auto racing. Unblessed by the year-round, nationwide professional sports leagues on which Americans lavish so much time, money, and attention, Western Europeans would throng to auto races like those at the Nuremberg Ring in Germany, Monza in Italy, and LeMans in France. They drew especially well among young males, the prime smoking group from the industry's point of view, and to reach them, Thomson poured Philip Morris money into Marlboro signage at stadiums and trackside displays as well as bannering the brand's logotype and colors on the high-powered vehicles and their drivers' racing jackets.

"To put our love into the sport," as Buzzi said, a bigger commitment was soon made: safety equipment such as barriers at the track's edge was contributed; ten-year contracts for signage were agreed to; and to help promote and market the sport big-time, Buzzi became personally involved with its promoters, including Italian carmaker extraordinaire, Enzo Ferrari—"a very tough customer," as Buzzi recalled. So enmeshed did the Philip Morris executive become that he found himself called upon to arbitrate squabbles over the terms in contracts to televise the races. Even as they were building the linkage between the Marlboro name and the sport, Buzzi and Thomson were trying to convince their superiors in New York that the race-car driver was the modern-day equivalent of the cowboy and, like him, the courageous lone adventurer who risked danger with a superpowered machine instead of a great snorting stallion under him. The Marlboro ads in European media never showed racing scenes, but the prominence of the brand logo at the events and as picked up unavoidably by the TV camera was giving it an image that appealed increasingly to thrill-hungry young smokers.

By 1973, Philip Morris was sponsoring its own five-car racing team that flew the Marlboro colors before millions. Except for a fluke victory accomplished with the help of a rainstorm in Morocco, Buzzi recounted, "We lost every race but got great attention." A reputation for losing, though, did not much advance the brand's standing, and after a couple of years, the company bought up some top drivers and, with an outlay that now reached into the millions per year, made the Marlboro team European champions. Thomson and Buzzi would trail along each weekend to cheer on their entry and assure proper display of the brand's name—the kind of obsessive involvement that would have quickly soured the company's top management if the Marlboro sales numbers had not kept pace with the lavish promotional spending.

Thus, success bred tolerance for the company's hotshot young European marketers, and Thomson was cut a great deal of slack, even to the once unthinkable point where he was able to buck the home-office directive to launch Marlboro 100s with the same gold roof on the package which appeared in the

U.S. version. Thomson and Buzzi argued vehemently that the brand's red-roof look was just beginning to gain widespread recognition across Europe, and a gold variation would blur its image, not to mention its growing reputation through the auto-racing program as a ballsy smoke. By the mid-'Seventies, Marlboro held one-fourth of the Italian cigarette market, had become the strongest foreign brand in Germany, and was even gaining acceptance from the French smoker.

Indeed, as the decade lengthened, Philip Morris brands were scoring big gains in sales and visibility around the world. A licensing deal was struck in partnership with the Spanish government. Accords were reached with the state tobacco monopolies throughout Eastern Europe, and sales were particularly good in Poland. The Marlboro name was dangling from lampposts all over Cairo, plastered across billboards, and painted, with the brand colors in the background, on innumerable kiosks, as Philip Morris launched a promotional war against Rothmans International for hegemony over the Egyptian market. In BAT-dominated Brazil the company opened a plant and launched Marlboro in the face of some derision toward the advertised Yankee cowboys who seemed like dudes compared to the rugged *vaqueros* of the Pampas. And in Hong Kong, the licensee was doing remarkably well as that oasis of capitalism became a center for Philip Morris export sales throughout the Orient, a considerable portion of the cigarettes smuggled onto teeming Asian streets in ways that the manufacturer chose to ignore.

Ronnie Thomson epitomized the high spirits and ceaseless energy of Philip Morris International (PMI). Thomson, in the view of John Murphy, second in charge of overseas operations, "might have become CEO of Philip Morris someday." Murphy fondly recalled how Thomson "loved to fight upward," *i.e.*, against those on top of him in the corporate hierarchy, starting with Murphy himself. But some at New York headquarters were less charmed by Thomson's often abrasive manner and standing request to plow European profits back into the building up of his domain instead of repatriating them—which, after all, was the main reason the company had gone into business abroad. For his part, Thomson behaved as if there were only one man in the Philip Morris organization he had to please—the chairman—and toward the rest he did not hesitate to exhibit disdain when he thought them dense.

There was also the matter of how New York perceived the zest with which its young European executives played as well as worked—the fast sports cars they favored, the hot tub on the roof at their glittery headquarters with its superb view of Lake Geneva, the swashbuckling way they commanded the best table at the finest restaurants in Berlin or Munich. Flashiness was not encouraged by Philip Morris overlords, especially not by those in charge of its tobacco operations, Ross Millhiser and Clifford Goldsmith, who, as Thomson himself put it, "thought the PMI lifestyle was a bit too grand." Thomson was less deferential to his immediate superior, PMI's president, Hugh Cullman, who in turn found his young hotshot "impatient, abrasive, and imperious—he drove me crazy. He'd do things without my clearance, and I'd hear about them after the fact. Some people in New York felt he was out of control."

Thomson came to feel he had done what he could to build an organization, got bored, and began, as he himself put it, "to drop grenades" during the monthly meetings of the top company people in New York. This self-destructive conduct would not be tolerated indefinitely, and when Revlon beckoned him to run its European operation, Thomson accepted, to the relief of all. But it did not work; he remained no lover of organizations and protocol, and in time, while still a young man, Ronnie Thomson became a Swiss citizen, set up shop as a financial, marketing, and personnel consultant in Geneva, bought a villa overlooking the lake, and continued to drive snappy sports cars.

V

IF PHILIP MORRIS'S overseas forays were reaping rewards by the early 'Seventies, the same could hardly be said for its non-tobacco ventures. Its early moves into packaging and adhesives manufacturing had been easy and sensible forms of vertical integration, but these industrial units gobbled up capital for returns at most one-third of what the core cigarette business earned, and they could not readily improve their margins without charging higher prices to their parent company, thus killing one of the chief benefits of their purchase. Far more sensible had been the plan to buy up makers of consumer products compatible with Philip Morris's marketing know-how and distribution system—laggards that could be turned around with the wizardry the company was now bringing to its soaring cigarette business.

The theory was unassailable when applied to, for example, American Safety Razor (ASR), whose products, like cigarettes, were cheap, used daily, and forever in need of replacement. But in practice, to build a mass following for its brands against dominant rivals Gillette and Schick took cash that Philip Morris had not been willing to spend and a unique selling proposition that the ASR marketers were never able to formulate. By 1977, after seventeen years of struggle, Philip Morris sold off ASR to the subsidiary's employees.

Clark chewing gum had been picked up for a few million in 1963 as an ideal vehicle for Philip Morris to enter the candy business, which used many of the same wholesalers who handled tobacco products. Again, though, Philip Morris was up against entrenched competitors: Wrigley had cornered the spearmint gum trade as Beech-Nut was preeminent with lovers of peppermint flavor and Dentyne had locked up the cinnamon crowd. To supplement its unexciting Teaberry mainstay, Clark came up with sour lemon and spent heavily to promote it. The trouble was that the citric acid added to the gum for its souring effect underwent a chemical reaction with the sugar dusting within each tightly wrapped stick, causing a buildup of carbon dioxide that turned the packages sausage-shaped or even round. And when Clark assayed the candy business with a new chocolate-covered, fruit-centered bar using a freeze-dry process, the product held up well enough in air-conditioned supermarkets, but when test-marketed as well at neighborhood food shops during a hot St. Louis summer, the bars wilted on the shelves. After a decade and an estimated $20 million in losses, Philip Morris dumped Clark but managed to recoup much of its investment from the sale of trademarks and manufacturing equipment.

None of these satellite ventures involved a large enough potential market to make a major difference in the financial fortunes of the parent company, yet they occupied an inordinate amount of top management's time and energy. In the view of Wallace McDowell, who in two decades with Philip Morris rose to executive vice president for operations, "There was reluctance to commit the cash and talents needed to make a go of these small businesses. There was no singleminded effort to do what was necessary, considering how they started behind the leaders in their field." Chairman Joseph Cullman would suggest in retrospect that "it was hard to pay enough attention" to the diversification program when his cigarette brands were now running so well, but neglect was no excuse for the simple truth, which with time Cullman readily admitted: "We failed."

With the TV advertising ban imminent and at least a part of the funds that had gone into the broadcast media available for new ventures outside the tobacco business, Philip Morris turned its efforts toward a product with a potential market large enough and a sales apparatus close enough to its basic business to justify finally a serious jump into diversification. Beer, like cigarettes, was an agriculturally based product, manufactured on high-speed equipment, consumed often, inexpensive and largely recession-proof as a low-cost pleasure, and dependent on advertising since there was little intrinsic difference between brands. Equally important, with the U.S. population growing and the demographics of beer drinking favorable, here was a field with a real upside opportunity if Philip Morris put serious money and talent into it.

In the wake of its recent setback in trying to take over British cigarette maker Gallaher, Philip Morris moved more stealthily in trying to buy up control of Canadian Breweries, featuring the Carling label, and bring its quality reputation into the U.S. market. But it was foiled by Rothmans International, which already held a piece of the company, and so Joe Cullman cocked a receptive ear when his phone rang at home one Sunday afternoon in early 1969 with an invitation from shipping baron Peter Grace to unburden him of his controlling interest in Miller Brewing, seventh-ranked of the four dozen U.S. beer makers with national distribution. Grace, who held 53 percent of Miller stock—the balance was owned by a foundation devoted to funding Catholic clerical orders—already had an offer of $120 million from PepsiCo, but he did not much like the payout terms and thus invited a last-minute counterbid by Philip Morris. Cullman asked how much time he had to respond. "Tomorrow," said Grace.

Philip Morris planners had done enough homework to know what Miller was and wasn't. Though light-years behind industry leaders Anheuser-Busch, Schlitz, and Pabst in profits and marketing prowess, lethargic Miller retained a reputation for selling a quality product, due in part to the slogan for its chief brand, Miller High Life: "The champagne of bottled beers." But those very words helped to explain what was wrong with the company's understanding of the suds-quaffing multitudes—beer drinkers thought champagne was something that swells drank out of glass slippers—and why Miller was operating at not much over half of its production capacity. Here was an old-line family enterprise now under a caretaker management and the perfect turnaround candidate for a Philip Morris that had learned from its past mistakes when wandering off the tobacco plantation. It paid Grace $127 million for his control of Miller and an additional $100 million to clear out the minority position of the charitable foundation. Then Cullman reached into his tobacco-executive ranks for a top-flight manager to sweep away the cobwebs from the sleepy Milwaukee brewery.

Told that his new assignment, in a gritty industrial town, was a reward for his high-speed, high-profile, globetrotting work as No. 2 man at PMI, big John Murphy protested at first that he didn't know a hop from a hoop, but the chance to run his own show was tantalizing. And besides, he recounted, "I was an Olympic-class beer drinker." He was also smart, versatile, and tested and had a presence that could be physically and verbally overwhelming—just the ticket to shake up the *Bräuhaus*.

Among Murphy's first discoveries was that High Life had a far lower per-customer take-away than the leaders and a higher proportion of female customers, partly because it was the only big brand sold in a clear bottle, not brown or green like its competitors, and thus had a reputation as a lighter brew with a visible effervescence, in keeping with its champagne image. In fact, Murphy soon found, Miller was heavier than most other beers because it used so much barley, was more bitter due to overhopping, and worst of all, "We had a country full of stale beer." Beer begins to lose its sparkle immediately upon leaving the brewery, and within a dozen days of its manufacture, the oxidation process takes a toll on taste detectable by true beer lovers; a lot of High Life was sitting on store shelves six months or longer.

The moribund management Murphy inherited might have passed for quaint if it had not been so hopeless. Marketing costs were sky-high, the advertising was awful (one commercial featured a player piano), the president devoted inordinate time to deciding which magazines the office should subscribe to and on which walls paintings should hang, and by 11:45 a.m. the brass in their sport jackets paraded en masse to the Wisconsin Club for lunch, "taking the same seats they'd taken for the past thirty-eight years," Murphy recounted, "with the same waitress asking, 'What'll you boys have today?'"

Soon heads began to roll. While the restaffing went on, Murphy addressed the root problem of fixing the product. He ordered a dating code to be printed on every label with a rigidly enforced "pull date" so that stale High Life would no longer clog retailers' shelves, and vendors who failed to cooperate were denied their supply of Miller. Next he sat down with Miller's brewmaster, Clement Meyn, who educated the company president about what hops are—namely, little pine-colored plants that grow on vines thirty to forty feet high and have buds that when boiled in giant brewing vats release a bitter acid that flavors the beer. They had no mysterious connection to the fermentation process but were "purely pepper," as Murphy put it, and he ordered the strong flavorant reduced, along with the barley content, to be replaced by corn in order to lighten Miller's taste. By 1972, "we had the brand turned," Murphy recalled, and now the trick was how to sell it.

One of Murphy's first packaging innovations stemmed from the discovery that not every buyer wanted to guzzle twelve ounces of beer—the standard fill—every time he uncapped a bottle. Instead of putting out High Life in six-packs of twelve ounces each, why not an eight-pack of seven ounces each? Such rank heresy produced a reaction natural to a manufacturing department unused to toeing anyone else's mark. "We can't pack 'em for you," Murphy was told. "Can't" was not a word in Murphy's colorful vocabulary; the production people were told to hire however many people were needed to hand-pack the new eight-unit configuration until the automatic equipment could be refitted. A lot of other equipment adjustments and replacements were also ordered, including new canning and glass works, hop-extracting facilities, and the basic breweries, at a cost that soon mounted into the tens of millions. By then Murphy had turned to the New York advertising agency of McCann-Erickson to reposition the lighter, fresher drink. Out went the old, faintly elitist sell of High Life as the proletariat's champagne; now it was to be a reward for all the regular folks who labored hard and played hard, working up an honest sweat and a powerful thirst. "If you've got the time," chimed the slick new commercials, "we've got the beer," and in place of the old "happy hour," they coined a new designation for the perfect end-of-the-day, wet-your-whistle interlude: "Miller Time". It was not notably clever, but there was a certain zippy, joyful earnestness to the pitch, and it worked, like the new seven-ounce bottles. After the first two years of Philip Morris ownership, when Miller sales actually slipped below 4 percent in market share as Murphy regrouped, volume began edging upward. The big boss, whom everyone called by his first name, was all over the place, and his lash, if selectively wielded, stung nevertheless.

To build up a real head of steam, Miller could not remain solely dependent on High Life. It tried Miller Malt, Miller Ale, and budget-priced Milwaukee Extra, but none of them caught on outside the company's home region. Murphy then turned to exploiting an asset that had come with a small Chicago brewery, Meisterbräu, he had bought—the name "Lite" in trademarked script lettering. A diluted beer, Lite had test-marketed surprisingly well in the blue-collar town of Anderson, Indiana, after its calorie content was cut from a standard 140 per bottle to 96. Such acceptance suggested to Murphy that a lot of "tonnage" drinkers really worried about their beer bellies but would never admit it, so that a less fattening brew might score well if not too big a fuss was made over its healthful attribute; the name alone would tell all. Such a product, in keeping with the trend to "light" cigarettes, less fatty milk, and "decaffeinated" coffee, might also appeal to beer buyers concerned about their weight.

Murphy knew full well, though, what had happened not long before when New York's Rheingold brewery had tried to market Gablinger's as a reduced-calorie beer. The thinned brew turned out to be so deficient in taste that the brand went nowhere. But Murphy had learned there were two ways to turn out a lighter product: just plain water it down or keep it in brewing vats longer to burn out more of the fermentable (and weight-adding) sugars. To produce a beer with reduced caloric content but not a readily detectable loss of taste, Murphy opted for the latter, if more costly, method.

In blind taste tests run for two years beginning in 1973, experimental Miller Lite outdid upscale Coors, its chief target. All the attention then shifted to how to make a splash with the new product in a way that got both the pleasure and the health message across. The problem was similar to the one in marketing Marlboro Lights, but the medical community, of course, had not charged beer with lethal effects unless chugged by the keg. McCann-Erickson's solution was the one that had worked so well for Benson & Hedges 100s when that brand still had television as its prime ad medium—humor. But the best-known precedent for the idea was not encouraging. Madison Avenue had been ecstatic over the hilarious deadpan wit of the campaign begun two decades earlier featuring broadcast zanies Bob Elliott and Ray Goulding as Bert and Harry Piel, the fictive brothers who ran the real-life Piels brewery. The public, too, loved the commercials but forgot to buy the beer.

McCann-Erickson's approach was broader and less cerebral, even gritty with a locker-room brand of joshing at barside among famous and not-so-famous athletes, ex-athletes, and their buddies, all quintessential beer drinkers. The subject of their zesty horseplay was nothing racier than the merits of new Lite, of which it was said once and only once during the commercial, "One third less calories." Instead of further hammering about the brand's healthful or dietary virtues, there was the telegraphic message "Tastes great—less filling," and the more inspired line, "Everything you want in a beer—and less." The playful but pointed vignettes caught on at once, and soon Miller was pumping in the ad dollars furiously as Philip Morris had never done with its earlier non-tobacco products; its outlays reached three dollars a barrel, twice the industry's average.

Suddenly, Murphy had a runaway success on his hands in Miller Lite. The brewery's profits, which had been just $6 million in 1974, rose to $29 million in 1975, as Miller overtook Coors for the No. 4 spot in the industry with a market share of nearly 9 percent. The next year, Miller passed Pabst, and by 1979, when it had also passed Schlitz to take second place in the beer business, Miller netted $181 million, returning a solid 8 percent on sales and accounting for 15 percent of Philip Morris's consolidated earnings—or about two-thirds of the entire international tobacco unit's bottom-line contribution. And by 1981, a decade after the Miller makeover had begun in earnest, its output hit 40 million barrels, an eightfold increase for the period after an investment for purchase and plant of about a billion dollars.

Murphy was of course buoyant over this success story. He had caught the competition napping with Miller Lite, and when Schlitz tried to answer with a light version of its own, it proved a listless entry. Industry behemoth Anheuser-Busch, not unlike Reynolds in the tobacco universe, had grown complacent and for years was unworried by Miller's gains until labor strife hurt the big St. Louis brewer; by the time it began to react at the end of the 1970s, Miller had grabbed off 60 percent of the reduced-calorie market. Murphy, meanwhile, was having the time of his life and attracting a lot of attention from the press. Unfortunately, he also began to attract the attention of August Busch, the head of Anheuser, who heard the same stories of Murphy's bravado that reached the Miller boss's superiors back in New York. Every time Miller gained a point of market share, the reports had it, Murphy would clang a ship's bell in his office to celebrate, then wipe his shoes on a floor mat beneath his desk that bore Anheuser's Budweiser logo. When these accounts of unseemly gloating reached "Gussie" Busch, the slumbering giant in St. Louis awoke and began to respond furiously.

V I

As JOSEPH CULLMAN entered his sixties and his company enjoyed growing stature as a moneymaker—and he himself ever more renown as a masterful manager—he seemed to undergo a revitalization of his energies. Throughout the 1970s, he was generally acknowledged as his industry's foremost spokesman. His peers in the corporate world displayed their admiration by inviting him onto their boards of directors (Ford Motor Company, Bankers Trust, and Levi Strauss). *Business Week* put him on its cover in 1974, noting how Philip Morris was running rings around its competition, and *Financial World* named him U.S. executive of the year for 1977.

Within Philip Morris itself, Cullman had taken on a more complex persona. "He was a pistol," summed up one younger executive in the personnel section at corporate headquarters, where he was greatly admired for his vigor but less so for an ego that had expanded in proportion to his achievements and a temperament tending to fray more often now with the burden accompanying his company's steadily weightier net worth. The chief executive's lifestyle was a source of fascination and endless speculation among his underlings, for he continued to play as hard as he worked, excelling at tennis, squash, golf, hunting big game, trout-fishing in Canada, ever on the go as he kept up with the trade and toured the outposts of his growing global empire. And as he aged, he remained very much a ladies' man. There was regret but no great surprise, therefore, when he announced to his board in 1974, at the age of sixty-two, that he was ending his thirty-nine-year marriage to Susan Lehman Cullman and would shortly wed a longtime acquaintance, the former Joan Straus Paley. A year after his second marriage, Cullman announced his intention to shed Joan and remarry Susan. But he didn't; instead, he enjoyed a somewhat unorthodox marriage to the second Mrs. Cullman, more or less living with her in New York but also apart from her in a suite at the Carlyle Hotel, meanwhile squiring other women, prominently including the first Mrs. Cullman, who continued in residence at Joe's former home in Westchester. He showed up at Philip Morris functions with one wife or the other and no explanations or advance advisory, necessitating the preparation of alternate "Mrs. Cullman" name tags— just in case. Cullman-watchers believed the chairman simply could not decide which wife he wanted, if not both—or neither. He finally divorced Joan in 1979, but remarried her in 1988.

Cullman's growing grandeur made him a more prickly customer for subordinates to deal with. There was the time, for example, when Joe was due in Miami Beach for a big tobacco distributors' convention, and Tom Littleton, then regional sales manager for Florida and part of the Philip Morris host party, was to pick up the chairman at the airport. The company had a big hospitality suite at the Fountainbleau hotel, where Cullman was also to stay, but the evening of his arrival, Philip Morris was throwing a gala dinner at the Doral, where the chief executive was supposed to preside and charm the customers. That afternoon, though, Clifford Goldsmith, then in charge of domestic tobacco operations, phoned Littleton from New York to say that Cullman, who had become notoriously finicky and jumpy, was not in a good mood and ought not, on his arrival, to be allowed under any circumstances to retire to his own suite, because the odds were he would never be lured out for the festivities at the Doral.

Littleton, already in a sweat over having to usher the boss around, grew damper still as the company jet arrived late, and Cullman remained on board another twenty minutes after the landing. When he finally emerged, Littleton bustled him into the waiting limousine and found Cullman, as advertised, in a funk. As the limo raced toward the site of the dinner, Littleton recounted, "Joe was kvetchy all during the ride—'It's too hot in here, it's too cold, it's too stuffy, it's too drafty.' " As the limo neared the beach, Cullman leaned forward to Littleton, who was in one of the jump seats, and gave the dreaded directive: he wished to stop by his hotel for a few minutes before going to the dinner. Littleton, by now a pool of perspiration, failed to pass the word to the chauffeur. As the limo raced past the Fountainbleau, Cullman asked his middle-rank sales executive with a flash of annoyance, "Didn't you hear what I said?" Littleton, gulping, said no, he hadn't heard, because he had a cold in his ear. Silence followed until they arrived at the dinner, where Cullman was at his most ingratiating. During dinner, however, he summoned Littleton to his side and said, "I know you heard me back in the car—what makes you think what you want is more important than what I want?" It was, without doubt, a rhetorical question. The chairman then told the weak-kneed Littleton, "Sit by me— you're going to take care of my every need this entire weekend"—a task zealously carried out until Cullman reboarded his jet and said, not unkindly, "Now we're even."

Littleton's punishment befit his crime but did not exceed it because Cullman thoroughly understood that the sales manager shared his boss's sense of devotion to their joint corporate mission: each had a job to do that night, and they did it, however unhappily. "He knew what to do, what moves to make, and when to make them," Littleton would remark years later, well after he had left Philip Morris, in tribute to Cullman. "He knew what good people were and how to let them do their work." His was not a naturally extroverted nature but one of a dutifully applied attentiveness. "He had a totally strategic personality," said Ronnie Thomson, whose own had never embraced Cullman's knack for gracefully handling people who riled him even when they were trying their best.

Cullman brought a shining optimism to his embattled company which sometimes blinded him to its most pressing problem. He felt able to advise his stockholders at their 1971 annual meeting that, with regard to the smoking and health issue, "We have entered a period of relative calm." And he himself was still giving no quarter in his public pronouncements on that subject, remarking on that same occasion: "A causal relationship of tobacco and various ills is increasingly open to question"—an assertion without scientific merit. If Cullman and his fellow industry executives were susceptible to charges of acting in a morally reprehensible manner, it was less for their continuing to purvey a product commonly understood by then to be a serious health hazard than for pretending it was otherwise in order to reassure those they lived off. Silence, even if taken for mute concession of the likely truth of the charges against cigarettes, would have been less heinous than blowing smoke in the public's face. Possibly Cullman had so conditioned himself to being combative and justifying his and Philip Morris's calling that he was no longer aware of just how objectionable his remarks on health and fitness sounded to those not financially dependent on tobacco. Looking fit and tan as he returned from his eighth African safari at the beginning of his last year as Philip Morris chairman, Cullman told the press, without seeming to recognize the irony, "I guess I'm sort of a physical cultist. . . . Someone who's fit can do a better job. And in a complicated world, there's nothing better than an exposure to the outdoors." Thus did a man who made a sizable living by selling arguably the most lethal product legally available counsel mankind on how to lead a healthful existence.

However uneasy in his role as an apparently shameless polemicist, Cullman had long since honed social skills allowing him to move easily through a corporate world in which few other Jews of his generation had risen to the top. That it was Jewish executives, with the notable exceptions of Jack Landry and John Murphy, who led Philip Morris to the heights of the tobacco industry was, in Cullman's view, "largely happenstance and certainly not intentional." The net effect of his heritage, he believed, was to make him and his company more liberal and tolerant than most in its social attitudes and wide open to diverse, even eccentric sorts of people. Cullman's broadmindedness was especially noticeable in PM's overseas division, where foreign nationals were regularly given great freedom of action. Philip Morris was a meritocracy, among whose beneficiaries were the likes of Ronnie Thomson, who once noted, "Philip Morris International was built on the best guy getting the job regardless of background or nationality."

As Cullman approached retirement age, speculation naturally intensified about the line of succession. The contest was plainly drawn in 1973, when George Weissman was advanced to the new position of vice chairman of the corporation, with special responsibility for all non-tobacco operations (particularly Miller Brewing), and Ross Millhiser was given Weissman's previous title as corporate president, with prime oversight of the tobacco business. The pair, both fifty-four at the time, had never been close, but each was smart enough not to let their differences in manner and temperament spill over into open incivility.

Weissman, generally seen within the company as the cooler and more calculating of the two, was contemplating broader entrepreneurial horizons for the company beyond tobacco. Millhiser, while probably the more intellectually adventurous, was the one who kept closer to the core business and was skeptical of the company's ability to thrive in any other sort of operation. If Weissman traveled in an entirely different social world from that of the Cullmans and the Millhisers, lacking their family connections and resources, he was nevertheless the most cultivated of the top Philip Morris people. It was he more than anyone else who pushed the company into becoming a highly visible patron of the arts, on the premise that such a role would help win it friends among opinion-shapers and counteract the unending bad news about smoking from the medical community. By the mid-'Seventies, the Philip Morris name was linked as major underwriting sponsor to events like the U.S. tour of La Scala's opera company and the National Endowment for the Humanities' exhibit "Two Centuries of Black American Art," and as a corporate contributor to such unexceptionably worthy institutions as the New York Public Library and the Henry Street Settlement House. Weissman was also the most politically active liberal in the place, having signed advertisements in opposition to the war in Vietnam and thereby earning a place he was proud of on Richard Nixon's infamous "Enemies' List". A civil rights advocate and conservationist as well, Weissman pushed the company to widen its minority hiring practices, and it was no accident that Cullman served as president of the Whitney Young Foundation, advancing educational opportunities among blacks. Possessed of the broadest smile and heartiest handshake in the company, Weissman had also indisputably proven himself an able administrator and superior judge of managerial talent.

For all of that, it was Millhiser who remained the favorite of the tobacco insiders. He had a profound knowledge of the product in all its phases and was no empire builder, as Weissman was suspected of being. There was little slickness to his jus'-folks personal style, and he was one of the few people in the company who could tease the board chairman to his face. At the same time, he was perceived as more emotionally volatile than his rival for chief executive, perhaps a bit eccentric in some of his maunderings. His practical side, though, forged a close bond with Clifford Goldsmith, his dedicated line officer, with whom he often argued, but between them they were running the smoothest tobacco operation in the world and winning medals for Cullman.

As 1977, the expected year of decision, dawned and Philip Morris executives chose up sides in the pending contest, Joe Cullman decided that things were going so well under his baton that he would stay on past his sixty-fifth birthday to conduct the company's affairs. This thunderbolt may have done wonders for Cullman's morale, but it was surely a crushing depressant for his would-be successors. On further reflection, the chairman decided that his indispensability should not extend beyond one more year.

13

Breeding a One-Fanged Rattler

SHORTLY after being chosen in the autumn of 1971 as chairman of British-American Tobacco, Richard P. Dobson passed a remark stunning in its candor for a prominent official in his industry. "It's hard to argue that filling your lungs with smoke can be actually good for you," he said. He quickly added, as if fearful of being dethroned on the spot, "But surely it is a question of moderation, and I do sincerely believe that the tobacco industry, in total, does more good than harm. I know more people who have liquor problems than tobacco problems."

Dobson's appeal to "moderation" by smokers, never uttered in any of the industry's advertising, seemingly had a commonsensical core, but upon closer examination, it rang hollow. What constituted "moderate" smoking—a cigarette or two a day, five to ten, a pack or fewer? Did that not depend rather on the size, weight, age, robustness, and degree of inhalation by the smoker? And if "moderation" was meant to imply a safe level of use, who had established it "surely," to use Dobson's telltale word, for *any* level of smoking? All that dozens of epidemiological studies had shown "surely" was that the more one smoked, the greater one's risk of eventually falling deathly ill from the habit. Other studies showed that few smokers in fact used cigarettes moderately; only about 10 percent smoked five cigarettes or fewer daily. And if "liquor problems," as Dobson styled them, were more apparent to him than "tobacco problems," it was only because the debilitating effects of alcohol abuse were so much swifter. The more pertinent fact, which he omitted, was that the incidence of immoderation was of an inverse ratio for drinkers and smokers: between 5 and 10 percent of the former became dependent alcoholics, while three-quarters of smokers consumed fifteen or more cigarettes a day.

More studied, and thus perhaps less innocent, in his expressed view of the uses and abuses of cigarettes was Philip Morris's research and development director, Helmut Wakeham. In addition to pushing his laboratories to produce what he called a "better"—he did not say "safer"—cigarette, Wakeham had asked for and been granted license from his superiors to probe why people smoked, the better to defend the product against its detractors by understanding its true appeal to consumers (and, in the process, market it more effectively). On the opening of his new research tower late in 1972, Dr. Wakeham, a nonsmoker, spoke to the Richmond press about the activities of his staff of 400. "According to the psychology of smoking, I'm not cut out to be a smoker," he said. "There are people who need the tension-relieving experience of a cigarette, and some need it more than others. . . . We think cigarettes help people to be less tense, but we don't know how."

Interest in such questions grew industry-wide now, as cigarettes were consumed in record quantities in the early and middle 'Seventies despite the ever graver cautions being sounded by the public-health community. In their efforts to identify the causes and rewards of smoking, behaviorists in the 1950s had focused on why youngsters chose in the first place to engage in a habit generally taken up by the end of the teenage years or not at all. Studies showed that many sampled cigarettes in very early adolescence, and that some 75 percent of smokers were fixed in the habit by the end of their high school years. Pacesetting investigations by Daniel Horn and others stressed the primacy of parental influences, either as role models or by degree of permissiveness, and added that a further key element was the perceived consolation that young smokers derived to ease feelings of social or intellectual inadequacy. By the 'Sixties, the smoking field was attracting more psychological inquiries but yielding few remarkable insights.

The relative worthlessness of such efforts was pointed up in a January 1968 article, "Smoking and Kids: Why Are We Failing?", in the house organ of the U.S. Clearinghouse on Smoking and Health. According to its author, *Encyclopaedia Britannica* science editor Anslie H. Drummond, Jr., the difficulty with motivational inquiries into youngsters' behavior was that they often responded as they thought adults wanted them to; more to the point with regard to smoking, they often were unable to identify the real reasons for taking up such a notorious custom—and even if they could, they might not choose to disclose it. But clearer to Drummond was the reason young people were unswayed by adult alarms over their imperiled futures if they smoked: "For the great majority, there is virtually nothing in their lives to help them integrate the meaning of lung cancer and death. . . ." Neither their smoking friends nor smoking parents had yet fallen victim to the habit, and if smoking grandparents had, the resulting diseases were common to older people and thus not readily blamed on or thought to be exclusively due to tobacco. By contrast, the perceived gratifications of smoking were immediate as well as mild and thus far more manageable when compared to other quick-acting but disabling drugs like euphoria-inducing cocaine or the mind-blurring, reflex-slowing sedatives, marijuana and alcohol, all fraught with antisocial implications. Their very mildness and perceived function as both stimulant and relaxant made cigarettes as useful to youngsters as to adults, and their cheapness, easy availability, and naughtiness made them still more so.

Perhaps the world's leading investigator into smokers' motives was M. A. H. Russell of the Addiction Research Unit at London's Institute of Psychiatry, who in the May 8, 1971, issue of the *British Medical Journal* delineated five types of smokers. Least caught up in the habit were "psychosocial" smokers who affected the use in adolescence or as a prop in social situations as adults, with a correspondingly low intake of nicotine. "Indulgent" smokers undertook the habit mostly for sensual or sensory rewards, of which the taste, smell, and "kick" at the back of the throat from inhaling were the most obvious. A third category used cigarettes largely for "tranquilization," in particular the calming effects of oral gratification "and the occupation of the hands to relieve anxiety and tension." Others favored smoking for its "stimulation" in sustaining the performance of or allaying fatigue from monotonous tasks like long-distance driving or for enhancing alertness, perseverance, and creativity in demanding cerebral tasks like writing or meeting a deadline in a hectic commercial transaction. Finally, there were plain and simple "addictive" smokers who lit up every twenty or thirty minutes primarily to avoid the dreaded symptoms of withdrawal. Russell did not notably elucidate just why and how smokers in each category derived their rewards or to what extent the categories overlapped. What mattered most, in Russell's view, was that "people who smoke at all sooner or later become regular, dependent smokers"—and only about 15 percent of them quit before reaching sixty.

A parallel avenue of sociological investigation was the hypothesis, favored by tobacco industry apologists like Wakeham, that smokers were basically different sorts of people from nonsmokers and may have been programmed that way from birth by a genetic code regulating the production of certain enzymes that governed emotional disposition and behavioral choices. Given that more than one-third of all U.S. adults smoked, could any valid generalization be offered about a "smoker's personality"? Surely all kinds of people smoked. But investigators throughout the 'Sixties and 'Seventies by and large corroborated certain tendencies apparent to any close observer of the smoke-wreathed human animal. Most smokers seemed to be more stressed and inordinately driven than nonsmokers, more impulsive and demonstrative and less in control of their emotions, conduct, and social and occupational environments. Many if not most smokers held a more fatalistic view of life than nonindulgers: your being could be snuffed out the next instant for any of a hundred reasons, thus take what pleasures you can from life without unduly fretting over the risk. In disproportionate numbers smokers felt saddened, if not cheated, by the hand fate had dealt them: impoverishment, too few brains or too little learning, inadequate social or professional opportunity, and/or loveless marriage. None of these explanations, though, especially a possible genetic predisposition to smoke, served to exonerate the cigarette itself from its lethal effects. Indeed, those most vulnerable to the habit were the ones best advised to try to flee from its ravages before it was too late.

Many smokers convinced themselves that a tobacco-free life would be unendurable; cigarettes served them with wonderfully protean versatility as both stimulant and relaxant. But how, psychologists pondered now, could the very same substance provide those diametrically opposed uses, especially when most observable bodily responses to smoking resembled the patterns of emotional arousal, *e.g.,* about a 15 percent increase in heartbeat rate, a jump of ten to twenty points in blood pressure resulting from a narrowing of the peripheral blood vessels? These phenomena acted to produce a surge of energy associated with the body's fight-or-flight reflex at moments of high anxiety and were thus useful to smokers, rescuing them from depression, boredom, or fatigue—in short, nicotine served as an "upper," like an amphetamine; how could it also trigger stress-relieving reactions by the body?

To find out, scientists began taking a more intensive look at the interplay of blood, nerves, and muscle tissue chemically activated by nicotine. A picture was assembled of how nerve cells formed a body-wide transmission system that could be both readily activated and deactivated by the particular properties of nicotine. When chemically charged, each nerve cell sent an impulse down its length to a fibrous extension, or axon, and relayed it to a receiver station, or dendrite, on the next nerve cell; the junction of these two, the synapse, is a microscopic gap that is crossed by the conversion of the nerve's electric impulse into a chemical secretion that serves as a neurotransmitter as it binds chemically on the surface of the dendrite, if it is receptive to the particular compound bearing its message, thus stimulating a chain reaction. These neurotransmitters vary in nature and do their work selectively in the reactions they trigger. Nicotine was found to act in a way imitative of one of the body's most important natural neurotransmitters—acetylcholine (ACT), a compound that is active as a stimulant where nerves and muscles meet and also serves to release other neurotransmitters, in particular those that travel to the adrenal glands near the kidneys. When aroused by neural receptors sensitive to ACT or nicotine, these glands release adrenaline with its highly stimulating effects on the circulatory and muscular systems, in the process raising the metabolic uptake of the body's fuels, *i.e.*, causing it to burn its food supply faster. A comparable, transient increase in brain-wave activity was also observed.

But there was nothing automatic about this neurological transmission process once it began; it had to be repeated, and so each nicotine-receptive dendrite, after dispatching the impulse, released a protein that broke up the key-and-lock bond between neurotransmitter and receptor, allowing some of the chemical compound to be taken back by the axon terminal in the adjacent nerve cell for further use and thus clearing the connection for the next impulse. Nicotine, as it happens, forms a stronger and longer-lasting bond at the junction point between nerve cells, and though the chemical secretion it activates is readily cleared away when small doses are relayed, the transmission site grows clogged when a lot of nicotine is taken up by the lungs and blood and floods the neural chain. The eventual effect of this process, some investigators found, is to block and finally halt the stimulating effects of nicotine entirely, thus slowing muscular activity, the heart in particular, and with it the delivery of oxygen throughout the body and brain—in short, causing a sedative effect. Thus, scientists have speculated that smokers consciously or subconsciously vary their nicotine dosage to mesh with their biorhythm and stress levels as the day wears on.

Nicotine, then, came to be understood through the work of many investigators, most prominent among them UCLA psychiatrist Murray Jarvik and Columbia psychologist Stanley Schachter, as possessing a dual or "biphasic" nature, initially stimulating but giving way upon heavier dosage to a depressant effect after inhibition of the neural release mechanism. And the more frequently the smoker found himself able to achieve the physiological reaction desired—at, say, 200 puffs a day—the more thoroughly he conditioned himself to want these effects and trained his body to tolerate them. Eventually one in four smokers pays with his or her life for this systemic fooling of nature.

II

AMONG the several dozen scientists gathered on the Caribbean island of St. Martin early in 1972 for a seminar, sponsored by the tobacco industry, on why people smoke was Duke-trained psychologist William L. Dunn, who had joined the research staff of Philip Morris eleven years earlier, when Helmut Wakeham saw value in probing the behavior of smokers. In a report to his company on the consensus among the psychologists at St. Martin, Dunn offered a stunningly simple answer to the profound question of why so many millions were driven to such self-destructive folly: "The primary incentive to cigarette smoking is the immediate salutary effect of inhaled smoke upon body function." The cigarette, he wrote, ought properly to be conceived of "not as a product but as a package. The product is nicotine. . . . Think of the cigarette pack as a storage container for a day's supply of nicotine." An integral part of the product's appeal, he went on, was its convenience—it was unobtrusively portable, instantly accessible, easily prepared for use and discard, its rate of consumption readily metered to dispense the desired level of nicotine; its psychoactive ingredients reached the brain rapidly—within seconds—and its acute effects lasted no more than thirty minutes. Here was the ideal mild stimulant-sedative.

This marvel, of course, had a serious short-term catch to it: you could not condition yourself to enjoy its multiple uses and then just take it or leave it. You had to keep taking it, every forty minutes or so, depending on one's level of addiction, or suffer the consequences of withdrawal. The symptoms, varying with the duration of one's abstinence, included edginess, irritability, hostility, depression, mood swings among all or several of these, oral fixation, craving, headache, constipation, and weight gain. However real the sedating effects of heavy smoking, they in fact merely masked the keen distress that would otherwise have affected the smoker if he quit. Nor could the conditioned customer easily reduce his or her tar and nicotine intake. A report on smoker psychology that Dunn himself co-authored in March 1977 said, "We find that our smokers [were] smoking cigarettes in 1972 that delivered significantly less tar and nicotine than in 1968. At the same time they were smoking more cigarettes as well as more of the rod [farther down the tobacco portion] from each cigarette. These findings suggest . . . that a tar and nicotine quota mechanism may be operative. That is, they may be smoking more . . . to compensate for the decreases in the tar and nicotine delivery of their cigarettes." In a deposition for a product liability suit ten years later, Dunn claimed that Philip Morris scientists had not concluded that the compensation theory was valid— and not surprisingly, for if they had, as Dunn's paper suggests they in fact did, it would have gone a long way toward demonstrating the pointlessness, if not downright deceit, of the industry's efforts to modify its product.

No doubt secondary to smoking's effects on the body's chemistry—but nonetheless a large part of its appeal—were the infinite forms of gratification arising from the sensuous nature of the act, starting with the gently crackling removal of the cellophane wrap and moving on to the tweezerlike extraction of the cigarette, the staccato tapping of it against the wrist or a firm surface, the becalming insertion into the mouth, the magical burst of flame, the searing intake to fill the void within, the rasp on the tracheal tissue on the way down, and finally the glorious expulsion of aromatic clouds to fill one's entire immediate surround. Then there was the ongoing busyness of the hands and mouth, using the little white cylinder as a wonderfully communicative device and personality surrogate: the languorous drag that bespoke of knowing cool, the leaning this way or that to flick an ash, the dismissive snuffing out of the deliciously reduced thing.

As far back as the 1950s, students of smoking behavior were reading psychic states into these manipulative and exhibitionist patterns (*e.g.*, handling a cigarette in a delicate or arty manner was thought to conceal a sense of inferiority). The cigarette was the all-purpose sublimation. That it continued to be so understood by smokers themselves was well captured by one who knew the price of this indulgence, New Haven surgeon-author Richard Selzer, who wrote in his 1976 book, *Mortal Lessons:* "[L]et no meddlesome man caution me against the extravagance, the injuriousness, of tobacco. . . . To deny me my smoke is to extinguish me as utterly as would death itself. . . . Smoking is good for the dumpish heart, lights up the gloomies. . . ."

I I I

WHILE many of smoking's perceived blessings were subjective, a few could be measured with clinical objectivity, such as the use of cigarettes to suppress the appetite and reduce weight. Nicotine had been shown to lower the level of insulin in the bloodstream and thus ease the smoker's craving for sweets. The nicotine-triggered effects of adrenaline on the stomach's musculature produced a transient effect of fullness that could somewhat allay the pangs of hunger. A Temple University study had determined that smokers, who on average weighed seven pounds less than nonsmokers, were lighter not because they ate less but because smoking had intensified their metabolic rate; a month after quitting, a cohort of ex-smokers showed an 8 percent drop in oxygen consumption and a 5 percent slowing of their heartbeat. By the late 1980s, researchers were finding that smokers experienced a disproportionately high expenditure of energy when they were engaged in light activity as opposed to when they were at rest. Just why this was so was unclear, but the association of smoking and slimness had an undeniable basis in fact.

Far more problematic, however, was the factual basis for the claim that smoking is an aid to mental acuity. To be sure, brain-wave arousal was measurable after small doses of nicotine, suggesting a rise in alertness, and laboratory experiments were showing smokers somewhat better able to remain attentive during the performance of long, boringly repetitive tasks. But in terms of a true heightening of cerebral powers, the evidence indicated that the effects of smoking may be more cosmetic than substantive. Rather than somehow sharpening the smoker's capacity to concentrate, analyze, or create, nicotine can place its users into a kind of intellectual cage or isolation booth, even a trancelike cocoon, that filters out environmental stimuli like light or noise or subconscious intrusions of memory, allowing little to distract the smoker from the mental task at hand. Thus, the smoking writer is freed of any diversions save the cigarette and its mindless use—"an innocuous channel for wandering attention," as psychologist Isidor Chein put it. The practical values of an uncluttered mind, even if not enhanced in brilliance, are manifold. Air traffic controllers, who need to avoid peripheral stimulants and distractions, have long been known to be notoriously heavy smokers, to cite one example. The perception, then, that smoking promotes keener mental faculties may have stemmed from a cloaking of the fact that the smoker's brain is simply registering and processing *less* information simultaneously, and in that insulated state focuses narrowly. It must be added that, however much of a spur smoking may be to the brain's activities, all bets are off very soon after the regular smoker stops smoking. To be precise, smoking as an isolated act has not been found to make anyone more mentally alert or less emotionally irritable; rather, not smoking makes the conditioned smoker less alert and attentive—and notably more distractable and irritable. The earnest smoker, therefore, was well advised not to flaunt the benefits of his habit but to acknowledge, as David Krogh wrote in his book, *Smoking: The Artificial Passion*, "If I don't smoke, I get upset," and that he is trapped in a constant cycle of arousal and incipient withdrawal, slaked only by his next cigarette.

One paradox of smoking behavior was particularly intriguing: how, when confronted with a cause of distress that activated the body's adrenal flow, did a smoker seem to attain relief by reaching for a cigarette, with its initially stimulating effects? Why, that is, use one stimulant to neutralize another?

Stanley Schachter, a Columbia psychologist who undertook research for Philip Morris, reported at the industry's 1972 Caribbean conference on an interesting experiment conducted by one of his graduate students, Paul Nesbitt. Dividing a group of subjects, male students between eighteen and twenty-six, into subgroups of nonsmokers, low-tar brand smokers, and high-tar smokers, Nesbitt instructed the latter two groups to inhale every thirty seconds while he administered electric shocks of increasing intensity every fifteen seconds for a full cycle of twenty-eight shocks—if his subjects could endure it. The premise of the experiment was that if cigarettes had a true tranquilizing effect, the smoking subjects would be able to absorb more shocks. The results bore out this expectation, and in a dose-response pattern: the more heavily dosed smokers tolerated the most shocks, so that calming seemed to be a direct function of the amount of nicotine absorbed. How so, though?

Nesbitt and Schachter proposed two possible explanations for what would become known in the literature of smoking and health as "Nesbitt's Paradox" (how can one stimulant blunt the effects of another?). Smoking, they hypothesized, established a base level of arousal in conditioned users, and the additional activation of certain bodily functions caused by the electric shock and the fear of the next one was superimposed over that basic excitation from smoking, which served to mask some of the cardiovascular and other effects that normally would have been triggered by disturbing events or environmental impingements, such as electric shocks. The stressed smoker will therefore reach for a cigarette and subconsciously attribute some of the arousal symptoms brought on by the frightening or disturbing situation to the similar but less intense physiological effects of smoking, the arousal level of which the smoker has long since become accustomed to—and so is less upset than the nonsmoker by the electric shock. By extension, the investigators went on, smoking served to modulate the intensity of highly emotional states, whether fear, anger, euphoria, or sexual arousal. Smoking can then be perceived as a tranquilizer not *despite* its short-term effects but *because* of them: the known level of excitation, that is, seemed to soften the blow or, at the other end of the emotional spectrum, to serve as ballast for the joyride and keep the passenger from spinning out of orbit.

While some investigators have confirmed Nesbitt's results and others have not, the explanation of the paradox underscores the overriding point about the apparent usefulness of cigarettes to those hooked on them: they serve most of all as a mood stabilizer, lifting their users from the dumps, keeping them from going off the deep end or getting lost in untethered bliss. Unlike more starkly mind- or mood-altering drugs taken for recreational use or out of bottomless desperation to escape life's grinding realities, cigarettes are used as a form of self-therapy to stay normal.

If the reasons young people take up smoking vary, starting with the lure of forbidden fruit, and their numbers would doubtless be smaller were they not under the delusion they will live forever, psychologists have helped public-health advocates understand why the lethal habit persists among tens of millions of adults who should know better. And indeed, they do; surveys have long shown that between half and 90 percent of smokers say they resent being in thrall to what they acknowledge as an addiction and would like to quit, at least in theory—if it were not so difficult to escape their bondage. Their fears of withdrawal symptoms are surpassed in many cases, furthermore, by the dread of assault from life's countless vicissitudes, which they have convinced themselves they could not cope with if denied a cigarette at the next stressful moment. Smokers are thus classic rationalizers and hiders from fact when unwelcome word arrives about the perils of the one thing they think lets them cope with life. They are the very model of the type described by Leon Festinger in his 1957 treatise, *A Theory of Cognitive Dissonance*—people who act in ways that deny knowledge of the consequences of hurtful or self-destructive acts.

Yet for all the conflict they endure over their dependency, most smokers deeply resent the ever more widely held suspicion by smoke-free society that they suffer from flawed characters or emotional instability because they persist

in what they shouldn't. The more articulate of them reply with two basic arguments. First, since life is so full of travail, with joy so rare and fleeting, heart-
break all too frequent, and monotony the common lot, what difference does it
make if smoking shortens our time on earth, so long as it also intensifies its
quality and makes it more tolerable? And if this coping device is just the
chimera of addiction, so be it. Second, admit it or not, everyone adopts such
coping mechanisms to survive, but the smoker's choice is just more evident—
and less destructive or antisocial than many others. Some nonsmokers cope by
taking out their frustrations on others, mocking them or nagging them, bullying or beating or even killing them. Some overeat or undereat; in a world that
seems otherwise unmanageable to them, they cope perversely by acting to distort the shape of their own bodies. Some attend to their work monomaniacally,
hiding out from the other demands of loveless lives. Some use hard drugs to
escape the hell of their existence. Smokers rationalize, almost parenthetically,
that if cigarettes were all that bad, no reputable company would market them
and no government would permit their use; ergo, all you nonsmoking busybodies, go tend to your own weed-infested gardens.

I V

I N terms of social action undertaken to curb the rising toll from smoking, a
stalemate prevailed throughout the 'Seventies. All that government had
done about this immensely popular and economically important product was to
require a tepid warning label on cigarette packages and in advertisements as
well as, in the latter case, disclosure of the toxic yields. True, the cigarette
companies were making available less potent versions of their accused product, but the swing-over by consumers to these often less flavorful brands was
slow and their therapeutic effects were far from certain. The likely impairment
to the public health went on hardly abated: millions quit the habit, but other
millions took their place—and tobacco profits soared.

One relatively small appendage of the American government, however, did
bestir itself in the 1970s. It was the most curious—critics called it the most
misguided—and surely most expensive government effort yet: a decade-long
attempt by the National Cancer Institute (NCI) to develop a truly less hazardous cigarette for those millions who could or would not quit the often
killing habit. Humane considerations dictated such an effort, its champions
said, noting that the industry itself could not be trusted to perfect such a product lest the attenuated brands prove a painless way station on the road to quitting altogether. To tobacco controllers, developing a "safer" cigarette seemed
like breeding a one-fanged rattlesnake, still deadly. But the pragmatists prevailed, and the industry quietly exulted.

The most persistent proponent of the concept was the world's most vocal investigator in the field. Twenty years after his breakthrough paper in 1950 on the higher prevalence of lung cancer among smokers, Ernst Wynder crusaded everywhere he went, declaring that cigarettes were a scourge the medical community had for too long taken lightly. Working in tight quarters with a small budget at Sloan-Kettering with Dietrich Hoffmann, the world's leading authority on the chemistry of tobacco, Wynder turned out a series of studies firmly establishing the link between smoking and cancer at many body sites besides the lung (among them, the larynx, esophagus, kidney, pancreas, and bladder). And the more the pair had measured the degree of toxicity of individual compounds among the thousands present in smoke, the more difficult the task of meaningfully modifying cigarettes looked. There were just too many potentially deadly substances to try to filter them out selectively, while modification of the product by diluting the tar and nicotine brought with it other potential perils, especially linked to the flavorants added to compensate for the loss of taste. Licorice, the most widely used casing, was 25 percent glycyrrhizin, a salt found to turn carcinogenic when burned; the same was true of cocoa powder, another popular cigarette flavoring. And when tobacco plants were doused with nitrate sprays to reduce cancer-breeding hydrocarbons like benzpyrene, the additive turned out to enhance the presence of nitrosamines, a tobacco-specific compound that was found to be highly carcinogenic in tests of laboratory animals.

Wynder, a sophisticated cosmopolite possessed of a patrician manner easily confused with condescension, was a well-read, well-connected scientist-entrepreneur, driven to make his mark. He once told Hoffmann, "I've had the two best things you can hope for in life, a German education and American opportunity," and he used the latter to the hilt. At Sloan-Kettering, he won the backing of the institute's medical director, Dr. Cornelius Rhoads, who was so taken with Wynder's work that he volunteered to have his own back painted with tobacco tar distillate, as in the mouse-skin bioassays Wynder had developed, to see if the spot turned tumorigenic (an allergic reaction cut short the experiment).

But Rhoads's successor, Frank Horsfall, conceding at most a minor link between smoking and disease, urged Wynder to tone down his antitobacco statements, tightened his budget, and demeaned his research until Wynder demanded and won a special review committee to endorse the ongoing value of his work. Horsfall kept after him, nevertheless, until after one 5 percent budget slash too many, Wynder had had enough. He used all his persuasive skills and far-flung contacts to build his own research establishment, the American Health Foundation (AHF), begun in 1969 with four employees (including the indispensable Hoffmann). Wynder proved a prolific fund-raiser, winning major backing from industrialist-philanthropist Norton Simon and the Dana and

Kellogg family foundations. In time, his health enterprise grew into a highly respected research institute with a staff of some 240 and offices in the stylish Ford Foundation headquarters in midtown Manhattan and on a small campus in Westchester, and turned out a series of useful publications including the scholarly journal *Preventive Medicine*, of which Wynder himself served as founding editor. AHF explored many fields, but it never stopped studying smoking and remained the world's leading private repository of knowledge on the subject.

Still, Wynder was viewed as a slightly disreputable operator by some scientists, most of whom specialized in a single discipline while Wynder was co-authoring some 400 articles on smoking that suggested an astonishing breadth of competence. His very versatility and virtuosity invited much skepticism and envy. One leading pathologist expert on the smoking issue granted Wynder a certain technical soundness but sniped, "He's as much a scientist as a bomber pilot is." Part of Wynder's uneasy standing was the single-mindedness of his pursuit in a field that many researchers found simplistic and merely a behavioral problem. Often Wynder shrilly preached to the already converted or the purposely unhearing and disclosed bitterness when little heeded. At times, he conducted himself with a flair not entirely in keeping with the conservative mores of his profession. A bachelor, he zipped about in an open sports car, squired many pretty women including well-known film actresses, frequented smart spots from Beverly Hills to the Hamptons, bought a duplex at New York's UN Plaza complex, and employed a gourmet chef for his entertaining. All of this did not endear him to the scientific establishment, but over time, admiration for Wynder grew, along with his influence. Recalled Frank J. Rauscher, Jr., a microbiologist who served as a top NCI officer in the 'Seventies, "He's a hard S.O.B.—he's good, he thinks he's good, and he'll tell you he's good. But there's nothing phony about Ernie Wynder and his flag-waving on smoking and health. He succeeded because he was needed."

Wynder was also among the first and surely the loudest of the voices in the health community to argue that smokers would not abandon their habit en masse no matter how grave the medical evidence against it, and since government could never, as a practical matter, outlaw tobacco use, it behooved academia and federal officials to join with the cigarette companies in pursuit of the least hazardous cigarette human ingenuity could devise. As one veteran industry lawyer recalled, "Here was the guy with the longest list of publications in the field saying in effect that cigarettes could and should be made safer. This gave encouragement to the manufacturers, who hung on his every suggestion." What did it matter, from the companies' standpoint, if they were pressured into marketing what the medical community judged to be a more acceptable sort of cigarette so long as the modified types sold? And if a new breed of cigarette were certified by government imprimatur to be authentically safer, smokers were less likely to quit and youngsters more likely to take up the habit. So the industry was cordial to Wynder, and he, in turn, ever eager to build his edifice, accepted research assignments from several cigarette companies so long as he was free to publish the findings.

As a self-appointed lobbyist for the less hazardous cigarette, Wynder stalked three prime targets in Washington during the 'Sixties—Senate Commerce Committee chairman Warren Magnuson's chief of staff, Michael Pertschuk; anyone who would listen at the FTC; and the National Cancer Institute. While lung cancer was by then recognized at the NCI as the most prevalent form of the disease, the institute's mission was not viewed as translating new knowledge into cancer control or prevention programs; it existed mainly for the best brains available to undertake basic research into the nature of the disease. Under John Heller, who directed the NCI throughout the 1950s with marked deference to the tobacco industry's defenders in Congress, the accumulating findings on smoking were viewed at the institute as so many scattered data points that did not register very heavily. Even in the early 'Sixties, some strategically placed NCI people were not sold on the need for urgency in addressing the smoking peril. But the 1964 report to the Surgeon General set off a warning gong at NCI. The head of its etiology research program, Carl G. Baker, recounted, "Most of our clinicians had not thought this thing through on causation and the chemistry of carcinogenesis." The Surgeon General's panel, in Baker's words, "woke up a lot of people," among them the new NCI director, Kenneth M. Endicott, a serious smoker who doubted that addicts like himself would ever be motivated to quit, however persuasive the health charges.

But it was precisely that conviction that made Endicott, a warm and somewhat rough-hewn man, innovative scientist, and hands-on administrator, ready prey for Wynder. Though many who enjoyed NCI's rarefied climate thought participation in a nuts-and-bolts endeavor like the development of a less hazardous cigarette was beneath their dignity, Wynder argued to Endicott that in view of the rising lung cancer toll, it was essential that NCI's mission be extended to include saving lives as well as discovering pristine truths. To the argument that development of a less dangerous smoke might serve only to condone continued use of the product and give would-be quitters an easy out, Wynder insisted that the dose-response data was still more persuasive and utopian dreams of mass abandonment of smoking served only to exacerbate the public-health peril.

Not everyone at NCI was smitten by Wynder's proposition. Among the serious doubters was Paul Kotin, then director of NCI's division of environmental health studies. "I thought the idea was . . . scientifically an absurdity," Kotin recounted. Reducing the toxic yields of a cigarette did not necessarily make it less hazardous, he told Endicott and Carl Baker, whom the NCI director named to explore the idea. "You can't tell what will happen by projecting a given level of carcinogenic material or promoters," Kotin contended, while insisting that there was no true threshold of safety for cancer since "any one molecule can react with another." It was a view shared by Endicott's deputy, Jesse Steinfeld, who noted that no given dosage was a surefire predictor of carcinogenesis: "It's a random hit"—which was to say that if the carcinogen did not assault that part of a cell's genetic material concerned with reproduction, the damage might be minimal, or even if the injury was serious, too much was and remained unknown about the DNA splicing process and how readily a given cell could repair itself.

Kotin, who knew the industry better than anyone else at NIH because he had worked with its people for fifteen years by then, wondered what made public-health officials think the tobacco companies would yield their sovereignty to NCI and actually market a cigarette blessed as less hazardous by government scientists. Why undertake that massive research effort when it was the industry's responsibility in the first place? The rank-and-file scientists below the policymaking level at NCI were equally dubious. Most of the benchmen had seen the ravaging effects of lung cancer and knew there was a far simpler and less costly way to reduce the peril: to educate the public not to smoke— and that was a job not for scientists at NCI but for the publicists at the institute's sister organization, the American Cancer Society.

In the end, the judgment had to rest on the relative merit of the proposition. No one was claiming that it was possible to produce an absolutely safe cigarette. The goal was to reduce the risks of smoking, not eliminate them, so that the bulk of the objections were beside the basic point Wynder was making. On reflection, Endicott was persuaded to go along with the less hazardous project at least in part because he recognized a politically viable proposition when he saw one. Jesse Steinfeld, deputy NCI director at the end of the 'Sixties, remembered accompanying Endicott to congressional appropriations sessions where they were confronted by tobacco-state lawmakers who demanded to know just how much the institute—and the HEW Department overall—was spending on "antismoking propaganda." To Steinfeld, "the covert, if not overt, message was that if you wanted your budget passed, you'd better go easy on smoking and health." But a program to develop a less hazardous cigarette seemed to have the dual virtue of engaging public-health concerns yet not threatening the tobacco industry. The task might more nearly resemble an engineering project than a venture on the cutting edge of science, but for Endicott it was a way simultaneously to promote and protect his domain, and he took it.

V

THE Less Hazardous Cigarette Working Group, as it was formally known, began its work in March 1968—the most promising idea to emerge from the presidentially created Lung Cancer Task Force, set up the year before under Kenneth Endicott to combat a disease by then assuming epidemic proportions. The working group, soon headed by NCI's Carl Baker, was composed of some of the brightest minds in the U.S. to address the smoking and health issue, including Ernst Wynder and Paul Kotin. What soon became apparent was the mundane nature of the scientific labor.

It was always possible that a startling breakthrough might occur—a particularly virulent form of carcinogen would be identified as the prime villain and a way found to filter it out of the smoke. But the reality was a painstaking regimen of separating the complex compounds in smoke and testing them for carcinogenicity and other toxic effects by skin-painting and other kinds of bioassay. As the more knowing minds at the industry's Council for Tobacco Research had long been aware, it was hard to attract top-flight scientists to research on smoking; much of the work was irksome, involving smelly smoking machines, the endless painting of mouse backs and tracking of tumors, and similar repetitive tasks that required more patience than insight. And there were few laboratories around the nation with the competence and experience to do such work well, among them Wynder's American Health Foundation and the Arthur D. Little lab in Cambridge, where Charles Kensler had long presided over the tobacco research done for Liggett & Myers. Thus, it was hardly a coincidence that both Wynder and Kensler were members of and key players on the less hazardous task force.

To make it work, then, Carl Baker knew that he could not wait for qualified applicants to ask for the assignment; he had to contract for the work with outside laboratories and let NCI personnel oversee their output. It was precisely the sort of coordinated, targeted effort that the tobacco industry's own designated body, the CTR, had never undertaken. The chief value of the NCI effort was precisely its focus and coordination, even if many within the institute looked down their noses at it. As Frank Rauscher, who headed the national cancer program in the mid-1970s, put it, "Though we didn't know how to do that sort of work, it was necessary science, and it couldn't be left to the tobacco industry, or it wouldn't get done."

And so it happened that the nation's leading cancer investigators found themselves in bed with the tobacco industry. The foreplay proved awkward in the extreme. While the industry had, on the face of it, little to lose from the affair, it was entered into with wariness and uncertainty about where it might lead. Philip Morris Chairman Joseph Cullman recalled his view of the government's less hazardous cigarette program as a possible form of product improvement: "We were happy to cooperate and hopeful something positive would emerge." But the industry could hardly have boycotted the effort without arousing a public outcry and congressional ire. If, on the other hand, it was too avid in its participation, the industry would appear to be conceding the need for such a modified cigarette. It was hard for the tobacco companies, moreover, to know how they would market such a product even if the government was a partner in its development. When Liggett developed a charcoal filter in the early 'Sixties which somewhat reduced the ciliatoxic gases in the Lark and American Tobacco tried a similar approach with Tareyton and Philip Morris with its Saratoga brand, the sales results had been unimpressive. It was a no-win situation for the manufacturers, in the view of Charles Kensler, whose ADL laboratory had played a significant role in the creation of Lark: "How do you know when you've taken everything [hazardous] out?" How, that is, could the industry ever claim it was selling a totally safe cigarette without massive exposure to liability suits? And how could any company boast of a less hazardous product without admitting in the same breath that all of its earlier offerings were *more* hazardous?

Still, the industry had to show up or forfeit the opportunity to affect the course of the federal program. From the opening session in 1968, there was tension in the air as thick as the smoke from Charlie Kensler's cigar and the cigarettes prominently brandished by the industry scientists. The latter seemed at first to be treading on eggshells, unwilling to concede the degree of the health peril claimed by the academics and government scientists in attendance. The company scientists' principal contribution in the early sessions was to insist that the name of their body be changed because of the implications of the term "less hazardous cigarette"; after that, the ad hoc committee was known simply as the Tobacco Working Group (TWG).

At first, according to TWG member Steinfeld, "the industry guys sat around saying not one word but taking notes feverishly." Their purpose, the non-industry people there assumed, was to report back in detail to their superiors and to assure them that the industry was not about to be bushwhacked by the public-health community. The industry scientists surrendered information highly selectively, none of it dealing with any biological findings that their own research had already yielded. The one area in which the company men were forthcoming was the chemistry of tobacco. As TWG Chairman Carl Baker recalled, "They were willing to tell us what they knew about what made up the smoke, the techniques they used to determine it, the size of the particles—nuts-and-bolts stuff they would share. . . . They were . . . useful—so long as you didn't ask them about biology. [And] I could never get the company people to admit that a lowered nicotine level would lead to reduced consumption. They got itchy—I could sense their uneasiness—on the addiction question."

Even by 1971, when Thomas B. Owen joined NCI as a contract administrator in what had come to be known as the Smoking and Health Program (SHP), there was still a palpable "Them Against Us" feeling in the air between the two sides. "The industry crowd wasn't telling us much about what they knew," Owen recounted. "I knew damned well we were talking about problems they had worked on two years earlier. . . . It took quite a while for our people to interface with them and understand that these guys wanted to prevent deaths, too, but couldn't afford to say so." One company scientist who participated in the ten-year program, Thomas Osdene of Philip Morris, recounted with delicacy, "It was rather a cumbersome situation—one put in one's expertise as one knew it—the politics could be rather horrendous." Too much of the research was carried out poorly, Osdene believed, "and there were never any clear-cut answers." For the industry scientists, "being there was like having one hand tied behind your back." They were there, during the life of the program, "to try to be helpful on the technical aspects . . . and not to let the government go down any blind alleys." Others, though, believing the whole enterprise to be a hopeless labyrinth, suspected that the longer government-paid investigators lingered within it, the better for the industry.

V I

RUNNING the Smoking and Health Program's less hazardous cigarette research effort was not a chore that delighted NCI's brainy overseers. The sort of person needed was ideally half diplomat, half detail-man, who was good at dealing with commercial laboratories, scrutinizing contracts, monitoring budgets, sweet-talking politicians, and riding herd on the prima donnas who made up the Tobacco Working Group. Unfortunately, Carl Baker had no one like that on his staff, and few at NCI aspired to the grinding assignment.

But Baker knew a journeyman microbiologist in his late thirties, Gio Batta Gori, a native of Italy, who had been educated at an uncelebrated medical school in his homeland and had worked with varying degrees of success at commercial and corporate labs in the Washington area, hoping to land a spot somewhere within the NIH complex. Personable and attractive, with smooth manners and quick wits, Gori was brought in as Baker's assistant in 1969 and viewed from the first as something less than a sterling addition to the institution. His medical training had been at a backwater school, he had no scholarly publications to speak of, and he brought no depth of knowledge on the nuances of cancer. But Baker, who was a far better scientist than a personnel manager, was willing to look past skepticism over Gori's credentials. "He had a broad

grasp of the issues on the scientific side and of the political realities," Baker recounted, "as well as a good managerial sense. . . . I found him a useful guy."

As long as Baker ran the NCI etiology program, he kept a fairly tight rein on
Gori. But when he succeeded Kenneth Endicott as director of NCI, his place
running etiology and monitoring the Smoking and Health Program was taken
by Frank Rauscher, who felt that the SHP was well launched and that Gori was
qualified to keep it moving forward. "I never viewed him as a scientist,"
Rauscher said of Gori, "but I was impressed by his managerial skill."

After the passage of the National Cancer Act in 1971, NCI's budget began
taking quantum annual leaps that eased residual grumbling within the institute
that the smoking program was siphoning needed funds from more worthy efforts. Increasingly Gori would socialize with Tobacco Working Group members, some of whom—like Wynder, Kensler, and the brilliant chemist Philippe
Shubik, who ran a large laboratory at the University of Nebraska—were also
prime contractors for the less hazardous cigarette program. Such a cozy
arrangement, which under ordinary circumstances would have run afoul of
conflict-of-interest standards, was countenanced in part because of the difficulty involved in finding suitable contractors and in part because the work
turned out by their labs was of superior quality. And it should have been, since
they were for the most part merely replicating their own earlier work but now
using the SHP's experimental cigarettes to conduct their studies. Nor did it
go unnoticed that Gori began to affect a few of the traits of his role model,
Wynder, driving a sporty car and traveling first-class while other NCI officers
settled for coach. His overall conduct earned him the enmity of an Italian
countryman at NCI with far more impressive credentials—Umberto Saffiotti,
Rauscher's assistant director in the carcinogenesis program and highly cautious about the efficacy of a "safer" cigarette. Saffiotti, among others, thought
of Gori more as an impresario than as an objective manager of his contractors,
playing the booster and even the propagandist for a program he was anxious to
build into his own bailiwick.

Characteristic of Gori's tub-thumping were remarks he delivered at the second world conference on smoking and health held in London in September
1971. By way of assuring his listeners that the goal of the NCI effort was no
abstract construct, he said that based on "epidemiological studies, smokers of
filter cigarettes delivering less tar and nicotine show a remarkably decreased
risk of disease; these studies give unequivocal proof in man that reduced tar
and nicotine provide a first model of a less hazardous cigarette." But two of the
three studies Gori cited in support of this gross overstatement had been led by
Wynder and Oscar Auerbach, neither of whom offered such definitive judgments, and the third study, by I. D. Bross, reported a significant reduction in
risk within two years after his subjects switched to lower-yielding brands—a
claim so premature as to be dubious on its face.

Gori's gift for currying favor with Congress earned him enhanced power at NCI. But critics feared that he had grown too chummy with the SHP contractors he was supposed to monitor: Gori's name appeared as co-author of some twenty articles growing directly out of the contract work under his supervision. Such publications fed concerns that Gori and his contractors enjoyed a mutually useful and manipulative relationship rather than one in which he stood apart from them as a rigorous arbiter of their work and the progress of the whole enterprise.

Gori extended his overreach. By the spring of 1974, remarks attributed to him in the unofficial *Cancer Newsletter* stated that the carcinogenic properties of tobacco smoke had been identified, and when reduced, "less cancer will result." He was further quoted as saying that the tobacco industry would be able to produce a cigarette "in no more than three years that could be smoked in moderation (up to a pack a day) with no harmful effects."

That was too much for Saffiotti, who, along with other circumspect investigators, saw lung cancer as an immensely complex disease in which each individual's genetic code and systemic vulnerability came into play along with environmental and occupational variables—all factors that, as Saffiotti later put it, "potentiate one another" and undercut the notion of panaceas. More research was required, along with confirming bioassays conducted over an adequate time span, Saffiotti asserted, dashing cold water on Gori's glowing 1974 picture of SHP's progress, and added, "Until we have those data, it is dangerous to lead people to believe there is a safer cigarette." Another influential NCI scientist, TWG member Marvin Schneiderman, was equally unhappy with Gori's facile evaluation, which he thought benefited the tobacco industry's marketing program. "It's not up to us to find a product they can market," he declared. "Are we the research arm of the tobacco industry?"

Gori's position was by now strong enough to weather such criticism. Saffiotti was regarded by some at NCI as a classic academic stickler who needed every last bit of rock-solid evidence in place before venturing a judgment, while Gori was arguing that public-health considerations demanded action as soon as possible, even if science had not yet reached a definitive conclusion. Still, Gori's remarks were of dubious scientific soundness. Nobody could say that smoking up to a pack of cigarettes a day constituted "moderation," and his endorsement of a threshold level of carcinogenic dosage—"no harmful effects"—was a hotly debated concept. Uneasiness persisted over Gori's incessant and as yet unwarranted optimism, and tensions surrounding his perceived deference to the industry within the SHP occasionally overflowed. The most notable occasion was a TWG meeting in October of 1974, when remarks by Robert Hockett, associate scientific director of the Council for Tobacco Research, in defense of the industry's resistance to the health charges against it, were assailed by member Philippe Shubik. "It shocks me that twenty years later," Shubik told the startled meeting, "you have not joined the community of men. You will go down in history denying facts well known to the scientific community." It angered him, Shubik thundered, that people "who are scientists and know better, offer the arrant nonsense that cigarettes are not a health threat," and he doubted that any among them truly believed that smoking was not "the primary cause of lung cancer."

By 1976, Gori had outflanked Saffiotti, his ranking *bête noire* within NCI, and taken over the added post of deputy director of the Division of Cancer Cause and Prevention. But in the December 17 number of *Science*, Gori crossed his Rubicon with an article bearing the almost sensational title of "Low-Risk Cigarettes: A Prescription." In it, he reported that the technology was now in place to reduce toxic components in cigarette smoke, and thus, "The feasibility of less hazardous cigarettes raises the question of whether there are limits of cigarette and smoke composition that may approach relative safety"—a threshold level, though Gori abstained from using the term. Such limits, he went on, "can be defined as smoke intake dosages at which the risk of disease in smokers approaches that of nonsmokers." These "critical values," as Gori termed them, could be estimated by dose-response analysis of various epidemiological studies, including those that formed the vital bases for the 1964 report to the Surgeon General. That threshold range for all smoke-caused diseases, he calculated, was a dosage equivalent to what a smoker derived from consuming two pre-1960 cigarettes, each containing 43 mg. of tar and 3 mg. of nicotine, per day or a daily pack of a brand yielding 4.3 mg. of tar and 0.3 mg. of nicotine per cigarette. The tables providing these figures were accompanied by extensive footnotes with mathematical formulas and abstract analytical analyses showing how he had reached these "critical values".

But having taken pains to establish the grounds for his calculations in defining "low-risk cigarettes," Gori then befogged the whole argument by stating, "It would be erroneous to interpret these critical values as indicators of safe smoking levels, since the experimental and statistical uncertainties of the [supporting epidemiological] studies are well known . . ."—he had alluded earlier in the article to their differences with respect to design, quality of data, number of subjects, and demographic characteristics. Those same difficulties had confronted statistician William Cochran when he assessed and synthesized them in making his essential contribution to the original Surgeon General's report. But these studies either were valid or were not valid in calculating the relative risks of consuming given dosages of tobacco smoke; Gori seemed to want to have it both ways. The same tendency confused his discussion of whether cigarettes satisfying his "critical values," which he equated with "the maximum number of cigarettes that the average individual could smoke daily without apparently increasing his expected risk of mortality significantly above that of the nonsmoker," were in fact safe or not. Those qualifying words "apparently" and "significantly" were his hedges. "Uncertainty, however," Gori went on, "should not be allowed to dilute the implication of these data, namely, that a rapid shift in cigarette consumption habits toward the proposed range of critical values would make it reasonable to expect that the current epidemic proportions of smoking-related disease could be reduced to minimal levels in slightly over a decade." But wasn't the certainty or uncertainty of the data the heart of the matter in determining whether one should risk smoking even relatively diluted cigarettes?

To understand the thin ice Gori was skating on, one may compare his article with another appearing at the same time, on the same subject, and pointing in the same general direction—" 'Tar' and Nicotine Content of Cigarette Smoke in Relation to Death Rates" in *Environmental Research* by an American Cancer Society team of epidemiologists including Cuyler Hammond, Lawrence Garfinkel, and Herbert Seidman. Drawing their conclusions from a study of more than a million subjects over a dozen years starting in 1959, the investigators reported that for those smoking the same number of cigarettes each day, users of lower-yielding cigarettes (defined as less than 17.6 mg. of tar and 1.2 mg. of nicotine) showed a 16 percent overall lower mortality risk than those using higher-yielding brands (of 25.8 mg. of tar and 2.0 mg. of nicotine or more), a 14 percent lower risk of heart disease, and a 26 percent lower risk of lung cancer. This was a far cry from claiming a reduced risk level approaching that of nonsmokers; indeed, the data in this latest ACS study explicitly stated that nonsmokers had a 34 percent lower overall mortality risk than smokers of lower-yielding cigarettes, a 40 percent lower risk of heart disease, and an 85 percent lower risk of lung cancer. "It is quite apparent that the reduction in the tar and nicotine content of cigarette smoke did *not* make cigarette smoking 'safe' for the men and women in this analysis," Hammond and his colleagues declared—and their data were based on actual smoking histories, not arithmetical computations drawn from hypothetical constructs about total daily dosages.

To be sure, Gori had his defenders, especially among industry-paid scientists and consultants like Charles Kensler of Arthur D. Little, who felt that Gori was unfairly criticized for simply following through on the ideas of Wynder and other ardent supporters of the less hazardous cigarette. Whether there was such a thing as a threshold level of safety in carcinogenic dosage was a matter of debate and opinion, Kensler argued, "but Gori knew all this and said, 'Let's look at the data,' and since all the population studies had dwelt on dose-response as the key supporting correlation, Gori focused on the bottom end of the exposure spectrum, where disease creation was minimal." To Kensler, Gori was simply being logical in pushing hard for attenuated cigarettes. "It was a damned courageous thing for him to do . . . [yet] all the establishment outfits jumped on him," primarily because Gori's program was viewed as perpetuating smoking, in Kensler's view.

At the end of January 1977, a month after his article ran in *Science, The New York Times* featured Gori's program in an article headlined "U.S. Trying to Help Out with a 'Safe' Cigarette." It spoke of the 150 varieties of experimental cigarettes that NCI had developed for the purpose of finding one within what Gori now termed "the tolerable range of risk." Indeed, he elaborated, there were some "ultra-low" tar brands already on the market—none was named—that if smokers used them exclusively, "We'd be in good shape, we'd have no problem." Did that mean they were safe to smoke? It surely sounded that way. But Gori put in his disclaimer: The only truly safe cigarette, he said, was "the one you don't smoke." Then why all this dancing around about "tolerable" levels of risk? The *Times* answer came in the comment that Gori and his project "are eager and compassionate propagandists for weaning the incurable smoker from high-risk smoking to low."

But who yet knew if the ultra-low-yielding brands on the market that Gori referred to would leave their users with, as he put it, "no problem"? Or whether the effect of the lower tar and nicotine levels, as recorded by smoking machines, was lost through the real-life habits of smokers? You could get a lot higher yield from a "low-yield" cigarette if you took more puffs and inhaled them longer and more deeply. And there were other ways to foil such manufacturers' devices for making cigarettes less dangerous as the addition of ventilation holes around the filter to dilute the delivery of carbon monoxide. Psychologist Lynn T. Kozlowski discovered that some smokers kept all those little holes covered with their fingers in order to derive the maximum flavor kick out of each puff. Such hole-blocking, Kozlowski reported in the November 1980 number of the *American Journal of Public Health*, could increase the yield of toxic by-products of smoking by as much as 300 percent. And who knew how much greater the increase was, if any, in toxicity from flavorings or anything else that cigarette makers felt they had to add—without reporting them to any outside regulatory body—to make the taste of their allegedly less hazardous cigarettes more acceptable to smokers accustomed to "full flavor"? A whole new generation would have to come of age before epidemiologists could track those smoking only lower-yielding brands and compare their mortality rates with those of nonsmokers and smokers of higher-yielding brands in order to calculate risk levels of allegedly less hazardous cigarettes. That did not mean that, in the interim, the effort to cut down yields was unworthy—only that high caution ought to be exercised in speaking of the promise such a modified cigarette might hold for smokers.

When Dr. Arthur C. Upton, a former chief of pathology at the Oak Ridge National Laboratories, took over as director of NCI in 1977, he had to address two principal concerns regarding the value of the less hazardous cigarette project. First, the contracts for the research were peer-reviewed either inadequately or not at all. "The sense was that there was too much favoritism, too much back-scratching, collusion, and at best irresponsible uses made of the money," said Upton, who ordered a gradual shift from contract research to grants made on a strictly merit basis. Second, there was Gori himself, who was seen by some as beyond the control of his divisional director and "not a credible spokesman," as Upton phrased the consensual assessment, "for the large cadre of technical people" who formed the backbone of NCI. "They questioned his ability and capacity to reflect what they were doing" and wondered if he was in beyond his depth. Upton himself found Gori to be "decent, thoughtful, decisive," and what he lacked in the way of scientific credentials, "he compensated for by his dedication to the job."

The delicacy of Gori's position under a new NCI chief, an outsider who did not care for bureaucratic boondoggling, was underscored by the growing realization that, for all the hopeful talk, his program had not yielded any notable breakthroughs. Summed up Frank Resnik, who had started as a research chemist at Philip Morris in the 'Fifties and ran operations at the company's research center in the 'Seventies, "NCI did a lot of work, but they didn't come up with anything more than the industry had." Many public-health officials were coming to the conclusion that NCI needed a broader focus if smoking was to be combated and not condoned in a dilute, but possibly still fatal, form.

VII

HISTORY is perhaps less likely to judge Jimmy Carter an ineffectual President than it is to note with astonishment how so obscure a figure ever came to occupy the White House. Similarly, Carter should be less faulted, perhaps, for having played a hypocritical game on the smoking issue than commended, given his political base in the same geographical region as the tobacco industry, for having allowed his administration to pay even lip service to the public-health need for curbing cigarette use.

An outsider in Washington and suspicious of the capital's power brokers, Carter surrounded himself for the most part with an inner circle of like-minded, down-home advisors. But to manage the government's most unwieldy bureau, the Health, Education, and Welfare Department, he chose as Secretary a classic, aggressive Washington insider. Robert Strauss, Democratic Party chairman, advised the President-elect, "If you pick Joe Califano, he'll irritate you every single day, but at the end of the day you'll look back and see he's been a great asset." And competence more than personal compatibility was what Carter needed to bring order to HEW, a potpourri of 150 programs,

150,000 employees, and a 36 percent slice of the federal budgetary pie. Administrative mistakes were routine, contracting and accounting procedures a muddle, and fraud and other abuses rampant.

Joseph Anthony Califano, Jr., a short, plumpish, Harvard-educated attorney, was known to be a good-humored and compassionate political activist who, as a powerful assistant to President Lyndon Johnson, had helped formulate and drive through the Great Society social programs. But Califano was also known as complicated, nakedly ambitious, and sometimes brutal in seeing that his orders were followed. A Brooklyn-born graduate of Holy Cross, he had made the law review at Harvard, joined the Wall Street firm of Dewey, Ballantine after military service, and gone to work for the Kennedy administration like many another high-minded young attorney, starting as an assistant counsel in the Pentagon under Robert McNamara. By the age of thirty-three, he was general counsel to the U.S. Army and soon on his way to the White House, where he served as a key aide until Nixon ousted the Democrats in 1968. Califano then became one of the most highly paid lawyers and effective lobbyists in Washington.

At HEW, Califano promptly showed his spine when he declined to staff his department with political pals of dubious talent sent to him by the White House staff chief, Hamilton Jordan, who early on took a dislike to him for failing to play ball. Califano put together a heavy agenda to help the ill, the needy, the poorly schooled, and others he thought had been neglected under eight years of Republican rule. The programs his department advanced were costly and controversial, and Califano soon found himself a convenient lightning rod for an ideologically moderate and politically insecure White House.

With so much else on his plate, Califano did not pay much attention to the smoking issue until toward the end of his first year running HEW. But he had asked his Surgeon General—a post that had lain dormant for four years—to look into the matter, and Julius B. Richmond, a soft-spoken pediatrician who, in keeping with his specialty, was a strong advocate of preventive medicine, suggested an aggressive attack on tobacco. Califano was receptive for two reasons. In drawing up his HEW program, he was repeatedly told that preventive medicine was the key to extracting maximum value from the government's investment in public-health measures. The drop then being achieved in heart disease, for example, was due in no small measure to new dietary and exercise habits taken up by a population freshly aware of their role in enjoying a full, hardy life. Califano, moreover, had been jarred into adjusting his own health habits two years earlier, after he asked one of his sons what he would like as a present for his eleventh birthday. The lad told his father, who had begun smoking at sixteen and was now up to three packs a day, that he would like no greater gift than Califano's quitting the habit. And he did, painfully.

But an administration program to combat smoking was sure to be a political hot potato. Indeed, one of the proposals offered the Secretary by Surgeon General Richmond's task force on tobacco control—ending the Department of Agriculture's $80 million price support program for a crop that did grave damage to the public health—ran into trouble as soon as word circulated in the capital that HEW was even contemplating such a recommendation. Agriculture Secretary Bob Bergland promptly made his opposition known in noting that his responsibility "begins and ends with the interests of the farmers. . . . The Department of Agriculture cannot involve itself in the health aspects of tobacco." Presumably Bergland would have opposed the added costs of milk pasteurization as an undue burden on dairy farming, had he held office at the time that advance in public health was made. A delegation of tobacco-state lawmakers hastened to the White House for assurances that the price support program was not about to be gutted.

On January 11, 1978, the fourteenth anniversary of the first report on smoking and health issued by the Surgeon General's office, Secretary Califano outlined an anticigarette program that was by far the most vigorous of any ever proposed by a U.S. official of Cabinet rank. Declaring smoking a major cause of an estimated 320,000 deaths a year in the U.S., nearly two-thirds of them a result of heart disease, Califano labeled cigarettes "Public Health Enemy No. 1" and said their users were committing "slow-motion suicide." He called upon every school in America to teach its students the dire risks of the habit; upon the Civil Aeronautics Board to ban smoking on all commercial flights; upon Congress to increase the federal excise tax on cigarettes (fixed at eight cents a pack for the preceding twenty-seven years); upon the broadcast networks to reinstate their free, prime-time antismoking announcements; upon his own vast agency to prohibit smoking on its premises except in explicitly designated areas, and upon other departments and the General Services Administration, which managed some 10,000 federal buildings across the nation, to follow suit. The Secretary also said he would soon move the practically defunct U.S. Clearinghouse on Smoking and Health back to Washington from its four-year exile to Atlanta and rename it the Office on Smoking and Health.

Public-health advocates like John Banzhaf's ASH and the consumer groups allied with Ralph Nader dismissed Califano's call as all gesture and little substance. HEW's proposed antitobacco budget of $25 to $30 million was denounced as a spit in the ocean to counter the billion dollars then being spent by the industry on advertising and promotion—and it was laughably small when compared even to the $250 million that HEW itself had squandered not long before on a mass inoculation campaign to head off a phantom swine flu epidemic. The Califano antismoking program was a popgun attack when heavy cannons were what the public-health community had in mind.

To the tobacco industry and its defenders, growing ever more paranoid,

Califano's words were a red flag. Kentucky's Senator Walter Huddleston, a reliable defender of his state's big Burley crop, reflexively denounced Califano for proposing "a massive propaganda campaign against cigarette smoking without having sufficient scientific evidence to justify it." North Carolina's Jesse Helms faulted the HEW Secretary for "demonstrating callous disregard for economic realities, particularly for the economy of North Carolina," while that state's governor, Jim Hunt, urged Califano to come for a visit so he could learn what the tobacco crop meant to Tarheel farmers. U.S. Representative Charlie Rose, not to be outdone in the stout defense of his constituents, promised, "We're going to have to educate Mr. Califano with a two-by-four, not a trip." The health worries of tens of millions of their countrymen did not enter into this elevated discussion.

The industry's own spokesmen stressed the claimed $50 billion that the tobacco companies contributed to the gross national product and the alleged 2.3 percent of U.S. employment accounted for by the smoking business. At one extreme, Califano was attacked crudely and in a personally offensive manner by Liggett & Myers's chairman, Raymond Mulligan, as "a silly ass." At the other end of the subtlety spectrum was a letter to the editor appearing in *The New York Times* from Philip Morris's president, Ross Millhiser, who argued that if cigarettes were not beneficial to smokers, there would not be so many of them, and cited several among the relatively short list of contrarian scientists who did not accept the health charges against smoking. "As for the lack of research on the 'harmful' effects of smoking," Millhiser went on, "the fact is there is good reason to doubt the culpability of cigarette smoking in coronary heart disease." The "fact," actually, was quite the opposite. Only thirteen months earlier, to cite just one study of many by then implicating smoking in heart disease, Oscar Auerbach had reported that autopsy studies on 1,056 men disclosed, upon microscopic examination, a rate of advanced atherosclerosis 4.4 times higher among men who smoked two or more packs of cigarettes a day than among nonsmokers, while somewhat more moderate thickening afflicted the heart vessels of 72.6 percent of those smoking one to two packs a day, compared with 29 percent among nonsmokers. Still more dubious than Millhiser's comments were the remarks of Philip Morris's honey-voiced chief publicist, James Bowling, who told *Business Week*, "I really believe the Califano type of thing is a tragic disservice to science. The real need is to find answers."

Far more surprising than the industry's response to the Califano program was the duplicitous game played by the White House under a President who had been an enlightened advocate of preventive public-health measures while governor of Georgia and whose own father, a heavy smoker, had died of lung cancer. The politically adept Califano had not looked for vocal White House support in promulgating his antismoking project. "It was too controversial," he recounted, "and not the kind of issue you dump on the White House doorstep." Carter, he knew, "wouldn't want to go out front on it."

The President and his people, apprised of Califano's antismoking initiative before it was launched, distanced themselves from the HEW Secretary's effort without disavowing it. A few weeks in advance of Califano's speech, Peter Bourne, a psychiatrist who served as special White House assistant on health issues, addressed the American Cancer Society's committee on smoking research and sounded more like a Tobacco Institute publicist than a public-health officer. Bourne spoke admiringly of the emotionally stabilizing effects of tobacco and cautioned against an excessive repression of smokers' "rights" by restricting the places where they could indulge their habit, as Califano would shortly propose with regard to federal office buildings. When Califano asked to deliver his initial antismoking speech from a White House rostrum, he was turned down. After the antismoking drive went public, Bourne continued to offer sniping comments, speaking of the "pleasure and relief factor" in smoking, questioning the cost-effectiveness of "programs designed to scare young people out of smoking," and needling that however much some people might favor the prohibition of tobacco, "we are 300 years too late"—as if a quarter-century of scientific findings on the hazards of smoking did not justify governmental steps to discourage the lethal habit. "The sole thing dictating what I did," Bourne later told a British journalist, "was what was in Carter's interest in maintaining his political base."

The administration declined to take up Califano's suggestion to all federal administrators to restrict smoking on their premises, and the President himself reassured the South generally and tobacco farmers specifically that they had little to fear from the HEW antismoking campaign. By the spring of 1978, the *Washington Monthly* was quoting well-placed Democratic officials as saying that the President and his staff were unhappy with Califano for "making war on [Carter's] voter base" and that the HEW Secretary's "loyalties just don't run to the President. His loyalties are to himself."

VIII

THE strategic core of Joseph Califano's effort to achieve a major shift in the social acceptability of smoking was the argument that the freedom of young people to make an informed choice in the matter was massively compromised by the tobacco industry's ceaseless campaign to glamorize its product and sow confusion and doubt about the grave risks that accompanied its use. He wrote to the nation's 16,000 school superintendents to push smoking education programs, to the broadcast networks to increase their public-service announcements, to life and health insurance companies to lower their premiums for nonsmokers, to the governor of every state to back laws restricting smoking in public places, and to medical groups to implore high-risk smokers, such as pregnant women, to avoid the danger they were courting. And every chance he got he spoke out against cigarettes, soon prompting bumper stickers to sprout in tobacco country that declared, "Califano Is Dangerous to Your Health."

One-man crusades rarely get very far, though, and so Califano turned to the only operation within his department's huge apparatus which was devoted to addressing the public on the smoking problem. "I was appalled by what I found," he recalled—the old U.S. Clearinghouse on Smoking and Health had become a tiny hovel at the Centers for Disease Control in Atlanta. Only two hands were left from the Clearinghouse's exuberant pioneer days as an effective public-education shop—the aging ex-director, Daniel Horn, no longer a strong functioning force, and his devoted technical information officer, the modest Donald Shopland.

Califano ordered a fresh effort, to operate out of the capital once again for improved access to national media, and renamed it the Office on Smoking and Health (OSH). To run it he chose John M. Pinney, who had no expertise in the subject and no compensating scientific or technical training. But the 1965 graduate of Yale was cocky and verbally slick and knew his way around Washington. His professional credentials consisted of two years as an administrative assistant in the HEW Secretary's office and five with the National Council on Alcoholism, the last three running its Washington office. So Pinney knew a thing or two about addiction and was politically adroit enough to take the OSH post only when it was yoked to his designation as an Assistant HEW Secretary, giving him direct access to Califano and Surgeon General Richmond. The latter, while seriously concerned about smoking, lacked the forcefulness to project the issue and delegated much of the task to the eager Pinney.

The new OSH director had a clear-eyed view of HEW's only other effort on the smoking problem, the National Cancer Institute's program under Gio Gori to develop a less hazardous cigarette: "It would be hard to have thought up a more ludicrous thing than this for the U.S. government to be spending public dollars on—for something the industry itself should have been doing. . . . [I]t was a waste of money and time when the bastards knew more than we knew, and the NCI could point to [its Smoking and Health Program] and say to Congress that it was doing something. I felt it was wrong and a sham."

To gear up his own operation, Pinney brought back the old Clearinghouse's gifted publicist, Robert Hutchings, who was rejuvenated by "the excitement of a new enterprise" that Pinney generated, with Califano as a spiritual and at times almost corporeal presence. "You could hear his voice coming over the phone down the hall," Hutchings remembered. But Pinney's budget was not large enough to accommodate a full-time medical officer or scientific director, a void that became all too noticeable as he set out to satisfy his primary command from Califano and Richmond—producing a new Surgeon General's report on smoking to be issued on the fifteenth anniversary of the original one and to set a new standard for accuracy and comprehensiveness.

"We designed the 1979 report to put an end to the controversy the industry kept alive over whether smoking was a health peril," Pinney recounted. "It had to be a single volume, no matter how large—I insisted on it—so that you could take it in and throw it down before a congressional committee and say, in effect, 'There it all is, gentlemen.'" Pinney had only nine months to produce that volume. The OSH staff was overwhelmed by the scope and depth of knowledge needed to carry out the assignment, and it was August by the time Pinney got the idea of summoning a reluctant Shopland, who had been involved in every Surgeon General's report from the first, back from Atlanta. Shopland found the effort "a shambles," especially the chapter on causality, which was loaded with technical detail but failed to spell out the degree of risk adequately, and the one on heart disease, which lacked hard data and illustrative tables. "If it hadn't been for Shopland," said Pinney, "I don't think we would have succeeded."

Shopland knew where to turn for authoritative writers, editors, and reviewers. His chief recruit was a brilliant, Harvard-educated pulmonologist, David M. Burns, then thirty-one, who had been the Clearinghouse's medical officer at the end of its residence in Washington and the beginning of its exile to Atlanta before he transferred to the University of California Medical Center at San Diego to pursue his specialty. Burns hurried to Washington to help Shopland unscramble the mess and then worked over the emerging text from his West Coast base. The team succeeded not least because Burns understood Shopland's unique skills. "He is a testament to the good things that can happen in government service to someone who's bright, conscientious, selfless, and focused," said Burns. "He put purpose and effort ahead of his own advancement, he sacrificed himself. . . . He could argue with Ph.D.'s at the NIH and deal with people who headed big programs, because he always had the facts and had them right. . . ." Shopland also wrote with what Burns called "a remarkable grasp of what the critical elements were," as the pair of them reshaped and reorganized the mass of material pouring in on them.

To raise the report to a higher level of scholarly acceptance required the enlistment of top-flight peer-reviewers, whose critical appraisals of the steadily growing mass of findings had to be integrated into the emerging text if it was to constitute a true scientific consensus. It was no easy task to find reviewers with both a detailed knowledge of the field and what Burns termed "a global view". He added, "And the science had to be watertight and not step beyond the evidence, because you knew it wasn't just going to slide by out there."

This high degree of scientific conservatism meant there could be no such thing as pride of authorship during the process. Writers, who were paid a few thousand dollars to compose a chapter, understood that they were participating in a group project and knew that the editors and peer-reviewers might pull their prose apart. The reviewers were not paid at all, Shopland recounted, "because we didn't want them to feel beholden," *i.e.*, to slant their critical evaluations in a way they may have felt the OSH preferred and thus assure themselves of a reward. In marked contrast to many of the scientists paid to vouch for the industry's denials or nitpick the medical evidence against smoking, those who worked on the Surgeon General's report did so not for monetary gain but largely for the professional recognition that came to them for weighing the case strictly on the merits of the evidence.

The 1979 Surgeon General's Report and those immediately succeeding it attained a breadth of scope, precision of balance, and degree of completeness rarely if ever matched in the annals of public-health literature. No other pathological process got reviewed with the same intensive, ongoing scrutiny for so many years as smoking and its ravages, and while the reports were largely incomprehensible to laymen, they effectively put an end to the scientific "controversy," which lingered in the public's mind only because the cigarette makers had the money, power, and brass to claim that there still was one.

IX

ALTHOUGH Jimmy Carter remained aloof from the public-policy issues surrounding smoking, he had made another appointment in addition to Califano that would eventually have an impact on government regulation of cigarettes. Asked by the President who could chair the Federal Trade Commission most ardently in the public interest, Ralph Nader had recommended the Senate Commerce Committee's chief counsel and staff director, Michael Pertschuk, who for thirteen years had helped shape consumer-friendly laws. Pertschuk cut a unique figure among Capitol Hill operatives, in his horn-rimmed glasses, turtleneck shirts, and tweed jackets. But a guileless manner and disarming humor were deceptive accouterments of a politically activist tendency with which he animated the commission as never before in its lackluster history.

Pertschuk did not give the smoking issue much priority at first, though he had had a major role in every measure, however ineffectual, the government had taken in the previous dozen years to regulate the cigarette companies. Part of this hesitancy stemmed from Pertschuk's uncertainty about what action the FTC could now undertake that would be tolerated by the industry and its allies in Congress. A toughened warning label was talked about, but few believed that any warning would do much good, and while some hyperactivists favored extending the broadcast ban to include all cigarette advertising, the most that realists were willing to propose was limiting cigarette print ads to the "tombstone" format of text without illustrative elements beyond a picture of the brand package. But the prospects for such a curb were bleak, and Pertschuk chose instead to press other battles, including those against abuses in the television advertising of children's products and the exploitation of the poor, gullible, and otherwise vulnerable by, among others, funeral directors, used-car dealers, mobile-home manufacturers, and life and health insurance companies.

All this out-front activity came at a time when the public was losing its sense of outrage over unethical business practices against consumers—a shift that Pertschuk had not detected. Instead of lubricating congressional concern with quiet backroom dealing of the sort he had mastered while working on Capitol Hill, Pertschuk assumed a noisy, even tactless tone in his pronouncements and soon was perceived in Congress as overreaching for power. Influential enemies began to tab the FTC chief as a nagging nanny to the nation.

With regard to the cigarette business, such "nannyism" in the form of state paternalism—*i.e.*, telling people to do what was good for them—had ample justification. Parents did not usually allow their children to suffer by learning from experience about the perils of electric sockets, household poisons, railroad crossings, and the like, and so the government, acting *in loco parentis*, had a vital role to play in warning youngsters about the risks of smoking. As James Fallows observed in his article "The Cigarette Scandal" in the February 1976 *Washington Monthly*, "The forces that draw children toward smoking in those awkward teenage years may be only temporary, but the consequences are not." That same year, the FTC had initiated an investigation to determine whether government actions had "effectively remedied deceptive practices" by the cigarette industry's advertising. Did the companies' marketing strategy amount to wholesale seduction of the innocent? Did their ads deal adequately with the probability or severity of the dangers of smoking? How much did the public really know and understand about this subject? Were the current warning labels useful? What further steps ought the government to take?

Pertschuk added impetus to the inquiry by insisting that the industry provide not only routine data on its advertising and promotion outlays but also any extant documents detailing advertising strategies, what efforts the cigarette manufacturers had undertaken to attract new smokers, and any research studies they had conducted about smoking behavior. When the industry balked at this as an invasion of privacy and its right to do business free of harassment, the FTC issued fifty-six subpoenas requiring the companies, their ad agencies, and research consultants to provide documentation of their marketing programs and strategies dating back to 1964. The commission offered assurances that all documents would be kept confidential, but the industry, dismissing the pledge as meaningless and the whole sweeping investigation as a fishing expedition, went to court and for more than two years kept Nanny Pertschuk and his staff at bay.

During that period, the commission staff persevered, and its findings were not encouraging. The per capita consumption of cigarettes by Americans eighteen or older had barely dropped, from 10.97 to 10.57 cigarettes a day, between 1970 and 1979, and smoking was on the rise among teenagers and women. Taking inflation into account, the cigarette companies were spending 50 percent more on advertising and promotion by 1979 than they had in 1967, and theirs had become the most heavily advertised product in the U.S. economy. R. J. Reynolds was the largest individual advertiser in American magazines, and almost half of all billboards across the land were pitching cigarettes.

Thematically, cigarette ads had not materially altered their practice of associating smoking with youthful vigor, sports and other strenuous activities, and social, professional, and sexual success. It was as if all the industry ad codes had never existed. Kool still tasted like "menthol mist" materializing from a picture-book waterfall or ocean spray, and "country fresh Salem" was still synonymous with "light mountain breezes" and "clear rippling waters." Camel Filter invoked boldness and adventure: "Some men taste it all." Old Gold displayed a young backpacker taking a smoking break while overlooking an expansive valley from a mountain crag. Winston was being pushed as a totem of adulthood; it was the brand that "may not be where you start. But when your taste grows up, Winston is for real." Brands aimed at the health-conscious were less subtle than earlier in implying a margin of safety: "With Vantage, I don't have as many problems with smoking." Lorillard went a step beyond that: "Considering all I'd heard, I decided to either quit or smoke True. I smoke True"—as if to say the alternatives were equally therapeutic. And, of course, nowhere in any cigarette ad, even in the government's warning label, was there a hint of the grave reality of the habit: one in seven U.S. deaths was thought to be smoke-related; pack-a-day smokers had a life expectancy six years shorter—and two-pack-a-day smokers eight years shorter—than nonsmokers; a smoker was 70 percent more likely to die at any given age than a nonsmoker; and 70 percent of lung cancer victims died within a year of detection.

The image merchants of Madison Avenue were more than capable, moreover, of upstaging the warning message from the Surgeon General. The FTC regulators, mostly lawyers, had naturally been inclined, as wordsmiths, to dwell on the textual content of cigarette ads rather than their visual aspects. But even untutored analysis of the industry's print advertising disclosed how effectively it had used overpowering graphics—bold imagery, lush landscapes, huge scale, vivid coloration, sharp contrast, simulated movement—to divert the reader's eye from the health warning. In an astute article titled "Graphic Propositions" in the *Tobacco Products Litigation Reporter*, Charles Zerner of the Massachusetts College of Art analyzed a number of 1974 cigarette ads and concluded that the cigarette makers' skillful disguising of the cautionary message and use of thematic implications contradictory to the warning label could well amount to a negligent failure to warn smokers. No company was more adept at this artifice than Philip Morris, and no brand more skillfully took the smoker's mind off the health risk than Marlboro. A classic instance was its ad in the February 2, 1974, issue of *Newsweek* showing a pair of horsemen set against a latticework of snow-clad birches in what Zerner described as "a landscape of poeticized winter-white images" over which the thick, white, Old West–style letters of the brand name "float like manufactured clouds above the environmental drama of Marlboro Man, horses and snow." The effect was to suggest that Marlboro was inextricably bound up with nature itself, that Marlboro smokers were rugged and capable, that inhaling Marlboro filled you with air as pure as wilderness and crisp as winter, and that "Marlboro Country," as Zerner put it, "is breathing room. In its immensity and exteriority it is . . . a pictorial counterbalance to what many smokers have come to experience and fear: the constricted, polluted, stained, and diseased interiority of cancerous lungs." Thus was the warning label trivialized.

The cigarette makers, moreover, made such heavy use of print advertising throughout the 'Seventies that they succeeded in further diluting the health community's message by simply buying off the message-bearers. In the January 1978 issue of the *Columbia Journalism Review*, R. C. Smith reported on a survey he had taken of press coverage of the smoking issue in periodicals during the seven years since the ban on broadcast advertising of cigarettes had gone into effect—a span during which the proportion of cigarette ads in magazines had doubled. Journalistic purists might have hoped that the press could keep its news columns fiercely independent of commercial considerations, thus allotting smoking the play it deserved among the pressing social concerns of the day. "Such simply has not been the case," Smith wrote, noting that his survey revealed "a striking and disturbing pattern. In magazines that accept cigarette advertising I was unable to find a single article, in seven years of publication, that could have given readers any clear notion of the nature and extent of the medical and social havoc being wreaked by the cigarette smoking habit." Neither *Time* nor *Newsweek*, to cite two of Smith's examples of flagrant nonfeasance, "has published anything resembling a comprehensive account of the subject," while carrying six to eight pages of cigarette advertising per issue. Smith was forced to conclude that "advertising revenue can indeed silence the editors of American magazines."

The inadequate press coverage of the smoking issue inevitably had its effect on the public's understanding of it, as FTC staff investigators learned when they conducted a pair of surveys of their own and uncovered privately taken opinion samplings by the Gallup and Roper polling organizations involving more than 8,000 consumers. The combined findings were that many people in fact did not know just how dangerous smoking was and what specific diseases it was causally linked to: 20 percent did not know smoking caused lung cancer, more than 30 percent were unaware of its link to heart disease, 40 percent of smokers thought only heavy smoking was dangerous, half of those polled did not know smoking could be addictive, and 60 percent did not know it caused emphysema. Nearly half the college-educated subjects in the sampling did not believe the statement that in industrialized nations cigarette smoking was the greatest single cause of excess deaths (*i.e.*, beyond normal actuarial probability); twice as many believed traffic accidents were a greater killer than smoking as those who knew the truth.

The FTC investigation moved into high gear after a January 1979 U.S. district court ruling in the commission's favor, giving it access to the tobacco companies' market research documents. The commission was fully within its rights, the court held, and did not have to specify its purpose in seeking the documents; the industry's cost of compliance, claimed to run into the millions, was minor relative to its financial position, the federal ruling added, "and when measured against the public interest of this investigation." Most cigarette makers, unafraid that the documents would hurt them since their lawyers had long since instructed tobacco executives not to commit sensitive words to paper, complied with the court order, but Brown & Williamson, in a fit of pique over what it called reckless bullying by a federal agency, overcomplied. It delivered a seven-ton truckload with 750,000 pages of documents, hoping to smother the FTC staff with a blizzard of irrelevant paper. The company's truculence was met by the commission staff's diligence; the most damaging evidence of the industry's eagerness to enlist young smokers was uncovered in nuggets panned from the Brown & Williamson mother lode. Among these was a report by Marketing & Research Counselors, Inc., hired by B&W's ad agency, Ted Bates, in 1975 to help plan the revitalization of the Viceroy brand and improve its appeal to youngsters. "For them, a cigarette, and the whole smoking process, is part of the illicit pleasure category. . . ," the consulting firm advised Bates. "To the best of your ability (considering some legal constraints) relate the cigarette to 'pot,' wine, beer, sex, etc. *Don't* communicate health or health-related points." FTC investigators determined that many of the ideas in this report for Bates found their way into the 1976 campaign for Viceroy, including two basic premises as spelled out by Brown & Williamson group project director V. C. Broach, in a March 3, 1976, report entitled "Viceroy Strategy". The campaign ought to provide consumers with a rationalization for smoking, Broach urged, and a "means of repressing their health concerns about smoking a full flavor Viceroy."

Despite findings by FTC investigators that Brown & Williamson employed these strategies and ideas embodied in the research by Bates and its consultants over a six-month campaign in three test markets, the company denied that it had ever heeded such advice and insisted, as did every other cigarette manufacturer before, during, and since the FTC probe, that it did not direct its advertising toward young people in the hope of recruiting them to smoking. None of them, though, ever explained how an industry that lost hundreds of thousands of customers to death each year and several million more who quit using its product could afford *not* to try to enlist customers of any age.

14

The Heights of Arrogance

Two-faced politicians, bent upon gaining and holding power and never spending it on risky causes, rarely beguile the electorate with a matched set of profiles in courage. The most they can manage, upon being unmasked, is to invite some laughter over the display of duplicity. So it was in August 1978 when Jimmy Carter, having publicly neither embraced nor disavowed his HEW Secretary's antismoking crusade, traveled to the heart of tobaccoland to damage the Senate reelection campaign of Republican right-winger Jesse Helms and to advance the President's own standing in the Tarheel State, thought to be pivotal to his own reelection prospects two years hence.

Carter told a crowd of tobacco warehousemen that he had planned to bring along that infamous former smoker, Joe Califano, until he discovered that North Carolina was not only the top tobacco-growing state "but that you produce more bricks than anyone in the nation as well." Instead of summoning the courage to justify the national need to relieve the health peril that their leading crop carried with it, Carter waxed poetic about "the beautiful quality of your tobacco," pledging his continued backing of the federal price support program for the crop and of the government's research "to make the smoking of tobacco even more safe than it is today."

That very day in Chicago, the American Medical Association's Education and Research Fund released *Tobacco and Health*, a 369-page, lavishly printed report on its study, initiated in 1964 and carried out through the tobacco industry's funding of 844 researchers at some one hundred institutions. The outcome of this prodigious labor proved to be nothing more than a grab bag of abstracts of the mostly unrelated studies, with a two-page summation dated fifteen months earlier, a sign of the urgency level of the project. Instead of a digest of findings from a carefully structured investigation that one might have supposed to be the ambition of the nation's largest medical organization, the summary noted merely that "the bulk of the research . . . supports the contention that cigarette smoking plays an important role in the development of chronic obstructive pulmonary diseases and constitutes a grave danger to individuals with preexisting diseases of the coronary arteries."

This revelation added nothing whatever to the findings fourteen years earlier by the original Surgeon General's committee on smoking and entirely skipped over any appraisal of the habit's link to lung cancer—on the excuse that the National Cancer Institute was adequately funding research on that subject. Most of the AMA-ERF studies listed in *Tobacco and Health* were at best tangentially related to the smoking and health question.

President Carter, advised of the AMA report while still genuflecting in North Carolina, promised to "read about it" back in the White House; nothing further was ever said of the findings, which, soft-pedaled though they were, made plain that beneath tobacco's "beautiful quality" lurked great danger. Nor was the AMA's virtual whitewash subjected to a deserved lashing for dereliction of professional duty by the government's little Office on Smoking and Health, whose director, John Pinney, recounted, "We didn't have the option to criticize the report." Such forthrightness would have plunged the Carter administration into deeper hot water in tobacco country, but the spirited band at the OSH was contemptuous nonetheless. "Why did it take them [the AMA-ERF] fourteen years to produce it? The whole thing was sinful," said Pinney.

Two days later the tobacco industry had still further reason to smile when the press got hold of an article awaiting publication at the AMA's flagship journal, *JAMA*. The author was Dr. Gio Gori, director and indefatigable hawker of the NCI's smoking and health program, who, as if impervious to the undertow of criticism charging that his enterprise was riddled with cronyism, had collaborated on the *JAMA* piece, "Toward Less Hazardous Cigarettes: Current Advances," with Cornelius J. Lynch, manager of NCI-funded smoking research at Enviro Control, Inc., of Rockville, Maryland, one of Gori's main contractors. Gori and Lynch claimed that cigarettes with a "tolerable risk" level were at hand, thanks to major (but unspecified) strides that had been taken in the past eighteen months.

This sensational claim grew out of the authors' calculations based on not only the tar (43 mg. on average) and nicotine yield of the average pre-1960 cigarette but also the dosages of four other known, major toxic components of tobacco smoke—carbon monoxide, nitrogen oxide, hydrogen cyanide, and acrolein—and their conclusion that two such cigarettes constituted the "critical level" of smoking (*i.e.*, no greater risk than from no smoking at all). Gori and Lynch then measured the amount of these six destructive ingredients in the smoke of twenty-seven current so-called low-tar (15 mg. or less) brands and interpolated to determine how many of the latter were needed to deliver the same concentration of these substances as were contained in two pre-1960 cigarettes. Thus, for Benson & Hedges Light, with a rating of 10.1 mg. of tar, the equivalent number of cigarettes would be 8.5, producing the total of 86 mg. of tar yielded by two pre-1960, "tolerable risk" cigarettes. Other brands in the Gori-Lynch calculations produced spectacularly higher equivalency figures: You could smoke twenty-three Carlton menthol cigarettes, seventeen Nows, eighteen Trues, and seven Pall Mall Extra Milds at the "tolerable risk" level, they said. To be sure, the authors added a disclaimer: Their calculations were "based on the assumption" that the smoker of these current, apparently less lethal brands "will not change his smoking habits in terms of depth of inhalation, frequency of puffing, and butt length." The article, when it appeared in the September 15, 1978, *JAMA*, concluded with the prescriptive comment that persuading the smoker "to wean himself to progressively less hazardous cigarettes may provide an alternative to smoking cessation that is perhaps more effective than the self-denial approaches of current antismoking messages"—like those (though the article did not cite him) by HEW Secretary Califano—"[and] reduce the current epidemic of smoking-associated diseases to a considerably less serious health problem."

In remarks to the Washington *Post* of August 10, 1978, Gori said, "I am not calling any cigarette safe," and noted that his calculations did not necessarily apply to any given individual's risk. But he stressed that recent technological developments now made it possible to speak of "tolerable" levels of smoking "from an overall public health standpoint." The *Post* accompanied its report on the Gori-Lynch findings with a double-column boxed listing of the twenty-seven low-tar brands tested and how many of each you could smoke at a "tolerable" risk. "We are not trying to endorse cigarettes or smoking in any way," Gori contended. "We are only trying to put the facts before the public."

But they were not facts; they were a theoretical hypothesis based on a set of untried assumptions. An angry Califano read about them and how the officer in his department charged with managing its smoking research program was saying things that seemed to cut the legs out from under his anticigarette drive. NCI director Arthur Upton remembered getting a phone call around midnight, soon after the *Post* had hit the street with the front-page headline, "SMOKING: Some Cigarettes Now 'Tolerable,' Doctor Says"—and it was not just any doctor. "He was mad as hops," Upton said, "and asking me who the hell Gio Gori is," as well as whether the NCI chief had read the offending study by Gori and Lynch. Upton had not, because the article had been passed on by an NCI reviewer some months before Upton had come to the institute and because Gori had not been astute or forthright enough to bring it to the new director's attention.

Upton roused his top biostatitician, Marvin Schneiderman, then vacationing in Maine, and sought his views on Gori's article. Schneiderman had indeed seen Gori's computations and told Upton that by his arithmetic, smoking two of the unfiltered, pre-1960 cigarettes a day was sufficient to double a smoker's risk of lung cancer. He thought Gori's claim was "overstated and wrong" and added his belief that there was simply no known threshold of safety for lung cancer. "My concern was that if we say there is a safe level of smoking, we're going to encourage kids to start smoking," Schneiderman recalled.

Upton's initial comment to the press on Gori's computations was a moderate rebuke, noting that "our present knowledge does not allow us to establish [any levels] below which smoking might be safe" and that "no cigarette now on the market can be considered wholly without risk to health." By the next day, though, Upton's distress was showing in the *Post*'s follow-up article. He lashed out at Gori's "assumptions" that anyone can smoke any given number of cigarettes at low risk, found the use of the term "tolerable" to be "unfortunate," and charged that Gori's statements "set back our cause, and even if we can correct the misinterpretation, we will have lost valuable momentum." Two weeks later, Upton told a writer for *Science* that the nub of the problem was that Gori's case depended upon the assumption that the risk of dying from smoking decreased "in exact proportion to the decreases in the concentration of those six toxic agents," but there was no evidence to support it. And there might well be other dangerous ingredients in cigarette smoke with effects as yet uncalculated.

Over at the Office on Smoking and Health, where they were scrambling to turn out a definitive Surgeon General's report by early January, the Gori article "came as a bombshell" to David Burns, the senior scientific editor. Gori's claims seemed "off the wall" to Burns and his colleagues and lacking in corroborative evidence in the form of smokers with actual histories of the cited "tolerable" doses. In dealing with millions of smokers, to speak as Gori had of abstract equivalency ratios of yields of toxic substances and "tolerable" risk levels was a very sticky business scientifically, "because you're still talking about a whole lot of deaths," said Burns. Gori's whole approach, in the view of OSH's technical officer Donald Shopland, amounted to "false reassuring of the public."

Besides grossly overselling his idea, Gori made a second mistake that was fatal for him. He did not accept critical advice by outside experts from whom he sought it and did not invite his own organization to undertake a stringent review of his paper, even when he knew that his parent department had adopted a strong antismoking policy. Having spurned the skeptical views of his NCI colleague Marvin Schneiderman, Gori turned to the keenly admired epidemiologist Jerome Cornfield at Johns Hopkins, who, according to Schneiderman, approved of some of Gori's paper but had serious misgivings about other parts of it. More revealing still was the view of Gori's role model, Ernst Wynder, who admired him as "a very clever fellow" and appreciated his help in funding smoking research by Wynder's American Health Foundation during its fledgling years. According to one close associate, Wynder told Gori "in no uncertain terms not to publish the article in that form, that it would bring down a firestorm around him, and provide his critics with the ammunition to blast him out of his little empire." Wynder himself acknowledged later that he thought it a great mistake for Gori to move beyond his theoretical construct by citing brand names and their equivalency values.

Within NCI's official channels, Gori had taken the path of least resistance. As he later explained it, "Internal review at the NCI was always performed by the experienced Dr. [Bayard] Morrison [the assistant director], who also approved this paper. Had it been published six months earlier, it would have been just another report. Instead, it came out at a time of abrupt policy changes." In fact, Morrison had passed on the paper in June of 1977, a full half-year before the HEW's antismoking initiative was announced by Califano and nine months before *JAMA* accepted Gori's article—plenty of time for Gori to have shown a study of such debatable conclusions to many of the other experts available to him on the NIH campus in Bethesda or even to have sought the advice of the review board of NCI's own journal. Instead, he relied on Morrison, a longtime NCI survivor and an adroit technocrat but, in the view of some, an inappropriate judge of a subject as controversial as the Gori-Lynch hypothesis. Morrison himself disputed the view that Gori was not enough of a scientist to have posited the tentative conclusions he had formulated: "You didn't have to be a Nobel laureate to be a perfectly adequate interpreter of the data. . . . There was real substance behind what he was saying, and it was not such a Machiavellian thing, after all. All his correlations and equivalents were scientifically determinable. . . ." What was not determinable, however, was the validity of the threshold concept of "tolerable" risk, upon which the whole paper was premised. Gori, perhaps fearing that his article would be quashed, chose not to call it to the attention of either NCI director Upton or his deputy director, Dr. Guy Newell, who said of the claim that the article had been sent through proper channels, "In my opinion, Dr. Gori misjudged how much end-running the [NCI] administration would tolerate."

In the view of Surgeon General Julius Richmond, Gori himself may not have been a captive of the cigarette manufacturers, but his years of salesmanship in behalf of "low-risk" smoking "were like a gift from heaven for the industry." *Business Week,* for example, had headlined its report on the Gori-Lynch article "A Cigarette Study the Industry Likes." By the end of

1978, Gori's star at NCI was in decline, he had been transferred from running the smoking research program, and the institute had begun the process of shifting its focus from modifying cigarettes to modifying the behavior of their users. Gori hung on for several years before departing for a post at the Franklin Institute and consulting work for cigarette maker Brown & Williamson.

II

ALTHOUGH Gori's endorsement of milder cigarettes as an alternative for those lacking the will to quit the habit upset many in the public-health community, smokers were grasping his point. Sales of Carlton, the brand Gori said could be smoked in the highest quantity with "tolerable" risk, jumped 50 percent in 1979. By that year, about 35 percent of smokers were using cigarettes in the low-tar range of 15 mg. or under—a big increase from the 2 percent smoking such brands only a dozen years earlier. And 11 percent of smokers were buying brands with 9 mg. or fewer. Between 1965 and 1980, the tobacco industry had brought down the yields of the sales-weighted average cigarette from 37 mg. of tar and 2 mg. of nicotine to 14 mg. of tar and under 1 of nicotine.

These figures did not set off a celebration, however, at the Office of Smoking and Health, precisely because Gori's proposition seemed mischievously seductive. His enticing message was interpreted, in the words of OSH's Don Shopland, by the typical listening smoker this way: "I may not like these weak smokes and may get a hernia drawing on them to extract any pleasure whatever, but wow! they're practically risk-free." Smokers not only felt they could consume more of the lower-yielding cigarettes but also were smoking them now, as Shopland put it, "down to their fingernails."

Such compensatory behavior was soon documentable. Where the average smoker had consumed twenty-two cigarettes a day in 1954, he or she was smoking thirty a day in 1978. This increase suggested that the quitting rate was higher among those who smoked less than average and/or that those buying the "less hazardous" brands were smoking more of them than of their previous, and presumably more hazardous, brands. Investigators in this period led by Lynn Kozlowski were putting together detailed evidence of smokers' compensatory devices. Although half of all cigarettes manufactured by 1980 had tiny holes in the filter overwrap in order to ventilate carbon monoxide and dilute tar and nicotine, some 40 percent of smokers were found to block the holes, consciously or not, while they smoked. A second major modification in cigarette manufacture—a faster burning rate, achieved by looser packing of the tobacco, more porous paper, and burn-enhancing chemical additives—further reduced tar and nicotine yields. But the typical smoker, who averaged about ten puffs per cigarette, could derive a lot more than the machine-rated yield of the low-tar brands by managing an extra drag or two from each or smoking them more intensively. Kozlowski estimated that someone smoking a low-tar cigarette the same way users of marijuana smoked theirs—inhaling deeply, holding the smoke down a while, and consuming every fraction of an inch—could derive as much as 70 mg. of tar from it.

However much any given smoker was compensating after switching down in brands, the sales trend toward the lower-yielding segment of the market was clear, and the industry competition heated up accordingly. But without television and radio advertising available to them, the cigarette companies found the going rough, especially when they tried to launch new, freestanding brands rather than extend their established lines with lower-yielding versions. One particularly unhappy example was R. J. Reynolds's 9-mg. entry in 1977—Real. In celebrating Real's "natural" goodness, RJR seemed to be trying to make tobacco into a health food of sorts, like granola or yogurt with perhaps a dusting of wheat germ, without noticing that smokers by and large were not exactly health faddists. Despite a $50 million ad campaign, 25 million sample packs, and 150 boxcars of promotional material, the brand struggled to get off the ground. Realizing the fatuousness of its health-food slant, Reynolds ditched the "natural" idea and replaced it with the ambiguous slogan "Low tar and taste." By 1980, Real was pronounced dead, and Reynolds was pushing line extensions to bolster its share at the low end of the yield spectrum.

The year Real died, Philip Morris decided to attack the ultra-low end of the market with a new brand. Carlton and distant runner-up Now, the only two entries in that 1-mg.-and-under category, commanded less than 3 percent of the market between them, so PM reasoned that it could make a big splash in that quiet little pond. But in bringing out heavily ventilated Cambridge, with 1 mg. in its soft-pack version and a mere 0.1 mg. in a box (so it could claim to be the lowest on the market), Philip Morris forgot all the lessons that had brought it close to the top of the industry. The packaging was unappealing, there was no unique selling proposition beyond the minimal yields, and its taste was barely detectable. Even a $60 million advertising send-off could not cure the built-in problem. "Everybody felt we had to do this," recalled Shepard Pollack, then president of Philip Morris USA, "but we probably outsmarted ourselves and overintellectualized the need. The brand had no parents [at the company] other than necessity. It was a flat, me-too offering." Cambridge sold fewer than a million packs a week for three years, and by 1983 was selling only half that. Philip Morris turned instead to Merit Ultra Lights with 4 mg. of tar and at least a *frisson* of flavor.

Far more needy than industry leaders Reynolds and Philip Morris to stake and hold a claim in the ultra-low field was Brown & Williamson, which in 1973 had overtaken American Tobacco for third place in market share but by

1980 had only 14 percent of the U.S. market, and that figure was softening. To reverse its slide, B&W put down a great many chips in the fall of 1980 on a new brand it called Barclay, which won a 1-mg. rating from the FTC's smoking machines. Barclay's purveyors said of it, "The pleasure is back," meaning that it had more flavor than other brands in its niche. Behind this claim was some interesting cigarette engineering. In place of the 20 to 250 little air holes that other low-tar brands had punched into the filter overwrap, Barclay had four air channels, little tunnels placed equidistantly around the circumference and running from intake holes about two-thirds down the filter, beneath the overwrap, which delivered the ventilating air directly into the smoker's mouth. Where the holes in other brands' filters diluted the smoke before it entered the mouth and speedily whooshed straight to the back of the oral cavity, missing the sensitive taste buds at the tip of the tongue, the as yet undiluted smoke in Barclay entered the mouth more slowly, mixing with the air brought there from the little subsurface tunnels and rolling more leisurely over the tongue to produce a keener taste sensation.

The device was promising enough for Barclay to aim for a quarter of the ultra-low market and for B&W to budget $150 million for the launch. Within nine months, Barclay had grabbed a 1.2 percent share, even better than the Louisville-based manufacturer had hoped, and its rivals were growing envious—and also suspicious. Reynolds and Philip Morris researchers tested Barclay and saw that the air tunnels in its elaborate filter produced a slightly ridged effect to the touch, tempting the fingers or the mouth encasing them to smooth the little bumps by crushing them down level with the rest of the filter overwrap. This, of course, destroyed their diluting effects and raised their yields well above the rating recorded by the FTC laboratory's smoking machines, which, devoid of tactile sensation, had no desire to exert pressure on the elevated air channels. In short, Barclay appeared to its competitors to have been intentionally designed to fool the FTC's testing devices in order to obtain a low-yield rating.

After urging Brown & Williamson to modify its ultra-low yield claims and being urged in return to go fly a kite, Philip Morris joined with Reynolds to protest Barclay's "design defect" to the FTC, arguing that whether it was deliberate or unintended, the brand in the hands and lips of real smokers produced a yield of 7 to 8 mg. of tar, not the 1 mg. Barclay claimed. B&W angrily denied the charge, complaining that it was the victim of "natural hostility from entrenched leaders" of its industry. To settle the squabble, the FTC named a three-man panel of independent experts, including Lynn Kozlowski, who concluded that the Barclay's air channels were "compromised with great regularity," and as he described the process, "lip pressure can cause the channels to buckle; place a Barclay carefully in your mouth and squeeze; you can 'hear-feel' the channels buckling. . . ." The net effect of the design flaw was a true tar yield in the 3- to 8-mg. range, the investigating panel reported to the FTC. Eventually the commission settled on a 3-mg. rating for Barclay, but by then, the initial momentum of the disputed brand had dwindled and, after peaking at a 1.3 market share, it tailed off badly.

III

ALTHOUGH the tobacco industry gradually reduced the toxic yields of cigarette smoke, the halfheartedness of the effort was vividly evidenced in the saga of an experimental project known as the palladium cigarette. It seemed so promising as a safer smoke, in the judgment of the scientists who long labored on it, that it might have rendered all other cigarettes on the market obsolete—and therefore constituted a great peril even to the company that had developed it.

No cigarette manufacturer was in greater need of such a breakthrough innovation than the company that had been known as the Liggett Group since 1973. That year, its chairmanship was turned over to Raymond Mulligan, who had successfully run the Alpo dog food line, one of Liggett's first acquisitions when it began diversifying in the late 1960s. Almost every aspect of Liggett's once blooming cigarette enterprise had wilted. The company proved better at diversifying than at selling cigarettes. It bought up only businesses that ranked first or second in their field and had managers who were eager to remain in place. By the mid-1970s, the Liggett Group had four other core businesses besides tobacco—pet foods, sporting goods and fitness equipment, soft drinks (several large Pepsi-Cola bottlers), and wines and spirits, including U.S. distribution rights to J&B scotch.

Indeed, it was doing so nicely in its new enterprises that Liggett had begun to shop around for a buyer for its 2 to 3 percent of the U.S. cigarette market. In 1977, it sold its overseas business to Philip Morris for $108 million, and its cigarette operations seemed to have entered their terminal phase, a cash cow to be milked as long as it lasted—except for one experimental program the company had been nursing along since the mid-'Sixties. Suddenly, this plodding effort was deemed capable of rescuing its tobacco business from the brink of extinction.

Liggett's chief scientist in this undertaking was James B. Mold, a tall, lean man reserved to the point of reticence, whose steel-framed glasses and precise manner made him seem the very model of a small-town pharmacist lifted bodily from a Norman Rockwell painting. A nonsmoker with a Ph.D. from Northwestern, Mold had joined Liggett in 1955 as head of organic chemistry research and harbored few doubts that cigarettes caused cancer; he knew from working on the development of Lark the ciliatoxic potency of smoke in attacking the lung's defenses. Mold eventually rose to the second-ranking post at Liggett's R&D labs in Durham and worked regularly with Dr. Charles Kensler of the Arthur D. Little research company (ADL) in Cambridge, which tested Liggett's experimental products.

Mold's ongoing task was to lower the tar and nicotine yields of Liggett's brands and to figure out how to neutralize their carcinogenic effect. In time, Mold concentrated on the propensity of the hydrocarbons in tobacco, when burned, to lose oxygen and in the process become "free radicals," outlaw molecules with an electron missing from their atomic structure and thus marked by an instability that left them on the prowl for similarly altered molecules. When they found each other, the resulting compound was no longer structurally volatile but had become carcinogenic in the binding process.

Mold and other scientists in the tobacco industry were trying to discourage this cancer-triggering outcome by the addition of a catalyst (a substance that speeds up molecular reactions) to cigarettes in order to achieve a more complete—or, in laymen's terms, a cleaner—burn, cutting down on the proliferation of free radicals, just as catalytic converters were coming into use in automobiles to reduce pollutants emitted during incomplete gasoline combustion. Over the years, Mold's department tested some 200 catalytic substances before hitting on the heavy metal palladium, a relative of platinum but about a third as costly. Added to tobacco in microscopic amounts, palladium was found to reduce the crop of tumors on mouse backs by 40 percent. Beyond concerns that palladium did not exist in adequate supply—most of it came from South Africa—to meet the demand if further testing proved its value to smokers, there were fears that it might have other, unsuspected effects that could neutralize its worth as a catalyst, or perhaps make cigarettes more hazardous. But extensive testing determined that the palladium consumed in a single smoker's lifetime would amount to no more than the smallest dot made with a pencil and, based on close examination of the skin, liver, spleen, and other organs of laboratory rats, left no residue; in short, the body apparently expelled the palladium before it had a chance to inflict damage.

A 40 percent reduction in tumor-generating activity was encouraging but not a smoker's savior, so Mold urged that the palladium be blended with a nitrate additive since nitrates were known to cut tumorigenesis by 5 to 10 percent. His choice was salts of nitrate derived from magnesium, a substance associated with human nutrition and readily soluble in the casings sprayed on blended tobacco. The combination of palladium and salts of magnesium nitrate was tested by the Liggett and ADL scientists and was found, by interfering with the binding process of the free radicals, to reduce tumors on painted mouse backs by 95 to 100 percent. That was the good news; the not so good news was that the combined additives somewhat increased the levels of nitric oxide, corrosive to the lungs but not carcinogenic, and of nitrosamines, compounds that promoted, if they did not cause, carcinogenesis. The solution was to further arm the palladium-treated cigarette with a charcoal filter that sharply cut down the nitric oxide in the smoke and to add air holes and improve the cellulose acetate filter—measures which effectively slashed the nitrosamines.

But Mold and his colleagues did not want to dilute the smoke so much that it was as tasteless as most ultra-low brands. Their goal, rather, was to wind up with a commercially promising cigarette that yielded in the range of 10 to 12 milligrams of tar, well within the "Light" cigarette segment, with levels of nitric oxide and nitrosamines no higher than the average for the ten top-selling brands. The tar yield of their experimental model, the Liggett scientists argued, was less important than the fact that it constituted a qualitatively reduced health hazard. Thus, by 1975 they emerged with a palladium cigarette that would probably cost five to ten cents a pack more than standard brands but might achieve a 100 percent reduction in tumorigenicity and a 50 percent drop in cocarcinogenic promoters—at least it did in laboratory rodents.

Confronted by a steadily shrinking market share for his tobacco business, Liggett chairman Mulligan decided that it was worth exploring the commercial prospects of this potential marvel and established a task force overseeing the palladium cigarette, code-named Tame. Efforts were made to improve its taste, more stringent testing of its long-range effects was undertaken at ADL's suggestion, and the palladium-magnesium nitrate catalyst was patented, though not without serious doubts about the wisdom of this action by Liggett's primary outside legal counsel, the New York firm of Webster & Sheffield. "They scared the shit out of Liggett about ruinous liability suits if the safer cigarette went into production," recalled an attorney with another outside firm in Liggett's hire at the time and privy to the thinking of Liggett's general counsel, Joseph Greer. Even if Tame, or whatever it was finally called, was patented and never marketed, Liggett's lawyers advised, there was possible exposure from disclosing knowledge of an apparently safer cigarette design and then negligently failing to bring it out for the public's health benefit. But since nobody really yet knew if the palladium cigarette would prove safer for human users, as it seemed to be for lab animals, the new product might be blamed, justly or not, for future deaths by those claiming that the reputedly improved product was nothing of the sort. Finally, there was the very real question of how to market the palladium cigarette without rendering obsolete all of Liggett's other brands.

For all of these legal concerns, Arthur Slote, head of Liggett's tobacco operations, saw the rest of his business going nowhere and urged Mulligan to give the palladium cigarette the green light. He did so on the proviso that the marketing effort would be lawyered to the hilt. Attorneys hovered over all aspects of the project, including the scientific meetings at which, as Mold recalled, "All paper that was generated—research progress reports, memoranda, notebooks, or what-all—were to be directed to the legal department and turned in at the end of the meeting. In other words, the legal department was imposing a privileged confidential lawyer-client relationship from then on over all our activity. . . . Whenever any problem came up in the project," as it did with one test result from ADL showing less of a reduction in tumors than earlier, "the legal department would pounce on it in an attempt to kill the whole thing. This happened time and time again."

For his part, Liggett house counsel Joe Greer, a gruff chain-smoker who would die of lung cancer, had his feet put to the fire by the house counsel of the other cigarette companies. Despite the industry's highly competitive marketing practices, its lawyers' ties encouraged a mutual monitoring process premised on the belief that there would be enough money in the pot for all of them if it was not shaken too hard, and so, as one outsider of counsel to the cigarette makers put it, they "forebore independent action" that might in any serious way threaten their shared interest in the status quo. When word of the palladium cigarette patent circulated, Greer's confrères told him Liggett would be pulling the rug out from under the rest of the industry if it proceeded with the experimental brand, and, given the collegiality among them, "Joe heard it," one of his legal confidants recounted. Plainly, it would have been in the interests of Liggett's competitors to discourage it from bringing the palladium brand to market and thereby possibly becoming overnight a major player in the industry once more. Added Mold: "They [competitors' counsel] convinced him it was not in Liggett's best interest to manufacture the palladium cigarette or to publicize its development."

But publicizing it was the only plausible way that Liggett would be able to market the presumably safer brand within the FTC rules, which since 1955 had knocked out explicit health claims in cigarette advertising unless adequately documented. That requirement could be met in the case of the palladium brand only by citing the results of Liggett's laboratory experiments with animals, which the tobacco companies had long argued could not be extrapolated to the human smoking experience. Even if it backpedaled in this regard, however, Liggett could hardly claim outright that, based on the evidence at hand, the new cigarette reduced lung cancer. "I would never have agreed to it," Mold later recounted. "You [could] only say this looks like it may have a beneficial effect." Or as Kensler put it, "This is potentially beneficial—that's all we ever said."

Liggett and ADL scientists thus had to set about winning a sympathetic hearing from the medical and public-health community for its palladium experiments in order not to run afoul of the FTC. Their strategy was to get their developmental findings reported in scholarly journals so they could be cited as corroborative evidence in advertisements if and when the palladium brand was marketed. Under the lawyers' directive, the initial scientific paper was drafted with Kensler listed as the leading author and other ADL researchers behind him, with Mold and other Liggett scientists unmentioned as the article was sent to *Cancer Research*, the journal of the American Association for Cancer Research. "It was my understanding," said Mold, "that Liggett did not want to be associated in public with this development," preferring ADL to get all or most of the credit, so no blame would redound to the company if it decided not to proceed with marketing the palladium brand. Forever after, Kensler would insist that Mold "had nothing to do with the palladium cigarette." Mold would later counter that "no way" was the palladium project an ADL initiative, as Kensler and Liggett claimed, and that ADL's role was primarily to test what Mold's laboratory had developed. Combining magnesium nitrate salts with the palladium, Mold added, was "my idea," though he conceded that, as project manager, he kept no notebook that might have corroborated his role.

To Kensler's surprise and annoyance, *Cancer Research* declined the article on the palladium project but did run an abstract of it. Kensler later said he was told that the journal review committee was dominated by antismoking scientists who felt that publicizing the palladium development would serve only to encourage people to keep smoking. A veteran member of the National Cancer Institute's Tobacco Working Group, Kensler would come to feel that prohibition-minded purists at the American Cancer Society, the Public Health Service, and in the health community at large opposed in principle all serious efforts to develop a less hazardous cigarette. Even Gio Gori, the NCI's chief proponent of that concept, was reluctant to lend his program's imprimatur to the palladium idea when Liggett and ADL brought it to him for corroborative tests. According to Mold, Gori said his budget would not allow such testing unless Liggett put down a million dollars for that purpose. Gori himself would later say merely, "Like many other ideas, the palladium [cigarette] was rapidly judged unpromising."

That same concern was intensively debated now inside Liggett, where the prospect of betting heavily on the palladium project looked more and more risky. "You had to be prepared to drop the rest of your product line," said one outside counsel on hand for the internal soul-searching. It would have been one thing to claim that the public had been warned of the smoking peril during the years the palladium cigarette was being developed and tested, "but it would have been a very [difficult] thing to claim good faith without incorporating the new health feature into the rest of the line." Yet the company was by no means so desperate that it was ready to risk exposing its non-tobacco business, by then accounting for 80 percent of the Liggett Group's revenues, to the uncertainties of marketing the experimental brand. And the company's existing brands still turned a profit; that they might be killing a lot more people than the newly developed product would was not readily factored into the debate when Chairman Mulligan assembled his executive committee at Liggett's Rockefeller Center offices late in 1977 to decide whether to start producing the palladium brand. Mold, summoned for the occasion and confronted by "a battery of lawyers," recalled that all of them proposed reasons why the undertaking should not proceed. "I was alone," he said. The decision was to continue the research—if word ever got out that it had been abandoned, as Mold divined the prevailing legal wisdom, "how would you explain why you'd stopped?"—and to seek scientific endorsements, even as Liggett executives explored the possibility of licensing the palladium process to a foreign manufacturer.

Kensler undertook missionary work among several top public and private health officials and academics, trying to pave the way for publication of the palladium findings. Articles were prepared for *Science* and *Preventive Medicine* with careful vetting by the Liggett lawyers, along with a paper by Kensler and Mold for delivery at the International Cancer Congress held in the fall of 1978 at Buenos Aires. Meanwhile, using such published reports—the only one at hand thus far was the abstract run by *Cancer Research*—Liggett's marketing people began working up sample ads for the palladium brand, now dubbed Epic, that they hoped would withstand the FTC requirement for scientifically supportable health claims. The most straightforward of the prepared ads stated, "This abstract appeared in the journal of the American Association of Cancer Researchers," gave the text and Liggett's name as sponsor of the research, and added blandly, "This process of treating tobacco is patented by new Epic cigarettes." A more deviously aggressive version stated, "It's worth trying just for the taste but—UNTIL THE GOVERNMENT CHANGES ITS POLICIES, WE CAN'T REALLY TELL YOU WHAT'S NEW ABOUT NEW EPIC." The most confrontational of all the proposed texts read, "We don't believe that mice-painting tests can be extrapolated to humans. But you may believe. And we think you deserve a choice. Which is why we now report . . . ," and gave details on how the Epic reduced cancerous tumors in mice up to 100 percent.

But these ads, prepared in September of 1978, were never brought to the FTC for its approval. And when Kensler and Mold showed up in Buenos Aires in October, ready to pass out publicity releases and hold a press conference in support of their presentation on the palladium development, the plug was pulled on them at the last second. Mold remembered their getting "a frantic call from New York" canceling the publicity blitz. No more than a few dozen scientists were on hand for their oral presentation, and the paper was only abstracted and not run in full in the published proceedings. House counsel Greer ordered articles approved for submission to *Science* and *Preventive Medicine* to be killed, the research and development staff was slashed severely, and efforts were intensified to find a taker abroad for the palladium concept. The Epic was stillborn.

The decision to put it aside was made by many at Liggett, prominently including a newcomer to the company, Kinsley V. Dey, who had taken overall charge of tobacco operations. Dey was unwilling to bet the whole store on Epic, and, as he told congressional investigators ten years later, "We could not substantiate the health claim," beyond the circumscribed and highly ambivalent manner of the sample ads cited above, so "[i]f you can't say anything about it, you can't put it in the marketplace. . . . If we could have found a way to do it fitting within the rules and regulations we had to live under, you betcha we would have marketed it." Dey was probably being more forthright when he added that if Liggett had marketed the palladium brand, the company believed it "would have been attacked from all sides—the government, health authorities, antismoking groups, and especially our competitors." Furthermore, Liggett was by then into heavy discussion with would-be buyers like Grand Metropolitan, a British conglomerate eager to get hold of its lucrative liquor franchises; why endanger an attractive buyout with all the uncertainties of the palladium option?

When Mold and Kensler were denied permission to attend a conference on the less hazardous cigarette with other leading authorities in the field, held in the fall of 1979 at the Banbury Center in Cold Spring Harbor, New York, the Liggett scientist had had enough. After more than a dozen years on the palladium project, during which he suffered two coronary attacks, Mold was heartbroken in more ways than one. The experience was "a total frustration" for him, one that he had endured because "it looked to me as if we were trying to do the right thing." In the end, they took the course safest only for the company's bottom line. For Mold, whose passionate belief in the palladium process had kept the project alive as long as it was, it amounted to a vivid lesson in how corporate capitalism deals with its technological innovators: "The creator has no options whatever. . . ."

The whole saga was not without its surreal aspects: "Here these guys develop a product that's really innovative—and therefore dangerous," said an outside attorney of counsel to Liggett during these years. "And thereafter half the executives in the place were trying to figure out how to bring it to market while the other half was trying to kill it."

I V

I N the fall of 1978, President Carter appeared at a softball game in his native Plains, Georgia, wearing a cap with the stitched inscription "Pride in Tobacco". Near the end of the year, U.S. House of Representatives Speaker "Tip" O'Neill warned the nation's most vocal antismoking advocate, HEW Secretary Joseph Califano, "You're driving the tobacco people crazy. These guys are vicious—they're out to destroy you."

Califano nevertheless made a media show out of the release of the 1,100-

page Surgeon General's report that the devoted little band at the Office of Smoking and Health had struggled to have ready by the fifteenth anniversary of the pioneering report that had been the public-health community's declaration of war on smoking. In the intervening years, as Surgeon General Julius Richmond wrote in the preface, the scientific evidence on the hazards of cigarette use had become "overwhelming". True, an average of 2 million Americans had quit each year since the 1964 report, lowering the percentage of smoking adults from 42 to 33 percent in that span, but the number of young people taking up the habit had not declined, and women, especially teenagers, were smoking more heavily now than then. The report placed the economic cost of cigarette smoking at $27 billion a year due to increased medical care, absenteeism, decreased work productivity, and smoking-related accidents; nonsmokers were said to bear a large portion of the bill through higher health insurance premiums, disability payments, and other tax-supported programs.

Of particular concern in the 1979 report was the news that the once-low death rate due to lung cancer among women, long cited by tobacco industry defenders as a disparity undermining all the population studies on the health risks of smoking, had risen threefold over the previous fifteen years. As Califano grimly put it at his press conference, "Women who smoke like men die like men who smoke." Pregnant women who smoked were on average 40 percent more likely than nonsmokers to give birth prematurely and about 30 percent more likely to lose their babies soon after birth. A second major area dealt with in the new report was the effects of carbon monoxide, hardly touched upon in the 1964 report but now understood to be one of the most harmful components of tobacco smoke and a "possible critical factor" in the onset of heart disease. The systemic toll taken by the toxic gas was most obviously manifested by the reduced pressure at which the blood, its hemoglobin depleted by the carbon monoxide in smoke, delivered oxygen to the body's tissues, dependent upon it for growth and sustenance; this was especially true of fetal tissue, which was often malnourished in expectant mothers who smoked and as a result had low-weight babies. A third subject on which investigators had gathered much new information was how emphysema likely developed. The hypothesis was based on the discovery that the disease was common in individuals deficient in alpha$_1$-antitrypsin, an enzyme that inhibits the effects of protease, another enzyme that gives elastic capability to the lung's little air sacs, allowing them to expand and contract. An inadequate supply of this inhibitor made the air-sac walls lose their resiliency, distend, and readily rupture, thus reducing the surface area of the lungs exposed to the bloodstream and lowering their capacity to deliver oxygen and remove gas wastes. This imbalance of enzymes was now believed to be fostered by cigarette smoke, which excited the macrophages, the lung's scavenger bodies, to synthesize and release too much protease.

The President made no comment about the weighty new report from the Surgeon General indicting smoking as America's foremost preventable health menace—but then none of Jimmy Carter's predecessors had ever urged his countrymen to forbear the killing custom; that was the job of the Surgeon General, who did not have to stand for reelection. But without presidential endorsement, the report was a vulnerable target for those with a vested interest in tobacco. North Carolina's state commissioner of agriculture, for example, told reporters after HEW's press conference, "I'm sick and tired of Joe Califano's ballyhooing the smoking and health question," and dismissed the new Surgeon General's report as "just another statement . . . 90 percent of it propaganda" and part of a "personal vendetta". Before anyone on the Tobacco Institute's staff could have read the volume, a spokesman called it "more rehash than research" and more of a "publicity stunt" than a serious scientific document.

In this latter characterization, the tobacco manufacturers did have a point of sorts, but at best a minor one. Arnold S. Relman, then editor of *The New England Journal of Medicine*, has suggested that it was not the function of the Surgeon General's report to present new data and findings, as his own magazine did; rather, the annual HEW reports to Congress were "public documents, public events, not scientific documents at all. . . ." But as one of the reports' leading organizers, Donald Shopland at the Office on Smoking and Health, noted, since the reports were "a legitimate response by the public-health community to a perceived peril," why not advance them directly into the arena of public consciousness as the occasion for media events? Too technical to be read in detail by laymen, the reports—especially the 1979 one and those over the next seven years—were accepted at face value by most of the public as balanced and accurate statements of the scientific consensus on smoking. The tobacco industry, without authentic evidence to the contrary, was reduced to trying to trivialize the reports by remarks like those by TI spokesman William Dwyer, who, referring to the 1979 document, quipped, "America, beware if Joe Califano ever decides to give up drinking and other pleasurable pursuits."

The cigarette makers, at such moments of authoritative rebuke, could have said nothing so long as they were left free to profit hugely from their certifiably dangerous product. Instead, they continued to behave as if silence were a confession of guilt. Thus, the day before the Surgeon General's report was issued, and without troubling to familiarize themselves with its contents, the Tobacco Institute published a 168-page booklet, *Smoking and Health, 1964–1979: The Continuing Controversy,* in rebuttal. The TI's president, Horace Kornegay, wrote in its preface: "The process of making public policy is better served when areas of scientific unknowns are illuminated by the light of reasoned deliberation rather than the heat of emotional rhetoric. . . . It is time for all parties to this [smoking and health] controversy to admit that there is much that is unknown."

This model of sanctimonious self-justification was censurable not merely because it was disingenuous on its face but because it soared so far beyond the boundaries of legitimate advocacy. The last thing the tobacco industry was interested in was "reasoned deliberation". If it had cared to join in a rational discourse on the scientific charges against it, it might at least have considered them on their merits as rendered in the new report before spieling off the same old mocking denials—the same dismissive allusions to "flawed population studies" and the rise in lung cancer as the result simply of "better diagnostic techniques". The last thing, furthermore, one could have fairly said of the Surgeon General's 1979 report, like those before and after it, was that it was heated by "emotional rhetoric". If anything, the government reports were too clinical to rouse the public over the enormity of their implications. Finally, by conceding nothing and challenging everything in their vehemence for self-preservation, the cigarette makers and their dependents fell well short of even marginally acceptable moral conduct. For while it was true, as the Tobacco Institute's attack literature argued, that much remained unknown about the specific mechanisms of how a cancer began to grow, why human arteries became clogged with lipids, or the exact pathogenesis of emphysema, these were towering irrelevancies when placed alongside the consensual understanding, beyond any reasonable doubt, arrived at by thousands of disinterested investigators, of how severely cigarette smoke insulted human tissue.

Ironically, one of the fiercest critics of the 1979 Surgeon General's report was John Banzhaf of Action on Smoking and Health (ASH). The report, he charged, was "criminally deficient and misleading," mostly a rehash, a gloss on the addictive nature of smoking—a finding that might "dramatically alter the way we deal with the entire smoking issue"—and "incredibly weak" on secondhand smoke. Banzhaf was also unremitting in his overall charge that HEW's antismoking campaign as voiced by Secretary Califano had been "completely ineffective," largely because he had asked people politely to act on the smoking peril—and "they have told him no." A glaring example, said Banzhaf, who had a tendency throughout his antismoking career to mistake the real enemy, was Califano's appeal by letter to the chief executives of the nation's 500 largest corporations, asking them to confront the smoking problem; the only response was the establishment of a separate nonsmoking section in a few company cafeterias. But what could a single Cabinet officer, unsupported by his President or a serious budgetary allocation for the purpose, really accomplish in a single year against a large industry outspending him hundreds of times over to persuade the public not to abandon a beloved social custom, however dangerous?

What Califano achieved was to ventilate the smoking issue as no federal official had before him—and in so doing put his political neck on the chopping block. In April 1979, Califano's friend Senator Edward Kennedy told him he would have to remove himself from the Cabinet well before the 1980 election, because Carter could not carry North Carolina and perhaps a lot of other Southern states if the HEW Secretary remained in office. Unable to please either side in the public-policy debate over smoking but successful in reaching countless multitudes in the middle ground, Califano became the thankless victim of his antitobacco crusade a few months later, when he was made to walk the plank by a President who could only commend him for his energetic performance in office. Tobaccoland cheered.

V

B Y the close of the 'Seventies, the tobacco industry was at the apex of its power and had never been more profitable. In both the social and political arenas the cigarette makers were triumphant largely because they faced no organized national opposition, only weak and scattered voices of protest. A 1978 report by a national commission on tobacco and health policy called the antismoking effort "minimal and symbolic" and noted that "in relation to the size and scope of the problem," only "a very small amount" of the $230 million raised annually by the three largest health voluntaries had gone to combat smoking. That same year, America's largest medical group, the AMA, had issued its report on tobacco and health, and it proved to be little more than glossy window dressing and a flagrant dereliction of the organization's professional responsibility. Few state laws had been enacted that materially curbed smoking in public beyond extreme cases like lighting up in elevators and on public transportation.

In Congress, nobody with power spoke out forcefully against smoking. Washington's two most skilled consumer advocates, Michael Pertschuk, chairing the FTC, and the unaffiliated, unquenchable Ralph Nader, had too many other battles to pursue. So well entrenched politically was the industry that the senior senator from the leading tobacco state—Jesse Helms—had little trouble extracting a pledge from his party's 1980 presidential candidate, Ronald Reagan, that if he was elected, his administration would countenance no antismoking crusade like Califano's. Nor was there a peep from any federal administrative figure after the decade's two most outspoken foes of smoking, Califano and Jesse Steinfeld, had been hounded out of office.

The only part of the federal government deeply involved in the health aspects of smoking was the National Cancer Institute, which had spent most of the 1970s and tens of millions of taxpayer dollars doing the industry's work for it by trying to develop a cigarette that could be endorsed—and was, by its director of smoking research—as a tolerable risk. Meanwhile, the ingredients of this documented hazard were less regulated than any other hazardous product.

When John Pinney, director of the Office on Smoking and Health, sought an agreement from the industry to disclose the additives in cigarettes and to introduce no others until the effects on consumers could be determined, he got nowhere. "The real outrage is that nobody lays a glove on this product," Pinney commented several years after leaving office. Best of all from the industry's standpoint, the public appeared little concerned about tobacco's dominion. The 1978 Roper poll taken for the Tobacco Institute found worry about cigarette use to be near the bottom of the list of the nation's social concerns, even though nine out of ten Americans believed smoking to be hazardous to the smoker's health and a majority believed it to be probably hazardous to bystanders.

Headquarters of the cigarette companies' united front was the Tobacco Institute, whose president since 1970, Horace Kornegay, was surrounded by some of the best lawyers, lobbyists, publicists, and scientific consultants money could buy. Their chief mission was to treat the soaring mountain of scientific evidence against their product as a mirage or a molehill and to reassure the public that eminent authorities contested the health charges, as if there were equal validity to each "side" of the ongoing cigarette "controversy". Senator Edward Kennedy, hardly its friend, remarked of the Tobacco Institute in 1979, "Dollar for dollar they're probably the most effective lobby on Capitol Hill." Added Nader's associate, Sidney Wolfe of the Health Research Group, "They have completely paralyzed Washington in terms of any significant ability to regulate cigarettes."

As if gearing up for incessant and intensified battle, the TI nearly doubled its staff to seventy operatives in 1978, opened satellite offices in California, Pennsylvania, Texas, Massachusetts, and New Jersey, and broadened its activities to include four full-time speakers who barnstormed the country addressing any business, fraternal, or civic group that would have them, and publication of a shelfload of rebuttal documents. Prominent among this attack literature was the bimonthly *Tobacco Observer*, which typically characterized its antismoking foes as "intolerant prohibitionists" composing "a joyless tribe . . . who want to manage everyone else's lives, perhaps because they have been incapable of managing their own." The newsletter was filled with apologetics like the article "Women and Cancer" in the February 1980 issue by a University of Texas professor emeritus, arguing that the rise in lung cancer among women was largely attributable to industrial pollutants and other occupational exposures now that there were more and more women in the workplace. In the TI's 1979 brochure "About Tobacco Smoke," carbon monoxide was dismissed as a common gas, and the amount of it contributed by cigarette smoke to the global air supply "is reported to be negligible"—thus omitting mention of its possibly critical role in polluting the bloodstream of inhaling smokers. For sheer artifice, this sort of deceptive propaganda won the admiration of the

American Cancer Society's vice president for public information, Irving Rimer, who found it handsomely produced and crisply written—"One expects an industry with their resources to go first-class," he remarked. But Rimer earnestly regretted the lack of candor in the TI's literature: "They might have confronted the evidence and said they were concerned about it and were going to do everything they could to reduce the carcinogenic contents . . . [and] remove any defects from the product that made it deleterious to the public health."

One of the TI's most effective operatives was William F. Dwyer, whose curly-headed good looks and pleasing voice gave him the demeanor of innocence and sincerity as he traveled the land from 1974 to 1979 reciting the gospels according to St. Nicotine. A 1950s Princeton dropout who had gone into politics as an aide to the Republican congressman from his conservative home district in Rochester, New York, Dwyer loved public speaking and was good at it, so in time he went to work for several federal agencies whose programs he would beguilingly explain and defend before business groups and the general citizenry. When Richard Nixon resigned the presidency, Dwyer decided he had had enough of politics and answered a blind ad for an industry group seeking a spokesman on a controversial subject. Himself a smoker, Dwyer was pleased by the prospect of traveling first-class for TI in an expense-account lifestyle to plump for tobacco. He underwent intensive indoctrination with industry scientists, technicians, lawyers, and publicists, who drove home two lessons to him: (1) "Nobody likes us," and (2) that almost certainly included smokers.

When he first went on the road, Dwyer was accompanied by members of Shook, Hardy & Bacon, a Kansas City law firm that specialized in defending tobacco companies against liability claims, and when he slipped by saying "there is no evidence" that smoking caused disease, he was corrected to say "there is no proof" of a causal link. The lawyers, Dwyer recalled, coached him to admit nothing and condition all his remarks, "so we cabined everything—the whole thing was a disclaimer" and never a thinly veiled pitch in behalf of the virtues of smoking or a claim of harmlessness. Typically a TI publicist would telephone a local Rotary Club program director to advise that an assistant to the institute's president—Dwyer had been given the exalted title to enhance his promotability—would be in his community on a given date not to push smoking but only to ask for a fair hearing on the industry's side of the health charges. "We were promoting the free market system," Dwyer recounted, "where people can decide for themselves whether or not to consume a particular product."

Before long, Dwyer had his patter down cold. "Smoking has been valued and vilified by popes and potentates—we accept that," his opening ran, but the industry could not accept the notion that its fully legal product ought to be foreclosed from the marketplace. "There are things the public hasn't heard," Dwyer would assert, because the industry's story had not been properly disseminated. "It was an appeal for fair play," he said. His notion of fair play, as expressed in talks to small groups and then much more widely amplified in press interviews and radio and television appearances scheduled around his prepared speech in any given community, included charges like:

> a widespread antitobacco industry is out to harass sixty million Americans who smoke and to prohibit the manufacture and use of tobacco products. . . . Outrageous and medically unsubstantiated assertions made by well-financed and highly organized groups opposed to smoking are disputed by many men and women of science.

What "widespread antitobacco industry" was that? Who was trying to prohibit the manufacture of tobacco products? Which "outrageous and medically unsubstantiated assertions" were those? And what were the names of the "many men and women of science" who disputed the health charges against smoking and were also innocent of taking the tobacco industry's pay?

Dwyer's knack for phrasemaking grew with time, as in his urging his listeners to be wary of "the shower-adjusters" among them—busybodies who would, "if we let them, try to take over our lives and adjust the temperatures in our showers next if they don't like the way we're living." His jousts with the media turned more and more one-sided, as he came to understand better how to manipulate them. Broadcast interviewers, he found, were rarely "real journalists" when compared to print reporters, who tended to be more prepared and persistent in their interrogations. Few of his questioners or opponents on a debate platform were as professionally equipped as Dwyer, and in time most antismoking organizations would not let their representatives appear on the same platform with the TI's glib pitchman. One prominent exception was the irrepressible John Banzhaf, every bit a match for the industry spokesmen; Dwyer found the ASH founder to be "a zealot" and their encounters devoid of all graciousness, possibly because for Banzhaf the encounter was more than a rhetorical contest.

By contrast, Dwyer savored the engagement: "I liked being in a battle—it was like a political contest—a head game. . . . I enjoyed the intellectual stimulation and the challenge of it." He suffered no guilt pangs, he said, for his work in behalf of what many took to be a rogue industry, and would point in justification to the government-mandated warning on every cigarette pack that each consumer was free to heed or not. "I really believed that these people had been told."

V I

B UT "these people" were continuously told a lot of other things as well. The Tobacco Institute started running a series of double-page advertisements in February 1979—a month after the big Surgeon General's report was issued—in the nation's three mass newsweeklies and *Parade*, the Sunday supplement, which showed the industry's mind-manipulators at their most adroit. The thrust of the ads was that smoking was not a grave health issue but merely one of several equally acceptable social options, none of which required intervention by government into the lives of a sensible and civil people.

Headlined "Freedom of Choice is the best choice," the first ad took the form of separate messages to smokers and nonsmokers. The former were offered commiseration: "If you've ridden any planes [lately], you've found yourself banished to the back of them, last to be served, last to leave," so it was only natural for them to feel they were being made into "social outcasts". But the whole notion of separating smokers from nonsmokers was much ado about very little, the ad went on to imply; in communities where nonsmoking diners were entitled to smoke-free accommodations, restaurant owners were finding scant demand for the segregated seating. "The point is that most nonsmokers think smokers are O.K.," the TI ad reassured the latter—as if it were the smokers as human beings rather than their smoking that were the object of disapproval.

In fact, government regulations did not require smoking sections to be in the rear of aircraft cabins or that smokers be the last to get service or to deplane. In fact, smoke-free sections in restaurants were growing in popularity as the public began to grasp the possible implications of the toxic content of environmental tobacco smoke (ETS), though its magnitude of deadliness remained uncalculated. And in fact, most nonsmokers did not think smoking was "O.K."; according to a large survey by the U.S. Public Health Service in 1975, 77 percent of those nonsmokers questioned found it annoying to be near a smoker in the act. None of this deterred the authors of the Tobacco Institute ads, which went on to trivialize smoking as "a small ritual," part of the "personal style" of those who practiced it, and whether "you prefer carrot juice or bottled water, beach buggies or foreign cars, tobacco smoking or chewing gum" hardly mattered. What did was how awful life would be "if we allowed a tiny handful of intolerant anti-smokers, and a small number of discourteous smokers, to break up the enjoyable harmony we find in each other's personal choice."

Smoking, though, was not a "small ritual"—harmlessness was implied by the diminutive—nor a charming personality trait but a compulsive, often debilitating habit that most smokers told pollsters they would gladly break if they could. Neither could sly representations reduce to "a tiny handful of intolerant anti-smokers" the increasing majority of the population that favored segregating smokers who indulged themselves in public, even if politicians were not yet ready to enact such restrictions. But when the tables were turned and the tobacco industry itself was done in by the dubious tactics of its enemies, it let out a loud bellow—or, as in the seduction of Philip Morris by an ardent anti-smoking advocate with access to a mass audience, went to great lengths to silence the tormentor.

Peter Taylor, a leading investigative reporter on British television, approached Philip Morris after he had made two 1975 documentaries, one entitled "Licensed to Kill" about the British tobacco industry and a second about a man dying of lung cancer, for ITV's popular "This Week," Britain's approximate counterpart to America's top-rated "60 Minutes". For yet another show on the perils of smoking, Taylor wanted to feature Philip Morris, which was of course aware of the antismoking pitch of the prior shows but said it was told their seeming one-sidedness was due to the failure of the British cigarette manufacturers to avail themselves of the proffered opportunity to appear and give their side of the story. Philip Morris was badly in need of a major plug in the British market, and since it was about to introduce Marlboro Lights there, the company had a keen incentive to grasp the hand Taylor was extending to it.

"He professed that he planned to contrast Philip Morris with the British cigarette companies," according to PM's James Bowling. The American company was to be presented to British viewers as a different kind of tobacco manufacturer, one with a conscience, and in the process the standing of its Marlboro line as the world's best-selling brand would be reinforced. Philip Morris agreed to cooperate on the proviso that its views would be fairly and accurately presented in the new Taylor documentary, which bore the working title "This Week—Philip Morris." "We expected a zap in there," Bowling recalled, "but also that there would be an upside."

Taylor and his film crew came to the U.S. in the fall of 1976 and were given access to company officials, footage of its manufacturing procedures, a tour of its research facilities, and abundant data on its enlightened labor policies, including the best wages, fringe benefits, and working conditions in the industry. What Philip Morris's top people did not know was that Taylor also obtained clips of old Marlboro television commercials from a pliable, low-level company official and that the British film crew took extensive footage of real-life cowboys, or at least Westerners who had worked with cattle professionally part of their lives and who also smoked and were now suffering gravely for it.

When Taylor's report aired in Britain later that fall, Philip Morris learned that it had been taken for a ride of sorts, as the title of the searing documentary made plain—*Death in the West: The Marlboro Story*. The format of the program was constant crosscutting among three kinds of footage in a free-flow narrated by Taylor's crisply dissecting voice. The first two were clips from the Marlboro commercials, showing sturdy wranglers smoking around campfires and chuck wagons or riding hell-for-leather across the range while the rousing anthem from *The Magnificent Seven* surged in the background, followed by pieces of Taylor's interviews with the six ailing real-life cowboys. One, a branding inspector from Wyoming who had worked with livestock all his life, told Taylor in a raspy voice, "I started smoking as a kid following these broncobusters. I thought that to be a man you had to have a cigarette in your mouth. It took me years to discover all I got out of it was lung cancer. I'm going to die a young man"—and he did, a few months after the filming, at the age of fifty-one. The only five-year survivor among the six smoking Westerners was a rancher from near Cimmaron, New Mexico, who had emphysema and whom Taylor's crew had filmed with an oxygen cylinder strapped to his saddle while he was rounding up cattle and describing the effect of his disease: "I just have to stop and gasp for breath, and it feels like someone has their fingers down in my chest cutting the air passage off."

In the third crosscut segment, Taylor gave Philip Morris the chance he had promised by allowing a pair of its top officers to make extended remarks in defense of their company and its product. One of them was the suavely confident James Bowling, with his authoritative newscaster's voice, who told the off-camera interviewer, "I am not in the business of killing people." He had read the scientific literature on smoking and would hardly continue the practice himself, or permit his wife and children to engage in it, if he thought cigarettes posed the peril alleged, Bowling said. His industry, he insisted, was the victim of scapegoating: "I think it is really comfortable for a lot of people, when they do not know, to be able to find a target, and cigarettes, because they are pleasurable, have been a very good target. . . ." Then, with contempt for the collective epidemiological data, Bowling answered Taylor's question about why most people who get lung cancer are smokers by asking in return, "Why do 98 percent of the smokers never get anything?" This, despite twenty-five years of research demonstrating that about one habitual smoker in ten contracted lung cancer and about one in four died of a disease to which smoking contributed materially. Asked point-blank if cigarettes were harmless, Bowling answered, "I do not know that they are harmful or harmless. What I am saying is I think someone should find out."

The company's second spokesman was its chief scientist, Helmut Wakeham, who within Philip Morris's walls had spoken out with candor that at times bordered on the courageous. But in *Death in the West* he said, "I think there is a great deal of doubt as to whether or not cigarettes are harmful." He later remarked, "None of the things which have been found in tobacco smoke are in concentrations which should be considered harmful." This prompted the following colloquy with Taylor:

Q. But the components themselves can be considered harmful, can they not?
A. Anything can be considered harmful. Apple sauce is harmful if you get too much of it.
Q. I do not think many people are dying from apple sauce.
A. They are not eating much.
Q. People are smoking a lot of cigarettes.
A. Well, let me say it this way. The people who eat apple sauce are dying. The people who eat sugar die. The people who smoke die. Does the fact that the people who smoke cigarettes die demonstrate that smoking is the cause?

Soon after *Death in the West* aired, Philip Morris moved against Thames Television, the production company, for an injunction to prevent further showings and any sale of the program, claiming that it had been fraudulently seduced into cooperating and its commercials had been deceitfully obtained and used in a manner constituting copyright infringement. Taylor argued that he had honored the spirit of his agreement with the company by allowing its representatives to have an ample on-air say and that the Marlboro commercials were freely given to him for use in the film.

While the British courts were mulling the matter, a smuggled copy of *Death in the West* reached the American Cancer Society, whose Irving Rimer considered it "the most effective attack ever done on the cigarette industry." The tape, its copyright somewhat clouded, found its way to the producers of "60 Minutes," who had a good deal of interest in airing it—until a judge on the High Court of Justice, Queen's Bench Division, ruled in June 1977 in favor of Philip Morris. The jurist, who noted that he was himself a smoker, commented that the program "gave me all the indications of intending as its purpose the complete discrediting of the defendants," starting with "the conscious concealment of the title." The judge said that while he did not doubt the value and importance of Taylor's message, he asked, "Can a civilized legal system survive side by side with the proposition that the end can always justify the means?"

In an out-of-court settlement, Philip Morris supposedly got all the prints of the program save one for the Thames Television archives and had quashed its further distribution; terms of the agreement were to be kept secret in order not to further prejudice the injured party's position. "60 Minutes" could not legally buy the rights to *Death in the West*, and so the best piece of antismoking advocacy ever fashioned was, for the time being, effectively silenced by the aggrieved party.

VII

THE tobacco industry had its apparent invulnerability to effective political regulation tested seriously for the first time in the late 1970s. The instigator, though, was not the public-health community, which perceived smoking as pathological behavior that had to be treated like a disease, but the emerging environmental protection movement, which saw tobacco smoke as the most visible, odoriferous, and pervasive indoor equivalent of outdoor air pollution. Whether indoors or out, other people's smoke was becoming a potent political and social issue as well as a health concern, because it was patently an imposition by self-indulgent smokers on the ability of nonsmokers to enjoy clean air, even as the well-behaved citizenry had the right not to have its eyes offended, say, by the indecent exposure of passersby or its eardrums rattled by loudspeakers in their neighborhoods.

Although the scientific evidence was thin regarding the gravity of the health peril from environmental tobacco smoke (ETS), common sense suggested that it was a genuine pollutant. Cigarette smoke was known by then to contain some forty carcinogenic materials in at least trace quantities, and smokers, who typically inhaled for about twenty-four seconds in consuming a cigarette, extracted only one-third of its total smoke effluent—the portion known as mainstream smoke (M/S). The remaining two-thirds, known as side-stream smoke (S/S), which drifted off into the surrounding air, was for a time more potent than M/S, which had had a portion of its toxic contents removed by the filter before it reached the smoker's lungs. Nitrosamines, for example, were 80 to 90 percent trapped by cellulose acetate filters but were measured in concentrations up to fifty times higher in side-stream smoke, which never passed through a filter.

Gauging the toxicity of ETS, which combined S/S and exhaled M/S, to determine its order of magnitude as a pollutant was no easy matter. The lingering duration of the smoke in any given chamber varied with its size, temperature, ventilation, number of smoking occupants, and other factors all affecting the rate of dilution. Still, the acute effects of ETS were manifest to those who suffered tearing eyes, sore throats, stuffy or runny noses, headaches, nausea, and other symptoms. Asthmatics beset by ETS risked respiratory distress in reaction, while heart patients with angina were at risk from the oxygen deprivation due to smoky air.

Thus, ETS was a ripe target for environmentally concerned nonsmokers, as the Roper pollsters had advised the tobacco industry, and nowhere did the issue arouse more distress than in California, the nation's prime social laboratory, an unruly arena for political experimentation that lured ideologues from both the radical and reactionary fringes. In such an environment, one-issue action groups flourished and often attained disproportionate power. So it was with the local antitobacco organizations in California, widely known by the acronym GASP (for Group Against Smoking Pollution).

Among the two dozen or so people who showed up one evening in the mid-'Seventies when the Berkeley GASP assembled was Paul Loveday, a young graduate of the University of California Law School, then practicing in San Francisco. Loveday was a Mormon by upbringing and had a physical sensitivity—as well as his sect's theological opposition—to tobacco smoke; he also had a yearning for social activism. In short order, he was chosen president of the Berkeley unit and found himself allied with two ardent co-workers, Peter Hanauer, a quiet, meticulous, rather philosophical law-book editor, and Tim Moder, a chemist disenthralled with his profession who turned his Berkeley home into the makeshift headquarters of what soon became a loose confederation of GASPs and other antismoking action groups throughout the state. These ranged from big units in places like San Diego and Santa Monica to small ones that Loveday and his colleagues helped colonize while Moder turned out a newsletter and other mailings. Their chief challenge as they traveled the state was to persuade audiences that, unlike some other single-issue causists, they were not fanatics—in this case, tobacco prohibitionists. As far as GASP was concerned, it was fine for the Marlboro cowboy to light up, Loveday would tell groups he addressed, "so long as he does it on his own range."

Young, energetic, full of themselves and their mission, the Berkeley antismoking activists soon moved beyond the educative function and set out on a course of social action. They besieged the Berkeley city council with letters, petitions, and in-person appeals for restrictions on smoking in all public indoor places and separate sections for nonsmokers in restaurants and workplaces. Tobacco industry representatives tried to tar GASP and its allies as zealots, but the company men were plainly interlopers and were badly outnumbered in a community with a rarefied social consciousness; and when the city's—and one of the nation's—best restaurants, Chez Panisse, signed on to the reform effort, the outcome was no longer in doubt. The restrictive measure, passed unanimously by the Berkeley council, was the toughest of its kind in the state and a model for other GASPs to pursue in California and elsewhere.

Buoyed by their own and similar local success stories, Loveday and his band of amateur activists tried to storm the legislature in Sacramento in quest of antismoking regulations like Berkeley's to apply to all of California, even calling for inclusion of the right of citizens' arrests of violators. But the cigarette industry, sensing a rising peril, focused its lobbyists' well-paid labors on the state's legislators and swatted down the GASPers' cheeky effort. Their crushing loss only inspired renewed enthusiasm, this time in a form that circumvented the industry's lock on the state lawmakers—a referendum under

California's public-initiative procedures, an exercise in direct democracy available when representative government was found unresponsive to perceived social needs.

To get on the 1978 ballot, they would need to gather 300,000 signatures by petition and mount an organizational effort far beyond anything GASP had attempted before. They got 600,000 names. Even so, the proposed Clean Indoor Air Act, as their Proposition No. 5 was termed, was not going to come easily in a state where Ronald Reagan, with his antiregulatory credo, had lately completed two terms as governor and a steamrolling antitax movement left voters in a sour mood toward activist programs like the antismoking initiative. But Prop Five, as the GASP-sponsored referendum was called for short, was no esoteric daydream of rabid environmentalists; instead, it struck a responsive chord with voters who could distinguish between risks they as individuals could take voluntarily, like skiing down a treacherous slope or driving without a seat belt, and risks that were imposed on their health and safety, like pesticides applied to their vegetables before harvesting or other people's smoke in their faces.

Loveday's clean-air coalition was bolstered by two important recruits among the leadership. The noisier of them was a technological virtuoso, Stanton A. Glantz, trained as an aeronautical engineer with a Stanford doctorate in applied mechanics and economics, who was on the University of California's medical faculty in San Francisco. He had been a political and environmental activist at Stanford and thus a natural enlistee in the emerging nonsmokers' rights movement, to which he brought political savvy, technical expertise, a pointed rhetorical style, and a feisty, somewhat obsessive disposition. But before Loveday and Hanauer unleashed him as their scientific guru, to explain the medical case for Prop Five in speaking engagements around the state, Glantz was asked to put aside his blue jeans and only suit—an orange one, his favorite color, that he was married in—for more respectable threads. Glantz, sometimes volcanic, complied and thus began a uniquely effective and long-running career as an antismoking activist.

The second key addition to the Prop Five advocates was Dr. Raymond Weisberg, a San Francisco internist and chairman of the public-affairs committee of the American Cancer Society's California branch. Weisberg was able to attract help from members of the California Medical Association, the American Lung Association, and other pillars of the medical establishment, thus overcoming the "kook" factor that Prop Five foes attributed to the effort. Weisberg also prevailed upon state ACS leaders to funnel some backdoor funding to the clean-air coalition—the only way the national organization, perennially fearful of political entanglements lest they offend contributors on the other side of the antismoking cause, would countenance the step. Even limited ACS backing of Prop Five made it easier to attract prominent figures in science, like former Atomic Energy Commission chairman Glenn Seaborg, and in Hollywood, like actor Gregory Peck, to the antismoking cause. Early polls showed voters favoring Prop Five by a surprising three-to-one ratio. But it was not a gut issue in that gubernatorial election year, and clean-air money was hard to come by; Loveday and Hanauer contributed several thousand dollars of their own to keep their statewide drive going.

The contest soon changed as the tobacco industry calculated that it stood to lose no less than $250 million of its California revenues if Prop Five passed. Five of the six companies assembled a war chest, with each one's contributions in keeping with its market share; only American Tobacco, self-styled industry militant, held aloof and got a free ride. With the aid of top lawyers, publicists, and political consultants, the industry soon realized that it could not prevail on the health issue, even though the scientific evidence on the nature of the ETS peril was hazy at best. Instead, the cigarette makers ridiculed the clean-air advocates as latter-day Carry Nations, strident busybodies intruding on the personal freedoms of the public. At the same time, they reached out to labor, racial minorities, and feminists by characterizing the antismoking restrictions as elitist, since smoking would be allowed in private offices but not in open areas at work sites, where secretaries, clerks, and other lower-level personnel were stationed. "Show me a worker who doesn't smoke," remarked the California head of the Oil, Chemical and Atomic Workers Union, "and I'll show you a worker who beats his wife." This allusion to the tobacco-allayed frustrations of blue-collar life was cited as well by the big teamsters, auto-workers, and longshoremen's unions in opposing Prop Five. The tobacco interests also appealed to Republican and antigovernment sentiments by claiming that the clean-air law would cost a great deal to implement and administer and confected a price tag to suit their needs: $250 million for the first year, when private businesses would be required to put up walls and partitions to establish nonsmoking sections, plus $43 million in government outlays, more than half for law enforcement. The industry won the support of San Diego's police chief, who said the new law would siphon off a portion of his manpower needed for combating serious safety hazards. Others argued that the proposed statute was somewhat arbitrary and capricious in that it barred smoking at rock but not jazz concerts, at amateur but not at professional sports events, and in taxis even if both driver and passenger did not object.

The clean-air coalition fought back, claiming that the restrictive measures would save the public a billion dollars in health-care costs and lost wages due to smoking-related illnesses. And the nimble-minded Stan Glantz uncovered an error in the tobacco industry's computations which he said inflated the claimed cost of "No Smoking" signage a thousandfold. But the correction was too complex for the public to grasp, no matter how lucidly Glantz tried to explain it, meanwhile allowing the debate to dwell on an issue damaging to the passage of Prop Five: the price the public would have to pay for its implementation. As the campaign ended, the tobacco ad dollars poured in; the industry spent $6 million to defeat Prop Five, more than twenty times the GASP-led coalition's outlay and more than the two gubernatorial candidates spent between them. The antismoking proposal lost by 54 percent to 46.

Viewing the outcome as a vigorous exercise in consciousness-raising, the clean-air coalition tried again two years later, but toned down the proposed restrictions a bit. Known as the Smoking and Nonsmoking Sections Initiative, Proposition 10 on the 1980 California ballot provided for separate areas in enclosed public places and indoor work sites, barred smoking in stores, permitted it anywhere outdoors, said the smoking and nonsmoking sections in offices did not have to be separated by walls or partitions, and made violations a civil, not a criminal, offense, to be enforced by health officers instead of the police. The antismoking camp slammed the tobacco industry with charges of having purchased victory in Prop Five and hiding now behind a paper organization called Californians Against Regulatory Excess (CARE); polls showed Prop Ten ahead by two to one just six weeks before the election. But with another advertising blitz by the companies in the homestretch, the separate smoking accommodations proposal went down again, 53 percent to 47.

The antismoking crusaders exacted retribution the following year against Philip Morris, which had spearheaded the industry's defense in the two California propositions. The clean-air coalition would soon reorganize as Californians for Nonsmokers' Rights, with Glantz as president. A celebrity of sorts by now, Glantz received by mail a pirated tape of Peter Taylor's *Death in the West*, suppressed under the court-approved settlement in Britain between Philip Morris and Thames Television. Convinced that the film should be shown in the U.S., Glantz went to a San Francisco law firm that agreed to handle the matter as a public service. On investigation, the tape was found to be in proprietary limbo: Thames had not copyrighted the original film in America, and Philip Morris had not obtained the copyright under its settlement agreement, probably believing it better public relations to have the British firm police any purloined copies and move against any attempted illicit showings. But Thames had no financial incentive for bringing an action against any U.S. exhibitor, and the First Amendment protection against prior restraint of speech or expression would shield at least an initial showing. Glantz further hedged the calculated risk he was about to take by explaining the entire matter to the general counsel of the University of California, his employer, which decided, according to Glantz, that he was performing a valuable community service and agreed to support him in the event that the filmmaker or the tobacco giant took him to court.

Glantz brought the tape to the three big health voluntaries, which all declined to sponsor a public showing, and to CBS, which again elected not to put it on "60 Minutes." Frustrated, Glantz took his problem to Michael Pertschuk at the FTC, who tried to have the antismoking film shown within the lawsuit-proof confines of the Senate Commerce Committee, where he had long wielded influence as a senior staffer, but those days were gone. He then fed the story of the suppressed tape to muckraking syndicated columnist Jack Anderson, who published it. The account persuaded San Francisco's NBC affiliate KRON-TV to view the tape and risk airing it. The ratings were good, and Philip Morris chose not to chance a public-relations black eye by taking the station, Glantz, or anyone involved to court. Subsequently, Boston's public TV outlet, WGBH, showed *Death in the West*, and soon the tape was made readily available through a private distributor to anyone who wanted to buy it, with royalties payable to the California Board of Regents and the nonsmokers' coalition. A special introduction explained how the American public was intended never to see the film.

VIII

PERHAPS the most contemptuous of the tobacco industry's chief executives toward its detractors in this period was Robert Heimann, who headed American Brands, as American Tobacco's parent was now known. During several depositions taken for liability suits in the mid-1980s, not long after he had retired from the company, Heimann disclosed what his thinking had been on the charges against smoking. American Tobacco had never bothered to assemble a panel of doctors or scientists to find out their opinion on the health hazards its product might present, Heimann said. Asked if he thought unlimited smoking might prove hazardous, Heimann replied that his company "never got into that subject of how much anybody should smoke. . . . What people want to do is their own decision, not our decision. We try to keep our product . . . in the best possible condition to produce pleasure on the part of our customers."

Lest the American Brands boss be supposed to have been utterly callous and indifferent to communal health concerns, it must be noted that Heimann told the trade magazine *Tobacco Journal* late in 1977 how his company tried to be "a good citizen". It did this not by worrying over any damage its product might do to consumers but by taking pains so that the water discharged into the James River from its plant at Bermuda Hundred, Virginia, was "a good deal purer than the same water when we drew it out." He was proud as well of the program run by the Council for Tobacco Research—which was as close as Heimann came to conceding that there was any problem that required research. "The beauty of this concept," Heimann told his interviewer, "[is] that the people who support it have nothing to say about the granting of the money. . . .

[I]t's not a public relations ploy. It doesn't amount to institutional advertising. It's not blowing your own horn. It's not attacking anybody. It's trying to be constructive."

But a likely more candid expression of American Tobacco's estimate of the CTR program was offered, not long after the published interview with Heimann, at a closed-door meeting in Lexington, Kentucky, on October 26, 1978, of the tobacco industry's research committee of lawyers and scientists. According to subpoenaed notes of that meeting, two American Brands attorneys, Arnold Henson and Janet Brown from the New York firm of Chaddbourne, Parke, stated that "CTR must be maintained but need[s] new people. It must be more politically oriented. . . . The approach must be steady, slow and conservative. They must find skeptical scientists. . . . The staff at CTR also need[s] to be more tobacco oriented with a skeptical view. . . ."

The alleged purity of the CTR's investigations into the links between smoking and disease had been a central tenet of the industry's publicly expressed code of conduct since 1954, when its joint research program was created. As a 1970 ad placed by the Tobacco Institute put it, "Completely autonomous, CTR's research is directed by a board of ten scientists and physicians. . . ." But a perhaps more revealing glimpse into how autonomous the CTR was, who ran it, and for what purpose was offered just a month after the Lexington meeting at another session of industry lawyers and scientists, this one in New York, according to a November 17, 1978, memo summarizing it by Robert Seligman, who had succeeded Helmut Wakeham as head of the Philip Morris research and development program. Seligman paraphrased the remarks at the meeting by veteran tobacco lawyer William Shinn of Shook, Hardy & Bacon describing the history of the tobacco companies' joint research council: "It was set up as an industry 'shield' in 1954. . . . CTR has helped our legal counsel by giving advice and technical information, which was needed at court trials. CTR has provided spokesmen for the industry at Congressional hearings. The monies spent on CTR provides [*sic*] a base for introduction of witnesses. . . ."

The Seligman memo for the PM files went on to note that the best way CTR spent its funds was on the "special projects" program run by the lawyers. "On these projects, CTR has acted as a 'front'; however, there have been times when CTR was reluctant to serve in that capacity." Most of all, Shinn felt, in remarks that Seligman's memo seems to imply were representative of the consensus, "It is extremely important that the industry continue to spend their dollars in research to show that we don't agree that the case against smoking is closed. . . . There is a 'CTR basket' which must be maintained for 'PR' purposes. . . ." Remarks seemingly corroborative of this assessment were offered three years later by CTR's veteran counsel, Edwin Jacob, who at a September 10, 1981, meeting of the industry's committee of general counsel said, according to notes made of the session, "When we started the CTR Special Projects, the idea was that the scientific director of CTR would review the project. If he liked it, it was a CTR special project. If he did not like it, then it became a lawyers' special project," which could be shielded from outside scrutiny under the privileged lawyer-client relationship. As Jacob added, noting several grantees by name, "With Speilberger, we were afraid of discovery for FTC and [in the case of] Aviado, we wanted to protect it under the lawyers. We did not want it out in the open."

The industry's direct involvement in these "special projects"—despite its repeated claims in public of a hands-off policy regarding the research it funded on smoking and health—was confirmed by one high-ranking Philip Morris scientist who sat on the manufacturers' "Technical Subcommittee," serving among other functions as liaison with and in oversight of CTR. The "special projects" were undertaken with and for the lawyers, according to the Philip Morris official, "to help them in their efforts to defend the industry. I see nothing sinister in all that—just a bunch of inept guys trying to play scientist." The CTR, he added, "had no program, just divisions of investigation" such as smoke chemistry, genetic studies, and carcinogenesis. Examples of CTR "special projects" for the 1979–81 period were found in industry documents marked "Personal and Confidential—For Counsel Only" and were produced in the course of litigation several years later. Among these were a grant of $30,000 to British psychologist Hans Eysenck for maintenance of a registry of twins to gather data in support of the "constitutional theory" that smokers were in effect born that way; $69,161 to Richard Hickey for studies on the relationship of air pollution "and other environmental variables" to chronic diseases; $61,500 to Arthur Furst to "study the effects of combined asbestos and benzopyrene on lungs of mice"; and $127,932 to Theodor Sterling for a "Retrospective Analysis of Environmental Contacts of Patients with Respiratory Cancer, Other Cancers, and Other Diseases." The projects had at least two important elements in common: all were aimed at blaming something besides tobacco smoke as a prime instigator in human pathogenesis, and each of the investigators wrote publicly or testified in court or before Congess (or both) in behalf of the cigarette industry's position on smoking and health.

Among the most egregious instances of "special projects" grant recipients carrying water for the tobacco industry in these years was Carl Coleman Seltzer, a fringe member of the Harvard academic community. Trained as an anthropologist, Seltzer was a longtime "research fellow" with the university's Peabody Museum, and though neither a medical doctor nor an epidemiologist with a specialty in public health, he wrote articles for more than thirty years, arguing that the scientific case against smoking was flawed and unproven. In 1979, the CTR gave him a "special" grant of $60,000 to continue his work on "constitutional differences between smokers and nonsmokers" and additional grants of $70,000 for each of the following two years; he later told *The Wall*

Street Journal he had received "well over a million" dollars for research under CTR's aegis in the course of his career.

Among the fruits of Seltzer's research was an article he contributed to the September 1980 *American Heart Journal* entitled "Smoking and Coronary Heart Disease: What Are We to Believe?" It had two main thrusts: (1) Research showing that those who quit smoking had a lowered coronary heart disease (CHD) risk was fatally flawed, because such studies "have made the false assumption that ex-smokers are representative of continuing smokers except for the change in the smoking habit." In a new study of 25,000 people enrolled in the Kaiser-Permanente health-care program in the San Francisco area (on which Seltzer was a co-investigator and the CTR a prime funder), the findings were that the ex-smokers, when tested before quitting, had "a lower CHD risk to begin with," thus contributing to their eventual CHD outcomes. And (2) claims in the 1979 Surgeon General's report that smoking was causally related to CHD were not validated by the evidence offered, and, as Seltzer put it, "The cold reality is that the mechanisms by which smoking . . . allegedly enhances CHD have not been established." The government's 1979 report seemed to concede as much, he argued, with statements like "Relatively little is known about the mechanisms by which smoking enhances atherogenesis or increases the risk of heart attack"; indeed, the report, Seltzer charged, was filled with speculation, surmise, hypotheses, and "facile postulations". Findings like Auerbach's showing that smokers had more severe atherosclerosis of the coronary arteries than nonsmokers did not in and of themselves prove that smoking was the cause. Therefore, this well-paid tobacco industry apologist concluded, "For the present, then, it is reasonable to believe that stopping smoking does not reduce the risk of CHD and that there is no established proof that cigarette smoking is causally related to coronary heart disease."

Close scrutiny of the study on which the first of these arguments was based reveals the shallowness—and false reassurance to smokers—of Seltzer's reading of the evidence. The differences found between ex-smokers and continuing smokers, as the cited study he co-authored for the *Journal of Chronic Diseases* disclosed (but Seltzer omitted in the more widely read *American Heart Journal*), "were quantitatively small," and this was true even for most indices by which CHD risk was assessed. Thirteen percent of white male continuing smokers had a history of hypertension, compared with 12 percent of the ex-smokers before they quit; 15 percent of the smokers had had electrocardiograms with abnormalities, compared with 14 percent of the quitters; and the ongoing smokers had an average cholesterol reading of 229, actually a point lower than the ex-smokers' average—and their hemoglobin ratings were the same. Even in the few "social-personal" characteristics cited in the Kaiser-Permanente study, there were scant differences: smokers consumed 3 percent more alcohol than those who later quit, for example, and 52 percent of the continuing smokers had some college education, compared with 56 percent of the quitters. The most significant difference cited appeared to be that about 36 percent of smokers drank six or more cups of coffee a day, compared with 26 percent of the ex-smokers. While it was true, and hardly surprising, that ongoing smokers consumed perhaps 40 to 50 percent more cigarettes than those who later stopped and that 86.3 percent of them inhaled, compared with 77.5 percent of quitters—which was to say those who ultimately quit had been lighter smokers—so what? To argue as Seltzer did that all or any of this meant that smokers and quitters were fundamentally different kinds of people, with significantly different levels of physiological vulnerability to the ravages of smoking and its pathogenic mechanisms, was simply unwarranted. Commented Dr. William B. Kannel, longtime former director of the NIH's Framingham Study, and a leading authority on the effects of smoking on CHD:

> Dr. Seltzer tends to select isolated pieces of data . . . that appear to support his biased point of view. He also tends to ignore data sets that do not support his own vested interest. The piece of evidence he refuses to confront is that those who quit smoking have only half the risk [of heart disease] of those who continue to smoke, regardless of how long and how much they have previously smoked.

As to Seltzer's reliance on the fact that science had not yet unraveled the precise nature of the mechanisms contributing to CHD, this was the same line pursued by the tobacco industry's pet scientists with regard to the incriminating evidence of smoking's causal links to lung cancer, obstructive pulmonary diseases, or anything else—namely, that they had not been proven beyond a scintilla of doubt. In fact, much was known, and still more was plausibly conjectured, about how smoking tipped the delicate balances of cellular biochemistry and compromised the body's defense mechanisms. None of these observed phenomena absolutely proved that smoking was causally related to heart disease, any more than the sizable grants Seltzer received from the tobacco industry proved that he was anything other than a totally objective, suitably skeptical scientist—but in both cases there were more than ample grounds for deep suspicion. In the estimate of Boston University medical professor Thomas S. Dawber, to cite one authority queried by *Medical World News* at the time of the 1980 article on CHD, Seltzer's conclusions were "nonsense".

Nonsensical or not, the research of many scientists and investigators like Seltzer was paid for by the industry to advance its own well-being and fend off criticism, yet the Tobacco Institute's 1982 pamphlet *Answers to the Most Asked Questions About Cigarettes* asked itself in query No. 12, "Do the tobacco companies control the research they sponsor?" and answered: "Absolutely not. Independent scientific advisors evaluate and fund research proposals by individuals and institutions. Awards are made with no strings attached. . . ."

I X

MOST businessmen who had achieved the financial results that Joseph F. Cullman III did during his twenty-one years at the helm of Philip Morris would have taken their bows and moved off to the wings without looking for fresh complications at the end of their performance. But from the moment Cullman announced in the spring of 1978 that he would step aside at the end of the year, it became apparent that he wanted to depart in a burst of glory.

This resolve was curious in light of the numbers. He had pushed his company from sixth to second place in its field, posting a higher net every year than in the year preceding, and for the final ten years of his tenure, that net had grown at a compounded annual rate of 20 percent. By 1978, it was earning twenty-three cents a year on every dollar of owner-invested capital, surpassing industry leader R. J. Reynolds in this critical measure of management skill. Over Cullman's last decade as CEO, no other company on *Fortune*'s annual list of the top five hundred U.S. corporations had brought its stockholders a greater total return in the form of rising dividend payments and enhanced value in the stock market. And in 1978, things were looking better than ever. Philip Morris USA had 28 percent of the American cigarette market and was closing in fast on RJR. Marlboro was outselling Winston by more than 2 million packs a day, and Merit had surpassed Vantage as the best-selling lowered-tar brand. Philip Morris International was now grossing three-quarters of the PM-USA total and twice as much as RJR, runner-up in foreign cigarette revenues.

And Cullman's major move to diversify out of tobacco was finally paying off; Miller Brewing's sales had shot up 482 percent over the last six years of his reign to gain 19 percent of the U.S. beer business and give PM, as in the cigarette trade, a strong No. 2 position. In the view of most financial analysts, Philip Morris was the smartest, best-run, and most sophisticated outfit in its industry.

Still, Cullman, at the age of sixty-six, remained driven; as he would later recount his final major move, "We were under a lot of pressure from the board to diversify further." How much pressure any corporate board could apply to a chairman with Cullman's track record was uncertain; what was clear was that in light of his earlier frustrations in trying to diversify profitably, Cullman relished Miller's growing success and saw it as a base for building a major beverage empire as an adjunct to Philip Morris's soaring worldwide tobacco business. Merger talks were arranged between Philip Morris and PepsiCo, another New York–based consumer goods outfit with superior marketing skills and a strong No. 2 position in its field. "We got pretty far into it," Cullman said, before both parties agreed that the deal was certain to be attacked on anti-trust grounds and so backed away.

But Cullman was enamored with the soft-drink industry as a natural complement to the tobacco and beer businesses, and his eyes came to rest on Seven-Up, maker of the lemon-lime drink that held 7 percent of the U.S. soda market and occupant of a very distant No. 3 position in market share behind Coca-Cola and PepsiCo. The two giants had all but a fraction of the cola business, which made up some 65 percent of the soft-drink market, while cola-less Seven-Up puttered along with sales of $250 million that netted about 10 percent. That the relatively small St. Louis–based soda maker faced a possible mauling from a pair of leviathans if it tried to move well beyond its niche did not much faze Cullman, who, after all, had come from far to the rear of the pack to challenge leviathans RJR and Anheuser-Busch for leadership in the tobacco and beer industries.

Early talks with the Seven-Up people proved fruitless; the soda company was not interested in a stock swap, only a buyout, and had been shopping the business widely. While the negotiations were inching along, though, Cullman began to encounter internal opposition to the idea of buying Seven-Up. PM's president, Ross Millhiser, believed that the company's moves out of the to-bacco business had served to dilute company earnings and strain its credit rating. He had a powerful ally in Clifford Goldsmith, then running PM-USA, who retained little faith in Cullman's turnaround philosophy of diversifying. Even the Miller Brewing victory had been achieved only with a massive infusion of fresh capital, and its margins remained well below those of PM's cigarette operations. Goldsmith told Cullman he thought it a serious mistake to enter the soda business "with a minority-preference product," even if it could be bought for a modest price; in the long run, it would cost a great deal to make it competitive with the market leaders.

There were serious structural problems as well with a Seven-Up takeover, Jetson Lincoln, PM's chief corporate planner, pointed out to the boss. The owners of the brand essentially just manufactured the syrup; it was the bottlers who sold the soda. This was entirely different from the beer business, in which the wholesalers had cancelable arrangements and only distributed the product. Soda bottlers, on the other hand, had long-term franchise agreements with precisely defined territories, and it was they who made the major capital investment to buy the syrup, mix the beverage, and bottle, sell, and advertise it. Most big bottlers were affiliated with either Coke or Pepsi and carried Seven-Up as a noncompetitive fill-in of their line. That meant that if Philip Morris ever intended to go big-time in the soda world by bringing out its own brand of cola, most of its regular bottlers would be unable to carry it. And if Coke and Pepsi got into a price war in the supermarket, Coke's modest lemon-lime entry,

Sprite, would also get involved, putting a heavy squeeze on Seven-Up's sales and margins, so a rough road could be expected if PM journeyed into soda. Buying Seven-Up thus struck PM's chief financial officer, Shepard Pollack, as "a bad idea."

For all this naysaying, Cullman had the strong backing of the other leading candidate to replace him at year's end—Vice Chairman George Weissman. He more than Cullman had closely monitored Philip Morris's overseas tobacco and domestic beer ventures, and as their earnings steadily improved, so had Weissman's confidence grown in the company's ability to move beyond its core business. Though few products on earth, he fully understood, were more profitable than cigarettes, tobacco was under a cloud, and the cloud was growing larger and stormier-looking. The soda business, moreover, had much in common with cigarettes and beer, Weissman argued to Cullman: all three were agriculturally based consumer products, low-priced and thus relatively recession-proof, and their marketing responded to imaginative advertising, packaging, and merchandising—all strong suits for Philip Morris. And the company already had an executive on hand who had displayed effective leadership in building a beverage business—the joyfully combative John Murphy.

Cullman decided to plow ahead, ordering his planning aide Jet Lincoln to put aside his own misgivings and prepare a favorable presentation on the proposed Seven-Up acquisition for the directors' meeting to be held the day before the annual stockholders' meeting, the last over which Cullman was to preside. The company overseers were divided as they had never been on a major decision during Joe Cullman's tenure. The tobacco executives on the board—Millhiser, Goldsmith, and marketing chief Jack Landry—remained steadfast in opposition, as the argument swayed back and forth. But in the end, no one had the strength to buck the still potent Cullman at the end of his spectacular career. Two months later, Philip Morris bought out Seven-Up for $514 million, its largest purchase ever.

The decision helped doom Millhiser's chances to succeed Cullman. The final choice was "a close call," as Cullman remembered it. "The board felt George was more open to diversification than Ross, who was a strong tobacco man and . . . dedicated to our staying mainly in that business." But the succession also played out as it did partly because the very strength of intellect that had propelled Millhiser into serious contention with Weissman caused concern among Philip Morris insiders. "The speed with which his mind flew from topic to topic could be off-putting," one high-ranking colleague recalled of Millhiser. "It was hard to get Ross to focus." Said another top company officer, "For all his brightness and love of words, he was not a very good communicator. . . . He didn't straight out identify a problem but approached it more anecdotally, as if the listener ought to intuit what needed to be done."

Weissman had never had a problem focusing or communicating. Son of an immigrant milliner, a poor boy who had attended City College by day and worked nights at Orbach's department store, he had charmed rather than shoved his way to the top of the business world. If possessed of a less original mind than Millhiser, Weissman at fifty-nine was the polished, consummate company loyalist, willing to undertake any assignment good-naturedly. His lanky build and craggy looks had once got him tagged by a financial writer as "a corporate Gary Cooper"; his weather-lined face gave him the appearance, fittingly, of the quintessential Marlboro Man. He lighted his cigarette with the flair of an actor and always managed to show the Marlboro pack while in the act.

Millhiser was given Weissman's former title of vice chairman but without the added designation of chief operating officer (COO), indicating that his standing in the power structure would be more ceremonial than real. Goldsmith, named president of the corporation, Millhiser's prior slot, was more the de facto COO and chief keeper of the tobacco flame. Socialite Hugh Cullman, whose success running Philip Morris International stemmed in large measure from his remarkably strong lieutenants, was thought unsuited to the trench warfare involved in running the company's day-to-day U.S. cigarette business. Instead, Hugh was named chairman of the nonexistent board of PM-USA and chief executive officer of the domestic unit, but the presidency and chief operating job went to Goldsmith's acolyte, Shepard Pollack, a crack finance man. Jack Landry was passed over, largely for fear that his drinking had burned him out; he was given company-wide oversight of marketing, a vague assignment that removed him from the front lines but kept him on call as a counselor to the company's golden boy and, many assumed, future CEO, James Morgan, who took over as marketing chief of PM-USA. Jim Bowling became Weissman's key executive assistant, the ultimate staff man, but without line power. The presidency of Philip Morris International went to the savvy, soft-spoken Cambridge man, Hamish Maxwell. As Cullman's successor, Weissman was supposed to keep this veteran lineup in place and driving toward the top in tobacco and beer—and while he was at it (and since he had campaigned for it), turn the problematic Seven-Up purchase into a silk purse.

Joe Cullman stepped aside as the Christmas holidays arrived, yet he never really left the premises. He traveled a lot and played more but was invited to keep his office, with the trophy elephant tusks in place, and he did. George Weissman had the keys to the cash register and all the trappings of power, but Cullman's shadow hovered nearby, and his substance remained highly visible on the board of directors. Had he been a brilliant merchandiser and astute manipulator of diversely gifted subordinates—or a monstrous merchant of death, stubbornly denying and defying the scientific evidence against smoking cigarettes, and minting profits all the while? Or was he both?

A fourth-generation tobacco man, Cullman had come of age when the medical case against smoking was based more on folklore and anecdote than persuasive documentation. How many businessmen this side of heaven would have willingly received the emerging verdict of science, bowed to it gracefully, and shuttered the shop that stood accused of poisoning so many of its customers? Such a concession was unthinkable to men who had risen to the top of the tobacco trade in the belief that they were servicing a clientele that by and large understood the product was not therapeutic for their internal systems, whatever calming or stimulating effects it worked on their psyches. The simple truth was that the cigarette makers were getting richer and richer as the scientific findings against them piled higher and higher, and before anyone fully grasped the situation, the choice seemed to have narrowed to abject confession and surrender to the health advocates or steadfast denial and rationalization. Cullman took the latter course and did so with somewhat less truculence than his opposite numbers at other cigarette companies. "Nobody could really identify what was in there [the cigarette smoke] that shouldn't be there," he would remark ten years into his retirement. His company nevertheless—and without ever conceding the reason—did partially respond to its critics by modifying the toxicity of its often lethal product. To use Cullman's retrospective words, "[W]e brought the numbers down . . . and we've done many things to come up with a cigarette that's more acceptable. . . . I never had a crumb of conscience."

Could he have felt anything else and kept functioning as the peerless tobacco purveyor of his generation? Actually, out of humanitarian concern he might have said nothing in derogation of the studied and disinterested judgment of medical science—namely, that he was selling a potentially deadly product. But businessmen are combatants, not healers, and when they press against or exceed the bounds of decency in their quest for gain, unhesitant to profit from the folly of others, should the exploited clientele and victimized society expect the perpetrators to restrain themselves out of some sudden divine visitation of conscience? Or must human nature be forcibly corrected when it goes awry?

If no one was garlanding Cullman as a paragon of compassion for his fellow man, the executives he left in place upon his retirement were even less inclined to concede culpability. The 1978 Philip Morris annual report, issued a few months after Cullman stepped down and the first to bear Weissman's signature as CEO, stated the official company position on smoking and health this way: "No conclusive medical or clinical proof has been discovered"; the antismoking charges still relied on statistical associations that did not establish cause; and "independent statisticians and biometricians have questioned the validity of the statistics in a number of these studies." On his retirement six years later, Weissman would go a good deal further than Cullman had ever ventured in both self-justification and reassurance of the public. "I've always felt science was on our side," he told the *Tobacco & Candy Journal*, ". . . and that we had more regard for the scientific truth as it existed. . . ."

Ross Millhiser, tobacco lover par excellence, would recount, in retirement, his experience at a World War II prison camp where he saw fellow captives of war trade badly needed food for the two or three cigarettes each was given among his daily rations and drew a lifelong lesson about the sustenance men extracted from their smokes: "I never lost faith in the business—you can't keep people frightened forever." In his sardonic manner, he expressed confidence that "the desire to die in good health will wane" and registered disdain for the American cultural norm "to live your life strictly to prolong it, eating only what's good for you and undertaking all of life's other activities that way. . . . Smoking is a contribution to living. You can say that I'm uninformed, obdurate, or blind, but I can't see where it's going to cause me to have cancer." The war in Vietnam, he was convinced, had "frustrated us as a society," causing the American people to feel "we aren't doing anything right anymore . . . and it's easy to take it all out on cigarettes."

This mentality, easily dismissed by outsiders as bunker paranoia, was still more forcefully voiced by Clifford Goldsmith. "We have been unfairly pilloried," he would say five years after retiring from Philip Morris, "and I'm sad because I know we're honorable people." He conceded that tobacco executives had a vested interest that made their views on smoking and health appear biased—"and we probably are, but I never had a moment's concern. . . . I felt we were performing a real service—that ours was a product helping the public through the rigors of living." From ancient times, human beings have ingested substances besides food to gain pleasure or achieve serenity—he cited opium, coca leaf–chewing, and crack as examples far worse than tobacco smoke—and added, "We have fulfilled a need, and it's very naive to assume that nonsmokers don't fulfill that need in other and more destructive ways," including self-consuming stress and a whole range of antisocial acts of aggression.

Far from apologizing, then, for the alleged devastation its product caused, Philip Morris, under a new chairman, a practiced hand at public relations, set out to convince the American public that it was animated by genuine social consciousness. Its philanthropic contributions under Weissman grew more numerous and visible, and special efforts were made to help minorities and their organizations (without mention of the fact that blacks and Latinos smoked in a somewhat heavier proportion than white Americans). In its gifts to both social causes and the arts, such as PM's sponsorship in 1979 of a touring show of a century of ceramics in the U.S., the company seemed guided by two criteria: urgent need on the part of the recipients, whose appreciation and complicity in PM's profit-seeking activities were thereby assured, and high visibility in the community.

Weissman's strong interest in the arts, stemming from exposure in his boyhood to opera records played on his family's phonograph, was a reflection as well of his attitude toward business. In time, he would speak of a "triple helix," an interweaving of interests whereby the arts needed the financial support of business, business needed the arts to improve the quality of its life, and the community at large needed both. "Our business activities must make social sense," he wrote in the 1979 annual report, "and our social activities must make business sense." And above all, "A Philip Morris unit must be an exemplary corporate citizen wherever it operates."

A few weeks before PM's annual report was issued in the spring of 1980, R&D vice president Robert Seligman exhibited his exemplary citizenship in a letter to Alexander Spears, his counterpart at Lorillard. He wrote that, as directed by Weissman's right-hand man, Jim Bowling, he was sending on "our recommendations for industry research which we prepared last year. . . . I have added a list of three subjects which I feel should be avoided." These were: "1. Developing new tests for carcinogenicity, 2. Attempt to relate human disease to smoking, 3. Conduct experiments which require large doses of carcinogen to show additive effect of smoking."

15

The Calling of Philip Morris

As the 1980 election year opened, FTC Chairman Michael Pertschuk, chief proponent of the staff's painstaking probe of cigarette advertising, found himself under mounting pressure to rein in the agency's four-year-old rule-making power to correct industrywide abuses. No one doubted the ebullient Pertschuk's sincerity or devotion to the public interest, but he was being painted now as a radical interventionist and enemy of American business. Sentiment was growing in Congress, stirred up by tobacco-state legislators like Kentucky's Senator Wendell Ford, to clip the FTC's wings before it turned into a ferocious bird of prey. Indeed, before Congress adjourned that year, those wings had been pinioned: the supposedly independent commission's power to issue sweeping rulings against practices violative of the public interest in any given industry was made subject to veto by either house of Congress. Pertschuk was plainly trying to breast a rising national tide against federal regulation of business, and he knew if a Republican became President, the FTC's options to move against the tobacco industry would be sharply curtailed.

Sensing urgency as the presidential nominating conventions loomed, the FTC chairman sent a memo to his staff on the need to accelerate the drafting of their report on the investigation into cigarette ads, noting that "too much time has passed (to which I've been a prime contributor). We must move to a decision before time slips out of our hands." To spur progress on the report, the agency in September brought in Matthew L. Myers, a product of the 'Sixties protest generation whose idealism had been tempered by years on the road as a troubleshooting litigator for the American Civil Liberties Union. Myers's mental toughness was put to the test at once as he encountered a staff of bright, young, dedicated people like himself who, as he recalled, "were surrounded by mounds of data, roomfuls of it, and didn't know what to do with it all."

Within two months, a draft report was hammered out. But then the Reagan landslide came in what Myers remembered as "a brutal blow" to his staff, greatly circumscribing the range of regulatory options the FTC might propose, no matter how convincing the staff report. Working seven-day weeks to fine-tune the report if possible before Reagan's political appointees were rooting out activism at the agency, Myers and his colleagues excised rhetorical flour-ishes and flat declarations of abuse by the cigarette companies—punches had to be pulled. To achieve any impact at all, Pertschuk and Myers wanted the five commissioners to adopt the report unanimously so that it might better withstand the scrutiny of the Reagan deregulators. Myers at once ran into "a huge damper," as he put it, in the person of that old, cigar-puffing warhorse, Paul Rand Dixon, nearing the end of his second decade on the commission and, still scarred by the rebuke he had suffered from Congress for his 1964 ini-tiative against the cigarette companies, "unwilling to do anything on tobacco." Dixon even wanted to keep the staff report to Congress secret. Commissioner Robert Pitofsky, a superior lawyer and stickler for precision in wording and airtight factuality, insisted the report be above reproach, and so the editing process proved anything but expeditious. The Reaganites arrived, Pertschuk was moved to the back bench, his place as FTC chairman taken temporarily by Daniel Clanton, a moderate Republican, and the text had to endure a painful combing by incoming senior staffers animated by a pro-business ideology. By that spring, the FTC's activist engines were running in reverse. In May, as the staff report on cigarettes was finally released, even Pertschuk had joined in a unanimous vote to end the FTC's proposed regulation of the nonprescriptive drug industry.

Five years in preparation, the 232-page FTC report turned out to be largely devoid of concrete policy proposals to Congress. Still, its muted findings could not be ignored altogether. Chief among them was that the eleven-year-old warning label on cigarette packs and in ads, stating merely that smoking was dangerous, "does not communicate information on significant, specific risks that have recently been identified" and was too abstract, read by only 3 percent of smokers, according to surveys, and "simply worn out." The cigarette mak-ers' ads, it was charged, "have continued to attempt to allay anxieties about the hazards of smoking" and in their graphic allure and seductive texts have served to "make it more difficult for the health warning to be effective and may fur-ther increase the possibility of deception. . . ." While voluntary restraint by the industry would be preferable to new government regulations, the report pointed out that the cigarette manufacturers had never acknowledged the health hazards of their product, had instead aggressively attacked the validity of the scientific evidence against them, and had agreed to warn the public only when threatened by imminent government actions.

The only plausible proposal in the staff report was to increase the size and change the shape (to a circle with an imposed arrow) of the health warning and to replace the present caution with a series of short, rotating messages of the sort used in Sweden—the "fortune cookie" approach, as the FTC staff called it—to inform the public more fully. But the proposal, along with the rest of the staff report, generated little attention from an administration elected on the promise to get government off the people's back. In such a climate, Matt Myers sought the united endorsement of the FTC report by the three big voluntary health societies as a means of attracting public notice and possibly stirring legislative action, but "I was told it was out of the question." Nor was the newly throttled FTC itself pushing the report with Congress. Myers left the agency in August, seeing scant hope for any forward movement in regulating cigarette ads under Reagan.

Another spirited young figure in the capital's tiny corps of antismoking political activists—John Pinney, director of the Office on Smoking and Health (OSH) at what was now called the Department of Health and Human Services (HHS)—came to the same conclusion. In Pinney's case, the decision to leave was hurried along by his new superiors' collective response to what he felt was "the best thing we had ever done" to educate the public on the perils of smoking. To reverse the uptrend in cigarette use by teenagers, especially among girls who were found to link smoking with slimness and sexiness, OSH accepted the offer of teenage film actress Brooke Shields for a series of short television messages on the theme that smoking was anything but sexy. It amounted to a million-dollar campaign all but donated to the government.

But when Pinney sent up the finished public service announcements for departmental review, he was advised that his HHS overseers found Shields to be an "inappropriate" role model for teenage Americans and her antismoking message thus valueless. Strongly suspecting that the HHS brass was fearful of upsetting the White House, where attitudinizing on "family values" was in vogue, if hardly honored in the practice, Pinney soon grew exasperated. He took the Shields messages to the American Heart Association, which found them too controversial to attach its hallowed name to, and the American Cancer Society said it would think it over. Frustrated after three spirited years revivifying OSH and instilling the Surgeon General's reports with new authority and focus, Pinney left.

Still more depressing to the prospects of the antismoking cause was Reagan's nominee for Surgeon General, a sixty-four-year-old evangelical Christian highly regarded as a pediatric surgeon in Philadelphia but a lightning rod for protest from the women's liberation movement due to his anti-abortion speeches—Dr. C. Everett Koop. So vehemently did this child-healer with the stentorian voice and full beard, which gave him the sound and look of an Old Testament prophet, deliver his "pro-life" message that congressional liberals were fearful that they might have a reactionary fanatic on their hands. The chief executive of the American Public Health Association pronounced Koop "almost uniquely unqualified to be Surgeon General," and in the Senate, Ted Kennedy, a power on public-health issues, charged that the nominee was deluded by "cruel, outmoded, and patronizing stereotypes" of women. But Kennedy could muster only twenty-three colleagues against Koop, and after the liberals had stalled the confirmation process as long as possible, the new Surgeon General was confirmed. He was hardly expected to be a forceful antismoking advocate.

I I

JAMES L. REPACE, a round-faced, gently spoken physicist with an infectious enthusiasm, came naturally by his aversion to polluted air. Since childhood he had suffered from asthma, which was aggravated by exposure to the cigarette smoke frequently emanating from his father, who would die from lung cancer at fifty-nine. Working at places where he could avoid smoke, Repace had become a clean-air and antismoking activist in his spare time. He helped fight a District of Columbia plan to put up incinerators not far from where he worked and joined with a citizens' group in Prince Georges County, Maryland, where he lived, and pushed for smoking restrictions in restaurants in Bowie, his hometown.

At one hearing, a local councilman asked Repace for hard data on the extent of pollution exposure from environmental tobacco smoke (ETS), and when he researched the question, he found little beyond anecdotal complaints. Because the Environmental Protection Agency (EPA) was empowered to deal only with outdoor pollutants, there were no accepted standards for indoor airborne breathable particles. This struck Repace as a serious lacuna in the scientific literature, since Americans spend an average of 85 to 90 percent of their lives indoors. And in the wake of the Mideast oil crisis of the early 'Seventies, national energy and fuel conservation measures had resulted in far more tightly sealed homes, with a substantial drop in ventilation rates, and many workplaces with permanently sealed windows and air-conditioning systems using recycled, stale air. Among indoor contaminants, colorless, odorless carbon monoxide was the most common and cigarette smoke the most readily detectable—and thus the most annoying to nonsmokers.

To measure the amount of cigarette smoke in confined areas, Repace undertook some basic and somewhat crude field research that no one else with his technical training had bothered to attempt. Using a piezobalance, a light-weight, noiseless device about the size of a woman's handbag, Repace counted the level of tiny air impurities known as respirable particulate (RSP) per cubic centimeter in real-world settings, starting with thirty-three indoor smoke-free sites to provide a basis for comparison; these included homes without smokers, nonsmoking sections of restaurants, public libraries, churches, and a bagel factory. The average of these RSP background levels was then subtracted from the RSP count he recorded in twenty-three smoky public places, among them eight restaurants, three cocktail lounges, two lodge halls during bingo games, a club during a dinner-dance, a bowling alley, a sports arena, and a hospital emergency room. While Repace could not take an accurate reading of the ventilation systems without the use of trace gases to measure how readily they were dissipated—impracticable under the circumstances without disclosing his mission and possibly affecting the random nature of his selection process—he nevertheless made every effort to place his gauge at tabletop level as close to the center of every room or hall he visited.

But what portion of the RSP measured could Repace reasonably attribute to cigarette smoking? The answer would surely have varied, depending upon how many smokers were in the room, how heavily they smoked, what the toxic yields of their cigarettes were, how large the room was, how well it was ventilated, its temperature and humidity, and other factors that were impossible for him to measure, given the time, money, and personnel constraints of the study. Instead Repace simplified the process by adopting the reasonable premise that smoking was a random process when it occurred among large groups of people, so he could rely on "equilibrium values," average figures based on known national data and standards. Thus, once he knew how many people were present at any of his sites, he could reasonably assume that one out of three was a smoker, that each of those smoked for about ten minutes and waited twenty minutes before lighting his or her next cigarette (assuring a more or less constant level of ETS), that each cigarette had an inhaled yield of 17.6 milligrams of tar (from which, based on the known level of mainstream smoke retained in the lungs and the emission rate of side-stream smoke, the quantity of ETS could be extrapolated), and that the known standards for ventilation systems as set down by the American Society of Heating, Refrigerating, and Air-Conditioning Engineers (ASHRAE) could be applied, neutralizing actual on-site differences for the purpose of his study. Taking all of this into account, Repace calculated that ETS, cigarette smoke in the air, was overwhelmingly the largest contributor to his RSP readings, provided that he avoided industrial neighborhoods and cooking facilities, from which combustible emissions could seriously skew his figures.

Conducted over a ten-week period in 1978, Repace's fieldwork disclosed that the pollution level was forty times higher inside a bowling alley than in the air outside, that the air in a bingo hall was fourteen times dirtier than that in the nonsmoking section of a restaurant, and that even in a heavily ventilated sports arena the air was four times more impure than either the air outside or in the smoke-free part of a selected restaurant. Plainly, then, a double standard was being employed by federal environmental air protectors. For if ETS, which contained four of the five pollutants held hazardous by the EPA—benzene, arsenic, coke oven emissions, and radionuclides (but not asbestos)—was coming out of smokestacks, it would have been held illegal. Repace computed the risk of exposure to lung cancer from the ETS levels he obtained to be 250 to 1,000 times above the acceptable level as set down by federal guidelines for carcinogens in air, water, and food.

While Repace's methods may have seemed primitive and his assumptions oversimplified, they were scientifically plausible, and by the time he and a friend, Alfred Lowrey, a theoretical chemist, finished refining the raw data, they felt they had an article worthy of submission to *Science*. In the interim between his fieldwork and the article's submission, Repace had gone to work in the EPA's air policy office and, mindful of the political sensitivity of government bureaus over anything to do with the tobacco industry, he cleared his study with agency lawyers and appended a disclaimer stating that the article did not reflect EPA's views. Nevertheless, his employment at EPA added to Repace's credentials, which no doubt helped steel the editors of *Science* against criticism of the Repace-Lowrey study, some unsolicited from scientists who had been shown the article by the journal's peer-reviewers. Chief among these was Professor Theodor Sterling of Simon Fraser University in British Columbia, who at that time was the recipient of grants totaling more than $400,000 for "special projects" approved by the industry lawyers overseeing the Council for Tobacco Research. Sterling wrote to *Science* that the Repace-Lowrey study suffered from poor methodology and mathematics, faulty equipment, and conclusions flawed by their failure to obtain background RSP and ventilation rates specific for every field location tested; that other variables were not accounted for; that the ETS level at any given site could not possibly be determined without taking into account the "aging" rate at which the smoke was diluted; and that other pollutants besides ETS were impossible to separate from the RSP readings.

Repace persuasively answered these charges, contending that they were largely beside the point—that the "aging" rate of ETS, for instance, could be calculated as a constant value since it took about three hours to clear 95 percent of the ETS from a room, during which time the smokers in it collectively lighted, smoked, and discarded cigarettes in a more or less continuous process. To the claim that the ETS level could not be inferred from RSP readings because other airborne pollutants were also present, he responded that the indoor pollution level is ten to one hundred times higher when people are smoking, by far the most significant source of respirable indoor air pollution.

Published in *Science* in May 1980, Repace's article—his first in a major journal—asserted that the RSP levels generated by smokers overwhelmed the effects of existing ventilation systems and that ETS "presents a serious risk to the health of nonsmokers. Since this risk is involuntary, it deserves as much attention as outdoor air pollution." The authors received 200 reprint requests almost at once, signaling that a new era of findings on smoking and health had opened.

But how could Repace state with such certainty that the ETS constituted a "serious risk" to society? The toxic ingredients may have been virtually identical to those that smokers drew into their lungs, but the dosage was obviously diluted, and who could say for sure if such a thinned dose was truly hazardous? Repace and Lowrey spent the next several years addressing that question, trying to link exposure rates of ETS to risk levels for contracting disease, in particular lung cancer. In its annual mortality toll, the U.S. Public Health Service put lung cancer deaths in 1982 at about 116,000, 85 percent attributed to the victims' active smoking habit. What portion of the more than 17,000 nonsmokers who died that year from lung cancer might have succumbed to the toxic intake from other people's smoke?

Repace attacked the question the only way he could as a practical matter— mathematically, using hypothetical constructs based on straightforward national tables and standards, rather than by costly epidemiological studies tracking specific population groups and their real-life exposure to ETS. Basic to his calculations was a 1980 study of disease and death rates among a group of Seventh-Day Adventists (SDA), the least smoke-exposed cohort Repace could find. Not only were there serious SDA strictures against smoking, but adherents of that faith socialized heavily among themselves, and an unusually large proportion of them worked for the church. The death rate from lung cancer among SDA wives was found in the study to be about 5.3 per 100,000, compared with about 12.7 among nonsmoking wives of smoking husbands in the non-SDA cohort chosen for comparison; Repace attributed the differential of 7.4 deaths per 100,000 entirely to the non-SDA wives' exposure to their husbands' smoking, even though the authors of the study had not, suggesting that factors such as diets low in meat among the SDA cohort might somehow have been involved. By multiplying the 7.4 differential figure by the exposed nonsmoking population over age thirty-five, Repace came out with an annual lung cancer death toll attributable to ETS of about 5,000 Americans. He then checked this against figures he derived from models or averages he used in determining the total national exposure to ETS. He assumed, by way of examples, that a third of adult Americans were smokers; that they smoked two cigarettes an hour in the course of a sixteen-hour waking day; that adults spent 90 percent of their time inside their homes or offices; that the average home (according to the National Association of Home Builders) contained 1,500 square feet with a height of 8 feet and that the average work site accommodated seven people per 1,000 square feet with a height of 10 feet; and that the U.S. workforce was divided about equally between white-collar workers, 80 percent of whom were exposed to ETS, and blue-collar workers, of whom only 50 percent were smoke-exposed due to safety or sanitary regulations. Further assuming that the RSP intake consisted largely of ETS, Repace concluded that the average nonsmoking American adult environmentally absorbed 1.43 milligrams of tar daily, or about the equivalent of one or two ultra-low-tar cigarettes smoked directly. He then divided the SDA-derived differential figure of 7.4 lung cancer deaths per 100,000 that he attributed to ETS by that 1.43-milligram exposure level and emerged with a risk exposure level of five deaths per 100,000 per milligram of tar absorbed per day per smoker—and that worked out to between 500 and 5,000 annual deaths, apparently corroborating the SDA-based calculations.

But could such a small average daily dosage of ETS-derived tar realistically cause that many deaths? If Gio Gori believed that there was a level of exposure to tobacco smoke below which the death risk was negligible, or at least unmeasurable, James Repace did not; indeed, he had, arguably, just measured it, even if in the abstract. Repace believed that each individual had a different genetic code from the next person, varying in body chemistry and delicately balanced immune systems and thus in vulnerability to disease. His own family illustrated this conviction painfully: his father had contracted lung cancer, his mother ovarian cancer, a brother suffered from Hodgkin's disease, and he himself and two of his four children had asthma. There was, to his way of thinking, a predisposition to disease among many in the population and no telling what the tipping point might be in the way of exposure to the disease-causing agents and mechanisms.

The plausibility of Repace's projected ETS death toll was enhanced by emerging studies on ETS-derived toxins residing in the bodily fluids of nonsmokers as measured by the amount of cotinine, the residue of nicotine after their bodies had metabolized it. Early cotinine studies tracking its presence in nonsmokers' blood and urine disclosed a quantity equivalent to the yield of one or two low-tar cigarettes a day, Repace suggested. But later studies put the figure considerably lower, closer to the yield from about one-sixth of a cigarette per day, or between .75 and 1 percent of the cotinine found in the bodies of active smokers. Even at that level, though, according to Repace's construct, the exposure was fatal for some, given the immense population at risk.

Submitted in 1984 to the journal *Environment International*, the Repace-Lowrey article, "A Quantitative Estimate of Nonsmokers' Lung Cancer Risk from Passive Smoking," withstood an unusually stringent peer-review process and a visit to the journal's editor, A. Alan Moghisi, by a four-man delegation of Tobacco Institute lawyers and scientists in their hire who tried to label the authors as antismoking fanatics and their work as hopelessly unscientific. Moghisi himself had some reservations but thought enough of the controversial study to run it, and the Tobacco Institute feared it enough to issue a forty-three-page rebuttal pamphlet, *Tobacco Smoke in the Air*, a few months after its early 1985 publication, charging it with too many theoretical or unwarranted assumptions. On the other hand, the *American Review of Respiratory Diseases* stated the following year, "Despite the simplifying assumptions of the risk estimates and the flaws in the epidemiological data from which they are derived, Repace and Lowrey's figures remain the best current estimates of lung cancer deaths from passive smoking."

Repace devoted much of his spare time to speaking out on the ETS problem, so the tobacco industry did its best to get him fired or demoted at the EPA. The Tobacco Institute fed information about Repace to a conservative Tennessee congressman (and later governor), Representative Don Sundquist, who was a member of the House subcommittee that controlled the EPA's purse strings. Sundquist addressed a four-page letter dated March 12, 1987, to the agency, objecting to Repace's "apparently inappropriate outside activities" that he said took up government time, his appearances as a "well compensated expert witness," and other antismoking efforts that "would seem to violate EPA guidelines."

Such a complaint from a well-placed congressman could not be ignored, and for the next year Repace's life became a hell as agency investigators examined every phase of his ETS studies. "Once you're caught up in an investigation, whether you're guilty or not has nothing to do with it," Repace said in recounting the experience. His usefulness as a government scientist was in limbo while he defended himself, showing that his outside antismoking efforts were indeed separate and apart from his office work, that any fees he received for speaking or testifying on ETS were appropriate and within his rights as a private citizen, and that every article he wrote carried a disclaimer stating that he was not speaking in behalf of the EPA—except for one that appeared in the British journal *Lancet*, whose editors left out the disclaimer. Eventually Repace was totally exonerated, but not before suffering a loss in standing with some of his uneasy superiors.

III

O F comparable importance to the Repace-Lowrey mathematical modeling studies in the growing effort to gauge the ETS risk—and comparably attacked for its alleged flaws—was a very different kind of investigation reported early in 1981 by Takeshi Hirayama, chief of epidemiology of the Research Institute at Tokyo's National Cancer Center. For fourteen years Hirayama and his associates followed 92,000 nonsmoking wives of smoking husbands to learn what their risk was of contracting lung cancer, compared to a similarly sized control group married to nonsmokers. The results of the Japanese spousal study were viewed as particularly significant because they were dose-related: nonsmoking wives married to ex-smokers or current smokers of up to fourteen cigarettes a day showed a 40 percent elevated risk of lung cancer over wives married to nonsmokers; those married to husbands smoking fifteen to nineteen cigarettes a day had a 60 percent higher risk; and those whose husbands smoked a pack or more a day had a 90 percent heightened risk. No such correlation was found for other diseases, and the data did not vary much between urban and rural areas, eliminating industrial pollutants as a confounding causal factor.

Accepted at their face value, Hirayama's findings amounted to stating that nonsmoking wives of smokers had a risk of getting lung cancer from ETS that was 4 to 9 percent of the risk they would have run if they themselves had been pack-a-day smokers (who had a 1,000 percent higher risk of suffering the disease than nonsmokers). That elevated range of risk amounted to a considerable menace when applied to all Japanese wives, for whom cigarettes were generally taboo, married to smoking husbands, who made up about 75 percent of all married Japanese men.

Hirayama's report did not go uncontested. Critics ripped into the Japanese spousal study for its alleged methodological and mathematical flaws, including failure to delineate its subjects' ages adequately (other than that they were all forty or older), to exclude occasional smokers from the nonsmoking category, and to determine how long the wives were present when their husbands smoked, what the degree of ventilation was, and the amount of exposure to airborne charcoal particles from traditional hibachi cooking. These and other objections were featured in a Tobacco Institute pamphlet that savaged the Hirayama study and prominently noted that the head of Hirayama's own institute said that Japanese husbands were not home enough to expose their wives to much cigarette smoke.

As the 1980s unfolded, other spousal studies proved to be less than fully corroborative of the Hirayama findings, and some contradicted them. Most important among the latter was a report in the June 1981 number of the *Journal of the National Cancer Institute* by the ACS's biostatistician, Lawrence Garfinkel, who, using older data but a far larger population base than the Japanese investigators, reported "very little, if any," elevated risk of lung cancer among nonsmoking wives of smoking husbands. In a 1984 follow-up report taking into account the workplace exposure to ETS of nonsmoking wives—as his 1981 article had not done—Garfinkel calculated that wives married to smokers of up to a pack a day and working wives had a 27 percent higher risk of lung cancer than nonsmoking, nonworking wives of nonsmokers. Yet he found, in a puzzling inconsistency with dose-response norms, that wives whose husbands smoked over a pack a day had only a 10 percent elevated risk. Garfinkel summed up the spousal risk as "small but real."

Evidence now emerged as well that ETS might affect breathing function and respiratory vulnerability to disease. California investigators James White and Herman Froeb followed some 2,000 nonsmokers chronically exposed at their work sites over a twenty-year period and found that their lung function was reduced by 5.5 percent and their air flow rate by 13.5 percent, or about the equivalent effects in smokers of up to half a pack a day from airways narrowed by hyperplasia. Industry critics picked apart the White-Froeb study, as they did almost every other negative finding, but in this case they were helped by other studies that did not support the California investigation. A consensus, though, formed with regard to the heightened risk of respiratory disease among infants and children in families with smoking parents and households with other smokers. A late 'Sixties study of 10,000 Israeli births had shown a 27 percent higher hospital admission rate for pneumonia and bronchitis among smokers' children; a British study found similarly elevated rates for the same diseases for the first two years of the infants' lives but not beyond. A 1978 study of 3,000 Finnish youngsters during their first five years disclosed a 70 percent higher chance of hospitalization for respiratory diseases among the offspring of smoking mothers. And a 1985 investigation of 1,144 American infants reported a 45 percent higher risk of bronchitis among smokers' children. On the other hand, no consistent relationship was reported between doctor-diagnosed cases of asthma and ETS exposure.

Much uncertainty, then, attached to the unfolding exploration of how great a peril secondhand smoke truly posed. In examining the literature to date, *Consumer Reports*, one of the very few periodicals that regularly and objectively covered smoking's effects on health, stated in its February 1985 issue that the evidence against ETS was "spare" and "often conflicting" except for the effects on the youngest children and small but measurable deficits in function in the developing lungs of fetuses in smoking mothers. Draconian social measures in the form of public smoking restrictions might stir civil contention before the effects of ETS could be authoritatively determined, the magazine suggested.

The following year, three careful and authoritative appraisals of the ETS peril were issued, two by federal government agencies and one by a blue-ribbon panel of establishment scientists. The first came from the Office of Technology Assessment (OTA), a unit that provided background information for Congress, and dwelled on smoking in the workplace. After noting that ETS was an irritant to the eyes and mucous membranes, the OTA report said of the studies thus far made, "The case is less clear for the contribution of passive smoking to chronic diseases. . . . These studies do not have the methodological strength of studies on direct smoking and cancer. . . ." It stressed that the classification of nonsmoking wives in spousal studies was a tricky business and found that some of the assumptions in the Repace-Lowrey studies, like basing the risk differential for lung cancer between Seventh-Day Adventists and other nonsmokers solely on ETS, were "inappropriate". Taken piece by piece, the results of some twenty ETS investigations were "equivocal," but taken as a whole, they prompted "stronger conclusions," for even if there were obvious difficulties in measuring actual dosage and exposure, these "do not invalidate the studies. . . . Despite the uncertainties of the evidence, the data are sufficient to warrant serious concern."

A similarly cautionary note was struck in a second report late in the year by a select committee of the National Research Council (NRC) for the august National Academy of Sciences, made at the request of the EPA and Office on Smoking and Health. Gauging the health hazards of ETS was difficult, the NRC panel observed, since there was as yet no strictly scientific way to measure human exposure to the pollutant. Even where the evidence appeared strongest—the risk from ETS exposure in infants and children—the picture was far from clear; it was debatable whether respiratory diseases and reduced function could be ascribed to a single type of exposure, such as ETS, or whether small decreases in breathing flow noted in children with smoking parents were temporary or might lead to permanent pulmonary dysfunction. Nonsmokers in general were reported by the consensus of studies to absorb from ETS the toxic equivalent of about one-fifth of a cigarette per day, which, assuming a linearity in dose-response relationships, translated into about 1 percent of the excess risk of lung cancer that active smokers faced and about 2 percent of their risk of heart disease.

But when the NRC study was reported in *The New York Times*, science writer Jane Brody did not cite this basis of comparison. In describing the heightened risk found in the consensus of the spousal studies, most of them below the levels observed in the Hirayama investigation, Brody wrote, accurately enough, that "nonsmoking spouses of smokers were 30 percent more likely to contract lung cancer than nonsmokers married to nonsmokers." True, but nonsmokers married to nonsmokers rarely contracted the disease; in fact, nonsmoking spouses married to smokers were found by the scientific consensus to have a heightened risk rate of lung cancer that was 2 to 3 percent of what it would have been if they themselves smoked a pack of cigarettes a day. Put another way, about 6 nonsmoking wives of nonsmoking husbands succumbed annually to lung cancer among every 100,000 in that category; if their husbands smoked, their death ratio from the disease rose to 8 per 100,000, or an increased risk of 1 in 50,000. The public-health community, including even its most conscientious members in the press corps, was not above using what Peter D. Finch, in a 1992 essay entitled "Creative Statistics," found to be distorting relative risk data rather than absolute figures. "Health activists often present their arguments in terms of relative risk to evoke fear . . . that will activate us to adopt a lifestyle which they have deemed to be desirable," Finch wrote as part of a booklet issued by the conservative Manhattan Institute. At any rate, the NRC study concluded that much more research was needed "if [public-health] policies are to be based on possible adverse health effects and not solely on the discomfort that passive smoking causes among the two-thirds of Americans who don't smoke."

The last, and most ambiguous, word on the subject came at the end of the year with publication of the Surgeon General's report on "The Health Consequences of Involuntary Smoking." Dr. Everett Koop had by then established himself, much to the amazement of the liberals who had opposed him and the conservative-fundamentalist camp that had championed his nomination, as a humane and powerful voice, calling for society-wide crusades against such scourges as AIDS (after having once referred to homosexuals as "antifamily") and cigarettes, whose makers he routinely termed purveyors of "death, disease, and deception." A barrel-chested thunderer with his grizzled, square-cut beard and steel-framed glasses, Surgeon General Koop was not easy to ignore when he wrote in the preface to his 1986 report:

> The relative abundance of data reviewed in this Report, their cohesiveness, and their biological plausibility allow a judgment that involuntary [i.e., secondhand] smoking can cause lung cancer in nonsmokers. Although the number of lung cancers due to involuntary smoking is smaller than that due to active smoking, it still represents a number sufficiently large to generate substantial public health concern.
>
> It is certain that a substantial proportion of the lung cancers that occur in nonsmokers are due to ETS exposure; however, more complete data on the dose and variability of smoke exposure in the nonsmoking U.S. population will be needed before a quantitative estimate of the number of such cancers can be made.

In fact, the data were neither abundant nor cohesive—and certainly not conclusive. And to state that ETS could plausibly kill people did not advance the scientific dialogue or social debate over whether restrictive measures were called for to curb smoking in public, as spitting had been outlawed at the beginning of the century. It was misleading, if not disingenuous in the extreme, to note merely that the number of lung cancer deaths from secondhand smoke was "smaller" than from active smoking when the most latitudinarian reading of the literature placed the annual toll for the disease attributable to ETS at one-twentieth as large. Nor was it "certain," as Koop's preface said, that a "substantial portion" of lung cancer deaths in nonsmokers was due to ETS; it was, no doubt, plausible and even likely, but in his own words, more data were needed before a "quantitative estimate" could be made authoritatively. The truth was that nobody yet knew the total human absorption of toxicity from ETS—there had been only calculated guesswork, a far cry from the overwhelming array of data, including quite precisely measurable dosages, on direct smoking.

At his press conference unveiling the report on ETS, Koop went a good deal further by stating that the health risk to nonsmokers from smoking colleagues in the workplace was so clear that everyone ought to be able to enjoy employment in a smoke-free environment. His new report, the Surgeon General added, would be "a turning point" comparable to the one marked by the original 1964 report. But a diligent reading of the 1986 text disclosed considerable equivocation in its findings, suggesting that Koop was indulging in hyperbole. The text noted, for example, that "healthy adults exposed to ETS may have small changes in pulmonary testing function but are unlikely to experience clinically significant deficits in pulmonary function as a result of ETS exposure alone. . . ." The spousal studies like Hirayama's on lung cancer risk from ETS, the report commented, were shadowed by doubts because "misclassification of exposure to ETS is inherent" and some degree of exposure to ETS "has been almost inevitable" among nonsmoking spouses, especially in the U.S., where so many wives worked or were otherwise away from home much of their time. Using the smoking habits of a spouse as the index of involuntary smoking might be a "convenient" measure, the report went on, but it was also "simplistic," and there was "no reason to believe that such exposure was limited to or governed by that source. . . . More accurate estimates for the assessment of exposure in the home, workplace and other environments are needed. Studies of sufficiently large populations should also be performed."

Why, then, since the jury was clearly still out, was the Surgeon General so denunciatory about the ETS peril? In the retrospective view of chemist Frank Resnik, who was then president of Philip Morris USA, Koop was "bending the research to accomplish his objective," which he had declared two years earlier to be a "smoke-free America by the year 2000." One prominent investigator on the dangers of smoking asked Koop at the time why he appeared to be overstating the findings of his scientific advisors, who were far more cautious in the text they had prepared to go out under the Surgeon General's imprimatur. Koop replied, according to this leading scientist, that as the nation's ranking public-health advocate, he had to be forceful in warning of the ETS threat in order to win the public's attention.

Without a doubt he succeeded, and without a doubt Koop was on the side of the angels, but without much doubt, either, he was in this instance using dubious means—shaky science—to justify the worthy end of achieving a healthier society. That same year, the *American Review of Respiratory Diseases* summed up the evidence this way: "[T]he existing data on passive smoking and lung cancer do not meet the strict criteria for causality of this association," adding that to reach that point "may be exceedingly difficult, if not impossible," due to methodological problems like measuring dosages and determining who was truly a nonsmoker. Even one of the soundest and most astute of the public-health investigators with an antismoking bent, economist Kenneth E. Warner of the University of Michigan, noted in his 1986 booklet, *Selling Smoke: Cigarette Advertising and Public Health,* that although a majority of the twenty or so studies done since 1980 had found a statistically significant elevated risk of lung cancer from ETS, "the likelihood that a lifelong nonsmoker will contract lung cancer is so small that a doubling of that risk remains relatively small." What made even that small risk significant, Warner did not fail to note, was that ETS exposure was so widespread, indeed nearly universal, that a substantial death toll "may be found in the aggregate."

A balanced appraisal, then, would have held that to try to calibrate the ETS hazard by linking it to the toll from active smoking was like comparing apples and oranges—or, to invoke a more apt metaphor, to try to quantify the peril of death by ranking the lethal power of a conventional bomb alongside that of a nuclear device. It was the wrong frame and scale of reference. More to the point was that the best or median guesses of the ETS lung cancer toll—the NRC study had put the figure at 2,400, or about half of Repace and Lowrey's outside number—were higher than the entire toll attributed to all other airborne pollutants regulated by the EPA. Donald Shopland, the longtime OSH technical information specialist and later acting director of the antismoking agency, conceded that the data indicting ETS were "much thinner," but also pointed out, "Everything is a small risk compared with direct smoking." ETS posed a much greater danger, for example, than asbestos exposure, believed to cause about thirty deaths a year across the U.S. and then costing almost a billion dollars annually to combat.

In short, the precise magnitude of the danger posed by other people's cigarette smoke was both uncertain and beside the point by the mid-1980s, so far as most in the public-health community were concerned. Their watchwords were preventive medicine, and linking ETS with direct smoking in order to alarm and mobilize the public against the still widely practiced habit served to counter the unstinting drumbeat of denial, distortion, and disinformation sounded by the tobacco industry in order to stay in business. As epidemiologist Lester Breslow, former dean of the UCLA School of Public Health, remarked, it is hard to awaken the people to a public-health peril, but once the arousal has begun, "it builds to a mighty wave, gathering force from almost any supporting evidence." Koop had won the people's attention on the smoking menace as no individual before him had, but "the turning point" he had spoken of was not to be found in the scientific evidence about ETS but in the public perception of what by any rigorous standard was a complex risk measurement. To Congressman Charles Whitley, retiring that year after five terms in the House representing North Carolina's tobacco-rich Third District, the 1986 Surgeon General's report and Koop's dissemination of it were "a very deliberate attempt to turn nonsmokers into antismokers" and thus the document was "a political, not a health, report." In truth, it was both, as purveyed by America's foremost public-health protector—and some felt that it was about time to put aside the velvet gloves in battling the tobacco interests.

I V

THE emergence of scientific evidence, however murky, on the dangers of ETS allowed the public-health and antismoking forces to open a second front that would prove far more difficult for the tobacco industry to withstand.

The cigarette makers had held off serious government restrictions by firming up their political alliances, challenging the scientific case, confusing the public, reassuring their customers—and no doubt salving their consciences by lowering the tar and nicotine yields of their product. As an antismoking movement began to coalesce during the 'Seventies and the public increasingly accepted the scientific consensus, the industry had taken to painting its foes as killjoys who would deny to millions worldwide a cheap and simple pleasure.

This defensive strategy worked so long as smoking was generally perceived as a self-indulgent, if perverse and self-destructive, practice that was indeed the smokers' business—and their right. If smoking killed them, it did so by inches, and the number of premature deaths, to go by the U.S. Public Health Service reports, had by now cumulatively amounted to so many millions that there was little sense of urgency in the popular mind about the nagging problem. Like the weather, people talked about it, and the habit similarly seemed almost a force of nature. In addition, an economic dependency on cigarettes affected so many—in the form of tobacco growers' livelihoods, manufacturers' salaries and wages, vendors' markups, governments' tax revenues, and stockholders' dividends—that the industry had essentially won the argument about whether money or health mattered more. Smoking and health remained a low-priority issue on most congressmen's agenda; a great many of their constituents still smoked, including any number of powerful people who did not relish being thought of or called weak-willed, possibly deviant, or even moronic addicts. Officeholders had discovered that it was much easier to lose votes by opposing something of paramount importance to a minority of voters than to gain votes by advocating a position—in this case, the regulation of smoking—of scant or no concern to the majority. In the words of ex-Congressman Charles Whitley, who went to work as a Tobacco Institute lobbyist and spokesman after leaving office, "Those hurt will know about it and will let you know."

Besides stigmatizing smokers, the ETS issue brought with it a fresh rationale for interventionist measures. If smokers were now viewed as violators of the social contract by imposing the unhealthful consequences of their pleasure-taking on others, then it might be quite acceptable to quarantine or even punish them as part of the broader social movement to cleanse the environment. Smoking near someone else was no more excusable than poisoning streams with industrial runoff or fouling the air with toxic smokestack emissions.

Even with this powerful added weapon, antismoking activists had to be organized and led, and nobody was as yet really doing that. The closest thing to a charismatic leader before Dr. Koop came to Washington was George Washington University law professor John Banzhaf, who ran his Action on Smoking and Health (ASH) effort as an adjunct to his teaching career and an extension of a not inconsiderable ego. By 1979, Banzhaf claimed a nationwide membership of some 60,000, who contributed an average of just six dollars apiece, so even ASH was no lavishly funded effort; it was a vehicle, rather, for its director to testify before congressional committees, appear on television, and exert what legal leverage he could against the cigarette companies, mostly by petitioning federal regulatory agencies to restrict smoking in public. Outside Washington, the grassroots GASPs (Groups Against Smoking Pollution), tiny, volunteer cells that generally depended for their survival on one or two deeply concerned individuals, pressed for local antismoking measures and tried, on shoestring budgets, to educate the public to the possible hazards of ETS.

The key to leadership if a national smoking control movement was to emerge resided not with these small, financially precarious units, but with the big voluntary health organizations, of which the American Cancer Society was by far the largest and best financed. The ACS, along with the American Heart Association (AHA) and the American Lung Association (ALA), had size, organization, and a universally acknowledged mission to educate the public. What they had no experience at, and little stomach for, was political crusading; what they shared was a determination to avoid controversy—and smoking remained an emotional, divisive issue. The Big Three's tax-exempt status, furthermore, might have been imperiled if they had overtly lobbied Congress on the smoking issue (or any other); the health voluntaries could have brought legal action against the cigarette companies or testified against them, but such measures were seen as antithetical to the voluntaries' basic task and might have cost them dearly.

Because the early epidemiological studies had disclosed so close and persuasive a link between smoking and lung cancer, the ACS with its 2 million members was the first to become involved in the issue among the Big Three. Even with a tightly hedged commitment, it had carried on the cause practically alone for two decades during which the scientific studies on smoking proliferated. The AHA, the most conservative of the three health voluntaries, was dominated by the wealthiest of medical practitioners—cardiac specialists—who viewed diet as the prime health risk for heart disease and generally were far more concerned with the latest techniques in valve replacement and other technological marvels than in advancing preventive medicine by aggressively discouraging smoking. The ALA, the smallest of the Big Three, was the most militant on the smoking issue, partly because it was most in need of a medical issue to perpetuate its existence after tuberculosis had been brought largely under control. But the three voluntaries rarely worked jointly on anything.

The prime policymaker at the ACS was Lane Adams, the suave ex-banker from Utah who served as its executive director for twenty-four years, beginning in 1959. A Republican and a Mormon, Adams exercised skillful, top-down control over his monolithic organization, with its fifty-six branches, and closely husbanded its power, which was unique. The ACS, when compared with any other health voluntary or even professional society, had huge numbers, organizational cohesion, continuity of leadership, discipline in policy-framing and execution, and a nearly sanctified standing in the public mind. Adams held the ACS aloof from compromising alliances or activities, took it out of the United Way fund-raising mechanism for many years, and insisted that the cancer society's mailing lists be jealously guarded. Perhaps because he was fiercely protective of the ACS's standing, Adams was no antismoking zealot.

But Adams, who said he never doubted the cancer peril from smoking as it was explained to him by the ACS's medical and scientific authorities, was finally willing to edge his organization toward the political stage when the federal laws were changed in 1976 to allow tax-exempt entities to maintain "safe harbors," or adjunct arms for lobbying, fundable up to a million dollars a year without tax exposure and subject to a 25 percent rate for more than that. The ACS formed a public-affairs committee but shied away from prompt, serious, and visible action on the tobacco-control front. Thus, when the California ACS, its most politically aggressive unit, sought national funds to put over the Proposition 5 smoking restrictions in 1978, Adams was reluctant, and a back-door approach was adopted. "I was not enthusiastic about legislation for non-smokers' rights, as favored by our activist California division," Adams recounted. "It was not the proper role for the ACS. . . . My position then was that we should stick to the medical aspects of this thing and help to do it by persuasion and reason. . . . The good will and reputation of the cancer society was our primary concern."

The effect of such wariness was to free the tobacco industry from political challenge by any powerful foe. The AHA and the ALA were no more eager than the ACS to submerge their identities in a united effort on the smoking issue. "We wouldn't talk to each other," recalled Scott Ballin, veteran member of the heart association's public-affairs department, who was on hand when the AHA opened its Washington office in 1980. The health voluntaries, at best a shadowy presence in the capital's legislative halls, had no access to the levers of power, and if a smoking control bill was filed in Congress, it was usually done by somebody without senior standing on a key committee. The cigarette companies, meanwhile, were at the pinnacle of their strength and influence. Lane Adams and his advisors were forced to recognize that the ACS's long-standing policy of nonconfrontation had proven largely ineffectual. Smoking was declining, but at a glacial pace, and not at all among women. The society's public-affairs committee now began to think seriously about becoming involved in the legislative process. At the same time, enough data had materialized with regard to the links between smoking and coronary and pulmonary diseases to define the common ground on which the ACS ought to be standing side by side with the AHA and the ALA; here was a pressing reason for the Big Three to set aside their territorial concerns and link arms.

Foremost among those pushing the cautious ACS leadership into the national political arena were Allan Jonas, an enlightened California realtor who worked well with the society's dominant Eastern element and emerged as national president in the early 1980s, and Charles "Mickey" LeMaistre, one of the ten members of the original Surgeon General's advisory committee on smoking and by then a superstar in the medical world's firmament. President of the University of Texas System Cancer Center and the M. D. Anderson Hospital in Houston, one of the three largest cancer-fighting facilities in the nation, the tall and handsome LeMaistre with his full head of white hair radiated a no-nonsense air that bespoke authority the moment he strode into a meeting room. Like Adams, he was a sound, deliberate man, very well organized and comfortable directing a big bureaucracy. Unlike the rather remote Adams, LeMaistre had a unique capacity for bringing and holding people together and never turned overbearing. He convinced Adams that the smoking control movement would get nowhere nationally unless concerted action was launched by the public-health community and spearheaded by the Big Three voluntaries. LeMaistre became the moving force behind a carefully orchestrated event held in New York in mid-November 1981, called the National Conference on Smoking or Health—the mere use of that "or" instead of the usual "and" suggested how carefully thought through the undertaking was— which drew representatives from twenty-one nationwide public-health organizations and several hundred of the most knowledgeable and committed professionals in the antismoking field.

From the first, frank words were spoken, led by conference chairman LeMaistre's introductory remarks: "Many of us have been critical of the lack of concerted action to decrease illness and death from smoking. Many of us have been critical of the agencies sponsoring this conference for failure to unite in a common cause. . . . Never before have we been afforded collectively such an opportunity . . . !" Former Surgeon General Luther Terry was equally pointed in criticizing the feminist movement for failing to protest the tobacco industry's splurge of brands and advertising aimed at women.

Perhaps the most stinging remarks delivered at the conference were those jointly authored by a pair of the smartest and best-informed activists on smoking in the public-health community—former Surgeon General Jesse Steinfeld and pulmonologist David Burns, then serving as the senior consulting editor on the Surgeon General's annual reports to Congress. Their paper blistered their medical colleagues nationwide for their failure to accept smoking as a serious health menace and to accord it the standing it warranted on the ladder of research priorities. Because no major concerted research effort had been mounted, Steinfeld and Burns noted, knowledge of the precise mechanisms by which cigarettes caused disease "remains fragmentary and incomplete." There was no "institutional memory" within the research establishment on smoking, since few younger researchers remained for long in the contentious smoking and health field, so that tired old ideas were continually being recycled. The only sustained federal research effort, the NCI's less hazardous cigarette program, could be characterized "with only mild exaggeration as product research for the cigarette industry." But the problem ran deeper. "The categorical nature of federal health funding allows the easy exclusion of smoking surveillance, behavior, and control as beyond any one group's mandate . . . [and] focuses research on the mechanisms of end organ involvement and therapy rather than on understanding and control of the risk factor." Complicating the picture were racial, socioeconomic, and occupational variables involved with tobacco issues, all of which helped cause "the current, near complete abdication by the federal government of its role in smoking research." Equally troubling to Steinfeld and Burns were the failure of the health voluntaries to coordinate their research efforts (or anything else) and a preoccupation with visibility and credit as part of their fund-raising function, which translated into "extremely conservative plans of action in avoidance of controversial issues." What was needed, above all, Steinfeld and Burns concluded, was a change in the mindset of policymakers and program-shapers in government, academia, and the voluntaries that "activity in the smoking area is political and budgetary suicide," and until that could be accomplished, "no amount of rhetoric and good intention" would reduce the smoking peril.

An agreement emerged from the conference, thrashed out during sessions that ran well into the small hours, to form the Coalition on Smoking or Health, a Washington-based office funded by the Big Three voluntaries—a larger membership was thought likely to prove too unwieldy—and aimed solely at advancing federal legislation and regulation. Four months later, with a modest appropriation in place, the Big Three hired Matthew Myers, the attorney who had played a central role in crafting the FTC's staff report on cigarette advertising, to run the Coalition. Myers was a knowing tactician good at winning rapport with the sometimes ego-driven Big Three officials who had been named to a steering committee charged with guiding the Coalition's legislative game plan.

Despite some ruffling of feathers among functionaries used to going their own way, the Coalition soon had its priorities in order: (1) to implement the FTC proposal for larger warning labels with rotating messages on cigarette packs and in industry advertising; (2) to raise the federal excise tax on cigarettes that had been stuck at eight cents a pack for thirty years; and (3) to end the federal tobacco price support program—although some argued that such an effort was both a political impossibility and a counterproductive gesture even if achieved, since it would likely raise leaf production and lower manufacturers' costs, with the savings perhaps passed on to consumers, who might then buy more cigarettes. Myers, on a short leash held by a triumvirate of Big Three vice presidents, had a single task: "to create political movement so that our agenda items would get a serious hearing on the Hill. That had never happened," Myers recounted. "There had never been a piece of antismoking legislation passed that the industry didn't want," all things considered. The cigarette companies' continued existence as purveyors of a legal product depended upon political power that they cultivated more assiduously than any other industry. "The tobacco-state congressmen were willing to fall on their swords over this," Myers recalled, "trading off votes with anybody for anything." But he had a sword of his own now, unlike any other ever wielded by an antitobacco commando.

V

SUCCESS came far more quickly than anyone at the Coalition on Smoking or Health could have guessed. "Lucky timing," said director Matt Myers.

It was a matter of numbers. By 1981, the eight-cent federal cigarette tax had shriveled in value through inflation to two and one-half cents in 1951 worth. When passed that year, the excise tax had amounted to 35 percent of the package price; three decades later, it was down to 13 percent of the consumer's cost. From the middle of the nineteenth century to the introduction of the income tax in 1913, tobacco revenues had accounted for between 10 and 20 percent of total federal tax receipts; by 1981 tobacco taxes came to less than 1 percent of the total. State taxes on cigarettes by then averaged a nickel more than the federal levy.

Aside from the mathematical case for pushing the federal tax back up toward where it had been in real-dollar value, there were several other good arguments that the Coalition brought to bear on Congress during its 1982 session. The cigarette tax was easy to collect at the point of sale—indeed, it was prepaid to manufacturers by wholesalers. And as a "sin" tax imposed on smokers who were already afflicted by guilt over their increasingly derided habit, a hike in the cigarette excise was unlikely to spark a consumer revolt. Nor was a doubling or more of the old levy likely to have a significant impact on sales to those same addicted users. Finally, the Reagan administration, elected on an antigovernment, antitax gospel, had dramatically slashed income taxes and now, with a recession cutting down on the pump-priming effect predicted, was badly in need of any remotely justifiable step to raise revenues. An increase in the cigarette tax could be masked as a kind of user's fee in view of the higher costs that smokers were said to force the rest of society to bear in the form of health benefits and insurance premiums.

The tobacco industry was caught somewhat off guard, then, as the Reagan White House averted its eyes from a doubling of the federal cigarette levy, which was counted on to bring in about $5 billion. But as with every other action the government had taken in an effort to discourage cigarette sales, the industry used this setback to its advantage. With classic hypocrisy, the companies entered a lip-service protest against the tax increase as discriminatory and regressive—since smokers were poorer on average than nonsmokers and paid a disproportionate piece of their income to feed their tobacco habit—and then used the higher federal levy, which went into effect at the beginning of 1983, as a cover to boost the price of cigarettes at a rate never before contemplated. Until then, the industry had raised prices at irregular intervals, mostly to keep pace with inflation and then a bit more. But starting in August of 1982, in anticipation of the higher federal tax, the cigarette makers put through a series of four piggyback hikes over a six-month period and kept raising prices thereafter in a semiannual ritual amounting to about a 10 percent yearly jump, far in excess of the inflation rate.

As expected, 1983 cigarette sales dipped a bit—something over 4 percent—and the industry pointed to the tax increase as the reason. But the average pack price rose from sixty-two cents in 1980 to ninety-six cents in 1984, allowing the manufacturers to realize delightfully wider profit margins and an industry-wide annual return on equity of well over 20 percent, twice the average for corporate America. Realists within the tobacco camp recognized that the U.S. government was taxing their product, even at sixteen cents a pack, far more lightly than most other industrial nations were. The tax hike, rather than a setback, actually helped the companies reach deeper into the pockets of their customers, who were understandably a bit fuzzy about how much of the higher price they were now paying was actually due to government punishment for their favorite dissipation and how much to the manufacturers' profiteering. Besides, as industry strategists grasped, the more government at any level relied on tobacco revenues, the less likely public officials would be to impose regulations materially discouraging cigarette sales.

V I

B Y 1979, seven years after he had moved to Winston-Salem as a kind of senior counselor and co-regent of the company, Paul Sticht ruled alone atop still prosperous and cash-rich R. J. Reynolds Industries, market leader of the tobacco world. Even the ever louder footsteps of runner-up Philip Morris did not greatly perturb the easygoing folks at RJR, satisfied so long as they held on to their one-third of U.S. cigarette sales and convinced that the challenger was grabbing market share from everyone else in the business but themselves.

A somewhat stiff and undemonstrative figure, not without a gentle sense of humor and a pleasing civility, Sticht enjoyed a magisterial hold on his board of directors while remaining remote from the company's day-to-day operations. Some saw in him a cunning Machiavellian, craving the power he had unexpectedly come into in a second corporate career and exercising far more sway than he had ever enjoyed as president of Federated Department Stores. Although he had no visceral feel for the rough-and-tumble tobacco business, the bespectacled Northerner in his tweed jacket and striped rep tie was in many ways an ideal choice to bring Reynolds into the industrial mainstream. An outsized company with small-town ways of thinking, uneasy in its global dealings, its managers unhappy when far from home, RJR continued to rely on its meat-and-potatoes sales force and had never developed the marketing finesse it needed to repulse the onrushing sophisticates from New York. Sticht brought the company a broader view of its potential and a sense of mission beyond tobacco, even as George Weissman had done in winning the CEO post at Philip Morris. But Weissman had a large pool of gifted tobacco merchandisers at his disposal; Sticht found the Reynolds company cupboard bare of first-rate talent and enlisted a growing number of executives from big, decidedly un-Southern outfits like Pillsbury, Lever Brothers, and American Cyanamid. Only three of these imports, though, would survive to play sustained roles well into the 'Eighties. Like him, none of the three knew the tobacco business before joining RJR; unlike him, they were all tough, lashing executives who issued sharp marching orders to the lethargic tobacco giant and motivated the ranks more by instilling fear than by inspiration or innovation.

His name had a Southern sound to it, but J. Tylee Wilson was a native of suburban northern New Jersey and a graduate of Lafayette College in Pennsylvania; he had been a top executive at the Chesebrough-Pond cosmetics and pharmaceutical house in Connecticut when Sticht brought him in to RJR in 1974 to pull together its international operations, including tobacco. Wilson was a tall, lean man with a narrow, patrician head and nervous mannerisms—he was forever fingering his shirt collar and brushing back his hair—that hinted at inner tensions. "He was a guy you could give a tough job to, and he'd get it done," Sticht remembered.

But Ty Wilson often did his job with the abrasive directness of an army drillmaster—a vestige of his military service, training infantrymen at Fort Benning, Georgia—and had a way of sometimes turning rude in social circumstances and indiscreet when he drank. Hardworking and buttoned up, he manifested little interest in company chitchat or give-and-take with even his more able subordinates. New York advertising executive Stanley Katz, who ran one of the agencies Reynolds had begun using to spark up its cigarette sales, found Wilson highly opinionated and harboring the attitude that the ad agencies had been handed too large a say in the company's marketing decisions. Boutique or niche brands of cigarettes that advanced market share by small increments held little fascination for him; the key for Wilson was in solid execution of core-brand sales. Those who failed to perform he did not hesitate to fire, including some he had befriended. When he called a meeting for 10 in the morning, you were well advised to be in your seat by 9:56—and if you were late, he damn well wanted to know why. Anxious subordinates due to make oral presentations in front of him were known to practice for days to get it just right. In short, Wilson was a demanding organization man who ran things by the book—and it was a book devoid of romance. He was named president of Reynolds in 1979, when Sticht became chief executive officer in title as well as in fact.

Quickly advanced along with Wilson was Edward J. Horrigan, equally tough, blunt, and hardworking, who was put in charge of domestic tobacco operations in 1980 after having worked on the international side for two years. A proud and combative Brooklynite who had won an athletic scholarship to the University of Connecticut and a medal for heroism in the Korean War, Horrigan was a bulldog of a man whom many found less than lovable; all, though, acknowledged his fierce loyalty to those who stood with him. He had come to Winston-Salem from Northwest Industries in Chicago, where he had been a ranking executive in the liquor division. Street-smart but sometimes inclined to miss the nuances of a problem area, the nonsmoking Horrigan threw all his considerable energies into rousing Reynolds Tobacco upon being named its president. When presented with the company's long-range plan book that showed it being overtaken within a few years by Philip Morris, "I ordered them to take that out of the book," Horrigan recounted; he thought predictions of their own downfall were "unconscionable".

For his key marketing and sales aide, Horrigan installed another rough battler out of metropolitan New York—Gerald Long, whose in-your-face managerial style and inelegant speech made clear what he expected from his subordinates. Some of them said of Long that he ate his young. "I may be a damn Yankee," he told the good ol' boys around him, "but I'm *your* damn Yankee." Wilson, Horrigan, and Long, those three unplayful musketeers, were a far cry from the Southern geniality and honeyed accent of a Bowman Gray and his courtly ilk; they were in fact a lot closer in manner and spirit to The Founder, cob-rough Dick Reynolds himself—only they had little feel for tobacco.

Horrigan, alternately called "Big Ed" (for his feisty presence, not his stature) and "Little Caesar" (never to his face), pushed hard for investment in the aging cigarette factories, an end to sloppy production habits, and a correction in false economies like the overuse of reconstituted leaf, which gave too harsh a taste to some brands. The company's prime need, though, was for marketing innovation instead of dependency on RJR's sales force. Horrigan, however, was more gifted as a manager than as a merchandiser; he killed off a number of also-ran brands, and when Wilson showed little enthusiasm for lavishing ad dollars on More, the long, brown-paper brand being aimed at upwardly mobile black women, or the new mint-flavored Bright, Horrigan directed the resources toward firing up the core brands. But there was little magic or imagery to the presentation, no "Marlboro Country" fantasyland—"armpit advertising" was what Stanley Katz privately called the new campaigns with a blue-collar pitch aimed right between the eyes. The dead-on, joyless ads "removed aspiration from the mix," Katz believed. And when they failed to ignite consumer activity, they were scrapped, and a full-scale drive was undertaken to reposition the whole Reynolds stable of brands for youth appeal instead of for the company's traditional older and aging clientele. Winston ads featured mountain climbers and helicopter pilots and text lines loaded with aspiration, like "America's Best" and "Excellence. The best live up to it." What any of it had to do with smoking was unclear. RJR's big menthol brand was said to stir "Salem Spirit" among skiers and other outdoors enthusiasts. Vantage put aside its siren song to the cerebral (*i.e.*, health-conscious) smoker and offered instead the "Taste of Success," showing young, well-heeled professionals as satisfied users. A boxed filter version of Camel was introduced, and considerable ad money went into Camel Lights, termed "Unexpectedly Mild" (as if to remind smokers that the hoary parent brand still packed a 19-milligram wallop of tar).

By 1984, RJR had become the nation's fourth heaviest advertiser, spending at a rate of more than half a billion dollars a year but still bringing little verve or originality to the effort. "All he cared about were the numbers," Katz said of Horrigan, whose outlay of energy, at least, he greatly admired. Cigarette sales were not advancing. To prod them, Horrigan and Gerald Long took a pair of radical measures that jarred the company's tobacco veterans.

The first amounted to a high-stakes scam. By the end of 1982, Philip Morris had closed to within a fraction of a single market share point of Reynolds, and Horrigan's dilemma intensified. As one big East Coast wholesaler characterized the fading industry leader's response, "When you're No. 1 and you see it slipping away, you'll do anything to hang on." What RJR did was to intensify its "trade-loading," a practice common in the food and beverage business for products with a long shelf life when prices were about to be raised. Jobbers were advised of the impending boost a month or so ahead of the effective date and invited, even encouraged, to load up on their inventory in the interim so they would have an abundant supply to sell to consumers at a wider profit margin when the new prices were posted. The frequent hikes the industry began to introduce around the increased federal cigarette tax provided the ideal environment to push the loading approach on the trade. It helped cigarette wholesalers who survived on sliver-thin profit margins—a 1 percent net on sales was considered splendid in a business where fierce competitive conditions prevented aggressive pricing to retailers; an extra fifty cents or so garnered per trade-loaded carton sold was a big help to jobbers. And since their cigarette inventories were returnable at a 100 percent refund, the only risk to wholesalers who trade-loaded heavily was the carrying charges on their excess orders.

For Reynolds the loading strategy was helpful in trying to protect the company's reported market share, which would have been hard to calculate if it were based on actual point-of-purchase sales in an industry where so many transactions occurred at small outlets like newsstands and corner groceries that lacked scanner technology and modern record-keeping capability. Instead, reported cigarette sales—and market shares—were calculated solely on manufacturers' shipments to wholesalers and corroborated by federal tax stamp sales. So long, then, as RJR was willing to absorb that eight-cent-per-pack (sixteen cents from 1983 on) stamp cost, all of its trade-loaded sales pushed onto wholesalers' shelves, however badly crowded, were listed as legitimate purchases. But they were not, in fact, net sales—they were only gross revenues, and the manufacturer eventually had to buy back any unsold inventory. To complement its "push" of product at trade-loading jobbers, Reynolds had to spend extra to spur consumer "pull" on those bulging inventories by more advertising, store displays, and couponing in the form of $1.50- or even $2-off stickers on cartons heaped on retail shelves, all in an effort to hold on to the critical one-third of the market that commanded the respect of store managers and Wall Street investors alike.

"Nobody worried that it was artificial," Jerry Long would later tell *Fortune* magazine, speaking of the trade-loading push and the fact that the reported sales resulting from it were conditional. The main trouble with trade-loading was that it was like check-kiting or borrowing from a loan shark—sooner or later you had to pay up or keep going deeper and deeper into the hole, where your remains were one day likely to be found. It might have worked well enough if cigarette sales had been growing, but Reynolds was loading into a gently but steadily eroding market in which several of its own brands were the worst sufferers. The only way for the company to sustain the appearance of holding its market share against still surging Philip Morris was to load more and more each time prices were raised, thereby building ever heavier inventories that too often turned stale on jobbers' shelves and tasted harsh when they finally reached consumers—or required a major payback to wholesalers when they returned the trade-loaded units unsold. Thus, RJR may have technically retained its lead in market share for two or three extra years through the loading device, but it was costing Reynolds more and more per sale. Overstock reached a mountainous 18 billion units by the end of the 1980s, the equivalent of about three market share points above the daunting truth. By then the cost of the gambit was no longer tolerable.

Still more troubling to the RJR veterans was the decision by their corporate officers, tobacco neophytes to a man, to break away from the single-tier pricing that had been in effect since the end of the Depression-era cigarette wars nearly half a century earlier. Little Liggett, down to a 3 percent share of the cigarette market by 1981, had taken the plunge into "generics," unadvertised brands cheaply packaged in plain black-and-white wrappers with bland names like Scotch Buy and Cost Cutter picked by supermarket chains that offered them at a discount of up to 30 percent below premium-priced brands. The savings became increasingly attractive to smokers as the cigarette companies kept jacking up their prices even after the U.S. economy drifted into a recession. The ever rising prices on regular brands, yielding higher profit margins to manufacturers, meant that Liggett could still make good money on its discount brands so long as it shaved marketing costs to the bone by plain packaging and no advertising.

The industry leaders, fearing a price war just when they were maximizing their profits, were not eager to follow Liggett into discount cigarettes. But they were also wary of letting Liggett steal a march on them and, by selling a lot of less profitable units, work its way back into the thick of the market share scramble. Reynolds's wishful position was expressed by James W. Johnston, the young executive vice president of RJR Tobacco under Horrigan, who told *Time* magazine, "In my judgment, you've got to have the link between the consumer and an identifiable brand name. I predict that the success of generics will be shortlived."

That earnest belief was mocked by Liggett's snappy sales figures for its discount units. Reynolds, increasingly desperate to preserve its hairline market-share lead over Philip Morris, compromised. It risked encouraging the discount movement in 1983 by bringing out Century, with twenty-five cigarettes per pack at the same price as regular twenty-per-pack brands, amounting to a discount of 20 percent per smoke. The Century 25s, using expanded leaf that allowed 10 percent less tobacco per cigarette, could be marketed to earn 70 percent of the profit margin of full-priced brands and seemed to be worth the gamble. They rapidly grabbed an encouraging 1 percent of the market, leading Horrigan and Long to conclude that if Reynolds was going to be a serious player in discount brands, it ought to become the dominant force in the sector. Horrigan told Ty Wilson he wanted to dust off Doral, the low-tar entry of a decade earlier that had failed to sustain itself, and bring it out as a discount brand with a recognizable name. Wilson, uneasy at the threat that discount sales posed to profits on full-priced brands, told Horrigan to go ahead if he was sure of himself. And if he proved wrong, Wilson added menacingly, his goose would be charred.

Doral took off at an even greater velocity than Century, and within a short time RJR held 40 percent of the discount sector. Jim Johnston, who had been too public in expressing his disagreement with both the discounting and trade-loading decisions, was fired. But neither of Horrigan's tactics, sacrificing profit margins for volume, could fend off Philip Morris for long; RJR's overall unit sales fell 10 percent in 1983, as the New York manufacturer swept by. Reynolds cigarette sales, due partly to the loading factor, remained steady over the next five years, but Philip Morris kept edging further and further ahead.

· V I I ·

FOR all its tobacco problems, R. J. Reynolds Industries was still swimming in profits. There was enough cash flow to cover any number of past mistakes, of which the most serious continued to be the disappointing earnings of Sea-Land, by the late 'Seventies the world's largest cargo-ship line in terms of gross tonnage carried and a highly cost-efficient operation. But many of its rivals had caught up with Sea-Land in container-ship technology and were subsidized by foreign governments, so that the Reynolds subsidiary often found itself being underbid by 20 to 30 percent. With its earnings dwindling or erratic, Sticht could not unload Sea-Land except for what he felt was a giveaway price; he saw no alternative to doctoring the carrier and biding his time until its fortunes changed.

To improve the company's return on the non-tobacco side, Sticht made a major move in 1979 by paying $618 million for Del Monte, a grand old name in the food business. The big but unexciting grower and canner of fruits and vegetables would add mass and, it was hoped, economies of scale to RJR's packaged foods business. Although the West Coast canner's earnings were, as Sticht recognized, "dead in the water," the prime causes—an antiquated plant and lack of growth capital, by Sticht's analysis—could be remedied. Early in 1981 he told a group of Wall Street analysts and portfolio managers visiting the premises of the giant food vendor, "Very little work has been done about how to sell a banana. We haven't even scratched the surface of merchandising fresh fruit." But as one of his listeners noted, fresh fruit has a troubling tendency—it rots if you don't sell it soon, and Del Monte was in an intensely competitive business with historically low margins, and its version of marketing wizardry was to expand into the thronged frozen-food field. After four years of struggling to justify RJR's big bet in food, prospects remained uncertain. Del Monte's chief financial officer conceded to *Forbes* early in 1984, "I don't think we can change the fundamentals of the processed food business, but we can use it as a building block to move into higher value-added food businesses."

Sticht did better in 1982 by picking up the Heublein liquor business for a pricey $1.2 billion, which bought U.S. distribution rights to such top-selling brands as Smirnoff and Harveys Bristol Cream and the lately revamped and upgraded Kentucky Fried Chicken fast-food chain. Far less capital-intensive than Sea-Land or Del Monte, Heublein also posted better profit margins. What was not lost upon Sticht throughout these checkered efforts at diversification was that almost nothing could compare with the cigarette business for profitability. With a new team in place to try to reenergize RJR's sluggish domestic performance in tobacco, the chairman pushed Tylee Wilson to expand overseas sales, which accounted for about 20 percent of total cigarette volume, most of it in the form of exports rather than through foreign manufacturing operations. The company remained skittish about foreign alliances and uncertain markets, like Iran, where RJR cigarettes had done very well until the shah was deposed. Hungry to score a coup in the international arena, Sticht donned his diplomat's hat and went after an overseas property that would have put his company right in the global running with Philip Morris, whose brands were outselling RJR's abroad by more than double.

Sticht's prey was the closest twentieth-century throwback to the young Buck Duke. Anthony Edward Rupert, called Anton, was an Afrikaner who had bootstrapped himself over a third of a century to become one of the world's leading cigarette merchants. A onetime lecturer in chemistry at the University of Pretoria, Rupert concluded that his best chance for business success lay in tobacco. And besides, he liked to smoke. A consumer of a pack and a half of cigarettes a day, he once told the press, "Smoking is a sign of drive. Most successful businessmen smoke frequently—it's a sign of their energy." And Rupert was nothing if not energetic.

Starting soon after World War II, when he was in his early thirties, Rupert opened a little cigarette plant in his native land with the dream of one day competing against mighty British-American Tobacco, whose lordly U.K. establishment rulers were of a type distinctly unbeloved among the Boers. Rupert's enterprise barely subsisted until he traveled to London and persuaded Rothmans of Piccadilly to license him to sell its deluxe line in South Africa. He did so well with it that within a few years he was able to buy out the parent firm. Soon after, his own technical training helped him develop one of the first king-size filter cigarettes—Rembrandt—and bring it to market even before filter brands became the hottest U.S. seller. Rembrandt flourished in British Commonwealth markets, and Rupert used his gains to grab off Carreras, the British manufacturer of the successful Craven A brand, at a bargain price. Before long, Carreras was the third largest U.K. vendor of cigarettes, though it stood far behind Imperial and Gallaher. In the meantime, Rupert with German tobacco baron Philip Reemtsma had successfully developed Peter Stuyvesant, the first non-U.S. blended cigarette, combining the light Virginia leaf favored by British Commonwealth smokers and the dark, stronger-tasting leaf preferred in continental Europe. Within a dozen years of beginning operations, Rupert was selling his cigarettes around the globe in ventures with foreign nationals in which he rarely took or sought a majority holding, partly out of fear of being tagged a predator. Instead, he relied on native managers and his own skills as a fearsome negotiator, shrewd marketer, and driving sales director who also kept a close eye on operating costs.

When Philip Reemtsma died, Rupert made a power play for control of the top German cigarette manufacturer, only to be swatted down by its directors and forced to settle for a lucrative price for selling the rights to the Stuyvesant brand in six nations starting with Germany. These funds helped Rupert to solidify his position in 1972 as the prime challenger in the world market to BAT. Using his Rothmans-Rembrandt-Carreras operations as a base, he put together a financial holding company known as Rothmans International, to which he added a controlling interest in the 159-year-old German firm of Martin Brinkmann—snatched away from eager bidder Philip Morris, which then began manufacturing on its own in Germany—and the leading Lowlands cigarette maker, Tabacafina. All together, Rothmans International operated forty-four factories in seventeen countries and employed 25,000 workers, overseen from Rupert's lair in Stellenbosch, a two-church, one-cinema village thirty miles east of Cape Town.

Sensitive to the world's growing censure of his country's apartheid racial policies and its possible negative impact on the popularity of the brands his companies sold, the publicity-shy Rupert considered taking on a safe minority partner with high public exposure. The two American cigarette giants, running neck and neck in their home market, were the obvious candidates. Rupert had clashed several times with Philip Morris, the first time at the end of the 'Sixties in a bidding war for control of Canada's Carling beer business; Rupert won, but the fight cost him more hard-earned cash than he liked. A few years later, he bested the New York–based outfit in its bid for Brinkmann in Germany, and in the late 'Seventies, he had once again skewered the American company, whose front-running position in the Australian market he successfully attacked by turning his Winfield brand into a twenty-five-to-the-pack discount entry and enlisting for his chief pitchman celebrity Paul Hogan, cast as a kind of cheeky outback version of the Marlboro cowboy. Still, Rupert recognized that Philip Morris had momentum and marketing smarts that RJR lacked, and he was hardly averse to trying to play the two big U.S. cigarette makers off against each other.

For both Reynolds and Philip Morris, Rothmans represented a juicy plum. RJR was the more needy of the pair in view of its shallow international penetration, and PM, still suffering from its corporate memory of how the British financial establishment had foiled its effort a dozen years earlier to take over Gallaher, was wary of intimate dealings with the redoubtable Rupert. But if Reynolds got in bed with him, so to speak, Philip Morris stood to lose a lot more than pride over the consummated affair. It would at once vault RJR into close competition globally with PM and make the battle to improve margins from its burgeoning overseas operations that much more difficult. Accordingly, Philip Morris International's chief, Hamish Maxwell, urged Chairman George Weissman to open talks with Rupert; Rothmans was doing well and could prove extremely useful to PM in areas where it lagged, such as Canada and especially Britain, where ever more stringent restrictions on cigarette advertising offered bleak prospects for the Philip Morris image-meisters. Rothmans, moreover, while very much an autocracy at the moment, would likely seek a buyer somewhere down the road, Maxwell supposed; Philip Morris ought to position itself for that day and meanwhile settle for a buy-in.

At a daylong exploratory meeting Weissman and Maxwell held with Rupert in London in the spring of 1980, the Philip Morris pair indicated that they had in mind an eventual controlling interest in Rothmans, but Rupert was receptive to nothing beyond the possibility of acquiring a junior partner. That fall, though, Rupert telephoned Weissman and proposed a dinner date at a quiet Manhattan hotel to renew their earlier exchange. Weissman begged off because he had to chair a meeting of his board of directors in Madrid the next morning. In his best poker-playing manner, Rupert said there was nothing urgent on his mind, and Weissman elected not to pursue the matter. But on that same day, Rupert saw Sticht, who made clear that Reynolds would be keenly interested in collaborating in some fashion with Rothmans. Their talks ran into 1981 and produced an understanding, at least in Sticht's mind, that Rothmans would remain a separate, freestanding entity for some years after a Reynolds buy-in but that a full takeover and integration into RJR would eventuate. "At no time was I told that the control question was a dealbreaker," Sticht recounted.

After a number of meetings elsewhere with Rupert, Sticht flew to South Africa for what he expected to be the clinching session. At the end of their deliberations, Sticht recalled, "I clearly thought we had a handshake on the deal," and then he headed home. But while the talks had been in progress, word was put out, partly due to SEC regulations to prevent rampant speculation in RJR stock, that a marriage of some sort between Reynolds and Rothmans was pending. The published reports, however, alluded to a takeover rather than a partnership, and Rupert's son, Johann, later recounted how he got an urgent call from a friend with whom he had become acquainted during a Wall Street apprenticeship. The friend, now at Lehman Brothers, Philip Morris's New York investment advisors, asked if the Reynolds situation was still fluid. The younger Rupert said he replied that "we're not sellers—we're looking to discuss a partnership," implying that the door was still open.

The word was flashed to Philip Morris, whose top brass, belatedly grasping the urgent need to stave off a major Reynolds initiative in the global cigarette market, winged into Cape Town, where Johann met them at the airport. The PM team was closeted with Rothmans's top financial people until three in the morning and then were taken the next afternoon to Stellenbosch, where Weissman asked Rupert if Rothmans was then actively negotiating with a third party. Weissman later said he was told there were no other negotiations going on—"and technically it was true—there was no one else there at the time." The PM chairman said in that case his company was interested and asked what the South African had in mind. Rupert replied that his price was $350 million for a 25 percent interest in Rothmans. Weissman gulped, said he thought that was a steep price based on the operating figures he and his colleagues had seen, but asked to ponder the matter overnight. On reflection, the Philip Morris team still concluded that the price was high, but in view of the importance of the Rothmans trademarks and prospects and the potential synergy of an amalgamated operation, what Rupert was asking was not all that outrageous. When the parties reassembled the next day, there was talk about how the partnership might actually operate, and after Weissman was satisfied that an entente cordiale would prevail, he made his offer: $275 million. Rupert's response was indelibly engraved in Weissman's memory: "Anton looked me in the eye, and I knew it was the end. So I said, 'Okay, let's not quibble.' And then Anton looked like he was in shock." For the $75 million concession in the blink of an eye, Weissman won right of first refusal on the purchase of any additional stock or trademarks that Rothmans elected to sell.

Philip Morris executives attributed their "Perils of Pauline" victory to a simple change of heart by Rupert, who negotiated better terms with the more adroit and enterprising of the two American giants. For Paul Sticht, the loss of a major stake in Rothmans was a heartbreaking setback. "I feel he reneged," he said a decade later. "The buy-in would have given us substantially more leverage internationally in terms of markets and brands."

Thus, on both the domestic and international tobacco fronts, Philip Morris dealt punishing blows to RJR under Sticht's stewardship. And some on Wall Street faulted him for ineptness on the non-tobacco side as well—for getting into lackluster Del Monte, for overpaying to get Heublein, for hanging on too long to Sea-Land. Insiders, too, grumbled that Sticht had failed to develop an integrated management, that the company was hopelessly compartmentalized, and that he thrived on a certain divisive mood that grew up around the question of who would shortly succeed him as CEO. A fairer appraisal would be that Sticht was too trusting—of the likes of Anton Rupert, for example, and of his own tobacco executives who had not leveled with him about their trade-loading strategy—and deserved more time for his diversification program to prove itself. But after he had rescued R. J. Reynolds from terminal provincialism during his eleven years as its sometimes diffident helmsman, his time ran out at the end of 1983. With some reluctance he submitted the name of Tylee Wilson to the board of directors to succeed him—there was nobody else inside the company who qualified as chief executive timber, and to have gone outside again for fresh talent would have been demoralizing. Sticht, though, stayed on as chairman of the board while handing over the CEO title to Wilson—"but that was always Sticht's board," one top Reynolds hand remarked, "and Ty never grasped that."

The year Sticht stepped aside, RJR's net income was $881 million, twice what it had been five years earlier—no shabby performance. Philip Morris, though, made $903 million that same year, the first time it had outearned its big Southern rival.

VIII

MORE outgoing and personable, less overtly intense than his predecessor, new Philip Morris chairman George Weissman enjoyed the luxury of retaining virtually intact a veteran team of managers who over the preceding twenty-five years had turned the company into the rising star of the tobacco industry. Most of the company's top executives were in the process of becoming multimillionaires as Philip Morris stock kept steadily gaining ground along with earnings. Miller Brewing had begun to pay off after a decade of tender loving care by management, thanks to vast infusions of capital and John Murphy's charismatic leadership. Earnings ratios were about one-third of those posted by tobacco sales, of course, and skimpy when measured by the size of the investment, but the Milwaukee-based operation was now solidly in the black. The big concern as the 1980s unfolded was the gamble on Seven-Up, which Weissman had pushed for en route to the CEO's desk.

The basic strategy was to push up the soda maker's share of a market in which lemon-and-lime drinks commanded only 10 percent of sales and then to try for major-league status by bringing out a new cola to compete seriously with Coke and Pepsi. It was a tall order. And to achieve it, ironically, Seven-Up would cast itself as the purveyor of the healthiest soft drinks on the market—the sort of claim that its new parent could never make for its cigarette brands.

To run Seven-Up, John Murphy's vice president for sales at Miller—Edward Frantel—was dispatched to the soda company's headquarters in St. Louis. Frantel was struck by the old "Uncola" advertising campaign that Seven-Up had used, without notable success. The idea of making a virtue of the brand's differentness was advanced by a spread in *Consumer Reports* noting that Seven-Up was the only true caffeine-free soda on the market. Though the article said that there was considerable disagreement about whether caffeine might be implicated in breast or pancreatic cancer and that moderate use of the chemical stimulant would not likely harm any healthy youngster, there was no debating that it also had certain nicotine-like effects, such as speeding up heart rate and constricting blood vessels. Frantel thought he had the peg he needed. He spent heavily on ads pitching Seven-Up as caffeine-free ("Never had it, never will"); it was not much to crow about, but it was a unique selling proposition.

Seven-Up's much bigger rivals recognized the challenge and hit back with their own caffeine-free entries and, more to the point, began pushing sugar-reduced Diet Coke and Diet Pepsi to weight-conscious quaffers. Seven-Up actually lost market share, though its revenues were climbing on the strength of the big ad backing. Frantel also looked to economize, but this, too, backfired. The company began substituting cheaper, crystal-clear fructose for slightly yellowish sucrose as the sweetener in Seven-Up, and although the drinker derived a satisfactory taste sensation from fructose at the front of the mouth, the punch faded fast, while sucrose held its sweetness longer—you could almost chew it before each swallow. The bottlers who mixed the syrup's ingredients, furthermore, did not all follow instructions uniformly, causing the product to have an inconsistent color as well as taste.

Whether out of impatience for progress, anger at Coca-Cola for pushing Sprite (its own lemon-lime entry) all the harder now, or overconfidence, Frantel and his team did not wait for Seven-Up to gain ground before launching their own cola in 1982—Like—which the company hoped would do for it what Lite had done in the 'Seventies for Miller Brewing. Again Frantel chose the health pitch: "You don't need caffeine. And neither does your cola." It was an approach that denigrated the rest of the soda world. Furthermore, the half of Seven-Up's bottlers who sold Coke or Pepsi could not also handle Like, even if they had wanted to. Philip Morris had to put up capital to buy eleven independent bottlers to market Like, and some of Miller's distributors were conscripted to get the new cola onto retailers' shelves. But those shelves were more crowded than ever now, and decent placement came at a premium price as the two cola kings began a market share war ruinous to second-tier brands like Seven-Up and Like. The combined market share for those two brands, which had edged up in 1982, took a pummeling the next year, falling to 5.3 percent, lower than it had been when Philip Morris bought the company, despite a cumulative outlay by then of nearly a billion dollars.

In retrospect, Weissman would concede that Philip Morris, or at least he and his predecessor, Joe Cullman, had been dazzled by "the challenge of it—a great trademark and reputation as a product. [But] we weren't up to it. Coke and Pepsi were not about to let us do what we had done in the cigarette and beer business." In the end, Seven-Up proved "a little bit of a disaster" for Philip Morris, as Weissman put it, and his successor would jettison it at the earliest seemly moment.

The problems at Miller were of a different magnitude. Having driven up its market share from 4 percent in 1970 to 22 percent by 1981 and spent $1.2 billion on six new breweries to keep pace with surging demand, the company suddenly hit a stone wall. Under pressure from corporate headquarters in New York to improve bottom-line performance—Miller was earning between 5 and 7 percent on sales—Murphy took the industry pricing lead even though his company was still a decided No. 2 behind Anheuser-Busch. Largely because Lite was a very hot brand, Miller made a pair of price rises stick as the industry reluctantly followed, and margins improved. But by 1981, Gussie Busch in St. Louis was counterattacking in earnest. Not only did the market leader decline to follow Miller's next price rise, forcing it to rescind the move and lose face, but the company also began to push hard with promotional discounts and other pricing weapons. Anheuser finally adopted advertising, too, that was as zesty as its growing challenger's "Miller Time" campaign, even if an obvious echo. Anheuser's pitch was more pointed and flattering: "For all you do, this Bud's for you." And they spent heavily on it. Miller Lite's barrelage, feeling the effects of the big Budweiser drive and of the price hikes that hurt with blue-collar customers, tailed off 40 percent between 1980 and 1984. In the premium market Miller's Löwenbräu was sniped at as an ersatz German beer and made little headway against Anheuser's Michelob. And when Bud Light finally debuted in mid-1982, it came on with bells, whistles, and flashing pyrotechnics that at once undercut Miller Lite's runaway domination in its low-calorie niche. The biggest Miller brewery yet, a $412 million leviathan slated to open in Trenton, Ohio, in 1983, was now superfluous. That year Miller produced a full 30 percent of Philip Morris's corporate volume but only 11 percent of its net, confirming it, even if then the second largest U.S. brewer, as a relative drag on the company's spectacular tobacco earnings.

Criticism was now heard that instead of sinking a billion dollars into Seven-Up and 2 billion into Miller during its thirteen-year diversification drive, Philip Morris would have earned more just investing the money in U.S. Treasury bills or buying back its stock to bolster investors' per-share equity. "We are operating people," Weissman answered, "we are not bankers," and urged shareholders to review the company's twenty-year record in determining if management had acted prudently to protect their long-term interests. For the company to have sat on its cash flow, he reflected half a dozen years later in his retirement office, would have been wrong: "You're not going to be a success doing nothing, you've got to keep moving—so you build one brewery too many—eventually we'll use that plant. . . . No one gets shot here [at Philip Morris] for making a mistake so long as it's an honest one and part of an overall strategy."

IX

TOBACCO remained the heart and soul of Philip Morris as it surged to the top of the industry in the early 'Eighties. Two of the key contributors to that rise, marketers Ross Millhiser and Jack Landry, had been moved to the sidelines, somewhat embittered by their failure to attain the apex of organizational power. The tobacco program passed now into the hands of technicians and theoreticians. Foremost on Weissman's team was Clifford Goldsmith, the perfectionist operations man who circled the globe tirelessly, inspecting and improving the company's proliferating production facilities. At home he took the lead in urging the company to expand its cigarette-making capacity at a time when the rest of the industry was slowing down. The new plant, less of a showplace than PM's huge Richmond manufacturing center, then operating at capacity, was put up in Cabarrus County, North Carolina, near Charlotte, the state's largest city, with its abundant labor supply.

At Goldsmith's side was Philip Morris USA President Shepard Pollack, a short man with a sizable brain, an indisputable talent for numbers, and an outgoing personality that he took on the road regularly to conventions and industry shows, to the amusement of wholesalers and others in the trade. One veteran Philip Morris sales director said of Pollack, "He was extremely funny—for an accountant." But Pollack did not delude himself, as Goldsmith did on occasion, that he was aces at moving the merchandise. The keeper of the flame in that department so critical to Philip Morris's rise was James Morgan, the talkative, chain-smoking golden boy of the organization, with his tousled hair and unstinting devotion to the Gospel According to St. Jack (Landry):

Get a great campaign with the right image and stick with it forever. Morgan was the clear heir apparent to Pollack to run PM-USA and, after that, the whole company—if he could just hold his horses. Some around New York headquarters, though, found that in contrast with Landry, his mentor, who would sit through a meeting and hear out everyone else in the room before ruling, Morgan as marketing vice president was inclined to gather his troops and peremptorily tell them how it was going to be. His chief subordinate was a very different character—glib, funny, charming Robert Cremin, whom Landry had brought in from the Leo Burnett ad agency to serve as head of brand management, with the idea that he might even succeed him in the marketing post. But Landry soon concluded that Cremin had a short attention span and an erratic work ethic, so the marketing job went to Morgan while Cremin, given his personable nature and fondness for high jinks, was put in charge of the sales force. Unfortunately, he failed to disguise what appeared to be a certain disdain for his social and intellectual inferiors, at times alluding to his sales force as "grunts" and "shit-kickers".

Propelled more by momentum now than inspiration, PM cigarette sales were monitored on a day-to-day basis by Cremin's obedient subordinate, sales director Jack Gillis, a veteran rep who stuck by the somewhat mechanical drill handed down by the New York marketing people and, in the view of a number of field men, poorly geared to the varying regional pull of the brands. Morale suffered from the perception that advancement was awarded to those who least questioned the centralized directives and most loudly kissed their overseers' rings. There was a perceptible loss of confidence and conviction, too, over the launching of new brands and line extensions. The Cambridge debacle, traceable possibly to uneasy consciences over the health issue, and surely to the company's reluctance to formulate an ultra-low-tar brand for people who didn't really want to smoke anymore, proved a costly misstep. And despite the growth of menthol brands, Philip Morris never sustained a freestanding entry in that sector, picking up the scraps instead in the form of line extensions of its main brands. It tried again now with Northwind, a mint-flavored variant, and had no better luck.

But its core business remained strong, and as Philip Morris's top brand sailed along at a smarter clip than anyone else's, a wariness set in against tinkering with the machinery. This was especially true when Liggett's discounted "generics" began selling well enough to command the industry's nervous attention. A few at PM urged an early and forceful entry into the lowered-price sector on the joint premise that multiple-tier pricing was common abroad and had to come to America sooner or later and that, with a higher U.S. cigarette tax imminent, pricing pressure was sure to grow. But most company executives did not relish the prospect of reduced margins from discount brands, perhaps a suitable expedient for survival by the likes of Liggett. A further factor militated against the notion: Philip Morris was not psychologically disposed to put out such an imageless product. One younger executive who went against the grain in pushing for an early Philip Morris move into generics was merchandiser Edwin J. McQuigg, who recalled, "They were not mentally prepared for it—to make a product visibly poorer, detectably inferior to their regular brands." The very notion violated Chairman Weissman's credo on smokers' love affairs with their brands: Cigarettes were "a personal statement about you . . . an expression of who [people] are or what they perceive themselves to be. . . ." So Philip Morris would not truck with faceless, colorless cheapies; Weissman doubted that generics would grab more than half of 1 percent of the cigarette market.

Instead, Philip Morris moved in the opposite direction. Goldsmith requested "the ultimate in a luxury look" for an extension of the upscale Benson & Hedges line, to be called DeLuxe Ultra Lights. Within a year of its 1982 debut, the brand, in designer Walter Landor's chic metallic silver box with a gold-foil laminate overlay, had captured 1 percent of the market—a rousing success and a nose-thumbing rebuke to the discount concept.

Encouraged, Philip Morris marketers decided to launch a full-price, free-standing brand, a perilous course in the age of TV-less cigarette advertising. Landry favored a kind of playful mentholated brand, to be called Raffles, after the famous hotel in Singapore and the British diplomat of the same name. Ever the imagist, Landry thought that the filmy allusions to travel, intrigue, and the exotic Orient might lend a light, even racy tone to the product. But Goldsmith and Morgan overruled him, believing there was a larger potential market for an American version of a big British hit that had also done well on the continent—John Player Special, dressed up in a suave black-and-gold package that reeked of elegance. Black, though, had been a taboo color for U.S. cigarette makers, sensitized to the health charges against their product, so in fashioning a gorgeous black box with the brand name in gold script, the marketing team pitched the new Player's brand at fun-loving yuppies with ads showing chic smokers at glitzy parties and swank cafés. But Player's ritzy black box absorbed a great deal of ink, and the moisture from it had a detectable effect on the brand's taste. Much time and money were spent correcting the problem, which slowed selling momentum. Beyond the smart package itself, moreover, the brand had no reason for existing, even as Cambridge had nothing going for it but its low yield. Player's got up to 0.7 percent of the market before tailing off into oblivion.

What the Philip Morris cigarette team proved best at in this period was aggressive pricing, which had the steroid-like effect of handsomely bulking up profits for much of the 1980s but would eventually serve to encourage the one thing the company wanted to avoid—price-cutting by hungry competitors. The 1983 U.S. cigarette tax rise had fueled steady upward pricing by providing ideal cover against consumer resentment of the moves as well as a price-driven profit opportunity for wholesalers, who welcomed the twice-a-year increases in order to trade-load, *i.e.*, buy cheap and sell high soon afterward. As Vincent Buccellato, Cremin's successor as sales vice president, later noted, "Outrageously ambitious profit margins could be sustained by equally aggressive pricing policies" without fear because of how the cigarette trade had traditionally operated at retail: "All prices gravitated to the highest level," in Buccellato's words, meaning that any boost made by one of the market leaders would automatically be adopted by retailers for all brands. Thus, so long as the economy boomed through the mid-'Eighties, Philip Morris and those who followed its lead were not viewed as price-gougers.

The results were dramatic. Between 1981 and 1985, the average price for a pack of cigarettes in the U.S. rose from 67 cents to $1.03; of this 36-cent increment, 11 cents went to pay higher federal and state excise taxes, 8 cents went to distributors to fatten their narrow margins, and the remaining 17 cents went to the manufacturer. The per-pack operations income thus soared from 8.2 cents in 1980 to 19.2 cents in 1985; by 1983, PM's operating revenues had soared 70 percent over three years earlier on a growth in unit sales of only 7.5 percent.

At the beginning of 1983, both RJR and Philip Morris played down the race for top market share in the tobacco business. Goldsmith said his company was "allergic to being the biggest. It's puffery. It means nothing." To charges that success was making the organization soft, he replied, "We're the opposite of complacent—we're nervous. . . ." By year's end, Reynolds had sold almost 14 billion fewer cigarettes nationwide than the year earlier, the severest hit suffered by its badly listing flagship brand, Winston, while Philip Morris steered through a stormy year for the industry to capture first place and end the North Carolina company's twenty-five-year reign as market leader. Shep Pollack, who loved a good party, refrained on this occasion, recalling, "There were no celebrations, no raises or awards." The company had triumphed by running scared; gloating was not in its nature.

Despite its long-sought triumph, however, the mood at Philip Morris had soured a bit. The breach within the executive ranks over the Seven-Up takeover never closed, and the old collegiality that had allowed sharply diverse personalities to reconcile their differences never returned. Among the company's tobacco people the sense grew that Weissman favored his beverage crowd, giving them excessive leeway while taking for granted those responsible for the core business—and its lush profits. Vice Chairman Millhiser, never close to Weissman, did not notably mellow toward him while lingering in corporate limbo. More overt tensions remained between Landry, at best semifunctional now, and Goldsmith, who was perhaps overfunctional. Goldsmith, as the company's de facto No. 2 officer, took on imperial trappings as he toured Philip Morris's global outposts. "They pulled the carpet out for him," recalled one high-ranking colleague, "and he'd come back to New York with new affirmations that he walked on water." Goldsmith would sometimes seem obsessively attentive to production glitches in, say, Sweden or Uruguay but indifferent to U.S. problems, and when a few like Pollack called him on it, they risked falling out of favor. Indeed, Goldsmith began to tell Pollack he was in the wrong job, and others, taking the cue, said they sensed a bit of slackening in Pollack's attention to every last detail and that he had become too flip. Then there was the Cremin problem. When his superiors came to the inescapable conclusion that he played more and better than he worked, they tearfully let the sales chief go. A more able younger executive, Wallace McDowell, who was strong in domestic operations and finance, quit in a clash with Goldsmith, reportedly over authority and prospects for advancement.

Most demoralizing of all was the sudden departure of the company's great future hope, James Morgan, pirated away by Warner Communications' Steve Ross to run his badly troubled video game subsidiary, Atari. The sweetener was said to be a seven-year contract worth $10 million and the chance to strut his managerial stuff. "I physically flinched when I heard about it," recalled Ellen Merlo, a Morgan colleague in marketing. Beyond regretting the loss of a personable and spirited co-worker, those who most admired Morgan noted that he had never really run anything and feared that he was not yet ready to be a CEO. Within eight months, before the forty-one-year-old Morgan could introduce any merchandising concepts or cut costs, Atari was sold out from under him, and Morgan found himself one of the best-paid unemployed young executives in America.

These stresses effectively left Philip Morris without adequately talented personnel to run the domestic tobacco business after Shep Pollack. The company's international tobacco people, in fact, were about to seize the reins of the nation's biggest cigarette maker.

X

To boost business in France, where Philip Morris had only a few percentage points of the market—compared with 30 percent in Italy, Switzerland, and Australia and a swiftly growing share in Germany—George Weissman went to Paris with a full corporate entourage in the fall of 1980. It had been twenty years since Joe Cullman put him in charge of the company's embryonic overseas sales, and his arrival now, in a London Fog raincoat, as he paused to light a Marlboro on the tarmac before heading to his suite at the Ritz, was noted by the French press and financial community. They knew he had come to try to sway the government to ease up on foreign competitors of the highly protected French national tobacco monopoly, yet it was hard not to take a liking to the low-key Philip Morris chairman. When a reporter at his press conference asked the world-class tobacco purveyor about his own choice in dissipations, Weissman replied, "Forty cigarettes a day, one or two beers"—then, remembering his audience, added without skipping a beat, "I also drink some wine."

Unobtrusively at Weissman's side throughout his Paris showing was the president of Philip Morris's international operations (PMI)—Hamish Maxwell, whose reserved manner was taken by some for introversion, by others for natural shyness. Almost everyone in the company thought he was smart because he listened intently, questioned incisively, said little more than he had to and no louder, and seemed to forget nothing he ever heard. In the view of Shep Pollack, who became president of PM-USA at the same time Maxwell took over PMI, the latter was "bright, driven, catholic in his knowledge, interests, and curiosity . . . and he held his cards very close indeed." While coming from a tobacco family and being competent in the financial and marketing aspects of the business without demonstrating a special flair for either, Maxwell had the crucial skill of winnowing wisdom from others' chaff. Subtle and politic, a precise user of both the spoken and written word, he worked most effectively in one-on-one exchanges rather than by force of command around a conference table. So quietly efficient an inside operator was he that one ranking company man said of Maxwell, "He could cut off your balls and have them in a jar before you knew you'd lost them."

His talents did not go unnoticed at corporate headquarters in New York, where a bit of a chill set in between the domestic and international tobacco people. The former felt that PMI's volume growth, building on relatively small bases, was unspectacular and that its profits were skimpy alongside the U.S. figures—that, in general, there was more sheen than substance to the overseas showing so far. For their part, PMI executives groused that PM-USA had been spoiled by the far easier conditions of doing business than prevailed overseas. PMI was forever operating at a huge pricing disadvantage, for example, when Marlboro had to be sold for one-third more than Gauloises, the French favorite, and 250 percent more than the leading Polish brand. Without benefit of the measured media that U.S. marketers used to gauge consumer pull and the American economies of scale, the international executives saw themselves, justifiably, as more versatile problem-solvers, having to confront more volatile economies and currencies, unstable if not corrupt governments, high cigarette taxes, rebel chiefs who threatened to burn their factory to the ground if tribute money was not forthcoming, and unskilled labor and sales forces, as in Indonesia, where it was hard to find field men who could both drive a motorcycle and read. Thus, the battle-scarred PMI corps was not eager to take orders from U.S.

executives, who they thought were too little exposed to the realities of doing global business.

Aware of the need to convert promise into achievement as he took over international operations, Hamish Maxwell believed that the key to the game was "to be tenacious and patient—but not passively patient," to keep his eyes open for opportunities like buying out Liggett's overseas business and buying into Rothmans, to press steadily against pricing inequities and for marketing access, to take calculated risks—and to own up when they didn't work out. "I was the one who urged us to get into Indonesia and Chile—and then to get out of them," he recounted.

The people under him whom Maxwell valued most were inventive, as ambitious for the company as for themselves, and, above all, dogged. In the case of Aleardo Buzzi, who would later succeed him as PMI president, years of working with auto-racing promoters helped break down barriers against U.S. brands, especially in Italy, where Merit as well as Marlboro became a top seller. Much of the time, Buzzi operated beyond the surveillance of the company's New York executives, from whom, as one admiring junior associate put it, "he was wonderfully protected by his poor command of English." In France, the company contended with tough advertising restrictions by distributing cigarette lighters embossed with the Marlboro name, and to overcome suffocating price controls, PMI executive Walter Thoma recalled how, on more than one occasion, "I had to knock on the French finance minister's door, get down on my knees, and tell him how poor a company Philip Morris was and how badly it needed a price increase." In Germany, where door-to-door deliveries from tobacco factory to retail outlets were routine—and more costly than the U.S. system of using wholesalers—PMI economized by hiring a delivery service that doubled as order-takers.

No PMI executive struggled longer or harder for a breakthrough than German-born Andreas Gembler, operating out of the company's European headquarters in Lausanne and roaming Eastern Europe from 1969 on in an effort to obtain licensing agreements with Communist governments to make and sell Marlboros through "courtesy shops" to tourists and a scattering of nationals. "You had to work at all levels," recalled Gembler, who dealt with everyone from Communist Party chairmen to workers on the factory floor after he finally succeeded in striking a deal. Every step—the tobacco leaf, the cigarette paper, the filters, the machinery—involved different offices, commissars, and endless skeins of red tape, and the very concept of a sales "royalty" by that name was resisted, especially in the Soviet Union, where it smacked of czarist exploitation; Gembler had to speak instead of "licensing fees." Throughout the years he had to avoid succumbing to the suspicion he was being toyed with by people with nothing better to do. And he had to be willing to settle for crumbs when offered, as in the mid-'Seventies, when it was proposed that in honor of the planned joint U.S.-Soviet *Apollo-Soyuz* space flight, Philip Morris market 10 billion commemorative cigarettes in each of the two nations as a good-will gesture. Since the brand would disappear from the market once the special run had been exhausted, the effort seemed unpromising to Philip Morris, which also explained how difficult it would be to guarantee the sale of what amounted to 2 percent of the fiercely competitive U.S. market without a large, costly advertising outlay. The Soviets, who did not have to truck with the decadent capitalist practice of advertising, settled for the company's promise to give the commemorative brand decent exposure in the U.S. Gembler, without a lot of other options to penetrate the Soviet market, got President Brezhnev to hold up the package on television and sold the Russians a billion units.

That small opening led to marathon negotiations for a contract to license Marlboro. Gembler would show up in the morning and endure a cadre of naysaying Soviet bureaucrats until the three-hour lunch break, when food and vodka were plentiful; afterward, the Red ranks thinned, spirits mellowed, and progress was made inch by inch, culminating in a 1978 contract. Once production actually began, Gembler and Philip Morris technicians stood by to teach and check up on factory hands used to being gauged by the quantity and not the quality of what they produced. "You couldn't leave them alone to make the Marlboro," Gembler remembered.

Half a world away, William L. Campbell faced an equally grinding challenge as head of Philip Morris's operations in Asia, where progress came sooner and in larger doses but only after costly mistakes. These were impressed upon Campbell in a five-page letter he received, on taking over the post, from one of his predecessors, Hamish Maxwell. PMI would do much better henceforth, Maxwell advised, by not trying, as it had earlier, to extract blood from stones—investing heavily in sales to teeming but desperately poor populations, like those in India and Indonesia—and concentrating instead on much smaller but more prosperous markets, like Taiwan, South Korea, Hong Kong, and Singapore.

The fate of PMI's Indonesia operation dramatized the point to Campbell. After complex negotiations to manufacture there, PMI confronted the realities of doing business in a culture where bribery was a routine cost; cigarettes could not be sold unless they bore excise tax stamps, and these could not be purchased without a payoff to tax officials. Such surcharges helped make the U.S. brands hopelessly expensive for the Indonesian masses, and PMI decided over time to close up shop. But to remove its machinery from the country, a punitive charge of $750,000 was levied—PMI had not stayed there long enough to suit the Indonesian authorities. When Campbell went to deliver the payment in person, the government officer assigned to collect it would not do so unless a sizable side gift was also given to him. The company declined, and six more months of haggling ensued.

Campbell made more headway in Hong Kong, where Marlboro had been handled by a British distributor who was lucky to gain a 1 percent share of the market; opportunities were missed for export sales from that bustling free-port bazaar. Campbell switched to an Asian distributor, the House of Ho, out of Shanghai, and things began to change. The Leo Burnett agency was then assigned to give the Marlboro Man a cultural makeover, since cowboys were perceived in Asia as little better than coolies and their brand preferences as necessarily a low-status smoke. The Marlboro wrangler got cleaned up, shown as more of a boss than a hand, and modernized: TV ads depicted him as driving a Jeep before he boarded a train for his trip to the Asian market. When Marlboro became the best-selling U.S. brand in 1976, the purchasable front pages of Hong Kong newspapers bannered the news, and so the cowboy became a symbol not of freedom and democracy but of Yankee-style commercial success and thus highly attractive among enterprising Asians. Marlboro was finally off and running seriously in East Asia, and exports from its Hong Kong licensee, many smuggled duty-free into any port where vendors were willing to risk it, grew substantially. The whole process was largely replicated in booming Singapore.

The Japanese market, too, opened a crack for PMI with the purchase of Liggett's foreign business, prominently including the charcoal-filter Lark, the most popular import there. In vain Campbell pressed Japanese officials to lighten punitive cigarette tariffs and excise taxes on imported brands and to allow U.S. makes to be distributed through the hundreds of thousands of vending machines available to Japan Tobacco, the national monopoly. A little progress was even made in China, where the demand for cigarettes vastly outstripped the supply. Campbell was enlisted for technological advice to the native plant managers and got taken on tours of the provinces, where he ate a lot of 4 a.m. breakfasts on very chilly mornings, heard a lot of patriotic music, and inspected much grit-encrusted machinery left over from pre–World War II days. Eventually he was rewarded with a grant to sell imported Marlboros and a small joint venture with the government to produce several Liggett brands, all for distribution through a handful of "friendship" stores around the country. The opportunity to export PM brands made from a Chinese plant to Asian markets was also offered, but since it would have undercut the company's own efforts to cultivate those areas for much better profit margins, the offer was politely rejected. "We didn't want to burn any bridges there," Campbell recounted, "or build any too fast."

Maxwell's feat in running PMI was to take a collection of complex and loosely confederated businesses, each essentially separate, and a bunch of

swashbuckling young executives and turn them into a coherent and more readily manageable business without killing the incentive of people used to a minimum of oversight. "The trick," as Maxwell himself later put it, "was to sustain
the vitality of the operations while running under a more clearly defined set of
responsibilities." That meant more financial data flowing to PMI headquarters
in New York, long-term sales and profit projections, brand introductions and
line extensions more carefully justified, and an end to managers' high-living.
Far more so than at PM-USA, you had to perform in the overseas territories or
you were cut loose.

Maxwell pulled the strings through a team of devoted technicians, including
R. William Murray and Geoffrey C. Bible, a pair of remarkably diligent numbers crunchers from Australia; Ehud Houminer, a brainy Israeli planner; and
the German-born Hans Storr, who established wide contacts throughout the
banking and financial communities and became a deft manipulator of international currencies. All would soon play central roles in running the parent company. To William Campbell, Maxwell's primary gift as a motivator was "to
demand excellence of you in a way you found tolerable—he didn't offend or
destroy you—he challenged you to do the job better. And he gave incredibly
good directions, however sparing." PMI profits forged ahead, more than doubling during Maxwell's five years at the helm.

While speculation rose throughout 1983 about who would succeed George
Weissman as chief executive, the year seemed to have a celebratory quality.
As befit the new industry leader, the company moved its headquarters one
block north to the newly completed Philip Morris Building, a twenty-six-story
slab of gray granite and glass and no great distinction except for its location—
on Forty-second Street, directly across from Grand Central Terminal—and an
enclosed block-long, four-floor-high pedestrian mall containing greenery, retail shops, and modern sculpture. The Whitney Museum was persuaded to des-
ignate the atrium area and a small adjacent gallery as its downtown branch and
fill it with sculpture. Company publicity called inclusion of the "museum"
within Philip Morris's domain an example of "how private enterprise can address the public interest to the betterment of society." It was the classic Weissman touch, manifest a few months later in a world-class public-relations coup:
exclusive sponsorship of a five-month tour of the Vatican's art treasures to
raise money for their restoration. The cost of the show to Philip Morris was $7
million, but its rewards, including good will among the faithful and a papal
blessing that tactfully omitted any suggestion of corporate mortal sins, were
priceless.

In bowing out, Weissman received many testimonials from the tobacco industry as a "class guy" after having posted annual average per-share earnings
gains of 18 percent without ever even hinting at any doubt or remorse about
the nature of his company's prime product. His cultural patronage was re-

warded by a post-tobacco career as chairman of the board of the nation's leading showcase for the performing arts—Lincoln Center. Even so, he could not dictate to the Philip Morris board of directors who his successor as CEO should be, as Joe Cullman had.

Weissman, it had been no secret, favored his fellow self-made native New Yorker, John Murphy, who had done so well helping put PMI together and then turning Miller Brewing into a winner before hitting the stone wall Anheuser-Busch had belatedly erected in his path. Few in the company doubted that Murphy was smart, excellent with figures, and an effective and at times even inspirational manager. But as a big man with a correspondingly outsized personality, he had displayed a flamboyance that edged over into arrogance at times, the kind of swagger that did not win him points with the more sedate denizens at corporate headquarters. While the relatively low profit margins at Miller and the failure to make a go of Seven-Up had mellowed Murphy somewhat, the tobacco people in New York feared that his advancement to the chairmanship would signal that the role of cigarettes was to be markedly diminished in the company's future.

As word of opposition to Weissman's choice circulated, the board meeting to elect his successor was twice postponed, and reports spread that the retiring chairman's second choice was an outsider, John Reed, executive vice president of Citibank and a Philip Morris director. But the prospect of his election was no more pleasing to the tobacco people, who as the heart of the enterprise thought they had first claim to the throne. Their spokesman, Clifford Goldsmith, too old at sixty-four to be a candidate himself, proved to have almost equal standing with Weissman in the eyes of the board, and his choice for chairman was a man almost the polar opposite of Murphy. After a long meeting, fittingly held in Lausanne, and a reportedly close vote, the board chose fifty-eight-year-old Hamish Maxwell to run Philip Morris. He would shortly perform spectacular corporate feats of the sort that might have been expected of his vanquished rival for the chairman's job.

16

Of Dragonslayers and Pond Scum

NOT since before the Depression had the gospel of laissez-faire been so enshrined as the state creed as it was when the Reaganites took command of and promptly throttled the machinery of government. A true free-enterprise system, inviting the open play of marketplace forces without dour bureaucrats fretting over deceitful business practices or rampant economic concentration, would surely generate the greatest good for the greatest number, the new administration was certain. This fundamental faith nourished corporate America's undeclared conviction, as exemplified by the conduct of the tobacco industry, that its own financial well-being was more important than anything on earth, not excluding the health of its customers.

The Reagan administration wasted little time in removing heads at the FTC, the putative protector of the consumer, where staff was reduced by one-third within a few years. At the Justice Department, not only was the antitrust division reined in but mergers, said to stimulate more efficient and profitable operations, were encouraged. One of the few liberal voices occasionally heard amid "the sour hum of reaction," as he put it, belonged to Michael Pertschuk, now a holdover FTC commissioner almost entirely shorn of power, who decried the reigning Republicans' "innate awe of the wonders of unfettered capitalist behavior" and their faith that business would police its own excesses, even if history offered scant evidence of any such impulse. The cigarette manufacturers' interests were now roundly championed by such high-riding conservative commentators as William Buckley, James Kilpatrick, Patrick

Buchanan, and William Safire, who argued that the health risks of smoking were a matter for each citizen to resolve without government interference.

Prominent among Ronald Reagan's virtues was that, once in office, he did what he had said he would do, such as keeping his promise to tobacco interests that "my own Cabinet officers will be far too busy with substantive matters to waste their time proselytizing against the dangers of cigarette smoking." His regulators took the cue. New FTC Chairman James C. Miller III told the press he had had no time to read the report of his staff's five-year investigation into cigarette advertising abuses, calling for toughened, more explicit, rotating health warnings on cigarette packs and in advertisements—and the full commission dawdled for nearly two years before responding to a request from Congress for its opinion of the proposal. "If people want to smoke," Miller remarked, "that's their business."

It was thus something of a surprise when, in March of 1982, Assistant Secretary of the Department of Health and Human Services Dr. Edward Brandt appeared before a House subcommittee considering a bill embracing the FTC staff proposal for expanded cigarette warnings and testified that the measure had "high priority" within the Reagan administration. Overnight the tobacco lobby besieged the White House, reminding its occupants of the President's promise to lay off their business, and when Brandt came before a Senate committee six days later to discuss the same antismoking bill, he backed off his earlier unequivocal endorsement. The White House would take no official stand on the new labeling bill, which languished for the next several years.

The bleak prospects for executive-branch backing of antismoking legislation were all the more poignant in view of remarks delivered by the nation's lately installed No. 1 health officer, Dr. Everett Koop, on the release of the 1982 Surgeon General's report to Congress. The consequences of smoking, he said, were "the most important public health issue of our time," and cigarettes were "the chief, single, avoidable cause of death in our society." Even so, Koop was not about to defy the White House and learned early on the vast gap between the license to wax rhetorical and the application of real political power. Over the ensuing seven years, Koop's would be the sole voice within the administration to speak out forcefully on the smoking peril. While he wielded no power himself and had only a tiny staff and budget—indeed no job, really, beyond serving as titular head of the Public Health Service's commissioned officers' corps and advisor to the HHS Department—he had a pulpit and brought to it a moral gravity as nobody in that post had before him. There was a self-dramatizing theatricality about Koop that captured the nation's attention. For one thing, he was a Surgeon General who really had been a surgeon, an autocrat of his own operating room, with the omniscience and self-certitude customary in one used to being entrusted with his patients' lives.

Like most surgeons who cannot taper off without risk of losing their skills, Koop channeled his professional drive into a public-health crusade rendered in the direct, unwavering tones of the missionary, but one who, his palpable vanity notwithstanding, never confused himself with God.

While a moral exemplar, Koop was a walking contradiction to the tenets of ideal health. He ate too much red meat and drank too many martinis and had become overweight and overstressed, the latter condition manifested by ulcers and frequent migraines. Yet at sixty-four, he was ready for the final challenge of his career. During the nine-month confirmation period when Koop was nastily pilloried, the Reaganites had applied their scalpels to the PHS's uniformed commissioned officers' corps, letting go 1,600 physicians and public-health workers, more than a quarter of the total, and ordering nearly all the PHS hospitals closed. Finding morale understandably low in the corps as he took office, Koop decided that it was fitting for the Surgeon General to don a uniform and so routinely appeared in public in navy blues or dress whites with a splash of gold braid. "I was fighting for recognition of a service that the Administration was trying to destroy," he recounted. "You can rally people around a uniform."

To the surprise of those at both ends of the political spectrum, the Surgeon General rapidly turned into an outspoken champion of issues neglected by most others in the federal government: the need to eat sensibly; the rights of the elderly; curbs on child abuse, domestic violence, and pornography; and the urgency of combating the new scourge of AIDS in an age when many on the political and religious right were inclined to believe that those so afflicted deserved their fate.

On no issue would Koop prove to be fiercer and more relentless in his opposition than smoking. He had smoked cigars for ten years—but never cigarettes—and had not planned to crusade against tobacco use until coming to government and discovering what he would later call in his memoirs "the incontrovertible truths about the health hazards of smoking." He was first dumbfounded by and shortly thereafter furious with the behavior of the tobacco industry for taking the "ridiculous position" that nothing had been proven about the health hazards of smoking, a stance he mocked in his many public appearances by saying he knew full well that each time he turned on a light switch, he set a lot of electrons moving along a wire—"but I can't prove it." He characterized the cigarette purveyors collectively as "a sleazy outfit" that deserved scorn "for attempting to obfuscate and trivialize this extraordinarily important public health information" and for instead flaunting "its ability to buy its way into the marketplace of ideas and pollute it with its false and deadly information." Never would he appear knowingly on the same platform with the industry's representatives to debate what they tried to fob off as "the smoking controversy."

Besides rhetoric, Koop seized on the annual release of the Surgeon General's reports as an ideal occasion to hammer home the case against smoking. The reports became almost the sole mission of the Office on Smoking and Health, which had its budget tightened anew and was again placed under the supervision of the Atlanta-based Centers for Disease Control. The new director, Joanne Luoto, was a young PHS careerist lacking both familiarity with the subject and the political savvy to run a tiny, sensitive agency with an outsized assignment. Though conscientious, Luoto deferred in substantive matters to the far more knowledgeable staff technical expert, Donald Shopland, and the senior scientific editor of the Surgeon General's reports, pulmonologist David Burns. Applying increasingly stringent peer-review standards to the reports, Shopland and Burns avoided enlisting evaluators who they felt might have social and political agendas beyond a purely scientific one, including those in the hire of both the tobacco industry and the health voluntaries. While they did engage some scientists funded by the Council for Tobacco Research, they did so with high caution. "It's hard to dance with the bear and continue to lead," Burns would later remark.

The first report on Surgeon General Koop's watch, the 1982 study devoted entirely to what the world knew about smoking and cancer, reached his desk only a few months after he began his job. When Shopland returned to Koop's office a few days after presenting him with the final manuscript, he was astonished to see that the pages were dog-eared and speckled with inquiries that the Surgeon General wanted answered before signing off on the hefty document and publicly endorsing its findings in strong language. The dimensions of the pathology were now catastrophically clear, the report indicated: 21 percent of all U.S. deaths were due to cancer, and 30 percent of those were attributable to smoking—a total of about 111,000 a year by then, a threefold increase over the preceding twenty years. Among the key recent findings noted in the report were a study by Richard Doll holding that air pollution was responsible for fewer than 5 percent of lung cancer cases, and bioassays with mice showing a detectable, if inconclusive, decline in the carcinogenic potency of smoke from cigarettes with lowered tar and nicotine yields.

The following year's report, devoted entirely to smoking and heart disease, asserted that tobacco use was the most serious risk factor, noted that heavy smokers were two or three times more prone to die from cardiac complications than nonsmokers, and examined the growing evidence on the likeliest mechanisms by which cigarettes contributed to atherosclerosis, the most prominent form of the affliction. The 1984 report was concerned only with chronic obstructive lung diseases and smoking, which was their "major cause" in the U.S. Some 95 percent of all smokers were found to be stricken with some degree of emphysema, the prime cause of which now appeared to be the excessive release in the lungs of the enzyme elastase by irritant-scavenging macrophages inflamed by cigarette smoke. Taken together, the three reports formed a triptych that put the scientific case against smoking beyond serious quarrel.

In May 1984, a few months after the release of the report on lung disease, Surgeon General Koop broke irreparably with the tobacco industry by delivering an address at the annual meeting of the American Lung Association entitled "Toward a Smoke-Free Society by 2000 A.D." In it he promised, with true missionary zeal, to minister to the plight of the nation's 53 million smokers: "We are not abandoning them, whether they appreciate it or not." He added that the abatement of tobacco use could not be achieved by his own or the administration's crusading; it had to be, rather, "the triumph primarily of private citizens and of the private sector." The speech led R. J. Reynolds's tobacco chief, Edward Horrigan, to write President Reagan on July 12 of that year to express his dismay "at the increasingly shrill preachments" of the Surgeon General "and his call for a second Prohibition," which amounted to "the most radical antitobacco posturing since the days of Joseph Califano."

Koop was able to command the media spotlight almost at will. "He was single-handedly responsible for reinvigorating the antismoking movement," said Guy L. Smith IV, then Philip Morris's vice president for corporate affairs. Smith thought the Surgeon General smart, sincere, and masterful in his use of the media, but he questioned Koop's "intellectual integrity" for often going beyond the careful language of the annual reports, especially the 1986 document on the hazards of secondhand smoke, which was "chockful of caveats that didn't appear in the Surgeon General's press release. His goal was to generate a good story, and the nuances—the statements hedged or mitigated in the text of the report—didn't work well for that purpose." Koop found such charges against him to be a case of a very charred pot calling the kettle black. "We felt we had enough to go on," he said of his casting ETS as a serious health peril.

II

As Everett Koop commanded the public eye and ear, a far less visible figure established himself on Capitol Hill as the tobacco industry's most dangerous foe. Ex-chain-smoker Henry A. Waxman had none of the sound, look, or glow of power that seemed to radiate from the Surgeon General, but the California congressman was skilled in its acquisition and deployment in a way that Koop, essentially a figurehead, could never hope to match.

Short, potbellied, and balding in his early forties, Waxman presented a mild exterior and sweet-tempered disposition that camouflaged his determination and toughness, qualities rare in an unabashed liberal committed to using government to help those who could not adequately help themselves. His grandparents had been fugitives from the Russian pogroms, his father had run a grocery in the Watts section of Los Angeles; and Waxman himself was the first member of his family to gain a college education, winning a law degree from UCLA. He soon entered the California legislature, did well, and, after moving to a far wealthier area embracing parts of west Los Angeles and Hollywood, where the well-heeled residents tended to be Democrats and generous campaign contributors, was elected to the U.S. House of Representatives in 1974, at the age of thirty-four, as part of the "Watergate Revolution" in Congress.

A protégé of maverick San Francisco Congressman Philip Burton, a master at forging unlikely alliances and fond of preaching that the point of politics was not self-expression but winning, Waxman carved a niche for himself on the House Subcommittee on Health and Environment, where he pushed for health services for the needy and consumer and environmental protection measures while impressing colleagues as affable, hardworking, and smart. The Americans for Democratic Action, guardians of liberalism at a time when that political creed was waning, gave his voting record a 95 percent approval rating. In 1979, at the outset of his third term in the House, Waxman made a reach for power startling for one so young and new to Washington. The vacant chairmanship of his subcommittee, which had jurisdiction over such politically potent matters as health insurance, hospital costs, air and water cleanliness standards, and the safety of food, drugs, and cosmetics, had been all but conceded to a moderate and well-regarded North Carolina Democrat, former federal judge Richardson Preyer. The Washington *Post* endorsed the diligent Preyer, who had six years of seniority over Waxman.

With ungentlemanly resolve, Waxman contested the key job, arguing that he better embodied the party leadership's political tenets and, more to the point, that Preyer, whose family held a fortune in stock in a major pharmaceutical company, was hardly an ideal choice to head the health subcommittee, especially at a time when it was contemplating a reform bill to facilitate the sale of unbranded drugs. Preyer's strong backing of the tobacco price support program and derogatory comments about the comprehensive 1979 Surgeon General's report on smoking further weakened his credentials to be chief House overseer of public-health issues. And Waxman was not above using a legal but suspect expedient to win the votes he needed to beat Preyer: he contributed some $50,000 of his own surplus campaign gifts to the war chests of forty fellow congressmen—"deserving progressives," he called them—including ten on his subcommittee's parent Energy and Commerce Committee, which decided the chairmanship issue in his favor.

If his prize was a touch tarnished because some critics said he had purchased it, Waxman at once set about disarming them by his conduct in the health subcommittee chairmanship. He was unfailingly courteous and accommodating to his colleagues, assembled a crack staff of workaholic aides, adjusted the parliamentary wheels and levers adroitly, and soon formed an unlikely cordial alliance with Republican Senator Orrin Hatch of Utah, chairman of the upper chamber's Labor and Human Resources Committee, holding jurisdiction over health issues. As certifiably conservative as Waxman was liberal, the tall, athletically lean Hatch had a transparent yearning for recognition as a statesmanlike achiever among his antismoking constituents back in Utah. Waxman found common ground with him in mutually advantageous legislative trade-offs.

In the age of Reaganomics, Waxman was able to fend off the budgetary ax-wielders who sought to roll back Medicaid benefits, close community health centers in poor neighborhoods, and gut family planning programs. Inch by inch against an inrushing tide, he managed to get disability coverage expanded during the Reagan years. In 1982, he demonstrated his grit in a battle with the formidable new chairman of his parent Commerce Committee—Michigan Democrat John Dingell, who had the biggest budget and staff of any House committee boss, with jurisdiction, it was said, over anything in America that moved, burned, or was sold. While Dingell's voting record was almost as sterlingly liberal as Waxman's, they were opposite sorts of operatives; the Michigander gloried in his role as power broker and loved the political process, part of which for him involved leveling a vindictive glower at anyone who defied him. The two were on an inevitable collision course because of the very different congressional districts they represented. Dingell's was the heart of auto-land, and the cars it churned out gave Waxman's district the most polluted air in the nation. When Dingell moved, in the deregulatory spirit of the day, to ease the auto emission standards in the federal Clean Air Act, Waxman used every device at his disposal to foil him. His success, assuring him of Dingell's enduring enmity, would hobble Waxman's efforts now, as he began to address the major health peril of smoking.

III

HENRY WAXMAN harbored genuine moral indignation over the way tobacco lobbyists and those who did their bidding in Congress declared that the cigarette industry was essential to the economic well-being of their region, just as Southern lawmakers had defended slavery during the first half of the nineteenth century. He was thus highly receptive to the approach of Matthew Myers, lobbyist for the Coalition on Smoking or Health, who proposed Waxman's sponsorship of a bill embracing the chief recommendations of the 1981 FTC staff report Myers had shepherded into being. The tobacco companies, Waxman wrote on the Washington *Post* op-ed page in August of

1982, "do an excellent job disguising the [health risk] warning with clever, thematic imagery suggesting the youthful, healthy or athletic attributes of smoking." He expected that his newly introduced Smoking Prevention Education Act would be hotly contested in Congress but hoped that "the days of plantation politics, when tobacco was king, are on the wane."

Using the full powers of his chairmanship, Waxman showcased hearings on the bill, giving antismoking forces maximum exposure and featuring celebrities like Bob ("Captain Kangaroo") Keeshan, who lamented the lure of cigarettes for children; actor John Forsythe of the top-rated TV series "Dynasty"; and the widow of Barney Clark, who testified that her husband had succumbed not because of the failure of the first artificial heart to be implanted in a human patient but due to the ravages he had suffered from smoking. An important new theme sounded at the 1983 hearings was the addictive nature of smoking, for if young smokers were quickly imprisoned by the habit, they were victims and hardly free and willing patrons of the tobacco companies. Director William Pollin of the National Institute on Drug Abuse (NIDA) testified that three out of four smokers polled said they wished they could quit the practice, that fewer than 2 percent of smokers used cigarettes only occasionally, and that smoking was "the most widespread example of drug dependence in this country," every bit as hard to break as the thralldom to heroin and cocaine. "Dependence" rather than "addiction" had become the preferred term among pharmacologists for the habituating effect of such psychoactive substances, which aroused the pleasure centers of the nervous system, reinforced a craving for them as they traveled through the body's chemical pathways, and promoted their compulsive use. Whatever the term, researchers were fast concluding that those who turned to alcohol, nicotine, or hard drugs to relieve psychological stress and emotional instability were in fact compounding their condition, because the absence of such addictive drugs only intensified anxiety and stress levels; instead of being a form of self-medication to help users control their lives, Pollin and others now contended, dependence on smoking represented a decided loss of control, with dire health consequences. Thus, in a society where instant gratification was every consumer's right and cigarettes were legal, cheap, and everywhere available, the public needed to be told on packages and in advertisements that they were also addictive.

But the tobacco manufacturers would not hear of it and chose instead to continue denying the health charges against them. Typical were the remarks of Lorillard's chief executive, Curtis Judge, who in testimony before Waxman's subcommittee insisted that the public was aware of "the claim that smoking is harmful" but nevertheless chose to disregard it. Waxman's bill "erodes the concept of individual decision-making," the Lorillard executive added, and called upon Congress to stop using smoking as a scapegoat for "the many factors associated with disease." Hearing this, Waxman retorted that if the industry thought the warning labels so useless, then perhaps Congress ought to repeal the 1965 labeling law. That, though, was the last thing the cigarette makers wanted, since the warnings were now their chief shield against liability suits.

In Waxman, the tobacco forces faced a more resourceful and committed adversary than any of his predecessors in Congress, and the presence of the health voluntaries' Coalition on Smoking or Health notably strengthened his hand. "It was clear," recounted the Coalition's Matt Myers, "that our people were not just going to go away." Timing, too, was assisting Waxman, as the once monolithic battlement the industry had built began showing fissures. Profit-minded cigarette makers were using less and less domestic leaf as consumption ebbed a percentage point or two each year, technology like freon-puffed tobacco allowed ever smaller quantities of leaf per cigarette, and more cheap foreign leaf was being imported. As a result, an increasing portion of the U.S. farmers' crop had to go under loan through the federal support program, and its growing burden on taxpayers at a time when other marginal government outlays were being cut was adding pressure in Congress to halt the absurd practice of subsidizing a lethal harvest. To survive at all, the tobacco support program needed fixing, but the matter was of far more concern to growers than cigarette makers, and Myers played skillfully on the divergent interests of the two as the legislative mills ground away during the first half of the 'Eighties.

The tobacco control bill emerging from Waxman's subcommittee toward the end of 1983 was tougher than the industry had anticipated. It provided that cigarette ads and packages carry, besides rotating warning labels, disclosure of the quantity of carbon monoxide as well as of tar and nicotine yielded by each brand. And a list of all ingredients added during the manufacturing process was to be provided to HHS officials for whatever investigatory steps they wished to take. This last provision had taken on more importance to public-health advocates who pointed out that 8 percent of every cigarette's ingredients consisted of non-tobacco additives—chemicals and plant extracts that affected moisture level, burn rate, and the taste and odor of the tobacco. As the tar and nicotine yields had edged downward, these additives, particularly the flavorants, played a greater role in the appeal of the product. Yet as the 1982 Surgeon General's report had underscored, there was no way to be certain that the newer additives did not promote cancer and thereby defeat the whole purpose of lowering yields. The industry, however, had steadfastly resisted full public disclosure of cigarette ingredients, claiming that they were trade secrets and of no interest to anyone but the competing companies. This was tantamount to a declaration that the cigarette business was privileged, since makers of crackers, salad dressings, cough syrups, and practically every other product in common use had to disclose their ingredients on the package under federal regulations. The tobacco industry had been exempted simply because it had political muscle. Waxman's bill was aimed at chopping the cigarette companies at least partway down to size in this regard. It also stated that while no other health warnings than those spelled out in the bill could be required by federal regulators or under any state law, the labels in and of themselves did not curtail the right of smokers to sue the manufacturers in common-law tort actions claiming damages because their cigarettes were unreasonably dangerous; local juries remained free to decide the merits, if any, of the claims.

The cigarette companies, for so long politically bunkered, saw Waxman's bill more as the wish list of a hyperliberal public-health advocate than an imminent threat to their privileged status. The Tobacco Institute's Horace Kornegay went to work on his former House colleague, John Dingell, whose Commerce Committee had to pass on the smoking bill after the health subcommittee approved it. Dingell, in no hurry to handle the barbed measure, doubted that warning labels had any impact on the public's buying behavior, and as a staunch defender of the automotive industry, beset like the tobacco companies by health and safety advocates, had a certain sympathy for the cigarette makers. It was an affinity skillfully massaged by the tobacco bloc's best operative, North Carolina's Representative Charlie Rose, whose deep drawl and somewhat unkempt appearance belied his aptitude as a gifted power broker. Rose had held his state's moderate congressional delegation as a bloc largely loyal to the House Democratic leadership's agenda, in marked contrast to many "boll-weevil" conservative Southern Democrats who voted with the Reagan administration. "We cooperate with the leadership," Rose wryly remarked, "and remind them from time to time of our needs."

He reminded Dingell now, not because he doubted that smoking was hazardous to health but out of concern for the financial survival of the many tobacco farmers among his constituents. Dingell, who had no love for Waxman, agreed to keep the smoking bill bottled up and give the industry time to cut the best deal it could for itself, provided that the tobacco lobby did not try to gut the bill when it reached the Senate.

Comforted by Dingell's strength in the House, the tobacco camp calculated that it was in a still stronger position in the Senate. But Orrin Hatch, ever sensitive to his antismoking Mormon constituency and eager to have his name as leading sponsor on a moderate tobacco control bill, had surprised the industry by staging hearings on the issue and then urging the administration to negotiate a series of warning labels acceptable to the cigarette companies. In the crunch, though, HHS officials backed away from a toughened warning and, instead of a series of rotating and more informative labels, signed on to a single, slightly more explicit message: "Cigarette smoking increases your risk of cancer and heart, lung and other serious diseases." Hatch, at heart a doctrinaire pro-business conservative, went along, much to the despair of the health lobbyists.

"Had the industry played its cards right," Matt Myers recalled, "that would have doomed us in the Senate."

But the tobacco forces now made the first of a series of miscalculations, believing that they would not need to compromise at all. As the bill was being marked up for a vote by Hatch's committee, the chairman asked Horace Kornegay if the final wording was agreeable to the tobacco people, and while health advocates held their breath, the Tobacco Institute's chieftain said that, alas, it was not. Hatch, who had nursed the deal through and staked his name on it, was humiliated. In short order, the committee passed a far more alarming label: "Cigarette smoking causes cancer, emphysema, and heart disease, may complicate pregnancy, and is addictive." It also required the industry to provide the government with a full list of additives to cigarette tobacco.

Jesse Helms, chairman of the Senate Agriculture Committee, ordered the toughened warning bill to be put on hold, and Dingell was keeping the lid on in the House as 1983 ended. At the Tobacco Institute, Kornegay confessed his puzzlement over where the industry's steadfast congressional support had gone after all the years and gifts and favors and horse-trading. "He didn't understand the changing times," remembered one TI operative. "He was a true believer who could look you in the eye and swear that cigarettes were a health additive." However well-intentioned and devoted, Kornegay had become a polarizing force and thus useless as a negotiator. But any successor still had to take orders from the industry's executive committee, hardly a resilient bunch. "Horace was not the only one who had lost touch," remarked the new choice to wheel and deal in Congress—Howard Liebengood, former chief aide to Senate Republican leader Howard Baker and the Senate's sergeant-at-arms for three years before coming to the Tobacco Institute.

Liebengood's charge was to get as many of the objectionable features as possible cleansed from the two versions that awaited release from committee for consideration by each chamber. Reconnoitering, he approached Dingell, whom he recalled saying to him, "I'm not going to skewer you guys," but held out in return for a pledge, which Liebengood delivered, for the industry to go along with the House version when whatever smoking bill might emerge reached the conference stage. The health forces' chief negotiator, Matt Myers, meanwhile set about trying to soften up opposition to a new labeling bill by the other key obstacle to such a measure in the House—Charlie Rose. Since Rose's priority was to keep alive the increasingly unpopular tobacco support program, which Myers's Coalition flatly opposed, common ground was elusive at first. But a narrow margin of it was found through Coalition support, in the name of public health, for a congressional measure banning the import of tobacco from nations that permitted it to be sprayed with carcinogenic pesticides. Rose appreciated the spirit of the gesture, which had the effect of supporting his tobacco farmers, but he and Myers played a cat-and-mouse game as long as the Coalition was on record in opposing continued federal crop supports for tobacco. Rose urged Dingell to keep the labeling bill under wraps, but meanwhile its provisions were being intensively negotiated.

Hatch, still peeved at the industry, had indicated he would go along with almost any antismoking bill that passed the lower chamber. But someone was needed to break the House logjam, and the brokering job fell to the earnest young Tennessee Congressman Albert Gore, Jr., whose constituency included a goodly number of tobacco farmers and whose family held a small, hereditary tobacco acreage allotment under the federal support program. Gore, running for the Senate that year, recognized the merits of the health issue and moved discreetly to bring the parties to an understanding. Impressed with Myers's square-shooting, Gore turned to Liebengood and asked him what the industry could not live with, not merely what it did not like. The tobacco lobbyist all but admitted that he could not negotiate with a free hand, because any concession that he might make had to be ratified by his employers, who were a very reluctant bunch.

Most attention was devoted to adjusting the warning labels—how many, how large, what shape, and how they would be worded. No matter what else, Liebengood made it plain, the industry would not sit still for language that included the words "death" or "addiction". And, as forecast, any ground Liebengood yielded was taken back after he consulted with his executive committee. Myers stayed in the game, winning points with Gore, who kept gently pressing the industry to compromise. Finally Gore advised Myers a deal could be struck if the health advocates would agree to language that explicitly barred liability suits against cigarette makers who met the new warning requirements—in short, federal preemption would not only block stronger warnings by any state or local jurisdiction but would also deny smokers the right to sue for damage to their health since they would have been alerted to the possibility by the labels. This was the opposite of the provision in the bill passed by Waxman's subcommittee.

Waxman's astute aide Ripley Forbes found that the sweeping preemption request drew surprisingly little resistance from the Coalition, probably because its constituent organizations included a great many doctors who bore a professional antipathy to lawyers and lawsuits, in particular those claiming medical malpractice, and were not eager to bolster the rights of litigants in general. Myers told Gore that if accepting explicit preemption was what it would take to seal the deal, he would accept it—only to be told soon thereafter that the industry still had another dozen or so "problems". By this point, Myers was ready to pull out of the negotiations and take his chances on a floor vote—assuming that Dingell ever freed the measure.

Exhibiting heroic patience, Gore managed to bring the parties to a settlement, which included more bitter medicine for Myers to swallow. The health community's much-sought warning that smoking was addictive would be stripped from the rotating messages; in its place the industry agreed to one stating merely that cigarette smoke contained carbon monoxide—without adding that it was a toxic gas. Three other warnings were agreed to: "Smoking Causes Lung Cancer, Heart Disease, Emphysema, and May Complicate Pregnancy"; "Smoking by Pregnant Women May Result in Fetal Injury, Premature Birth and Low Birth Weight"; and "Quitting Smoking Now Greatly Reduces Serious Risks to Your Health." The warnings were to appear in type half again as large as previously. The preemption issue would not be elaborated upon in the new bill, leaving the scope and the interpretation of the language in the earlier warning laws up to the courts. And the industry would have to turn over each year to OSH a complete list of the additives it used in manufacturing cigarettes, but it did not have to state which ingredients were used in what quantity in any particular brand—and the list had to be kept under lock and key, to be scrutinized only by authorized government researchers who could report their findings to HHS officials, who in turn might make regulatory proposals to Congress if the additives were found dangerous.

After the health camp accepted the package, Liebengood, pleased with the bargain he had struck, took it to his masters, only to find them wringing their hands. "They weren't used to getting pushed around," Liebengood recounted; "they were used to sweetheart bills—and this wasn't one." He argued that this was the best bill the industry could hope for, that nothing better would emerge from the Senate, and that the company chiefs would gain favor in Congress by appearing responsive to the health community's concerns. The companies' answer: No deal.

Gore, snookered as Hatch had been by the industry's treachery, went to Charlie Rose with his tale of double-dealing, and the shrewd North Carolinian, fearful that the manufacturers' conduct would fire up Congress to the point where it would not only pass a tougher antismoking law but also wipe away the tobacco crop support program, went to Dingell. The redoubtable House Commerce Committee head, overseer of 40 percent of the bills enacted by the lower chamber, resented the way the tobacco people were toying with the legislative process and ordered the Waxman bill freed. Gore's version was quickly substituted for it, and the measure was passed by acclamation. Even then, the industry executives tried, despite repeated pledges by its operatives to accept the House version, to get the bill shot down in the Senate. They failed.

Although the 1984 law did nothing to restrict the manufacture or marketing of cigarettes, it represented a turning point in the industry's hold on the federal legislative machinery. Its lobbyists were perceived by a growing number of lawmakers as duplicitous agents of to-the-bitter-end moguls, and smoking was no longer an issue that could only embarrass everyone in Congress. The 1984 act, moreover, marked the emergence of Henry Waxman as what one Philip

Morris attorney called "a very dangerous adversary." His persistence matched his patience, and he would keep after the tobacco industry over the following decade, repeatedly holding hearings on antismoking measures for which he could never muster a majority of his subcommittee membership, yet each time he advanced the antismoking cause by ventilating it for an ever-widening segment of the public. And he did not grow jaded as the fight lengthened—a prime virtue in the eyes of battle-scarred consumer advocate Ralph Nader, who termed Waxman "something special" and a notable exception to "the high attrition rate among progressives in Congress."

Just how slowly the tobacco industry would be made to yield ground at the federal level was evidenced by the fate of one provision of the 1984 act—the companies' surrender of the list of tobacco additives. For ten years—during which Congress would pass only one other real tobacco control measure, a two-stage ban on smoking during all domestic airline flights—the list of added ingredients was locked away in a safe in the OSH office while that tiny bureau, starved on a budget that barely allowed it to prepare the Surgeon General's reports and conduct a minimal antismoking educational program, could never find the money or resolve to have the additives investigated by qualified scientists. Finally, in 1994, with the first avowedly antismoking President in the White House, an activist FDA commissioner suggested that cigarette manufacturers appeared to be manipulating the nicotine level of the product, with the help of additives, to keep smokers addicted.

This seemingly startling disclosure—of manufacturing procedures well known to public-health investigators for more than thirty years and testified to by the yields listed in cigarette ads and monitored by the FTC since 1967—allowed Waxman to pressure the industry into making public its long-secret list of additives. Included among the nearly 600 substances listed were irritants like ammonia; ethyl 2-furoate, known to cause liver damage in laboratory animals; and Sclareol, which induced convulsions when combined with certain other substances. But the industry issued the familiar assurances that these ingredients were safe in the amount present in cigarettes—precisely what they had long contended about all the compounds yielded during the smoking process. Yet such is the nature of massive media attention that these newly identified additives, composing a fraction of the ingredients in each cigarette, were treated as a major revelation and potentially grave health menace while the tobacco itself, making up more than 90 percent of every cigarette and long known when burned to produce dozens of carcinogens and toxic substances, was ignored as very old news.

IV

Not blind to the slippage in their mastery of Capitol Hill, the lords of tobacco struck a deal in 1985 to narrow the divergence between their own
interests and those of the prime source of their political power—the growers.

For nearly half a century the federal tobacco price support system had
brought a decent livelihood to more than half a million farm families while assuring the manufacturers of a ready supply of the world's best leaf. The system
worked because the farmers accepted acreage allotments and crop quotas that
kept the leaf supply in close balance with the demand and guaranteed them a
floor price geared to their costs of doing business. As a result, a tiny percentage—as low as 2 percent in some years—of the crop went unsold and had to be
taken up under government loan by the farmer cooperatives, which eventually
sold off most of the surplus. The industry contended that the program
was not a subsidy but a boon to all parties, since 99 percent of the loans were
repaid and the cumulative total of $200 million in lost principal and forgiven
interest over nearly fifty years of the system's operation was dwarfed by the
cigarette excise taxes—$7 billion in 1981 alone—that federal and state trea-
suries reaped.

The situation remained stable so long as cigarette consumption kept rising
in the U.S., along with demand for American leaf by foreign manufacturers
who prized its taste and texture. The public's willingness to sustain the support
program to benefit tobacco farmers and manufacturers at minimal governmental cost vied with its awareness that the program helped sustain a health hazard
under increasing censure. By the early 'Eighties, though, that precarious tolerance tipped over into discernible unhappiness with the arrangement. The price
of U.S. tobacco leaf, artificially sustained by the support program, had climbed
to as high as twice the going rate in developing countries, like Brazil and Zim-
babwe, where the crop was becoming a mainstay of the domestic economy and
labor was much cheaper. Imports soared twentyfold between 1960 and 1980,
when they made up one-third of the leaf used in American cigarettes. Demand
for U.S. leaf was further reduced by increasing use of reconstituted tobacco
sheets and puffed leaf, allowing 523 cigarettes to be made from a pound of tobacco, compared with 382 only a dozen years earlier. On top of all this, per
capita smoking was now dropping by a percentage point or two annually in response to the health charges.

These conditions damaged tobacco growers, especially small ones; the
larger ones were now benefiting from modernized means of harvesting and
curing the crop, like mechanical pickers and metal bulk barns where the leaf

was no longer tied into "hands" and hung up to dry. Even so, tobacco required 200 man-hours of work per acre, and U.S. leaf was pricing itself out of the market except for the richest buyers like Japan, which paid up for the genuine article. But even with exports accounting for up to 40 percent of the U.S. crop, the harvest by the early 1980s was only two-thirds of what it had been three decades earlier. The proportion of the crop going unsold and put under government loan rose now along with antismoking sentiment. Senator Bob Packwood of non-tobacco-growing Oregon conveyed the national sentiment when he remarked that it was "unconscionable to allow Americans to go hungry while supporting an inedible and unhealthy crop like tobacco. . . ."

The fight to end tobacco supports was joined in earnest in 1981. The program's most enlightened defenders like Charlie Rose did not bother anymore to deny the health charges against the leaf; their concern was the economic survival of the farm families still dependent on tobacco—about 250,000 of them in twenty-two states. If the support program was shut down and the growing quotas eliminated, Rose and his comrades argued, planting would almost surely expand and seriously depress prices, abetting only the largest growers, who would probably survive by contracting directly with the cigarette companies. But unless the program was revised, even its most ardent backers saw, only the manufacturers would benefit from the widening gulf between U.S. and overseas leaf prices. The cigarette makers, though, could not let their growers dwindle to the point where there were too few to assure the industry of an adequate supply of high-quality domestic leaf and, equally important, enough political clout in Congress.

The tobacco congressmen struck a bargain with the Democratic leadership by which the doubled cigarette sales tax was put through on a provisional three-year basis, while the tobacco support program was continued on the condition that it inflict no net cost on U.S. taxpayers beyond the $15 million a year required to administer it. The growers agreed to cover the cost of any ultimately unsold leaf taken under loan so that the expense of the inventory held in farmers' cooperatives, already over a billion pounds, could be brought under control. The Agriculture Department was given the right to slash the support price by about one-third, which meant that the growers would absorb the shortfall due to reduced demand for leaf and ever-rising costs for their fuel, fertilizer, bank interest, and other necessities. But cigarette companies were left free to buy abroad as they chose, keeping downward pressure on U.S. prices, so that more of the American crop went unsold and under loan—up to 25 percent now—and growers had to pay a penalty of about twenty-five cents a pound, or more than 15 percent of the sales price, under the no-net-cost-to-taxpayers formula. By 1985 federal loans to growers from the Commodity Credit Corporation had hit $3.5 billion, with $1 billion of that in the form of an unsalable stockpile and likely to go unrepaid. More growers were being driven to the brink of bankruptcy even as the cigarette companies were coining unprecedented profits.

Putting aside a deep enmity, the populist Charlie Rose, the growers' champion, and economic royalist Jesse Helms, who held the fort for the manufacturers, pushed a deal through Congress in 1985 which headed off an irreparable breach within the tobacco industry. Its leadership agreed to a permanent doubling of the federal excise tax on cigarettes—indeed, congressional sentiment was running high for an even stiffer boost—and the manufacturers conceded the need to relieve the growers' distress by splitting the costs with them for all future loans on unsold crop that could not be repaid. They also agreed to bail out the government by buying up the huge stockpile of unsold tobacco held by growers' cooperatives over the next five years at a discount of 10 percent on the newer leaf and as much as 90 percent on the older leaf, thus assuring the manufacturers an abundant supply of cheaper leaf and reducing their buying needs when the new crops came to auction. But in order not to inflict still further pain on farmers, the cigarette makers agreed to advise the Agriculture Department confidentially of their individual buying needs for the coming year so that the growers' overall quota could be adjusted accordingly; the companies also pledged to buy no less than 90 percent of their stated needs.

"We saw that our political base was going to disappear," recalled Frank Resnik, then president of Philip Morris-USA, "so we made a decision that cost us a lot of money." But relatively speaking, the companies' concession was a modest enough investment in good will and political survival; only 8 percent of the cost of state-of-the-art manufacturing and marketing of cigarettes was represented by tobacco. A year into the new support program jointly funded by growers and manufacturers, tobacco acreage in the U.S. fell to half of what it had been only a decade earlier. For the tobacco industry to retain political influence, it would have to move beyond dependency on a regional power base and invest seriously in other forms of enterprise.

V

UNTIL the 'Eighties, the core of the tobacco issue had been the health of smokers, but with the emergence of scientific evidence, however fragmentary, that environmental tobacco smoke imperiled nonsmoking bystanders, the debate broadened to include social issues and grew more charged. A decade earlier, you were considered rude or a crank if, out of annoyance at having your eyes and nose offended at close quarters, you asked a smoker to refrain in an elevator or other confined place. Many smokers declined to oblige, assuming that it was their right to feed their habit when and where they chose and thereby breeding a latent resentment among nonsmokers. Their distress mounted with the disclosures about ETS from the medical community and led to outbursts edged with real anger. Comedian Steve Martin captured the change in mood in one of his monologues by remarking that when friends asked him, "Do you mind if I smoke?" he now replied, "Not in the least—do you mind if I fart?"

It was not war yet, exactly, but there was a clear lowering of tolerance for smokers, who were increasingly seen as trampling on nonsmokers' assertedly God-given right to breathe clean air. The tobacco industry was forcibly being made aware of the shift in sentiment by antismoking activists like bioengineering professor Stanton Glantz of San Francisco, who recalled, "Our movement undercut the social support network for smoking by implicitly defining it as an antisocial act."

Although the nascent nonsmokers' rights movement was still largely perceived as peripheral to the main issue of smoking as posing a serious peril to those who indulged in it and thus represented a frittering away of the health community's scarce antismoking resources, in bellwether California the disparate Groups Against Smoking Pollution (GASPs) had captured public attention. Their confederation changed its name in 1981 to Californians for Nonsmokers' Rights (CNR), drawing sustenance from new data on ETS in studies like those by Repace and Hirayama. The precise nature and strength of these findings was somewhat beside the point. "We were just waiting for science to tell us what we already knew," remarked one longtime activist—namely, who was violating whose rights; the extent and medical consequences of the violation were nuance. Also fueling the issue were new data on the economic costs of smoking. Seattle University economist William L. Weis, for example, reported in 1983 that smokers devoted 6 percent of their workday to the ritual, took 50 percent more sick days, and made 50 percent greater use of the health-care system than nonsmokers. If they hired only the latter instead, Weis added, employers would shave their personnel costs by 20 percent, their insurance premiums by 30 percent, their office maintenance by 50 percent, and their disability outlays by 70 percent, for a claimed total saving of as much as $4,600 per worker a year. Tobacco industry spokesmen denounced these figures as ludicrously inflated and noted, by way of rebuttal, that the disproportionately higher number of sick days attributed to smokers was readily explained by the fact that there were more smokers in the lower-paid blue-collar sector of the workforce, where it was the often tedious nature of the labor—not smoking—that prompted the higher sick-day claims. Another frequently noted report came from the congressional Office of Technology Assessment in 1985, placing the cost of health care for smoking-related diseases at $22 billion a year and adding to it another $43 billion in lost productivity in the form of wages unpaid to smoking workers absent from the job due to illness, for an annual total cost of $65 billion, or $2.17 per pack of cigarettes sold. It was far from clear, though, just what proportion of the overall social cost was borne by smokers themselves.

However debatable the particulars, the growing vilification of smokers and smoking contributed to the passage in San Francisco in mid-1983 of the nation's first truly restrictive rules against smoking in the workplace in a major metropolitan area. The measure, intended to accommodate the wishes of both smokers and nonsmokers, called for separate work areas for each if even a single nonsmoker requested it. CNR and other nonsmoking crusaders viewed work-site regulations as far more important than rules governing restaurants, stores, and public gathering places, because the latter involved shorter exposure to ETS and because where one dined out or shopped or took cultural nourishment involved voluntary choices, while where one worked often involved far less, if any, choice. Inconveniencing smokers, moreover, by limiting the time and/or places they could smoke was viewed as sound public-health policy aimed at discouraging a harmful habit. And the San Francisco ordinance left enforcement of a segregated workplace up to health officials and peer pressure, not police. Reading polls that showed the public favored the step by a two-to-one margin, Mayor Dianne Feinstein rebuffed objections from the tobacco industry, unions, and some other elements among Democrats who argued that the restrictions were an elitist concept, and signed them into law. Within a month, the cigarette makers, knowing that San Francisco as a tourist mecca attracted worldwide media coverage, gathered 30,000 signatures in protest of the new smoking restrictions and put the issue up to a citywide referendum.

Once more the industry confected a front group, this time called San Franciscans Against Government Intrusion, and argued, in a campaign that cost more than a million dollars, that the workplace smoking regulations would drive people apart; the San Francisco *Examiner* agreed, telling readers that city-supervised smoking was "a recipe for antagonism and frustration" and that the issue was more properly a matter for resolution between workers and employers.

Given the compact political arena and saturation media attention, CNR and its allies figured that a war chest of $150,000 would be adequate to win, but they never reached that sum. The size of the antismoking kitty mattered less, though, than the passion brought to the effort and the message CNR was broadcasting against the cigarette makers. "These sleazebags were pouring money into our state so they could keep on killing hundreds of thousands," one activist said, summing up the spirit of their cause, "and everything they said was a lie." The antismoking television ads showed a cowboy, who was decidedly not a Marlboro Man, riding to the top of one of the city's picturesque hills, dismounting, and asserting, "Tell the cigarette companies to butt out of

San Francisco." The smoking control effort, little abetted by the health voluntaries, was assisted by large, progressive local employers like Bank of America
and Levi Strauss, which had already instituted workable separate smoking and
nonsmoking areas, and by local NBC affiliate KRON-TV, which had aired
the anti-Marlboro documentary, *Death in the West*, the year before and now
drew attention to the industry's artifice by insisting that its commercials bear a
tag line identifying the real sponsor and not just the front group. For all that,
the industry barely missed buying yet another victory; the law was upheld by
only 1,259 votes.

Though narrowly endorsed at the polls, the San Francisco ordinance provided a major lift nationwide for the nonsmokers' rights movement and established three precepts to guide its advance: (1) The tobacco companies could be
beaten, especially at the local level, where they could be verifiably cast as
predators. (2) A focused and limited antismoking law was more workable and
useful than a weak, broad one. (3) The industry's endorsement of "common
courtesy" as a substitute for smoking restrictions was a code term for continued knuckling under to inconsiderate smokers, since most nonsmokers preferred to avoid a confrontation. The key to clean indoor air was to create, by
statute, an environment empowering nonsmokers. The idea was taking hold
throughout California, not only in liberal cities like San Francisco but also in
conservative places, from San Diego in the south to Ukiah in the north. Of the
eighty-nine cities and counties in the U.S. with tough work-site smoking regulations by the end of 1985, three-quarters were in California.

Spearheading this effort was CNR, the grassroots complement to John
Banzhaf's ASH, which operated within a narrow federal orbit. What was most
needed in view of the limited reach of the national smoking control laws was
intensified local effort, field hands and voices to form a genuine social movement dealing with a life-and-death issue. Surgeon General Koop served as a
national beacon for the cause, and the reports issued in his name drew ever-
widening respect. But the movement took flight only when animated by passionately devoted leaders like CNR's Glantz, as compulsive a worker as he
was a talker, who dreamed up most of his group's arresting ideas, had a mind
both inventive and encyclopedic, raised a lot of its money, wrote its pithy
newsletter (usually including his picture), and loosed its fiercest rallying cries.
The trouble with having such an immensely productive leader, though, was
that he could turn into a thorny autocrat and be as much an impediment as an
inspiration. "Stan decided everything," recalled one of Glantz's not unadmir-
ing colleagues, "and to him everyone else was incompetent." When a few full-
timers were brought in to give CNR more programmatic coherence, Glantz
seemed unable to trust them or delegate responsibility and soon had the staff
rattled by his constant directives. It was not until the emergence of a pair of

young recruits, who had joined CNR in a junior capacity in 1984 when each was twenty-seven, that the operation turned less chaotic, expanded its mission, and changed its name to Americans for Nonsmokers' Rights (ANR).

Michael Pertschuk's long-running wrestling match with the tobacco companies was at best a mixed incentive for his son, Mark, a graduate of American University law school, who had joined CNR's office in Berkeley to assist with its legislative and lobbying efforts. Endowed like his father with abundant brains, humor, and integrity, Pertschuk *fils* was inclined to turn confrontational when dealing with base adversaries and meretricious arguments. He stood up to Glantz and after a couple of years was willing to tell CNR's directors that if the organization was going to go national and function efficiently, its charismatic leader would have to stand aside. Glantz, to his credit, seemed to understand that despite only good intentions, he was driving everyone else crazy, and the leadership passed to Pertschuk and an associate, the incendiary Julia Carol, a passionate foe of smoking.

While Pertschuk operated as legislative strategist for the country's largest nonsmokers' rights organization, Carol served as its spiritual den mother, nurturing its rank and file and preaching that the struggle was not between smokers and nonsmokers but between the rest of society and the rogue vendors of cigarettes. "The majority of the public now sees the industry as pond scum," she would remark, but reserved the larger portion of her fervor for cheering on and guiding those around the country she lovingly called "the movement people," the ones who had long operated out of their living rooms or garages to put the antismoking crusade together stick by stick. "They aren't all real good at saying less instead of more," she wrote of them in a 1989 internal memo on grassroots activism, ". . . [and] they'll run miles for you at the drop of a hat, but they'll also tell you you're full of shit if you say something they don't agree with. . . . They need to be appreciated. They need to be energized." And Julia Carol was gifted at energizing people, getting them to write individualized letters—never form ones—to officeholders when a smoking control bill was approaching a critical point in the legislative process, and helping GASPs and other allied groups around the country understand when and how the tobacco lobbyists were trying to cut the heart from pending measures.

Decisive in CNR's conversion into a national program was the appearance at the end of 1986 of the Surgeon General's report on ETS, which gave state and local legislators courage to enact smoking restriction laws that science now approved. Requests for help on how to get smoking control measures passed flowed in to CNR's busy little shop from all over the country, and the younger Pertschuk and Carol were quick to urge use of the Surgeon General's document as a vital weapon. "All you had to do was hold up the report," they recounted, "and say [to opponents], 'Go argue with him,' and the point was made. The report didn't just give us a weapon—it ended the debate."

But even before the report was issued, the movement was in full stride: thirty-five states had by then restricted smoking on public transit, thirty-one in elevators, twenty-nine in cultural and recreational facilities, twenty-seven in schools, nineteen in libraries; twenty-two had segregated smokers in public office buildings, and nine in private ones. The trend would intensify, and helping orchestrate it at the other end of the country from ANR's humming headquarters in California was a larger and better-financed suite of offices in Washington with the deceptively tame name of the Advocacy Institute. Brainchild of co-founder Michael Pertschuk, who declined to cash in on his priceless experience as a Senate committee staff director and FTC commissioner and become a gilt-edged hired gun for industry, the institute was created from foundation grants, private gifts, and rare human resources to serve as a strategic think tank for public-interest causes trying to move federal lawmakers and regulators. Primary item on the Advocacy Institute's agenda was the war on tobacco. Pertschuk and his staff, functioning as the Smoking Control Advocacy Resource Center (SCARC), networked globally by telephone, computer, and print bulletins with health advocates now on the move everywhere to challenge the dominion of the cash-rich cigarette makers.

V I

A FTER California, the most avid antismoking campaign in America was being carried on in the commonwealth of Massachusetts, particularly in the Boston area with its concentration of leading medical and educational facilities. The effort had begun in the early 'Seventies with a group composed largely of Harvard and MIT faculty people loosely linked to John Banzhaf's ASH, which they had helped establish with their names and seed money. But since ASH devoted itself to combating tobacco in the federal arena, the Massachusetts contingent formed an independent GASP, funded by charitable crumbs from the wealthy suburban complex that included Newton, Brookline, and Cambridge. The shoestring operation survived with the help of a vital gift from Boston's Deaconess Hospital: office space, a telephone, and a photocopy machine. Mainstay of the effort was another young attorney, soft-spoken Edward L. Sweda, Jr., who, while attending Suffolk Law School, lost his father to colon cancer and asked himself, "What could I best do to fight the disease?"

Sweda's attention was drawn to the tobacco industry, whose executives, he came to feel, were "a greater danger to society than any of the criminals I encountered in my practice." To combat them, he helped local GASP and other antismoking units around the state agitate for tobacco control ordinances, of which the easiest to gain acceptance for were separate sections in restaurants. But some communities were receptive to farther-reaching measures, like Newton, the first town in Massachusetts to put through workplace restrictions on smoking, and Amherst, which banned the free sampling of cigarettes and smoking advertisements on public transit facilities. In his quarterly newsletter and speaking engagements, Sweda called for lower health insurance premiums for nonsmokers; he helped organize suits against store owners who were lax about selling cigarettes to underage smokers, and he lobbied the Boston Red Sox to take down the Marlboro sign looming over the right-field stands at Fenway Park—"the most notorious pro-cancer billboard in Massachusetts," he called it—and Boston University to stop leasing its facilities to the Virginia Slims tennis tour. The Red Sox said no, but the university, after resisting for two years, agreed.

In bone-chilling cold outside the Worcester Arena and in summer heat in front of the Newport Casino in nearby Rhode Island, Sweda picketed cigarette-sponsored events while wearing a black-hooded Grim Reaper costume made to fit his lanky build. As he marched, one hand wielded a wooden scythe with which Death cut down his harvest, and the other hoisted placards with earnest but inoffensive messages like "Virginia Slims and Tennis Don't Make a Match." Handing out leaflets at a Marlboro-funded country music festival, he told the hovering media, "The only appropriate music at a cigarette-sponsored event is 'Taps'." And he was not above utilizing a bit of hyperbole to press home his point, as in a Massachusetts GASP pamphlet containing the assertion inside that "if you work near smokers, your lungs suffer the same harm as if you smoked up to ten cigarettes a day"—a gross overstatement.

Sweda's chief preoccupation was his eight-year struggle to get a clean indoor air act through the state legislature. Ranged against him, so far as he could determine, were five full-time and eight part-time tobacco company lobbyists. By 1986, Sweda had managed to win a vote in the House two years running but was stymied by Senate President William Bulger, of South Boston, who once made the loutish remark "I don't give a damn about nonsmokers' rights," and kept the smoking control bill from reaching the Senate floor. That autumn, the counterculture weekly Boston *Tab*, in a front-page exposé, stated that the tobacco companies had given Bulger $10,000 in campaign gifts and speaking honoraria. The disclosure had its effect, and at the very end of the following legislative session in January 1988, Bulger stepped aside and let the people's will prevail. "Victory!" the GASP newsletter exulted in reporting the new statute that banned smoking statewide in retail food stores and mandated separate smoking and nonsmoking sections in government buildings (the state legislature alone excepted), airport waiting rooms, restaurants with seventy-five or more seats, health and child-care centers, and state-owned college dormitories. A collateral bill barring student smoking in all public schools was achieved with the help of youngsters whom Sweda recruited as junior lobbyists.

By the end of the year, the Massachusetts GASP could claim, besides the state control law, antismoking ordinances in fifty-four communities across the state, a membership of 2,000, a full-time executive director—not Sweda, who remained a volunteer—and an annual budget of $50,000, about the salary of one of the tobacco industry's array of lobbyists.

V I I

A T Boston's Northeastern University, an antismoking project was born in 1984 devoted to fulfilling the tobacco industry's worst fears by trying to foment product liability suits that would drain their deep corporate pockets. Such suits were to be patterned after those then bringing ruin to the asbestos industry, whose companies, like the cigarette manufacturers, had long known the health risks of their product but had minimized, denied, or suppressed the information, thereby exposing many to injury and death. But the potential stakes in tobacco litigation loomed vastly larger.

The agent provocateur behind this effort, dubbed the Tobacco Products Liability Project (TPLP), was Richard A. Daynard, a slender, bearded Northeastern law professor of no luminous achievement but a powerful yearning, as he turned forty, to put his steel-trap mind to social use. A graduate of Columbia College and Harvard Law School with a doctorate in urban planning from MIT thrown in, Daynard had specialized in consumer protection law and come to the conclusion that the perils of smoking dwarfed all other consumer concerns—only the threat of nuclear holocaust struck him as a greater menace to humanity—yet none was being more nonchalantly grappled with by society.

Accordingly, he had become president of Massachusetts GASP and drafted the state's first work-site smoking control statute for Newton, but, foreseeing an endless campaign to put across such measures in the state's 350 other municipalities, Daynard sought a more telling way to combat the health problem. Given the tobacco industry's record of fierce resistance to legislative action against it, he honed a strategy relying on the judicial branch of government, which seemed less susceptible to the companies' infiltration. Johns-Manville, the giant of the asbestos industry, had been sued by 25,000 claimants and lately pushed into bankruptcy—an obvious model for the campaign Daynard was envisioning. Whatever their immediate financial results, similar suits against the cigarette companies were, according to TPLP's statement of its mission, "the best way to force into the media and the public consciousness a strong emotional awareness of tobacco's true degree of danger by focusing on the suffering of particular individuals, thereby helping to counteract the $2 billion spent annually . . . which promotes this catastrophic epidemic." A court finding for even a single plaintiff victimized by smoking—and there had never been one in American judicial history—was held likely to open the floodgates to thousands of similar actions.

Daynard was convinced he could carry off this campaign on the strength of three legal arguments. First, liability suits under state common law had not been preempted by either the 1965 or the 1970 federal cigarette labeling acts because neither had been conceived as a comprehensive piece of legislation "but as a minimal step"—the smallest that Congress could take and still pose as guardian of the public health. Congress's labeling laws had merely prevented a myriad of such warning notices from being required by state and local jurisdictions, thus accommodating the industry in the conduct of its business. Second, the companies' assumption-of-risk defense was fatally flawed by the addicting nature of cigarettes, which the industry did not warn against; indeed, it denied as much. Nicotine addiction made the use of cigarettes anything but a voluntary lifestyle preference, Daynard contended; smokers, rather, were captives of an industry that knowingly ensnared them, usually at an age when they lacked understanding of the possible deadly consequences of tobacco dependency. And third—and most pertinent, because the companies (a) had failed to warn their customers adequately before the warning labels had been mandated by Congress, and (b) had willfully acted since then to undermine the force of the warnings by denying or minimizing the scientific charges against smoking and continuing to advertise the pleasures of the custom—the industry at the very least shared responsibility for the physical damage that cigarettes inflicted. The risk of smoking, that is, ought to be assumed not solely by the buyers of so deviously marketed a product but by the makers as well, who were running a dirty business.

Fueled by a $30,000 annual grant from the Rockefeller Family Fund, the TPLP operated out of a cluttered office with a staff of six part-timers and a view of the Northeastern gymnasium. A self-proclaimed academy of instruction in the doctrine and execution of liability actions against the cigarette industry, Daynard and his crew acted as a referral service for litigators, aggrieved claimants, and public-health professionals, feeding them a stream of ideas and keeping them posted through the *Tobacco Products Litigation Reporter*, a periodic compendium of the latest legal opinions and rulings, complaints, briefs, statutes, theories, and book reviews relating to smoking, health, and the law. Daynard prosecuted no cases personally, but made himself available gratis to any member of the trial lawyers' bar pursuing the tobacco merchants.

By the late 'Eighties, more than 150 suits had been filed against the industry, whose lawyers were scurrying around courthouses everywhere to keep the liability dike from bursting open. Daynard served as the plaintiff lawyers' tactician, cheerleader, publicist, and cross-pollinator, trying to get the attorneys, invariably working on a contingency basis (no fee but a hefty piece, up to one-third, of any award for damages), to share costs, intelligence, and documents by way of combating the millions the companies were spending on whole phalanxes of lawyers to stymie litigants. All this action drew the admiration of Ralph Nader, who had felt there was not much his own group could do to protect smokers beyond the warning labels. "We gave up too soon," Nader remarked in saluting Daynard's challenge to the industry's assumption-of-risk defense by claiming the shared responsibility of both seller and buyer. Despite many setbacks, Daynard would keep doggedly after his prey and cost them millions in defense outlays.

V I I I

IN downtown Boston, not far from Daynard's lair, a young state public-health officer was giving fits to a fast-growing sector of the tobacco industry that had until then attracted little attention from the antismoking movement, largely because it emitted no smoke and seemed relatively benign.

At the beginning of the twentieth century, smokeless tobacco, usually taken as a chew held cudlike in the cheek or as a dip of moist, sweetened, finer-grained snuff placed between the front of the bottom teeth and the interior of the lower lip, was the most popular form of tobacco consumption in America. Tobacco-drenched saliva, the principal by-product, had made spitting (and spittoons) a gross national institution until the practice in public was outlawed as a health menace; cigarettes were then seen as a safer, and less unsightly, alternative. By the last quarter of the century, though, the situation was reversed. In the early 1980s, smokeless tobacco was being used by an estimated 10 to 12 million Americans, one-third of them under the age of twenty-one, most of whom saw it as a safe substitute for cigarettes, since no tars or toxic gases were inhaled during its use. Smokeless was most popular in non-urban areas, where a big chaw bulging in the cheek and a flat circular snuff can bulging in a back jeans pocket were taken for signs of budding virility and considered as American as country music, say, or baseball—indeed, nearly one of three major leaguers used snuff.

The dominant entry in the smokeless field, Connecticut-based United States Tobacco (UST), was pushing all the harder now, as cigarettes were increasingly subject to health charges and social opposition. Free of advertising codes and marketing compunctions, UST and its competitors showed famous athletes enjoying smokeless and reassuring novice users, as one televised commercial did, by telling them at first they might experience slight irritation around the gums, "but learning is part of the fun, and things pass with practice, and in two weeks you'll be a pro." Pointed promotions of the product among the young included providing schools with free driver-education films showing cars placarded with brand labels, licensing toy and clothing manufacturers to emblazon their products in similar fashion, tobacco-spitting contests at country fairs, and the introduction of Skoal Bandits as a "starter" brand.

But how much safer, if at all, was smokeless tobacco than its burned and inhaled form? Given the newness of the smokeless vogue and the long incubation period of cancer, heart, and other chronic killer diseases, investigators had not had time to conduct epidemiological studies. Still, of the 20,000 or so annual deaths from oral cancer by the mid-'Eighties, the Public Health Service attributed 10 to 15 percent to the use of smokeless and pointed to the heightened risk of mouth cancer based on findings to date: moderate users were fatally afflicted at more than four times the rate of nonusers, and heavy users had a fiftyfold higher risk. Smokeless, furthermore, was strong in nicotine, quickly absorbed through the oral mucosa to produce a kick comparable to cigarette smoking. A serious user—taking eight or ten dips daily—was getting the nicotine equivalent of a pack and a half to two packs of cigarettes a day. Nicotine, though, was not implicated in cancer but in heart disease, uncommon in younger people and, at any rate, a condition with multiple causes. A far more suspicious ingredient in smokeless were nitrosamines, cancer promoters present without need of combustion and in amounts ranging from several hundred to as high as 14,000 times more than the levels approved by the FDA for foods like beer and bacon. In such concentrations, nitrosamines—the effects of which were partially combated by filters on cigarettes—were likely accelerators of dysplasia in the form of oral lesions, or leukoplakia, whitish patches on the tongue or mouth lining that sometimes turned malignant. Just what biochemical processes caused this transformation was not yet clear, and laboratory animals dosed with nitrosamines had been able to slough off the carcinogenic effects. In short, the medical case against smokeless was not airtight, and the product remained essentially unregulated.

The situation began to change following the death in February 1984 of nineteen-year-old Sean Marsee, who seven years earlier had been handed a sample of Copenhagen, a leading smokeless brand, while attending a rodeo in his native Oklahoma. A schoolboy track star, Sean liked the product in part because it did not affect his wind as smoking cigarettes might have, and he soon became addicted. In time, he contracted tongue cancer, endured three increasingly mutilating courses of surgery, and died. His mother, who kept her single-parent household together by working as a nurse, sued UST on the claim of having failed to warn Sean of the hazards of snuff-dipping.

Among those whose attention was captured by the Marsee suit was Gregory N. Connolly, director of dental health at the Massachusetts Department of Public Health and, because his brother was state attorney general in the administration of Governor Michael Dukakis, well connected politically. Funny, fast-talking, and well-educated (Holy Cross, Tufts Dental, and a Harvard doctorate in public health), Connolly started working for the state in 1980, when he was thirty-one, as smokeless began to emerge as an oral hygiene issue. After Marsee died, Connolly decided to dramatize the problem by finding five young dippers and chewers with resulting severe gum disease and taking their cautionary tale to the Boston *Globe*. The story wound up next to the comics, far from what Connolly had hoped for in the way of serious attention. To escalate the issue, he pushed his department and the state administration to back a law categorizing smokeless tobacco as a toxic substance and requiring it to carry a warning label. Scraping together $15,000 to fly in medical experts and celebrity athletes who used snuff, Connolly stage-managed lively legislative hearings, helped get *Reader's Digest* and "60 Minutes" to carry stories on Marsee and the smokeless problem, and packaged hearings in nine other state legislatures.

Aroused now, the smokeless companies marshaled legal talent to meet the sudden regulatory challenge. "But we neutralized the industry lobbyists through use of the media," Connolly recounted, and soon he was avidly soliciting the health voluntaries for support, urging Surgeon General Koop to undertake a special report on smokeless, and petitioning Henry Waxman to hold House hearings on a smokeless warning label bill. As the dynamic engine of this effort, Connolly found himself jaw to jaw with industry lawyers who, he recalled, alternately flattered him by suggesting that he switch sides and threatening him with professional and even physical damage if he persisted in his crusade. In 1985, he prevailed over the tobacco industry's hold on Beacon Hill, as Massachusetts became the first state to require a warning label for smokeless.

Connolly then carried the fight to Washington, testifying at Waxman's hearings and joining with the House health subcommittee chairman's legislative aide Ripley Forbes on a strategy to beat UST in Congress, where the industry was terming the proposed warning label "a draconian measure." Forbes urged Connolly and his colleagues to push hard in every state legislature where a smokeless bill was pending and to make sure the warnings were each worded slightly differently, so that the industry would be faced with the prospect of fifty different mandated labels and a perhaps ruinously costly packaging burden. Soon twenty-three states were actively considering smokeless warnings— California alone was mulling ten different variations—and Connolly gleefully advised his adversaries, "We're going to fry you guys across the country."

Late in the 1985 congressional term, the Senate passed a smokeless labeling bill stripped of a proposed "addictive" warning, even as the cigarette bill a year earlier had been watered down. But the health forces in the House, led by Waxman and reinforced by the antitobacco lobbying efforts of Connolly and Matt Myers, sensed that without a warning label of the sort the cigarette industry had had for nearly twenty years to shield them against liability suits, the smokeless manufacturers faced a powerful threat to their solvency from litigants like Sean Marsee's mother, whose case was now nearing trial. Waxman's aide Forbes thus put together a package that included a ban on broadcast advertising for smokeless, which had boomed the product over the past decade; a larger and more noticeable label than on cigarette packs; and, most grating of all to the companies, a "savings" clause explicitly stating that the warnings did not stop liability suits from being brought.

Recalling the success of the cigarette manufacturers in softening the 1984 labeling bill and supposing that they would benefit from the borrowed strength of a united industry, the smokeless lobbyists told Forbes, Connolly, and Myers that there was no way they would accept a "savings" clause, which seemed an open invitation to stricken customers to sue them. In that event, the industry would get no bill whatever, they were told, and smokeless tobacco would be left to the mercies of the state legislatures, which might well tear them to pieces if Massachusetts was any guide. On the last night of the congressional session, the industry folded. The bill was signed early in 1986, and a few months later, Surgeon General Koop reported that the use of chewing tobacco and snuff was an unsafe alternative to smoking, a cause of mouth cancer in 3 to 5 percent of users, and a promoter of nicotine dependency and serious gum diseases, but did not declare it the primary cause of oral cancer.

That inability to fix sure blame on smokeless as a lethal causative agent doomed the plaintiff's case in the Marsee trial, played out in an Oklahoma federal court soon thereafter. The courtroom proceedings were notable for defendant UST's supreme disdain for the rest of society's concern about the health hazards of tobacco products. Company officials unapologetically noted that they had not looked into the dangers of nitrosamines until 1984; the vice president in charge of research claimed not to know what a carcinogen was or the meanings of the words "safety" and "danger" in the context of how tobacco might relate to health, and the former chief executive of UST remarked at one point, "I am not aware that anyone has said that snuff causes cancer," adding that it was not his company's policy—massive evidence to the contrary notwithstanding—to market smokeless tobacco to teenagers. The jury was not convinced that young Marsee had died from using the product and found for UST.

"These are very evil people," Gregory Connolly said of tobacco industry executives a few years after his legislative triumphs over smokeless had whetted his appetite for the antismoking (and antichewing and antidipping) fray. Tobacco in its manufactured form, he said, "has got to be prohibited eventually." Connolly would go on to play an important role, as an advisor to international tobacco control efforts, in the outlawing of smokeless throughout Western Europe, and by the mid-'Nineties was running the new Massachusetts office on smoking control with an annual budget, derived from a stiff state cigarette tax approved by referendum, of nearly $60 million, bigger than the entire federal effort.

I X

THE new breed of antismoking activists, while well trained in the physical and social sciences, made their contribution not in laboratories or legislative corridors but at the barricades as unabashed agitators against an entrenched foe, as self-styled dragonslayers who used words as their cutting weapon. One of the best and most incessant of them was Amherst man Alan Blum, a deft writer and arresting speaker, who, at the age of thirty while a resident in family medicine at the University of Miami, launched Doctors Ought to Care (DOC) as a vehicle to combat the smoking scourge.

The son of a heavy-smoking physician who had suffered a heart attack in his early forties, Blum had become fascinated with and sickened by old cigarette advertisements, in particular those that employed pseudo-scientific claims and white-coated models to persuade the public that smoking was harmless. He collected an archive on the subject and grew convinced that the industry's sales technique was "aimed virtually entirely at children to gain their social acceptance of the product." And while he saw the point of pushing for clean indoor air laws and higher cigarette taxes, he thought such measures primarily punished smokers, who were the wrong target. A specialist in family medicine, Blum had a more direct expedient in mind: "I'd put the manufacturers in jail—for going after the kids—on a child molestation ground."

There was only a small element of hyperbole in his satiric onslaught against what he came to view as a savage industry, let off the hook far too easily and "laughing all the way to the bank in a society that finds it of at best tangential interest that their product kills so many every year—which is why I'm a revolutionist and obsessive on this subject." In organizing DOC, a loose alliance of medical practitioners who shared his distress over this neglected killer and were willing to alert their communities to it, Blum sought to fight back by using the industry's own weapons. He applied dues money and other contributions to DOC to buying billboards and signs on benches at bus stops and led picketers with placards that unsubtly lampooned cigarette ads (*e.g.*, "You've coughed up long enough, baby. Emphysema Slims," and "Benson & Hedges Destroys Healthy Bodies 12 Ways") and then turned to advocacy journalism, practiced largely in professional publications. As an AMA Fellow in medical journalism, he produced a cutting commentary in the February 22, 1980, *JAMA* entitled "Medicine vs. Madison Avenue," in which he shredded the tobacco companies for their claim that it was not advertising that sold cigarettes to youngsters but peer pressure; Blum noted that "peer pressure can be bought, as any rock music impresario, toy maker or market research expert will corroborate. . . ."

Blum raged particularly at the professional sports community, which he thought ought to place physical well-being on a pedestal but instead seemed to be in cahoots with the cigarette makers by leasing them advertising space in their stadiums and arenas where youthful spectators could not miss the message. Not only did almost every major league ballpark have a giant cigarette billboard, Blum pointed out, but they were artfully positioned for maximum exposure during telecasts of the games, like the one at Shea Stadium in New York which filled almost the entire backdrop when the field-level camera showed a runner leading off first base. This practice was, for Blum, "in violation of the law against showing cigarette advertising on television"; that the manufacturers were paying someone other than the broadcasting companies to deploy their signage did not alter the effect of nose-thumbing at a federal prohibition.

Battling the tobacco industry became the dominant mission in Blum's life. He traveled wherever he was welcomed to give witty talks and slide shows vilifying the purveyors, wrote cogently vituperative articles and letters to the editor, and appeared on talk shows, as if single-handedly trying to instruct the nation about what truly imperiled its collective health. As he wrote in the 1982 annual edition of the *Encyclopedia of Preventive Medicine:* "Public outcry (egged on by banner headlines) over a mere handful of cases of botulism, toxic shock syndrome, or Legionnaires' disease can close businesses. One million cars can be recalled because of one death due to a malfunction of a single automobile. Yet newspapers run full-page advertisements for the product that has been described by the World Health Organization as the single most preventable cause of death and disability."

But Blum spoke loudest and most compellingly to his fellow practitioners through DOC, using its newsletter and member meetings to lament, for example, that not one of the 9,000 courses listed in the catalogues of U.S. medical schools was devoted to the treatment or prevention of smoking and that seldom was it a topic dealt with on grand rounds at teaching hospitals. Doctors, he argued, ought to mentor their younger patients on the perils of smoking by stressing not the ultimate price they might pay for it but the social unattractiveness of "zoo breath" and the impairment of their athletic skills; to quit smoking themselves and ban it from their waiting rooms, along with magazines they subscribed to that carried cigarette ads; to urge hospitals with which they were affiliated and pharmacies they dealt with not to dispense cigarettes; and to send a postcard black-edged for bereavement to the congressman of every patient who died from a smoking-related disease.

Blum's crowning, and ultimately self-immolating, editorial feat came when he was named in 1983 to edit the *New York State Journal of Medicine* and devoted the entire contents of its December issue that year to "The World Cigarette Pandemic." Normally a conservative academic publication, the magazine—for one issue—turned into a grab bag of fire-breathing pieces on the biochemical, political, economic, legal, and ethical aspects of tobacco use, attracting contributions from five Surgeon Generals, former HEW Secretary Califano, and leading investigators and public-health activists in the field. Although very uneven, the issue was lively and full of unfamiliar items, like the calculation that Americans spent 40 percent as much on cigarettes as they did on buying cars, the advisory that *The New York Times* and Time Inc. bought space in the tobacco trade press thanking the industry for its advertising patronage, and the disclosure that fully one-quarter of Philip Morris's stock was held by banks, suggesting how intimately the cigarette companies had been consorting with the financial as well as the political establishment. The cumulative effect of this special issue was "stunning," in the opinion of the *Columbia Journalism Review*, and showed what the mainstream press could have done if it had truly wanted to explore the tobacco story.

Having made his point, Blum was incapable of leaving off. He devoted a second issue, in June 1985, of his journal to the same subject, this time concentrating on the international aspects of tobacco exploitation—a topic rarely written about—and had so much material left over that he was preparing a third special issue when he was summoned the day after Christmas 1985 and summarily fired without severance. His superior, by way of explanation, told him only, "I don't like your journal," Blum recounted, but conceded that he had come to be viewed as a zealot on smoking and thus an unsound choice to run such a publication. But he continued, at considerable personal expense, to hector the industry. He bought a single share of Philip Morris stock, for instance, and made a point of showing up at the company's annual meetings to protest practices that he found unforgivable, such as exporting cigarettes without health warnings on the pack to developing countries that did not require them. Never subdued or deferential to critics who found him almost pathetically eager to be credited with the growth of antismoking sentiment he had in fact done much to foment, Blum invested still more of himself in building DOC even while holding a tenured place on the Baylor medical faculty in Texas.

A less flamboyant antismoking crusader, befitting her conservative political views, was Elizabeth M. Whelan. With a master's degree in public health from Yale and a doctorate from Harvard, she wrote widely for popular consumption on diet, child care, and other health matters during the 'Seventies but found that whenever she dealt with tobacco, her prose was toned down by editors. If she termed smoking a serious hazard, for example, the reference might be fixed to read "very, very heavy smoking," or cut out altogether. Such indulgence by editors, with an eye to a major source of their magazines' advertising, led to what Whelan considered "an incredible inversion of priorities," as irritants like red dye No. 2 and air pollution were blown into major health perils by the media, and cigarettes were all but exonerated. "The elephants were running wild," she reflected, "while we were busy crushing the ants."

In 1978, when she was thirty-five, Whelan enlisted the backing of famed Harvard nutritionist Fredrick Stare, a former professor of hers, and other academic eminences to open her own enterprise, somewhat grandly called the American Council on Science and Health, devoted to educating consumers. Funded by non-profit foundations and decidedly profit-seeking corporations, some in the food business, opening Whelan to conflict-of-interest charges, her office generated studies, pamphlets, reports, and a newsletter that were clear, informative, and objective. From the first, smoking was one of her council's major concerns, as she kept after the subject in ways others ignored by writing in her newsletter, *Healthwatch*, on, for example, the inadequacy of the cigarette companies' disclosure of the additives in their manufacturing process and how the U.S. government had long been guilty of pushing surplus American tobacco in Third World nations in the guise of economic aid.

Because she felt that her fellow conservatives suffered from a "complete inability to deal effectively with cigarettes" due to their doctrinaire distaste for government intervention in matters best left to private resolution, Whelan reached out to them, in part through articles in *The Wall Street Journal.* A particular source of sadness to her was that many conservatives were avowedly "pro-life" in their opposition to abortion but seemingly anti-life in their failure to combat the hazards of smoking. Whelan's most noteworthy effort was a sustained but not shrill diatribe in book form—*A Smoking Gun: How the Tobacco Industry Gets Away with Murder*—issued in 1984 by a small Philadelphia publisher. The most stinging volume on the subject by an American since Senator Maurine Neuberger's *Smoke Screen* twenty-one years earlier, it blended history and analysis of the cigarette companies' conduct, which she called "a unique problem that demands a unique solution," yet feared it would not be addressed because "Americans today do not want to talk about cigarettes." In a chapter entitled "Fourteen Ploys That Can Kill You," she battered most of the industry's pet defenses, such as the claim that the health charges against it were merely an association of factors and did not prove causation. The companies, she wrote, "would have us believe that statistics are just a group of numbers looking for an argument."

x

DURING the congressional testimony by health advocates on the 1984 cigarette labeling bill, no organization was more conspicuous by its absence than the group widely regarded as the voice of the American medical profession—the AMA—with more than 300,000 physicians, over half the national total, as members. AMA policy in tolerance of smoking had for decades been a notorious example of self-serving cynicism in the eyes of those who felt that doctors were, or ought to be, exemplars of altruism.

Practitioners in a high-stress profession, many physicians had been heavy smokers. Industry-manned tables distributing free cigarettes were a fixture at medical meetings and conventions throughout the first half of the century and beyond, and if doctors did not openly condone smoking by their patients, they were slow to denounce it. The AMA had been particularly dilatory in this regard, indeed unconscionably so. At the first congressional hearings on smoking and health in 1957, its spokesman contended that a man would have to inhale 100,000 cigarettes a day to absorb a dose equivalent to what was being painted on the shaved backs of mice in bioassays to test the carcinogenic potency of tobacco. The AMA leadership had opposed the health warning labels on cigarette packs seven years later, when Congress first seriously considered the idea, and then allowed the tobacco industry to buy time and the AMA's good name in its abortive fourteen-year study of the hazards of smoking— part of the crass exchange for winning protobacco lawmakers' opposition to Medicare.

But there had come a sea change by the 1970s, as a new breed of doctors, reflecting the idealism and revulsion with materialism of the previous decade, emerged from medical school. A number were even prepared to practice within health maintenance organizations rather than as individuals. Smoking had by then dropped sharply within the profession to perhaps as low as 10 percent, and those who chose to join the AMA were bringing to it a fresh sense of social awareness.

A shining example of the new AMA breed was Ronald M. Davis, trained in medicine at the University of Chicago and devoted to improving society by working within its established power centers. Elected at the age of twenty-four to the House of Delegates, the AMA's version of representative democracy, Davis served on the governing councils of first the medical student and then the resident physician sections, speaking out on policy issues like smoking, about which he felt the AMA had been grievously backward. In 1984, he became the first resident physician with full voting authority to serve on the AMA's ruling sixteen-member board of trustees, where he spoke up spiritedly but respectfully to his elders. Among his suggestions was that the AMA get out in front on the smoking issue, and in 1985 the association sent a spokesman to testify before Congress—in favor of making the higher federal cigarette sales tax permanent.

Later that year, the AMA board weighed a proposal from its membership to endorse an extension of the ban on broadcast advertising of cigarettes to include all forms of advertising of the product. Davis forcefully pushed the idea and successfully expanded it to include a ban on all forms of promotion, including cultural and sports events that carried the name of cigarette brands. When U.S. Representative Mike Synar of Oklahoma introduced a House bill to impose the sweeping ban, it was young Ronald Davis who was sent to testify in its favor in 1986. The nation could no longer afford to allow cigarettes to be "the heaviest advertised consumer product in our society," he asserted. "In terms of health costs alone it is unjustifiable; but, more importantly, in terms of human suffering and loss it is unconscionable. . . ."

After his residency AMA trustee Davis joined the preventive medicine training program at the Public Health Service's Centers for Disease Control, and during a stint in the Dominican Republic to oversee government immunization efforts, he was struck by the saturation advertising of cigarettes, including street signs that bore the Marlboro design, colors, and logo. More than ever he was convinced of the predatory nature of the tobacco manufacturers. Soon thereafter, the director's job at the Office on Smoking and Health had to be filled. Many around the country in the antismoking cause favored the appointment of Donald Shopland, its acting director and the executive editor of the Surgeon General's reports, who was unmatched in his dedication to the tobacco control movement. But the Public Health Service required the OSH director to hold academic credentials that Shopland had never acquired. The job went instead, with the full endorsement of the AMA, to its rising star, Ronald Davis, who in 1987, at the age of thirty, found himself in the forefront of the new generation of antismoking advocates now beginning to bring the tobacco industry down, if hardly to its knees.

Another young activist in the public-health field, Joe B. Tye III, an Iowan trained as a hospital administrator, put his mark on the antismoking movement in two distinctive ways. In 1985, while completing his MBA training at Stanford, he established a program to nip the smoking problem in the bud; Tye called it Stop Teenage Addiction to Tobacco, or STAT. Its principal vehicle was a highly graphic quarterly newsletter in the form of a tabloid paper which went after the cigarette makers for what he saw as their transparent advertising pitch to young people and lamented the widespread indifference to enforcing state laws against the sale of cigarettes to underage buyers.

As a communicator, Tye was more a broad-axed propagandist than a neat dart-thrower. But he was also capable of excoriating the tobacco lords in a more philosophical vein, as in an article he contributed to the special June 1985 issue of Alan Blum's *New York State Journal of Medicine*, placing the cigarette industry against the broader backdrop of business conduct and trying to define its particular brand of roguery. The ultimate consequences of the way cigarettes were sold, Tye argued, were "so pernicious" as to constitute corporate violence, which he defined as behavior producing "an unreasonable risk of physical harm to consumers, employees, or other persons as a result of deliberate decision-making by corporate executives or culpable negligence on their part." Such violence was distinguishable from more familiar forms "by the absence of malevolent intent . . . [or] a deliberate conspiracy to cause injury, but results from subordination of concern for human safety to monetary considerations."

But if, as Tye charged, the cigarette companies were committing corporate violence, how exactly was their behavior different from or worse than the bottom-line ethic that came naturally to so many aggressive businessmen? Or were their crimes simply variants of the malfeasance of, say, General Motors in marketing its Corvair and Ford its Pinto, each with known design defects that the carmakers could have eliminated at small cost but instead denied and delayed fixing, thereby causing deaths and injuries? The cigarette makers, though, did not design in a defect that made their product more dangerous—it just turned out that way because of the toxic properties of the cured leaf when burned and could be made safe only by altering the very essence of the product. The tobacco companies in fact had acted—too slowly and too little, to be sure—to try to modify the toxicity of cigarettes by offering smokers a wide range of nicotine and tar potency, thereby feeding the scientifically plausible inference that the weaker yields were, to some undemonstrable degree, less hazardous. The cigarette manufacturers, furthermore, could not fairly be accused of the sort of gross managerial negligence involved in Union Carbide's failure to safeguard equipment used to manufacture highly toxic pesticides, resulting in a heavy human toll in Bhopal, India, or in Metropolitan Edison's faulty monitoring of the nuclear reactors at Three Mile Island in Pennsylvania, where the consequences could have been catastrophic. Nor had the tobacco companies shown a flagrant disregard for the health of their own employees by failing to safeguard them from the toxic ingredients that went into their products, as a number of leading chemical manufacturers had habitually done. Nor had the tobacco companies knowingly and wantonly dumped the residue of their manufacturing process and fouled the environment, like General Electric, which for twenty years had poured PCBs, recognized as a dangerous toxin, into the Hudson River and badly polluted it. Nor had the tobacco people doctored their research as the A. H. Robins Company did by fudging the data presented to the FDA on the efficacy of its Dalkon Shield as a contraceptive device and then, despite warnings by its own scientists, withholding information from the public on the pain and disease the device could and did inflict. The perils of smoking, by contrast, had been long and well documented by outside investigators.

The violence committed by the cigarette companies was to be found, rather, as Tye and others saw it, in their continuously disappointing the expectation by society "that when significant evidence suggests that a product is dangerous, those engaged in selling it should adhere to a standard of conservatism, whether they believed the evidence or not." The potential health risks from smoking did not need to imply the inevitability of harm; the duty to alert the public fully of it "arises as soon as there is credible evidence, not when the last shred of doubt in the manufacturer's mind is resolved," Tye wrote. Instead, the cigarette industry had steadfastly declined to warn about the risk of its own accord, and, worse still, Tye added, through its advertising, promotions, and pseudo-scientific publications, "the industry has conducted major publicity campaigns to create doubt in the public mind" about the relationship between smoking and disease—no mere passive negligence in the form of omitted disclosures but overt acts of calculated deception. By insisting on an unobtainable level of knowledge of human pathology as a requisite for dealing forthrightly with the public, Tye contended, the cigarette companies could reasonably be said to have behaved both violently and fraudulently, even if out of fear that to have acted otherwise might well have put them out of business.

X I

A s their enemies grew in number, resolve, skills, and effectiveness, the cigarette companies resisted all the more fiercely, sometimes with new weapons.

Nothing better illustrates the industry's unrelenting tactics than its response in the form of booklets, issued by the Tobacco Institute, that challenged each emerging Surgeon General's report, no matter how authoritatively and carefully wrought or what the weight of evidence against smoking. The TI's rebuttal to the 1982 report on cancer, for example, regurgitated the same discredited arguments that the industry and its apologists had been dispensing for almost thirty years, starting with the suggestion that there really might not have been an upsurge in lung cancer—or if so, it had been greatly exaggerated. And although the TI's reply pamphlet to the 1983 Surgeon General's report argued that "the mechanisms by which smoking may relate to heart disease are not known" and the TI reply to the 1984 report contended that the causes of chronic obstructive lung disease were "multiple and poorly understood," the truth was that the causes and the mechanisms in both cases had become far better understood.

A yet more heinous instance of the Tobacco Institute's deception could be found in a 1983 pamphlet seizing upon the findings of the Public Health Service's lately reported "Mister Fit" study (after the acronym for its full name, the Multiple Risk Factor Intervention Trial). A twenty-year investigation undertaken by the government at a cost of more than $100 million, MRFIT monitored 12,000 subjects between thirty-five and fifty-seven who were divided into two groups, one receiving its usual health care and the other given special counseling with regard to the three leading risk factors in heart disease (smoking, high blood pressure, and fatty diet). The prime purpose was to learn if those given the added attention would correct their destructive habits—that is, quit smoking, reduce their stress levels, and eat more healthful foods—and thus suffer less heart disease.

As it turned out, the smokers among those receiving special health counseling did quit at almost twice the rate of those in the regular-care group, but, as the Tobacco Institute crowed, "there was no significant difference in the mortality rate between the two groups" (meaning the special-care and regular-care cohorts), and indeed, the death rate for all causes, not just heart disease, was slightly lower among those receiving the usual health care. The TI's implication was that there was no correlation between smoking, quitting, and the rate of heart disease. In fact, while MRFIT showed that the care intervention did not have any notable effect on overall death rates, it also confirmed what earlier studies had shown—that smokers, whether receiving regular or special health-care treatment, suffered about a 70 percent heightened risk of heart disease and that those who quit substantially reduced their risk over time. The TI revealed neither point.

The industry was also displaying fresh skill at enlisting accomplices and exploiting their reputable names. In 1984, for example, the National Association of State Boards of Education put its imprimatur on a pair of slick pamphlets entitled *Helping Youth Decide* and *Helping Youth Say No: A Parents' Guide to Helping Teenagers Cope with Peer Pressure.* The Tobacco Institute paid for the publications because, according to its spokesman, "the industry does not want youngsters smoking cigarettes"—he did not say why. The booklets themselves were hardly more instructive. The one intended to guide parents contained no substantive discussion of, or any reference to, the specific health hazards of smoking or the reasons why youngsters should refrain other than to urge on them the "need for patience" before taking up customs reserved for adults. Such a characterization of smoking served, of course, to glorify it as forbidden fruit, placing the custom alongside drinking and sexual activity among the normal, acceptable forms of adult conduct. The closest *Helping Youth Say No* came to noting the health risks of smoking was a case scenario that began, "Bill's best friends start smoking and encourage him to join them. What are his alternatives?" By year's end, the Tobacco Institute bragged that 100,000 copies of the booklets had been distributed—evidence, presumably, of the industry's purity of heart against juvenile smoking.

At the Tobacco Institute's executive committee meetings, where the rotating chairmanship was held for several years in the early 'Eighties by Reynolds Tobacco chief Edward Horrigan, concern grew that smokers were fast becoming second-class citizens and social outcasts. Although RJR had lost the industry's lead in market share, the feisty Horrigan was no quitter and, if anything, grew more determined to display his company's clout within tobacco councils. Arguing that antismoking sentiment had "clearly reached a point beyond reason," Horrigan called on his fellow executives to undertake an institutional advertising campaign, based loosely on the sort of "advertorials" that Mobil Oil had done so well on newspaper op-ed pages—a set of running rebuttals to their enemies that would support and reassure smokers and defuse the growing impact of the secondhand smoke issue. Some of his fellow tobacco chieftains agreed with Horrigan's view that "You can't be intimidated and stay in this business," and were willing to join in his proposed united-front campaign— until, as Horrigan recounted it, they got back to their headquarters and were talked out of the idea by their lawyers. His own two superiors, Reynolds Industries chairman Paul Sticht and president Tylee Wilson, were not enthusiastic about the concept, either, but Horrigan bulled it through as an RJR-only venture, poured himself into the effort (budgeted at $7 million) and made sure that every word was fine-combed by a battery of admen, marketers, and lawyers.

The RJR counterpunch began to land in the spring of 1984, when the first ad appeared under the headline "Can we have an open debate about smoking?" Horrigan's idea of openness was to insist that a "causal relationship" between smoking and disease had not yet been proven. The follow-up ads were a bit more inspired, the most effective one featuring side-by-side messages from prototypical smokers to nonsmokers ("We're on the spot. Smoking is something we consider to be a very personal choice, yet it's become a very public issue. We're confused. . . . We're not criminals . . .") and vice versa ("We feel a little powerless. Because you can invade our privacy without even trying. Often without noticing. And sometimes when we speak up and let you know how we feel, you react as if we were the bad guys . . ."). The spread said in small italics that it was "brought to you in the interest of common courtesy."

This raised-fist campaign crossed the line between advocacy and deception, however, with an ad headlined "Of Cigarettes and Science," which dwelled on the MRFIT study, just as the Tobacco Institute pamphlet had the year before. The Reynolds text said, "After 10 years, there was no statistically significant difference between the two groups in the number of heart disease deaths"— allowing readers to infer in the overall context of the ad that it was referring to the effect on smokers and quitters, not merely on the regular and special treatment groups. As the FTC asserted, when it finally got around to issuing a complaint against RJR for the misleading ad two years later, the company had conspicuously failed to disclose that "men in the study who had quit smoking had a significantly lower rate of coronary heart disease than men who continued to smoke."

Philip Morris, meanwhile, was pioneering with a less cerebral form of brainwashing, this one involving subliminal advertising. For a reported payment of $42,000 the company bought twenty-two exposures of the Marlboro logo in the 1980 movie *Superman II*, aimed largely at the youth market. While neither the extraterrestrial man of steel nor his mild-mannered, earthbound alter ego, Clark Kent, was seen to light up, his girlfriend, Lois Lane, a reporter and role model for teenage girls, had a Marlboro pack on her desk and was shown puffing merrily away. At one point in the film, a character was tossed into a van with a large Marlboro sign on its side, and in the climactic scene the superhero battled numerous foes amid a maze of Marlboro billboards until he zoomed off in triumph, leaving in his wake a solitary taxi with a Marlboro sign on top. So effective was this technique deemed that the company next teamed up with Liggett, its partner in world rights to Lark cigarettes, to buy multiple plugs for that brand in the James Bond thriller *License to Kill* at a cost of $350,000. The method was used in other films by other manufacturers, attracted in part by the added exposure of the brand names on millions of home screens when the movies were shown on television—yet another circumvention of the federal ban on broadcast advertising of cigarettes. The practice continued for several years, until congressional investigators began making unfriendly noises about it, largely because the plugola game was employed in films for which a sizable part of the intended viewership was eighteen and under—a market the tobacco manufacturers swore they were not interested in soliciting.

Even as Philip Morris lobbyists were fighting to remove any reference to tobacco dependency from the rotating warning labels in the federal cigarette legislation being considered in 1983 and 1984, company researchers were coming up with interesting findings on that subject. Starting in the late 'Seventies, its scientists had begun intensified studies of the pharmacological properties of nicotine, looking for an artificial substitute without its negative effects like elevated heartbeat. Among their suspicions was that a second substance in tobacco smoke—acetaldehyde—was as addictive as nicotine, and the two together might be a more powerful addicting agent than either separately; further, that a synthetic compound known as 2-prime methylnicotine caused animals to behave as if they were undergoing a nicotine high without experiencing rapid heartbeat. An important corroborative study was also proving fruitful. Associate senior scientist Victor J. DeNoble, a psychologist who had joined Philip Morris in 1980 and was put in charge of the nicotine explorations, worked with rats that self-administered the substance by depressing a lever for small, rapid doses equivalent to that in a human cigarette puff. The animals became increasingly fond of the nicotine and learned how, when the task of obtaining it was made harder, to depress the lever six or seven times to obtain their momentary fix and to ignore another lever that yielded only a placebo. DeNoble's rats conditioned themselves to absorb nearly a hundred nicotine jolts in a twenty-four-hour period. He wrote up his findings in a paper entitled "Nicotine as a Positive Reinforcer in Rats," of scientific interest because so vivid a demonstration of self-administered addictive behavior from nicotine had not been achieved before with rodents.

Shortly after DeNoble sent off his paper to the scientific journal *Psychopharmacology* in May of 1983, a Little Ferry, New Jersey, woman named Rose Cipollone, dying from lung cancer, filed a product liability suit against three cigarette makers, Philip Morris among them, accusing them of failing to warn her properly of the addictive nature of smoking and its potential lethal effects. DeNoble was summoned to New York to brief top Philip Morris executives on his laboratory's findings. The highly suggestive conduct of his nicotine-dosed animals worried the Philip Morris brass. One of their rank, according to DeNoble, asked him rhetorically, "Why should I risk a billion-dollar [business] on rats pushing a lever to get nicotine?" On August 30, 1983, DeNoble wrote the editor of *Psychopharmacology* to advise that "due to factors beyond my control I must withdraw our manuscript. . . ." Publication was suppressed because, accordingly to an account by DeNoble ten years later, his lab was "generating information that the company did not want generated inside the company [and] it was information that would not be favorable to the company in litigation." Consideration was given to moving DeNoble's staff and facilities to Switzerland, where the work could have been done at arm's length from the company, with the scientists funded as independent contractors. Instead, on April 5, 1984, just a few weeks before Mrs. Cipollone's lawyers filed a massive request for company research documents, DeNoble was told to close down his laboratory, to kill the animals, to suspend all further investigation of possibly less toxic or harmful alternatives to nicotine, never to try to publish or discuss his work on addicting rats, and to find work elsewhere. DeNoble tested the company's resolve in the matter by submitting his paper, slightly revised, once more the following year to *Psychopharmacology* and was promptly threatened with a court injunction.

About the same time that DeNoble's work was running its course, Philip Morris scientists were undertaking another project that might have proved similarly vexing to the public, had it not been similarly shielded from its view. The effort, aimed at developing a fire-retardant cigarette, was called Project Hamlet (as in "To burn or not to burn . . .") and was carried out as Congress was expressing concern over the more than 1,000 deaths, many more injuries, and hundreds of millions in property damage traceable each year to some 40,000 cigarette-ignited fires. Public-health officials spearheaded by Andrew McGuire of the trauma center at San Francisco General Hospital had argued that cigarettes could be made far less incendiary if the tobacco was cut finer and packed tighter, the paper was less porous, and additives to quicken the burn rate were dropped. By 1987, the R&D team at Philip Morris had developed a less flammable version of Marlboro, found by a panel of seventy-seven consumers to be

as acceptable in taste as the regular brand. Yet the company did not share details of this development with a special federal commission convened to study
the problem, but instead joined with other industry officials in insisting before
the inquiry board that the experimental fire-retardant cigarettes their companies had explored were too hard to draw on or had an unsatisfactory taste,
making them commercially unviable.

Perhaps the most egregious example of the tobacco industry's reprehensible
tactics in this period was a study undertaken by the Council for Tobacco
Research (CTR)—in itself a rare initiative—and presented to the public as
something very different from what it actually was: a hugely expensive investigation, flawed in design and mangled in execution, which might have seriously embarrassed the industry if it had been allowed to be completed.

Published by CTR itself in a handsome blue cloth binding in November of
1984, the 187-page study entitled *Chronic Exposure of Mice to Cigarette
Smoke* was described in a press release carried in the February 1985 issue of
the Tobacco Institute's house organ, the *Tobacco Observer*, and by the wire
services as a nine-year investigation undertaken by Microbiological Associates
of Bethesda, Maryland, under contract to the industry's research council at a
cost of $12 million. In the course of the study, 10,000 mice and the smoke
from 800,000 cigarettes were used by researchers who performed a reported
11,000 daily manipulations of the test animals, dosing and later autopsying
them, studying their tissue under the microscope, and evaluating the data—in
short, the last word in completeness and thoroughness, or so it was implied—
as part of what CTR's scientific director, Sheldon Sommers, called in the fore-
word "a determined effort to develop a suitable animal model" for inhalation
tests to learn if tobacco smoke caused cancer. The key finding, Sommers
wrote, was that the vast experiment "did not produce any squamous cell lung
cancer, a type often reported to be associated with smoking in humans." The
only hint that the smoke might not have been exactly therapeutic was the disclosure that "[t]he incidence of alveolar adenocarcinoma was not different between smoke-exposed and sham-tested [put in the same stock-like holders,
though not exposed to the smoke], but appeared sooner in the former." Even
this vaguely cautionary information seemed to be outweighed by the further
news that some type of cancer occurred in 27 percent of the smoke-exposed
mice but in 29 percent of the sham-tested animals. The overall message,
though not explicitly stated, apparently was that the smoke exposure had not
harmed the test animals. The 1984 CTR annual report called special attention
to the study, as it had done to no other before. Upon careful review, however,
the investigation appears to have been based on inadequate science and
presented to the public in a misleading and confusing way that was close to
fraudulent.

To start with, there was no indication that the findings had ever been peer-reviewed by outsiders; the report was published by the CTR itself. The same industry that had howled fourteen years earlier when Oscar Auerbach's study on smoking beagles was made public before it appeared in a scholarly journal was now bringing forth as legitimate science its own self-certified work. Then there was the matter of Sommers's introductory claim that the study was a "determined effort" to find a suitable animal model for such inhalation studies when (a) no other species but mice was used and (b) it had been well known among experimental biologists for more than twenty-five years that small animals were notoriously poor subjects for such studies because most of them inhaled shallowly when administered smoke and allowed so little of it to reach their lungs that cancers were most unlikely to develop there. Investigators like the Leuchtenbergers and Homburger, on the other hand, had found laryngeal cancers in smoke-dosed hamsters, yet the CTR study neither used hamsters nor examined the larynx tissue in their subject mice. More to the point, mice were known to react badly to being immobilized for inhalation tests and, if dosed too strongly, were prone to die of asphyxiation from the carbon monoxide in the smoke or go into convulsions due to nicotine poisoning. In the case of the Microbiological Associates study contracted for by CTR, researchers apparently failed to conduct dose-response tests to set a tolerable level of smoke, and as a result, by the thirty-second week of the scheduled two-year investigation, 52 percent of the smoke-exposed mice and 19 percent of the sham-tested ones had died from what the report termed "exposure-related problems"—either systemic stress and agitated head movement or "improper air-smoke flow leading to suffocation." So severe was the agitation problem that some of the animals had to be "rested" from the test to allow their wounds to heal, yet when the research laboratory developed padded holders to reduce the mice's self-inflicted abrasions, the CTR disallowed their use. This huge premature death toll meant that many fewer smoke-exposed animals were left in the study, greatly skewing the outcome since the subject animals most likely to develop cancers did not live long enough for the pathology to take hold.

Even so, some 77 percent of the smoke-exposed mice developed pulmonary lesions, compared with less than half that percentage among the unexposed animals, and such cellular alterations, as Auerbach and others had posited in work with both dogs and human tissue, might well have turned into malignancies if the mice had lived long enough. Furthermore, despite the impression given by the CTR that all the test animals had been autopsied, fewer than half the smoke-exposed animals were, compared with 82 percent of the unexposed subjects—and none of the smoke-exposed animals that had died prematurely were autopsied, so the investigators could not tell how many of them might have had presymptomatic cancers or precancerous lesions. The first half of the investigation, moreover, was halted after fifteen months, nine short of its planned duration, on orders from CTR's overseers and without explanation to the commercial laboratory conducting the project. The high premature death toll was the likely reason; for the second part of the study, the smoke dosage was cut to one-fifth of what had been administered during the first stage—in order, probably, to spare many more of the subject mice, but probably too low an amount to induce cancer.

In the view of Carol Henry, director of inhalation toxicology and in charge of the CTR-ordered study at Microbiology Associates, even with all the flaws and skews the early results were building "a very strong case" that cigarette smoke could induce cancers in lab animals. This was unthrilling news to tobacco industry lawyers, who, according to a disclosure nearly a decade afterward by a former CTR associate science director, John Kreisher, "worried like hell" about it. CTR insisted that its lawyers be present in the laboratory during the latter stages of the project—yet another highly suspect factor in the undertaking.

The author of this book was presented with a copy of the CTR-published *Chronic Exposure of Mice to Cigarette Smoke* by a retired Philip Morris top executive with the suggestion that he consult it to satisfy himself on the relationship of smoking and cancer. After enlisting expert assistance, I wrote to the CTR to ask if it would explain some of the problems with the study discussed above, but in a December 11, 1991, letter in reply, the council's president, R. F. Gertenbach, stated, "Our practice has been to let research funded by CTR speak for itself and not to become involved in discussions about the details or results of that research."

17

Chow Lines

THE last Philip Morris chief executive to have joined the company in the days before the Marlboro Man saddled up, Hamish Maxwell celebrated his ascension by buying a Maserati, not a palomino.

It was an uncharacteristic impulse for the modest Scotsman, never a showy sort. In his private life he withstood the lure of a Manhattan penthouse residence, retaining his Brooklyn Heights apartment with its expansive view of the New York harbor and skyline and enjoying an occasional night on the town, in the company of his wife, Gigi, a Wellesley graduate of surpassing charm. The couple typically went to the opera or an art gallery followed by dinner at a trendy spot in Tribeca. An unpompous man with a dry British wit useful for relieving a tight moment, he was not easily impressed with either himself or the accomplishments of his company. One close colleague viewed him as "the ultimate student," unafraid to ask a lot of questions about how his two immediate predecessors, more outgoing men, had coped with the industrial giant Philip Morris had grown into. "You could watch by Hamish's body language and see as time went on that he had become comfortable with the position and the knowledge that he deserved the job . . . and there wasn't anybody better qualified for it."

Indeed, after thirty years, Maxwell knew his steadily advancing company inside out, and on top of that, as another associate noted, "He was very smart—and enjoyed being very smart," to the point where some subordinates found his formidable intellect intimidating, as they tried to anticipate what their somewhat sphinxlike chairman was likely to inquire of them that they had not thought through adequately. Far more a strategic analyst than a charismatic field general of the sort Joe Cullman had been, or a pleasing cheerleader in the George Weissman mold, Maxwell drove his troops not by lashing them but by issuing directives and painstakingly following up on their execution. The results were one of the bravura performances in the annals of American corporate management.

Hamish Maxwell was not a callous man. His occasional brief remarks about the health charges against smoking, however, while less combative and absolute than those of his predecessors and rival tobacco chieftains, conceded little and could sound almost cavalier. Early in 1985, a year after becoming head of the company, he said of the medical findings against cigarettes, "What I feel is that living is hazardous. Most of the things you want to do are more hazardous than just breathing. As time goes on, smoking will be seen in that context." Four years later, not long before he underwent heart bypass surgery, Maxwell, a pack-a-day smoker, cracked, in an unintended echo of a famous Mark Twain witticism denying the addictive nature of tobacco, that he would quit smoking "for a month or so, every so often, just to show that I can." Maxwell granted that for the industry to keep insisting that nothing had been proven about the health allegations against smoking "sounds Neanderthal" and that his company's public pronouncements "are affected by our concern over lawsuits." It was better, he believed, to say nothing than "to make people madder at us than they already are. . . . Over the years we've been about as straightforward as you can be under the circumstances." And if smoking brought perils with it, he felt that "people are or have been made aware of them . . . [and] have the right to decide for themselves if they want to take a risk. . . ."

Maxwell's ruling concern was that his company not grow complacent following its arrival at the mountaintop; his driving ambition was to channel Philip Morris's huge cash flow, among the highest of any U.S. company, in a way that would eventually free the business from dependency on a product whose appeal was visibly, if gradually, eroding in its home market. Meanwhile, he would press the aggressive cigarette-pricing policy set in motion by George Weissman and Shepard Pollack which seemed to defy the law of supply and demand and allowed profit margins to approach 40 percent and free cash flow to accumulate at the rate of $5 million a day.

American cigarettes had long been a one-price item, and the price was sharply lower proportionately than for far more heavily taxed cigarettes in other industrialized nations. But Maxwell, used to multi-tier pricing in the cigarette business overseas, was sure that the practice had to come eventually to the U.S. as well—after all, a range of prices was common to almost all other products worldwide, whether toothpaste or automobiles. Once the U.S. Congress raised the tax in 1983, opening the door to state legislatures to jack up tobacco excise tax levies as well, there was no telling how high and how fast cigarette taxes might rise. Maxwell and his top marketers nonetheless continued to raise prices on a semiannual basis, using taxes as a scapegoat and relying on their competitors to follow suit, since retailers generally priced all brands to follow the market leader's level. If a real price war eventuated, Maxwell was confident that Philip Morris had the resources and talent to prosper in the discount sector as well, but what was the point of prematurely encouraging the growth of that lowered-price tier? So, with the benefit of state-of-the-art manufacturing facilities and the availability of cheap foreign leaf to hold U.S. tobacco costs in line, Philip Morris was able to keep milking its miraculous cash cow, raising prices at twice the rate of inflation—with only a minimal impact on sales to its captive customers. In a momentary lapse of corporate pretense at the end of the decade, the company's chief of tobacco operations, Vice Chairman William Murray, said of this brazen pricing policy, "We've done it because we thought we could get away with it—and we have. That's what you're in business to do."

Still, all that money brought its own set of problems. What Maxwell had on his hands, if one did not dwell on the rosy view, was a badly unbalanced company; 92 percent of its profits came from tobacco, an industry facing an ever louder public clamor over the health toll it exacted. If the company's cash was not put to creative use fast, it would soon likely attract corporate raiders, greenmailers, leveraged-buyout artists, and other predators enjoying their own heyday. The treasure trove from tobacco was also inviting lawsuits from aggrieved customers, further depressing Philip Morris stock, already selling at a price/earnings ratio comparable to that of companies with only half its per-share net. PM's major forays into diversification—its beverage operations—had not proven much of a help; Seven-Up was barely breaking even now and facing bleak prospects, while Miller Brewing, though safely in the black, had been overbuilt and its earnings were just about enough to cover the interest charges on all the capital that had been invested in it. As far as some on Wall Street were concerned, the company would have been better off if it had socked its surplus funds into U.S. Treasury bills. When Maxwell's new chief corporate planner, Ehud Houminer, made the rounds to get acquainted with the big New York investment and brokerage houses, he was chastened by the response. "You guys are just a big cash machine," he was told, garnering few plaudits for the company as marketing marvels. The continuing attacks from the antismoking camp and the constant threat of endlessly draining lawsuits caused a downgrading of the company's prospects, despite the surging numbers in its quarterly earnings reports and the steady annual dividend increases of 20 percent or more. Philip Morris was a tightrope walker in Wall Street's eyes as long as it remained essentially a one-product company.

Maxwell's choices, then, were to keep milking his cow as long as possible, paying out ever more in dividends and buying back stock to raise earnings-per-share still higher—letting the animal enjoy its golden years, so to speak, before sending it to the slaughterhouse—or to convert the creature into a quite different being with the benefit of high cigarette profits for as long as they lasted. As a charter member of the new class of organizational managers who thrived as skillful manipulators of corporate machinery, Maxwell elected to build his empire, free of the delusion that he was the Sun-King. "Managements are paid on the basis of revenues, not profits," according to Roy D. Burry, a veteran Wall Street financial analyst and tobacco industry specialist. For Maxwell, the challenge would be to increase both his gross and net rapidly without seriously diluting the return on his company's invested capital.

II

As a corporate manager, Hamish Maxwell did not feel compelled to articulate his mastery of the house. Cordial but firm, he was at his best in front of a knowing audience, like the society of San Francisco financial analysts, whom he once addressed at the Mark Hopkins Hotel, where Paine Webber's Emanuel Goldman, among the nation's leading authorities on the food and tobacco industries, found himself spellbound by the Philip Morris chairman's comforting voice, never loud or rushed, rarely reaching for striking language or imagery, "yet he had the room riveted . . . giving a sense he was in control but not in any grating way."

He led not by trying to micromanage a company about to reap tens of billions in revenues a year but by managing his managers, mostly in one-on-one meetings that ran as long as necessary. He regularly bypassed the top echelon to obtain direct input from his middle management so that he would not become dependent on a handful of advisors. Maxwell's prevailing mood was known intramurally as "constructive discontent," another way of saying he hated smugness and preferred to see the glass as half empty rather than half full. "He never made you immortal," one ranking company colleague remarked of the chairman's stinginess in dispensing praise. "His encouragement was always personal and subtle, not public and blatant. It was typical of him to send a subordinate a news clipping with a note saying, 'Since you're doing such a fine job, I thought this item might be of interest to you. . . .' You knew you were doing things well by his lights when one year your name showed up on the Maxwells' Christmas card list."

A hard-to-satisfy workaholic, he was also at times a hard-to-read communicator, given to cryptic suggestions like "We ought to be looking at—" that had a way of being taken for an outright command. But missed signals were a small problem; swollen heads and exhibitionist personalities were not, and individual ambition had to wear the seemly guise of aspiration for the company's fortunes. Thus, Maxwell sent Shep Pollack packing—the brainy head of PM-USA was just not his type of executive—after providing him with a plump retirement package, and replaced him with a beloved company man, chemist Frank Resnik, up from a career in R&D at Richmond. Never one of the brighter stars in the company firmament and devoid of marketing skills, Resnik had strong political and professional contacts in Washington that made him a useful figurehead. He was also malleable, taking and carrying out the chairman's instructions and not resenting the oversight of battle-tested Maxwell loyalists from the company's international operation who were now handed key posts of power.

To fill the void left by the departure for supposedly greener fields of popular company princeling Jimmy Morgan, Maxwell gave Resnik his top marketer from PMI, William Campbell. Affable and upbeat, with a somewhat volatile temperament, Campbell was viewed as bright if not shrewd. He was also a Canadian, a nationality thought to be more acceptable to PM-USA people under renewed pressure to sustain the division's growth in market share and not eager for directives by foreigners when the domestic tobacco operation had, by any standard, been a rousing success to that point. At the corporate level, Maxwell brought in his two key Australian aides, accountants William Murray and Geoffrey Bible, somewhat humorless men but able at their craft, fanatical workers, and undeviating in their loyalty to the chairman. A literal-minded fact-squeezer, Murray ran PMI for a time until being elevated to vice chairman in charge of worldwide tobacco operations. The little notebook he carried became something of a company joke; in it Murray was said to record with precision every instruction that Maxwell gave him—and then faithfully, at times coldly, saw to it that the orders were carried out. Bible, who took over running PMI from Murray, was regarded as a highly competent financial man with a focused mind, a thin skin, and a forceful, if not endearing, managerial style. The two Aussies, perfect conduits for Maxwell's contained force, were the sort of men good at running a company rather than building it. A different sort of key staff man, Ehud Houminer, an Israeli who had graduated from the University of Pennsylvania's Wharton School, probably came closer than anyone else in the organization to qualifying as a genius—a condition he did not try to hide. Having done well under Maxwell at PMI in Europe, Houminer was made top corporate planner and assigned to help the chairman figure out how best to expand the business beyond cigarettes.

To complaints—raised in hushed tones that rarely reached Maxwell's ears—that he had surrounded himself with too many organization men and not enough freethinkers, the chairman might have pointed to his chief financial officer. German-born, American-educated Hans Storr had been with the company almost as long as Maxwell but had never been a favorite of his and was widely expected to be replaced as CFO. But Maxwell soon saw that Storr was, in the words of Shep Pollack, his predecessor as CFO, "smart as hell and worked like a dog." He was also astute at anticipating changes in interest and currency exchange rates and exploiting them. Having convinced Maxwell that the growing U.S. trade deficit had to soften the dollar on international exchanges, Storr deposited $2 billion of Philip Morris funds in overseas banks and thus earned some $400 million for the company in the mid-'Eighties while cementing links with foreign bankers that would shortly prove of great value.

To secure the corporate profit base in U.S. cigarette sales before launching his diversification program, Maxwell mandated as PM-USA's marketing target an annual share gain of no less than 1 percent of the domestic pie—and the use of whatever means were needed to achieve it. This included a modified version of the trade-loading that RJR was now living off, but Philip Morris faced a far smaller risk of inventory pileup since its brands continued to defy the sales slippage affecting the rest of the industry. Marlboro stayed strong, accounting for three out of every five packs of Philip Morris brands sold and sprinting ahead in the vital eighteen-to-twenty-four-year-old sector, where its customer share rose from about 40 percent in the early 'Eighties to nearly 70 percent by the end of the decade. PM's main problem now was to obtain retail shelf exposure in proportion to its sales in order to avoid running out of stock all the time. Such an allocation of selling space, desirable on its face to the retail outlets as well, was greatly complicated by Reynolds's dominance at the store level, where its big sales force patrolled constantly and its regional sales directors had long cultivated supermarket and other chain-store executives. The RJR-provided carton racks were still accepted as a convenience by store managers, thus assuring that its own brands, if no one else's, would be fully stocked, even though they were not moving off the shelves nearly as fast as the Philip Morris makes. Reynolds was also now discounting feverishly, through price-off coupons and stickers, to prevent further erosion of its market share.

Philip Morris, then, had a great deal of catching up to do organizationally if it hoped to rout Reynolds. But it also had a compelling story to tell the chains. Cigarettes were perhaps the most profitable item in their stores, and 90 percent of those profits flowed from sales and only 10 percent from "push money" (placement and display fees) from rivals who paid for their space on the Reynolds racks. In the biggest stores, this ancillary income could reach $1,000 a month, but by grabbing it, Philip Morris's sales force now argued, store managers were sacrificing a far larger take from lost sales of hot PM brands, which kept running out because they were not given enough shelf space.

To push this argument, sales vice president Vincent Buccellato urged top management to spend for a larger and more persuasive field force and to offer retailers Philip Morris racks to break Reynolds's lock on the concept. But stores willing to make the switch soon learned that RJR would not do what all of its rivals had been compelled to do when Reynolds had been king of the hill—pay up for assured space and position on their arch foe's racks. This response blunted the PM challenge, since it meant that stores would reap less push money from a Philip Morris rack; throughout the 'Eighties, RJR clung to more than 70 percent of the store racks and its preferred positioning. But Philip Morris's aggressive pricing was cutting into carton sales, the staple of supermarket cigarette activity, and single-pack sales rose at the front of the store, where PM was investing heavily in displays and neutralizing RJR's rack advantage. All-out war was waged now at retail outlets between the two industry leaders for cigarette signage, ranging from door and window decals to newspaper racks bearing cigarette logos—usually either Marlboro or Winston—to elaborate, fluorescent-lighted clock fixtures mounted over the checkout register. Most daunting to Reynolds hopes was the growth of cigarette sales in the convenience-store market. The proliferation of the 7-Eleven chain and its imitators, helped by the oil companies, which were funding the expansion of their filling stations into the convenience grocery and sundries business, was good news for Philip Morris, since the typical convenience outlet customer was a young male, earning good pay, who bought one pack of cigarettes at a time—and it was Marlboro, in one of its dozen versions (or "packings," to use the industry term), more often than not. And because the new convenience chains did not invite the sort of long-running institutional ties that RJR had enjoyed with supermarkets, Philip Morris was able to use its money for strong signage and displays without having to worry about Reynolds racks.

As a result of these trends, so favorable to Philip Morris's full-priced brands, the rest of the industry, Reynolds included, turned more and more to the discount sector, especially in the convenience-store market. Brands like RJR's Doral, Brown & Williamson's Richland, and American Tobacco's Capri were selling well, even if at reduced margins, allowing Reynolds to sustain its unit sales through the mid-'Eighties, but Philip Morris continued to post fractional gains in units, enough to satisfy Hamish Maxwell's command to gain a point a year in overall market share.

Abetting this effort was a Philip Morris innovation aimed at fixing the company's out-of-stock woes at the nation's 250,000 retail outlets, where clerks with marginal literacy and a notoriously high turnover rate lacked the skills and incentive to keep PM's forty-five to fifty packings fully stocked, costing the company tens of millions in lost sales. Philip Morris also understood that wholesalers, already losing ground to chains that bought directly from the cigarette makers, were being pinched further by heavier carrying charges on their inventories, often swollen by trade-loading, and by the whipsaw tactics of retailers, who made as much as 20 percent on their cigarette markups (compared with the 1 percent or less that the jobbers eked out) but continually pushed for longer discounts. To help rescue wholesalers, many hanging by a thread, and advance their own cause, Philip Morris in the late 'Eighties conceived its "Masters" sales program, which paid wholesalers a cash bonus for, first, putting their operations on a more systematic basis—PM offered guidance in computerized inventory control and financial record-keeping—and, second, making sure that the distribution and retail pipeline was always fully stocked with all packings of Philip Morris brands, not just the leading sellers, and that these were well displayed. The PM sales force was assigned to keep constant check on how well the wholesalers were performing and whether they were really earning the eight- or nine-cents-per-carton bonus payment. Sweepstakes prizes, including fancy paid vacations, were awarded to the best performers in the Masters program, which netted the largest and most efficient jobbers as much as half a million dollars a year in bonus money. RJR aped the effort with its "Winners" version, but it was less ambitious and amounted to little more than an added volume discount.

For a time, its Masters program helped keep Philip Morris's full-priced brands moving relatively well—and much better than its rivals'—but a sizable downturn in the economy finally forced the industry leader to quit holding itself aloof from the discount sector. By the end of the 'Eighties, RJR held one-third of the discount cigarette business, and the PM-USA managers knew they would have to yield a portion of their sensational profit margins on full-price brands (approaching 50 percent) to keep Reynolds from running wild in the off-price sector, by then accounting for about 15 percent of cigarette sales and about to double that—and more—in the early 1990s. PM began pushing hard into the discount market with a pair of its retired failures, Alpine and Cambridge, retrofitted as off-price brands, and brought out a new "branded generic" called Buck, an even lower-priced "sub-generic," Bristol, and black-and-white Basic as a supermarket house brand. By 1989 Philip Morris had gained about a quarter of the discount sector, and while this quick incursion was a mixed blessing (because every pack it sold at discount might result in one less full-priced pack sold), it served, as Maxwell would later acknowledge, "to take the curse off of our aggressive pricing of the top-name brands." By the end of the 'Eighties, PM held a historically huge 42 percent overall share of the cigarette business, while Reynolds, finally abandoning trade-loading as a ruinously expensive and artificial device, dropped to just under 29 percent. This growing dominance provided Philip Morris with the wherewithal to transform its corporate profile.

III

To transform Philip Morris truly—and not simply to recostume it as a nicotine-stained trollop masquerading in finery to gain respectability—would
take a change in the corporate mind-set, used to fat tobacco profits compared
to which earnings from almost all other businesses looked anemic. And cigarette making was a delightfully simple form of enterprise, measured against
other consumer goods. "It's a lovely business, because it's so relatively easy,"
Hamish Maxwell reflected in his retirement years. "Cigarettes have tremendous brand loyalty, you don't have to bring out new products every five minutes, new advertising campaigns can actually hurt you," and there was scant
technological innovation required after the manufacturing speed reached
nearly 10,000 units per minute. In short, cigarettes had spoiled the company's
managers who, by 1984, were contemplating massive entry into some other
field.

Ehud Houminer, as Maxwell's designated brainstormer, had been given a
few basic guidelines as he scanned the economic terrain from Philip Morris's
Park Avenue aerie. First, no more turnaround situations. The company had
more or less succeeded, at an extravagant price, with Miller Brewing, but it
had failed in a string of other attempts, among them ASR, Clark Gum, and,
most distressingly, Seven-Up, even then bleeding badly despite multiple cash
transfusions. What was wanted now was a company already a major factor in
its field, and the field ought to be a vast one, with plenty of growing room. The
beer business, by comparison, was too limited, and Miller, having gained more
than one-fifth of the market, had finally aroused industry leader Anheuser-
Busch sufficiently to halt further penetration of its dominion. The idea now
was "to buy the biggest business we could afford," Houminer recounted, and
the move was supposed to command a strong consensus within Philip Morris
in contrast to the contentious Seven-Up purchase.

But what industry, and which company? "I studied zillions of industries,"
said Houminer, and the one he kept coming back to was food. Not just little
corners of it, like the beer or soft-drink business—the whole larder. He reasoned that Philip Morris ought to stick to what it knew and did best—consumer products in general and the processing of agricultural products in
particular. The manufacturing, packaging, and marketing of food were cousins
of the cigarette business, and it was a huge industry with sales running into the
hundreds of billions of dollars annually. While it was hard to gain entry to it,
the food business offered many opportunities for maneuver and growth—and
whatever acquisition PM now made would be only a start, for Maxwell was
determined that, given the resources at his disposal, Philip Morris should be-

come a principal player, and preferably the share leader, in whatever field the company entered. "It didn't matter which company," Houminer recounted, so long as it was profitable and had a pedigree in the form of famous trademarks and a global potential far from fully realized; more dynamic management could always be enlisted, if need be.

Food offered advantages to Philip Morris investors as well as to its executives. Even though profit margins in the food business were, at 10 percent or so, far below those in tobacco, Wall Street valued the former's earnings at almost twice the P/E ratio of the cigarette companies; food was a stable, socially essential, and wholesome form of commerce, rarely drawing liability suits. And here was a way for the No. 1 cigarette purveyor to plant high and benign hedges of respectability around its fortresslike headquarters, where a siege mentality prevailed; it would no longer be classified as a rogue operation. Through food, it would also gain influence with the media, especially the broadcasting industry, where food advertising was a prime contributor to profits, and as manufacturers of indisputably healthful and legitimate products, the company would gain political strength as well by acquiring some outfit with a big payroll outside the Tobacco Belt and in the mainstream of the economy.

The problem was how to achieve all of that without a major dilution of per-share earnings. The answer, hardly invented by Philip Morris but strongly embraced now by Houminer and resident financial chief Hans Storr, was maximum use of leveraging—buying earnings that were higher than what it cost to acquire them. Equity would not be diluted if the great expedition into food was funded not by the sale of new stock or the exchange of PM shares for those of the targeted company—both steps that would broaden the equity base and require a greater payout of dividends—but with borrowed funds that could be readily obtained at favorable rates, given Philip Morris's cascading cash flow and increasing dominance in the cigarette business. The company could safely afford to depart from the fiscally sound 50/50 debt/equity ratio it had hewed to, running it up at least temporarily as high as 75/25 without imperiling its pristine credit standing. Thus, once PM settled on its takeover candidate, it could put down a relatively small portion of the purchase price in the form of cash from surplus and borrow the rest on a short-term payback schedule, not likely to prove burdensome in view of what Storr foresaw as dropping interest rates. The newly acquired company's earnings could then be used to cover interest charges, entirely tax-deductible and thus relieving downward pressure on overall earnings, and PM's cash flow, mounting by the year, would be applied to pay down a big piece of the loan principal, which could be entirely repaid within three or four years. As the debt service then shrank, more and more of the acquired company's earnings could be brought to the bottom line. And even if, after the purchase price was entirely paid off, the return on equity capital was not as great as that from the tobacco operations, Wall Street would reward Philip Morris investors by boosting the price of its stock, because the company by then would be heavily into the food business and would no longer be viewed as primarily a hot but suspect tobacco operator. The stockholders' total return—dividends plus stock price enhancement in the market—would be at least as high as if the company had stuck with tobacco exclusively and paid out more and more of the profits as dividends until the goose died and there were no more golden eggs.

With this basic concept in place, Storr moved smoothly in international banking circles, seeking to build a hefty war chest in the form of loan commitments for the takeover venture. This was no small task, for he could not divulge the names of Philip Morris's likely prey without risking a leak that might drive up the purchase price unbearably; thus, the loan pledges were made blind and necessarily tentatively, pending news of the actual takeover target. American banks were uneasy about such dealings, partly out of fear that the loan commitment might represent a conflict of interest—*i.e.*, if the target company was already a client of theirs—and no doubt partly because of Philip Morris's less than glittering record when it had diversified in the pre-Maxwell era. Storr turned more to overseas lenders, especially Japanese banks awash in credits from their nation's bulging balance-of-trade payments surplus. Within a year, Storr had built a $6 billion takeover chest.

But which company in the food business? Why not the biggest, Philip Morris asked itself, and so rested its gaze on General Foods Corporation (GF), a goliath with $7.5 billion in annual sales and 56,000 employees. By the numbers alone, a takeover of GF would mean a major reconfiguring of its corporate structure for PM, then grossing $14 billion a year with a payroll of 68,000. But if it could be accomplished, would GF be worth the price it could command?

General Foods was a high-class operation, certainly, run by well-bred people in a country-club atmosphere in suburban Westchester County north of New York. Its management, though, was viewed as sleepy and overly reliant on its great old trademarks; indeed, 75 percent of its sales came from brands that were top in their field, including Jell-O gelatin desserts, Maxwell House coffee, Birds Eye frozen foods, Log Cabin syrup, and Oscar Mayer bacon. And even its laggard product lines, like Post breakfast cereals, included some great old names like Grape-Nuts, which dated back to the nineteenth century. In internal documents and discussions about their prey, Philip Morris executives code-named GF "Brew" after its top rank among U.S. coffee sellers; about one-third of its sales were derived from the beverage. The trouble was that, as with cigarettes, per capita consumption of coffee had peaked in the 'Sixties, and the volatility of coffee-bean harvests kept the retail prices on a roller coaster. Though its largest grossing product, coffee yielded only 21 percent of the food company's net, making it a decided drag on earnings.

Overall, Wall Street found GF to be an underachiever and unaccountably in the doldrums. It had doubled its net over the 'Seventies, keeping pace with inflation and then some, but during the first half of the 'Eighties its revenues had only inched ahead, and dividends had actually failed to keep pace with inflation. Management was seen as too soft, slow, overgrown, and expensive. Its executives were said to take Friday afternoons off in nice weather and had lavished $50 million on a new headquarters building in Rye Brook, near Long Island Sound—an industrial palace of gleaming white aluminum sheathing that resembled a Disney version of the Taj Mahal remodeled as a world-class resort hotel. To make up for stagnant sales of its established brands, GF had spent $2 billion on plant improvements and the purchase of new lines like Ronzoni pastas, Entenmann's bakery goods, and Oscar Mayer with its fast-growing Louis Rich turkey business, popular with increasing numbers of health-conscious Americans and economically more profitable than chicken because the bigger birds yielded one-third more meat per man-hour of processing. There were other signs as well that GF was waking up to the changes in U.S. dietary habits. It had moved into convenience foods, a boom item now that more than half of all married women held jobs outside their homes, and was doing well with a new entry in the health-food field—Fruit & Fibre cereals—but it was fighting an uphill battle against Kellogg and General Mills, because it had failed to market and innovate with vigor for too long.

GF, then, appeared to be rallying itself. With talk of annual earnings increases of 3 to 5 percent after inflation, it made an enticing package for Hamish Maxwell and his advisors. Still, they were not mesmerized by it. Food was a complicated business, and GF's in-place management was lackluster, but the company would give Philip Morris a very large foot inside the door of a highly respectable industry—and their cigarette profits could buy them time to appraise the food managers who came with the deal, to learn from them, and if need be, to replace them. But the transformation could not be accomplished peremptorily, for Maxwell wanted PM, as newcomers to the industry, to avoid being tarred as a bunch of corporate roughnecks.

By 1985, Wall Street was expecting a shakeout in the crowded and murderously competitive food industry. Sluggish General Foods seemed a likely takeover candidate, and its stock price rose. If and when Philip Morris walked off with it, the resulting combination would become the nation's largest consumer products company, surpassing Procter & Gamble. But before PM acted, its vanquished chief tobacco adversary, Reynolds, grabbed the honor by snatching up a glittering trophy of its own.

IV

IN 1984, its first year under the lash of chairman Tylee Wilson, R. J. Reynolds Industries put up numbers that were every bit as good overall as Philip Morris's under its new boss, Hamish Maxwell, even though PM had knocked RJR off its tobacco pedestal.

Wilson acted promptly to do what predecessor Paul Sticht had felt the time was never ripe to get done: jettison its cash-gobbling Sea-Land shipping subsidiary by spinning it off to its employees. Del Monte, after being slimmed down through thirty-eight plant closings, was doing better now, pushing new lines of canned goods like sugar-free fruits and low-salt vegetables. Kentucky Fried Chicken was expanding, too, especially abroad, and when RJR entered the soda business, it did not make the same mistake Philip Morris had with Seven-Up; Reynolds steered clear of Coke and Pepsi by buying up Canada Dry and Sunkist, which sold mostly mixers and flavor drinks that the industry leaders did not bother with. By earning 7 percent on its non-tobacco business, a good deal better than Philip Morris had managed to do with Miller and Seven-Up, RJR posted overall figures remarkably close to PM's—a consolidated profit margin of just under 20 percent and a 25 percent return on equity. More successful than Philip Morris so far per dollar invested in the food business, Reynolds was now casting about the same waters as its New York rival, and early in 1985 Ty Wilson put in an exploratory call to the chairman of the fourth-ranking company in the food industry: Nabisco.

Holding on hard to a 40 percent share of the cookie and cracker market through such household-name brands as Premium saltines, Ritz crackers, Fig Newtons, Lorna Doone, Chips Ahoy!, and top-selling Oreo, Nabisco was somewhat smaller than General Foods but more profitable; its margin on sales and return on equity were 5.4 percent and 19.1 percent, respectively, compared with GF's 3.7 percent and 16.8. Even so, Nabisco had shared GF's reputation as a somewhat stodgy and conservative outfit. The same could not be said, however, of its CEO, R. Ross Johnson, who had held the job for only three years when RJR's Wilson phoned him up to talk merger.

Johnson was Wilson's polar opposite. The RJR chief was a rigid and methodical professional manager with an often impolitic directness. Johnson, at fifty-three, the same age as Wilson, was breezy, wisecracking, and gregarious, a talker and tinkerer rather than a corporate martinet, with the rangy, wavy-haired good looks of a fashion model in his mod aviator glasses, wide ties, and leather outer coat. He was a consummate gamesman, good on the golf course and even better at corporate politics, disarming everyone he encountered with a deep-throated laugh and a self-deprecating manner. Claiming that he had no functional skills as a businessman, Johnson in fact had a decided knack for detecting soft spots in monthly sales and earnings reports, sensing when he could obtain top dollar by selling off a troubled division, and buttering up older executives or those who outranked him before reaching for their mantle when they faltered. Adept as neither a manager nor a marketer, he was too impatient to fix the ailing parts of whatever company he ran, preferring to replace them with new, more amusing ventures. He thrived on action, rarely bothering to project where a business ought to be headed five years down the road. He was part Falstaff in a business suit, part Peter Pan with a mean golf swing, and part piranha scenting blood in roiled waters.

Just four years before Ty Wilson summoned him, Johnson had had a similar call from Nabisco while he was running Standard Brands, a sizable consumer goods outfit whose Canadian subsidiary he had revitalized and thus got himself switched to the fast track. Despite his limousine lifestyle in a horse-and-buggy company run by a tyrannical and somewhat sour overlord, Johnson's on-line performance and pleasing personality won him pals among fellow Standard Brands executives. A palace coup landed him in the CEO's job, where he busily pruned and added, and before his limitations as a manager could become apparent, he and his company were brought in to Nabisco to liven up the place and fatten earnings. By turns antic and brutish, Johnson charmed and shoved his way upward; within three years of the merger, he again had become CEO of the company that had taken over his. Wholly a pragmatist, Johnson specialized in firehouse management as Nabisco's boss, planning little but responding quickly to emergencies, like Kellogg's challenge to Shredded Wheat, a Nabisco mainstay, and Procter & Gamble's sortie into the cookie business with a soft, chewy line that Johnson repulsed by bringing out a similar line dubbed Almost Home.

In proposing a Reynolds takeover of Nabisco, Wilson found Johnson likable—everyone did—and supposed him manageable. Mostly, he was impressed by Nabisco's financial sheet, which Johnson, a trained accountant, knew how to massage into sinewy shape. The amiably reached takeover package of cash, stock, and bonds totaled $4.9 billion, then the richest U.S. corporate marriage ever outside the oil business, and made RJR Nabisco, as the new company was soon to be called, the second largest consumer products company on earth, trailing only Unilever. Johnson became president and chief operating officer, with a pledge from Wilson that he would step aside after a few years and cede his sporty adjutant the chairmanship.

Demoted in the process was Reynolds President Edward Horrigan, the combative, un-mod fireplug who was no match in style or quick-wittedness for Johnson. The latter now descended on Winston-Salem like a lubricious "Professor" Harold Hill come to River City, Iowa, to disarm the natives. The town was agog as he breezed in with his beauteous blond second wife, who was half his age, bounced around in a Jeep to show he was a down-to-earth guy, had folks in for dinner instead of waiting for them to break the ice, outplayed most of the local talent on the golf course, and on the weekend jetted all over the country to play famous courses and consort with celebrated sports figures. His executive style was also unnerving to staid Reynolds executives, who were not used to bosses who habitually arrived late at meetings—people did not pay attention to you if you were punctual, Johnson once suggested—and did not join in the usual pre-business chat about family and fishing. Johnson and his Nabisco crew, based in suburban New Jersey, were privately disdainful of the bloated staffing and slow and easy ways of the dominant tobacco division. His impatience would occasionally spill over in the form of his pet put-down of a subordinate's unprofound analysis: "That was a blinding glimpse of the obvious."

Nabisco benefited from RJR's cash riches by a plant modernization program and adapted the cigarette business's knack for line extensions with, for example, mint-flavored and giant-sized versions of the Oreo cookie. But Johnson, as the company's food czar, craved a more exciting game. His impatience with dawdling divisions soon manifested itself as Wilson authorized the sell-off of Del Monte's frozen food line, the KFC fast-food chain, the soda business, Morton salt, the Patio and Chun King specialty food lines, and—just a few weeks after RJR had bought up the big Almaden winery—Heublein and the whole alcohol business, unloaded in part because of Johnson's capricious view that a liquor company without a leading Scotch brand was like a baseball team without a shortstop.

Wilson, meanwhile, was self-destructing in the chairmanship. He seemed not to sense the precariousness of his standing with the Reynolds board, whose members were unappreciative of what they perceived in him to be a certain high-handedness and irreverence toward them. Tensions rose, along with concerns about how the chairman comported himself socially. "We were not comfortable with him," recalled board executive committee chairman Paul Sticht, who had reluctantly endorsed him for the job, "and Ross Johnson was doing a pretty good job of undermining Wilson by then."

Matters reached a critical point when board members learned that the RJR tobacco people had spent tens of millions over five years on a top-secret experimental cigarette project code-named "Spa" without ever apprising the directors. Housed in bunkerlike quarters in downtown Winston and intended to reverse RJR's sagging cigarette market share, Spa was a kind of successor to Liggett's abandoned palladium brand, likewise designed to be a less hazardous smoke, but the Reynolds effort was far more inventive: it would reduce the toxic by-products of the combustion process by virtually eliminating them; instead of burning, the tobacco was warmed by a glowing charcoal rod that would never get hot enough to ignite it and thus produced almost no smoke.

The trick was to get it to taste enough like a regular cigarette and then present it to the public in a way that did not tacitly cast the company's established brands as health perils. The project was kept hush-hush to the point where RJR public-relations head David Fishel was ordered to deny its existence, telling press inquirers in 1985, "I don't know anything about it. We don't know of anything that makes a cigarette unsafe, so how could we be working toward a safer cigarette?" In fact, many people at RJR knew about Spa, and not a few outside the company, but RJR's board was not let in on the secret project, funded under the chairman's discretionary prerogatives and hidden in the corporate research budget. When confronted, Wilson and Horrigan somewhat lamely cited their fears of preliminary disclosure of the effort and possible leaks from board members, all of which amounted to a statement of no-confidence in the directors, at whose pleasure Wilson served—and they were not pleased.

At this juncture, Ross Johnson, by now well wired into Wilson's problems with the board, let the directors know that he did not plan to remain long in the No. 2 managerial slot at the company. The directors were thus forced to choose, in effect, between retaining the truculent, hard-nosed Wilson and the quick brown fox who had flashed into view, bedazzling in the Oleg Cassini sportswear ads for which he posed, emblematic of the contrast between Johnson and the frumpy Reynolds style of life and doing business. The gladsome newcomer may have made them nervous, but he was a welcome change from Wilson, and there was no gainsaying his financial track record, despite an inclination to elect radical surgery in place of tender loving care for the ailing parts of any business he ran. Within fourteen months of his arrival at RJR, Ross Johnson was named to replace the man who had enlisted him.

Once in charge, Johnson lost little time revealing his disdain for the Reynolds corporate culture. In a symbolical move, he sold off Prince Albert pipe tobacco, the product that had been the foundation of the company's explosive growth at the beginning of the century. Then, quipping that Winston-Salem was a great town for raising a family but inconvenient to serve as headquarters for a corporate giant, he ordered the top managerial staff slashed by two-thirds and moved to a characterless glass tower in a suburban Atlanta mall, presumably for better flight connections with the Nabisco executive team up north and contractors, bankers, and anyone else from the faster-paced world wanting to do business with the company. Though its 12,000 or so manufacturing jobs were not affected by the shift, Winston's pride was badly wounded. Then there was the added display of arrogance in a sybaritic, late-night-and-long-weekend lifestyle that Johnson pursued. Reynolds executives soon had at their disposal a ten-plane RJR air force with thirty-six full-time pilots, housed in a costly new hangar facility, while their fast-stepping chairman set a standard for peripatetic extravagance: he had five homes, several of which he managed to visit each week, and held memberships in twenty-four country clubs—all, of course, suitable for advancing his business interests. His fondness for hobnobbing with star athletes was not unrelated to the millions the company lavished on a single golf tourney, the Dinah Shore Open. A few million here or there, Johnson was heard to say more than once, were lost in the sands of time. His managerial methods seemed similarly arbitrary and feckless. For no compelling reason, for example, the Nabisco unit producing Planters peanuts and Life Savers was assigned to the tobacco division, and executives were shifted around often and chaotically, like so many toy soldiers, to the point where a Johnson-inspired gag ran through the company corridors to the effect that nobody had a fixed job and title anymore, only a temporary assignment.

But Johnson was wily enough to mute effective criticism by lathering up potential adversaries. Chief among these was Ed Horrigan, who had not trusted Johnson from the first but now found himself artfully cosseted with higher pay and more power—full sway over the tobacco business, which Johnson knew little about and needed Horrigan, or someone both energetic and pliable, to preside over—plus perks like his own private plane and the latchkey to an RJR executive apartment in New York. If Horrigan had never had it so good, the same could be said for more than thirty other top RJR Nabisco executives, whose remuneration now averaged well over $400,000 a year. The all-important board of directors was similarly romanced. The fee for their attending meetings was raised to a $50,000 annual nugget; directors received gifts of 1,500 shares of restricted company stock; and side deals and rewards were doled out to key board members, like a $250,000 annual consultant's fee to Sticht, who had never been a wealthy man, and smaller ones to others, along with endowed professorships named for them at Duke. It was all very flattering, and Johnson's spendthrift indulgences seemed to have scant impact on the RJR bottom line. In 1987, his first full year at the helm, earnings per share rose 23 percent.

Yet Johnson was antsy about Wall Street's continuing reluctance to bid up RJR's stock to a price commensurate with its earnings. Security analysts were uneasy about Johnson's future path and RJR's ongoing loss of ground in tobacco to Philip Morris, whose stock was priced notably higher, even though Reynolds was outpacing it in the food business, which the New York company had entered in a big way a few months after RJR's mid-1985 buyout of Nabisco.

V

As rumors intensified on Wall Street that General Foods, with its gold-plated trademarks but bloated overhead, low-margin coffee business, and sluggish earnings growth, was a prime takeover candidate, influential Kidder, Peabody tobacco and food analyst Roy Burry wrote that he doubted Philip Morris would be dumb enough to be the buyer. That got him a quick summons to Hamish Maxwell's office, where the PM chairman asked, "Roy, what would you have me do?"

To any other course of action, as Burry remembered, Maxwell had a plausible if not entirely persuasive counterargument. For Philip Morris to pay off all debts, slowly contract its business, and raise dividends at a still faster rate than the 20 to 25 percent annual hikes PM was already managing would not really have been a service to its stockholders, Maxwell contended, since they would then have to pay higher income taxes on their dividends, which already reflected the government's corporate income tax bite. Better to build investors' equity by retaining earnings and acquiring strong new assets, even if the added operations posted lower margins than the tobacco business—as almost every other form of enterprise did. Stock buybacks, instead of further diversification, also brought with them a serious problem: the smaller the stockholder base—that is, the more tightly the company was held and the more nearly it resembled a private operation—the more of a target for carping do-gooders and critics it would become. Finally, for Philip Morris to plunge its surplus cash into a capital-intensive business, particularly in the technologically exotic fields, was exceedingly chancy, as RJR's misadventures in the shipping business had shown. Such industries were usually competitive in the extreme and often highly cyclical; they guzzled cash for state-of-the-art plant and equipment, and, as Maxwell explained to Burry, "We have to be able to talk to these people"—no small matter, particularly in the high-tech fields, where the vocabulary, frames of reference, and profit margins were so different.

And so Maxwell proceeded with a preemptive, all-cash tender offer of $120 a share for General Foods, a premium of nearly 50 percent above the market price. No one else could or wanted to match it, as Hans Storr reeled in his loan pledges, some 70 percent of which came from foreign banks, to meet the buyout price of $5.8 billion and make Philip Morris the biggest U.S. consumer products company, a title RJR Nabisco had held for just three months. A number of analysts wrote that PM had overpaid for General Foods—the price was 3.5 times book value (the difference between a company's assets and liabilities), compared with the 3.2 ratio Reynolds had paid for higher-earning

Nabisco. But Maxwell insisted that it was a fine catch and that the GF brands had great global potential. Probably a more candid assessment was Storr's retrospective remark that "From day one we realized General Foods was a company with real problems that would be a big headache."

To help focus Philip Morris's attention on absorbing its huge acquisition, Maxwell sold off troubled Seven-Up in 1986 for about half the money PM had sunk into the spirited, though somewhat bullheaded, effort. Maxwell let the new food executives function with minimal restraint and, while watching, learned the hard truth about their new business—it was not one enterprise but many, each product line with its own agricultural sources, government oversight of sanitary conditions and ingredients, and manufacturing, pricing, distribution, and competitive dynamics. Jell-O, in short, was not interchangeable with Sanka, or dry cereals with cured ham.

Even as they learned, though, Philip Morris executives grew disenchanted with the General Foods management, which got better pay and more perks than they did but, as one top younger PM sales executive put it, "They were dead from their ankles up. . . . Their arrogance was exceeded only by their sloth." The GF plants, in the eyes of Philip Morris operations people, used to immaculate facilities, were sloppy, and, far worse, the bellwether product line—Maxwell House and other coffee brands—had been diluted in quality in a conscious decision to economize by buying cheaper beans and cutting corners in the processing. As a result, Folgers and other competitors had cut deeply into GF's coffee business.

Maxwell began to clean house by advancing younger managers who addressed the coffee problem, especially the taste of Sanka, with a new, costly decaffeination process; then he sold off GF's unrewarding sideline ventures like toys and a seed business, pruned 2,000 jobs from the payroll, and restructured the whole operation. But there were no miracle cures. Results for 1986 showed GF accounting for 40 percent of Philip Morris's revenues but only 20 percent of the profit. And in 1987, things did not change appreciably. The move into big-time food was no disaster, surely; GF was netting 7 percent on $10 billion in sales and legitimizing Philip Morris's overall corporate identity, as the stock market reacted more favorably to the General Foods venture than results could yet justify. But when youthful GF chairman Philip Smith accepted an invitation to run Pillsbury without a superchief like Maxwell hovering over his shoulder, there was no rush to replace him.

Instead, Maxwell explored his options. Among these was listening politely to overtures from his fleet archrival, Ross Johnson, always on the prowl for new worlds to conquer. The former cordiality between RJR and Philip Morris had frayed over the years with the latter's ascendancy. But, as Maxwell recounted, "Ross was everyone's pal—he was willing to talk about anything and everything," even while sulking about the undeservedly low price at which his company's stock was trading. The two were miles apart in manner and temperament, Johnson a quick study but the shallow, impetuous hare to Maxwell's pensive and patient tortoise, with a vision of where he wanted to take his company. Johnson struck him as "a restless man who liked to make deals better than live with a situation." Johnson proposed that the two companies pool their overseas tobacco business or perhaps their food divisions, with the RJR Nabisco chairman running the latter. Maxwell, aware that only one chief executive survived whenever Johnson was involved in a merger, did not take the bait. As a consolation prize, he urged Johnson not to fret unduly over how his company was faring in the daily gyrations of the stock market so long as he was advancing its earnings smartly each year.

V I

S PURNED by his savvy competitor, Ross Johnson turned to his chief subordinate, Edward Horrigan, to push ahead with RJR's pet developmental program, the "smokeless" Spa cigarette. If it worked, Johnson figured, it could truly revolutionize the tobacco industry and put RJR back on top, driving its stock price up where it belonged. Horrigan, feisty as ever and sharing his chairman's ambition, did not require much prodding to advance the timetable for the project.

But Horrigan was apprehensive about Spa. It was too big an idea for the company to risk falling on its face by pushing out an inadequate or legally vulnerable product. Johnson, a high-stakes roller, was ready to toss caution to the wind, even if it proved ill. "Ross wanted it so bad you wouldn't believe it," Horrigan recalled of Johnson's enthusiasm for the daring departure. "He treated [the experimental version] almost recklessly, leaving samples around on airplanes." Plainly he wanted word to get out that his company was about to hatch something enormous. Horrigan's claimed preference was to ease the smokeless brand into small test markets, working out the bugs before chancing a national rollout. Meanwhile, and not by accident, word spread on Wall Street about the internal debate, and Reynolds's lawyers advised that securities regulations required general disclosure of the planned new product as a "material" factor that might affect the stock's orderly trading. And so, in September 1987, amid much media hype, the company staged a New York press conference, complete with information kits, charts, and cutaway diagrams of the new cigarette. The chief claim for it was that it looked, lit, tasted, and smoked like other cigarettes but had no ash, produced virtually no smoke after the first puff or two, and if left alone, would extinguish itself rather than igniting any surface with which it came into contact.

It was an ingenious contraption, a cylinder of tobacco wrapped around a carbon rod that was ignited and burned down, warming the air drawn in by the smoker's inhalation and passing over a small aluminum capsule implanted in the center containing beads of tobacco extracts, nicotine in particular, and flavorants. A cellulose acetate filter was attached, but what value it had for an essentially smokeless cigarette was not explained. In lawyer-crafted language, Horrigan stated that since the tobacco did not burn, the compounds normally produced by cigarettes "are eliminated or greatly reduced, including most compounds that are often associated with the smoking and health controversy. Simply put, we think that this is the world's cleanest cigarette . . . [and] addresses the desires and perceptions of many of today's smokers."

But when he tried to elaborate on the nature and purpose of the radical device, Horrigan lapsed into language that disclosed the manufacturer's dilemma in presenting it to the public. "We're not saying it's a safe or safer cigarette," he said. "We're saying many allegations about the burning of tobacco and elimination of those compounds should be greatly reduced with this product." Beneath that double-talk was the unmistakable implication that here was a less hazardous cigarette—otherwise, why was Reynolds going to market it? Just to meet "the perceptions of many of today's smokers"? That would make the product a mere piece of trickery.

That the company was truly trying to address the scientific and medical communities' concerns without putting itself out of business was suggested a few days later by a Reynolds attorney, Peter Hutt, a member of the Washington firm of Covington & Burling. At a private session with top HHS Department officials arranged through Vice President George Bush's office, Hutt explained, according to Office on Smoking and Health director Ronald Davis (and corroborated later by Surgeon General Koop), that the new product would provide "important health benefits by reducing the risk of cancer in smokers." And if the public took to the innovative brand, RJR's researchers would work "to find ways to reduce the nicotine and carbon monoxide levels so as to reduce the risk of heart disease," Hutt repeatedly said, trying to reassure, if not obtain an outright endorsement from, key federal public-health authorities. "I was rather surprised that [Hutt] referred to cancer [and] chronic lung and heart disease as problems related to smoking," Davis recounted, and the OSH head asked the Reynolds attorney if he was speaking for the company. When Hutt said yes, Davis asked if the potential health benefits attributed to the new product had been part of the public press briefing in New York the week before. "He said they were not and asked in effect not to be quoted as saying that smoking was hazardous." Davis, though pledging not to quote him publicly, did record Hutt's remarks in a memorandum, which Tobacco Products Liability Project Director Richard Daynard learned of from Davis and obtained after threatening to invoke the Freedom of Information Act.

What followed was a dramatization of the moral ambivalence of the antismoking movement toward any serious effort by the tobacco industry to produce an authentically—or at least plausibly—less dangerous cigarette. Citing Davis's account of the HHS meeting, Daynard accused the company of towering hypocrisy for denying in public what it conceded in private about the severe hazards of smoking. Hutt and the company rushed out a reply that Davis had misquoted the lawyer, who, it was claimed, had referred only to the *alleged* risks of smoking and yielded nothing to the charges against the product. Once again the industry was bowing to its lawyers' directives and sacrificing its credibility out of dread of the legal repercussions of telling the truth in plain English.

But even the truth might not advance its cause, RJR found out when it tried to meet with American Cancer Society officers to explain how they hoped the new product might reduce the threat of disease. ACS realists like public-relations director Irving Rimer thought the door ought to be opened to RJR, whose invention might actually modify the dangers of smoking for the hopelessly hooked. The fear prevailed, however, within ACS councils as well as at other antismoking strongholds that if the product really accomplished what the manufacturer implied, it would serve primarily to allow smokers who should quit to continue the habit and also to encourage others, younger and more impressionable, to take it up as not so dangerous as previously charged. The ACS was not about to endorse the RJR "smokeless" cigarette.

While the company said it would keep working on the product to hasten its future marketing, criticism of the concept accumulated. Elizabeth Whelan of the American Council on Science and Health hit at the industry's long record of denial by needling, "How can [Reynolds] claim they took out the harmful elements when [they also claim] we don't know what causes the harm?" ASH's John Banzhaf registered unhappiness with the smokeless nature of the new gadget—its chief virtue—by noting, "Now when someone lights up, you can see and avoid the smoke. With the new cigarette . . . it will be harder to avoid." Gregory Connolly of the Massachusetts public-health department pointed out that the new product might reduce the tar yield, but with the nicotine and carbon monoxide left in, there was still plenty of toxicity to endanger its users. The American Heart Association's Scott Ballin said that the undisclosed chemicals and additives used in the RJR product's "flavor capsule" might add a fresh carcinogenic or other health peril. And Congress's foremost smoking foe, Henry Waxman, put in, "It doesn't sound like a great advance to have another product that causes heart problems."

But others understood that this demonizing of Reynolds for putting forth a cigarette arguably less lethal than the industry standard was not constructive. The smokeless brand presented a dilemma to "Americans who dream of a smoke-free society," a *New York Times* editorial noted, because with smoking in decline and the rights of nonsmokers finally being recognized, "a less dangerous cigarette could slow, perhaps even reverse, these welcome, healthy trends." But not to allow the sale of the Reynolds experimental brand "would condemn hard-core nicotine addicts and those who breathe their secondary smoke to the greater hazard of conventional cigarettes," the *Times* added. "Moralistic opposition to anything labeled tobacco cannot substitute for reasoned debate on how best to reduce nicotine addiction."

Reynolds, though, had never suggested that its new product would cut down on its addictiveness; indeed, there had been no concession that smoking was at all addictive. Michael Pertschuk's Advocacy Institute picked up on this shortcoming when, in a March 1988 "action alert" to its smoking control network of public-health advocates, it advised that the company would soon test-market the experimental brand unless the FDA could be persuaded that the product was essentially a drug-delivery device masquerading as a cigarette. Pertschuk, uncrowned leader of the tobacco control movement, argued that because (1) the company's patent application conceded that the presence of tobacco was optional in its mechanical operation, (2) the extracts used in the flavor capsule contained unknown and unexamined chemicals, and, most of all, (3) the manufacturer's hope was to reduce the cancers caused by smoking, the FDA ought to classify the Reynolds smokeless cigarette as a drug and keep it off the market until its safety could be assured.

Here, truly, was a perfect opportunity for the FDA to exert its jurisdiction over cigarettes, long withheld on the grounds that they were neither a food nor a drug and that their makers neither intended nor claimed any therapeutic value for them. But what then? It was surely disingenuous to call for the FDA to ban the smokeless RJR cigarette until its safety was proven; it would take a generation of epidemiological surveys after its introduction to determine whether the product actually reduced the dangers of smoking. What the FDA could probably do, short of banning the Reynolds smokeless cigarette—or any other—was to place limits on tar, nicotine, and carbon monoxide yields. But this might appear to countenance as medically acceptable any brand meeting the prescribed lowered levels of toxicity when nobody knew whether even the lowest habitual intake of tobacco toxins was safe.

Pressure mounted on the FDA to act—somehow. The Coalition on Smoking or Health petitioned the agency to keep the RJR product off the market, the AMA joined in the request, and six top federal health officers, including Surgeon General Koop, added their voices. The FDA, though, temporized as RJR researchers addressed some of the criticisms aimed at its smokeless cigarette. In a 743-page book distributed to every congressman and many public-health officials, Reynolds dealt with the nicotine issue by stating that its level in the adjusted product, as measured in the urine of test subjects, was lower than that in 97 percent of cigarettes then on the market. Although such claims did not allay the most vociferous objections or win an FDA waiver, the company's drumbeat grew louder. Wall Street got interested, as Ross Johnson had intended; Kidder, Peabody's analyst Roy Burry predicted that the soon-to-be-marketed RJR smokeless brand "could add three to seven percentage points to annual rates of tobacco earnings growth during the coming decade" and, if successful, "could alter the industry's economics, worldwide consumption trends, and relative company positions."

Named Premier instead of Spa, its old in-house code name, the Reynolds smokeless entry was test-marketed in early autumn of 1988 with whizbang electronic store displays and a two-packs-for-one offer. Such costly merchandising raised the price tag of the project, counting all the years of research, special manufacturing equipment, and promotional hoopla, to almost $300 million, making it a candidate for the most expensive U.S. consumer product introduction ever. But Premier still had a few problems, and a buying public used to instant gratification was not forgiving.

There was the taste, for one thing, and the smell, for another; both were bad if you failed to follow the instructions on a little leaflet inside the package. It said to light the cigarette with a pure butane flame; the impurities in a regular sulphur safety match or other kinds of lighters reacted badly with the carbon rod, the cigarette's heating element, producing little black specks that gathered in the filter system and made it taste, as its first customers testified, "as if you'd lighted the wrong end." One venturous buyer told inquiring reporters that his Premier smelled "like burning tennis sneakers," while another suggested the experience was "as if you'd just opened a grave on a warm day." Some complained that, assuming you could tolerate the taste and smell, it was hard to drag on, and one leading Wall Street analyst commented that a blowtorch, not a butane lighter, was required to get the thing going. This problem was traceable to the quarter-inch overwrap at the front end of the Premier, needed to sheath the carbon rod and allow it to be lit without the flame contacting the tobacco. As with the obligatory butane lighter, Horrigan would later concede, "You had to overexplain it."

Mechanics aside, even as an intellectual concept, the Premier presented would-be consumers with problems. Smoking is a complex interplay of psychological and pharmacological factors, but at its core is—well, smoke. Without it, without the feel of its going down and the sight of its being expelled as a pungent miasma, you were just sucking tobacco-flavored warm air. And there was no ash to assure the smoker that he was in fact consuming anything—just a tiny receding red dot when viewed head-on. "I've been smoking the hell out of this," one early customer reported in frustration, "and it won't go away." And at the end, assuming you knew when you had reached it, you couldn't even stub out the Premier with ritualistic vigor; you had to break it apart, sometimes causing the little metal flavor capsule to clank into the ashtray like an unexpectedly discovered Soviet bugging device.

Why, with so many apparent drawbacks, had Reynolds even test-marketed the Premier? "We went to market at least a year before any of us wanted to," Horrigan would later acknowledge. One explanation might have been to beat the competition, but RJR officials privately believed that they had a three-to-five-year lead over any rival version of a smokeless cigarette. A rationalized answer was Horrigan's belief that consumers would be patient while the manufacturer responded to their objections and would understand that so radical an innovation would take some getting used to, just as decaffeinated coffee, sugar-free soda, and low-fat milk had tasted funny to buyers when they were introduced. But most of all, in the opinion of those closest to the disastrous marketing of Premier, the reason was Ross Johnson's uncontainable desire to score a big hit and get his company's stock price up.

Instead, the product became an overnight laughingstock, grist for stand-up comedians and talk show hosts. Few customers in the test cities were willing to try a second pack, and almost no stores reordered. Within weeks of its unveiling, Premier had taken its place alongside the Edsel in the pantheon of American marketing catastrophes.

VII

THWARTED by smokers' rejection of the Premier and the stock market's persistent failure to value RJR Nabisco for what he thought it was worth, Ross Johnson turned to the fastest game of his action-packed career. Since the investment community had not properly rewarded him, he would demonstrate Wall Street's obtuseness by taking his company private. His method, in vogue among plungers with a great deal of nerve and at least some cash at their disposal, was the leveraged buyout.

LBOs, as the business world termed the practice, were based on use of the target company's own assets and earning power as the prime collateral for a loan of whatever size was required, at whatever rates were necessary, to buy out the stockholders and run the company in rugged entrepreneurial style. No need to placate Wall Street with glowing quarterly reports, no frittering of cash on dividend payments to unappreciative stockholders, no paternalistic concerns like retaining deadwood managers or plump fringe benefits to make employees happy and secure. Once privately held, the operation could slash payrolls, cut other costs to the bone, sell off weak-sister divisions, and direct all the resulting savings and revenue to paying down the often grotesquely swollen debt incurred in the buyout. A large piece of the debt was usually in the form of "junk" bonds, high-yielding subordinated instruments backed mostly by the earning power of the business, which became burdened now with incessant pressure to meet the heavy charges and was chronically threatened with bankruptcy if revenues took an untimely dip. The upside of leveraged buyouts, of course, was that the takeover management, with a direct stake in its success, could run the show with maximum efficiency—and brutally if necessary—until it paid off most of the debt, and if it elected, could then take the leaner company back public and make a bundle on the transaction.

Some 500 companies had undergone the supposedly therapeutic process in the three years before Ross Johnson turned to Wall Street investment bankers and brokers for lessons in how to join in the biggest self-rewarding orgy since the nineteenth-century robber barons were rampant. What was wrong with LBOs—and generally a matter of indifference to their perpetrators—was that instead of building equity in corporate America and an efficient, globally competitive industrial plant, the greed machine was piling up huge debts from the bidding wars that the buyouts set in motion, grossly inflating values, making fortunes for a few key players in the takeover group—along with their bankers, brokers, and lawyers—and for investors intrepid enough to buy up the junk bonds that were usually at the heart of the deals. The results sometimes were that the targeted trophy was shorn of its patina, heads rolled, plants closed, whole communities went into shock and despair, and the surviving enterprise, groaning with debt, was starved for funds to make capital improvements and even to maintain the existing plant; new product development and technological progress suffered. Yet the U.S. Treasury helped to underwrite the game, losing out on corporate income taxes that were no longer being paid to it by buyout managements, who were able to deduct the full cost of their outsized interest payments on the loan with which they had captured their companies. Nor were there any dividends left to tax, though stockholders did have to pay up for whatever capital gains they realized from the buyout price. An LBO engineered by entrenched management was, moreover, a particularly suspect undertaking, thick with conflict-of-interest problems. For if the point of the deal was a leaning down of operations, why couldn't the in-place management, authorized to make whatever economies and sell-offs were needed, have done the job without resorting to taking the company private? In the case of RJR Nabisco, the answer was that Ross Johnson had little stomach for cutting costs and tempering his high-living ways. His skill was not solving problems but getting rid of them; he was a dealmaker and a parlayer of assets, not a creator of wealth by developing and marketing goods and services. If Wall Street would not value RJR for what it was worth, then Johnson would walk off with the package himself and cash it in at full liquidation value, even if that meant risking dismemberment of the enterprise.

Accordingly, Johnson engaged a top Wall Street firm to represent him, selected a management team of six other executives to join him, including Horrigan, and worked out an intricate deal with the giant investment house of

Shearson Lehman Hutton. Under it, the Johnson team would in effect be allotted up to 18.5 percent of the equity in the bought-out RJR Nabisco, pieces of which could be distributed to others outside the core management at Johnson's discretion—or not at all. The value of the management agreement, depending on how close the privatized company could come to hitting its performance incentives, was calculated to be as much as $2.5 billion over the first five years, with Johnson's personal take as much as $100 million. Johnson's team would get three of the seven board seats, one more than Shearson; the other two would go to independent directors. If major parts of the company had to be ditched to pay off the purchase price, so be it; Johnson fully expected to sell a sizable portion of the food business, starting with Del Monte. And if the buyout effort failed—if the board of directors he had so deftly cultivated now recommended against his proposition to the stockholders or another group outbid him—he would still walk away with a king-size severance package as one of the settlement costs to unseat him. It looked like a no-lose gamble to Ross Johnson, the non-company man.

But Johnson was a rookie when it came to playing with the big boys of Wall Street. He did not grasp that his role in so vast a transaction could not be merely to negotiate himself a goodly piece of the action and then retire to the sidelines to let his bankers do whatever punching and kicking might be needed. Whoever was putting up the money got to call the tune, even if Johnson had been the agent provocateur behind the effort. He also misjudged how the RJR board of directors felt about him. If he supposed that his steady cultivation had purchased from them a willingness to suspend the rules of the game or bend them in ways to facilitate his raid on his own company, he soon learned otherwise. For all his pledges of concern about the interests of stockholders, employees, and the corporate welfare, Johnson's governing impulse was, in the end, recognized as thinly varnished self-interest.

The titanic struggle for possession of RJR Nabisco, the largest takeover battle yet in U.S. financial history, was played out over forty days beginning in mid-October of 1988. It was front-page news across the country and would be chronicled in a best-selling book that appeared soon after the event—*Barbarians at the Gate*. The trigger of the hostilities was the price per share that Johnson's group offered to shareholders—$75, too low a premium over the market price of $55, to accomplish its purpose. Others, too, could calculate the liquidation value of the RJR Nabisco empire and figure how much more it might be worth in pieces than as a tobacco-driven money machine slowly running out of steam. Chief among the takeover specialists drawn to the prey was Kohlberg Kravis Roberts & Company, headed by the stern and daring Henry Kravis, a dealer credited with both rectitude and sharklike tendencies, who was far more disciplined and infinitely more calculating a player than Ross Johnson. The RJR board, pledged by law to obtain the best possible deal for its shareholders, opened up the bidding. In the end, Johnson had succeeded in getting his stock's price up, all right—to a winning bid of $109 a share, or almost twice what it had been before the LBO was announced—only it was Kravis's firm that made the bid. The price, larger than the treasuries of whole nations, was nearly $25 billion, almost $19 billion of it represented by a complex package of debt instruments, most notably junk bonds.

The last person Kravis needed to make this immense gamble pay off was the airy chief executive officer who came with the prize. Wall Street had had Ross Johnson for lunch, but it tipped him lavishly; he descended from corporate Olympus on a golden parachute worth $53 million and left behind a once proud company, brimming with debt, fearful of imminent bloodletting all over the payroll, at the mercy of hard-eyed New Yorkers, and unlikely ever again to challenge Philip Morris for supremacy in the cigarette business.

VIII

PLAYED out almost simultaneously with, but far less publicly than, the RJR buyout was exactly the opposite sort of scenario, orchestrated by Philip Morris's chairman. Unlike Ross Johnson, Hamish Maxwell had elected to build his business, not to cash it in. And unlike RJR, his company was being amply rewarded by Wall Street for its problematic entry into the food business. Its stock had risen and split two for one within a year of the GF takeover as domestic tobacco margins kept growing, the international unit kept adding to its position in Europe—No. 1 in market share since 1982—and formerly closed or greatly restricted markets in the Far East were in the process of being forced open through the friendly services of the U.S. Trade Representative. And the company's big, new stake in food legitimized Philip Morris as never before. Maxwell, relishing his expanded empire, went shopping again.

His keenest need was for dynamic management of his food business, and he thought he saw it in place at the company Wall Street valued higher than any other in the food industry—Kraft, Inc. Based in suburban Glenview a dozen or so miles north of Chicago, the big food processor had sales of $10 billion, the largest piece in the dairy products business, which it dominated with such brands as Kraft and Velveeta cheese, Philadelphia Brand cream cheese, Breakstone's butter and sour cream, Parkay margarine, Miracle Whip salad dressing, and Breyers and Sealtest ice cream. Its per-share net had advanced 11 percent after inflation in 1987, far ahead of General Foods' performance and among the best in the industry. It would mesh perfectly, moreover, with GF, since there was virtually no duplication in their respective product lines, and many obvious economies could be realized in marrying the two food businesses; the refrigerated trucks that delivered Oscar Mayer's meat products, to cite one example, could equally accommodate Kraft's dairy line. To add to its allure in Maxwell's eyes, Kraft was also the second-ranking entry in the U.S. food service business, supplying restaurants and institutional cafeterias, and recorded more sales overseas than any other American competitor.

Perhaps Kraft's most important quality, from the Philip Morris perspective, was a managerial style and philosophy palpably different from General Foods'. The latter seemed to be distracted by the form of things—frilly business practices, exotic R&D, elaborate training programs, little of which seemed to be converted into higher earnings. Kraft, on the other hand, was very much a sales- and operations-directed company, not unlike Reynolds Tobacco in its heyday, with a bottom-line awareness that succeeded because, as one top veteran there put it, "We don't have a lot of smartassed M.B.A.'s standing around here." The only real knock against Kraft as a strong takeover candidate for Philip Morris was that its heavy dependence on dairy products made it vulnerable to changing dietary habits.

Kraft was run in 1988 by its sixty-year-old chairman, lawyer John M. Richman, and president and chief operating officer, Michael A. Miles, eleven years his junior and with the company since only 1982. Miles was widely rated the coming marketing and managerial superstar of the food industry. Cool, thoughtful, and articulate, he had majored in journalism at Northwestern and had worked for ten years as an account executive at the Leo Burnett ad agency in Chicago. Among his clients was Heublein's Kentucky Fried Chicken subsidiary, which badly needed managerial help, and, liking both chicken and Louisville, where KFC was headquartered, Miles took up the challenge the company offered him. Preaching McDonald's founder Ray Kroc's back-to-basics formula of quality, service, cleanliness, and value, Miles rose to the KFC presidency in six years and turned the operation around. Its growing success was one of the reasons RJR had paid more than a billion dollars for Heublein in 1982, but when Reynolds could find no challenging use for him, Miles was glad to be offered the Kraft presidency. Richman soon found in him a rare blend of manager, communicator, analyst of both products and people, and, above all, "a man who doesn't like to lose."

As Kraft president, Miles enlivened the company's advertising, redeployed talent, pushed for divestitures of distracting and less profitable non-food units like Tupperware plastic kitchen containers and Duracell batteries, and moved vigorously into fresh marketing avenues with 350 new products or line extensions. Special stress was put on "light" dairy lines for the weight-conscious, like Light n' Lively yogurt and low-fat versions of its cream cheese and salad dressing. Miles spent money as well for some things not always measurable in earnings reports, like the hundred scientists enlisted to improve reduced-fat technology and a $35 million, two-year effort to develop tamperproof packaging. "He's crucial to the value of Kraft," his former boss at Heublein, Hicks Waldron, said of Miles.

That value was very much on Hamish Maxwell's mind as he sat down with his outside banking advisors and the Philip Morris planning brain trust in mid-1988 to determine how best to lay siege to Kraft. While the bloom was decidedly off the rose in Wall Street's harvest of mergers and acquisitions following the stock market's nosedive the previous October, it had not wilted altogether. Keener strategizing was the order of the day, though, in a more unforgiving bargaining climate. Bidding too low, as Ross Johnson discovered, succeeded only in stirring up your prey and inviting other bidders to the fray. Too high a bid, on the other hand, in an attempted preemptive strike ran the equal risk of exhausting the predator's bankroll before adding the sweetener almost certain to be required to close the deal. Not wanting to be perceived as the aggressor in a knock-down takeover fight of the sort that had not been needed to win over the docile General Foods management, Maxwell and his advisors concluded that the way to win Kraft was to come in with a strong, all-cash bid hard for shareholders and the target management to spurn and for other bidders to match or top, and then to be prepared to pay whatever more it took. The truth was that Kraft had precisely what Maxwell wanted—solid and steadily growing earnings, famous brands to add to the General Foods collection, able management, global reach, low debt, and, for good measure, an overfunded pension plan.

Its own virtues were well known to Kraft's management, and it was no secret that Philip Morris wanted to expand its commitment to the food industry. For several years Richman and his top executives had been meeting periodically with their New York counsel, staging "war games" to prepare for any takeover thrust, but the bigger Kraft became and more highly valued by the stock market, the less likely the threat seemed. Only a few entities had the money and need to risk a hostile takeover, and Philip Morris was the one usually cast as the model villain at Kraft's skull sessions.

Even so, Richman was shaken during a Monday morning meeting with his executives in mid-October 1988 when he was handed a note saying that Hamish Maxwell had phoned and asked him, with British restraint, to please call back because "it is reasonably urgent." Richman had met Maxwell at food industry events since Philip Morris had taken over GF and found him likably undemonstrative; he had never given the Kraft chairman a clue as to his intentions. Now, as he heard Maxwell out, Richman thought the PM chairman sounded cordial but scripted when he expressed regret that legal necessities dictated that the takeover move assume the form of a "tender" offer to Kraft shareholders, giving them twenty days to accept or reject the bid price. Technically, there was no pressing reason for the tender offer—Maxwell could have tried negotiating directly with Kraft's management and board. But a tender was swifter, and perhaps kinder because more honestly confrontational than protracted bargaining, which could readily turn bitter, since the targeted management had no wish to be ousted. Maxwell's offer was ninety dollars a share, nearly 50 percent higher than the market price and twenty-two times Kraft's 1988 estimated earnings. The bid, which Richman thought was "high and clever," was worth $11.5 billion. The only costlier one had been Chevron's $13.3 billion buyout of Gulf Oil.

Kraft's New York lawyers and financial advisors took over three floors at its suburban Chicago headquarters for the next two weeks, as company officials met with them late into the night to plot a response to the assault by Philip Morris. And the clock was running. What kept the tension level tolerable for the Kraft executives was the understanding that they were not exactly being threatened by a savage marauder who would wolf them down and leave only a pile of bones in their memory. The high price of the tender offer was surely a compliment, albeit a backhanded one, for the way Kraft had been managed. "We were being acquired for all the right reasons—our franchises and our people—to be built on and not sold off piecemeal," Richman recognized. Even so, they were not about to surrender without a fight; the goal was to extract every last dollar they could from their unwelcome New York admirer.

Kraft had several choices in trying to repel Maxwell's advances. Its top officers could have tried to engineer a leveraged buyout of their own, as Ross Johnson was even then attempting at RJR. But that would have involved such extreme dislocations and pressures that the company might be wrenched to pieces in the effort. Nor did its core management feel compelled to own the company in the hope of vastly greater financial rewards—and, surely, in the face of grave risks. Alternatively, Kraft could have tried to enlist a "white knight," another and presumably friendlier bidder who might defeat Philip Morris and leave current management in place. But as Richman knew, "There were not many out there that could afford it," and few who had Hamish Maxwell's incentive. "It never seemed to us that there would be another likely contender."

Conceivably, though, Kraft might have driven off its insistent suitor by insulting it with a "merchants of death" defense. It could have denounced PM as a bunch of immoral killers trying to extend their deadly grip and marshaled the antismoking movement under its banner in an all-out public-relations campaign. The idea was hashed over in the Kraft crisis center for several hours, but neither Richman nor Miles had the heart for what would have amounted to a lie so far as they were concerned. "It was not a moral issue for us," Richman recounted. "It was a straight business decision. Smoking has its risks—we all know that, and nobody made any bones about it." Miles, known to be an ex-smoker and rumored to be uncomfortable about the prospect of working for the nation's leading cigarette seller, later denied harboring such sentiments. "I had no qualms [about the takeover] from the product point of view," he said. "I had fear of the unknown about Kraft's being taken over by anyone." Upon familiarizing himself with the literature on smoking, he would tell interviewers several years later that "the risks attributed to cigarettes are greatly exaggerated" and that the causation charge had never been proven to his satisfaction. Smoking, like abortion, was a matter best left to the individual, Miles believed. Their personal convictions aside, the damning of Philip Morris might have had consequences inimical to Kraft investors. "The most you could probably have hoped for," Richman calculated, "was the well would be so poisoned that maybe Philip Morris would go away—and you would have deprived your stockholders of a very attractive offer."

Kraft's only realistic response to the takeover bid was a recapitalization of its assets to give its shareholders a plump dividend, big enough for them to accept in place of the Philip Morris proffer but not so rich as to drive the company deep into paralyzing debt. A leveraged "recap," as the Wall Street patois termed it, pledged the company's assets for the loan to pay out the big bonus to stockholders without actually buying out their equity interest, which remained in the form of a "stub," or small piece of the overall recapitalization until the loan could be paid down. The arrangement would surely have required rigorous economies and a sell-off of weaker units (and possibly some strong ones), but it was preferable to limply surrendering the company intact.

But how high would Kraft have to go to stave off Philip Morris? Not all Kraft people were convinced the sky was the limit for Maxwell, no matter what his resources. Some believed that he might go to $100 a share, but no higher. "We really believed the Philip Morris offer was inadequate in the world in which we lived," Richman recalled. "This was not just a struggle on our part to remain independent and to drive up their price." Richman's management team had no illusions, knowing, as he put it, that "we weren't going to be doing business at the same old stand. But it was by no means obvious that we wouldn't succeed in the recap proposal," so long as it was "a legitimate, competitive offer." Deep down, though, Richman felt that Philip Morris would keep on coming.

He gave Miles the critical job of formulating an operating plan on which the recap could be based; how much could Kraft extract in earnings from each of its units compared with what it would bring if put on the auction block? "There was no thought given to saying, in effect, 'We'll figure all of that out later,' " said Richman. "We had to be able to live with it." The offer to Kraft shareholders, announced a week after the Philip Morris tender, was a package said to be worth $110 a share—or $14 billion for the whole bundle, the largest recap proposed in American corporate annals. Each holder was to receive

$84 per share in a cash dividend, $14 in junk bonds, and the rest in the equity "stub," its value placed at $12 in accordance with an overall debt/equity ratio of 90 percent. In presenting the package, Richman portrayed Kraft as the victim in a situation "not of our making" but part of a prevailing temper in the economic community that favored "short-term financial gratification over steady, long-term growth." The recap, he was confident, would work but would "require herculean efforts by our employees."

But Wall Street analysts and traders scrutinized the Kraft package with concern. The value of the junk bonds in it was debatable because they were of the "cram down" variety, not to be sold on the open market but foisted on shareholders with the maturity and interest rate to be determined. Nor was the true value of the stock "stub" beyond debate. The true value of the package was between $100 and $103, according to the Street consensus. Quickly exploiting this appraisal, Maxwell issued a statement suggesting that there were serious questions about the "feasibility" and "real value" of the Kraft counteroffer. In contrast, he said, the Philip Morris tender offer would keep Kraft intact and not require it to mortgage its future.

The next day, Richman fired back that Maxwell's "disparaging remarks" had been "totally consistent with Philip Morris's pressure tactics to buy Kraft on the cheap." Pressure it surely was, but there was nothing cheap about Maxwell's offer. Indeed, it was Richman's offer that was the more suspect, as Kraft's stock price peaked at $102, well below the level that Richman said the recap package was worth. Meanwhile, Maxwell stayed his hand, in no hurry to raise his offer against the recap, and investors began to wonder if Philip Morris would counter at all. Slowly Kraft shares began to dip. They fell below 100, the suspected Philip Morris resistance level, to 96½ when the market closed at the end of the second week of the tender offer. It was low enough to bestir the watchful PM chairman. He signaled his Wall Street counselors to contact Richman's people and suggest a meeting of the principals. Philip Morris was not about to match Kraft's recap number, but it would come close enough, Richman heard, to justify the session.

Maxwell jetted into Chicago's O'Hare Field that same evening and came to Kraft's airport hotel suite for a face-to-face showdown. Although their advisors were hovering in the wings, the meeting was mostly just between Maxwell and Richman. The two chairmen were hardly a pair of frothing bears locked in combat to the death. Their earlier public exchange, it was understood by the parties, had been as sharp as need be yet as civil as could be. Soda and cookies were the refreshments.

Richman had come into the room with his mind fixed on $106 a share. Maxwell, who struck the Kraft CEO as astute and deceptively low-key throughout the course of the evening, opened at $104, and Richman, having extracted another $1.75 billion for his company above the initial tender, breathed easier. He said $106 would be more like it, and Maxwell, too, knew there would be a meeting of the minds—but since each half-dollar he raised the per-share ante would tack on $62 million to the final price, he was in no hurry. They talked of many things—about their companies, about how Philip Morris had no intention of moving Kraft from its Illinois moorings, about managing the food business, with promises neither sought nor made that Kraft people would run a giant Kraft-General Foods division, although both parties understood that was one of the prime motives for the transaction. Maxwell raised his offer fifty cents, and they talked some more, and then he raised it again and they called in one of Kraft's financial people to discuss the pension fund—and by 1 a.m. Maxwell put out his hand and agreed to Richman's price.

The final figure came to $13.1 billion. When the deal was disclosed to the press over the weekend, Maxwell was asked if he had any further immediate acquisition plans. "No," said the Philip Morris chairman, "this is enough for this year." His newly expanded company became the seventh biggest in the nation in terms of revenues and the largest single advertiser—the latter distinction spurring cries of alarm from public-health advocates, fearing that the media would be all the more readily muzzled on the smoking issue. The company soon issued a statement pledging that it would not apply its growing musculature in so unseemly a fashion.

Among the 47,000 new employees Hamish Maxwell had acquired in the Kraft deal, perhaps the single most important was Michael Miles. But Miles was not overdosed with hubris; he was not even certain that he had a job with the takeover management. Reassurance was quick in coming. Maxwell had him fly to New York toward the end of the week in which the deal was sealed and apologized that he could not place the Kraft president on the Philip Morris board of directors just yet in view of Richman's designation as vice chairman—it would have been a bit too much Kraft representation too soon. Miles was promptly named, though, to coordinate the new Kraft General Foods operation (no hyphen), whose products would now capture one out of every ten dollars spent in U.S. grocery stores.

I X

THE job that Michael Miles won, running the largest U.S. food company, had been coveted by the man who had played a central role in projecting Philip Morris into the midst of that industry—chief corporate planner Ehud Houminer. Having masterminded the General Foods and Kraft deals, Houminer could conceive of no more stimulating challenge for him than running the food enterprise.

Intellect was never Houminer's problem. "He was a brilliant and enjoyable man in private exchanges," said one colleague from their days together at Philip Morris International. "But he didn't understand that you needed other people's skills to run an organization. He'd always worked only for Hamish." Maxwell, known to prize brains and modesty as prime virtues in his executives, settled for only the first in Houminer's case, and probably suspecting that his crack Israeli staff man had been stricken by one of his occasional episodes of egomania in asking for the top food job in the nation without ever having run anything before, said no. But he had a nice consolation prize for Houminer—the presidency of PM-USA, where unit sales were only creeping ahead and, reports had it, the chairman felt that complacency had taken hold. Houminer might serve as his lash and keep the company's biggest money-maker trim and driven.

It was one of Maxwell's few mistakes as chief executive. Houminer trusted nobody and was thought to be constitutionally incapable of accepting counsel from his intellectual inferiors, *i.e.*, everyone he dealt with. "He had to prove every hour of every day how bright he was," recalled one top subordinate. "He took other bright people and drained them and spit them out, like Dracula." Houminer was heard to berate most of the staff he inherited for incompetence and could not understand why the company had to waste money on the Masters program, rewarding wholesalers for doing what they should have done in the first place, and on larcenous placement fees to retailers who should have been eager to give prominent display to Philip Morris's top-selling brands. "It stuck in Ehud's craw that we were No. 1 in the marketplace," recounted his sales vice president, Vincent Buccellato, "but couldn't call the tune for the industry." Houminer frightened and offended jobbers with claims of Philip Morris's infallibility and invincibility, and if some of them could not survive without a dole from the company, that was unfortunate. "He was not thought of as our friend," said Ronald Sosnick, a major West Coast wholesaler. He also made life miserable for many working under them, forever carping, sometimes showing them up at high-level meetings, and finally carrying penny-pinching to the point of obsession. In the end, several of Maxwell's trusted younger executives went to the chairman and told him that the situation was out of control. Since PM-USA's unit sales had done no better under Houminer, there could be no pragmatic justification for retaining him. He was replaced after a year and a half by the personable and mercifully less scintillating William Campbell, a Maxwell devotee.

The stock market loved Maxwell and his confident direction of Philip Morris's torrent of surplus cash. With its position in the food business solidified by the Kraft acquisition, the company's stock doubled in price, and by the middle of 1989 it announced a 22 percent dividend increase and a four-for-one stock split. On top of the two-for-one split only three years earlier and previous splits, the action meant that each share of PM stock bought in 1966 was now worth 192 shares in 1989 dollars.

Nor was the company resting on its laurels. Finding arch tobacco rival RJR reeling from debt after the leveraged buyout, Philip Morris moved to widen its market share lead by adding to its sales force and persisting in aggressive pricing, which served to hurt Reynolds's fading full-price brands and drive it deeper into the discount business, where lower margins threatened to drain off the cash flow the new Kravis ownership needed to pay down its immense debt. "I can assure you that we plan to take advantage of any opportunities that the changed situation [at RJR] may bring," Philip Morris vice chairman William Murray told *The Wall Street Journal*, a hint of relish in his words. The company was on such a roll that even when a situation did not work out quite as envisioned, it made money. Its $350 million investment in Rothmans in 1981, in the hope of eventually buying out the South African company's founder and controlling force, Anton Rupert, and meanwhile preventing RJR from becoming a major player in the international cigarette business, had led nowhere in particular. Rothmans remained a distant third behind leaders Gallaher and Imperial in the British market; joint selling efforts by Rothmans and Philip Morris like the one attempted in Malaysia had proven ineffective; and Rupert, at seventy-three, was showing no willingness to part with his jewel. Maxwell, confident that his company's growing penetration of the European market made its large minority holding of Rothmans stock superfluous, cashed it in for $860 million, a half-billion-dollar capital gain.

A *Fortune* magazine survey reported in January of 1990 found Philip Morris to be the second most admired American corporation, largely because it had given its investors just what they were after. Over the 'Eighties, the company had posted an average return on equity capital of 30 percent a year, the highest in U.S. industry for the period, and annual per-share gains in net of more than 20 percent (compared with 16 percent for Ford, the most lucrative American automaker, and 7 percent for no-longer-so-blue-chip IBM). And Hamish Maxwell's appetite had not yet slaked. Presented with an inviting opportunity later that year to add to his swiftly coalescing food empire—precisely the sort of move that RJR could no longer entertain, given its groaning debt burden—the Philip Morris chairman snatched it.

Klaus J. Jacobs, by avocation a Swiss Olympic equestrian and leader in the scouting movement, was also a complex and combative entrepreneur, of the Anton Rupert stripe, out to build an empire in the coffee and chocolate business. Grandnephew of the founder of the Jacobs coffee business, launched in Hamburg late in the nineteenth century, he took over the family enterprise after establishing a holding company in Zurich in 1974. Eight years later, he shocked the confectionery world by purchasing the leading Swiss chocolate makers, Suchard and Tobler, Belgium's celebrated Côte d'Or chocolates,

Italy's Du Lac, and Palvides of Greece, all added to Jacobs's leading market position in both the chocolate and coffee business in Germany, France, and Austria. For good measure he plowed $720 million into U.S. candymaker E. J. Brach, best known for its jelly beans, and inquired of Hamish Maxwell whether he might care to part with General Foods' problem-ridden coffee business.

Maxwell did not encourage Jacobs, but then, in an unexpected turn, the Swiss tycoon discreetly reapproached the Philip Morris chairman to ask if he might be interested in buying control of his entire operation, Jacobs Suchard AG, then grossing $4.7 billion. The company was netting just 4 percent on its sales, but Maxwell had several reasons to covet it. Profit margins in the European food business traditionally ran behind those in the U.S. market because of the smaller scale of operations and higher distribution expenses due to trade barriers. But those barriers were expected to begin falling in 1992 as the European Economic Community became a reality and a huge transnational market beckoned. The acquisition, moreover, would add substantially to the Kraft General Foods (KGF) presence on the Continent, making the Philip Morris food venture the third largest in Europe, where the industry was growing at a faster rate than in the U.S. And the price was right—$3.7 billion, or about twenty times earnings. Just why the volatile Jacobs was prepared to sell so soon after his flurry of buying was unclear; financial analysts suspected that his resources had been overextended, especially by the Brach purchase, which was losing heavily.

Whatever Jacobs's reasons, Maxwell found Jacobs Suchard—*sans* Brach, which was not included in the deal—a solid enterprise and said he would proceed provided that the Swiss company was not shopped around. The transaction was accomplished expeditiously, and entirely with Philip Morris's own funds. Thus, Maxwell's empire grew by 16,000 new employees spread over the twenty countries where Jacobs Suchard operated, and his global sales surged past $50 billion by the close of 1990. Food now accounted for more than half of the company's revenue and two-thirds of the payroll though only one-third of the net. But signs were encouraging of higher profitability on the food side, as Michael Miles was able to do enough cost-cutting to post a 25 percent gain in KGF earnings on a rise of just over 3 percent in sales. Tobacco, though, was still king at Philip Morris, as Marlboro sales accounted for 26 percent of the U.S. cigarette business; the brand was rated the largest-grossing branded consumer product on earth for the moment. And the company's overall return on equity hit the spectacular annual rate of 33 percent.

Even so, a few purists complained that the Maxwell-Houminer-Storr strategy of leveraging on the huge free cash flow from cigarette margins had, by strict accounting standards, not worked. The $5.4 billion it had netted on sales of $79 billion from its food acquisitions over the 1985–90 period fell $337 million short—applying the 9 percent average prime lending rate in effect over that span—of the borrowing charges on the $22.8 billion that the company had paid to become a food titan. That is, the strategy amounted, in practice, to deleveraging. This was, however, a rarefied and exceedingly narrow view. In fact, the company had paid back most of the borrowed principal, so that earnings, if sustained, would soon increasingly outstrip debt charges; meanwhile, Wall Street had kept bidding up the price of Philip Morris stock, as the architects of the food strategy had foreseen, so that investors were realizing a bonanza in terms of total return (dividends plus stock price enhancement)—at least on paper. If Maxwell had overpaid, he had gained a whole new world and future for his company.

All of this success, and perhaps his own recent heart surgery, may have contributed to a slight softening in the company line about the health charges against smoking as noted in the 1990 annual report, the last one to bear Hamish Maxwell's signature. The formal Philip Morris position now was:

> We have acknowledged that smoking is a risk factor in the development of lung cancer and certain other human diseases, because a statistical relationship exists between smoking and the occurrence of these diseases. Accordingly, we insist that the decision to smoke, like many other lifestyle decisions, should be made by informed adults. We believe that smokers around the world are well aware of the potential risks associated with tobacco use, and have the knowledge necessary to make an informed decision.

Never before had a major tobacco manufacturer acknowledged the hazardous nature of its product; the concession in the form of a warning on the cigarette pack, attributed to the Surgeon General, had been made only under duress from Congress. To be sure, Philip Morris had not exactly donned a hair shirt, and one could argue with the failure of the company report to concede anything beyond a statistical link in view of the overwhelming body of clinical and histological evidence. But it was no longer a die-hard denial: the annual report left it to smokers to decide the merits of their habit while recognizing the peril it presented to them. Had the industry said no more—and no less—over the years as medical science was lodging its charges, its moral position would have been strengthened. Or at least it would have had a basis for claiming one.

X

PHILIP MORRIS may have been the darling of Wall Street, but on Main Street a growing segment of the public viewed the company as peddlers of a deadly substance. To improve this image as soon as possible after he became chairman, Hamish Maxwell named a bulky, creative Tennessean, Guy L. Smith IV, to be vice president for corporate affairs, and told him to "make something happen."

A former newspaperman in Knoxville and later press secretary to that city's mayor, Smith had won high grades as a publicist over an eight-year stint with the company's beverage subsidiaries, Miller Brewing and Seven-Up. Summoned to corporate headquarters for the ultimate challenge any public-relations man could hope to face, he brought to the task several useful assets— charm, guile, not even a scintilla of perceptible guilt, and a very large budget. His tactics were mostly diversionary, in more than one sense. At their core they were an elaboration of the program that George Weissman, a past master at the craft, had persuaded Joe Cullman to embrace: associate the company at every opportunity with positive social values, institutions, and ideas, and if it behaved like a sterling corporate citizen, people would overlook the unfortunate tendency of the core product to shorten life expectancy.

Smith focused his efforts on staging or sponsoring public spectacles and practicing strategic philanthropy. The former took "mass-and-class" forms— sports and popular music events to attract the widest audience possible, and high-art, even avant-garde, exhibitions and performances to reach the monied and educated elite who ran much of society or shaped its opinions. The philanthropic outlays had to be highly visible, reach people who badly needed the help, and present at least the appearance of altruism. A subcategory of giving allowed for coalition-building in the form of ad hoc grants to recipient groups whose mission or plight was transparently useful to the company.

Beginning after the broadcast ban on tobacco commercials took effect in 1971, the company's investment in sports sponsorship was essentially a repackaging of the *verboten* cigarette ads, combining a heavy on-site presence with far-flung visibility through televised signage at arenas. At its least complicated, this meant renting space for and erecting giant billboards or scoreboards at major league ballparks and flaunting the Marlboro brand name—only Dodger Stadium in Los Angeles and Wrigley Field in Chicago did not permit such displays. At its most involved, it meant heavy outlays— Philip Morris's Virginia Slims tourney, for example, cost $17 million in annual prize money alone by the late 'Eighties—and saturation brainwashing of the crowd. Of PM's trackside effort during the Marlboro Grand Prix, targeting young males who were the brand's most desirable customers, marketing services vice president Ellen Merlo explained, "We have samplers and sweepstakes booths, we give away branded merchandise, we have signage around the track. We have a media center where we supply information about [the] . . . car series. We make the drivers available for interviews. . . ."

All of these colorful efforts were aimed at associating smoking with the wholesome ambience of athletic prowess, youth, strength, and the excitement of nonlethal combat, obscuring the habit's link to disease. They also purchased easy access to young people without the obvious appearance of targeting them, as well as the complicity of sports administrators. The president of baseball's American League, Bobby Brown, a former New York Yankee infielder and a physician, told *Washington Monthly* writer Jean DeParle in September 1989 that "it's unrealistic for tobacco advertising to be removed from baseball parks," because the companies would just put up the ads somewhere else—as if that excused their presence there, or any other site offered a comparably large captive viewership in person or via telecasts of the games. Television people were hardly more discerning or contrite. The ABC network's sports program director, Lydia Stephans, said of Philip Morris's access to millions of potential customers through its sponsorship of the televised Virginia Slims tennis circuit, "I think it's clever. They've found a loophole. . . ." And the athletes themselves, recognizing their meal ticket, testified unapologetically to the company's brazenness and their own gratitude for it. "Virginia Slims is our sponsor," said Pam Shriver, who made millions from the sport, " 'cause they're a great sponsor. Too bad they're a cigarette company."

Philip Morris pranced so gracefully through the world of the visual and performing arts that *The Wall Street Journal* was driven to anoint it in 1988 as "a twentieth-century corporate Medici, the art world's favorite company." Its outlay as patron of the arts was in the $10-to-$15-million-a-year range by the late 'Eighties—about one-fifth of what it spent on sports promotion. The identity linkage here was more subtle but was not lost on the cognoscenti. Posters, programs, catalogues, and ads prominently mentioned the company as prime benefactor of as many as twenty art exhibitions a year, ranging from regional museum shows to traveling international retrospectives, and dozens of regional and repertory theatrical companies around the nation. Most notable in this latter category was the company's support of the leading cultural institution in Hamish Maxwell's home borough—the Brooklyn Academy of Music, which received ongoing grants to help establish its New Wave Festival, one season featuring a nine-hour, three-part adaptation of the 100,000-verse Sanskrit epic, *The Mahabharata*, staged by British director Peter Brook and requiring among its props a fiery pyre, a pool of water, and thirty-five cubic yards of mud. Brook was feted at a luncheon hosted by Philip Morris, which immodestly noted, in a 1990 report, its role as "an arts patron on the cutting edge of contemporary sensibility."

The company's most constant presence in the art world took the form of chief patron of the dance. It contributed significant amounts to the Joffrey and Alvin Ailey troupes, the American Ballet Theatre, and some fifty smaller companies, sustaining virtually an entire art form and displaying its generosity to a high-powered elite that consisted of not only authentic dance-lovers but also a wider circle of lacquered arts patrons, opinion-creators, showbiz celebrities, and their fawning hangers-on. There was, of course, nary a whisper about the product during any of this. "I don't talk about health and smoking in the middle of an art show," Philip Morris chairman George Weissman would remark. "We hope people will come away with favorable impressions of the company—that we are cultured human beings like everyone else, not a bunch of barbarians."

No less skillfully deployed was the company's social philanthropy, budgeted at about 1 percent of pretax corporate earnings and concentrated upon those in earnest need of funding and recognition. By the late 1980s, this program came to about $50 million annually. Other leading philanthropic companies gave more in proportion to their revenues—some twice as much as Philip Morris—but none achieved greater visibility for its gifting. Seventy percent of PM's 3,000 grants in 1990 were for under $10,000; typical were $5,000 gifts to the New York chapter of the American Civil Liberties Union and the Hispanic Bar Association of Pennsylvania. Larger gifts went to a wide array of nonprofit causes, from seed money for the nation's first "multimaterial" recycling facility outside Atlanta to sustaining grants to New York City's Holy Apostles Soup Kitchen. Most emphasis was placed on educational causes, with gifts ranging from a small grant for disadvantaged preschoolers in Little Rock to multimillion-dollar donations to the Gateway literacy project in Philadelphia.

Calling the public's attention to these less visible boons required some ingenuity. In the case of a million-dollar grant to the New York Public Library for the cleaning of 3.5 million volumes, the company spread around bookmarks that noted the project and instructed library patrons on how to care for their own collections. Less subtle was a two-page ad in *The New York Times Magazine* discussing Strive, an East Harlem job-training and placement program for disadvantaged youth. In Strive, the ad explained, Philip Morris had found some hope in a neighborhood of crime, drugs, and family violence, "and we're proud to support their efforts." That support amounted to gifts totaling $75,000 over three years, doubtless admirable in and of itself but more than a touch suspect in light of the cost of the horn-tooting *Times* ad, which came to about the same amount as the contribution itself.

Antismoking advocates charged Philip Morris with seeking "innocence by association" through its strategic gift-giving to cultural institutions and social causes, but in this effort to improve its appearance and win recognition as a good citizen, how was the company different from any other? "Let's be clear about one thing," George Weissman had said in 1980. "Our fundamental interest in the arts is self-interest." The difference, of course, resided in the hazardous nature of its product, so that Philip Morris stood accused of passing out blood money in seeking expiation from the society it victimized. Even if its philanthropy sprang from a guilty conscience, though, did that make the program reprehensible and its recipients tainted?

The moral problem seemed to crystallize in either of two circumstances—when the company pretended to noble instincts and when its beneficiaries denied all social responsibility for the activities that had generated the money bestowed on them. "If we gave a million dollars to Mother Teresa, they'd find something wrong with it," remarked Philip Morris spokesman Tom Ricke in 1988. "We do it because it's the right thing to do." If doing right was indeed Philip Morris's guiding star, however, tobacco industry spokesmen would not have made a career of challenging every new finding by science that regular use of their product could lead to grave medical consequences. The far more debatable issue that Ricke opened up was whether his designated paragon, Mother Teresa, given her mission to salvage the lives of perhaps the most hopeless souls on earth, ought to have accepted a donation from his company if it had in fact been offered. Should any individual, agency, or institution devoted to saving or enhancing life have faced an ethical dilemma in accepting funds derived from sales of a product that certifiably hastened death for millions?

For some of Philip Morris's beneficiaries, to hear them tell it, the question never arose. The company made a point of selecting causes in dire need of financial support and without the luxury to be fussy about their benefactors. "To tell you the truth, I'm not that interested," Alison Dineen, fellowship director of the Women's Research and Educational Institute, responded when asked if she suffered any qualms about accepting tobacco money. "I'm just glad they [Philip Morris] fund us." Said a spokesman for the Ailey dance troupe, "If it were not for the support of the Philip Morris Companies, we would be forced to curtail many of our activities." On another occasion, the Ailey's general manager, Peter Brown, suggested—with perhaps a touch of hyperbole—just how unselective his group had to be to survive, telling *The Wall Street Journal*, "We would accept money from the Mafia if they offered it." Behind such a remark was the implication that no one who helped the genuinely deserving needy could be all that bad. Indeed, the worthiness of the recipient organization's mission overrode all other considerations that might have decently excluded a donation as compromising. "If you deny us the support of enlightened members of the private sector," the Ailey's William Hammond asked on another occasion, "where is the money to come from?" Enlightenment, in such a view, consisted largely (if not entirely) of adequate appreciation of the recipient group's contribution to humanity; the giver's contribution—or destructiveness—was irrelevant. Noted Karen Brooks Hopkins, vice president of the Brooklyn Academy of Music, a prime recipient of Philip Morris largesse, "There are so many people who do absolutely nothing for the arts. Let's go after them. . . ."

Carried to its ultimate, this line of rationalization denied the existence of such a thing as dirty money. As James Kraft, the Whitney Museum's assistant director of development, once phrased it, "Very few fortunes in the world were achieved through goodness." Philip Morris's George Weissman put it a touch more archly: "Only the gurus on top of the Himalayas are clean." Valid up to a point, such observations served, however, to relieve beneficiaries of any need to reach moral judgments; not all riches are amassed by equal feats of ruthlessness or oppression—and some souls are actually cleaner than others even at altitudes less lofty than Tibet's. Such a judgmental process would necessarily be fraught with difficulty and perhaps even pain, as the Metropolitan Museum of Art's vice president for development, Emily Rafferty, implied in commenting, "If we got into the middle of this [form of moral evaluation], we would question everything." The far easier path, of course, was to question nothing, avoiding tiresome considerations of decency and mindlessly accepting all gifts as sanitized by the recipient's need.

Although much was made of the no-strings aspect of such cultural philanthropy, there were inevitable small paybacks. When Philip Morris needed a suitable site for the awards ceremony for an essay contest it had run on the splendor of the First Amendment (and its claimed right to advertise cigarettes and anything else legal), the New York Public Library, its volumes now pleasingly dust-free, readily obliged its donor. Lincoln Center, the nation's prime showcase for the performing arts, on whose board George Weissman was a powerhouse, let its jazz festival bear the name of the sponsor, Marlboro. The Ailey troupe protested to Surgeon General Koop that he was unjustly pillorying Philip Morris, its "enlightened [and] generous patrons," and contended, "A nation has a cultural health as well as a physical health"—as if to imply that the latter could somehow, sometimes, justifiably be held hostage by the former.

What the eager recipients of tobacco money lost sight of—or averted their eyes from—was the real service they were performing in return. Thomas P. F. Hoving, former director of the Metropolitan Museum of Art and a willing vessel in his day for the flow of tobacco bounty, put it bluntly by charging that his own and other such eminent institutions had been "prostituting themselves" by allowing cigarette makers to trade on the cultural centers' status as pillars of the community and to bask in the sunlight of communal approval like honorable citizens who made their living with clean hands. How could any worthy social enterprise, from soup kitchen to world-class museum, entirely escape the charge of selling its soul when it let a rogue industry purchase absolution with ill-got lucre?

The moral dilemma was forcefully stated for the antismoking movement by the Advocacy Institute's Michael Pertschuk, who argued in his 1987 pamphlet, *Smoke Signals*, that the tobacco companies were waging a campaign for legitimacy by masquerading as the Good Corporate Citizen when in reality they were "death and disease merchants . . . profiteers from human misery . . . drug pushers. Culture can survive without providing a cloak of legitimacy for an industry that kills. . . ." But when an Advocacy Institute associate of Pertschuk expressed this view to a top officer at a leading New York museum, he was told, "Oh, grow up!"

Harsh social realities, then, generally routed any serious consideration of whether tainted means should be embraced to advance worthy ends—such as, in the case of the African-American community, survival itself. Philip Morris was an early contributor to black causes and steadily expanded this program, giving to the NAACP, the Urban League, and the United Negro College Fund, sponsoring black cultural events, patronizing black-run banks and insurance companies, and advertising prominently in black media. Did the fact that a higher percentage of black Americans smoked than whites constitute an ulterior motive—racial targeting—on the company's part? A better question was whether African-Americans battling for social justice knew or cared that their fellow blacks died at a disproportionately higher rate from smoking-related diseases—40 to 50 percent higher in the case of lung cancer—than white Americans and thus might plausibly oppose tobacco company exploitation as genocidal.

On the surface, the black community's approach to the question was little different from the cultural community's. Donald Hesse, vice president for development of the Urban League, told *Common Cause* magazine in March 1989 why it accepted tobacco money: "We're really trying to do a lot with very little. . . . How do we keep the doors open?" His organization's criteria for accepting contributions from a company, he said, were that "it does not ask us to endorse their product and is a legal entity." Mafia money, at least, was out. And nothing as gauche as an implied product endorsement was purchasable (unlike Lincoln Center's Marlboro Jazz Festival). But the black community was susceptible to exploitation in a subtler fashion, one that suggested what might lie behind Philip Morris's otherwise estimable show of interracial concern. At a two-day 1985 conference in New York for 200 black editors and publishers, sponsored by Philip Morris, keynoter (and veteran company officer) Hugh Cullman asserted: "Today tolerance for my smoking may be under attack. Tomorrow it may be tolerance for someone else's right to pray or choose a place to live. So the real issue isn't smoking against nonsmoking—it's discrimination against tolerance."

Thus was posited a bond of victimization between all smokers and all blacks. Just how effective this sort of bonding could be was detectable in remarks delivered the year after the editors' conference by John Holoman, president of the *Herald Dispatch*, serving the black community in Los Angeles, who denounced recent antismoking regulations as discriminatory and dreamed up by "people with a lot of free time on their hands" who wrongly assumed black support for their cause. Kissing off the health hazards of smoking as decidedly secondary to African-American concerns about hypertension, sickle-cell anemia, teenage pregnancy, and the ravages of narcotics, Holoman charged that the real enemy was not cigarettes but the continuing American failure to correct long-standing social injustices. Besides, he said, "the strident exhortations to restrict smokers" hurt an important American industry that had been good to blacks. This same note of kinship was sounded by Harlem's Representative Charles Rangel, who said he found no ulterior motive in the tobacco industry's courting of blacks—an argument, he claimed, that was "only raised by health groups and white liberal groups as far as I know. . . ." Added another prominent African-American politician (and a heavy taker of campaign contributions from tobacco), California Assembly Speaker Willie Brown, "I'm not concerned about smoking—it's not my issue. I'm concerned about substance abuse."

But that was precisely why—beyond the industry's claim that blacks and smokers were equally subjected to intolerance—the cigarette companies were so strongly suspected of targeting black Americans as customers: they had too much else to worry about to ponder the possible blessings of a smoke-free society by the year 2000. As University of California sociologist Troy Duster discovered while directing an intervention trial in smoking cessation among black youngsters in the San Francisco Bay area for the National Cancer Institute, his subjects were preoccupied with "crack and the rejection and irrelevance of their labor." Indeed, they resented efforts, however well intended, to discourage them from smoking, one of the few cheap, legal pleasures easily available to them. Trying to convince them that they were injuring themselves by persisting in their tobacco habit, Duster began to feel, was as far removed from reality as Malthus's instruction to the teeming and overfertile poor to refrain from the procreative act.

Any suggestion that they were exploiting the miseries of the black underclass evoked cries of indignation from the cigarette companies. They insisted that they were in no way deviating from their standard marketing and philanthropic practices in dealing with the African-American sector of the population. Its ad and promotional allocation to the black community, Philip Morris said, came to 12 percent of the total, just a bit more than its proportional share of the population. A Reynolds spokesman declared it "highly offensive" to suggest that blacks were being taken advantage of by the tobacco industry and were somehow incapable of reaching the same judgment as the rest of the nation about the desirability of smoking.

It was precisely that judgment, though, that the prevalent social pathologies afflicting the black subculture could skew, as Duster and other sensitive observers understood, casting African-Americans as unwitting accomplices of the tobacco industry's political agenda as well as its commercial prey. A case in point was the vocal but ultimately unsuccessful effort during the mid-'Eighties by Hazel Dukes, president of the New York state conference of NAACP branches, to oppose office smoking restrictions proposed by the New York City Council. Dukes argued that the public-health measure was steeped in racial bias, because under the workstation arrangements outlined in the proposal, smoking would be forbidden in the open and shared office areas, where blacks were disproportionately numbered among the secretaries and clerks, while being permitted in closed or private offices, usually occupied by white executives. When *The New York Times* editorialized in print what others were thinking—that the tobacco industry was buying political allies by its heavy donations to the black community—Dukes answered angrily, "Our opposition is based on a long tradition of confronting discrimination that the white mainstream and majority press often ignore." In parroting the industry line, the NAACP spokeswoman saw no difference between discrimination based on behavior found to be antisocial and unhealthy (*e.g.*, smoking in close proximity to nonsmokers) and discrimination based on factors entirely beyond an individual's control (*e.g.*, race, national origin, age, appearance, physical handicap). She had also missed the truly troubling point that if blacks were numerically preponderant in open office spaces where smoking was to be restricted, it was precisely the black nonsmokers among them who were being most heavily victimized by exposure to secondhand smoke.

A growing number of black leaders, though, were coming to understand their community's vulnerability to the smoking peril and began speaking out against an easily overlooked form of victimization. One of black America's most prominent medical practitioners, Harold Freeman, chief of surgery at Harlem Hospital and the 1988 president of the American Cancer Society, accused the tobacco companies of trying by its philanthropy and patronage to buy silence from the black community, "already suffering a disproportionate burden of disease and death," and converting it into "a special target for a lethal product." U.S. Representative John Conyers, Jr., of Michigan, in his thirteenth term in the House, noted the prevalence of sickness and death in black America from the products behind tobacco philanthropy: "There's no way we can compartmentalize our lives conveniently to say, 'Thanks so much for your promotion,' and ignore the statistics." The case was more vehemently stated in 1988 by Reed V. Tuckson, commissioner of public health for the District of Columbia, who labeled the tobacco industry's philanthropic programs among blacks a "predatory strategy" with the sole goal of making money: "They go to the people of color; they go to women; they go to the poor. . . . There is a meanness to this greed that is unprecedented in its intensity, tenacity, and consequences. It is unjustified by any standard of humanity. . . ."

XI

CHIEF Philip Morris publicist Guy Smith was able to afford a magazine all his own—a weapon of particular utility in an age in which broadcast sound bites were inadequate to spell out detailed views on complex issues. Having its own megaphone also allowed the company to encourage its customers and reassure them that their smoking did not make them morons or malefactors.

Overcoming internal objections by company lawyers fearful the publication would say too much that could come back to haunt them in court, Smith launched *Philip Morris Magazine* late in 1985 with a free circulation of 125,000, culled largely from names of those who had bought brand-monogrammed merchandise from PM. During the next six years, it evolved into a four-color, forty-eight-page bimonthly with a claimed circulation of 13 million and became the costliest item in the corporate affairs budget. The circulation list also provided a splendid data base whenever the company needed to enlist political support against antismoking initiatives.

Smith felt that in order for the magazine to work, it had to be "more than a corporate hype sheet," so he splashed it with lively graphics, name writers, and a cheery tone that allowed its propaganda content to be easily sugar-coated. Each issue was a studiously low-brow celebration of a wholesome, outdoorsy American lifestyle in which smoking was a natural but not overly prominent component. Amid this fluff one also came upon surveys purporting to find that 96 percent of smokers indulged for the sheer pleasure of it and that only 2 percent of restaurant-goers objected to smoking by others while they ate—figures wildly at odds with more disinterested surveys on those questions; a salute to Defense Secretary Caspar Weinberger for preserving the sale of cigarettes at military commissaries, presumably as an act of patriotism; a screed by a self-proclaimed health-conscious vegetarian, asserting disbelief of any link between smoking and disease and preaching moderation in all things; and a letter from a man who said he walked six to nine miles daily without ill effects from the two packs of cigarettes and twenty cups of coffee he consumed.

Smith also moved to gain intellectual respectability for the industry by en-listing, through the Tobacco Institute and the services of its leading outside public-relations counselor, the Washington office of Ogilvy & Mather, a stable of social scientists from respectable quadrants of academia. Mostly econo-mists of the supply-side persuasion, these scholars dealt with the smoking issue largely in terms of political and econometric theory. The informal group, which was very well rewarded for its efforts, according to one former

Ogilvy & Mather publicist who worked on the agency's tobacco account, was headed by a former high-ranking FTC official, economist Robert D. Tollison, then director of George Mason University's Center for the Study of Public Choice, a think tank for the dissemination of libertarian values, in particular free-market pragmatism as antidote to the misguided intrusiveness of welfare-state activism.

A prime example of this group's contribution was a 1986 book of essays, edited by Tollison and subsidized by the industry, entitled *Smoking and Society: Toward a More Balanced Assessment.* In his introduction, Tollison argued that there was "a useful scholarly case to be made that the conventional wisdom about smoking behavior is either wrong, unproven, built upon faulty analysis, or pushed well beyond the point of common sense." Tollison's contributors conceded virtually nothing to the evidence of ravaging effects of the habit and dwelled instead on its perceived high value to users. Sherwin Feinhandler's essay, "The Social Role of Smoking," held that the use of cigarettes "helps the smoker cope with the demands of life, eases and promotes his or her social interactions and is a valuable aid to the establishment of a sense of identity." At the root of "the vehemence of the antismoking campaign," he added, was the suddenly widened context of environmental pollution, in which "the cigarette has become a tiny representation of the industrial smokestack"—in short, a scapegoat for a far more legitimate object of alarm. A more withering view of the antismoking movement was ventured by Boston University sociologist Peter L. Berger, who portrayed many of its members as "singleminded, aggressive, even absolutist"; given to the language of hyperbole (*e.g.*, smoking termed an "epidemic," "pestilence," and "the single most preventable cause of death"), and so consumed by their "quasi-religious goal" of robust health as "the formulaic key to a long and pleasurable life" that they were inclined to engage in "emotional violence" toward those who did not share such a "virtually sacred" goal.

Tollison himself co-authored a second and more telling volume in 1988, *Smoking and the State*, also funded by the Tobacco Institute, in which he argued that smokers willingly pay the price for the risk of damaged health and in fact make less—not more—use of welfare-state medical benefits, because they die younger than nonsmokers. He also railed against the paternalism implicit in cigarette excise taxes, aimed at protecting the "unwashed" from their "sins" and turning them into easy political targets long conditioned to hearing about the irresponsibility of their habit and thus incapable of mounting a counteroffensive.

Whatever pity had formerly been reserved for the self-destructive tendencies of smokers was transformed over the course of the 'Eighties into a growing intolerance of the sort that Tollison, Berger, and even some who were not in the tobacco industry's pay had begun to characterize as health fascism. Energized by the claim that environmental tobacco smoke posed a proven health peril to nonsmoking bystanders, the intensified vilification of smokers caused them to be denied the use of cigarettes while guests in nonsmoking homes (and admonished for their weakness, in the bargain), stared at and sometimes insulted in restaurants although abiding by the rules of the establishment, relegated to separate work areas, and even faced with a hiring bias on the ground that their habit made them an economically poorer risk than nonsmokers—a test rarely applied to other risky off-the-job preferences like a fat-drenched diet, mountain-climbing, or driving fast. Carrying the issue to an extreme, a few illiberal employers even required their avowedly nonsmoking employees to submit to testing of their urine for traces of metabolized nicotine. That antismoking sentiment might be getting out of hand was suggested in an August 12, 1991, *Time* cover story headlined "Busybodies: New Puritans," which noted that some 6,000 U.S. companies were by then refusing to hire confessed smokers and lamented that, under the delusion that laws and restrictions were necessary to protect people from themselves, many Americans had lost sight of a bedrock national virtue—tolerance.

XII

B ESIDES the unrelenting derogation of their product and the prospect of being sued out of existence by its users, nothing alarmed the tobacco companies more during the latter part of the 'Eighties than the rising call for an outright ban on all advertising and promotion of cigarettes. The industry's outlay for this purpose, more than $2 billion annually, was its lifeline, preserving the surface respectability of smoking by associating it with pleasurable and life-enhancing activities as a counterweight to the health charges against it.

In seeking to extend the 1971 ban on broadcast advertising of tobacco, the antismoking forces were arguing that the First Amendment ought not to serve as a license for the cigarette makers to lie and distort the truth about their deadly wares. The broadcast ban had escaped the constitutional strictures against governmentally muzzled speech because the airwaves were held to be public property and therefore subject to regulation for the common good; because electronic media suffused the popular culture, allowing impressionable children easy access; and because cigarettes were held to be a uniquely dangerous product that could not, as a practical matter, be outlawed. But to ban *all* advertising and promotion of a legal product, however dangerous, raised harder questions.

The First Amendment, clearly understood to ensure individual expression free of restraint by the state, indisputably protected political opinions, artistic statements, and assertions of religious or any other innermost convictions. But commercial speech had traditionally been viewed as a different and lesser species, falling within the government's constitutional powers to regulate business. Indeed, commercial speech was treated as a form of commercial activity, and thus it was of the essence that contracts, the public offering of merchandise or services, and warranties pertaining to them—all forms of communication between buyer and seller—be truthful and safeguarded by the government under its charge to protect the general welfare. Utterances by corporations were especially held subject to government regulation since, as artificial persons created mainly to make money, their speech was considered less fragile than individuals' and their power disproportionate in the arena of ideas as well as commerce. The twentieth century witnessed a codification not only of what businesses could not say (as manifested, for example, by FTC regulations against false, misleading, or unfair advertising) but also in certain cases of the forms of speech they had to adhere to (as prescribed, for example, by the Securities Act of 1933 with regard to the public offering of securities only through a statutorily formatted prospectus, registration statement, and tombstone advertising).

Hope of extending this trend to an all-out ban on cigarette ads and promotions using brand names was dealt a blow, however, by the Supreme Court's 1976 ruling in *Virginia State Board of Pharmacy v. Virginia Citizens Consumer Council, Inc.* upholding the previously denied right of pharmacists to advertise the price of prescription drugs. Advertising of legal products that was truthful and not misleading was entitled to First Amendment protection, the high court held, striking a balance between the public's right to information about goods and services, the seller's right to state it, and the government's right to regulate commercial activity. "Advertising, however tasteless and excessive it sometimes may seem, is nevertheless dissemination of information," the Justices wrote, and in the interest of facilitating the "numerous economic decisions" at the heart of the free-enterprise system, "the free flow of commercial information is indispensable." But cigarette advertising, according to anti-smoking activists, conveyed precious little information and a great deal of overblown lifestyle imagery that was inherently deceitful for failing to disclose clearly the health peril from the product, thus undercutting the small statutory warning included in tobacco ads.

The commercial free-speech doctrine was elaborated four years later by the Supreme Court in a fashion that encouraged tobacco control advocates. In *Central Hudson Gas & Electric v. Public Service Commission*, the Justices struck down the effort by a state agency to encourage fuel conservation by barring a utility company's advertisements promoting the use of electrical products; in the process the high court set down a four-part test for government-imposed restrictions on commercial speech. These could be justified only if the ads were untruthful or deceptive, or if the government had a substantial interest in the matter, the restriction directly advanced that stated interest, and it was narrowly tailored to achieve that objective. Tobacco industry lawyers thereupon trotted out their old contention that if the avowed government interest in a cigarette ad ban was to reduce consumption, it would not advance that interest, because advertising did not broaden the cigarette market but only shifted smokers around in their choice of brands, and, besides, such a ban would plainly be too sweeping a measure, serving only to deny smokers useful information.

The Supreme Court seemed to help the industry by its 1983 ruling in *Bolger v. Youngs Drug Products*, overturning a ban on the unsolicited mailing of circulars for the sale of contraceptives, because they might fall into the hands of young people or children. The adult population could not be reduced to reading solely what was fit for children, the Justices held; only ads explicitly and exploitively directed at children could be barred. Thus, the antismoking advocates' contention that cigarette advertising ought to be ended because it served to entice children seemed to be shaken. The tobacco industry pressed home its basic argument: If a product is legal, so must the advertising of it be.

By 1986, Congressman Mike Synar was pushing a comprehensive cigarette ad ban bill and attracting serious interest in the idea. In backing it, the American Medical Association, awakening from its long sleep on the smoking issue, commissioned a pair of top Columbia law professors, Vincent Blasi and Henry Paul Monoghan, to make the legal case for such a ban in view of the twists and turns of the Supreme Court in determining whether commercial speech merited First Amendment shielding. The professors argued that since falsity and deception were adequate grounds for ad restrictions, one needed to go no further in applying the *Central Hudson* test; cigarette advertising, flamboyantly promotional in nature, was far more deceptive than informative. And since the government had "a clear and substantial public interest in reducing cigarette consumption," an advertising ban made much more sense as public policy than "a vastly more intrusive interference with personal freedom" in the form of banning the product itself.

The Supreme Court zigzagged once more in the 1986 5-to-4 ruling in *Posadas de Puerto Rico Associates v. Tourism Company of Puerto Rico*, unsettling the tobacco companies and civil liberties champions alike. The *Posadas* opinion stemmed from the Puerto Rican government's effort, dating back nearly forty years, to attract tourism by legalizing casino gambling. In order to discourage Puerto Rican residents from participating, it forbade casino ads addressed to the native population. Without bothering, under the *Central Hudson* test, to examine whether the statute directly advanced a legitimate government interest, the majority opinion by Chief Justice William Rehnquist held that "it would be a strange constitutional doctrine" that conceded to a legislature the power to outlaw a product or activity but denied it authority to ban advertising of same. Though Puerto Rico's casino gambling was legal, Rehnquist wrote,

> it is precisely because the government could have enacted a wholesale prohibition of the underlying conduct that it is permissible for the government to take the less intrusive step of allowing the conduct, but reducing the demand through restrictions on advertising. . . . Legislative regulation of products or activities deemed harmful, such as cigarettes . . . has varied from outright prohibition . . . to legislation . . . with restrictions on stimulation of its demand. . . . To rule out the latter, intermediate kind of response would require more than we find in the First Amendment.

Antismoking advocates were gleeful. Professors Blasi and Monoghan declared that *Posadas* explicitly confirmed that the First Amendment "does not confer a constitutional right to advertise such an intrinsically and gravely harmful product" as cigarettes, which were deceptively advertised and remained legal only because of the historical accident that their use was "diffused widely before the hazards of tobacco were well understood." A total prohibition, while now scientifically justifiable, was politically implausible, the antismoking movement recognized, but "no constitutional imperative," observed the Blasi-Monoghan treatise, required that "a legislature must do everything or nothing at all." Columnist George Will, one of that rare breed, an antismoking conservative, endorsed the Rehnquist ruling by noting that cigarette ads "are not seminars; they are inducements" and that it would be "perverse to argue" that a legislature could ban a product or activity "but cannot regulate commercial speech that stimulates demand for the product or activity."

But one man's perversion is the next man's passion. Speaking for many civil libertarians, Harvard's Laurence Tribe assailed the sweeping implications of the *Posadas* ruling when he wrote that "the strange constitutional doctrine" that Rehnquist had dismissed as an illogical impediment to barring advertising when a legislature could outlaw the product or activity itself "is called the First Amendment." To University of Chicago law professor Philip Kurland, Rehnquist's *Posadas* opinion invited a grave undermining of the First Amendment, since virtually all economic conduct was subject to government regulation, up to and including total prohibition, and by that standard, all advertising was censurable. Rehnquist, in blurring the traditional distinction in First Amendment readings between speech and conduct, had found advertising to be the latter, Kurland wrote, and if government was thus entitled to regulate it, then the commercial free-speech doctrine was illusory and as good as dead.

Freedom of speech itself, then, regardless of content, was arguably a more hallowed and valuable liberty than the right to sell a particular product or activity, and it by no means necessarily followed that the silencing of speech—any speech—was a less oppressive form of intervention by government than outlawing an objectionable product or activity. The question was explored widely in the press while Synar's cigarette ad ban bill languished in Congress. In a March 7, 1987, symposium in *The Nation*, the American Civil Liberties Union's executive director, Ira Glasser, argued that the health peril associated with cigarettes was not an adequate reason to except the product from First Amendment protection: "Once danger becomes a permissible basis for abridging speech, the only question is, Who defines what is dangerous? . . . Indeed, the purpose of the First Amendment is precisely to remove such discretion from government officials, including judges." The amendment had suffered terrible erosion in the name of national security in the McCarthy era—grim testament "to the tendency of courts to allow illegitimate government claims of danger to justify censorship," Glasser wrote. "When they come after abortion clinic ads, using as precedent the liberal arguments in favor of banning cigarette ads, it will be too late to invoke the protection of the First Amendment." Michael Pertschuk, a careerist in practical politics, responded that such disquisitions on the nature of cigarette advertising were "unworldly," while Peter Hanauer, president of Americans for Nonsmokers' Rights, argued that the question really turned on the "uniquely dangerous" nature of cigarettes, a product "that is harmful when used in precisely the manner for which it is intended."

In the shadow of this debate, three of the most astute smoking control advocates co-authored a paper in the winter 1987 issue of the *Journal of Public Health Policy* which revealed the transparency of the tobacco industry's claim that no governmental interest would be directly advanced by banning cigarette advertising, because such expenditures were not intended to attract new smokers, only to switch present smokers over from rival brands (see, for example, page 23 of *The Great American Smoker's Manual*, a Philip Morris publication intended to rebut Pertschuk's *Smoke Signals*: "Cigarette advertising is aimed only at people who smoke . . .").

In their article, "Tobacco Advertising and Consumption: Evidence of a Causal Relationship," Joe Tye, Kenneth Warner, and Stanton Glantz noted that cigarette smokers exhibit "one of the most tenacious brand loyalties of any consumer product"—only about 10 percent of them switched annually, and then often to other brands from the same manufacturer. Citing industry figures for 1983, the authors went on, "A simple calculation shows that brand-switching alone could never justify the enormous advertising and promotion expenditures" of the tobacco companies, which paid out $1.9 billion, it claimed, so it could switch over 5.5 million smokers (one-tenth of the total number). That worked out to a $345 outlay per switcher in order to reap gross revenues from that switching smoker of $347, even assuming that all switchers came from other companies—hardly the case. Thus, no new profits could accrue from a transaction for that purpose alone, leaving only two economically viable motives for the huge expenditure. One was to hold on to customers who might be lured away by rival companies—a problem that might have been eliminated, of course, if none of the companies bothered or was permitted to advertise—as well as to those tempted to quit under the barrage of health charges. The second motive, of course, was to attract new customers, many of them necessarily adolescents, since most surveys agreed that about 90 percent of smokers began the practice by the age of twenty. And, contrary to repeated industry claims, Tye *et al.* listed many studies that found a reinforcing link between the impact of cigarette advertising on children and future use of the product (*e.g.*, "Out of the Mouths of Babes: The Opinions of Ten- and Eleven-Year-Old Children Regarding the Advertising of Cigarettes" by D. A. Fisher and P. Magnus in *Community Health Studies* in 1981, pages 22–26).

Whatever the legal, social, economic, or psychological justifications for entertaining a ban on cigarette ads and promotion, only the political will of duly elected legislators could make it happen. And that will, by the close of the 'Eighties, was not there. Even some antismoking activists were sympathetic to the view expressed by leading First Amendment attorney Floyd Abrams, hired to help protect the tobacco industry from such a blow: "[I]t is at the heart of the First Amendment that we do not lightly strike out at speech to deal with social problems. We try to persuade people . . . with more speech."

XIII

Not all of the publicity and promotional gambits that Guy Smith dreamed up for Philip Morris were inspired. There was the misbegotten 1988 exhibition in muscle-flexing, for example, when the company budgeted $5 million for an advertising campaign proclaiming the collective might of American smokers ("$1 trillion is too much financial power to ignore," the first one was headlined) by way of announcing that their customers were damned angry and weren't going to take it anymore. Just whom or what the flag-waving ads were targeting was unclear—possibly smokers themselves, to remind them that they were not alone in a hostile world.

But it was the American flag, not the company banner, that Smith waved in pulling off one of the more daring public-relations exploits in the annals of ballyhoo. Not only did he succeed in wrapping Philip Morris in the Bill of Rights and its cherished guarantees of tolerance—for smokers and smoking, along with other sometimes reviled groups and acts, it was implied though never stated—but even got the government of the United States to join in.

Spurred by fears that the proposed Synar bill banning cigarette ads might catch fire, Smith launched a 1986 essay contest in defense of the First Amendment and against attempted encroachments upon it; prize money totaled $80,000, with $15,000 to the national winner and, by way of maximizing publicity, $1,000 to the winner in each state. A year later, to announce the contest winner, the company issued an attention-grabbing press kit. It took the form of a glossy black brochure bearing on its cover in deep red a picture of the Order of Lenin, the Soviet Union's highest medal, and the words "One world-famous newspaper without cigarette advertising." Inside was a copy of *Pravda* and a 444-page volume, *American Voices: Prize-Winning Essays on Freedom of Speech, Censorship and Advertising Bans.* The stunt steamed up Congressman Synar, who as chief sponsor of the ban bill termed its linkage to Soviet oppression "the basest, grossest form of redbaiting to protect their multi-million-dollar investment." Smith, having struck a raw nerve, responded by adding innuendo to insult; the press kit did not imply that backers of the ban were "communists or anything else. . . . I'm certain they're all card-carrying Americans. . . . The purpose is to make the point that advertising bans are a form of censorship, and everything that goes into *Pravda* is censored."

Although Synar's bill was stymied in Congress, the ad ban idea would not die, and so when a letter crossed Smith's desk the following year from Don W. Wilson, the Archivist of the United States, seeking corporate support for the bicentennial celebration of the Bill of Rights to be marked in 1990, the wily publicist seized on it. Here was the ideal occasion to run up the company's tattered ensign in defense of its continued right to advertise.

Wilson, a 1987 political appointee who had worked for both the Eisenhower and Ford presidential libraries, believed that the U.S. Archives were "an unrecognized national treasure" and that his mission was "to take it to the people and not let it become a passive warehouse intimidating to the public." Disappointed by the Archives' low visibility during the bicentennial of the Constitution the year he arrived, he wanted to mount a major national exhibit to honor the Bill of Rights, the original of which was housed on his premises. Since Congress was disinclined to parcel him special funding for so marginal a purpose, Wilson began soliciting top corporate givers, even as other federal repositories like the Smithsonian and the National Gallery had done with success. He received polite turndowns from General Motors, IBM, and other corporate heavyweights but got more positive feedback from Philip Morris USA, which wanted to organize a conference around the First Amendment as the focus of its salute to a Bill of Rights exhibit. Wilson knew that Congress had been mulling a bill to ban cigarette advertising and feared that the PM-USA interest in the undertaking was "too pointed and too narrow," but when no other company came forward and a New York intermediary said he had a corporate client worth meeting with, Wilson found himself being spirited away to Guy Smith's Park Avenue office.

The company was now prepared to celebrate the whole Bill of Rights, and the distinction between Philip Morris's tobacco unit and its larger corporate parent was stressed to the Archivist; it was the latter entity that was prepared to undertake a major participatory role, as it had done with so many other leading cultural and social causes, and would forgo the use of any of the company's brand names and logos, so nobody could complain that it was pushing a controversial product in promoting the Bill of Rights exhibition. "I was very impressed with their forthrightness," Wilson recounted. "Smith was very clear about his motives—that the image-building aspect of the project was good for the company. And he said, 'You may get some flak over this.' " Wilson found that the company had a high standing as corporate philanthropist and that other federal showcases had not been tarred by accepting Philip Morris funding. The negotiations warmed.

Smith's vision of the event turned out to surpass Wilson's ambitious hopes. The company would not only pay for an exhibit at the old U.S. Archives building on Pennsylvania Avenue, replete with recordings of presidential voices, but would also mount an elaborate road show, bearing the document to every state under the joint Philip Morris and Archives banners. Because the national repository could not, of course, let the original of the sacred relic out of its hands, the company would have to settle for one of the original copies, themselves precious documents. Philip Morris went to its home manufacturing base of Virginia, where a copy was housed in the state library, which, according to later press releases, "graciously" lent the document for the tour. Graciously, perhaps, but not gratis: the company agreed to donate $250,000 to the library, pay the cost for a staff member to accompany the document and ensure its safekeeping throughout the projected two-year tour, and other considerations. Besides this elaborate traveling display, the company also planned to offer the public, via print and broadcast advertising, free reproductions of the Bill of Rights along with educational materials about it.

Any other company or organization could have done the same thing, of course, since the use of such a document was not available for exploitation on an exclusive basis, but the imprimatur of the U.S. Archives as sponsor of the bicentennial promotion proved purchasable. The price that Wilson set was $500,000—the cost of putting together the exhibition in Washington—and an additional $100,000 contribution to a corporate sponsorship endowment for future commemorative events. Wilson's staff was to review the company's traveling version of the exhibit and any materials Philip Morris planned to distribute in order to certify their accuracy and to guarantee that the project was not being grossly commercialized.

As the preparations advanced, Wilson felt reassured by the quality of every aspect of the company's efforts, from the excellence of the printing job on the reproduced Bill of Rights, to be sent to anyone who wanted a copy, to the roster of national organizations that had been enlisted as supporters of and hosts for the traveling exhibition, including the Veterans of Foreign Wars, the Daughters of the American Revolution, the Boy Scouts of America, the Kiwanis, and state and local bar associations. The proposed layouts for the ads prepared for the celebration by Ogilvy & Mather seemed duly uplifting yet spare and to the point. Typical was one bearing a large photograph of Franklin Roosevelt and his words in appropriately big type, "Those who have enjoyed such privileges as we enjoy forget in time that men have died to win them." A text block, unsullied by a hint of commercialism, read, "Today, as we approach the bicentennial of the Bill of Rights, let us all, as President Roosevelt asked of us . . . rededicate its principles and its practice." Who could object to that? The corporate payoff came in the relatively small-sized tag line at the bottom: "Join Philip Morris and the National Archives in celebrating the 200th anniversary of the Bill of Rights. For a free copy of this historic document," readers were invited to phone an 800 number or write to the company's Washington office.

Archivist Wilson looked at the proposed ads with open eyes. "I said to myself, 'There's risk here.' But we were going to reach millions with the message, identifying the document with the Archives." That it was similarly identifying it with Philip Morris, the nation's leading cigarette maker, was secondary; after all, they were paying for the linkage, and no one else had been willing to. The only uneasiness that the company's handling of preparations aroused in Wilson came from the belated discovery that the mailing tube enclosing the requested copies of the Bill of Rights (accompanied by a letter from PM chairman Hamish Maxwell) was imprinted with the names and logos of some of Philip Morris's leading products—Miller Lite, Birds Eye, Jell-O, and Oscar Mayer among them. But the company had had the sense to spare him embarrassment by omitting the brand names of its cigarettes.

Wilson would not be spared the embarrassment of his own folly, though, when news of the deal with Philip Morris reached the public. The first burst of ire was directed at the company for making off with one of the nation's enduring symbols of its liberty. Michael Pertschuk spoke for the tobacco control movement when he said that Philip Morris "should be treated like the Medellín drug cartel, not the Founding Fathers." Sidney Wolfe of Public Citizen thought the projected campaign "smears the Bill of Rights with the blood of all Americans killed as a result of smoking Marlboros and other Philip Morris cigarettes"—precisely the kind of line that a number of company insiders had feared the project would invite. Wilson and his misguided agency came in for abuse, too. As *The New York Times* editorialized, it was a noble idea for any company to commemorate the Bill of Rights, "but why on earth should a federal agency help it do that?" The government had allowed itself to be taken in by lending its "priceless prestige" to "a shabby transaction," the *Times* concluded. An Archives spokeswoman responded that the agency had thought it "very appropriate to stretch the taxpayers' dollars this way. My understanding is that we were dealing with Philip Morris the corporation, not a smoking company." Guy Smith concurred: "If [the public] think[s] well of the company through our support of the Bill of Rights, it follows that they'll think well of our products. . . . This has nothing to do with cigarettes, nor will it ever." Marketing experts saw through the scheme and thought it masterful. Said Al Ries of the Greenwich, Connecticut, consulting firm of Trout & Ries, "This is clever, subliminal advertising that really says, 'Smokers have rights, too.' "

By the time the Philip Morris Bill of Rights road show set out in the fall of 1990, most of the criticism of the sellout had abated, and the campaign's television commercials, patterned after its print ads, were image-building, as Smith had envisioned. When the specially designed truck bearing the elaborately displayed Virginia copy of the Bill pulled into Barre, Vermont, its first stop, it was accompanied by an honor guard of twenty-six former marines and greeted by local dignitaries and prominent press coverage. Attendance, particularly by schoolchildren, was good; visitors were invited to offer their impressions in a thirty-second videotape, and educational kits bearing the corporate name were dispensed at the site and through schools. Anticipating some protests, Smith had ordered a "speakers' corner" set aside near, but not too near, the mobile exhibition. At the first stop, antismoking protesters were hardly visible, but gay rights activists noisily challenged Philip Morris's contributions to homophobic Senator Jesse Helms. Smith looked on impassively, then purred to reporters, "This is what [the First Amendment is] all about. They're entirely entitled to their opinion—it's a minority opinion."

Threatened with a huge publicity triumph by its arch enemy, the antismoking movement belatedly tried to frustrate it. The problem was not to appear unpatriotic while denouncing the Philip Morris tour as a cynical public-relations stunt. The "antis," as the industry called its foes, networked frantically through Pertschuk's Advocacy Institute to organize a national protest, with the help of the company's tour itinerary, which allowed the timely staging of counterevents. Thus, the night before the Philip Morris entourage arrived in Albany, New York, the antis stole its thunder with a candlelight vigil lamenting the lethal nature of the sponsor's core product, and while they were at pains not to discourage the public from viewing the Bill of Rights, the diversionary purpose behind the tour was duly noted. A leaflet entitled *The Philip Morris Bill of Wrongs* denounced what it characterized as the company's efforts to squelch others' First Amendment rights, such as a suit brought against Alan Blum's DOC claiming copyright infringement for selling T-shirts imprinted "Killer Time—We're Having a Party," satirizing "Miller Time" ads, and the barring of Olympic diving champion and ex-smoker Greg Louganis from the company-funded U.S. Olympic training center at Philip Morris's Mission Viejo real estate development, because he had served as an antismoking spokesman for the American Cancer Society.

The antismoking movement's most effective device to undermine the company tour was a fifteen-foot-high replica of the Statue of Liberty, fashioned by the Washington state chapter of DOC. The statue, christened Nicotina, held up a lit cigarette in her right hand instead of the torch of liberty; chained to her left arm was a pack of cigarettes. Embedded in the pedestal, a cluster of Philip Morris brand cigarettes, butts, and ashtrays, was a digital counter tracking the number of smoking-related deaths that had, according to Public Health Service data, occurred since the Bill of Rights tour began. The company was not amused. Despite efforts to have her shunted from view, as at the Kansas statehouse grounds, where legislators apparently unfamiliar with the First Amendment tried to have Nicotina banned as an unpatriotic form of protest, the statue got hauled all over the nation by one antismoking group after another and often found its way into the press coverage of the company exhibit. By the end of the tour in the spring of 1991, Nicotina had tolled 521,558 American deaths attributed to smoking.

No one could say whether Philip Morris, for its investment in the Bill of Rights ploy, put at between $30 million and $50 million, had gained more celebrity than notoriety. What was known was that more than 4 million copies of the Bill of Rights were sent out under the company's letterhead.

18

Melancholy Rose

ALTHOUGH forces hostile to the tobacco industry grew as the 'Eighties unfolded, the cigarette makers had suffered little damage to their pocketbooks. True, U.S. unit sales kept sliding, but the market had proven well able to absorb steady price rises to compensate, and foreign sales were advancing smartly. In 1983, though, the industry's worst nightmare threatened to become a reality—a carefully mounted lawsuit by a smoker claiming damages due to the manufacturers' alleged failure to have dealt in a timely and forthright fashion with the question of how gravely smoking cigarettes imperiled human health.

For three decades, as medical evidence gathered on that topic, company lawyers had stood vigil against such assaults on the industry's bulging cash register from aggrieved claimants with little to lose and an available attorney willing to represent them on a contingency-fee basis. Not a cent in damages was surrendered by cigarette manufacturers. And their legal position appeared to be strengthened even as the consumer protection movement helped liberalize product liability law and encourage claims against negligent manufacturers. But since such negligence was often difficult and costly to prove, the doctrine of comparative fault had spread, abetted by another new legal concept: strict liability. As posited in the nationally authoritative American Law Institute's *Restatement of Torts* and examined by the profession over the first half of the 'Sixties, strict liability had shifted the law's attention from the conduct of the contending parties—*i.e.*, what did each know and what was their resulting responsibility for any harm caused by the product?—to the nature of the product itself. Some products were unavoidably dangerous, like sharp tools, tall stepladders, and medicines with strong side effects, but some were said to be "unreasonably" so on the ground that the risks accompanying their use were greater than their utility. Legal sages wrote at length on how to apply this risk/utility test to a given product. But the *Restatement*, in its often invoked "Comment i," called for denying an award for damages when the danger of a product "is contemplated by the ordinary consumer who purchases it, with the ordinary knowledge common to the community as to its characteristics. . . ." Cigarettes were explicitly cited in this hallowed text as an example of such an exempted product, even if they ultimately ravaged their users. In effect, the legal profession's philosophers were saying that cigarettes posed so notorious a health risk that their very danger protected them from liability claims by the forewarned consumer; tobacco manufacturers could not be expected to serve as perpetual health insurers for customers who fell ill.

This apparent reward for constituting a flagrant health hazard was reinforced by Congress in passing the 1966 cigarette labeling law. The single nationwide warning on all packs (and five years later in all advertisements as well) was designed to prevent chaos in the marketing of cigarettes and did not, on its face, seem to strike at the continued vitality of state common-law provisions for liability actions in which smokers could claim before juries that cigarette makers had injured them. The 1970 revision of the labeling act, however, in wording hardly contested by public-health advocates, barred not only all other warnings but any requirements or prohibitions with regard to smoking and health in the advertising and promotion of cigarettes "imposed by State law." Tobacco lawyers would insist that Congress was implicitly preempting all forms of state law, whether statutory, administrative, or common-law doctrine evolved from court filings, and whether enforced by injunctions, fines, or the award of damages. But were damages truly a form of state regulation if awarded because juries felt that claimants had not been adequately informed of the risks of smoking? If so, Congress would seem to have frustrated all hope of recovery by aggrieved smokers who had fallen ill from the habit after the warnings were mandated and thus handed the tobacco companies an impenetrable shield against liability, of a sort granted no other industry—odd public policy indeed, considering that no other industry's product was accused of taking so heavy a toll on human life.

Because the federal warning labels were not affixed until the late 'Sixties, claimants were of course free to sue cigarette companies on the ground of negligence for failure to warn before then. But only two dozen suits were brought during the 1970s, with only one reaching a jury—and again the industry prevailed. Legal scholars and public-health advocates were meanwhile developing a counterargument to the contention that universal knowledge of the hazards of smoking precluded liability suits. Could it be fairly said, they asked, that smokers who were felled by their habit had made an informed choice to take it up when (1) most did so in their callow youth, (2) most became compulsive users because of the undisclosed addicting power of nicotine, and (3) most were confirmed in their dependency by the industry's massive advertising and promotion, which glamorized the product, dismissed or minimized the health charges brought against it, and otherwise acted to subvert the force of the federal warning label? Perhaps the congressional warning was adequate to immunize the tobacco companies, allowing them to stand mute, to say no more about the risks their product entailed—taking the Fifth Amendment, as it were, against self-impeachment. But the cigarette makers had not let it go at that. They had spoken out repeatedly to reassure the public by stating their disbelief that smoking cigarettes was harmful, by associating them in their advertisements with a vigorous and pain-free lifestyle, and by insisting that the health consequences of smoking were being vigorously explored by industry-financed research, the results of which would be fully disclosed if they proved germane. Suppose, though, that the manufacturers knew that their product was extremely hazardous, but nevertheless kept saying otherwise to their customers—or were in fact not researching the matter purposefully and objectively, and were even suppressing findings in order not to scare off smokers? Surely, these legal commentators suggested, Congress could not have intended to confer upon the tobacco manufacturers the right to say anything at all about their product to lull or mislead the public. If the industry elected to speak out on the health issue, even if not required to, thanks to the labeling laws, surely it was obliged to tell the truth or face the consequences from suits for fraud, negligence, and intentional tort. The *Restatement*'s Comment i, moreover, exempting cigarettes from liability claims, was merely prescriptive and lacked the force of law; it remained for individual jurisdictions to determine what constituted an "unreasonably dangerous" product and the communitywide state of awareness of that peril.

This skeptical view of the legal invulnerability of the cigarette companies was bitingly rendered by a University of Houston law professor, A. A. White, writing the lead article in his school's May 1972 law review under the title "The Intentional Exploitation of Man's Known Weaknesses." Ever since the 1964 report to the Surgeon General, White argued, "only the obstinately blind or the willfully ignorant" could remain in doubt about the lethal nature of smoking, and thus it was proper for the law to look not only to the conduct of the presumably forewarned consumer but also to that of the manufacturers who had "aggressively promoted the use of this dangerous product . . . deliberately and continuously over the years despite . . . possession of overwhelming evidence that faceless tens of thousands would die annually from the captive use of their product." The congressional warning, furthermore, was inadequate on its face, falling "far short of conveying to the user the total relevant facts," while the industry's advertising constituted a fraud or at most a half-truth, never hinting at the tragic effects of cigarettes and pandering to the natural rebelliousness of youth in its "period of adventurous indiscretion." Since the tobacco manufacturers knew the high danger of smoking, their conduct "is callous as well as willful and wanton," so why should they alone among U.S. industrialists be declared free to take the lives of their customers? They ought, instead, White concluded, to be subject to damages as a cost of doing business until they halted their deceptive practices and made a genuinely less lethal product, if possible—or go out of business.

A decade would pass before American case law caught up with Professor White's juridical indignation and those who shared it. A robust and expanding application of tortious liability was brought to bear, meanwhile, on defective product design and failures to warn adequately, as juries returned hefty and in some cases angrily punitive damages. Nowhere was this tendency more advanced than in New Jersey, where that state's supreme court held in its 1982 ruling on *Beshada v. Johns-Manville* that liability could be found even if the full risk to health was unknown, or claimed to be so, by the manufacturer. Cigarette makers had long argued that causation had not been proven in the relationship of smoking to disease, but, as announced in *Beshada*, the law no longer required 100 percent certainty and held instead that the duty to warn arose when information became available "from which a reasonable inference might be drawn that there is a likelihood the product carries with it some type of *potential* hazard. . . ." The following year, in *O'Brien v. Muskin*, the New Jersey high court dramatically extended the scope of the state's product liability law in a case where the plaintiff asked for damages after diving into an aboveground swimming pool and injuring his head when his hands slid on the slippery vinyl pool liner. The court held that even though the plaintiff could not point to an alternative safer liner material or better design for the pool, a jury could find the product to be unreasonably dangerous—even if not defective—and to have failed the risk/utility test, given the marginal nature of swimming pools among life's necessities. The manufacturer would thus have to be willing to shoulder the burden of liability damages or quit the swimming-pool business. Particularly relevant to cigarette smoking was the added holding in *O'Brien* that in such cases of unreasonably dangerous but not defectively made products—and contrary to Comment i in the *Restatement of Torts*—manufacturers could not insulate themselves from liability claims "merely by placing warnings on their products . . . [and] regardless of the number of people those products maim or kill."

The potential impact of these rulings on liability claims against tobacco companies was not lost on New Jersey practitioners, among them a young, smart, and highly combative Morristown attorney named Marc Z. Edell. Son of a vitamin manufacturer and a native of West Orange, Edell had been sent off to New York Military Academy, where he acquired self-discipline and a martial bearing. After taking a business degree at Boston University, he went to unaffiliated New York Law School and became a driven and dogged attorney—"a pit bull," one latter-day colleague called Edell, not a large man—with dreams of stardom as a trial lawyer. Characteristically, he earned a first-degree black belt in karate, a skill he savored "because there's no backing up in it. It's all attack . . . there's no place to hide."

He began to learn his craft by defending pharmaceutical companies and did well at it. Soon he represented an asbestos company as that embattled industry fell into chaos over disclosures that it knew, a generation before warning workers about it, of the health peril that inhaling the fibrous material presented those who came into close contact with it. In the litigation process, Edell became expert in bronchial pathology, noting how much more prevalent lung cancer was among smokers than nonsmokers. He himself had once smoked, liked the smell, and as a self-controlled person believed that addictions such as smoking could be conquered if the will was there to do so. But as the asbestos damage awards began to mount—seventeen companies would be made to pay out $7 billion over the dozen years following the *Beshada* verdict—Edell saw a potential bonanza in pressing similar liability actions against the tobacco companies as well as the chance of a lifetime to grab fame.

To win, though, he would have to argue that damages awarded by juries for inadequate warnings to smoking victims were not a form of state action— impermissible under the federal cigarette labeling laws; rather, damages had to be cast as compensatory in nature, which might influence but did not coerce manufacturers to alter their conduct (in this case, to change their warning labels or simply pay the damages and carry on as before—the choice was theirs). Rather than relying on this fragile argument, Edell felt that he now had a far stronger weapon in the *Beshada* and *O'Brien* rulings. The adequacy of the cigarette warning labels was beside the point, the New Jersey courts had held, in the case of a product so unfixably dangerous that no plausible claim of utility could justify its use and no warning could immunize its manufacturer from liability suits.

Even with this new cudgel in hand, though, Edell had to face the intimidating practicalities of charging the ramparts of the tobacco kingdom. Product liability plaintiffs generally had limited financial resources, so their lawyers had to be prepared to sustain cases at their own expense in the hope of collecting a share, usually between one-quarter and one-third, of any damages awarded. Defense counsel, mindful that a single verdict against it could stir an avalanche of litigation that might bury the tobacco industry as it had the asbestos companies, were prepared to go to almost any length not to lose. Their tactics were to try to scare off or exhaust claimants long before their cases ever reached a jury, and to assist them they had a veritable standby army of scientific and medical experts as well as investigators not above using brutally aggressive means to uncover almost every aspect of a plaintiff's life, from dietary habits to degree of marital bliss. Plaintiffs' depositions were likely to be grueling, and industry lawyers were adept at tossing up mountains of legal debris—infinite procedural motions and objections, all designed to drain the pocketbooks and patience of claimants' attorneys and discourage the grieving families of claimants from sustaining the battle.

At age thirty-three, though, Edell was a battler, and after weighing all the discouragements with his older partners, he went shopping for a client prepared to face the ordeal. One partner discussed the project over dinner with a friend of his, a New York pulmonologist, who suggested that Edell visit a patient of his who had already undergone two lung cancer operations and was undergoing chemotherapy. On a warm August afternoon in 1983, Edell drove to the nearby working-class suburban town of Little Ferry to call at the immaculate home of fifty-seven-year-old Rose Cipollone (pronounced Chip-a-loan), a short, dark-haired woman going round with age. Even in depleted health, she struck him as spirited and frank. "I was laying it on the line, not trying to woo her," Edell recounted, "and telling her it would be extremely burdensome for her . . . putting the worst face on it, sort of testing her. You don't want to cajole someone who doesn't have the fortitude—you don't take on someone who just happens to be convenient for you at the moment."

They dwelled, of course, on her smoking habit; Rose Cipollone had averaged about a pack and a half of cigarettes a day since the age of sixteen. Their exchange was the beginning of Edell's education in tobacco and its enticements. "I was as ignorant as the rest of the public about the nature of nicotine addiction. People with a reasonable amount of self-discipline find it hard to understand how others can't control themselves." Their conversation grew so animated, Edell recalled, that "I didn't realize how sick she was." In fact, Rose was dying. Two weeks passed before the call came into his office advising that she was prepared to bring a liability suit against the three cigarette makers whose brands she had smoked for twenty-five years before government-ordered warning labels went on the packs.

One advantage Edell enjoyed with Rose as his client were studies showing that women smokers encountered considerably more difficulty breaking the habit, investigators believed, because they generally exercised less control over the circumstances of their lives than men and had to endure more stresses in juggling their multiple roles as workers, homemakers, mothers, and lovers. Society allowed men, moreover, to vent their aggressions and frustrations in overt ways denied to women, such as keen competitiveness, long frowned on as unfeminine. A metabolic stimulant, smoking also served as a weight control and thus a beauty aid, to many women's thinking, as well as a symbol of their liberation from male oppression—a notion cultivated by tobacco manufacturers for more than half a century. But even as cigarettes may have been a consolation to women for one form of powerlessness, they also induced another kind of enslavement—to the addicting powers of nicotine. Many of these emotional factors had come into play in Cipollone's life.

Rose Defrancesco grew up on New York's Lower East Side, one of four children, in the midst of the Depression; her father, a barber, was a smoker, but her mother was not, finding the habit unladylike. Because her father's shop accepted posters promoting Hollywood's latest films, Rose was given passes to the neighborhood Loews theater and often after school would attend that dreamland, enraptured by glamorous queens of the silver screen like Bette Davis, Joan Crawford, and Norma Shearer. Rose noticed two things in particular about her film idols: they always seemed to be wearing evening gowns, not regular dresses like she did, and they smoked a lot. She cadged old fan magazines from the neighborhood junk collector and clipped them to make scrapbooks devoted to her favorite stars, and she dressed herself in a downstairs neighbor's grown-up clothes, rolling up little paper tubes in emulation of filmdom's cigarette-wielding temptresses. But smoking was forbidden to the Defrancesco children; she became a nail-biter instead and confined her performing artistry to a self-taught talent playing the piano for her music-loving but poor family. After her father died of a stroke at fifty—her mother blamed it largely, and probably correctly, on his smoking—Rose at sixteen followed her older sister and began to smoke, buying two or three cigarettes at a time at the corner candy store and indulging in them in the girls' room at her high school. She picked Chesterfields, because she thought they were glamorous and ladylike, and ads for the brand stressed their mildness. Smoking seemed "cool, grown up—fantastic," she would tell the tobacco company lawyers who deposed her in 1984. She dropped out of school early in her senior year to help her family make ends meet, working as a packer for a scarf manufacturer, a secretary for the New York Philharmonic, and a billing clerk. By eighteen she was a pack-a-day smoker.

She was twenty-one when she met handsome, strapping Antonio Cipollone at a street festival near her home. Tony, who had emigrated from Sicily as a teenager, shared Rose's love for music; they soon married, and Tony proved a devoted husband, laboring as a rigger at U.S. navy yards and later as a cable-splicer for U.S. Steel, eventually running his own small wire business on the side. They had three children, moved from the city to New Jersey, and lived a pleasant, modest suburban life. There was only one source of dissension in their marriage—her smoking.

"He hated it," Rose readily acknowledged. "He didn't like the smell—he didn't like my smell. . . ." She was a class mother for the PTA, she played the organ at their church, she hosted dinner and card parties at her home, she did the bookkeeping for Tony's business, and she kept their snug home spotless—

and she smoked all the while. The first thing she did every morning was to put a pot of coffee on and light up a cigarette—Tony, who put in twelve-hour workdays, had long since gone to his job—and would go through thirty or forty cigarettes before her last one just before she went to bed (she never smoked in the bedroom itself). She did her best to keep the smoke away from Tony, who said it was bad for his hay fever allergy and told her over and over it was not good for her health, either. When she ran out of cigarettes, Rose, who did not drive, tended to panic. Sometimes she would call the local food market for groceries the family did not really need just so she could have cigarettes delivered with the order. And if she ran out at night, she would dispatch Tony to the store for a pack. Sometimes he returned with the wrong brand, and Rose made him go back for hers. When she was pregnant for the first time, she had tried to quit—with moderate success—but during labor she consumed a whole pack and never again tried to quit. Tony promised her he would buy her a fur coat if she would quit; she didn't, but her adoring spouse got her the coat anyway.

Rose was health-conscious enough to switch in 1955 from Chesterfield to Liggett's new filter brand, L&M, having noticed ads "talking about the filter tip, that it was milder and a miracle, it would keep the stuff inside a trap—whatever." She saw "all this brown in the bottom of the filter. . . . I figured, 'Gee, that's good,' " and believed L&M would be a cleaner, fresher smoke. Liggett's lawyers asked her, after her suit had been filed, whether she had concluded that the brand was safer.

> A. No, there was advertising that made the determination for me.
> Q. The advertising didn't say those cigarettes were safer . . . ?
> A. They gave me that impression that they were. . . . They would say "milder, low tar, low nicotine."
> Q. So you assumed that meant safer?
> A. I assumed that meant safer.
> Q. But they didn't say they were safer?
> A. If you say so.

When the Surgeon General's 1964 report appeared, Rose was fully aware of it. But, she admitted, "I didn't want to hear it. I never gave any thought to giving it up. I liked to smoke—I liked the way I looked—[it] gave me something to do. . . ." The government report frightened her a bit, certainly, but she was "sure that if there was anything that dangerous that the tobacco people wouldn't allow it and the government wouldn't let them. . . . The tobacco companies wouldn't do anything that was going to kill you . . . so I figured until they proved it to me . . . I didn't have to take it seriously. I'm being very honest with you. Maybe I didn't want to believe it." Even when the warning labels went on, she refused to believe it. The antismoking commercials ordered by the FCC soon followed, and Tony often pointed them out to her. She remembered one that went, "Smoking—it's a matter of life and breath," and got lectured by her granddaughter, who told her, "Grandma, smoking kills." Yet she kept on.

Rose Cipollone, in short, had a textbook case of what academics termed "cognitive dissonance". A pair of social psychologists, Harold Kasarjian and Joel Cohen, both of whom would testify in the *Cipollone* trial, had suggested in the autumn 1965 issue of *California Management Review* how smokers dwelled in a constant state of disequilibrium because their dependency conflicted with the human impulse to survive and continued "in the face of undeniable and overwhelming evidence that cancer is directly attributable" to smoking. "Information can be denied, distorted or forgotten in the service of dissonance reduction," Kasarjian and Cohen wrote, while arguments supporting the perverse conduct or belief are sought out and prized.

This denial of the undeniable became harder for Rose as she entered her forties, and her health declined. She suffered from hypertension, had her gallbladder removed and later underwent a hysterectomy, endured a pleurisy attack, and began to be racked with smoker's cough, a symptom of chronic bronchitis. But none of this affected her passion for nicotine. Rose did switch brands in 1968, not to a low-tar cigarette but to Philip Morris's new Virginia Slims, because "I thought they were very glamorous. . . . They were long, and it represented beautiful women. . . ." The lissome models in the Slims ads "really got to me," so she went out and bought the kind of lounging pajamas featured in the brand's ads. Four years later, she switched to another Philip Morris brand, Parliament, with its seemingly antiseptic recessed filter, but after two years she took the advice of her doctor, who told her that if she had to smoke, she ought to use True, Lorillard's low-tar brand. But she smoked more of them than of her previous brands, thus defeating any conceivable therapeutic effect. She never asked a physician to help her quit or contemplated joining a cessation clinic. Whenever Tony stuck an article under her nose detailing new evidence of the perils of her compulsion, she would insist that the health charges had not been proven as yet and quip that if you strapped a monkey to a smoking machine for twenty-four hours a day, of course it would sooner or later come down with something dreadful.

In truth, she read and understood the cautionary articles and grew concerned as her hacking cough persisted. "I was saying novenas I was so scared sometimes that I was getting sick," she said at her deposition, "and I used to make all kinds of promises to God if he didn't let me have cancer that I wouldn't do this and I wouldn't do that. . . . But I never kept the promise, and that's terrible. . . ." Her denial made everything simpler. "I didn't want to believe there was a risk. You've got to remember—I was addicted. I smoked. I smoked a lot. . . . You just don't stop smoking like that. It's very difficult." She told the drug abuse expert whom Marc Edell sent to question her, "I didn't think about quitting because I didn't think I could bear it."

By attributing her smoking to an addiction, Rose had convinced herself she was the victim of a pathological condition. But medical science stopped short of characterizing drug dependency as a diseased state; there was no readily determinable threshold beyond which one could be pronounced as addicted. The 1982 statement to Congress by the National Institute on Drug Abuse (NIDA) had listed as the four most common characteristics of addiction a psychoactive effect on the user's brain and body chemistry, compulsive use despite knowledge of the possible consequences, physical and psychological symptoms of distress during abrupt withdrawal, and a strong tendency to relapse. But the layman's understanding of the word sufficed: to the public, "addiction" meant an activity that once begun was very difficult to stop.

Nobody, though, in or out of science said addictions were impossible to break. In the case of cigarettes, it was estimated that one-third of users tried to quit each year, and probably no more than one-fifth of those who tried succeeded for good. But that amounted to somewhere between 30 and 40 million Americans who had stopped smoking in the span between the issuing of the 1964 Surgeon General's report and Marc Edell's first meeting with Rose Cipollone nearly two decades later. By then a whole literature of smoking cessation had grown up, testifying that tobacco dependency was not a disease but a form of self-destructive behavior that could be remedied. Jane Brody of *The New York Times* summed up the consensus in a February 23, 1977, article in her paper: "No matter how strong this habit [of smoking] or how frequently it is reinforced, anyone who wants to badly enough can break it." "Wanting to," not the knowledge that it was bad for you, was the key; the rest was largely a matter of technique. Many articles and books were written on how to break the mechanics of the habit, how to intrude on its rituals and substitute others, how to satisfy the oral craving that contributed to an average six-pound weight gain by quitters during their first year off cigarettes (frequent drinks of water, carrot sticks, dried prunes, and sugar-free hard candy being the most often recommended replacements for nicotine).

Cigarette makers could thus justifiably argue that the charge of addiction was an excuse by the weak-willed, who based the fact that they *had* not quit smoking on the claim that they *could* not quit, as if they were in the unbreakable clutches of an iron monster, and therefore deserved forgiveness for, or at least understanding of, their behavior. By calling it addiction, in short, smokers were denying responsibility for their conduct. And how did this differ fundamentally from the alcoholic motorist who caused a fatal crash and then blamed it on the liquor manufacturer? Or the junkie who robbed, maimed, or killed in the process of feeding his habit and then claimed that he himself had been victimized by the degraded social condition of his life? In the end, the tobacco industry held, no individual could blame societal forces, and certainly not the allurements of the marketplace, for the consequences of smoking when quitting was plainly possible. Rose Cipollone, moreover, was not merely asking to be excused for her smoking by attributing it to an addiction—she was going to court to ask reparations from those who had, she claimed, knowingly foisted it on her.

Rose's luck ran out in 1981, when a routine chest X ray disclosed a three-centimeter lesion at the rear of the upper lobe of her right lung. A bronchoscopy with a flexible tube proved negative, but Rose returned soon for a thoracotomy, in which the lung is deflated, an incision is made between the ribs, and the chest spread open. This time the surgeon found the tumor by feeling it and removed a piece for biopsy; the tissue was judged malignant, though there was some dispute over whether the cancer was an atypical carcinoid, a rare form of the disease, or the more common, fast-growing small-cell type. The affected lobe was removed in August. For eight months Rose had no further symptoms, but then she began wheezing and coughing up bloody sputum. Diagnosis showed that her middle and lower right lobes were now involved as well—the surgery had not got all the cancer. In a second operation they took out, with the rest of her lung, lymph nodes and major pulmonary arteries and began a course of chemotherapy to minimize the chances of recurrence. The chemo treatment induced an overwhelming nausea, and though Rose, unable to eat for days sometimes, tried hard to endure it—"she wanted to live so bad," Tony later said—she called off the regimen.

She remained clinically free of disease for fifteen months, until August 1983, when, soon after having met Marc Edell, she began complaining of pain in her abdomen and legs. High-resolution X rays detected a ten-centimeter mass behind the liver, just above the kidneys; when removed, the malignancy was diagnosed as metastasized lung cancer. Now chemotherapy was mandatory. Rose suffered no less wrenching nausea than earlier, as well as chronic intestinal upset, hair loss, and an esophagal spasm so severe she feared that she was having a heart attack. Frightened and anxious, she underwent hypnosis to still anticipatory fears of the chemo treatments, which she took from September through June 1984. At the end of February, near the close of the four-day deposition by tobacco lawyers that had utterly drained what little strength remained in her, she had begun to display symptoms of metastasis in her brain; she had trouble speaking, and bright light bothered her. Edell, finally understanding how far gone his client was, did not have the heart to depose her himself on tape, to be played eventually in the courtroom. Soon Rose's enlarged liver was found to be riddled with multiple cancers; in September, radiographic studies of her head showed similar effects. "She had tubes all over her, drainage, everything—it was a mess," Tony recalled. She survived on morphine now, screaming for it an hour and a half after the last shot. Tony, who rarely left her bedside, learned how to administer the painkiller so that he could take Rose home for a while. But she could not remain there.

Tony got to her room by five in the morning on October 21, 1984, and the doctor said she did not have long. Rose and Tony talked until the priest came a little after nine. The doctor made a final visit, and then Tony took Rose in his arms, and she said, "Tony, I love you," and he said, "I love you, too," and Rose said, "I know," and tears fell from her eyes until she closed them, forever. Tony sent the doctor away, screamed and cried, and when the doctor later proposed an autopsy, Tony said no, "because too many times she had been stabbed and cut and everything. I [didn't] want nobody to touch her. . . . We had a beautiful relation."

Several times during the later stages of her illness, Rose had told her young attorney that she wanted out of the liability suit he had filed in her behalf, but in the end she told Tony she wanted the case to go forward after she was gone. More than three years would pass before she got her posthumous day in court.

II

THREE days after Rose Cipollone died, her attorney arrived at the Park Avenue offices of Philip Morris to depose the newly crowned industry leader's retired chairman—Joseph Cullman. Half Cullman's age and looking younger still despite his neat mustache, Marc Edell was ushered into a very large conference room and shown to a chair at one end of a very long table; the senior statesman of the tobacco business sat at the other. Deployed between them was a squadron of company lawyers, their sheer number enough to intimidate a fainthearted adversary. Edell, unaccompanied, scanned the scene and decided that he had better let his massed adversaries know he was no pushover. He moved his chair the length of that immense table until he was sitting directly across from Cullman, with whom he proceeded to have "a nice, friendly chat," as the young attorney recalled it, before interrogating him.

While Philip Morris appeared to have the least exposure of the three defendants in *Cipollone v. Liggett Group, Philip Morris, and Loews* (the hotel and insurance conglomerate that had purchased Lorillard in 1969) since Rose Cipollone had smoked its brands for only six years, all of them after the warning label was required by law, its allies in the case were by now relatively small potatoes in the industry, so no one complained about PM's assumption of the role as *primus inter pares*. The captaincy of their joint effort was assigned to Murray H. Bring, a partner from Arnold & Porter, Philip Morris's formidable Washington counselors. A 1956 Phi Beta Kappa graduate of the University of Southern California, Bring served as editor in chief of the *New*

York University Law Review and a law clerk for two years to Earl Warren, Chief Justice of the United States, before joining the State Department as a junior officer and then the Justice Department, where he rose to director of policy planning in the antitrust division. A partner at Arnold & Porter since 1967, he excelled as a strategic thinker adept at orchestrating legal talent in complex cases, defining the terrain, and melding the sometimes contentious views of his colleagues. "He's simply a brilliant lawyer," commented Robert Pitofsky, of counsel to Arnold & Porter, and Georgetown law dean before chairing the FTC. "He's the most careful, thorough lawyer I've ever run into—for him everything is in the details." Bring was also a lover of theater and opera, a collector of modern art, highly active in civil liberties, the Legal Aid Society, and other professional causes, and a onetime heavy smoker who had tailed off in the years before he began to represent Philip Morris and took up the habit anew. There was no hint of hesitancy in the vigor with which he coordinated the efforts of the two dozen or so lawyers, with all the supporting paralegal, clerical, and expert advisory personnel they needed, to deny the heirs of Rose Cipollone compensation for the suffering and shortened life that her love affair with the cigarette had cost her.

Bring's defense strategy was not particularly innovative; there were just many more operatives than usual to carry it out. In essence, the defendants' position was that (1) smoking had not been absolutely proven as the cause of any disease, including Rose Cipollone's lung cancer, and (2) even if there was a strong statistical association between them, she had a rare kind of lung cancer not often found in smokers. But (3) even if her smoking had caused her premature death, by her own admission she had long known all about the health charges against cigarettes, had been warned repeatedly of the risks by various relatives starting with her mother, and had never made a serious effort to stop smoking even after the government-mandated warning label was put on each pack and in every cigarette ad. Therefore, (4) what reason was there to believe that any warnings that the manufacturers of her brands might have given before Congress had required them would have in any way deterred her from smoking? (5) Congress, moreover, in fashioning the warning label and defining it as adequate to meet the public-health concerns of the nation, had implicitly intended to block liability suits under state common law; damages awarded by juries sitting in such cases were tantamount to state regulation. To allow state judges and juries to determine the adequacy of the congressionally mandated warning and the propriety of the industry's advertising and promotion efforts as they related to health questions was to promote precisely the "diverse, nonuniform, and conflicting" array of warnings nationwide that Congress had explicitly intended to prevent from hobbling the industry's ability to conduct its business. The Supreme Court had on several occasions struck down the award of damages by state courts which served to frustrate the legislative purposes of Congress. As to the application of strict-liability standards favored by the New Jersey courts, the three defendants asserted that (6) cigarettes readily passed the risk/utility test for unfixably dangerous products on the grounds that they provided succor for millions around the world as their pacifier of choice, yielded a rich harvest of excise and income taxes at the federal, state, and even local levels, and contributed significantly to the American economy all the way from Tobacco Row to Madison Avenue.

The one obvious hole in this cluster of defenses was the question of how Rose Cipollone could be said to have made an informed decision to smoke, and thus to have assumed the full risk of her behavior, when her thinking was colored by the manufacturer's longtime contention that the scientific case against the perils of smoking remained unproven. Why should she have understood for a certainty what the tobacco companies would not admit to be so—namely, that smoking killed a lot of the people who enjoyed it? It was a classic blame-the-victim defense by an industry that had spent billions of dollars in advertising, promotion, and written rebuttals to the Surgeon General in order to allay the anxieties of their customers and becloud the consensual scientific case that had convicted cigarettes as slow-motion killers. The heart of the industry's defense could have been paraphrased, "Rose Cipollone knew the risks, even if we do not accept the medical community's conclusions about them." The cigarette makers insisted on having it both ways.

As the defendants' lead counselor, Bring recognized this apparent contradiction in their argument but had little trouble finessing it. He had mastered the industry's knack for selective citation of the evidence and used that aptitude with lawyerly precision. It had never been scientifically established that smoking was the cause of any human disease, Bring said, at once adding that "any honest scientist will admit that a statistical link doesn't establish causation. . . ." This contention airily disregarded the linkage as massively elaborated by two decades of chemical and biological studies, clinical observations, and laboratory investigations since the original, and compelling, advisory report to the Surgeon General. But for the tobacco industry to concede anything beyond a statistical correlation between smoking and disease—the risk that Bring called "common knowledge"—would have been to chance being sued out of business.

"Put yourself in our place back then," Bring reflected after the *Cipollone* case had ended. Tobacco was a big, prospering industry, a part of American folklore and basic lifestyle, when there was a sudden burst of publicity highly critical of its chief product. The manufacturers' first response, Bring said, was "to initiate research and to support independent investigators" to look into the charges. The skin-painting bioassays with mice were the only real substantiation for the view that cigarette smoke might be carcinogenic, but the dosages administered to the laboratory animals were "totally unrealistic" and many researchers believed that almost any organic substance when burned and made into a condensate might cause comparable tumors in mice. Yet the industry adopted the skin-painting technique itself because "you don't ignore the possibility" that its findings were applicable to the human smoking experience, "and so you continue to test and try to . . . modify your product" to reduce the tumors in test animals, "but that doesn't mean you admit that causation has been proven—only that it might be true." There was "unrest among the smoking public, and the industry felt it was possible" that tobacco tars were a cause of lung cancer, "and if there was such a possibility, we ought to reduce the tars," a process that had evolved over the years and met with the public's approval. But in so doing, "the industry wasn't conceding that its product was the culprit—only that the charge could be true. . . . The industry is justified in saying that the link hasn't been proven. But we don't deny that the risk exists, nor have we said that smoking doesn't cause lung cancer—we've never denied the statistical association. Anything short of the industry's concession that the case has been proven is not considered news. . . . We've been operating in a constant state of siege." Not a day had passed since 1955 when lawsuits were not pending against the industry, and its lawyers, highly conservative by nature, tended to urge their clients to concede as little as possible for fear that plaintiffs' counsel "will twist anything you say or use it against you."

This neatly evasive positioning failed to address one further plaintiff's claim for which the industry had no ready legal defenses. What if, instead of dealing in a forthright way with the public, as Bring contended they had done, the cigarette companies had striven ceaselessly, as Houston law professor White had suggested a decade before, to subvert the warnings by medical science and the U.S. government? What if, in order to confuse the public, the industry had nitpicked the findings of public-health investigators for minor imperfections while distorting the major—and undeniable—thrust of such studies? What if it had misrepresented the virtues of its products in seductive advertisements while failing to acknowledge the true severity of the risks? What if it had, through joint undertakings by its trade association and committees, conducted research it claimed sought answers to the health charges against it but in fact skirted the issue—or even terminated investigators who came uncomfortably close to evidence that incriminated smoking? What if the tobacco companies had knowingly suppressed important health information while continuing to protest that the case against them was unproven? What if what they were saying all along was at odds with what their own scientists believed to be the case—scientists who failed ever to offer a halfway plausible alternative explanation for the overwhelming body of corroborative evidence linking smoking and disease? Marc Edell set out to establish just such a case of conspiracy against the industry through the pretrial discovery process.

The task required, more than anything else, tireless pursuit. The industry lawyers rigorously fought Edell before yielding up a single document, filing endless motions and objections while insisting that the plaintiff's requests amounted to harassment, invasion of privacy, and nothing more than a fishing expedition for anything that might appear remotely embarrassing to the tobacco merchants. The trick for Edell, beyond perseverance, was to avoid a pyrrhic victory in the form of a blizzard of paper of the sort that had nearly buried FTC investigators in the late 'Seventies after a similar court battle for documents. But Edell's experience representing an asbestos company had taught him that corporations did save sensitive and potentially revealing documents if one knew where to look for them; his requests were thus not of an umbrella type but for the files of specific executives dealing with specified subjects. Defense lawyers succeeded in getting Edell's requests, put before a magistrate hardly sympathetic to his case, narrowed to documents generated within the forty-two years that Rose had smoked and dealing only with the brands she smoked, the diseases she suffered, and corporate activities within the New York metropolitan area where she lived. Even so, that amounted to a great deal of terrain to probe. More than half a million documents were eventually produced for Edell's examination; he ordered—and his firm had to pay for—copies of 100,000 of them.

"It was like having a great pile of candy to feast on," Edell recounted. The industry files were produced on a rolling basis, not all at once, so the tiny plaintiff's team of Edell, a pair of associates, and a few paralegals could sift through them over several years while other pretrial skirmishes were fought out. The industry provided copies as far as possible removed from the original documents, because, as Edell noted, "the original has a texture that can be revealing—a front, a back, either with notations on it, or it may come in a manila folder where there are notes—it's been handled." Often he was given incomplete or illegible documents and had to press to obtain a copy that was whole and readable. He and his team had to travel down a lot of empty roads as they pored over their booty, but they acquired skills along the way that facilitated their quest. They became adept, for example, at finding and filling in gaps in correspondence, learning how to check for a letter from the files of Company A for which they had found a response from Company B—an advantage they enjoyed over the defendant companies who were reluctant to pool their files. There was nothing magical about the process; it was mostly a matter of ceaselessly pushing onward. "He's like a bulldog," plaintiff's paralegal Michele Brown said of Edell during the pretrial phase. "He never gives up—he's so damned compulsive. He strives to be perfect at work and at play—in karate he had to be a black belt, a brown belt wasn't enough. . . ."

Edell's adversaries, to quote one leading tobacco attorney, viewed him as "a very good, very ambitious young lawyer who saw the case as his avenue to a national reputation. He was so driven in his desire to be the first plaintiff's lawyer to score a big hit against the tobacco industry that he'd put in almost any amount of work necessary to get the job done."

Edell was vitally helped in the early pretrial stages by the rulings of the U.S. district court judge whom fate had dealt him to preside in *Cipollone*. H. (for Hadden) Lee Sarokin, a high-domed jurist with a fringe of remaining pale hair and horn-rimmed glasses, had brought with him to the federal bench in 1979 a nimble mind, a patient and gracious courtroom manner, and a supple, sometimes barbed pen. A Dartmouth graduate who had helped pay his way through Harvard Law School by playing the drums for bands in the Boston area—and a recreational drummer he remained afterward—Sarokin became a prominent New Jersey private practitioner whose clients included former college and professional basketball star Bill Bradley. When Democrat Bradley made his bid in 1978 for the U.S. Senate, Sarokin served as finance chairman of the campaign; Bradley's triumph was followed within the year by Sarokin's nomination as a federal judge. Critics found him an overly liberal and opinionated jurist; admirers saw in him a staunch defender of civil rights and liberties and champion of social justice. He drew attention by holding that the Kiwanis International could not terminate a local chapter for admitting women in a state that banned sex discrimination by statute and won still more fame for freeing the once prominent boxer Rubin "Hurricane" Carter, after nineteen years in jail on a triple-murder conviction, following disclosures that the prosecution had withheld material evidence and that the trial process had been racially poisoned.

The tobacco industry lawyers felt Sarokin's sting in July 1985 when, after he had ruled a number of times to open up the discovery process beyond the dictates of the magistrate assigned to oversee it, he approved of Edell's use of the documents in seven other liability cases he was by then handling for smoking claimants as well as of his sharing them with other litigators and making them public. Sarokin wrote that while he was passing no judgment as to whether the documents in question—Edell would eventually introduce some 300 of them as evidence in *Cipollone*—disclosed any conspiracy or chicanery on the defendants' part, the court could not be a party to their suppression. Product formulas, marketing strategy, and other matters affecting the day-to-day operations of the cigarette companies could remain private, but what part, if any, the companies played "in concealing or misrepresenting information regarding the risks of smoking is not entitled to such protection." Then, noting the David-and-Goliath nature of the legal encounter before him, Sarokin added, "The court cannot ignore the might and power of the tobacco industry and its ability to resist the individual claims asserted against it. There may be some claimants who do not have the resources or such able and dedicated counsel as in this case to pursue the thorough investigation which these cases require. To require that each and every plaintiff go through the identical long and expensive process would be ludicrous."

This ruling, which the industry appealed to the Third Circuit and lost, capped off Edell's chief triumph in the case. The documents he obtained and ventilated represented the first glimpse by outsiders into the cigarette industry's internal understanding of the health issue and substantiated the suspicion that what company executives were apprised of by their scientists varied markedly from their pronouncements on the subject. Perhaps the most illuminating documents were the memoranda in the early 1960s by Philip Morris R&D chief Helmut Wakeham, who had urged his superiors to allow his department to develop a "medically acceptable" cigarette (see chapter 8, section IV) and not to waste the company's energies denying the heart of the charges in the 1964 report to the Surgeon General in the absence of persuasive evidence to the contrary (see chapter 9, section IV). Through his depositions of high-ranking company officials, Edell also succeeded in obtaining disclosures of the industry's inability or unwillingness to face up to the health issue. Liggett's former president and CEO Milton Harrington, who headed the company when the pioneer Surgeon General's report appeared in 1964, was the very model of insouciance on the subject.

Q. What, if anything did you do in response to the Surgeon General's report . . . ?

A. I read the report.

Q. What else did you do?

A. Nothing.

    . . .

Q. You didn't discuss it any further with any other executive at Liggett & Myers?

A. Not that I recall.

Q. Did Liggett & Myers do anything in response to the Surgeon General's report?

A. Not that I recall.

Q. Did you form any impression as to . . . the validity of the Surgeon General's report?

A. No, because that wasn't up to me to do that. . . . I wasn't asked what my personal opinion was.

Q. Was there anyone at Liggett in 1964 who was responsible for setting policy for the company with respect to cigarette smoking and health?

A. I don't know. I didn't have that responsibility at that time.

    . . .

Q. Well, did Liggett & Myers have a corporate position with respect to the issue of cigarette smoking in 1964, 1965?

A. Well, I don't know of any policy we had about it.

    . . .

Q. What does the phrase "smoking and health" mean to you, sir?

A. Not anything particularly, really. The only time that really I began to think about—if you are talking about smoking and health—what is the warning labeling and all that stuff. I didn't think about anything about smoking and health other than smoking was not harmful to you in any way.
    . . .

Q. Was it your understanding you could not warn the public further about the potential health hazards of cigarettes because the warning was mandated by Congress?

A. We didn't care to warn the public about anything. We just had to put that warning on. It wasn't because we liked to, it was just something we had to do. . . .

Still more precious to Edell than this confession of nonfeasance was the testimony of two whistle-blowers he uncovered in an industry noted for its secrecy even on the part of disgruntled former employees. One whom Edell solicited was James Mold, the retired head of Liggett's long-running and ultimately abandoned palladium cigarette project. When Edell telephoned Mold at his home in Durham, North Carolina, the town where Buck Duke got his start, the scholarly and dedicated scientist indicated that he was willing to recount how the company had spent nearly twenty years and millions of dollars on the "safer" cigarette, only to keep it off the market out of fear of liability claims against the company based on the inference that the rest of the product line was therefore unsafe (see chapter 14, section III). "Am I really hearing this stuff right?" Edell said he asked himself as Mold spun his startling tale. The young lawyer, unused to asking questions of a tobacco industry official who actually wanted to tell him something damaging, was so fearful that the palladium story and his witness would evaporate that he asked the court stenographer to provide him with a copy of the tape recording she had made as a backup before he left North Carolina. Liggett lawyers would first try to show up Mold in court as a tattler nursing sour grapes because he was never promoted to the top R&D job at the company and then argue that the palladium cigarette's safety advantages were unproven. Independent investigator Freddy Homburger told his almost equally harrowing story of how he had been cut off by the Council for Tobacco Research after reporting evidence of laryngeal cancers in his laboratory hamsters and being pressured not to publish his findings; he, too, was disparaged by the industry lawyers as a scientist of dubious competence (see chapter 11, section II).

What did all of Edell's findings amount to? He had discovered no evidence about the lethal nature of cigarette smoking buried in the industry's cellar, or about the pathological mechanisms tobacco smoke set in motion, that was not already largely known to the scientific and public-health communities. What Edell had uncovered were numerous indications that the tobacco industry had not been dealing straightforwardly with the public but had been acting in deceptive ways to ease its customers' growing anxieties over the health charges. Whether that constituted a criminal conspiracy would be left to the jury to decide.

III

B ESIDES granting Rose Cipollone's counsel wide latitude in the discovery process, Judge Lee Sarokin made a ruling a year into the case that seemed to suggest even more clearly where his sympathies lay. He denied a motion by the tobacco companies' defense team arguing that liability suits like Mrs. Cipollone's had been prohibited by Congress when it crafted the warning label legislation.

Neither the language of the 1966 and 1970 labeling statutes nor anything in their legislative history, Sarokin held, revealed congressional intent to foreclose liability in tort claims; if so intended, the acts would have stated that explicitly, and even if they were interpreted to mean that the cigarette manufacturers needed to affix no stronger warnings in order to fend off claimants with an assumption-of-risk defense, the industry was still exposed to liability charges for collateral efforts "to neutralize or negate the effects of the warning" by trying to convince the public that the health risk of smoking was minimal and causation unproven. Any damages a jury might award were not tantamount to a "requirement or prohibition" under state law, as Congress meant those terms, but served to shift the burden of losses suffered by use of a dangerous product to "those who are in a position to either control the danger or to make an equitable distribution of the losses when they do occur." The federal cigarette labeling laws, moreover, said only that it was illegal not to place the specified warning on all packages, thereby fixing a level of conduct below which the manufacturers should not fall; the statutes were "silent as to additional information or warnings that might also be included. . . . [I]t would be unfortunate if those directed to do no less, assume they need to do no more." With this aphoristic bent, Sarokin gave the defendants a final jab, remarking, "[L]egal minimums were never intended to supplant moral maximums."

Philip Morris counsel Bring called Sarokin's sixty-page ruling a "brilliant job of crafting an opinion with very little to support it." The U.S. Court of Appeals for the Third Circuit agreed with Bring's assessment and, in an almost offhand three-page reversal of Sarokin's opinion, held that common-law damage awards by state juries did have the effect of requirements that were capable of creating an obstacle to "the accomplishment of congressional objectives." It concluded that any liability suit based on the adequacy of the manufacturers' warning after the congressional mandate went into effect in 1966 was barred.

Some legal commentators thought the Third Circuit reversal was motivated at least in part by fear that, if encouraged, such liability suits by aggrieved smokers would bollix up the federal judicial system for years, even as suits by injured asbestos workers had threatened to—and there was a far larger number of potential smoker-plaintiffs. Whatever covert motives the circuit judges may have harbored, their ruling on its face left Judge Sarokin "in vehement disagreement" with what he saw as the unconscionable implications of their reading of Congress's intentions. In spelling out what causes of action remained to the plaintiff, the district judge wrote that "the cigarette industry evidently can continue to deny or refute the risks of cigarette smoking with impunity and immunity so long as the little rectangle with the necessary language appears in its advertising and on its cigarette packages." In a parting blast at his appellate overseers, Sarokin thundered that under the circuit opinion, the cigarette makers' concealment of the truth from the public

> is deemed to be an activity which Congress impliedly intended to protect in enacting this [labeling] legislation. In essence, without any express authority from Congress, a single industry, for the first time in our country's history, may speak what is untrue, may conceal what is true, and may avoid liability for doing so merely by affixing certain mandated warnings to its products and advertising.

However soaring Sarokin's language, his reading of the Third Circuit reversal was as expansive as his reading of the federal labeling laws had been narrow. The circuit had not held that anything the tobacco companies said about the health risks of their product after the labeling began was permissible; it held that the adequacy of the warning could not be challenged. "He interpreted the Circuit ruling much too broadly," Edell said after the trial. "I think he was intimidated." Whatever caused Sarokin's sharp swing in reaction to the overruling, the plaintiff's ability to introduce evidence of the industry's conduct on the health issue over the final eighteen years of Rose Cipollone's life (*i.e.,* after the warning labels were required) was now sharply reduced.

Edell suffered an equally severe blow almost on the eve of the trial. During the summer of 1987, a year in which the tobacco industry spread a million dollars in campaign contributions among the members of the New Jersey legislature, the lawmakers of that state had passed a "tort reform" law, partly in reaction to excessive jury awards to claimants in product liability actions. It was hardly accidental, with the *Cipollone* trial imminent and threatening the financial security of the cigarette makers as no tobacco case ever had, that the industry's lobbyists had taken the lead in trying to end New Jersey's national leadership in the pro-consumer reading of liability law.

The "reform" in effect wrote into law the "Comment i" language of the *Restatement of Torts*, which had said that "Good [*i.e.*, unadulterated] tobacco is not unreasonably dangerous merely because the effects of smoking may be harmful," for it was universally understood that the custom was risky and ought therefore not to be subject to liability claims. The New Jersey Supreme Court had decisively declined to accept the logic of that view, which served to reward manufacturers by shielding them precisely *because* their products were so dangerous that everybody knew it. Instead, the New Jersey high court had held such products to strict-liability standards, insisting on a risk/utility test and casting aside warnings as a complete defense. In 1987, however, the state legislature turned a decade of rulings by the state courts on their head by outlawing liability suits over unavoidably dangerous products that were understood by the community at large to involve high risk; alcoholic beverages, guns, meat, and dairy products were cited as examples along with tobacco.

The only real question about the 1987 law was when it would go into effect. According to its own text, the act was to become effective immediately, except that "any new rules" which it established were to apply only to liability suits filed on or after the date of enactment. This language seemed to say that *Cipollone* and other tobacco liability cases that Edell had filed as long ago as four years earlier were not covered by the new statute, and that strict-liability standards could still be applied to those claims. That the statute was intended to be a sharp departure from the prevailing New Jersey common law—and thus constituted a "new rule," as the tort revision act specified in exempting suits previously filed—was explicitly stated by the bill's sponsor, by the accompanying statement from the New Jersey Senate's judiciary committee, and by the Democratic legislators' staff analysis. But the defense lawyers in *Cipollone* pointed instead to a statement by the State Assembly's insurance committee, claimed by the plaintiff's counsel to have been drafted by a well-known Morristown attorney who was a registered lobbyist for the tobacco industry, which said the new product liability law was merely putting into statutory language what the New Jersey courts had previously embraced—namely, the "Comment i" exemption of unfixably dangerous products so known to the public. This was plainly an incorrect reading of the status of product liability law in New Jersey, but if accepted, would have meant that Edell's cases could be denied strict liability as a cause of action.

Astonishingly, given Sarokin's prior rulings in *Cipollone*, he accepted the defense's interpretation of the legislative intent, even though he found it "offensive . . . that a litigant in the midst of ongoing litigation can prevail upon the legislature to eliminate a cause of action pending against it, particularly if that legislation is procured through the submission of intentionally misleading facts." But it was not a "fact" that the liability revision was merely codifying previous state common law, as Edell now desperately argued in appealing to

Sarokin to reconsider his ruling. Interpretive statements by legislative committees were not a part of any statute nor could they usurp the power of the courts
to interpret the judicial meaning of a body of common-law rulings, the plaintiff's counsel said. The Assembly committee statement, moreover, had been
"drafted by a special interest group, without hearing or debate . . . and released
after the bill had already been voted on by the Senate," Edell stressed.

But Sarokin felt he had no choice; strict-liability and risk/utility causes
were retroactively cut out from Edell's case. Some felt that the judge, his sympathies in the case being no secret, was bending over backwards to be fair to
the defense in order to avoid further reversals of his rulings.

I V

MARC EDELL's hopes of becoming the first trial lawyer to beat the tobacco companies were further threatened by a pair of liability suits that
reached their juries before his case did. One of them was brought by the flamboyant Melvin Belli, who in Louisiana in 1958 had argued the first tobacco liability case to reach a jury. In late 1985 he filed a claim of $100 million in
behalf of Mark Galbraith, a three-pack-a-day smoker who had died at sixty-
nine, against R. J. Reynolds Tobacco in Santa Barbara, California, county
court. It was the first such action to go before a jury in fifteen years, and Belli
made a typical splash, arriving in the coastal city with his entourage aboard a
yacht and wearing cowboy boots.

But *Galbraith* was not one of Belli's better efforts. One problem was that
the deceased plaintiff, who had long suffered from multiple afflictions including tuberculosis and heart disease, was said to have died from arteriosclerosis
and pulmonary fibrosis with lung cancer held to be also contributory—all
smoking-related diseases, but the first two were multicausal, and no autopsy
had been performed that might have implicated smoking more centrally. Belli,
moreover, had uncovered no enlightening industry documents, as Edell had,
and was peeved when the latter said he was unable to share the fruits of his
own discovery until his trial court had ruled on his request to do so. Belli was
hampered, too, by the county judge, who tossed out the Surgeon General's reports as hearsay evidence, and examples of the defendant's advertisements intended to show how they constituted express or implied warranties of smoking
safety were never introduced. Finally, there was substantial testimony that the
plaintiff had, like Rose Cipollone, spurned many warnings by family and
friends to desist from heavy smoking and was fully cognizant of the risks of
continuing. The jury found for the defense, 9 to 3, holding that neither causation nor addiction had been proven.

A more promising case for the plaintiff was argued in Holmes County, Mississippi, in January 1988, just before *Cipollone* was heard. Nathan Horton, a fifty-year-old African-American carpenter and contractor who smoked Pall Malls, had filed in May 1986 for $17 million in damages from American Tobacco, not on the claim that he had been improperly warned of the risks by the company but because its cigarettes had been adulterated by the use of fertilizers and pesticides in excess of the government-approved limits—a charge that the company said was true for several years but denied was the cause of Horton's death from lung cancer eight months after launching his case.

There were several reasons to believe that the plaintiff might prevail in the trial of *Horton v. American Tobacco*, postponed twenty-two times. To start with, Mississippi had one of the most liberal comparative fault statutes of any state, so that a plaintiff demonstrating even 5 percent responsibility for injuries due to the manufacturer's actions could be awarded damages. Then there was the fact that blacks made up the majority of the population in Holmes County. The jury consisted of eleven blacks and one white, and half of its members were unemployed; some observers felt that the jury might relish punishing an establishment white corporation in behalf of a black plaintiff. Horton's lawyer told the court, "We accept our responsibility. The American Tobacco Company refuses to accept theirs, and that's what this lawsuit is all about." In an emotional appeal, Horton's wife would testify at the trial that her husband had tried to quit smoking on several occasions by buying candy but had never managed to go more than a few days before lapsing. Of his illness she said, "His nights were so long. Sometimes I would wake up, and he would just be staring up and . . . crying, tears rolling down his face. I would try to hug him, and he would say it hurt too much."

After hearing witnesses for the defense deny that smoking had been proven causally related to lung cancer, the jury deliberated for eleven hours, and then the judge called a mistrial "for reasons I do not feel would be advantageous to anyone" to reveal—certainly a novel theory of justice even in remotest Mississippi. Rumors of jury-tampering soon swirled, along with reports of how American Tobacco had spread a lot of money around Holmes County. One "consultant" for jury selection admitted to improper contact with three jurors during the course of the trial but said that their conversations had had nothing to do with the substance of the case and that two of the three were in fact siding with the plaintiff at the time the trial was halted. No tampering charges were proven, and two and a half years later the case was retried, this time in the university town of Oxford, Mississippi, before a jury of eight whites and four blacks. The jury held that the company had been "irresponsible" in monitoring the quantities of fertilizers and pesticides used in growing its tobacco, but it awarded not a dollar to the heirs of Nathan Horton.

V

MARC EDELL's youthful stamina was put to the test throughout the final pretrial year of the *Cipollone* case. He had moved from his old firm to the posh offices of Budd Larner Gross Rosenbaum Greenberg & Sade in suburban Millburn by the time the trial began in February 1988. While Budd Larner's partners, hopeful of large future rewards, were willing to sustain Edell's effort to humble the lords of tobacco, the unreimbursed bill for time and expenses had passed $2 million and was still mounting. Yet Edell's was a minimal operation; his team consisted largely of his dedicated legal associate, Cynthia Walters, and a gifted paralegal, Nelson Thayer. Nonstop twelve-hour days became routine as they struggled with a constant flurry of court papers, industry documents grudgingly released after last-minute hassling, and draining skirmishes over the defense's ceaseless efforts to narrow the plaintiff's case.

Ranged against Edell's tiny band was the industry's legal legion, numbering close to a hundred people including the support staff, drawn primarily from three firms: Arnold & Porter in Washington, representing Philip Morris; Webster & Sheffield, the white-shoe Manhattan firm that had long handled Liggett's legal business; and Shook, Hardy & Bacon, the Kansas City firm specializing in tobacco cases and arguing now for the Lorillard division of Loews. The defense's unanointed chief strategist, Murray Bring, had by then joined Philip Morris as an associate general counsel; within half a year he would become general counsel, senior vice president, a board director, and one of the most powerful figures in an industry now facing unprecedented legal challenges.

Judge Sarokin's courtroom, in a nondescript federal office building on Newark's once flourishing Broad Street, held seats for only seventy-five spectators, many of them occupied throughout the trial by tobacco industry observers and members of the defense team supplementing the five or six litigators involved in the proceedings on any given day. Because media attention had been lavished on the *Horton* trial, which had just come to an aborted end, the press by and large gave slim coverage to *Cipollone* until its final stages. Hardly a dozen reporters were on hand as the trial opened, and neither *The New York Times*, arguably the nation's foremost daily, nor *The Wall Street Journal*, its most widely read financial publication, saw fit to provide running coverage of the sharpest challenge ever mounted against an industry accused by medical science of being the deadliest on earth. Only the Washington *Post*, among national media, paid continuous attention, due in large measure to the insistence of its veteran consumer affairs specialist, Morton Mintz, who grasped the significance of the documents Edell was introducing.

His main problem, Edell understood, would be to convince the six-member jury, only one of them a current smoker, that anyone who, in that day and age, had continued to smoke and then fallen fatally ill from the habit deserved to be compensated monetarily. Edell thus opened his long-rehearsed remarks by telling the jury this case was about an industry that, instead of warning the plaintiff and her fellow smokers of the dangers of its product, said, "Mrs. Cipollone, if you trusted us . . . if you believed our statements in the press, if you believed our advertisements—if you were stupid enough to believe us, then you deserve what you get." Conceding that Rose Cipollone had had a choice in electing to smoke, he argued that it was not an informed choice but one made when she was a teenager and that quickly led to a powerful addiction. The tobacco industry, Edell insisted, had also made a choice: it could have chosen to warn its customers long before the U.S. government made it do so in 1966—by which time Rose had been smoking almost twenty-five years. The cigarette makers, "unlike Rose Cipollone," knew all the facts about the health hazards of smoking, but instead of warning the public, "they embarked on a campaign to deceive, confuse and mislead people."

Opening for the defense was its lead courtroom performer, Peter Bleakley, a former FTC and Justice Department litigator before joining Arnold & Porter, where he had tried a number of complex corporate cases. At fifty-one, he was easily the most accomplished trial lawyer in the courtroom, expertly wielding a soft tenor voice that could be quickly honed to a nice cutting edge to menace hostile witnesses. Tobacco was as old as the Western Hemisphere, Bleakley told the jury, and reports of its harmful effects had been prominently spread since the days of James I nearly four centuries earlier. Everyone was familiar with the term "coffin nails," referring to cigarettes, he said, thus blurring the distinction between the almost entirely anecdotal notoriety of tobacco over much of its history and the body of evidence that medical science had uncovered only since the midpoint of the twentieth century. The tobacco industry, once apprised of the serious charges against it, had begun research in earnest in 1954 and had continued ever since, but even a third of a century later, the defense lawyer said, the causes of cancer remained a mystery to science. Rose Cipollone knew all about the health charges against smoking, Bleakley asserted; she was "an intelligent, inquiring, well-read woman aware of what was going on around her in the world," and therefore "that is the issue" in the case.

Edell first put on the stand his most remarkable and useful witness, one who had no personal connection with Rose. A tall, slender associate professor of economics from Massachusetts Institute of Technology, Jeffrey E. Harris was also a Harvard-educated physician who for twelve years had devoted one day a week to primary in-patient care at Massachusetts General Hospital. Over the four previous years Harris had also immersed himself in libraries, sopping up everything he could on the chemical, medical, and economic aspects of the tobacco business and conveying the essence of his findings to Edell.

Though he was not a board-certified practitioner in any field of medicine or the author of notable books or articles on any subject, Harris was accepted by Judge Sarokin as an expert witness on almost every aspect of the tobacco industry and, over repeated objections by the defense, Sarokin granted him immense latitude to tell the jury what he had learned. What followed was, in effect, nearly a weeklong lecture, on what science had come to know about the health effects of smoking, what the tobacco industry knew or should have known about it, and what it did and did not do in response. Like a lively classroom instructor, Harris used graphic aids in the form of blowups or slide-projected copies of important scientific articles, from which he cited highlights, then bounced off the witness stand to enter their titles at the appropriate spot on a "time line" of Rose Cipollone's life. Edell would cut into Harris's presentation from time to time with a question about terminology or a request for an elaboration in order to maintain the appearance of a question-and-answer exchange, but essentially the bearded MIT professor was laying out Edell's case for him. The more substance it took on with Harris's almost clinical delivery, the more the defense lawyers objected to his performance. But Sarokin would not rein him in, and Harris tellingly contrasted the tobacco companies' conduct with that of the canning industry, which had adopted new sterilizing methods when botulism was traced to its careless procedures, and the pharmaceutical industry, which had put a skull-and-crossbones warning on preparations found to be toxic when ingested. Such measures were in marked contrast to the conduct of Philip Morris, Harris said, which in the 'Thirties had introduced the humectant diethylene glycol—a compound later found to be harmful to the kidneys—based on a minimum of testing (see chapter 4, section IV).

Harris proved even more effective on cross-examination. The young professor never grew flustered and gave pointed questions long, detailed answers that only made the defense look worse. When Bleakley asked him, for example, if early Argentine investigator A. H. Roffo's studies into the carcinogenic properties of burned tobacco (see chapter 4, section VII) were not compromised by his stated hatred of smoking, Harris replied, "As a doctor who saw a lot of people dying of cancer, I think that would be understandable." And when asked if Ernst Wynder's skin-painting bioassays with mice (see chapter 6, section VI) were not fatally marred by unrealistically high dosages of tobacco smoke condensate, Harris asked in turn why the tobacco companies' researchers had utilized the same testing technique for carcinogenic activity for so many years. The industry as a whole, he declared, should have initiated serious research into the health charges by the late 'Thirties, and since the scientific case firmly establishing cigarette smoking as a lethal health hazard was a *fait accompli* by the late 'Fifties, there was no justification after that for the industry's holding out for unquestionable "proof". "Do we have to know the cause of lung cancer in order to do something about it?" he asked.

Edell took perhaps his biggest chance in the case by calling to the stand the tobacco industry's leading figure since the death of American Tobacco's George Washington Hill. Joseph Cullman was just a few weeks shy of his seventy-fifth birthday when he appeared in Judge Sarokin's court for a grilling that lasted more than two days. At the time, the retired chairman of Philip Morris held 325,000 shares of his company's stock, worth about $30 million. Cullman remarked after the trial, "My conscience was absolutely clean—we didn't conceal, delude, or withhold anything from the public." The industry, he said, had handled itself "in an exemplary way . . . and in this landmark case I was glad to stand up and be counted." He savored the challenge that Edell represented, "but he didn't make my life easy." If the defense lawyers were concerned about whether Cullman could, at his age, stand up to Edell's relentless questioning, they were soon put at ease. Shook, Hardy's young lawyer Steven C. Parrish, then representing Lorillard but later to become general counsel for Philip Morris's U.S. tobacco division, remembered how, during one break in the trial, Cullman had become so engaged in conversation in the marbled hall outside the courtroom that he failed to notice that the jury had reassembled and was awaiting his return to the witness stand. Alerted, "Joe nearly sprinted all the way from the hall back to the stand," Parrish said, "and gave a little jump into his chair at the end," to the jurors' amusement.

Certainly compared to the other two retired chief executives of the defendant companies who testified in the trial—Liggett's Milton Harrington and Lorillard's Curtis Judge—Cullman seemed a model of corporate civility and candor. Surely, he said, he and his fellow Philip Morris executives were fully aware of the health charges against smoking and had, accordingly, set in motion research into the chemical properties of tobacco, but the carcinogenic initiators and promoters found in the smoke were "minuscule"; even so, the company undertook to reduce the tar and nicotine levels in its brands, although he insisted, "There was nothing at that time—and there still isn't—that proves causally that cigarettes cause lung cancer." He conceded that smoking was a difficult habit to break but denied that it was addictive, and when shown a report by Philip Morris researcher William Dunn calling cigarettes mostly a delivery system for nicotine (see chapter 13, section II), Cullman simply said he disagreed with that characterization.

But Edell began to bore in on him, pressing to learn why exactly the company had modified its products in the wake of scientific findings that they posed a serious health hazard. "We reduced the tar and nicotine because there was a demand in the marketplace for a cigarette that reduced tar and nicotine—smokers wanted it," Cullman said.

> Q. That's the purpose—that was your motivation—so you could sell your cig-arettes. There was a demand out there, you knew it from your consumer surveys that people wanted a filter cigarette with less tar and nicotine, correct?
>
> A. I think that's a fair statement.
>
> Q. And that's why you put them on the market. It wasn't in an effort to reduce heart disease and reduce cancer—isn't that right?
>
> A. . . . I think we were trying to do anything we could to satisfy the large mar-ket of smokers out there and also their desire to continue to smoke and also to give them a cigarette that would be reduced in tar and nicotine which they would view as being somewhat better for them.

The company was thus responding to its critics by lowering the yield numbers without knowing of or claiming any health benefit in the process, he said, adding, "and we were doing it all the time, but we were not allowed to adver-tise [the fact]. We were prevented from doing this by the FTC. . . . It was my distinct understanding that the FTC prevented us from making any health claims about the cigarettes." Edell pounced on that.

> Q. But you could have told them there were health detriments—there was no prohibition to tell your customers that there were detriments, that there were hazards to your cigarettes, right?
>
> A. I don't know. I was there, and I'm not sure that you were there, and I don't recall—
>
> Q. I've looked at the law, Mr. Cullman.
>
> A. . . . My answer is we abided by the regulations of the Federal Trade Com-mission—they were very tough—and that we had to abide by their instruc-tions to us.
>
> Q. And that is your testimony, Mr. Cullman—that those instructions by the Federal Trade Commission prevented you from advising your consumers of the potential health hazards of your products? A simple yes or no, sir.
>
> A. My answer to that is yes.

There was, of course, no such FTC prohibition—only a rule against making affirmative declarations of health benefits that could not be documented. Asked if Philip Morris could not have told the public about its internal research into the properties of tobacco smoke, Cullman said that statements made out-side its formal advertising might nonetheless be taken for such and would have been similarly forbidden. This, too, was either an invention or misinterpretation. Edell put it more baldly in his summation, calling Cullman "very smooth, very polished, very sophisticated . . . probably one of the greatest marketing men the tobacco industry has ever known, [yet] he sat there and looked you straight in the eye and told you, 'We didn't warn them because the FTC wouldn't let us' "—and that, declared Edell, was "a straight lie."

Although Edell was permitted by the court to explore the industry's post-1966 conduct relating to its research into the health question, he had trouble impaling its witnesses even with the help of documents that seemed to suggest something other than an unswerving pursuit of the scientific truth. Cullman, for example, was shown the internal 1972 memo by Tobacco Institute Vice President Fred Panzer (see chapter 11, section II) describing the industry's strategy, of "creating doubt about the health charge without actually denying it." Cullman said merely that he disagreed with Panzer.

A more slippery response greeted Edell's introduction of a 1974 memo by Lorillard's research director, Alexander Spears, to his CEO, Curtis Judge, stating that the Council for Tobacco Research's program (see chapter 11, section II) avoided the core of the health problem and was devoted instead to "purposes such as public relations, political relations, position for litigation. . . ." Confronted with this letter that he himself had written fourteen years earlier, Spears, a thirty-year Lorillard veteran, said that his real objection to CTR's program was its reliance on the grant method and that "certain areas of research . . . were not conducive to that approach," citing smoke inhalation studies with animals, which he felt required "a large, cohesive effort by an organization rather than individual investigators"; thus, he thought CTR "ought to be doing contract research." Edell, with narrowed gaze, asked Spears where in his memo there was any discussion of what he had just told the court; Spears insisted that his methodological objection was all he had intended to convey.

Because Spears had so casually brushed aside the plain English of his earlier sharp criticism, Edell decided not to put on Spears's opposite number from Philip Morris, Helmut Wakeham, to explain the hortatory memos he had directed to his bosses in the 'Sixties urging an all-out drive to produce less hazardous cigarettes. Wakeham's documents would speak better for themselves, Edell calculated, than if the imposing Philip Morris scientist were to take the stand and try to twist his own written words to meet the exigencies of a liability lawsuit. It would prove a costly miscalculation, because the references to Wakeham's pointed recommendations were lost sight of in the long, complex trial.

Edell did better in getting on the record the saga of Freddy Homburger and his finally soured relationship with the Council for Tobacco Research and in disputing the testimony from former CTR scientific director Sheldon Sommers that the council's research grants had nothing to do with the industry's lawyers or any ulterior motives they may have had in defending tobacco manufacturers from liability actions. Minutes produced from CTR files of meetings attended by both scientists and lawyers to discuss "special projects" for just such purposes (see chapter 14, section VIII) could not be denied, nor could James Mold's tale of how Liggett developed and finally suppressed its apparently less hazardous palladium cigarette. At the close of the plaintiff's case, however, Judge Sarokin once again narrowed Edell's claims by ordering the jury to disregard all the evidence about the palladium cigarette and Liggett's failure to implement a safer alternative design of its product—grounds for a negligence claim—because the court found no persuasive evidence that Rose Cipollone would have smoked such a brand even if Liggett had marketed it. In fact, she said in her deposition that she had switched at least two times to brands that she perceived to be less hazardous to her health.

The patchwork nature of the disclosures in the internal industry documents that Edell put into the record worked against him. They could not be presented in an orderly fashion, indeed had to be shoehorned into the case in many instances, thanks to a tolerant judge, only to be denied or dismissed as the views of subordinate employees well below the corporate policymaking level. The press, like the jury, was unable to discern the pattern of denial and diversion Edell sought to attribute to the industry; only Mintz's dispatches in the Washington *Post* drew attention to the industry documents in detailed fashion, much to the annoyance of a New York public-relations firm that Arnold & Porter had hired to perform damage control during the course of the trial. Its chief operative, buoyantly fraternizing with the attending reporters when he was not hectoring them, was publicist John Scanlon, who along with Shook, Hardy lawyer Charles Wall tried to give a pro-industry spin to each day's testimony. They would supply texts and transcripts to facilitate the reporters' task of deadline filing, then the next morning present blue-penciled critiques of published accounts in which an anti-industry bias was detected. Mintz was a particular target of this spin-doctoring since he got the most ink of any covering journalist and wrote for one of the nation's most influential newspapers. Scanlon sent an aide to tell Mintz, according to the reporter's account of the conversation, that "his people" were unhappy with Mintz's coverage of the anti-industry witnesses Edell was parading before the jury and that the publicity agency was "going to take this to the highest levels in Washington," meaning Mintz's editors at the *Post*. "I took this as a threat," Mintz recounted, but he did not relent in his coverage of the anti-industry revelations.

At the end of the trial Scanlon made good on his threat, writing a four-page letter to Mintz's immediate superior documenting how the reporter's coverage was heavily weighted with testimony by the plaintiff's witnesses. The charge was correct, because in Mintz's view, the witnesses and documents Edell was presenting were hard news, while the defense case consisted largely of familiar recitals by longtime recipients of tobacco money and a protracted examination of Rose Cipollone's medical history in order to plant doubt among the jury that smoking had caused her lung cancer. Scanlon charged that Mintz's news judgment produced "patently unfair and biased coverage of the case" by a journalist with a "well-known anti-corporate bias" who was "so much of an anti-tobacco advocate that it is patently impossible for him to ever apply . . . standards of objectivity on this issue."

The worst that could have been said of Mintz's fair and accurate reporting on the trial was that it was selective. But selectivity among all available material is the essence of journalism; not all related facts, statements, or opinions are equally deserving of comparable treatment or inclusion in a given day's story. Certainly there were no fiery castigations of the industry's conduct in Mintz's articles. The same, however, could not be said of the opinion Judge Sarokin issued in response to the defense's motion for a directed verdict to dismiss the plaintiff's suit on the ground that the evidence Edell had presented had fallen so far short of the charges as not to deserve the jury's consideration.

The evidence that Rose Cipollone had died from smoking-caused lung cancer was "overwhelming," the judge wrote; the question of who was responsible for that outcome had to be viewed "in light of the activities of the defendants during this same time period. . . . The defendants and others in the tobacco industry not only failed to warn of the risks of smoking but to the contrary suggested that cigarette smoking was safe and harmless and, indeed, that this contention even had the support of medical doctors." Evidenced by documents from the defendants' own files, the tobacco manufacturers had "entered into a sophisticated conspiracy . . . organized to refute, undermine, and neutralize information coming from the scientific and medical community and, at the same time, to confuse and mislead the consuming public." In connection with the defendants' decision to lower the tar and nicotine content of their cigarettes and advertise the action, the manufacturers "did not and do not concede any relevance to health for fear of making an admission. Rather they contend that such products are merely an accession to a baseless consumer concern—an effort to placate and humor a misguided public which believes in a risk that does not exist." More pointedly still, Sarokin noted the defense's position that Cipollone "was sufficiently warned by what these defendants contend was unproven and unreliable, and is barred from recovering from them if or because she believed what *they* said about the subject of smoking and health" (italics in original). Based on the evidence as a whole, a jury could "reasonably conclude" that the defendants had participated in a conspiracy "vast in its scope, devious in its purpose and devastating in its results."

All that Sarokin had needed to write was "Motion denied." Instead, the judge wrote in such a way that he appeared to be venting his rage toward gross corporate malefactors. Most press reports of his opinion barely noted his repeated mitigating phraseology—"a jury could thus reasonably conclude from the evidence . . ."—and dwelled on the scorching lines that followed. *The Wall Street Journal* headlined the story "Judge Says Tobacco Industry Hid Risks," while one leading local paper, the *Record* of Bergen County, New Jersey, where a number of the jurors lived, headed its account "Judge Finds Conspiracy by Tobacco Firms." Asserting that Sarokin must or should have known that his words would be taken as judgment of the plaintiff's claims, the defense moved—for the third time during the four and a half years the case had consumed—to have him removed as the presiding judge and called for a mistrial on the ground that the jurors had almost certainly read the judge's words in the press even though they had not been present in the court when they were spoken.

Sarokin declined to take himself out of the case for exercising his judicial prerogative to write an opinion that he believed the evidence before him warranted, and a poll of the jury showed that none of its members had read or heard anything about his heated ruling. The defense, never in much doubt about where Sarokin's heart resided in the case, could only lament what Murray Bring would afterward call "a diatribe against the industry—even before he heard our evidence."

V I

T HE defense's evidence consisted for the most part of a procession of witnesses contesting the exact type of lung cancer that Rose Cipollone had died from. Her attorney, fearful that the rest of his case could founder if he did not thoroughly clinch the causation issue, let himself be led down this diversionary pathway for weeks of highly technical testimony, the net effect of which was to befog the question in the jurors' minds. One of the defense team's attorneys confided after the trial, "It would have been risky but gutsy if Marc had sidestepped the whole technical argument by telling the jury, 'Whether she had an atypical carcinoid or oat-cell lung cancer isn't the point— Rose Cipollone died of lung cancer, and you all know what caused it.' "

The defense, of course, was playing a two-faced game. The industry's position had steadfastly been that it remained unproven that smoking caused *any* form of lung cancer—or, for that matter, any other disease. Why, then, were the company lawyers trying to convince the jury that she had had one kind of lung cancer instead of another? But Edell did not hammer at this subterfuge. Nor could he overcome the basic vulnerability in his own case—namely, trying to blame his client's death on the industry's failure to warn her early enough about the risks of smoking when, as he also contended, she was hopelessly addicted to cigarettes almost from the first and thus powerless to break her dependency. How, in that event, could any industry warnings have helped her? Besides, she did not even try to quit after the warnings were introduced by law; what evidence was there that she would have quit if they had been on the packs and in ads earlier? Edell's own expert witness on drug addiction conceded on the stand that his interview with Rose did not enable him to deny that she could have quit smoking, although years of reinforcement of the addiction had reduced "her flexibility". Even after her first lung cancer operation, he noted, she continued sneaking cigarettes, hiding them from Tony in her piano bench. Such testimony, defense attorney Bleakley recalled later, "was just what we wanted—we didn't need our own witness" on the addiction question.

Rose's failure even to attempt the travail of quitting also undermined Edell's ability to take advantage of a potentially huge break that occurred outside the courtroom during the closing stages of the trial. Surgeon General Koop released his annual report on smoking and health, this one devoted entirely to nicotine addiction. In it, Koop finally put to rest the judgment made in the original 1964 report that chronic smoking was more akin to a bad habit than a serious medical problem waiting to happen. "Cigarettes and other forms of tobacco are addicting," the 1988 report asserted; the pharmacological and behavioral processes contributing to it "are similar to those that determine addiction to drugs such as heroin and cocaine." The medical profession and the public at large were urged once and for all to set aside any lingering conception of smoking as a nasty little trait like nail-biting and of smokers as weak-willed and self-indulgent. The Tobacco Institute lost no time in dismissing the report by asserting it "runs counter to common sense, as proved by the fact that people can and do quit smoking when they make the decision. . . ." The *Cipollone* jury, as it soon turned out, agreed.

In the end, Edell was victimized perhaps less by his client's smoking history than by his own conscientiousness. His ambition was to bring down the whole industry—he saw no other way to win damages for his client; as a result, he tried to crowd too much into one trial, too much history, science, medicine, marketing, and psychology; too many witnesses who droned on too long; too many documents, the import of which was not made clear or threaded together. It was an overwhelming presentation for one jury to digest, and it was not helped by the defense's constant objections. Judge Sarokin, sensitive to industry charges that he was a less than neutral arbiter, entertained many of these objections in lengthy sidebars during which the jury was excused from the courtroom. These repeated interruptions broke the flow of Edell's argument and unduly prolonged the entire proceeding. And while Edell never stopped trying to expand his case into a vilification of an entire industry allegedly conspiring against the public for the better part of a century, the defense kept trying to narrow the case to the questions of what and when Rose Cipollone knew about the risks of smoking. Documents revealing what the industry knew, when it knew it, and what it did and did not do about it were all but ignored by the defense lawyers or trivialized as out-of-context remarks by underlings.

Peter Bleakley closed effectively for Philip Morris: "I suggest to you that there isn't anybody who's ever smoked who didn't know . . . that there were claims that cigarette smoking is bad for you." But Philip Morris had acted responsibly once those claims were linked to scientific charges, Bleakley asserted, by slashing the tar and nicotine yields of its brands in half between 1950 and 1966—"They changed their product"—and by entering into ongoing research on the health issue. The jury was not there to make any sweeping social judgments, Bleakley said, about whether smoking was good or bad or cigarette manufacturers spent too much on advertising or too little on research, because that was not the point of the Cipollone suit. "[M]ake no mistake about it, ladies and gentlemen, that is what this case is all about—money," whether Tony Cipollone, who had come to court every day in his royal blue sleeveless sweater and stood vigil over the proceedings, was entitled to collect damages from any of the defendants in behalf of his beloved Rose. Her death at fifty-eight, the star defense counsel concluded, was tragic, to be sure, and "There is no one in this courtroom that doesn't hope that medical science very soon will figure out . . . what exactly causes cancer—lung cancer—and how to cure it."

Drained by his herculean effort, Marc Edell managed a five-hour summation in which he tried to tie together the immense package of charges he had taken years to assemble. Alas, he lacked the courtroom command, the rhetorical grace, and, at the end, the sheer energy to heap moral indignation upon the defendants. But he soldiered on to the end, telling the jury:

> You represent the American people. . . . You have the power to regulate one of the most powerful industries in the world. In this courtroom there are no deals . . . just the truth. . . . You can tell the tobacco industry it is okay to withhold information . . . to distort information . . . to mislead people . . . to lie to people—it's okay. Or, as the first jury ever to see the internal workings of this industry [you] can say, "That is it. We have had enough . . . this is not acceptable behavior."

But the jury did not do that. After four and a half days of deliberation, it emerged with a somewhat confusing verdict that, when finally disentangled, was a sizable, if costly, victory for the cigarette makers. The newspapers and evening news telecasts, at last aware of the dimensions of *Cipollone v. Liggett*, led off their reports of the day's events with the sensational fact that for the first time, a tobacco company would have to pay damages to the family of a stricken smoker. Liggett was held to have been negligent for its failure prior to 1966 to warn smokers adequately of the health risks presented by their brands and for advertising that was interpretable as a warranty of product safety. Yet the jury awarded no damages to the estate of Rose Cipollone, because the company was found to have been only 20 percent responsible for her death—her own behavior was preponderantly at fault, and New Jersey law required a finding of at least 50 percent responsibility by the defendant for damages to be awarded. Almost as a consolation prize, however, the jurors awarded Tony Cipollone $400,000, apparently for having been a dutiful and concerned husband to the deceased claimant. Philip Morris and Lorillard, whose brands Rose smoked after the 1966 warnings began, were let off entirely. As to the claim of an industry-wide conspiracy to confuse and mislead the American public in order to sustain glittering profits, the jury found no fraud or intentional tort. All the illuminating documents amounted to no more than disparate fragments, hinting at deceptive conduct, perhaps, but far from conclusive and never firmly pinned to top executives, only to subordinates with the temerity at times to speak the truth.

Edell, regretful that he had never deposed Rose himself so that a more sympathetic presentation might have been made of her plight, nevertheless professed to be "very, very happy" with the outcome. "We won where nobody else has won before," he said, and while the monetary rewards did not begin to cover the nearly $3 million that the plaintiff's case had cost to sustain, Edell had other smoking claimants' cases lined up ready to build on the evidentiary and procedural gleanings of *Cipollone*. Not to be lost sight of was the enormous legal bill that the tobacco industry had had to absorb over the duration of the case; estimates ranged between $30 million and $50 million.

Still, Murray Bring could claim a substantive victory for the industry, which soon set about appealing the somewhat bizarre jury verdict and getting the $400,000 award vacated. Liggett's lawyers argued that Judge Sarokin had erred in failing to instruct the jury that in order for it to find a breach of the warranty that the company's pre-1966 advertising (*e.g.,* "Just what the Doctor Ordered") was said to have constituted, the plaintiff would have had to rely on it in her decision to begin or to continue smoking—it was not enough to show merely that the offensive ads existed—and Rose Cipollone's lawyers had not so proven. The award to Tony Cipollone, moreover, was said to be entirely inappropriate in view of the jury's failure to hold Liggett more than 20 percent responsible for causing the claimant's death. Edell, for his part, appealed on the grounds that Sarokin had erred in stripping away the heart of his intentional tort case in disallowing evidence on the defendants' alleged post-1966 behavior to subvert the warning labels and in applying retroactively the 1987 New Jersey tort "reform" law. The Third Circuit eventually agreed with both parties' appeals, holding that Sarokin had failed to instruct the jury properly on the warranty question, that the $400,000 award of damages was not justifiable under law—once again, the industry's record of never having paid a penny in damages was intact—and that the trial judge had read too much into the appeals court's earlier reversal of Sarokin's opinion that the federal labeling laws had not preempted smokers' liability suits based on failure-to-warn claims. Edell was free to seek a retrial and pursue his fraud and conspiracy case using post-1966 evidence. Meanwhile, the New Jersey Supreme Court, in a hearing on *Dewey v. Reynolds Tobacco*, the second of Edell's cigarette liability cases ready for trial, ruled that, despite the holdings of five circuit tribunals of the U.S. Court of Appeals, state common-law suits by smokers could proceed on the claim of inadequate post-1966 warnings and that Edell's cases against the tobacco companies could not be blocked retroactively by the New Jersey legislature. The stage was set for the U.S. Supreme Court to resolve these conflicting decisions.

The Justices heard the arguments twice, the second time to accommodate the high court's newly arrived member, Clarence Thomas. In mid-1992, the Supreme Court held, seven votes to two, for the tobacco industry's position that the 1970 revision of the federal cigarette labeling law was so worded that any award of damages by state juries on the claim of inadequate health warnings by the cigarette manufacturers in their packaging, advertising, and promotion would frustrate the congressional intent of establishing a single nationwide warning program. Nor could it be persuasively argued that the depiction of attractive and vigorous people in cigarette advertising was part of a scheme to undermine the federally mandated warnings; vendors had historically and naturally used such images to help sell their wares. But the Court's decision was by no means an unalloyed victory for the industry. The Justices also agreed with Edell's contention that the trial court had unfairly stripped away his post-1966 conspiracy claim—that the industry had concealed or misrepresented the truth on the smoking and health issue—on the invalid premise that because the plaintiff's failure-to-warn claim had to be limited to the industry's ads and promotion prior to that date, the intentional tort charges had to be similarly confined. As Justice John Paul Stevens wrote, "Congress offered no sign that it wished to insulate cigarette manufacturers from long-standing rules governing fraud. . . ." The case was remanded for retrial on that issue, and Edell announced his intention to show that the companies had indeed conspired to mislead the public.

But Edell had two problems to overcome. The first, which was soon to prove fatal, was the need for a continuing subsidy by his law firm, whose members had to make a cold assessment of Edell's chances of prevailing. That estimate was necessarily colored by the second of Edell's obstacles: even if he could put together a convincing case of industry-wide deception, could he get a jury to conclude that Rose Cipollone, or any of his other claimants, had begun and kept on smoking *because* of the companies' misconduct?

Edell's hopes had been buoyed four months before the Supreme Court decision, when Judge Sarokin, who was also assigned to *Haines v. Liggett Group*, another tobacco case, had ruled in favor of Edell's effort to obtain documents from the Council for Tobacco Research, and especially those dealing with its "special projects," involving company lawyers and research scientists to whom they gave grants. Based on documents Edell had uncovered in *Cipollone*, Sarokin held that a "reasonable jury could conclude" that the tobacco companies had "sought to discredit or neutralize the adverse information [on smoking and health] by proffering an independent research organization," whose primary purpose was in fact "directed at finding causes other than smoking for the illnesses being attributed to it"—and that the CTR's "announcement of proposed independent research into the dangers of smoking and its promise to disclose its findings was nothing but a public relations ploy—a fraud—to deflect the growing evidence against the industry. . . ." As he had also done during the *Cipollone* trial in denying the defense's motion for a dismissal of the case, Sarokin rose to rhetorical heights of indignation in stating an opinion that could have been offered at a far lower pitch. His February 2, 1992, ruling began:

> . . . All too often in the choice between the physical health of consumers and the financial well-being of business, concealment is chosen over disclosure, sales over safety, and money over morality. Who are these persons who knowingly and secretly decide to put the buying public at risk solely for the purpose of making profits and who believe that illness and death of consumers is an appropriate cost of their own prosperity!
>
> As the following facts disclose, despite some rising pretenders, the tobacco industry may be the king of concealment and disinformation.

Edell was thus empowered to present nearly 1,500 documents to a special master Sarokin was to name to determine if they were protected under the attorney-client privilege or, because the industry lawyers may have been parties to wrongful acts, could be used in pursuit of the claimant's charges of conspiracy.

Later that year, the Third Circuit finally bowed to the tobacco industry's repeated efforts to get Judge Sarokin out of its hair. He was ordered removed as the judge in pending tobacco liability cases because his opinion on the admissibility of documents in *Haines* contained language that gave the appearance of bias against the defendant companies. Sarokin registered surprise and unhappiness at this rebuke, saying that he thought it was his judicial duty to speak the truth in his opinions so long as they were based on an adequate factual record before his court. Some of Sarokin's friends and admirers, of whom there were legion, believed privately that, in venting his frustration over the outcome to date in *Cipollone* and the dubious prospect of other smoking claimants' cases, he had veered from the narrow path of dispassion into the thickets of judicial, not to say injudicious, retribution. But to the more passionate elements in the antismoking camp, Sarokin's reprimand seemed without justification. Richard Daynard, chief architect of the products liability crusade against the tobacco industry, commented, "He called it straight and did it in a way that was highly quotable. I had always thought that one of the functions of judges was to show moral indignation. . . ."

The loss of Sarokin, despite some of his restrictive rulings in *Cipollone*, was a severe setback for Edell. His successor in the tobacco liability cases would probably not be as tolerant in matters like qualifying experts and the admissibility of evidence—a problem that would arise at once now, because the Third Circuit, in removing Sarokin, had also vacated his opinion allowing the CTR documents to be considered in support of conspiracy charges against the cigarette makers. Then, too, Tony Cipollone had died, and his and Rose's children were unenthusiastic about pursuing the case in their mother's name. Edell's firm had grown even more unenthusiastic about carrying on the problematic, expensive, and seemingly endless struggle. With reluctance, Marc Edell ended his undermanned fight to humble the tobacco lords. But he had cost them millions in expenses and generated a body of evidence in their own words and writings which testified to an American industry's long unwillingness to deal straightforwardly with the society that licensed it.

19

Smooth Characters

B Y THE closing years of the twentieth century, the nonsmoking majority of Americans was wasting little sympathy on the 25 to 30 percent of their countrymen who continued to puff away, even as the Centers for Disease Control were reporting that the habit stole twelve years of life from the average smoker taken by a tobacco-caused illness. Victims of smoking had been told, and told repeatedly, that their bodies might not withstand the systemic abuse that the indulgence inflicted upon them decade after decade. AIDS sufferers, by contrast, were widely mourned because most of them had not known of the peril when they contracted the disease, were stricken when young, and died long before their time.

If Rose Cipollone had had a choice, as the cigarette manufacturers argued, in exposing herself to the well-known potential hazards of smoking, the industry could not claim as much for those assaulted by other people's smoke. However diluted it might be compared with active smoking and however inconclusive the scientific data thus far on its effects, secondhand smoke was coming to be widely viewed as an unacceptably antisocial imposition. Smokers almost everywhere were being reprimanded, restricted, and reviled as environmental polluters—assailants of innocent bystanders. A 1987 AMA survey found that 87 percent of nonsmokers and nearly half of smokers themselves believed that the former had the right to a smoke-free environment, even as smokers had the right to keep jeopardizing their own health in private. A poll that same year by the Centers for Disease Control showed that 75 percent of the respondents believed that environmental tobacco smoke (ETS) was harmful to nonsmokers, and 70 percent said they were annoyed by other people's smoke. And a Gallup poll disclosed that 84 percent of the adult population favored either separate smoking sections or a total ban on smoking in public areas; even two years earlier, according to a Gallup survey, 87 percent wanted smokers segregated at work sites—and four out of five smokers, probably guilt-ridden as much over the damage they might be doing to themselves as over what they might be inflicting on others, concurred. A U.S. government survey in 1987 found that 77 percent of smokers said they would like to quit— up from 66 percent a decade earlier.

"Human behavior responds to context," remarked psychologist Ellen Gritz, a leading editor of the Surgeon General's reports during the 1980s, and the social context by that decade's end had turned smoking into deviant conduct. Smokers found themselves more and more under assault everywhere they turned—by their loved ones, their friends, their doctors, their employers and workmates, the schools and churches in their communities, the media, and the government. They were suddenly being interfered with anyplace they went outside their homes—on almost all forms of public transportation on their way to work, at the workplace itself, whenever they dined out or shopped, wherever they went for cultural stimulation, and even at sporting events in the open air.

Although the federal government, run by deregulators during the dozen years of the Reagan and Bush administrations, mostly kept its hands off the cigarette makers, state and local governments were now launching a broad-ranged assault on smoking. By 1989, after a decade-long battle with tobacco interests whose position was championed by conservative Republican lawmakers, the New York state legislature became the eleventh in the nation to pass a comprehensive clean air and smoking control act. Among the strongest in the U.S., the law confined smoking to set-aside areas in offices, restaurants, theaters, and transportation facilities and banned it in schools, hospitals, many retail stores, and indoor sports arenas. That same year, as a further disincentive to smoking, thirteen states raised their excise tax on cigarette sales.

The prime arena for the smoking control movement was the workplace. Here politicians were far more hesitant to tread, since for the most part it was private property, but by the end of the 1980s about half of all U.S. companies had established some sort of smoking rules on their premises. The old reasons, mostly to guard against fire and protect sensitive equipment, were now supplemented by health considerations, as more and more firms contemplated a total ban on smoking. One of the first large companies to take that step—Boeing, the Seattle aircraft manufacturer—phased in the prohibition for its 85,000 workers over several years after its chief executive remarked, "When we provide a better operating atmosphere for our high-tech machinery than for the people who operate [it], then it's time to reassess policies." Outright bans were believed to have the dual advantage of cutting maintenance and insurance costs and improving productivity, since smokers in offices with set-aside areas were often found to be preoccupied by thoughts of their next cigarette break. Total bans ran into resistance, though, from unions and employee groups who objected to the loss of an activity they had long taken for granted. More enlightened companies seeking a smoke-free work environment offered smokers counseling and cessation programs. Pacific Northwest Bell, for example, 4,000 of whose 15,000 employees were smokers, found that 7.5 percent of them were off tobacco six months after availing themselves of the company-funded quitting clinics. Perhaps equally encouraging, smokers who continued the habit had cut their daily consumption from twenty-three cigarettes to seventeen.

This apparent fringe benefit was one of the chief, if rarely announced, purposes of the widening crusade against ETS. As the 1989 Surgeon General's report acknowledged, smoking restrictions, while serving to reduce the health risks for those involuntarily exposed, "may have the side effect of discouraging tobacco use by reducing opportunities to smoke and changing public attitudes about the social acceptability of smoking." Former OSH veteran officer Donald Shopland, by then coordinating smoking intervention programs for the National Cancer Institute, noted that one of the primary benefits of the new laws was to provide "a more supportive environment for people trying to quit." ASH's founder, John Banzhaf, added that if you were a smoker no longer surrounded by other smokers in a restricted workplace, "you're not getting visual and oral cues to smoke," and if every time you craved a cigarette, you had to get up, possibly ask permission, and take an inconvenient trek to a designated smoking area, you began to harbor serious doubts about the pleasures of your dependency.

For many smokers who did not want to quit, the social pressures to do so went well beyond inconvenience and discouragement. A reporter for the Long Island newspaper *Newsday*, part of a trade in which serious dragging on a cigarette was long a badge of hard-boiled grace under pressure, summed up the sentiment of all besieged smokers when the practice was banned in his city room: "This is a process of humiliation." Throughout the country smokers felt the change. At social gatherings they slipped out onto balconies or into backyards to indulge rather than face possible abuse for befouling the indoor air. At restaurants, even when obeying the separate seating rules, they hid their cigarettes under the table and waved away the smoke to avoid the dirty looks of smoke-sensitive patrons. And at offices and plants, those desperate for a cigarette were disappearing into hallways, stairwells, and rest rooms, hovering outside building entrances, even hunching against outside walls to avoid the raw elements, and if allowed to indulge in a ghettoized quadrant within the cafeteria, some gulped down two or three cigarettes' worth of smoke within the time normally allotted for one. *The Wall Street Journal* reported that some executives were finding their path to career advancement impeded by their smoking affliction, which their superiors inclined to view as a symptom of deficient self-control or weak character. But at all levels, smokers sensed the growing animosity. Said one employee at a New York publishing company devoted to medical journals: "People make you feel like you've got some filthy habit."

This perception was reinforced by a television commercial produced by the New York agency of Saatchi & Saatchi for Northwest Airlines. It showed a cabinful of passengers standing and cheering the voice-over announcement that the airline had gone entirely smoke-free. For this antic presentation, the admaker was promptly fired by another of its accounts, RJR Nabisco, even though the agency had been handling only food products for the big cigarette maker. Such vengeful acts, however, could not change the prime sociological fact of cigarette marketing a century after Buck Duke had introduced America to the joys of the little smokes: just as peer pressure had once worked to spread the cigarette habit across the land, and then the globe, now it was operating in reverse.

I I

FEARFUL for its livelihood, the tobacco industry counterattacked broadly by declaring smoking to be a civil and human right that the cigarette-haters were out to crush. In institutional advertisements that ignored the health issue, the industry called out for tolerance of their customers' lifestyle preferences and "individual choice"—a thinly coded pitch to ally smokers with other abused minorities and casting smoking control advocates as bullies, not just busybodies and killjoys. If their foes prevailed, said the Tobacco Institute's veteran spokesman Walker Merryman, "[w]e end up with a product that's too expensive to buy, too inconvenient to use, and that you can't tell anybody about. . . . [Y]ou might as well call that Prohibition."

The strategic thrust of the cigarette manufacturers' counterattack was to present themselves as accommodationists and to campaign for soft "clean in-door air" laws that set aside no-smoking zones in virtually all public places statewide and thus reestablished smoking as socially acceptable. What the smoking control movement was after, of course, was precisely the opposite arrangement: all indoor areas to be declared smoke-free unless otherwise specified. The industry-authored bills in their ideal form added a preemptive feature, whereby the statewide smoking regulations, however tepid, superseded all local measures, thus allowing the tobacco lobbyists to fight one battle at a time in any given state and not to have to scatter their resources combating brushfires in every municipal and county jurisdiction.

An instance of the industry's strategy at its most effective was the contest played out in the late 'Eighties in Pennsylvania, where Pittsburgh had led the way in antismoking regulations with a strong law limiting the practice in offices, restaurants, and other public places and requiring employers to provide sizable smoke-free areas. Philadelphia, Harrisburg, and Erie, among other cities in the state, adopted versions of the Pittsburgh restrictions. But after the tobacco lobby pressured the legislators, Pennsylvania put on its books a statewide law preempting every municipal antismoking regulation except Pittsburgh's and obliging only restaurants with seventy-five or more seats to set aside a no-smoking section and employers to set some sort of smoking policy, even if it amounted to minimal restrictions or none whatever. One Pennsylvania Democratic state senator who had fought for nine years for meaningful smoking controls called the industry-backed law "a marshmallow but better than nothing." More farsighted antismoking advocates saw such compromises as surrender.

Whenever possible, the industry tried to tack on to the state clean indoor air laws—or to push separately for—statutorily guaranteed "smokers' rights," intended to prevent infrequent but disturbing instances of discrimination by employers who refused to hire smokers, even if they agreed to abide by company smoking rules while on the job, or fired them if they were discovered to smoke during non-working hours, even in their own homes. Such displays of intolerance, rationalized as economically prudent, provided the tobacco interests with a perfect opportunity to shove aside legitimate concerns about secondhand smoke and to plead instead for justice for victimized smokers. Nearly one-third of the states passed some form of "smokers' rights" legislation, including New Jersey, where Philip Morris lobbyists wrote the law, which included barring insurance companies from charging higher premiums to smokers. One measure of the shrewdness of this industry tactic was the way it split elements within the smoking control movement. While the New Jersey chapter of the Coalition on Smoking or Health, made up of the three big health voluntaries in that state, and the vigorous GASP organization there strongly opposed the smokers' rights bill as the legislature was considering it, others in the anti-smoking camp feared that the industry lobbyists might succeed in trapping health advocates by tarring them as biased militants. Over the Advocacy Institute's electronic internet, for example, John Slade, a professor at Robert Wood Johnson Medical School in New Brunswick, New Jersey, and a leader of the American Society of Addiction Medicine, warned his colleagues:

> In conceding this issue to the tobacco industry, we give them what they otherwise have a hard time finding: a credible issue. . . . Sure, many people, including most news organizations, see their rhetoric as transparently emanating from 120 Park Avenue [Philip Morris's New York headquarters], but that does not rob the issue of the kernel of truth that we advocate discrimination against

people who smoke simply because they smoke. . . . Why are we advocating less protection for people addicted to nicotine? Do we imagine that people are not really hooked? . . . There are important strategic, legal, humane, and public health reasons to shift gears and to advocate job protection for people who are handicapped by nicotine addiction.

Big tobacco did not hesitate to dig into its deep pockets to resist the social tide through the purchase and manipulation of the political process. Although some in the antismoking movement were in awe of the industry's reputedly adroit lobbying operations, Congressman Henry Waxman's legislative aide Ripley Forbes, who often crossed swords with the industry's hired hands, remarked, "There's no magic in it, it's a very basic issue—their power and influence starts and ends with their money."

Just how much money the industry spent in this connection can only be guessed at based on clues provided by the few disclosure rules imposed on the lobbying game. Probably the least of the expenditures were the campaign contributions through political action committees (PACs), intended to assure tobacco lobbyists of a hearing by, if not the votes of, their congressional recipients. While cigarette PACs contributed a reported $2.5 million to congressmen during the 1991–92 term, for the same period Philip Morris alone spent about half that much on its Washington-based federal lobbyists, and the Tobacco Institute, with a headquarters staff of around 75 and an additional 125 contract lobbyists in the states, cost the industry another $5 to $10 million a year. Its lobbying bill in the states, where antismoking forces were proving more active and successful than in Washington, was much higher cumulatively. In California alone during the 1989–90 term of the state legislature, the cigarette companies spent a reported $4 million on campaign gifts and fees to more than two dozen lobbyists working the statehouse in Sacramento. The $600,000 reportedly spent by the industry during the 1993 session of the New York state legislature amounted to more than any other industry or special interest group devoted to political persuasion in Albany. Bulging war chests were also provided to finance fights against challenges deemed critical to the industry, like the $3.3 million spent in 1994 on trying to stave off a tripling of the cigarette tax in Michigan and an estimated $12.5 million the same year in California to win an industry-initiated referendum for a statewide smoking control program that would have overridden all 300 or so local regulations. (The industry lost both fights.)

With such resources readily available, tobacco lobbyists could throw lavish entertainments like the annual "legislative conference" at deluxe golf resorts in Palm Springs, California, where congressmen were offered what amounted to three- or four-day, all-expenses-paid vacations worth $3,000 to $5,000 in return for an hour or two devoted to political science. These outings regularly attracted three or four dozen congressmen, among them House Speaker Jim Wright, Ways and Means (*i.e.*, tax-writing) Committee Chairman Dan Rostenkowski, and minority leader Robert Michel. The Congressional Black Caucus received $155,000 in tobacco money in 1993, and large gifts went as well to the Hispanic caucus and the Senate Employees Child Care Center. The industry could also pinpoint its friends and enemies in state and local legislative bodies and reward or punish them accordingly, as, for example, when it helped pay for plane and limousine travel for California Assembly Speaker and tobacco ally Willie Brown (in addition to campaign contributions that would have embarrassed some elected officials) and mounted a recall campaign against an Albuquerque councilman who had sponsored the passage of a strong smoking restriction law in New Mexico's largest city (the councilman survived).

On top of its pursuit of favor with public officeholders, the industry stepped up its efforts to enlist political, cultural, and ideological allies wherever it could find them, ranging from antigovernment libertarians to labor unions to abortion-rights advocates—"choice" had been their bannered slogan before the tobacco lobby seized upon it—to the American Civil Liberties Union. The ACLU claimed not to have been swayed by the $500,000 it had received from tobacco companies between 1987 and 1992, when that supposedly most principled of organizations sent its spokesmen before congressional committees to oppose a contemplated ban on cigarette advertising and, in the process, to argue that there was no evidence that advertising encouraged smoking or that its suppression would discourage it.

The Tobacco Institute, while continuing as a clearinghouse for intelligence reports on antismoking sentiment and legislative activities around the nation, served less and less as the spearhead for the industry's defensive efforts. TI continued to host weekly skull sessions run by lawyers from Covington & Burling on how to target the industry's lobbying, but the shape, pace, and locus of the industry's lobbying operations were now being largely determined by its market leader.

Philip Morris and R. J. Reynolds between them held nearly three-quarters of the American cigarette market. PM, though, was selling half again as many cigarettes as RJR by the 1990s—by 1995, it was selling twice as many—and the latter was temporarily in the hands of New York financiers, preoccupied with reducing their immense debt burden before it crushed them. Third-place Brown & Williamson had quit the Tobacco Institute for a number of years, partly out of pique over the Barclay brand squabble, and so remained outside the industry's councils. American Tobacco and the Lorillard division of Loews maintained their long-standing policies of saying virtually nothing about the controversial aspects of the cigarette business. And the Liggett Group, though it brought in the combative former RJR tobacco chief Edward Horrigan in the early 'Nineties to try to revitalize its operations, was just too small a factor, with only a few percentage points of the market, to be influential. Increasingly, Philip Morris was running the show.

The company's lobbying operations, almost certainly far larger than the Tobacco Institute's, were directed out of Washington, although its New York executives were constantly involved and retained the last word. Masterminding the nationwide program was a small team of lawyers at Arnold & Porter headed by Jack Quinn and a tightly supervised satellite group at APCO Associates, a subsidiary providing business and political counsel but no legal services to clients, under Neal Cohen. The hush-hush Quinn-Cohen joint apparatus, devoted to monitoring Philip Morris's nationwide lobbying, was believed to be costing the company several million dollars in fees a year by the early 'Nineties, exclusive of the expenses to run PM's own Washington lobbying office, a low-visibility layout on G Street. The battle was being waged in so many places that Philip Morris pressed its own workforce, an army now numbering some 160,000, into service as its eyes and ears in the field. But the weapons were placed in the hands of outside paid lobbyists who prowled every state capital to block or blunt antismoking measures.

Details of this ongoing campaign were of course not made public, but its scope, methods, and cost could be inferred from documents anonymously delivered to Alan Blum's DOC headquarters in Dallas and dealing with Philip Morris's 1989 lobbying efforts in its Southwest region. That year in Missouri, for example, PM spent $134,000 on campaign gifts to legislators and state political parties and $85,000 on its two leading lobbyists. For this investment the lobbying team succeeded in killing a proposed rise in the state cigarette tax and new restrictions on smoking, but it could not pry a proposed smokers' rights bill out of committee. PM's chief agent in Arizona, due to receive a fee of $53,000 in 1990, was commended for "a great job with his first session as our lobbyist. He is best friends with the Speaker and use[d] personal clout to kill our cigarette tax." The $13,000 spent on a gala reception for Arizona legislators at the opening session seemed a sound investment since they later defeated proposed new public smoking restrictions, a ban on cigarette vending machines, and an enlargement of the health warning on cigarette billboards. In Louisiana, where the company's top lobbyist was down for a $77,000 fee the following year, the report noted approvingly, "We are members of all the groups. Particularly helpful is the Association of Business and Industry, which fronted the products [tort reform] stuff." The PM group there was credited with keen tactical acumen for knowing when to back off after it decided not to push for designated smoking and nonsmoking areas in government buildings "because all legislation that would adversely affect smokers had been killed." The regional report card gave high marks, too, to the Oklahoma lobbying team, because it had both blocked a tax increase and managed to have smoking areas designated in all state buildings "and seems to be able to hold [the legislature's] leadership to coming out in the press against a cigarette tax every time the Governor brings it up, which is often."

These efforts were minuscule when compared with the Philip Morris program in Texas, where it spent $441,000 in 1989 on lobbyists and consultants, aside from such off-the-books outlays as $10,000 for a "legislative buck hunt" and a similar amount on a dance honoring the African-American community in Dallas. By a quaint parliamentary maneuver adopted at the beginning of every term, no more than 11 votes in the 31-member Texas Senate were needed to block the call-up of any given piece of legislation for a vote by the upper chamber of the legislature, which was more liberal than the 150-member, strongly pro-business House and dominated by the influence of the consumer-oriented, litigiously disposed Texas Trial Lawyers Association. Thus, PM's chief lobbyist (proposed 1990 salary: $63,000) and his team "will always concentrate on the Senate," the company field report noted, "but there are things we can do in the House that will be of major benefit to us. We will continue to cater to the Speaker and his pet projects, as well as to the five or six committee chairs that have [helped] and will help us. . . ."

To win political influence with lawmakers, PAC contributions to their campaigns were only the most visible ploys, according to one former APCO employee, "because there were so many other ways to approach the policymakers in a given state." Among these were entertainment, consulting fees, honoraria for speeches, and gifts to charities designated by the targeted lawmakers and other officials. A classic example of this last device was the Philip Morris philanthropic program in Wisconsin, where during the decade following U.S. Senator Robert Kasten's 1981 arrival in Washington, the company spread around 5,000 charitable gifts worth $6 million. The fact that Kasten, who received more in campaign gifts from PM than any other senator, came from Milwaukee, headquarters of the company's Miller Brewing operations, was probably not a coincidence.

The key to purchasing influence at the state level was personal friendships. PM lobbyists and their Washington and New York overseers spent endless hours trying to identify the closest past and current associates of the power wielders in each capital "and how to get them on the APCO payroll," said the former operative, a lawyer on lease to the lobbying controllers. When necessary, these key contacts would be lured away from their previous positions, but if they were already private practitioners of the law or public relations, they would typically be put on retainer for a year at a time, even when the vital contact work might involve setting up only a single meeting.

The process at its most painstaking and costly unfolded in Texas in the course of a six-year effort, from 1987 through 1993, when Philip Morris lobbyists engineered "tort reform" in the nation's second most populous state. To corral the right influence-peddlers, according to the APCO dropout who was on hand during part of this grueling effort, the company's Washington operatives were heard to remark repeatedly, "We'll pay whatever's necessary." He added, "They never balked if the bill came to $20,000 instead of $10,000 to hire a strategic friend, and some went for more than that." During the Texas tort reform battle, as many as fifty "consultants" a year were enlisted to promote the legislation, which was simultaneously advanced by an ad hoc front group dubbed the Texas Civil Justice League (TCJL), the nation's largest tort reform coalition, consisting at its peak of more than one hundred trade and professional organizations, chambers of commerce, and health-care providers. Their purpose was to revise the state's allegedly permissive personal injury claim code, which sometimes allowed plaintiffs to win huge damage awards from runaway, antibusiness juries—an injustice said to have cost the state some 80,000 jobs and $8 billion in corporate revenues because companies had either left Texas for that reason or declined to come to it. The TCJL's tort reform measure was put forward in 1987, the same year in which such bills were bustled through the California and New Jersey legislatures on the eve of their adjournments, providing in essence that products that could not be made safe ought not to be the manufacturers' responsibility after purchase by forewarned customers. Consumer advocates assailed the "tort reform" proposal as a lobbyist-driven outrage, and the contest was joined.

According to one knowledgeable Democratic member of the Texas House of Representatives, the TCJL "employed dozens of the highest paid, most effective lobbyists in the state" to push the tort revision effort, freely spending millions over the course of the project since under Texas law, it was not a lobby but a trade group and, as such, was not required to disclose where its funds came from, only approximately how much each lobbyist spent. The system all but invited abuse, and in the case of the TCJL, according to one of its foes, "served as nothing more than a method for laundering the lobbying money paid by the pharmaceutical, insurance, and tobacco industries, among others." Though claiming to be a broad-based coalition, the TCJL "was Philip Morris's show," said the ex-APCO man who witnessed its activities. The industry leader's name was never mentioned in the press as the prime mover in the tort law drive.

The TCJL effort achieved partial success during the 1987 legislative session: claimants held to be 50 percent or more responsible could not be awarded damages, and claims were capped at $200,000 or four times actual losses like hospital costs and lost wages, whichever was higher. But those limitations fell well short of a satisfying victory, and so the drive was renewed in 1989 under chief lobbyist Jack Gullahorn, a Dan Quayle look-alike and a disarmingly smooth member of one of the most powerful law firms in Texas—Akin, Gump, Strauss, Hauer & Feld. Gullahorn had eighteen other clients beside the TCJL that he lobbied for at that time, including Texaco, several banks, the fireworks and billboard industries, and the Gulf Coast Conservation Association, and was so well connected around Austin, the state capital, that in the days before mobile phones were commonplace, a pay telephone booth just outside the Texas House chamber was set aside largely for his personal use and decorated with flowers, family photos, and a deer head in humorous tribute to his influence.

Gullahorn's key connection in the tort revision drive was Dallas attorney Dan Matheson, who during Republican Governor Bill Clements's first term (1978–82) headed the state's Washington office for federal relations. Clements, a somewhat laconic figure who some felt was more at home with his country club set than in the governor's office, lost his first bid for reelection, but won a second term in 1986. Matheson, though considered close to Clements, did not serve in his second administration, and during the regular 1989 session Gullahorn turned to him to lead the tort law revision effort. The TCJL lobbyists had failed to win strong support from the executive branch by the time Clements agreed to place the tort issue on the agenda for a special legislative session. In an August 4, 1989, memo marked "Highly Confidential" and addressed to Arnold & Porter's Quinn and Cohen in Washington and Philip Morris attorney David Zelkowitz at corporate headquarters in New York, Gullahorn outlined the proposed strategy, which began:

1. Educating the Governor and his staff.

   A. Choose a primary peer spokesman. Ed Vetter [chairman of the Texas Commerce Department] is the preferred choice. Dan [Matheson] would outline the best strategy for educating Ed and requesting that he lead the delegation to the Governor and explain the economic importance of the issue. Should Vetter decline, we would have identified an alternate leader.

After that, the memo proposed, the primary spokesman would head a team from business groups who would further educate the governor on the shortcomings of the present law, after which a third contact group, drawn from the governor's friends and confidants, would personally call upon Clements to press the issue.

Despite such elaborate planning, pro-consumer legislators blocked passage of the TCJL-backed bill. By the time the legislature reconvened in 1991, a new governor presided over Texas—moderate Democrat Ann Richards—and her lieutenant governor, Bob Bullock, who presided over the state Senate, had once headed the Texas attorney general's consumer and antitrust division. Prospects for tort revision seemed bleak, and indeed got nowhere that term.

But Gullahorn persevered. He added new groups to his coalition, got learned articles published seeming to authenticate the grim effect on Texas business of plump awards by juries to product liability claimants, and helped install as head of the TCJL the former chief deputy to Lieutenant Governor Bullock when he had served as state comptroller in the late 1970s. Bullock's parliamentarian, moreover, was the father of an RJR lobbyist, one of twenty-eight who were helping push the TCJL cause (including six for Philip Morris) by the time the legislature convened to consider what Ralph Nader had tagged "the 1993 Wrongdoers' Protection Bill." By then Bullock was not only aboard Gullahorn's wagon but pushing hard to turn tort revision into law—an effort bolstered immeasurably by the defeat in the 1992 election of three pro-consumer members of the Senate, destroying the thin protective margin that had denied victory to the TCJL forces for four years. Fearing they would be overwhelmed and denied virtually all causes of product liability claims, the trial lawyers' association succumbed to the Bullock-brokered deal that removed tobacco, liquor, and firearms from the list of actionable products. The victory probably cost the cigarette companies $5 to $10 million.

"This is the biggest gift any legislature has ever given the tobacco industry," declared DOC's Alan Blum, who went on to blast Bullock for having accepted campaign funds from the industry and proceeded to do its bidding. Bullock's spokeswoman replied that the $7,500 he had taken in tobacco PAC money in 1990 was peanuts compared to what others accepted, "and it would be incorrect to conclude that it bought anything. Bob Bullock has always considered himself a consumer advocate."

Such efforts as the Texas triumph served to safeguard tobacco companies' treasuries against raids by claimants but did not help smokers escape a spreading web of restrictions by state and local authorities. The earlier wave of clean indoor air acts inevitably prompted a demand for more sweeping laws to create smoke-free environments. States on the cutting edge of social legislation, like California, New York, Washington, and Maryland, were banning or rigidly confining smoking almost everywhere people congregated, and many other states were moving in that direction. By 1995, according to *Common Cause* magazine, more than 600 local jurisdictions had joined in a patchwork quilt of antismoking restrictions across America. Some 100 communities had banned the sale of cigarettes by vending machines. Columbus, Ohio, a conservative, midsize city, barred smoking in its stores, theaters, and bowling alleys, while New York City implemented perhaps the most stringent smoking control law of any U.S. metropolis, banning the practice in most public places except small restaurants, offices occupied by three or fewer people, and set-aside zones that met fixed high-ventilation levels. By then more than three-quarters of all

American corporations with 750 or more employees had either banned smoking outright or sharply limited it, even if state laws did not call for such measures, and more than half of smaller businesses had done the same.

III

A LTHOUGH the belief in secondhand smoke as a serious health menace had become the most potent contributor to the nation's deepening war on cigarettes, just how real a peril it was had not been definitively determined. The three authoritative reports in 1986—by the U.S. Surgeon General, the National Academy of Sciences, and the congressional Office of Technology Assessment—had all agreed that further serious research was needed before a true appraisal of the ETS risk could emerge. Smoking control advocates, though, their patience exhausted from decades of evasion and denial by the tobacco industry about the health risks of direct smoking, would not wait for definitive evidence on ETS.

The fact remained, however, that it was proving difficult to develop epidemiological data on ETS drawn from real-life conditions. How heavy a dose of toxic substances smokers themselves directly ingested had long been readily calculable, but no one had been able to figure out practicable ways to determine—except theoretically—dilution rates of ETS and how to classify just who was or wasn't exposed to it at least to some degree in a society where it was next to impossible to avoid the stuff. It was also questionable science, however tempting, to extrapolate risk ratios at low exposures from the effects observed at higher exposures. As a 1994 study for the Congressional Research Service noted, "The existence of an exposure threshold for disease onset below which many passive smokers fall is not implausible. Many organisms have the capacity to cleanse themselves of some level of contaminants"—which was why public-health policymakers usually did not insist that every unit of air or water pollution be scrubbed from the environment.

By the late 'Eighties, the population studies on ETS remained few, involved a low number of subjects (usually fifty or fewer), and revealed relatively weak links to cancer—they consistently showed a 20 to 30 percent heightened risk for exposed nonsmokers, compared to the risk for those reporting no exposure from spouses or at their workplaces; an increased risk of 100 to 200 percent was generally regarded as significant evidence of causation by epidemiologists. Few antismoking advocates candidly noted the disproportionate bases of the risks being claimed. Only one or two nonsmokers per thousand died of lung cancer, while fifty to one hundred smokers per thousand succumbed to it; by stressing the risk of ETS exposure, the smoking control movement was effectively trivializing the risk from direct smoking, which was thirty to forty times greater. It was an incendiary, effective, but questionable tactic for those on the side of the angels.

What the antismoking camp most needed was a finding by the Environmental Protection Agency that ETS qualified as what the EPA termed a Group A carcinogen, meaning that it was found to cause at least 1 death per 100,000, the measure by which asbestos, radon, and a dozen other substances were branded human killers and thus subject to government regulation. By such a finding, ETS would be elevated to an official public menace, given the all but universal exposure to it by the American public, and it would hardly matter how relatively slight the risk from it might be for any healthy individual; in the process, the industry's chief defense—that ETS had not been shown to be a legitimate health risk but was, for some, a source of annoyance, readily mitigated by courtesy on both sides—would be destroyed.

Thus, as the EPA in the late 1980s undertook a formal risk assessment of ETS, the tobacco industry was much vexed at the prospect. If the agency pronounced secondhand smoke carcinogenic to man, the Labor Department's Occupational Safety and Health Administration (OSHA) would be standing by to issue smoking regulations, which the EPA was not empowered to do, for the proprietors and managers of the nation's businesses. To strengthen its hand, the tobacco industry decided to encourage research on ETS rather than just stand by helplessly—and, it would be charged, negligently—while unsympathetic government investigators carried on the quest. If the companies had undertaken the research in their own laboratories, had arrived at unfavorable findings, and then had suppressed them, they would have risked charges of fraudulently deceiving the public. If, on the other hand, their own findings exonerated ETS as a serious health peril, they would surely have been disparaged as the work of predisposed scientists. Their decision, therefore, implemented in 1988, was to establish the Center for Indoor Air Research (CIAR), in the dubious tradition of the Council for Tobacco Research, overseen by an advisory board of scientists from leading universities who made grants to investigators unaffiliated with the industry. Maddeningly, as Philip Morris house counsel Steven Parrish commented, "[W]e get criticized for trying to buy off scientists, even though the grants are given with no strings attached." But CIAR did not function beyond the industry's close surveillance, as one top Philip Morris scientist conceded, having served on the industry's "oversight committee" for CIAR, which he characterized as "a creature of the industry."

CIAR's agenda was heavily laden with projects contending that many other factors besides ETS, such as faulty ventilation systems and a rogues' gallery of other contaminants less visible and aromatic than smoke, caused the real problem with indoor air. But CIAR also sponsored studies of authentic value by reputable investigators, such as the American Health Foundation report "Determination of Nicotine Metabolites by Immunochemical Methods," a step toward measuring ETS dosages. The industry, though, also crossed to the shady side of the street by contributing millions of dollars, according to reports by NBC News and *The New York Times*, to a Fairfax County, Virginia–based private company called Healthy Buildings International, which ostensibly conducted objective indoor air pollution tests and reported their findings to owners or tenants. A number of whistle-blowers once employed by the company charged that the data gathered during its inspections, which almost never faulted ETS as a major pollutant, were routinely doctored to reduce the measured level of ambient smoke and that its representatives, coached by tobacco industry personnel, made frequent public appearances during which they downplayed ETS as a serious health threat. Asked about these disclosures, the Tobacco Institute admitted that it had given funds to Healthy Buildings, which it called "a fine firm."

In gearing up for its ETS evaluation, the EPA enlisted a sixteen-member panel of experts, including six who had received industry grants, to counsel its scientific advisory board. They gave every sign of approaching the task judiciously. The agency was then aspiring to Cabinet-level status and thus was eager to be viewed not as a bunch of antibusiness, power-hungry bureaucrats but as prudent guardians of the public interest, in touch with everyday realities. One result was that over the ensuing four years of the Bush presidency, EPA allowed itself to be pressured and interfered with by tobacco industry lawyers and officials in what Michael Pertschuk, guru of the smoking control movement, called "a classic failure of bureaucratic nerve." But the delays and hesitations in issuing the EPA risk assessment on ETS were at least partly due to the seriousness of the tobacco industry's objections to the evaluation process.

At first the EPA took pains to be warily cordial when the tobacco industry lawyers approached them and offered help in the ETS risk assessment. That the agency feared the industry's wolfish intent, though, was made clear when a high official wrote to the tobacco lawyers in February of 1988, ". . . We are neither seeking the advice of the tobacco industry nor opening a formal line of communication." Yet a month later, EPA sent industry lawyers the draft of a handbook the agency was drawing up for employers and institutional administrators entitled "Understanding Indoor Air Pollution"—a curious procedure in view of the agency's own concurrent risk assessment of ETS; why not wait for the completion of the latter before undertaking the former?

The industry lawyers' reply to the invitation to review the handbook gave EPA officials a clearer understanding of what they were in for. Many of the assertions in the draft of the booklet were unfounded, the tobacco people said, and the suggestion that eliminating ETS will "get rid of relevant pollutants is simply wrong." On the contrary, a large number of studies "show that poor ventilation is by far the most important cause of indoor air pollution," the industry spokesman added, and the 1986 Surgeon General's report had not concluded that ETS was "a leading cause of lung cancer in nonsmokers," as the EPA booklet said, and because of all the foregoing inaccuracies, it "seriously misrepresents the consensus of the scientific community." Later in the year, Tobacco Institute lawyers took further issue with the draft of an EPA "fact sheet" on ETS, part of the agency's series on indoor pollutants. They claimed to be particularly upset by the assertion, "plainly without justification," that "ETS contributes 80 to 90 percent of the pollution present" in buildings where smoking was permitted, and pointed out that the Surgeon General had determined that no previously healthy person was likely to develop chronic lung disease on the basis of "involuntary smoke exposure in adult life."

The war of words escalated the following spring, when the TI enlisted Virginia's U.S. Senator John Warner, who wrote EPA to ask why the handbook was being written by Robert Rosner, director of the Smoking Policy Institute in Seattle, whom Warner called "an outspoken and vehement antismoking advocate," and why both the handbook and the fact sheet were being written before the risk assessment had been completed, implying a prejudicial mind-set on the part of the agency. An assistant administrator, William G. Rosenberg, replied to the senator that Rosner was familiar with the subject and that his writings would be closely edited but that "whether or not there are health effects associated with ETS is no longer in question." Just how serious those effects were, however, was precisely the question being investigated.

Pressure on the agency grew and the exchanges became more pointed by mid-1989, when the Tobacco Institute's attorney, John Rupp of Covington & Burling, told Rosenberg that the TI had received "numerous calls from smokers around the country" who had lost their jobs, been shunted to undesirable locations, or been denied the opportunity to compete for a job because the person in charge of their office "had decided that ETS has been proven to be a health hazard." While it was true that the TI had been allowed to comment on the handbook and fact sheet drafts, "at no time has there been an opportunity for a scientific discussion of fundamental issues regarding ETS," Rupp wrote, adding, "All opposing data and views are simply ignored. We cannot understand how such an approach can be justified." The price the industry was now paying for all the years it had acted to confuse the public through its disinformation efforts was revealed by Rosenberg's response: "Frankly, the tobacco industry's argument . . . would be more credible if it were not so similar to the tobacco industry's position on direct smoking, despite the estimated 50,000 studies linking smoking with disease in humans."

But the two situations were not comparable. Public impressions to the contrary, no investigator had produced evidence remotely approaching in strength and consistency findings like those incriminating direct smoking by Wynder, Hammond and Horn, Doll and Hill, and Auerbach. The industry could thus retain the hope that a large-scale study might fail to show a correlation between lung cancer occurrence and exposure to ETS among nonsmokers. Such results, however, might not find their way into scientific journals because of a phenomenon known as "publication bias"; studies that produced negative results or did not report a statistically significant relationship were generally assigned a low priority among submissions.

But in the spring of 1990, a Philip Morris scientist, Thomas J. Borelli, who bore the suggestive title of "manager of scientific issues," was scouring about for unpublished studies on ETS and, while consulting the University Microfilms International Dissertation Information Service, struck gold. Not only did he find a doctoral dissertation done at Yale by Luis Varella, a Mexican postdoctoral physician, but the study was larger than any U.S. investigation yet reported in the scientific press. And the results were cause for joy within the tobacco industry. As Borelli noted, after making 300 copies of the dissertation and sending it to the EPA, ACS, HHS, and concerned scientists around the nation, "Varella looked at 439 lung cancer cases in nonsmokers"—implying that he had been the primary and original investigator, since no other names were cited—and found "no statistically significant increased risk of lung cancer in nonsmokers exposed to tobacco smoke in the workplace or in social situations." Nor had Varella found any elevated risk among nonsmokers due to spousal smoking, which was the key measure of dosage in the Hirayama and other studies that had reported an elevated risk of, on average, about 30 percent above that for unexposed nonsmokers.

The size of Varella's sampling and the Yale imprimatur gave his findings special cachet, and in mid-June, Philip Morris's John Nelson, vice president for corporate affairs, crowed in a letter published in *The New York Times* that Varella's study was the most prominent recent addition of evidence to the body of work on ETS in which "no study of exposure to tobacco smoke in the workplace or public places has demonstrated a scientifically significant risk to nonsmokers" and that eighteen of twenty-three studies that dealt with the effects of spousal smoking had failed to report such a risk. It followed, to Nelson's way of thinking, that the nonsmoking majority ought to willingly accommodate smokers' needs by providing them with ample designated areas or properly ventilated public places to carry away ETS.

The full story about Varella's dissertation, which Borelli did not disclose, possibly because it did not alter the validity of its conclusions, was that it was derived entirely from data gathered during 1981–85 under an NCI grant to investigators headed by Dwight T. Janerich, director of epidemiology for New York State before transferring in 1986 to Yale Medical School. There Varella approached him about the possibility of using his group's raw data for his own doctoral thesis. Since it was not unusual for students to work on part of large existing data sets, Janerich and the rest of Varella's advisory committee approved the arrangement. Varella finished his work in 1987, when it was judged to be of a high order, approved, and copied by University Microfilms for the benefit of mankind—if anyone was interested in looking it up. Janerich, meanwhile, immersed in new assignments at Yale and without a grant to complete the ETS study, which had produced a great deal of raw data, was able to attend to it only sporadically, and so it had languished—until Borelli drew attention to it somewhat indirectly by publicizing Varella's treatment of a portion of the data.

The Philip Morris scientist was not the only one keenly interested in Varella's dissertation. The year before Borelli came upon it, an EPA advisor, Kenneth G. Brown, working with the review panel involved in the ETS risk assessment, learned of its existence and the surrounding circumstances and wrote to Janerich, identifying his link to the EPA and asking for further data but without indicating any urgency or stressing the official nature of his inquiry. Janerich, taking the request to be informal and somewhat offhand, was not eager to share his group's findings with a casual inquirer before they had been refined and published. Borelli learned from the EPA that Brown's request to Janerich had not been complied with and, unable to understand why the Yale epidemiologist had not published anything on the timely subject, grew "concerned that the data was being 'dredged' in order to find a statistical relationship," as he later put it.

This concern seemed not entirely groundless after Janerich broke into print in the September 6, 1990, issue of the *New England Journal of Medicine* with an article entitled "Lung Cancer and Exposure to Tobacco Smoke in the Household." Its stress was entirely different from what Borelli had pulled out of Varella's thesis and circulated to the scientific world. About the only significant added risk that Varella had reported from the Janerich group's data was due to exposure in the subjects' homes at the equivalent level of 150 "person-years," meaning the number of years a nonsmoker spent in a residence multiplied by the number of smokers in that household, so that a nonsmoker who lived for fifteen years in a home with ten smokers or, say, thirty years with five smokers—a lot of other people's smoke, indeed—ran an elevated risk of contracting lung cancer. In Janerich's report, given wide press attention, this household exposure was broken down to show that while during adulthood nonsmokers enduring even as many as fifty to seventy-four "smoker years" (the term Janerich substituted for Varella's "person-years") of ETS exposure showed no increased risk of lung cancer, nonsmokers with twenty-five or more smoker years of exposure during childhood or adolescence showed a doubled risk of lung cancer. Janerich's paper, citing nine co-authors including Varella, who had died by this time, attributed 17 percent of lung cancer cases in nonsmokers to childhood and adolescent exposure to ETS, although he noted that "we know of no specific mechanism that would explain our findings." But other studies had shown children of smokers to be significantly more susceptible to respiratory diseases, and such exposure, Janerich *et al.* speculated, "might initiate changes that eventually lead to lung cancer when the exposed children become adults."

Almost entirely lost sight of in the press reports on the Janerich study, no doubt because the study itself minimized the point, was that it contradicted most of the previous ETS studies with regard to the effects of spousal smoking. Not only was no heightened risk found attributable to either spousal smoking or workplace exposure, even at high levels, but "a statistically significant inverse association between ETS and lung cancer" was discovered in social settings. Janerich conceded, "The apparent protective effect of exposure in social settings is difficult to explain," and later speculated that smoke-susceptible people perhaps avoided, consciously or otherwise, smoky social situations. The thrust of the Janerich study, then, although neither it nor those reporting on it said as much, was that only reasonably heavy exposure to ETS during a nonsmoker's pre-adult years seemed linked to an increased risk of lung cancer. But even this finding, while potentially important and inviting follow-up studies, suffered from a serious shortcoming: the questionable accuracy of the "smoker years" figures. Most of Janerich's subjects were close to seventy when interviewed and asked to remember who in their homes smoked for how many years during their childhood—no small feat of memory at a distance of half a century or longer, and one that was possibly further skewed by the more acute sensations and reactions to surrounding phenomena during the childhood years of discovery. Janerich owned up on that score as well: "The possibility of recall bias and other methodological problems may influence the results." Still, he expressed confidence that his group's findings "support the conclusion that exposure to ETS can cause lung cancer."

If the epidemiological evidence for that judgment remained hazy and ambiguous, other studies published by 1990 were suggesting biological mechanisms that might be traceable to ETS as a cause of various pulmonary and cardiac diseases. A University of Arizona researcher, exposing rabbits to ETS for only fifteen minutes a day over a twenty-day span, found that the animals' lung tissue had become permeable, opening the organ to microbes and toxins that promoted disease formation. Other investigators had found that exposure to unfiltered side-stream smoke made platelets, the tiny fragments in the blood that caused it to clot, grow less mobile and thus stickier and more prone to clot in plaque-clogged arteries. Toxins and carcinogens in ETS, moreover, were believed to cause abrasion, through chemical or mechanical interaction, in the inner linings of arterial walls, producing damage sites inviting to blood fats that could settle and cause blockage. Children exposed to smoke since birth were discovered to register elevated cholesterol levels and reduced HDL, a protein associated with a lowered incidence of heart disease. Based on the far greater frequency of heart ailments than of lung cancer and in view of both the plausibility of these triggering mechanisms in ETS and several population studies showing an elevated risk of heart disease in nonsmokers exposed to ETS, comparable to the risk levels found for lung cancer, epidemiologists and other public-health investigators were now attributing between 35,000 and 40,000 coronary deaths a year to secondhand smoke.

This news served only to compound the tobacco industry's anxiety as the EPA began to circulate a preliminary draft of its ETS risk assessment, which the Tobacco Institute, in a December 4, 1990, broadside, attacked as "an uncritical condensation of only selected studies" and accused of failing to include the lately published Janerich study, which on balance seemed to the tobacco camp largely to exonerate ETS as a carcinogen. The elevated risk of lung cancer found in the nine U.S. studies so far on nonsmokers exposed to ETS was just 8 percent when compared to unexposed nonsmokers, the TI said.

Seeming to ignore the industry's scientific arguments, a revised draft of the EPA risk assessment was circulated in April 1991 and drew a careful, blistering fourteen-page letter, signed by U.S. Representative Thomas J. Bliley, Jr., a Republican from Richmond, manufacturing home of Philip Morris, whose hand was apparent in the congressman's letter. Bliley had run his family's century-old funeral home before serving as mayor of Richmond and moving on to Congress in 1981; antismoking advocates found it fitting that the tobacco industry's latest champion was a former undertaker. A ranking minority member of the House Energy and Commerce Committee, with its oversight of Henry Waxman's subcommittee on environment and health, Bliley protested in his letter that EPA had failed to apply a "weight of the evidence" test to the ETS question; that the agency had failed to factor in four recent major studies on the subject—two from China, one from Japan, and Janerich's—which did not support the EPA draft's claimed higher risk of lung cancer from ETS, and that he could not understand how spousal smoking could serve as the critical gauge of ETS exposure "when every epidemiological study published to date uses a different formula for defining" what constituted spousal exposure.

Bliley's complaint could not be shrugged off lightly, and EPA said it would reconsider its data, thus further delaying the assessment. That many others in the public-health community had already made up their minds about the ETS danger, however, was suggested by a declaration two months after the Bliley letter by the National Institute on Occupational Safety and Health (NIOSH), part of the U.S. Public Health Service, that secondhand smoke was a workplace hazard that all employers ought to take steps to reduce to the lowest possible level, preferably barring it altogether, and offering workers who smoked classes and other incentives to help them quit.

But reports spread that at EPA itself, the industry's steady drumfire had taken its toll. The agency was said to be under growing pressure from within the Bush administration to bury or materially soften the ETS risk appraisal, and new personnel had reportedly been assigned to take a fresh look at the data. In 1992 three large new studies appeared that could only further complicate the ongoing assessment. In the premier January issue of the journal *Epidemiology, Biomarkers and Prevention*, investigators headed by Louisiana State University epidemiologist Elizabeth T. H. Fontham studied 420 nonsmoking women with lung cancer in five metropolitan areas—a subject group about as large as Janerich's—and reached almost exactly the opposite findings: no elevated risk from childhood exposure to ETS but a 30 percent rise from spousal smoking and slightly higher from work-site exposure. In the September 16, 1992, number of the *Journal of the National Cancer Institute*, Florida investigator Heather Stockwell reported a small, statistically insignificant increase in lung cancer risk among 210 nonsmoking women subjects but a more than doubled risk for those with twenty-two smoker years of exposure in childhood or forty years in adulthood, partially corroborating Janerich's data (which had shown no elevated risk from adulthood exposure). To add to the ever larger body of conflicting findings, Ross C. Brownson of the Missouri Department of Health examined 432 lifetime nonsmokers and discovered no increased lung cancer risk associated with childhood exposure to ETS, but at the high exposure level of forty or more "pack years" (meaning years of exposure to a pack-a-day smoker) found a 30 percent higher risk—yet none in a dose-related pattern at lower levels.

If this round of new reports seemed to yield more conflict than agreement regarding cancer, far more uniform—and indicting—findings were accumulating with regard to ETS and heart disease. By 1994, a dozen epidemiological studies dating back to 1985 and involving 3,131 subjects, more than the total in the thirty lung cancer studies on ETS exposure until then, showed a consistent 30 percent elevated risk of heart disease. Since there were ten times as many cardiac deaths as from lung cancer, the overall toll from ETS exposure was coming to be seen as much graver than previously supposed. The CDC was estimating it to be on the order of 12 to 15 percent of the lives claimed by direct smoking. The likely underlying mechanisms, too, were coming to be better understood in ETS-linked heart disease. The presence of endothelial cell carcasses detected in the blood of nonsmokers was attributed to carcinogenic agents found in ETS and held responsible for damage to the arterial walls where plaques were rooting. Studies found the loss of platelet activity in the blood, a condition which encouraged clotting, to be as high as 80 percent after repeated exposure to ETS. And eight weeks of exposure was enough to cut in half the efficacy of enzymes affecting the heart's ability to convert oxygen into "energy molecules" like adenosine triphosphate, which served as a little chemical battery to fuel the heart muscle's ability to contract.

Rather than producing a diluted dosage of smoke and thus having a minimal pathological effect, ETS was now being charged by some investigators with having a much greater systemic impact on nonsmokers than was implied by extrapolations in the form of equivalent doses from smoked cigarettes— usually put at one or two ultra-lights a day for the average nonsmoker. As Stanton Glantz stressed in testimony before OSHA officials in August 1994, whereas smokers' bodies adapted to the toxic and abrasive effects and reduced oxygen supply due to their chronic inhalation, nonsmokers' systems were more sensitive when exposed to ETS, even though absorbing much smaller doses. As an example, he noted that the tendency to greater stickiness and clot-formation in nonsmokers' blood often proved irreversible after even compara-tively brief exposures, because, as he put it, "The process saturates at low doses." As a result, the tobacco industry's fondness for minimizing the ETS peril by measuring it as a fraction of the doses from directly smoked cigarettes "will lead to gross underestimates of the risks of passive smoking to the car-diovascular system."

I V

ALTHOUGH hard-core smokers remained the prime target of the tobacco control movement, serious attention now began to be paid to how to halt adolescents from taking up the practice in the first place or, at the least, to make it harder for them to do so. Surveys confirmed the public-health commu-nity's worry that youngsters did not grasp the hazards involved. More than a third of them did not know that pack-a-day users ran a resulting high risk of se-rious illness, and 95 percent of teen smokers said they intended to quit in the foreseeable future when in fact only one-quarter of them would do so within eight years of first lighting up.

Forty-four states had laws on the books, many of them long-standing, against the sale of tobacco products to underage customers, with eighteen be-ing the most common cutoff age. But unlike the far more vigilantly exercised laws governing the sale of alcoholic beverages to minors, the curb on tobacco sales was laxly regarded, if at all. Signs declaring such sales illegal, required by eleven states, were rarely posted. Store clerks, often youngsters themselves, almost never bothered asking for identification cards. Witnesses to underage sales almost never reported such violations to the police, and in the thoroughly unlikely event that a purveyor was found in violation of the law, fines were minimal. What message was adult society sending to youngsters, furthermore, when it granted them easy access to cigarettes via freestanding, unattended vending machines but forbade the sale of beer and liquor in that fashion? Smoking, in short, was regarded as far less hazardous to the community than drinking was.

To rectify this impression, public-health authorities in Massachusetts under-

took a "sting" experiment, sending an eleven-year-old to try to purchase cigarettes at one hundred locales around the state; the youngster succeeded at fifty-
nine out of ninety-three stores and six out of seven vending-machine sites. And
only four of the locations had signs posted saying such sales were prohibited,
as the law required. Edward Sweda of the Massachusetts GASP took this instructive effort one step further by sending two obviously underage children to
buy cigarettes from a Store 24 chain outlet and, after they succeeded, brought
suit on their behalf. The vendor settled out of court in 1990—the first such acknowledgment in the nation that tobacco sales to underage youngsters were no
laughing matter—and led other such chains, like Southland Corporation's big
7-Eleven convenience stores, to announce new monitoring procedures. The
Massachusetts legislature put through a far tougher version of the rules, requiring the licensing of tobacco vendors, steeper fines for underage sales, and license suspension for repeated offenders. President Bush's Secretary of Health
and Human Services, Louis Sullivan, called on the states to emulate the Massachusetts model and urged public-health offi-cials rather than police authorities to enforce bans on cigarette sales to minors, but no federal initiative, such
as a national age limit on cigarette sales, was contemplated.

Sampling, too, was now subjected to consciousness-raising. Giveaways had
become increasingly favored in the cigarette companies' promotional budgets
as advertising allocations continued their relative decline. Most state laws applied only to sales, not gifts, of cigarettes to youngsters, so the manufacturers
handed them out with impunity, often in settings such as outside rock concerts
and not far from schools, where the samplers, usually under contract to the tobacco companies (and thus not in their direct employ), were sure to encounter
the next generation of smokers and speed them on their way. Joe Tye's organization, Stop Teenage Addiction to Tobacco (STAT), caught Lorillard in the act
of sampling youngsters with Newports from a van painted green and orange
and bearing the brand's slogan, "Alive with Pleasure," in large, equally attention-getting letters on the streets of the nation's capital. When Tye reported his
carefully documented sightings to the cigarette company, it declined to respond at first, but when Tye persisted, Lorillard stated, "We do not give cigarettes to children," and blamed the incident on the carelessness of its hired
dispensers. Slowly recognizing the indefensibility of the practice and the impossibility of screening out underage recipients, the companies began to drop
the marketing scheme in the early 1990s, just as governmental bodies were
starting to bar it.

Although the tobacco companies devoted a growing portion of their marketing expenditures to display allowances for retailers, incentive payments to
wholesalers for monitoring out-of-stock shortages, and price-cutting rebates to
buyers, cigarette advertising still served as a primal lure to young customers
who would replace those who died or quit. The ad message, whatever its varia-

tions, was always the same: smoking makes you beautiful, adventurous, and sexy, provides pleasure without penalty or pain, and turns kids into grown-ups. And as psychologists William McCarthy and Ellen Gritz noted in a joint 1988 paper, "[t]he sheer ubiquitousness" of tobacco ads—in the press, on billboards, and at sports arenas—"encourages the teenager to think that smoking is a nearly universal phenomenon."

By far the most popular brand in the twenty-four-and-under sector of the cigarette market, winning about seven out of every ten sales, Marlboro had built its appeal to youth by tirelessly projecting its cowboy imagery, a manifestation of independence from the programmed adult world. To challenge Marlboro's youth appeal, the key to the brand's command of one-quarter of the entire U.S. cigarette market, R. J. Reynolds Tobacco decided in 1988 to rejuvenate its moribund pioneer brand, Camel, then celebrating its seventy-fifth birthday. With little more than 3 percent of the market, Camel was favored mostly by older, blue-collar, and rural smokers. The company offered milder line extensions and flip-top box versions of the brand and then hit upon the most arresting advertising campaign since Philip Morris discovered "Marlboro Country".

To get around a French government ban on the use of human figures in cigarette ads in the early 'Seventies, RJR used a cartoon version of the listless camel on the front of the brand pack—known as Old Joe in company lore (see chapter 3, section I)—and gave him a friskier persona. While Old Joe, as a dashing dromedary in French Foreign Legion garb, had not done wonders for Camel in the French market, RJR now trotted out the cartoon camel to appeal to younger U.S. smokers by turning him into a "smooth character," as the ad copy called him—the quintessential party animal, done up in a tuxedo and sunglasses, with a cigarette adangle from his pendulous lips and a bevy of adoring (human) beauties nearby.

The sexual overtones of the campaign were underscored by the none too subtle resemblance of smooth Joe's face to the male genitalia. It was all as "plain as the nose on your face," wrote a Harvard professor, expert in Freudian iconography, on *The New York Times* op-ed page. Reynolds officials professed bewilderment that the creature was being taken for anything other than a heroically posed gadabout, a lover of sun 'n' surf, a flashy racing-car driver, or the leader of a five-camel blues band known—suggestively, according to Joe's critics—as the Hard Pack. "I was not amused by it," James Johnston, fired a decade earlier but recalled in 1989 by the takeover Kravis management to run the RJR domestic tobacco operation, said of the uproar the ad campaign was causing. Johnston ordered Old Joe's looks to be made less testicular, but when the ad agency artists presented him drawings of a fifteen-stage evolution of the animal, his phallic appearance had not notably changed. "That's what camels really look like," Johnston was told, and he decided Old Joe was not about to be tampered with to placate puritanical fantasies. Besides, Madison Avenue loved the lively roué. The new Old Joe was odd-looking and amusing enough to win high marks from the creative end of the business for breaking out of the sameness that had long dulled cigarette advertising.

Reynolds budgeted $75 million a year to advertise and promote Joe Camel. A huge, illuminated "smooth character" billboard went up in Times Square, a block from where the famous Camel sign with its wafting smoke rings had gone up early in World War II and had remained for a generation. And the company aggressively promoted Joe's likeness in a whole line of such youth-oriented merchandise as T-shirts and sweatshirts, posters, mugs, and beach sandals, purchasable with "C-Notes," bills featuring Joe in a George Washington wig and available in exchange for empty packs of Camel.

Tobacco control advocates pounced on the Joe Camel campaign as evidence of the industry's contempt for public concern about the health issue and a transparent pitch to young people—surely the cartoon character and his likeness adorning low-priced recreational gear were not targeted at adult buyers, they argued. The Coalition on Smoking or Health petitioned the FTC to halt the Joe Camel ads as unfair advertising, luring the underaged to purchase a hazardous product. And Surgeon General Koop's successor, Antonia Novello, urged Reynolds to rein in Old Joe as a public-health menace and called upon the nation's newspaper and magazine publishers to turn down Camel ads and upon retailers not to display point-of-sales materials featuring the lusty pitchman. But RJR steadfastly denied that the campaign was aimed at underage buyers—to concede as much would have been to plead guilty to fostering illegal sales—and granted only that the marketing program was directed toward young adults whom it was trying to switch from rival brands. Nobody could prove otherwise.

Protestations of intent aside, Reynolds was succeeding fabulously in winning recognition for its cheeky cartoon Camel mascot among youngsters well under the legal smoking age. Several studies reaching that conclusion in the December 11, 1991, issue of *JAMA* showed, among other findings, that 30 percent of three-year-olds and 90 percent of six-year-olds questioned knew that the Joe Camel image was connected with cigarettes, and that 98 percent of high schoolers grasped Joe's link to the Camel brand (compared with 67 percent of adults who made the linkage). Still, RJR's Johnston insisted, "Advertising is irrelevant to a young person's decision to begin smoking," and his ad agency executives argued that cartoon characters like the "Jolly Green Giant" and Owens Corning's "Pink Panther" were used to push products without generating a passion for string beans or insulating material among children. Still, for whatever reason, beginning smokers were found by surveys to favor overwhelmingly the most heavily advertised brands.

If the effectiveness of the Joe Camel campaign was measured not by the notoriety it aroused but by its effect on sales, then the effort was proving hardly worth the antagonism it engendered and the fuel it provided for those calling on Congress to ban cigarette advertising altogether. Camel's market share in the twenty-four-and-under sector climbed from 4.4 percent to 7.9 percent at its height, but in 1993, five years into the cartoon campaign, the brand's overall share had risen only about 1 percentage point to just over 4. By the following year, when the FTC finally decided not to act against Reynolds's use of Joe Camel, priapic or not, the brand's share was back under 4 percent.

V

To counter the cigarette companies' efforts to shore up their eroding consumer base—between 400,000 and 500,000 were said to be dying from smoking or ETS every year, more than a million quit annually, and 15 million tried to—by enlisting young smokers, preventive medicine authorities urged a more aggressive intervention and educational campaign. By far the most successful effort along these lines was undertaken in California, where tobacco control advocates had long been stymied by state lawmakers indifferent to the problem, or worse. "When the tobacco industry says 'Jump,' " remarked Mark Pertschuk of the Berkeley-based Americans for Nonsmokers' Rights (ANR), "the California Legislature says, 'How high?' " Its most powerful figure, Assembly Speaker Willie Brown, accepted some $200,000 from tobacco-funded political action committees over a five-year period in the late 'Eighties and early 'Nineties and was known to have worked closely with industry officials to help foil antismoking legislation. Thus, while California led the nation in the number of local smoking restrictions, there was no substantive statewide program in place.

To end this bottleneck, nonsmokers' rights groups framed Proposition 99, to be passed on directly by California voters in 1988. "Prop 99" called for raising California's low ten-cent-a-pack cigarette tax by twenty-five cents, the largest tobacco excise increase ever contemplated by any U.S. governmental jurisdiction. The revenues from it were to be devoted to an antismoking educational campaign, cancer research, medical services for indigents, and reforestation of areas ravaged by cigarette-ignited fires.

The cigarette manufacturers, with 10 percent of their domestic market imperiled by the threatened huge tax rise, responded with a war chest estimated at $15 million and a no-holds-barred advertising campaign. In a typical industry-paid ad, an alleged undercover police officer stated that the big cigarette tax jump "will create major crime" by increasing tobacco smuggling from out of state through gangs who could clear $13,000 per vanload of contraband smokes, enough to buy "thirty-two pounds of marijuana, enough crack for

1,280 kids, or 185 handguns." But the invention of such bogeymen boomeranged. California law enforcement officers who had initially opposed the cigarette tax hike objected to the tobacco industry's fabricated argument and withdrew their opposition. More to the point, the nonsmoking public, heavily in the majority, liked the tax increase because its burden fell entirely on smokers and its yield would be a windfall for the state's public-health and environmental protection needs. Prop 99 sailed to victory with 58 percent of the voters in favor.

The smoking control movement, starved for funding nationwide and surviving through the dedication of a handful of workers, suddenly found itself awash in California gold. The twenty-five-cent tax increase produced $150 million to educate state residents on the perils of smoking and help them quit—a figure fifty times as high as the total for those purposes in the other forty-nine states. And the money, astonishingly, was put to effective use. Three hundred public-health officers went on the payroll statewide to train and oversee local health workers in tobacco control programs set up in each of California's fifty-eight counties and 1,000 school districts. Nothing like this had ever been attempted. A fourteen-month advertising campaign budgeted at almost $30 million and supervised by California's Department of Health Services was launched in 1990; conducted in eight languages, it involved 69 television stations, 147 radio stations, 130 newspapers, and 775 billboards. Antismoking activists had feared that these public-service ads would prove bland and stingless, but they displayed imagination and wit, and contained scalding criticism of the cigarette companies, whose executives were portrayed in them as cynical and manipulative. Perhaps the most notable of the commercials showed a simulated, smoke-wreathed conference of tobacco officials, one of whom was saying that they had a multibillion-dollar problem on their hands: "We need more cigarette smokers. Pure and simple. Every day 2,000 Americans stop smoking, and another 1,100 also quit. Actually, technically, they die. That means that this business needs 3,000 fresh, new volunteers every day. . . ." The unseen speaker then gave a laugh and added, "We're not in this for our health." Some of the commercials were beamed at ethnic communities, like one in Spanish that said simply, "Our children grow up wanting to be like us. . . . Don't let them inherit our bad habits. For your family's sake don't smoke." Youngsters in the black community were appealed to with an antismoking recitation in rap, which went in part: "We used to pick it/now they want us to smoke it . . . /tobacco blacks it's killin' many/the ages start from fifteen to twenty/cancer it be givin'/keeping brothers from livin'/six feet under the ground/they are diggin' . . . /cigarettes are killing black men/faster than whites."

Such a head-on assault alarmed the cigarette makers, not least of all because of how it vilified them as well as their product. Asserted the Tobacco Institute's veteran spear-carrier, Walker Merryman, "This is a very nasty, scandalous personal attack on people in the tobacco industry," and he went on to complain that the state government of California was spending millions of the public's tax dollars on "a propaganda campaign". The shoe was plainly on the other foot now, and it fit. The California antismoking attack was indeed personal—that was part of the point of it—for if Rose Cipollone, to cite one of hundreds of thousands who succumbed annually to smoking-related diseases, had exercised her *personal* choice in electing to smoke and paid the price for it, so, too, did tobacco industry executives make a *personal* choice in devoting their careers to the manufacture and marketing of a product known to be a grave health menace. Why should these highly paid businessmen have been immune to the consequences of their actions and have escaped public scorn? And if California's antismoking ads were tax-funded propaganda, then what was the tobacco industry's own advertising—and wasn't it being paid for in part by tax-deductible dollars that amounted to a public subsidy in the billions?

The effects of the big cigarette tax rise and the antismoking drive it paid for were immediate and sensational. California smokers began quitting at twice the national rate, and by 1991 the percentage of smokers in the state had dropped from 25 to 21, one of the lowest figures in the nation. Indeed, the antismoking effort was proving so successful that the industry began putting on the heat every way it could to undermine the program. One result was that the state's new governor, Pete Wilson, with the connivance of tobacco industry friends in the legislature, acted to plug his budgetary shortfall by commandeering some of the cigarette tax revenues—a move that antismoking forces went to court to challenge. But Wilson soon proved to be no friend of the tobacco industry. In 1993, he issued an executive order banning smoking in all buildings owned or leased by the state, and the following year signed one of the most restrictive smoking control measures in the nation. Philip Morris moved at once to try to blunt the sweeping bill, which marked the end of the tobacco lobby's long dominance over the legislature in Sacramento, by spending millions to mount a referendum on what was styled the California Uniform Tobacco Control Act, a euphemism for snuffing out all local smoking laws and replacing them with a single, statewide, and much-watered-down measure. With a 71 percent vote against, California voters that fall kept the nation's most populous state in the antismoking vanguard.

VI

A T the national level, the smoking control effort languished. Eighteen years were to pass between the first significant federal regulatory measure—the 1970 broadcast ban on cigarette advertising—and the next one—a ban on smoking by airplane passengers on flights of two hours or shorter. And even then, the new restriction was something of a fluke, a nearly spontaneous display of congressional pique that cut across party lines and traditional alliances.

Reagan appointees at the Federal Aviation Administration and Department of Transportation had been sitting on the idea of an in-flight smoking ban for several years when spadework to take the concept out of the hands of the deregulators and present it to Congress for enactment was begun by Americans for Nonsmokers' Rights, which viewed midair smoking as a classic instance of nonsmokers' victimization. But ANR, while growing in numbers and effectiveness, was still small and far away from Washington, so it leagued with the Coalition on Smoking or Health and the 50,000-member flight attendants union, which saw itself as uniquely vulnerable to the smoke in the recirculated air that crews had to breathe throughout their workweek. The in-flight smoking ban got nowhere, though, until the spring of 1988 when a stalwart advocate arose in the person of U.S. Representative Richard J. Durbin, an Illinois Democrat in his third term in the House.

A Springfield attorney and skilled parliamentarian, Durbin without warning tacked on an amendment to an appropriations bill being considered by the House transportation subcommittee, on which he sat, calling for a cutoff of federal funds to any airport servicing planes that did not impose a smoking ban on domestic flights of two hours or under. Durbin's amendment failed in subcommittee, five votes to three, and was buried by a twenty-three-to-eleven tally when he proposed it to the full Appropriations Committee. And since the idea had no backing from the House's Democratic leadership, it was left for dead, and the tobacco lobby breathed easy.

But Durbin heard informally from many House colleagues, who were among the nation's most frequent fliers, shuttling between Washington and their home constituencies almost every weekend, that his proposal appealed to them. No one had to lecture them on the unpleasantness of ETS, and no bombardment of technical data from tobacco lobbyists could convince them that the stuff, however much filtered in flight, was harmless. Durbin went to his friend Claude Pepper, chairman of the House Rules Committee, and obtained a procedural waiver so that his amendment could be brought directly to the House floor for a two-hour debate and vote. He had four days before the scheduled airing to gather a majority for the ban.

ANR's directors, Mark Pertschuk and Julia Carol in Berkeley, went to work on their membership list of 15,000, telephoning and sending express letters to try to generate an instant cascade of appeals by nonsmokers to their congressmen. The whole network of GASP units across the country was similarly mobilized, and by the time Durbin took the House floor to push his amendment, the message had been delivered. Throughout his remarks Durbin pointed to members of the flight attendants union, present in their uniforms in the House gallery, whose health concerns gave the measure an urgency that outweighed the discomfort of congressmen. The ban passed, 198 to 193, and went to the Senate, where, despite a three-month lull during which the tobacco lobby feverishly worked its wiles, the antismoking sentiment was ascendant. Key to this surprising development was New Jersey Democrat Frank Lautenberg, chairman of the Senate's transportation subcommittee, who made clear to his colleagues that the in-flight smoking ban was a priority item for him and that those who bucked him in the matter risked a lean diet of pork when transportation projects in their home districts came up for Senate funding. The measure, to last for two years and then face reconsideration in view of the public's response, carried by a vote of 84 to 10. The ban, despite the loud lamentations of some smokers, was made permanent in 1990 and was extended to all domestic flights.

Just how remarkable the airborne ban was could be gauged by the congressional response to a report it received, in the same month it outlawed smoking on planes, from a fifteen-member federal study commission, which for three years had been considering the feasibility of manufacturing fire-safe cigarettes. Five of the commission members represented the tobacco companies, which had insisted that cigarettes that burned at low enough temperatures to reduce the ignition hazard when coming into contact with flammable materials could not be produced without the introduction of new and costly equipment. But the federal study commission was able to achieve its goal by no more exotic means than experimental cigarettes with a reduced circumference, a lower than normal density of tobacco, less porous paper, and no citrate additive to speed up burning. The cumulative effect of these features was to drop the ignition temperature to the point where, as the commission report concluded, "[i]t is technically feasible and may be commercially feasible to develop cigarettes that will have a significantly reduced propensity to ignite upholstered furniture or mattresses."

Even so, the tobacco companies still argued that such a fire-safe cigarette would be burdensome to market because it was hard to draw on—one company man likened it to trying to drink a milk shake through five straws laid end to end—and had an unsatisfactory taste. Another three years ought to be allotted for the manufacturers to test-market the experimental cigarette, the industry said. Commission member Andrew McGuire, head of San Francisco's Trauma Foundation and the moving force behind the fire-retardant cigarette effort, called this "an unconscionable delay" and pointed out that the tobacco industry had raised precisely the same objections about reduced draw and taste before introducing filter and lowered-tar brands when medical evidence threatened its very survival. But cigarette-ignited fires in the late 'Eighties were taking a relatively low 1,500 lives a year and causing some 7,000 serious injuries (although McGuire contended that the toll was much higher, citing a seven-year Maryland study that traced almost half of all fire deaths to cigarette smoking). For such a modest reduction in mortality, the industry was reluctant to risk introducing a manufacturing technique that would remind consumers of still one more way that smoking imperiled human life. The tobacco companies had bought political clout, moreover, through sizable contributions to such groups as the National Volunteer Fire Council, which stood with the industry in stressing the need for public education, not a new cigarette design, in the war to reduce fire hazards. Congress caved in and granted the additional delay, stalling any meaningful industry response to the safety need well into the 1990s.

If Congress mostly malingered in the matter of serious strictures on the manufacture, sale, and use of cigarettes, the tobacco industry was the beneficiary of a yet more pleasing indifference by the executive branch during the dozen years that deregulatory fundamentalism prevailed at the Reagan-Bush White House. Neither President lifted a finger to encourage smoking control legislation, and the ardent antitobacco preachments of the Surgeon Generals who served them were permitted so long as they were understood to be merely prescriptive for healthful private behavior, not a call for action by government. The only detectable difference between the two administrations on smoking policy was that dinner guests in the Reagan White House were still offered cigarettes when the meal was over, while Barbara Bush did not extend that questionable kindness.

Evidence of the Reagan-Bush unconcern about the tobacco issue abounded. In 1987, for example, the FTC shut down the laboratory it had run for twenty years to monitor the tar and nicotine yields of most cigarette brands, ostensibly to save the $750,000 a year it cost to provide the public with the only reliable measurement of those toxic substances. The task was handed over to an industry-run laboratory—the equivalent of assigning the fox to guard the hen coop—with an occasional checkup visit by a government inspector. The FDA and EPA were hardly more vigorous in their policing of tobacco products. In 1990, for example, the two agencies moved swiftly and jointly to order Perrier mineral water off the nation's retail shelves when it was discovered that each bottle contained minute amounts of toxic benzene. Cigarette packs, meanwhile, which the 1986 Surgeon General's report stated had up to 2,000 times more benzene than each Perrier bottle, remained exempt from such preventive measures. The EPA had by then formulated nine rules and OSHA had put out six regulations governing pollution by carcinogenic substances believed to claim, among them, a total of 1,000 lives a year, but neither agency had formulated anything to deal with secondhand tobacco smoke, which public-health investigators said took from 3,000 to 5,000 lives annually by lung cancer alone. The EPA did finally undertake reviews to determine if ETS could in fact be lethal, but would not declare its findings until literally the final hours of the Bush administration. The only Cabinet member who registered concern about smoking in those years was Bush's HHS Secretary, Dr. Louis Sullivan, an African-American, who would manage an outburst now and then about how unscrupulous cigarette makers were targeting minorities with their advertising and promotion, but he publicly proposed no federal legislation to modify these or any other practices by the industry. When Sullivan did grow bold enough to fashion a government-wide executive order that would have made all federal office buildings smoke-free except for certain designated areas, his proposal sat in the White House awaiting presidential implementation that never came.

The closest the Reagan-Bush executive branch did come to an antismoking initiative was its countenancing a program at the National Cancer Institute, under the leadership of a skilled and passionate bureaucrat, veteran public-health officer Joseph Cullen, who guided a series of sixty studies on why smokers take up the habit and how best to help them stop it. Based on the results, NCI in 1991 launched the costliest ever federal antismoking effort, a seven-year, seventeen-state, $135 million drive aimed at cutting the adult smoking population from around 28 percent to 15 by the century's end. It was a project that somehow fell between the cracks, escaping congressional ire largely because it was aimed at modifying the behavior of smokers and not the conduct of the cigarette business. And it was abundantly compensated for, to the extent that it menaced the tobacco companies' fortunes, by the highly active role played by Reagan-Bush federal trade officials in prying open large, lucrative, and previously impenetrable Asian markets for U.S. brands.

Even as U.S. cigarette consumption ebbed by one or two percentage points a year over the last two decades of the twentieth century, the industry ever more hungrily scouted and infiltrated markets abroad. Pacesetting Philip Morris sold two cigarettes overseas for every one that it peddled domestically. Some 70 percent of PM's foreign sales were in Western Europe, where by the mid-'Eighties it had become the continent's leading cigarette purveyor. But it was fast becoming a saturated market, fiercely contested by international and domestic manufacturers; the future lay elsewhere.

American cigarette makers were doing well enough in the open markets of the Philippines, Hong Kong, Malaysia, and Singapore, but the rest of the Pacific Rim nations remained out of their reach, practically speaking, due to high tariff barriers and punitive excise taxes on imported brands. These East Asian countries—Japan, Taiwan, South Korea, and Thailand—with a combined population larger than the U.S., were prosperous, smoked cigarettes heavily, and, thanks in large part to the cheapness of their labor, were flooding American shores with quality goods that contributed to an ever-widening unfavorable balance of U.S. trade and helped transform America into a debtor nation.

By Reagan's second term, his economic masterminds were receptive to any plan that might ease the nation's trade imbalance and spiraling U.S. debt—and the tobacco companies, deeply devoted to a laissez-faire government policy toward their domestic operations, were only too eager to enlist federal officials to help them penetrate the alluring East Asian markets. The effort began in earnest with the enlistment of the U.S. Trade Representative (USTR) of a wealthy Nebraskan, Clayton K. Yeutter, who had held high posts in the Nixon-Ford Agriculture and Transportation departments before becoming president of the Chicago Mercantile Exchange. Yeutter's chief weapon to aid the American tobacco industry was Section 301 of the 1974 revision of the U.S. Trade Act, empowering the President to slap retaliatory tariffs on imports from nations that discriminated against U.S. goods seeking access to their markets. Between 1985 and 1990 the USTR's office processed seventy-nine Section 301 complaints, and none more ardently than the six it brought in behalf of U.S. cigarette exporters. That he retained, among other assets (including a 2,500-acre ranch), tobacco company stocks or options worth between $30,000 to $100,000 at the time he was promoting U.S. cigarette sales abroad did not rise to the level of a conflict of interest, USTR Yeutter would explain when he was appointed Secretary of Agriculture by President Bush and given an elaborate Inauguration Week party in 1989 by a grateful Philip Morris.

Yeutter's prime target was Japan, a smoker's paradise and the second largest cigarette market in the non-Communist world. Two-thirds of its men (but a mere 7 percent of its women) used cigarettes at a per capita rate as high as Americans did. Japan Tobacco, Inc., the monopoly owned by the national finance ministry, turned over 60 percent of the retail price as an excise tax—three times the tax bite for U.S. cigarettes. The government also issued statements commendatory of smoking, *e.g.*, that it helped smokers think more clearly and suffer less stress in a nation with a compulsive work ethic and a large population on a tightly packed archipelago. Not surprisingly, Japanese cigarettes bore the most tepid of warning labels: "For your health don't smoke too much." The government sponsored no research on the subject; television advertising of cigarettes was permitted, and nearly half of Japan's doctors smoked.

As a huge tax producer, Japan's native tobacco industry was closely protected. Facing a 90 percent tariff, foreign brands held only 2 percent of the market. The state monopoly was obliged to buy up every leaf raised by Japan's 13,000 politically potent tobacco growers, at a cost two to three times that of U.S. leaf, which seemed a bargain to Japan Tobacco, buyer of 20 percent of American raw-tobacco exports. This sizable purchase, however, scarcely made a dent in the huge trade surplus, reaching some $20 billion a year by the mid-'Eighties, that Japan's automotive and electronics industries were piling up by imports to the U.S., with a tariff levied at only 20 percent. When the USTR leaned gently on the Japanese government, asking the courtesy of a reciprocal tariff level for American cigarettes, Tokyo replied by lowering its levy to 35 percent and increasing the number of retail outlets available to foreign brands by one-third. But it also imposed a 57 percent excise tax on imported cigarettes on top of a 20 percent surcharge Japan Tobacco demanded for its handling and distribution costs, and U.S. brands were still not allowed access to the ubiquitous vending machines on Japan's city streets.

This transparent evasiveness prompted Yeutter to enlist one of the U.S. tobacco industry's foremost congressional defenders, Senator Jesse Helms, then the ranking Republican member of the Senate Foreign Relations Committee, who in July 1986 wrote directly to Japanese Prime Minister Yasuhiro Nakasone reminding him of the cost to the American people of maintaining a defense umbrella over the Pacific Rim and adding pointedly that his allies in Congress "will have a better chance to stem the tide of anti-Japanese trade sentiment if and when they can cite tangible examples of your doors being opened to American products." But he mentioned only one: "I urge that you establish a timetable for allowing U.S. cigarettes a specific share of your market. I suggest a total of 20 percent. . . ."

Given what it had to lose, Japan chose to open its cigarette market to foreigners. Some 95 percent of the imported brands' sales were American, in large part because the U.S. companies were more inventive and intensive users of TV advertising. The typical Japanese cigarette commercial showed a solitary smoker savoring his brand; the American makers stressed the social aspects of smoking, as in groups singing while puffing away, or juxtaposed it with sports prowess, such as auto-racing drivers who lighted up after the finish. Philip Morris's leading brand in Japan—Lark—was linked with adventure and intrigue, and Marlboro was given a charcoal-filter version to meet Japanese tastes. Some Japanese grumbled that their government had made a blood sacrifice of its people to assuage the American tobacco predators, as U.S. brands grabbed almost 10 percent of the market within the first year of the opening, and the number kept growing, though at a slowed rate. Overall cigarette consumption rose, especially among those under twenty, whose smoking rate jumped sixfold between 1978 and 1990, by which time Philip Morris had a sales and promotion staff of 400 working the country. Four years later it was selling 44 billion units there, representing more than one-eighth of the Japanese market and the equivalent of nearly 20 percent of its U.S. sales.

Taiwan, a nation one-seventh as populous as Japan but blessed by a trade surplus with the U.S. proportionately far larger, was thus still more dependent on American friendship for its prosperity and survival in the shadow of mainland China. But its cigarette market was even more tightly closed than Japan's to foreign brands, which held a scant 1 percent of the trade and sold for three times the price of the government monopoly brands. While Taiwan could not risk threatened reprisals from the USTR if it did not relent, it fought hard to preserve a ban on television advertising of cigarettes and sharply limited their visibility in print media.

Despite Taiwanese expressions of concern that young people not be targeted by the foreign tobacco companies, their promotional blitz seemed to pinpoint the youth market. Stickers, signage, and billboards for foreign brands were plastered over storefronts and kiosks, seventeen cigarette posters were counted at one time on walls close to Taipei's largest high school, and sampling among teenagers was widespread at video game arcades, disco night spots, and fashion shows. Nor could the state tobacco monopoly match such marketing innovations as direct-drop delivery to retailers by the U.S. companies while the government required shopkeepers to make a time-consuming trip to a central depot to pick up their cigarette supply. Within the first year of open access, Taiwan's leading domestic brand, called Long Life, dropped in market share from 90 percent to 72; within two years, high school smoking had increased 50 percent. And when aroused Taiwanese health officials pushed hard to crack down on promotional efforts by U.S. importers, calling for an end to sampling, a ban on cigarette ads in magazines aimed at young readers, and larger warning labels to appear on the front instead of the sides of packages, the USTR argued that such a proposal was intended to limit access by foreign competitors and represented an unacceptable revision of the trade pact U.S. officials had extracted. Carla Hills, Yeutter's successor at USTR, wrote to authorities in Taipei in 1992 that they would be wise to discontinue their efforts to rein in American tobacco promotion "at a time when Taiwan is seeking active consideration of its GATT [General Agreement on Tariffs and Trade] application," and added they ought also to be mindful that "cigarette exports have made a significant contribution to reducing the global U.S. trade deficit." Behind such thinly veiled bullying was constant pressure by the tobacco companies, exemplified by Philip Morris's director of international trade relations, Donald Nelson, who suggested that the Taiwanese were protesting aggressive U.S. marketing practices "not because they have an inferior product but because we are doing something insidious. It's just not true."

South Korea, whose citizens were subject to the equivalent of a $1,000 fine if caught smoking an American cigarette, was far more resistant to USTR efforts to allow in U.S. brands. To arm themselves for the siege, RJR Tobacco signed up President Reagan's former national security advisor, Richard Allen, and Philip Morris followed by enlisting ex-Reagan White House deputy staff chief Michael Deaver for a fee of $250,000 to lobby the South Koreans, whose military security against their bristling North Korean neighbors was assured by the sizable presence of American troops. In a happy coincidence of interests, Deaver, an intimate of the Reagans, was perceived as useful to the government in Seoul, which paid him nearly half a million dollars to lobby Congress and the White House against passage of legislation intended to protect the U.S. tex-

tile industry from the likes of cheap Korean goods. Several years of hard negotiating were required before tariffs and taxes were lowered enough to allow
U.S. cigarettes to compete with South Korean government brands. Within a
year of the American incursion, unprecedented cigarette promotion in the form
of sports sponsorships, sampling, and magazine advertising helped drive up
smoking among South Korean boys from 18 to 30 percent. When the textile
protection bill aimed at Asian imports reached President Reagan's desk, he
vetoed it.

In pushing their complaint against barriers to U.S. cigarettes in Thailand,
with a population 40 percent as large as Japan's but with far lower per capita
cigarette consumption, the U.S. tobacco companies would not settle for the
same passive sales customs as the Thai state monopoly; instead, they wrote in
their petition to USTR Hills, "Sufficient advertising and promotion will be
necessary to repair the results of previous unfair Thai practices as well as providing a commercially competitive environment." Hills took up their cause,
explaining to tobacco control advocates, "We are not pushing cigarettes on
other countries, but where they allow cigarette consumption we say they ought
not to ban ours. . . . As long as cigarettes remain a legal commodity in the
United States and abroad, there is no legal basis to deny cigarette manufacturers assistance in gaining market access."

Fearful that sophisticated forms of consumer persuasion would be loosed on
their vulnerable society, the incensed Thais took their case to antismoking
forces in Washington, where they found ready allies. "Free trade is not a license to export lung cancer and ride roughshod over the antismoking laws of
other nations," declared Ted Kennedy, chairman of the Senate Labor and Human Resources Committee, and Michael Pertschuk's Advocacy Institute asked
in print, by way of an analogy, how the American people would feel if the
Colombian government, in behalf of its enterprising drug cartel, insisted that
the U.S. government allow advertising and promotion of cocaine as well as
Juan Valdez's coffee. Only when the Thais proposed that the issue be resolved
by GATT officials did Hills relent under pressure from tobacco control forces
at home. In 1990, GATT ruled that Thailand had to admit foreign cigarette
brands but could restrict marketing techniques in light of public-health considerations, provided that the rules were applied uniformly to domestic as well as
foreign brands.

The sole semblance of conscience manifested within the Reagan administration over the leagued efforts by government and industry to bring the pleasures and perils of American cigarettes to Asia's multitudes was Everett
Koop's passionate protest. "There is a higher good," the Surgeon General declared in 1988, "than the greed market. I think it is reprehensible for this
wealthy nation to export disability, disease, and death to the Third World."
Later that year the chief facilitator of that enterprise, Clayton Yeutter, com-

mended Koop in writing for his "aggressive efforts to sensitize the American people to the health dangers of this troublesome habit" and said that he himself believed addiction to smoking to be "a terrible human tragedy." The USTR then concluded his patronizing moral instruction to Koop, "However, what we are about in our trade relationships is something entirely different." Yeutter had apparently meant that addiction to smoking *by Americans* was "a terrible human tragedy"—or he was a shameless hypocrite—for two years later, during a press conference while he was Secretary of Agriculture, he commented about one of his apparently favorite crops, "I just saw the figures on tobacco exports a few days ago, and, my, have they turned out to be a marvelous success story."

Bush's top health officials proved craven and impotent in the face of such boosterism. Koop's successor as Surgeon General, Antonia Novello, occasionally flayed the tobacco companies for pursuing the youth market, but her priorities were apparent when she stated, in answer to press inquiries about why she had not opposed the USTR efforts to spread the sale of U.S. cigarettes to previously restricted markets, that such intrusiveness by the nation's ranking public-health officer would have been "disrespectful to my party." Traveling to Perth, Australia, in 1990 for the triennial World Conference on Tobacco and Health, Assistant HHS Secretary James O. Mason delivered a rousing keynote address, charging U.S. cigarette makers with playing "our free-trade laws and export policies like a Stradivarius violin" and calling it "unconscionable" for them "to be peddling their poison abroad." But when summoned by Congressman Waxman to repeat the charge before his House health subcommittee, Mason canceled his appearance and a departmental letter arrived instead, explaining that it was not appropriate for a health official to discuss trade matters. When Mason's boss, HHS Secretary Sullivan, who had approved his subordinate's speech in Perth, was asked on "Meet the Press" to explain the apparent policy reversal, he said that the issue was "one of equity in trade. What Dr. Mason has said in Australia is entirely consistent with what I have said."

More truthfully reflecting the smoking policies of the Bush presidency, Vice President Dan Quayle told a North Carolina audience in July 1990 that "Tobacco exports should be expanded aggressively because Americans are smoking less. . . . We're not going to back away from what public health officials say and what reports say. But on the other hand, we're not going to deny a country an export from our country because of that policy." Thus was a generation of findings that smoking was destructive of human health degraded by two American Presidents while actively carrying the banner of U.S. tobacco companies into foreign parts when ample humanitarian grounds existed for pressing their cause less fervently, if at all.

This unseemly overseas initiative by the government compounded the injury then being dealt to the antismoking campaign domestically by official federal indifference. The most hurtful setback at the national level was the 1989 departure of Surgeon General Koop, who had brought moral weight and a believable voice to the issue. Only Henry Waxman in Congress played a comparable, if less audible, role in the broad public airing of the hazards of smoking throughout the 'Eighties. But for all his skills in the pulpit, Koop had been unable or unwilling to persuade the White House to undertake control measures.

Eighteen months after Koop's departure, the only other forceful antismoking advocate in the federal administration, Ronald Davis, director of the Office on Smoking and Health, ended four years of frustration in that job and soon held the ranking public-health post for the state of Michigan. A team player, Davis had nonetheless bridled under the executive branch's disdain for his mission, typified by a budget that did not even allow him to carry out studies into the possible dangers of the tobacco additives that the industry was using, according to lists it provided to his office under the 1984 cigarette labeling law. His role was limited to cross-pollinating among the myriad of private antismoking organizations—ASH, GASP, ANR, DOC, STAT, AMA, the Advocacy Institute, the American Council on Science and Health, the American Health Foundation, and the Coalition of the ACS, AHA, and ALA, among others, which formed a movement Davis felt was hopelessly dispersed and duplicative—and urging state and local lawmakers and health officials to deal more vigorously with smoking, even if the federal government he worked for was doing next to nothing about the peril. "Anything that would have required federal legislation was tossed out," Davis said in recounting the strictures on him. "It was a pass-the-buck approach. It's much easier to make recommendations to the states than to Congress."

Practically speaking, there was no nationally coordinated smoking control movement, only a lot of groups with their own agendas, membership lists, newsletters, fund drives, and egos. Together, they generated a considerable din, orchestrated only occasionally (as in the push for the airline smoking ban), but mostly they were in disarray. The oldest entity, John Banzhaf's ASH, was by now relatively well funded but had become peripheral and idiosyncratic in approach; younger, poorer antismoking groups wanted Banzhaf to exercise real leadership by turning ASH into the legal arm of the tobacco control movement—or get out of the way. Americans for Nonsmokers' Rights was growing in skill and reach but lacked funding and an ongoing presence in Washington. After nearly ten years of existence, the coalition of the big three health voluntaries remained "a case of arrested development," in the opinion of the Advocacy Institute's Michael Pertschuk, the coach of and father confessor to the tobacco control movement but not an active lobbyist himself. The Coalition's three parents had proven unwilling to cede to it any policymaking power of its own, kept its operating budget to a pitiable $150,000 a year, and declined to broaden its membership, claiming that any such increase would make its workings cumbersome but in truth worrying that the large voluntaries' identities would be submerged in the process. The Coalition's skilled lobbyist, Matthew Myers, had his hands tied by its steering committee, and even when he proposed a modest and seemingly unexceptionable step, like a drive to outlaw the brazen circumvention of the 1970 federal ban on cigarette advertising in the broadcast media by preventing tobacco signage at arenas and stadiums where sports events were regularly televised, his overseers said no.

The one organization that might have lent meaningful muscle to the Coalition was the American Medical Association. But the AMA did not relish the prospect of seeing its star dimmed within a larger constellation, while the health voluntaries felt that the AMA's commitment to the smoking issue was mostly lip service. In fact, it had done no follow-up lobbying in behalf of the total cigarette ad ban it had urged on Congress in 1986. To try to forge coherence within the muddled smoking control community and to fashion national legislative priorities to present to the 101st Congress, the AMA funded a weekend-long conference in Houston at the end of January 1989 attended by all the major antismoking activists and a number of enlistees in the newly formed Tobacco Task Force, composed of fifty-two congressmen. "Never before has such a broad-based coalition assembled," declared U.S. Representative Michael Anderson, Texas Democrat and a host of the affair. After all the brave talk, though, what emerged was another long shopping list of goals; too many bills with too many unattainable provisions got introduced, and while this multiplicity kept the tobacco lobbyists scrambling, never knowing which proposal congressional sentiment might coalesce behind, it also failed to narrow the playing field to a manageable size. Particularly divisive was the high priority assigned to a ban on all tobacco advertising—an idea that split the liberal community, usually more antismoking than not, over First Amendment concerns.

The result was disastrous. Instead of seeking half a loaf or even a quarter, the usually skilled Henry Waxman loaded up an omnibus Tobacco Control and Health Protection Act that he introduced in 1990. The immense package would have limited cigarette advertising to the black-and-white-only "tombstone" format (without human or cartoon figures), banned sponsorship of cultural and sports events using cigarette brand names, added a warning label about addiction, listed the toxic content on every pack as well as the tobacco additives, and funded antismoking commercials on television. But Waxman could not muster a majority for the bill within his subcommittee. A slimmed version of the bill, including the addiction label, a ban on cigarette sampling and vending machines unless under visual supervision, and reduced funding for alcohol and drug abuse programs in states that did not seriously enforce a federal age limit of eighteen on the sale of tobacco products, did gain a subcommittee majority.

But the measure never reached the House floor, where it might well have carried, because Commerce Committee Chairman John Dingell, Waxman's nemesis, sat on it.

Waxman's astute aide on smoking legislation, Ripley Forbes, commented in the wake of this glaring failure by the public-health community to check the tobacco forces, "There is an almost terminal problem of focus—and there hadn't been sufficient tactical thinking on how to mount and put through legislation." Without genuine White House support, moreover, the prospect for substantive federal antismoking regulation was dim to invisible at the beginning of the final decade of the twentieth century.

VII

THE cigarette makers were cheered as well by an epochal political upheaval abroad that fired up their expansionist impulses. Eastern Europe and the great Soviet Eurasian land mass had yielded capitalist tobacco manufacturers a sorry harvest despite two decades of assiduous cultivation, and then so swiftly did the old order crumble at the opening of the 1990s that the international tobacco companies at first found the situation nearly too good to be true. Although the Communist nations, which couldn't get enough to smoke, had now sent their commissars packing, free-market corporations were naturally wary of investing in the suddenly liberated societies before the roots of political democracy and economic stability could take hold. But that metamorphosis might take years, decades, generations even; meanwhile, a lot of cigarettes could be sold by whoever got there quickly.

In contrast to East Asia, where invading U.S. cigarette makers faced widespread resentment on grounds of imperiling public health and wounding national pride, the masses within the former Soviet bloc were starved for consumer goods and welcomed the early arrival of U.S. products as symbols of their spiritual emancipation and hope for a more materially abundant future. Under the Soviet economy, cigarette production had been hampered by antiquated plants, a shortage of replacement parts, undertrained and poorly motivated labor, and inefficient manufacturing logistics—instead of going to self-contained factories, for example, harvested tobacco was sent by rail over vast distances for processing at a single site and then reshipped to widely dispersed cigarette-making facilities. Thus, even in a society desperately short of creature comforts, hungry for almost any form of solace under tyranny, and unfazed by health fears about smoking when severe environmental contaminants of every kind were rampant, the Soviet system could not sustain cigarette production at its rated 400 billion units a year. Output had fallen to about half that figure in the last years of the Red empire, causing a cigarette shortage so severe that Soviet ruler Mikhail Gorbachev was forced to stave off rioting by emergency bulk purchases from foreign manufacturers—20 billion units from Philip Morris was the largest single order—paid for with Russian oil, gold, and diamonds.

As the Iron Curtain disintegrated, no outside tobacco manufacturer was better positioned to exploit the event than Philip Morris, which had tirelessly pursued licensing arrangements throughout the Soviet bloc, if only to show its flag and win good will. But rather than charging in to seize any advantage it could, PM moved selectively, adapting strategies to the often chaotic circumstances. The effort began in the spring of 1990 in East Germany, a market about one-quarter the size of West Germany's, where Philip Morris had achieved the largest share. Its chief German rival, Reemtsma, anxious to reestablish its tobacco hegemony in a soon-to-be-reunified Germany, bought up the leading East German brand, Cabinet, took away jobs by moving its manufacturing to facilities in West Germany, and promptly altered its taste to the American-style blend that had gained dominance there. Sensing that East German smokers would need time to acquire a taste for the milder U.S. blend, Philip Morris formulated a different plan. It bought out the Dresden factory with which it had long had a licensing arrangement—a run-down, turn-of-the-century factory with stained-glass windows and iron stairway railings—and made it more cost-effective but kept its top brand, called f/6, intact, even its strong taste and stodgy packaging, on the premise that with the moorings torn loose from so many other aspects of their daily lives, East Germans would like to cling to at least one pleasurable part of their past. With the slogan "F/6: The Taste Remains," Philip Morris, on a minimal investment, soon seized first place in the East German market with a 45 percent share while slowly nurturing a taste for Marlboro and its other U.S. brands.

In Czechoslovakia, a market about the same size as East Germany, PM took a bolder tack. It paid a steep $413 million, one-third more than RJR's bid, for AS Tabak, the state monopoly, and gained a commanding position in a Middle European locale that could give it a tactical advantage geographically if and when a large, centralized manufacturing facility became practical. Here, too, PM pushed the leading domestic brand, Start, but smartened up the package. In Hungary, however, where it faced more competition, Philip Morris let Reemtsma and BAT buy up more costly plants, settled on a $30 million outlay for its former licensee and, in that more Western-oriented society, vigorously promoted Marlboro. Kiosks all over Budapest were festooned in Marlboro red, white, and black. At a big rock concert in the Hungarian capital, girls clad in the brand's colors merrily handed out samples—and anyone who lit up on the spot got a pair of white sunglasses as an added premium. In Poland, with the highest per capita consumption of cigarettes in Europe, RJR staked a large claim by investing $50 million in a plant of its own; Philip Morris, meanwhile, reinforced its fifteen-year licensing agreement with a plant in Cracow, standing ready to invest in it whenever the Polish government might elect to privatize its state-owned tobacco industry. In the smaller adjacent Baltic states market, though, PM made a $40 million commitment to upgrade and control two-thirds of Lithuania's largest cigarette factory.

In contrast to a level of euphoria in the Eastern European states over their release from thralldom under the Soviet yoke, the mood was darker and the sense of political and economic disarray deeper in the former USSR. When Philip Morris tried to fill the void left by malfunctioning local factories with imported Marlboros, it drove down the old black-market price, and soon kiosks around Moscow that were offering the top U.S. brand went up in flames—the handiwork of organized thugs who emerged as a frightening reality in the former police state. Rather than relying on extortionate payoffs to the new Russian mob, PM and other foreign companies began to invest in the struggling new market economy by buying and renovating old plants or, in a far riskier move, building new ones. Outspending all its Western rivals—BAT, Rothmans, RJR, and Reemtsma—Philip Morris allocated some $1.5 billion among eight manufacturing sites within the first four years after the breakup of the Soviet empire.

National health officials, more humane than their Communist predecessors, began to insist early on that cigarette purveyors be reined in. But while Western Europe, under its newly functioning economic union, was imposing a single standard of tobacco regulations, including advertising bans and a phased mandatory reduction in the tar yield to 12 milligrams per cigarette by the late 'Nineties, the fledgling democratic governments of Eastern Europe set down widely varying rules and standards, with enforcement lax at first in most countries. Soon, though, there was a perceptible tightening, as in Russia, where cigarette commercials were being taken off television by 1995 as an unwelcome by-product of the nation's still fragile freedom of speech. Meanwhile, cigarette sales proliferated, and Philip Morris was shortly reporting a narrow profit on its new operations and quantum leaps in sales (tripling in Eastern Europe, for example, from 1993 to 1994). Indeed, the company's international tobacco operations were posting unit gains of 10 percent a year, far more than compensating for the erosion of its American market. PM's overseas net seemed likely to surpass its domestic cigarette profits before the year 2000.

For all that, the most prized cigarette market of all—China, with one-quarter of its 1.2 billion people believed to be smokers and comprising more than 30 percent of the world's smoking population by the early 1990s—remained tantalizingly out of reach to the international tobacco companies. Only a trickle of foreign brands was sold under close government scrutiny, mostly to tourists, as the Chinese Communist leaders jealously guarded the cigarette trade as their largest single source of tax revenues and prime fount of capital formation.

The ambitions of American and other tobacco companies to part the Bamboo Curtain served as a standing reminder to the Chinese of the vicious practices of British merchants in the first half of the nineteenth century to finance their purchases of tea and silk by persuading their government to help them foist imported opium on a resistant and still largely feudal society. Shooting their way into the Chinese market when necessary in what became known as the Opium Wars, London entrepreneurs, like their latter-day counterparts in the U.S. cigarette business, justified their incursions into often hostile Asian markets as contributions to their own nation's balance of trade. Nicotine had replaced opium as the best-selling drug in China by the early part of the twentieth century, when British-American Tobacco crushed the native cigarette industry through ruthless pricing practices, dubious legal maneuvers, and purchased political influence. BAT dominated the market until World War II forced it to close down, and the Communist takeover thereafter ended foreign economic activity altogether.

But smoking knew no political favorites nor was its economic exploitation restricted to predatory capitalism. The leaders of Red China, in particular Chairman Mao Tse-tung and Premier Chou En-lai, were legendary smokers, and cigarettes were one of the few consumer products kept in cheap and ready supply, though by no means adequate to fulfill the demand for a mild opiate by a vast populace struggling for national cohesion and social justice within a rigidly conformist state. And it had long since become a widespread sign of civility in China to pass around cigarettes at the beginning of state, community, and family functions. It scarcely mattered that the leaf raised by some 90,000 Chinese tobacco growers made for a harsh smoke, with twice the tar and nicotine levels of U.S. cigarettes and rarely mitigated by filter tips. They came in pretty packs with a thousand different names, like Panda, Peony, Butterfly, Golden Orchid, and Sailing Boat, produced by nearly a hundred clanking old factories run by the national Ministry of Light Industry and sold in the 1980s at the subsidized price of twenty to thirty cents a pack. Even so, the tobacco habit, practiced mostly by men in a resolutely sexist society, claimed 15 percent or so of the typical Chinese household's income. Enlisting technological assistance from American tobacco companies anxious for any toehold in that immense but closed market, China succeeded in doubling its cigarette output between 1978 and 1986 and once again by the early 'Nineties, as production reached a reported 1.7 trillion units a year, three and a half times total U.S. consumption. Far from inviting foreign capitalists to dip into this seemingly bottomless market, China's economic ministers began casting eyes on the world export market, especially in other Communist states that could not satisfy their peoples' appetite for smoking.

In a society where starvation had chronically threatened a large portion of its multitudes, few worried about the health risks of smoking—and, indeed, not many Chinese could afford to smoke heavily enough to be at high risk from the practice. But with production and creature comforts on the rise, the effects slowly began to take hold. One large prospective study running from 1972 to 1981 disclosed a lung cancer toll comparable to that afflicting U.S. smokers—8.8 times higher than for nonsmokers and an 80 percent higher mortality rate. Official concern about the problem emerged with the ascension of Prime Minister Li Peng, a nonsmoker, whose health overseers were newly attentive to predictions by Western scientists that unless the nation's passion for smoking was soon moderated, some 2 million Chinese could die annually from tobacco-related diseases by the end of the first quarter of the twenty-first century. Efforts slowly began to reduce the toxic yields of Chinese cigarettes, educate young people on the wasting consequences of habitual use, disallow smoking on public transit, and limit its advertising.

Covetous of an immense consumer supply that now seemed to be receding from their reach, Western cigarette makers did the only thing they could while playing a waiting game—built fame for their brand names by advertising them without ever showing or mentioning cigarettes or smoking. Thus, Philip Morris sponsored a national soccer league for a time, and one of the more popular radio programs in China was "The Marlboro Music Hour," featuring a generation of gyrating American heartthrobs from Elvis Presley to Michael Jackson. Following U.S. comedy shows on Chinese television, commercials displayed the names of BAT's brand State Express 555 and footage from the old "Marlboro Country" ads—rousing music, snorting stallions, and all, though the average Chinese couldn't get near the product.

Partly in return for President Bush's support of a "most-favored nation" status—*i.e.*, the lowest tariff rates—for the swiftly growing export of Chinese goods to the U.S. despite Beijing's continuing practice of political suppression, American trade officials in the closing days of the Bush administration won an agreement from Beijing to admit a large number of U.S. products for sale in China by 1995. Included on the list were cigarettes. But it was an agreement in principle only; the details remained to be worked out. Just how difficult that might prove in the case of cigarettes, a mainstay of the Chinese economy, became apparent by the summer of 1994, as China hiked its tobacco tariffs and hinted at raising the cigarette excise tax; later in the year, on the eve of the supposedly new open-market policy, the National People's Congress voted tougher restrictions on cigarette advertising, banning it on billboards and in films and further limiting smoking in such public places as transit waiting rooms, meeting halls, and sports stadiums. Health warnings were being drafted for inclusion on all cigarette packs, and the government announced that in 1997 Beijing would be the site of the tenth world conference on smoking and health, with the theme "Tobacco—the Growing Epidemic."

Even so, Western tobacco companies were hopeful. As Philip Morris's Geoffrey Bible, a veteran of the international tobacco wars, confidently noted, "There is already much awareness of branded products in China—and people everywhere aspire to the gold standard." The door to the world's largest smoking market was opening, if only a millimeter at a time. The immediate problem of cultivating it would not be government restrictions so much as low Chinese incomes, a dire shortage of hard currency to pay for imports, and the widespread piracy of famous foreign products. Such problems would persist even if communism withered and a market economy replaced it in the new millennium. But sooner or later, access would come, assuring the proliferation of U.S. and other global brands, sustaining tobacco profits, and seducing millions more to an early death.

20

Blowing Smoke

WHEN Hamish Maxwell completed his farewell address to Philip Morris stockholders at their April 1991 annual meeting in Richmond, Joseph Cullman, the retired chairman and chief catalyst of the company's ascent to the top ranks of American industry, jumped up from his front-row seat to lead the applause. Maxwell was the best chief executive PM had ever had, Cullman would later say, because he had not only solidified the company's leadership in the domestic tobacco market and extended it abroad but also engineered the takeover of three giant food companies to make Philip Morris the largest U.S. entry in that industry as well—and accomplished the feat without excessive acrimony, indeed with some civility. "A masterly move," Cullman called it, "done with great style and polish."

Wall Street agreed, having bid up Philip Morris stock so steadily that company shareholders had earned a 40 percent compounded total return on their equity over the seven years of Maxwell's chairmanship. As a sign of gratitude, the PM board rewarded the retiring CEO with a good-bye gift worth $24 million in compensation, stock, and options. But the triumphs of one generation's leadership can speedily devolve into pressing problems for the next, and in Philip Morris's case the nature of the challenge was foreseeable. Almost overnight Maxwell had created a titanic business by diverting the excess cash from fabulously profitable tobacco operations to shape a far larger, potentially more enduring enterprise. But after two decades during which the company's profits had doubled on average every four years, how could the corporate machinery continue to churn out earnings of such magnitude and at such a velocity, particularly in light of the far lower operating margins in the keenly competitive food industry?

During the first months of 1991, Wall Street wondered aloud who would take charge at Philip Morris, the hottest and most controversial moneymaker in corporate America. Although the tobacco side of the business still had promising growth prospects abroad, the whole thrust of Maxwell's master plan had been to make tobacco the fuel to turn PM into a global colossus in the food business, a sure winner over the long run on an increasingly overpopulated planet. The new PM chairman, then, probably ought to be a food man, and Maxwell was confident that he already had the right one on board in Michael Miles, the lanky Midwesterner he had coveted as part of the Kraft, Inc., acquisition.

There were a number of qualities in Miles that Maxwell greatly admired: a good analytical mind, an aggressive marketing style, a gift for public speaking but a disinclination to gab freely in private, and a controlled intensity in his methodical approach to every problem. "Well, did you have a great year, Mike?" Miles recalled Maxwell asking him in their review session at the end of his first year running Philip Morris's complex food operations. "I've never had a year I could honestly call great," Miles answered truthfully but with a laugh, knowing full well that his boss was a man of the glass-is-half-empty school of incentive management.

Two years later, after Miles had demonstrated skills as an economizer by cutting out some duplicative functions, facilities, and personnel in PM's sprawling food business and gifts as a marketer by extending product lines, particularly appealing to the growing number of health- and diet-conscious consumers, Maxwell had no trouble in winning unanimous approval from his directors for the low-key Chicago man with the no-nonsense style and impeccable chief executive's bearing. The only real concern about Mike Miles was whether, as a nonsmoker, he had the knowledge and the mettle to run a company whose core was still tobacco. Surely there seemed to be enough talent left on the tobacco side to provide Miles with the know-how to keep the industry leader advancing. In William Murray, Maxwell was bequeathing to Miles a devoted detail man who might have been a serious contender for the CEO post but for a dogged, by-the-numbers approach to management. Murray became Miles's chief subordinate, even as he had been Maxwell's, and czar of tobacco operations, with Murray's fellow Australian, Geoffrey Bible, in charge of the overseas business. The spirited William Campbell continued at the helm of the U.S. cigarette unit; the iconoclastic David Dangoor was advanced from the international side to oversee domestic marketing; and James Morgan, ardent articulator of Philip Morris image-marketing and five-year PM dropout after quitting to run Atari, was back at Maxwell's invitation in corporate planning and available for regular consultation. So were Maxwell, George Weissman, and Joe Cullman, all retaining offices at 100 Park Avenue, just across the street from Miles's executive suite.

Still, turning over direction of the company to a non-tobaccoman was a revolutionary step, as the press noted when Miles's election was announced in the spring of 1991. Asked if the continuing medical, social, and political agitation over smoking did not concern him and whether his selection did not in fact signal a turn away from tobacco by Philip Morris, Miles replied, "The cigarette business is great, profitable, and growing, so it looks like the future to me. I just wish we could produce similar economics in the food business." Why was it, then, reporters pressed him, that he himself did not smoke? His answer presaged lingering suspicions over his claimed serenity in playing the role of the capitalist world's chief peddler of cigarettes, a product accused of annually killing multitudes: "I used to smoke, and for some reason that I can't even remember now, I lost my taste for it. . . . I used to eat a lot of scallops and don't anymore. It's just one of those things." Millions of smokers had quit over the previous two decades as the health charges grew louder, but probably very few of them could not remember the reason—including Hamish Maxwell, who stopped the year before, after undergoing heart bypass surgery. At the stockholders' meeting a few weeks after his election, Miles was reminded of the difficult position he had won for himself when a Philip Morris shareholder stood up to lament the fate of the company's chief rival, RJR, after it had been taken over by what he called "the biscuit makers," meaning executives from Nabisco. He told the PM management arrayed on stage that it was tobacco that had made the company what it now was, adding, "I would hate to see Philip Morris turned over to the salad-and-mayonnaise makers." Former mayo-maker Miles rose and in his best abbreviated style answered, "Comment taken—please don't be concerned."

But Miles was never to become an eager defender of smoking, beyond insisting on everyone's right to do so without a busybody government or anyone else interfering. And he was anything but confrontational in his approach to tobacco's embattled status, replacing the joyfully combative Guy Smith as PM's top public-relations man. Even when the company might have generated some favorable publicity over a decision it made early in 1992 to placate its critics—the placement of health warning labels on all packs of cigarettes PM exported to the few remaining nations that did not require them on their domestic brands—there was no announcement; the press learned of the move from a disgruntled stockholder, a clergyman who had long urged the humane step on management and was apprised that it had finally been done. Miles was probably right in his the-less-said-the-better approach; to have trumpeted the change would surely have invited criticism of the company's long delay in making it.

Once in office, Miles encountered difficulty almost from the first in gunning the company full throttle when the rest of the U.S. economy was mired in re-

cession. American business was feverishly cutting costs, bringing unprecedented layoffs in the white-collar sector, a growing sense of national economic
insecurity, and a suddenly acute price consciousness among consumers about
what they were paying for everyday products, food and cigarettes prominent
among them. Philip Morris's inordinate pricing power, based on its stable of
more than 3,000 products, many of them household names, was now under
siege by no-name generic and private-label rivals sprouting on store shelves at
discount prices.

The problem was more pressing at first on the food side of the business,
where Miles had already effected the easy "synergies," his favorite buzzword
for economies like central purchasing of advertising for all corporate products
in order to obtain the lowest rates, and manufacturing efficiencies like saving a
million dollars a year by reducing the size of the caps on Miracle Whip jars.
Faced with narrowing margins due to price warfare on supermarket shelves
and volatile commodity costs, Miles elected to follow the lead of Procter &
Gamble and risk a loss in market share to gain higher profitability by slashing
promotional outlays in the form of "placement allowances" to retailers for desirable shelf display and off-price couponing to appease consumers. The decision meant slowed growth, if any, for Kraft General Foods (KGF) brands, the
prices of which were cut cautiously when at all, but margins slowly firmed up.
Meanwhile, high-volume but thin-margin product lines were peeled off, like
Birds Eye frozen fruits and vegetables and KGF's 15 percent share of the U.S.
ice-cream business, under the Breyers and Sealtest labels, being hard hit by
specialty and regional competitors like Häagen-Dazs and Ben & Jerry's.
Unilever took the lagging ice-cream business off Miles's hands for $115 mil-
lion, and he turned instead to more promising projects, like building up KGF's
11 percent share of the high-margin breakfast cereal market, a distant third to
leaders Kellogg and General Mills, by paying debt-laden RJR $450 million for
its venerable but somewhat faded Nabisco Shredded Wheat trademark. Miles
was also determined to turn around KGF's low-profit food-service business,
catering to restaurants and institutional cafeterias with bulk sales of cheese,
mayonnaise, and other staples.

Increasingly, Miles also had to face up to the constant and often costly com-
plexities of the food-processing business. This meant keeping constant vigil
over not only inefficient and outmoded plants but even state-of-the-art installa-
tions like the turkey-processing facility put up in California to replace the old
system by which the birds, after they were decapitated and their feathers
steamed off, got dunked into a cold-water bath to await evisceration and dismemberment; the result was a kind of "fecal soup," in which bacteria proliferated. To eliminate this unsanitary birdbath, the company installed an expensive
cold-air process developed by German technology and approved by the U.S.
Department of Agriculture for temporarily storing the poultry. Unfortunately,

the system did not work. "It was back to fecal soup," Miles somewhat grimly recounted later. But instead of constructing a whole new configuration of the plant at a time when the demand for turkey was on the wane, the installation was closed down as part of a $400 million KGF write-off during Miles's first year in office.

Such setbacks were inevitable for PM's huge $20 billion food business. But often when one sector slumped, another was likely to compensate. The same was true of Miller Brewing, where its leading brand, Lite, was losing its luster but Miller Genuine Draft continued to advance, gaining seventh place among all brands. Even in a struggling economy, then, Philip Morris was able to generate enough surplus cash flow not only to finish paying off the debt from its huge acquisitions in the food business but to continue investing in expanded facilities and new ventures. The chief difference was that now Miles spent more surgically and less spectacularly than his predecessor, and mostly overseas in much smaller moves.

This continuing expansion was more apparent on the tobacco side, where PM acted as aggressively as prudence allowed in the republics of the former Soviet Union and its lately freed Eastern European vassals as well as in countries like Turkey, where it spent $400 million for a large new plant and was soon selling more cigarettes than it did in Japan and France combined; in Brazil, where it had bought out RJR's manufacturing operations and was now pushing hard to improve on its 17 percent market share, still far behind BAT's 80 percent but at least a legitimate contender now; and in Vietnam, where by late 1994 PM became one of the first U.S. companies to open a manufacturing operation. The company was equally active in expanding on the food side abroad, where the KGF-Jacobs Suchard food empire was a mishmash of loosely federated licensees, distributors, and partners. Under Miles and Geoffrey Bible, structural coherence was sought along with what the latter termed "critical mass" by concentrating on three product lines: coffee, candy, and cheese. PM, already a major factor in the European coffee business, soon acquired top processors in Spain, Italy, and the Czech Republic; by 1994, it was selling twice as many roasted and ground beans as its nearest competitor on the Continent. In the confectionery business it moved more boldly by paying $1.5 billion for the biggest Scandinavian candymaker, Norway's Freia Marabou, to gain 15 percent of the continental market, just behind Mars, and then closed in further by outbidding Hershey to win Terry's Group, a leading British maker of boxed chocolates and toffee, for $320 million, gaining 6 percent of the candy business in a nation with a pulsating sweet tooth. Leading confectioners were shortly added in Eastern Europe.

In the beer business, where Miller ranked as the world's second largest producer, PM acted to improve its puny overseas sales—Anheuser-Busch was grossing three times its foreign revenues—by buying up 8 percent of Mexico's leading brewer, makers of the Dos Equis brand, for $160 million and a 20 percent share of Canada's top entry, Molson Breweries, including rights to its U.S. import of the Molson brand, third-ranking among foreign labels that held 4 percent of the American market. Holdings in both foreign companies were likely to be expanded at the earliest opportunity, along with other promising candidates to solidify its power in the worldwide beer and candy business, like the Dutch brewer Heineken and the giant British confectioner and soft-drink producer Cadbury Schweppes.

II

MICHAEL MILES's severest problem running Philip Morris turned out to be sliding sales in its most profitable line of business: the American cigarette division. After so many years of clear sailing and ever escalating margins, reaching a sublime 50 percent on premium brands by the early 1990s on the strength of incessant price increases of 10 percent a year, there had seemed to be no limit to what the consumer traffic would bear. Even when the discount sector of the market began growing, PM had responded by offering its own lower-priced entries yet increasing their prices at twice the rate of its full-priced line to keep profit margins presentable. The main challenge had been how to prevent Marlboro, with a quarter or so of the cigarette market, from being squeezed into about half that proportion of the available retail shelf space and having to rely on closely monitored turnover of the stellar brand.

By Miles's first year at the helm, though, the good old days were plainly over in Marlboro Country. The brand had lost 2.5 percent of its unit sales between 1988 and 1990, as the discount brands were capturing 20 percent of the market. In 1991, the erosion grew more serious. The older generation of smokers, knowing that one brand of cigarette was very like every other, resented paying two dollars or more for a pack and was turning to the cheaper brands, while for younger smokers, Marlboro was losing some of its appeal—it was the brand their parents smoked, and cowboys were old-fashioned, like Western movies. Camel, with its fun-loving mascot, Old Joe, was attracting a lot of attention from novice smokers. For the first time, Marlboro was offered in Christmas giveaway promotions. But it was not only Marlboro that was going into decline; all premium-priced brands except Camel were hurting, in particular Reynolds's Winston and Salem, which RJR tobacco chief James Johnston was trying hard to resuscitate with glossier packages, improved blending, more puffs per butt, and a tighter wrap to ensure freshness, none of which seemed to help.

To check Marlboro's decline, PM in mid-1991 rolled out its first major line extension in twenty years, since the introduction of Marlboro Light, which had developed into almost as big a seller as original Marlboro Reds. Company marketers thought there might be a niche they could fill between the flagship Marlboro Red and Light, which had about two-thirds of the former's tar and nicotine yield and appealed heavily to women. Why not Marlboro Medium, with yields slightly above Lights but offered in a package almost identical to the Reds and advertised in a slightly coyer fashion—without cowboys, only pictures of their boots or spurs to suggest a diminished strength to the smoke? The introduction was lavishly promoted through ads and incentives to wholesalers; the idea was to keep Marlboro buyers from defecting to rival full-priced brands or the discount sector, even if at the expense of Marlboro Red's sales. Within a year, Medium had taken a 1.5 percent share of the market but succeeded only in slowing, not stopping, Marlboro's overall slide.

Fresh thought was now given to revisiting the ultra-light sector of the market—brands yielding six or fewer milligrams of tar—and particularly the bottom end of it, dominated by American Tobacco's Carlton and RJR's Now, with yields of about one milligram; all together, this niche held barely 3 percent of the market. Philip Morris had virtually abandoned it after the failure of Cambridge as a minimal-yield entry a decade earlier. "We had other fish to fry," PM-USA head William Campbell recounted. Merit Ultra Lights, with a 5-milligram yield, had done well and taken 2 percent of the market, but what if Philip Morris tried seriously now to stir smokers' interest in a supermild brand, on the unspoken premise that it would be perceived as a safer product and stake out a good deal broader market than Carlton and Now held, if marketed with the old Philip Morris verve?

The scientific evidence in support of such a product remained sketchy but plausible. In the mid-'Eighties, Neal Benowitz and other investigators, measuring yields by trace elements of nicotine in smokers' blood and urine (and taking into account any increase in their smoking habits due to compensation), found that users of ultra-low brands were experiencing a 50 percent drop in nicotine absorption and 30 percent less than the average yield of carbon monoxide. And in highly preliminary estimates by Wynder and others, smokers using or switching to low-yield brands showed a 25 to 35 percent reduction in their risk rate for lung cancer but no discernible gain in fending off heart disease. But whether these sizable drops were enough to sustain a significant or even measurable reduction in disease formation could not be authoritatively determined without a major epidemiological study, perhaps covering the entire smoking life of subjects who used only the weakest brands.

Even so, Philip Morris marketers, however much they preferred to believe that it was the growing social stigma of smoking more than health fears which were depressing sales, brought out Merit Ultima in 1992 in a sky-blue pack with a metallic finish and white lettering meant to suggest a mild product. It got pushed hard with futuristic ads using computer-like dot printing that hinted at technological innovation and declared, simply, "Surpassing flavor at only 1 mg. of tar" (and 0.1 of nicotine)—the Carlton-Now rock-bottom dosage level. Nevertheless, Ultima, like Medium for the Marlboro line, slowed but could not halt Merit's attrition.

Philip Morris might have prevented some of the continuing erosion of its full-priced sales if it had chosen to stop raising prices in the teeth of a recession and buyer resistance to costlier name brands. Or it might have even cut prices, as its KGF division had done with its Cracker Barrel cheese brand when faced with heavily discounted no-name house brands in the supermarkets. Instead, PM-USA opted to defend its aggressive pricing with premiums. These ranged from T-shirts with brand logos, given away by the millions per year for cutouts of the package bar code to prove purchase, to Virginia Slims' new "V-Line" of women's wear, which included a supple black leather jacket with a surplus of zippers (as a reward for a year's worth of smoking at a pack-a-day rate), to the still more elaborate Marlboro Team Adventure promotion, offering outdoor gear like sleeping bags and insulated jackets bearing the brand imprimatur and giving contest winners a free trek through "Marlboro Country" in a four-wheel R/V, on a whitewater raft, and, of course, on horseback.

Amid all this frenetic effort to defend a relentless pricing policy for its top brands, PM continued to guard its rear by accommodating customers who no longer could or would pay high prices for a name alone. It offered three brands at a mid-level discount—Cambridge, Alpine, and Buck—and the more deeply discounted Bristol and the supermarket black-and-white label, Basic. By the end of 1991, Philip Morris had actually seized the share lead from Reynolds in the discount sector of the market, which was now accounting for one out of every four packs sold.

But in 1992, RJR, determined if not desperate to pay off its leveraged buy-out debt before it ruined the new owners, decided to heavily mine the low end of the volatile cigarette market. The new management had no stockholders to satisfy, no lofty return-on-equity rate to sustain; its priority was to generate sales dollars, at however slender a profit margin, in order to get out of debt as quickly as possible. Thus, RJR set up a dummy subsidiary called Forsyth Tobacco, named for the North Carolina county where the company was based, in order to mask the provenance of new brands priced radically low—Monarch at ninety-nine cents and private labels like Austin, sold at eighty-nine cents by the Circle K convenience stores in the Southwest, and America's Highway, offered at only sixty-nine cents by British Petroleum's filling stations. RJR also heavily couponed its premium-priced brands, especially Camel, to try to check severe hemorrhaging of its market share in that besieged sector. Mostly, though, the executives at Winston-Salem hoped to run away with the discount sector, where Brown & Williamson was offering its GPC Approved brand for a dollar, and American Tobacco and Liggett were placing almost all their bets as well. With a whole new breed of superdiscount brands selling at one-half to as low as one-third the cost of the full-priced brands, the sector Philip Morris so thoroughly dominated, sales in the premium market could move only at an accelerated downward pace. For its part, Philip Morris did all it could to stave off a massive switchover to the cheap brands; why should it grab a nickel-a-pack profit, which the Monarch and other deep-discount brands averaged, when it could earn ten to eleven times as much on every pack of Marlboro it sold?

In what amounted to a full-fledged price war led by RJR, some 30 percent of all cigarette sales in 1992 were registered in the discount sector, where Reynolds had retaken the lead with a 36 percent share. The lower prices seemed to be encouraging Americans to keep smoking, or at least to slow their quitting rate. Per capita cigarette consumption, which had dropped by 4 percent in each of the two previous years, was off now by only 1 percent. Philip Morris brands dropped 3 percent overall in unit sales, but Marlboro was off almost twice that percentage and the other full-priced brands were similarly hurting; its deep-discount Basic brand had become PM's second best seller. Reynolds, on the other hand, showed a 3 percent increase overall; even full-priced Camel was up a few points; and the other companies had recorded still higher gains, all of them in the discount sector. But there was some solace for Philip Morris in its 9 percent net income rise on U.S. cigarette sales, which, while well under its usual pace of advance, contrasted with RJR's 19 percent drop in net income due to sharply reduced margins on its rising discount sales. On the strength of the performance of its food and international tobacco units, PM was able to declare a 23 percent increase in its annual dividend rate, almost as if nothing had changed.

There was real trouble, though, lurking in the fourth-quarter U.S. cigarette sales trend for 1992. PM brands were off 9 percent in units while its competitors had all posted gains of that magnitude or more. And the downward spin continued into the new year. By March of 1993, Marlboro units were off an additional 8 percent as the discount sector for the industry approached a 40 percent market share, and some tobacco analysts were predicting that it would command fully half the industry sales before long. It was beginning to look as if RJR's strategy had been correct. PM-USA President Campbell admitted "surprise" at the swiftness of the discount sector's growth, but neither he nor anyone else at the industry leader's headquarters was willing to acknowledge that he had contributed to the trend by having pushed up prices too high for too long.

Michael Miles understood and approved of the PM pricing game, which had amounted to a calculated decision to hold margins as high as possible for as long as possible and then retrench when and if necessary—as the company had in effect done after holding aloof from the discount sector because a leap into the price-cutting fray would have succeeded only in cutting profitability. Now, though, Miles saw that the company, relying on the domestic tobacco division for nearly half its profits, risked irreparable losses to its market share if it kept on playing a strictly bottom-line game. Averse as they all were to tampering with the price of Marlboro, the fuel that generated about half of PM's $60-billion-a-year gross, Miles felt he had no choice but to approve an experimental cut of forty cents a pack in the Portland, Oregon, market—a slash of nearly 20 percent. The results were encouraging: defectors began drifting back to the No. 1 brand, for which many would pay a premium so long as it was not exorbitant.

Without warning to the financial community or tobacco wholesalers, who might have made a run on the company by trade-*un*loading (*i.e.*, returning portions of their heavy Marlboro inventories for what they had paid instead of absorbing the loss in value due to the impending price cut), Philip Morris announced on April 2, 1993, that it was temporarily dropping the nationwide price on Marlboro by forty cents, or its equivalent through coupons or other incentives, and freezing the price on all its other top brands. The company conceded that the income lost by the big price slash would come almost entirely out of profits, which it expected to fall by a huge $2 billion for 1993 as a result.

Coming in the wake of mounting public hostility toward smoking being stirred up by the new Clinton White House, which had indicated it would seek a major increase in the federal tax levy on cigarettes to help pay for the administration's proposed health-care reform package, the news from 120 Park Avenue sent Wall Street reeling. In stock trading that April day, soon dubbed "Marlboro Friday" by the financial community, Philip Morris dropped 14³/₄ points, or 23 percent of its value—an astounding $13 billion paper loss to its 100,000 stunned shareholders. Big "MO," as Philip Morris was designated on the New York Stock Exchange trading tape, fell below $50 a share after having sold as high as $85 the year before.

As often happened, investors were overreacting to an unanticipated event. Wall Street brokers and analysts, however, did little better. Spoiled for so long by PM's unbroken skein of spectacular profitability, some of them turned now into doomsayers and blamed the company for acting in a panicky fashion after having clung too long to its high-pricing policy in a down economy with consumers on a bargain-hunting bent. Few saw it as simply and pithily as the company's former chief executive in Europe, Ronald Thomson, who remarked privately of the big Marlboro price cut, "They just got a bit too greedy, and now they have to pay some of it back." In truth, Wall Street may have expected Philip Morris to keep scoring unstoppable gains, but the company's top marketers knew they were playing a temporizing hand at best by defying the economic laws of pricing. Their aggressive policy had indeed been instrumental in transforming the company, but in hindsight its executives had waited too long to ease off in premium-brand pricing, inviting rivals to undercut PM's share dominance while still allowing them to turn a decent profit in a greatly expanded discount sector. The result was that when the erosion of full-priced brands reached the point where Philip Morris management could no longer tolerate it, the corrective action seemed traumatic.

There was one large side benefit to the PM price slash, even if its abruptness had unsettled investors far too severely for the good of the company stock. The price cut dealt a deft and punishing blow to RJR for having plunged so deeply into discounting and forgetting the lesson that earlier generations of tobacco executives had come to recognize: a price war would hurt them all; there was no need for rash measures in their oligopolistic industry, where the pie was large enough and the clientele sufficiently captive that all could prosper, more or less, if the pricing line held. But Reynolds, unable to halt the Philip Morris juggernaut, had chosen to wage war on the industry leader and settle for thinner per-unit profits from what it hoped would become a good deal larger slice of the market. Such thinking assumed PM would hew to its ever upward full-price policy, no matter what. The simple fact, though, was that Philip Morris was far better able to absorb the reduced margins of a pricing war than Reynolds, which had to give up nine cents of every sales dollar to meet the interest charges on its LBO debt, against only three cents that PM had to allot to debt service. Similarly, the price-slashing left RJR with fewer profits to shelter at the effective 8 percent income tax rate it was paying, thanks to its huge debt charges, while PM, at a 32 percent tax rate, was giving up less proportionately since it had to hand over a much larger piece of its profits to the government. All that aside, the Marlboro price cut seemed likely to have a negative impact on RJR's gross tobacco revenues, reducing the capacity of Henry Kravis and his partners to replace draining junk-bond yields, some with interest accruing at a potentially disastrous rate, with equity instruments. Stock warrants that RJR Holdings, the KKR-run parent company, had issued at 11¼ as a debt-retiring device dropped to half that value in the wake of the PM move. Little wonder that Kravis, in remarks at Harvard Business School a few weeks after Philip Morris announced the Marlboro cut, called it "the dumbest decision in corporate history. . . . They have ruined one of the best names in the world and created permanent damage." What PM had ruined was RJR's attempt to waylay it. Michael Miles, seeking to reassure his stockholders at the annual meeting held at about the same time that Kravis made his disparaging comment, promised to make further cuts if required to stem PM's loss of market share.

To implement the new pricing program, Miles made a pair of fateful personnel moves. Hard-driving Geoffrey Bible, veteran of cigarette price wars in Australia and Germany, where PM had allowed itself to be undersold too long before striking back, was advanced to worldwide czar of the company's tobacco operations, effectively moving past his titular overseer, William Murray, while James Morgan was restored to the post of senior vice president for marketing at PM-USA, the key job he had held at the time he left the company a decade before. The feisty Bible denied charges that the company had been too greedy in its pricing policy, calling the Marlboro cuts merely "an acknowledgment of our current economic conditions." In reality, they were an acknowledgment that Philip Morris could not exercise absolute pricing power in a time of economic duress for many of its customers.

Morgan, who had played a useful role during the heyday of Marlboro's growth, gave the brand a bigger advertising push and made sure there was no suggestion in its always spare copy that its price had been slashed, lest the brand's gold-plated image be cheapened. He also helped revamp PM's discount strategy. Its Basic brand, the former low-priced supermarket entry, was pushed up by a dime to $1.40 a pack, or forty cents below the average price now for Marlboro; Alpine and Cambridge, which had been pegged in between, were cut to the same price as Basic and given some small promotional support while Buck and Bristol were left to wither. In short, there were now just two PM cigarette price levels, and the company elected to put virtually all of its discount-sector effort into Basic, investing it with what Morgan liked to call "brand equity". The Basic line was extended to the full range of "packings," dressed in a smarter yet still quite basic-looking package, and advertised with what Morgan called "a bit of twinkle"—spartan layouts showing, for example, a pack inside a baseball mitt and headlined "Your Basic catch" or with a Walkman mini-CD player clamped on it and headlined "Your Basic concert"—and promoted with what the industry called "trinkets," T-shirts and flashlights bearing the brand logo, for example. All of this was to see if the old Philip Morris brand-image magic could work for a product with a sales twist no more unique than a variant of the old Miller Lite pitch, "Tastes good, costs less."

While the company waited to learn if these collective measures would correct its tailspin, management made a number of economy moves in anticipation of the expected drop in net from the deep cigarette price cut. Some 14,000 jobs were to be slashed, about an 8 percent reduction in the payroll, and forty food plants closed. A stock buyback program aimed at enhancing per-share equity value was suspended as well, and, most shockingly, for the first time in twenty-five years there was to be no increase in the dividend during 1993. The stock price, accordingly, stayed in the doldrums.

III

No subject more thoroughly arrested the attention of the tobacco manufacturers than the trend to sharply higher cigarette taxes, with their dampening effect on sales. To raise prices aggressively in the hope of richer profits was the prerogative of risk-taking entrepreneurs, but to be forced to do so for the benefit of government was to serve as a revenue collector with no hope of gain and plenty to lose.

Yet the nonsmoking public, even in the antitax Reagan-Bush era, had seemed only too glad to punish self-indulgent smokers whose habit jacked up the insurance costs for the rest of society and stood accused of disproportionate use of health-care services, 43 percent of which were paid for by federal and state tax-derived funds. The combined federal-state levy on American cigarettes, which had averaged twenty cents a pack in 1980, had risen to forty-six cents by 1992, the highest for any product relative to its selling price and three times as high as the tax on gasoline. Even so, the U.S. cigarette tax was among the lowest in the industrial world; the equivalent levy in 1992 stood at $4.07 a pack in Denmark, $3.25 in Canada, $3.24 in Great Britain, $2.23 in Germany, $1.52 in France, $1.49 in Italy, and $1.08 in Japan. The trend line in the U.S., though, was cause for alarm in the industry camp. In 1993, right after the Environmental Protection Agency officially ruled that secondhand smoke was capable of killing, fifteen states raised their cigarette tax, and in 1994 several imposed quantum leaps in the tobacco excise—Washington State by twenty-five cents, Arizona by forty cents, and Michigan by fifty cents for a total cigarette levy in that state of ninety-nine cents, then the highest in the nation.

Even these increases, however, were dwarfed by the prospect that accompanied the arrival in the White House in 1993 of the first avowedly antismoking President. As governor of Arkansas, Bill Clinton had vetoed a smokers' rights bill as trivializing authentic civil rights concerns. New First Lady Hillary Clinton, practically the moment she set foot in the nation's executive mansion, declared it a smoke-free zone—an important symbolic breakthrough for the tobacco control movement. In making clear, furthermore, that health-care reform was the keystone of his legislative agenda, Clinton said that the goal could be achieved without resorting to any increase in taxes—except for one. "I think health-related taxes are different," he explained. "I think cigarettes, for example, are different. We are spending a ton of money in private insurance and government tax payments to deal with the health-care problems occasioned by bad health habits—and particularly smoking."

How high was the national medical bill for smoking-related diseases? In 1994, the Centers for Disease Control placed the figure at $50 billion annually, or twice the previous estimate for direct medical costs attributable to smoking; the new figure represented 7 percent of the entire U.S. health bill. But public-health and antismoking groups, in calculating the net dollar cost to society, never mentioned the $12 billion or so that smokers paid in the form of federal and state cigarette taxes; instead, they called for a two-dollar-a-pack increase in the federal excise levy to cover the alleged $50 billion smokers' health-care cost. Tobacco-state congressmen made it clear to the White House that so huge an increase, roughly doubling the price of a pack of cigarettes, would lose the President their support for any health-care reform bill he put forward, and the Clinton administration's proposed figure was pared to seventy-five cents—still more than tripling the federal cigarette levy.

But the tobacco industry now drew attention to evidence gathered by econometricians, biostatisticians, and other analysts that the net figure for health costs attributable to smoking-caused diseases was being much exaggerated by tobacco control advocates. The most highly regarded work on the true health-cost burden smokers were imposing on the rest of society was a 1991 study sponsored by the Rand Corporation and published by Harvard University Press—*The Cost of Poor Health Habits* by Willard G. Manning *et al.* The Manning study added up the higher lifetime medical costs for smokers, the deficit in life insurance premiums they paid in as compared with the total pay-out to their beneficiaries, the property damage from cigarette-ignited fires, and the tax revenues that prematurely dying smokers did not pay to finance health and retirement programs—but out of fairness the study also calculated the *savings* that smokers provided by being fated to die younger than nonsmokers. Smokers received far less in retirement and health-care benefits from the government's Social Security and Medicare programs, drew far less in payments from private pension funds, and made far less use of private nursing homes. When all of these factors were taken into account, the Manning study as updated to 1995 dollar values found the net cost to the rest of society due to smoking-related diseases to be thirty-three cents per pack, not the two dollars the government's CDC claimed—and well under the fifty-two cents a pack in federal and state taxes which smokers were paying in 1994.

The Congressional Research Service, operated by the Library of Congress, examined the Manning study and several others on the same subject and found, in a 1994 report entitled "Cigarette Taxes to Fund Health Care Reform: An Economic Analysis" by Jane G. Gravelle and Dennis Zimmerman, that the Manning methodology was the most thorough and its "spillover" cost figure of thirty-three cents a pack was the median for all studies on the subject, thereby casting doubt on the fairness of a heavy additional tax on smokers alone to pay for the new Clinton health-care program. The Gravelle-Zimmerman report also remarked:

> Some argue these estimates of net external costs [due to smoking-related illness and not borne by smokers themselves] are inaccurate because they do not account for the intangible costs of premature death (*e.g.,* the grief of family and friends). . . . Pleasure driving, many recreational activities, some dietary practices, and some occupations, to name just a few activities, involve the same actuarially-validated risks of premature death and grief. In fact, we do not impose taxes on these activities.

Still more doubt was cast on the equity of a massive jump in the tobacco excise by a paper prepared for a November 1994 conference of the National Bureau of Economic Research by Duke economist W. Keith Viscusi. In "Cigarette Taxation and the Social Consequences of Smoking," Viscusi argued that although the tar and nicotine yields of cigarettes had dropped to about 25 percent of the levels of a half-century earlier, most of the mortality calculations still in use were drawn from epidemiological studies dating back to the 1950s and 1960s, based on lifetime smoking experiences with brands probably far more toxic than those in current use. Even granting that some smokers of low-tar brands compensated and extracted more hazardous yields than the machine-tested ratings for their brands, Viscusi concluded that smokers on balance were actually *saving* twenty-three cents a pack more than they were costing the rest of society because they had the misfortune to die younger. Strictly as sound fiscal policy, he jocularly added, "cigarette smoking should be subsidized rather than taxed." If the escalating mortality figures for secondhand smoke being put forward lately by smoking control advocates were taken at face value—and Viscusi made his doubts about them plain—he found the net health costs of smoking to be a break-even proposition, even before taking into account the excise taxes that smokers were paying.

I V

In the first week of 1993, within days of the end of the Bush administration, which had guarded and indeed advanced the interests of the tobacco industry, and months after a panel of outside scientific advisors had signed off on it for a second time, EPA administrator William Reilly finally released his agency's risk assessment on secondhand smoke—more than five years after it was begun. Whether he was at last approving findings that the lame-duck White House had long pressured him to delay for political reasons or he was overcoming doubts he himself had about the verdict was unclear. The fact, though, was that Reilly released the report at the last possible moment of his tenure.

For all the objections that had been raised by the cigarette makers, there was little equivocation in the final version of the risk assessment. The Group A classification of ETS as lethal to man was the least of it. Airborne cigarette smoke was labeled "a serious and substantial public health risk," responsible for approximately 52,000 deaths a year—15,000 due to various kinds of cancer and the rest from heart disease (not addressed by the EPA review)—as well as being implicated in from 150,000 to 300,000 cases of pneumonia and bronchitis in infants up to eighteen months old and a complicating factor for between 200,000 and 1 million youngsters afflicted with asthma.

The EPA's judgment did not go entirely unchallenged. The presumably nonpartisan Congressional Research Service advised the Senate that "statistical evidence does not appear to support a conclusion that there are substantial health effects from passive smoking." Such a caveat, of course, was precisely why the EPA assessment so infuriated the tobacco industry, which had long and speciously argued that there was *nothing but* statistical evidence to support the health charges against direct smoking. The industry's case against the EPA findings was most expansively and persuasively argued on the pages of the March 1994 issue of *Forbes MediaCritic* by Jacob Sullum, managing editor of the conservative magazine *Reason*, who contended that the press had uncritically accepted the EPA indictment of ETS and had promoted it into an essential prop for the smoking control movement by inviting the public to infer that the data against secondhand smoke was just as incriminating as the case against direct smoking. Sullum's analysis, marred by too much reliance on quoted authorities who had long taken the tobacco industry's money, nevertheless drew attention as few other commentators had to the obvious limitations behind the scientific charges against ETS, starting with the weakness of the association by epidemiological standards and the fact that in only six of the thirty lung cancer studies had the reported risk differential risen to the level of statistical significance (meaning that the odds were at least twenty to one against the results being a chance occurrence).

After Philip Morris showcased the Sullum article in a five-day series of full-page advertisements in several leading newspapers, the Clinton-backed EPA strongly defended its ETS stand. The EPA's June 1994 counterattack, "Setting the Record Straight," called it "an indisputable fact" that ETS was "a real and preventable health risk." Few objective observers questioned that view; the issue was how severe the risk was and whether the EPA had rushed to judgment in endorsing the high death toll attributed to ETS by the Centers for Disease Control and other public-health investigators, especially since the bulk of the total was blamed on multicausal heart disease through plausible but still speculative pathological agents and processes. That the EPA was not above playing the propagandist in its own defense was suggested by its broadside when it spoke of "the remarkable consistency" of the results of the studies on ETS. If there was any characteristic that marked the findings, particularly in the larger studies on lung cancer risk due to ETS exposure, it was the inconsistency of the results—except the weakness of the associations, where they were found to exist at all. The frequent absence of dose-relatedness, which had been the key to the findings against direct smoking, served only to strengthen the suspicion that the EPA was exaggerating its case.

Once the EPA had finally spoken on ETS, however, it was not about to retreat, and the rest of government and most of the public-health community now took the scientific case against secondhand smoke to be a given. The

CDC, for example, issued a slick pamphlet on the subject in which it asserted that "secondhand tobacco smoke causes thirty times as many lung cancer deaths as all other cancer-causing air pollutants regulated by the EPA." It failed to note that the latter figure was estimated to be about one hundred deaths annually. That is not an inconsiderable number of human lives, certainly, nor could any conscientious investigator outside the tobacco industry's pay dismiss the likely pathological potency of ETS. Still, the government agencies seemed nearly as capable in this instance of blowing smoke at the public to cloud the scarcity of cold, clinical science in support of the indictment of ETS as a substantial public-health risk as the cigarette companies had habitually been in denying and distorting the overwhelming scientific case against direct use of their product.

As predicted, the EPA branding of ETS set off a chain reaction of governmental and private measures to discourage smoking, starting with the proposed huge increase in the cigarette excise tax to help pay for the Clinton health-care reform program. It was followed by the Waxman House health subcommittee's approval of the sweeping Smoke-Free Environment Act, which would have virtually banned smoking in all nonresidential sites in the nation, including every office entered by ten or more people per week. But the measure got sat on when it reached the full House Commerce Committee, where tobacco-state congressmen among others held it hostage against the pending health-care reform program. Meanwhile, the Clinton administration indicated its readiness to act against smoking by administrative edict. The Labor Department, through OSHA, proposed a ban on smoking, except in set-aside and properly ventilated rooms, at some 6 million work sites across America and scheduled a series of public hearings on its proposed new rule that drew a loud and sustained protest by the tobacco industry, bent on indefinitely delaying implementation of the step. Congress, however, actually passed a requirement, more symbolic than substantive, that any school district receiving federal funds had to ban smoking in its buildings. The Department of Defense banned smoking in all military workplaces, starting with the inside of tanks. More tellingly, U.S. Trade Representative Mickey Kantor, who had once worked for the tobacco industry in fighting a ban on smoking in Beverly Hills restaurants while a Los Angeles lawyer, held a series of meetings with top HHS Department officials and then announced an about-face in the government's trade policy on cigarettes. The USTR would no longer aggressively try to force open foreign markets for U.S. tobacco companies, Kantor said, adding, "We will not challenge the health-based regulations of other countries as [they] were challenged in the past concerning tobacco products," especially their advertising restrictions so long as they were applied to domestic as well as imported brands. But Bill Clinton refrained from the one act he could have accomplished with a stroke of the pen early in his term of office: order smoking banned in all federal office buildings—a proposal that HHS had urged George Bush to institute, without success.

V

NOTHING better illustrated the power of an antismoking president to energize the tobacco control movement than the action taken early in 1994 by the one person in the federal government with the statutory authority to end the long-standing travesty that had allowed society's most dangerous consumer product to escape serious regulation.

The federal Food and Drug Act of 1906 and its later amended versions had handed oversight powers to the Food and Drug Administration with regard to the licensing, manufacturing, labeling, selling, and advertising of thousands of everyday consumer goods, but it was never established that tobacco products qualified as a food or a drug. The definition of a drug eligible for FDA governance was expanded by Congress under the Food, Drug, and Cosmetic Act as amended in 1938 to refer to a substance or device that was, according to the language in a Senate committee report accompanying the passage of the amendment, "intended for use in the cure, mitigation, treatment or prevention of disease" and included non-food products and cosmetics that were "intended to affect the structure and function of the body."

To base the policing powers of the FDA on manufacturers' stated intentions in marketing a product instead of on its measurable effects on customers' health was absurd on its face. By the same logic, the state ought to have been denied the right to press charges against a drunk driver who ran over a pedestrian or against a robber who killed a store clerk, because neither of them had intended to take a life. Forty years of scientific investigation had documented the systemic pathological impact of smoking on the "structure and function of the body," regardless of the cigarette manufacturers' avidly advertised intention to provide pleasure only—pain was never mentioned. Yet historically the FDA itself insisted that the agency had no power to intervene so long as the cigarette companies made no explicit health claims.

No way out of this legalistic bind was formulated until 1988, when Matthew Myers of the Coalition on Smoking or Health filed a pair of petitions with the FDA urging it to regulate all low-tar cigarettes as well as the new Reynolds "smokeless" brand, Premier, on the premise that these modified products were clearly *intended* to mitigate or prevent disease formation, as 1935 Senate committee language required. The Coalition's argument was not easy to ignore, for in marketing lower-yielding cigarettes—and, indeed, all filter-tip brands—by manufacturing innovations for more than a third of a century, the tobacco industry could have had but two purposes: (1) to respond to health charges, essentially dose-related, by reducing the toxicity and widely reported pathological effects from the use of their product, or (2) to satisfy consumers' perception that purposely weakened cigarettes were less hazardous—or might well be, as Rose Cipollone had testified to be her belief when switching to lighter brands. It was a distinction without a difference; either way, the manufacturers' *intention* was to market a product that did in fact, or appeared to, mitigate or prevent disease and thus qualified under law as suitable for FDA regulation.

But the Coalition petitions were left on the table as the FDA stalled, partly because, as a dependency of the HHS Department, rather than an independent agency like the FTC or FCC, it was beholden to the antiregulatory policies of the Reagan-Bush White House, and partly because, if the Coalition's logic was applied closely, only low-tar, filtered, and otherwise modified forms of cigarettes would qualify for FDA regulation while the old, filterless, and unaltered high-yielding brands might escape the regulatory net. Thus, the question stood on hold in 1990 when Bush appointed thirty-nine-year-old pediatrician David A. Kessler, a newcomer to government bureaucracy, to administer the FDA as its one-man commissioner. He was an odd choice for a President who had been a paragon of passivity in addressing the social ills and health needs of the nation.

A Phi Beta Kappa graduate of Amherst, with a medical degree from Harvard and a law degree from the University of Chicago, the bearded, brilliant Kessler had served six years as hospital administrator at New York's Albert Einstein College of Medicine before being tapped for the top FDA post. Reputedly instilled with high scruples and a sincerity that political infighting was sure to challenge, Kessler inherited an understaffed and underfunded agency charged with regulating products that registered a trillion dollars in sales annually. Hopelessly backlogged with applications for approval of new drugs and devices, the FDA had lately been further demoralized by a scandal over lax oversight of generic drugs. Kessler shortly showed that the FDA might no longer be a toothless tiger when he made an example of Procter & Gamble by fining it for selling orange juice labeled "fresh" when it was in fact made from concentrate; he then banned nearly all breast implants as a health hazard and began to implement a new and complex set of food labeling regulations. There was too much else on his plate for Kessler to address the cigarette question, which, at any rate, was hardly a priority with the Bush people.

But the new, young commissioner assigned several dozen scientists, lawyers, and other agency staffers to look into the FDA's power to regulate tobacco products, and cigarettes in particular as a drug-delivery system, even if the manufacturers did not admit that was their intention. The subject, though under continuing scrutiny, was left on hold until a new—and antismoking—president took over.

When Kessler finally felt it was timely to act, his tactic was fresh but the claim of its sudden availability as a weapon was in effect a shrewd contrivance. Instead of worrying about the entire product, the FDA commissioner dwelled on the known habituating effects of its chief druglike ingredient, nicotine, which, in turn, allowed the long-term pathological effects of smoking to develop. In a February 25, 1994, letter to Scott Ballin, by then chairman of the Coalition on Smoking or Health, Kessler asserted, "Evidence brought to our attention is accumulating that suggests that cigarette manufacturers may intend that their products contain nicotine to satisfy an addiction on the part of some of their customers," and it was the FDA's further understanding that the companies "commonly add nicotine to cigarettes to deliver specific amounts of nicotine." If his agency made a finding to this effect and could prove it in court, "it would have a legal basis on which to regulate these products. . . ."

That nicotine was the ingredient in tobacco that induced a habitual craving for, dependency upon, or addiction to smoking cigarettes—call it what you will—had been common scientific knowledge for much of the twentieth century. That manufacturers had been controlling or manipulating the amount of nicotine their customers ordinarily derived from their cigarettes had been known for forty years, ever since the introduction of filter tips, to students of the subject, and to any portion of the public that thought for a moment about it. Independent tests run by Consumers Union and *Reader's Digest* starting in the 1950s had revealed the variations in tar and nicotine yields by brands—surely not random or accidental but the result of technological advances by their makers. From 1967, the FTC had tested and regularly reported on these varying yields, and since 1971, every cigarette advertisement had been required to disclose the nicotine and tar yields of its brand. Plainly, the manufacturers had *intended* to vary the delivery levels of nicotine, with its body-altering effects, and on this premise, the FDA could at any time in the preceding generation have claimed that cigarettes were a drug as statutorily defined and gone to court to defend the agency's right to regulate it. But it would have needed a determined commissioner, ready to confront a powerful industry with die-hard support in Congress, and a President likewise committed. And there had been neither until now.

On February 28 and March 7, just after Kessler went public with his nicotine stratagem, the ABC News television program "Day One" presented what it called the tobacco industry's "last best secret . . . never before disclosed to consumers or the government"—that manufacturers were "spiking" or "fortifying" their cigarettes with extraneous nicotine for the express purpose of keeping their customers hooked. The closest the ABC programs came to documenting the spiking charge was an on-camera interview with an unidentified (and unidentifiable) former RJR manager, who said, "They [Reynolds] put nicotine in the form of tobacco extract into a product to keep the consumer happy." The clear implication was that this nicotine dosage exceeded what came naturally in the tobacco plant and that this seemingly sinister power to control the nicotine content was immoral if not downright criminal. Nowhere was a hint given that various strains of tobacco and indeed different leaves from the same plant, depending on their location on the stalk, naturally contained different amounts of nicotine and had long been blended by the manufacturers to vary the nicotine level—or that the artificial and mechanical means of lowering that level had been no secret for decades. Instead, "Day One" put on skilled smoking control advocate Clifford E. Douglas, then an ACS lobbyist, who said, "The public doesn't know the industry manipulates nicotine—takes it out, puts it back in, and uses it as if it were sugar being put in candy. They don't have a clue." Clues, though, they had aplenty, unless smokers elected to believe that the wide variance in reported and advertised nicotine levels was merely one of Mother Nature's dubious little gifts to mankind. The only legitimate question, really, was whether the tobacco companies were turning out *unnaturally* nicotinized cigarettes—juiced up, that is, beyond what grew in the fields, *even if* the government-tested yields had long been reported to the public.

To justify their assertions that the industry was or might be spiking cigarettes, ABC and the FDA pointed to the companies' use of reconstituted tobacco leaf (RL), developed more than forty years before, long disclosed in books and articles, and described in the 1979 Surgeon General's report. RL was salvaged as an economy measure from stems, lower in nicotine than the leaves, and scraps that had broken off during curing and were reconfigured in paperlike sheets that, after shredding, composed about one-third of the modern cigarette. During the RL process, solubles including nicotine were extracted from the mostly cellulose fibrous parts of the leaf; the nicotine was then returned to the reconstituted leaf along with some flavorings, preservatives, and a moisturizing agent. But according to one company, Philip Morris, which quickly filed a $10 billion defamation suit against ABC, "no nicotine whatsoever not found in the original natural tobacco materials is introduced in the production of reconstituted tobacco sheets," which "contain approximately 20 to 25 percent less nicotine" than the natural materials because of what was lost during the extraction process "and is not replaced" (underscoring in the original text). The company's complaint added flatly, "Philip Morris never had, and does not now add, any nicotine whatsoever in the process of manufacturing cigarettes. To claim that these processes constitute 'spiking' or 'fortifying' of cigarettes with nicotine to 'hook' smokers, to 'keep people smoking' is an egregious falsehood. To the contrary . . . the only adjustment of the nicotine content of cigarettes that is involved in the manufacturing process is the *reduc-*

tion of nicotine levels" (emphasis in original). Would it have been justifiable to claim that a dairy company was spiking natural milk with fat because it knew how to process skim or 1 percent milk but did not limit its output to those reduced fat varieties, a PM publicist asked as the suit against ABC neared the trial stage. It was a persuasive argument, which, coupled with the absence of hard evidence that the manufacturers were juicing up the product beyond what nature wrought—except by genetic experiments to develop nicotine-rich strains of tobacco leaf, often with help by Department of Agriculture scientists (the resulting yields of which, at any rate, were reported by FTC testing and not hidden from the public)—caused the TV network to recant in August 1995 with two on-air apologies and pick up PM's legal expenses to get it to drop its slander suit. That ABC's parent, Capital Cities, was about to be acquired by the Disney organization to form the world's largest entertainment conglomerate no doubt helped speed the settlement.

The "spiking" charge might have carried more weight if it had been informed by disclosures just two months after the ABC-PM settlement by *The Wall Street Journal*, in a page-one October 18, 1995, report based on Brown & Williamson documents it had received from whistle blowers. These claimed that Philip Morris's, and particularly Marlboro's, dominance in the cigarette business stemmed in large part from the skillful admixture of ammonia compounds to its tobacco that served to intensify the potency of the nicotine in its brands without measurably increasing the quantity. According to a 1991 B&W "handbook" for its leaf blenders and product developers and a second analysis a year later on Marlboro's runaway success, the additions of ammonia, a substance occurring naturally in tobacco, served as an "impact provider" by quickening the rate at which nicotine was absorbed in smokers' systems— a finding corroborated, according to the *Journal*, by a number of top non-industry pharmacologists who contended that the quicker the nicotine absorption, the more satisfying and reinforcing its psychological (and, by extension, its addicting) effect. Other cigarette makers were also said to have adopted the practice.

In response to the *Journal* disclosures, tobacco company officials denied that the ammonia additives, which they readily acknowledged, were intended to increase the *amount* of nicotine smokers absorbed—but that had not been the charge, of course. PM scientists said the main value of the ammonia added was to keep the reconstituted leaf in its brands' blends from falling apart by generating the release of gluelike pectins. Reynolds spokesmen said their primary task in developing cigarettes was "to sell sensory impact," not addiction, as the public-health community was now charging, and the ammonia additives helped RJR brands to "smoke smoother." But a former associate director of the Council for Tobacco Research, John Kreisher, may have come much closer to the truth when he remarked to the *Journal*, "Ammonia helped the industry lower the tar and allowed smokers to get more bang with less nicotine. It solved a couple of problems at the same time."

Thus, the industry may not have been precisely "spiking" the tobacco in its cigarettes with more nicotine, but it may well have been performing prodigies of chemical engineering to reduce the carcinogenic potency of cigarette smoke (*i.e.*, through lowered tar yields) without comparably modifying its addicting properties, as the reduced nicotine yields measured by FTC-approved smoking machines plainly implied. In short, this would not have been an entirely good-faith effort by the cigarette makers to modify their product. Even if the newly revealed B&W documents were creditable, though, no one was saying just how much more potent the ammonia made the nicotine, probably because the impact was largely subjective and possibly beyond the reach of scientific calibration.

When FDA Commissioner Kessler later appeared before the Waxman House subcommittee in spring 1994 to elaborate on his letter to the Coalition, his carefully channeled premise was apparent. Contrary to the industry's effort to frame the debate on smoking in terms of the right of each American to use the product or ignore it, Kessler stated that the cigarette manufacturers "may be controlling smokers' choice by controlling the levels of nicotine in their products in a manner that creates and sustains an addiction in the vast majority of smokers." This would represent a deceptive practice, to the FDA commissioner's thinking, since "most people assume that the nicotine in cigarettes is present solely because it is a natural and unavoidable component of tobacco." Kessler also pointed to dozens of patent applications that the tobacco companies had filed for processes to enhance the nicotine content of their cigarettes, but he did not go on to charge that these processes were in fact being used in tobacco manufacturing (though he would cite the long use of certain strains of leaf genetically developed to be extra-rich in nicotine).

Why, though, if the cigarette makers had mastered sophisticated production techniques to calibrate their nicotine yields, did they not remove the substance altogether, at least from some brands? Kessler suggested the answer to this most pointed of his questions by stating, "What appears to be true is that smokers become accustomed to, and associate, the sensory impact of nicotine (burning in the throat) with the resulting psychoactive effects of nicotine and thus look for these sensory signals in a cigarette; this is called 'conditioned reinforcement.' " Or, as a layman might have put it, smokers would not have derived a "kick" out of entirely denicotinized cigarettes. But while it was certainly true that manufacturers knew, from their own laboratories' studies and many published by outsiders, that nicotine was an addicting drug that surely helped sell their product to hooked customers, they could also point to the fact that they had long been marketing brands with sharply reduced levels of the addicting agent. And the further fact was that only about one of every eight cigarettes sold fell into this ultra-low yield category of 0.6 milligram of nicotine or less, probably because such reduced yields did not satisfy the very yen Kessler had described.

Kessler confronted the option that the companies had provided—to "smoke down"—by essentially dismissing it as a marketing device. "It is a myth that people who smoke low nicotine cigarettes are necessarily going to get less nicotine than people who smoke high nicotine cigarettes," he asserted, because smokers choosing the former brands could and did compensate "by altering puff volume, puff duration, inhalation frequency, depth of inhalation, and number of cigarettes smoked." The manufacturers, Kessler added, achieved their lowered yields with devices that could be compromised by smokers but not by the FTC's smoke-testing machines, such as ventilation holes around the filter and faster burn rates. This problem could have been avoided by removing more or all of the nicotine during the leaf processing instead of designing the nicotine reduction into the manufactured cigarette and its filter. In short, the whole industry was open to the charge of trying to fool the testing machines, as Brown & Williamson had been accused of doing with its Barclay brand.

The chief executives of the tobacco industry's cigarette-making subsidiaries came before the Waxman subcommittee a few weeks later to answer Kessler's charges and implications. There was a disingenuous, almost surreal quality about the whole hearing on the part of the interrogators as well as of the witnesses. Chairman Waxman and his fierce antismoking ally, Congressman Synar, seemed to attack their prey with postured indignation over the allegedly fresh revelations of nicotine manipulation when both plainly understood—or should have—that ample evidence had long existed to bring the cigarette-manufacturing process under federal regulation if only the bureaucratic will had been there or Congress had so directed. The tobacco executives, as was their wont, were still less candid, declaring that the evidence remained inconclusive that smoking caused any disease or addiction and conceding that they controlled the nicotine yields in their cigarettes but only to affect their taste. They might better have acknowledged that they had lowered tar and nicotine yields to meet the health charges against cigarettes, even if they had done so in a way that still permitted smokers to compensate who were determined or felt compelled to do so. They might further have admitted that for a great many, if not most, smokers, cigarettes were a very hard habit to break once begun, though millions of longtime smokers had quit—and those fearing their susceptibility to addiction were perhaps best advised to stick to the ultra-low brands.

Perhaps the closest the tobacco executives came to a persuasive response to the Kessler and health subcommittee charges was the argument raised by Philip Morris USA President William Campbell: "If we were supposedly intent on adding nicotine to cigarettes, why would Philip Morris have spent over $300 million to develop a process to denicotinize tobacco and launch 'Next,' a near zero nicotine brand?" An equally good question in return would have been why had Philip Morris marketed Next so hesitantly and uninventively—could it, for example, have been given a duller name?—and brought it out only in selective test markets with little fanfare, almost as if the company wanted the brand to fail so that it could point to the halfhearted effort as evidence that there was no real market support for a denicotinized brand.

The net effect of Kessler's testimony and the Waxman subcommittee's exchange with tobacco executives was to put Congress and the industry on notice that the FDA commissioner was repositioning his agency with regard to government oversight of cigarette manufacturers. He would not act precipitously, making it clear that he was seeking further technical advice on the addicting nature of smoking as well as guidance from Congress, which held the ultimate power to define how the FDA could exercise its control over cigarettes. Washington insiders, watching Kessler maneuver, quipped that the young FDA lion, uneager to risk an overreach of power even if it could be defended as sound public-health policy, was really saying to Congress, "Stop me before I regulate"—meaning that unless Congress put down markers for him, he would have no choice but to ban cigarettes altogether as a drug-delivery system, whatever else they were.

That summer an FDA advisory panel told Kessler that, lest any doubt remained, nicotine was indeed an addicting drug and the main reason people smoked. The most constructive step the FDA might therefore take, Kessler was advised by addiction experts, would not be to ban cigarettes entirely, thereby precipitating a national trauma among smokers and illegal traffic in the product, but to impose a regimen on the manufacturers to reduce the maximum tar and nicotine yields by stages over a period of years—ten or fifteen perhaps, so the effect would hardly be noticeable—and drop dosages to below the probable threshold for addiction for most smokers. Kessler and aides hinted that they would consider such a measure as well as rules to cut sharply into underage smoking.

Confronted with the sudden appearance of a regulatory monster breathing fire in their direction, industry officials grumbled that this whole new FDA initiative had been trumped up and there was nothing at all new about the charges. Philip Morris attorney Steven Parrish summed up the companies' position by remarking, "If Dr. Kessler wants people to try to quit smoking, he ought to tell them to try, because they can quit, and not characterize them as addicts doomed to fail. . . ."

VI

MICHAEL MILES'S calculated gamble to slash the price of Marlboro and then of the other Philip Morris premium brands as well in March 1993 brought swift results. By December, Marlboro gained back 3½ market share points, ending the year with just under a quarter of the U.S. market once again. And Basic doubled its volume during the year, winning a 5.3 share of the market to become the nation's No. 3 brand and the leader in the discount sector. Reynolds, having suffered a 58 percent drop in its third-quarter earnings as a result of the price cuts that Philip Morris had forced it to make on its own premium brands, late in the year announced a modest 2.7 percent price rise for all its brands—and Philip Morris was glad to go along. A truce had been called in the price war.

For all of 1993, PM's net fell at about the rate predicted: 37 percent overall on a 46 percent drop in earnings for the company's U.S. cigarette business, and while its unit sales for the year were off 9 percent, most of that drop had come before the price cuts kicked in. For Reynolds, the news was far worse: not only were its units down 3.5 percent for the year, but its operations had slipped into the red. Slowly, Wall Street began to recognize that Philip Morris, unlike General Motors, IBM, Sears, and other such corporate titans also once thought to be invincible, had not sat around letting itself be undersold by hungry challengers until it was too late to recover its commanding market position.

The new year brought tobacco industry executives, ever eager to spot a silver lining in their perpetually clouded skies, some signs to gladden them. The annual federal government health survey of 40,000 or so Americans showed, despite a continued drop of about 2 percent a year in the per capita consumption of cigarettes, that the proportion of the nation's adults who still smoked was stabilizing at just under 26 percent. The proportion of smokers under eighteen was 19 percent and had stood fixed at that figure for a decade, even in the face of pressing efforts by doctors, educators, and public-health workers to discourage youngsters from taking up the habit. There was anecdotal evidence now, furthermore, that among educated and affluent young adults, "social smoking"—lighting up a few cigarettes a day or a week during dates or parties to enjoy the taste of burned tobacco and the sensation of flirting briefly with danger—was catching on. And U.S. unit sales for the year would actually increase for the first time in a decade. By any standard, an industry with more than 45 million customers spending $55 billion or so a year on its products remained a serious force in the national economy.

At Philip Morris's Park Avenue headquarters, there was still more cause for cheer. Sales figures piling up throughout the first half of the year were thoroughly confirming the pricing and marketing decisions of the previous spring. PM's midyear cigarette unit sales were up 17 percent, while RJR's had slumped 6 percent; for the second quarter, Marlboro's market share hit 28 percent—its best ever.

Yet Wall Street analysts and investors were still unconvinced that tobacco stocks represented a good bet, even if the blue chip among them was showing every sign that it had weathered the crisis over slashed cigarette prices. The twin perils of far stricter government regulation and litigation regarding the health consequences of smoking had not abated; actually, both were looking more fearsome by the month. The FDA, OSHA, and the House subcommittee on environment and health were moving purposefully toward making the industry face up to the hazardous nature of its product. And while it was growing less and less likely that individual claimants like Rose Cipollone could persuade any jury in America to compensate them for injuries suffered after decades of smoking, a blizzard of new, broader-based suits with the potential for huge awards to the litigants was now swirling about the tobacco manufacturers. These included a class action in the name of 40,000 flight attendants claiming damage to their health from ETS exposure; suits by three sovereign states to recover their share of Medicaid payments to victims of smoking-related diseases, and a "mega-suit" brought by a consortium of leading product liability lawyers from more than fifty firms, each pledging $100,000 to their joint war chest, and filed in the name of millions of Americans who had allegedly become addicted to cigarettes due to the deceitful practices of their manufacturers.

It was not unnatural, therefore, in the early months of 1994, particularly after FDA Commissioner Kessler had speculated aloud that he might soon find nicotine an addicting drug requiring regulation by his agency, that executives at Philip Morris were fearful that the tobacco part of their business would permanently depress the value of their stock on Wall Street. Financial analysts and institutional investors with a heavy position in PM stock, including several big California and New York pension funds and the Teamsters Union, began actively calling for the split-up of the company into separate tobacco and food entities on the theory that (1) the stock market would value the separated enterprises a good deal higher as an investment package than it did the existing company, if for no other reason than (2) its non-tobacco assets could thereafter be protected from claims over injuries from smoking. The idea had been considered by the chief instigator of the tobacco-food marriage—former chairman Hamish Maxwell—as early as 1990, but the political and legal climate had not yet turned so tempestuous. His successor had been hopeful that the industry might enjoy a respite of benign neglect during the early years of his tenure, but the arrival of the Clintons in the White House had dashed that dream. As he contemplated the merits of a breakup of Philip Morris, Michael Miles recognized that such a proposal would be "a challenge to Hamish's previous direction." Yet Maxwell himself, very much on the scene as chairman of the PM board of directors' executive committee though discreetly hovering at the periphery of the company's daily operations, was by no means unalterably opposed to reconfiguring the edifice he had erected. "I had no strong sense that the company structure had to be forever," he recounted.

The depressed price of its stock aside, there were several practical reasons for its managers to consider dismembering Philip Morris. The company might already have extracted optimum value from the strategy of aggressive tobacco pricing in order to acquire a major stake in another, far vaster industry. For despite his continuing efforts to meld the two businesses, Miles was coming to the conclusion that "the synergies maybe weren't there, after all." Tobacco, as he put it later, was "a screw-it, do-it" culture more intuitive than the food business "with its forty-four product categories, each subject to quantitative analysis." As an outgrowth of this inherent difference and the divergent management styles it bred, senior counselor Maxwell had noted that the two sides of the house he had constructed "were not altogether happy with each other's business."

Chief among those suspected, both within and outside the company, of being unthrilled with its double identity was its nonsmoking CEO. Press speculation that Miles was, as he himself phrased it, "not a champion of the most profitable product in the house," was fed by his failure to defend it publicly and his near-invisibility as a prominent global industrialist. He had given no press interviews during a year in which the cigarette business was in tumult on both the political and marketing fronts, and rarely did he address Wall Street analysts on the company's financial performance. PM-USA President William Campbell, several notches below the top in company authority, was assigned to joust with tobacco industry critics, while Miles came to be perceived as a remote figure, uncommunicative with his subordinates as well as the outside world. He would on occasion reply to cracks about his seeming aloofness and cold-fish personality by saying he thought of himself as "businesslike," and would, in retrospect, explain why he had not thought it seemly to play "the media hound—maybe I should have." He attributed his minimal public presence to the conviction that "a corporation should speak with its results—its profits—not through press releases and interviews," which, at any rate, he felt were often misreported or distorted. He insisted that he was never discomforted by the health charges against smoking, which to him were not different in kind from those against cholesterol-rich cheese, the bellwether product of Kraft, of which he had been president. But such a view failed to acknowledge that dairy products had high nutritional value and that the danger from their fat content could be readily mitigated by moderate use; the same could not be persuasively said for smoking.

Miles's unease over the perception of tobacco as a rogue industry and the difficulty of meeting the ultimate public-relations challenge it presented was detectable in his response to a request by *The New York Times Magazine* for access to Philip Morris executives for an article that appeared in the March 20, 1994, issue by trenchant social commentator Roger Rosenblatt and entitled "How Do Tobacco Executives Live with Themselves?" According to knowledgeable insiders, Miles had to be talked into letting Rosenblatt interview the company's executives on so sensitive a topic. Most notably missing from the roster of PM officials with whom Rosenblatt met—and large photographs of whom appeared with the text—was CEO Miles. The article, which dealt only with Philip Morris, was notable for the access granted to Rosenblatt, its length—on the order of 10,000 words, certainly the most extensive (and likely the first) printed examination of the inner moral struggle of the industry's executives—and its curious effect, perhaps the opposite of the writer's intention, of letting his subjects portray themselves as not entirely insensitive human beings rather than as a den of fanged merchants of death. In answering the question of "[h]ow good, smart, decent individuals manage to contribute to a wicked enterprise," Rosenblatt, who made no secret of his antismoking attitude, wrote that "in dealing with these Philip Morris executives, I felt the presence of the company within the person. In the end, I felt that I was speaking with more company than person, or perhaps to a person who could no longer distinguish between the two."

But in the extraordinarily long quotations from the PM executives, perhaps interpretable by antismoking advocates as self-satirizing, their blameworthiness was cast into doubt by seeming candor, such as that exhibited by PM-USA general counsel Steven Parrish, who told how upset he had become one Sunday upon returning home from church with his family and turning on his television set to hear commentator Sam Donaldson say on "This Week with David Brinkley" that he didn't understand how any tobacco executive could look himself in the mirror every morning. Parrish went on to narrate how his daughter had come home from school and asked him, in preparation for a classroom assignment on drugs, what he thought about cigarettes.

And I told her that a lot of people believe that cigarette smoking is addictive but I don't believe it. And I told her the Surgeon General says some 40 million people have quit smoking on their own. But if she asked me about the health consequences, I would tell her that I certainly don't think it's safe to smoke. It's a risk factor for lung cancer. For heart disease. But it's a choice. We're confronted with choices all the time. Still, I'd have to tell her that it might be a bad idea. I don't know. But it might be.

More argumentative but no less reasonable-sounding were remarks by David Dangoor, executive vice president of Philip Morris International:

> You know, actually, it sounds crude and simplistic, but ultimately it's not up to the tobacco industry to deal with the cigarette issue. The final solution to the cigarette issue, that's up to society. If they want to ban cigarettes, you know, we live in a democracy, it should be done in a democratic way and discussed how the hell to deal with the economic consequences, and that's not meant as a threat. It's just a fact.

Not until the closing section of the very long article, dealing with the confession of guilt by a former Tobacco Institute lobbyist who later contracted throat cancer, was the ravaging effect of the cigarette business dwelled upon. And yet Michael Miles told subordinates that he felt the Rosenblatt piece reflected badly upon the company and chided those who had prevailed upon him to go along with it.

Convinced by then that cigarettes had been stigmatized beyond repair and that, as he later put it, "the food side of the business might do better on its own" in terms of Wall Street's valuation, Miles discussed the split-up idea openly with current and former PM executives. Although his espousal of the move was taken as further evidence "to the smoking side of the house . . . to doubt even more" the CEO's comfort level with tobacco, Miles noted, "at the end of the day Hamish himself was pretty reconciled to the split-up." And, according to Maxwell, so were most of the other Philip Morris executives on the company's nineteen-member board, "but the rest of them needed convincing."

The subject of the internal debate but little of its substance was reported in the press during the spring of 1994, with some accounts placing Miles and Maxwell on opposite sides of the issue. But probably the major barrier to that giant step was advice from PM lawyers that it was just too late to try to break off the food assets from the tobacco side because plaintiffs who had already filed class actions and multimillion-dollar suits against the company would surely press additional suits to block the split-up and prevent major corporate assets from eluding their claims—a prospect that could involve the company in a long, distracting set of lawsuits beyond its already weighty caseload. After a six-and-a-half-hour meeting late in May, the board issued a statement that the breakup proposal had been taken off the table "for the foreseeable future." As the 1994 annual report later elaborated, splitting the food from the tobacco business would have proven "very complicated, both legally and structurally . . . and the resulting uncertainties would be very disruptive" without clear, compensating gains. Shareholder groups, disgruntled at the time with the performance of PM stock, still languishing in the 50s, and tantalized for months by their anticipated enrichment from a split-up, howled.

Four weeks later, over a weekend and without making a public appearance, Michael Miles resigned. His only explanation was that "I thought it was better to return the company to lifetime executives with tobacco juice in their veins."

Some at corporate headquarters had heard that Miles was feeling heat from his old set of Chicago friends who were appalled that he had sold his soul to the devil in his capacity as the world's leading private purveyor of cigarettes. Some speculated that, having come to regret that sellout to Satan, Miles saw in the breakup of Philip Morris a way to escape from tobacco and resume his career as a leader in the food business, an industry he loved and understood—and if he could thus regain control of a much enlarged food enterprise from the tobacco predators who had seized Kraft six years earlier, the retribution would be sweet. Still others supposed there was just too much on his plate that was unpalatable: irate stockholders, a ceaseless din from antismoking activists, never-ending lawsuits, and the likelihood that he would soon have to engage the whole issue of smoking and health in person and probably on the national stage, before congressional committees—"something he really didn't want to do," a fellow PM director said.

Whatever his precise reasons, just a few months shy of three full years at the helm, Miles left 120 Park Avenue and went home to Illinois—and peace.

VII

THE Philip Morris board lost little time in reaching past the company's second in command, William Murray, to elevate his quick-witted, energetic countryman, Geoffrey Bible, to chief executive officer. Thirty-five years after leaving his hometown of Canberra, the Australian capital, at the age of twenty-two, Bible attained a pinnacle of corporate power beyond his dreams.

Lacking Joseph Cullman's social advantages and self-assurance, George Weissman's charm and presence, Hamish Maxwell's savoir-faire and cunning, and Michael Miles's American rootedness, Bible had parlayed his training as a chartered accountant into a career as a peripatetic troubleshooter for PM, willing to take on any assignment and expedite it handily if not brilliantly. A short, peppery man who had had to work at mastering interpersonal skills, he most resembled Cullman in mold and manner among his modern predecessors as PM chairman. He shared Cullman's dynamism, decisiveness, capacity to absorb and retain information, and, when he needed to, the knack of making subordinates sweat. But he was just as capable of sending an underling a congratulatory bottle of champagne with a warm note for a job well done. More to the point, Bible was an unapologetic, pack-a-day smoker, and if, as a churchgoing Catholic, he had any qualms about the cigarette business, he likely resolved them on Sundays. "None of us has weak knees about the product," he remarked to an interviewer soon after becoming CEO. "We manufacture and market it in the most honorable way. . . . We break no rules or laws." He thought the company had "a wonderful spirit and marvelous camaraderie," and told the press from the first, "It is our intention to defend our industry and our customers briskly and strenuously."

The change from his predecessor's above-the-battle style became apparent almost at once. The company was soon running full-page ads challenging the EPA's ruling that secondhand smoke was lethal, and pressed a suit against the agency for applying dubious science and exceeding its statutory powers. It was also pursuing court actions against Capital Cities for its ABC Network's "Day One" charge that PM and other tobacco companies spiked their cigarettes, against the city of San Francisco for unreasonably restrictive smoking regulations, and against the state of Florida for a new law that would allegedly strip the company of due process in defending liability claims by the government to recover its medical outlays for sick smokers. And when New York City considered adopting the severest smoking restrictions in the nation, PM hinted that it might have to abandon the metropolis that had always been its American home if the antitobacco environment grew too oppressive—and did not discourage the cultural institutions it had funded from leaning on city officials with pointed reminders of just how vital Philip Morris was to the artistic life of the Big Apple.

Wall Street was relieved that an unabashed tobaccoman was back at the helm, and felt still better later, when, based on the steadily improving results in its domestic cigarette business, PM boosted its dividend rate nearly 27 percent and announced a two-year, $6 billion resumption of its stock buyback plan. By year's end, the company's per-share earnings had made up the ground lost during the 1992–93 tumble in cigarette market share and the profit squeeze from the resulting price cuts; PM-USA's market share was at a record 47 percent, Marlboro had nearly 30 percent of the total, and Philip Morris was selling four out of every five full-priced cigarettes bought by Americans. The company extended its dominance into 1995, posting a gain in units as well as revenues while the rest of the industry tailed off; little talk was heard now of a company breakup as PM's stock price pushed over 70 by mid-spring and soon soared toward 90, past its pre-"Marlboro Friday" level. Even a voluntary recall of 8 billion units, at first attributed to contaminants in the plasticizer used in its cigarette filters and expected to cost the company more than $100 million, did little to slow PM's advance. Indeed, the action had the salutary effect of making the manufacturer appear to be a zealous watchdog of its customers' well-being, as Alan Blum sniped, "They've taken a product that kills you and have recalled it because it makes you dizzy."

To strengthen his hand in areas where he was least accomplished, Bible advanced James Morgan, his most passionate and gifted marketer, to the presi-

dency of PM-USA, and gave general counsel Murray Bring, the house intellectual and chief legal tactician, the added title of executive vice president in
charge of worldwide regulatory issues and public relations, thus recognizing
the company's likely long-term entanglement in the political and legal realms.

By the close of his first season running the company, Bible's career as an international executive stood him in good stead. Increasingly, Philip Morris
needed a global outlook, for while the home cigarette business remained its
corporate profit center, the company was selling almost three times as many
cigarettes overseas, international tobacco profits had nearly caught up to the
domestic net, and the United States, as Bible saw it, was "beginning to look
like an island of extremism" due to the smoking control measures Americans
were adopting. On top of a 20 percent annual growth rate in foreign tobacco
profits, PM's share of the cigarette business was surging almost everywhere
abroad: 37 percent, for example, in reunited Germany, Europe's biggest and
most lucrative tobacco market; a similar share in Bible's homeland, Australia,
where it had regained first place; 88 percent in Turkey; 46 percent in Mexico;
29 percent in France; and close to 14 percent of the world's No. 3 cigarette
market, Japan. While per-capita cigarette consumption had fallen off 10 to 12
percent in the lucrative Western European market, where PM reigned in the
1985–1995 decade, and tougher tobacco control regulations were being
adopted, some 34 percent of the adult European Union population continued to
smoke—more than one-third higher than the 25 percent figure for the U.S. Enforcement of the new antismoking rules, morever, tended to be lax in France,
Italy, and Spain, where the national governments still ran the tobacco business,
and in Greece and Germany, where cigarettes accounted for 5 to 6 percent of
all tax revenues. In Eastern Europe and the dismantled Soviet Union, Philip
Morris was sweeping ahead unstoppably by late 1995, at a pace exceeding the
combined sales of its two largest rivals, RJR and BAT, and amounting to
nearly 60 percent of its U.S. unit volume—and this was largely with imported
merchandise and before newly built or renovated local factories had come on
stream. Beyond that, PM vigilantly awaited political and economic breakthroughs in other vast markets where it as yet sold few or virtually no cigarettes, like China, India, Pakistan, Indonesia, and Nigeria. By late 1995 the first
Marlboros to be made in China were being produced in Shanghai.

On the food side, Bible displayed his impatience with the sluggish rate of
growth in the North American market, where Kraft General Foods was the
largest grossing purveyor. Younger executives were put in charge, the Kraft
and General Foods divisions were consolidated under the Kraft name alone for
greater efficiency, and efforts were intensified to weed out and sell off what
Bible called "the hippos," lethargic performers like the food-service unit,
which was grossing $4 billion, or some 17 percent of North American food
revenues, but earned far less proportionately. Bible got rid of it for $700 mil-

lion at the earliest opportunity and soon after peddled Kraft's lagging baked-goods business (the Lender's bagel unit excluded) for $865 million. Abroad, he pushed for further organizational tightening and expansion of business beyond Europe, particularly into Asia and Latin America, where PM's food lines had a modest presence. Efforts were intensified, for example, to create an appetite for coffee in Japan and yogurt in China—products little known in those societies.

Bible's confidence that Philip Morris would derive far more mileage from its core tobacco business was justified by the relative weakness of its chief U.S. rivals. The prime achievement of runner-up RJR Nabisco was that it had managed in six years since the LBO to retire about 60 percent of its $25 billion debt by aggressive conversion of its high-yielding bonds. And KKR, the New York takeover artists who had nearly choked on the RJR buyout, had maneuvered themselves out of the picture by selling off or transferring most of its equity interest. On the operational side, though, only RJR's Nabisco food business sparkled, proportionately outearning PM's far more complex food operations. Its tobacco brands, despite earnest efforts, continued to lose ground to PM, and its profit margins in particular suffered on a comparative basis. But RJR was far from ready to surrender, hoping that innovative marketing might yet bring about a reversal of its fortunes. Five years after the disastrous introduction of its foul-smelling, hard-drawing "smokeless" Premier brand, it announced the development of a presumably improved version, called Eclipse. Like its predecessor, though, it had the look more of a nicotine-delivery system than a cigarette and seemed certain to invite examination by the newly aroused FDA if the company decided to market the experimental brand.

RJR was less likely to find itself struggling in the last years of the twentieth century against front-running Philip Morris than with third-ranking Brown & Williamson, whose parent, British-American Tobacco, paid $1 billion in 1994 to buy out fading American Tobacco's 6 percent share of the U.S. cigarette market. The move, which gave expanded B&W about a 17 percent share—within five or six points of RJR—also had a retributive aspect to it. AT's marauding founder, Buck Duke, who had played the central role in the creation of BAT at the beginning of the century, had ceded international rights to the U.S. giant's brands to his British partners in their joint venture; now, at the end of the century, BAT was returning the favor by buying up the last remnant of Duke's U.S. tobacco empire and adding it to its own American subsidiary.

Still more important to Philip Morris's near-term prospects were the political developments that lightened Geoffrey Bible's heart during his early months as chief executive. The proposed Clinton health-care reform program, perceived by a majority of Americans as overly complex, intrusive, and costly, was scuttled by Congress—and with its inglorious demise went the prospect of a large increase, or perhaps any at all, in the federal cigarette tax. The health-care debacle foreshadowed the Democratic disaster at the polls in November 1994, as voters handed control of both houses of Congress to antiregulatory Republicans for the first time in forty years.

Gloom now descended like an immense cloud of cigar smoke on the tobacco control movement. Chairmanship of the Commerce Committee, the most powerful in the House, passed to Virginia's Thomas Bliley, ardent protector of his hometown's largest employer, Philip Morris; all further efforts to investigate, regulate, and harass the tobacco industry would end in the 104th Congress, so far as he was concerned, Bliley asserted. At Commerce's subcommittee on health, Henry Waxman was out as chairman and his close antitobacco ally, Mike Synar, was out of Congress altogether, having lost his seat in the Oklahoma primary. On the Senate side, things looked nearly as bleak. Bob Dole was back as majority leader, having first won the job in 1981 by bargaining for Jesse Helms's support with what many suspected had been a promise to tread softly on tobacco issues; Dole had been rewarded with large campaign contributions from the cigarette companies and gifts to his charitable foundation for the handicapped. Tobacco control stalwart Ted Kennedy was replaced as chair of the Labor and Human Resources Committee by Nancy Kassebaum, an opponent of FDA regulation of tobacco.

True, the Clinton White House could still take executive action to discourage smoking, like the Justice Department's successful suit in the spring of 1995 to bar televised cigarette signs from Madison Square Garden—the first federal enforcement of the twenty-five-year-old ban on broadcast advertising of tobacco products (and prompting Philip Morris to announce removal of all its cigarette signs at sports arenas where they could be seen on camera). But the balance of power in the capital had shifted to Capitol Hill, where Congress ordered a postponement of any new regulatory measures and debated a national tort "reform" bill to end all liability claims against unfixably dangerous products—steps that greatly heartened the tobacco industry. If FDA administrator Kessler had been looking to Congress for guidance before claiming jurisdiction over the making and selling of cigarettes, he was now unlikely to get it. The new and powerful House Speaker, Newt Gingrich, termed Kessler "a bully and a thug," threatening swift comeuppance from the Republican majority unless he proposed only the mildest of antismoking measures.

Even so, in August 1995, after carefully preparing the scientific and legal groundwork for the long-overdue action, Kessler won President Clinton's strong endorsement of FDA oversight of cigarettes as essentially nicotine-delivery devices and therefore a drug. This historic outreach of federal jurisdiction, proposing regulations far more sweeping than any that Congress or the FTC had ever imposed on the tobacco industry, was staked out at a presidential press conference in which Clinton, at his compassionate best, framed the effort as a public-health initiative—in effect, a program of preventive medicine directed not at irretrievably addicted adult smokers but at impressionable teenagers being lured into the habit in increasing numbers by the cigarette manufacturers' ever greater outlays on youth-oriented sports and entertainment events and recreational merchandise. "Our children face a health crisis that is getting worse," said the President, citing surveys that found one in five high school seniors to be a daily smoker and a sharp uptrend in the lower grades as well. "We need to act ... before another generation of Americans is condemned to fight a difficult and grueling personal battle with an addiction that will cost millions of them their lives."

In framing the proposed regulations on the marketing—but not the ingredients—of cigarettes, FDA lawyers sent the White House an 800-page rationale for the agency's claim of jurisdiction, reversing its position of 1980, the last time it evaluated its authority to take the politically embroiling step. Since the earlier reluctance relied on statutory history that defined as a drug only products and devices so intended by their sellers, the FDA's legal corps now asserted that "to require a showing of subjective intent—which would limit the relevant evidence to what is in the mind of the manufacturer or vendor as shown by express representation [*i.e.,* product labeling or advertising], promotional claims, or otherwise—would frustrate [the] legislative policy goals" of the 1938 Food, Drug, and Cosmetics Act and the 1960 Federal Hazardous Substances Act. Citing agency regulations first promulgated in 1952, in which the concept of "objective intent" was introduced (and thereby suggesting that the grounds for staking out jurisdiction had been available that long if only the agency had chosen to claim them), FDA lawyers argued that in deciding what was or was not a drug, the agency was free to draw upon "the totality of the relevant evidence showing the seller's awareness of how its product is actually used and affects the structure or function of the body, *regardless of how the product is labeled or advertised* . . . [italics added]." As precedents for regulating tobacco products, the agency now pointed to other actions it had taken in the past dozen years, including juridiction over vaginal products for over-the-counter use, and said, "If an active ingredient is present in a therapeutic concentration, the product is a drug, even if that product does not claim to produce the effect which will result from the action of the . . . ingredient." Fluorides and hormones were other examples of such "active ingredients". Since 1980, the Surgeon General "and virtually every major public health organization have concluded that nicotine in tobacco products leads to addiction," the FDA said. Its own intensive investigation, ordered by Commissioner Kessler, had further revealed "a wealth of evidence consisting of industry statements, research and actions acknowledging nicotine's drug effects" and resulted in overwhelming findings that "consumers use the products predominantly . . . for its significant pharmacological" and other psychoactive effects "such as relaxation and stimulation [and] weight regulation."

The proposed FDA measures were far more sweeping than tobacco-control advocates could have hoped for, given the hostile political climate in which they were announced. Included were a federal ban on cigarette sales to anyone under eighteen, preempting the diverse state bans, and requirement of photo identification as proof of age; the abolition of cigarette sales by vending machines and mail order; prohibition of cigarette billboards within 1,000 feet of schools and limitation of ads in print media with more than 2 million readers or more than 15 percent of their readership among those under eighteen to a black-and-white, text-only format; and, perhaps most frightening of all to the industry, a halt to brand-name sponsorship of sports and entertainment events and the sale or giveaway to youngsters of promotional merchandise bearing brand names or logos.

In anticipation of the FDA move, Philip Morris led the industry with a big increase in its political contributions to congressmen during the first half of 1995 and renewed its intermittent avowals of uninterest in the teenage market by now placing a label on all its cigarette packs stating they were not to be sold to underage customers. A new PM ad campaign, intending to show that FDA action was unnecessary, again declared that youngsters should not begin smoking until they were old enough to make a reasoned decision about its claimed risks.

It was less the likely impact of the proposed FDA regimen on U.S. cigarette sales, about 3 percent of which were derived from underage smokers, that greatly alarmed the tobacco companies than the principle being laid down by the agency—namely, that it had the power to regulate the manufacture and sale of cigarettes, even if it had not chosen to exercise it earlier, and, once established, that power could warrant severe restrictions in the future, such as maximum allowable tar and nicotine yields. Not surprisingly, the industry filed suit at once in a North Carolina federal district court to challenge the lawfulness of the FDA initiative and thereby threatened to delay indefinitely the implementation of the new regulations. As this book went to press, it was uncertain whether the antiregulatory Congress would move to strike down the FDA action, almost certainly inviting a presidential veto; agree to a modified version of the regulatory package; or leave the issue to the courts to decide. In the end, though, greater federal government oversight of cigarettes—an addicting product that could almost certainly never be either banned outright or certified as safe for human consumption—appeared inevitable.

VIII

IF the national political tide had shifted enough to give the cigarette manufacturers strong hope of at least temporary surcease from the proddings of the smoking control movement, they nevertheless remained under the long shadow of litigation, that chronic potential spoiler of their financial well-being. And the mid-'Nineties wave of suits, brought by resourceful attorneys representing vast claimant pools and even whole states, was likely to stretch into the twenty-first century. The Department of Justice, too, was finally bestirring itself through investigations, fueled by pilfered internal industry documents, into the possibly fraudulent habitual behavior by the cigarette companies in denying and suppressing their knowledge of the effects of smoking.

The tobacco industry was primed to meet these ever larger challenges as a cost of doing business, and it did not lack for plausible, even persuasive, defenses. The "mega-suit," for example, *Castano v. American Tobacco*, the claim behind which one of the plaintiff lawyers paraphrased as, "You addicted me, and you knew it was addicting, and now you say it's my fault," differed primarily in emphasis from the claim in Rose Cipollone's case, which the jury did not buy. While new evidence had emerged in the interim showing that Philip Morris and B&W, among others, had done research on the addictive nature of nicotine and had neither disclosed it to the public nor warned against the addicting potency, many similar findings by investigators outside the industry had long since been made and published. Public-health advocates, moreover, had for years advised that nicotine was as addicting as heroin and cocaine, yet the Surgeon General had not declared smoking to be addicting until 1988. The point was that whether one categorized smoking as a practice, a habit, an indulgence, a vice, a dependency, or an addiction, it was commonly known—and had been for decades—to be hard to stop once begun. Nor could anyone say for certain how much of a daily dose served to induce addiction; tolerances differed from person to person, and the industry had in fact made available brands with extremely low dosages. How, then, to justify a claim that the cigarette makers had massively imposed an intentionally addicting product on an innocent public that had little knowledge or choice in the matter?

Equally defensible were the suits for reimbursement of medical expenses filed by the states of Mississippi, Minnesota, and West Virginia and being contemplated by Florida, which in effect demanded that, for smoking-caused illnesses, the cigarette manufacturers assume the states' role as health insurers of their citizens. Was this any more reasonable than demanding that automakers and oil companies reimburse the states for their highway maintenance and driving-caused injury costs? Although the state suits said their claims were not based on injuries suffered by individual smokers, tobacco industry lawyers could point to precedent holdings that third-party payers had no greater claims than those receiving the health care, so that the state cases arguably amounted to personal injury claims in disguise, of the sort preempted by the federal cigarette labeling laws and upheld by the Supreme Court in *Cipollone*. There was growing evidence, as well, that the states might not be net losers due to smokers' call on public health-care funds in view of their shorter life spans (and thus reduced use of public services generally) and what they paid in the form of cigarette taxes. As for the class action by flight attendants and similar suits contemplated over diseases said to be linked to environmental tobacco smoke, industry lawyers could argue that (1) ETS had not been officially declared lethal or a serious threat to healthy people until the EPA's 1993 risk assessment was issued; (2) the EPA conclusions were based on data that some disinterested observers believed to be at best a marginal indictment of ETS as an authentic peril to health (though it was surely an annoyance); and (3) if ETS was found to be a health threat to flight personnel, why were cigarette makers liable rather than the owners of the airlines who controlled the working conditions within their planes?

But, for all the legal brainpower their money could hire, the tobacco manufacturers had to face the likelihood, perhaps the certainty, that someday some jury—and sooner probably than later—would reach a verdict against the industry that would, upon final appeal, be sustained. And then the cigarette makers, who, as the evidence presented in this book strongly suggests, well understood the health charges against them and had by utterance and action tried for forty years to blind the public to the severity of the risks of smoking, could well be dealt with unkindly—and in a grievously costly fashion. Other massive blows might follow, ending the industry's flow of riches.

Would it not, then, make more sense for the tobacco industry, rather than fighting to the bitter end, to abandon its lush but precarious existence beside the ever-rumbling volcano and make peace with the American public, the majority of whom scorns smoking, little pities those enslaved to it, and views with contempt the companies living off it? Would it not greatly benefit both the public health and an industry under constant dread of disaster from litigants and regulators to reach an accommodation? Such an arrangement, sure to be denounced by the more zealous wing of the antismoking movement as a gift to Mammon and resisted by industry diehards incapable of conceding their past culpability, might relieve the severest effects of a deadly product that, practically speaking, cannot be outlawed.

The linchpin of such an agreement—indeed, the only inducement that might bring the industry to the bargaining table—would be a blanket (and retroactive) exemption by Congress from all personal injury claims by smokers against the cigarette manufacturers (except those suits involving contaminated ingredients). In return for this immense grant of relief, the tobacco industry could be asked to agree to the following measures:

1. The twenty-four-cent federal excise tax on cigarettes would go to fifty cents and thereafter become an ad valorem tax not to exceed 50 percent of the wholesale price. Based on 1995 data, such a tax would yield between $12 and

$14 billion, about twice the present U.S. cigarette tax revenue, to be used to pay for all the costs incurred by the subsequent provisions of this agreement; any surplus would go to defray the cost of the Medicare program.

2. FDA would have oversight of the manufacturing and marketing of cigarettes, including the power to set maximum tar and nicotine yields, to be reduced over a ten-year span to 5.0 and 0.5 milligrams, respectively. This level would cut but not eliminate the addictive properties of nicotine and the "kick" smokers derive from the habit, nor could it prevent compensatory smoking behavior, the nature and risk of which would be spelled out on inserts in every cigarette package. While such a ceiling on toxic yields might invite the creation of a black market for stronger cigarettes, these would be officially classified as illicit drugs, and efforts to police their sale would be preferable to not trying to reduce dangerously high dosages. The FDA would monitor dosage levels in its laboratories.

3. Every cigarette package would carry that brand's tar and nicotine yield and a list of other ingredients the FDA believed perilous to smokers' health, even if found only in trace amounts. Warning labels would also state that smoking was addicting for many people, that smokers live on the average approximately eight fewer years than nonsmokers, and that carbon monoxide— now indicated in one of the four rotating warning labels as merely an ingredient in smoke—is a poison linked to heart disease.

4. Cigarette advertisements would be restricted to the "tombstone" format, in black and white only, with no illustrations permitted other than a small picture of the pack. Nor could cigarette brand names be used in promotions, including logos on merchandise or as the sponsor of cultural exhibitions, artistic performances, or sports events. Advertising and promotional outlays by tobacco companies would no longer be tax deductible—a measure aimed at both discouraging the propagation of smoking and reducing the high profitability of the tobacco business.

5. Free sampling of cigarettes and their sale in vending machines would be forbidden. Sale of cigarettes would be allowed only in state-licensed stores, and those selling to buyers under the age of eighteen would face painful fines and, for repeated violation, loss of their sales licenses.

6. The federal support program for the tobacco crop, an enticement to hazardous public-health practices, would be discontinued. Tobacco growers would be eligible for up to three years for federal grants to compensate for the resulting shortfall in their incomes, based on the average crop prices they had received over the preceding five years. The money to ease the burden on farmers during this transition period would come from the increased federal cigarette excise tax (see #1 above).

7. The Office on Smoking and Health would function as a separate entity within the U.S. Public Health Service to educate the public on the perils of

smoking through school and other community programs and paid advertisements using both print and broadcast media. OSH might also operate quit clinics for smokers using hospitals or other health facilities. Further reports by the
U.S. Surgeon General on the health consequences of smoking would cease;
they have performed their function well.

8. Smoking in all locations where the public congregates, indoors and outdoors, would be restricted to confined and properly ventilated areas.

The tobacco industry could surely survive this regimen, undoubtedly better
than some of its customers. The legislative package could be designed and
wrapped with a bow by a Republican-controlled Congress, more likely to be
sensitive to the companies' concerns and generous about the provisions. But
if a Republican majority proved unwilling to broker such a negotiation or impose it on an obstinate industry, then surely a future, probably Democratic-
controlled Congress in league with a resolute President could do so. Such a
rational and civilized remedy, though, is probably too much to hope for as
slayer of an incubus that has defied all reason, thrived on greed and folly, and
driven poor mortals to grasp onto it for succor in a fashion their Maker never
designed their bodies to long endure.

A Note on Sources and
Acknowledgments

This narrative has been drawn from sources too numerous and disparate to account for in every instance, given the fact that the subject is a common social habit and ubiquitous item of commerce indulged in by hundreds of millions of people. The chief primary sources utilized were some 500 studies by scientific investigators examining the properties of tobacco and the health consequences of smoking and interviews with nearly 300 individuals who have been closely connected with advancing or thwarting the activities of the American cigarette industry. The main secondary sources were readings in the sprawling body of literature on the subject, including several hundred books and several thousand articles in the daily and periodical press. What was most notable about these secondary sources was how few manifested a disinterested and critical assessment of the evidence related to the health aspects of smoking. Much of the literature, furthermore, took the form of either industry boosterism by paid apologists and those too passionately devoted to smoking to bear hearing it ill spoken of, or of sharp assaults on the custom as an inexcusable scourge, with scant acknowledgment of, or interest in, its perceived pleasures and benefits— and none at all regarding the quandary in which the tobacco industry found itself, partly of its own doing, as the medical case against smoking grew ever more persuasive.

The author's most difficult task, accordingly, was to try to suspend moral judgment as long as possible in sifting through this immense and untidy collection of materials in order to craft a coherent social narrative about an industry that was, after all, a thriving enterprise well before a conclusive scientific consensus on the hazards of its products was achieved. My intent throughout has been to bring an unpremeditated approach to a subject that has historically generated a good deal more heat than light.

Of particular value to the book was the access kindly and cannily granted the author by the Philip Morris Companies, Inc., whose growth from the smallest of the six chief competitors in the U.S. cigarette business to its present dominance as the world's leading private-enterprise purveyor forms a prominent strand of this history. The company allowed me to interview sixty of its past and present executives, some on more than one occasion, with the understanding that the book would fairly convey their views on the health question without necessarily embracing all or any of them. Most of the interviews were conducted with house legal counsel present; a list of questions for each session was submitted in advance, but the exchanges themselves were not limited to those topics about which prior notice had been given. House counsel, during hundreds of hours of discussion, intervened on only two occasions, claiming that the topic raised was pending before the courts or Congress. Not surprisingly, other interviews with former Philip Morris officials arranged beyond the company's purview were more productive. In large part my purpose was to try to understand better how the company prospered, especially as the news from the scientific community grew worse and worse. That irony is one of the central themes of this work.

To have freighted the text with sourcing for all of its assertions would have required a companion volume perhaps equally forbidding in size. Instead, attribution of some of the main sources is given within the narrative itself, along with the place and date of publication of some of the most important scientific findings; a limited number of other sources, including books not listed in the Selected Bibliography, are cited in the Chapter Notes. Quoted comments, unless otherwise indicated, are drawn mostly from the author's interviews, as suggested by the attributive verbs "recalled," "recounted," "remembered," and the like.

The authority relied on in chronicling the comparative sales performances of the cigarette companies is John C. Maxwell, Jr., the veteran financial analyst and unofficial tollkeeper for the tobacco industry, a member of the Richmond-based brokerage and investment firm of Wheat, First Securities, Inc., who generously allowed me use of his data without revealing exactly how he had come by it—apparently a combination of tax revenue stamp reports, company-provided figures, and wholesaler corroboration. Maxwell's numbers have generally held up as the most reliable gauge of the industry's shipments, if not net sales figures. I was also courteously provided with many of the Tobacco Institute's publications, quoted herein. The Federal Trade Commission's annual reports to Congress, as mandated by the 1965 cigarette labeling law, on the advertising and promotional expenditures and practices of the tobacco industry are the best source for this information, though they necessarily rely on the hard-to-verify claims of the companies themselves. The readiest source of information on the activities of antismoking lawmakers and litigants is the *Tobacco Products Litigation Reporter*, published since December 1985 with personnel based at Northeastern Law School; its contents, though, are often excerpts rather than complete texts and sometimes skewed by an avowed anti-industry perspective.

Some of the most noteworthy material in the book is derived from documents produced in the course of the discovery process for *Cipollone v. Liggett et al.*, which came to trial during the early stages of my research. In many cases the documents are cited by plaintiff's exhibit number in the Chapter Notes.

My interview notes and other research materials are to be on permanent file in the Manuscripts and Archives Section of Sterling Memorial Library, Yale University.

*   *   *

Many people lent me assistance in this undertaking, which consumed six and a half years, in part due to a rash of unfolding events on the legal, political, and financial fronts, all affecting the status of the cigarette. My principal aide and sorely tried sounding board throughout this wearing process was Phyllis Kluger, who gathered and initially evaluated most of the scientific documents consulted. Susan S. Angell prepared skillful memoranda on the political and legal aspects of the book. Michael Pertschuk of the Advocacy Institute and Donald Shopland of the National Cancer Institute were founts of wisdom on the modern history of the tobacco control movement. John C. Maxwell, Jr., of Wheat, First Securities (see above) kindly provided me with industry marketing data, and Joe Tye of Stop Teenage Addiction to Tobacco shared materials on the marketing and advertising practices of the industry. Attorney Marc Edell, chief plaintiff's counsel in *Cipollone*, and his associate Cynthia Walters and legal aide Nelson S. T. Thayer, Jr., were generous with time, insights, and materials. Alexander Holtzman, associate counsel of Philip Morris, and his assistant, Anne Doherty, were unfailingly courteous in response to many inquiries. Elizabeth Whelan of the American Council on Science and Health allowed me early access to her own research files. Anne Mintz, *Forbes* librarian, and Linda Smith of the Lexington, Kentucky, *Herald-Leader* helped me obtain highly useful clippings. Joan Garb of Buckingham, Pennsylvania, undertook often tiresome readings on the historical background of the subject. My old friend James C. Freund offered insights on some of the late-breaking corporate takeover maneuvers within the tobacco industry. Lisa Bero and Dr.

John Slade provided instructive and valuable scientific scrutiny. Others who helped in various ways were Clifford Douglas, Mark Pertschuk, Janet Holt, Morton and Anita Mintz, Carole Nebiolo, Andrew Mytelka, Daniel Kornstein, Jolie Goodman Khalsa, Fraser Lewis, Molly Ivins, Victor Navasky, and the late John Bogart. Without their invaluable collective help, my want of expertise would have made the project unthinkable. Finally, I am grateful for the editorial acumen applied to this book by Jonathan B. Segal of Alfred A. Knopf, Inc.

R. K.
Skillman, New Jersey

Selected Bibliography

American Medical Association/Education and Research Foundation. *Tobacco and Health.* AMA/ERF, 1978.

Badger, Anthony J. *Prosperity Road: The New Deal, Tobacco, and North Carolina.* University of North Carolina Press, 1980.

Borgatta, Edgar F., and Robert R. Evans, eds. *Smoking, Health and Behavior.* Aldine, 1968.

Brecher, Ruth and Edward, *et al. The Consumers Union Report on Smoking and the Public Interest.* Consumers Union, 1963.

Burrough, Bryan, and John Helyar. *Barbarians at the Gate: The Fall of RJR Nabisco.* Harper & Row, 1990.

Calfee, John E. *Cigarette Advertising, Health Information and Regulation Before 1970.* Bureau of Economics, Federal Trade Commission, 1985.

Califano, Joseph A., Jr. *Governing America: An Insider's Report from the White House and the Cabinet.* Simon & Schuster, 1981.

Coles, L. B. *The Beauties and Deformities of Tobacco-Using.* Ticknor, Reed & Fields, 1853.

Corina, Maurice. *Trust in Tobacco: The Anglo-American Struggle for Power.* London: Michael Joseph, 1975.

Corti, Count. *A History of Smoking.* London: George A. Harrap, 1931.

Cox, Edward, *et al.*, eds. *The Nader Report on the Federal Trade Commission.* Richard W. Baron, 1969.

Diehl, Harold S. *Tobacco and Your Health: The Smoking Controversy.* McGraw-Hill, 1969.

Doron, Gideon. *The Smoking Paradox: Public Regulation in the Cigarette Industry.* Abt Books, 1979.

Dunn, William L., Jr., ed. *Smoking Behavior: Motives and Incentives.* V. H. Winston, 1973.

Eysenck, H. J. *Smoking, Health and Personality.* London: Weidenfeld & Nicholson, 1965.

———. *Smoking, Personality and Stress: Psychosocial Factors in the Prevention of Cancer and Cardiovascular Disease.* New York: Springer-Verlag, 1991.

Farnum, Henry W. *Our Tobacco Bill: A Tentative Social Balance Sheet.* Unpopular Review, 1914.

Festinger, Leon. *A Theory of Cognitive Dissonance.* Stanford University Press, 1957.

Finger, William R., ed. *The Tobacco Industry in Transition: Policies for the 1980s.* D.C. Heath/Lexington Books, 1981.

Fink, Bruce. *Tobacco.* Abingdon, 1915.

Fisher, Ronald A. *Smoking: The Cancer Controversy.* London: Oliver & Boyd, 1959.

Ford, Henry. *The Case Against the Little White Slaver.* Privately published, 1916.

Fritschler, A. Lee. *Smoking and Politics: Policymaking in the Federal Bureaucracy.* Prentice-Hall, 1969.

Gahagan, Dolly D. *Smoke Down and Quit: What the Cigarette Companies Don't Want You to Know About Smoking.* Ten Speed Press, 1987.

Gerstein, Dean R., and Peter K. Levison, eds. *Reduced Tar and Nicotine Cigarettes: Smoking Behavior and Health.* National Academy Press, 1985.

Goldstein, Tom. *A Two-Faced Press?* Twentieth Century Fund, 1986.

Gori, Gio B., and Fred G. Bock, eds. *The Banbury Report: A Safe Cigarette?* Cold Spring Harbor Laboratory, 1980.

Harvard Institute for the Study of Smoking Behavior and Policy. *Policy Implications of the 1986 Surgeon General's Report on Involuntary Smoking.* Harvard University Press, 1987.

———. *The Cigarette Excise Tax.* Harvard University Press, 1985.

Heimann, Robert K. *Tobacco and Americans.* McGraw-Hill, 1960.

Henningfield, Jack E. *Nicotine: An Old-Fashioned Addiction.* Chelsea House, 1985.

Infante, G. Cabrera. *Holy Smoke.* Harper & Row, 1985.

International Agency for Research on Cancer. *Tobacco Smoking,* vol. 38 of *IARC Monographs on the Evaluation of the Carcinogenic Risk of Chemicals to Humans.* World Health Organization, 1986.

Jacobson, Bobbie. *The Ladykillers: Why Smoking Is a Feminist Issue.* London: Pluto Press, 1981.

James I, King. *A Counter-Blaste to Tobacco.* Rodale Press, 1954 reprint of original 1604 treatise.

James, George, and Theodore Rosenthal, eds. *Tobacco and Health.* Charles C. Thomas, 1962.

Jenkins, John A. *The Litigators.* Doubleday, 1989.

Johnson, Paul R. *The Economics of the Tobacco Industry.* Praeger, 1984.

Kenyon, Otto Allen. *Theory and Facts of Cigarette Smoking.* Axton-Fisher Company, 1934.

Kohlmeier, Louis M. *The Regulators: Watchdog Agencies and the Public Interest.* Harper & Row, 1969.

Koop, C. Everett. *Koop: The Memoirs of America's Family Doctor.* Random House, 1991.

Krogh, David. *Smoking: The Artificial Passion.* W. H. Freeman, 1991.

Larson, Paul S., and H. Silvette. *Tobacco: Experimental and Clinical Studies: A Comprehensive Account of the World Literature*, Supplement I. Williams and Wilkins, 1968.

Lewine, Harris. *Goodbye to All That.* McGraw-Hill, 1970.

McKeown, Thomas. *The Role of Medicine: Dream, Mirage, or Nemesis?* Princeton University Press, 1979.

Magnuson, Warren G., and Jean Carper. *The Dark Side of the Marketplace.* Prentice-Hall, 1968.

Meyer, John A. *Lung Cancer Chronicles.* Rutgers University Press, 1990.

Meyers, William. *The Image-Makers: Power and Persuasion on Madison Avenue.* Times Books, 1984.

Miles, Robert H. *Coffin Nails and Corporate Strategies.* Prentice-Hall, 1982.

Mokhiber, Russell. *Corporate Crime and Violence: Big Business Power and the Abuse of the Public Trust.* Sierra Club, 1988.

Mullen, Charles. *Cigarette Pack Art.* London: Gallery Press, 1979.

Myers, Matthew L., et al., eds. *Staff Report on the Cigarette Advertising Investigation.* Federal Trade Commission, 1981.

Nath, Uma Ram. *Smoking: Third World Alert.* Oxford University Press, 1986.

National Cancer Institute. *Review and Evaluation of Smoking Cessation Methods: The U.S. and Canada, 1978–1985.* U.S. Public Health Service, 1987.

National Research Council. *Environmental Tobacco Smoke: Measuring Exposures and Assessing Health Effects.* National Academy Press, 1986.

Neuberger, Maurine B. *Smoke Screen: Tobacco and the Public Welfare.* Prentice-Hall, 1963.

Northrup, Eric. *Science Looks at Smoking: A New Inquiry into the Effects of Smoking on Your Health.* Coward-McCann, 1957.

Ockene, J. K., ed. *The Pharmacologic Treatment of Tobacco Dependence: Proceedings of the World Congress, November 4–5, 1985.* Harvard Institute for the Study of Smoking Behavior and Policy. Harvard University Press, 1986.

Office of Technology Assessment. *Passive Smoking in the Workplace.* U.S. Congress, 1986.

Olshansky, Richard W. *No More Butts: A Psychologist's Approach to Quitting Cigarettes.* Indiana University Press, 1977.

Pack, Frederick J. *Tobacco and Human Efficiency.* Deseret News, 1918.

Pertschuk, Michael. *Giant Killers.* Norton, 1987.

Posner, Richard A. *Regulation of Advertising by the FTC.* American Enterprise Institute, 1973.

Reynolds, Patrick, and Tom Shachtman. *The Gilded Leaf: Triumph, Tragedy and Tobacco.* Little, Brown, 1989.

Robert, Joseph C. *The Story of Tobacco in America.* Knopf, 1949.

———. *The Tobacco Kingdom: Plantation, Market and Factory in Virginia and North Carolina.* Duke University Press, 1938.

Royal College of Physicians. *Smoking and Health.* American Cancer Society, 1962.

Sims, Albert E., ed. *The Witching Weed.* Crowell, n.d.

Sobel, Robert. *They Satisfy: The Cigarette in American Life.* Anchor/Doubleday, 1978.

Strasser, Susan. *Satisfaction Guaranteed: The Making of the American Mass Market.* Pantheon, 1989.

Taylor, Peter. *The Smoke Ring: Tobacco, Money and International Politics.* Pantheon, 1984.

Tennant, Richard B. *The American Cigarette Industry: A Study in Economic Analysis and Public Policy.* Yale University Press, 1950.

Tilley, Nannie M. *The Bright Tobacco Industry, 1860–1929.* University of North Carolina Press, 1948.

———. *The R. J. Reynolds Tobacco Company.* University of North Carolina Press, 1948.

Tollison, Robert D., ed. *Clearing the Air: Perspectives on Environmental Tobacco Smoke.* D. C. Heath/Lexington Books, 1988.

———, ed. *Smoking and Society: Toward a More Balanced Assessment.* D. C. Heath/Lexington Books, 1986.

———, and Richard E. Wagner. *Smoking and the State: Social Costs, Rent Seeking, and Public Policy.* D. C. Heath/Lexington Books, 1988.

Troyer, Ronald J., and Gerald E. Markle. *Cigarettes: The Battle over Smoking.* Rutgers University Press, 1983.

U.S. Surgeon General. *Smoking and Health: Report of the Advisory Committee to the Surgeon General.* U.S. Public Health Service, 1964.

———. *The Health Consequences of Smoking.* U.S. PHS, 1971.

———. *The Health Consequences of Smoking.* U.S. PHS, 1972.

———. *Smoking and Health.* U.S. PHS, 1979.

———. *The Health Consequences of Smoking for Women.* U.S. PHS, 1980.

———. *The Health Consequences of Smoking: The Changing Cigarette.* U.S. PHS, 1981.

———. *The Health Consequences of Smoking: Cancer.* U.S. PHS, 1982.

———. *The Health Consequences of Smoking: Cardiovascular Diseases.* U.S. PHS, 1983.

———. *The Health Consequences of Smoking: Chronic Obstructive Lung Disease.* U.S. PHS, 1984.

———. *The Health Consequences of Smoking: Occupational Exposures.* U.S. PHS, 1985.

———. *The Health Consequences of Smoking: Involuntary Smoking.* U.S. PHS, 1986.

———. *The Health Consequences of Using Smokeless Tobacco.* U.S. PHS, 1986.

———. *The Health Consequences of Smoking: Nicotine Addiction.* U.S. PHS, 1988.

———. *Reducing the Health Consequences of Smoking: Twenty-five Years of Progress.* U.S. PHS, 1989.

———. *The Health Benefits of Smoking Cessation.* U.S. PHS, 1990.

Wagner, Susan. *Tobacco Country.* Praeger, 1971.

Warner, Kenneth E. *Selling Smoke: Cigarette Advertising and Public Health.* American Public Health Association, 1986.

Whelan, Elizabeth M. *A Smoking Gun: How the Tobacco Industry Gets Away with Murder.* Stickley, 1984.

White, Larry C. *Merchants of Death: The Tobacco Industry in America.* Peach Tree/Morrow, 1988.

Whiteside, Thomas. *Selling Death: Cigarette Advertising and Public Health.* Liveright, 1971.

Winkler, Joseph K. *Tobacco Tycoon: The Story of James Buchanan Duke.* Random House, 1942.

Winter, Ruth. *The Scientific Case Against Smoking.* Crown, 1980.

Wood, Frank Z. *What You Should Know About Tobacco.* Zondervan, 1944.

Woofter, T. J., Jr. *The Plight of Cigarette Tobacco.* University of North Carolina Press, 1931.

Wynder, Ernst L., and Dietrich Hoffmann. *Tobacco and Tobacco Smoke: Studies in Experimental Carcinogenesis.* Academic Press, 1967.

Zagona, Salvatore V., ed. *Studies and Issues in Smoking Behavior.* University of Arizona Press, 1966.

Notes

Foreword : A Quick Drag

John Hollander's evocative article "Notes of a Redeemed Smoker" appeared in *Harper's* of April 1969. The Samuel Johnson quotation is cited by Tennant in his *The American Cigarette Industry*, by far the best account of the subject in the era before medical science began to report steadily on the health perils of the product.

Chapter 1 : Adoring the Devil's Breath

I Most of the pre-twentieth-century histories of tobacco are anecdotal and sketchy, and none dwells on the health problem in a reliable fashion. For general historical background on the earlier American aspects, the best works are Robert's *The History of Tobacco in America* and Tilley's *The Bright Tobacco Industry*. The subsequent literature on smoking and health is voluminous; for an overview of the evolving consensus, one might consult *The Consumers Union Report on Smoking and the Public Interest*, Diehl's *Tobacco and Your Health*, Krogh's *Smoking: The Artificial Passion*, and especially the 1989 Surgeon General's Report, *Reducing the Health Consequences of Smoking: Twenty-five Years of Progress*.

II The Columbus quotation is from *Learning Mechanisms and Smoking*, edited by William A. Hunt (Aldine, 1970), p. 156. The graceful introductory essay by Jerome Brooks to the Arents Collection at the New York Public Library is useful for understanding the important role of tobacco in England and her American colonies as well as the early natural history of the crop.

III   For an example of the exchanges in the *Lancet*, the first substantive published scientific exploration of the health question—though narrow in scope because the cigarette was not yet in common usage—see the March 14, 1857, issue.

IV   For a colorful and graphic rendering of the early manufacturing history of the cigarette, see *Smoke Signals: Cigarettes, Advertising, and the American Way of Life* by Jane Webb Smith, produced for an exhibition at the Valentine Museum in Richmond in 1990 (and distributed through the University of North Carolina Press).

V   Winkler's *Tobacco Tycoon: The Story of James Buchanan Duke* is the standard biography and not entirely idolatrous. See also *James Buchanan Duke: Master Builder* by John Gilbert Jenkins (Doran, 1927); *James Buchanan Duke, 1856–1925* by Watson Smith Rankin (Newcomen Society, 1952); and *"Sold American!"*, a company-written history of the first fifty years of American Tobacco. For a more objective view, see *Fortune*'s December 1936 issue and Corina's *Trust in Tobacco*. A *New York Times* (*NYT*) editorial nicely stated the prevailing view on the pernicious effect of cigarettes on January 29, 1884; a contrasting view from its pages five years later is cited by Jerome Brooks in *The Philip Morris Century* on p. 59 of the first volume (1956); the work, commissioned by the company, is unpublished but is included in my papers.

VI   The prime source on RJR is Tilley's turgid but essential *The R. J. Reynolds Tobacco Company*, done largely under company scrutiny; it breaks off in 1964, just when the competition with PM was warming up. For human interest on Richard Joshua Reynolds, see also *The Gilded Leaf*, co-authored by his grandson Patrick; and *Barbarians at the Gate* by Burrough and Helyar, more a Wall Street than a tobacco saga.

Chapter 2 : The Earth with a Fence Around It

I   Principal documents on the growth and conduct of the tobacco trust are the *Report of the Commissioner of Corporations on the Tobacco Industry* issued on February 25, 1909, by the Department of Commerce and Labor; and the May 29, 1911, opinion of the U.S. Supreme Court in *U.S. v. American Tobacco* (221 U.S. 105).

II   Among the early twentieth-century periodical literature on the medical and moral objections to cigarettes, see especially "The Cigarette Habit: A New Peril" in the February 18, 1904, number of *The Independent*; the May 26, 1906, *Harper's Weekly*; the August 1912 *Harper's*; and "Smoking" in the April 1916 *Atlantic Monthly*.

IV   Corina's *Trust in Tobacco* is the leading account of Duke's incursion into Britain and the resulting birth of BAT.

VI   Among the voluminous literature on the subject, see *The Federal Antitrust Policy* (1954) by Hans Torelli and *The Legislative History of the Federal Antitrust Laws and Related Statutes* (1978) by Earl Kintner.

Chapter 3 : It Takes the Hair Right Off Your Bean

I   See chapter 4 of Tilley's history of Reynolds Tobacco for the most detailed account of the birth of Camel.

II   Among the sources used on George Washington Hill were chapter 28 of *Biography of an Idea: Memoirs of Public Relations Counsel Edward L. Bernays* (1963); "Cigarettes and Candy" in the February 13, 1929, *New Republic*; "Good Taste in Advertising" in the

March 1930 *Fortune*; "George Washington Hill: He Makes America Sit Up and Buy" in the January 1, 1933, *Forbes*; "The American Tobacco Co." in the December 1936 *Fortune*; and "How Hill Advertises Is at Last Revealed" in *Printer's Ink* for November 17, 1938. *"Sold American!"*, the company's own joyous account of its success during the first half of the twentieth century—when it dominated the cigarette business—describes the birth of Lucky Strike and has instructive graphics on advertising and packaging.

III Michael Schudson's insights are in the chapter "The Emergence of New Consumer Patterns: A Case Study of the Cigarette" from his book *Advertising: The Uneasy Persuasion* (Basic Books, 1984).

IV See "Is a Tobacco Crusade Coming?" by L. James Brown in the October 1920 *Atlantic Monthly*, "Should Tobacco Be Prohibited?" in the March 1921 *Current Opinion*, and "The Triumph of the Cigarette" by Carl Avery Werner in the December 1925 *American Mercury*.

VI For a highly critical but revealing tour through the annals of tobacco hucksterdom, see Joe Tye's *Sixty Years of Deception: An Analysis and Compilation of Cigarette Ads in Time Magazine, 1925–1985*, issued privately in photocopy form by the Health Advocacy Center in 1986. Tye's organization is now called STAT (Stop Teenage Addiction to Tobacco) and headquartered in Springfield, Massachusetts.

Chapter 4 : The Golden Age of Malarkey

I Tennant has the best account of the pricing wars in the early 1930s, pp. 294–357. See also "Camels of Winston-Salem" in the January 1931 *Fortune*, "One Out of Every Five Cigarettes" in the November 1932 *Fortune*, and "Cigarettes Hit New High" in the July 9, 1936, *Printer's Ink*. On the condition of tobacco farmers just before and during the early years of the Depression, Woofter's *The Plight of Cigarette Tobacco* is rich in appalling detail; Badger's *Prosperity Road* tells of the farmers' and the government's response in the tobacco heartland of North Carolina. For an overview of the New Deal and the AAA program of price supports and allotments, see Robert's *The Story of Tobacco in America*, pp. 202–18, and Johnson's *The Economics of the Tobacco Industry*, p. 26–45.

II Clay Williams and William Esty are featured in "$57,000,000 Worth of Whizz and Whoozle" in the August 1938 *Fortune*; no other source compares with this magazine in critical financial coverage until *Forbes* from the 1960s on.

III Sylvester (Pat) Weaver and, to a lesser extent, Emerson Foote provided valuable firsthand accounts of Hill's conduct. On the birth of the modern Pall Mall, see the November 11, 1939, *Business Week* (*BW*), and for AT's surge in this era, see the July 15, 1941, *Sales Management*. An essential source on the conduct of the tobacco industry in the 'Thirties is the proceedings in the twenty-eight-week antitrust trial, *U.S. v. American Tobacco*, heard in U.S. district court in Lexington, Kentucky, beginning on June 2, 1941. The most complete account is in the pages of the Lexington *Herald-Leader*. See also "Behind the Cigarette Verdict" in the November 8, 1941, *BW* and especially the 1946 U.S. Supreme Court decision in *American Tobacco v. U.S.* (328 U.S. 781).

IV AND V The most useful sources on the early years of Philip Morris as a U.S. company are the authorized but unpublished *The Philip Morris Century* by Jerome E. Brooks, written in five volumes, and covering the years through 1977 (the company kindly provided me with the largely uncritical text, except for volume IV, which I was told was lost), and the company profile in the March 1936 *Fortune*. Johnny Roventini, the original Philip Morris pageboy, was alive and well when I interviewed him in January 1989 in Joseph Cullman's office.

VII   Besides the sources cited in the text, a useful compendium of the research on tobacco and health is *Tobacco: Experimental and Clinical Studies: A Comprehensive Account of the World Literature*, edited by P. S. Larson and H. Silvette; the original edition was issued by Williams & Wilkins in 1961, and the first supplement in 1968, as the volume of studies increased markedly; they are known not quite affectionately by students in the field as "the green monster" and "the red monster," respectively. While succinctly enough stated, these monographs are treated in a way that fails to distinguish adequately the truly important findings from the morass of routine studies. The tobacco industry supported the composition and probably the publication of these reference works. Franz Hermann Müller's seminal study appeared in translation in the September 30, 1939, *Journal of the American Medical Association* (*JAMA*).

Chapter 5 : "Shall We Just Have a Cigarette on It?"

II   For an example of Hill's use of radio talent to sell his products, see the April 22, 1945, *NYT*.

III   On the famous Camel sign in Times Square, see the October 1990 issue of *Avenue*, a New York controlled-circulation magazine. A valuable study on the wholesaling and retailing aspects of the business is the unpublished 1951 doctoral dissertation in economics at Ohio State University—"The Marketing of Tobacco Products"—by W. Arthur Cullman, brother of PM's Joseph Cullman.

IV   On PM during the 'Forties, see especially *The Philip Morris Century*, pp. 260–370, and the October 1949 *Fortune*.

V   The texts of the FTC decisions discussed here are rich in detail about the extravagance—indeed, the mendacity—of the tobacco companies' advertising in the 1930s and 1940s. See *In re P. Lorillard*, 46 F.T.C. 735 (1950), 46 F.T.C. 853, and 186 F.2d 52 (4th Cir. 1950); *In re Reynolds Tobacco*, 46 F.T.C. 706 (1950) and 192 F.2d 535 (7th Cir. 1951); *In re American Tobacco*, 47 F.T.C. 1393 (1951); and *In re Philip Morris*, 49 F.T.C. 703 (1952) and 51 F.T.C. 857 (1955).

VI   The initial Doll-Hill report ran in the September 30, 1950, issue of the *British Medical Journal*.

VII   On the Cullman family, see *Four Generations: Memoirs of Frances Nathan Wolf* (privately published in 1939); "Benson & Hedges" in the May 1950 *Fortune*; *Mister Junior* by Lael Tucker Wertenbaker (Pageant, 1960); and the August 15, 1965, *Forbes*.

Chapter 6 : The Filter Tip and Other Placebos

I   On Clarence Little's career before joining the tobacco industry, see *Crusade: The Official History of the American Cancer Society* by Walter Ross (Arbor House, 1987), an inadequate treatment of its subject; a pamphlet by Little, "Cancer: A Study for Laymen," undated but probably done in the late 'Thirties, while he was managing director of the cancer society, in which he wrote that it was "difficult to see" how smoking could not cause "a certain amount of irritation"; the July 31, 1979, *NYT* on the fiftieth anniversary of Jackson

Memorial Laboratory; and *Current Biography* for December 1944. The most informative account of the creation of the Kent brand and its original asbestos-containing "Micronite" filter appears in the Winter 1987 number of the *Alicia Patterson Foundation Reporter* by Myron Levin, a Los Angeles *Times* science writer and probably the most knowledgeable U.S. journalist on smoking and health. See also the March 22, 1952, *BW* and the June 1952 *Consumer Reports* (*CR*). In September 1995 a California state court jury awarded an ex-smoker of Kent $2 million on his claim of suffering an asbestos-induced form of lung cancer.

II On Hammond and his landmark prospective study, see the June 1957 *Current Biography*; his obituary in the November 4, 1986, *NYT*; Lawrence Garfinkel's tribute in the January–February 1988 issue of *Ca* magazine (an ACS publication); and Hammond's article "The Effects of Smoking" in the July 1962 *Scientific American*, the best periodical summary on the subject prior to the pioneer 1964 report by the Surgeon General's advisory committee. Interviews with Charles Cameron, Clifton Read, and Irving Rimer of the ACS were especially helpful; Daniel Horn would not see me.

IV The February 1953 *CR* tested and compared yields of the first generation of filter-tip brands.

V On RJR's Whitaker and the creation of the Winston brand, see especially the November 17, 1952, *Time*; December 1957 *Fortune*; and the April 1, 1954, and June 15, 1961, *Forbes.*

VI Wynder's article on the experimental production of carcinoma on the shaved backs of mice with distilled cigarette smoke tars ran in the December 1953 issue of *Cancer Research.* Four decades of the industry's objections to the Wynder skin-painting study were well summarized in an April 29, 1993, letter to the author by PM's Helmut Wakeham.

VII The intramural documents relating to the creation of the Tobacco Industry Research Committee and its public-relations purposes were disclosed, along with many others cited subsequently in this book, in the course of the discovery process in *Cipollone v. Liggett et al.* The publication of the documents, the trial, and appeals of the verdict up to the U.S. Supreme Court occurred fortuitously in the course of the author's research, which was thereby greatly enriched; they also added several years to the time required to complete the project. On the TIRC, see plaintiff's exhibit 2700. On the March 1954 meeting of Liggett scientists and advisors, see *Cipollone* exhibit 453.

VIII The first report on the Doll-Hill study of doctors' mortality in relation to their smoking habits ran in the June 26, 1954, *British Medical Journal.*

IX AND X These sections and much of the subsequent treatment of Philip Morris were drawn from extensive interviews with company personnel, including most of the key figures in the marketing area. On the Cullmans' arrival at PM, see "Cullmanation" in the November 1, 1953, *Forbes*; and on Parker McComas, see "Mr. President" in the July 1, 1954, *Forbes.* On the creation of Marlboro, the single richest source is "The Road to Marlboro Country," the introductory essay by Scott Ellsworth, written in August 1987, to his tape-recorded interviews with many of the company and Burnett ad agency executives connected with the Marlboro campaign, under the auspices of the Smithsonian Institution's oral history project on famous advertising campaigns. On Leo Burnett, see "Reaching for the Stars" in the March 1954 *TV Age*; a strong nuts-and-bolts article on copywriting in the November 7, 1955, *Advertising Age*; and his obituary in the June 8, 1971, Chicago *Tribune.*

Chapter 7 : The Anguish of the Russian Count

I   *Reader's Digest*, the leading antismoking crusader among U.S. periodicals, focused its wrath on the largely cosmetic effects of the filter tips in articles by Lois Miller and James Monahan in its issues of July and August 1957. On the July 1956 DuPuis memo, see plaintiff's exhibit 600A in *Cipollone*.

II   Bowman Gray's dismissal of the importance of tar and nicotine levels is quoted on p. 153 of *The Consumers Union Report on Smoking and the Public Health*, a compact 1963 volume that lucidly summarizes the clash between marketing wizardry and health concerns within the tobacco industry on the eve of the first Surgeon General's report.

III   The studies by pathologist Oscar Auerbach represent the single most indicting body of laboratory research on the systemic ravages of cigarette smoke. Their publication began with "The Anatomic Approach to the Study of Smoking and Bronchogenic Carcinoma: A Preliminary Report on Forty-one Cases" in *Cancer*, vol. 9 (1956): pp. 76–83; then see the *New England Journal of Medicine* (*NEJM*), vol. 256 (1957): pp. 97–104; *NEJM*, vol. 267 (1962): pp. 111–25; *NEJM*, vol. 269 (1963): pp. 1045–54; and *NEJM*, vol. 273 (1965): pp. 775–79.

IV   Harold Dorn's large corroborative study is reported in detail in the July 1959 *Public Health Reports*, vol. 74, no. 7. See also the findings by Haenszel and Shimkin reported in the *Journal of the National Cancer Institute* (*JNCI*) in June 1956 and November 1958. The forty-four-month wrap-up of the first giant Hammond-Horn study for the ACS ran in *JAMA* for March 8 and 15, 1958.

V   Lilienfeld's study on the emotional characteristics of smokers ran in *JNCI*, vol. 22 (1959): pp. 259–82. For Horn's study on smoking among Portland high school students, see the November 1959 *American Journal of Public Health*, pp. 1497–1511. The text of the Ad Hoc Study Group report was carried in the June 7, 1957, *Science*. Surgeon General Burney's statement, the most forthright to that date by a federal official, appeared in the November 28, 1959, *JAMA*. For the proceedings of the September 1960 symposium at the New York State Academy of Preventive Medicine, see *Tobacco and Health*, edited by George James and Theodore Rosenthal.

VI   Clarence Little's April 1955 TIRC memo is among the *Cipollone* documents (plaintiff's exhibit 8762); typical of his statements arguing that more research was needed before any judgment could be reached on the smoking-health peril is the guest editorial he wrote for the March 1956 *Cancer Research*. Darkis's derogatory remark about the TIRC is on p. 112 of CU's *Report on Smoking and the Public Interest*. Hill & Knowlton's July 2, 1959, memo to Bowman Gray was plaintiff's exhibit 2702A in *Cipollone*. For a discussion of other instances, statements, and opinions dealing with the questionable purpose and legitimacy of the industry-funded research by the TIRC and its successor, CTR, see, for example, *infra* in this section; chapter 8, section VI; chapter 10, section VI; chapter 11, section II; chapter 14, section I on the AMA-ERF study funded by the tobacco industry, and section VIII; and chapter 16, section XI on the CTR's own study on smoke inhalation by mice.

IX   DuPuis's September 30, 1959, memo to the PM board was plaintiff's exhibit 320 in *Cipollone*.

Chapter 8 : Grand Inquisitors

III The Jerome Brooks quotation is taken from page 3 of *The Philip Morris Century, Second Continuation Through 1965.*

IV Most revealing of all the industry documents ventilated in *Cipollone* were Philip Morris research director Helmut Wakeham's memos to the company's top officers; in calling for development of a "medically acceptable" cigarette, they reveal a sophisticated understanding of the growing scientific evidence against smoking and the obligation of a socially concerned corporation to respond. See in particular Wakeham's memo of November 15, 1961 (No. 608 among *Cipollone* plaintiff's exhibits); the October 24, 1963, memo to CEO Cullman re "those areas where the cigarette industry might be most subject to criticism" (exhibit 323); and the November 21, 1963, memo entitled "Project 0100—Objectives for '64" (exhibit 610). These and other documents were made available to the public by the Tobacco Products Liability Project at Northeastern Law School, presided over by Richard Daynard. Cullman's comment that he believed cigarettes would be exonerated of the health charges against them appeared in the November 29, 1963, *NYT*. Whiteside's articles in *The New Yorker* were collected in his 1971 book, *Selling Death: Cigarette Advertising and Public Health.* Bowling's PM memo on Dr. Horsfall was plantiff's exhibit 430 in *Cipollone.*

V Kensler's tardy report on the ciliatoxic properties of smoke ran in the November 28, 1963, *NEJM.*

VI Brown & Williamson's concerns about the health risks of their cigarettes and explorations of a modified-yield product in the 1960s and 1970s were detailed in a series of articles by reporter Philip J. Hilts in the *NYT* of June 16–18, 1994, based on documents apparently stolen from company files by a former employee. These disclosures are not treated at length here because the efforts essentially paralleled those by other companies, which the *Times* virtually ignored when they were revealed during the *Cipollone* trial nearly six years earlier (and discussed elsewhere in these pages). In its July 19, 1995, issue, *JAMA* ran an extensive analysis of the B&W documents by Stanton Glantz and colleagues, who incorrectly state that the purloined papers "provide our first look at the inner working of the tobacco industry during the critical period in which the scientific case that smoking is addictive and kills smokers solidified." A number of documents that surfaced in *Cipollone* seven years earlier and are widely citied in these notes deserve that distinction, but the B&W documents are surely the largest cache of industry data thus far revealing that what its officials knew about their product diverged widely and perhaps fraudulently from what they were telling the public. The Heimann study on allegedly low mortality rates in the tobacco industry was discussed in the April 12, 1961, *NYT* and drawn in part from "Smoking Habits and Mortality Among Workers in Cigarette Factories" by H. B. Haag and H. R. Hanmer in *Industrial Medicine*, vol. 26 (1957), pp. 559–62. Cornfield *et al.* demolished the industry's defensive arguments in their January 1959 *JNCI* article, the most vigorous indictment of smoking to appear in any scholarly journal until then. Barney Walker's derogation of the previous American Tobacco management was in the January 19, 1964, *NYT*.

VII The excerpt from Bob Newhart's famous Sir Walter Raleigh monologue came from a tape provided by the comedian-actor's office and is hereby gratefully acknowledged; it was included in two recordings he made in 1963—*The Best of Newhart* and *The Button Down Mind on TV*. The files of the Surgeon General's Advisory Committee at the U.S.

Archives have been rather badly cannibalized. Useful materials were provided by Peter Hamill, whom I interviewed, as well as SGAC members Emanuel Farber, Charles LeMaistre, and Leonard Schuman.

VIII   For Joseph Berkson's objections to the methodology in the epidemiological studies on smoking and lung cancer, see *Proceedings of the Staff Meetings of the Mayo Clinic* for July 27, 1955 (vol. 30, no. 15); the *Journal of the American Statistical Association*, vol. 53 (1958): pp. 28-38; *The Mayo Clinic Proceedings* for April 15, 1959 (vol. 34, no. 8); and his letter in the April 14, 1962, *Lancet*.

Chapter 9 : Marlboro Mirage

I   Stanley Cohen's prescient comments on the difficulty of regulating the tobacco industry ran in the November 7, 1963, *Advertising Age*.

II   Issued on June 22, 1964, the FTC's proposed "Trade Regulation Rule for the Prevention of Unfair or Deceptive Advertising and Labeling of Cigarettes in Relation to the Health Hazards of Smoking and Accompanying Statement on Basis and Purpose of Rule" is a persuasive indictment of the industry's excesses in huckstering; that this bureaucratic initiative was substantially watered down by Congress in the 1965 Federal Cigarette Labeling and Advertising Act is a glaring example of legislative spinelessness in response to a clear warning by public-health officials. On this subject, see Fritschler's 1969 book, *Smoking and Politics*.

IV   Wakeham's February 18, 1964, memo was plaintiff's exhibit 324 in the *Cipollone* trial.

V   Fortas's remarks at the Justice Department meeting of June 12, 1964, are taken from an internal Lorillard memo by an attending company attorney, dated the following day. See also quotation from same source in the following section.

VI   On *Pritchard v. Liggett & Myers Tobacco Co.*, see 295 F.2d (3d Cir. 1961), *aff'd on rehearing*, 350 F.2d 479 (3d Cir. 1965), *cert. denied*, 382 U.S. 987 (1966), *modified*, 370 F.2d 95 (3d Cir. 1966), *cert. denied*, 386 U.S. 1009 (1967).

VII   The AMA's February 28, 1964, letter from Blassingame to the FTC opposing the labeling law was plaintiff's exhibit 1312 in *Cipollone*. The industry's efforts to avoid congressional regulation are illustrated by the transcript of hearings before the Committee on Interstate and Foreign Commerce of the House of Representatives, 88th Cong., 2d sess., June 23, 24, 25, 29, and July 2, 1964, and 89th Cong., 1st sess., March 22, 23, 24, 25, 29, and April 1, 2, and 6, 1965.

VIII   On the creation of "Marlboro Country" and how it departed from the previous "Marlboro Man" campaign, see the article by Robert Henderson in *The New Yorker* of June 28, 1958, and a simulated article in that same magazine's November 15, 1958, issue, "The Marlboro Story" by Leo Burnett (in fact a three-page advertisement); "The Higher Meaning of Marlboro Cigarettes" by Bruce Lohof in the *Journal of Popular Culture*, vol. III, no. 3 (Winter 1969): pp. 41-50; "In Search of the Marlboro Man," a series by Jim Carrier in the Denver *Post*, January 13–27, 1991; and especially Scott Ellsworth's archive on the Marlboro campaign, an oral history project under the auspices of the Smithsonian's Museum of History and Technology.

Chapter 10 : Three-Ton Dog on the Prowl

I Robert Wald's intramural memo was dated December 28, 1965, suggesting how rapidly Lorillard's disenchantment with Meyner set in.

II The best single source on the sorry performance of the Cigarette Advertising Code and the National Association of Broadcasters' dealing with the tobacco companies in the 1960s is Warren Braren's testimony before the House Commerce Committee on June 10, 1969; the published transcript includes the confidential September 1966 report by the New York office of the NAB Code Authority on broadcast cigarette advertising. On John Banzhaf: The chain of events began with his December 1, 1966, letter to WCBS-TV and his formal complaint of January 15, 1967; for the legal record, see *Banzhaf v. FCC*, 405 F.2d 1082 (D.C. Cir. 1968), and *Capital Broadcasting Co. v. Mitchell*, 333 F.Supp. 582 (1971), and on his personality and activities, see March 24, 1969, *NYT*; the February 5, 1970, *Washington Evening Star*; "John Banzhaf and the Giants" in *Listen*, vol. 21, no. 7; "The Man Behind the Ban on Cigarette Commercials" in the March 1971 *Reader's Digest*; the December 1973 *Current Biography*; and "Gadfly and Hound" in the August 31, 1984, Washington (D.C.) *City Paper*.

IV For Robert Barney Walker's efforts to revitalize American Tobacco, see *Forbes* of November 1, 1956, on Hahn's shortcomings, and June 15, 1958, on the Hit Parade brand flop; *BW* of January 11, 1964, on the Carlton debut; and the January 19, 1964, *NYT* personality sketch on Walker; also *Barron's* of October 5, 1964; *Sales Management* of May 21, 1973; the *NYT* of November 8, 1966; and Walker's obituary in the January 18, 1973, *NYT*.

VI On CTR's fifteenth-anniversary denial of a "demonstrated causal link" between smoking and any disease, see that organization's press release of February 3, 1969 (*Cipollone* plaintiff's exhibit 2920B); Wakeham to Roper on December 9, 1965, on the AMA/ ERF's shortcomings (*Cipollone* plaintiff's exhibit 1315); Wakeham to Clements, *Cipollone* exhibit 923B. On the "special projects" committee of the CTR, see Alvan Feinstein to Edwin Jacob, November 23, 1965 (*Cipollone* exhibit 527); Addison Yeaman's letter of January 3, 1966, with list of "special projects" (*Cipollone* exhibit 538); and the February 11, 1993, *Wall Street Journal* (*WSJ*) for its front-page exposé. Carl Thompson's instructive memo of October 18, 1968, to the Tobacco Institute's new press chief, William Kloepfer, is *Cipollone* exhibit 2725. George Weissman's dismissive remarks about the health peril of smoking appeared in the April 1968 *Dun's Review*.

IX, X, AND XI The widest-ranging periodical article on PM in this breakthrough period is "The Marketing Merlins of Philip Morris" in the April 1968 *Dun's Review*; see also *Forbes* for July 15, 1966, November 15, 1968, and July 1, 1969. On the Gallaher takeover failure, see the *Financial Times* of July 9 and 17, 1968; the *WSJ* and the (London) *Times* of July 17 and 19, 1968; the *Daily Telegraph* of July 19, 1968; the *Observer* of July 21, 1968; and *Time* of August 2, 1968.

Chapter 11 : Stroking the Sow's Ear

I On the smoking beagles episode, see the July 31, 1969, *NEJM* editorial, "Unpublicized Results"; the May 1 and 9, 1979, *NYT*, for Cullman's blast and the paper's editorial supporting his request for disclosure of the data; TI's June 23, 1970, release, suggesting that none of the dogs was stricken, and its October 12, 1970, release, in which TI president Kornegay speculates that the study may have been a hoax. *Nature* of April 30, 1971, has the best concise report. Auerbach provided copies of his exchange with *NEJM* and *JAMA* editors, the letter inviting Sommers's telegram in response, and the comments by *JAMA*'s reviewers on their concerns about the study. Wakeham's February 1971 memo was plaintiff's exhibit 330 in *Cipollone*.

II Panzer's May 1972 memo to Kornegay was plaintiff's exhibit 1105 in *Cipollone*, Ramm's November 1970 memo to the CTR was exhibit 511, and Spears's June 1974 memo to Judge was exhibit 939. The shutdown of RJR's "mouse house" was detailed in the September 26, 1992, Greensboro (N.C.) *News & Record* by Justin Catanoso and Taft Wireback. Kloepfer's intramural memo of September 7, 1971, to Kornegay saying that AMA's executive director Howard felt that the link with the tobacco industry was a great liability but politically expedient was plaintiff's exhibit 1327 in *Cipollone*. Alexander Spears, whose testimony at the trial unpersuasively tried to contradict his June 1974 memo faulting the industry's overall research program as evasive of the main health problem (*Cipollone* exhibit 939), was serving as president and chief operating officer of Lorillard as this book was being completed. Zahn's memo on how he torpedoed Homburger's press conference was *Cipollone* exhibit 1205A.

V Whiteside's exchange with the FDA is dealt with in his *Selling Death*, pp. 123–35.

VI Wynder's dismissal of ETS as a health risk because the toxic dosage was too small is quoted in the TI's April 1978 "Special Report: Smoking and the Public."

Chapter 12 : Let There Be Light

On PM's 1970s performance, discussed in latter parts of chapter, see, for example, *Forbes* for November 1, 1971, March 1, 1974, and May 15, 1976; the cover story in *BW* for January 27, 1973, and "Philip Morris: The Hot Hand in Cigarettes" in *BW* for December 6, 1976; *Financial World* for March 15, 1976, and March 15, 1977, celebrating Cullman as the top corporate executive for the preceding two years; and the December 17, 1975, *NYT* heralding the debut of Merit.

Chapter 13 : Breeding a One-Fanged Rattler

I Dobson's concession is on p. 279 of Corina's *Trust in Tobacco*. Wakeham's defense of the tranquilizing power of cigarettes was in the December 30, 1971, Richmond *News Leader*.

II On William Dunn's writings, his intramural memo on the St. Martin conference of 1972 portraying cigarettes as essentially a nicotine-delivery system was plaintiff's exhibit 5171 in *Cipollone*. His comment on compensation, whereby smokers may increase the number of lower-yielding cigarettes they smoke to maintain stable intake, is on p. 26 of his November 20, 1987, deposition in *Cipollone*. See as well his introduction and other contributions to *Smoking Behavior*, a 1973 volume he edited drawing on the participants in the St. Martin conference, including Stanley Schachter's essay on "Nesbitt's Paradox," a plausible speculation about how cigarettes may serve as both stimulant and sedative (see section III of this chapter).

VI For the prevailing sentiment about "less hazardous" cigarettes, including the views of Gori and Wynder, see the proceedings of the second World Conference on Tobacco and

Health in London in 1971 as reported in the June 1972 *JNCI*. Gori's remarks that an "incremental improvement could be made now" in cigarette smoke to reduce dramatically the health risks of smoking moderately were reported in the April 19, 1974, *Cancer Newsletter*. Contrast Gori's article in the December 17, 1976, *Science* with the one in the December 1976 *Environmental Research* by Hammond, Garfinkel, *et al.*

VII Auerbach's clinical findings about smoking and heart disease and his conjecture that the carbon monoxide and nicotine in cigarette smoke work together to promote atherosclerosis ran in the December 1976 *Chest*. Bourne's defense of his conduct is quoted on p. 213 of Taylor's *The Smoke Ring*. For Califano's account of these events, see pp. 182–97 of his *Governing America.*

IX Zerner's "Graphic Propositions" appeared in the November 1986 *Tobacco Products Litigation Reporter*. Wakeham's remarks at the February 17, 1971, seminar on how well smokers were informed about the risks they were taking are in *Cipollone* plaintiff's exhibit 330. For its consulting firm's advice to Brown & Williamson on appealing to youth, see pp. 179–81 of Taylor's *The Smoke Ring.*

Chapter 14 : The Heights of Arrogance

I On Gori's overstated claim for "safer" cigarettes and the resulting shutdown of the NCI program, see in particular the Washington *Post* for January 13 and August 10, 11, 14 and 15 (op-ed-page article by Daniel Greenberg), 1978; the August 28, 1978, *BW*; and the September 1, 1978, *Science.*

II On the fight over the Barclay, see "The $150 Million Cigarette" in the November 17, 1980, *Fortune*; *BW* for July 12, 1981; the January 1983 *Consumer Reports*; and *F.T.C. v. Brown & Williamson Tobacco Corp.* (580 F.Supp. 981, 984 D.D.C. 1983).

III James Mold told the sad story of Liggett's palladium cigarette when he was deposed for *Cipollone* at the Durham County (North Carolina) courthouse on January 11, 1988; the videotape of his testimony was played at the trial on February 11, 1988. Mold retold it before the House subcommittee on hazardous materials on June 8, 1988; Liggett's Kinsley Dey gave the company's version on that date. For a detailed account, see the Greensboro (N.C.) *News & Record* for September 27, 1992. The *NYT* and most other papers essentially ignored this story when it was disclosed during the *Cipollone* proceedings yet gave lavish space to Brown & Williamson's less intensive effort to make a "safer" cigarette in this same time frame, probably because the *Times* felt it had an exclusive in the latter instance.

V The *Tobacco Observer*'s derogatory characterization of the antismoking activists is cited in Troyer and Markle's *Cigarettes* on p. 104.

VI Taylor gives his version of the "Death in the West" saga on pp. 53–64 of his *The Smoke Ring*. Justice Ackner of Britain's High Court of Justice, Queen's Bench Division, issued his muzzle order in *Philip Morris v. Thames Television Ltd.* on June 1, 1977.

VIII Heimann's claim of good citizenship by the tobacco industry and defense of the CTR appeared in the December 22, 1977, *Tobacco Journal*. The discussion of how the tobacco industry lawyers and scientists worked together on "special projects" is drawn largely from Judge Sarokin's pretrial motion ruling of February 6, 1991, in *Haines v. Liggett Group* in the U.S. District Court of New Jersey—the opinion that got him removed from the tobacco cases. One may argue with a number of his procedural rulings in the tobacco cases, but Sarokin's consistent actions in ventilating for public inspection documents revelatory of the companies' hypocritical, if not fraudulent, behavior were uniquely valuable for the writing of this book. Seltzer's comment about the collective grants he had received from the tobacco industry appeared in the February 11, 1993, *WSJ*. The article he co-authored, "Characteristics Predictive of Coronary Heart Disease in Ex-Smokers Before They Stopped Smoking: Comparison with Persistent Smokers and Nonsmokers," ran in the *Journal of Chronic Diseases*, vol. 32 (1979): pp. 175–90. Kannel's assessment of Seltzer was made in an April 23, 1993, letter to the author. Seltzer declined to be interviewed for this book.

IX Weissman's remarks to the effect that he believed science was on the industry's side appeared in the July 17, 1984, *Tobacco & Candy Journal*. Seligman's recommendations were found in Sarokin's ruling in *Haines* (cited above in notes on section VIII of this chapter).

Chapter 15 : The Calling of Philip Morris

II The breakthrough Repace-Lowrey article appeared in *Science*, vol. 208, no. 464 (1980). Their quantitative analysis of nonsmokers' lung cancer risk from ETS ran in *Environment International*, vol. 11 (1985): pp. 3–22. The editorial favorably noting their work was in the *American Review of Respiratory Diseases*, vol. 133 (1986): pp. 1–3.

III Hirayama's article, "Non-Smoking Wives of Heavy Smokers Have a Higher Risk of Lung Cancer: A Study from Japan," was in the January 17, 1981, *British Medical Journal*. The White-Froeb study, "Small-Airways Dysfunction in Nonsmokers Chronically Exposed to Tobacco Smoke," was in the March 27, 1980, *NEJM*. Jane Brody's article on the National Research Council's report on ETS appeared in the November 15, 1986, *NYT*. Finch's "Creative Statistics" was a chapter in *Health, Lifestyle and Environment: Countering the Panic*, a 1991 publication of the Manhattan Institute. The passage quoted from Koop's introduction to the 1986 Surgeon General's report is on p. x of the front matter.

VI Long's candid comments about the trade-loading practice were in "The $600 Million Cigarette Scam" in the December 4, 1989, *Fortune.*

VIII On PM's struggles in the soda and beer businesses in the early 'Eighties, see *BW* for February 15, 1982, and June 11, 1983; *Fortune* for May 1982; *Forbes* for June 6, 1983, and January 16, 1984; and the *WSJ* for June 30, 1982.

Chapter 16 : Of Dragonslayers and Pond Scum

III Chapter 2 of Pertschuk's *Giant Killers* is an engaging retelling of the struggle to pass the 1984 cigarette labeling law.

VIII For an extended discussion of the *Marsee* case, see chapter 5 of White's *Merchants of Death*, a strong antismoking treatise; and "The Artful Dodgers" by Morton Mintz in the October 1986 *Washington Monthly*.

X For background on the AMA's position on lobbying, see Frank D. Campion's *The AMA and Health Policy Since 1940* (Chicago Review Press, 1984).

XI On the "Mister Fit" study, see the September 24, 1982, *JAMA* for a report by the Multiple Risk Factor Intervention Trial Research Group. On PM's and other companies' payments for product exposures in movies, see the *NYT* for July 13, 1989; the American Council on Science and Health's *News & Views* for January 1984; STAT's *Tobacco Youth*

Reporter for Autumn 1988; Americans for Nonsmokers' Rights' *Update* for Spring 1990; and *Tobacco on Trial* for April 30, 1992. On Victor DeNoble's research into the addictive nature of nicotine while a PM scientist, see Congressman Waxman's March 31, 1994, statement and accompanying documents he issued as chairman of the House subcommittee on health; the April 29, 1994, *NYT*; and the April 29 and May 16, 1994, *WSJ*. On PM's Project Hamlet, company documents dating back to 1981 identify the challenge of the undertaking as: "How to decrease the transfer of heat generated by the smouldering cigarette to a substrate." Typical of the interoffice memos on the subject are those from B. L. Goodman to R. K. Greene dealing with "Methodology for Project Hamlet; Mock-up Rate Procedure" (January 18, 1984) and "Project Hamlet; The Effect of Wrapper Perforation" (September 30, 1986). Public-health investigators were sent copies of the PM "Hamlet" file by company insiders. See also "Cigarette Ignition Behavior of Commercial Upholstery Cover Fabrics" by G. H. Damant *et al.* in the March 1982 *Journal of Consumer Product Flammability*, pp. 31–34.

Chapter 17 : Chow Lines

IV The best source on the RJR takeover of Nabisco, Ross Johnson, and the leveraged buyout is, of course, *Barbarians at the Gate*, a spirited and informed piece of storytelling, although questions remain about the authors' re-creation of quoted conversations between principal figures in these events—which make up a significant proportion of the contents— since they neither were present nor had access to transcripts of the exchanges. On the Nabisco deal, see also the June 3, 1985, *WSJ* and the June 17, 1985, *BW*. On RJR's experimental "smokeless" Spa brand and the Premier, dealt with in more detail in section VI, see the *NYT* for September 14, 15, 18, and 27 (editorial), 1987, August 30, September 8 and 10 (editorial), and October 9, 1988, and March 1, 1989; the *WSJ* for September 18, 1987, March 2, April 12, August 16 and 30, September 8, October 21, and December 5 and 12, 1988; and in particular March 10, 1989; *Time* for September 28, 1987; *BW* for October 10, 1988, and *U.S. News & World Report* for September 28, 1987, and October 3, 1988.

V On PM's takeover of General Foods, see *Fortune* for January 10, 1983; *Forbes* for May 20, 1985; the *WSJ* for September 25, 1985; the *NYT* for September 30 and October 1, 1985; *BW* for October 14, 1985; and *Time* for October 7, 1985.

VII On the RJR buyout by KKR, see in particular *BW* for May 23, 1988; *Fortune* for July 18, 1988; the *NYT* for October 30 and December 2 and 5, 1988; *Time* for December 5, 1988; *Newsweek* for December 12, 1988; and *Manhattan, Inc.* for December 1988. *Barbarians at the Gate* is the definitive account, so the episode is merely sketched here.

VIII On the PM takeover of Kraft, see in particular the *NYT* for October 18, 23, 24, 26, 27, and 31 and November 3 and 14 (editorial), 1988; the *WSJ* for October 20, 1988, and February 21, 1989; and *BW* for October 31 and November 7, 1988.

IX On the Jacobs Suchard deal, see *Forbes* for April 2, 1990; and the *Financial Times* for June 22, 23, 25, and July 11, 1990; the *NYT* for June 23, 1990; and the *Economist* for June 30, 1990.

X On the tobacco industry's efforts to purchase friends in the cultural and philanthropic establishment, see "Tobacco Companies' Gifts to the Arts: A Proper Way to Subsidize Culture?" in the March 8, 1987, *NYT*; "Strange Alliances: Lobbying for Tobacco" in the August 15, 1987, *National Journal*; "Big Tobacco Buying New Friendships" by Myron

Levin in the May 12, 1988, Los Angeles *Times*; and the leader "Blowing Smoke: Tobacco Firms, Pariahs to Many, Still Are Angels to the Arts" in the June 8, 1988, *WSJ*. The best piece on the industry's involvement with sports sponsorships is "Sports May Be Hazardous to Your Health" by Jason De Parle in the September 1989 *Washington Monthly*, a fiercely antismoking publication. On the race angle, contrast the letter by New York State NAACP leader Hazel Dukes in the June 9, 1986, *NYT* and the speech by Los Angeles *Herald Dispatch* publisher John Holoman reported in the January 1986 *Tobacco Observer* with the June 17, 1988, speech by District of Columbia health commissioner Reed Tuckson and remarks by Harlem Hospital surgeon Harold Freeman in the May 1, 1989, *NYT* article headlined "An Uproar Over Billboards in Poor Areas." See also "Blacks Debate on Tobacco Industry Influences" in the January 17, 1987, *NYT*; "Are Blacks the Targets of Cigarette Makers?" by John Henry in the December 18, 1988, New York *Daily News*, and "Tobacco Companies Find Harlem Wary" in the September 8, 1990, *NYT*. PM's role as arts patron and good corporate citizen is described in company publications including *In the Public Interest* (1988) and *Philip Morris and the Arts: A 30-Year Celebration.*

XII The leading cases on First Amendment protection of commercial speech are *Virginia State Board of Pharmacy v. Virginia Citizens Consumer Council, Inc.*, 425 U.S. 748 (1976); *Central Hudson Gas & Electric Corp. v. Public Service Commission*, 447 U.S. 557 (1980); and *Posadas de Puerto Rico Associates v. Tourism Co. of Puerto Rico*, 478 U.S. 328 (1986). See also *National Commission on Egg Nutrition v. F.T.C.*, 570 F.2d 157 (7th Cir. 1977), *cert. denied*, 439 U.S. 821 (1978); *F.T.C. v. Brown & Williamson Tobacco Corp.*, 778 F.2d 35 (D.C. Cir. 1985); and *In re R. J. Reynolds Tobacco Co.*, 111 F.T.C. 539 (March 4, 1988). On *Posadas*, see Laurence Tribe in *American Constitutional Law* at 903 (1988).

XIII The *NYT* editorial criticizing the U.S. Archives for granting its imprimatur to the PM Bill of Rights bicentennial anniversary campaign ran on November 19, 1989. See also "A Principle Tested unto Death" by Keltner Locke in the November 19, 1987, *St. Louis Post-Dispatch.*

Chapter 18 : Melancholy Rose

I Perhaps the most latitudinarian state ruling advancing the strict-liability doctrine was *O'Brien v. Muskin*, 94 N.J. 169, 469 A.2d 298.

II The testimony of Liggett's Milton Harrington was played on videotape for the *Cipollone* jury on February 17, 1988.

III Judge Sarokin's pretrial opinion arguing that the federal cigarette labeling laws did not preempt Rose Cipollone's claims that she was inadequately warned by the tobacco companies was issued September 20, 1984; the Third Circuit's reversal came on April 7, 1986. Sarokin's resulting, barely muted rage in the opinion clarifying the remaining causes for action was issued on December 9, 1986. Sarokin's ruling that the New Jersey tort revision act applied retroactively to *Cipollone* is explored at p. 160 in Jenkins's *The Litigators*, more than one-fourth of which is devoted to Marc Edell and his handling of *Cipollone.*

IV The most extensive coverage of the *Galbraith* and *Horton* trials was in the local press. On *Galbraith v. R. J. Reynolds Tobacco*, tried in California Superior Court, see the Santa Barbara *News-Press*'s daily accounts from November 17, 1985, until the end of the month. On *Horton v. American Tobacco*, tried in the Holmes County (Mississippi) Circuit

Court, see accounts in the Jackson *Clarion Ledger* from January 6 to 29, 1988, and the *Greenwood Commonwealth* from January 5 to 31, 1988; also the *NYT* for August 16, 1987, and January 29, 1988; the Washington *Post* for January 25, 1987, January 5, 6, 29, and 30, 1988, and September 2, 1990; the *WSJ* for December 31, 1987, and February 1 and 22, 1988; the Atlanta *Constitution* for January 6 and 21, 1988; and the Los Angeles *Times* for January 6 and 30 and February 18, 1988.

V AND VI   Joseph Cullman's confrontational testimony in the *Cipollone* trial occurred on February 23, 24, 25, and 29, 1988. Sarokin's heated ruling on the defendants' motion to dismiss was delivered on April 21, 1988. Summations were on June 1, 2, 3, and 6, 1988. The U.S. Supreme Court ruled on *Cipollone v. Liggett Group* (No. 90-1038) on June 24, 1992.

Chapter 19 : Smooth Characters

I   On the antismoking movement in the latter 1980s, see, for example, "New Laws and Potential Savings Move Employers to Cut Smoking on the Job" in the *NYT* for March 14, 1985; " 'No Smoking' Sweeps America" in *BW* for July 27, 1987; "Assault on Smokers Growing Every Year" in the Boston *Globe* for September 22, 1987; "Smoking Rules Spread Like Wildfire" in the Washington *Post* for December 9, 1987; "Antismoking Groups Grow More Sophisticated" in the *WSJ* for February 26, 1990; and "Common Courtesy and the Elimination of Passive Smoking" in *JAMA* for April 25, 1990.

II   On the cigarette companies' lobbying activities in the states, the best-documented example is California, where the tigerish Stanton Glantz and the Institute for Health Policy Studies at the University of California monitor the publicly reported activities; see, for example, "Political Expenditures by the Tobacco Industry in California State Politics" by Glantz and Michael Evans Begay, a March 1991 monograph in the institute's series. On the industry's counterstrategies such as soft "clean-air" acts and state preemption of local initiatives, see the Advocacy Institute's SCARC report covering activities for February–August 1989. On the TI's golf-resort junkets for congressmen, see as an example the article in the January 17, 1988, Louisville *Courier-Journal*. Summaries of the industry's political initiatives and defense tactics may be found in Michael Pertschuk's lecture "New Fronts in the Tobacco Wars," delivered at the UCLA Faculty Center on February 21, 1991; "Tobacco Money, Tobacco People, Tobacco Politics," a joint report of the Advocacy Institute and the Public Citizen's Health Research Group, by Bruce Samuels, Clifford Douglas, Sidney Wolfe, and Philip Wilbur, issued in August 1992, and a companion report, "The Congressional Addiction to Tobacco," issued by the same groups two months later. For a pithy digest of the PM and other industry documents given to Alan Blum's DOC and released to the public, see the October 22, 1992, speech by Pertschuk, "Smoking Gun Speaks: The Tobacco Industry's Buy-America Strategy," delivered in Minneapolis to the seventh national conference on disease prevention and control.

III   The Congressional Research Service's skeptical view of the health effects of ETS was reported in the May 29, 1994, Washington *Post*. On Healthy Buildings International, see the December 21, 1994, *NYT*. Borelli's concerns about the Janerich study were stated in a March 31, 1992, memo he wrote in answer to the author's questions about how he handled the Varella thesis. Janerich presented his side of it in a July 7, 1992, letter to the author. For the first comprehensive report on the links between ETS and cardiac diseases, see "Passive

Smoking and Heart Disease: Epidemiology, Physiology, and Biochemistry" by Stanton Glantz and William Parmley, delivered at the seventh World Conference on Tobacco and Health in Perth (April 1–5, 1990). For an update on the same subject, see Glantz's lucid testimony before OSHA on August 11, 1994, and a report by A. Judson Wells in the August 1994 *Journal of the American College of Cardiology.*

IV See especially "Teenagers' Responses to Cigarette Advertising" by William McCarthy and Ellen Gritz, a paper presented at the April 1994 meeting of the Western Psychologists Association. On the infamous Joe Camel ads, see the *NYT* for November 11 and December 15 (editorial) and 20, 1991; and " 'Joe Camel': An X-Rated Smoke" by Marjorie Carter on the op-ed page of the March 21, 1992, *NYT.*

V On California's Prop 99 and its early aftermath, see "Toward a Tobacco Free California," a status report issued in December 1990 by the state's departments of health services and education.

VI On the U.S. government's efforts to advance cigarette export sales by American tobacco manufacturers, see "Tobacco, Politics, and U.S. Trade Policy" by Gregory Connolly in the September–October 1987 issue of the American Council on Science and Health *News*; "Tobacco Roads: Delivering Death to the Third World" by Morton Mintz in the May 1991 *Progressive*; "America's New Merchants of Death" in the April 1993 *Reader's Digest*; and "Opium War Redux" by Stan Sesser in the September 13, 1993, *New Yorker.* On Yeutter and Hills, see also "America's Frontline Trade Officials," a 1990 pamphlet by Charles Lewis under the auspices of the Center for Public Integrity. On smoking in Japan, see the *WSJ* for October 19, 1987, and September 23, 1991; and the *NYT* for October 17, 1993. On Dan Quayle's remarks about opening world markets to U.S. tobacco companies, see the Asheville (North Carolina) *Citizen-Times* for July 19, 1990, p. 1CL.

VII On smoking in China, see Michael Pertschuk's article in the October 17, 1976, Washington *Post*; "The Tobacco Trap" in *International Monitor*, a Nader Group periodical, for July–August 1987; Judith Mackay's "Letter from Hong Kong" in the January 6, 1989, *JAMA* and her "China's Tobacco Wars" in the January–February 1992 *International Monitor*; and Richard Peto's reports on smoking in China, including the 1986 World Health Organization study "Tobacco: A Major International Health Problem." Particularly helpful on the international cigarette wars in general are Philip L. Shepherd's chapter entitled "Transnational Corporations and the International Cigarette Industry" in *Profits, Progress, and Poverty*, edited by R. S. Newfarmer (University of Notre Dame Press, 1985); and Nath's *Smoking: Third World Alert.*

Chapter 20 : Blowing Smoke

II Kravis's derogatory comment about the Marlboro price cut was reported in the April 30, 1994, *WSJ.*

III In addition to the studies cited on the health-care costs of smoking, see "The Taxes of Sin: Do Smokers and Drinkers Pay Their Way?" in the March 17, 1989, *JAMA.*

V For a précis of the legal background of the FDA's avoidance of tobacco regulation, see "Who's Minding the Tobacco Store?: It's Time to Level the Regulatory Playing Field" by John Slade and Scott Ballin, in *Tobacco Use: An American Crisis*, a booklet prepared for the January 9–12, 1993, conference of that title held in Washington sponsored by, among others, HHS, the CDC, and the AMA. Kessler laid out his position on nicotine in testimony before Waxman's House subcommittee on health on March 25, 1994; the tobacco company executives replied on April 14 of that year.

INTERVIEWS

The author conducted interviews for this book with the following individuals, in person for the most part but in a few instances by telephone or taped recording (designated by the letter T), by letter (L), or through a researcher (R). Those interviewed on the condition of anonymity are necessarily omitted.

Lane W. Adams
Susan Arnold
Oscar Auerbach
Ralph L. Axselle, Jr.
Carl G. Baker
Scott D. Ballin
John F. Banzhaf III
Rebecca Barfield
Glenn Barr
Glenn Bennett
Neal L. Benowitz
Max L. Berkowitz
Geoffrey C. Bible
Richard J. Bing
Peter Bleakley
Stephen J. Bloom
Alan Blum
James C. Bowling
Warren Braren
Edward Brecher
Lester Breslow
Murray H. Bring
Byron W. Brown, Jr.
Vincent Buccellato
Leroy E. Burney
David M. Burns
Roy D. Burry
Aleardo G. Buzzi
William G. Cahan
Joseph A. Califano, Jr.
Charles S. Cameron
William L. Campbell
Stig Carlson
Julia Carol
Barry Case
Jim Charles

David Cohen
Stanley Cohen
Gregory N. Connolly
Morgan Cramer III
Gordon Crenshaw
Ed Crews
Joseph W. Cullen
Edgar M. Cullman
Hugh Cullman
Joseph F. Cullman III
W. Arthur Cullman
David E. R. Dangoor
Alan C. Davis
John W. Davis III
Ronald M. Davis
Frank Daylor
Richard A. Daynard
Edward DeHart
Clifford E. Douglas
Troy Duster
Marc Z. Edell
Philip Elman
Emmanuel Farber
Jonathan E. Fielding
David B. Fishel
Emerson Foote
Ripley Forbes
Yancey W. Ford, Jr.
Barbara Fox
James C. Freund
Lawrence Garfinkel
Henry Geller
Andreas Gembler
Lawrence Gerzog
John J. Gillis
Stanton A. Glantz

Irving Glasser
Emanuel Goldman
Clifford H. Goldsmith
Helen Golenzer (L)
Lawrence G. Goodman
Myrna G. Goodman
Gio B. Gori (L)
David T. Greenberg
Thomas C. Griscom
Ellen P. Gritz
Peter V. Hamill
Dwight E. Harken
William Harlan
Jeffrey E. Harris
Wirt H. Hatcher, Jr.
Keith Henderson
Jan L. Hitchcock
Dietrich Hoffmann
Arthur I. Holleb
Alexander Holtzman
Freddy Homburger
Edward J. Horrigan
Ehud Houminer
Robert Hutchings
Robert V. P. Hutter
Dwight T. Janerich (L)
Sharon Jaycox
J. Paul Jeblee
James W. Johnston
Allan K. Jonas
Daniel P. Jordan
Manfred L. Karnovsky
Stanley H. Katz
Charles J. Kensler
David A. Kessler
William Kloepfer

Peter H. Knapp
C. Everett Koop
Lynn Koslowski
Paul Kotin
Victor Kramer (R)
Abe Krash
Walter Landor
John T. Landry
James Latimer
Charles A. LeMaistre
Elizabeth Levin
Michael Levin
Morton L. Levin
Howard Liebengood
Jetson E. Lincoln
C. Thomas Littleton
Diane Crouch Littleton
Joseph Lloyd
Paul Loveday
F. Dennis Lowry
William J. McCarthy
W. Wallace McDowell, Jr.
Andrew McGuire
Edwin J. McQuigg
Hamish Maxwell
John C. Maxwell, Jr.
Edward A. Merlis (T)
Ellen Merlo
Walker Merryman
Michael A. Miles
Ross R. Millhiser
Morton Mintz
Toby Moffitt (T)
James D. Mold
Charles Morgan, Jr.
James J. Morgan
Bayard H. Morrison III
John A. Murphy
R. William Murray
Matthew L. Myers

Gertrude Mytelka
Herman Mytelka
Ralph Nader
Guy R. Newell (L)
Kenneth P. Offord (L)
Anne Marie O'Keefe
Thomas S. Osdene
Richard H. Overholt
Thomas B. Owen
William W. Parmley
Steven C. Parrish
Mark Pertschuk
Michael Pertschuk
Harold Pillsbury (R)
John M. Pinney
Robert Pitofsky
Shepard Pollack
Lee Pollak
Frank J. Rauscher, Jr.
Clifton Read
Arnold S. Relman
James L. Repace
Frank E. Resnik
John M. Richman
Julius B. Richmond
Irving Rimer
Ruth Roemer
Johnny Roventini
Umberto Saffiotti
Thomas C. Schelling
Michael D. Schlain
Suely Schlain
Marvin A. Schneiderman
Richard Schoenkopf
Leonard M. Schuman
S. Bufford Scott
Herbert Seidman
Richard Selzer
Donald R. Shopland
Ira Singer

Guy L. Smith IV
Zachary Smith
Ronald B. Sosnick
Stephen Spain
Jesse L. Steinfeld
Steven D. Stellman
J. Paul Sticht
Joseph Stokes III
Hans G. Storr
Peter Strauss
Edward L. Sweda, Jr.
Keith Tarr-Whelan
William F. Taylor (L)
Janet (Mrs. Luther L.) Terry
Walter Thoma
Ronald H. Thomson
Robert D. Tollison
Joe B. Tye (T)
Earl Ubell
Arthur C. Upton
Richard G. Vail
Charles B. Wade, Jr.
Helmut R. R. Wakeham
    (T, L)
Robert L. Wald
John T. Walden
Cynthia Walters
Henry A. Waxman
Sylvester (Pat) Weaver (T)
Raymond Weisberg
Elizabeth K. Weisburger
George Weissman
Elizabeth M. Whelan
Charles Whitley
Judith Wilkenfeld
Don W. Wilson
Ernst L. Wynder
Raymond Yesner
Michael Zarski

Index

A NOTE ABOUT THE AUTHOR

Richard Kluger began a career in journalism at *The Wall Street Journal*, and was a writer for *Forbes* magazine and then the New York *Post* before becoming literary editor of the New York *Herald Tribune* during its final years. In book publishing he served as executive editor at Simon and Schuster and editor in chief at Atheneum. A full-time writer since 1974, he is the author of two other works of social history—*Simple Justice*, an account of the epochal 1954 Supreme Court decision outlawing school segregation, and *The Paper*, on the life and death of the *Herald Tribune*; each was nominated for the National Book Award. The best known of his six novels are *Members of the Tribe* and *The Sheriff of Nottingham*. Kluger and his wife, Phyllis, have two sons, have written two novels together, and live near Princeton, New Jersey, where they met while he was attending the university as a member of the class of 1956.

A NOTE ON THE TYPE

The text of this book was set in Times Roman, a typeface designed by Stanley Morison for *The Times* (London), and first introduced by that newspaper in 1932.

Among typographers and designers of the twentieth century, Stanley Morison was a strong forming influence, as typographical adviser to the English Monotype Corporation, as a director of two distinguished English publishing houses, and as a writer of sensibility, erudition, and keen practical sense.

Composed by Creative Graphics, Inc.,
Allentown, Pennsylvania

Printed and bound by
R. R. Donnelley & Sons,
Harrisonburg, Virginia

Designed by Dorothy Schmiderer Baker